Criminal Procedure for the Criminal Justice Professional

Eighth Edition

JOHN N. FERDICO, J.D.

Member of the Maine Bar
Former Assistant Attorney General and
Director of Law Enforcement Education for the State of Maine

WADSWORTH
™
THOMSON LEARNING

Australia · Canada · Mexico · Singapore · Spain
United Kingdom · United States

WADSWORTH
★
THOMSON LEARNING
™

Executive Editor: Criminal Justice: SABRA HORNE
Criminal Justice Editor: SHELLEY MURPHY
Development Editor: TERRI EDWARDS
Assistant Editor: DAWN MESA
Editorial Assistant: LEE MCCRAKEN
Marketing Manager: JENNIFER SOMERVILLE
Marketing Assistant: KARYL DAVIS
Print/Media Buyer: TANDRA JORGENSEN
Permissions Editor: BOB KAUSER

Production Service: MATRIX PRODUCTIONS
Text Designer: JOHN WALKER
Copy Editor: SUSIE FRANKLIN DEFAZIO
Cover Designer: BILL STANTON
Cover Image: IMAGE BANK (CONSTITUTION),
TONY STONE IMAGES
Compositor: COLORTYPE, SAN DIEGO
Text and Cover Printer: R. R. DONNELLEY, WILLARD

For more information, contact
Wadsworth/Thomson Learning
10 Davis Drive
Belmont, CA 94002-3098
USA

For more information about our products, contact us:
Thomson Learning Academic Resource Center
1-800-423-0563
http://www.wadsworth.com

International Headquarters
Thomson Learning
International Division
290 Harbor Drive, 2nd Floor
Stamford, CT 06902-7477
USA

UK/Europe/Middle East/South Africa
Thomson Learning
Berkshire House
168-173 High Holborn
London WC1V 7AA
United Kingdom

Asia
Thomson Learning
60 Albert Complex, #15-01
Singapore 189969

Canada
Nelson Thomson Learning
1120 Birchmount Road
Toronto, Ontario M1K 5G4
Canada

Library of Congress Cataloging-in-Publication Data
Ferdico, John N.
    Criminal procedure for the criminal justice professional/
John N. Ferdico.—8th ed.
    p. cm.
Includes index.
ISBN 0-534-56025-3
1. Criminal procedure—United States. I. Title
KF9619.F47 2001

2001026166

BRIEF CONTENTS

PREFACE

Criminal Procedure for the Criminal Justice Professional was originally published in 1975 as *Criminal Procedure for the Law Enforcement Officer*. Its primary emphasis was on providing practical guidelines for law enforcement officers with respect to the legal aspects of their daily duties. Over the years, in response to suggestions and comments from professors and students who have used it, many changes have been made to enhance the book's suitability for use as a classroom text. Chapters dealing with individual rights under the Constitution and basic underlying concepts have been added; and chapters dealing with evidence, testifying in court, and investigation of crime have been eliminated. Review and discussion questions have been included to stimulate discussion and to expand students' understanding beyond the principles and examples used in the text. In the 1990s, several pedagogical devices were added to the book to enhance understanding of the law of criminal procedure:

■ Chapter Objectives and Outline—statements of student learning goals, followed by a profile of the chapter's major topics. These appear at the beginning of each chapter and are designed to provide purpose, structure, and context.

■ Key Points—concise, clear statements of the essential principles of criminal procedure. These appear at the end of major sections of chapters and serve as mini-summaries of those sections. Their purpose is to aid the student in "separating the wheat from the chaff" and to expedite review by boiling down complexities into simple statements of fundamentals.

■ Key Holdings from Major Cases—essential principles from U.S. Supreme Court cases, usually presented in the form of quotations. These appear at the end of chapters. Their purpose is to familiarize students with judicial language and to give them a sense, in the words of the Supreme Court, of the historical development of particular aspects of criminal procedure. These holdings also serve as summaries of important principles.

■ Real-Life Fact Situations—verbatim statements of fact situations from actual reported court cases. These appear at the end of chapters and are designed to supplement the sometimes theoretical Review and Discussion Questions by challenging students to apply their knowledge to practical, everyday circumstances.

■ Glossary—definitions of major terms used in criminal procedure law taken from Ferdico's *Criminal Law and Justice Dictionary*.

The purpose of the various modifications made to the book has been to provide the student with a broad and sophisticated understanding of the law of criminal procedure while maintaining a practical, real-life orientation. The Eighth Edition of *Criminal Procedure for the Criminal Justice Professional* retains all these features, expanding and revising them when necessary. In addition, every chapter has been thoroughly reviewed, corrected, and updated to reflect modern developments in the law. Revisions include discussions of all relevant U.S. Supreme Court cases decided since the publication of the Seventh Edition and all amendments to relevant legislation and court rules. Also, all forms and exhibits have been reviewed and updated where necessary.

The most important *new* feature of the Eighth Edition of *Criminal Procedure for the Criminal Justice Professional* is the *complete integration of the text with the Internet*. This means that, first of all, every U.S. Supreme Court case, federal statute, or federal court rule is accompanied by an Internet reference in the margin next to it. This enables the student to consult an entire Supreme Court case, including dissenting and concurring opinions. Casebooks, which merely present selected excerpts from Supreme Court opinions, are effectively rendered obsolete by this new feature. Internet access to federal statutes and court rules enables the student to develop a broader contextual understanding of particular statute or rule provisions and also enables him or her to keep current with statute or rule changes as Web sites are updated.

Of equal importance to these Internet references to cases, statutes, and rules is the addition of *over four hundred Internet references* to a great variety of materials dealing with all aspects of criminal procedure law. These Internet references include scholarly articles, commentaries, reports, practical advice and guidelines, law outlines, legal documents, speeches, and various other resources. Each Internet reference appears in the margin next to the corresponding discussion of the particular topic in the text, which it supplements, explains, or augments. This provides the student, again literally at his or her fingertips, with a wealth of information on criminal procedure law to enhance and deepen understanding of the material.

In addition, the Real-Life Fact Situations contain all-new fact situations taken from recent state and federal court decisions. A major improvement from the Seventh Edition, however, is the addition of an Internet reference to the entire court opinion for each fact situation presented. Now the student can analyze the fact situations and find out immediately via the Internet how the court resolved the issues in each case.

One final new feature is titled Case in Point. This feature is similar to the Real-Life Fact Situations with this exception: each Case in Point presents a verbatim fact situation from a state or lower federal court opinion that interprets a *recent* U.S. Supreme Court decision that is new to the Eighth Edition. In chapters for which no new U.S. Supreme Court decisions have been handed down, the Case in Point presents a case that interprets one of the most recent U.S. Supreme Court decisions. This new feature gives the student the opportunity to clarify the meanings and appreciate the implications of sometimes obscure and confusing new Supreme Court opinions. As with the Real-Life Fact Situations, an Internet reference is provided for each Case in Point.

Although not a feature of the book itself, a Web site supporting this book will be available to all students upon publication of the book. The address of this Web site is www.wadsworth.com/cj/ferdico0253. This Web site will be used to update the information in the text with new cases, statutes, and rules and to provide other current information relating to the developing law of criminal procedure. The Web site will also notify students of new Internet references relating to criminal procedure and criminal justice in general. Students and professors are encouraged to notify the author of new postings on the Internet that have come to their attention, and of problems accessing Web sites listed in the text that have changed their addresses or have been removed from the Internet. All communications with the author should be directed to the following email address: (jferdico@gwi.net).

Because racial profiling has become a controversial and much-discussed topic in recent years, the Eighth Edition adds a new section in Chapter 7 dealing with this issue, accompanied by eleven Internet references discussing various aspects of the problem. The Eighth Edition also adds discussions of over fifty new cases decided by the U.S. Supreme Court and other federal and state courts. Many of these new cases replace old and archaic cases with modern examples illustrating important legal principles. Some of these new cases establish precedents in criminal procedure law or provide instructive examples of the operation of existing law. The recent U.S. Supreme Court decisions discussed in this edition are:

Pennsylvania Board of Probation v. Scott, in Chapter 3, dealing with the application of the federal exclusionary rule to the introduction at parole revocation hearings of evidence seized in violation of parolees' Fourth Amendment rights.

Minnesota v. Carter, in Chapter 3, dealing with the reasonable expectation of privacy of a temporary, commercial visitor in a home he or she is visiting.

Wilson v. Layne, in Chapters 4 and 5, dealing with the police practice of bringing members of the media or other third parties into a home during the execution of a warrant.

United States v. Ramirez, in Chapter 5, dealing with reasonable suspicion to justify a "no-knock" entry into premises.

Illinois v. McArthur, in Chapter 5, dealing with the right of the police to prevent a person from entering his or her home while a search warrant is being obtained.

Sacramento v. Lewis, in Chapter 7, dealing partially with the Fourth Amendment seizure implications of an accidental crash following a hot pursuit by police.

Florida v. J.L., in Chapter 7, dealing with whether an anonymous tip that a person is carrying a gun is sufficient to justify a stop and frisk of that person.

Illinois v. Wardlow, in Chapter 7, dealing with a suspect's presence in a high-crime area and unprovoked flight as factors in developing reasonable suspicion to stop the suspect.

Indianapolis v. Edmond, in Chapter 7, dealing with the legality of a highway checkpoint program the primary purpose of which was the discovery and interdiction of illegal narcotics.

Bond v. United States, in Chapter 7, dealing with the legality of a police officer's physical manipulation of a bus passenger's carry-on luggage.

Knowles v. Iowa, in Chapter 8, dealing with the legality of Iowa's "search incident to citation" exception to the Fourth Amendment's warrant requirement.

Flippo v. West Virginia, in Chapter 10, rejecting a "homicide scene" exception to the warrant requirement.

Florida v. White, in Chapter 11, dealing with seizure of the *vehicle itself* under the *Carroll* doctrine.

Maryland v. Dyson, in Chapter 11, holding that a separate finding of exigency is not required under the *Carroll* doctrine.

Wyoming v. Houghton, in Chapter 11, dealing with the search of passengers' belongings under the *Carroll* doctrine.

Dickerson v. United States, in Chapter 13, dealing with the constitutional basis for the *Miranda* decision.

Texas v. Cobb, in Chapter 13, reaffirming that the Sixth Amendment right to counsel is "offense specific."

Acknowledgments

I am grateful to the following criminal justice instructors for their time and effort in reviewing the Eighth Edition and providing helpful comments and suggestions for this book's improvement: Kenneth Agran, University of California Irvine; Alan W. Clarke, Ferris State University; Craig Hemmens, Boise State University; William Hyatt, Western Carolina Weslyan; Judy Hails Kaci, California State University Long Beach; David Kramer, Bergen Community College; Milo Miller, Southeast Missouri State; Thomas O'Connor, North Carolina Weslyan; Gene Straughan, Lewis-Clark State College; and John Wyant, Illinois Central College. I also wish to thank again the following professors for their reviews of previous editions of this text: Jack E. Call, Joseph Robert Caton, Charles Dreveskracht, Jack Elrod, David V. Guccione, James Hague, G. G. Hunt, Susan Jacobs, Richard Janikowski, Elizabeth Lewis, Joseph G. Sandoval, Susette M. Talarico, and Alvin J. T. Zumbrun. My appreciation also extends to the staff at Wadsworth Publishing Company and those who worked with them at all stages of the production of the Eighth Edition. Special thanks go to Brian MacMaster, Chief Investigator for the Maine Attorney General's Office, for his valuable and competent assistance in editing and updating the manuscript for the Eighth Edition. His contribution reflects his many years of experience in all aspects of the law enforcement profession and his insights as a teacher of various topics related to criminal justice. Finally, and most important, I express my deepest appreciation to my wife, Barbara Duff, for her skilled editing and helpful suggestions in the preparation of the manuscript. Also, many thanks go to her and to my son, Rocky, for their loving support and understanding through my absences and preoccupation in the preparation of the Eighth Edition. When the task sometimes seemed overwhelming, their presence gave me the solace and encouragement to carry on.

JOHN N. FERDICO

INTRODUCTION

A crime is an act committed or omitted in violation of a law specifically prohibiting or commanding it. Crimes differ from other prohibited behavior in that, upon conviction, an adult may be penalized by fine, incarceration, or both; a corporation may be penalized by fine or forfeiture; and a juvenile may be adjudged delinquent or transferred to a criminal court for prosecution. Generally, a crime consists of conduct that violates the duties a person owes to the community or society, as distinguished from a private wrong committed against one or more persons or organizations. Criminal law is the body of law that defines what acts or omissions constitute crimes and provides for the punishment of that behavior. Criminal procedure can be defined as the body of laws and rules governing the process of detecting and investigating crime and gathering evidence against, apprehending, prosecuting, trying, adjudicating, sentencing, and punishing persons accused of crimes.

Criminal Procedure— Complex and Dynamic

The law of criminal procedure is not only complex, but also constantly changing. The criminal justice professional, and especially the law enforcement officer, is expected to understand these complexities and keep abreast of the changes. More important, criminal procedure law must be applied to a variety of situations that do not always neatly conform to established principles. To compound the problem, criminal procedure law is derived primarily from judicial opinions that are often written in a rambling, legalistic style that even lawyers and judges have trouble comprehending. The result is a gap in communication and understanding between those who make the rules (judges) and those who must enforce and apply them (law enforcement officers and other criminal justice professionals). Violations of citizens' rights by criminal justice personnel who are not aware of or do not heed court-imposed limitations on their activities often cause the failure of prosecutions and the reversal of convictions.

This book is an attempt to bridge the gap in communication and comprehension between judges and criminal justice professionals. All who operate within the criminal justice system need understandable guidelines for performing their particular functions within the system. For example, law enforcement officers need clearly defined rules and procedures for conducting arrests, searches and seizures, interrogations, and lineups. Also, all criminal justice personnel should be familiar with the language and reasoning of the courts defining rights and obligations in the criminal justice area. Nonlawyers, however, should not be expected to read through long, involved opinions of every state and federal case that affects them and to extract principles of law to guide them in the execution of their duties. They already carry a heavy enough burden. Therefore, this book attempts to reduce the complexity of the law of criminal procedure into simple, straightforward guidelines and recommendations, illustrated with examples of actual cases. Quotations from cases are used if they are written in clear, understandable language.

Criminal Procedure—The Constitution and the Courts

Most of the principles governing criminal procedure are derived from the United States Constitution, constitutions of individual states, and court decisions interpreting those constitutions. This book begins with a discussion of individual rights under the U.S. Constitution and an overview of the criminal court system. The remainder (and greater portion) of the book examines specific areas of criminal procedure, presented primarily through appellate court decisions. An *appellate court* is a court that hears appeals from lower courts, usually trial courts. An *appeal* in a criminal case is a request to an appellate court by either the defendant or the prosecution to review alleged errors by the trial court or alleged official misconduct or violation of rights by one of the participants in the criminal justice process. Most appeals are by convicted defendants attempting to overturn their convictions. After the appellate court reviews the allegations presented, it issues a written opinion explaining its decision.

Most of the principles in this book are illustrated by decisions of the U.S. Supreme Court. The Supreme Court plays a significant role in the development of the law of criminal procedure, because criminal procedure is prominently featured in the Constitution and because the Supreme Court has the ultimate responsibility for interpreting the Constitution. Of the twenty-three separate rights set out in the first eight amendments to the Constitution, more than half concern criminal procedure. Although the Supreme Court has had little to say about some constitutional rights, it has, since the early 1960s especially, developed complex and comprehensive bodies of law around other constitutional rights. Lower federal courts and state appellate courts have responded to this development with increased activity of their own in the criminal procedure arena in recent years. Decisions of these lower courts are used in this book primarily to give examples of important principles and to clarify the law in areas about which the U.S. Supreme Court has not spoken, or has spoken only superficially or sketchily. In rare situations, a lower court case may be used to set out a principle or doctrine not addressed by the U.S. Supreme Court or to illustrate a state court's disagreement with and departure from guidelines established by the Supreme Court. The reader is apprised in the text of these uses of lower court decisions.

Because most criminal procedure principles and doctrines derive from U.S. Supreme Court decisions interpreting the Constitution, the reader should know how to recognize these cases. Here is an example of a U.S. Supreme Court case citation: *Miranda v. Arizona,* 384 U.S. 436, 86 S.Ct. 1602, 16 L.Ed.2d 694 (1966). The title of the case appears in italics. The designation "384 U.S. 436" means that the *Miranda* case appears in volume 384 of the *United States Reports,* beginning at page 436. The *United States Reports* is the official published collection of U.S. Supreme Court decisions. "S.Ct." refers to the *Supreme Court Reporter,* a compilation of U.S. Supreme Court decisions published by West Publishing Company, Eagan, Minnesota. "L.Ed.2d" refers to the *U.S. Supreme Court Reports Lawyer's Edition,* Second Series, published by Lawyers Cooperative Publishing, Rochester, New York. These published collections of Supreme Court decisions can be found in law libraries. All U.S. Supreme Court decisions in this book are cited according to this format and are accompanied by an Internet reference in the margin, as mentioned above.

This book uses the West Publishing Company Reporter System for all citations for lower federal and state court decisions. For example, *United States v. Galindo-Gonzales,* 142 F.3d 1217 (10th Cir. 1998), means that the *Galindo-Gonzales* case appears in volume 142 of West's *Federal Reporter,* Third Series, beginning at page 1217. "10th Cir." means that the case was decided by the U.S. Court of Appeals for the Tenth Circuit. All decisions of U.S. Courts of Appeals appear in West's *Federal Reporter.* Decisions of the U.S. District Courts appear in West's *Federal Supplement.* A typical citation to that reporter is: *United States v. Wilbon,* 911 F.Supp. 1420 (D.N.M. 1995). "D.N.M." indicates that the case was decided by the U.S. District Court for the District of New Mexico. A typical state court citation is: *State v. Morato,* 619 N.W.2d 655 (S.D. 2000). "N.W.2d" means that the case appears in West's *Northwestern Reporter,* Second Series. West Publishing Company publishes state court decisions in reporters covering different regions of the United States. The designation "S.D." means that

the case was decided by the South Dakota Supreme Court. A more detailed discussion of citations and the reporter systems is beyond the scope of this book.

How to Read an Appellate Court Opinion

Since the Internet references in the margins of this text provide access to the complete opinions of all U.S. Supreme Court cases and some lower federal appellate court and state appellate court opinions, a brief explanation on how to read a court opinion may be useful to the student. In rough outline, a court opinion in a criminal case consists of the title of the case, the procedural background, the facts, the issue, the decision or holding, the reasoning for the decision, and the case's disposition. Each of these will be described briefly.

Title   The title of an appellate case is usually expressed by listing the name of the party bringing the appeal (the *appellant*) followed by "v." and the name of the party against whom the appeal is brought (the *appellee*). The "v." is an abbreviation of the Latin word *versus,* which means against. Therefore, *Bond v. United States* means that a person named Bond is appealing against the U.S. government. Likewise, *Wyoming v. Houghton* means that the state of Wyoming is appealing against a person named Houghton. Note that at the *trial* stage of judicial proceedings the government is always listed first because, in the United States, the government initiates all criminal prosecutions. If a case is before an appellate court by petition rather than by means of an appeal, the party initiating the petition is called the *petitioner* and the party against whom it is brought is called the *respondent. Habeas corpus* proceedings (see Chapter 2) are brought before appellate courts by petition. The titles of *habeas corpus* cases have the names of two persons, such as *Fay v. Noia,* rather than the name of a governmental entity and a person. One of the persons is a prisoner or other person being restrained who is challenging the legality of his or her detention. The other person is the prison administrator or jailer who is holding the prisoner.

Procedural Background   The procedural background of a case is the set of legal procedures that have already taken place in the case, along with the results of those procedures. In other words, it is a record of the courts that have dealt with the case and the decisions those courts have made. A brief statement of the procedural background of a case is often presented immediately after the title of the case. For example, in the U.S. Supreme Court case of *Bond v. United States,* 529 U.S. 334, 120

S.Ct. 1462, 146 L.Ed.2d 365 (2000), discussed in Chapter 7, the following statement appears after the title:

> Defendant was convicted in the United States District Court for the Western District of Texas, Harry Lee Hudspeth, Chief Judge, of conspiracy to possess, and possession with intent to distribute, methamphetamine, and he appealed denial of his motion to suppress. The Court of Appeals, 167 F.3d 225, affirmed. After granting *certiorari*, The Supreme Court, Chief Justice Rehnquist, held that law enforcement officer's physical manipulation of defendant's carry-on bag on bus violated Fourth Amendment.
>
> Reversed.
>
> Justice Breyer filed dissenting opinion in which Justice Scalia joined.

A more detailed statement usually appears in the body of the court opinion. For example, in the *Bond* case, the following statement expands upon the one quoted above:

> Petitioner was indicted for conspiracy to possess, and possession with intent to distribute, methamphetamine in violation of 84 Stat. 1260, 21 U.S.C. § 841(a)(1). He moved to suppress the drugs, arguing that Agent Cantu conducted an illegal search of his bag. Petitioner's motion was denied, and the District Court found him guilty on both counts and sentenced him to 57 months in prison. On appeal, he conceded that other passengers had access to his bag, but contended that Agent Cantu manipulated the bag in a way that other passengers would not. The Court of Appeals rejected this argument, stating that the fact that Agent Cantu's manipulation of petitioner's bag was calculated to detect contraband is irrelevant for Fourth Amendment purposes. 167 F.3d 225, 227 (C.A.5 1999) (citing *California v. Ciraolo*, 476 U.S. 207, 106 S.Ct. 1809, 90 L.Ed.2d 210 [1986]). Thus, the Court of Appeals affirmed the denial of the motion to suppress, holding that Agent Cantu's manipulation of the bag was not a search within the meaning of the Fourth Amendment. 167 F.3d, at 227. We granted *certiorari*, 528 U.S. ____, 120 S.Ct. 320, 145 L.Ed.2d 250 (1999), and now reverse. 529 U.S. at 336, 120 S.Ct. at 1464, 145 L.Ed.2d at ____.

From these two quotations, the student can determine with what crime the defendant was charged, how different courts dealt with his case, and what was the final result. Unfamiliar terms in these quotations are explained below and in the Glossary at the end of this text.

Facts   The facts set out the essentials of what happened in the case and answer questions such as: Who is the defendant? What law did the defendant allegedly violate? Who was the victim, if any? How did the police respond to the alleged criminal activity? What did the police do to detect the crime, identify the perpetrator, investigate the scene of the crime, interview suspects and other witnesses, and apprehend the defendant? Although this book is concerned primarily with the conduct of the police, many criminal cases also analyze and evaluate the conduct of the prosecuting attorney, the defense attorney, and the trial judge. Students should read the statement of facts in a court opinion very carefully because a careful analysis of the facts will determine whether the police, prosecutor, defense counsel, or judge violated a constitutional provision, statute, or court rule protecting some right of the defendant. As will become apparent in later chapters, violations of defendants' rights can result in evidence being excluded from court, dismissal of charges, new trials, and various other sanctions.

Issue   The issue in a criminal case is essentially the legal question to be resolved by the court. Sometimes the court will state the issue early in the court's opinion. For example, in the *Bond* case (quoted above), Chief Justice Rehnquist stated the issue in the first paragraph of the opinion: "This case presents the question whether a law enforcement officer's physical manipulation of a bus passenger's carry-on luggage violated the Fourth Amendment's proscription against unreasonable searches. We hold that it did." 529 U.S. at 335, 120 S.Ct. at 1463, 146 L.Ed.2d at ____. Many cases have several legal issues to be resolved by the appellate court, some of which involve complex and esoteric questions of court procedure, evidence law, or statutory interpretation of interest mostly to lawyers and judges. Issues of primary interest to criminal procedure students usually involve claims by the defendant that the police at some point in the proceedings violated his or her constitutional rights. Typical claims are that the defendant's rights were violated by means of an illegal arrest, search, interrogation, or identification procedure. The appellate court's duty is to resolve the legal issues arising from these claims after hearing the arguments of the opposing parties.

Decision or Holding   The appellate court's decision or holding is simply the court's resolution of the issue in the case. Sometimes, as the quote in the preceding paragraph indicates, a court will announce its holding at the beginning of its opinion. A court may also announce its holding further along in the opinion or at the end, after discussing its reasoning. For example, in *Wilson v. Layne*, 526 U.S. 603, 614, 119 S.Ct. 1692, 1699, 143 L.Ed.2d 818, ____ (1999), the Court announced the following holding several pages into the opinion: "We hold that it is a violation of the Fourth Amendment for police to bring members of the media or other third parties into a home during the execution of a warrant when the presence of the third parties in the home was not in aid of the execution of the warrant." Examples of the holdings of major U.S. Supreme Court decisions appear throughout this text under "Key Holdings from Major Cases" at the end of Chapters 3 through 14.

Reasoning   The court's reasoning is simply the totality of its arguments justifying its holding. Courts often go to great lengths to justify their holdings; therefore, the court's reasoning may constitute the greater portion of the court opinion. In its reasoning, a court will compare the case before it with cases previously decided by that court or other courts. Also, courts will bolster their reasoning by quoting at length from opinions in previously decided cases. Previously decided cases that are recognized as authorities or rules for disposition of future similar or analogous cases are called *precedents*. The reason why courts go to such lengths to align their opinions with previous court opinions is the doctrine of *stare decisis*. That doctrine states that when a principle of law has been decided by a court, that principle will be adhered to by that court and by inferior courts in future cases in which the facts are substantially the same, even though the parties may be different. The object of the doctrine of *stare decisis* is uniformity, certainty, and stability in the law. *Stare decisis* is a compelling but not absolute doctrine. Principles announced in former decisions may be overturned, but only on a showing of good cause or if they conflict with a statutory or constitutional provision.

Disposition   Common dispositions in criminal cases include affirmed, reversed, and remanded. *Affirmed* simply means that the appellate court agrees with the opinion of the lower court from which the appeal came and allows that opinion to retain its validity. *Reversed* means that the appellate court disagrees with the opinion of the lower court from which the appeal came and sets aside or invalidates that opinion. *Remanded* means that the case is sent back to the court from which it came for further action consistent with the appellate court opinion. Reversals are often accompanied by a remand to the lower court.

Concurring and Dissenting Opinions   Many appellate court decisions contain not only a majority opinion, but also one or more concurring or dissenting opinions. The *majority opinion*, as its name indicates, is one in which a majority of the judges on the court agree on both the result and the reasoning. It is the official opinion of the court and is the law in the case. A *concurring opinion* is a separate opinion of one or more judges that generally agrees with the result of the majority opinion but disagrees with the reasoning and states its own reasons supporting the result. A *dissenting opinion* is a separate opinion of one or more judges who disagree with the result of the majority opinion. A dissenting opinion usually points out the deficiencies of the majority opinion and explains the reasons for arriving at a different result.

Note that this rough guide to reading a court opinion is just that, a rough guide. Many aspects of court opinions have been left out or dealt with summarily. As the student progresses through this text and reads the court opinions listed in the Internet references, he or she will become more familiar with legal terms and the structure and style of court opinions.

Internet Guide to the Study of Criminal Procedure

The Internet is a rich source of information for enhancing and broadening the student's understanding of the specific topic of criminal procedure and the entire field of criminal justice. New technology has not only increased the speed with which laws and cases are generated but has also multiplied the range of issues dealt with by the criminal justice system. In addition to creating new problems, new technology has also brought new answers and new tools for the criminal justice professional. The Internet is one such essential tool for the criminal justice student to keep up with rapidly changing problems and solutions. This guide focuses on the potential uses of the Internet for the criminal procedure/criminal justice student. It points out particular Web sites that have proven useful to the author in the preparation of this edition and refers the student to Web sites that provide links to the great variety of criminal justice resources on the Internet.

There are seven broad categories of information for which the Internet can provide useful resources to the criminal procedure/criminal justice student. They are research; constitutions, court decisions, statutes, and court rules; scholarly articles; practical advice and guidelines; law outlines; state and local events, activities, and news; and organizations providing educational, informational, and employment services. Each of these categories will be discussed separately, although they often overlap when referring to particular topics or particular Web sites.

Research   In general, to quickly find specific information on a particular topic using the Internet, the best place to start is a reputable search engine. A search engine is simply a Web site that looks for specific information stored on the Internet. Each search engine is different from every other search engine, and trying a variety is the best way to find out which one suits the user's needs. The author has found the Google search engine (www.google.com) particularly valuable, because of its speed and its uncanny ability to find exactly what is being sought and list it among the top ten or fifteen search results. For example, assume that a student wants information on racial profiling. If the words "racial profiling" were typed in the Google search box and the search implemented, in less than a second over 48,000 results would appear. The top ten or fifteen of these results would give a variety of Web sites presenting basic information on racial profiling. Assume further that a student wanted to know what the attorney general of New Jersey was doing about racial profiling. If the words "racial profiling New Jersey Attorney General" were typed in the Google search box and the search implemented, again in less than a second, over two thousand results would appear. The top ten or fifteen of these results would give a variety of web sites specifying the New Jersey attorney general's approach to the problem of racial profiling. Google also allows for more advanced search techniques, as do other popular search engines such as Altavista (www.altavista. digital. com), Ask Jeeves (www.askjeeves.com), Botspot (www. botspot.com), Deja News (www.dejanews.com), Excite (www.excite.com), Hotbot (www.hotbot.com), Go (www.go.com), Lycos (www.lycos.com), Northern Light (www.northernlight.com), Webcrawler (www. webcrawler.com), and Yahoo! (www.yahoo.com). For more advanced legal searches, the student is referred to the 'Lectric Law Library's Web site, "Legal Research Using the Internet" (www.lectlaw.com/files/lws56.htm).

Constitutions, Court Decisions, Statutes, and Court Rules

For a student of criminal procedure, or any legal topic for that matter, the U.S. Constitution, state constitutions, court decisions, statutes, and court rules provide the fundamental information upon which texts, lectures, articles, commentaries, and editorials are based. Because of the importance of these primary legal sources and because the law is constantly changing, students need ready access to these materials. The author has found two Web sites invaluable in accessing constitutions, court decisions, and statutes and has referred to them often in the margin notes of this text. These Web sites are Findlaw (www.findlaw. com), and the Legal Information Institute at Cornell University (www.law.cornell.edu/index.html). These Web sites are relatively easy to navigate and no further instructions will be given here. Students are encouraged to access these Web sites and browse the sites to familiarize themselves with the wealth of information available. Of particular interest is the annotated U.S. Constitution (findlaw.com/ casecode/constitution), many parts of which are referenced in the margins of this text next to the discussion of related topics. The Federal Rules of Criminal Procedure can be found at the University of Kansas Law Library Web site (www.law.ukans.edu/research/frcrimI.htm). The Federal Rules of Evidence can be found as part of the Cornell Legal Information Institute Web site (www.law.cornell.edu/rules/ fre/overview.html). Cornell's Legal Information Institute also provides email notification of U.S. Supreme Court decisions as they are handed down along with a summary of the decision and a link to the full text of the opinion. To receive this email service, use the form at (www3.law. cornell.edu/lii/). To receive email notification of each day's legal news, go to law.com (www.law.com) and follow the directions for obtaining email service. Although most of the news provided by this service is unrelated to criminal procedure or criminal justice, it is a good way to keep current on developments in the law. Findlaw is also a source for email notification of the latest decisions of the U.S. Supreme Court, all the federal circuit courts, and certain appellate courts in California, Florida, New York, and Texas. To subscribe to these daily email notifications and other newsletters of interest, go to Findlaw Newsletters (newsletters.findlaw.com).

Scholarly Articles

Scholarly articles on various aspects of criminal procedure law are becoming increasingly available on the Internet as more law schools publish their law reviews online. Nevertheless, these articles are often difficult to find without looking for information on a specific topic with the aid of a search engine. Two dependably consistent sources of high-quality articles on criminal procedure topics, however, are the monthly *FBI Law Enforcement Bulletin* (www.fbi.gov/publications/leb/leb.htm) and the *Quarterly Review*, published by the Federal Law Enforcement Training Center (www.fletc.gov/legal/qrtrly_ rev.htm). Every issue of these publications usually has at least one article on a contemporary issue in criminal procedure law along with other valuable material. Note that recent issues of the *FBI Law Enforcement Bulletin* are published in PDF (portable document format) and require the latest edition of Adobe Acrobat Reader to access them. Adobe Acrobat Reader can be downloaded free of charge from the Adobe Web site (www.adobe.com/products/ acrobat/readstep2.html). To receive the *Quarterly Review* via email the student should send his or her email address to (blemons@fletc.treas.gov) and request electronic delivery of this publication.

Practical Advice and Guidelines

Many governmental and nongovernmental entities provide information in the form of manuals, handbooks, guidebooks, advice columns, and step-by-step procedures to criminal justice personnel and private citizens on criminal procedure topics. One excellent example is the manual entitled "Searching and Seizing Computers and Obtaining Electronic

Evidence in Criminal Investigations" (www.cybercrime. gov/searchmanual.htm) published by the Criminal Division of the U.S. Department of Justice. Another good example is the series of publications issued by the District Attorney's Office in Alameda County, California (www.co.alameda.ca.us/da/pov/POV_index.htm), dealing with topics ranging from "Citizens' Arrests" and "Testifying in Court," to "*Miranda* Custody" and "Bodily Intrusion Searches." Web sites for these and similar publications can be found in margin references throughout this book. Many state and local governmental entities have comparable publications tailored to the law of that particular jurisdiction. Each student should contact his or her state's attorney general's office, local district attorney's offices, and local law libraries to determine if online publications providing advice and guidelines are available in his or her state or locality. Links to directories of state and local governmental offices for all fifty states are available at the Web site "State and Local Government on the Net" located at (www.piperinfo.com/state/index.cfm).

Law Outlines   Law outlines of varying quality dealing with criminal procedure and related topics are available on the Internet. These outlines, although necessarily sketchy in content, may assist the student in organizing complex legal material and also help provide broad overviews of or unique organizing principles for the material. Among the best are those provided by Emanuel Publishing Company (lawschool. lexis.com/emanuel/index.html). Outlines on criminal procedure, criminal law, constitutional law, and evidence are available through this Web site. References to sections of these outlines appear in the margins throughout this book. Other criminal procedure law outlines that may be useful to students can be found at the following Web sites:

(barney.gonzaga.edu/~mkaser/law/crimpro.html)

(www.pitt.edu/~lawwomen/outlines/ crimpromccarthylt.doc.)

(www.pitt.edu/~lawwomen/outlines/crimprowen.doc)

(www.law.nyu.edu/mirskyc/criminalprocedure/ crimpro.html)

State and Local Events, Activities, and News   Web sites announcing state and local events, activities, and news relating to criminal justice and criminal procedure may be the same Web sites as those providing scholarly articles or practical advice or guidelines. An example in the author's home state is the *Maine Law Officer's Bulletin*, published monthly since November 1999 by Brian MacMaster, chief investigator for the Maine attorney general's office (www.mainechiefs.org/officersbulletin.htm). All past issues of the *Bulletin* are available at (www.state.me.us/

ag/investigations/Bulletin). Recent issues have provided summaries of the latest court decisions of the Maine Supreme Judicial Court, the U.S. Supreme Court, and various federal circuit courts; articles on criminal procedure topics; announcements of classes and seminars occurring throughout the state; notice of important bills affecting the criminal justice community before the Maine legislature; and news about people and events related to the criminal justice system. Another example is the North Carolina Justice Academy Web site (www.jus.state.nc.us/NCJA), which provides training announcements, employment information, legal commentaries, support services, and a variety of other resources. Students should check with local authorities to see what types of criminal justice Web sites are available online in their states or localities. Information about useful criminal justice Web sites will be made available at www.wadsworth.com/cj/ferdico0253, the Web site supporting this book. Recommendations of useful Web sites and any other suggestions that would benefit the criminal justice community should be sent to the author at (jferdico@gwi.net).

Organizations Providing Educational, Informational, and Employment Services   Literally hundreds of organizations provide educational, informational, and employment services. Listing them is beyond the scope of this basic guide. Fortunately, this work has already been done by Dr. Cecil Greek of Florida State University. The Web site maintained by Dr. Greek is called "Criminal Justice Links" (www.criminology.fsu.edu/cjlinks) and is probably the most comprehensive compilation of links to criminal justice resources on the Internet. The student is encouraged to browse this Web site to appreciate the astounding variety of information available. Other Web sites providing links to educational, informational, and employment services are sponsored by various governmental and educational agencies. Two examples are the Villanova Legal Express (vls.law.villanova.edu/library/ express/) from the Villanova University Law Library and "More Legal and Governmental Links" (www.state.me. us/legis/lawlib/morelink.htm) from the Maine State Law and Legislative Reference Library. Exploration of the links in any of these Web sites will lead the student to information and services that best meet his or her needs. Some Web sites provide links tailored to a particular area of interest. For example, for students intending to become law enforcement officers, "Officer.Com" (www.officer. com) provides links to news, information, and services relating to that profession. Another such Web site is About.com's "Law Enforcement" page (lawenforcement. about.com/careers/lawenforcement/mbody.htm).

Part I

Framework for the Study of Criminal Procedure

Chapter 1
Individual Rights under the
United States Constitution

Chapter 2
An Overview of the
Criminal Court System

Chapter 3
Basic Underlying Concepts

Individual Rights under the United States Constitution

Outline

Objectives

■ **Understand the historical context which gave birth to the concern for the individual rights embodied in the United States Constitution.**

■ **Explain how the legislative, judicial, and executive branches of government are involved in the protection of the constitutional rights of citizens.**

■ **Understand the individual rights protected by the original Constitution of 1788, and the terms** *habeas corpus, bill of attainder, ex post facto law,* **and** *treason.*

■ **Explain the general nature and limits of the rights embodied in the Bill of Rights, especially: the First Amendment freedoms of religion, speech, press, assembly, and petition; the Fourth Amendment prohibition against unreasonable searches and seizures; the Fifth Amendment protection against double jeopardy and self-incrimination and the right to due process of law; the Sixth Amendment rights to a speedy and public trial, notice of charges, confrontation with adverse witnesses, compulsory process for favorable witnesses, and assistance of counsel; and the Eighth Amendment rights against excessive bail and fines and against cruel and unusual punishment.**

■ **Understand the concepts of due process and equal protection as guaranteed by the Fourteenth Amendment.**

The law of criminal procedure can be described as rules designed to balance the important governmental functions of maintaining law and order and protecting the rights of citizens. These functions, common to every government that is not totally authoritarian or anarchistic, are conflicting because an increased emphasis on maintaining law and order will necessarily involve greater intrusions on individual rights. Conversely, an increased emphasis on protecting individual rights will impede the efficient maintenance of law and order. For example, a policy overprotective of individual rights is likely to result in an atmosphere conducive to increased violation of and disrespect for the law. Those with a propensity toward crime will perceive that restrictions on police authority to arrest, detain, search, and question will decrease their likelihood of getting caught and that complex and technical procedural safeguards designed to ensure the fairness of court proceedings will enable them to avoid punishment if they do get caught. To the detriment of all, the ultimate result is a society in which people do not feel secure in their homes or communities and in which illegal activity abounds in government, business, and other aspects of daily life.

On the other hand, enforcement of criminal laws would be much easier if criminal suspects were presumed guilty; if they had no privilege against self-incrimination; if their bodies, vehicles, and homes could be searched at will; and if they could be detained for long periods of time without a hearing. Life in many totalitarian countries today is characterized by such governmental abuses, and the citizens of these countries live in daily fear of official intrusion into the home, the disappearance of a loved one, or tight restrictions on movement, speech, and association.

Because the United States was born as a direct response to eighteenth century British abuses against the early colonists—although those abuses were certainly not as severe as the government oppression under present-day dictatorships—our form of government has always reflected a strong commitment to the protection of individual rights from governmental abuse. This commitment was embodied in the original Constitution of 1788 and in the Bill of Rights, adopted shortly thereafter. Our discussion of individual rights begins with a brief history of events leading to the Constitution's adoption.

History

On September 17, 1787, a convention of delegates representing all the original thirteen states except Rhode Island proposed a new Constitution to the Continental Congress and the states for ratification. The rights expressed and protected by this Constitution, and by the amendments adopted four years later, were not new. Some had roots in the societies of ancient Rome and Greece, and all were nurtured during almost six hundred years of English history since the signing of the Magna Carta.

As colonists under English rule, Americans before the Revolution were familiar with the ideas that government should be limited in power and that the law was superior to any government, even the king. As the Declaration of Independence shows, the colonists rebelled because the English king and Parliament refused to allow them their historic rights as free English citizens. In September 1774, delegates from twelve colonies met in the First Continental Congress to petition England for their rights "to life, liberty, and property" and to trial by jury; "for a right peaceably to assemble, consideration of their grievances, and petition the King"; and for other rights they had been denied. The petition was ignored, and soon afterward fighting broke out at Lexington and Concord. Meanwhile, citizens in Mecklenburg County, North Carolina, declared the laws of Parliament to be null and void and instituted their own form of local government with the adoption of the Mecklenburg Resolves in May 1775. In June 1776, a resolution was introduced in the Continental Congress, and a month later, on July 4, 1776, the Thirteen United Colonies declared themselves free and independent. Their announcement was truly revolutionary. They listed a large number of abuses they had suffered, and justified their independence in these historic words: "We hold these truths to be self-evident, that all men are created equal, that they are endowed by their Creator with certain Inalienable Rights, that among these are Life, Liberty and the pursuit of Happiness."

Two years later, in July 1778, the newly independent states joined in a united government under the Articles of Confederation, which was our nation's first Constitution. It soon became clear, however, that the Articles of Confederation did not adequately provide for a working, efficient government. Among their other weaknesses, the articles gave Congress no authority to levy taxes or to regulate foreign or interstate commerce. In May 1787, a convention of delegates, meeting in Philadelphia with Congress's approval, began to consider amendments to the articles, but soon realized that a new system of government was necessary. After much debate, and several heated arguments, a compromise Constitution was negotiated.

Although we now honor the delegates' wisdom, they themselves had a different opinion of their work. Many were dissatisfied, and a few even thought a new Constitution should be written. No delegate from Rhode Island attended the convention or signed the document on September 17, 1787, when the proposed Constitution was announced. Delaware was the first state to accept this Constitution, ratifying it on December 7, 1787, by a unanimous vote. Not all states were as pleased, and in some states the vote was extremely close. For a while it was not certain that a sufficient number of states would ratify. A major argument against ratification was the absence of a Bill of Rights. Only after it became generally agreed that the first order of business of the new government would be to propose amendments for a Bill of Rights was acceptance of the Constitution obtained by a sufficient number of states. On June 21, 1788, New Hampshire became the ninth state to sign on, and ratification of the new Constitution was completed. By the end of July 1788, the important states of Virginia and New York had also ratified the Constitution.

On September 25, 1789, Congress proposed the first ten amendments to the new Constitution—the Bill of Rights. With the proposal of these guarantees, North Carolina and Rhode Island, the last of the thirteen original colonies, ratified the Constitution. Ratification of the Bill of Rights was completed on December 15, 1791. Since that date, the Bill of Rights has served as our nation's testimony to its belief in the basic and inalienable rights of the people and in limitations on the power of government. Together with provisions of the original Constitution, it protects that great body of liberties that belongs to every citizen.

For ease of discussion, the remainder of this chapter treats the original Constitution separately from the Bill of Rights and later amendments.

lcweb2.loc.gov/const/mdbquery.html
www.yale.edu/lawweb/avalon/artconf.htm#art2
These document collections include the Articles of Confederation and other important early documents in U.S. history
supreme.findlaw.com/documents/consthist.html
A short history of the United States Constitution

For new and updated weblinks, go to www.wadsworth.com/cj/ferdico0253

The Original Constitution

The Constitution of 1789 has served as the fundamental instrument of our government for almost all of our country's history as an independent nation. Drawn at a time when there were only thirteen states, dotted with small towns, small farms, and small industry, the Constitution has provided a durable and viable instrument of government

library.thinkquest.org/11572/cc/
cases/marbury.html
A brief essay on the case of *Marbury v. Madison*
www.supremecourtus.gov/
about/constitutional.pdf
An article that briefly explains
the concept of judicial review

Marbury v. Madison
laws.findlaw.com/us/5/137.html

despite enormous changes in technology and in the political, social, and economic environments.

The Constitution was originally designed to serve a weak country on the Atlantic seaboard; it now serves a continental nation of fifty states, a federal district, and numerous territorial possessions with over 275 million people producing goods and services at a rate thousands of times faster than in 1789. Nevertheless, the framework for democratic government set out in the Constitution has remained workable and progressive. Similarly, the rights of individuals listed in the Constitution and its twenty-seven amendments have retained an extraordinary vitality despite being tested in situations that could not have been envisioned by the Founding Fathers. Freedom of the press, for example, was originally understood only in the context of the small, primitive printing presses of the late eighteenth century. Yet today that freedom applies not only to modern presses but also to radio, television, motion pictures, and computers—all products of the twentieth century.

The purpose of this chapter is to explain how these basic individual rights have been applied and to develop sensitivity to these rights as a prelude to the study of criminal procedure, under which these rights confront the countervailing demands of society for enforcement of the law and efficient detection and prevention of crime.

Each branch of the government—legislative, judicial, and executive—is charged by the Constitution with the protection of individual liberties. Within this framework, the judicial branch has assumed perhaps the largest role. Chief Justice John Marshall, speaking for the Supreme Court in the early case of *Marbury v. Madison*, 5 U.S. (1 Cranch) 137, 2 L.Ed. 60 (1803), declared that it was the duty of the judiciary to say what the law is, and that this duty included expounding and interpreting the law. Marshall stated that the law contained in the Constitution was paramount and that other laws that were repugnant to its provisions must fall. It was the province of the courts, he concluded, to decide when other laws were in violation of the basic law of the Constitution and, where this was found to occur, to declare those laws null and void, and thus unconstitutional. This is the doctrine known as **judicial review,** which became the basis for the application of constitutional guarantees by courts in cases brought before them.

> Judicial review is the exercise by courts of their responsibility to determine whether acts of the other two branches are illegal and void because those acts violate the constitution. The doctrine authorizes courts to determine whether a law is constitutional, not whether it is necessary or useful. In other words, judicial review is the power to say what the constitution means and not whether such a law reflects a wise policy. Adherence to the doctrine of judicial review is essential to achieving balance in our government. . . . Judicial review, coupled with the specified constitutional provisions which keep the judicial branch separate and independent of the other branches of government and with those articles of the constitution that protect the impartiality of the judiciary from public and political pressure, enables the courts to ensure that the constitutional rights of each citizen will not be encroached upon by either the legislative or the executive branch of the government. *State v. LaFrance*, 471 A.2d 340, 343–44 (N.H. 1983).

Congress has played an important role in the protection of constitutional rights by enacting legislation designed to guarantee and apply those rights in specific contexts. Laws that guarantee the rights of Native Americans, afford due process to military service personnel, and give effective right to counsel to poor defendants are examples of this legislative role.

Finally, the executive branch, which is charged with implementing the laws Congress enacts, contributes to the protection of individual rights by devising its own regulations and procedures for administering the law without intruding on constitutional guarantees.

To properly understand the scope of constitutional rights, one must realize that our government is a federal republic, which means that an American lives under two governments: the federal government and the government of the state in which that person lives. The authority of the federal government is limited by the Constitution to the powers specified in the Constitution; all remaining governmental power is reserved to the states. The federal government is authorized, for example, to settle disputes among states, conduct relations with foreign governments, and act in certain matters of common national concern. The states hold the remainder of governmental power, to be exercised within their respective boundaries.

www.aclu.org/library/pbp9.html
Brief history of the Bill of Rights by the American Civil Liberties Union

The Bill of Rights

Only a few individual rights were specified in the Constitution when it was adopted in 1788. Indeed, the principal design of the original Constitution was not to specify individual rights, but to state the division of power between the new central federal government and the states. Shortly after its adoption, however, ten amendments—called the Bill of Rights—were added to the Constitution to guarantee basic individual liberties. These liberties include freedom of speech, freedom of the press, freedom of religion, and freedom to assemble and petition the government.

The guarantees of the Bill of Rights originally applied only to acts of the federal government and did not prevent state and local governments from taking action that might threaten civil liberty. As a practical matter, states had their own constitutions, some containing their own bills of rights that guaranteed the same or similar rights as those guaranteed by the Bill of Rights against federal intrusion. These rights, however, were not guaranteed by all the states; if they did exist, they were subject to varying interpretations. In short, citizens were protected only to the extent that the states themselves recognized their basic rights.

In 1868, the Fourteenth Amendment was added to the Constitution. In part, that amendment provides that no state shall "deprive any person of life, liberty, or property without due process of law." Not until 1925, in the case of *Gitlow v. New York*, 268 U.S. 652, 45 S.Ct. 625, 69 L.Ed. 1138, did the Supreme Court interpret the phrase "due process of law" to mean, in effect, "without abridgement of certain of the rights guaranteed by the Bill of Rights." Since that decision, the Supreme Court has ruled that a denial by a state of certain rights contained in the Bill of Rights represents a denial of due process of law. The members of the Court, however, have long argued about which of and to what extent the provisions of the Bill of Rights are applicable to the states. Essentially three major due process positions, with many variations, have evolved over the years:

Gitlow v. New York
laws.findlaw.com/us/268/652.html

1. The "total incorporation" approach held that the due process clause of the Fourteenth Amendment made the entire federal Bill of Rights applicable to the states. This view never commanded a majority of the court and was rejected repeatedly in *Twining v. New Jersey*, 211 U.S. 78, 29 S.Ct. 14, 53 L.Ed. 97 (1908); *Palko v. Connecticut*, 302 U.S. 319, 58 S.Ct. 149, 82 L.Ed. 288 (1937); and *Adamson v. California*, 332 U.S. 46, 67 S.Ct. 1672,

Twining v. New Jersey
laws.findlaw.com/us/211/78.html

Palko v. Connecticut
laws.findlaw.com/us/302/319.html

Adamson v. California
laws.findlaw.com/us/332/46.html

91 L.Ed. 1903 (1947). In *Twining,* the Court noted, however, that "it is possible that some of the personal rights safeguarded by the first eight Amendments against National action may also be safeguarded against state action, because a denial of them would be a denial of due process of law. . . . If this is so, it is not because those rights are enumerated in the first eight amendments, but because they are of such a nature that they are included in the conception of due process of law." 211 U.S. at 99, 29 S.Ct. at 19–20, 53 L.Ed. at 106.

2. The possibility mentioned in the *Twining* quote became known as the "fundamental rights" or "ordered liberty" approach to due process, which was adopted by the Court in *Palko, Adamson,* and other cases and prevailed until the early 1960s. Under this approach, the Court found no necessary relationship between the due process clause of the Fourteenth Amendment and the Bill of Rights. The due process clause was said to have an "independent potency" which existed apart from the Bill of Rights. Due process was viewed as prohibiting state action that violated those rights that are "implicit in the concept of ordered liberty," that are "so rooted in the traditions and conscience of our people as to be ranked fundamental," that represent "fundamental fairness essential to the very concept of justice," or some similar phrase suggesting fundamental rights. Under the fundamental rights–ordered liberty approach, the Court looked to the "totality of the circumstances" of the particular case to determine what right, or what aspect or phase of a right, is "fundamental."

3. The "selective incorporation" approach combines aspects of the other two approaches and has prevailed since the early 1960s. This approach accepts the basic tenet of the fundamental rights–ordered liberty approach (that Fourteenth Amendment due process protects only rights that are "fundamental"). Also, under selective incorporation, every right in the Bill of Rights was not necessarily considered fundamental, and some rights outside the Bill of Rights might be considered fundamental. But the selective incorporation approach rejected the examination of the "totality of the circumstances" to determine whether particular aspects or phases of rights in the Bill of Rights were or were not fundamental. Instead, if a right was determined to be fundamental, it was incorporated into the Fourteenth Amendment through the due process clause, and deemed applicable to the states to the same extent as to the federal government. As the Court said in *Duncan v. Louisiana,* "Because we believe that trial by jury in criminal cases is fundamental to the American scheme of justice, we hold that the Fourteenth Amendment guarantees a right of jury trial in all criminal cases which—*were they to be tried in a federal court*—would come within the Sixth Amendment's guarantee" (emphasis added). 391 U.S. 145, 149, 88 S.Ct. 1444, 1447, 20 L.Ed.2d 491, 496 (1968). The reference in this quotation to the American scheme of justice is not without significance, as is pointed out in footnote 14 of the *Duncan* opinion:

> In one sense recent cases applying provisions of the first eight amendments to the States represent a new approach to the "incorporation" debate. Earlier the Court can be seen as having asked, when inquiring into whether some particular procedural safeguard was required of a State, if a civilized system could be imagined that would not accord the particular protection. . . . The recent cases, on the other hand, have proceeded upon the valid assumption that state criminal processes are not imaginary and theoretical schemes but actual systems bearing virtually every characteristic of the common-law system that has been developing contemporaneously in England and in this country. The question thus is whether given this kind of system a particular procedure is fundamental—whether, that is, a procedure is necessary to an Anglo-American regime of ordered liberty. . . . Of immediate relevance for this case are the Court's holdings that the States

Duncan v. Louisiana
laws.findlaw.com/us/391/
145.html

must comply with certain provisions of the Sixth Amendment, specifically that the States may not refuse a speedy trial, confrontation of witnesses, and the assistance, at state expense if necessary, of counsel. . . . Of each of these determinations that a constitutional provision originally written to bind the Federal Government should bind the States as well it might be said that the limitation in question is not necessarily fundamental to fairness in every criminal system that might be imagined but is fundamental in the context of the criminal processes maintained by the American States.

At present, the following guarantees of the Bill of Rights have been applied to the states under the terms of the Fourteenth Amendment: the First, Fourth, and Sixth Amendments; the self-incrimination, double jeopardy, and just compensation clauses of the Fifth Amendment; and the guarantee against cruel and unusual punishment of the Eighth Amendment. The only guarantees specifically concerning criminal procedure that have *not* been applied to the states are the right to indictment by grand jury in the Fifth Amendment and the prohibition against excessive bail or fines in the Eighth Amendment.

To place these rights in a broader perspective, one should realize that they make up only the core of what are considered to be **civil rights**—the privileges and freedoms that are accorded all Americans by virtue of their citizenship. Many other civil rights are not specifically mentioned in the Constitution but nonetheless have been recognized by the courts, have often been guaranteed by statute, and are embedded in our democratic traditions. The right to buy, sell, own, and bequeath property; the right to enter into contracts; the right to marry and have children; the right to live and work where one desires; and the right to participate in the political, social, and cultural processes of the society in which one lives are a few of the rights that must be considered as fundamental to a democratic society as those specified by the Constitution.

Despite the premise that the rights of American citizenship are incontrovertible, the rights guaranteed by the Constitution or otherwise are not absolute rights in the sense that they entitle citizens to act in any way they please. Rather, to be protected by the law, people must exercise their rights in such a way that the rights of others are not denied. Thus, as Justice Oliver Wendell Holmes pointed out, "Protection of free speech would not protect a man falsely shouting 'Fire' in a theater and causing a panic." Nor does freedom of speech and press sanction the publication of libel and obscenity. Similarly, the rights of free speech and free assembly do not permit one to engage knowingly in conspiracies to overthrow by force the government of the United States. Thus, civil liberties carry with them an obligation on the part of all Americans to exercise their rights within a framework of law and mutual respect for the rights of others.

This obligation implies not only a restraint on the part of those exercising these rights but a tolerance on the part of those who are affected by that exercise. Thus, cit- izens may on occasion be subjected to annoying political tirades, disagreeable entertainment, or noisy protest demonstrations. They may feel aggravated when a defendant refuses to testify or when they see a seemingly guilty defendant go free because certain evidence was not admissible in court. But these frustrations or inconveniences are a small price to pay for the freedom American citizens enjoy. If the rights of one are suppressed, it is, in the final analysis, the freedom of all that is jeopardized. Ultimately, a free society is a dynamic society, in which thoughts and ideas are forever challenging and being challenged. In such a society, there is a risk that the wrong voice will be listened to or the wrong plan followed. But a free society is one that learns by its mistakes and can freely pursue the happiness of its citizens.

caselaw.findlaw.com/data/
constitution/article01/
46.html#1
Comprehensive discussion (with
annotations) of Article I, Section
9, Clause 2
caselaw.findlaw.com/data/
constitution/article01/
47.html#2
caselaw.findlaw.com/data/
constitution/article01/
53.html#6
Comprehensive discussion (with
annotations) of the bill of attainder provisions of Article I, Section 9, Clause 3 and Article I,
Section 10, Clause 1
caselaw.findlaw.com/data/
constitution/article01/
47.html#3
caselaw.findlaw.com/data/
constitution/article01/
53.html#7
Comprehensive discussion (with
annotations) of the *ex post facto*
provisions of Article I, Section 9,
Clause 3 and Article I, Section
10, Clause 1

Individual Rights in the Original Constitution

■ Article I, Section 9, Clause 2

The Privilege of the Writ of Habeas Corpus shall not be suspended, unless when in Cases of Rebellion or Invasion the public Safety may require it.

This guarantee enables a person whose freedom has been restrained in some way to pe-tition a federal court for a writ of **habeas corpus** as a means of testing whether the re-straint was imposed in violation of the Constitution or laws of the United States. Petitioning for a writ of *habeas corpus* is the procedure by which a federal court is en-listed to inquire into alleged illegal detention and requested to issue an order directing authorities to release the petitioner. This right under the Constitution applies to all cases in which a person is confined by governmental authority. It can be suspended only when the president, pursuant to congressional authorization, declares that a na-tional emergency requires its suspension and probably only when the courts are phys-ically unable to function because of war, invasion, or rebellion. *Habeas corpus* is an important safeguard to prevent unlawful imprisonment and is discussed in further de-tail in Chapter 2.

■ Article I, Section 9, Clause 3

No Bill of Attainder . . . shall be passed [by the federal government].

■ Article I, Section 10, Clause 1

No State shall . . . pass any Bill of Attainder. . . .

Historically, a **bill of attainder** is a special act of a legislature that declares that a per-son or group of persons has committed a crime and that imposes punishment without a trial by court. Under our system of separation of powers, only courts may try a per-son for a crime or impose punishment for violation of the law. Section 9 restrains Con-gress from passing bills of attainder, and Section 10 restrains the states.

■ Article I, Section 9, Clause 3

No . . . ex post facto Law shall be passed [by the federal government].

■ Article I, Section 10, Clause 1

No state shall . . . pass any . . . ex post facto Law. . . .

Beazell v. Ohio
laws.findlaw.com/us/269/
167.html

These two clauses prohibit the states and the federal government from enacting any *ex post facto* law, literally a law passed "after the fact." "[A]ny statute which punishes as a crime an act previously committed, which was innocent when done; which makes more burdensome the punishment for a crime, after its commission, or which deprives one charged with crime of any defense available according to law at the time when the act was committed, is prohibited as *ex post facto.*" *Beazell v. Ohio,* 269 U.S. 167, 169–70, 46 S.Ct. 68, 68–69, 70 L.Ed. 216, 217 (1925). However, laws that retroactively deter-mine how a person is to be tried for a crime may be changed so long as the substantial rights of the accused are not curtailed. Laws are not *ex post facto* if they make punish-ment less severe than it was when the crime was committed. A common example in contemporary times of statutory changes that are not prohibited as *ex post facto* under this provision of the Constitution is the elimination of statutes of limitations—the time period in which the state must commence a criminal action. There is an increasing tendency for state legislatures to remove such limitations on sexual crimes that involve young victims.

■ **Article III, Sections 1 and 2**

(Article III, Sections 1 and 2, of the Constitution deal with the judicial system of the United States and are too long to be reproduced here.)

Article III, Section 1, of the Constitution outlines the structure and power of our federal court system and establishes a federal judiciary that helps maintain the rights of American citizens. Article III, Section 2, also contains a guarantee that the trial of all federal crimes, except that of impeachment, shall be by jury. The Supreme Court has interpreted this guarantee as containing exceptions for "trials of petty offenses," cases rightfully tried before a court martial or other military tribunal, and some cases in which the defendant has voluntarily relinquished the right to a jury. The right to a jury trial is discussed further in Chapter 2.

Section 2 also requires that a federal criminal trial be held in a federal court sitting in the state where the crime was committed. Thus, a person is protected against being tried without his or her consent in some part of the United States far distant from the place where the alleged violation of federal laws occurred.

■ **Article III, Section 3**

Treason against the United States, shall consist only in levying War against them, or in adhering to their Enemies, giving them Aid and Comfort. No Person shall be convicted of Treason unless on the Testimony of two Witnesses to the same overt Act, or on Confession in open Court.

The Congress shall have power to declare the Punishment of Treason, but no Attainder of Treason shall work Corruption of Blood, or Forfeiture except during the Life of the Person attainted.

Treason is the only crime defined by the Constitution. The precise description of this offense reflects awareness by our forebears of the danger that unpopular views might be branded as traitorous. Recent experience in other countries with politically based prosecutions for conduct loosely labeled treason confirms the wisdom of the Constitution's authors in expressly stating what constitutes this crime and how it shall be proved.

■ **Article VI, Clause 3**

[N]o religious Test shall ever be required as a Qualification to any Office or public Trust under the United States.

Together with the First Amendment, this guarantee expresses the principle that church and government are to remain separate and that religious beliefs are no indication of patriotism, ability, or the right to serve this country. Thus, a citizen need not fear that religious affiliations or convictions may legally bar him or her from holding office in the United States.

Individual Rights in the Bill of Rights

■ **Amendment I**

Congress shall make no law respecting an establishment of religion, or prohibiting the free exercise thereof; or abridging the freedom of speech, or of the press; or the right

caselaw.findlaw.com/data/constitution/article03/01.html#1

caselaw.findlaw.com/data/constitution/article03/09.html#1

Comprehensive discussion (with annotations) of Article III, Sections 1 and 2

www.wcl.american.edu/pub/journals/lawrev/48/fountaine.pdf

Article, "Article III and the Adequate and Independent State Grounds Doctrine" by Cynthia L. Fountaine

caselaw.findlaw.com/data/constitution/article03/24.html#1

Comprehensive discussion (with annotations) of Article III, Section 3

caselaw.findlaw.com/data/constitution/article06/04.html#1

Comprehensive discussion (with annotations) of Article VI, Clause 3

www.cardozo.yu.edu/cardlrev/
v21n4/McConnell.PDF
Article, "Why is Religious Liberty
the 'First Freedom'?" by Michael
W. McConnell

of the people peaceably to assemble, and to petition the Government for a redress of grievances.

Freedom of Religion

Two express guarantees are given to the individual citizen with respect to religious freedom. First, neither Congress nor a state legislature (by virtue of the Fourteenth Amendment) may "make any law respecting an establishment of religion." This means that no law may be passed that establishes an official church that all Americans must accept and support, or to whose tenets all must subscribe, or that favors one church over another. Second, no law is constitutional if it "prohibits the free exercise" of religion. Citizens are guaranteed the freedom to worship in any way they choose.

The Supreme Court described the establishment clause as providing a "wall of separation between church and state." *Everson v. Board of Education,* 330 U.S. 1, 16, 67 S.Ct. 504, 512, 91 L.Ed 711, 723 (1947):

Everson v. Board of Education
laws.findlaw.com/us/330/1.html

> The "establishment of religion" clause of the First Amendment means at least this: Neither a state nor the Federal Government can set up a church. Neither can pass laws that aid one religion, aid all religions, or prefer one religion to another. Neither can force nor influence a person to go to or remain away from church against his will or force him to profess a belief or disbelief in any religion. No person can be punished for entertaining or professing religious beliefs or disbeliefs, for church attendance or non-attendance. No tax in any amount, large or small, can be levied to support any religious activities or institutions, whatever they may be called, or whatever form they may adopt to teach or practice religion. Neither a state nor the Federal Government can, openly or secretly, participate in the affairs of any religious organizations or groups and vice versa. 330 U.S. at 15–16, 67 S.Ct. at 511–12, 91 L.Ed. at 723.

Lemon v. Kurtzman
laws.findlaw.com/us/403/
602.html

In *Lemon v. Kurtzman,* 403 U.S. 602, 612–13, 91 S.Ct. 2105, 2111, 29 L.Ed.2d 745, 755 (1971), the Court sought to refine these principles by focusing on three tests for determining whether a statute or government practice is permissible under the establishment clause: (1) it must have a secular purpose, (2) its principal or primary purpose must be one that neither advances nor inhibits religion, and (3) it must not foster an excessive government entanglement with religion. Thus, Court decisions have held that a state may not require prayer in the public schools, nor may a state supplement or reimburse parochial schools for teachers' salaries and textbooks. To permit or authorize such activities would constitute governmental support of the religious organization affected. On the other hand, the Court held that it is permissible for public schools to release students, at the students' own request, from an hour of class work so that those students may attend their own churches for religious instruction; or for a state to provide free bus transportation to children attending church or parochial schools if transportation is also furnished to children in the public schools. Furthermore, the Court upheld the tax-exempt status of church property used exclusively for worship purposes, and it has sanctioned federal aid programs for new construction at church-related universities. It also held that the establishment clause does not prevent a state from designating Sunday as a day of rest.

Freedom to worship, as interpreted by the Supreme Court, must not conflict with otherwise valid government enactments. For example, a man may not have two wives and escape conviction for bigamy by attributing his conduct to his religious beliefs. Nor could a person commit an indecent act or engage in immoral conduct and then validate the actions on grounds of religious freedom. The Supreme Court also has declared that it is an unconstitutional invasion of religious freedom to exclude from public schools children who, because of their religious beliefs, refuse to salute the American flag. The Court further ruled that requiring Amish children to attend public schools beyond the eighth grade was an impairment of the free exercise clause, since such attendance prevented education in the traditional Amish religious framework.

Freedom of Speech

As a general rule, citizens may freely speak out on any subject they choose. In addition, they may join organizations, wear buttons, buy books, carry signs that represent their views, and take their cases to court when they feel they have been wronged.

The Supreme Court has ruled, however, that the protections afforded by the First Amendment do not extend to all forms of expression. Highly inflammatory remarks made to a crowd that advocate violence and clearly threaten the peace and safety of the community, or present a "clear and present danger" to the continued existence of the government, are not protected. Obscenity, too, has been judged unprotected by the First Amendment, although the Court has held that the mere possession of obscene materials in the home may not be punished.

Courts have also recognized that "symbolic speech," which involves more tangible forms of expression, falls within the protection of the First Amendment. Wearing buttons or clothing with political slogans, displaying a sign or a flag, or burning a flag as a mode of expression are examples of symbolic speech. The wearing of black armbands by secondary school students to protest the Vietnam War was ruled to be activity protected by the First Amendment, so long as the activity was not disruptive or injurious to the rights of other students. Displaying a black flag to protest organized government is also protected. On the other hand, burning draft cards to protest the Vietnam War was held not to be protected, since it could be shown to disrupt or undermine the operation of the Selective Service System. Courts have also been reluctant to overturn public schools' grooming and dress codes when the schools could show that the codes were designed to prevent disruption or distraction of classes.

Finally, the courts have frequently condemned the type of censorship imposed by requiring official approval or a license in advance for speaking. Nevertheless, although a citizen is free to make speeches on public streets, he or she may be prevented from doing so when using a loud and raucous amplifier in a hospital zone or when the location chosen is such that the address is likely to interfere with traffic movement.

Freedom of the Press

Freedom of the press is a further guarantee of the right to express oneself, in this case by writing or publishing one's views on a particular subject. The Founding Fathers recognized the importance of a free interplay of ideas in a democratic society and sought to guarantee the right of all citizens to speak or publish their views, even if those views were contrary to those of the government or society as a whole. Accordingly, the First Amendment generally forbids censorship or other restraints on speech or the printed word. Thus, a school board's dismissal of a teacher who had protested school board activities in a letter to the editor of the local newspaper was held to infringe on the teacher's First Amendment rights in the absence of evidence that the teacher's activity caused significant disruption or interference with the delivery of educational services. And a state court order, issued in anticipation of the trial of an accused mass

www.aclu.org/issues/cyber/
burning.html#executivesum
Article, "Fahrenheit 451.2: Is
Cyberspace Burning?"
www.aclu.org/library/
pbp10.html
Paper on freedom of expression
presented by the American Civil
Liberties Union
www.law.upenn.edu/conlaw/
issues/vol1/num1/strossen.htm
Article, "Freedom for Speech" by
Nadine Strossen
vjolt.student.virginia.edu/
graphics/vol2/home_art3.html
Article, "Protecting the Core
Values of the First Amendment
in an Age of New Technologies:
Scientific Expression vs. National
Security" by E. John Park
vjolt.student.virginia.edu/
graphics/vol1/home_art7.html
Article, "The Impact of Cyberspace on the First Amendment"
by Mark S. Kende
vjolt.student.virginia.edu/
graphics/vol2/home_art2.html
Article, "The Use of Encrypted,
Coded and Secret Communications is an 'Ancient Liberty' Protected by the U.S. Constitution"
by John A. Fraser

caselaw.findlaw.com/data/
constitution/amendment01/
Comprehensive discussion (with
annotations) of the First
Amendment

murderer, restraining the press and broadcast media from reporting any confessions or incriminating statements made by the defendant or from reporting other facts "strongly implicative" of the defendant was similarly struck down.

As with speech, however, freedom to write or publish is not an absolute right of expression. The sale of obscene materials is not protected, nor are printed materials that are libelous. The Supreme Court has ruled, however, that public figures cannot sue for defamation unless the alleged libelous remarks were printed with knowledge of their falsity or with a reckless disregard for the truth.

The Court has also ruled that the publication of a secret study into the origins of the United States' involvement in the Vietnam War could not be prevented because of the First Amendment guarantee. The Court indicated, however, that freedom of the press might not extend to similar matters that could be shown to have a more direct and substantial bearing on national security.

Finally, broadcasting, including radio, television, and motion pictures, receives the protections of the free press guarantee, but is also subject to its limitations. The burgeoning development of computers and the Internet are providing unique First Amendment challenges to the courts, and will continue to do so.

The Right to Assembly and Petition

American citizens, whether they are meeting for political activity, religious services, or other purposes, have the right to assemble peaceably. Public authorities cannot impose unreasonable restrictions on such assemblies, but they can impose limitations reasonably designed to prevent fire, health hazard, or traffic obstruction. The Supreme Court emphasized that freedom of assembly is just as fundamental as the freedoms of speech and press. Thus, although no law may legitimately prohibit demonstrations, laws or other governmental actions may legitimately restrict demonstrations to certain areas or prohibit the obstruction and occupation of public buildings.

Picketing is also protected under the free speech guarantee. It may, however, be reasonably regulated to prevent pickets from obstructing movement onto and from the property involved. Picketing on private property has been upheld, but only where the property is open to the public and the picketing relates to the business being conducted on the property. Thus, the distribution of antiwar handbills on the premises of a privately owned shopping center has been held to be unprotected. Yet, antiabortion pickets or demonstrations outside health care facilities that provide abortion services have been held to be protected under the free speech guarantee.

The right of petition is designed to enable citizens to communicate with their government without obstruction. When citizens exercise their First Amendment freedom to write or speak to their senators or members of Congress, they partake of "the healthy essence of the democratic process."

■ Amendment II
A well regulated Militia, being necessary to the security of a free State, the right of the people to keep and bear Arms, shall not be infringed.

caselaw.findlaw.com/data/
constitution/amendment02/
Comprehensive discussion (with
annotations) of the Second
Amendment

The Second Amendment's "right of the people to keep and bear arms" has engendered some of the most spirited public debate since the adoption of the Bill of Rights. Two poles of interpretation have emerged. One theory holds that the clause was primarily meant to convey individual rights, like other parts of the Bill of Rights. A contrasting theory contends that the Second Amendment was spelling out the right of the states, independent of a central federal government, to establish and maintain state militias.

During the era of the Founding Fathers, it was deemed of paramount importance for citizens to have the right to protect themselves against both disorder in the community and attack from foreign enemies. Some believe that this right to bear arms has become much less important in recent decades because of the ongoing presence of well-trained military and police forces, and that people no longer need to have their own weapons available. Along these lines, the Supreme Court has held that the state and federal governments may pass laws prohibiting the carrying of concealed weapons, requiring the registration of firearms, and limiting the sale of firearms for other than military uses.

In spite of the ongoing controversy, Congress continues to enact statutes that directly affect a citizen's legal ability to purchase, receive, possess, or transport firearms. Indeed, since 1939 when the U.S. Supreme Court in *United States v. Miller*, 307 U.S. 174, 59 S.Ct. 816, 83 L.Ed. 1206, upheld a federal statute barring the possession of sawed-off shotguns, a host of other statutes affecting the private ownership of firearms have been enacted. Many of these statutes have been deemed by the U.S. Supreme Court not to be in violation of the Second Amendment. Those subscribing to the theory that the Second Amendment "right to bear arms" clause was meant to be an expression of the rights of the states to maintain a militia often point to the *Miller* case. In *Miller*, the Court declared, "[W]e cannot say that the Second Amendment guarantees the right to keep and bear such an instrument [sawed-off shotgun]. Certainly it is not within judicial notice that this weapon is any part of the ordinary military equipment or that its use could contribute to the common defense." 307 U.S. at 178, 59 S.Ct. at 818, 83 L.Ed. at 1209. More recently, Congress has enacted legislation that bars possession of a firearm by any citizen previously convicted of a misdemeanor crime of domestic violence, supplementing an existing law stating that felons could not possess firearms. And the Supreme Court, primarily in *per curiam* decisions, has refused to invalidate either the prohibition itself or the retroactive effect of these laws, under which persons convicted many years ago of "qualifying" misdemeanors cannot today possess firearms because of the intervening federal prohibition.

What does seem clearly defined with respect to the "right to bear arms" clause of the Second Amendment, however, is that the restraint applies only to the federal government, and not to the states or to private interests. As far back as 1886, in *Presser v. Illinois*, 116 U.S. 252, 265, 6 S.Ct. 580, 584, 29 L.Ed. 615, 619, the Supreme Court said that "a conclusive answer to the contention that this amendment prohibits the legislation in question lies in the fact that the amendment is a limitation only upon the power of Congress and the National Government, and not upon that of the state." As a result of this and other similar judicial determinations, the states have essentially been left unfettered to establish their own schemes of regulations or state constitutional provisions respecting the purchase, possession, or transportation of firearms.

Just exactly what that the Founding Fathers intended to protect by the Second Amendment will continue to cause public debate and consume legal and political resources until the U.S. Supreme Court offers a definitive resolution.

■ **Amendment III**

No Soldier shall, in time of peace be quartered in any house, without the consent of the Owner, nor in time of war, but in a manner to be prescribed by law.

www.constitution.org/mil/
rkba1982.htm
"The Right to Keep and Bear Arms: Report of the Subcommittee on the Constitution of the U.S. Senate, Ninety-Seventh Congress, Second Session."
www.uchastings.edu/clq/
maltradf.html
Article, "The Right of the People to Keep and Bear Arms: The Common Law Tradition" by Joyce Lee Malcolm

United States v. Miller
laws.findlaw.com/us/307/
174.html

keepandbeararms.com/
newsarchives/xcnewsplus.asp?
cmd=view&articleid=708
(Article, "A Brief Overview of the Right to Keep and Bear Arms" by Charles Mosteller)
A brief explanation, with legal references, as to why the Second Amendment is an individual right

Presser v. Illinois
laws.findlaw.com/us/116/
252.html

www.2ndlawlib.org/journals/
dowdesp.html#fnb
Article, "The Right to Keep and Bear Arms: A Right to Self-Defense against Criminals and Despots" by Robert Dowlut
www.law.ua.edu/lawreview/
Article, "The Revolutionary Second Amendment" by Brent McIntosh. (Click on "Recent Issues" and then click on "Volume 51, No. 2 (Winter 2000)"

caselaw.findlaw.com/data/
constitution/amendment03/
Comprehensive discussion (with
annotations) of the Third
Amendment
caselaw.findlaw.com/data/
constitution/amendment04/
Comprehensive discussion (with
annotations) of the Fourth
Amendment

Before the Revolution, American colonists had, against their will, frequently been required to provide lodging and food for British soldiers. The Third Amendment prohibited the continuation of this onerous practice.

■ Amendment IV

The right of the people to be secure in their persons, houses, papers, and effects, against unreasonable searches and seizures, shall not be violated, and no Warrants shall issue, but upon probable cause, supported by Oath or affirmation and particularly describing the place to be searched, and the persons or things to be seized.

In some countries, even today, police officers may invade a citizen's home, seize the citizen's property, or arrest the citizen whenever they see fit. In the United States, the Fourth Amendment protects the person and his or her property from *unreasonable* search and seizure by governmental officers. In general, although there are exceptions to the rule, a police officer may not search the home of a private citizen, seize any of the citizen's property, or arrest the citizen without first obtaining a court order, called a **warrant.** Before the warrant will be issued, the police officer must convince a neutral and detached magistrate that there is **probable cause**—defined by the U.S. Supreme Court as a *fair probability*—either that the person involved has committed a crime or that evidence of a crime is in a particularly described place.

Because most of this book deals with the topics of arrest, search and seizure, and probable cause, further discussion of the Fourth Amendment appears in the chapters dealing with those topics.

■ Amendment V

No person shall be held to answer for a capital, or otherwise infamous crime, unless on a presentment or indictment of a Grand Jury, except in cases arising in the land or naval forces, or in the Militia, when in actual service in time of War or public danger; nor shall any person be subject for the same offense to be twice put in jeopardy of life or limb; nor shall be compelled in any criminal case to be a witness against himself, nor be deprived of life, liberty, or property, without due process of law; nor shall private property be taken for public use, without just compensation.

Indictment by Grand Jury

The Fifth Amendment requires that before a person is tried in *federal* court for an infamous crime, he or she must first be indicted by a grand jury. The grand jury's duty is to make sure that there is probable cause to believe that the accused person is guilty. This provision prevents a person from being subjected to a trial when there is not enough proof that he or she has committed a crime.

Generally, an infamous crime is a **felony** (a crime for which a sentence of more than one year's imprisonment can be imposed) or a lesser offense that is punishable by confinement in a penitentiary or at hard labor. An indictment is not required for a trial by court martial or by other military tribunal. Furthermore, the constitutional requirement of grand jury indictment does not apply to trials in state courts. *Hurtado v. California,* 110 U.S. 516, 4 S.Ct. 111, 28 L.Ed. 232 (1884). However, when states do use grand juries in their criminal proceedings, the Supreme Court has ruled that the grand juries must be free of racial bias. The grand jury is discussed in further detail in Chapter 2.

Hurtado v. California
laws.findlaw.com/us/110/
516.html

Freedom from Double Jeopardy

The clause "nor shall any person be subject for the same offense to be twice put in jeopardy of life or limb" is often referred to as the **double jeopardy** clause. The U.S. Supreme Court has recognized three separate guarantees embodied in the double jeopardy clause: "It protects against a second prosecution for the same offense after acquittal, against a second prosecution for the same offense after conviction, and against multiple punishments for the same offense." *Justices of Boston Municipal Court v. Lydon,* 466 U.S. 294, 306–07, 104 S.Ct. 1805, 1812, 80 L.Ed.2d 311, 323 (1984). Note that the double jeopardy clause "protects only against the imposition of multiple criminal punishments for the same offense." *Hudson v. United States,* 522 U.S. 93, 99, 118 S.Ct. 488, 493, 139 L.Ed.2d 450, 458 (1997). It does not protect against criminal prosecution of a person after the person has been penalized in a civil proceeding. The double jeopardy protections were explained in *Ohio v. Johnson,* 467 U.S. 493, 498–99, 104 S.Ct. 2536, 2540–41, 81 L.Ed.2d 425, 433 (1984):

> [T]he bar to retrial following acquittal or conviction ensures that the State does not make repeated attempts to convict an individual, thereby exposing him to continued embarrassment, anxiety, and expense, while increasing the risk of an erroneous conviction or an impermissibly enhanced sentence. . . . [P]rotection against cumulative punishments is designed to ensure that the sentencing discretion of courts is confined to the limits established by the legislature.

Jeopardy attaches in a jury trial when the jury is impaneled and sworn and in a nonjury trial when the judge begins to hear evidence. Jeopardy attaches to all criminal proceedings, whether felony or misdemeanor, and to juvenile adjudicatory proceedings, even though they are civil in nature.

There are many exceptions to these general rules protecting a person from double jeopardy. Some of the important exceptions are mentioned here. First, a second trial for the same offense may occur when the first trial results in a mistrial (for example, deadlocked jury), if there is a "manifest necessity" for the mistrial declaration, or "the ends of public justice would otherwise be defeated." *Richardson v. United States,* 468 U.S. 317, 324, 104 S.Ct. 3081, 3085, 82 L.Ed.2d 242, 250 (1984). Generally, the double jeopardy clause does not bar reprosecution of a defendant whose conviction is overturned on appeal.

> While different theories have been advanced to support the permissibility of retrial, of greater importance than the conceptual abstractions employed to explain the . . . principle are the implications of that principle for the sound administration of justice. Corresponding to the right of an accused to be given a fair trial is the societal interest in punishing one whose guilt is clear after he has obtained such a trial. It would be a high price indeed for society to pay were every accused granted immunity from punishment because of any defect sufficient to constitute reversible error in the proceedings leading to conviction. *United States v. Tateo,* 377 U.S. 463, 466, 84 S.Ct. 1587, 1589, 12 L.Ed.2d 448, 451 (1964).

Reprosecution after a conviction is reversed on appeal is prohibited, however, if the reason for the reversal was insufficiency of the evidence to support the conviction. *Burks v. United States,* 437 U.S. 1, 98 S.Ct. 2141, 57 L.Ed.2d 1 (1978). Double jeopardy does not arise when a single act violates both federal and state laws and the defendant is exposed to prosecution in both federal and state courts. This is called the

Justices of Boston Municipal Court v. Lydon
laws.findlaw.com/us/466/294.html

Hudson v. United States
laws.findlaw.com/us/000/96-976.html

Ohio v. Johnson
laws.findlaw.com/us/467/493.html

Richardson v. United States
laws.findlaw.com/us/468/317.html

United States v. Tateo
laws.findlaw.com/us/377/463.html

Burks v. United States
laws.findlaw.com/us/437/1.html

www.state.co.us/gov_dir/cdps/
academy/ar797.htm
Article, "Double Jeopardy—Two
Bites of the Apple or Only One?"
by Charles A. Riccio, Jr.

Heath v. Alabama
laws.findlaw.com/us/472/
82.html

Ashe v. Swenson
laws.findlaw.com/us/397/
436.html

Malloy v. Hogan
laws.findlaw.com/us/378/1.html

Doe v. United States
laws.findlaw.com/us/487/
201.html

dual sovereignty doctrine, and it also applies to prosecutions by two different states. In *Heath v. Alabama,* 472 U.S. 82, 106 S.Ct. 433, 88 L.Ed.2d 387 (1985), the U.S. Supreme Court held that the key question under this doctrine was whether the two entities seeking to prosecute the defendant for the same criminal act are separate sovereigns that derive their power to prosecute from independent sources. Because local governments are not sovereigns for double jeopardy purposes, the double jeopardy clause prohibits successive prosecutions by a state and a municipality in that state or by two municipalities in the same state. A criminal prosecution in either a state court or a federal court does not exempt the defendant from being sued for damages by anyone who is harmed by his or her criminal act. Finally, a defendant may be prosecuted more than once for the same conduct if that conduct involves the commission of more than one crime. For instance, a person who kills three victims at the same time and place can be tried separately for each killing.

The double jeopardy clause also embodies the **collateral estoppel doctrine.** The U.S. Supreme Court explained that collateral estoppel "means simply that when an issue of ultimate fact has once been determined by a valid and final judgment, that issue cannot again be litigated between the same parties in any future lawsuit." *Ashe v. Swenson,* 397 U.S. 436, 443, 90 S.Ct. 1189, 1194, 25 L.Ed.2d 469, 475 (1970). The collateral estoppel doctrine is often applied in civil suits brought by a citizen against a police officer where (1) the citizen has been previously convicted of a crime associated with the same event providing the basis for the lawsuit, and (2) as part of the conviction, the court determined that the citizen had acted with a particular state of mind. To the extent that the plaintiff's state of mind becomes significant in the civil litigation, the plaintiff is *estopped* (precluded) from litigating the state of mind issue because of the collateral estoppel doctrine. In other words, because the issue of state of mind has previously been determined "by a valid and final judgment" (the criminal conviction), the issue cannot be relitigated.

Privilege against Self-Incrimination

The Fifth Amendment protects a person against being incriminated by his or her own compelled **testimonial communications.** This protection is applicable to the states through the due process clause of the Fourteenth Amendment. *Malloy v. Hogan,* 378 U.S. 1, 84 S.Ct. 1489, 12 L.Ed.2d 653 (1964). To be testimonial, a "communication must itself, explicitly or implicitly, relate a factual assertion or disclose information" that is "the expression of the contents of an individual's mind." *Doe v. United States,* 487 U.S. 201, 210 n.9, 108 S.Ct. 2341, 2347 n.9, 101 L.Ed.2d 184, 197 n.9 (1988). Therefore, the privilege against self-incrimination is not violated by compelling a person to appear in a lineup, produce voice exemplars, furnish handwriting samples, be fingerprinted, shave a beard or mustache, or take a blood-alcohol or breathalyzer test. With respect to the requirement that the communication be incriminating, the U.S. Supreme Court said:

> The privilege afforded not only extends to answers that would in themselves support a conviction under a . . . criminal statute but likewise embraces those which would furnish a link in the chain of evidence needed to prosecute the claimant for a . . . crime. . . . But this protection must be confined to instances where the witness has reasonable cause to apprehend danger from a direct answer. . . . To sustain the privilege, it need only be evident from the implications of the question, in the setting in which it is asked, that a responsive answer to the question or an explanation of why it cannot be answered

might be dangerous because injurious disclosure could result. The trial judge in appraising the claim must be governed as much by his personal perception of the peculiarities of the case as by the facts actually in evidence. *Hoffman v. United States,* 341 U.S. 479, 486–87, 71 S.Ct. 814, 818, 95 L.Ed. 1118, 1124 (1951).

Hoffman v. United States
laws.findlaw.com/us/341/
479.html

In other words, not only the compelled confession to the commission of a crime is protected under the Fifth Amendment. Also protected are incriminating admissions that, while not sufficient in and of themselves to support a conviction, would provide "a link in the chain of evidence needed to prosecute" the person. An example of the latter may be statements that a suspect was at or near the scene of a crime.

The protection against self-incrimination enables a person to refuse to testify against himself or herself at a criminal trial in which the person is a defendant and also "privileges him not to answer official questions put to him in any other proceeding, civil or criminal, formal or informal, where the answers might incriminate him in future criminal proceedings." *Minnesota v. Murphy,* 465 U.S. 420, 426, 104 S.Ct. 1136, 1141, 79 L.Ed.2d 409, 418 (1984). The privilege also applies to the compelled preparation or offering of incriminating documents. *United States v. Doe,* 465 U.S. 605, 104 S.Ct. 1237, 79 L.Ed.2d 552 (1984). When a defendant chooses not to testify at trial, neither the prosecutor nor the trial judge may make any adverse comment about the defendant's failure to testify. *Griffin v. California,* 380 U.S. 609, 85 S.Ct. 1229, 14 L.Ed.2d 106 (1965). Moreover, the defendant is entitled to a jury instruction that no inference of guilt may be drawn from the failure to testify. The *Miranda* safeguards to secure the privilege against self-incrimination when a defendant is subjected to custodial interrogation are discussed in detail in Chapter 13.

Minnesota v. Murphy
laws.findlaw.com/us/465/
420.html
United States v. Doe
laws.findlaw.com/us/465/
605.html
Griffin v. California
laws.findlaw.com/us/380/
609.html

Under the Fifth Amendment privilege, a witness at a civil or criminal proceeding is protected from answering questions when the answers might be incriminating in some future criminal prosecution. If authorized by statute, however, the prosecution may compel the witness to testify by granting immunity from prosecution. The type of immunity usually granted is *use immunity,* which prevents the prosecution from *using* the compelled testimony and any evidence derived from it in a subsequent prosecution. If a witness has been granted immunity and still refuses to testify, he or she can be held in contempt of court.

The Right to Due Process

The words **due process of law** express the fundamental ideas of American justice. A due process clause is found in both the Fifth and Fourteenth Amendments. While originally construed as a restraint only upon the federal government, later interpretations by the U.S. Supreme Court have established that the restraint is similarly applicable to the states. "The Due Process Clause of the Constitution prohibits deprivations of life, liberty, or property without 'fundamental fairness' through governmental conduct that offends the community's sense of justice, decency and fair play." *Roberts v. Maine,* 48 F.3d 1287, 1291 (1st Cir. 1995). Timely notice of a hearing or trial that adequately informs the accused of the charges against him or her is a basic concept included in due process. Other rights repeatedly recognized as within the protection of the due process clause include the right to present evidence in one's own behalf before an impartial judge or jury, the right to be presumed innocent until proven guilty by legally obtained evidence, and the right to have the verdict supported by the evidence presented at trial.

The due process clauses of the Fifth and Fourteenth Amendments also provide other basic protections against the enactment by states or the federal government of arbitrary

www.shadeslanding.com/
firearms/cramer.haynes.html
Article, "The Fifth Amendment,
Self-Incrimination, and Gun Registration" by Clayton Cramer
www.richmond.edu/~jolt/v2i1/
sergienko.html
Article, "Self-Incrimination and
Cryptographic Keys" by Greg S.
Sergienko; examines the Fourth
and Fifth Amendment's protection against the compulsory production of cryptographic keys to
decipher computer documents
and the scope of the Fifth
Amendment immunity against
compelled production
www.co.alameda.ca.us/da/pov/
immunity.shtml
Article, "Immunity," from the
District Attorney's Office of
Alameda County, California.

www.wld.com/conbus/weal/
wdueproc.htm
Article, "Due Process of Law,"
excerpted from *West's Encyclopedia of American Law*

members.aol.com/
abtrbng.sdp.htm
Article, "Substantive Due
Process"

www.ascusc.org/jcmc/vol2/
issue1/due.html#
Article, "Due Process and Cyber-
jurisdiction" by David R.
Johnston

www.wld.com/conbus/weal/
wemindom.htm
Article, "Eminent Domain," excerpted from *West's Encyclopedia
of American Law*

www.pegasus.rutgers.edu/
~record/drafts/domain.html
Article, "Eminent Domain:
Whose Property Is It Anyway?"
by Ivan Paneque

www.law.indiana.edu/ilj/v72/
no4/long.html
Article, "The Expanding Importance of Temporary Physical
Takings: Some Unresolved Issues
and an Opportunity for New Directions in Takings Law" by
Dennis H. Long

caselaw.findlaw.com/data/
constitution/amendment05/
Comprehensive discussion (with
annotations) of the Fifth
Amendment

and unreasonable legislation or other measures that would violate individuals' rights. Thus, constitutional limitations are imposed on governmental interference with important individual liberties—such as the freedom to enter into contracts, engage in a lawful occupation, marry, and move without unnecessary restraints. To be valid, governmental restrictions placed on one's liberties must be reasonable and consistent with due process. (See the discussion of incorporation in this chapter under "Bill of Rights.")

The Right to Just Compensation

The power of the government to acquire private property is called *eminent domain*. The Fifth Amendment requires that the government may only take a person's property for public use, and the full value of the property must be paid to the owner. Thus, property cannot be taken by the federal government from one person simply to be given to another. The Supreme Court has held, however, that it is permissible to take private property for such purposes as urban renewal, even though ultimately the property taken will be returned to private ownership, since the taking is for the benefit of the community as a whole. To qualify for just compensation, property does not have to be physically taken from the owner. If governmental action leads to a lower value of private property, that action may constitute a "taking" and therefore require payment of compensation. Thus, the Supreme Court held that disturbing the egg-laying habits of chickens on a man's poultry farm by the noise of low-level flights by military aircraft from a nearby air base lessened the value of that farm and that, as a result, the landowner was entitled to receive compensation equal to his loss.

■ **Amendment VI**

In all criminal prosecutions, the accused shall enjoy the right to a speedy and public trial, by an impartial jury of the State and district wherein the crime shall have been committed, which district shall have been previously ascertained by law, and to be informed of the nature and cause of the accusation; to be confronted with the witnesses against him; to have compulsory process for obtaining witnesses in his favor, and to have the Assistance of Counsel for his defence.

The Right to a Speedy and Public Trial

Barker v. Wingo
laws.findlaw.com/us/407/
514.html

The right to a speedy and public trial requires that, after arrest or indictment, the accused be brought to trial without unnecessary delay and that the trial be open to the public. Intentional or negligent delay by the prosecution that prejudices the defendant's right to defend himself or herself has been held to be grounds for dismissal of the charges. *Barker v. Wingo*, 407 U.S. 514, 92 S.Ct. 2182, 33 L.Ed.2d 101 (1972). In the *Barker* case, the Court identified four factors that courts should assess in determining whether a particular defendant has been deprived of the right to a speedy trial: "Length of delay, the reason for the delay, the defendant's assertion of his right, and prejudice to the defendant." 407 U.S. at 530, 92 S.Ct. at 2192, 33 L.Ed.2d at 117. The Court said that the length of the delay was to some extent a "triggering mechanism." If there is no delay that is prejudicial on its face, judicial inquiry into the other three factors is not necessary. The Court also said that prejudice should be assessed in the light of defendants' interests that the speedy trial right was designed to protect: (1) to prevent oppressive pretrial incarceration; (2) to minimize anxiety and concern of the accused; and, most important, (3) to limit the possibility that the defense will be impaired.

While the Sixth Amendment guarantees a criminal defendant the right to a public trial, the First Amendment implicitly provides the press and the general public the right to attend criminal trials. Therefore, the "right to an open public trial is a shared right of the accused and the public, the common concern being the assurance of fairness." *Press-Enterprise Co. v. Superior Court,* 478 U.S. 1, 7, 106 S.Ct. 2735, 2739, 92 L.Ed.2d 1, 9 (1986). In addition to ensuring fairness, the constitutional commitment to public trials helps maintain confidence in the criminal justice system, promote informed discussion of governmental affairs, ensure that judges and prosecutors perform their duties responsibly, encourage witnesses to come forward, and discourage perjury. *Waller v. Georgia,* 467 U.S. 39, 104 S.Ct. 2210, 81 L.Ed.2d 31 (1984). Although a defendant may waive the Sixth Amendment right to a public trial and request a closed proceeding, such a request must be balanced against the First Amendment rights of the press and the public to have access to criminal trials.

Press-Enterprise Co. v. Superior Court
laws.findlaw.com/us/478/1.html

Waller v. Georgia
laws.findlaw.com/us/467/39.html

Trial by an Impartial Jury

The guarantee of trial by an impartial jury supplements the earlier jury trial guarantee contained in Article III of the Constitution. Jury trials are discussed further in Chapter 2.

The Right to Notice of Charges

The Sixth Amendment requirement that a person "be informed of the nature and cause of the accusation" means that an accused person must be given notice regarding exactly how he or she has allegedly broken the law, to provide the person with an opportunity to prepare a defense. This means that the indictment or information must be sufficiently specific in setting forth the charges to enable the defendant to plead and prepare a defense. (The indictment and information are discussed in detail in Chapter 2.) This also means that the crime must be established by statute beforehand so that all persons are aware of what is illegal before they act. (See the earlier discussion of *ex post facto* laws under "Individual Rights in the Original Constitution.") Also, the statute must not be so vague or ambiguous that it does not make clear the exact nature of the crime.

The Right to Confrontation with Witnesses

The **confrontation** clause guarantees the accused the right to confront hostile witnesses at his or her criminal trial. This right is designed to promote the truth-finding function of a trial by "ensur[ing] the reliability of the evidence against a criminal defendant by subjecting it to rigorous testing in the context of an adversary proceeding before the trier of fact." *Maryland v. Craig,* 497 U.S. 836, 845, 110 S.Ct. 3157, 3163, 111 L.Ed.2d 666, 678 (1990). This rigorous testing is accomplished both through the defendant's face-to-face confrontation during the witness's testimony and through the opportunity for cross-examination. Therefore, the defendant is entitled to be present at all important stages of the criminal trial, unless the right to be present is waived (1) by voluntarily being absent from the courtroom, *Taylor v. United States,* 414 U.S. 17, 94 S.Ct. 194, 38 L.Ed.2d 174 (1973), or (2) by continually disrupting the proceedings after being warned by the court. *Illinois v. Allen,* 397 U.S. 337, 90 S.Ct. 1057, 25 L.Ed.2d 353 (1970):

Maryland v. Craig
laws.findlaw.com/us/497/836.html
Taylor v. United States
laws.findlaw.com/us/414/17.html
Illinois v. Allen
laws.findlaw.com/us/397/337.html

It is essential to the proper administration of criminal justice that dignity, order, and decorum be the hallmarks of all court proceedings in our country. The flagrant disregard

www.law.cornell.edu/rules/fre/
overview.html
Federal Rules of Evidence in
their entirety
lawschool.lexis.com/emanuel/
web/evid/index.htm
(Scroll down to "Chapter 6:
Confrontation and Compulsory
Process")
Chapter 6 of Emanuel Publish-
ing's "Evidence: Capsule
Summary"

in the courtroom of elementary standards of proper conduct should not and cannot be tolerated. We believe trial judges confronted with disruptive, contumacious, stubbornly defiant defendants must be given sufficient discretion to meet the circumstances of each case. No one formula for maintaining the appropriate courtroom atmosphere will be best in all situations. We think there are at least three constitutionally permissible ways for a trial judge to handle an obstreperous defendant like Allen: (1) bind and gag him, thereby keeping him present; (2) cite him for contempt; (3) take him out of the court-room until he promises to conduct himself properly. 397 U.S. at 343–44, 90 S.Ct. at 1061, 25 L.Ed.2d at 359.

The defendant's right to the opportunity for cross-examination permits the defendant to test both the witness's credibility and the witness's knowledge of relevant facts of the case.

> The opportunity for cross-examination . . . is critical for ensuring the integrity of the fact-finding process. Cross-examination is "the principal means by which the believability of a witness and the truth of his testimony are tested." Indeed the Court has recognized that cross-examination is the "greatest legal engine ever invented for the discovery of the truth." *Kentucky v. Stincer,* 482 U.S. 730, 736, 107 S.Ct. 2658, 2662, 96 L.Ed.2d 631, 641 (1987).

Kentucky v. Stincer
laws.findlaw.com/us/482/
730.html

Cross-examination is discussed further in Chapter 2.

In general, the admission of **hearsay evidence** is prohibited by the confrontation clause, because the defendant cannot confront the absent declarant. Hearsay evidence is defined by Rule 801(c) of the Federal Rules of Evidence as "a statement, other than one made by the declarant while testifying at the trial or hearing, offered in evidence to prove the truth of the matter asserted." The U.S. Supreme Court has held that the confrontation clause does not prohibit the admission of hearsay evidence if the prosecution establishes (1) that it is unable to procure the witness's attendance at trial, despite good-faith efforts, and (2) that the evidence introduced bears sufficient "indicia of reliability." *Ohio v. Roberts,* 448 U.S. 56, 100 S.Ct. 2531, 65 L.Ed.2d 597 (1980). A statement is reliable if it falls within one of the established exceptions to the **hearsay rule** or if the prosecution shows that it is "trustworthy" in the totality of the circumstances.

Ohio v. Roberts
laws.findlaw.com/us/448/
56.html

Guarantee of Compulsory Process

The **compulsory process** clause guarantees the defendant's right to compel the attendance of favorable witnesses at trial, usually by means of a court-issued subpoena. To obtain compulsory process, the defendant must show that the witness's testimony would be relevant, material, favorable to the defendant, and not cumulative. *United States v. Valenzuela-Bernal,* 458 U.S. 858, 102 S.Ct. 3440, 73 L.Ed.2d 1193 (1982). Cumulative evidence is evidence that is of the same kind as evidence already offered as proof of the same factual matter, and is generally disallowed because it does little more than contribute to inefficiency. Cumulative evidence should not be confused with corroborating evidence, which is evidence that supplements or strengthens evidence already presented as proof of a factual matter.

United States v. Valenzuela-Bernal
laws.findlaw.com/us/458/
858.html

The Right to Representation by Counsel

Finally, the Sixth Amendment provides a right to be represented by counsel in all criminal prosecutions that may result in imprisonment. "[A]bsent a knowing and intelligent waiver, no person may be imprisoned for any offense, whether classified as petty, misdemeanor, or felony unless he was represented by counsel at his trial." *Argersinger v. Hamlin*, 407 U.S. 25, 37, 92 S.Ct. 2006, 2012, 32 L.Ed.2d 530, 538 (1972). As the quotation implies, by knowingly and intelligently waiving the right to counsel, a defendant has the right to conduct his or her own defense in a criminal case. This is known as a *pro se* defense. "[I]t is one thing to hold that every defendant, rich or poor, has the right to the assistance of counsel, and quite another to say that a state may compel a defendant to accept a lawyer he does not want." *Faretta v. California*, 422 U.S. 806, 832–33, 95 S.Ct. 2525, 2540, 45 L.Ed.2d 562, 580 (1975).

The right to counsel attaches at the initiation of adversary judicial criminal proceedings "whether by way of formal charge, preliminary hearing, indictment, information or arraignment." *Kirby v. Illinois*, 406 U.S. 682, 689, 92 S.Ct. 1877, 1882, 32 L.Ed.2d 411, 417 (1972). A person is entitled to the assistance of counsel, however, only at a "critical stage" of the prosecution "where substantial rights of a criminal accused may be affected." *Mempa v. Rhay*, 399 U.S. 128, 134, 88 S.Ct. 254, 257, 19 L.Ed.2d 336, 340 (1967). Thus, courts have accorded this right at

- Preindictment preliminary hearing—*Coleman v. Alabama*, 399 U.S. 1, 90 S.Ct. 1999, 26 L.Ed.2d 387 (1970)
- Postindictment pretrial lineup—*United States v. Wade*, 388 U.S. 218, 87 S.Ct. 1926, 18 L.Ed.2d 1178 (1967)
- Postindictment interrogation—*Massiah v. United States*, 377 U.S. 201, 84 S.Ct. 1199, 12 L.Ed.2d 246 (1964)
- Arraignment—*Hamilton v. Alabama*, 368 U.S. 52, 82 S.Ct. 157, 7 L.Ed.2d 114 (1961)
- Interrogation after arraignment—*Brewer v. Williams*, 430 U.S. 387, 97 S.Ct. 1232, 51 L.Ed.2d 424 (1977)
- First appeal as a matter of right—*Douglas v. California*, 372 U.S. 353, 83 S.Ct. 814, 9 L.Ed.2d 811 (1963)

The right to counsel is also assured at all stages of the trial process. In addition, prior to the initiation of adversary judicial criminal proceedings, a person has a *Fifth* Amendment right to counsel during custodial interrogation (see Chapter 13).

For many years, the guarantee of representation by counsel was interpreted to mean only that defendants had a right to be represented by a lawyer if they could afford one. In the 1930s, however, the U.S. Supreme Court began to vastly expand the class of persons entitled to the right to counsel in preparing and presenting a defense. In *Powell v. Alabama*, 287 U.S. 45, 53 S.Ct. 55, 77 L.Ed. 158 (1932), the Court held that the right to counsel was so fundamental that the due process clause of the Fourteenth Amendment required states to provide all defendants charged with capital crimes with the effective aid of counsel. Six years later, *Johnson v. Zerbst*, 304 U.S. 458, 58 S.Ct. 1019, 82 L.Ed. 1461 (1938), held that the Sixth Amendment required all federal defendants to be provided legal counsel for their defense, unless the right to counsel was properly waived. That decision raised the question of whether the constraint on the federal courts expressed a rule so fundamental and essential to a fair trial, and thus to due process of law, that it was made obligatory on the states by the Fourteenth Amendment. The Supreme Court said no in *Betts v. Brady*, 316 U.S. 455, 62 S.Ct. 1252, 86 L.Ed. 1595 (1942). The Court held that

the Fourteenth Amendment prohibits the conviction and incarceration of one whose trial is offensive to the common and fundamental ideas of fairness and right, and while want of counsel in a particular case may result in a conviction lacking in such

Argersinger v. Hamlin
laws.findlaw.com/us/407/25.html

Faretta v. California
laws.findlaw.com/us/422/806.html
Kirby v. Illinois
laws.findlaw.com/us/406/682.html
Mempa v. Rhay
laws.findlaw.com/us/399/128.html

Coleman v. Alabama
laws.findlaw.com/us/399/1.html
United States v. Wade
laws.findlaw.com/us/388/218.html
Massiah v. United States
laws.findlaw.com/us/377/201.html
Hamilton v. Alabama
laws.findlaw.com/us/368/52.html
Brewer v. Williams
laws.findlaw.com/us/430/387.html
Douglas v. California
laws.findlaw.com/us/372/353.html

Powell v. Alabama
laws.findlaw.com/us/287/45.html
Johnson v. Zerbst
laws.findlaw.com/us/304/458.html

Betts v. Brady
laws.findlaw.com/us/316/455.html

fundamental fairness, we cannot say that the amendment embodies an inexorable command that no trial for any offense, or in any court, can be fairly conducted and justice accorded a defendant who is not represented by counsel. 316 U.S. at 473, 62 S.Ct. at 1262, 86 L.Ed.2d at 1607.

Twenty-one years later, the Court changed its mind and finally recognized that "lawyers in criminal courts are necessities, not luxuries." In *Gideon v. Wainwright*, 372 U.S. 335, 83 S.Ct. 792, 9 L.Ed.2d 799 (1963), the Supreme Court overruled *Betts v. Brady,* holding that the Sixth Amendment imposed an affirmative obligation on the part of the federal *and* state governments to provide at public expense legal counsel for those who could not afford it, in order to have their cases adequately presented to the court. In addition, indigents were given the right to a free copy of their trial transcripts for purposes of appealing their convictions.

The Sixth Amendment right to counsel is a right to the *effective* assistance of counsel. "The very premise of our adversary system of criminal justice is that partisan advocacy on both sides of a case will promote the ultimate objective that the guilty be convicted and the innocent go free." *Herring v. New York,* 422 U.S. 853, 862, 95 S.Ct. 2550, 2555, 45 L.Ed.2d 593, 600 (1975). The absence of effective counsel undermines faith in the proper functioning of the adversarial process. In *Strickland v. Washington,* 466 U.S. 668, 104 S.Ct. 2052, 80 L.Ed.2d 674 (1984), the Court held that to establish a claim of ineffective assistance of counsel, a defendant must show (1) that counsel's representation fell below an objective standard of reasonableness and (2) that there is a reasonable probability that, but for counsel's unprofessional errors, the result of the proceeding would have been different. A reasonable probability is a probability sufficient to undermine confidence in the outcome. In *Lockhart v. Fretwell,* 506 U.S. 364, 113 S.Ct. 838, 122 L.Ed.2d 180 (1993), the Court refined the *Strickland* test to require that not only would a different trial result be probable because of attorney performance but that the actual trial result was fundamentally unfair or unreliable.

■ Amendment VII

In suits at common law, where the value in controversy shall exceed twenty dollars, the right of trial by jury shall be preserved, and no fact tried by a jury, shall be otherwise re-examined in any Court of the United States, than according to the rules of the common law.

The Seventh Amendment applies only to federal civil trials and not to civil suits in state courts. Except as provided by local federal court rules, if a case is brought in a federal court and a money judgment is sought that exceeds twenty dollars, the party bringing the suit and the defendant are entitled to have the controversy decided by the unanimous verdict of a jury of twelve people.

■ Amendment VIII

Excessive bail shall not be required, nor excessive fines imposed, nor cruel and unusual punishments inflicted.

The Right to Bail

Bail has traditionally meant the money or property pledged to the court or actually deposited for the release from custody of an arrested or imprisoned person as a guarantee of the person's appearance in court at a specified date and time. Accused persons who are released from custody and subsequently fail to appear for trial forfeit their bail to the court.

Gideon v. Wainwright
laws.findlaw.com/us/372/335.html

Herring v. New York
laws.findlaw.com/us/422/853.html
Strickland v. Washington
laws.findlaw.com/us/466/668.htm

Lockhart v. Fretwell
laws.findlaw.com/us/506/364.html

www.nlada.org/indig/mj97/p-under.htm
Article, "Underfunded and Unconstitutional" by John Haldridge, about effective assistance of counsel
caselaw.findlaw.com/data/constitution/amendment06/ Comprehensive discussion (with annotations) of the Sixth Amendment
lawschool.lexis.com/emanuel/web/crimpro/crimpro08.htm Outline of the law on the right to counsel
caselaw.findlaw.com/data/constitution/amendment07/ Comprehensive discussion (with annotations) of the Seventh Amendment

The Eighth Amendment does not specifically provide that all citizens have a right to bail but only that bail will not be excessive. A right to bail has, however, been recognized in common law and in statute since 1789. Excessive bail was defined in *Stack v. Boyle*, 342 U.S. 1, 4–5, 72 S.Ct. 1, 3, 96 L.Ed. 3, 6 (1951):

> From the passage of the Judiciary Act of 1789 . . . to the present . . . federal law has unequivocally provided that a person arrested for a non-capital offense *shall* be admitted to bail. This traditional right to freedom before conviction permits the unhampered preparation of a defense, and serves to prevent the infliction of punishment prior to conviction. . . . Unless this right to bail before trial is preserved, the presumption of innocence, secured only after centuries of struggle, would lose its meaning.
>
> The right to release before trial is conditioned upon the accused's giving adequate assurance that he will stand trial and submit to sentence if found guilty. . . . Like the ancient practice of securing the oaths of responsible persons to stand as sureties for the accused, the modern practice of requiring a bail bond or the deposit of a sum of money subject to forfeiture serves as additional assurance of the presence of an accused. *Bail set at a figure higher than an amount reasonably calculated to fulfill this purpose is "excessive" under the Eighth Amendment.* (Emphasis supplied.)

The excessive bail clause "has been assumed" to be applicable to the states through the Fourteenth Amendment. *Schilb v. Kuebel*, 404 U.S. 357, 92 S.Ct. 479, 30 L.Ed.2d 502 (1971). Under many state constitutions, when a capital offense such as murder is charged, bail may be denied altogether if "the proof is evident or the presumption great."

In 1966, Congress enacted the Bail Reform Act to provide for pretrial release of persons accused of noncapital federal crimes. Congress sought to end pretrial imprisonment of indigent defendants who could not afford to post money bail and who were, in effect, confined only because of their poverty. The act also discouraged the traditional use of money bail by requiring the judge to seek other means as likely to ensure that the defendant would appear when the trial was held.

The Bail Reform Act of 1984 substantially changed the 1966 act to allow an authorized judicial officer to impose conditions of release to ensure community safety. This change marked a significant departure from the basic philosophy of the 1966 act: namely, that the only purpose of bail laws was to ensure the defendant's appearance at judicial proceedings. The 1984 act also expanded appellate review and eliminated the presumption in favor of bail pending appeal. Most significantly, however, the 1984 act allowed an authorized judicial officer to detain an arrested person pending trial if the government could demonstrate by clear and convincing evidence after an adversary hearing that no release conditions "will reasonably assure . . . the safety of any other person and the community." In *United States v. Salerno*, 481 U.S. 739, 107 S.Ct. 2095, 95 L.Ed.2d 697 (1987), the U.S. Supreme Court held that pretrial detention under the act, based solely on risk of danger to the community, did not violate due process or the Eighth Amendment.

Freedom from Cruel and Unusual Punishment

The prohibition against the infliction of cruel and unusual punishment is concerned with punishments imposed after a formal adjudication of guilt. The prohibition is applicable to the states through the due process clause of the Fourteenth Amendment. *Robinson v. California*, 370 U.S. 660, 82 S.Ct. 1417, 81 L.Ed.2d 758 (1962). The cruel and unusual punishment clause of the Eighth Amendment limits the punishment that

Stack v. Boyle
laws.findlaw.com/us/342/1.html

Schilb v. Kuebel
laws.findlaw.com/us/404/
357.html

www.napsa.org/docs/
1984bailref.pdf
Monograph on the Bail Reform
Act of 1984 published by the
Federal Judicial Center

United States v. Salerno
laws.findlaw.com/us/481/
739.html

Robinson v. California
laws.findlaw.com/us/370/
660.html

faculty.ncwc.edu/toconnor/
410/410lect16.htm
Article, "Cruel and Unusual
Punishment," discussing the history of that constitutional
prohibition

Ingraham v. Wright
laws.findlaw.com/us/430/
651.html
Coker v. Georgia
laws.findlaw.com/us/433/
584.html

Solem v. Helm
laws.findlaw.com/us/463/
277.html

Gregg v. Georgia
laws.findlaw.com/us/428/
153.html

www.capdefnet.org/3_intro_to_
8th.htm
Article, "Introduction to the
Eighth Amendment: An
Overview of Constitutional Principals Relevant to Capital Cases"
by John H. Blume and Mark E.
Olive
caselaw.findlaw.com/data/
constitution/amendment08/
Comprehensive discussion (with
annotations) of the Eighth
Amendment

Griswold v. Connecticut
laws.findlaw.com/us/381/
479.html

may be imposed on conviction of a crime in three ways. First, the clause "imposes substantive limits on what can be made criminal and punished as such." *Ingraham v. Wright*, 430 U.S. 651, 667, 97 S.Ct. 1401, 1410, 51 L.Ed.2d 711, 728 (1977). The U.S. Supreme Court held that a statute making the condition or status of narcotics addiction a crime was unconstitutional because it imposed punishment of personal characteristics rather than illegal acts. *Robinson,* supra. Also, a person may not be punished in retaliation for exercising a constitutional right. *United States v. Heubel*, 864 F.2d 1104 (3d Cir. 1988). Second, the cruel and unusual punishment clause proscribes certain kinds of punishment such as torture and divestiture of citizenship. Third, the clause prohibits punishment that is excessive in relation to the crime committed. In *Coker v. Georgia*, a case holding that the state may not impose a death sentence on a rapist who does not take human life, the Court said that a "punishment is 'excessive' and unconstitutional if it (1) makes no measurable contribution to acceptable goals of punishment and hence is nothing more than the purposeless and needless imposition of pain and suffering; or (2) is grossly out of proportion to the severity of the crime." 433 U.S. 584, 592, 97 S.Ct. 2861, 2866, 53 L.Ed.2d 982, 989 (1977). In *Solem v. Helm*, 463 U.S. 277, 103 S.Ct. 3001, 77 L.Ed.2d 637 (1983), the U.S. Supreme Court set forth three criteria for analyzing the proportionality of sentences:

> [A] court's proportionality analysis under the Eighth Amendment should be guided by objective criteria, including (i) the gravity of the offense and the harshness of the penalty; (ii) the sentences imposed on other criminals in the same jurisdiction; and (iii) the sentences imposed for the commission of the same crime in other jurisdictions. 463 U.S. at 292, 103 S.Ct. at 3011, 77 L.Ed.2d at 650.

The cruel and unusual punishment clause does not prohibit capital punishment. *Gregg v. Georgia*, 428 U.S. 153, 96 S.Ct. 2909, 49 L.Ed.2d 859 (1976). Mandatory death statutes leaving the jury or trial judge no discretion to consider the individual defendant and his or her crime are cruel and unusual, however. The Court also held that standards and procedures might be established for imposing death that would remove or mitigate the arbitrariness and irrationality characteristic of many death penalty laws. (Further discussion of the many Supreme Court cases decided in recent years dealing with capital punishment is beyond the scope of this text.)

■ Amendment IX

The enumeration in the Constitution, of certain rights, shall not be construed to deny or disparage others retained by the people.

The Ninth Amendment emphasizes the Founding Fathers' view that powers of government are limited by the rights of the people and that it was not intended, by expressly guaranteeing in the Constitution certain rights of the people, to grant the government unlimited power to invade other rights of the people.

The Supreme Court has on at least one occasion suggested that this amendment is a justification for recognizing certain rights not specifically mentioned in the Constitution or for broadly interpreting those that are. The case involving the Ninth Amendment was *Griswold v. Connecticut*, 381 U.S. 479, 85 S.Ct. 1678, 14 L.Ed.2d 510 (1965), in which a statute prohibiting the use of contraceptives was voided as an infringement of the right of marital privacy. At issue was whether the right to privacy was a constitutional right and, if so, whether the right was one reserved to the people under the Ninth Amendment or only derived from other rights specifically mentioned in the Constitution.

Courts have long recognized particular rights to privacy that are part of the First and Fourth Amendments. As the Court in *Griswold* said, the "specific guarantees in the Bill of Rights have penumbras, formed by emanations from those guarantees that help give them life and substance." 381 U.S. at 484, 85 S.Ct. at 1681, 14 L.Ed.2d at 514. Thus, freedom of expression guarantees freedom of association and the related right to be silent and free from official inquiry into such associations. It also includes the right not to be intimidated by government for the expression of one's views. The Fourth Amendment's guarantee against unreasonable search and seizure confers a right to privacy because its safeguards prohibit unauthorized entry onto one's property and tampering with one's person, property, or possessions.

The court in *Griswold* ruled that the Third and Fifth Amendments, in addition to the First and Fourth, created "zones of privacy" safe from governmental intrusion and, without resting its decision on any one of these or on the Ninth Amendment itself, simply held that the right of privacy was guaranteed by the Constitution.

■ Amendment X

The powers not delegated to the United States by the Constitution, nor prohibited by it to the States, are reserved to the States respectively, or to the people.

The Tenth Amendment embodies the principle of federalism, which reserves for the states the remainder of powers not granted to the federal government or withheld from the states.

Later Amendments Dealing with Individuals

■ Amendment XIII

Section 1. Neither slavery nor involuntary servitude, except as a punishment for crime whereof the party shall have been duly convicted, shall exist within the United States, or any place subject to their jurisdiction.
Section 2. Congress shall have power to enforce this article by appropriate legislation.

The Thirteenth Amendment prohibits slavery in the United States. It has been held that certain state laws were in violation of this amendment because they had the effect of jailing a debtor who did not perform his or her financial obligations. The Supreme Court has ruled that selective service laws, which authorize the draft for military duty, are not prohibited by this amendment.

The courts have also justified certain civil rights legislation that condemned purely private acts of discrimination but that did not constitute "state action," on the basis of the authority granted in Section 2 of this amendment and Section 5 of the Fourteenth Amendment, which is similar. An example is the civil rights legislation of 1866 and 1964 designed to end discrimination in the sale or rental of real or personal property. These discriminatory practices were seen as "badges of servitude," which the Thirteenth Amendment was intended to abolish.

■ Amendment XIV

Section 1. All persons born or naturalized in the United States, and subject to the jurisdiction thereof, are citizens of the United States and of the State wherein they reside. No State shall make or enforce any law which shall abridge the privileges or immunities of citizens of the

caselaw.findlaw.com/data/ constitution/amendment09/ Comprehensive discussion (with annotations) of the Ninth Amendment

caselaw.findlaw.com/data/ constitution/amendment10/ Comprehensive discussion (with annotations) of the Tenth Amendment

caselaw.findlaw.com/data/ constitution/amendment13/ Comprehensive discussion (with annotations) of the Thirteenth Amendment

caselaw.findlaw.com/data/
constitution/amendment14/
15.html#1
Comprehensive discussion (with
annotations) of Fourteenth
Amendment due process

*United States; nor shall any State deprive any person of life, liberty, or property, without
due process of law; nor deny to any person within its jurisdiction the equal protection of the
laws. . . .*

*Section 5. The Congress shall have power to enforce, by appropriate legislation, the
provisions of this article.*

The Right to Due Process

The Fourteenth Amendment limits the states from infringing on the rights of individuals. The Bill of Rights—the first ten amendments—does not specifically refer to actions by the states but applies only to actions by the federal government. Through judicial interpretation of the phrase "due process of law" in the Fourteenth Amendment, many of the Bill of Rights guarantees have been made applicable to actions by state governments and their subdivisions, such as counties, municipalities, and cities. Under this principle, certain rights and freedoms are deemed so basic to the people in a free and democratic society that state governments may not violate them, even though states are not specifically barred from doing so by the Constitution. (See the discussion of incorporation of guarantees in the Bill of Rights, through the due process clause of the Fourteenth Amendment, in this chapter under "The Bill of Rights.") In determining whether state action violates the due process clause, a court considers

> [f]irst, the private interest that will be affected by the official action; second, the risk of
> an erroneous deprivation of such interest through the procedures used, and the probable value, if any, of additional or substitute procedural safeguards; and finally, the
> Government's interest, including the function involved and the fiscal and administrative burdens that the additional or substitute procedural requirement would entail.
> *Mathews v. Eldridge,* 424 U.S. 319, 335, 96 S.Ct. 893, 903, 47 L.Ed.2d 18, 33 (1976).

Mathews v. Eldridge
laws.findlaw.com/us/424/
319.html

The Fifth Amendment, discussed earlier, also contains a due process clause that applies to actions of the federal government.

The Right to Equal Protection of the Laws

In addition to the due process clause, the Fourteenth Amendment also prohibits denial of the **equal protection of the laws.** This requirement prevents any state from making unreasonable, arbitrary distinctions between different persons as to their rights and privileges. Because "all people are created equal," no state law could, for example, deny red-haired men the right to drive an automobile. A state may, however, make reasonable classifications, such as denying minors the right to drive.

Some classifications, such as those based on race, religion, and national origin, have been held to be patently unreasonable. Thus, racial segregation in public schools and other public places, laws that prohibit the sale or use of property to certain races or minority groups, and laws that prohibit interracial marriage have been struck down. Furthermore, the Supreme Court has held that purely private acts of discrimination can be in violation of the equal protection clause if they are customarily enforced throughout the state, whether or not there is a specific law or other explicit manifestation of action by the state.

The equal protection clause has been interpreted to mean that a citizen may not arbitrarily be deprived of the right to vote and that every citizen's vote must be given equal weight to the extent possible. Thus, the Supreme Court held that state legislatures and local governments must be strictly apportioned in terms of their populations in such a way as to accord one person one vote.

Section 5 of the Fourteenth Amendment provided the authority for much of the civil rights legislation passed by Congress in the 1960s.

■ Amendment XV

Section 1. The right of citizens of the United States to vote shall not be denied or abridged by the United States or by any State on account of race, color, or previous condition of servitude.

Section 2. The Congress shall have power to enforce this article by appropriate legislation.

■ Amendment XIX

Section 1. The right of citizens of the United States to vote shall not be denied or abridged by the United States or by any State on account of sex.

Section 2. Congress shall have power to enforce this article by appropriate legislation.

■ Amendment XXVI

Section 1. The right of citizens of the United States, who are eighteen years or older, to vote shall not be denied or abridged by the United States or any State on account of age.

Section 2. The Congress shall have power to enforce this article by appropriate legislation.

Together these three amendments ensure the right to vote, which is the keystone of our democratic society, and which may not be denied any citizen over the age of eighteen because of race, color, previous condition of servitude, or gender. The Twenty-sixth Amendment, which lowered the voting age for all elections from twenty-one to eighteen years of age, became law on July 1, 1971. These amendments, together with the Fifth and Fourteenth, prohibit any arbitrary attempt to disenfranchise any American citizen.

■ Amendment XXIV

Section 1. The right of citizens of the United States to vote in any primary or other election for President or Vice President, for electors for President or Vice President, or for Senator or Representative in Congress, shall not be denied or abridged by the United States or any State by reason of failure to pay any poll tax or other tax.

Section 2. The Congress shall have power to enforce this article by appropriate legislation.

The Twenty-fourth Amendment prohibits denial of the right to vote for federal officials because a person has not paid a tax. This amendment was designed to abolish the requirement of a poll tax, which, at the time of its ratification, five states imposed as a condition to voting. The Supreme Court subsequently held that poll taxes were unconstitutional under the equal protection clause of the Fourteenth Amendment on the basis that the right to vote should not be conditioned on one's ability to pay a tax. Accordingly, poll taxes in any election, state or federal, have been prohibited.

caselaw.findlaw.com/data/
constitution/amendment14/
18.html#1
Comprehensive discussion (with annotations) of the equal protection clause of the Fourteenth Amendment
caselaw.findlaw.com/data/
constitution/amendment15/
caselaw.findlaw.com/data/
constitution/amendment19/
caselaw.findlaw.com/data/
constitution/amendment26/
Comprehensive discussion (with annotations) of the Fifteenth, Nineteenth, and Twenty-sixth Amendments
caselaw.findlaw.com/data/
constitution/amendment24/
Comprehensive discussion (with annotations) of the Twenty-fourth Amendment

Conclusion

In addition to the specific constitutional rights outlined in this chapter, certain safeguards for the individual are inherent in the structure of American government. The separation of powers among legislative, executive, and judicial branches of government is the basis for a system of checks and balances—which prevents excessive concentration of power, with the inevitable threat to individual liberties that accompanies such concentration. With respect to legislative power itself, the existence of two houses of Congress—each chosen by a different process—is itself a protection against ill-advised laws that might threaten constitutional rights. Similarly, our federal system, which divides authority between the national government and the various state governments, has provided a fertile soil for the nourishment of constitutional rights.

No matter how well a constitution may be written, the rights it guarantees have little meaning unless there is popular support for those rights and that constitution. Fortunately, that support has historically existed in the United States. Indeed, in this country the most fundamental protection of personal liberty

rests in the well-established American traditions of constitutional government, obedience to the rule of law, and respect for the individual. These traditions provide the groundwork for the entire body of law dealing with criminal procedure and should be foremost in the minds of students of and participants in the American criminal justice system. The remainder of this book shows how the criminal justice system operates to achieve a balance between the protection of individual rights guaranteed by the Constitution and the maintenance of the rule of law and public order in our society.

Review and Discussion Questions

1. How has the Constitution been able to remain a durable and viable instrument of government despite the enormous changes that have occurred in our society since its adoption? Discuss this issue in terms of specific changes.

2. Discuss generally the most important roles and functions under the Constitution of each of the following: the three branches of the federal government, the state governments, the average citizen, and the law enforcement officer. Explain the interrelationships among some of those roles and functions.

3. The Constitution speaks predominantly in terms of the protection of individual rights from governmental abuse or abridgment. What corresponding obligations and burdens must each citizen undertake or bear to ensure that everyone remains free to exercise these rights to their full extent?

4. Name three constitutional sources for the protection of the right to privacy, and explain how they differ.

5. If a state legislature passed a law requiring all bookstores that have, in the last six months, sold or advertised for sale pictures of the pope to be closed down and their owners immediately arrested and jailed, what provisions of the Constitution might be violated?

6. If a terminally ill cancer patient wishes to refuse medical treatment and die a "natural" death because of religious beliefs, can that person be required under state law to undergo treatment? What if the wish to die is not based on a reli-

gious belief, but the person is a minor or mentally incompetent? What if the cancer was caused by exposure to radiation and the person wishes the death to be a political statement on the dangers of nuclear power and nuclear war?

7. Discuss the constitutional issues involved in compelling a journalist to reveal a confidential source of information when the source would be useful to the government in a criminal investigation or helpful to a criminal defendant at trial. Should the government be able to obtain a search warrant to look into files, audit tapes, or view films in the possession of the news media to find evidence of crime?

8. Should members of the news media have greater access than that of the general public to court proceedings and court records? What about greater access to prisons to interview prisoners? What about greater access to police investigative files?

9. Would the Fifth Amendment privilege against self-incrimination prohibit the government from any of the following: requiring all participants in a lineup to speak certain words; requiring a person to produce income tax records; threatening a person with a reduction in pay in his government job if he does not make incriminating testimonial admissions about a matter not related to his job?

10. What does the term *checks and balances* mean? What aspects of the Constitution other than separation of powers help fulfill the purposes of checks and balances?

Chapter 2

An Overview of the Criminal Court System

Outline

■ **Explain the structure of the court system of the United States and of the student's state.**

■ **Trace the progress of a criminal case through its various stages from initial complaint through appeal and postconviction remedies.**

■ **Understand the meanings of the following terms: acquittal, affidavit, appeal, appellate jurisdiction, arraignment, arrest warrant, bench trial, beyond a reasonable doubt, burden of proof, challenge for cause, complaint, court of general jurisdiction, court of limited jurisdiction, cross-examination, deposition, direct examination, discovery, grand jury,** *habeas corpus,* **indictment, information, instruction, judgment, jury nullification, motion,** *nolo contendere,* **original jurisdiction, peremptory challenge, plea, preliminary examination, probation, rebuttal, rule of four, sentence, subpoena, summons, transactional immunity, trial** *de novo,* **true bill, use immunity, venue, verdict,** *voir dire,* **writ of** *certiorari.*

The law enforcement officer's daily duties include enforcing the laws, keeping the public peace, and investigating and preventing crime. To perform these duties properly, officers must be sensitive to the constitutional rights of all persons (discussed in Chapter 1) and be familiar with the criminal laws of their jurisdictions. Just as important, officers must understand the law dealing with arrest, search and seizure, confessions, and pretrial identifications. Most of the remainder of this book is concerned with these legal topics.

Most law enforcement officers are not as familiar with the rules and procedures that govern the course of a prosecution beyond the investigatory or arrest stage. Law enforcement officers play an important role in this process, often as chief witnesses for the prosecution. Nevertheless, outside their roles as witnesses, officers are often ignored as their cases move through pleadings, motions, jury selection, trial, and appeal. To many officers, the entire process may look like a complex legal jumble involving the prosecuting attorney, the defense attorney, and the judge. Because law enforcement officers are an integral part of the criminal justice system, and because their early actions in a case vitally affect its outcome at nearly all stages of the prosecution, they should have a basic understanding of what happens to the case, and why, when it reaches the prosecutor and the courts. Other criminal justice professionals, who are usually less involved in a criminal case than are law enforcement officers, can also function more effectively within the criminal justice system if they have a general knowledge of that system's structure and operation.

Criminal court procedure in most states is governed by court rules and statutes. These are designed for use by judges and attorneys to ensure the just and efficient processing of criminal offenders. Many of the rules and statutes are quite complex and do not directly concern law enforcement officers or other criminal justice professionals. Accordingly, this chapter highlights pertinent court procedures and legal terms to provide a comprehensive view of how the system works, without dwelling too heavily on details that are of little direct concern to the criminal justice professional.

So far as possible, this chapter presents the different stages of criminal court procedure in chronological order, following a criminal case from beginning to end. The discussion is limited to court procedures for serious offenses and does not cover procedures for traffic violations and other less serious misdemeanors. Wherever certain aspects of criminal court procedure are covered in another chapter, reference is made to that chapter. Because the information in this chapter is general, and because criminal court procedure differs by state, do not take this information presented as a final authority; be sure to consult your own state's pertinent statutes or rules.

Structure of the Court System

Before discussing the preliminary proceedings in a criminal case, this chapter first outlines the basic structure of the federal court system and a typical state court system and then briefly describes the criminal trial jurisdiction of the different courts. As used here, the term **jurisdiction** simply means the authority of a court to deal with a particular type of case.

The federal court system is larger and more complex than any state court system, but their basic structures are similar. Both the federal and the state systems consist of courts that have original jurisdiction over criminal matters and courts that have appellate jurisdiction. **Original jurisdiction** means the authority to deal with a case from beginning to end, including trying the case as well as passing judgment on the facts and the law. **Appellate jurisdiction** means the authority to deal with a case, not in its initial stages but only after it has been finally decided by a lower court of original jurisdiction, and then only to revise or correct the proceedings of the lower court.

Courts are further classified as **courts of limited jurisdiction** and **courts of general jurisdiction.** A court of limited jurisdiction is a court whose trial jurisdiction either includes no felonies or is limited to less than all felonies and that may or may not hear appeals. A court of limited jurisdiction is limited to a particular class or classes of cases. It often has jurisdiction over misdemeanor or traffic cases, over the initial setting of bail and preliminary hearings in felony cases, and occasionally over felony trials in which the penalty prescribed for the offense is below a statutorily specified limit. A court of general jurisdiction is a court that has trial jurisdiction over all criminal offenses and that may or may not hear appeals. A court of general jurisdiction has original jurisdiction over all felonies and frequently has appellate jurisdiction over the decisions of a court of limited jurisdiction. An appellate court may review the decisions of a court of general jurisdiction.

www.clarkprosecutor.org/html/
police/police2.htm
Article, "Effective Courtroom
Performance for Police Officers"

*For new and updated weblinks,
go to* www.wadsworth.com/
cj/ferdico0253

Federal Courts

The U.S. district courts are the trial courts of general federal jurisdiction. Each state has at least one district court, while some of the larger states have as many as four. There are a total of ninety-four district courts in the fifty states, the District of Columbia, the Commonwealth of Puerto Rico, and the territories of Guam, the U.S. Virgin Islands, and the Northern Mariana Islands. District courts may have divisions (for example, Eastern and Western Divisions of North Dakota), usually in districts covering a large geographic area, and may have several locations where the court hears cases. With the exception of the territorial courts, all district court judges are appointed for life by the president with the advice and consent of the Senate. Congress authorizes judgeships for each district based in large part on its caseload. At this writing, there are 636 district court judges. Usually only one judge is required to hear and decide a case in a district court. The district courts have original jurisdiction over criminal cases, and the great majority of federal criminal cases begin in the district courts. Cases from the district courts are reviewable on appeal by the applicable court of appeals. Each district court has one or more bankruptcy judges, a clerk, a U.S. attorney, a U.S. marshal, probation officers, court reporters, and a support staff.

Each district court also has one or more U.S. magistrate judges. Magistrate judges are appointed for eight-year terms by district court judges and are required to be members of the bar. A magistrate judge, at the designation of the district court judge, may issue search warrants, hear and determine certain kinds of pretrial matters, conduct preliminary examinations and other hearings, and submit for the court's approval proposed findings and recommendations on motions. Perhaps the most important power magistrate judges possess is the authority to conduct misdemeanor trials with the defendant's consent and to conduct trials in civil cases with the consent of the parties involved. Since the enactment of the Federal Magistrates Act in 1968, Congress has expanded the services magistrate judges may perform. As a result, magistrate judges are playing an increasingly significant role in the administration of the justice in the federal system.

The U.S. courts of appeals (often referred to as circuit courts) are intermediate appellate courts created by Congress to relieve the U.S. Supreme Court of considering all appeals in cases originally decided by the federal trial courts. The courts of appeal are empowered to review all final decisions and certain interlocutory decisions of district

www.uscourts.gov/
Official Web site of the federal
courts maintained by the Administrative Office of the U.S.
Courts

www.uscourts.gov/UFC99.pdf
Handbook, "Understanding the
Federal Courts"; explains the
structure, function, and makeup
of the U.S. federal courts

www.ncmd.uscourts.gov/
glossary.htm
"Glossary of Frequently Used
Terms in the Federal District
Court System"; includes a short
description of civil actions and
criminal actions

www.law.emory.edu/FEDCTS/
Provides access to decisions of
federal courts

www.supremecourtus.gov/
Official Web site of the U.S.
Supreme Court; comprehensive
information about the Court's
history, procedures, rules, and
justices

courts. They also have the power to review and enforce orders of many federal administrative bodies. The decisions of the courts of appeals are final, except that they are subject to discretionary review or appeal in the U.S. Supreme Court.

The United States is divided geographically into twelve judicial circuits, including the District of Columbia. Each circuit has a court of appeals. Each of the fifty states is assigned to one of the circuits, and the territories are assigned variously to the first, third, and ninth circuits. A thirteenth federal circuit court, the U.S. Court of Appeals for the Federal Circuit, was created by act of Congress in 1982 with nationwide jurisdiction to hear appeals in patent and contract cases and various other matters. Appeals court judges are appointed for life by the president with the advice and consent of the Senate. Each court of appeals has from six to twenty-eight permanent circuit judgeships, depending on the amount of judicial work in the circuit. At this writing, there are 179 judges in the thirteen judicial circuits. One of the justices of the U.S. Supreme Court is assigned as a circuit justice for each of the thirteen judicial circuits. Each court of appeals normally hears cases in panels consisting of three judges but may sit *en banc* with all judges present. *En banc* refers to a session of a court in which all the judges of the court participate, as opposed to a session presided over by a single judge or a mere quorum of judges. The judge who has served on the court the longest and who is under sixty-five years of age is designated as the chief judge and performs administrative duties in addition to hearing cases. The chief judge serves for a maximum term of seven years.

The U.S. Supreme Court is composed of the chief justice of the United States and such number of associate justices as may be fixed by Congress. By act of Congress in 1948, the number of associate justices is eight. Power to nominate the justices is vested in the president of the United States, and appointments are made with the advice and consent of the Senate. Article III, Section 1, of the Constitution further provides that "[t]he Judges, both of the supreme and inferior Courts, shall hold their Offices during good Behaviour, and shall, at stated Times, receive for their Services, a Compensation, which shall not be diminished during their Continuance in Office."

The U.S. Supreme Court is the appellate court of last resort, meaning that it is a court from which no appeal is possible. The Court has original jurisdiction in certain limited areas, but its greatest workload is to review the decisions of the lower federal courts and the highest state courts. The Supreme Court exercises its appellate jurisdiction through the granting of a **writ of *certiorari,*** which means that the Court, upon petition of a party, agrees to review a case decided by one of the circuit courts of appeals or the highest court of a state. A vote of four Supreme Court justices is required to grant *certiorari* to review a case (sometimes referred to as the rule of four). *Certiorari* is granted at the Court's discretion when a case presents questions the resolution of which will have some general "importance beyond the facts and parties involved." *Boag v. MacDougall,* 454 U.S. 364, 368, 102 S.Ct. 700, 702, 70 L.Ed.2d 551, 555 (1982) (REHNQUIST, J., dissenting). For example, the Court may grant *certiorari* in cases involving important and unsettled questions of federal law or in situations involving confusion among the state and federal courts. Note that failure to grant *certiorari* is not an affirmation in disguise of the lower court's decision. It simply means that the petitioner failed to persuade four of the nine justices to hear the appeal. Legislation effective in 1988 essentially eliminated the Supreme Court's former so-called mandatory or obligatory appeal jurisdiction. With very minor exceptions, petitioning for a writ of *certiorari* is now the only path to Supreme Court review of federal and state court decisions. Exhibit 2.1 depicts U.S. courts with criminal jurisdiction.

Boag v. MacDougall
laws.findlaw.com/us/454/
364.html

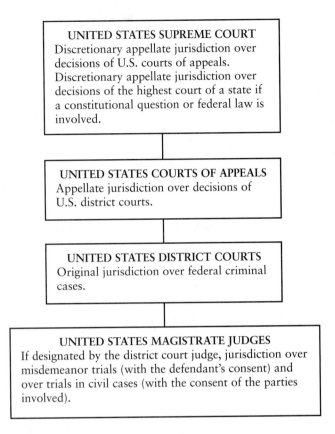

air.fjc.gov/history
A history of the federal judiciary

United States Courts with Criminal Jurisdiction

■ EXHIBIT 2.1

In addition to the courts described above, the federal court system also includes a number of specialized courts that have been established to hear particular classes of cases. Examples are the U.S. Court of International Trade and the U.S. Court of Federal Claims. Courts outside the judicial branch of government include the U.S. Court of Military Appeals and the U.S. Tax Court. There are also quasi-judicial boards or commissions that have special and limited jurisdiction under specific federal statutes.

State Courts

A typical state court system has the same basic structure as the federal system. Courts of original jurisdiction are usually divided into (1) courts of limited jurisdiction whose trial jurisdiction either includes no felonies or is limited to less than all felonies and (2) higher courts of general jurisdiction with trial jurisdiction over all criminal offenses, including all felonies. The courts of limited jurisdiction are usually established on a local level and may be called municipal courts, police courts, magistrate courts, district courts, or something similar. These courts have jurisdiction over misdemeanor cases, traffic cases, initial setting of bail and preliminary hearings in felony cases, and occasionally felony trials in which the penalty prescribed for the offense is below a statutorily

```
┌─────────────────────────────────────────┐
│         NEBRASKA SUPREME COURT           │
│  Highest appellate court. May exercise   │
│  original jurisdiction in certain cases. │
│  Hears discretionary appeals from the    │
│  court of appeals.                       │
└─────────────────────────────────────────┘
                      │
┌─────────────────────────────────────────┐
│      NEBRASKA COURT OF APPEALS           │
│  Intermediate appellate court. Hears     │
│  appeals from district courts except     │
│  for cases involving the death penalty or│
│  life imprisonment or cases raising      │
│  constitutional questions.               │
└─────────────────────────────────────────┘
                      │
┌─────────────────────────────────────────┐
│        NEBRASKA DISTRICT COURTS          │
│  Trial courts of general jurisdiction.   │
│  Try all felony cases. Hear and determine│
│  appeals from county courts and juvenile │
│  courts.                                 │
└─────────────────────────────────────────┘
```

NEBRASKA COUNTY COURTS	SEPARATE JUVENILE COURTS
Trial courts of limited jurisdiction. Try misdemeanors, including traffic and municipal ordinance violations. Conduct preliminary hearings in felony cases. Function as juvenile courts, except in Douglas, Lancaster, and Sarpy Counties.	Established in Douglas, Lancaster, and Sarpy Counties. Same juvenile jurisdiction as county courts.

Courts with Criminal Jurisdiction in Nebraska
■ EXHIBIT 2.2

specified limit. The courts of general jurisdiction have original jurisdiction over all criminal offenses and are usually established on a county or regional level. They may be called circuit courts, district courts, superior courts, or something similar. Generally, the most serious criminal cases are tried in these courts.

In some states, courts of general jurisdiction may also exercise a limited appellate jurisdiction over certain cases appealed from the courts of limited jurisdiction. Such appeals result in a **trial *de novo*** in the court of general jurisdiction. A trial *de novo* is a new trial or retrial in which the whole case is examined again as if no trial had ever been held in the court of limited jurisdiction. In a trial *de novo*, matters of fact as well as law may be considered, witnesses may be heard, and new evidence may be presented, regardless of what happened at the first trial. Some states also have lower-level specialized courts, such as juvenile courts, traffic courts, or family courts, which may have criminal jurisdiction or partial criminal jurisdiction.

From the court of general jurisdiction, a case may proceed through an intermediate appellate court until it reaches the highest court (or the court of last resort) of the state, usually called the state supreme court. If a case involves important constitutional issues or questions of federal law, it may finally reach the U.S. Supreme Court for review. Generally the state supreme court also has the power to prescribe rules of pleading, practice, and procedure for itself and the other lower courts of the state. Exhibit 2.2 depicts the courts with criminal jurisdiction in Nebraska.

Preliminary Proceedings

This chapter focuses on the progress of a felony case through the criminal court system. A brief note about misdemeanor cases is useful at the outset to emphasize the differences between the two types of cases. Generally, **misdemeanors** are crimes for which the maximum possible sentence is less than one year's imprisonment. Misdemeanors are tried in courts of limited jurisdiction. Although misdemeanor proceedings are similar to felony proceedings, they are usually less formal and more abbreviated. For example, jury trials are available but unusual in misdemeanor cases, and six-person juries are common. Also, in some jurisdictions, if the defendant pleads guilty, misdemeanor charges may be disposed of at the initial appearance before the magistrate. Because misdemeanor proceedings differ greatly from jurisdiction to jurisdiction, and because they are similar in many ways to felony proceedings, the remainder of this chapter focuses primarily on felony proceedings. Exhibit 2.3 gives a general view of the progress of a case through the criminal justice system; the reader may wish to refer to it as an aid to understanding the following material.

The Complaint

A criminal process against a defendant formally begins with a **complaint.** The word *formally* is used here because a person can be arrested for an offense before a complaint is filed or a warrant is issued. Such an arrest would be considered the beginning of the criminal process. However, because an arrest without a warrant is considered an exception to the basic warrant requirement, the complaint is still considered the formal beginning of proceedings. Also, a person may be arrested based on a report of, or a law enforcement officer's observation of, the commission of a crime, but for various reasons the prosecutor decides not to charge the defendant. The most common reason for releasing without prosecution is insufficient evidence, but other reasons may be the minimal harm caused by the offense, disinclination of the victim to press charges, and adequate alternative remedies, such as restitution to the victim. Once the decision to charge is made, however, the next step is the filing of the complaint.

The complaint can serve a dual purpose in a criminal proceeding. If the defendant has been arrested without a warrant, the complaint is prepared, signed, and filed at the defendant's initial appearance before the magistrate. The complaint serves as the charging document on which the preliminary examination will be held. If the defendant has not been arrested and is not before the court, the complaint serves as the basis for determining whether there is probable cause (fair probability) to justify issuing a warrant for his or her arrest.

www.courts.net/
Court directory for U.S. courts; provides access to Web sites maintained by courts nationwide

profs.lp.findlaw.com/ legalresearch/ch12/index.html Article dealing with all aspects of state courts by Kent C. Olson

www.lawsource.com/also/ Provides links to Web sites for the courts and other governmental agencies for all fifty states

www.webpack.net~tca3sec/ mcharged.htm Article, "You Have Been Charged With a Misdemeanor— What Happens Now?"

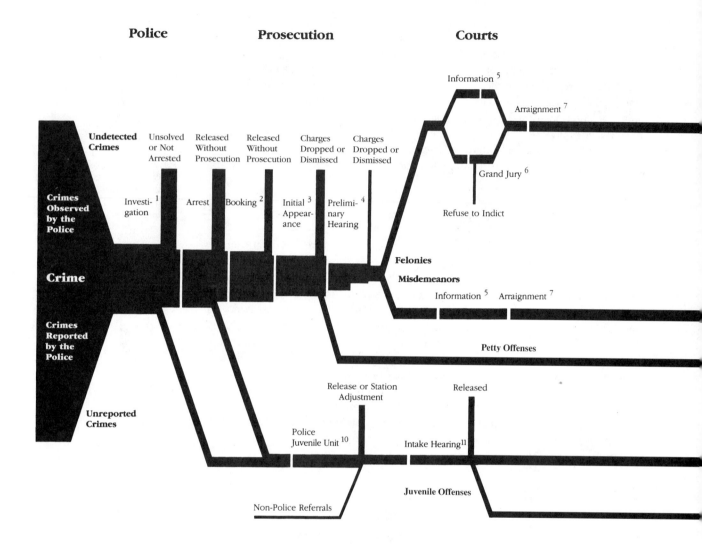

1.   May continue until trial.
2.   Administrative record of arrest. First step at which temporary release on bail may be available.
3.   Before magistrate, commissioner, or justice of peace. Formal notice of charge, advice of rights. Bail set. Summary trials for petty offenses usually conducted here without further processing.
4.   Preliminary testing of evidence against defendant. Charge may be reduced. No separate preliminary hearing for misdemeanors in some systems.

5.   Charge filed by prosecutor on basis of information submitted by police or citizens. Alternative to grand jury indictment; often used in felonies, almost always in misdemeanors.
6.   Reviews whether government evidence sufficient to justify trial. Some states have no grand jury system; others seldom use it.

General View of the Criminal Justice System
■ EXHIBIT 2.3

Corrections

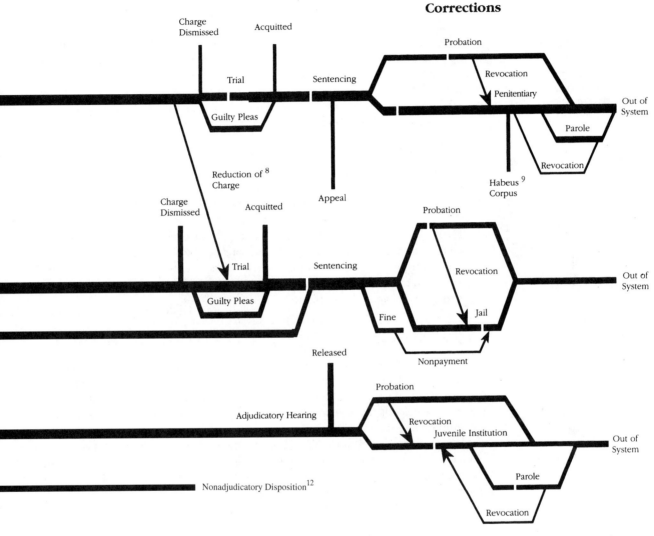

7. Appearance for plea; defendant elects trial by judge or jury (if available); counsel for indigent usually appointed here in felonies. Often not at all in other cases.

8. Charge may be reduced at any time prior to trial in return for plea of guilty or for other reasons.

9. Challenge on constitutional grounds to legality of detention. May be sought at any point in process.

10. Police often hold informal hearings, dismiss or adjust many cases without further processing.

11. Probation officer decides desirability of further court action.

12. Welfare agency, social services, counseling, medical care, etc., for cases where adjudicatory handling not needed.

Report by the President's Commission on Law Enforcement and Administration of Justice: The Challenge of Crime in a Free Society 8, 9 (1967).

www.totse.com/en/law/
justice_for_all/accused2.html
Handbook, "What You Should
Know If You're Accused of a
Crime" by Joyce B. David; focuses on New York law but provides a good overview of criminal
court procedure

www.co.eaton.mi.us/ecpa/
process.htm
Article, "Anatomy of a Michigan
Prosecution"; follows a case from
the commission of a crime
through an appeal

www.texasbar.com/pubinf/
legalinfo/cjp.htm
Detailed description of the Texas
criminal justice process

The complaint must be made on oath or affirmation, must state the essential facts of the offense being charged, must be in writing, and must be made before a judicial officer authorized to issue process in criminal cases. This officer is usually called a **magistrate.** The information in the complaint does not have to be derived from personal observation or experience, but it may be based on information from others or circumstantial evidence. Nevertheless, the evidence put forth in the complaint must be strong enough to convince the magistrate that there is probable cause to believe that an offense has been committed and that the defendant committed it. (Probable cause is discussed in Chapters 3 and 6.)

Affidavits

Information that is not contained in the complaint or that comes from witnesses other than the complainant may be brought to the court's attention in the form of an **affidavit.** An affidavit is a sworn written statement of the facts relied on in seeking the issuance of a warrant. An affidavit need not be prepared with any particular formality. It is filed with the complaint, and together these documents can provide a sufficient written record for a reviewing court to examine in determining whether probable cause existed for the issuance of a warrant.

Warrant or Summons Issued on the Complaint

Once the magistrate has determined from the complaint and accompanying affidavits that there is probable cause to believe that an offense has been committed and that the defendant committed it, the magistrate issues either a summons or an arrest warrant for the defendant's appearance in court. If the defendant is already before the court, no summons or warrant is necessary.

Once the summons or warrant is issued, the law enforcement officer must serve the summons or execute the warrant by arresting the defendant and bringing the defendant before a judicial officer as commanded in the warrant. A detailed discussion of arrest warrant procedure appears in Chapter 4.

Initial Appearance before the Magistrate

Once a person has been arrested, either with or without a warrant, he or she is required by statute to be brought before a magistrate "without unnecessary delay," or "forthwith," or some similar statutory language. The details of this procedure are also discussed in Chapter 4.

Preliminary Examination

At the **preliminary examination** (also called the preliminary hearing), the magistrate must determine whether there is probable cause to believe that an offense was committed and that the defendant committed it. The purpose of the preliminary examination is to provide another judicial determination of the existence of probable cause and to protect the defendant from a totally baseless prosecution. Rule 5(c) of the Federal Rules of Criminal Procedure provides that the preliminary examination "shall be held within a reasonable time but in any event not later than 10 days following the initial appearance if the defendant is in custody and no later than 20 days if the defendant is not in custody. . . ." The rule also provides that "the preliminary examination

Complete text of Rule 5 of the
Federal Rules of Criminal
Procedure
www.law.ukans.edu/research/
frcrimI.htm#II
(Scroll down to Rule 5)

shall not be held if the defendant is indicted or if an information against the defendant is filed in district court before the date set for the preliminary examination."

The preliminary examination is a formal adversarial proceeding conducted in open court with a transcript made of the proceedings. The U.S. Supreme Court held that the preliminary examination is a critical stage of a criminal prosecution, and, as such, the defendant is entitled to have an attorney present at the hearing. *Coleman v. Alabama,* 399 U.S. 1, 90 S.Ct. 1999, 26 L.Ed.2d 387 (1970). Indigent defendants who cannot afford an attorney must be provided one at the government's expense. The preliminary examination consists mainly of the presentation of evidence against the defendant by the prosecuting attorney. The Court in *Coleman v. Alabama* described the defense attorney's function:

Coleman v. Alabama
laws.findlaw.com/us/399/1.html

> First, the lawyer's skilled examination and cross-examination of witnesses may expose fatal weaknesses in the State's case that may lead the magistrate to refuse to bind the accused over. Second, in any event, the skilled interrogation of witnesses by an experienced lawyer can fashion a vital impeachment tool for use in cross-examination of the State's witnesses at the trial, or preserve testimony favorable to the accused of a witness who does not appear at the trial. Third, retained counsel can more effectively discover the case the State has against his client and make possible the preparation of a proper defense to meet that case at the trial. Fourth, counsel can also be influential at the preliminary hearing in making effective arguments for the accused on such matters as the necessity for early psychiatric examination or bail. 399 U.S. at 9, 90 S.Ct. at 2003, 26 L.Ed.2d at 397.

If probable cause to believe that the defendant committed the offense is found, the defendant is bound over either to the grand jury or, in jurisdictions that allow prosecution by information, to the trial court for adjudication. The magistrate may admit the defendant to bail at the preliminary examination or may continue, increase, or decrease the original bail. (Bail is discussed in further detail in Chapter 1.) If no probable cause is found, the magistrate dismisses the complaint and releases the defendant. A dismissal at this stage does not invoke the constitutional safeguard against double jeopardy. This means that the prosecution may recharge the defendant and submit new evidence at a later preliminary examination. Nor does a dismissal prevent the prosecution from going to the grand jury and obtaining an indictment in states that have both grand jury and preliminary hearing procedures.

Exhibit 2.4 compares the preliminary examination with grand jury proceedings.

Indictment and Information

In felony cases, the **indictment** or the **information** replaces the complaint as the document that charges the defendant with an offense and on which the defendant is brought to trial. The indictment and the information are very similar in nature and content. Rule 7(c)(1) of the Federal Rules of Criminal Procedure defines each as a "plain, concise and definite written statement of the essential facts constituting the offense charged." The main difference between the indictment and the information is that the indictment is returned by a grand jury and signed by the foreperson of the grand jury and the prosecuting attorney. The information is signed and sworn to only by the prosecuting attorney, without the approval or intervention of the grand jury. Laws governing when the indictment or the information is used vary in different

Complete text of Rule 7 of the Federal Rules of Criminal Procedure
www.law.ukans.edu/research/frcrilII.htm
(Scroll down to Rule 7)

consumerlawpage.com/article/
grand.shtml
Article, "Grand Jury Indictment
versus Prosecution by Information: An Equal Protection–Due
Process Issue"

GRAND JURY PROCEEDINGS	PRELIMINARY EXAMINATION
Primary function is to determine whether there is probable cause to believe that the defendant committed the crime or crimes charged.	Primary function is to determine whether there is probable cause to believe that the defendant committed the crime or crimes charged.
If probable cause is found, indictment against the defendant is returned.	If probable cause is found, the defendant is bound over to the grand jury or to the trial court for adjudication.
Held in the grand jury room in closed session.	Held in open court.
Held in secret.	Open to the public.
Informal proceeding.	Formal judicial proceeding.
Nonadversarial proceeding in which grand jury hears only evidence presented by the prosecution.	Adversarial proceeding in which both the prosecution and defense may present evidence.
No judge or magistrate presides.	Judge or magistrate presides.
Defendant has no right to be present or to offer evidence.	Defendant has the right to be present and to offer evidence.
Defendant has no right to counsel.	Defendant has the right to counsel.
Power to investigate crime on grand jury's own initiative.	No power to investigate crime.
Power to subpoena witnesses and evidence.	No subpoena power.
Power to grant immunity.	No power to grant immunity.

Grand Jury vs Preliminary Exam

■ EXHIBIT 2.4

jurisdictions. An example of a typical indictment appears in Exhibit 2.5. Note the language "a true bill" in the example. This means that the grand jury found probable cause to justify the prosecution of the defendant. If the grand jury had rejected the prosecutor's accusations and found no grounds for prosecution (which is rare), it would have endorsed on the indictment form "no true bill," "not a true bill," "no bill," or some similar language.

A variety of technical statutes and rules deal with drafting, amending, and dismissing indictments and informations. These provisions are of direct concern only to judges and attorneys and are not discussed here.

```
                    UNITED STATES DISTRICT COURT
                         DISTRICT OF MAINE

UNITED STATES OF AMERICA     )
                             ) Criminal Number
            VS.              ) (21 U.S.C. §§841(a)(1), 841(b)(1)(B),
                             ) 853(a); 18 U.S.C. §2)
ROY L. PAINE                 )
```

INDICTMENT

The Grand Jury Charges:

Count One

On or about February 15, 1996, in the District of Maine,

ROY L. PAINE

defendant herein, did unlawfully, knowingly and intentionally manufacture and aid and abet the manufacture of in excess of one hundred (100) marijuana plants, a Schedule I controlled substance listed in Title 21, United States Code, Section 812, in violation of Title 21, United States Code, Sections 841(a)(1) and 841(b)(1)(B) and Title 18, United States Code, Section 2.

Count Two

On or about February 15, 1996, in the District of Maine,

ROY L. PAINE

defendant herein, did unlawfully, knowingly and intentionally possess with intent to distribute and aid and abet the possession with intent to distribute in excess of one hundred (100) marijuana plants, a Schedule I controlled substance listed in Title 21, United States Code, Section 812, in violation of Title 21, United States Code, Sections 841(a)(1) and 841(b)(1)(B) and Title 18, United States Code, Section 2.

A Typical Indictment
■ EXHIBIT 2.5

Sufficiency of Indictment

An indictment is sufficient if it adequately informs the accused of the facts and elements of the charge so that the accused is able to prepare an adequate defense or enter a plea of double jeopardy in a subsequent prosecution for the same offense. In determining the sufficiency of an indictment, courts construe the indictment in a commonsense manner and generally ignore technical errors or omissions. An indictment

---

Count Three

In committing violations of Title 21, United States Code, Section 841(a)(1) which are punishable by imprisonment for more than one year, to wit: the offenses charged by Counts One and Two of this indictment,

ROY L. PAINE

defendant herein, used and intended to use real property located off the John Tarr Road in the Town of Bowdoin, County of Sagadahoc and State of Maine which is better described in a deed from Guy Dwyer to the said ROY L. PAINE, defendant herein, dated November 9, 1985 and recorded in the Sagadahoc County Registry of Deeds at Book 733 and Page 231, including any buildings and structures located thereon, to commit and facilitate the commission of said offenses, and by virtue of the commission of said felony offenses, ROY L. PAINE, defendant herein, is forfeit of any and all interest in the said real property and such interest is vested in the United States of America and is forfeitable thereto pursuant to Title 21, United States Code, Section 853.

A TRUE BILL.

_____
Foreperson

_____
Assistant U.S. Attorney   A TRUE COPY
Dated: ATTEST: William S. Brownell, Clerk

                                 By _____
                                              Deputy Clerk

A Typical Indictment *(continued)*
■ EXHIBIT 2.5

Hamling v. United States
laws.findlaw.com/us/418/
87.html

that uses exact statutory language is usually held to be sufficient. *Hamling v. United States*, 418 U.S. 87, 94 S.Ct. 2887, 41 L.Ed.2d 590 (1974). A defendant can obtain more specific details about the crime charged by requesting the court to require that the government provide a bill of particulars. The grant or denial of this request is within the discretion of the trial court. A "bill of particulars" is a document giving the accused specific details of the charges made by the prosecutor.

Joinder and Severance

Statutes and court rules permit the joinder of offenses or defendants in the same indictment or information. Rules 8 and 14 of the Federal Rules of Criminal Procedure are illustrative:

■ **Rule 8. Joinder of Offenses and of Defendants**

(a) Joinder of Offenses. Two or more offenses may be charged in the same indictment or information in a separate count for each offense if the offenses charged, whether felonies or misdemeanors or both, are of the same or similar character or are based on the same act or transaction or on two or more acts or transactions connected together or constituting parts of a common scheme or plan.

(b) Joinder of Defendants. Two or more defendants may be charged in the same indictment or information if they are alleged to have participated in the same act or transaction or in the same series of acts or transactions constituting an offense or offenses. Such defendants may be charged in one or more counts together or separately and all of the defendants need not be charged in each count.

Complete text of Rule 8 of the Federal Rules of Criminal Procedure
www.law.ukans.edu/research/frcriIII.htm
(Scroll down to Rule 8)

■ **Rule 14. Relief from Prejudicial Joinder**

If it appears that a defendant or the government is prejudiced by a joinder of offenses or of defendants in an indictment or information or by such joinder for trial together, the court may order an election or separate trials of counts, grant a severance of defendants or provide whatever other relief justice requires. In ruling on a motion by a defendant for severance the court may order the attorney for the government to deliver to the court for inspection *in camera* any statements or confessions made by the defendants which the government intends to introduce in evidence at the trial. (A detailed discussion of joinder and severance is beyond the scope of this text.)

Complete text of Rule 14 of the Federal Rules of Criminal Procedure
www.law.ukans.edu/research/frcrimIV.htm
(Scroll down to Rule 14)

Duplicity and Multiplicity

A **duplicitous indictment** or information is one that unites two or more separate and distinct offenses in the same count. By obscuring the exact charge, duplicitous indictments or informations may violate the defendant's constitutional right to notice of charges and may impair the defendant's ability to plead double jeopardy in a subsequent prosecution. A **multiplicitous indictment** or information is one that charges the commission of a single offense in several counts. The evil of a multiplicitous indictment or information is that it may lead to multiple sentences for the same offense, or it may have some psychological effect on a jury by suggesting that the defendant has committed more than one crime. If a duplicitous or multiplicitous indictment or information is prejudicial to the defendant and the prejudice is not corrected, the indictment may be dismissed.

Prosecutorial Discretion

In our criminal justice system, the Government retains "broad discretion" as to whom to prosecute. . . . "[S]o long as the prosecutor has probable cause to believe that the accused committed an offense defined by statute, the decision whether or not to prosecute, and what charge to file or bring before a grand jury, generally rests entirely in his discretion." *Wayte v. United States,* 470 U.S. 598, 607, 105 S.Ct. 1524, 1530, 84 L.Ed.2d 547, 555–56 (1985).

Wayte v. United States
laws.findlaw.com/us/470/598.html

A prosecutor also has broad discretion in determining when to bring charges, whether to investigate, and whether to grant immunity or to plea-bargain. The prosecutor may dismiss charges against a person without giving reasons. Prosecutorial discretion is not absolute, however. It is subject to judicial review in cases in which selective prosecution or vindictive prosecution is alleged.

Selective prosecution is a violation of the equal protection clause of the Constitution. To establish selective prosecution, a defendant bears a heavy burden to show that others similarly situated were not prosecuted *and* that the defendant's prosecution was "deliberately based upon an unjustifiable standard such as race, religion, or other arbitrary classification." *Bordenkircher v. Hayes*, 434 U.S. 357, 364, 98 S.Ct. 663, 668–69, 54 L.Ed.2d 604, 611 (1978).

Vindictive prosecution violates due process. Vindictive prosecution occurs when a prosecutor increases the number or severity of charges to penalize a defendant who exercises constitutional or statutory rights. In *Blackledge v. Perry*, 417 U.S. 21, 94 S.Ct. 2098, 40 L.Ed.2d 628 (1974), a case involving a felony charge brought against a defendant who exercised a statutory right to appeal from a misdemeanor conviction for the same offense, the Court said the real basis of the vindictiveness rule is that "the fear of such vindictiveness may unconstitutionally deter a defendant's exercise of the right to appeal or collaterally attack his first conviction. . . ." 417 U.S. at 28, 94 S.Ct. at 2102, 40 L.Ed.2d at 634. In *United States v. Goodwin*, 457 U.S. 368, 381, 102 S.Ct. 2485, 2492–93, 73 L.Ed.2d 74, 85 (1982), the Court recognized a distinction between alleged vindictiveness before trial and alleged vindictiveness during or after trial:

> There is good reason to be cautious before adopting an inflexible presumption of prosecutorial vindictiveness in a pretrial setting. In the course of preparing a case for trial, the prosecutor may uncover additional information that suggests a basis for further prosecution or he simply may come to realize that information possessed by the State has a broader significance. At this stage of the proceedings, the prosecutor's assessment of the proper extent of prosecution may not have crystallized. In contrast, once a trial begins—and certainly by the time a conviction has been obtained—it is much more likely that the State has discovered and assessed all of the information against an accused and has made a determination, on the basis of that information, of the extent to which he should be prosecuted. Thus, a change in the charging decision made after an initial trial is completed is much more likely to be improperly motivated than is a pretrial decision.

Grand Jury

The Fifth Amendment provides that "[n]o person shall be held to answer for a capital, or otherwise infamous crime, unless on a presentment or indictment of a Grand Jury." As explained in Chapter 1, this Fifth Amendment requirement applies only to the federal government, although the states have developed their own varying laws and rules regarding the use of the **grand jury.** The primary duty of the grand jury is to receive complaints in criminal cases, hear the evidence put forth by the state, and return an indictment when the jury is satisfied that there is probable cause that the defendant has committed an offense. The concurrence of a specified number of grand jurors is required to return an indictment.

The grand jury is unique in that

> the whole theory of its function is that it belongs to no branch of the institutional Government, serving as a kind of buffer or referee between the Government and the people. . . . Although the grand jury normally operates, of course, in the courthouse and under judicial auspices, its institutional relationship with the Judicial Branch has traditionally been, so to speak, at arm's length. Judges' direct involvement in the function-

Bordenkircher v. Hayes
laws.findlaw.com/us/434/357.html

Blackledge v. Perry
laws.findlaw.com/us/417/21.html

United States v. Goodwin
laws.findlaw.com/us/457/368.html

www.proskauer.com/pubs/articles/cpe.html
Article, "Curbing Prosecutorial Excess: A Job for the Courts and Congress" by Arnold I. Burns, Warren L. Dennis, and Amybeth Garcia-Bokor

www.abanet.org/ceeli/conceptpapers/crimprocedure/crimpro1.html#2
Article, "An Analysis of the Control of Prosecutorial Discretion and Plea Bargaining in the United States" by Andrew L. Sonner

ing of the grand jury has generally been confined to the constitutive one of calling the grand jurors together and administering their oaths of office. *United States v. Williams,* 504 U.S. 36, 47, 112 S.Ct. 1735, 1742, 118 L.Ed.2d 352, 365 (1992).

The grand jury usually consists of sixteen to twenty-three jurors, selected from their communities according to law to serve during the criminal term of the appropriate court. Either the prosecution or the defendant, on the grounds of improper selection or legal disqualification, can challenge the composition of a grand jury. Bias in grand jury selection results in dismissal of the indictment. In *Rose v. Mitchell,* the U.S. Supreme Court said:

> Selection of members of a grand jury because they are of one race and not another destroys the appearance of justice and thereby casts doubt on the integrity of the judicial process. The exclusion from grand jury service of Negroes, or any group otherwise qualified to serve, impairs the confidence of the public in the administration of justice. As this Court repeatedly has emphasized, such discrimination "not only violates our Constitution and the laws enacted under it but is at war with our basic concepts of a democratic society and a representative government." 443 U.S. 545, 555–56, 99 S.Ct. 2993, 3000, 61 L.Ed.2d 739, 749 (1979).

Grand jury proceedings are nonadversarial and are traditionally conducted in secrecy. During deliberations or voting, no one other than the jurors is allowed to be present. When the grand jury is taking evidence, however, the attorneys for the state, the witnesses under examination, and, when ordered by the court, an interpreter and an official court reporter may be present. Matters occurring before the grand jury, other than the deliberations or the votes of any juror, may be disclosed to the prosecuting attorney for use in performing his or her duties. Otherwise, these matters are to be kept secret, unless the court orders that they be disclosed.

The reasons for keeping grand jury proceedings secret were summarized by the U.S. Supreme Court in *United States v. Procter & Gamble Co.,* 356 U.S. 677, 681 n.6, 78 S.Ct. 983, 986 n.6, 2 L.Ed.2d 1077, 1081 n.6 (1958):

> (1) to prevent the escape of those whose indictment may be contemplated; (2) to insure the utmost freedom to the grand jury in its deliberations, and to prevent persons subject to indictment or their friends from importuning the grand jurors; (3) to prevent subornation of perjury or tampering with the witnesses who may testify before grand jury and later appear at the trial of those indicted by it; (4) to encourage free and untrammeled disclosures by persons who have information with respect to the commission of crimes; (5) to protect innocent accused who is exonerated from disclosure of the fact that he has been under investigation, and from the expense of standing trial where there was no probability of guilt.

The grand jury also has broad investigative powers:

> Traditionally the grand jury has been accorded wide latitude to inquire into violations of criminal law. No judge presides to monitor its proceedings. It deliberates in secret and may alone determine the course of its inquiry. The grand jury may compel the production of evidence or the testimony of witnesses as it considers appropriate, and its operation generally is unrestrained by the technical procedural and evidentiary rules governing the conduct of criminal trials. *United States v. Calandra,* 414 U.S. 338, 343, 94 S.Ct. 613, 617, 38 L.Ed.2d 561, 568–69 (1974).

United States v. Williams
laws.findlaw.com/us/504/
36.html

Rose v. Mitchell
laws.findlaw.com/us/443/
545.html

lawschool.lexis.com/emanuel/
web/crimpro/crimpro09.htm
Outline of law relating to grand jury proceedings and other aspects of criminal court procedure
freedomlaw.com/GRANDJRY.
html
Article, "Why Grand Juries Do Not (and Cannot) Protect the Accused" by Andrew D. Leipold
wcr.sonoma.edu/v2n2/
fukurai.html
Article, "Where Did Hispanic Jurors Go? Racial and Ethnic Disenfranchisement in the Grand Jury and the Search for Justice?" by Hiroshi Fukurai

United States v. Procter & Gamble Co.
laws.findlaw.com/us/356/
677.html

United States v. Calandra
laws.findlaw.com/us/414/
338.html

The grand jury can use its broad subpoena power to compel witnesses to testify or provide physical evidence. The Fourth Amendment prohibits unreasonably vague or overbroad subpoenas for documents, and some courts hold that the evidence sought must be relevant to the investigation. Failure to obey a subpoena is punishable as contempt of court. A grand jury can also grant **immunity** to compel testimony from witnesses who exercise their Fifth Amendment privilege against self-incrimination and refuse to testify. So-called use immunity protects a witness from use of his or her testimony and any evidence derived from the testimony in future prosecutions. Transactional immunity, on the other hand, protects a witness only from prosecution for crimes to which his or her compelled testimony relates. Exhibit 2.4 compares grand jury proceedings with the preliminary examination.

Waiver of Indictment

In some jurisdictions, a defendant who does not wish to be prosecuted by indictment may waive the indictment and be prosecuted by information. The waiver of an indictment procedure is of great advantage to a defendant who wishes to plead guilty or *nolo contendere.* (These pleas are discussed in further detail later in this chapter.) In effect, the waiver of indictment procedure enables a defendant to begin serving a sentence sooner instead of having to wait for a grand jury, which sits only during the criminal term of court. The defendant can thereby secure release from custody at an earlier date than by going through the indictment procedure.

Warrant or Summons Issued on the Indictment

An indictment may sometimes be found against a defendant before the defendant has been taken into custody and brought before the court. In these cases, on the request of the prosecuting attorney or by direction of the court, the clerk shall issue a summons or a warrant for the arrest of each defendant named in the indictment. This process indicates no change of procedure for law enforcement officers, who are required to execute the warrant or serve the summons in the same way as they would any other warrant or summons. Procedures for executing an arrest warrant or serving a summons appear in Chapter 4.

Arraignment and Preparation for Trial

The next step in the criminal proceeding, after the indictment or information, is the **arraignment.** A defendant who has been arrested often confuses the meaning of the term *arraignment* with the term *initial appearance before a magistrate.* Part of the reason for the confusion is that, in misdemeanor proceedings in courts of limited jurisdiction, the two procedures are combined. The essence of the arraignment is that the defendant is called on to plead to the charge after the magistrate reads the substance of the charge. In misdemeanor proceedings, if there is no requirement of prosecution by indictment or information, the complaint is read to the defendant, and the plea is made to the complaint. However, in courts in which prosecution must be by indictment or information, the indictment or information is read to the defendant, and the plea is made to the indictment or information. Therefore, in courts that require prosecution by indictment or information, the arraignment proceeding must be separate from the initial appearance before the magistrate.

Pleas

In general, the pleas available to the defendant vary in different jurisdictions. Three of the most common pleas are as follows:

- Not guilty
- Guilty
- *Nolo contendere* (no contest)

A plea of not guilty puts in issue all the material facts alleged in the indictment, information, or complaint. A defendant has a right to refuse to plead at all, in which case the court must enter a plea of not guilty. Refusing to plead is sometimes called standing mute, and it may occur for various reasons, such as obstinacy, dumbness, insanity, mental illness or retardation, or ignorance of the language used in the proceedings.

To plead guilty or **nolo contendere,** the defendant must obtain the court's consent. Both these pleas simply mean that the defendant does not wish to contest the charge but will submit to the judgment of the court. A guilty plea may constitute an admission of guilt by the defendant and may be used against him or her in a civil action based on the same facts. A plea of *nolo contendere,* however, is not an admission of guilt and cannot be used against the defendant in a civil action.

By pleading guilty, a defendant waives many constitutional rights. Therefore, the court may not accept a plea of guilty or *nolo contendere* in a felony proceeding unless the court is satisfied, after inquiry, that the defendant committed the crime charged and that the plea is made knowingly and voluntarily with the advice of competent counsel. This inquiry by the court is often referred to as a "Rule 11 proceeding." Rule 11 of the Federal Rules of Criminal Procedure and similar state provisions establish guidelines for courts in making these and other determinations. Relevant portions of Rule 11 follow.

■ Rule 11. Pleas

(a) Alternatives.

(1) In General. A defendant may plead not guilty, guilty, or nolo contendere. If a defendant refuses to plead, or if a defendant organization, as defined in 18 U.S.C. § 18, fails to appear, the court shall enter a plea of not guilty.

(2) Conditional Pleas. With the approval of the court and the consent of the government, a defendant may enter a conditional plea of guilty or nolo contendere, reserving in writing the right, on appeal from the judgment, to review of the adverse determination of any specified pretrial motion. A defendant who prevails on appeal shall be allowed to withdraw the plea.

(b) Nolo Contendere. A defendant may plead nolo contendere only with the consent of the court. Such a plea shall be accepted by the court only after due consideration of the views of the parties and the interest of the public in the effective administration of justice.

(c) Advice to Defendant. Before accepting a plea of guilty or nolo contendere, the court must address the defendant personally in open court and inform the defendant of, and determine that the defendant understands, the following:

(1) the nature of the charge to which the plea is offered, the mandatory minimum penalty provided by law, if any, and the maximum possible penalty provided by law, including the effect of any special parole or supervised release term, the fact that the court is required to consider any applicable sentencing guidelines but may depart from those guidelines under some circumstances, and, when applicable, that

Complete text of 18 U.S.C. § 18
caselaw.findlaw.com/scripts/
ts_search.pl?title=18&sec=18
Complete text of Rule 11 of the
Federal Rules of Criminal
Procedure
www.law.ukans.edu/research/
frcrimIV.htm

www.abanet.org/ceeli/
conceptpapers/CrimProcedure/
crimpro2-5.html
Article, "Guilty Pleas and the
Public Interest: The Judicial
Role" by Abraham S. Goldstein

the court may also order the defendant to make restitution to any victim of the offense; and

(2) if the defendant is not represented by an attorney, that the defendant has the right to be represented by an attorney at every stage of the proceeding and, if necessary, one will be appointed to represent the defendant; and

(3) that the defendant has the right to plead not guilty or to persist in that plea if it has already been made, the right to be tried by a jury and at that trial the right to the assistance of counsel, the right to confront and cross-examine adverse witnesses, and the right against compelled self-incrimination; and

(4) that if a plea of guilty or nolo contendere is accepted by the court there will not be a further trial of any kind, so that by pleading guilty or nolo contendere the defendant waives the right to a trial; and

(5) if the court intends to question the defendant under oath, on the record, and in the presence of counsel about the offense to which the defendant has pleaded, that the defendant's answers may later be used against the defendant in a prosecution for perjury or false statement; and

(6) the terms of any provision in a plea agreement waiving the right to appeal or to collaterally attack the sentence.

(d) Insuring That the Plea is Voluntary. The court shall not accept a plea of guilty or nolo contendere without first, by addressing the defendant personally in open court, determining that the plea is voluntary and not the result of force or threats or of promises apart from a plea agreement. The court shall also inquire as to whether the defendant's willingness to plead guilty or nolo contendere results from prior discussions between the attorney for the government and the defendant or the defendant's attorney.

(e) Plea Agreement Procedure. [Paragraph (e) is reproduced in the next section, "Plea Bargaining."]

(f) Determining Accuracy of Plea. Notwithstanding the acceptance of a plea of guilty, the court should not enter a judgment upon such plea without making such inquiry as shall satisfy it that there is a factual basis for the plea.

(g) Record of Proceedings. A verbatim record of the proceedings at which the defendant enters a plea shall be made and, if there is a plea of guilty or nolo contendere, the record shall include, without limitation, the court's advice to the defendant, the inquiry into the voluntariness of the plea including any plea agreement, and the inquiry into the accuracy of a guilty plea.

(h) Harmless Error. Any variance from the procedures required by this rule which does not affect substantial rights shall be disregarded.

The court must also ensure the defendant's competency to plead guilty. This determination involves the same considerations as the determination of competency to stand trial, discussed later in this chapter.

Complete text of Rule 32 of the
Federal Rules of Criminal
Procedure
www.law.ukans.edu/research/
frcriVII.htm

A defendant may withdraw a guilty plea with the court's permission. Rule 32(e) of the Federal Rules of Criminal Procedure and similar state provisions govern this procedure:

(e) Plea Withdrawal. If a motion to withdraw a plea of guilty or nolo contendere is made before sentence is imposed, the court may permit the plea to be withdrawn if the defendant shows any fair and just reason. At any later time, a plea may be set aside only on direct appeal or by motion under 28 U.S.C.A. § 2255.

Complete text of 28 U.S.C.
§ 2255
caselaw.findlaw.com/scripts/
ts_search.pl?title=28&sec=
2255

In some jurisdictions, a plea of not guilty by reason of insanity may be entered. This plea is required if the defendant intends to raise the defense of insanity. A defendant may plead not guilty and not guilty by reason of insanity to the same charge. When a plea of not guilty by reason of insanity is entered, the court may, on petition, order the defendant committed to an appropriate institution for the mentally ill for examination. The insanity plea is rarely raised in a misdemeanor proceeding.

Plea Bargaining

The disposition of criminal charges by agreement between the prosecutor and the accused, sometimes loosely called "plea bargaining," is an essential component of the administration of justice. Properly administered, it is to be encouraged. If every criminal charge were subjected to a full-scale trial, the States and the Federal Government would need to multiply by many times the number of judges and court facilities.

Disposition of charges after plea discussions is an essential part of the process and a highly desirable part for many reasons. It leads to prompt and largely final disposition of most criminal cases; it avoids much of the corrosive impact of enforced idleness during pretrial confinement for those who are denied release pending trial; it protects the public from those accused persons who are prone to continue criminal conduct even while on pretrial release, and, by shortening the time between charge and disposition, it enhances whatever may be the rehabilitative prospects of the guilty when they are ultimately imprisoned.

This phase of the process of criminal justice, and the adjudicative element inherent in accepting a plea of guilty, must be attended by safeguards to insure the defendant what is reasonably due in the circumstances. Those circumstances will vary, but a constant factor is that when a plea rests in any significant degree on a promise or agreement of the prosecutor, so that it can be said to be part of the inducement or consideration, such promise must be fulfilled. *Santobello v. New York*, 404 U.S. 257, 260–62, 92 S.Ct. 495, 498–99, 30 L.Ed.2d 427, 432–33 (1971).

Santobello v. New York
laws.findlaw.com/us/404/
257.html

The federal government and most states have developed statutes or rules governing the plea bargaining process. Many states model their provisions after Rule 11(e) of the Federal Rules of Criminal Procedure:

(e) Plea Agreement Procedure.

(1) In General. The attorney for the government and the attorney for the defendant—or the defendant when acting pro se—may agree that, upon the defendant's entering of a plea of guilty or nolo contendere to a charged offense or to a lesser or related offense, the attorney for the government will:

(A) move to dismiss other charges; or

(B) recommend, or agree not to oppose the defendant's request for a particular sentence or sentencing range, or that a particular provision of the Sentencing Guidelines, or policy statement, or sentencing factor is or is not applicable to the case. Any such recommendation or request is not binding on the court; or

(C) agree that a specific sentence or sentencing range is the appropriate disposition of the case, or that a particular provision of the Sentencing Guidelines, or policy statement or sentencing factor is or is not applicable to the case. Such a plea agreement is binding on the court once it is accepted by the court.

The court shall not participate in any discussions between the parties concerning any such plea agreement.

(2) Notice of Such Agreement. If a plea agreement has been reached by the parties, the court shall, on the record, require the disclosure of the agreement in open

court or, on a showing of good cause, in camera, at the time the plea is offered. If the agreement is of the type specified in subdivision (e)(1)(A) or (C), the court may accept or reject the agreement, or may defer its decision as to the acceptance or rejection until there has been an opportunity to consider the presentence report. If the agreement is of the type specified in subdivision (e)(1)(B), the court shall advise the defendant that if the court does not accept the recommendation or request the defendant nevertheless has no right to withdraw the plea.

(3) Acceptance of a Plea Agreement. If the court accepts the plea agreement, the court shall inform the defendant that it will embody in the judgment and sentence the disposition provided for in the plea agreement.

(4) Rejection of a Plea Agreement. If the court rejects the plea agreement, the court shall, on the record, inform the parties of this fact, advise the defendant personally in open court or, on a showing of good cause, in camera, that the court is not bound by the plea agreement, afford the defendant the opportunity to then withdraw the plea, and advise the defendant that if the defendant persists in a guilty plea or plea of nolo contendere the disposition of the case may be less favorable to the defendant than that contemplated by the plea agreement.

(5) Time of Plea Agreement Procedure. Except for good cause shown, notification to the court of the existence of a plea agreement shall be given at the arraignment or at such other time, prior to trial, as may be fixed by the court.

(6) Inadmissibility of Pleas, Plea Discussions, and Related Statements. Except as otherwise provided in this paragraph, evidence of the following is not, in any civil or criminal proceeding, admissible against the defendant who made the plea or was a participant in the plea discussions:

(A) a plea of guilty which was later withdrawn;

(B) a plea of nolo contendere;

(C) any statement made in the course of any proceedings under this rule regarding either of the foregoing pleas; or

(D) any statement made in the course of plea discussions with an attorney for the government which do not result in a plea of guilty or which result in a plea of guilty later withdrawn.

However, such a statement is admissible (i) in any proceeding wherein another statement made in the course of the same plea or plea discussions has been introduced and the statement ought in fairness be considered contemporaneously with it, or (ii) in a criminal proceeding for perjury or false statement if the statement was made by the defendant under oath, on the record, and in the presence of counsel.

Blackledge v. Allison
laws.findlaw.com/us/431/
63.html

In general, plea agreements are treated as contracts. If the defendant breaches the agreement, the prosecution may not only reprosecute the defendant but also bring more serious charges. For example, in *Bordenkircher v. Hayes,* 434 U.S. 357, 98 S.Ct. 663, 54 L.Ed.2d 604 (1978), the U.S. Supreme Court found no due process violation when the prosecutor carried out a threat made during plea negotiations to reindict the defendant on more serious charges if the defendant did not plead guilty to the original charge. If the defendant alleges that the prosecution breached a plea agreement and the allegations are not "palpably incredible" or "patently frivolous or false," the defendant is entitled to an evidentiary hearing. *Blackledge v. Allison,* 431 U.S. 63, 97 S.Ct. 1621, 52 L.Ed.2d 136 (1977). If the defendant establishes such a breach, the court may allow the defendant to withdraw the plea, may alter the sentence, or may require the prosecution to honor the agreement.

Motions

A **motion** is an oral or written request asking a court to make a specified finding, decision, or order. Many standard motions are available, but an attorney may also fashion unique motions in response to particular circumstances requiring court action. Some of the most common standard pretrial motions are: motion to be admitted to bail, motion to quash a grand jury indictment, motion to inspect grand jury minutes, motion to challenge the sufficiency of the indictment, motion for a competency hearing, motion for discovery, motion for a continuance, motion for change of venue, motion to dismiss an indictment, motion for joinder or severance of codefendants, and motion to withdraw a guilty plea. Most of these motions are discussed elsewhere in this chapter or are primarily of concern to judges and attorneys and, therefore, beyond the scope of this book.

Two pretrial motions, however, are central to criminal procedure law: (1) the motion to suppress evidence and (2) the motion to suppress a confession. These motions are made by defendants who believe they are aggrieved by either an unlawful search and seizure or an unlawfully obtained admission or confession. Some jurisdictions do not allow one or both of these motions to be made before trial. The purpose of a motion to suppress is twofold:

- To enable the defendant to invoke the exclusionary rule and prevent the use of illegally obtained evidence at trial
- To enable the court to resolve the issue of the legality of a search and seizure or confession without interrupting the trial

The hearing on the motion to suppress is often the point in the proceedings at which the court carefully scrutinizes a law enforcement officer's performance in a case. If the defendant is able to prove that an officer illegally obtained evidence, and if the evidence is essential to the prosecution's case, suppression of the evidence is likely to result in a dismissal of charges or the granting of a motion for judgment of acquittal. Therefore, law enforcement officers must know the law not only at the time they conduct a search and seizure or obtain a confession, but also when they may be called on to justify their actions at a hearing on a motion to suppress.

Depositions

When a witness is unable to attend a criminal trial and it is shown that his or her testimony is material to a just determination of the case, the court may order that a **deposition** of the witness be taken at any time after the filing of an indictment or information. Obtaining a deposition involves taking the out-of-court testimony of a witness and preserving that testimony in writing for later use in court. A deposition is used only in exceptional circumstances and not for the mere convenience of a witness or party. Either the prosecution or the defendant may request it, and the opposing party may attend the taking of the deposition.

A deposition, or a part of a deposition, may be used at a trial or hearing if it appears that any of the following circumstances exist:

- The witness who gave the deposition is dead.
- The witness is out of the jurisdiction (unless the party offering the deposition caused the witness's absence).
- The witness is unable to attend or testify because of sickness or infirmity.

Complete text of Rules 12.1 and 16 of the Federal Rules of Criminal Procedure
www.law.ukans.edu/research/
frcrimIV.htm
(Scroll down to Rule 12.1 and Rule 16)
Complete text of Rule 26.2 of the Federal Rules of Criminal Procedure
www.law.ukans.edu/research/
frcrimVI.htm
(Scroll down to Rule 26.2)

■ The party offering the deposition is unable to procure the attendance of the witness by subpoena.

Furthermore, depositions may be used even if the witness does testify at the trial, but only for the purposes of contradicting or impeaching the witness's testimony.

Discovery

Discovery, also called pretrial discovery, is a procedure, largely governed by statute or court rule, whereby the defendant or the prosecution is enabled to inspect, examine, copy, or photograph items in the possession of the other party. Discovery in federal cases is governed by Rules 12.1, 16, and 26.2 of the Federal Rules of Criminal Procedure. Among the items subject to discovery are tangible objects, tape recordings, books, papers (including written or recorded statements made by the defendants or witnesses), and the results or reports of physical examinations and scientific tests, experiments, and comparisons. The general purpose of discovery is to make the criminal trial "less a game of blindman's bluff and more a fair contest with the basic issues and facts disclosed to the fullest practical extent." *United States v. Procter & Gamble Co.,* 356 U.S. 677, 682, 78 S.Ct. 983, 986–87, 2 L.Ed.2d 1077, 1082 (1958).

Ordinarily, to obtain the right to discovery, a party must make a timely motion before the court and must show that the specific items sought may be material to the preparation of its case and that its request is reasonable. Nevertheless, jurisdictions differ considerably with respect to both the conditions under which discovery is allowed and the items subject to discovery. Some jurisdictions do not allow discovery at all. Others allow discovery only for the defendant, in an effort to correct the imbalance between the investigative resources of the prosecution and the defendant, thereby enabling the defendant to prepare a more adequate defense. A recent development is automatic informal discovery for certain types of evidence, without the necessity for motions and court orders. The state of the law governing discovery is constantly changing, but the trend appears to be in favor of broadening the right of discovery for both the defense and the prosecution.

"There is no general constitutional right to discovery in a criminal case. . . ." *Weatherford v. Bursey,* 429 U.S. 545, 559, 97 S.Ct. 837, 846, 51 L.Ed.2d 30, 42 (1977). Nevertheless, to protect defendants' due process rights, courts have created constitutional rules requiring disclosure of evidence in certain situations. In *Brady v. Maryland,* 373 U.S. 83, 87, 83 S.Ct. 1194, 1196–97, 10 L.Ed.2d 215, 218 (1963), the U.S. Supreme Court held that "the suppression by the prosecution of evidence favorable to an accused upon request violates due process where the evidence is material either to guilt or punishment, irrespective of the good faith or bad faith of the prosecution." In *United States v. Bagley,* 473 U.S. 667, 682, 105 S.Ct. 3375, 3383, 87 L.Ed.2d 481, 494 (1985), the Court held:

Weatherford v. Bursey
laws.findlaw.com/us/429/
545.html
Brady v. Maryland
laws.findlaw.com/us/373/
83.html
United States v. Bagley
laws.findlaw.com/us/473/
667.html

> The evidence is material only if there is a reasonable probability that, had the evidence been disclosed to the defense, the result of the proceeding would have been different. A "reasonable probability" is a probability sufficient to undermine confidence in the outcome.

As the Court explained in *Kyles v. Whitley,* 514 U.S. 419, 434, 115 S.Ct. 1555, 1566, 131 L.Ed.2d 490, 506 (1995), "[t]he question is not whether the defendant would more likely than not have received a different verdict with the evidence, but whether in its absence he received a fair trial, understood as a trial resulting in a verdict worthy of

Kyles v. Whitley
laws.findlaw.com/us/000/
u10294.html

confidence." That case required disclosure of exculpatory evidence to the defense, even if the police have not revealed the evidence to the prosecutor. According to the Court, prosecutors are responsible for ensuring that police communicate relevant evidence to the prosecutor's office. *Giglio v. United States*, 405 U.S. 150, 92 S.Ct. 763, 31 L.Ed.2d 104 (1972), held that the prosecutor must also disclose information that may be used to impeach the credibility of prosecution witnesses, including law enforcement officers. Such information could include the prior criminal records or other acts of misconduct of prosecution witnesses, or such information as promises of leniency or immunity offered to prosecution witnesses. In *United States v. Henthorn*, 931 F.2d 29 (9th Cir. 1991), the Court held that the government has a duty to examine the personnel files of testifying law enforcement officers for *Brady* material; for example, information that could compromise the credibility of those law enforcement officers, including past accusations of misconduct.

Giglio v. United States
laws.findlaw.com/us/405/
150.html

The *Brady* rule does not, however, require the prosecution to make its files available to the defendant for an open-ended "fishing expedition" or to disclose inculpatory, neutral, or speculative evidence or evidence that is available to the defendant from other sources through the defendant's own efforts. Also, the prosecution has no *Brady* obligation to provide the defense potentially exculpatory information that would not be admissible in court. Thus, in *Wood v. Bartholomew*, 516 U.S. 1, 116 S.Ct. 7, 133 L.Ed.2d 1 (1995), the U.S. Supreme Court held that there is no requirement to turn over the results of a polygraph examination of a witness because such information is not admissible in a court of law.

Wood v. Bartholomew
laws.findlaw.com/us/000/
u10235.html

Subpoena

The term **subpoena** describes the process used to secure the attendance of witnesses or the production of books, papers, documents, or other objects at a criminal proceeding. It is the primary vehicle by which the defendant exercises the Sixth Amendment right to "compulsory process for obtaining witnesses in his favor" (see Chapter 1). The subpoena is usually issued by a judicial officer, and it commands the person to whom it is directed to attend a trial, hearing, or deposition for the purpose of testifying at the proceeding or bringing a named document or object. As discussed earlier, the grand jury also has broad subpoena powers. A law enforcement officer or any other adult person who is not a party to the proceedings can serve a subpoena. A typical form for a subpoena in a criminal case appears in Exhibit 2.6.

Competency to Stand Trial

The test for determining competency to stand trial is whether the defendant "has sufficient present ability to consult with his lawyer with a reasonable degree of rational understanding—and whether he has a rational as well as factual understanding of the proceedings against him." *Dusky v. United States*, 362 U.S. 402, 402, 80 S.Ct. 788, 789, 4 L.Ed.2d 824, 825 (1960). Due process requires a court to hold a competency hearing if there is sufficient doubt regarding a defendant's competency. "[E]vidence of a defendant's irrational behavior, his demeanor at trial, and any prior medical opinion on competence to stand trial are all relevant in determining whether further inquiry is required. . . ." *Drope v. Missouri*, 420 U.S. 162, 180, 95 S.Ct. 896, 908, 43 L.Ed.2d 103, 118 (1975).

Dusky v. United States
laws.findlaw.com/us/362/
402.html

Drope v. Missouri
laws.findlaw.com/us/420/
162.html

When a court finds that a defendant is incompetent to stand trial, criminal proceedings against the defendant are suspended until such time as the defendant may be

AO 89 (Rev. 11/91) Subpoena in a Criminal Case

United States District Court

_____ DISTRICT OF _____

SUBPOENA IN A CRIMINAL CASE

V.

CASE NUMBER:

TO:

☐ YOU ARE COMMANDED to appear in the United States District Court at the place, date, and time specified below to testify in the above case.

PLACE	COURTROOM
	DATE AND TIME

☐ YOU ARE ALSO COMMANDED to bring with you the following document(s) or object(s):

U.S. MAGISTRATE JUDGE OR CLERK OF COURT	DATE
(By) Deputy Clerk	

ATTORNEY'S NAME, ADDRESS AND PHONE NUMBER:

A Typical Subpoena
■ EXHIBIT 2.6

found competent. If future competency is highly probable, the defendant may be committed to a mental institution for a reasonable period of time to determine future competency. During this period, the court may order periodic examination of the defendant to determine whether competency has been regained. After such a reasonable time,

AO 89 (Rev. 11/91) Subpoena in a Criminal Case

PROOF OF SERVICE			
RECEIVED BY SERVER	DATE	PLACE	
SERVED	DATE	PLACE	
SERVED ON (PRINT NAME)		FEES AND MILEAGE TENDERED TO WITNESS ☐ YES ☐ NO AMOUNT $_____	
SERVED BY (PRINT NAME)		TITLE	

DECLARATION OF SERVER

    I declare under penalty of perjury under the laws of the United States of America that the foregoing information contained in the Proof of Service is true and correct.

Executed on _____   _____
         Date   *Signature of Server*

                _____
           Address of Server

ADDITIONAL INFORMATION

A Typical Subpoena *(continued)*
■ EXHIBIT 2.6

the government must either institute civil commitment proceedings or release the defendant. *Jackson v. Indiana*, 406 U.S. 715, 92 S.Ct. 1845, 32 L.Ed.2d 435 (1972).

    A claim that a defendant is incompetent to stand trial must be distinguished from the claim that a defendant is not guilty by reason of insanity. The former concerns only the defendant's mental fitness at the time of trial and is unrelated to any determination of guilt. The latter is a defense to prosecution on the ground that the defendant was mentally impaired at the time that an alleged crime was committed.

Jackson v. Indiana
laws.findlaw.com/us/406/
715.html

Venue

One final pretrial matter to be considered is **venue.** Venue is often confused with **jurisdiction.** Jurisdiction refers to the authority of the court to deal with a particular type of case. For instance, a municipal court may have jurisdiction over misdemeanor offenses. Venue, on the other hand, merely refers to the place at which the authority of the court should be exercised. Article III, Section 2, Paragraph 3, of the U.S. Constitution states that "[t]he Trial of all Crimes . . . shall be held *in the State where the said Crimes shall have been committed,* . . ." and the Sixth Amendment requires that "[i]n all criminal prosecutions, the accused shall enjoy the right to a speedy and public trial, by an impartial jury *of the State and district wherein the crime shall have been committed,* which district shall have been previously ascertained by law. . . ." (emphasis supplied). A typical state statute or rule requires that the trial of certain types of cases be held in the geographic division of the court in which the offense was committed. Most jurisdictions also have special rules relating to the proper venue for an offense that is committed on a boundary of two counties or for an offense partly committed in one county and partly in another. (These technicalities are not discussed here.)

Sometimes, because of heavy publicity or intense community feeling, a defendant may wish to have his or her case tried in a different place than the one authorized by statute. To accomplish this, a defendant may make a motion for a change of venue. The motion usually must be made before the jury is impaneled or, in cases in which there is no jury, before any evidence is received. The defendant must give adequate reasons in support of the motion. Typical grounds for granting a motion for change of venue are:

- Such prejudice prevails in the county where the case is to be tried that the defendant cannot obtain a fair and impartial trial there.
- Another location is much more convenient for the parties and witnesses than the intended place of trial, and the interests of justice require a transfer of location.

The Trial

The Sixth Amendment to the U.S. Constitution guarantees a defendant in a criminal prosecution the right to a speedy, public, and impartial trial by jury. The right to a jury trial was made applicable to the states through the due process clause of the Fourteenth Amendment in *Duncan v. Louisiana:*

Duncan v. Louisiana
laws.findlaw.com/us/391/145.html

> Because we believe that trial by jury in criminal cases is fundamental to the American scheme of justice, we hold that the Fourteenth Amendment guarantees a right of jury trial in all criminal cases which—were they to be tried in federal court—would come within the Sixth Amendment guarantee. 391 U.S. 145, 149, 88 S.Ct. 1444, 1447, 20 L.Ed.2d 491, 496 (1968).

This guarantee means that a defendant must be provided a jury trial in all criminal prosecutions except those for petty offenses. In *Baldwin v. New York,* the U.S. Supreme Court held that "no offense can be deemed 'petty' for purposes of the right to trial by jury where imprisonment for more than six months is authorized." 399 U.S. 66, 69, 90 S.Ct. 1886, 1888, 26 L.Ed.2d 437, 440 (1970). A defendant who is prosecuted in a single proceeding for multiple counts of a petty offense, however, does not have a con-

Baldwin v. New York
laws.findlaw.com/us/399/66.html

stitutional right to a jury trial, even if the aggregate of sentences authorized for the offense exceeds six months. *Lewis v. United States,* 518 U.S. 322, 116 S.Ct. 2163, 135 L.Ed.2d 590 (1996). For an offense punishable by a sentence of six months or less, a defendant has a constitutional right to a jury trial only if the additional statutory penalties "are so severe that they clearly reflect a legislative determination that the offense in question is a 'serious' one." *Blanton v. City of North Las Vegas,* 489 U.S. 538, 543, 109 S.Ct. 1289, 1293, 103 L.Ed.2d 550, 556 (1989). There is no right to jury trial in juvenile court proceedings. *McKeiver v. Pennsylvania,* 403 U.S. 528, 91 S.Ct. 1976, 29 L.Ed.2d 647 (1971). Defendants who do not wish to be tried by a jury may, with the approval of the court, waive in writing their right to a jury trial. The waiver must be voluntary, knowing, and intelligent. A defendant has no absolute constitutional right to a trial without a jury.

Lewis v. United States
laws.findlaw.com/us/000/
u20025.html

Blanton v. City of North Las Vegas
laws.findlaw.com/us/489/
538.html
McKeiver v. Pennsylvania
laws.findlaw.com/us/403/
528.html

Trial without a Jury

A trial without a jury is also called a **bench trial** or a **nonjury trial.** When a case is tried without a jury, the judge must perform the jury's functions of weighing the evidence, determining the credibility of witnesses, and finding the facts, in addition to performing his or her regular duties as judge. The judge must also make a finding that the defendant is guilty or not guilty based on the evidence presented. Outside the performance of these jury functions in a nonjury trial, the judge's other regular duties are essentially the same in either a jury or a nonjury trial. Therefore, the remainder of this chapter is concerned primarily with jury trials.

Selection of Jurors

Once it has been determined that the trial will be by jury, the next step in the criminal proceeding is the selection of the jurors. The jurors will perform the crucial tasks of finding the facts, determining the credibility of witnesses, weighing the evidence, and ultimately issuing a verdict of guilty or not guilty. Because of the importance of the jury's function, detailed rules governing the selection of jurors have been devised. These rules are designed to protect the prosecution or the defendant from having a person who is prejudiced against its cause sitting as a member of the jury during the trial.

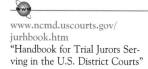

www.ncmd.uscourts.gov/
jurhbook.htm
"Handbook for Trial Jurors Serving in the U.S. District Courts"

The jury is selected by the court through an examination of prospective jurors on the **jury panel.** The **jury panel** (also called the *venire*) is a list of members of the community considered eligible for jury service. Most states have minimum qualifications for juror eligibility based on factors such as age, residence, normal intelligence, and literacy in English. The list is compiled by local officials, often according to statute. It must be indiscriminately drawn and must not systematically exclude any class of persons. The U.S. Supreme Court held that "the selection of a petit jury from a representative cross section of the community is an essential component of the Sixth Amendment right to a jury trial." *Taylor v. Louisiana,* 419 U.S. 522, 528, 95 S.Ct. 692, 697, 42 L.Ed.2d 690, 697 (1975). Federal law and the law of most states requires that no citizen be excluded from service as a juror on account of race, color, religion, gender, national origin, or economic status.

Taylor v. Louisiana
laws.findlaw.com/us/419/
522.html

The examination of prospective jurors on the panel is commonly referred to as ***voir dire,*** a term that means "to speak the truth." The usual method of examination is to question the prospective jurors about their feelings and views on various matters. The trial judge generally has broad discretion in conducting the *voir dire.* The judge may allow the parties or their attorneys to conduct the examination, or the judge may elect to personally conduct the examination.

The purpose of the examination or *voir dire* is to determine whether any prospective juror is prejudiced about the case in any way. Typical questions relate to whether prospective jurors know the defendant, the attorneys, or any of the witnesses; whether they have read about the case in the newspapers; whether they have racial, nationality, or gender biases; and whether they have formed any opinions on the case. If either attorney wishes to have a prospective juror dismissed on the basis of these questions or for any other reason, the attorney may issue a challenge to that juror. Two types of challenges are available. One is a **challenge for cause** and is directed toward the qualifications of a juror. Most jurisdictions have statutes or rules setting out the permissible grounds for a challenge for cause. Typical grounds are:

- The juror is related to one of the parties.
- The juror has given or formed an opinion in the case.
- The juror has a bias, prejudice, or particular interest in the case.

Each party has available an unlimited number of challenges for cause, assuming that the grounds for such a challenge can be established to the judge's satisfaction.

The other form of challenge is known as the **peremptory challenge.** Peremptory challenges are available to each party as a means for dismissing prospective jurors who may be qualified but for some other reason are considered undesirable by one party's attorney. No reason need be given for a peremptory challenge. Peremptory challenges must be exercised with great care. It is often difficult to determine from a few questions whether a prospective juror will be receptive or antagonistic to a party's position. Furthermore, the number of peremptory challenges available to each side is limited in number. While a peremptory challenge does not require a stated cause or reason, there are limitations to its use. For example, the prosecutor's use of peremptory challenges to deliberately produce racially unbalanced juries is unconstitutional.

> [T]he State's privilege to strike individual jurors through peremptory challenges, is subject to the command of the Equal Protection Clause. Although a prosecutor ordinarily is entitled to exercise peremptory challenges "for any reason at all, as long as that reason is related to his view concerning the outcome" of the case to be tried . . . the Equal Protection Clause forbids the prosecutor to challenge potential jurors solely on account of their race or on the assumption that black jurors as a group will be unable impartially to consider the State's case against a black defendant. *Batson v. Kentucky,* 476 U.S. 79, 89, 106 S.Ct. 1712, 1719, 90 L.Ed.2d 69, 82–83 (1986).

Batson v. Kentucky
laws.findlaw.com/us/476/
79.html

J.E.B. v. Alabama ex rel. T.B.
laws.findlaw.com/us/000/
u10411.html

In *J.E.B. v. Alabama ex rel. T.B.,* 511 U.S. 127, 114 S.Ct. 1419, 128 L.Ed.2d 89 (1994), the U.S. Supreme Court held that the equal protection clause forbids intentional discrimination on the basis of gender, just as it prohibits discrimination on the basis of race. Therefore, the use of peremptory challenges to strike potential jurors solely on the basis of gender is unconstitutional.

> Discrimination in jury selection, whether based on race or on gender, causes harm to the litigants, the community, and the individual jurors who are wrongfully excluded from participation in the judicial process. The litigants are harmed by the risk that the prejudice which motivated the discriminatory selection of the jury will infect the entire proceedings. . . . The community is harmed by the State's participation in the perpetuation of invidious group stereotypes and the inevitable loss of confidence in our judicial sys-

tem that state-sanctioned discrimination in the courtroom engenders. 511 U.S. at 140, 114 S.Ct. at 1427, 128 L.Ed.2d at 104.

Since *Batson v. Kentucky* in 1986, courts have continued to limit the unfettered use of peremptory challenges. For example, in *Powers v. Ohio*, 499 U.S. 400, 111 S.Ct. 1364, 113 L.Ed.2d 411 (1991), the prosecutor's exclusion of black potential jurors was challenged under *Batson* by a white defendant. The Court held that the equal protection clause precludes a prosecutor from challenging potential jurors either solely because of their race or on the assumption that jurors of that race, as a group, will be unable to consider the case impartially. The principles of *Batson* have likewise been extended to civil cases. *Edmonson v. Leesville Concrete Co.*, 500 U.S. 614, 111 S.Ct. 2077, 114 L.Ed.2d 660 (1991).

Powers v. Ohio
laws.findlaw.com/us/499/400.html

Edmonson v. Leesville Concrete Co.
laws.findlaw.com/us/500/614.html

Batson and its progeny have resulted in parties being entitled to an evidentiary hearing to determine the propriety of peremptory challenges against members of a protected group. This hearing is called a *Batson/Edmonson* hearing. The party who objects to the peremptory challenge presents a **prima facie case** of discrimination, and then the burden shifts to the party who raised the peremptory challenge to counter with a neutral explanation as to why the original challenge was nondiscriminatory in nature. At that point in the hearing, the moving party—the one objecting to the peremptory challenge—is given an opportunity to demonstrate that the defense offered by the other party is pretextual.

Once all the challenges available to both the prosecution and the defense are exercised, a jury is chosen and sworn in by the judge. In some cases, additional jurors are selected as alternates; they hear the evidence just as the other jurors do but do not enter deliberations unless one of the regular twelve jurors becomes ill, dies, or is unable to serve for some other reason. After administering an oath to the jurors, the judge admonishes the jurors to discuss the case with no one until the jury goes into deliberations to decide the case after hearing all the evidence. Once the jury is so impaneled, the constitutional safeguard of double jeopardy attaches. (See the discussion of the Fifth Amendment in Chapter 1.)

Jury Composition

Historically, juries have been composed of twelve members. In *Williams v. Florida*, however, the U.S. Supreme Court held that a six-member jury satisfied the Sixth Amendment:

Williams v. Florida
laws.findlaw.com/us/399/78.html

> The purpose of the jury trial . . . is to prevent oppression by the Government. . . . Given this purpose, the essential feature of a jury obviously lies in the interposition between the accused and his accuser of the common-sense judgment of a group of laymen, and in the community participation and shared responsibility which results from this group's determination of guilt or innocence. The performance of this role is not a function of the particular number of the body which makes up the jury. To be sure, the number should probably be large enough to promote group deliberation, free from outside attempts at intimidation, and to provide a fair possibility for obtaining a representative cross-section of the community. But we find little reason to think that these goals are in any meaningful sense less likely to be achieved when the jury numbers six, than when it numbers 12—particularly if the requirement of unanimity is retained. And, certainly the reliability of the jury as a fact-finder hardly seems likely to be a function of its size. . . .

Similarly, while in theory the number of viewpoints represented on a randomly selected jury ought to increase as the size of the jury increases, in practice the difference between the 12-man and the six-man jury in terms of the cross-section of the community represented seems likely to be negligible. 399 U.S. 78, 100–02, 90 S.Ct. 1893, 1905–7, 26 L.Ed.2d 446, 460–61 (1970).

In *Ballew v. Georgia,* 435 U.S. 223, 98 S.Ct. 1029, 55 L.Ed.2d 234 (1978), the Court held that a five-person jury violated the Sixth Amendment.

Ballew v. Georgia
laws.findlaw.com/us/435/
223.html

Presentation of Evidence

Once the jury has been impaneled, the presentation of evidence begins with the opening statement of the prosecuting attorney. The prosecuting attorney outlines what the government intends to prove by the evidence to be presented. Usually, the defense counsel then makes an opening statement to the jury outlining what the defense intends to prove. Sometimes, however, the defense counsel will wait until the prosecutor has presented the government's evidence before giving an opening statement, thereby concealing the defense strategy until the government has disclosed its case.

After the opening statement or statements are given, the prosecutor begins introducing the government's proof. The prosecution is entitled to present its evidence first in a criminal case because it is the plaintiff and therefore has the **burden of proof.** Because the accused is presumed innocent of the allegations against him or her, the duty to establish the truth of the allegations is upon the prosecution from the beginning to the end of the trial. Furthermore, the due process clause requires the prosecution to prove beyond a reasonable doubt all the elements included in the definition of the crime with which the defendant is charged. If the prosecution fails to meet this burden of proof on any element, the defendant must be acquitted. *In re Winship,* 397 U.S. 358, 90 S.Ct. 1068, 25 L.Ed.2d 368 (1970).

In re Winship
laws.findlaw.com/us/397/
358.html

Reasonable doubt is a term requiring little interpretation, although various courts have attempted to formulate somewhat involved definitions that add little beyond its plain meaning. It is sufficient to say that proof beyond a reasonable doubt requires that the guilt of the defendant be established to a reasonable, but not absolute or mathematical, certainty. Probability of guilt is not enough. In other words, to satisfy the "beyond a reasonable doubt" standard, the jury must be satisfied that the charges against the defendant are almost certainly true.

Rules of Evidence

The rules of evidence govern which evidence will be admissible in court and which will be excluded. These rules deal with matters such as relevancy, privileges, presumptions, witnesses, expert testimony, hearsay, authentication, and judicial notice. (A discussion of the rules of evidence is beyond the scope of this text.)

Order of Presentation of Evidence

lawschool.lexis.com/emanuel/
web/evid/index.html
"Evidence: Capsule Summary" by
Emanuel Publishing Corporation
www.law.cornell.edu/topics/
evidence.html
Provides links to federal and
state evidence rules and court
decisions on the law of evidence

The order of presentation of evidence begins with the **direct examination** or examination in chief of the prosecution's first witness. This witness is someone the prosecution calls and expects to give evidence favorable to the government's position. The examination of the witness is designed to produce evidence that will prove the prosecution's case against the defendant. A law enforcement officer is usually involved as a witness for the prosecution, sometimes as its only witness.

When the prosecutor is through questioning the prosecution's witness, the defense counsel has a right to question the same witness. This is known as **cross-examination.** Its purpose is either to discredit information given by the witness or to impeach the person's credibility as a witness. This is done by showing inadequacy of observation, confusion, inconsistency, bias, contradiction, and the like. In some jurisdictions, the defense attorney on cross-examination is limited to questioning the witness only on matters raised by the prosecutor during direct examination. In other jurisdictions, the defense attorney is not so limited, and the witness may be cross-examined concerning any matter that is relevant and material to an issue in question. The judge determines what is relevant and material, and may also limit cross-examination if questions are prejudicial, cumulative, confusing, or lacking a sufficient factual base. (See the discussion of the Sixth Amendment in Chapter 1 for additional material on cross-examination.)

After cross-examination, the prosecutor may wish to reexamine the prosecution's witness in order to rehabilitate him or her in the eyes of the jury. This is called **redirect examination.** Unlike cross-examination, the scope of redirect examination is limited to the matters brought out in the previous examination by the adverse party. This same rule applies if the defense counsel wishes to conduct a recross-examination. This order of presenting evidence by direct examination, cross-examination, redirect, and recross is followed for all the prosecution's witnesses until all the government's evidence has been presented.

Motion for Acquittal

After the prosecutor has presented the government's evidence, the defense counsel may move for a judgment of **acquittal.** A judgment of acquittal will be granted by the judge—even in jury trials—in cases in which the evidence is insufficient to sustain a conviction on the offense or offenses charged. This usually means the judge has decided that reasonable persons could not conclude that guilt has been proven beyond a reasonable doubt. If the motion is not granted at the close of the prosecution's evidence, the defense may then offer its evidence. The motion for acquittal may be renewed at the close of all the evidence, or, at the judge's discretion, it may be renewed after the jury returns a verdict or is discharged without having returned a verdict.

The Defendant's Evidence

Assuming that the court does not grant a motion for judgment of acquittal at the close of the prosecution's evidence, the defense counsel then has an opportunity to present evidence. The defense may put forth one or more of several possible defenses to refute the proof offered by the prosecution. Among the defenses available to the defendant are alibi, insanity, duress, self-defense, and entrapment. In presenting any of these defenses, the defense counsel may call witnesses on direct examination. The prosecutor has a right to cross-examine each of the defense witnesses, just as the defense counsel had a right to cross-examine the prosecution's witnesses.

Defendants may choose to testify in their own behalf or to exercise their constitutional privilege against self-incrimination and not testify. Defendants who do testify are treated much like any other witness. If a defendant chooses not to testify, the prosecuting attorney is not permitted to comment to the jury upon the failure to testify. *Griffin v. California,* 380 U.S. 609, 85 S.Ct. 1229, 14 L.Ed.2d 106 (1965).

Griffin v. California
laws.findlaw.com/us/380/
609.html

Rebuttal by the Prosecution

Assuming that a motion for judgment of acquittal is not granted at the close of defendant's evidence, the prosecution is entitled to present rebuttal proof at this time. Rebuttal proof is designed to controvert evidence presented by the defense and to rebut any special defenses raised. Rebuttal proof is limited to new material brought out in the defendant's presentation of evidence. Law enforcement officers may be called as witnesses again at this stage of the prosecution to correct any errors or misleading impressions that might be left after the defendant's presentation of evidence. After rebuttal, the defense may present additional evidence.

Closing Arguments

After all the evidence has been presented, both the prosecutor and the defense attorney are allotted certain amounts of time, usually specified by statute or rule, for final argument. In the final argument, attorneys for each side attempt to convince the jury (or in nonjury cases, the judge) of the correctness of their positions. The prosecutor presents the government's argument first and is followed by the attorney for the defense. The prosecutor is then allowed to present a short rebuttal. Much leeway is given for the attorneys for both sides to use their wit and imagination to win the jury over to their respective positions. However, the attorneys are required to confine themselves to a discussion of the evidence presented and reasonable inferences to be derived from that evidence.

Instructions to the Jury

After the final arguments and before the jury retires for deliberations, the judge must give **instructions** to the jury regarding the law of the case. Attorneys for both sides are given an opportunity to submit written requests to the judge for particular instructions that they wish to be given. In a typical case, the instructions cover such matters as the respective responsibilities of the court and the jury, the presumption of innocence and the burden of proof, various evidentiary problems, a definition of the offense or offenses charged, additional clarification of the critical elements of those offenses, any defenses that are available in the case, and the procedures to be followed in the jury room. The exact content of the instructions is a matter for the judge's discretion, but the attorneys are given an opportunity to object to any portion of the charge or any omission from it.

The judge may summarize the evidence for the jury members, help them recall details, and attempt to reduce complicated evidence into its simplest elements. However, the judge may not express any opinion on any issue of fact in the case or favor either side in summarizing the evidence. Furthermore, when a jury has no sentencing function, it should be instructed to "reach its verdict without regard to what sentence might be imposed." *Rogers v. United States*, 422 U.S. 35, 40, 95 S.Ct. 2091, 2095, 45 L.Ed.2d 1, 7 (1975).

Rogers v. United States
laws.findlaw.com/us/422/
35.html

The principle that juries are not to consider the consequences of their verdicts is a reflection of the basic division of labor in our legal system between judge and jury. The jury's function is to find the facts and to decide whether, on those facts, the defendant is guilty of the crime charged. The judge, by contrast, imposes sentence on the defendant after the jury has arrived at a guilty verdict. Information regarding the consequences of a verdict is therefore irrelevant to the jury's task. Moreover, providing jurors sentencing information invites them to ponder matters that are not within their province, distracts them from their factfinding responsibilities, and creates a strong possibility of confusion. *Shannon v. United States*, 512 U.S. 573, 579, 114 S.Ct. 2419, 2424, 129 L.Ed.2d 459, 466–67 (1994).

Shannon v. United States
laws.findlaw.com/us/000/
ul0384.html

Verdict

After receiving instructions, the jury retires to the jury room to begin deliberations on a **verdict.** The verdict is the decision of the jury as to the defendant's guilt or innocence. In federal cases, court decisions and Rule 31(a) of the Federal Rules of Criminal Procedure require a unanimous verdict for conviction. In state jury trials, however, a verdict of fewer than twelve members of a twelve-member jury satisfies the Sixth Amendment. *Apodaca v. Oregon*, 406 U.S. 404, 92 S.Ct. 1628, 32 L.Ed.2d 184 (1972), held that conviction by ten votes of a twelve-member jury in a state court did not violate the Sixth Amendment right to a jury trial. And *Johnson v. Louisiana*, 406 U.S. 356, 92 S.Ct. 1620, 32 L.Ed.2d 152 (1972), held that conviction by nine votes of a twelve-member jury in a state court did not violate the due process guarantee of the Fourteenth Amendment. If, however, the state uses six-member juries, the verdict must be unanimous. *Burch v. Louisiana*, 441 U.S. 130, 99 S.Ct. 1623, 60 L.Ed.2d 96 (1979). If the jurors are so irreconcilably divided in opinion that they are unable to agree on a verdict, a **hung jury** results. The jurors are then dismissed, and the case must be either retried or dismissed. If, however, an agreement is reached on a verdict, the jurors return to the courtroom, and the verdict is read in open court by the jury foreperson. Any party, or the court itself, may then request a poll of the jury. This simply involves asking each juror whether he or she concurs in the verdict. The purpose of polling the jury is to make sure that the verdict was not reached as a result of the coercion or domination of one juror by others or as a result of sheer mental or physical exhaustion of a juror. If, during the poll, it is found that any juror did not concur in the verdict, the whole jury may be directed to retire for further deliberations or may be discharged by the judge.

Apodaca v. Oregon
laws.findlaw.com/us/406/
404.html
Johnson v. Louisiana
laws.findlaw.com/us/406/
356.html
Burch v. Louisiana
laws.findlaw.com/us/441/
130.html

Complete text of Rule 31 of the Federal Rules of Criminal Procedure
www.law.ukans.edu/research/
frcrimVI.htm
(Scroll down to Rule 31)

Jury nullification is the power of a jury to acquit regardless of the strength of the evidence against a defendant. An acquittal is, of course, final and cannot be appealed by the prosecution. Nor can the prosecution bring charges based on the same offense against the defendant again. Nullification usually occurs when the defendant is particularly sympathetic or when the defendant is prosecuted for violating an unpopular law. In a decision that rejected the appellants' request to have the jury informed of its power of nullification, the court said:

> The way the jury operates may be radically altered if there is alteration in the way it is told to operate. The jury knows well enough that its prerogative is not limited to the choices articulated in the formal instructions of the court. The jury gets its understanding as to the arrangements in the legal system from more than one voice. There is the formal communication from the judge. There is the informal communication from the total culture—literature (novel, drama, film, and television); current comment (newspapers, magazines and television); conversation; and, of course, history and tradition. The totality of input generally convey adequately enough the idea of prerogative, of freedom in an occasional case to depart from what the judge says. *United States v. Dougherty*, 473 F.2d 1113, 1135 (D.C.Cir. 1972).

www.ce9.uscourts.gov/web/
sdocuments.nsf/crim
"Manual of Model Criminal Jury Instructions"; comprehensive model jury instructions for federal judges with explanations and annotations
www.fija.org/juror-handbook.
htm
"Jurors' Handbook: A Citizen's Guide to Jury Duty"; focuses on the jury nullification power

Some states require their courts to instruct juries on the power of nullification, and the issue continues to be debated.

Sentence and Judgment

After the defendant's guilt or innocence has been determined, either by verdict of the jury or by a judge without a jury, the judge must enter a judgment in the case. The **judgment** is merely the written evidence of the final disposition of the case, signed by the judge. A judgment of conviction sets forth the plea, the verdict or findings, and the adjudication and sentence. If the defendant is found not guilty or for some other reason is entitled to be discharged, the judgment is entered accordingly, and the defendant is guaranteed by the double jeopardy clause of the Constitution to be free forever from any further prosecution for the crime for which he or she was tried. (See Chapter 1 for a discussion of double jeopardy.) If the defendant is found guilty, the judge must pass sentence on the defendant before entering judgment.

The determination of the **sentence** is perhaps the most sensitive and difficult decision the judge has to make, because of the effect it will have on the defendant's life. For this reason, most jurisdictions have laws directing and guiding the judge in this determination. In general, sentencing courts have broad discretion to consider various kinds of information. 18 U.S.C.A. § 3661 states in its entirety, "No limitation shall be placed on the information concerning the background, character, and conduct of a person convicted of an offense which a court of the United States may receive and consider for the purpose of imposing an appropriate sentence." A sentencing court may even consider conduct of which a defendant has been acquitted, so long as that conduct has been proved by a preponderance of the evidence. *United States v. Watts*, 519 U.S. 148, 117 S.Ct. 633, 136 L.Ed.2d 554 (1997).

Rule 32(a)(1) of the Federal Rules of Criminal Procedure and similar state provisions require judges to impose sentence without unnecessary delay. This protects the defendant from a prolonged period of uncertainty about the future. In addition, Rule 32(c)(3) provides that, before imposing sentence, the judge must "(B) afford defendant's counsel an opportunity to speak on behalf of the defendant;" and "(C) address the defendant personally and determine whether the defendant wishes to make a statement and to present any information in mitigation of the sentence." The purpose of these provisions is to enable the defendant and defense counsel to present any information that may assist the court in determining punishment. The prosecution is also given an equivalent opportunity to speak to the court.

In addition, in most jurisdictions, the victim of the crime is provided an opportunity to participate at sentencing either by an oral statement in open court or by written statement to the court. The court, in its discretion, may allow others, such as the victim's family and friends and members of the victim's community, to participate at sentencing. After imposing sentence, the court is required to notify the defendant of the defendant's right to appeal, including any right to appeal the sentence.

Another typical provision designed to assist the court in fixing sentence either allows or mandates the court to consider the report of a presentence investigation before the imposition of sentence. This report is prepared by a probation and parole board or similar agency and contains the prior criminal record of the defendant and such other information on personal history and characteristics, financial condition, and the circumstances affecting the defendant's behavior that may be helpful to the court in imposing sentence. The presentence investigation report may also include specific sentence recommendations, information on the effects of the offense on the victims, and available alternatives to imprisonment.

The Constitution also restricts the information that the judge may properly consider in determining sentence. Examples are:

Complete text of 18 U.S.C.
§ 3661
caselaw.findlaw.com/scripts/ts_
search.pl?title=18&sec=3661

United States v. Watts
laws.findlaw.com/us/000/
u20050.html

Complete text of Rule 32 of the
Federal Rules of Criminal
Procedure
www.law.ukans.edu/research/
frcriVII.htm

- Due process prohibits a judge from relying on materially untrue assumptions. *Townsend v. Burke,* 334 U.S. 736, 68 S.Ct. 1252, 92 L.Ed. 1690 (1948).

- Due process prohibits a judge from vindictively imposing a harsher punishment on a defendant for exercising constitutional rights. *North Carolina v. Pearce,* 395 U.S. 711, 89 S.Ct. 2072, 23 L.Ed.2d 656 (1969).

- The First Amendment prohibits a judge from considering the defendant's religious or political beliefs. *United States v. Lemon,* 723 F.2d 922 (D.C.Cir. 1983). In *Wisconsin v. Mitchell,* 508 U.S. 476, 113 S.Ct. 2194, 124 L.Ed.2d 436 (1993), however, the U.S. Supreme Court held that, although the First Amendment protects the defendant's "abstract beliefs" from being considered at sentencing, a sentence may be enhanced because the defendant intentionally selected the victim on account of the victim's race. The court explained that the "Constitution does not erect a per se barrier to the admission of evidence concerning one's beliefs and associations at sentencing simply because those beliefs and associations are protected by the First Amendment." 508 U.S. at 486, 113 S.Ct. at 2200, 124 L.Ed.2d at 445.

- The Eighth Amendment prohibits the imposition of excessive fines and the infliction of cruel and unusual punishments on persons convicted of a crime. (See Chapter 1 for a discussion of the Eighth Amendment.)

The court has a number of alternatives open to it with respect to sentencing, depending largely on individual criminal statutes. Some criminal statutes have mandatory sentences, some have fixed maximum sentences, some have fixed minimum sentences, and others leave the matter of sentencing to the judge. Therefore, depending on the offense for which the defendant has been convicted, the court may have very broad discretion in fixing sentence or no discretion whatsoever. In a few jurisdictions, the jury has the power to fix the sentence as well as to determine guilt or innocence.

In federal courts, sentencing is determined through the use of guidelines promulgated by the U.S. Sentencing Commission under the Sentencing Reform Act of 1984. The guidelines (18 U.S.C.A. Appendix Chapters 1–7) consist of a grid of forty-three offense levels and six criminal history categories. They became effective on November 1, 1987, and apply to offenses committed on or after that date. The Sentencing Reform Act abolished indeterminate sentencing and parole and created a sentencing structure that attempts to establish similar sentences for similarly situated defendants and varies the sentence imposed to reflect differences in the severity of the criminal conduct. The act also creates a sentencing method in which the sentence imposed by the judge generally determines the actual time that the convicted person will serve in prison. Restitution is a mandatory sentence for conviction of certain crimes. Judges are allowed to depart from the sentencing guidelines when a defendant has provided substantial assistance in the investigation or prosecution of another person and to correct perceived unjust effects of the guidelines in extraordinary cases. (A detailed discussion of the Sentencing Reform Act is beyond the scope of this text.) Prosecutors in state cases often employ these federal sentencing principles or similar guidelines in fashioning sentencing recommendations for the judge.

The court also has the power to place a defendant on **probation** for certain offenses. Probation is usually controlled by statute. It is a procedure by which a person found guilty of an offense is released by the court, subject to conditions imposed by the court, without being committed to a penal or correctional institution. Probation of a defendant is usually effected in one of two ways. The court may sentence the defendant,

Townsend v. Burke
laws.findlaw.com/us/334/
736.html
North Carolina v. Pearce
laws.findlaw.com/us/395/
711.html
Wisconsin v. Mitchell
laws.findlaw.com/us/508/
476.html

www.ussc.gov/2000guid/
TABCON00.htm
"2000 Federal Sentencing Guideline Manual"; contains the federal sentencing guidelines and policy statements effective November 1, 2000
www.ussc.gov/training/
intro599.pdf
"An Introduction to Federal Guidelines Sentencing" by Lucien B. Campbell and Henry J. Bemporad
www.ussc.gov/training/
tipsart.pdf
Article, "Federal Sentencing Advocacy: Tips for Beginning Practitioners" by Donald A. Purdy & Gustavo A. Gelpi
www.uakron.edu/lawrev/
witten.html
Article, "Sentence Entrapment and Manipulation: Government Manipulation of the Federal Sentencing Guidelines"

suspend the execution of the sentence, and place the defendant on probation with the provision that if the defendant is found to have violated the terms of the probation, he or she can then be remanded to serve the underlying suspended sentence. Alternatively, the court may continue the matter for sentencing for no more than two years and during that period place the defendant on probation with the provision that a violation of probation may result in the court then passing sentence on the underlying verdict. A defendant placed on probation is usually under the control and supervision of a probation and parole board or similar agency, although still under the jurisdiction of the court.

In some jurisdictions, a different type of probation may be imposed by the court for cases that involve the violation of certain statutes concerning controlled or illegal drugs or narcotics. In these cases, the court may impose sentence, place the defendant on probation, and require as a condition of probation that the defendant participate in programs at an approved drug treatment facility.

In federal cases, probation is governed by the Sentencing Reform Act of 1984, which treats probation as a sentence in its own right and not as a suspension of sentence. The act specifically limits the offenses for which probation may be granted and imposes mandatory conditions that the person on probation not commit another crime and not possess illegal controlled substances. If the conviction is for a felony, the act requires that one or more of the following be imposed as conditions of probation: a fine, an order of restitution, or community service.

The *U.S. Sentencing Commission Guidelines Manual* recommends that the following conditions be imposed on all probationers: restricted travel without prior permission, regular reporting to a probation officer, answering all inquiries of the probation officer, supporting all dependents and meeting other family responsibilities, working at a regular occupation, notifying the probation officer of change in residence or employment, refraining from possession of drugs and drug paraphernalia and excessive use of alcohol, not frequenting places where illegal drugs are sold, not associating with those known to engage in criminal activity, permitting a probation officer to visit at any time, notifying the probation officer of any arrest, not becoming a government informant without court permission, and notifying any applicable third party of the probationer's criminal record. The *Guidelines Manual* suggests that the following special conditions be imposed if appropriate: prohibition on ownership of weapons, restitution, fines, credit limitations, financial disclosure, community confinement, home detention, community service, occupational restrictions, participation in a mental health or substance abuse program, intermittent confinement, and curfew.

Complete text of Rule 32.1 of the Federal Rules of Criminal Procedure
www.law.ukans.edu/research/frcriVII.htm
(Scroll down to Rule 32.1)

Probation revocation and modification are governed by the Sentencing Reform Act of 1984 and Rule 32.1 of the Federal Rules of Criminal Procedure. In general, probation can be revoked at any time before the end of the probationary period for any violation of probation conditions that occurs during the probation period. The burden of proof that the government must satisfy for probation violations is typically preponderance of the evidence, a standard substantially less than proof beyond a reasonable doubt, and the standard typically applicable to civil lawsuits.

Posttrial Motions

After judgment has been entered, several motions are still available to the defendant to challenge the court's decision. One of these is the motion for judgment of acquittal, sometimes called a motion for "judgment notwithstanding the verdict." The statutes or rules in some jurisdictions provide that this motion can be made after the jury has been discharged so long as it is made within a specified time after the discharge. Courts do not usually grant such a motion unless

- the prosecution's evidence was insufficient or nonexistent on a vital element of the offense charged; or
- the indictment or information did not state a criminal offense under the law of the jurisdiction.

Another motion open to the defendant is the motion for a new trial. This motion may be made in addition to a motion for acquittal. When it is made alone, it is sometimes deemed to include a motion for acquittal. In the latter case, if the defendant moves for a new trial, the court in granting it may either enter a final judgment of acquittal or grant a new trial. The court may grant a new trial if it is required in the interest of justice. The usual ground for granting a new trial is insufficient evidence to support the verdict. Some courts have also considered errors of law and improper conduct of trial participants during the trial under the motion.

Another ground for granting a motion for a new trial is the discovery of new evidence, which carries with it the procedural difference of an extended time period during which the motion may be made. The time period varies among different jurisdictions, but is usually longer than the period for a motion based on any other ground. This longer period allows a reasonable amount of time for the discovery of new evidence. To justify the granting of a motion for a new trial on the ground of newly discovered evidence, it must be shown that the new evidence was discovered after the trial, that it will probably change the result of the trial, that it could not have been discovered before the trial by the exercise of due diligence, that it is material to the issues involved, and that it is not merely cumulative or impeaching.

In some jurisdictions, by motion of either the defendant or the court, the defendant may obtain a revision or correction of sentence. The power to revise a sentence is granted to enable the trial court to change a sentence that is inappropriate in a particular case, even though the sentence may be legal and was imposed in a legal manner. This power to revise a sentence includes a limited power to increase as well as reduce the sentence.

In contrast to the power to revise, the power to correct a sentence is granted to enable the court to change a sentence because the sentence was either illegal or imposed in an illegal manner. An example of an illegal sentence is one that was in excess of the statutory maximum. An example of an illegally imposed sentence is one in which the defendant was not personally addressed by the judge and given an opportunity to be heard before sentencing, when such a procedure is required by statute. The court must exercise both its power to revise and its power to correct a sentence within specific time periods, or the powers are lost. A federal court's power to correct a sentence is limited by the Sentencing Reform Act of 1984.

Remedies after Conviction

There are two major forms of relief for a defendant after being convicted of a crime: **appeal** and *habeas corpus.* Each is discussed separately here.

Appeal

A defendant has a right to **appeal** after being convicted of a crime and after the trial judge has decided all posttrial motions. The appeal procedure varies among different jurisdictions and is not detailed here. It involves, among other things, the filing of a notice of appeal, the designation of the parts of the trial record to be considered on appeal, the filing of a statement of points on appeal, the filing of briefs, and the arguing of the briefs before the appellate court. If a defendant is unable to afford a lawyer to handle the appeal, provision is made by statute or court rule for a lawyer to be appointed by the court free of charge.

In some jurisdictions, by statute, the prosecution is also given a right to appeal adverse decisions of the trial court. The prosecution's right to appeal, however, is usually much more limited than the defendant's right. Typical statutes allow appeal by the prosecution of adverse rulings made before the jury hears the case or in cases in which the defendant has appealed. The procedure for appeal by the prosecution is essentially the same as it is for appeal by the defendant.

The appeal procedure is not a retrial of the case, nor is it ordinarily a reexamination of factual issues. The determination of factual issues is the function of the jury or, in a nonjury case, the lower court judge. The appellate court's function in an appeal is primarily to review the legal issues involved in the case. The following example illustrates this point:

> Suppose a law enforcement officer obtained a confession from a defendant but forgot to give the *Miranda* warnings before a custodial interrogation. During the case's trial, the trial judge erroneously permitted the officer who obtained the confession to read it to the jury over the objection of the defense. The jury convicted the defendant. On appeal, the defendant argues that the trial judge committed an error of law in allowing the jury to hear the confession.
>
> The appellate court would very likely reverse the conviction on the basis of the error of law made by the trial judge. Along with reversal, the usual procedure is to remand the case (send it back to the trial court for a new trial) with instructions to exclude the confession from the jury in the new trial. A different jury would then hear the evidence in the case, without the illegally obtained confession, and render another verdict. Therefore, even though a conviction is reversed on appeal, it does not necessarily mean that the defendant is acquitted and can go free. It usually means simply that the defendant has won the right to be tried again.

Generally, to obtain appellate court review of an issue, the appealing party (appellant) must preserve its claim by making a specific timely objection at or before trial. This is called the contemporaneous objection rule. If the appellant failed to make a timely objection, the appellate court will consider the claim only if it constitutes "plain error." Plain errors are defects seriously affecting substantial rights that are so prejudicial to a jury's deliberations "as to undermine the fundamental fairness of the trial and bring about a miscarriage of justice." *United States v. Polowichak*, 783 F.2d 410, 416 (4th Cir. 1986).

On the other hand, even though the appellant preserved its claim by timely objection and the appellate court found that an error occurred in the trial court, the appellate court may still affirm the conviction if it finds that the error was "harmless." This so-called harmless error rule avoids "setting aside of convictions for small errors or defects that have little, if any, likelihood of having changed the result of the trial." *Chapman v. California*, 386 U.S. 18, 22, 87 S.Ct. 824, 827, 17 L.Ed.2d 705, 709 (1967). If the error was of constitutional dimensions, the appellate court must determine "beyond a reasonable doubt that the error complained of did not contribute to the verdict obtained." 386 U.S. at 23, 87 S.Ct. at 828, 17 L.Ed.2d at 710. If the error was not of con-

Chapman v. California
laws.findlaw.com/us/386/
18.html

stitutional dimensions, the appellate court must determine with "fair assurance after pondering all that happened without stripping the erroneous action from the whole that the judgment was not substantially swayed by the error. . . ." *Kotteakos v. United States,* 328 U.S. 750, 765, 66 S.Ct. 1239, 1248, 90 L.Ed. 1557, 1566–67 (1946).

Most types of error are subject to harmless error analysis, including classic trial errors involving the erroneous admission of evidence. *Arizona v. Fulminante,* 499 U.S. 279, 111 S.Ct. 1246, 113 L.Ed.2d 302 (1991). Some types of error, however, involve rights so basic to a fair trial that they can never be considered harmless. Examples of these types of errors are:

- Conflict of interest in representation throughout the entire proceeding. *Holloway v. Arkansas,* 435 U.S. 475, 98 S.Ct. 1173, 55 L.Ed.2d 426 (1978).
- Denial of the right to an impartial judge. *Chapman v. California,* 386 U.S. 18, 87 S.Ct. 824, 17 L.Ed.2d 705 (1967).
- Racial discrimination in grand jury selection. *Vasquez v. Hillery,* 474 U.S. 254, 106 S.Ct. 617, 88 L.Ed.2d 598 (1986).
- Failure to inquire whether a defendant's guilty plea is voluntary. *United States v. Gonzalez,* 820 F.2d 575 (2d Cir. 1987).

If the appellate court finds that the trial court committed no errors of law or only harmless errors, it will affirm the defendant's conviction. The defendant may, however, still have a chance for further appeal. If the appeal was heard in an intermediate appellate court, an additional appeal to the highest appellate court in the jurisdiction is possible. If the defendant's appeal was heard in the highest appellate court in a state, an appeal may be made to the U.S. Supreme Court. Note that the U.S. Supreme Court and the highest appellate courts of some states have discretionary jurisdiction and may select the cases they will hear. Defendants have no right to compel such a court to hear their appeals.

Appeals may be taken only from cases that have come to a final judgment. This means that an appellate court will not decide any legal issues, nor will it review the denial of any motions until the trial court has finally disposed of the case. The reason for this rule is to prevent unnecessary delays in the conduct of trials that would result if the parties could appeal issues during the course of a trial. (There are some minor exceptions to the final judgment rule, but they are not discussed here.)

When an appellate court decides a case, it delivers a written opinion to explain and justify its decision. In this way the higher court explains the trial judge's errors and also informs the party losing the appeal that it has lost and why. The decisions of the appellate courts are compiled and published in books of reported court decisions, which can be found in law libraries. Attorneys and judges use these reported decisions as authorities for arguing and deciding future cases that raise issues similar to those already decided.

Habeas Corpus

FEDERAL *HABEAS CORPUS* FOR STATE PRISONERS   State prisoners who challenge the fact or duration of their confinement on constitutional grounds and seek immediate or speedier release may petition for a writ of *habeas corpus* (also known as the Great Writ) in federal district court. The federal statute governing the *habeas corpus* remedy is 28 U.S.C.A. § 2254. (A state prisoner who challenges the conditions of confinement or attempts to obtain damages should seek relief by means of a civil action under 42 U.S.C.A. § 1983.)

Kotteakas v. United States
laws.findlaw.com/us/328/750.html

Arizona v. Fulminante
laws.findlaw.com/us/499/279.html

Holloway v. Arkansas
laws.findlaw.com/us/435/475.html

Vasquez v. Hillery
laws.findlaw.com/us/474/254.html

profs.lp.findlaw.com/habeas/index.html
Article, "Federal *Habeas Corpus* Review: A Brief Overview" by Todd Maybrown

Complete text of 28 U.S.C. § 2254
caselaw.findlaw.com/scripts/ts_search.pl?title=28&sec=2254

Complete text of 42 U.S.C. § 1983
caselaw.findlaw.com/scripts/ts_search.pl?title=42&sec=1983

Since the Judiciary Act of February 5, 1867, *habeas corpus* has been available to state prisoners "in all cases where any person may be restrained of his or her liberty in violation of the Constitution or of any treaty or law of the United States." Initially, the constitutional grounds for which *habeas corpus* relief could be granted were limited to those relating to the jurisdiction of the state court, but the U.S. Supreme Court extended the scope of the writ to all constitutional challenges by its decision in *Fay v. Noia*, 372 U.S. 391, 83 S.Ct. 822, 9 L.Ed.2d 837 (1963).

Fay v. Noia
laws.findlaw.com/us/372/
391.html

Although in form the Great Writ is simply a mode of procedure, its history is inextricably intertwined with the growth of fundamental rights of personal liberty. For its function has been to provide a prompt and efficacious remedy for whatever society deems to be intolerable restraints. Its root principle is that in a civilized society, government must always be accountable to the judiciary for a man's imprisonment: if the imprisonment cannot be shown to conform with the fundamental requirements of law, the individual is entitled to his immediate release. Thus there is nothing novel in the fact that today *habeas corpus* in the federal courts provides a mode for the redress of denials of due process of law. Vindication of due process is precisely its historic office. 372 U.S. at 401–02, 83 S.Ct. at 828–29, 9 L.Ed.2d at 846–47.

Brecht v. Abrahamson
laws.findlaw.com/us/507/
619.html

In *Brecht v. Abrahamson*, 507 U.S. 619, 623, 113 S.Ct. 1710, 1714, 123 L.Ed.2d 353, 363 (1993), the Court held that the standard for determining whether *habeas corpus* relief must be granted for constitutional trial errors is whether the error "had substantial and injurious effect or influence in determining the jury's verdict."

In 1976, the U.S. Supreme Court limited federal *habeas corpus* review of state prisoners' claims of violations of federal constitutional rights, holding that "where the State has provided an opportunity for full and fair litigation of a Fourth Amendment claim, a state prisoner may not be granted federal habeas corpus relief on the ground that evidence obtained in an unconstitutional search or seizure was introduced at his trial." *Stone v. Powell*, 428 U.S. 465, 494, 96 S.Ct. 3037, 3052, 49 L.Ed.2d 1067, 1088 (1976). With that limitation, however, other constitutional claims of state prisoners may be heard in a federal *habeas corpus* proceeding even though a state court has fully adjudicated the claims. *Townsend v. Sain*, 372 U.S. 293, 83 S.Ct. 745, 9 L.Ed.2d 770 (1963). Furthermore, "Stone's restriction on the exercise of federal habeas jurisdiction does not extend to a state prisoner's claim that his conviction rests on statements obtained in violation of the safeguards mandated by *Miranda v. Arizona*. . . ." *Withrow v. Williams*, 507 U.S. 680, 681, 113 S.Ct. 1745, 1748, 123 L.Ed.2d 407, 413 (1993).

Stone v. Powell
laws.findlaw.com/us/428/
465.html

Townsend v. Sain
laws.findlaw.com/us/372/
293.html

Withrow v. Williams
laws.findlaw.com/us/507/
680.html

Prisoners must exhaust available state remedies before a federal court will consider their constitutional claim on *habeas corpus*. This rule means that, if an appeal or other procedure to hear a claim is still available by right in the state court system, the prisoner must pursue that procedure before a federal *habeas corpus* application will be considered. Federal *habeas corpus* review may likewise be barred if a defendant is unable to show cause for noncompliance with a state procedural rule and to show some actual prejudice resulting from the alleged constitutional violation. *Wainwright v. Sykes*, 433 U.S. 72, 97 S.Ct. 2497, 53 L.Ed.2d 594 (1977).

Wainwright v. Sykes
laws.findlaw.com/us/433/
72.html

In 1996, Congress, in response to the bombing of the federal building in Oklahoma City, passed the Antiterrorism and Effective Death Penalty Act. The *habeas corpus* provisions of that act establish a one-year limitation on filing *habeas corpus* petitions and provide new procedures governing the disposition of second or successive petitions. Before the district court will hear a second or successive petition, the petitioner is required to obtain an authorization order from a three-judge panel in the appropriate court of appeals. The grant or denial of an authorization order cannot be appealed to the U.S. Supreme Court and is not subject to rehearing. In *Felker v. Turpin*, 518 U.S. 651, 116 S.Ct. 2333, 135 L.Ed.2d 827 (1996), the Court found the "gatekeeping" requirements constitutional but found nothing in the law to limit or remove its authority to hear original petitions for *habeas corpus*, thereby preserving its own power to review.

Felker v. Turpin
laws.findlaw.com/us/000/
u20029.html

The remedies available to courts deciding *habeas corpus* petitions include reclassifying a petitioner's conviction or ordering the state to retry or resentence a petitioner. Release of the prisoner is granted only if the state fails to comply with the court's order of relief. *Burkett v. Cunningham*, 826 F.2d 1208 (3rd Cir. 1987).

HABEAS CORPUS RELIEF FOR FEDERAL PRISONERS In 1948, Congress enacted a statute (28 U.S.C.A. § 2255) that was designed to serve as a substitute for *habeas corpus* for federal prisoners. The primary purpose of the statute was to shift the jurisdictions of the courts hearing *habeas corpus* applications. The statute did not change the basic scope of the remedy that had been available to federal prisoners by *habeas corpus*. Section 2255 provides, in part:

Complete text of 28 U.S.C. § 2255
caselaw.findlaw.com/scripts/ts_search.pl?title=28&sec=2255

> **Section 2255. Federal custody; remedies on motion attacking sentence.** A prisoner in custody under sentence of a court established by Act of Congress claiming the right to be released upon the ground that the sentence was imposed in violation of the Constitution or laws of the United States, or that the court was without jurisdiction to impose such sentence, or that the sentence was in excess of the maximum authorized by law, or is otherwise subject to collateral attack, may move the court which imposed the sentence to vacate, set aside or correct the sentence. . . .
>
> An application for a writ of habeas corpus in behalf of a prisoner who is authorized to apply for relief by motion pursuant to this section, shall not be entertained if it appears that the applicant has failed to apply for relief, by motion, to the court which sentenced him, or that such court has denied him relief, unless it also appears that the remedy by motion is inadequate or ineffective to test the legality of his detention.

prof.findlaw.com/habeas/
checklist.html
Checklist for the Antiterrorism and Effective Death Penalty Act of 1996

In *Hill v. United States*, 386 U.S. 424, 428, 82 S.Ct. 468, 471, 7 L.Ed.2d 417, 421 (1962), the U.S. Supreme Court held that a petitioner is not entitled to *habeas corpus* relief under Section 2255 unless the violation of federal law was a "fundamental defect which inherently results in a complete miscarriage of justice [or] an omission inconsistent with the rudimentary demands of fair procedure." The Section 2255 remedy is similar to the *habeas corpus* remedy for state prisoners, discussed earlier. (Although there are some significant distinctions between the two remedies, they are beyond the scope of this text and not discussed here.)

Hill v. United States
laws.findlaw.com/us/386/
424.html

STATE POSTCONVICTION RELIEF Almost all states have postconviction procedures permitting prisoners to challenge constitutional violations. These procedures may derive from statutes, court rules, or the common law. Many of these state remedies are as extensive in scope as federal *habeas corpus* for state prisoners. Other states provide much narrower remedies. (The differences in postconviction remedies among the states are beyond the scope of this text and not discussed here.)

Summary

The purpose of this chapter is to provide law enforcement officers and other criminal justice professionals with a better understanding of some of the legal terms and procedures involved in a criminal case, from the initial report of a crime through an appeal to the U.S. Supreme Court. Although much of the information is not immediately useful for carrying out daily duties, it can help enhance the criminal justice professional's perception of his or her role in the entire criminal justice system and the importance of properly performing that role to the effective and just operation of the system.

Review and Discussion Questions

1. Draw a diagram of the hierarchy of federal and state courts with criminal jurisdiction in your state. Indicate whether each court has original or appellate criminal jurisdiction, and explain any peculiarities in the jurisdiction of each court (for example, whether it handles only misdemeanors, or whether it has a limited appellate jurisdiction).

2. Draw a diagram of the progress of a felony case in your state from warrantless arrest through appeal to the U.S. Supreme Court. Assume that, at each stage of the proceedings, the decision is adverse to the defendant, who then seeks relief at the next highest tribunal.

3. Discuss the differences and similarities among a complaint, an affidavit, an indictment, and an information.

4. Why is the arraignment sometimes confused with the initial appearance before the magistrate?

5. What is the grand jury, and what is its function? Discuss the similarities and differences between grand jury proceedings and a preliminary examination.

6. What pleas are available to a person charged with a crime, and what is the effect of each?

7. What is the difference between jurisdiction and venue, and between a challenge for cause and a peremptory challenge?

8. Why is a motion to suppress important to a law enforcement officer?

9. Explain the meaning of burden of proof in a criminal case, discussing the standard of proof in this type of case.

10. Name and briefly describe three ways in which a defendant can obtain relief from the courts after a verdict of guilty.

Chapter 3

Basic Underlying Concepts

Before discussing in detail the law of criminal procedure—arrest, search and seizure, admissions and confessions, and pretrial identification—it is helpful to lay some further groundwork by presenting four basic concepts fundamental to criminal procedure. The concepts discussed here are the exclusionary rule, privacy, probable cause, and reasonableness. Later in this book, they will be developed in greater detail and clarified by examples. Because these concepts are so pervasive and so essential to an understanding of criminal procedure, discussing them at the outset should make the following chapters more meaningful.

Exclusionary Rule

The **exclusionary rule** requires that any evidence obtained by police using methods that violate a person's *constitutional* rights must be excluded from use in a criminal prosecution against that person. This rule is judicially imposed and arose relatively recently in the development of our legal system. Under the common law, the seizure of evidence by illegal means did not affect its admissibility in court. Any evidence, however obtained, was allowed as long as it satisfied other criteria for admissibility, such as relevance and trustworthiness. The exclusionary rule was first developed in 1914 in the case of *Weeks v. United States,* 232 U.S. 383, 34 S.Ct. 341, 58 L.Ed. 652, and was limited to a prohibition on the use of evidence illegally obtained by federal law enforcement officers. Not until 1949, in the case of *Wolf v. Colorado,* 338 U.S. 25, 27–28, 69 S.Ct. 1359, 1361, 93 L.Ed. 1782, 1785, did the U.S. Supreme Court rule that the Fourth Amendment was applicable to the states through the due process clause of the Fourteenth Amendment:

> The security of one's privacy against arbitrary intrusion by the police—which is at the core of the Fourth Amendment—is basic to a free society. It is therefore implicit in the "concept of ordered liberty" and as such enforceable against the States through the Due Process Clause.

The Court, however, left enforcement of Fourth Amendment rights to the discretion of the states and did not require application of the exclusionary rule. That mandate did not come until 1961, in the landmark decision of *Mapp v. Ohio,* 367 U.S. 643, 655, 81 S.Ct. 1684, 1691, 6 L.Ed.2d 1081, 1090, in which the Court said:

> Since the Fourth Amendment's right of privacy has been declared enforceable against the States through the Due Process Clause of the Fourteenth, it is enforceable against them by the same sanction of exclusion as is used against the Federal Government. Were it otherwise, then just as without the *Weeks* rule the assurance against unreasonable federal searches and seizures would be "a form of words," valueless and undeserving of mention in a perpetual charter of inestimable human liberties, so too, without that rule the freedom from state invasions of privacy would be so ephemeral and so neatly severed from its conceptual nexus with the freedom from all brutish means of coercing evidence as not to merit this Court's high regard as a freedom "implicit in the 'concept of ordered liberty.'"

As discussed in Chapter 1, the Supreme Court has made other constitutional guarantees in the Bill of Rights applicable to the states through the due process clause of the Fourteenth Amendment. For example, the Fifth Amendment privilege against self-incrimination was made applicable to the states in *Malloy v. Hogan,* 378 U.S. 1, 84 S.Ct.

Weeks v. United States
laws.findlaw.com/us/232/383.html
Wolf v. Colorado
laws.findlaw.com/us/338/25.html
Mapp v. Ohio
laws.findlaw.com/us/367/643.html

Malloy v. Hogan
laws.findlaw.com/us/378/1.html

1489, 12 L.Ed.2d 653 (1964), and the Sixth Amendment right to counsel was made applicable to the states in *Gideon v. Wainwright*, 372 U.S. 335, 83 S.Ct. 792, 9 L.Ed.2d 799 (1963). The manner in which the exclusionary rule is used to enforce the rights guaranteed in these amendments and others is discussed in detail in later chapters.

The U.S. Supreme Court has also invoked the exclusionary rule to protect certain "due process of law" rights that are not specifically contained in the Constitution or its amendments. For example, a confession that has been coerced and is therefore involuntary will be excluded from evidence because it is a violation of due process of law. Similarly, pretrial identification procedures that are not fairly administered may be violations of due process of law.

The exclusionary rule was designed to deter police misconduct. It follows that evidence illegally obtained by persons other than the police will not be rendered inadmissible in court—that is, such evidence is admissible. In *Burdeau v. McDowell*, 256 U.S. 465, 41 S.Ct. 574, 65 L.Ed. 1048 (1921), a private citizen illegally seized certain papers from another private citizen and turned them over to the government. The Court said:

> The papers having come into the possession of the government without a violation of petitioner's right by governmental authority, we see no reason why the fact that individuals, unconnected with the government, may have wrongfully taken them, should prevent them from being held for use in prosecuting an offense where the documents are of an incriminatory character. 256 U.S. at 476, 41 S.Ct. at 576, 65 L.Ed. at 1051.

If, however, police instigate, encourage, or participate in an illegal search or other constitutional violation, and if the private citizen acts with the intent of assisting the police, he or she will be considered an agent of the government. The evidence thus gathered will be subject to the exclusionary rule as if it had been gathered by a governmental official. *United States v. Lambert*, 771 F.2d 83, 89 (6th Cir. 1985).

Alternatives to the Exclusionary Rule

Theoretically, there are several alternatives to the exclusionary rule. An illegal **search** and **seizure** may be criminally actionable, and an officer performing an illegal search or seizure may be subject to prosecution. However, examples of officers being criminally prosecuted for overzealous law enforcement are extremely rare. An officer who makes an illegal search and seizure is subject to internal departmental discipline procedures, which may be backed up in the few jurisdictions that have adopted them by the oversight and participation of police review boards. Again, however, examples of disciplinary actions are exceedingly rare.

Persons who have been illegally arrested or have had their privacy invaded will usually have a tort action available under state statute or common law. Moreover, law enforcement officers acting under color of state law who violate a person's Fourth Amendment rights are subject to a suit for damages and other remedies in federal courts under a federal civil rights statute (42 U.S.C. § 1983). While federal officers and others acting under color of federal law are not subject jurisdictionally to this statute, the Supreme Court has held that a right to damages for violation of Fourth Amendment rights arises by implication out of the guarantees secured and that this right is enforceable in federal courts. *Bivens v. Six Unknown Named Agents of the Federal Bureau of Narcotics*, 403 U.S. 388, 91 S.Ct. 1999, 29 L.Ed.2d 619 (1971). Lawsuits under Section 1983 are much more prevalent in recent times because of a succession of U.S. Supreme Court cases that clarified provisions of that section and provided a mechanism by which the

Gideon v. Wainwright
laws.findlaw.com/us/372/
335.html

Burdeau v. McDowell
laws.findlaw.com/us/256/
465.html

www.uncp.edu/home/
vanderhoof/geolr.html#
Exclusionary
Short summary of the law relating to the exclusionary rule
lawschool.lexis.com/emanuel/
web/crimpro07.htm
General overview of the law relating to the exclusionary rule
caselaw.findlaw.com/data/
constitution/amendment04/
06.html#1
Comprehensive discussion (with annotations) of the exclusionary rule.
www.co.alameda.ca.us/da/pov/
npsearch.htm
Article, "Non-Police Searches" from the District Attorney's Office of Alameda County, California; explains what makes a person a police agent for purposes of the exclusionary rule

For new and updated weblinks, go to www.wadsworth.com/
cj/ferdico0253

Complete text of 42 U.S.C. § 1983
caselaw.findlaw.com/scripts/ts_
search.pl?title=42&sec=1983

Bivens v. Six Unknown Named Agents of the Federal Bureau of Narcotics
laws.findlaw.com/us/403/
388.html

firms.findlaw.com/idf/
memo1.htm
Article, "A Guide to Civil Rights
Liability Under 42 U.S.C.
§ 1983: An Overview of
Supreme Court and Eleventh
Circuit Precedent"

Anderson v. Creighton
laws.findlaw.com/us/483/
635.html

plaintiff in such a suit can recover significant legal costs if he or she prevails. Moreover, there are no limits on money damages in Section 1983 suits, making these actions more popular than tort actions under state laws, which usually place limits on liability.

Nevertheless, a number of legal and practical problems stand in the way of a truly effective damage remedy. Law enforcement officers have available to them the usual common law defenses, the most important of which is the claim of good faith. Federal officers are entitled to qualified immunity based on an objectively reasonable belief that a warrantless search later determined to violate the Fourth Amendment was supported by probable cause or exigent circumstances. *Anderson v. Creighton*, 483 U.S. 635, 107 S.Ct. 3034, 97 L.Ed.2d 523 (1987). And on the practical side, those subjected to illegal arrests and searches and seizures are often disreputable people toward whom juries are unsympathetic, or they are indigent and unable to bring suit. The U.S. Supreme Court, therefore, has emphasized exclusion of unconstitutionally seized evidence in subsequent criminal trials as the only effective enforcement method. Some argue today that civil tort redress, without its present limitations, against law enforcement officers who violate individual constitutional rights in gathering incriminating evidence may be a viable alternative to the exclusionary rule.

Federal-State Conflict

Mapp v. Ohio did not require the states to follow all interpretations of federal courts in the area of criminal procedure but only interpretations dealing with constitutional guarantees. Some of the rulings handed down by the U.S. Supreme Court are based on the Court's statutory authority to promulgate rules for the supervision of federal law enforcement. These rulings apply only in federal courts. In *Ker v. California*, 374 U.S. 23, 83 S.Ct. 1623, 10 L.Ed.2d 726 (1963), the Court explicitly stated that *Mapp* established no assumption by the Supreme Court of supervisory authority over state courts, and it therefore implied no total obliteration of state laws relating to arrests and searches in favor of federal law. The Court went on to say:

> The States are not thereby precluded from developing workable rules governing arrests, searches and seizures to meet "the practical demands of effective criminal investigation and law enforcement" in the States, provided that those rules do not violate the constitutional proscription of unreasonable searches and seizures and the concomitant command that evidence so seized is inadmissible against one who has standing to complain. 374 U.S. at 34, 83 S.Ct. at 1630, 10 L.Ed.2d at 738.

The practice of state courts affording the accused greater protection under state law than that required by the U.S. Constitution is sometimes called the new federalism. It is derived from the well-established rule that state court decisions based on "adequate and independent state grounds" are immune from federal review. *Murdock v. Memphis*, 87 U.S. (20 Wall.) 590, 22 L.Ed. 429 (1875). Under this rule, state courts are free, as a matter of state constitutional, statutory, or case law, to expand individual rights by imposing greater restrictions on police than those imposed under federal constitutional law. State courts may not, however, decrease individual rights below the level established by the U.S. Constitution. Nor may state courts impose greater restrictions on police activity as a matter of federal constitutional law when the U.S. Supreme Court specifically refrains from imposing such restrictions. *Oregon v. Hass*, 420 U.S. 714, 95 S.Ct. 1215, 43 L.Ed.2d 570 (1975).

A state court has several options in responding to a U.S. Supreme Court decision that raises issues of federal law:

Ker v. California
laws.findlaw.com/us/374/
23.html

Murdock v. Memphis
laws.findlaw.com/us/87/
590.html

Oregon v. Hass
laws.findlaw.com/us/420/
714.html

- Apply the ruling as it thinks the Supreme Court would. This might include adopting the ruling as a matter of state law.
- Factually distinguish the case before it from the Supreme Court case, whereupon the decision would be subject to reversal by the Supreme Court.
- Reject the Supreme Court ruling on adequate and independent state grounds by interpreting the state constitution or state statutes to provide rights unavailable under the U.S. Constitution as interpreted by the Supreme Court. This approach clearly expresses disapproval of the Supreme Court ruling and insulates the state court decision from Supreme Court review. When the state court opinion is ambiguous as to whether it is based on an adequate and independent ground, the Supreme Court applies the so-called plain statement rule:
- [W]hen . . . a state court decision fairly appears to rest primarily on federal law, or to be interwoven with the federal law, and when the adequacy and independence of any possible state law ground is not clear from the face of the opinion, we will accept as the most reasonable explanation that the state court decided the case the way it did because it believed that federal law required it to do so. If a state court chooses merely to rely on federal precedents as it would on the precedents of all other jurisdictions, then it need only make clear by a plain statement in its judgment or opinion that the federal cases are being used only for the purpose of guidance, and do not themselves compel the result that the court has reached. In this way, both justice and judicial administration will be greatly improved. If the state court decision indicates clearly and expressly that it is alternatively based on bona fide separate, adequate, and independent grounds, we, of course, will not undertake to review the decision. *Michigan v. Long,* 463 U.S. 1032, 1040–41, 103 S.Ct. 3469, 3476, 77 L.Ed.2d 1201, 1214 (1983).

  In recent years, many state courts, reacting against the Burger and Rehnquist Courts' reluctant and sparing approach to protecting the rights of the accused, have resorted to this option to keep alive the Warren Court's active commitment to the protection and expansion of individual rights.

Michigan v. Long
laws.findlaw.com/us/463/
1032.html

One example of this trend is the case of *South Dakota v. Opperman,* 428 U.S. 364, 96 S.Ct. 3092, 49 L.Ed.2d 1000 (1976). In that case, the South Dakota Supreme Court ruled that an automobile inventory conducted by South Dakota law enforcement officers violated the Fourth Amendment, but the U.S. Supreme Court reversed the decision, holding that the police conduct was reasonable. On remand, the South Dakota Supreme Court, in *State v. Opperman,* 247 N.W.2d 673 (S.D. 1976), decided that the police inventory procedure violated the South Dakota Constitution and held that the evidence seized was inadmissible. This South Dakota court's decision is noteworthy because the search and seizure provision of the South Dakota Constitution is essentially similar to the Fourth Amendment of the U.S. Constitution and because neither the prosecution nor the defense in the case had raised the issue of the state constitution. (Other examples of the new federalism are presented in later chapters dealing with particular areas of conflict.)

South Dakota v. Opperman
laws.findlaw.com/us/428/
364.html

caselaw.findlaw.com/data/
constitution/article03/
14.html#11
Comprehensive discussion (with annotations) of Supreme Court review of state court decisions

Criticism of the Exclusionary Rule

The exclusionary rule has, throughout its existence, been the object of criticism and attempted reform. In recent years, no less a public authority than the chief justice of the U.S. Supreme Court has complained of the ineffectiveness of the exclusionary rule to achieve its purpose: the deterrence of police misconduct. In his dissent in the case of *Bivens v. Six Unknown Named Agents of the Federal Bureau of Narcotics*, 403 U.S. 388, 416–18, 91 S.Ct. 1999, 2015, 29 L.Ed.2d 619, 638–39 (1971), Chief Justice Warren E. Burger said:

> The rule does not apply any direct sanction to the individual official whose illegal conduct results in the exclusion of evidence in a criminal trial. With rare exceptions law enforcement agencies do not impose direct sanctions on the individual officer responsible for a particular judicial application of the suppression doctrine. . . . Thus there is virtually nothing done to bring about a change in his practices. The immediate sanction triggered by application of the rule is visited upon the prosecutor whose case against a criminal is either weakened or destroyed. The doctrine deprives the police in no real sense; except that apprehending wrongdoers is their business, police have no more stake in successful prosecutions than prosecutors or the public.
>
> The suppression doctrine vaguely assumes that law enforcement is a monolithic governmental enterprise. . . . But the prosecutor who loses his case because of police misconduct is not an official in the police department; he can rarely set in motion any corrective action or administrative penalties. Moreover, he does not have control or direction over police procedures or police actions that lead to the exclusion of evidence. It is the rare exception when a prosecutor takes part in arrests, searches, or seizures so that he can guide police action.
>
> Whatever educational effect the rule conceivably might have in theory is greatly diminished in fact by the realities of law enforcement work. Policemen do not have the time, inclination, or training to read and grasp the nuances of the appellate opinions that ultimately define the standards of conduct they are to follow. The issues that these decisions resolve often admit of neither easy nor obvious answers, as sharply divided courts on what is or is not "reasonable" demonstrate. Nor can judges, in all candor, forget that opinions sometimes lack helpful clarity.
>
> The presumed educational effect of judicial opinions is also reduced by the long time lapse—often several years—between the original police action and its final judicial evaluation. Given a policeman's pressing responsibilities, it would be surprising if he ever becomes aware of the final result after such a delay. Finally, the exclusionary rule's deterrent impact is diluted by the fact that there are large areas of police activity that do not result in criminal prosecutions—hence the rule has virtually no applicability and no effect in such situations.

The criticism and attempts at reform of the exclusionary rule have resulted in limitations on the application of the rule and refusals to further extend the application of the rule beyond the criminal trial context. For example, in *United States v. Calandra*, 414 U.S. 338, 94 S.Ct. 613, 38 L.Ed.2d 561 (1974), the Supreme Court held that the Fourth Amendment did not prevent the use of illegally obtained evidence by a grand jury. In *United States v. Janis*, 428 U.S. 433, 96 S.Ct. 3021, 49 L.Ed.2d 1046 (1976), the Court held that illegally obtained evidence need not be suppressed at trial in a civil case brought by the United States. In *Harris v. New York*, 401 U.S. 222, 91 S.Ct. 643, 28 L.Ed.2d 1 (1971), the Court allowed the use of illegally obtained evidence to impeach the defendant's testimony at trial. In *Pennsylvania Board of Probation v. Scott*, the Court held that "the federal exclusionary rule does not bar the introduction at parole revocation hearings of evidence seized in violation of parolees' Fourth Amendment rights." 524 U.S. 357, 364, 118 S.Ct. 2014, 2020, 141 L.Ed.2d 344, 352 (1998). And in *Stone v. Powell*, 428 U.S. 465, 494, 96 S.Ct. 3037, 3052, 49 L.Ed.2d 1067, 1088 (1976), the Court held that "where the State has provided an opportunity for full and

United States v. Calandra
laws.findlaw.com/us/414/338.html

United States v. Janis
laws.findlaw.com/us/428/433.html

Harris v. New York
laws.findlaw.com/us/401/222.html

Pennsylvania Board of Probation v. Scott
laws.findlaw.com/us/000/97-581.html

Stone v. Powell
laws.findlaw.com/us/428/465.html

fair litigation of a Fourth Amendment claim, a state prisoner may not be granted federal habeas corpus relief on the ground that evidence obtained in an unconstitutional search or seizure was introduced at his trial." The *Stone v. Powell* decision is noteworthy not only because it limited the application of the exclusionary rule but also because it strengthened the authority of state courts in interpreting the Fourth Amendment.

Despite the recent limitations on the application of the exclusionary rule by these various Supreme Court decisions, the basic holding of *Mapp v. Ohio* remains good law, and the basic tenets of the exclusionary rule remain valid legal doctrine. Any further limitations or changes in the exclusionary rule will depend largely on the makeup of the Supreme Court and the opportunities presented to the Court in the cases brought before it.

www.cato.org/pubs/pas/
pa-319es.html
Article, "In Defense of the
Exclusionary Rule" by Timothy
Lynch

Fruit of the Poisonous Tree Doctrine

The exclusionary rule is not limited to evidence that is the direct product of illegal police behavior, such as a coerced confession or the items seized as a result of an illegal search. The rule also requires exclusion of evidence that is obtained *indirectly* when one's constitutional rights are violated. This type of evidence is sometimes called **derivative evidence** or secondary evidence. In *Silverthorne Lumber Co. v. United States,* 251 U.S. 385, 392, 40 S.Ct. 182, 183, 64 L.Ed. 319, 321 (1920), the U.S. Supreme Court invalidated a subpoena that had been issued on the basis of information obtained through an illegal search:

*Silverthorne Lumber Co. v.
United States*
laws.findlaw.com/us/251/
385.html

> The essence of a provision forbidding the acquisition of evidence in a certain way is that not merely evidence so acquired shall not be used before the Court but that it shall not be used at all. Of course this does not mean that the facts thus obtained become sacred and inaccessible. If knowledge of them is gained from an independent source they may be proved like any others, but the knowledge gained by the Government's own wrong cannot be used by it in the way proposed.

Thus, the prosecution may not use in court evidence obtained directly *or indirectly* from an unconstitutional search. The prohibition against using this derivative or secondary evidence is often called the rule against admission of "fruit of the poisonous tree," the tree being the illegal search and the fruit being the evidence obtained as an indirect result of that search. The fruit, or the evidence indirectly obtained, is sometimes referred to as tainted evidence. Although the rule against the admission of fruit of the poisonous tree was originally developed in applying the exclusionary rule to unconstitutional searches, it has been applied equally to evidence obtained as the indirect result of other constitutional violations. Thus, evidence may be inadmissible if it is acquired indirectly as a result of an illegal stop, an illegal arrest, an illegal identification procedure, or an involuntary confession.

The **fruit of the poisonous tree doctrine** applies only when a person's *constitutional* rights have been violated. Neither the exclusionary rule nor the fruit of the poisonous tree doctrine applies when a violation of rights is *not* of constitutional dimensions. Nevertheless, the fruit of the poisonous tree doctrine may apply in different ways depending on the type and severity of the underlying violation of constitutional rights. As the U.S. Supreme court stated with respect to the fruit of the poisonous tree doctrine, "unreasonable searches under the Fourth Amendment are different from unwarned interrogation under the Fifth Amendment." *Dickerson v. United States,* 530 U.S. 428, 120 S.Ct. 2326, 2335, 147 L.Ed.2d 405, 418 (2000). (See the discussion of *Oregon v. Elstad* on page 494–95.

Dickerson v. United States
laws.findlaw.com/us/000/
99-5525.html

INDEPENDENT SOURCE   Several exceptions to the fruit of the poisonous tree doctrine are recognized, allowing the admission of tainted evidence under certain conditions. One exception already referred to in the *Silverthorne* case is the **independent source doctrine.** This exception allows the admission of tainted evidence if that evidence was also obtained through a source wholly independent of the primary constitutional violation. The independent source exception is compatible with the underlying rationale of the exclusionary rule: the deterrence of police misconduct. As stated by the U.S. Supreme Court:

> The independent source doctrine teaches us that the interest of society in deterring unlawful police conduct and the public interest in having juries receive all probative evidence of a crime are properly balanced by putting the police in the same, not a worse, position than they would have been in if no police error or misconduct had occurred. *Nix v. Williams,* 467 U.S. 431, 443, 104 S.Ct. 2501, 2509, 81 L.Ed.2d 377, 387 (1984).

Nix v. Williams
laws.findlaw.com/us/467/
431.html

In a case applying the independent source doctrine, law enforcement officers illegally entered an apartment, secured it, and then remained there for about nineteen hours until a search warrant arrived. Despite the illegal entry, the U.S. Supreme Court admitted the evidence found during the execution of the warrant. The Court found an independent source for the tainted evidence because the information on which the warrant was based came from sources entirely separate from the illegal entry and was known to the officers well before that entry. The Court held that "[w]hether the initial entry was legal or not is irrelevant to the admissibility of the challenged evidence because there was an independent source for the warrant under which that evidence was seized." *Segura v. United States,* 468 U.S. 796, 813–14, 104 S.Ct. 3380, 3390, 82 L.Ed.2d 599, 614 (1984). In *Murray v. United States,* 487 U.S. 533, 108 S.Ct. 2529, 101 L.Ed.2d 472 (1988), federal agents made an unlawful search of a warehouse. They then obtained a warrant to search the warehouse without revealing the unlawful search to the issuing magistrate. The Supreme Court upheld the trial court's denial of motions to suppress evidence found in the warehouse:

Segura v. United States
laws.findlaw.com/us/468/
796.html

Murray v. United States
laws.findlaw.com/us/487/
533.html

> Knowledge that the marijuana was in the warehouse was assuredly acquired at the time of the unlawful entry. But it was also acquired at the time of entry pursuant to the warrant, and if that later acquisition was not the result of the earlier entry there is no reason why the independent source doctrine should not apply. Invoking the exclusionary rule would put the police (and society) not in the same position they would have occupied if no violation occurred, but in a worse one. 487 U.S. at 541, 108 S.Ct. at 2535, 101 L.Ed.2d at 483.

ATTENUATION   Another exception to the fruit of the poisonous tree doctrine was first established in *Nardone v. United States,* 308 U.S. 338, 60 S.Ct. 266, 84 L.Ed. 307 (1939), and is referred to as the **attenuation doctrine.** This doctrine states that, even where the tainted evidence would not have been discovered except through the constitutional violation, there being no independent source, the evidence may still be admissible if the means of obtaining the evidence were sufficiently remote from and distinguishable from the primary illegality. The key question, as posed in *Wong Sun v. United States,* 371 U.S. 471, 488, 83 S.Ct. 407, 417, 9 L.Ed.2d 441, 455 (1963), is "whether granting establishment of the primary illegality, the evidence to which instant objection is made has been come at by exploitation of that illegality or instead by means sufficiently distinguishable to be purged of the primary taint." If the tainted evidence is obtained by means sufficiently distinguishable from the primary illegality, the causal connection

Nardone v. United States
laws.findlaw.com/us/308/
338.html

Wong Sun v. United States
laws.findlaw.com/us/371/
471.html

between the primary illegality and the evidence indirectly derived from it is said to be attenuated, and the evidence is admissible even though tainted. The rationale behind this exception is that the deterrent purpose of the exclusionary rule is not served where an officer could not have been aware of the possible benefit to be derived from his or her illegal actions at the time he or she took those actions.

In the *Wong Sun* case, narcotics agents illegally broke into Toy's laundry and followed Toy into his living quarters, where they arrested and handcuffed him. Almost immediately thereafter, Toy told the agents that Yee had been selling narcotics. The agents subsequently seized heroin from Yee, who told them that it had been brought to him by Toy and Wong Sun. Wong Sun was illegally arrested, arraigned, and released on his own recognizance. Several days later, Wong Sun returned voluntarily and made an oral confession to a narcotics agent.

Toy argued that his statement and the heroin later seized from Yee were fruit of the illegal entry into his dwelling and his illegal arrest. The Court agreed and held both inadmissible. Wong Sun claimed that his statement was the fruit of his illegal arrest. The Court disagreed:

> We have no occasion to disagree with the finding of the Court of Appeals that his arrest, also, was without probable cause or reasonable grounds. At all events no evidentiary consequences turn upon that question. For Wong Sun's unsigned confession was not the fruit of that arrest, and was therefore properly admitted at trial. On the evidence that Wong Sun had been released on his own recognizance after a lawful arraignment, and had returned voluntarily several days later to make the statement, we hold that the connection between the arrest and the statement has "become so attenuated as to dissipate the taint." 371 U.S. at 491, 83 S.Ct. at 419, 9 L.Ed.2d at 457.

The U.S. Supreme Court has set out three factors for courts to consider in determining whether the connection between the primary illegality and the resulting evidence has been sufficiently attenuated: (1) the time elapsed between the illegality and the acquisition of the evidence, (2) the presence of intervening circumstances, and (3) the purpose and flagrancy of the official misconduct. *Brown v. Illinois,* 422 U.S. 590, 95 S.Ct. 2254, 45 L.Ed.2d 416 (1975). (See the discussion of the *Brown* case in Chapter 4 under "Effect of Illegal Arrest.")

Brown v. Illinois
laws.findlaw.com/us/422/590.html

Courts applying the attenuation doctrine make a distinction between physical and verbal evidence. In *United States v. Ceccolini,* 435 U.S. 268, 98 S.Ct. 1054, 55 L.Ed.2d 268 (1978), the Supreme Court held that because of the cost to the truth-finding process of disqualifying knowledgeable witnesses, the exclusionary rule should be invoked with much greater reluctance when the fruit of the poisonous tree is the testimony of a live witness rather than an inanimate object. Therefore, a court will not exclude the testimony of a witness discovered as the result of a constitutional violation, unless the court finds a more direct link between the discovery and the violation than is required to exclude physical evidence. Furthermore, the court must find that the constitutional violation is the kind that will be deterred by application of the exclusionary rule. In a case illustrating the kind of constitutional violation that should be deterred, police obtained an involuntary statement from the defendant for the very purpose of discovering the defendant's crimes and witnesses to testify to those crimes. The court held that legitimate concerns for the deterrence of police misconduct compelled the application of the exclusionary rule to the testimony of sexually abused children who were revealed through the defendant's coerced statement. *Commonwealth v. Lahti,* 501 N.E.2d 511 (Mass. 1986).

United States v. Ceccolini
laws.findlaw.com/us/435/268.html

INEVITABLE DISCOVERY   Another exception to the fruit of the poisonous tree doctrine is the **inevitable discovery doctrine.** This doctrine is "in reality an extrapolation from the independent source doctrine. . . ." *Murray v. United States,* 487 U.S. 533, 539, 108 S.Ct. 2529, 2534, 101 L.Ed.2d 472, 481 (1988). Whereas the independent source doctrine allows the admission of tainted evidence if the tainted evidence was also obtained from an independent source, the inevitable discovery doctrine allows admission of the evidence if it would inevitably have been discovered in the normal course of events. Under this exception, the prosecution must establish by a preponderance of the evidence that, even though the evidence was actually discovered as the indirect result of a constitutional violation, the evidence would ultimately or inevitably have been discovered by lawful means—for example, as the result of the predictable and routine behavior of a law enforcement agency, some other agency, or a private person.

The U.S. Supreme Court specifically adopted the inevitable discovery doctrine in *Nix v. Williams,* 467 U.S. 431, 104 S.Ct. 2501, 81 L.Ed.2d 377 (1984). In that case, police initiated a search for a ten-year-old girl who had disappeared. While the search was going on, the defendant was arrested and, in response to illegal questioning, led police to the girl's body. The search was called off, but the girl's body was found in a place that was essentially within the area to be searched. Although the defendant's illegally obtained statements, leading to the discovery of the body, rendered evidence relating to the body inadmissible, the Court allowed the admission of the evidence under the inevitable discovery doctrine. The Court found that the volunteer search parties were approaching the actual location of the body, that they would have resumed the search had the defendant not earlier led the police to the body, and that the body would inevitably have been found.

The Court justified its adoption of the inevitable discovery doctrine using the rationale underlying the independent source exception:

> [I]f the government can prove that the evidence would have been obtained inevitably and, therefore, would have been admitted regardless of any overreaching by the police, there is no rational basis to keep that evidence from the jury in order to ensure the fairness of the trial proceedings. In that situation, the State has gained no advantage at trial and the defendant has suffered no prejudice. Indeed, suppression of the evidence would operate to undermine the adversary system by putting the State in a worse position than it would have occupied without any police misconduct. 467 U.S. at 447, 104 S.Ct. at 2511, 81 L.Ed.2d at 389–90.

Furthermore, in response to the defendant's contention that the prosecution must prove the absence of bad faith on the part of the police, the Court said that such a requirement

> would place courts in the position of withholding from juries relevant and undoubted truth that would have been available to police absent any unlawful police activity. Of course, that view would put the police in a worse position than they would have been in if no unlawful conduct had transpired. And, of equal importance, it wholly fails to take into account the enormous societal cost of excluding truth in the search for truth in the administration of justice. 467 U.S. at 445, 104 S.Ct. at 2509–10, 81 L.Ed.2d at 388.

Finally, the Court dismissed arguments that the inevitable discovery doctrine will promote police misconduct. A police officer who is faced with an opportunity to obtain evidence illegally will rarely, if ever, be in a position to calculate whether the evidence sought would inevitably be discovered. Even when an officer is aware that evidence will inevitably be discovered, there will be little to gain from taking dubious shortcuts to obtain the evidence. Other significant disincentives to obtaining evidence illegally include the possibility of departmental discipline and civil liability.

Lower courts have been careful to scrutinize claims of inevitable discovery. For example, in *United States v. Satterfield*, 743 F.2d 827, 846 (11th Cir. 1984), the court stated:

> To qualify for admissibility, there must be a reasonable probability that the evidence in question would have been discovered by lawful means, and the prosecution must demonstrate that the lawful means which made discovery inevitable were possessed by the police and were being actively pursued *prior* to the occurrence of the illegal conduct.

In the *Satterfield* case, despite the claim by police that they would have undoubtedly found a shotgun during a search of the defendant's home, no warrant was sought until several hours after an illegal search that uncovered the weapon. Therefore, the police did not possess before the illegal action the legal means that would have led to the discovery of the shotgun. The shotgun was ruled inadmissible.

Occasionally, courts will find inevitable discovery based on the behavior not of law enforcement officers but ordinary civilians. In *State v. Miller,* 680 P.2d 676 (Or. 1984), a law enforcement officer obtained, in violation of *Miranda,* the defendant's statement that he had "hurt someone" in his hotel room. The officer conducted a warrantless search of the hotel room and discovered a dead body. The court held that evidence of the discovery of the body was admissible despite the *Miranda* violation, because the maid would inevitably have discovered the body and would normally be expected to come forward and cooperate with police authorities.

www.fbi.gov/publications/leb/19 97/sept697.htm
Article, "The Inevitable Discovery Exception to the Exclusionary Rule" by Edward M. Hendrie

Good-Faith Exception

In *United States v. Leon,* 468 U.S. 897, 104 S.Ct. 3405, 82 L.Ed.2d 677 (1984), the U.S. Supreme Court adopted another exception to the exclusionary rule: the **good-faith exception** for searches conducted pursuant to a warrant. Under this exception, whenever a law enforcement officer acting with objective good faith has obtained a search warrant from a detached and neutral judge or magistrate and has acted within its scope, evidence seized pursuant to the warrant will not be excluded, even though the warrant is later determined to be invalid. The Court reasoned that excluding such evidence would not further the purposes of the exclusionary rule—deterrence of police misconduct—since the officer is acting as a reasonable officer would and should act under the circumstances. In determining what is good faith on the part of an officer, the Court said:

> [O]ur good-faith inquiry is confined to the objectively ascertainable question whether a reasonably well-trained officer would have known that the search was illegal despite the magistrate's authorization. In making this determination, all of the circumstances— including whether the warrant application has previously been rejected by a different magistrate—may be considered. 468 U.S. at 922–23 n.23, 104 S.Ct. at 3421 n.23, 82 L.Ed.2d at 698 n.23.

The Court described several circumstances under which an officer would not have reasonable grounds for believing that a warrant was properly issued:

- In issuing the warrant, the magistrate or judge was misled by information in an affidavit that the affiant knew was false or would have known was false except for a reckless disregard of the truth (see Chapter 5).

United States v. Leon
laws.findlaw.com/us/468/ 897.html

- The issuing magistrate wholly abandoned a neutral and detached judicial role and acted either as a "rubber stamp" or as an arm of the prosecution (see Chapter 5).
- The warrant was based on an affidavit so lacking in indicia of probable cause as to render official belief in its existence entirely unreasonable (see Chapter 6).
- The warrant was so facially deficient—failing to particularize the place to be searched or the things to be seized—that the executing officers could not reasonably presume it to be valid (see Chapter 5).

Under such circumstances, not only would the warrant be declared invalid, but also any evidence seized pursuant to the warrant would be ruled inadmissible.

The U.S. Supreme Court cited an example of good-faith behavior in *Massachusetts v. Sheppard,* the companion case to *United States v. Leon:*

Massachusetts v. Sheppard
laws.findlaw.com/us/468/
981.html

> The officers in this case took every step that could reasonably be expected of them. Detective O'Malley prepared an affidavit which was reviewed and approved by the District Attorney. He presented that affidavit to a neutral judge. The judge concluded that the affidavit established probable cause to search Sheppard's residence . . . and informed O'Malley that he would authorize the search as requested. O'Malley then produced the warrant form and informed the judge that it might need to be changed. He was told by the judge that the necessary changes would be made. He then observed the judge make some changes and received the warrant and the affidavit. At this point, a reasonable police officer would have concluded, as O'Malley did, that the warrant authorized a search for the materials outlined in the affidavit. 468 U.S. 981, 989, 104 S.Ct. 3424, 3428, 82 L.Ed.2d 737, 744 (1984).

Arizona v. Evans
laws.findlaw.com/us/000/
u10310.html

In *Arizona v. Evans,* 514 U.S. 1, 115 S.Ct. 1185, 131 L.Ed.2d 34 (1995), the Court found that the officer acted in good faith in arresting under authority of a warrant, even though the warrant had been quashed (annulled) several weeks before. In that case, when the defendant was stopped for a minor traffic violation, he told the officer that his license had been suspended. The officer checked his cruiser's computer data terminal, which revealed an outstanding misdemeanor warrant for the defendant's arrest. The officer arrested the defendant, searched his car, and found marijuana. Later, police were informed that the arrest warrant had been quashed seventeen days prior and that court personnel had not properly notified the police. Since there was no indication that the arresting officer was acting in any other way than objectively reasonable when he relied on the computer record, the Court applied the good-faith exception and refused to exclude the evidence, despite the clerical error by court personnel. The Court said that the exclusion of evidence at trial would not sufficiently deter future errors so as to warrant such a severe sanction.

> First . . . the exclusionary rule was historically designed as a means of deterring police misconduct, not mistakes by court employees. . . . Second, respondent offers no evidence that court employees are inclined to ignore or subvert the Fourth Amendment or that lawlessness among these actors requires application of the extreme sanction of exclusion. . . . Finally, and most important, there is no basis for believing that application of the exclusionary rule in these circumstances will have a significant effect on court employees responsible for informing the police that a warrant has been quashed. Because court clerks are not adjuncts to the law enforcement team engaged in the often com-

petitive enterprise of ferreting out crime, . . . they have no stake in the outcome of particular criminal prosecutions. 514 U.S. at 14–15, 115 S.Ct. at 1193, 131 L.Ed.2d at 46–47.

Some courts, when reviewing suppression rulings, now proceed directly to the good-faith issue and bypass the question of whether probable cause supported the warrant. For example, in *United States v. McLaughlin*, 851 F.2d 283, 284–85 (9th Cir. 1988), the court said:

> We need not decide whether the warrant was based on probable cause, because we find that even if the warrant lacked probable cause, the evidence was properly admitted under the exception to the exclusionary rule announced in *United States v. Leon*. . . . The officers in this case relied on the determination of a neutral magistrate that they had probable cause to search. . . . We cannot say that their reliance was objectively unreasonable. There is no evidence that the affidavit upon which the warrant was based contained any knowing or reckless falsehood, or that the magistrate abandoned his judicial role. The warrant, even if not based on probable cause, was not so deficient that no officer could reasonably have believed it to be valid, and the affidavit did not lack all indicia of probable cause.

In *Illinois v. Krull*, 480 U.S. 340, 107 S.Ct. 1160, 94 L.Ed.2d 364 (1987), the U.S. Supreme Court extended the good-faith exception to the exclusionary rule, holding that the exclusionary rule does not apply to evidence obtained by police who acted in objectively reasonable reliance on a statute that authorized warrantless administrative searches but that was subsequently found to violate the Fourth Amendment. Following the approach used in the *Leon* case, the Court said that applying the exclusionary rule in this situation would have as little deterrent effect on an officer's actions as would excluding evidence when an officer acts in objectively reasonable reliance on a warrant.

> Unless a statute is clearly unconstitutional, an officer cannot be expected to question the judgment of the legislature that passed the law. If the statute is subsequently declared unconstitutional, excluding evidence obtained pursuant to it prior to such judicial declaration will not deter future Fourth Amendment violations by an officer who has simply fulfilled his responsibility to enforce the statute as written. 480 U.S. at 349–50, 107 S.Ct. at 1167, 94 L.Ed.2d at 375.

Note that several states have opted not to embrace the good-faith exception. For example, the Georgia Supreme Court said:

> [W]e declined to adopt the "good faith" exception to the exclusionary rule . . . holding that because the Georgia legislature has statutorily protected the right to be free from unreasonable search and seizure . . . "the State of Georgia has chosen to impose greater requirements upon its law enforcement officers than that required by the U.S. Supreme Court." *Davis v. State*, 422 S.E.2d 546, 549 n.1 (Ga. 1992).

The discussion of the exceptions to the exclusionary rule serves to highlight an important feature of the rule: The exclusionary rule does not necessarily bar or stop a prosecution. At most, it will cause the suppression of evidence obtained as the direct or indirect result of a constitutional violation. If, however, that evidence is essential to the prosecution's case against a defendant, the prosecution may decide that it is futile to continue the prosecution. If, on the other hand, the prosecution has sufficient other evidence, either legally obtained or falling within one of the exceptions to the exclusionary rule, the prosecution may go forward despite the illegal police conduct.

www.richmond.edu/~jolt/v2i1/stinger.html
Article, "Arizona v. Evans: Adapting the Exclusionary Rule to Advancing Computer Technology" by C. Maureen Stinger
www.lectlaw.com/files/cjs09.htm
Article, "'Good Faith'—Police Reliance on Computerized Information" by Gary L. Gerszewski

Illinois v. Krull
laws.findlaw.com/us/480/340.html

Standing

Rakas v. Illinois
laws.findlaw.com/us/439/
128.html

To invoke the exclusionary rule to challenge the admissibility of evidence, a defendant must have **standing.** A defendant has standing when his or her own constitutional rights have been allegedly violated. In *Rakas v. Illinois,* a police search of a car yielded a box of rifle shells in the glove compartment and a sawed-off rifle under the passenger seat. The U.S. Supreme Court held that the petitioners, who were passengers in the car and had no ownership interest in the rifle shells or sawed-off rifle, had no legitimate expectation of privacy in the area searched. Therefore, they suffered no invasion of their Fourth Amendment rights and had no standing to object to the intrusion.

> "Fourth Amendment rights are personal rights which, like some other constitutional rights, may not be vicariously asserted." . . . A person who is aggrieved by an illegal search and seizure only through the introduction of damaging evidence secured by a search of a third person's premises or property has not had any of his Fourth Amendment rights infringed. . . . And since the exclusionary rule is an attempt to effectuate the guarantees of the Fourth Amendment, . . . it is proper to permit only defendants whose Fourth Amendment rights have been violated to benefit from the rule's protections. *Rakas v. Illinois,* 439 U.S. 128, 133–34, 99 S.Ct. 421, 425, 58 L.Ed.2d 387, 394–95 (1978).

Katz v. United States
laws.findlaw.com/us/389/
347.html

In *Rakas,* the U.S. Supreme Court went on to say that "capacity to claim the protection of the Fourth Amendment depends not upon a property right in the invaded place but upon whether the person who claims the protection of the Amendment has a legitimate expectation of privacy in the invaded place." 439 U.S. at 143, 99 S.Ct. at 430, 58 L.Ed.2d at 401. A subjective expectation of privacy is legitimate if it is "one that society is prepared to recognize as 'reasonable.'" *Katz v. United States,* 389 U.S. 347, 361, 88 S.Ct. 507, 516, 19 L.Ed.2d 576, 588 (1967). For example, the Supreme Court held that a person's status as an overnight guest is alone enough to show that the person had an expectation of privacy in the home that society is prepared to recognize as reasonable. The Court said:

> To hold that an overnight guest has a legitimate expectation of privacy in his host's home merely recognizes the everyday expectations of privacy that we all share. Staying overnight in another's home is a longstanding social custom that serves functions recognized as valuable by society. We stay in others' homes when we travel to a strange city for business or pleasure, when we visit our parents, children, or more distant relatives out of town, when we are in between jobs or homes, or when we house-sit for a friend. We will all be hosts and we will all be guests many times in our lives. From either perspective, we think that society recognizes that a houseguest has a legitimate expectation of privacy in his host's home. *Minnesota v. Olson,* 495 U.S. 91, 98, 110 S.Ct. 1684, 1689, 109 L.Ed.2d 85, 94 (1990).

Minnesota v. Olson
laws.findlaw.com/us/495/
91.html

Jones v. United States
laws.findlaw.com/us/362/
257.html
New York v. Burger
laws.findlaw.com/us/482/
691.html
United States v. Padilla
laws.findlaw.com/us/508/
77.html

In contrast, a person who is merely present in someone else's home with the consent of the householder may not claim a legitimate expectation of privacy in the home. *Jones v. United States,* 362 U.S. 257, 80 S.Ct. 725, 4 L.Ed.2d 697 (1960). Furthermore, "[a]n expectation of privacy in commercial premises . . . is different from, and indeed less than, a similar expectation in an individual's home." *New York v. Burger,* 482 U.S. 691, 700, 107 S.Ct. 2636, 2642, 96 L.Ed.2d 601, 612 (1987). Even a coconspirator or a codefendant in a crime has no standing to object to a search, unless that person has a reasonable expectation of privacy in the place to be searched. *United States v. Padilla,* 508 U.S. 77, 113 S.Ct. 1936, 123 L.Ed.2d 635 (1993). Based on these principles, the U.S. Supreme Court held that a temporary, commercial visitor has no reasonable expectation of privacy

Case in Point

Interpreting *Minnesota v. Carter*

On December 24, 1998, defendants Nerber and Betancourt-Rodriguez went to La Quinta Inn in Seattle to conduct a narcotics transaction with confidential informants. The informants brought defendants to Room 303. The FBI and the King County Police had rented the room for the operation and installed a hidden video camera without first obtaining a warrant. The parties entered the room at 9:54 A.M., the informants gave defendants one kilogram of sample cocaine, and the defendants briefly "flashed" money in a briefcase. The informants left the room at 10:00 A.M., telling defendants they would return to deliver 24 more kilograms of cocaine. They did not return, however, because they believed defendants intended to rob them. For three hours thereafter, law enforcement agents used the surveillance equipment to monitor defen-

dants' activities in the hotel room. They observed the other two defendants—Betancourt and Alvarez—enter the room, and watched as the defendants brandished weapons and sampled cocaine. All four defendants left the hotel at approximately 1:00 P.M. and were arrested shortly thereafter.

A grand jury returned an indictment charging all four defendants with narcotics offenses and two with possessing a firearm during the commission of a narcotics offense. Defendants moved to suppress the evidence derived from the video surveillance. In light of *Minnesota v. Carter,* should the motion to suppress be granted? *United States v. Nerber,* 222 F.3d 597 (9th Cir. 2000).

Read the court opinion at:
laws.findlaw.com/9th/9930161.html

---

in a home he or she is visiting. In *Minnesota v. Carter,* 525 U.S. 83, 119 S.Ct. 469, 142, L.Ed.2d 373 (1998), while the defendants and the lessee of an apartment bagged cocaine in the apartment, a law enforcement officer investigating a tip observed them by looking through a drawn window blind. The defendants did not live in the apartment, had never visited that apartment before, and their visit only lasted a matter of hours. Their singular purpose there was to package cocaine. After respondents were arrested, they moved to suppress evidence obtained from the apartment and their car, arguing that the officer's initial observation was an unreasonable search in violation of the Fourth Amendment. The U.S. Supreme Court ruled they could not invoke the Fourth Amendment:

> If we regard the overnight guest in *Minnesota v. Olson* as typifying those who may claim the protection of the Fourth Amendment in the home of another, and one merely "legitimately on the premises" as typifying those who may not do so, the present case is obviously somewhere in between. But the purely commercial nature of the transaction engaged in here, the relatively short period of time on the premises, and the lack of any previous connection between respondents and the householder, all lead us to conclude that respondents' situation is closer to that of one simply permitted on the premises. We therefore hold that any search which may have occurred did not violate their Fourth Amendment rights.
>
> Because we conclude that respondents had no legitimate expectation of privacy in the apartment, we need not decide whether the police officer's observation constituted a "search." 525 U.S. at 91, 119 S.Ct. at 474, 142 L.Ed.2d at 381.

The topic of privacy is discussed further in the following section.

Privacy

In a criminal case, for the Fourth Amendment to be applicable to a particular fact situation, there must be a seizure or a search and seizure accompanied by an attempt by

Minnesota v. Carter
laws.findlaw.com/us/000/97-1147.html

www.theatlantic.com/issues/2000/10/budiansky.htm
Article, "Rescuing Search and Seizure" by Stephen Budiansky; questions modern interpretations of the Fourth Amendment and the exclusionary rule

the prosecution to introduce what was seized as evidence in court. Whether there was a search or seizure within the meaning of the Fourth Amendment and, if so, whether the search or seizure violated someone's constitutional rights depend upon the nature of the interest that the Fourth Amendment protects. Under the common law, it was clear that the security of one's property was a sacred right and that protection of that right was a primary purpose of government. In an early English case, the court said:

> The great end for which men entered into society was to secure their property. That right is preserved sacred and incommunicable in all instances where it has not been taken away or abridged by some public law for the good of the whole. . . . By the laws of England, every invasion of private property, be it ever so minute, is a trespass. No man can set foot upon my ground without my license but he is liable to an action though the damage be nothing. . . . *Entick v. Carrington*, 19 Howell's State Trials 1029, 1035, 95 Eng.Rep. 807, 817–18 (1765).

The protection of property interests as the basis of the Fourth Amendment was adopted by the U.S. Supreme Court, and until relatively recently, analysis of Fourth Amendment issues centered on whether an intrusion into a "constitutionally protected area" had occurred. Three cases involving electronic surveillance illustrate this approach. In *Olmstead v. United States*, 277 U.S. 438, 48 S.Ct. 564, 72 L.Ed. 944 (1928), one reason for the Court's holding that wiretapping was not covered by the Fourth Amendment was that there had been no physical invasion of the defendant's premises. The Court said:

Olmstead v. United States
laws.findlaw.com/us/277/
438.html

> The evidence was secured by the use of the sense of hearing and that only. There was no entry of the houses or offices of the defendants. . . . The intervening wires are not part of his house or office, any more than are the highways along which they are stretched. 277 U.S. at 464–65, 48 S.Ct. at 568, 72 L.Ed. at 950.

Silverman v. United States
laws.findlaw.com/us/365/
505.html
Clinton v. Virginia
laws.findlaw.com/us/377/
158.html

In *Silverman v. United States*, 365 U.S. 505, 81 S.Ct. 679, 5 L.Ed.2d 734 (1961), however, a spike mike was pushed through a common wall until it hit a heating duct, and the Court held that the electronic surveillance was an illegal search and seizure. And in *Clinton v. Virginia*, 377 U.S. 158, 84 S.Ct. 1186, 12 L.Ed.2d 213 (1964), the Court ruled as inadmissible evidence obtained by means of a mechanical listening device stuck into the wall of an apartment adjoining the defendant's. The rationale for the *Silverman* and *Clinton* cases was that the listening devices had actually physically invaded the target premises, even though the invasion was slight.

This emphasis on property concepts in interpreting the Fourth Amendment began to lose favor in the 1960s. Justice William O. Douglas, concurring in the *Silverman* case, said that "our sole concern should be with whether the privacy of the home was invaded." 365 U.S. at 513, 81 S.Ct. at 683, 5 L.Ed.2d at 740. In a later case, the Court said:

Warden v. Hayden
laws.findlaw.com/us/387/
294.html
Katz v. United States
laws.findlaw.com/us/389/
347.html

> The premise that property interests control the right of the Government to search and seize has been discredited. . . . We have recognized that the principal object of the Fourth Amendment is the protection of privacy rather than property, and have increasingly discarded fictional and procedural barriers rested on property concepts. *Warden v. Hayden*, 387 U.S. 294, 304, 87 S.Ct. 1642, 1648, 18 L.Ed.2d 782, 790 (1967).

Finally, in *Katz v. United States*, 389 U.S. 347, 88 S.Ct. 507, 19 L.Ed.2d 576 (1967), another electronic surveillance case, the Court dispensed with the requirement of an actual physical trespass in applying the Fourth Amendment. The issue was the admissibility of telephone conversations overheard by FBI agents who had attached an electronic listening and recording device to the *outside* of a public telephone booth. The Court said:

> [T]his effort to decide whether or not a given "area," viewed in the abstract, is "constitutionally protected" deflects attention from the problem presented by this case. For the Fourth Amendment protects people, not places. What a person knowingly exposes to the public, even in his own home or office, is not a subject of Fourth Amendment protection. . . . But what he seeks to preserve as private, even in an area accessible to the public may be constitutionally protected. 389 U.S. at 351–52, 88 S.Ct. at 511, 19 L.Ed.2d at 582.

The Court held that the government's activities in electronically listening to and recording the defendant's words violated the privacy on which the defendant justifiably relied while using the telephone booth and thus constituted a search and seizure within the meaning of the Fourth Amendment. The Court added, "The fact that the electronic device employed to achieve that end did not happen to penetrate the wall of the booth can have no constitutional significance." 389 U.S. at 353, 88 S.Ct. at 512, 19 L.Ed.2d at 583.

The *Katz* case signaled a major shift in the interpretation of the Fourth Amendment away from a property approach toward a privacy approach. Court decisions since the *Katz* case no longer focus on whether there has been a physical intrusion into a constitutionally protected area. Now the formula for analysis of Fourth Amendment problems is that "wherever an individual may harbor a reasonable 'expectation of privacy,' . . . he is entitled to be free from unreasonable governmental intrusion." *Terry v. Ohio*, 392 U.S. 1, 9, 88 S.Ct. 1868, 1873, 20 L.Ed.2d 889, 899 (1968). It would seem that such a sweeping change in the interpretation of the Fourth Amendment would result in a large-scale reversal of earlier decisions. Yet, as Justice John Marshall Harlan noted in his concurring opinion in the *Katz* case, the determination of what protection the Fourth Amendment affords to people requires reference to a "place." Therefore, many of the pre-*Katz* decisions are not necessarily changed or overruled by the *Katz* decision. These cases should, however, be evaluated in terms of not only the reasoning employed in them but also the new standard announced in *Katz*. In later chapters considering the Fourth Amendment, both pre- and post-*Katz* cases are discussed, to help the reader gain as complete an understanding as possible of this continually developing area of the law.

In analyzing Fourth Amendment issues, most courts take the approach suggested by Justice Harlan in his concurring opinion in the *Katz* case. Justice Harlan said that "there is a twofold requirement, first that a person has exhibited an actual (subjective) expectation of privacy and, second, that the expectation be one that society is prepared to recognize as 'reasonable.'" 389 U.S. at 361, 88 S.Ct. at 516, 19 L.Ed.2d at 588. If these requirements are satisfied, any governmental intrusion on the expectation of privacy is a search for purposes of the Fourth Amendment. Reflecting Justice Harlan's approach, the U.S. Supreme Court defined the terms *search* and *seizure* as follows:

> A "search" occurs when an expectation of privacy that society is prepared to consider reasonable is infringed. A "seizure" of property occurs when there is some meaningful interference with an individual's possessory interests in that property. *United States v. Jacobsen*, 466 U.S. 109, 113, 104 S.Ct. 1652, 1656, 80 L.Ed.2d 85, 94 (1984).

Terry v. Ohio
laws.findlaw.com/us/392/1.html

United States v. Jacobsen
laws.findlaw.com/us/466/
109.html

Maryland v. Macon
laws.findlaw.com/us/472/
463.html

The case of *Maryland v. Macon,* 472 U.S. 463, 105 S.Ct. 2778, 86 L.Ed.2d 370 (1985), illustrates the application of these definitions. A county police detective, who was not in uniform, entered an adult bookstore. After browsing for several minutes, the detective purchased two magazines from a salesclerk, paying for them with a marked fifty-dollar bill. The detective then left the store and showed the magazines to his fellow officers, who were waiting nearby. The officers concluded that the magazines were obscene, reentered the store, and arrested the salesclerk. In determining whether there had been a search, the Court said:

> [R]espondent did not have any reasonable expectation of privacy in areas of the store where the public was invited to enter and to transact business. . . . The mere expectation that the possibly illegal nature of a product will not come to the attention of the authorities, whether because a customer will not complain or because undercover officers will not transact business with the store, is not one that society is prepared to recognize as reasonable. The officer's action in entering the bookstore and examining the wares that were intentionally exposed to all who frequent the place of business did not infringe a legitimate expectation of privacy and hence did not constitute a search within the meaning of the Fourth Amendment. 472 U.S. at 469, 105 S.Ct. at 2782, 86 L.Ed.2d at 376–77.

In determining whether there had been a seizure, the Court said:

> [R]espondent voluntarily transferred any possessory interest he may have had in the magazines to the purchaser upon the receipt of the funds. . . . Thereafter, whatever possessory interest the seller had was in the funds, not the magazines. At the time of the sale the officer did not "interfere" with any interest of the seller; he took only that which was intended as a necessary part of the exchange. 472 U.S. at 469, 105 S.Ct. at 2782, 86 L.Ed.2d at 377.

Therefore, no seizure occurred for the purposes of the Fourth Amendment.

In *Warden v. Hayden,* 387 U.S. 294, 304, 87 S.Ct. 1642, 1649, 18 L.Ed.2d 782, 790 (1967), the U.S. Supreme Court observed that the "principal" object of the [Fourth] Amendment is the protection of privacy rather than property and that "this shift in emphasis from property to privacy has come about through a subtle interplay of substantive and procedural reform." Nevertheless, the Court did not suggest that this shift in emphasis had eliminated the previously recognized protection for property under the Fourth Amendment. In *Soldal v. Cook County , Ill.,* 506 U.S. 56, 113 S.Ct. 538, 121 L.Ed.2d 450 (1992), the Court ruled that the Fourth Amendment protects against unreasonable seizures of property, even though neither privacy nor liberty is also implicated and even though no search within the meaning of the amendment has taken place. The *Soldal* case involved the forcible repossession of a mobile home by deputy sheriffs and the owner of a mobile home park. The Court said:

Soldal v. Cook County, Ill.
laws.findlaw.com/us/506/
56.html

> [T]he reason why an officer might enter a house or effectuate a seizure is wholly irrelevant to the threshold question of whether the [Fourth] Amendment applies. What matters is the intrusion on the people's security from governmental interference. Therefore, the right against unreasonable seizures would be no less transgressed if the seizure of the house was undertaken to collect evidence, verify compliance with a housing regulation, effect an eviction by the police, or on a whim, for no reason at all. . . . [I]t would be "anomalous to say that the individual and his private property are fully protected by the Fourth Amendment only when the individual is suspected of criminal behavior." 506 U.S. at 69, 113 S.Ct. at 548, 121 L.Ed.2d at 463–64.

In this book, the primary concern is with governmental actions that are sufficiently intrusive as to be considered searches and seizures, and with the legality of those actions. Generally, to be legal, a search or seizure must be reasonable. For most searches or seizures, this reasonableness requirement means that they must be conducted under the authority of a valid warrant, or they must fall within a recognized exception to the warrant requirement. Parts Two and Three of this book deal with the warrant requirement and its exceptions.

Note that privacy, as one of the basic rights guaranteed to individuals in our society, encompasses much more than the protections offered by the Fourth Amendment, even as interpreted under the *Katz* formula. This point is perhaps best stated in the *Katz* decision itself:

> [T]he Fourth Amendment cannot be translated into a general constitutional "right to privacy." That Amendment protects individual privacy against certain kinds of governmental intrusion, but its protections go further, and often have nothing to do with privacy at all. Other provisions of the Constitution protect personal privacy from other forms of governmental invasion. But the protection of a person's general right to privacy—his right to be let alone by other people—is, like the protection of his property and of his very life, left largely to the law of individual States. 389 U.S. at 350–51, 88 S.Ct. at 510–11, 19 L.Ed.2d at 581.

Probable Cause

The Fourth Amendment to the U.S. Constitution introduces the concept of **probable cause:**

> The right of the people to be secure in their persons, houses, papers, and effects, against unreasonable searches and seizures, shall not be violated, and no Warrants shall issue, but upon probable cause, supported by Oath or affirmation, and particularly describing the place to be searched, and the persons or things to be seized.

From this language, it is apparent that probable cause is necessary for the issuance of an arrest or search warrant. It is not so apparent that the other clause of the Fourth Amendment declaring the right of the people to be secure against "unreasonable searches and seizures" is also founded on probable cause. In general, that clause governs the various situations in which police are permitted to make warrantless arrests, searches, and seizures. These warrantless police actions are usually held to be unreasonable, if not based on probable cause. As the U.S. Supreme Court explained, if the requirements for warrantless arrests, searches, and seizures were less stringent than those for warrants, "a principal incentive now existing for the procurement of . . . warrants would be destroyed." *Wong Sun v. United States,* 371 U.S. 471, 479–80, 83 S.Ct. 407, 413, 9 L.Ed.2d 441, 450 (1963).

To explain what probable cause means, it is helpful to start with the Supreme Court's often-cited definition of probable cause to arrest set forth in *Brinegar v. United States:*

> Probable cause exists where "the facts and circumstances within their [the arresting officers'] knowledge and of which they had reasonably trustworthy information [are] sufficient in themselves to warrant a man of reasonable caution in the belief that" an offense has been or is being committed [by the person to be arrested]. 338 U.S. 160, 175–76, 69 S.Ct. 1302, 1310–11, 93 L.Ed. 1879, 1890 (1949).

www.rbs2.com/privacy.htm
Article, "Privacy Law in the USA" by Ronald B. Standler

www.pegasus.rutgers.edu/
~record/drafts/flir.html
Article, "Reasonable Expectation of Privacy: Protecting Individual Privacy in the Face of Intrusive Surveillance Technology" by James P. McGovern

www.adelphi.edu/~sbloch/
privacy.html
Article, "Privacy and Liberty in the Computer Age"

www.infowar.com/class_1/
class_1.shtml
Links to hundreds of articles on all aspects of privacy

Note: After this book had gone to press, the U.S. Supreme Court held in *Kyllo v. United States,* (decided June 11, 2001) that when the government uses a device that is not in general public use (a thermal imaging device), to explore details of a private home (relative amounts of heat) that would previously have been unknowable without physical intrusion, the surveillance is "search" under the Fourth Amendment and is presumptively unreasonable without a warrant.

Read the court opinion at:
laws.findlaw.com/us/000/
99-8508.html

Brinegar v. United States
laws.findlaw.com/us/338/
160.html

The Court noted that probable cause has come to mean more than bare suspicion. In a more recent case, the Court defined probable cause to search as "a fair probability that contraband or evidence of a crime will be found in a particular place." *Illinois v. Gates*, 462 U.S. 213, 238, 103 S.Ct. 2317, 2332, 76 L.Ed.2d 527, 548 (1983). The Court also said:

> Perhaps the central teaching of our decisions bearing on the probable cause standard is that it is a "practical, nontechnical conception." . . . "In dealing with probable cause, . . . as the very name implies, we deal with probabilities. These are not technical; they are the factual and practical considerations of everyday life on which reasonable and prudent men, not legal technicians, act." 462 U.S. at 231, 103 S.Ct. at 2328, 76 L.Ed.2d at 544 (1983).

Illinois v. Gates
laws.findlaw.com/us/462/213.html

Note that although these definitions seem to make a distinction between arrests and searches, the same quantum of evidence is required to establish probable cause to search and probable cause to arrest. The distinction only applies to the type of information needed. Probable cause to search requires a belief that certain items are contraband or fruits, instrumentalities, or evidence of crime, and are in a particular place or on a particular person. Probable cause to arrest requires a belief that a particular person has committed or is committing a crime.

As discussed in detail in later chapters, many arrests and searches are conducted without a warrant. The quantum of evidence required to establish probable cause for a warrantless arrest or search is somewhat greater than that required under authority of a warrant. The reason that a greater degree of probable cause may be required in the warrantless situation is that the Supreme Court has expressed a strong preference for arrest warrants (*Beck v. Ohio*, 379 U.S. 89, 85 S.Ct. 223, 13 L.Ed.2d 142 [1964]) and for search warrants (*United States v. Ventresca*, 380 U.S. 102, 85 S.Ct. 741, 13 L.Ed.2d 684 [1965]). This preference is so strong that less persuasive evidence will justify the issuance of a warrant than would justify a warrantless search or warrantless arrest. In *Aguilar v. Texas*, the Supreme Court said that

Beck v. Ohio
laws.findlaw.com/us/379/89.html
United States v. Ventresca
laws.findlaw.com/us/380/102.html
Aguilar v. Texas
laws.findlaw.com/us/378/108.html

> when a search is based upon a magistrate's, rather than a police officer's, determination of probable cause, the reviewing courts will accept evidence of a less "judicially competent or persuasive character than would have justified an officer in acting on his own without a warrant," . . . and will sustain the judicial determination so long as "there was a substantial basis for [the magistrate] to conclude that [seizable evidence was] probably present. . . ." 378 U.S. 108, 111, 84 S.Ct. 1509, 1512, 12 L.Ed.2d 723, 726 (1964).

The warrant procedure is preferred because it places responsibility for deciding the delicate question of probable cause with a neutral and detached judicial officer. Thereby, law enforcement is served, because law enforcement officers are enabled to search certain places and seize certain persons or things when the officers can show a fair probability that those persons, places, or things are significantly connected with criminal activity. The Fourth Amendment rights of citizens are also served by the warrant procedure, because the decision to allow a search and seizure is removed from the sometimes hurried and overzealous judgment of law enforcement officers engaged in the competitive enterprise of investigating crime.

Whether law enforcement officers are applying for a warrant or are determining their authority to arrest or search without a warrant, they must have sufficient information to establish probable cause. Probable cause may arise through facts or information that an officer has personally observed or gathered. It may also be based on apparently reliable information from third parties such as the victim, other police agencies, witnesses, reporters, and informants, or even on information from the defendant. Chapter 6 contains a detailed discussion of what information may and may not be considered in arriving at probable cause. It also contains procedures to assist the law enforcement officer in establishing probable cause, both when the information comes from informants and when it does not.

Probable cause is evaluated by examining the collective information in the possession of the police at the time of the arrest or search, not merely the personal knowledge of the arresting or searching officer. Therefore, if the police knowledge is sufficient in its totality to establish probable cause, an individual officer's actions in making a warrantless arrest or search upon orders to do so will be justified, even though that officer does not personally have all the information on which probable cause is based. *United States v. Thevis*, 469 F.Supp. 490 (D.Conn. 1979).

> [L]aw enforcement officers in diverse jurisdictions must be allowed to rely on information relayed from officers and/or law enforcement agencies in different localities in order that they might coordinate their investigations, pool information, and apprehend fleeing suspects in today's mobile society. In an era when criminal suspects are increasingly mobile and increasingly likely to flee across jurisdictional boundaries, this rule is a matter of common sense: it minimizes the volume of information concerning suspects that must be transmitted to other jurisdictions and enables police in one jurisdiction to act promptly in reliance on information from another jurisdiction. *United States v. Nafziger*, 974 F.2d 906, 910–11 (7th Cir. 1992).

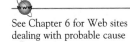

See Chapter 6 for Web sites dealing with probable cause

Even if the collective knowledge of the police is not sufficient to establish probable cause, the officer arresting upon orders will be protected from civil and criminal liability.

Reasonableness

The final basic underlying concept to be discussed is reasonableness. The Fourth Amendment does not prohibit all searches and seizures, only those that are unreasonable. Reasonableness has therefore been called the touchstone of the Fourth Amendment.

> The fundamental command of the Fourth Amendment is that searches and seizures be reasonable, and although "both the concept of probable cause and the requirement of a warrant bear on the reasonableness of a search, . . . in certain limited circumstances neither is required." . . . Thus, we have in a number of cases recognized the legality of searches and seizures based on suspicions that, although "reasonable," do not rise to the level of probable cause. . . . Where a careful balancing of governmental and private interests suggests that the public interest is best served by a Fourth Amendment standard of reasonableness that stops short of probable cause, we have not hesitated to adopt such a standard . . . Determining the reasonableness of any search involves a twofold inquiry: first, one must consider "whether the . . . action was justified at its inception," . . . second, one must determine whether the search as actually conducted "was reasonably related in scope to the circumstances which justified the interference in the first place." *New Jersey v. T.L.O.*, 469 U.S. 325, 340–41, 105 S.Ct. 733, 742–43, 83 L.Ed.2d 720, 734 (1985).

New Jersey v. T.L.O.
laws.findlaw.com/us/469/
325.html

Other Fourth Amendment considerations, such as warrants, probable cause, exigency, and good faith, while necessary depending on the particular circumstances, are factors subservient to reasonableness. The U.S. Supreme Court has pointed out that reasonableness does not necessarily mean correctness.

> It is apparent that in order to satisfy the "reasonableness" requirement of the Fourth Amendment, what is generally demanded of the many factual determinations that must regularly be made by agents of the government—whether the magistrate issuing a warrant, the police officer executing a warrant, or the police officer conducting a search or seizure under one of the exceptions to the warrant requirement—is not that they always be correct, but that they always be reasonable. *Illinois v. Rodriguez*, 497 U.S. 177, 185–86, 110 S.Ct. 2793, 2800, 111 L.Ed.2d 148, 159 (1990).

Illinois v. Rodriguez
laws.findlaw.com/us/497/177.html

Also, the Court has said that "[t]here is no formula for the determination of reasonableness. Each case is to be decided on its own facts and circumstances." *Go-Bart Importing Co. v. United States*, 282 U.S. 344, 357, 51 S.Ct. 153, 158, 75 L.Ed.2d 374, 382 (1931).

Go-Bart Importing Co. v. United States
laws.findlaw.com/us/282/344.html

The outcomes of cases in which the U.S. Supreme Court has applied a reasonableness balancing test have varied with the particularities of the cases and the philosophies of individual Supreme Court justices. Examples can be found in the discussion of administrative searches in Chapter 5, the discussion of stop and frisk in Chapter 7, and elsewhere in this book. Essential to an understanding of the concept of reasonableness is an appreciation that it is a flexible standard to be liberally construed for the protection of individual freedom.

> Implicit in the Fourth Amendment's protection from unreasonable searches and seizures is its recognition of individual freedom. That safeguard has been declared to be "as of the very essence of constitutional liberty" the guaranty of which "is as important and as imperative as are the guaranties of the other fundamental rights of the individual citizen * * *." [Citations omitted.] While the language of the Amendment is "general," it "forbids every search that is unreasonable; it protects all, those suspected or known as to be offenders as well as the innocent, and unquestionably extends to the premises where the search was made * * *." *Go-Bart Importing Co. v. United States*, 282 U.S. 344, 357, 51 S.Ct. 153, 158, 75 L.Ed. 374 (1931). Mr. Justice Butler there stated for the Court that "(t)he Amendment is to be liberally construed and all owe the duty of vigilance for its effective enforcement lest there shall be impairment of the rights for the protection of which it was adopted." Ibid. He also recognized that "(t)here is no formula for the determination of reasonableness. Each case is to be decided on its own facts and circumstances." Ibid. [Citations omitted.]
>
> This Court's long-established recognition that standards of reasonableness under the Fourth Amendment are not susceptible of Procrustean application is carried forward when that Amendment's proscriptions are enforced against the States through the Fourteenth Amendment. And, although the standard of reasonableness is the same under the Fourth and Fourteenth Amendments, the demands of our federal system compel us to distinguish between evidence held inadmissible because of our supervisory powers over federal courts and that held inadmissible because prohibited by the United States Constitution. We reiterate that the reasonableness of a search is in the first instance a substantive determination to be made by the trial court from the facts and circumstances of the case and in the light of the "fundamental criteria" laid down by the Fourth Amendment and in opinions of this Court applying that Amendment. Findings of rea-

sonableness, of course, are respected only insofar as consistent with federal constitutional guarantees. As we have stated above and in other cases involving federal constitutional rights, findings of state courts are by no means insulated against examination here. [Citations omitted.] While this Court does not sit as in nisi prius to appraise contradictory factual questions, it will, where necessary to the determination of constitutional rights, make an independent examination of the facts, the findings, and the record so that it can determine for itself whether in the decision as to reasonableness the fundamental—i.e., constitutional—criteria established by this Court have been respected. The States are not thereby precluded from developing workable rules governing arrests, searches and seizures to meet "the practical demands of effective criminal investigation and law enforcement" in the States, provided that those rules do not violate the constitutional proscription of unreasonable searches and seizures and the concomitant command that evidence so seized is inadmissible against one who has standing to complain. . . . Such a standard implies no derogation of uniformity in applying federal constitutional guarantees but is only a recognition that conditions and circumstances vary just as do investigative and enforcement techniques. *Ker v. California*, 374 U.S. 23, 32–34, 83 S.Ct. 1623, 1629–30, 10 L.Ed.2d 726, 737–38 (1963).

caselaw.findlaw.com/data/constitution/amendment04/01.html #4
Comprehensive discussion (with annotations) of the concept of reasonableness in the Fourth Amendment

It is fitting to conclude this chapter with a quotation from Justice Brennan that succinctly summarizes the essence of the Fourth Amendment and neatly ties together the concepts of privacy, probable cause, and reasonableness:

The Fourth Amendment was designed not merely to protect against official intrusions whose social utility was less as measured by some "balancing test" than its intrusion on individual privacy; it was designed in addition to grant the individual a zone of privacy whose protections could be breached only where the "reasonableness" requirements of the probable cause standard were met. Moved by whatever momentary evil has aroused their fears, officials—perhaps even supported by a majority of citizens—may be tempted to conduct searches that sacrifice the liberty of each citizen to assuage the perceived evil. But the Fourth Amendment rests on the principle that a true balance between the individual and society depends on the recognition of "the right to be let alone—the most comprehensive of rights and the right most valued by civilized men." *New Jersey v. T.L.O.*, 469 U.S. 325, 361–62, 105 S.Ct. 733, 753, 83 L.Ed.2d 720, 747–48 (1985).

Summary

This chapter is designed to round out the reader's preparation for the detailed study of the law of criminal procedure. Chapter 1 introduced the Constitution, the wellspring from which flow all the rules and principles to follow. Emphasis was placed on the constitutional sources of individual rights and the inevitable conflict between the protection of individual rights and the maintenance of law and order. Future chapters deal with specific examples of this conflict and show how the delicate balance among these competing interests is maintained.

Chapter 2 presented an overview of the criminal court system, the arena in which the balancing takes place and in which the reasonableness, appropriateness, and thoroughness of the law enforcement officer's activities are ultimately tested.

Chapter 2 was designed to give an overall picture of the criminal justice system as a backdrop for a more integrated understanding of the law of criminal procedure.

Finally, this chapter introduces the basic concepts of the exclusionary rule, privacy, probable cause, and reasonableness, which wind through the following chapters of this book. The law enforcement officer or other criminal justice professional who knows the potentially devastating effects of the exclusionary rule; who is sensitive to the constitutional rights of all citizens, especially to their reasonable expectation of privacy; who understands the meaning and importance of probable cause; and who embraces the concept of reasonableness as a guide is well on the way to appreciating the constitutional restraints that characterize the operation of our criminal justice system. Succeeding chapters will provide the details of criminal procedure, the knowledge of which enables a criminal justice professional to function effectively within that system.

Key Holdings from Major Cases

Wolf v. Colorado (1949). "The security of one's privacy against arbitrary intrusion by the police—which is at the core of the Fourth Amendment—is basic to a free society. It is therefore implicit in the 'concept of ordered liberty' and as such enforceable against the States through the Due Process Clause." 338 U.S. 25, 27–28, 69 S.Ct. 1359, 1361, 93 L.Ed. 1782, 1785.

Mapp v. Ohio (1961). "Since the Fourth Amendment's right of privacy has been declared enforceable against the States through the Due Process Clause of the Fourteenth, it is enforceable against them by the same sanction of exclusion as is used against the Federal Government. Were it otherwise, then just as without the *Weeks* rule the assurance against unreasonable federal searches and seizures would be 'a form of words,' valueless and undeserving of mention in a perpetual charter of inestimable human liberties, so too, without that rule the freedom from state invasions of privacy would be so ephemeral and so neatly severed from its conceptual nexus with the freedom from all brutish means of coercing evidence as not to merit this Court's high regard as a freedom 'implicit in the "concept of ordered liberty."'" 367 U.S. 643, 655, 81 S.Ct. 1684, 1691, 6 L.Ed.2d 1081, 1090.

"[A]s to the Federal Government, the Fourth and Fifth Amendments and, as to the States, the freedom from unconscionable invasions of privacy and the freedom from convictions based upon coerced confessions do enjoy an 'intimate relation' in their perpetuation of 'principles of humanity and civil liberty [secured] only after years of struggle.' . . . They express 'supplementing phases of the same constitutional purpose—to maintain inviolate large areas of personal privacy.' . . . The philosophy of each Amendment and of each freedom is complementary to, although not dependent upon, that of the other in its sphere of influence—the very least that together they assure in either sphere is that no man is to be convicted on unconstitutional evidence." 367 U.S. at 657, 81 S.Ct. at 1692, 6 L.Ed.2d at 1091.

"Having once recognized that the right to privacy embodied in the Fourth Amendment is enforceable against the States, and that the right to be secure against rude invasions of privacy by state officers is, therefore, constitutional in origin, we can no longer permit that right to remain an empty promise. Because it is enforceable in the same manner and to like effect as other basic rights secured by the Due Process Clause, we can no longer permit it to be revocable at the whim of any police officer who, in the name of law enforcement itself, chooses to suspend its enjoyment. Our decision, founded on reason and truth, gives to the individual no more than that which the Constitution guarantees him, to the police officer no less than that to which honest law enforcement is entitled, and, to the courts, that judicial integrity so necessary in the true administration of justice." 367 U.S. at 660, 81 S.Ct. at 1694, 6 L.Ed.2d at 1093.

Malloy v. Hogan (1964). The protection of the Fifth Amendment's privilege against self-incrimination is "to be enforced against the States under the Fourteenth Amendment according to the same standards that protect those personal rights against federal encroachment." 378 U.S. 1, 10, 84 S.Ct. 1489, 1495, 12 L.Ed.2d 653.

Gideon v. Wainwright (1963). "[I]n our adversary system of criminal justice, any person haled into court, who is too poor to hire a lawyer, cannot be assured a fair trial unless counsel is provided for him. . . . [L]awyers in criminal courts are necessities, not luxuries. The right of one charged with crime to counsel may not be deemed fundamental and essential to fair trials in some countries, but it is in ours. From the very beginning, our state and national constitutions and laws have laid great emphasis on procedural and substantive safeguards designed to assure fair trials before impartial tribunals in which every defendant stands equal before the law. This noble ideal cannot be realized if the poor man charged with crime has to face his accusers without a lawyer to assist him." 372 U.S. 335, 344, 83 S.Ct. 792, 796–97, 9 L.Ed.2d 799, 805.

Murdock v. Memphis (1874). The U.S. Supreme Court will not review state court judgments that rest on "adequate and independent state grounds" even if there are also federal grounds. 87 U.S. (20 Wall.) 590, 22 L.Ed. 429.

Silverthorne Lumber Co. v. United States (1920). "The essence of a provision forbidding the acquisition of evidence in a certain way is that not merely evidence so acquired shall not be used before the Court but that it shall not be used at all. Of course this does not mean that the facts thus obtained become sacred and inaccessible. If knowledge of them is gained from an independent source they may be proved like any others, but the knowledge gained by the Government's own wrong cannot be used by it in the way proposed." 251 U.S. 385, 392, 40 S.Ct. 182, 183, 64 L.Ed. 319, 321.

Wong Sun v. United States (1963). Not "all evidence is 'fruit of the poisonous tree' simply because it would not have come to light but for the illegal actions of the police. Rather, the more apt question in such a case is 'whether granting establishment of the primary illegality, the evidence to which instant objection is made has been come at by exploitation of that illegality or instead by means sufficiently distinguishable to be purged of the primary taint.'" 371 U.S. 471, 488, 83 S.Ct. 407, 417, 9 L.Ed.2d 441, 455.

Nix v. Williams (1984). "The independent source doctrine teaches us that the interest of society in deterring unlawful police conduct and the public interest in having juries receive all probative evidence of a crime are properly balanced by putting the police in the same, not a worse, position than they would have been in if no police error or misconduct had occurred." 467 U.S. 431, 443, 104 S.Ct. 2501, 2509, 81 L.Ed.2d 377, 387.

"[I]f the government can prove that the evidence would have been obtained inevitably and, therefore, would have been admitted regardless of any overreaching by the police, there is no rational basis to keep that evidence from the jury in order to ensure the fairness of the trial proceedings. In that situation, the State has gained no advantage at trial and the defendant has suffered no prejudice. Indeed, suppression of the evidence would operate to undermine the adversary system by putting the State in a worse position than it would have occupied without any police misconduct." 467 U.S. at 447, 104 S.Ct. at 2511, 81 L.Ed.2d at 389–90.

United States v. Leon (1984). The Fourth Amendment exclusionary rule does not "bar the use in the prosecution's case-in-chief of evidence obtained by officers acting in reasonable reliance on a search warrant issued by a detached and neutral magistrate but ultimately found to be unsupported by probable cause." 468 U.S. 897, 900, 104 S.Ct. 3405, 3409, 82 L.Ed.2d 677, 684.

Arizona v. Evans (1993). "[T]he exclusionary rule was historically designed as a means of deterring police misconduct. . . ." 514 U.S. at 14, 115 S.Ct. at 1193, 131 L.Ed.2d 46–47.

Illinois v. Krull (1987). "The application of the exclusionary rule to suppress evidence obtained by an officer acting in objectively reasonable reliance on a statute would have as little deterrent effect on the officer's actions as would the exclusion of evidence when an officer acts in objectively reasonable reliance on a warrant. Unless a statute is clearly unconstitutional, an officer cannot be expected to question the judgment of the legislature that passed the law. If the statute is subsequently declared unconstitutional, excluding evidence obtained pursuant to it prior to such judicial declaration will not deter future Fourth Amendment violations by an officer who has simply fulfilled his responsibility to enforce the statute as written." 480 U.S. 340, 349–50, 107 S.Ct. 1160, 1167, 94 L.Ed.2d 364, 375.

Rakas v. Illinois (1978). "'Fourth Amendment rights are personal rights which, like some other constitutional rights, may not be vicariously asserted.' . . . A person who is aggrieved by an illegal search and seizure only through the introduction of damaging evidence secured by a search of a third person's premises or property has not had any of his Fourth Amendment rights infringed. . . . And since the exclusionary rule is an attempt to effectuate the guarantees of the Fourth Amendment, . . . it is proper to permit only defendants whose Fourth Amend-

ment rights have been violated to benefit from the rule's protections." 439 U.S. 128, 133–34, 99 S.Ct. 421, 425, 58 L.Ed.2d 387, 394–95.

Minnesota v. Olson (1990). A person's "status as an overnight guest is alone enough to show that he had an expectation of privacy in the home that society is prepared to recognize as reasonable." 495 U.S. 91, 96–97, 110 S.Ct. 1684, 1688, 109 L.Ed.2d 85, 93.

Minnesota v. Carter (1998). A temporary, commercial visitor has no reasonable expectation of privacy in a home he or she is visiting. 525 U.S. 83, 119 S.Ct. 469, 142, L.Ed.2d 373.

United States v. Padilla (1993). Even a coconspirator or a codefendant in a crime has no standing to object to a search, unless that person has a reasonable expectation of privacy in the place to be searched. 508 U.S. 77, 113 S.Ct. 1936, 123 L.Ed.2d 635.

Katz v. United States (1967). "[T]he Fourth Amendment protects people, not places. What a person knowingly exposes to the public, even in his own home or office, is not a subject of Fourth Amendment protection. . . . But what he seeks to preserve as private, even in an area accessible to the public may be constitutionally protected." 389 U.S. 347, 351–52, 88 S.Ct. 507, 511, 19 L.Ed.2d 576, 582.

United States v. Jacobsen (1984). "A 'search' occurs when an expectation of privacy that society is prepared to consider reasonable is infringed. A 'seizure' of property occurs when there is some meaningful interference with an individual's possessory interests in that property." 466 U.S. 109, 113, 104 S.Ct. 1652, 1656, 80 L.Ed.2d 85, 94.

Soldal v. Cook County, Illinois (1992). "[T]he reason why an officer might enter a house or effectuate a seizure is wholly irrelevant to the threshold question of whether the [Fourth] Amendment applies. What matters is the intrusion on the people's security from governmental interference. . . . [I]t would be 'anomalous to say that the individual and his private property are fully protected by the Fourth Amendment only when the individual is suspected of criminal behavior.'" 506 U.S. 56, 69, 113 S.Ct. 538, 548, 121 L.Ed.2d 450, 463–64.

Brinegar v. United States (1949). "Probable cause exists where the facts and circumstances within their [the arresting officers'] knowledge and of which they had reasonably trustworthy information [are] sufficient in themselves to warrant a man of reasonable caution in the belief that an offense has been or is being committed [by the person to be arrested]." 338 U.S. 160, 175–76, 69 S.Ct. 1302, 1310–11, 93 L.Ed. 1879, 1890.

Illinois v. Gates (1983). Probable cause to search is "a fair probability that contraband or evidence of a crime will be found in a particular place." 462 U.S. 213, 238, 103 S.Ct. 2317, 2332, 76 L.Ed.2d 527, 548.

"Perhaps the central teaching of our decisions bearing on the probable cause standard is that it is a 'practical, nontechnical conception.' . . . 'In dealing with probable cause, . . . as the very name implies, we deal with probabilities. These are not technical; they are the factual and practical considerations of everyday life on which reasonable and prudent men, not legal technicians, act.'" 462 U.S. at 231, 103 S.Ct. at 2328, 76 L.Ed.2d at 544.

Aguilar v. Texas (1964). "[W]hen a search is based upon a magistrate's, rather than a police officer's, determination of probable cause, the reviewing courts will accept evidence of a less 'judicially competent or persuasive character than would have justified an officer in acting on his own without a warrant,' . . . and will sustain the judicial determination so long as 'there was a substantial basis for [the magistrate] to conclude that [seizable evidence was] probably present. . . .'" 378 U.S. 108, 111, 84 S.Ct. 1509, 1512, 12 L.Ed.2d 723, 726.

New Jersey v. T.L.O. (1985). "The fundamental command of the Fourth Amendment is that searches and seizures be reasonable, and although 'both the concept of probable cause and the requirement of a warrant bear on the reasonableness of a search, . . . in certain limited circumstances neither is required.' . . . Determining the reasonableness of any search involves a twofold inquiry: first, one must consider 'whether the . . . action was justified at its inception,' . . . second, one must determine whether the search as actually conducted 'was reasonably related in scope to the circumstances which justified the interference in the first place.'" 469 U.S. 325, 340–41, 105 S.Ct. 733, 742–43, 83 L.Ed.2d 720, 734 (1985).

Illinois v. Rodriguez (1990). "It is apparent that in order to satisfy the 'reasonableness' requirement of the Fourth Amendment, what is generally demanded of the many factual determinations that must regularly be made by agents of the government—whether the magistrate issuing a warrant, the police officer executing a warrant, or the police officer conducting a search or seizure under one of the exceptions to the warrant requirement—is not that they always be correct, but that they always be reasonable." 497 U.S. 177, 185–86, 110 S.Ct. 2793, 2800, 111 L.Ed.2d 148, 159.

Review and Discussion Questions

1. Explain why the application of the exclusionary rule does not necessarily mean that the prosecution is ended and that the defendant goes free.

2. Discuss the probable effectiveness in deterring illegal police conduct of the following suggested alternatives to the exclusionary rule: criminal prosecution of law enforcement officers; administrative discipline of officers; bringing civil actions for damages against officers.

3. Explain why a state court may refuse to follow certain holdings of the U.S. Supreme Court.

4. Give three reasons in support of the exclusionary rule and three reasons in support of its abolishment.

5. Discuss three theories under which evidence may be admissible in court even though it is fruit of the poisonous tree.

6. What did Justice Harlan mean when he said, in his concurring opinion in *Katz v. United States*, that the answer to the question of what protection the Fourth Amendment affords to people requires reference to a place?

7. Should a person in a telephone booth be given the same degree of Fourth Amendment protection as a person in his or her bedroom? As a person in his or her garage? As a person in his or her automobile?

8. Although *Katz v. United States* dispensed with the requirement of an actual physical trespass to trigger the Fourth Amendment, is a physical trespass always an intrusion on a person's reasonable expectation of privacy?

9. Compare the standard of probable cause against the following statements of degree of certainty: absolutely positive; pretty sure; good possibility; beyond a reasonable doubt; reasonable suspicion; preponderance of the evidence; reasonable probability; strong belief; convinced.

10. Why do reviewing courts accept evidence of a "less judicially competent or persuasive character" to justify the issuance of a warrant than they would to justify officers acting on their own without a warrant?

Arrest, Search Warrants, and Probable Cause

lawschool.lexis.com/emanuel/web/
crimpro/crimpro02.htm
General overview of the law relating to
arrest, search warrants, and probable
cause

www.uncp.edu/edu/home/vanderhoof/
m-trial/4-amend.html
Article, "All about Search and Seizure";
an overview of Fourth Amendment law

www.pitt.edu/~lawwomen/outlines/
crimsc.htm
Outline of criminal procedure; brief
summaries of all major cases

www.freeadvice.com/articles/
arrest_don'ts_dinday.htm
Article, "Ten Things Not to Do if
Arrested" by Brian Dinday

Chapter 4

Arrest

Outline

Objectives

- **Define the elements of a formal arrest.**

- **Understand the distinctions among the terms** *seizure, stop,* **and** *seizure tantamount to arrest* **(de facto arrest).**

- **Understand the difference between an arrest warrant and a summons; explain why arrests made pursuant to a warrant are preferred.**

- **Differentiate between the warrantless arrest authority for misdemeanors and for felonies.**

- **Know the procedures for effecting a formal arrest.**

- **Know the law relating to citizen's arrest and fresh pursuit.**

- **Know the limitations on the use of force in making arrests, self-defense, and entry of dwellings.**

- **Know the legal requirements and procedures for dealing with an arrested person after the arrest is made.**

- **Understand the consequences of an illegal arrest.**

The power of arrest is the most important power possessed by a law enforcement officer. An officer who arrests a person deprives that person of the freedom to carry out daily personal and business affairs. Also, an arrest initiates against that person the process of criminal justice, which may ultimately result in that person's fine or imprisonment. Because an arrest potentially has an extremely detrimental effect on a person's life, liberty, and privacy, the law governing arrest provides many protections to ensure that a person will be arrested only when reasonable and necessary. These protections take the form of severe limitations and restrictions on the law enforcement officer's exercise of the power of arrest. The law governing arrest is based on guarantees in the Fourth Amendment to the U.S. Constitution, which provides as follows:

> The right of the people to be secure in their *persons*, houses, papers and effects, against unreasonable searches and *seizures*, shall not be violated and no Warrants shall issue, but upon probable cause, supported by Oath or affirmation, and particularly describing the place to be searched and the *persons* or things *to be seized*. (Emphasis added.) U.S. Const., Amend. 4.

There is a common misunderstanding that the Fourth Amendment applies only to searches and seizures of material things and not to people. The word *persons* has been emphasized in the preceding passage to indicate clearly that this amendment is not restricted to material things; it protects individuals from illegal seizures of their persons. (Note that although the Fourth Amendment does not specifically mention arrest, an arrest is a type of seizure and is clearly governed by the Fourth Amendment.) With the Fourth Amendment as a backdrop, the discussion now turns to defining arrest and exploring the law enforcement officer's powers and duties with respect to arrest.

Definition of Formal Arrest

Arrest is a difficult term to define, because it is used in different senses. In its narrow sense, sometimes called a formal or technical arrest, arrest can be defined as "the taking of a person into custody for the commission of an offense as the prelude to prosecuting him for it." *State v. Murphy,* 465 P.2d 900, 902 (Or.App. 1970). In its broader sense, sometimes called a seizure tantamount to arrest, a *de facto* arrest, or an arrest for constitutional purposes, arrest refers to any seizure of a person significant enough to resemble a formal arrest in important respects. This chapter refers to the narrow sense as a formal arrest and to the broad sense as a seizure tantamount to arrest, or simply an arrest. (Seizures tantamount to arrest are discussed in the next section.) The discussion of formal arrest begins with a listing of the basic elements necessary for a formal arrest:

- A purpose or intention of a law enforcement officer to take a person into the custody of the law
- Exercise of real or pretended authority
- Detention or restraint of the person to be arrested, whether by physical force or by submission to assertion of authority
- Understanding by the person to be arrested that it is the intention of the arresting officer then and there to arrest and detain him or her

Each of these elements is discussed separately.

Intention to Arrest

To satisfy the first requirement of formal arrest, a law enforcement officer must intend to take a person into the custody of the law. This intention is the basic element that distinguishes a formal arrest from lesser forms of detention. Examples of lesser forms of detention are:

- Restraining a person who is behaving in a manner that is dangerous either to self or others
- Briefly stopping a person to seek information or to render assistance
- Serving a subpoena or other process such as a summons or notice to appear in court
- Asking a suspect or witness to appear at the station house for questioning
- Briefly stopping a vehicle to inspect license, equipment, or load

Although this is not a complete list, it illustrates the type of situation in which the law enforcement officer does not intend to take the person into the custody of the law and in which there is no formal arrest. (Ways in which lesser forms of detention can develop into the constitutional equivalent of a formal arrest are discussed in the next section on seizures tantamount to arrest.)

One further detention situation deserves mention: when a police officer detains a person under suspicious circumstances and conducts a brief, general on-the-scene investigation about possible criminal conduct. This type of encounter is commonly referred to as a **stop.** Because a separate body of law has developed to govern such encounters, the stop is discussed separately in Chapter 7. For purposes of this chapter, the ordinary stop does not involve an intention to arrest and therefore does not constitute a formal arrest.

Real or Pretended Authority

A law enforcement officer's taking a person into custody must be under real or pretended authority. **Real authority** is simply the legal right to make a formal arrest either with or without a warrant. That right may derive from the warrant itself or from the officer's observing the commission of a crime or having probable cause to believe that a particular person committed, or was in the process of committing, a particular crime. An example of pretended authority is an officer making a formal arrest without the legal right to do so but erroneously assuming that right. The arrest is still technically a formal arrest despite the officer's error. This authority requirement distinguishes arrest from the situation in which a person is seized and detained without any type of apparent or claimed authority. An example is a kidnapping, in which a person is seized but no one claims any kind of authority to arrest.

Detention or Restraint

An arrest requires either physical force . . . or, where that is absent, submission to the assertion of authority. *California v. Hodari D.*, 499 U.S. 621, 626, 111 S.Ct. 1547, 1551, 113 L.Ed.2d 690, 697 (1990).

California v. Hodari D.
laws.findlaw.com/us/499/
621.html

PHYSICAL FORCE   To constitute an arrest, the mere grasping or application of physical force with lawful authority, whether or not it succeeds in subduing the arrestee, is sufficient. The following was quoted with approval by the U.S. Supreme Court in the *Hodari D.* case:

There can be constructive detention, which will constitute an arrest, although the party is never actually brought within the physical control of the party making an arrest. This is accomplished by merely touching, however slightly, the body of the accused, by the party making the arrest and for that purpose, although he does not succeed in stopping or holding him even for an instant. . . . A. Cornelius, *Search and Seizure* 163–64 (2d ed. 1930) 499 U.S. at 625, 111 S.Ct. at 1550, 113 L.Ed.2d at 696.

To say that an arrest is effected by the slightest application of physical force, despite the arrestee's escape, is not to say that, for Fourth Amendment purposes, there is a continuing arrest during the period the person is not in custody. A seizure is a single act and not a continuous fact.

SHOW OF AUTHORITY   An arrest may be accomplished without any physical touching if the officer makes a show of authority and the person to be arrested submits. The following was also quoted with approval in the *Hodari D.* case:

Mere words will not constitute an arrest, while, on the other hand, no actual, physical touching is essential. The apparent inconsistency in the two parts of this statement is explained by the fact that an assertion of authority and purpose to arrest followed by submission of the arrestee constitutes an arrest. There can be no arrest without either touching or submission. Perkins, *The Law of Arrest*, 25 Iowa L.Rev. 201, 206 (1940) 499 U.S. at 626–27, 111 S.Ct. at 1551, 113 L.Ed.2d at 697.

A suspect who flees upon being informed of the intention to arrest is not seized for purposes of the Fourth Amendment because the suspect has not submitted to authority. In a case illustrating this point, the court determined that "a fleeing suspect—even one who is confronted with an obvious show of authority—is not seized until his freedom of movement is terminated by intentional application of physical force or by the suspect's submission to the asserted authority. We have also recognized that neither a police officer who chases a suspect unsuccessfully nor an officer who yells stop at a fleeing suspect has effected a seizure." *United States v. $32,400.00 in United States Currency*, 82 F.3d 135, 139 (7th Cir. 1996).

Understanding by the Arrestee

The final element of formal arrest is that the law enforcement officer's actions in making an arrest must result in the arrested person's understanding that an arrest is being made. The officer's notifying the person of the arrest ordinarily conveys this understanding. Surrounding circumstances, however, such as handcuffing or other physical restraint or confinement, may make the fact of arrest obvious to the arrested person. The officer may never say a word, but the circumstances convey the idea anyway. If the arrested person is unconscious, under the influence of drugs or alcohol, or mentally impaired, the requirement of understanding may be delayed or eliminated.

The element of understanding as necessary for a formal arrest to occur has been the subject of several court decisions in recent years. Problems concerning this issue arise when an encounter between the police and a person does not quite fit the description of a formal arrest, but the intrusion on the person's freedom of action is significantly greater than an ordinary, brief investigative detention or other minimal street encounter. The next section discusses such seizures, which, although not formal arrests, may be tantamount to arrests for the purposes of Fourth Amendment protection.

Key Points

1. The requirements for a formal arrest are a law enforcement officer's intention to take a person into the custody of the law to answer for an alleged crime, under real or pretended authority, accompanied by detention or restraint of the person and an understanding by the person that an arrest is being made.

2. The "detention or restraint" requirement of a formal arrest may be satisfied either by actually touching the person to be arrested or by the person's submitting to the officer's show of authority.

Seizures of the Person Tantamount to an Arrest

A law enforcement officer carrying out his or her daily duties of investigating crime, enforcing the laws, and keeping the public peace will have varying degrees of contact with members of the public. These contacts may range in intensity from the briefest observation or questioning to a full-fledged formal arrest with the use of force. With respect to the most minimal of these police contacts, the U.S. Supreme Court has stated:

> [L]aw enforcement officers do not violate the Fourth Amendment by merely approaching an individual on the street or in another public place, by asking him if he is willing to answer some questions, by putting questions to him if the person is willing to listen, or by offering in evidence in a criminal prosecution his voluntary answers to such questions. . . . Nor would the fact that the officer identifies himself as a police officer, without more, convert the encounter into a seizure requiring some level of objective justifications. . . . The person approached, however, need not answer any question put to him; indeed, he may decline to listen to the questions at all and may go on his way. . . . He may not be detained even momentarily without reasonable, objective grounds for doing so; and his refusal to listen or answer does not, without more, furnish those grounds. . . . If there is no detention—no seizure within the meaning of the Fourth Amendment—then no constitutional rights have been infringed. *Florida v. Royer*, 460 U.S. 491, 497–98, 103 S.Ct. 1319, 1324, 75 L.Ed.2d 229, 236 (1983).

Florida v. Royer
laws.findlaw.com/us/460/
491.html

Some encounters with members of the public, however, are more intrusive than those described in the previous paragraph and involve greater encroachments on a person's freedom of movement and privacy. One example of such an encounter is a so-called "*Terry*-type" investigative stop, which is a brief detention of a person for investigative purposes, sometimes accompanied by a limited search for weapons called a frisk. Officers may stop a person only if they have a reasonable and articulable suspicion that criminal activity is afoot. Officers may frisk a person they have stopped only if they have a reasonable and articulable suspicion that the person is armed and dangerous. Both the stop and the frisk must be reasonable under the circumstances. (Stop and frisk are discussed in Chapter 7.)

caselaw.findlaw.com/data/
constitution/amendment04/
01.html#6
Comprehensive discussion (with annotations) of arrests and other detentions

*For new and updated weblinks,
go to* www.wadsworth.com/
cj/ferdico0253

At a still higher level of intrusiveness are police contacts with members of the public involving a detention or temporary seizure of a person that restrains his or her freedom of action more than a brief investigatory stop but does not satisfy the four elements of a formal arrest (discussed earlier). The missing element is usually the officer's intention to arrest. In these instances, courts often hold that despite the lack of a formal arrest, the seizure is so similar to a formal arrest in important respects that it should be allowed only if supported by probable cause to believe a crime has been or is being committed. In 1981, the U.S. Supreme Court stated "the general rule that every arrest, and every seizure having the essential attributes of a formal arrest, is unreasonable unless it is supported by probable cause." *Michigan v. Summers*, 452 U.S. 692, 700, 101 S.Ct. 2587, 2593, 69 L.Ed.2d 340, 348.

Michigan v. Summers
laws.findlaw.com/us/452/
692.html
Dunaway v. New York
laws.findlaw.com/us/442/
200.html

The leading case on this subject is the U.S. Supreme Court case of *Dunaway v. New York*, 442 U.S. 200, 99 S.Ct. 2248, 60 L.Ed.2d 824 (1979). In the *Dunaway* case, the defendant was picked up at his neighbor's home by the police and taken to the police station for questioning about an attempted robbery and homicide. Although the defendant was not told that he was under arrest, he would have been physically restrained had he attempted to leave. The police did not have probable cause to arrest the defendant. He was given *Miranda* warnings, and he waived his right to counsel. He was questioned, and he eventually made statements and drew sketches incriminating himself. His motions at trial to suppress the statements and sketches were denied, and he was convicted.

On appeal, the Supreme Court examined the seizure of the defendant and held that the police violated his constitutional rights under the Fourth and Fourteenth Amendments. The seizure was much more intrusive than a traditional stop and frisk (see Chapter 7) and could not be justified on the mere grounds of "reasonable suspicion" of criminal activity. Whether or not technically characterized as a formal arrest, the seizure was in important respects indistinguishable from a formal arrest. Instead of being questioned briefly where he was found, the defendant was taken from a neighbor's home to a police car, transported to a police station, and placed in an interrogation room. He was never informed that he was free to go and would have been physically restrained had he refused to accompany the officers or tried to escape their custody. That the defendant was not formally placed under arrest, was not booked, and would not have had an arrest record if the interrogation had proven fruitless did not make his seizure something less than an arrest for purposes of Fourth Amendment protections. Because it was unsupported by probable cause, Dunaway's seizure was illegal.

Therefore, even though an officer does not intend to formally arrest a person, a court may find that the officer's actions in seizing the person are tantamount to an arrest if they are indistinguishable from an arrest in important respects. A seizure tantamount to an arrest is also known as a *de facto* arrest. If an officer seizes or significantly detains a person, beyond a mere stop or other minor investigatory detention, the seizure or detention may be considered an arrest for purposes of the Fourth Amendment, even if the officer does not comply with all the requirements of a formal arrest. As such, the seizure or detention will be ruled illegal unless it is supported by probable cause.

In a case similar to *Dunaway*, in which police took a burglary-rape suspect against his will from his home to the police station for fingerprinting, the U.S. Supreme Court reiterated its principles regarding seizures tantamount to arrests:

> [W]hen the police, without probable cause or a warrant, forcibly remove a person from his home or other place in which he is entitled to be and transport him to the police station, where he is detained, although briefly, for investigative purposes . . . such seizures, at least where not under judicial supervision, are sufficiently like arrests to invoke the

traditional rule that arrests may constitutionally be made only on probable cause. *Hayes v. Florida*, 470 U.S. 811, 816, 105 S.Ct. 1643, 1647, 84 L.Ed.2d 705, 710 (1985).

Hayes v. Florida
laws.findlaw.com/us/470/811.html

The Court did not rule out, however, the possibility that an investigative seizure on less than probable cause might be permissible if judicially authorized.

> [U]nder circumscribed procedures, the Fourth Amendment might permit the judiciary to authorize the seizure of a person on less than probable cause and his removal to the police station for the purpose of fingerprinting. . . . [S]ome States . . . have enacted procedures for judicially authorized seizures for the purpose of fingerprinting. The state courts are not in accord on the validity of these efforts to insulate investigative seizures from Fourth Amendment invalidation. 470 U.S. at 817, 105 S.Ct. at 1647, 84 L.Ed.2d at 711.

Many issues involving seizures tantamount to arrest arise as a result of investigative detentions of suspected drug law violators on the public concourses of airports. In one such case, *Florida v. Royer*, 460 U.S. 491, 103 S.Ct. 1319, 75 L.Ed.2d 229 (1983), the U.S. Supreme Court concluded that the detention of the defendant was tantamount to an arrest. In that case, narcotics agents had adequate grounds to suspect the defendant of carrying drugs, based on his traveling under an assumed name and his appearance and conduct fitting the "drug courier profile." The agents therefore had the right to temporarily detain the defendant, within the limits of the *Terry* case, in order to confirm or dispel their reasonable suspicions. The agents, however, not only asked the defendant for his identification and to accompany them to another room. They told him they were narcotics agents and had reason to believe he was carrying illegal drugs, they kept his identification and airline ticket, they took him to a small room where he found himself alone with two police officers, they retrieved his checked luggage from the airline without his consent, they never informed him he was free to board his plane if he so chose, and they would not have allowed him to leave the interrogation room even if he had asked to do so. Under these circumstances, the Court held that the officers' conduct was more intrusive than conduct that would constitute an investigative detention authorized by the *Terry* case. The detention was therefore a seizure tantamount to an arrest, and since the officers did not have probable cause to arrest, it was an illegal seizure. The defendant's consent to a search of his luggage in the interrogation room was tainted by the illegal seizure; thus, the search of the luggage was also illegal as a "fruit of the poisonous tree" (see Chapter 3).

Florida v. Royer
laws.findlaw.com/us/460/491.html

When a suspect is in a motor vehicle, police may have more leeway in stopping the suspect for investigation before the stop rises to the level of an arrest. In *United States v. Jones*, 759 F.2d 633 (8th Cir. 1985), the court found no seizure tantamount to arrest where two officers, acting on reasonable suspicion that a fleeing man was involved in a burglary, blocked the suspect's car with theirs, drew their guns, forcefully ordered the suspect out of his vehicle, and repeatedly demanded identification. Noting the danger inherent in the situation, the court said, "Blocking generally will be reasonable when the suspect is in a vehicle because of the chance that the suspect may flee upon the approach of police with resulting danger to the public as well as to the officers involved." 759 F.2d at 638.

In contrast, though, in *United States v. Hill*, 91 F.3d 1064 (8th Cir. 1996), the court held that "a de facto arrest occurs when the officers' conduct is more intrusive than necessary for an investigative stop. . . . We must consider such factors as the duration of a stop, whether the suspect was handcuffed or confined in a police car, whether the suspect was transported or isolated, and 'the degree of fear and humiliation that the police conduct engenders.'" 91 F.3d at 1070.

Key Points

3. A seizure of a person that is in important respects indistinguishable from a traditional formal arrest is illegal unless it is supported by probable cause to believe that the person has committed or is committing a crime.

Arrest Authority under a Warrant

Even though the authority of law enforcement officers to arrest without a warrant in proper circumstances has been recognized for a long time, arrests made under the authority of a warrant have always been preferred. The warrant procedure is favored because it places the sometimes delicate decision of determining whether there is probable cause to justify an arrest in the hands of an impartial judicial authority. The U.S. Supreme Court said that "the informed and deliberate determinations of magistrates empowered to issue warrants . . . are to be preferred over the hurried action of officers . . . who may happen to make arrests." *Aguilar v. Texas,* 378 U.S. 108, 110–11, 84 S.Ct. 1509, 1512, 12 L.Ed.2d 723, 726 (1964). This preference for warrants attempts to avoid placing the responsibility for determining probable cause on law enforcement officers who, in their eagerness to enforce the law and investigate crime, may be tempted to violate constitutional rights.

Aguilar v. Texas
laws.findlaw.com/us/378/
108.html

If a warrant is proper on its face and the officer does not abuse authority in executing the arrest, the officer is protected against civil liability for false arrest or false imprisonment, even though it is later determined that the issuance of the warrant was illegal. The officer is not so protected when making warrantless arrests.

Although law enforcement officers often consider warrants a hindrance, warrants protect officers in an important way. If a warrant is proper on its face and the officer has not abused authority in obtaining or executing the warrant, the officer has some protection against civil liability for false arrest or false imprisonment, even though it is later determined that the issuance of the warrant was illegal. This general protection, however, provides a qualified, not absolute, immunity for the law enforcement officer. In *Malley v. Briggs,* 475 U.S. 335, 106 S.Ct. 1092, 89 L.Ed.2d 271 (1986), a Rhode Island state trooper applied for an arrest warrant for marijuana possession, the judge issued the warrant, and the defendants were arrested. The charges were subsequently dropped, however, when the grand jury failed to find probable cause to indict. Respondents then brought a damages action in Federal District Court under 42 U.S.C. 1983, alleging that the officer, in applying for the arrest warrants, violated their rights under the Fourth and Fourteenth Amendments. The U.S. Supreme Court held that a law enforcement officer applying for a warrant has qualified immunity from liability for damages if the officer's actions were "objectively reasonable." Under that standard, "[o]nly where the warrant application is so lacking in indicia of probable cause as to render official belief in its existence unreasonable . . . will the shield of immunity be lost." 475

Malley v. Briggs
laws.findlaw.com/us/475/
335.html

Complete text of 42 U.S.C.
§ 1983
caselaw.findlaw.com/scripts/ts_
search.pl?title=42&sec=1983

U.S. at 344–45, 106 S.Ct. at 1098, 89 L.Ed.2d at 281. The Court said that the question is "whether a reasonably well-trained officer in petitioner's position would have known that his affidavit failed to establish probable cause and that he should not have applied for the warrant. If such was the case, the officer's application for a warrant was not objectively reasonable, because it created the unnecessary danger of an unlawful arrest." 475 U.S. at 345, 106 S.Ct. at 1098, 89 L.Ed.2d at 281.

A law enforcement officer has authority to arrest under a warrant whether or not the officer has possession of the warrant. If a proper judicial authority has validly issued the warrant, any officer may arrest under the warrant's authority.

Arrest Warrant

The **arrest warrant** is (1) a written order, (2) issued by a proper judicial authority, (3) in the name of the government, (4) upon probable cause, (5) directing the arrest of a particular person or persons. Typical forms for an arrest warrant appear in Exhibits 4.1 and 4.2. Note that Exhibit 4.2 is a combination form that can be used as a complaint, a summons, an arrest warrant, or an order of detention. The person issuing the arrest warrant could be a judge, a magistrate, a complaint justice, a justice of the peace, or a clerk of the court. Every jurisdiction authorizes different judicial officers to issue warrants. (For the remainder of this chapter, the term **magistrate** is used to designate the judicial officer authorized to issue arrest warrants.) The warrant is issued on the basis of a sworn complaint, charging that a particularly described suspect has committed a crime. The person swearing out the complaint is usually a law enforcement officer or, in some cases, the victim of the crime.

Complaint

The **complaint** must state the essential facts constituting the offense charged, including the time and place the offense was committed and the name of the suspect or a reasonably definite description of the suspect if the name is not known. The complaint must be sworn to and signed by the person charging the offense (the complainant). A warrant issued on an unsworn complaint is void, and any arrest made under such a warrant is illegal. Typical complaint forms appear in Exhibits 4.2 and 4.3.

Besides serving as an application for an arrest warrant, in some jurisdictions the complaint is the charging instrument for misdemeanor cases or for the initial appearance or preliminary examination. In felony cases, the complaint is replaced as the charging instrument by the indictment or information. (The complaint is discussed in further detail in Chapter 2.)

Probable Cause

Before an arrest warrant can be issued, the magistrate must be satisfied from the complaint that there is **probable cause** to believe that the offense charged in the complaint was committed by the accused. (Probable cause is discussed briefly in Chapter 3 and in detail in Chapter 6.) If the complaint form has insufficient space, a separate **affidavit** or affidavits detailing the facts and circumstances on which probable cause is based must be filed with the complaint. An affidavit need not be prepared with any particular formality and may be merely a sworn statement of the facts on which the complainant relies in seeking the issuance of a warrant. The magistrate may require additional affidavits of other persons having pertinent and reliable information bearing

www.nolo.com/encyclopedia/
faqs/crim/arrestint.html
Frequently asked questions about arrests, arrest warrants, and interrogations

jec.unm.edu/Benchbk/
Magistrate/2-2-2.htm
Outline of New Mexico's requirements for complaints and arrest warrants
www.faculty.ncwc.edu/
toconnor/arraign.htm
Information on how to file complaints (deals with North Carolina law)

AO 442 (Rev. 5/93) Warrant for Arrest

United States District Court

DISTRICT OF _____

UNITED STATES OF AMERICA

V.

WARRANT FOR ARREST

CASE NUMBER: _____

To: The United States Marshal
and any Authorized United States Officer

YOU ARE HEREBY COMMANDED to arrest _____
Name

and bring him or her forthwith to the nearest magistrate judge to answer a(n)

☐ Indictment ☐ Information ☐ Complaint ☐ Order of Court ☐ Violation Notice ☐ Probation Violation Petition

charging him or her with (brief description of offense)

in violation of Title _____ United States Code, Section(s) _____

_____   _____
Name of Issuing Officer   Title of Issuing Officer

_____   _____
Signature of Issuing Officer   Date and Location

Bail fixed at $ _____ by _____
                                                      Name of Judicial Officer

RETURN
This warrant was received and executed with the arrest of the above–named defendant at _____

DATE RECEIVED	NAME AND TITLE OF ARRESTING OFFICER	SIGNATURE OF ARRESTING OFFICER
DATE OF ARREST		

Typical Arrest Warrant Form
■ EXHIBIT 4.1

on probable cause. All the information on which probable cause is based must appear in the original complaint and the affidavits submitted in support of it. The reason for this requirement is to maintain a record of the evidence presented to the magistrate issuing the warrant, if the validity of the warrant is later questioned.

```
AO 442 (Rev. 5/93) Warrant for Arrest
```

THE FOLLOWING IS FURNISHED FOR INFORMATION ONLY:

DEFENDANT'S NAME: _____

ALIAS: _____

LAST KNOWN RESIDENCE: _____

LAST KNOWN EMPLOYMENT: _____

PLACE OF BIRTH: _____

DATE OF BIRTH: _____

SOCIAL SECURITY NUMBER: _____

HEIGHT: _____   WEIGHT: _____

SEX: _____   RACE: _____

HAIR: _____   EYES: _____

SCARS, TATTOOS, OTHER DISTINGUISHING MARKS: _____

_____

_____

FBI NUMBER: _____

COMPLETE DESCRIPTION OF AUTO: _____

_____

INVESTIGATIVE AGENCY AND ADDRESS: _____

_____

_____

Typical Arrest Warrant Form *(continued)*
■ EXHIBIT 4.1

Requirements of Arrest Warrant

The arrest warrant must conform to certain requirements, which vary among different jurisdictions. The following list is representative of what an arrest warrant must contain:

- The caption of the court or division of the court from which the warrant issues
- The name of the person to be arrested, if known; if not known, any name or description by which the person can be identified with reasonable certainty. The warrant must show on its face that it is directed toward a particular, identifiable person to satisfy the Fourth Amendment requirement that a warrant particularly describe the person to be seized.
- A description of the offense charged in the complaint. This description should be in the language of the appropriate statute or ordinance. The important consideration, however, is that the description be in words definite enough for the defendant to readily understand the charge. Stating that the defendant is

State of Minnesota   County of   Court

CCT	SECTION/Subdivision	U.O.C.	GOC	CTY. ATTY. FILE NO.	CONTROLLING AGENCY	CONTROL NO.

COURT CASE NO.   DATE FILED

√if more than 6 counts (see attached)

Complaint   SUMMONS
WARRANT
ORDER OF DETENTION

State of Minnesota
VS.   PLAINTIFF,   FELONY
GROSS MISDEMEANOR

NAME: first, middle, last   Date of Birth   SJIS COMPLAINT NUMBER

DEFENDANT.
COMPLAINT

The Complainant, being duly sworn, makes complaint to the above-named Court and states that there is probable cause to believe that the Defendant committed the following offense(s). The complainant states that the following facts establish PROBABLE CAUSE:

THEREFORE, Complainant requests that said Defendant, subject to bail or conditions of release be:
(1) arrested or that other lawful steps be taken to obtain defendant's appearance in court; or
(2) detained, if already in custody, pending further proceedings;
and that said Defendant otherwise be dealt with according to law.
COMPLAINANT'S NAME: COMPLAINANT'S SIGNATURE:

Being duly authorized to prosecute the offense(s) charged, I hereby approve this Complaint.
DATE: PROSECUTING ATTORNEY'S SIGNATURE:

PROSECUTING ATTORNEY:
NAME/TITLE: ADDRESS/TELEPHONE:

FORM B.1

Combination Form, Page 1
■ EXHIBIT 4.2A

charged merely with a "felony" or a "misdemeanor," for example, is insufficient and will invalidate the warrant.

■ The date of issuance
■ The officer or officers to whom the warrant is directed, together with a command that the defendant be brought before the proper judicial official

Court Case #:   *PAGE   of*

FINDING OF PROBABLE CAUSE

From the above sworn facts, and any supporting affidavits or supplemental sworn testimony, I, the Issuing Officer, have determined that probable cause exists to support, subject to bail or conditions of release where applicable, Defendant(s) arrest or other lawful steps be taken to obtain Defendant(s) appearance in Court, or his detention, if already in custody, pending further proceedings. The Defendant(s) is/are thereof charged with the above-stated offense.

SUMMONS

THEREFORE You, THE ABOVE-NAMED DEFENDANT(S, ARE HEREBY SUMMONED to appear on the day of   , 19   at   AM/PM before the above-named court at   to answer this complaint.

IF YOU FAIL TO APPEAR in response to this SUMMONS, a WARRANT FOR YOUR ARREST shall be issued.

WARRANT

EXECUTE IN MINNESOTA ONLY

To the sheriff of the above-named county; or other person authorized to execute this WARRANT; I hereby order, in the name of the State of Minnesota, that the above-named Defendant(s) be apprehended and arrested without delay and brought promptly before the above-named Court (if in session, and if not, before a Judge or Judicial Officer of such Court without unnecessary delay, and in any event not later than 36 hours after the arrest or as soon thereafter as such Judge or Judicial Officer is available) to be dealt with according to law.

ORDER OF DETENTION

Since the above-named Defendant(s) is/are already in custody;

I hereby order; subject to bail or conditions of release, that the above-named Defendant(s) continue to be detained pending further proceedings.

Bail:

Conditions of Release:

This COMPLAINT – SUMMONS, WARRANT, ORDER OF DETENTION was sworn to subscribed before, and issued by the undersigned authorized Issuing Judicial Officer this   day of   , 19

JUDICIAL OFFICER:

Name:

Title:

Signature:

Sworn testimony has been given before the Judicial Officer by the following witnesses:

STATE OF MINNESOTA   COUNTY of

Clerk's Signature or File Stamp:

State of Minnesota

Plaintiff,

vs.

Defendant(s)

RETURN OF SERVICE

I hereby Certify and Return that I have served a copy of this COMPLAINT - SUMMONS. WARRANT. ORDER OF DETENTION upon the Defendant(s) herein-named.

Signature of Authorized Service Agent:

FORM J-1

Combination Form, Page 2
■ EXHIBIT 4.2B

■ The signature of the issuing magistrate, together with a statement of the magistrate's official title

An officer to whom a warrant is directed should read the warrant carefully. If the warrant satisfies the requirements listed here, the officer may execute the warrant without fear of civil liability arising from a challenge to the validity of the warrant.

```
AO 91 (Rev. 5/85)  Criminal Complaint   ●
```

United States District Court

_____ DISTRICT OF _____

UNITED STATES OF AMERICA
V.

CRIMINAL COMPLAINT

CASE NUMBER:

(Name and Address of Defendant)

I, the undersigned complainant being duly sworn state the following is true and correct to the best of my

knowledge and belief. On or about _____ in _____ county, in the

_____ District of _____ defendant(s) did, (Track Statutory Language of Offense)

in violation of Title _____ United States Code, Section(s) _____.

I further state that I am a(n) _____ and that this complaint is based on the following
                                        Official Title

facts:

Continued on the attached sheet and made a part hereof: ☐ Yes   ☐ No

_____
Signature of Complainant

Sworn to before me and subscribed in my presence,

_____ at _____
Date   City and State

_____ _____
Name & Title of Judicial Officer   Signature of Judicial Officer

A Typical Criminal Complaint Form
■ EXHIBIT 4.3

Summons

A magistrate may issue a **summons** instead of an arrest warrant in certain situations. The requirements for a summons are generally the same as those for a warrant, except that a summons directs the defendant to appear before a court at a stated time and place rather than ordering the defendant's arrest. Court rules and statutes usually pro-

```
AO 83 (Rev. 12/85) Summons in a Criminal Case
```

United States District Court

_____ DISTRICT OF _____

UNITED STATES OF AMERICA V.	**SUMMONS IN A CRIMINAL CASE**

CASE NUMBER: _____

(Name and Address of Defendant)

YOU ARE HEREBY SUMMONED to appear before the United States District Court at the place, date and time set forth below.

Place	Room
	Date and Time
Before:	

To answer a(n)
☐ Indictment　☐ Information　☐ Complaint　☐ Violation Notice　☐ Probation Violation Petition

Charging you with a violation of Title _____ United States Code, Section(s) _____

Brief description of offense:

_____　　_____
Signature of Issuing Officer　　　　　　Date

_____
Name and Title of Issuing Officer

A Typical Summons Form, Page 1
■ EXHIBIT 4.4A

vide that, if a defendant fails to appear in response to a summons, a warrant will be issued for his or her arrest. Typical summons forms appear in Exhibits 4.2 and 4.4.

The summons is usually used when the offense charged in a complaint is a misdemeanor, a violation of a municipal ordinance, or some other petty offense. If the offender is a citizen with "roots firmly established in the soil of the community" and can be easily found for serving a warrant if the summons is ignored, the summons

AO 83 (Rev. 12/85) Summons In a Criminal Case

RETURN OF SERVICE	
Service was made by me on:	Date

Check one box below to indicate appropriate method of service

☐ Served personally upon the defendant at: _____
_____

☐ Left summons at the defendant's dwelling house or usual place of abode with a person of suitable age and discretion then residing therein and mailed a copy of the summons to the defendant's last known address. Name of person with whom the summons was left: _____

☐ Returned unexecuted: _____
_____
_____

I declare under penalty of perjury under the laws of the United States of America that the foregoing information contained in the Return of Service is true and correct.

Returned on _____   _____
　　　　　　　Date　　　　　　　　　　　　　Name of United States Marshal

　　　　　　　　　　　　　　　　　　　　_____
　　　　　　　　　　　　　　　　　　　　(by) Deputy United States Marshal

Remarks:

1) As to who may serve a summons see Rule 4 of the Federal Rules of Criminal Procedure.

A Typical Summons Form, Page 2
■ EXHIBIT 4.4B

www.law.ukans.edu/research/
frcriml.htm#II
Rule 4 of the Federal Rules of
Criminal Procedure; *Arrest Warrant or Summons Upon Complaint*
courtlink.utcourts.gov/rules/
urcerp/06.htm
Utah Rules of Criminal Procedure; warrant of arrest or
summons

procedure, rather than formal arrest, is a more efficient and less intrusive means of inducing the defendant to appear in court.

The term **summons** may be confusing because it is often used to describe a citation, ticket, or notice to appear issued by a law enforcement officer, especially in traffic cases. Such a notice is *not* a summons in the legal sense, because it is not issued by a magistrate on the basis of a complaint. A citation, ticket, or notice to appear merely gives notice to offenders that they may be arrested if they do not voluntarily appear in court to answer the charges against them.

Key Points

4. An arrest warrant is a written order to arrest a person, issued by a proper judicial authority on the basis of a sworn complaint charging the commission of a crime, supported by a statement of facts and circumstances establishing probable cause.

5. A summons is similar to an arrest warrant, except that it directs a person to appear in court rather than ordering the person's arrest.

Arrest Authority without a Warrant

Law enforcement officers are often faced with the decision of whether to apply for an arrest warrant or to arrest without a warrant. Since officers often have to make an immediate determination of this question, they must have a clear working knowledge of the law governing arrest without a warrant.

Generally, authority to arrest without a warrant depends on the difference between a **felony** and a **misdemeanor.** In most jurisdictions, a felony is defined as any crime that is or may be punished by death or imprisonment in a state prison. Since most jurisdictions do not provide for imprisonment in the state prison unless the term of the sentence is one year or more, a crime is probably not a felony unless the penalty is at least one year's incarceration. Note that it is the punishment that *may* be imposed under the statute defining the crime that determines whether a crime is a felony or misdemeanor, not the penalty that is actually imposed. *Therefore, a felony can be defined as any crime for which the punishment could possibly be imprisonment for a term of one year or more. All crimes that do not amount to a felony are classified as misdemeanors.*

Jurisdictions differ greatly as to which specific crimes are classified as felonies and which are misdemeanors. Law enforcement officers must familiarize themselves with the classifications of crimes as felonies or misdemeanors in their jurisdictions.

lawschool.lexis.com/emanuel/ web/crimpro/crimpro03.htm General overview of the law relating to warrantless arrest

Misdemeanors

In most jurisdictions, unless otherwise provided by statute, a law enforcement officer may arrest without a warrant for a misdemeanor only when the misdemeanor is "committed in the officer's presence." Ordinarily, this means that the officer must personally observe the misdemeanor being committed before making an arrest. However, sight is not the only means of perceiving the commission of a crime. Therefore, courts have generally held that a misdemeanor is committed in an officer's presence if the officer is able to perceive it through any of the five senses: sight, hearing, touch, taste, or smell. For example, an officer had authority to make a warrantless misdemeanor arrest when he heard, through a door, a person dial a telephone and accept a bet on a horse race. *People v. Goldberg,* 280 N.Y.S.2d 646, 227 N.E.2d 575 (N.Y. 1967). In another case, an officer's smelling alcohol on a driver's breath justified a conclusion that a misdemeanor was being committed in the officer's presence. *State v. Hines,* 504 P.2d 946 (Ariz.App. 1973). And an officer's sense of touch justified a warrantless misdemeanor arrest of a citizen who hit the officer in the face during an investigation of a

Note: After this book had gone to press, the U.S. Supreme Court held in *Atwater v. Lago Vista,* (decided April 24, 2001) that a law enforcement officer who perceives a person committing even a very minor criminal offense in the officer's presence may, without violating the Fourth Amendment, make a full custodial arrest of the person.

Read the court opinion at: laws.findlaw.com/us/000/ 99-1408.html

domestic quarrel in the citizen's home. *Hoover v. Garfield Heights Municipal Court*, 802 F.2d 168 (6th Cir. 1986). Furthermore, an officer investigating crime may enhance his or her senses in various ways.

> Permissible techniques of surveillance include more than just the five senses of officers and their unaided physical abilities. Binoculars, dogs that track and sniff out contraband, search lights, fluorescent powders, automobiles and airplanes, burglar alarms, radar devices, and bait money contribute to surveillance without violation of the Fourth Amendment in the usual case. *United States v. Dubrofsky*, 581 F.2d 208, 211 (9th Cir. 1978).

The "presence" requirement may even be satisfied by the defendant's admission of guilt. *People v. Ward*, 252 N.W.2d 514 (Mich.App. 1977). But information from other witnesses may not be used to satisfy the presence requirement:

> When the basis of the officer's belief that the defendant has committed a misdemeanor is information imparted to him by, say, victims, witnesses or informers, he must present the evidence to a magistrate and seek an arrest warrant. He may not act on his own appraisal of the reasonableness of the information. *People v. Dixon*, 222 N.W.2d 749, 751 (Mich. 1974).

An officer must perceive the commission of a misdemeanor *before* arresting the offender. If the officer arrests on mere suspicion or chance that a misdemeanor is being committed, the arrest is illegal, even if later developments show that a crime did take place. *In re Alonzo C.*, 151 Cal.Rptr. 192 (Cal.App. 1978).

An officer also has no authority to arrest without a warrant for a past or completed misdemeanor, even if the offender is still at the crime scene. If the misdemeanor was completed before the officer arrived, it could not have been committed in the officer's presence. In this situation, the officer may either

- issue a citation to the suspected offender or
- identify the offender and apply for an arrest warrant.

The rule allowing warrantless arrests only for misdemeanors committed in the officer's presence is based on the common law and is not required by the Fourth Amendment. (Note: The **common law** is a body of unwritten law developed in England and based on court decisions. It receives its binding force from traditional usage, custom, and universal acceptance.) "The United States Constitution does not require a warrant for misdemeanors not occurring in the presence of the arresting officer." *Fields v. City of Houston, Tex.*, 922 F.2d 1183, 1189 (5th Cir. 1991). Absent a constitutional warrant requirement, the states may enlarge the authority to arrest for misdemeanors without a warrant through statute or state constitutional amendment.

MISDEMEANOR ARRESTS ON PROBABLE CAUSE   In recent years, various state legislatures have increasingly enacted laws making exceptions to the general rule that an arrest without a warrant for a misdemeanor is authorized only for offenses committed in an officer's presence. These laws authorize arrests on probable cause for certain types of misdemeanors, such as crimes related to domestic violence, certain assaults and threats, shoplifting, driving while intoxicated, fish and game violations, and liquor violations. Because the laws of each state are different, each law enforcement officer must determine the misdemeanors, if any, for which his or her state law allows warrantless arrests on probable cause.

www.clew.org/CLEW/Trn/
DVDraft398.html
Detailed guidelines for handling domestic violence cases in San Diego County, California; includes information on misdemeanor arrests on probable cause

PROMPTNESS OF ARREST   An arrest without a warrant for a misdemeanor committed in an officer's presence must be made promptly and without unnecessary delay. The officer must set out to make the arrest at the time the offense is perceived and must continue that effort until the arrest is accomplished or abandoned.

> The arrest for misdemeanors committed or attempted in the presence of officers must be made as quickly after commission of the offense as the circumstances will permit. After an officer has witnessed a misdemeanor, it is his duty to then and there arrest the offender. Under some circumstances, there may be justification for delay, as for instance, when the interval between the commission of the offense and the actual arrest is spent by the officer in pursuing the offender, or in summoning assistance where such may reasonably appear to be necessary. . . . If, however, the officer witnesses the commission of an offense and does not arrest the offender, but departs on other business, or for other purposes, and afterwards returns, he cannot then arrest the offender without a warrant; for then the reasons for allowing the arrest to be made without a warrant have disappeared. *Smith v. State,* 87 So.2d 917, 919 (Miss. 1956).

Reasonable delay in making a warrantless misdemeanor arrest that is closely connected with the offense itself or with an attempted flight by the offender will usually not invalidate the arrest. Examples of reasonable delays are delays to summon assistance in making the arrest, plan strategy to overcome resistance to arrest, pursue a fleeing offender, or take safety precautions. If an officer delays a warrantless misdemeanor arrest for reasons unconnected with the process of arrest, however, the arrest will be unlawful. These types of delay require the officer to obtain a warrant and to arrest in accordance with the warrant.

Felonies

A law enforcement officer may make a warrantless public arrest for a felony if, at the time of arrest, the officer has probable cause to believe that a felony has been committed and that the person to be arrested is committing or has committed the felony. The U.S. Supreme Court said:

> Law enforcement officers may find it wise to seek arrest warrants where practicable to do so, and their judgments about probable cause may be more readily accepted where backed by a warrant issued by a magistrate. . . . But we decline to transform this judicial preference into a constitutional rule when the judgment of the Nation and Congress has for so long been to authorize warrantless public arrests on probable cause rather than to encumber criminal prosecutions with endless litigation with respect to the existence of exigent circumstances, whether it was practicable to get a warrant, whether the suspect was about to flee, and the like. *United States v. Watson,* 423 U.S. 411, 423–24, 96 S.Ct. 820, 827–28, 46 L.Ed.2d 598, 608–09 (1976).

United States v. Watson
laws.findlaw.com/us/423/
411.html

Some states, however, either by statute or by court interpretation of the state constitution, place greater restrictions on the arrest authority of law enforcement officers. In *People v. Hoinville,* 553 P.2d 777 (Colo. 1976), the court held that a state statute providing that "[a]n arrest warrant should be obtained when practicable" required police officers to obtain a warrant whenever possible.

www.nolo.com/encyclopedia/
articles/crim/when_arrest.html
Article, "Knowing When an
Arrest is Legal"; brief explanation
of probable cause

FELONY ARRESTS ON PROBABLE CAUSE   Assuming that most states allow warrant-less felony arrests on probable cause, the key terms that law enforcement officers must understand to determine their authority to arrest without a warrant are *felony* and *probable cause*. Felony was defined earlier in this chapter as any offense for which the punishment could possibly be imprisonment for a term of one year or more. Probable cause was defined in Chapter 3 and is discussed in greater detail in Chapter 6. For purposes of this discussion, probable cause to arrest is a *fair probability* that the person to be arrested is committing or has committed a crime. Note that before making a warrant-less arrest, a law enforcement officer must have specific facts or circumstances connecting the person to be arrested with a particular felony. If the officer is unable to later justify the arrest by articulating the facts and circumstances supporting probable cause, the arrest is likely to be declared illegal.

If an officer making an arrest has probable cause to believe that a felony has been committed and that the defendant committed it, it makes no difference whether the officer turns out to be right or wrong in making the arrest or whether the defendant is later acquitted of the crime for which the arrest is made. The officer is still justified in making the arrest, and it is a legal arrest. On the other hand, if the officer, on mere suspicion or chance, makes a warrantless arrest without probable cause, the arrest is illegal whether the defendant is guilty or not. Therefore, probable cause is the main consideration in determining the validity of an arrest.

PROMPTNESS OF ARREST   Unlike a warrantless arrest for a misdemeanor, which must be made immediately, a warrantless arrest for a felony may be delayed. Also, it makes no difference whether or not the felony was committed in the officer's presence. *United States v. Drake,* 655 F.2d 1025 (10th Cir. 1981). Delay may be justified for a variety of reasons, so long as the delay is not designed to prejudice an offender's constitutional rights. Reasons justifying delay include an inability to locate the defendant, the need to complete additional undercover investigation, a desire to avoid alerting other potential offenders, and the need to protect the identity of undercover agents or informants.

> The police are not required to guess at their peril the precise moment at which they have probable cause to arrest a suspect, risking a violation of the Fourth Amendment if they act too soon, and a violation of the Sixth Amendment if they wait too long. Law enforcement officers are under no constitutional duty to call a halt to a criminal investigation the moment they have the minimum evidence to establish probable cause, a quantum of evidence which may fall far short of the amount necessary to support a criminal prosecution. *Hoffa v. United States,* 385 U.S. 293, 310, 87 S.Ct. 408, 417, 17 L.Ed.2d 374, 386 (1966).

Hoffa v. United States
laws.findlaw.com/us/385/
293.html

Some courts hold that a person has no constitutional right to be arrested, suggesting that a warrantless felony arrest may be delayed indefinitely. *United States v. Hudgens,* 798 F.2d 1234 (9th Cir. 1986). The safest procedure for the law enforcement officer, however, is to arrest soon after a crime is committed unless there are good reasons for delay.

> [A] point can be reached where the delay is so great that the prejudice to the defendant caused by it—due to faded memories of parties and witnesses, loss of contact with witnesses, and loss of documents—becomes so great that due process and fundamental fairness require that the charges be dismissed. *People v. Hall,* 729 P.2d 373, 375 (Colo. 1986).

> ### Key Points
>
> 6. A law enforcement officer may make a warrantless public arrest for a felony if, at the time of arrest, the officer has probable cause to believe that a felony has been committed and that the person to be arrested is committing or has committed the felony. An officer may arrest without a warrant for a misdemeanor only when the misdemeanor is committed in the officer's presence, or unless otherwise provided by statute or state constitution.
>
> 7. An arrest without a warrant for a misdemeanor committed in an officer's presence must be made as quickly after commission of the offense as the circumstances will permit. An arrest without a warrant for a felony on probable cause, however, may be delayed for various reasons, so long as the delay is not designed to prejudice the offender's constitutional rights.

Effecting a Formal Arrest

To effect a formal arrest, a law enforcement officer must satisfy the basic requirements of a formal arrest. To summarize, these requirements are a law enforcement officer's intention to take a person into the custody of the law to answer for an alleged crime, under real or pretended authority, accompanied by detention or restraint of the person and an understanding by the person that an arrest is being made. Other aspects of effecting an arrest include notice, time of day, warrant requirements, service of a summons, assistance, and the use of discretion.

Notice

The notice a law enforcement officer is required to give when making an arrest is usually governed by statute and differs from state to state. The following is a list of typical information to be included in that notice:

- Notice that the person is under arrest. "The obvious purpose of informing the suspect he is under arrest is not to make the arrest legal but to indicate to the person being arrested that his detention is legal, so that he will not resist." *Pullins v. State,* 256 N.E.2d 553, 556 (Ind. 1970).
- Notice of the officer's authority to arrest. This can be accomplished by the officer's announcing his or her identity as a law enforcement officer. This announcement is not necessary, however, if the officer's authority is already known to the defendant or is obvious from the display of a badge, uniform, or other indicia of authority. *State v. Erdman,* 292 N.W.2d 97 (S.D. 1980).
- Notice of the cause of the arrest. An otherwise lawful arrest is not rendered unlawful, however, if the arresting officer states the offense inaccurately or imprecisely, particularly where the officer acts in good faith and the defendant is not prejudiced by the error. *State Department of Public Safety v. Rice,* 323 N.W.2d 74 (Minn. 1982).

An officer may dispense with giving any notice before making an arrest when one or more of the following are true:

- It would endanger the officer to do so. *United States v. Manfredi,* 722 F.2d 519 (9th Cir. 1983).

- It would adversely affect the making of the arrest. *People v. Bigham,* 122 Cal.Rptr. 252, 49 Cal.App.3d 73 (Cal.App. 1975).
- The offense is being committed in the officer's presence. *Dillard v. State,* 543 S.W.2d 925 (Ark. 1976).
- The person to be arrested is reasonably likely to escape. *United States v. Nolan,* 718 F.2d 589 (3rd Cir. 1983).
- It would result in the destruction or concealment of evidence. *State v. Mueller,* 552 P.2d 1089 (Wash.App. 1976).

Time of Day

An arrest, with or without a warrant, may be made on any day of the week and at any time of the day or night, unless otherwise provided in the warrant or by statute. *State v. Perez,* 277 So.2d 778 (Fla. 1973). Unlike the execution of a search warrant, generally no specific provision in an arrest warrant is required to authorize a nighttime arrest (see Chapter 5). Note, however, that some states limit the time during which a *misdemeanor* warrant may be served, unless another time period is specifically authorized in the warrant.

Executing an Arrest Warrant

Several additional considerations are involved in effecting an arrest when the arrest is carried out under authority of a warrant. First, when officers are directed to serve a warrant of arrest, their belief in the guilt of the defendant or their personal knowledge of facts pertaining to the offense is immaterial. There is no requirement that the offense be committed in their presence or that they have probable cause to believe that the defendant committed the offense. Officers are simply required to carry out the command as stated in the warrant, and the only questions of concern are (1) whether the person to be arrested is the person identified in the warrant and (2) whether the warrant is valid on its face.

When the accused is identified in the warrant by name or description, a law enforcement officer is required to exercise reasonable diligence to make sure that no one else but the person designated in the warrant is arrested. If the person being arrested claims not to be the person identified in the warrant and there is a reasonably simple and direct means of checking that claim, the officer who arrests without checking may be civilly liable for false arrest or false imprisonment. The officer must be reasonably careful in determining whether the person arrested is the person identified in the warrant.

A warrant that is invalid on its face gives the law enforcement officer executing it no protection and no authority to arrest. The officer is bound to examine the warrant if it is available and acts at his or her peril in executing it if it is obviously invalid on its face. An arrest warrant is invalid on its face if one or more of the following are true:

- The court issuing the warrant clearly has no jurisdiction.
- The warrant fails to adequately indicate the crime charged.
- The warrant fails to name or describe any identifiable person.
- The warrant is not signed by the issuing magistrate.
- The warrant is not directed to the officer who is about to execute it. (If the warrant is directed to all law enforcement officers in the jurisdiction, any sworn officer may execute it. If, however, the warrant is directed only to the sheriff of a particular county, only that sheriff or a deputy sheriff may execute it.)

Once an officer determines that a warrant is valid on its face, the officer must carry out the warrant's commands and arrest the person identified in the warrant. The officer no longer has any personal discretion and is merely carrying out an order of the court:

> When the warrant purports to be for a matter within the jurisdiction of the justice (magistrate), the ministerial officer is obliged to execute it, and of course must be justified by it. He cannot inquire upon what evidence the judicial officer proceeded, or whether he committed an error or irregularity in his decision . . . the constable has nothing to look to but the warrant as his guide. . . . *Alexander v. Lindsey*, 55 S.E.2d 470, 473–74 (N.C. 1949).

Most states allow arrest warrants for violations of state law to be executed at any place within the boundaries of the state. However, a law enforcement officer of one state may not go into another state to arrest under a warrant except in fresh pursuit (discussed later in this chapter).

Officers arresting with a warrant should give the same notice, discussed earlier, that they would ordinarily give in making any arrest. In addition, officers should have the warrant in their possession at the time of arrest and should show the warrant to the person arrested. In some states, however, officers may make a legal arrest pursuant to a warrant even though they do not possess the warrant. They must, however, inform the defendant of the offense charged and the existence of the warrant. If the defendant requests, officers must produce the warrant as soon as possible.

Like a warrantless felony arrest, an arrest made under a warrant (for a felony or misdemeanor) need not be made immediately. Officers have considerable discretion as to the time of making an arrest under a warrant. They may have lawful strategic reasons for delay, or they may wish to select a time when the arrest can be accomplished with the least difficulty. "[T]he general rule is that, while execution should not be unreasonably delayed, law enforcement officers have a reasonable time in which to execute a warrant and need not arrest at the first opportunity." *United States v. Drake*, 655 F.2d 1025, 1027 (10th Cir. 1981). If, however, an officer fails to execute an arrest warrant with the purpose of allowing any person charged with or convicted of a crime to escape, the officer may be criminally liable for that failure.

An officer executing an arrest warrant must make a return of the warrant. The return is made by entering on the warrant the date of the arrest, signing the warrant, and filing the warrant with the court. (See the arrest warrant forms in Exhibits 4.1 and 4.2.) Failure to return an arrest warrant may invalidate the arrest and subject the officer to civil liability for false arrest or false imprisonment.

Service of a Summons

As discussed earlier, a magistrate may, under certain circumstances, issue a summons instead of an arrest warrant. A summons is served by personally delivering a copy to the defendant or by leaving it at the defendant's home or usual place of abode with some person of suitable age and discretion who resides there. It may also be served by mailing it to the defendant's last known address. As with an arrest warrant, most states provide that a summons for a violation of state law may be served at any place within the state. In addition, a summons must be returned by the officer serving it to the proper magistrate before the return date appearing on the summons. (See the summons forms in Exhibits 4.2 and 4.4.)

Case in Point

Interpreting *Wilson v. Layne*

On November 21, 1997, at approximately 1:30 A.M., Donna Polk and Christopher Bell returned to the Washington Plaza Hotel after a late dinner with friends. Polk, an African-American woman, is the Executive Director of the Nebraska Urban Indian Health Coalition in Lincoln, Nebraska. Bell, who is Native American, is a law-school graduate and, at the time these claims arose, was a member of the Board of Directors of the American Indian Health and Family Services of Southeastern Michigan, Inc. The plaintiffs were staying at the Washington Plaza Hotel while attending the Indian Health Service Round Table Symposium in Washington, D.C. As the plaintiffs walked through the hotel lobby, Det. Valdes and Aponte intercepted them.

According to the plaintiffs, Det. Valdes and Aponte, who were both dressed in plainclothes, identified themselves as MPD officers. The plaintiffs also claim that when Det. Valdes flashed a badge to identify himself, Aponte made a similar gesture with an official emblem, which the plaintiffs assumed was a police badge. Det. Valdes did nothing to dissuade Aponte's conduct, although it occurred in his presence. To the contrary, the plaintiffs allege that when Det. Valdes later took Polk out of the hotel, he encouraged Aponte to keep Bell behind an imaginary line in the hotel, which Aponte so did.

In fact, Aponte was neither an MPD officer nor employee, but rather had accompanied Det. Valdes that evening as a "civilian ride-a-long." During the MPD's internal investigation of the incident (prompted by a complaint filed by Bell with the MPD), Aponte admitted that in the past he had accompanied Det. Valdes on several tours of duty, though he had never completed the proper ride-a-long authorization forms. The evening in question was no exception. Indeed, the MPD's investigation revealed both that Aponte had failed to complete the requisite paperwork, and that Det. Valdes had not attempted to verify whether Aponte was authorized to participate in the ride-a-long program—an MPD requirement.

Unaware that Aponte was not a police officer, Bell inquired several times as to why the officers had stopped him and Polk in the lobby of the hotel. Aponte did not reply, but instead repeated his requests for Bell's identification. Aponte then ordered Bell to remain behind an imaginary line inside the hotel. After five minutes, when Bell began to move, Aponte ordered him to "stay behind the line," and held up his hands in a gesture to prevent Bell's free movement. At the same time, Det. Valdes "grabbed" Polk's arm and escorted her outside the hotel where he kept her "against her will," even while she insisted that she was a guest at the hotel.

Det. Valdes explains that he noticed Polk entering the hotel because she fit the description of a prostitute whom the MPD suspected of robbery. According to Det. Valdes, Polk matched the description of the prostitute in both her physical build and her attire ("a red sweater, a short skirt, high boots and black stockings"). Contrary to Polk's assertion that he "physically" took her outside the hotel, Det. Valdes states that he merely asked Polk to step outside, she complied, and after a brief interview, he became satisfied that she was not the suspect he was seeking. Polk recalls that Det. Valdes never informed her that he was investigating a robbery, or that she fit the description of a robbery suspect. He did, however, accuse her of being a prostitute, an accusation which Polk claims he made solely because of her race.

The plaintiffs allege that the defendant's actions—effectuated with the assistance of a civilian but without probable cause, reasonable suspicion, or a warrant—constituted an unlawful stop and seizure in violation of their constitutional rights. Defendant Valdes responds that he had a reasonable, good-faith basis on which to conduct an investigatory stop and thus enjoys qualified immunity for his actions. He further asserts that the court must dismiss the plaintiff's common-law claims of battery, false arrest, and false imprisonment as untimely and for failure to state a claim. In light of *Wilson v. Layne*, should the defendant's motion to dismiss be granted? *Polk v. District of Columbia*, 121 F.Supp.2d 56 (D.D.C. 2000).

Read the court opinion at:
www.dcd.uscourts.gov/99-3088.pdf

Assistance

Law enforcement officers may request private citizens to aid them in making an arrest. The laws of some jurisdictions require that any person called on by a law enforcement officer to assist the officer in executing his or her official duties, including the arrest of another person, is legally obligated to obey the officer. Refusal to aid an officer may be punishable under state law.

When private citizens act in aid of a known law enforcement officer, they have the same rights and privileges as the officer. While so acting, they have the status of a temporary law enforcement officer, including the right to use force and to enter property. If the person called on acts in good faith, he or she is protected from liability even if the officer was acting illegally. "It would be manifestly unfair to impose civil liability upon a private person for doing that which the law declares it a misdemeanor for him to refuse to do." *Peterson v. Robison,* 277 P.2d 19, 24 (Cal. 1954).

While a law enforcement officer may request a person to assist in the execution of a warrant, the U.S. Supreme Court has held "that it is a violation of the Fourth Amendment for police to bring members of the media or other third parties into a home during the execution of a warrant when the presence of the third parties in the home was not in aid of the execution of the warrant." *Wilson v. Layne,* 526 U.S. 603, 614, 119 S.Ct. 1692, 1699, 143 L.Ed.2d 818, 830 (1999). Thus, it is recommended that officers should not permit a third party to accompany them inside a residence for any purpose unless (1) the resident voluntarily consents to the third party's entry or (2) the third party's presence is reasonably necessary for police to carry out their duties. If third parties are enlisted to help in the execution of a warrant, the purpose of their presence should be spelled out in the application for the warrant and in the warrant itself.

Wilson v. Layne
laws.findlaw.com/us/000/
98-83.html

Discretion

Even though a law enforcement officer clearly has the ability and authority to arrest, good police practice may call for the arrest to be delayed or not to be made at all. It is beyond the scope of this book to give detailed guidelines in this area, but a brief discussion is necessary to set out general principles.

A law enforcement officer's primary duty is to protect the public at large. Therefore, when an arrest may cause great risk of harm to the public or will only cause embarrassment to a person who poses no real threat to the community, proper police practice may call for delay or restraint in exercising the power of arrest. For example, when a crowd is present, it is often unwise to arrest a person or persons who are creating a minor disturbance. An arrest may aggravate the disturbance and possibly precipitate a riot or civil disorder. Less drastic ways to handle the matter should be explored, even though legal grounds for an arrest may exist. The same considerations apply to minor squabbles and disturbances by intoxicated persons who are creating no danger and may need no more than help in getting home. *An arrest is a significant restraint on a person's freedom and should always be justified by circumstances.*

Some law enforcement agencies have policies covering discretion to arrest. Where no policies exist, officers must use their common sense and good judgment. *Authority to arrest does not necessarily mean duty to arrest.*

www.fbi.gov/publications/leb/
2000/jul00leb.pdf
Article, "Media Ride-Alongs: Fourth Amendment Constraints" by Kimberly A. Crawford (page 26 of the July 2000 *FBI Law Enforcement Bulletin*)
www.jus.state.nc.us/NCJA/
layne.htm
Discussion of *Wilson v. Layne* with advice for law enforcement officers from the North Carolina Justice Academy
pegasus.rutgers.edu/~record/
articles/vol24/24rlr6/
peeping.html
Article, "Covering the Peep Hole: The American Culture of Voyeurism and the First Amendment in the wake of *Wilson v. Layne*" by Xan Kaitlin Desch

Key Points

8. Unless there are extenuating circumstances, an officer arresting a person should give notice that the person is under arrest as well as notice of the officer's authority and the cause of arrest.

9. If an arrest warrant is valid on its face, a law enforcement officer must execute the warrant within a reason-

able time according to its terms, and the officer has no personal discretion in this matter.

10. Warrantless arrests are discretionary and should always be justified by the circumstances.

prairielaw.com/articles/chnl26/
artcl1329.asp
Article, "Making a Citizen's
Arrest" by Sarah Rupp
www.co.alameda.ca.us/da/pov/
citizen_arrests.htm
Article, "Citizen's Arrests" from
the District Attorney's Office in
Alameda County, California

Place of Arrest

In most states, law enforcement officers acting under authority of a warrant may make an arrest at any place within the state where the defendant may be found. Similarly, officers may serve a summons at any place within the state.

However, with respect to warrantless arrests, "[a]s a general rule, a police officer acting outside his or her jurisdiction does not act in his or her official capacity and does not have any official power to arrest." *State v. Slawek,* 338 N.W.2d 120, 121 (Wis.App. 1983). Thus, sheriffs may not arrest without a warrant beyond the counties in which they have been elected, nor may municipal police officers arrest without a warrant beyond the limits of the cities in which they have been appointed. On the other hand, the authority of state law enforcement officers is statewide, and their power to arrest without a warrant runs throughout the state. However, a law enforcement officer of one state has no authority to arrest in another state. Two exceptions to the rule that an officer may not arrest without a warrant outside his or her jurisdiction should be noted:

- Arrests made as a private citizen
- Arrests made in fresh pursuit

Citizen's Arrest Authority

Law enforcement officers have the same authority as private citizens to arrest without a warrant. Under the common law rule in force in most states, a private citizen may arrest a person if the citizen has probable cause to believe that the person has committed a felony. In *State v. Slawek,* 338 N.W.2d 120 (Wis.App. 1983), Chicago, Illinois, police officers in unmarked cars followed the defendants' van into Wisconsin on information that the defendants were involved in residential burglaries. The officers observed the defendants commit a burglary in Wisconsin and arrested them. There were no Wisconsin precedents on the issue of the citizen's arrest authority of police officers. Nevertheless, the court found the arrests legal based on an extensive line of cases from other states. Those cases upheld the validity of an extraterritorial arrest made by a police officer who lacked the official authority to arrest when the place of arrest authorizes a private person to make a citizen's arrest under the same circumstances. The court noted that "the reasoning which permits an officer to make a citizen's arrest in an adjoining jurisdiction within the same state also allows an officer from a different state to make a citizen's arrest in a neighboring state under those circumstances when the state allows private persons to make arrests." 338 N.W.2d at 122 n.1.

A private citizen may use the same degree of force as a law enforcement officer in making an arrest. (See the discussion of use of force later in this chapter.) If, however, the private citizen is mistaken and no felony was *actually committed,* the citizen is subject to civil liability for false arrest or false imprisonment. In contrast, a law enforcement officer who arrests for a felony based on probable cause is protected from civil liability, even if the officer is mistaken.

Under the common law, private citizens have a *duty* to arrest for felonies *committed in their presence.* Also, private citizens *may* arrest for "breach of the peace" misdemeanors *committed in their presence.* A breach of the peace misdemeanor can be defined generally as a misdemeanor that causes or threatens direct physical harm to the public.

Therefore, in a state where the common law rule on citizen's arrest is followed, a law enforcement officer may arrest as a private citizen without a warrant in the previously described circumstances anywhere in the state. Furthermore, unless neighboring states have modified the common law rule by statute, a law enforcement officer may also arrest outside the borders of his or her state as a private citizen. However, the officer making a felony arrest on probable cause as a private citizen risks civil liability if the officer cannot prove that a felony was actually committed.

Fresh Pursuit

Under the common law and most statutes, law enforcement officers may make a lawful arrest without a warrant beyond the borders of their jurisdiction in cases of **fresh pursuit.** Fresh pursuit means an officer's immediate pursuit of a criminal suspect into another jurisdiction after the officer has attempted to arrest the suspect in the officer's jurisdiction. The common law allowed a warrantless arrest in fresh pursuit only in felony cases, but today most state statutes allow warrantless arrests for both felonies and misdemeanors. For a warrantless arrest in fresh pursuit to be legal, all of the following conditions must be met:

- The officer must have authority to arrest for the crime in the first place.
- The pursuit must be of a fleeing criminal attempting to avoid immediate capture.
- The pursuit must begin promptly and be maintained continuously.

The main requirement is that the pursuit be fresh. The pursuit must flow out of the act of attempting to make an arrest and must be a part of the continuous process of apprehension. The pursuit need not be instantaneous, but it must be made without unreasonable delay or interruption. There should be no side trips or diversions, even for other police business. However, the continuity of pursuit is not legally broken by unavoidable interruptions connected with the act of apprehension, such as eating, sleeping, summoning assistance, or obtaining further information.

Fresh pursuit may lead a law enforcement officer outside the boundaries of his or her state. Ordinarily, an officer has no authority beyond that of a private citizen to make arrests in another state. However, many states have adopted the Uniform Act on Fresh Pursuit or similar legislation, which permits law enforcement officers from other states, entering in fresh pursuit, to make an arrest. The Uniform Fresh Pursuit Law of Iowa is typical:

> Any member of a duly organized state, county, or municipal law enforcing unit of another state of the United States who enters this state in fresh pursuit, and continues within this state in such fresh pursuit, of a person in order to arrest the person on the ground that the person is believed to have committed a felony in such other state, shall have the same authority to arrest and hold such person in custody, as has any member of any duly organized state, county, or municipal law enforcing unit of this state, to arrest and hold in custody a person on the ground that the person is believed to have committed a felony in this state. Iowa Code Ann. § 806.1.

Because some states extend the privilege to make an arrest in fresh pursuit to out-of-state officers only on a reciprocal basis, a law enforcement officer must be familiar with not only the statutes in his or her own state but also the fresh pursuit statutes of all neighboring states.

A law enforcement officer who makes an arrest in fresh pursuit under such a statute in a neighboring state must take the arrested person before an appropriate judicial officer in that state without unreasonable delay. Some states allow an arresting officer from another state to take a person arrested in fresh pursuit back to the officer's home state after the arrested person is brought before an appropriate judicial officer. Other states

www.laaw.com/managi~1.htm
Article, "Managing the Risk: Law Enforcement Jurisdictional Issues" by Michael A. Brave and Steven D. Ashley

allow this only upon **extradition** or waiver of extradition. Extradition is a procedure whereby authorities in one state (the demanding state) demand from another state (the asylum state) that a fugitive from justice in the demanding state, who is present in the asylum state, be delivered to the demanding state. Most states have adopted the Uniform Criminal Extradition Act, which provides uniform extradition procedures among the states.

Key Points

11. In general, a law enforcement officer has no authority to make warrantless arrests outside the geographic limits of the jurisdiction for which he or she has been elected or appointed.

12. As a private citizen, a law enforcement officer may arrest outside his or her jurisdiction for felonies on probable cause and for felonies and "breach of the peace" misdemeanors if committed in the officer's presence.

13. A law enforcement officer may arrest outside his or her jurisdiction in "fresh pursuit." Fresh pursuit means an officer's immediate and continuously maintained pursuit of a criminal suspect into another jurisdiction after the officer has attempted to arrest the person in the officer's own jurisdiction.

Use of Force

www.txk9cop.com/force.htm
Article, "Use of Force" by Robert
C. Phillips; discussion based on
both federal and California laws
and court decisions
www.fmew.com/archive/police
Article, "When Police Officers
Kill" by Jody M. Barringer
www.laaw.com/uof6acc.htm
Article, "How Much Force is
Acceptable?" by Michael A.
Brave
www.fbi.gov/library/leb/1997/
oct975.htm
Article, "Police Use of Non-
deadly Force to Arrest" by John
C. Hall
www.law.ua.edu/lawreview/
mcilwain.htm
Article, "The Qualified Immunity
Defense in the Eleventh Circuit
and Its Application to Excessive
Force Claims" by Christopher
McIlwain
www.law.indiana.edu/ilj/v73/
no4/06.htm
Article, "Cooling the Hot Pur-
suit: Toward a Categorical
Approach" by Travis N. Jensen

A law enforcement officer's right to use force to make an arrest depends on the degree of force used and the context in which it is used. This section examines various aspects of arrest and discusses the degree of force appropriate in each situation.

Felony Arrests

Under the common law rule, a law enforcement officer could use any reasonably necessary *nondeadly* force to arrest for a felony. Most jurisdictions retain this rule today, by either statute or court decision: "[T]he use of any significant force . . . not reasonably necessary to effect an arrest—as where the suspect neither resists nor flees or where the force is used after a suspect's resistance has been overcome or his flight thwarted—would be constitutionally unreasonable." *Kidd v. O'Neil*, 774 F.2d 1252, 1256–57 (4th Cir. 1985).

The common law rule also allowed officers to use *deadly* force to arrest any fleeing felony suspect. Under the rule, an officer was not required to retreat from effecting an arrest to avoid extreme measures, but was required to press on and use all necessary force to bring the offender into custody. The use of deadly force was therefore permitted as a last resort if the only alternative was to abandon the attempt to arrest.

An examination of the history of the common law rule reveals that it originated in an era when all felonies were capital crimes punishable by death, all felons were considered dangerous, defendants had meager rights, and few of those arrested and tried for felonies escaped conviction and death. Consequently, the use of deadly force to apprehend fleeing felons was viewed merely as a more timely and less costly implementation of the eventual penalty for their offenses.

In addition, police as such did not exist at that time; the responsibility for apprehending fleeing felons fell upon the unarmed and untrained citizens who responded to the hue and cry. Weapons were primitive, and the use of force often meant hand-to-hand combat, which was seldom deadly, although it posed significant danger to the arresting person.

Today, most felonies are not punishable by death; fewer felons are convicted or executed; and police are organized, trained, equipped with sophisticated weapons, and capable of killing accurately at a distance and under circumstances posing little danger to officers or others, especially if the felon is unarmed. Operation of the common law rule under these changed circumstances would allow police to kill persons merely suspected of offenses that, upon conviction, would very likely result in only brief imprisonment or even probation.

Although it is generally agreed that police should be able to use as much force as necessary to protect themselves and the public against violent offenders, the common law rule on deadly force has been much criticized as overly broad to fulfill these legitimate functions. As a result, the U.S. Supreme Court in 1985 declared unconstitutional Tennessee's statute that codified the common law rule. The Court reasoned that the statute authorizing police to use deadly force to apprehend *any* fleeing felony suspect, regardless of the particular circumstances, violated the Fourth Amendment's guarantee against unreasonable seizures. Killing a suspect, the Court noted, is the ultimate seizure.

> The use of deadly force to prevent the escape of all felony suspects, whatever the circumstances, is constitutionally unreasonable. It is not better that all felony suspects die than that they escape. Where the suspect poses no immediate threat to the officer and no threat to others, the harm resulting from failing to apprehend him does not justify the use of deadly force to do so. It is no doubt unfortunate when a suspect who is in sight escapes, but the fact that the police arrive a little late or are a little slower afoot does not always justify killing a suspect. A police officer may not seize an unarmed, nondangerous suspect by shooting him dead. . . . Where the officer has probable cause to believe that the suspect poses a threat of serious physical harm, either to the officer or to others, it is not constitutionally unreasonable to prevent escape by using deadly force. Thus, if the suspect threatens the officer with a weapon or there is probable cause to believe that he has committed a crime involving the infliction or threatened infliction of serious physical harm, deadly force may be used if necessary to prevent escape, and if, where feasible, some warning has been given. *Tennessee v. Garner*, 471 U.S. 1, 11–12, 105 S.Ct. 1694, 1701, 85 L.Ed.2d 1, 9–10 (1985).

Even before the Supreme Court decision in the *Garner* case, criticism of the common law rule on deadly force in felony cases resulted in abolition of the rule in many jurisdictions and in changes such as Section 3.07(2)(b) of the Model Penal Code, which reads as follows:

> The use of deadly force is not justifiable under this Section unless:
> (i) the arrest is for a felony; and
> (ii) the person effecting the arrest is authorized to act as a peace officer or is assisting a person whom he believes to be authorized to act as a peace officer; and
> (iii) the actor believes that the force employed creates no substantial risk of injury to innocent persons; and
> (iv) the actor believes that:

www.ci.seattle.wa.us/seattle/spd/images/forg.htm
Report, "A Less Lethal Options Program for Seattle Police Department"; in-depth report on deadly force and recommended alternatives
www.fbi.gov/publications/leb/1998/febleb.pdf
Article, "Improving Deadly Force Decision Making" by Dean T. Olson (page 1 of the February 1998 *FBI Law Enforcement Bulletin*)
www.fbi.gov/publications/leb/2000/oct00leb.pdf
Article, "Reviewing Use of Force" by Sam W. Lathrop (page 16 of the October 2000 *FBI Law Enforcement Bulletin*)

Tennessee v. Garner
laws.findlaw.com/us/471/1.html

(A) the crime for which the arrest is made involved conduct including the use or threatened use of deadly force; or

(B) there is substantial risk that the person to be arrested will cause death or serious bodily injury if his apprehension is delayed.

Some states have adopted this section of the Model Penal Code or variations of it. The policies of other states on the use of deadly force are unclear.

Officers should make every effort to clearly ascertain the law on deadly force in their states and the policy in their departments, but at a minimum, officers must comply with the standards of the Supreme Court as set out in the *Garner* case. Very serious consequences can result from the unwarranted use of deadly force, such as death or injury to the officer or other persons, or both civil and criminal liability of the officer.

Misdemeanor Arrests

As with felonies, most states retain the common law rule allowing law enforcement officers to use any reasonably necessary nondeadly force to arrest for a misdemeanor. However, an officer is *never* justified in using deadly force to arrest for a misdemeanor. *State v. Wall*, 286 S.E.2d 68 (N.C. 1982). *The rule is that it is better that a misdemeanant escapes rather than a human life be taken.* The use of deadly force on a misdemeanant is excessive force constituting an assault. An officer who kills the suspect may be guilty of murder or manslaughter.

Self-Defense

Whether an offense is a felony or misdemeanor, a law enforcement officer making a lawful arrest may use any force reasonably necessary under the circumstances, including deadly force, if the officer reasonably believes that the person to be arrested is about to commit an assault and that the officer is in danger of death or serious bodily injury. The law enforcement officer's duty is to be the aggressor and to press forward to bring the person under restraint. This cannot be accomplished by purely defensive action on an officer's part. Therefore, if an officer has lawful authority to arrest, the officer is not required to back down in the face of physical resistance to the arrest. *State v. Williams*, 148 A.2d 22 (N.J. 1959). An officer faced with the choice of abandoning an arrest or using deadly force in self-defense has the right to use deadly force if necessary for self-protection.

Resisting Arrest

boalt.org/CCLR/v2/ v2hemmensnf.htm Article, "Resisting Unlawful Arrest in Mississippi: Resisting the Modern Trend" by Craig Hemmens; inludes a detailed history of the right to resist arrest www.fbi.gov/publications/leb/ 1999/jun99leb.pdf Article, "Assessing the Patterns of Citizen Resistance During Arrests" by Darrell L. Ross (page 5 of the June 1999 *FBI Law Enforcement Bulletin*)

Resisting arrest is a crime involving a person's opposing a law enforcement officer by direct, forcible means to prevent the officer from taking the person into custody. Under statutes defining the crime, indirect interference or hindrance of an officer will usually not support a conviction. Resistance requires active opposition such as shooting, striking, pushing, or otherwise struggling with the officer. Mere flight, concealment, or other avoidance or evasion of arrest will not constitute resistance.

The fact that the accused sought to escape the officer by merely running away was not such an obstruction as the law contemplates. While it is the duty of every citizen to submit to a lawful arrest, yet flight is not such an offense as will make a person amenable to the charge of resisting or obstructing an officer who is attempting to make an arrest, as there is a broad distinction between avoidance and resistance or obstruction. *Jones v. Commonwealth*, 126 S.E. 74, 76–77 (Va. 1925).

Nor will verbal objections, protests, or threats unaccompanied by force constitute resisting arrest. However, a serious threat, accompanied by apparent ability and present intention to execute it, that prevents an officer from acting because of reasonable fear of serious bodily injury, may constitute resistance to arrest.

Under the common law rule, the crime of resisting arrest requires that the arrest be lawful. If an arrest is unlawful, the person being arrested has the *right* to resist. A person being arrested also has a right to resist if the person making the arrest is not an officer of the law or if the officer does not proceed in a lawful manner in making the arrest. Therefore, it is very important for law enforcement officers making an arrest to

- establish their identity, if not already known or obvious; and
- explain their purpose and authority.

Under the common law rule, a person threatened with an illegal arrest may not only resist the arrest but may use any force reasonably necessary for self-defense and prevention of impending injury. *State v. McGowan,* 90 S.E.2d 703 (N.C. 1956). Since the impending injury resulting from an arrest is ordinarily only a brief unlawful detention, the degree of force a person may use is strictly limited. A person who uses more force than is reasonably necessary for the purpose may be guilty of an assault and battery on the officer. Deadly force is rarely justified to resist an unlawful arrest, except when a person has reasonable grounds to fear death or serious bodily injury at the hands of an officer.

The law on resisting arrest and other interferences with law enforcement officers varies among jurisdictions. For example, some jurisdictions prohibit a private citizen from using force to resist an arrest made by one whom the citizen knows or has good reason to believe is an authorized police officer engaged in the performance of official duties, whether or not the arrest is illegal. If, however, the officer uses excessive and unnecessary force in effecting the arrest, the citizen may respond or counter with reasonable force for self-protection.

> Despite his duty to submit quietly without physical resistance to an arrest made by an officer acting in the course of his duty, even though the arrest is illegal, his right to freedom from unreasonable seizure and confinement can be protected, restored and vindicated through legal processes. However, the rule permitting reasonable resistance to excessive force of the officer, whether the arrest is lawful or unlawful, is designed to protect a person's bodily integrity and health and so permits resort to self-defense. Simply stated, the law recognizes that liberty can be restored through legal processes but life or limb cannot be repaired in a courtroom. And so it holds that the reason for outlawing resistance to an unlawful arrest and requiring disputes over its legality to be resolved in the courts has no controlling application on the right to resist an officer's excessive force. . . .
>
> Two qualifications on the citizen's right to defend against and to repel an officer's excessive force must be noticed. He cannot use greater force in protecting himself against the officer's unlawful force than reasonably appears to be necessary. If he employs such greater force, then he becomes the aggressor and forfeits the right to claim self-defense to a charge of assault and battery on the officer. . . . Furthermore, if he knows that if he desists from his physically defensive measures and submits to arrest the officer's unlawfully excessive force would cease, the arrestee must desist or lose his privilege of self-defense. *State v. Mulvihill,* 270 A.2d 277, 280 (N.J. 1970).

As illustrated by the *Mulvihill* case, the modern trend is away from the common law rule allowing resistance to any illegal arrest, because of the dangers inherent in the rule and because the consequences of an illegal arrest are at most a brief period of detention

www.perkel.com/pbl/city/
briefsup.htm
Supplemental brief filed in U.S.
District Court dealing with physical entry of the home to arrest

during which arrested persons can resort to nonviolent legal remedies for regaining their liberty.

Entry of Dwellings

Under the common law, the right of a law enforcement officer to enter a dwelling to arrest depended on whether the officer had legal authority to arrest. Legal authority to arrest, with or without a warrant, carried with it the authority to forcibly enter any dwelling and search for the suspect who the officer had probable cause to believe was in that dwelling.

> An agent must have probable cause to believe that the person he is attempting to arrest, with or without a warrant, is in a particular building at the time in question before that agent can legitimately enter the building by ruse or any other means. To hold otherwise is to grant the agent a license to go from house to house employing ruse entries in violation of the right of privacy of the respective occupants. *United States v. Phillips*, 497 F.2d 1131, 1136 (9th Cir. 1974).

This authority to enter a dwelling house to arrest applied even to misdemeanor arrests.

The common law rule is no longer valid. In recent years the U.S. Supreme Court has decided cases dealing with the entry of dwellings to arrest. The general rule now is that a law enforcement officer may not enter a dwelling to arrest a person without a warrant, unless there is consent or **exigent circumstances.** Whether an arrest warrant or search warrant is required for entry depends on whether the dwelling to be entered is the suspect's home or someone else's home.

Entry of a Suspect's Home

Payton v. New York
laws.findlaw.com/us/445/
573.html

In *Payton v. New York*, 445 U.S. 573, 100 S.Ct. 1371, 63 L.Ed.2d 639 (1980), the U.S. Supreme Court held that, absent exigent circumstances or consent, a law enforcement officer may not make a warrantless entry into a suspect's home to make a routine felony arrest. The Court said that the physical entry of the home is the chief evil against which the wording of the Fourth Amendment is directed and that the warrant procedure minimizes the danger of needless intrusions of that sort. The Court went on to say that an arrest warrant requirement, although providing less protection than a search warrant requirement, was sufficient to interpose the magistrate's determination of probable cause between a zealous officer and a citizen. The Court concluded that "an arrest warrant founded on probable cause implicitly carries with it the limited authority to enter a dwelling in which the suspect lives when there is reason to believe the suspect is within." 445 U.S. at 603, 100 S.Ct. at 1388, 63 L.Ed.2d at 661. Therefore, absent consent or exigent circumstances, a law enforcement officer must have at least an arrest warrant to lawfully enter a suspect's home to arrest the suspect.

With respect to the *Payton* requirement that an officer executing an arrest warrant at the suspect's home have "reason to believe the suspect is within," the following quotation from the 11th Circuit Court of Appeals is informative:

> [I]n order for law enforcement officials to enter a residence to execute an arrest warrant for a resident of the premises, the facts and circumstances within the knowledge of the law enforcement agents, when viewed in the totality, must warrant a reasonable belief that [1] the location to be searched is the suspect's dwelling, and that [2] the suspect

is within the residence at the time of entry. . . . In evaluating this on the spot determination, as to the second *Payton* prong, courts must be sensitive to common sense factors indicating a resident's presence. For example, officers may take into consideration the possibility that the resident may be aware that police are attempting to ascertain whether or not the resident is at home, and officers may presume that a person is at home at certain times of the day—a presumption which can be rebutted by contrary evidence regarding the suspect's known schedule. *United States v. Magluta*, 44 F.3d 1530, 1535 (11th Cir. 1995).

In *United States v. Beck*, 729 F.2d 1329 (11th Cir. 1984), the court held that FBI officers and local police had reason to believe that Beck was in his apartment when the officers entered it to execute an arrest warrant. There were no outward signs of life in the apartment the evening before the search or the next morning, and as the agents had not monitored Beck's apartment, they were not aware of his comings and goings. Despite these evidentiary shortcomings, the court observed that Beck's car was parked near the home and that it was reasonable to believe that a person would be home sleeping at 7:30 A.M., which would account for the lack of outward signs of life. Finally, the court noted that the lack of response to the officer's knock and announcement did not indicate that no one was at home "since it was reasonable to expect a fugitive to hide or flee if possible." 729 F.2d at 1332. *In United States v. De Parias*, 805 F.2d 1447 (11th Cir. 1986), the court held that agents reasonably believed that the suspects were at home, since the apartment manager informed agents that the De Pariases were at home if a certain car was parked in front of the apartment.

In *United States v. Holland*, 755 F.2d 253 (2d Cir. 1985), the court held that the *Payton* rule did not apply to vestibules and common areas of multiple-tenant buildings, because there can be no expectation of privacy in those areas and because police protection is needed in those areas. In that case, the court upheld a nonconsensual, nonemergency arrest of a defendant who answered the doorbell in the vestibule of his two-apartment building. The arresting officer had probable cause to believe that the defendant was involved in illegal drug sales.

Entry of a Third Person's Home

In *Steagald v. United States*, 451 U.S. 204, 101 S.Ct. 1642, 68 L.Ed.2d 38 (1981), the U.S. Supreme Court held that an arrest warrant does not authorize law enforcement officers to enter the home of a third person to search for the person to be arrested, in the absence of consent or exigent circumstances. To protect the Fourth Amendment privacy interests of persons not named in an arrest warrant, a search warrant must be obtained to justify the entry into the home of any person other than the person to be arrested. The Court said:

> In the absence of exigent circumstances, we have consistently held that [law enforcement officers' determinations of probable cause] are not reliable enough to justify an entry into a person's home to arrest him without a warrant, or a search of a home for objects in the absence of a search warrant. We see no reason to depart from this settled course when the search of a home is for a person rather than an object.
>
> A contrary conclusion—that the police, acting alone and in the absence of exigent circumstances, may decide when there is sufficient justification for searching the home of a third party for the subject of an arrest warrant—would create a significant potential for abuse. Armed solely with an arrest warrant for a single person, the police could

www.cwu.edu/~millerj/academic/methods/readings/hall1.htm
Article, "Entering the Premises to Arrest: The Threshold Question" by John C. Hall; examines when an actual crossing of the threshold has occurred and the distinction between actual and constructive entry

www.co.alameda.ca.us/da/pov/rameyweb.htm
Article, "*Ramey*: Entering a Home to Make an Arrest" from the District Attorney's Office in Alameda County, California; discusses the California case of *People v. Ramey*, a precursor to *Payton v. New York*

Steagald v. United States
laws.findlaw.com/us/451/204.html

search all the homes of that individual's friends and acquaintances. . . . Moreover, an arrest warrant may serve as the pretext for entering a home in which the police have suspicion, but not probable cause to believe, that illegal activity is taking place. 451 U.S. at 215, 101 S.Ct. at 1649, 68 L.Ed.2d at 46–47.

This requirement places a heavy practical burden on law enforcement officers, causing them to seek both an arrest warrant and a search warrant in many situations. An alternative, suggested by the Supreme Court, is that in most instances the police may avoid altogether the need to obtain a search warrant simply by waiting for a suspect to leave the third person's home before attempting to arrest the suspect. When the suspect leaves either the home of a third person or his or her own home and is in a public place, officers may arrest on probable cause alone. Neither an arrest warrant nor a search warrant is required to support an arrest made in a public place.

Some courts have allowed exceptions to the requirement of a search warrant to enter a third person's home to arrest a suspect. *United States v. Donaldson*, 793 F.2d 498 (2d Cir. 1986), held that a search warrant was not required when the third-party homeowner knowingly allowed a fleeing felon to enter his home. And *United States v. Riis*, 83 F.3d 212 (8th Cir. 1996), held that a search warrant was not required to arrest a suspect at the home of a third party when police reasonably believed that the suspect was the third party's girlfriend and that she possessed common authority over the home.

Exigent Circumstances

www.lectlaw.com/def/e063.htm
Comprehensive definition of
"exigent circumstances"

Welsh v. Wisconsin
laws.findlaw.com/us/466/
740.html

In neither the *Payton* nor *Steagald* cases did the Supreme Court specify the nature of the exigent circumstances that would justify a warrantless entry of a home to make an arrest. In *Welsh v. Wisconsin*, 466 U.S. 740, 753, 104 S.Ct. 2091, 2099, 80 L.Ed.2d 732, 745 (1984), however, the Court held:

> [A]n important factor to be considered when determining whether any exigency exists is the gravity of the underlying offense for which the arrest is being made. Moreover, although no exigency is created simply because there is probable cause to believe that a serious crime has been committed . . . application of the exigent-circumstances exception in the context of a home entry should rarely be sanctioned when there is probable cause to believe that only a minor offense . . . has been committed.

Illinois v. McArthur
laws.findlaw.com/us/000/
99-1132.html

In the *Welsh* case, the warrantless arrest of the defendant in his home for a "nonjailable" traffic offense (operating a motor vehicle while under the influence of an intoxicant) was held illegal. The need to obtain a blood sample quickly for blood-alcohol testing was not considered a sufficient exigency. In *Illinois v. McArthur*, __ U.S. __ , 121 S.Ct. 946, 148 L.Ed.2d 838 (2001), the U.S. Supreme Court held that the need to preserve evidence of "jailable offenses" (possession of marijuana and drug paraphernalia) was sufficiently urgent or pressing to justify the police in keeping the defendant from entering his home. The Court noted, however, that "[t]emporarily keeping a person from entering his home, a consequence whenever police stop a person on the street, is considerably less intrusive than police entry into the home itself in order to make a warrantless arrest or conduct a search." __ U.S. at __ , 121 S.Ct. at 953, 148 L.Ed.2d at 851 . Note that the Court did *not* decide whether the need to preserve evidence would have justified a greater restriction for a "jailable offense" or the same restriction for a "nonjailable" offense. The resolution of these issues awaits a case that presents them.

In *Minnesota v. Olson,* 495 U.S. 91, 110 S.Ct. 1684, 109 L.Ed.2d 85 (1990), the U.S. Supreme Court approved the Minnesota Supreme Court's standard for determining whether exigent circumstances exist. The Minnesota court observed that "a warrantless intrusion may be justified by hot pursuit of a fleeing felon, or imminent destruction of evidence . . . or the need to prevent a suspect's escape, or the risk of danger to the police or to other persons inside or outside the dwelling." 436 N.W.2d at 97. Furthermore, "in the absence of hot pursuit there must be at least probable cause to believe that one or more of the other factors justifying the entry were present and that in assessing the risk of danger, the gravity of the crime and likelihood that the suspect is armed should be considered." 495 U.S. at 100, 110 S.Ct. at 1690, 109 L.Ed.2d at 95–96. Applying this standard, exigent circumstances justifying the warrantless entry into a home were determined not to exist in the *Olson* case in which

- although a grave crime was involved, the defendant was known not to be the murderer;
- the police had already recovered the murder weapon;
- there was no suggestion of danger to the two women with whom the defendant was staying;
- several police squads surrounded the house;
- the time was 3 P.M. Sunday;
- it was evident the suspect was going nowhere; and
- if he came out of the house, he would have been promptly apprehended.

A case in which the U.S. Supreme Court found that **hot pursuit** of the perpetrator of a serious crime constituted exigent circumstances is *Warden v. Hayden,* 387 U.S. 294, 87 S.Ct. 1642, 18 L.Ed.2d 782 (1967). In that case, police officers had reliable information that an armed robbery had taken place and that the perpetrator had entered a certain house five minutes earlier. The Court held that the officers

acted reasonably when they entered the house and began to search for a man of the description they had been given and for weapons which he had used in the robbery or might use against them. The Fourth Amendment does not require police officers to delay in the course of an investigation if to do so would gravely endanger their lives or the lives of others. Speed here was essential, and only a thorough search of the house for persons and weapons could have insured that Hayden was the only man present and that the police had control of all weapons which could be used against them or to effect an escape. 387 U.S. at 298–99, 87 S.Ct. at 1646, 18 L.Ed.2d at 787.

When the arrest of a suspect is set in motion in a public place, but the suspect retreats into his or her home, the right of officers to enter the home in hot pursuit is governed by the case of *United States v. Santana,* 427 U.S. 38, 96 S.Ct. 2406, 49 L.Ed.2d 300 (1976). In that case, police officers drove to the defendant's house after receiving information that she had in her possession marked money used to make a heroin buy arranged by an undercover agent. The defendant was standing in the doorway of her house holding a paper bag as the police pulled up within fifteen feet of her. The officers got out of the car, shouting "Police," and the defendant retreated into the vestibule of her house where she was apprehended. When the defendant tried to pull away, envelopes containing heroin fell to the floor from the paper bag. Some of the marked money was found on her person.

The Court held that, while standing in the doorway of her house, the defendant was in a "public place" for purposes of the Fourth Amendment. Since she was not in an

Minnesota v. Olson
laws.findlaw.com/us/495/91.html

www.co.alameda.ca.us/da/pov/scene_searches.htm
Article, "Crime Scene Searches"; discusses extensively exigent circumstances as justification for entering a crime scene

Warden v. Hayden
laws.findlaw.com/us/387/294.html

United States v. Santana
laws.findlaw.com/us/427/38.html

www.fbi.gov/publications/leb/
1996/sept966.txt
Article, "Creating Exigent Circumstances" by Edward M. Hendrie; discusses the creation of
exigent circumstances by the
police

area where she had any expectation of privacy and she was exposed to public view, speech, hearing, and touch, it was the same as if she had been standing completely outside her house. When police sought to arrest her, they merely intended to make a warrantless arrest in a public place upon probable cause. Under *United States v. Watson*, 423 U.S. 411, 96 S.Ct. 820, 46 L.Ed.2d 598 (1976), such an arrest would not violate the Fourth Amendment. By retreating into a private place, the defendant could not defeat an otherwise proper arrest that had been set in motion in a public place. Since the officers needed to act quickly to prevent the destruction of evidence, a true hot pursuit took place, even though it entailed only a very short chase. Thus, the warrantless entry to make the arrest was justified, as was the search incident to that arrest.

A case in which the court found that the risk of danger to persons inside a dwelling constituted exigent circumstances is *State v. York*, 464 N.W.2d 36 (Wis.App. 1990). In that case police, acting on a missing persons report, went to the home of the missing persons and detected the odor of a decomposing body emanating from an open window. Warrantless entry of the home was justified because the officers had reason to believe there might be another living victim in the area in need of assistance. The court pointed out that "the criterion is the reasonableness of the belief of the police as to the existence of an emergency, not the existence of an emergency in fact." 464 N.W.2d at 40. (See pages 381 through 384 for a discussion of limitations on searches of murder scenes and for a broader discussion of emergency entries of dwellings and observations of evidence under the plain view doctrine.)

Officers, of course, cannot deliberately create exigent circumstances to subvert the warrant requirements of the Fourth Amendment. In considering claims of manufactured exigency, courts "distinguish between cases where exigent circumstances arise naturally during a delay in obtaining a warrant and those where officers have deliberately created the exigent circumstances." *United States v. Webster*, 750 F.2d 307, 327 (5th Cir. 1984). In *United States v. Hultgren*, 713 F.2d 79 (5th Cir. 1983), the court held that exigent circumstances arose naturally when the transmitter worn by a confidential informant participating in a drug buy suddenly failed. Concern for the confidential informant's safety justified the warrantless entry. On the other hand, a warrantless entry was held to be illegal because of manufactured exigency in *United States v. Scheffer*, 463 F.2d 567 (5th Cir. 1972), in which codefendants who had already been arrested were helping agents catch other members of a drug conspiracy. Agents sent the cooperating defendants into a residence to consummate a drug deal and then made a warrantless entry to arrest the residents. The court refused to accept the government's argument that the agents lacked the time to obtain a warrant, because the agents controlled the timing of the drug buy.

Forced Entry

Assuming police officers have legal authority to enter a dwelling, they should first knock on the door, announce their authority and purpose, and then demand admittance before they force their way into the dwelling to arrest someone inside. This principle is an element of the reasonableness inquiry under the Fourth Amendment.

> Given the longstanding common-law endorsement of the practice of announcement, we have little doubt that the Framers of the Fourth Amendment thought that the method of an officer's entry into a dwelling was among the factors to be considered in assessing the reasonableness of a search or seizure. . . . [W]e hold that in some circumstances an officer's unannounced entry into a home might be unreasonable under the Fourth

Amendment. *Wilson v. Arkansas*, 514 U.S. 927, 934, 115 S.Ct. 1914, 1918, 131 L.Ed.2d 976, 982 (1995).

Wilson v. Arkansas
laws.findlaw.com/us/000/
u10280.html

If their demand to enter is refused or met with silence, officers may enter forcibly after waiting a reasonable time under the circumstances.

> The requirement of prior notice of authority and purpose before forcing entry into a home is deeply rooted in our heritage, and should not be given grudging application. . . . Every householder, the good and the bad, the guilty and the innocent, is entitled to the protection designed to secure the common interest against unlawful invasion of the house. The petitioner could not be lawfully arrested in his home by officers breaking in without first giving him notice of their authority and purpose. Because the petitioner did not receive that notice before the officers broke the door to invade his home, the arrest was unlawful, and the evidence seized should have been suppressed. *Miller v. United States*, 357 U.S. 301, 313–14, 78 S.Ct. 1190, 1198, 2 L.Ed.2d 1332, 1340–41 (1958).

Miller v. United States
laws.findlaw.com/us/357/
301.html

In this context, forcible entry of a dwelling does not necessarily mean only the violent breaking down of a door or the smashing of a window. The U.S. Supreme Court stated that "[a]n unannounced intrusion into a dwelling . . . is no less an unannounced intrusion whether officers break down a door, force open a chain lock on a partially open door, open a locked door by use of a passkey, or . . . open a closed but unlocked door." *Sabbath v. United States*, 391 U.S. 585, 590, 88 S.Ct. 1755, 1758, 20 L.Ed.2d 828, 834 (1968). Also, refusal of admittance is not restricted to an affirmative refusal but is determined from the totality of the circumstances. As stated in *United States v. James*, 528 F.2d 999, 1017 (5th Cir. 1976), "Failure to respond within a reasonable time [is] tantamount to a refusal. A reasonable time is ordinarily very brief." Furthermore, officers' knowledge that the occupants are drug dealers justifies a shorter wait before entry.

Sabbath v. United States
laws.findlaw.com/us/391/
585.html

> Those within might reasonably be thought to be unusually attuned to a law-enforcement knock at the door, and ready to respond promptly in one form or another. As common sense, and bitter experience, would suggest, the law has "uniformly . . . recognized that substantial dealers in narcotics possess firearms and that such weapons are as much tools of the trade as more commonly recognized drug paraphernalia." *United States v. Payne*, 805 F.2d 1062, 1065 (D.C. Cir. 1986). . . . Once police officers seeking to enter a drug traffickers' enclave have announced their identity and authority, they stand before the door blind and vulnerable. In such a danger-fraught situation, the officers may quite reasonably infer refusal more readily than under other circumstances. *United States v. Bonner*, 874 F.2d 822, 824 (D.C.Cir. 1989).

The U.S. Supreme Court held that although an officer's unannounced entry into a home might, in some circumstances, be unreasonable under the Fourth Amendment, not every entry must be preceded by an announcement.

> The Fourth Amendment's flexible requirement of reasonableness should not be read to mandate a rigid rule of announcement that ignores countervailing law enforcement interests. . . . [T]he common-law principle of announcement was never stated as an inflexible rule requiring announcement under all circumstances. *Wilson v. Arkansas*, 514 U.S. 927, 934, 115 S.Ct. 1914, 1918, 131 L.Ed.2d 976, 982 (1995).

Therefore, the failure to knock, announce, and demand admittance before forcibly entering may be excused in the following situations:

www.fletc.gov/legal/
archive_dir.htm
Article, "The Knock and
Announce Rule: 'Knock, Knock,
Knocking on the Suspect's
Door'" by John Besselman; first
of three articles in the October 2,
2000, issue of *Quarterly Review:
Legal Commentary for Federal Law
Enforcement Officers*

■ When the officer's purpose is already known to the offender or other person upon whom demand for entry is made. As the Supreme Court stated in the *Miller* case:

> It may be that, without an express announcement of purpose, the facts known to officers would justify them in being virtually certain that the petitioner already knows their purpose so that an announcement would be a useless gesture. 375 U.S. at 310, 78 S.Ct. at 1196, 2 L.Ed.2d at 1338.

■ When the personal safety of the officer or other persons might be imperiled. "[T]he presumption in favor of announcement would yield under circumstances presenting a threat of physical violence." *Wilson v. Arkansas,* 514 U.S. 927, 936, 115 S.Ct. 1914, 1918–19, 131 L.Ed.2d 976, 983 (1995).

■ When the delay to knock and announce might defeat the arrest by allowing the offender to escape. *State v. Fair,* 211 A.2d 359 (N.J. 1965).

■ When a prisoner escapes from an officer and retreats into the prisoner's dwelling. "Proof of 'demand and refusal' was deemed unnecessary in such cases because it would be a 'senseless ceremony' to require an officer in pursuit of a recently escaped arrestee to make an announcement prior to breaking the door to retake him." *Wilson v. Arkansas,* 514 U.S. 927, 936, 115 S.Ct. 1914, 1919, 131 L.Ed.2d 976, 983 (1995).

■ When knocking and announcing might allow persons inside to destroy evidence. In *Ker v. California,* 374 U.S. 23, 83 S.Ct. 1623, 10 L.Ed.2d 726 (1963), the U.S. Supreme Court held that an unannounced entry into the defendant's apartment was proper when evidence of narcotics activity would otherwise have been destroyed. However, officers must be able to justify an unannounced entry by the particular facts of a case. In the *Ker* case, not only did the officers reasonably believe that the defendant was in possession of narcotics, but the defendant's furtive conduct in eluding officers shortly before the arrest gave the officers grounds to believe that he might have been expecting the police. In *United States v. Stewart,* 867 F.2d 581 (10th Cir. 1989), the officers' justification for their unannounced entry consisted only of generalities about drug dealers that bore no relation to the particular premises or the particular circumstances. Finding the unannounced entry illegal, the court stated:

Ker v. California
laws.findlaw.com/us/374/23.html

> None of these facts specifically pertained to the defendant or the defendant's house. No officer had any information to the effect that the house had been barricaded or fortified or if the occupants were monitoring activity in the surrounding area. Most importantly, no effort was made to determine who was in the house at the time the entry was made. 867 F.2d at 585.

(See the discussion on page 185 of *Richards v. Wisconsin,* holding that there is no automatic exception to the "knock and announce" requirement in drug cases.)

Key Points

14. In general, a law enforcement officer may not use deadly force to arrest or prevent the escape of a felon, unless the felon poses a threat of serious physical harm, to either the officer or others.

15. A law enforcement officer may use any reasonably necessary nondeadly force but may never use deadly force to arrest for a misdemeanor. It is better that a misdemeanant escapes rather than a human life be taken.

16. A law enforcement officer making a lawful arrest (for either a misdemeanor or a felony) may use any force reasonably necessary under the circumstances in self-defense, including deadly force, if the officer reasonably believes that the person to be arrested is about to commit an assault and that the officer is in danger of death or serious bodily injury.

17. Resisting arrest is a crime involving a person's opposition by direct, forcible means against a law enforcement officer to prevent being taken into custody.

18. Absent exigent circumstances or consent, a law enforcement officer may not make a warrantless entry into a suspect's home to make a routine felony arrest.

19. Absent exigent circumstances or consent, an arrest warrant does not authorize a law enforcement officer to enter the home of a third person to search for the person to be arrested. A search warrant must be obtained to justify the entry into the home of any person other than the person to be arrested.

20. Exigent circumstances that would justify a warrantless entry of a dwelling to arrest are hot pursuit of a fleeing felon, imminent destruction of evidence, the need to prevent a suspect's escape, and the risk of danger to the police or to other persons. In assessing the risk of danger, the gravity of the crime and the likelihood that the suspect is armed should be considered.

21. If an arrest is begun in a public place, officers may enter a dwelling without a warrant in hot pursuit, to complete the arrest.

22. Absent extenuating circumstances, before law enforcement officers may lawfully force their way into a dwelling to arrest someone inside, they should first knock on the door, announce their authority and purpose, and then demand admittance and be refused admittance.

Disposition of an Arrested Person

The arrest of a person initiates a series of administrative and judicial procedures dealing with the person and his or her property. These procedures vary among jurisdictions, but all basically deal with the same issues; namely, the protection of the person and property of the arrestee, notification of and opportunity to exercise certain rights, safety and security of law enforcement officials and places of confinement, identification, further investigation, record keeping, and avoidance of civil liability. Booking is usually the first of these procedures to take place after arrest.

Booking

Booking is a police administrative procedure officially recording an arrest in a police register. Booking involves, at the minimum, recording the name of the person arrested; the name of the officer making the arrest; and the time of, place of, circumstances of, and reason for the arrest. The meaning of booking, however, is sometimes expanded to include other procedures that take place in the station house after an arrest. For more serious offenses, booking may include a search of the arrested person (including in some cases a search of body cavities), fingerprinting, photographing, a lineup, or other identification procedures. The arrested person may be temporarily detained in a jail or lockup until release on bail can be arranged. For less serious offenses, the arrested person may be released on personal recognizance, under which the person agrees to appear in court when required but is not required to pay or promise to pay any money or property as security.

Booking is usually completed before the arrested person is taken for his or her initial appearance before the magistrate. It may, however, take place after the initial appearance, or parts of the booking procedures may take place both before and after the initial appearance. Booking procedures vary among different jurisdictions and among different law enforcement agencies within a particular jurisdiction.

Initial Appearance before the Magistrate

After arresting a person, with or without a warrant, and after the complaint has been filed, a law enforcement officer must take the person before a magistrate or deliver the person according to the mandate of the warrant. Statutes in different jurisdictions require that this be done promptly, using terms such as *immediately, without unnecessary delay, forthwith, within a specified time period,* or other similar language. These statutes confer a substantial right on the defendant and create a corresponding duty on law enforcement officers.

The reasons behind the rule requiring arrested persons to be brought before a magistrate without unnecessary delay are these:

- To verify that the person arrested is the person named in the complaint
- To advise the arrested person of the charges, so that the person may prepare a defense
- To advise the arrested person of his or her rights, such as the right to a preliminary hearing, the right to counsel, and the right to remain silent
- To protect arrested persons from being abandoned in jail and forgotten by, or otherwise cut off from contact with, people who can help them
- To prevent secret and extended interrogation of arrested persons by law enforcement officers
- To give the arrested person an early opportunity to secure release on bail while awaiting the final outcome of the proceedings. If the person has been bailed earlier, the magistrate will simply review that bail. Release on personal recognizance upon the defendant's promise to appear, without any pledge or deposit of money or property, may also be granted at the initial appearance.
- To give the arrested person an opportunity to speedily conclude proceedings on charges of minor offenses by pleading guilty to the charges, paying fines, and carrying on with his or her life
- To obtain a prompt, neutral "judicial determination of probable cause as a prerequisite to extended restraint of liberty following arrest." *Gerstein v. Pugh,* 420 U.S. 103, 114, 95 S.Ct. 854, 863, 43 L.Ed.2d 54, 65 (1975). Not all states provide for a judicial determination of probable cause at the initial appearance before a magistrate.

Gerstein v. Pugh
laws.findlaw.com/us/420/
103.html

There is no single preferred pretrial procedure, and the nature of the probable cause determination usually will be shaped to accord with a State's pretrial procedure viewed as a whole. . . . It may be found desirable, for example, to make the probable cause determination at the suspect's first appearance before a judicial officer, . . . or the determination may be incorporated into the procedure for setting bail or fixing other conditions of pretrial release. In some States, existing procedures may satisfy the requirement of the Fourth Amendment. Others may require only minor adjustment, such as acceleration of existing preliminary hearings. Current proposals for criminal procedure reform suggest other ways of testing probable cause for detention. Whatever procedure a State may adopt, it must provide a fair and reliable determination of probable cause as a condition for any significant pretrial restraint of liberty, and this determination must be made by a judicial officer either before or promptly after arrest. 420 U.S. at 123–25, 95 S.Ct. at 868–69, 43 L.Ed.2d at 71–72.

In *County of Riverside v. McLaughlin,* 500 U.S. 44, 111 S.Ct. 1661, 114 L.Ed.2d 49 (1991), the U.S. Supreme Court held that, to satisfy the "promptness" requirement of *Gerstein,* a jurisdiction that chooses to combine probable cause determinations with other pretrial proceedings must do so as soon as is reasonably feasible, but in no event later than forty-eight hours after arrest. This is not to say that the probable cause determination in a particular case passes constitutional muster simply because it is provided within forty-eight hours. As the Court said:

County of Riverside v. McLaughlin
laws.findlaw.com/us/500/44.html

> Such a hearing may nonetheless violate *Gerstein* if the arrested individual can prove that his or her probable cause determination was delayed unreasonably. Examples of unreasonable delay are delays for the purpose of gathering additional evidence to justify the arrest, a delay motivated by ill will against the arrested individual, or delay for delay's sake. In evaluating whether the delay in a particular case is unreasonable, however, courts must allow a substantial degree of flexibility. Courts cannot ignore the often unavoidable delays in transporting arrested persons from one facility to another, handling late-night bookings where no magistrate is readily available, obtaining the presence of an arresting officer who may be busy processing other suspects or securing the premises of an arrest, and other practical realities. 500 U.S. at 56–57, 111 S.Ct. at 1670, 114 L.Ed.2d at 63.

The Court went on to say that, in situations in which an arrested person does not receive a probable cause determination within forty-eight hours, the burden shifts to the government to demonstrate the existence of a bona fide emergency or other extraordinary circumstance. The Court specifically stated that neither intervening weekends nor the fact that in a particular case it may take longer than forty-eight hours to consolidate pretrial proceedings qualifies as an extraordinary circumstance.

jec.unm.edu/Benchbk/Magistrate/2-2-3.htm
New Mexico's requirements for the initial appearance before the magistrate

Safety Considerations

In *Washington v. Chrisman,* 455 U.S. 1, 102 S.Ct. 812, 70 L.Ed.2d 778 (1982), the U.S. Supreme Court held:

Washington v. Chrisman
laws.findlaw.com/us/455/1.html

> [I]t is not "unreasonable" under the Fourth Amendment for a police officer, as a matter of course, to monitor the movements of an arrested person, as his judgement dictates, following the arrest. The officer's need to ensure his own safety—as well as the integrity of the arrest—is compelling. Such surveillance is not an impermissible invasion of the privacy or personal liberty of an individual who has been arrested. 455 U.S. at 7, 102 S.Ct. at 817, 70 L.Ed.2d at 785.

In the *Chrisman* case, the officer arrested a college student for possession of alcoholic beverages by a person under age twenty-one, and the student asked permission to go to his room to get his identification. The officer accompanied the student to his room, and while in the room, the officer observed marijuana in plain view. The Court held that the officer had a right to remain literally at the student's elbow at all times and that no showing of exigent circumstances was necessary to authorize the officer to accompany the student into the room. The Court said:

> Every arrest must be presumed to present a risk of danger to the arresting officer. . . . There is no way for an officer to predict reliably how a particular subject will react to arrest or the degree of potential danger. Moreover, the possibility that an arrested person will attempt to escape if not properly supervised is obvious. 455 U.S. at 7, 102 S.Ct. at 817, 70 L.Ed.2d at 785.

www.laaw.com/finalre2.htm
Article, "Liability Constraints on
Human Restraints" by Michael
A. Brave and John G. Peters;
explores the risks of using hand-
cuffs and other restraints
www.fbi.gov/publications/leb/
1996/may966.txt
Article, "Suspect Restraint and
Sudden Death" by Donald T.
Reay, M.D.

Protection and Welfare of an Arrested Person

When delay in taking an arrested person before a magistrate is unavoidable, the officer must keep the arrested person safely in custody for the period of the delay. The officer may reasonably restrain the person to prevent escape and may even confine the person in a jail or other suitable place. Handcuffs may be used at the officer's discretion, depending on the person's reputation or record for violence, the time of day, the number of other persons in custody, and the duration of the detention.

The officer is responsible for the health and safety of the arrested person, including providing adequate medical assistance, if necessary. Any unnecessary use of force or negligent failure to prevent the use of force by others against the arrested person may subject the officer to criminal or civil liability.

Station-House Search

Illinois v. Lafayette
laws.findlaw.com/us/462/
640.html

When a person is arrested and taken into custody, police may, as part of the routine administrative procedure incident to booking and jailing the person, search the person and any container or article in his or her possession. In *Illinois v. Lafayette*, 462 U.S. 640, 103 S.Ct. 2605, 77 L.Ed.2d 65 (1983), the U.S. Supreme Court held that station-house inventory searches were an incidental step following arrest and preceding incarceration. The justification for these searches does not rest on probable cause; thus, the absence of a warrant is immaterial to the reasonableness of the searches. The Court said that the governmental interests justifying a station-house inventory search are different from, and may in some circumstances be even greater than, those supporting a search incident to arrest (see Chapter 8). Among those interests are prevention of theft of the arrested person's property; deterrence of false claims regarding that property; prevention of injury from belts, drugs, or dangerous instruments such as razor blades, knives, or bombs; and determination or verification of the person's identity. Furthermore, it does not matter that less intrusive means of satisfying those governmental interests might be possible. The Court said:

> It is evident that a stationhouse search of every item carried on or by a person who has lawfully been taken into custody by the police will amply serve the important and legitimate governmental interests involved.
>
> Even if less intrusive means existed of protecting some particular types of property, it would be unreasonable to expect police officers in the everyday course of business to make fine and subtle distinctions in deciding which containers or items may be searched and which must be sealed as a unit. 462 U.S. at 648, 103 S.Ct. at 2610, 77 L.Ed.2d at 72.

A station-house inventory search need not be conducted immediately upon the arrested person's arrival at the station house. The U.S. Supreme Court held that a seizure of a prisoner's clothing in the morning, several hours after his arrest and incarceration the previous evening, was reasonable. No substitute clothing had been available at the time of arrest and, therefore, the normal processes incident to arrest and custody had not been completed.

United States v. Edwards
laws.findlaw.com/us/415/
800.html

> [O]nce the accused is lawfully arrested and is in custody, the effects in his possession at the place of detention that were subject to search at the time and place of his arrest may lawfully be searched and seized without a warrant even though a substantial period of time has elapsed between the arrest and subsequent administrative processing, on the one hand, and the taking of the property for use as evidence, on the other. *United States v. Edwards*, 415 U.S. 800, 807, 94 S.Ct. 1234, 1239, 39 L.Ed.2d 771, 778 (1974).

Sometimes, especially when a vehicle is involved, officers must take positive action to protect the defendant's property or become civilly liable for damages for failure to do so. To protect against liability of this nature, many law enforcement agencies have adopted standard procedures for impounding arrested persons' vehicles and making an inventory of their contents. (For a further discussion of impoundment and inventory of vehicles, see Chapter 11.)

Identification and Examination of an Arrested Person

Pretrial procedures for identifying and examining an arrested person may take many different forms. One form is confrontation of the arrested person with victims or witnesses of the crime, sometimes accomplished through the use of a police lineup or showup. The arrested person has no right to object to being viewed by witnesses for identification purposes and also has no right to demand to be placed in a lineup. (For a discussion of pretrial identification techniques and the right to counsel, see Chapter 14.)

Law enforcement officers may take fingerprints, footprints, or photographs of the arrested person for purposes of identification or evidence. Officers may also obtain voice exemplars or have a dentist examine a defendant's mouth for a missing tooth for identification purposes.

> [T]he Fourth Amendment does not protect "what a person knowingly exposes to the public even in his home or office. . . . Like a man's facial characteristics, or handwriting, his voice is repeatedly produced for others to hear. No person can have a reasonable expectation that others will not know the sound of his voice, any more than he can reasonably expect that his face will be a mystery to the world." This doctrine is applicable as well to a missing tooth. *United States v. Holland,* 378 F.Supp. 144, 155 (E.D.Pa. 1974).

Law enforcement officers may physically examine arrested persons for measurements, scars, bruises, tattoos, and so on, and may require persons to disrobe against their will.

> Such procedures and practices and tests may result in freeing an innocent man accused of crime, or may be part of a chain of facts and circumstances which help identify a person accused of a crime or connect a suspect or an accused with the crime of which he has been suspected or has been accused. The law is well settled that such actions, practices, and procedures do not violate any constitutional right. *Commonwealth v. Aljoe,* 216 A.2d 50, 52–53 (Pa. 1966).

These various forms of identifying and examining arrested persons may be accomplished by force, if necessary, but the methods used may not be such as to "shock the conscience," offend a "sense of justice," or run counter to the "decencies of civilized conduct." *Rochin v. California,* 342 U.S. 165, 72 S.Ct. 205, 96 L.Ed. 183 (1952). In the *Rochin* case, three officers, suspecting that Rochin was selling narcotics, entered Rochin's home and forced their way into the bedroom occupied by Rochin and his wife. When asked about two capsules on a bedside stand, Rochin put them in his mouth. After an unsuccessful struggle to extract them by force, the three officers took Rochin to a hospital. There, a medicine to induce vomiting was forcibly administered. Rochin vomited the two capsules, which were later found to contain morphine. This evidence was admitted at trial over Rochin's objection and he was convicted. The Supreme Court, finding that the conduct of the officers "shocked the conscience" and thereby violated the due process clause of the Fourteenth Amendment, reversed the conviction.

Rochin v. California
laws.findlaw.com/us/342/
165.html

Briethaupt v. Abram
laws.findlaw.com/us/352/
432.html
Schmerber v. California
laws.findlaw.com/us/384/
757.html

www.fbi.gov/publications/leb/
1999/feb99leb.pdf
Article, "Due Process and Deadly
Force: When Police Conduct
Shocks the Conscience" by John
C. Hall (page 27 of the February
1999 *FBI Law Enforcement
Bulletin*)

Winston v. Lee
laws.findlaw.com/us/470/
753.html

www.co.alameda.ca.us/da/pov/
Bodily_intrusion.htm
Article, "Bodily Intrusion
Searches" from the District
Attorney's Office of Alameda
County, California; presents
guidelines for these searches with
an emphasis on California law
www.law.asu.edu/kaye/pubs/dna/
ncfdna-report1-000122.htm
Article, "The Constitutionality of
DNA Sampling on Arrest" by
D. H. Kaye

The U.S. Supreme Court held that there is no denial of due process of law in taking a blood sample with proper medical supervision from a person who is unconscious and unable to give consent. *Breithaupt v. Abram*, 352 U.S. 432, 77 S.Ct. 408, 1 L.Ed.2d 448 (1957). Also, in *Schmerber v. California*, the Court held that there is no violation of the Fifth Amendment privilege against self-incrimination or the Fourth Amendment protection against unreasonable searches and seizures when a blood sample is taken without consent from an arrested person in lawful custody. The Court said that the privilege against self-incrimination "protects an accused only from being compelled to testify against himself, or otherwise provide the State with evidence of a testimonial or communicative nature, and that the withdrawal of blood and use of the analysis in question in this case did not involve compulsion to these ends." 384 U.S. 757, 761, 86 S.Ct. 1826, 1830–31, 16 L.Ed.2d 908, 914 (1966). The Court found that the Fourth Amendment standard of reasonableness was satisfied when (1) "there was plainly probable cause for the officer to arrest petitioner and charge him with driving an automobile under the influence of intoxicating liquor," and (2) the facts "suggested the required relevance and likely success of a test of petitioner's blood for alcohol. . . ." The blood sample was taken in a hospital by a physician following accepted medical procedures. Also, the officer "might reasonably have believed that he was confronted with an emergency" and that there was a need for immediate action because the sample was needed to measure the blood's alcohol content, which would quickly dissipate. The Court said:

> [W]e reach this judgment only on the facts in the present record. The integrity of an individual's person is a cherished value of our society. That we today hold that the Constitution does not forbid the State's minor intrusions into an individual's body under stringently limited conditions in no way indicates that it permits more substantial intrusions or intrusions under other conditions. 384 U.S. at 772, 86 S.Ct. at 1836, 16 L.Ed.2d at 920.

In a case involving a more substantial intrusion, the Supreme Court refused, on Fourth Amendment grounds, to allow the prosecution to compel an armed robbery suspect to undergo a surgical procedure under a general anesthetic for removal of a bullet lodged in his chest. *Winston v. Lee*, 470 U.S. 753, 105 S.Ct. 1611, 84 L.Ed.2d 662 (1985). The Court applied the same balancing test used in *Schmerber* and found that the potential threat to the suspect's health and safety, combined with the extensive intrusion on the suspect's personal privacy and bodily integrity, were not counterbalanced by a compelling need for evidence. Of particular importance was the Court's finding that the prosecution had substantial additional evidence that the suspect was the person who committed the robbery. The Court said:

> The Fourth Amendment is a vital safeguard of the right of the citizen to be free from unreasonable governmental intrusions into any area in which he has a reasonable expectation of privacy. Where the Court has found a lesser expectation of privacy . . . or where the search involves a minimal intrusion on privacy interests . . . the Court has held that the Fourth Amendment protections are correspondingly less stringent. Conversely, however, the Fourth Amendment's command that searches be "reasonable" requires that when the State seeks to intrude upon an area in which our society recognizes a significantly heightened privacy interest, a more substantial justification is required to make the search "reasonable." Applying these principles, we hold that the proposed search in this case would be "unreasonable" under the Fourth Amendment. 470 U.S. at 767, 105 S.Ct. at 1620, 84 L.Ed.2d at 673.

Key Points

23. A state must provide a fair and reliable judicial determination of probable cause as a condition for any significant pretrial restraint on liberty either before arrest or as soon as is reasonably feasible after arrest, but in no event later than forty-eight hours after arrest.
24. A law enforcement officer may monitor the movements of an arrested person, as his or her judgment dictates, to ensure the officer's safety and the arrest's integrity.
25. Once a person is lawfully arrested and in custody, police may, as part of the routine administrative procedure incident to booking and jailing the person, search the person and any containers or articles in his or her possession.
26. An arrested person may be subjected to various identification and examination procedures, including the obtaining of a blood sample, so long as the reasonableness requirement of the Fourth Amendment is satisfied. Reasonable force may be used for these purposes if the methods do not "shock the conscience," offend a "sense of justice," or run counter to the "decencies of civilized conduct."

Effect of Illegal Arrest

Jurisdiction to try a person for a crime is not affected by an illegal arrest.

> [T]he power of a court to try a person for crime is not impaired by the fact that he had been brought within the court's jurisdiction by reason of a "forcible abduction." . . . [D]ue process of law is satisfied when one present in court is convicted of crime after having been fairly apprised of the charges against him and after a fair trial in accordance with constitutional procedural safeguards. There is nothing in the Constitution that requires a court to permit a guilty person rightfully convicted to escape justice because he was brought to trial against his will. *Frisbie v. Collins,* 342 U.S. 519, 522, 72 S.Ct. 509, 511–12, 96 L.Ed. 541, 545–46 (1952).

Frisbie v. Collins
laws.findlaw.com/us/342/519.html

The doctrine that the manner in which a defendant is brought to trial does not affect the power of the court to try him or her is known as the *Ker-Frisbie* doctrine. Its principle was previously enunciated in the 1886 U.S. Supreme Court case of *Ker v. Illinois* in which the Court declared that "forcible abduction is no sufficient reason why the party should not answer when brought within the jurisdiction of the court which has the right to try him for such an offense, and presents no valid objection to his trial in such a court." 119 U.S. 436, 444, 7 S.Ct. 225, 229, 30 L.Ed. 421, 424.

Ker v. Illinois
laws.findlaw.com/us/119/436.html

However, although an illegal arrest does not affect jurisdiction to try an offender, the exclusionary rule may affect the trial adversely. The exclusionary rule, as it relates to arrest, states that any evidence obtained by exploitation of an unlawful arrest will be inadmissible in court in a prosecution against the person arrested. Therefore, if the only evidence that the state has against an armed robbery suspect is a gun, a mask, and a roll of bills taken during a search incident to an unlawful arrest, the offender will very likely go free because these items will be inadmissible in court. (The exclusionary rule is discussed in detail in Chapter 3.)

A confession obtained by exploitation of an illegal arrest will also be inadmissible in court. In *Brown v. Illinois,* the defendant was illegally arrested in a manner calculated to cause surprise, fright, and confusion and taken to a police station. He was given *Miranda* warnings, and he waived his rights and made incriminating statements, all

Brown v. Illinois
laws.findlaw.com/us/422/590.html

www.nesl.edu/annual/vol3/
alien.htm
Article, "The United States'
Extraterritorial Abduction of
Alien Fugitives: A Due Process
Standard" by Anthony J.
Donegan
www.pit.edu/~lawrev/58-4/
articles/miller.htm
Article, "The Limits of U.S.
International Law Enforcement
after *Verdugo-Urquidez:* Resur-
recting *Rochin*" by Randall K.
Miller

Taylor v. Alabama
laws.findlaw.com/us/457/
687.html

within two hours of the illegal arrest. The Court held that officers could not avoid the effect of the illegal arrest by simply giving the arrested person the *Miranda* warnings. *Miranda* warnings do not alone sufficiently deter a Fourth Amendment violation. The Court said:

> The *Miranda* warnings are an important factor, to be sure, in determining whether the confession is obtained by exploitation of illegal arrest. But they are not the only factor to be considered. The temporal proximity of the arrest and the confession, the presence of intervening circumstances, . . . and, particularly, the purpose and flagrancy of the official misconduct are all relevant. . . . And the burden of showing admissibility rests, of course, on the prosecution. *Brown v. Illinois,* 422 U.S. 590, 603–04, 95 S.Ct. 2254, 2261–62, 45 L.Ed.2d 416, 427 (1975).

The prosecution has a difficult burden in curing the effect of an illegal arrest on a subsequent confession. In *Taylor v. Alabama,* 457 U.S. 687, 102 S.Ct. 2664, 73 L.Ed.2d 314 (1982), police made an investigatory arrest without probable cause, based on an uncorroborated informant's tip, and transported the defendant against his will to the station for interrogation in the hope that something would turn up. The defendant was in police custody the entire time, and the police repeatedly questioned him, took his fingerprints, and subjected him to a lineup without counsel present. The Court held that there was no meaningful intervening event to break the causal connection between the arrest and the confession, even though (1) six hours elapsed between the arrest and the confession and (2) the confession may have been voluntary for purposes of the Fifth Amendment in the sense that *Miranda* warnings were given and understood, the defendant was permitted a short visit with his girlfriend, and the police did not physically abuse the defendant.

Many factors must be considered to determine whether a confession is obtained by exploitation of an illegal arrest; thus, it is difficult to predict how a particular court will rule. For example, despite only a two-hour lapse between an illegal arrest and a confession, in *People v. Vance,* 185 Cal.Rptr. 549 (Cal.App. 1982), the court held the defendant's confession admissible because of the following circumstances:

- Proper *Miranda* warnings were given,
- the defendant was confronted with information that tied him to the crimes,
- the defendant was allowed to speak privately with his common-law wife, and
- there was no purposeful or flagrant police activity.

Because circumstances in the police's control often determine the admissibility of a confession following an illegal arrest, officers should do everything possible to ensure that a confession is a product of the suspect's free will.

If the evidence is not the *product* of the illegal arrest, however, the exclusionary rule does not apply. The indirect fruits of an illegal arrest should be suppressed only when they bear a sufficiently close relationship to the underlying illegality. In *New York v. Harris,* 495 U.S. 14, 110 S.Ct. 1640, 109 L.Ed.2d 13 (1990), police officers, who had probable cause to believe that the defendant committed murder, entered his home without first obtaining an arrest warrant in violation of *Payton v. New York* (see pages 134–35). The officers read him his *Miranda* rights and obtained an admission of guilt. After the defendant was arrested, taken to the police station, and again given his *Miranda* warnings, he signed a written inculpatory statement. The first statement was inadmissible because it was obtained in the defendant's home by exploitation of the *Payton* violation. The statement taken at the police station, however, was admissible. That statement was *not* the product of being in unlawful custody; neither was it the

New York v. Harris
laws.findlaw.com/us/495/
14.html

fruit of having been arrested in the home rather than someplace else. The police had a justification to question the defendant prior to his arrest. Therefore, his subsequent statement was not an *exploitation* of the illegal entry into his home. Moreover, suppressing a station-house statement obtained after a *Payton* violation would have minimal deterrent value, since it is doubtful that the desire to secure a statement from a suspect whom the police have probable cause to arrest would motivate them to violate *Payton*. The Court therefore held that "where the police have probable cause to arrest a suspect, the exclusionary rule does not bar the State's use of a statement made by the defendant outside of his home, even though the statement is taken after an arrest made in the home in violation of *Payton*." 495 U.S. at 21, 110 S.Ct. at 1644–45, 109 L.Ed.2d at 22.

Finally, a law enforcement officer may be subject to civil liability for false arrest or false imprisonment if an arrest is illegal or is made with excessive or unreasonable force.

 **Key Points**

27. Jurisdiction to try a person for a crime is not affected by an illegal arrest.

28. In general, evidence that is obtained by exploitation of an illegal arrest and is a product of that arrest will be inadmissible in court in a prosecution against the person arrested.

Summary

A formal arrest can be defined as the taking of a person into custody for the commission of an offense as the prelude to prosecuting him or her for it. The basic elements constituting a formal arrest are (1) an intention to take a person into the custody of the law, (2) exercise of real or pretended authority, (3) detention or restraint of the person to be arrested, and (4) an understanding of the officer's intention by the person to be arrested. Even though these basic elements are not all present, courts may find that an encounter between a law enforcement officer and a person entails such a significant intrusion on the person's freedom of action that it is in important respects indistinguishable from a formal arrest. Such an encounter, sometimes called a seizure tantamount to arrest or a *de facto* arrest, must be supported by probable cause or it is illegal. The test to determine whether a seizure is tantamount to arrest is whether, in view of all the circumstances surrounding the encounter, a reasonable person would have believed that he or she was not free to leave.

Although warrantless arrests on probable cause are permitted, courts always prefer arrests made under the authority of an arrest warrant. An arrest warrant is a written judicial order directing a law enforcement officer to arrest a particular person. The warrant is issued by a magistrate on the basis of a complaint stating the essential facts constituting the offense charged, if the magistrate is satisfied that the offense was committed and that the person to be arrested committed it. The magistrate may also issue a summons that merely directs the defendant to appear rather than ordering an arrest.

Law enforcement officers may make a warrantless public arrest for a felony if they have probable cause to believe that a felony has been or is being committed and that the person to be arrested has committed or is committing the felony. Officers may make a warrantless public arrest for a misdemeanor, however, only if (1) the misdemeanor was committed in their presence or (2) a state statute or constitution allows warrantless arrests on probable cause for certain misdemeanors. A warrantless misdemeanor arrest for offenses committed in the officer's presence must be made immediately, but a warrantless felony arrest may be delayed for various reasons, so long as the defendant's rights are not prejudiced by the delay.

When law enforcement officers make an arrest, they should notify the person arrested that he or she is under arrest and notify that person of the officers' authority and the cause of the arrest. If the arrest is made under authority of a warrant, officers should examine the warrant to make sure it is valid on its face before carrying out its commands. When the arrest warrant is executed, officers should return the warrant as directed and explain what they have done in carrying out its commands.

Officers have no official authority to arrest without a warrant outside their jurisdiction—the geographic area for which they were elected or appointed. Nevertheless, even though outside their jurisdiction, they have the authority of any private citizen to arrest for breach of the peace misdemeanors committed in their presence and for felonies on probable cause. They may also arrest outside their jurisdiction in fresh pursuit of a criminal who has fled their jurisdiction, if the pursuit is begun promptly inside the jurisdiction and maintained continuously.

Officers may use only the amount of force reasonably necessary under the circumstances to effect an arrest. Deadly force may be used only as a last resort and then only in specifically limited circumstances. Deadly force may never be used to accomplish an arrest for a misdemeanor. But officers may use deadly force in self-defense to protect themselves from death or serious bodily injury, and officers need not abandon an attempt to arrest in the face of physical resistance to the arrest.

Officers may not enter a dwelling to arrest a person without a warrant unless there is consent or exigent circumstances. An arrest warrant is required to enter a suspect's home to arrest the suspect. A search warrant is required to enter the home of a third person to arrest a suspect. Exigent circumstances that would justify a warrantless entry of a dwelling to arrest are hot pursuit of a fleeing felon, imminent destruction of evidence, the need to prevent a suspect's escape, and the risk of danger to the police or other persons. In assessing the risk of danger, the gravity of the crime and the likelihood that the suspect is armed should be considered. If an arrest is begun in a public place, officers may enter a dwelling without a warrant in hot pursuit, to complete the arrest. Before officers may lawfully enter a dwelling forcibly to arrest a person, they must be refused admittance after knocking, announcing their authority and purpose, and demanding admittance. Failure to knock and announce is excused if an officer's purpose is already known or if knocking and announcing would cause danger to the officer or other persons, cause the escape of the suspect, or result in the loss or destruction of evidence.

Duties of the officer after an arrest is effected include the following: booking; bringing the arrested person before a magistrate without unnecessary delay; ensuring the health and safety of the prisoner while in the officer's custody; conducting a station-house inventory search of the prisoner, which may include searching and seizing any container or object in the prisoner's possession; and conducting identification procedures, including fingerprinting, photographing, physical examinations, and lineups.

Although an illegal arrest will not affect the jurisdiction of the court to try a person, any evidence obtained as the product of the exploitation of an illegal arrest will be inadmissible in a criminal proceeding against the defendant. In addition, the law enforcement officer may be both civilly and criminally liable for making an illegal arrest or using excessive force.

Key Holdings from Major Cases

California v. Hodari D. (1990). "An arrest requires either physical force . . . or, where that is absent, submission to the assertion of authority." 499 U.S. 621, 626, 111 S.Ct. 1547, 1551, 113 L.Ed.2d 690, 697.

Michigan v. Summers (1981). It is "the general rule that every arrest, and every seizure having the essential attributes of a formal arrest, is unreasonable unless it is supported by probable cause." 452 U.S. 692, 700, 101 S.Ct. 2587, 2593, 69 L.Ed.2d 340, 348.

Hayes v. Florida (1985). "[W]hen the police, without probable cause or a warrant, forcibly remove a person from his home or other place in which he is entitled to be and transport him to the police station, where he is detained, although briefly, for investigative purposes . . . such seizures, at least where not under judicial supervision, are sufficiently like arrests to invoke the traditional rule that arrests may constitutionally be made only on probable cause." 470 U.S. 811, 816, 105 S.Ct. 1643, 1647, 84 L.Ed.2d 705, 710.

Aguilar v. Texas (1964). "[T]he informed and deliberate determinations of magistrates empowered to issue warrants . . . are to be preferred over the hurried action of officers . . . who may happen to make arrests." 378 U.S. 108, 110–11, 84 S.Ct. 1509, 1512, 12 L.Ed.2d 723, 726.

United States v. Watson (1976). "Law enforcement officers may find it wise to seek arrest warrants where practicable to do so, and their judgments about probable cause may be more readily accepted where backed by a warrant issued by a magistrate. . . . But we decline to transform this judicial preference into a constitutional rule when the judgment of the Nation and Congress has for so long been to authorize warrantless public arrests on probable cause rather than to encumber criminal prosecutions with endless litigation with respect to the existence of exigent circumstances, whether it was practicable to get a warrant, whether the suspect was about to flee, and the like." 423 U.S. 411, 423–24, 96 S.Ct. 820, 827–28, 46 L.Ed.2d 598, 608–09.

Hoffa v. United States (1966). "The police are not required to guess at their peril the precise moment at which they have probable cause to arrest a suspect, risking a violation of the Fourth Amendment if they act too soon, and a violation of the Sixth Amendment if they wait too long. Law enforcement officers are under no constitutional duty to call a halt to a criminal investigation the moment they have the minimum evidence to establish probable cause, a quantum of evidence which may fall far short of the amount necessary to support a criminal prosecution." 385 U.S. 293, 310, 87 S.Ct. 408, 417, 17 L.Ed.2d 374, 86.

Wilson v. Layne (1999). "[I]t is a violation of the Fourth Amendment for police to bring members of the media or other third parties into a home during the execution of a warrant when the presence of the third parties in the home was not in the aid of the execution of the warrant." 562 U.S. 603, 614, 119 S.Ct. 1692, 1699, 143 L.Ed.2d 818, 830.

Tennessee v. Garner (1985). "The use of deadly force to prevent the escape of all felony suspects, whatever the circumstances, is constitutionally unreasonable. It is not better that all felony suspects die than that they escape. Where the suspect poses no immediate threat to the officer and no threat to others, the harm resulting from failing to apprehend him does not justify the use of deadly force to do so. . . . Where the officer has probable cause to believe that the suspect poses a threat of serious physical harm, either to the officer or to others, it is not constitutionally unreasonable to prevent escape by using deadly force. Thus, if the suspect threatens the officer with a weapon or there is probable cause to believe that he has committed a crime involving the infliction or threatened infliction of serious physical harm, deadly force may be used if necessary to prevent escape, and if, where feasible, some warning has been given." 471 U.S. 1, 11–12, 105 S.Ct. 1694, 1701, 85 L.Ed.2d 1, 9–10.

Payton v. New York (1980). "[A]n arrest warrant founded on probable cause implicitly carries with it the limited authority to enter a dwelling in which the suspect lives when there is reason to believe the suspect is within." 445 U.S. 573, 603, 100 S.Ct. 1371, 1388, 63 L.Ed.2d 639, 661.

Steagald v. United States (1981). "In the absence of exigent circumstances, we have consistently held that [law enforcement officers' determinations of probable cause] are not reliable enough to justify an entry into a person's home to arrest him without a warrant, or a search of a home for objects in the absence of a search warrant. We see no reason to depart from this settled course when the search of a home is for a person rather than an object." 451 U.S. 204, 213, 101 S.Ct. 1642, 1648, 68 L.Ed.2d 38, 46.

Welsh v. Wisconsin (1984). "[A]n important factor to be considered when determining whether any exigency exists is the gravity of the underlying offense for which the arrest is being made. Moreover, although no exigency is created simply because there is probable cause to believe that a serious crime has been committed . . . application of the exigent-circumstances exception in the context of a home entry should rarely be sanctioned when there is probable cause to believe that only a minor offense . . . has been committed." 466 U.S. 740, 753, 104 S.Ct. 2091, 2099, 80 L.Ed.2d 732, 745.

Minnesota v. Olson (1990). "[A] warrantless intrusion may be justified by hot pursuit of a fleeing felon, or imminent destruction of evidence . . . or the need to prevent a suspect's escape, or the risk of danger to the police or to other persons inside or outside the dwelling." 436 N.W.2d 97. Furthermore, "in the absence of hot pursuit there must be at least probable cause to believe that one or more of the other factors justifying the entry were present and that in assessing the risk of danger, the gravity of the crime and likelihood that the suspect is armed should be considered." 495 U.S. 91, 100, 110 S.Ct. 1684, 1690, 109 L.Ed.2d 85, 95–96.

Warden v. Hayden (1967). Police officers without a warrant in hot pursuit of an armed robbery suspect "acted reasonably when they entered the house and began to search for a man of the description they had been given and for weapons which he had used in the robbery or might use against them. The Fourth Amendment does not require police officers to delay in the course of an investigation if to do so would gravely endanger their lives or the lives of others." 387 U.S. 294, 298–99, 87 S.Ct. 1642, 1646, 18 L.Ed.2d 782, 787.

United States v. Santana (1976). Law enforcement officers who attempt an arrest in a public place may, under the *Hayden* "hot pursuit" rule, follow the person to be arrested into a dwelling in order to effectuate the arrest. 427 U.S. 38, 96 S.Ct. 2406, 49 L.Ed.2d 300.

Miller v. United States (1958). "The requirement of prior notice of authority and purpose before forcing entry into a home is deeply rooted in our heritage, and should not be given grudging application. . . . Every householder, the good and the bad, the guilty and the innocent, is entitled to the protection designed to secure the common interest against unlawful invasion of the house. The petitioner could not be lawfully arrested in his home by officers breaking in without first giving him notice of their authority and purpose. Because the petitioner did not receive that notice before the officers broke the door to invade his home, the arrest was unlawful, and the evidence seized should have been suppressed." 357 U.S. 301, 313–14, 78 S.Ct. 1190, 1198, 2 L.Ed.2d 1332, 1340–41.

Sabbath v. United States (1968). "An unannounced intrusion into a dwelling . . . is no less an unannounced intrusion whether officers break down a door, force open a chain lock on a partially open door, open a locked door by use of a passkey, or . . . open a closed but unlocked door." 391 U.S. 585, 590, 88 S.Ct. 1755, 1758, 20 L.Ed.2d 828, 834.

Gerstein v. Pugh (1975). "Whatever procedure a State may adopt, it must provide a fair and reliable determination of probable cause as a condition for any significant pretrial restraint of liberty, and this determination must be made by a judicial officer either before or promptly after arrest." 420 U.S. 103, 124–25, 95 S.Ct. 854, 868–89, 43 L.Ed.2d 54, 71–72.

County of Riverside v. McLaughlin (1991). "[A] jurisdiction that provides judicial determinations of probable cause within 48 hours of arrest will, as a general matter, comply with the promptness requirement of *Gerstein*. . . . Such a hearing may nonetheless violate *Gerstein* if the arrested individual can prove that his or her probable cause determination was delayed unreasonably." 500 U.S. 44, 56–57, 111 S.Ct. 1661, 1670, 114 L.Ed.2d 49, 63.

Washington v. Chrisman (1982). "[I]t is not 'unreasonable' under the Fourth Amendment for a police officer, as a matter of course, to monitor the movements of an arrested person, as his judgment dictates, following the arrest. The officer's need to ensure his own safety—as well as the integrity of the arrest—is compelling. Such surveillance is not an impermissible invasion of the privacy or personal liberty of an individual who has been arrested." 455 U.S. 1, 7, 102 S.Ct. 812, 817, 70 L.Ed.2d 778, 785.

Illinois v. Lafayette (1983). "It is evident that a stationhouse search of every item carried on or by a person who has lawfully been taken into custody by the police will amply serve the important and legitimate governmental interests involved." 462 U.S. 640, 648, 103 S.Ct. 2605, 2610, 77 L.Ed.2d 65, 72.

United States v. Edwards (1974). "[O]nce the accused is lawfully arrested and is in custody, the effects in his possession at the place of detention that were subject to search at the time and place of his arrest may lawfully be searched and seized without a warrant even though a substantial period of time has elapsed between the arrest and subsequent administrative processing, on the one hand, and the taking of the property for use as evidence, on the other." 415 U.S. 800, 807, 94 S.Ct. 1234, 1239, 39 L.Ed.2d 771, 778.

Ker v. Illinois (1886). "[F]orcible abduction is no sufficient reason why the party should not answer when brought within the jurisdiction of the court which has the right to try him for such an offense, and presents no valid objection to his trial in such a court." 119 U.S. 436, 444, 7 S.Ct. 225, 229, 30 L.Ed. 421, 424.

Frisbie v. Collins (1952). "[T]he power of a court to try a person for crime is not impaired by the fact that he had been brought within the court's jurisdiction by reason of a 'forcible abduction.' . . . [D]ue process of law is satisfied when one present in court is convicted of crime after having been fairly apprised of the charges against him and after a fair trial in accordance with constitutional procedural safeguards. There is nothing in the Constitution that requires a court to permit a guilty person rightfully convicted to escape justice because he was brought to trial against his will." 342 U.S. 519, 522, 72 S.Ct. 509, 511–12, 96 L.Ed. 541, 545–46.

Brown v. Illinois (1975). "The *Miranda* warnings are an important factor, to be sure, in determining whether the confession is obtained by exploitation of illegal arrest. But they are not the only factor to be considered. The temporal proximity of the arrest and the confession, the presence of intervening circumstances, . . . and, particularly, the purpose and flagrancy of the official misconduct are all relevant." 422 U.S. 590, 603–04, 95 S.Ct. 2254, 2261–62, 45 L.Ed.2d 416, 427.

New York v. Harris (1990). "Where the police have probable cause to arrest a suspect, the exclusionary rule does not bar the State's use of a statement made by the defendant outside of his home, even though the statement is taken after an arrest made in the home in violation of *Payton*." 495 U.S. 14, 21, 110 S.Ct. 1640, 1644–45, 109 L.Ed.2d 13, 22.

Review and Discussion Questions

1. Is it possible to formally arrest an insane or extremely mentally retarded person? Explain.

2. Name several ways in which a law enforcement officer or officers can prevent a routine encounter with a person on the street from being considered a seizure tantamount to arrest.

3. Give three practical reasons why a law enforcement officer should obtain an arrest warrant if possible.

4. How is a law enforcement officer's authority to arrest affected by time?

5. Is it valid to say that if an officer has strong probable cause to arrest someone, the officer may arrest the person anywhere in the country? Explain.

6. Under what circumstances may a law enforcement officer use deadly force, and what are the potential consequences of an illegal use of deadly force? Name several circumstances under which little or no force should be used to make an arrest.

7. Do law enforcement officers have a broader right to self-defense when they are assaulted while making an arrest than when they are assaulted while simply walking or cruising their beats?

8. Assume that a law enforcement officer has probable cause to arrest a defendant for armed assault and probable cause to believe that the person is hiding in a third person's garage, which is attached to the house. What warrants, if any, does the officer need to enter the garage to arrest the defendant? What if the officer is in hot pursuit of the defendant? What if the defendant is known to be injured and unarmed?

9. Give reasons to support an argument that a law enforcement officer should never have to knock and announce before entering a dwelling to arrest a dangerous felon or a drug offender.

10. If a law enforcement officer has probable cause to arrest, does the officer have to make an arrest? If not, what alternatives to arrest are available, and under what circumstances should they be used?

Real-Life Fact Situations

1 Officer Jerry Symonds, a police officer with the Village of Woodridge in Du Page County, testified that he was on duty on May 23, 1999, at approximately 1:40 A.M. when he saw a car traveling southbound on Lemont Road at a high rate of speed. Defendant was driving the car Officer Symonds observed, and Officer Symonds was outside of Woodridge when he saw defendant. Officer Symonds testified that defendant was "perhaps" in Woodridge at the time he first observed him. Specifically, Officer Symonds testified that he "[did not] know if [defendant] was in town or out of town. It was that close." Officer Symonds watched as the car got closer to him, and he activated his radar when no other cars were around defendant's car. At the time the radar was activated, defendant was not in any municipality.

The radar showed that defendant was driving 67 miles per hour, and the posted speed limit was 45 miles per hour. Officer Symonds made a U-turn, activated his emergency equipment, drove approximately 80 miles per hour to catch defendant, and eventually stopped defendant approximately a half a mile away in Cook County. After the stop, Officer Symonds notified his dispatch and conducted an investigation. Based on this investigation, Officer Symonds placed defendant under arrest for driving while under the influence of alcohol.

The trial court denied defendant's petition and found that Officer Symonds properly arrested defendant. The court stated that, assuming defendant was outside Woodridge, Officer Symonds was acting as a private citizen when he arrested defendant for speeding, and Officer Symonds only made the arrest after he observed defendant traveling at a high rate of speed. The trial court noted that after making that observation Officer Symonds activated his radar to determine defendant's precise speed. This timely appeal followed.

Defendant argues that Officer Symonds lacked the authority to arrest him because Officer Symonds was outside his jurisdiction at the time he made the arrest and the officer did not have any statutory authority to make the arrest outside his jurisdiction. The State contends that the arrest was a proper citizen's arrest. Specifically, the State argues that the arrest was proper because Officer Symonds first observed defendant driving at a high rate of speed, an observation that a private citizen could make, and then used his radar to determine defendant's precise speed. The State claims that an officer's use of the powers of his office after observing criminal activity does not invalidate the arrest. Did Officer Symonds have the authority to arrest the defendant? *People v. Kirvelaitis*, 734 N.E.2d 524 (Ill.App. 2000).

Read the court opinion at:

www.state.il.us/court/opinions/AppellateCourt/2000/
2ndDistrict/August/HTML/2990859.htm

2 The controversy concerns a City of Overland Park police officer who was working off-duty as a security guard. Officer Kevin Duncan worked as a full-time police officer. In his spare time, he worked as a security guard at the Oak Park Mall, where his duties included patrolling the parking lot, responding to calls for assistance or emergency-type situations, and doing routine security activities such as locking the doors. During the time Officer Duncan was employed at the mall, he was armed and dressed as an Overland Park police officer. The evidence indicates that Officer Duncan received no money from the City of Overland Park for working off-duty. The only exception would be an occasion when circumstances required him to make an arrest.

On the day in question, Officer Duncan was working at his mall job when he was dispatched to Nordstrom's. At Nordstrom's, another security guard showed him a photograph of defendant and informed him that defendant was currently in the store. The other security guard had been informed by an Overland Park detective that there was a warrant outstanding for defendant's arrest. The security guard was asked to notify the police if he saw defendant. After receiving this information, Officer Duncan contacted the Overland Park police dispatch and verified there was an outstanding misdemeanor warrant for defendant's arrest.

Officer Duncan then watched defendant until he left the store, approached him, and identified himself as an Overland Park police officer. He informed defendant of the outstanding warrant and asked for identification. Defendant refused to identify himself, whereupon Officer Duncan handcuffed him and removed his wallet. After verifying that defendant was the same individual who was wanted in the misdemeanor warrant, Officer Duncan placed defendant under arrest and, during the search incident to the arrest, removed a $20 bill from defendant's wallet. When the bill was unfolded, it was found to contain a white powdery substance that was later confirmed to be cocaine. After finding the cocaine, Officer Duncan called for an on-duty police officer to respond to the scene who took defendant into custody.

Defendant filed a motion to suppress introduction of the cocaine into evidence at his trial. The motion was based on the fact that the police officer was acting as a security guard or as a private citizen and had no authority to arrest or to search defendant. . . .

The record contains the Overland Park Police Department policy manual guidelines for off-duty employment. The guidelines say, among other things, that an officer who is working off-duty is not acting in his or her capacity as a law enforcement officer. The guidelines go on to provide that officers employed as security personnel are not to provide on-duty response when the matter can be handled by requesting the assistance of an on-duty law enforcement officer. Officer Duncan testified that he did not know about this provision of the manual guidelines.

The trial court found that Officer Duncan was acting as a police officer, that he had the authority to arrest defendant, and that the cocaine found during the search incident to the arrest should not be suppressed. Should the cocaine be suppressed? *State v. Epps*, 9 P.3d 1271 (Kan.App. 2000).

Read the court opinion at:
www.kscourts.org/kscases/ctapp/2000/20000825/83434.htm

3 In March 1996, Gutierrez entered a fast-food restaurant in Bay City, Texas, and, using a receipt that belonged to another customer, he requested to be given free food. When he was told he could not have the food, he cursed one of the managers, who was black, and called her a racial epithet. The manager told him to leave and then called the police, who arrived after Gutierrez already had departed.

Gutierrez returned to the restaurant about an hour later; the manager again called the police. This time, Officer Hadash arrived and recognized the man as Gutierrez, whom he approached, and an altercation ensued. According to Hadash, Gutierrez jumped off a stool and started swinging his fists, striking Hadash several times. Hadash apparently did not strike Gutierrez at this time, because he was busy blocking his assailant's blows. Other witnesses also said Gutierrez struck Hadash, and it is undisputed that Hadash and Gutierrez eventually ended up struggling on the floor.

Officer Mirelez arrived and, seeing the fight, tried to assist Hadash. The two officers struggled to restrain Gutierrez, who continued fighting. Although different witnesses provided slightly varying accounts as to the sequence of events, it is undisputed that one or both of the officers dragged Gutierrez outside and sprayed him with pepper spray. It is uncertain how many times he was sprayed or how much spray was used. And although one witness stated that the officers sprayed Gutierrez while inside the restaurant, all other witnesses stated that this occurred after Gutierrez was taken outside.

Next, the officers placed Gutierrez face down on the pavement and eventually were able to handcuff him. According to the officers, Gutierrez was still struggling at that point. But, according to one witness, Maria Juarez, Gutierrez did not appear to be struggling at the time he was dragged outside. Juarez stated that after Gutierrez was taken outside, she watched the incident from the store and saw Gutierrez on the ground, face down, handcuffed.

One of the officers had his knee on Gutierrez's back and "kept pushing Mr. Gutierrez [*sic*] neck and head to the ground" with a stick. Mirelez confirmed placing his right shin across Gutierrez's back while attempting to restrain Gutierrez. Neither Hadash nor Mirelez mentioned using a baton, however.

After Gutierrez was cuffed, three other officers arrived— Sergeant Garcia, Officer Hempel, and Officer Sherrill. Accord-

ing to Garcia, when he arrived he observed Hadash and Mirelez on top of Gutierrez. Then, when Sherrill and Hempel arrived, Garcia told them to put Gutierrez into a patrol car. Garcia advised Hadash that Gutierrez could go to the hospital to be decontaminated from the pepper spray, but Hadash declined, because the jail was closer and more secure, and because Gutierrez had been combative.

When Sherrill and Hempel arrived, Gutierrez was lying on his stomach and was no longer struggling. The officers had to carry him to place him in the car; he did not walk on his own. The officers placed him in the car head-first. Sherrill had to go to the other side of the vehicle to pull Gutierrez through, placing him on his stomach with his head turned toward the front of the vehicle. Sherrill reported that Gutierrez appeared to have passed out. According to Garcia, he did not attempt to assess whether Gutierrez was injured, nor did he speak to him.

Hadash then drove Gutierrez to the county jail. He recalled hearing "a couple of groans and grunts" during the trip but did not speak to Gutierrez during that time.

When Hadash arrived, he was met by two jailers, who again had to assist Gutierrez out of the car. Gutierrez was not combative; indeed, Hadash did not know whether he was even conscious at that point. The jailers carried Gutierrez into the jail, half dragging him, and laid him face down. At that point, Hadash looked at Gutierrez and told Garcia that it appeared Gutierrez was not breathing.

The officers removed Gutierrez's handcuffs and turned him over, and Hadash began CPR. Once his breathing was revived, Gutierrez was transported to the hospital, where he slipped into a coma and eventually died.

Gutierrez's sister (Wagner) and his daughter (Irma Gutierrez) sued the city and the officers, alleging violations of Gutierrez's civil rights pursuant to § 1983. The complaint set forth claims of, *inter alia*, excessive force and a failure to respond to Gutierrez's medical needs. Although the original complaint named Bay City and every male officer of the Bay City police force, the claims eventually were dismissed against all but Bay City and Mirelez, Sherrill, Garcia, Hadash, and Hempel, the officers involved in the arrest.

The officers moved for summary judgment on the basis of qualified immunity, and the court granted summary judgment on the excessive force claims as to Sherrill, Garcia, and Hempel, because they arrived after the altercation was over. The court denied summary judgment in all other respects. Should officers Mirelez and Hadash be protected from liability for damages because of qualified immunity? *Wagner v. Bay City, Tex.*, 227 F.3d 316 (5th Cir. 2000).

Read the court opinion at:
www.ca5.uscourts.gov/opinions/pub/99/99-40175-cv0.htm

4 On October 29, 1998, Lieutenant Alvin Pair of the Greensville County Sheriff's Department sent a confidential informant to Room 117 of the Dixie Motel in order to make a controlled purchase of cocaine. Pair searched the informant beforehand to determine that he had no drugs on his person and gave him a marked twenty dollar bill to use to purchase cocaine. Police surveillance was positioned outside the motel room while the informant knocked on the door. Robert Ferguson, a codefendant, opened the door, stepped outside the room, looked around, and allowed the informant to enter, closing the door after the informant was inside. Soon thereafter, Ferguson walked out of the room again and looked around, whereupon the informant exited the room, got into his car, drove a short distance away, and met the police. The informant gave the police the crack cocaine he had just purchased, and a search of his person established that he no longer had possession of the marked twenty dollar bill.

Pair and two other officers "immediately went back to Room 117." Pair knocked on the door. One of the occupants asked who was there. Pair identified himself and said, "Police, open the door." The immediate reply from inside the room was, "wait a minute." Pair then heard voices, movements and a commode being flushed, whereupon he knocked on the door again. Ferguson opened the door and, after he and Weathers exited the room and were placed in custody, the officers entered. They searched the room and found cocaine located in and around the commode. The marked bill was found on Weathers' person, together with additional cash and a single-edged razor.

On July 22, 1999, Weathers was tried for possession of cocaine with intent to distribute and was convicted on that charge. This appeal followed. Should Weathers' motion to suppress the seized evidence be granted? *Weathers v. Commonwealth,* 529 S.E.2d 847 (Va.App. 2000).

Read the court opinion at:
www.lawyersweekly.com/vacoa/1795992.htm

5 On September 10, 1997, at approximately 7:15 P.M., Milwaukee Police Officer Diane Arenas, Wauwatosa Police Detective Keith Werner, and two other Milwaukee police officers arrived at an apartment building located at 2867 South Kinnickinnic Avenue in the City of Milwaukee. The officers believed that Blanco was staying in apartment # 118 at that location. The officers had an arrest warrant for Blanco for the crime of attempted first-degree homicide, while armed. The officers did not directly proceed to the apartment where Blanco was believed to be, but conducted further investigation. An officer showed Blanco's picture to the apartment manager, who stated that Blanco might be staying in apartment # 118. An occupant of the apartment building told an officer that Blanco had just been outside the apartment building smoking a cigarette before the police arrived. Another occupant told the police that he had seen Blanco enter apartment # 118 just before the police arrived.

At approximately 8:00 P.M., the officers knocked on the apartment door, announced that they were police officers, and that they were there to arrest Blanco, pursuant to a felony arrest warrant. A female, later identified as Al-Shammari, refused to allow the officers to enter. During this time period, another officer observed Blanco attempt to leave the apartment through a window. Blanco aborted the attempt, however, when he saw the police. The police called for assistance from the Tactical Enforcement Unit.

The immediate area was secured, surrounding apartments were evacuated, and the police were granted entry to an apartment immediately above and identical to the Al-Shammari apartment. As a result of this access and a review of the layout of the apartment, police were aware that there was a crawl space above the bathtub where someone could hide. Communications were repeatedly attempted with Al-Shammari to have Blanco turn himself over to the police. During this time, the police heard noises and activity coming from Al-Shammari's bathroom, including an inordinate amount of toilet flushing, and voices and sounds near the crawl space above the bathtub. The police also heard repeated use of the garbage disposal in Al-Shammari's kitchen. As a result, the water was turned off to the Al-Shammari apartment.

At approximately 10:30 P.M., after their unsuccessful efforts to have Al-Shammari consent to entry, or Blanco voluntarily submit to arrest, the six-man Tactical Enforcement Unit entered the apartment by use of a key obtained from the building manager. Officer Gilbert Carrasco was the first to enter. He held his shield in front of him in anticipation of some type of resistant force. Upon entry, three individuals were located: Al-Shammari, Blanco, and Rogelio Fuentez. The three were handcuffed and taken into custody. Carrasco proceeded to the bathroom to perform a protective sweep of that room. He testified that he was concerned that someone may have been hiding in the crawl space located above the bathtub. The board covering the crawl space was secured to the ceiling with four screws. Carrasco asked another officer for a screwdriver and he then removed the panel. Upon doing so, a bag containing marijuana fell on his head. He checked the crawl space for suspects, but it was empty.

As a result of the discovery of the contraband, the police obtained a search warrant for the premises and discovered additional marijuana, a total of 20.4 pounds, scales, $1,745 in cash, three pagers, a cellular telephone, and a .380 caliber pistol. After being properly charged for the drug offenses, Blanco and Al-Shammari both filed motions seeking to suppress the evidence. Should the evidence be suppressed? *State v. Blanco,* 614 N.W.2d 512 (Wis.App. 2000).

Read the court opinion at:
www.wisbar.org/WisCtApp2/2q00/98-3153.htm

6 Officer Dave Tertipes of the Moline, Illinois, police department responded to a call on June 25, 1998, to meet the manager of an apartment complex concerning "pictures of naked children." On his arrival, the manager gave Tertipes a magazine entitled "Ophelia Editions" that had been found in the hallway of the apartment complex where Moore lived. The magazine was addressed to "Chris Moore."

The cover of the magazine featured a drawing of a clothed girl in a provocative pose who appeared to be about 10 to 12 years old and described the contents as "Fine Art—Photography—Literature—Non-Fiction." The twenty-eight page magazine was a catalogue accompanied by descriptions and sample photos of about eighty other publications, including picture books of nude children and stories of children engaged in sex. The magazine contained a disclaimer purportedly affirming that the contents had been reviewed by an attorney and did not contain "lascivious exhibition[s]" of persons under eighteen. Tertipes, who had no special training in identifying child pornography, found at least three photographs that he considered illegal under the state child pornography law. The catalogue also contained many written descriptions of sexual contact with and among minors.

Based on this review, Tertipes knocked on Moore's apartment door and identified himself to Moore, who invited him to enter. Tertipes asked Moore about the magazine, and Moore admitted to ordering the magazine over the Internet. Moore characterized himself as a nudist who "likes to view the human body in its natural state." Tertipes asked Moore to come to the police station, and Moore initially complied voluntarily. Once in the car, Moore asked if he could leave. Tertipes consulted with his supervisor who said, "He doesn't have a choice. Bring him down." Tertipes placed Moore under arrest.

Once Moore arrived at the station, Lt. Steve Brockway took over the investigation. Brockway, who had previous training and experience in child sexual abuse and pornography cases, reviewed the magazine and concluded that it contained child pornography. Brockway read Moore his *Miranda* rights. Following a detailed explanation of his rights, Moore agreed to waive his rights and signed a voluntary waiver form. During questioning, which lasted about two hours, Moore referred to himself as a nudist but eventually admitted that he had a proclivity toward sex with children and possessed other depictions of child pornography at his apartment.

Brockway informed Moore that he thought he had probable cause to obtain a search warrant and asked Moore if he would consent to a search of his apartment and vehicle. Moore agreed and signed a form consenting to the warrantless search of his home and vehicle. No evidence indicated that Moore was incapable of voluntary consent or that Moore was threatened or coerced in any way. After signing the form, Moore ceased the interview.

The police executed the warrant and found an album containing eighty-nine photographs of minor boys posed provocatively or engaged in sexual acts and a stack of computer-generated photos of boys engaged in sexual acts. Police seized Moore's computer, which contained images of child pornography and e-mail correspondences detailing Moore's efforts to arrange meetings with children for the purpose of engaging in sex. Other publications, including some that were advertised in "Ophelia Editions," were also found.

Subsequently, Moore challenged the legality of the search under the Fourth Amendment. Moore presents two reasons why the search should be suppressed. First, he argues that police lacked probable cause to arrest him, and therefore, his consent to the search of his apartment was involuntary. Second, he contends that as a matter of law, the police should seek probable cause review from a neutral magistrate before executing an arrest. Should the fruits of the search be suppressed? *United States v. Moore*, 215 F.3d 681 (7th Cir. 2000).

Read the court opinion at:
www.ci.keene.nh.us/police/Moore.html

Chapter 5

Search Warrants

Outline

Objectives

■ **Know the general history of the development of the Fourth Amendment and of the law of electronic surveillance.**

■ **Know how to obtain a search warrant, including the following: who issues search warrants; grounds for issuance; what may be seized; how to describe the person or place to be searched and the things to be seized**

■ **Know how to execute a search warrant, including the following: who may execute a search warrant; when a search warrant may be executed, allowable delays, and how long the search may last; gaining entry to premises; authority to search persons not named in the warrant; allowable scope of the search and seizure; duties after the search is completed**

■ **Know the differences between an administrative search warrant and a criminal search warrant.**

■ **Know the meaning of and rationale justifying "special needs" searches.**

Like the law of arrest, the law governing search warrants is based on guarantees in the Fourth Amendment to the U.S. Constitution:

> The right of the people to be secure in their persons, houses, papers and effects, against unreasonable searches and seizures, shall not be violated, and no Warrants shall issue, but upon probable cause, supported by Oath or affirmation, and particularly describing the place to be searched and the persons or things to be seized. U.S. Const., Amend. 4.

Whereas the main concern of the previous chapter on arrest was the *seizure* of the *person,* this chapter's concern is with a broader array of matters, including the search of persons *and* places and the seizure of a variety of things. A search can be defined as an examination or inspection of a location, vehicle, or person by a law enforcement officer or other authorized person for the purpose of locating objects or substances relating to or believed to relate to criminal activities or wanted persons. In recent years, courts have increasingly analyzed search and seizure issues in terms of violation of the right of privacy and have expanded the definition of search to include any official intrusion into matters and activities about which a person has exhibited a reasonable expectation of privacy. The U.S. Supreme Court definitions of **search** and **seizure,** set out in Chapter 3, are repeated here for emphasis.

> A "search" occurs when an expectation of privacy that society is prepared to consider reasonable is infringed. A "seizure" of property occurs when there is some meaningful interference with an individual's possessory interests in that property. *United States v. Jacobsen,* 466 U.S. 109, 113, 104 S.Ct. 1652, 1656, 80 L.Ed.2d 85, 94 (1984).

Probable cause, which is a common aspect of both arrest and search and seizure law, is discussed in detail in Chapter 6.

History

The Fourth Amendment to the Constitution was adopted in response to abuses of governmental search and seizure authority originating in England in the seventeenth and eighteenth centuries. The early development of legally authorized searches and seizures under English common law is somewhat obscure. It appears that search warrants were first used in cases involving stolen property. The use of warrants to recapture stolen goods became widespread and increasingly violated citizens' privacy.

Eventually, the use of warrants was extended to the enforcement of other laws. For example, in the eighteenth century, the government issued general warrants to enforce strict libel laws. A general warrant is one that fails to specify the person or place to be searched or the person or item to be seized, and that leaves the time and manner of the search to the discretion of the searching officer. Law enforcement officers abused these general warrants, and soon no person or property was free from unlimited search conducted at the whim of an officer on the mere suspicion that the person possessed literature critical of the king or others in high places.

Despite their unpopularity with the citizenry, these abusive practices were transplanted to the American colonies. In the mid–eighteenth century, Parliament enacted legislation authorizing general searches, called *writs of assistance,* to be conducted against the colonists to enforce the Trade Acts. Writs of assistance authorized royal customs officers to search houses and ships at will to discover and seize smuggled goods or goods on which the required duties had not been paid. The colonists' reaction against

United States v. Jacobsen
laws.findlaw.com/us/466/
109.html

the writs of assistance was strong and was one of the major causes of the American Revolution. As stated in the 1886 U.S. Supreme Court case of *Boyd v. United States:*

> The practice had obtained in the colonies of issuing writs of assistance to the revenue officers, empowering them, in their discretion, to search suspected places for smuggled goods, which James Otis pronounced "the worst instrument of arbitrary power, the most destructive of English liberty and the fundamental principles of law, that ever was found in an English law book"; since they placed "the liberty of every man in the hands of every petty officer." This was in February, 1761, in Boston, and the famous debate in which it occurred was perhaps the most prominent event which inaugurated the resistance of the colonies to the oppressions of the mother country. "Then and there," said John Adams, "then and there was the first scene of the first act of opposition to the arbitrary claims of Great Britain. Then and there the child Independence was born." 116 U.S. 616, 625, 6 S.Ct. 524, 529, 29 L.Ed. 746, 749 (1886).

The experiences of the Founding Fathers with general warrants and writs of assistance caused them to insist on including in the basic charters of the states and nation suitable guarantees against unreasonable searches and seizures. A prohibition against searches conducted at the whim of a law enforcement officer without any restrictions on the person or place to be searched or the person or item to be seized was first embodied in the Virginia Bill of Rights, adopted in 1776. By the close of the Revolutionary War, most of the states had adopted similar provisions. The present Fourth Amendment to the Constitution, with its emphasis on the protection of warrants issued upon probable cause, was included in the Bill of Rights in 1791. Today, every state's constitution contains a similar provision.

The U.S. Supreme Court stated the policy underlying the warrant requirement of the Fourth Amendment:

> The point of the Fourth Amendment, which often is not grasped by zealous officers, is not that it denies law enforcement the support of the usual inferences which reasonable men draw from evidence. Its protection consists in requiring that those inferences be drawn by a neutral and detached magistrate instead of being judged by the officer engaged in the often competitive enterprise of ferreting out crime. Any assumption that evidence sufficient to support a magistrate's disinterested determination to issue a search warrant will justify the officers in making a search without a warrant would reduce the Amendment to a nullity and leave the people's homes secure only in the discretion of police officers. . . . When the right of privacy must reasonably yield to the right of search is, as a rule, to be decided by a judicial officer, not by a policeman or Government enforcement agent. *Johnson v. United States,* 333 U.S. 10, 13–14, 68 S.Ct. 367, 369, 92 L.Ed. 436, 440 (1948).

Although several exceptions to the warrant requirement have been established over the years (see Part three of this book), warrants are clearly preferred and reviewing courts will accept evidence of a less "judicially competent or persuasive character than would have justified an officer in acting on his own without a warrant." *Jones v. United States,* 362 U.S. 257, 270, 80 S.Ct. 725, 736, 4 L.Ed.2d 697, 708 (1960).

The Fourth Amendment's drafting history shows that its purpose was to protect the people of the United States against arbitrary action by their own government and not to restrain the federal government's actions against aliens outside U.S. territory. "The people" protected by the Fourth Amendment and several other amendments "refers to a class of persons who are part of a national community or who have otherwise

Objectives *(continued)*

■ Have a general understanding of Title III of the Omnibus Crime Control and Safe Streets Act of 1968, including the following: familiarity with the conflicting demands for more effective law enforcement and individual privacy rights; knowledge of several ways in which Title III provides for judicial supervision of electronic surveillance; understanding of the similarities and differences between an interception order under Title III and an ordinary search warrant; knowledge of specific ways in which Title III protects individual rights, especially privacy rights; understanding of the types of interceptions of wire, oral, or electronic communications that are excepted from the coverage of Title III

www.nolo.com/chapter/KYR/ KYR_store_ch2_b.html Discussion of law relating to search warrants with examples

For new and updated weblinks, go to www.wadsworth.com/ cj/ferdico0253

Boyd v. United States laws.findlaw.com/us/116/ 616.html
Johnson v. United States laws.findlaw.com/us/333/ 10.html
Jones v. United States laws.findlaw.com/us/362/ 257.html

United States v. Verdugo-Urquidez
laws.findlaw.com/us/494/
259.html

developed sufficient connection with this country to be considered part of that community." *United States v. Verdugo-Urquidez*, 494 U.S. 259, 265, 110 S.Ct. 1056, 1061, 108 L.Ed.2d 222, 233 (1990). The *Verdugo-Urquidez* case held that the Fourth Amendment does not apply to a search and seizure by U.S. agents of property owned by a nonresident alien and located in a foreign country. The Fourth Amendment does, however, protect legal, resident aliens from unreasonable searches and seizures conducted on U.S. soil, since legal, resident aliens enjoy substantially the same constitutional rights as do U.S. citizens. *Yick Wo v. Hopkins*, 188 U.S. 356, 6 S.Ct. 1064, 30 L.Ed. 220 (1886). Whether illegal aliens enjoy the protection of the Fourth Amendment is a matter open to dispute.

Yick Wo v. Hopkins
laws.findlaw.com/us/188/
356.html

Definition

caselaw.findlaw.com/data/
constitution/amendment04/
01.html
Comprehensive discussion (with annotations) of the history and scope of the Fourth Amendment

A **search warrant** is (1) an order in writing, (2) issued by a proper judicial authority, (3) in the name of the people, (4) directed to a law enforcement officer, (5) commanding the officer to search for certain personal property, and (6) commanding the officer to bring that property before the judicial authority named in the warrant. A search warrant is similar to an arrest warrant, which is an order to take a person into custody and bring the person before the proper judicial authority. In this chapter, the terms of the preceding definition are clarified, and important relationships between search warrants and arrest warrants are highlighted.

Obtaining a Search Warrant

Law enforcement officers must conform to established laws and procedures in applying for a search warrant. Otherwise, the application will be denied or, if a warrant is issued, the warrant will be invalidated later by a court. In either instance, valuable evidence will be unavailable to be used in the prosecution of a criminal case. Search warrant procedures vary among different jurisdictions and are found in various statutes, rules, and court decisions. The laws and procedures common to most jurisdictions are summarized and discussed in this chapter.

www.lectlaw.com/files/
cri12.htm
Article, "Search Warrant Applications" by Andrew Grosso

Who May Issue Search Warrants

Only judicial officers who have been specifically authorized to do so may issue search warrants. Most jurisdictions give this authority to judicial officers such as clerks of court, magistrates, complaint justices, justices of the peace, and judges. Law enforcement officers need to know which judicial officers are authorized to issue search warrants in their jurisdictions. These judicial officers may be different from those authorized to issue arrest warrants. A search warrant issued by a person without authority has no legal effect, and a search made under such a warrant is illegal. For convenience, the term *magistrate* is used in this chapter to designate an official authorized to issue search warrants.

Shadwick v. City of Tampa Bay
laws.findlaw.com/us/407/
345.html

In *Shadwick v. City of Tampa*, 407 U.S. 345, 92 S.Ct. 2119, 32 L.Ed.2d 783 (1972), the U.S. Supreme Court, rejecting the notion that all warrant authority must reside exclusively in a lawyer or judge, upheld a city charter provision authorizing municipal court clerks to issue arrest warrants for municipal ordinance violations. The Court concluded that "an issuing magistrate must meet two tests. He must be neutral and detached, and he must be capable of determining whether probable cause exists for the requested arrest or search." 407 U.S. at 350, 92 S.Ct. at 2123, 32 L.Ed.2d at 788. In other cases, the Court found that the following persons were not sufficiently "neutral and detached" to issue warrants:

- A state attorney general who was also the state's chief investigator and was later to be the chief prosecutor at trial. *Coolidge v. New Hampshire,* 403 U.S. 443, 91 S.Ct. 2022, 29 L.Ed.2d 564 (1971).
- A magistrate who received a fee for issuing a search warrant but received nothing for denying a warrant application. *Connally v. Georgia,* 429 U.S. 245, 97 S.Ct. 546, 50 L.Ed.2d 444 (1977).
- A magistrate who participated in a search, helping officers determine what to seize. *Lo-Ji Sales, Inc. v. New York,* 442 U.S. 319, 99 S.Ct. 2319, 60 L.Ed.2d 920 (1979).
- Officials of the executive branch of government. *United States v. U.S. District Court,* 407 U.S. 297, 92 S.Ct. 2125, 32 L.Ed.2d 752 (1972).

Coolidge v. New Hampshire
laws.findlaw.com/us/403/443.html
Connally v. Georgia
laws.findlaw.com/us/429/245.html
Lo-Ji Sales, Inc. v. New York
laws.findlaw.com/us/442/319.html
United States v. U.S. District Court
laws.findlaw.com/us/407/297.html

Grounds for Issuance

Before issuing a search warrant, the magistrate must have probable cause to believe that items subject to seizure are in a particular place or on a particular person at the time the warrant is issued. A law enforcement officer applying for a search warrant must supply the magistrate with the grounds for issuance of the warrant. This is done by means of an affidavit, which is merely a written declaration or statement of facts sworn to before the magistrate. Exhibit 5.1 is a typical form for an affidavit for a search warrant.

If a law enforcement officer knowingly and intentionally, or with reckless disregard for the truth, makes false statements in an affidavit supporting a request for a search warrant, the warrant may not issue or, if it is, evidence seized under the warrant may be suppressed. In *Franks v. Delaware,* 438 U.S. 154, 98 S.Ct. 2674, 57 L.Ed.2d 667 (1978), the U.S. Supreme Court held that a defendant may challenge the veracity of an affidavit used by the police to obtain a search warrant. The Court said:

caselaw/findlaw.com/data/constitution/amendment04/02.html#2
Discussion (with annotations) of the requirement that the warrant be issued by a neutral and detached magistrate

Franks v. Delaware
laws.findlaw.com/us/438/154.html

> [W]here the defendant makes a substantial preliminary showing that a false statement knowingly and intentionally, or with reckless disregard for the truth, was included by the affiant in the warrant affidavit, and if the allegedly false statement is necessary to the finding of probable cause, the Fourth Amendment requires that a hearing be held at the defendant's request. In the event that at the hearing the allegation of perjury or reckless disregard is established by the defendant by a preponderance of the evidence, and, with the affidavit's false material set to one side, the affidavit's remaining content is insufficient to establish probable cause, the search warrant must be voided and the fruits of the search excluded to the same extent as if probable cause was lacking on the face of the affidavit. 438 U.S. at 155–56, 98 S.Ct. at 2676–77, 57 L.Ed.2d at 672.

www.faculty.ncwc.edu/toconnor/warrant.htm
General information about affidavits and warrants

In *United States v. Johns,* 851 F.2d 1131 (9th Cir. 1988), the court found that a so-called *Franks* hearing was required when the defendants made a substantial preliminary showing that they never engaged in any activities at a storage unit that could have produced the odors the officers allegedly smelled. Two expert witnesses swore the officer's affidavit was necessarily false because it was scientifically impossible to smell what the officers claimed to have smelled given the contents of the storage space searched under the warrant. Without the alleged falsities, the probable cause support for the search warrant collapsed because the remainder of the affidavit merely described the

AO 106 (Rev. 7/87) Affidavit for Search Warrant   ⊕

United States District Court

_____ DISTRICT OF _____

In the Matter of the Search of
(Name, address or brief description of person, property or premises to be searched)

**APPLICATION AND AFFIDAVIT
FOR SEARCH WARRANT**

CASE NUMBER:

I _____ being duly sworn depose and say:

I am a(n) _____ and have reason to believe
                                    Official Title

that ☐ on the person of or ☐ on the property or premises known as (name, description and/or location)

in the _____ District of _____
there is now concealed a certain person or property, namely (describe the person or property to be seized)

which is (state one or more bases for search and seizure set forth under Rule 41(b) of the Federal Rules of Criminal Procedure)

concerning a violation of Title _____ United States code, Section(s)_____.
The facts to support a finding of Probable Cause are as follows:

Continued on the attached sheet and made a part hereof.   ☐ Yes   ☐ No

_____
Signature of Affiant

Sworn to before me, and subscribed in my presence

_____   at   _____
Date   City and State

_____   _____
Name and Title of Judicial Officer   Signature of Judicial Officer

A Typical Affidavit for a Search Warrant
■ EXHIBIT 5.1

location and ownership of the storage unit. In *United States v. Pace*, 898 F.2d 1218 (7th Cir. 1990), the court found that the rule of the *Franks* case also prohibits the officer from deliberately or recklessly *omitting* material information from the application. That court held, however, that the failure to advise the magistrate that another magistrate had denied the warrant was not a material fact when the affidavit was sufficient to show probable cause and the second magistrate was neutral and detached. In addition, if a warrant application is so lacking in indicia of probable cause as to render official belief in its existence unreasonable, the officer making the application may be held liable for damages in a civil suit. *Malley v. Briggs*, 475 U.S. 335, 106 S.Ct. 1092, 89 L.Ed.2d 271 (1986). A mere allegation of such impropriety, however, is not enough. "A mere allegation standing alone, without an offer of proof in a sworn affidavit of a witness or some other reliable corroboration, is insufficient. . . . When no proof is offered that an affiant deliberately lied or recklessly disregarded the truth, a *Franks* hearing is not required." *United States v. Mathison*, 157 F.3d 541, 548 (8th Cir. 1998).

Malley v. Briggs
laws.findlaw.com/us/475/335.html

The following discussion covers in detail the information that must be presented to the magistrate to establish grounds for the issuance of a search warrant.

PROBABLE CAUSE Some jurisdictions require that an affidavit contain *all* the information upon which a magistrate is to base a finding of probable cause to issue a search warrant. *Valdez v. State*, 476 A.2d 1162 (Md. 1984). Other jurisdictions allow supplementation of a defective or incomplete affidavit by sworn oral testimony given before the magistrate. *State v. Hendricks*, 328 N.E.2d 822 (Ohio 1974). Several jurisdictions permit issuance of search warrants over the telephone but still require that the information called in by the affiant to the magistrate be taken under oath and recorded. For example, Rule 41(c)(2)(A) of the Federal Rules of Criminal Procedure authorizes the issuance of warrants based on sworn testimony communicated by telephone or other appropriate means, including facsimile transmission, "[if] the circumstances make it reasonable to dispense, in whole or in part, with a written affidavit." Exhibit 5.3, appearing later in the chapter, is a typical form for a search warrant upon oral testimony.

Complete text of Rule 41 of the Federal Rules of Criminal Procedure
www.law.ukans.edu/research/frcrimIX.htm
(Scroll down to Rule 41)

It is recommended that all the information on which probable cause is based be included in the written affidavit. This forces the law enforcement officer to think carefully about the case before applying for a warrant, and it provides a complete record for a court to review the magistrate's decision if the warrant is later challenged. This chapter proceeds on the assumption that a written affidavit is the exclusive vehicle for applying to a magistrate for a search warrant.

An affidavit for a search warrant should inform a magistrate (1) that a criminal offense has been or is being committed and (2) that seizable evidence relating to that offense is in a particular place at a particular time. The amount of proof required to persuade the magistrate to issue a search warrant is essentially the same as that required for the issuance of an arrest warrant or that required before an officer may arrest without a warrant for a felony. The constitutional term used to describe this amount of proof is *probable cause*. (Probable cause is discussed in Chapter 3 and explained in further detail in Chapter 6.) In applying for a search warrant, the essential requirement is that the underlying facts and circumstances on which probable cause is based must be stated in the affidavit. These facts and circumstances must show "a fair probability that contraband or evidence of a crime will be found in a particular place." *Illinois v. Gates*, 462 U.S. 213, 238, 103 S.Ct. 2317, 2332, 76 L.Ed.2d 527, 548 (1983). An officer's mere conclusions, beliefs, or opinions will not suffice to establish probable cause. "The source and credibility of evidence in support of a warrant request is considered in the totality of the circumstances analysis, and a warrant is proper so long as the evidence as a whole creates a reasonable probability that the search will lead to the discovery of evidence." *United States v. Humphrey*, 140 F.3d 762, 764 (8th Cir. 1998).

Illinois v. Gates
laws.findlaw.com/us/462/213.html

Probable cause to search differs in two important respects from probable cause to arrest. First, probable cause to search and probable cause to arrest will usually arise out of different sets of facts. To find probable cause to arrest, a magistrate must find sufficient facts to show that an offense was committed and that a particular suspect committed it. Probable cause to search requires sufficient facts to show that particular items are connected with criminal activity and that they will be found in a particular place. Therefore, the same set of facts and circumstances might provide probable cause to arrest, but not probable cause to search, and vice versa.

Another difference between probable cause to arrest and probable cause to search is that time is a very important factor in determining probable cause to search. If there is too long a delay between the time when the information on which probable cause is based is gathered and the time when the search is executed, there may no longer be good reason to believe that the property is still at the same location. Probable cause is said to be "stale" in this situation.

> Staleness is not measured merely on the basis of the maturity of the information but in relation to (1) the nature of the suspected criminal activity (discrete crime or "regenerating conspiracy"), (2) the habits of the suspected criminal ("nomadic" or "entrenched"), (3) the character of the items to be seized ("perishable" or "of enduring utility"), and (4) the nature and function of the premises to be searched ("mere criminal forum" or "secure operational base"). *United States v. Bucuvalas,* 970 F.2d 937 (1st Cir. 1992).

In *United States v. Wagner,* 989 F.2d 69 (2d Cir. 1993), the information supporting probable cause to search the suspect's home was (1) a single small purchase of marijuana from the suspect in her home more than six weeks before the search, (2) a recorded statement of the suspect as to who was her source for that marijuana, and (3) an unsubstantiated assertion that the suspect's home was owned by the source. On these facts, the court could not find that the suspect engaged in continuing criminal activity in her home as a member of the source's drug distribution network. Therefore, since marijuana is the type of property that is likely to disappear or be moved, probable cause was found to be stale at the time the warrant was issued and the search conducted.

The length of time that an item of property is likely to remain at a given location depends on the nature of the property, the nature of the criminal activity, the duration of the criminal activity, the criminal suspects, and many other factors. In *United States v. Laury,* 985 F.2d 1293 (5th Cir. 1993), probable cause to search a suspected bank robber's home for instrumentalities and evidence of the crime was found not to be stale although nearly two months had passed since the date of the robbery. In that case, the affiant, an expert in bank robbery investigation, stated that bank robbers tend to keep evidence of the crime in their homes for a long time, sometimes several years.

Evidence of continuing crimes, especially white-collar crimes, is also likely to stay in one place for a long time. The U.S. Supreme Court found that business records of an illegal real estate scheme would probably remain at their location for an extended period of time after the business transactions had taken place.

> The business records sought were prepared in the ordinary course of petitioner's business in his law office or that of his real estate corporation. It is eminently reasonable to expect that such records would be maintained in those offices for a period of time and surely as long as the three months required for the investigation of a complex real estate scheme. *Andresen v. Maryland,* 427 U.S. 463, 479 n.9, 96 S.Ct. 2737, 2747 n.9, 49 L.Ed.2d 627, 641 n.9 (1976).

Andresen v. Maryland
laws.findlaw.com/us/427/
463.html

Other examples of continuing crimes, evidence of which is likely to stay in one place for a long time, are the cultivation and distribution of illegal drugs (*United States v. McKeever,* 5 F.3d 863 [5th Cir. 1993]) and gun control violations (*United States v. Maxim,* 55 F.3d 394 [8th Cir. 1995]).

ITEMS SUBJECT TO SEIZURE   Laws and court rules authorizing a warrant to be issued to search for and seize certain types of property vary among different jurisdictions. Rule 41(b) of the Federal Rules of Criminal Procedure is typical and is reproduced here:

(b) Property or Persons Which May Be Seized With a Warrant. A warrant may be issued under this rule to search for and seize any (1) property that constitutes evidence of the commission of a criminal offense; or (2) contraband, the fruits of crime, or things otherwise criminally possessed; or (3) property designed or intended for use or which is or has been used as the means of committing a criminal offense; or (4) person for whose arrest there is probable cause, or who is unlawfully restrained.

Categories 1 and 4 of Rule 41(b) require further discussion. Examples of "(1) property that constitutes evidence of the commission of a criminal offense" are clothing, blood, hair, fingerprints, and business records. Evidence of crime was added to the list of seizable items in response to the U.S. Supreme Court decision in *Warden v. Hayden,* 387 U.S. 294, 87 S.Ct. 1642, 18 L.Ed.2d 782 (1967). That case abolished the former rule that search warrants could not be used as a means of gaining access to a person's house or office and papers solely for the purpose of searching for mere evidence to be used against the person in a criminal proceeding.

One limitation on the seizure of mere evidence is that the evidence to be seized must be nontestimonial. This requirement protects persons from being compelled to be witnesses against themselves in violation of Fifth Amendment rights. It was originally assumed that private personal papers and business records could not be seized under this limitation because of their testimonial nature. The U.S. Supreme Court held, however, that a seizure of personal papers or business records from persons under a search warrant does not necessarily compel those persons to be witnesses against themselves. *Andresen v. Maryland,* 427 U.S. 463, 96 S.Ct. 2737, 49 L.Ed.2d 627 (1976). The Court quoted an earlier case stating that "'a party is privileged from producing the evidence, but not from its production.'" 427 U.S. at 473, 96 S.Ct. at 2745, 49 L.Ed.2d at 638. The Court held that the defendant in the *Andresen* case was not compelled to be a witness against himself because he was not required to say or to do anything during the search. If law enforcement authorities had attempted to subpoena the records, however, the defendant could have refused to give up the records by exercising his Fifth Amendment rights. The Court said:

[A]lthough the Fifth Amendment may protect an individual from complying with a subpoena for the production of his personal records in his possession because the very act of production may constitute a compulsory authentication of incriminating information, . . . a seizure of the same materials by law enforcement officers differs in a crucial respect—the individual against whom the search is directed is not required to aid in the discovery, production, or authentication of incriminating evidence. 427 U.S. at 473–74, 96 S.Ct. at 2745, 49 L.Ed.2d at 638.

Bank records have even less protection. In *United States v. Miller,* 425 U.S. 435, 96 S.Ct. 1619, 48 L.Ed.2d 71 (1976), the U.S. Supreme Court held that a person's bank records are not private papers of the kind protected against compulsory production by the Fifth Amendment. Also, by choosing to deal with a bank, people lose their expectation of Fourth Amendment protection against government investigation:

The checks are not confidential communications but negotiable instruments to be used in commercial transactions. All of the documents obtained, including financial statements and deposit slips, contain only information voluntarily conveyed to the banks and

caselaw.findlaw.com/data/ constitution/amendment04/ 02.html#6
Comprehensive discussion (with annotations) of property subject to seizure

Warden v. Hayden
laws.findlaw.com/us/387/ 294.html

www.techlawonline.com/ articles/a-esearch.htm
"Current Legal Standards for Access to Papers, Records, and Communications: What Information Can the Government Get About You, and How Can They Get It?"
www.fletc.gov/legal/ archive_dir.htm
Article, "Answering Machine Tapes: Search Warrant or Title III Court Order?" by Robert Cauthen (third of three articles in the October 2, 2000 issue of *Quarterly Review: Legal Commentary for Federal Law Enforcement Officers*
www.cybercrime.gov/ searchmanual.htm#II
Federal guidelines for searching and seizing computers with a warrant

United States v. Miller
laws.findlaw.com/us/425/ 435.html

consumerlawpage.com/article/
privacy.shtml
Article, "Privacy, Banking
Records and the Supreme Court:
A Before and After Look at
Miller" by Richard Alexander
and Roberta K. Spurgeon

exposed to their employees in the ordinary course of business. 425 U.S. at 442, 96 S.Ct. at 1624, 48 L.Ed.2d at 79.

The *Miller* case concerned a subpoena, but either a search warrant or subpoena could be used to obtain a person's bank records without violating the person's Fifth Amendment right against compulsory self-incrimination. Note that the *Miller* case does not automatically grant unrestricted access to bank records. Access may be restricted by state or federal statute.

Both the *Andresen* and *Miller* cases serve to highlight a basic principle regarding obtaining papers as evidence in criminal cases: "There is no special sanctity in papers, as distinguished from other forms of property, to render them immune from search and seizure, if only they fall within the scope of the principles of the cases in which other property may be seized, and if they be adequately described in the affidavit and warrant." *Gouled v. United States*, 255 U.S. 298, 309, 41 S.Ct. 261, 265, 65 L.Ed. 647, 652 (1921). Nevertheless, officers seizing items such as business records or personal papers under a warrant may request the defendant's assistance but may not compel assistance in any way. Otherwise the evidence may be suppressed because of a violation of the defendant's Fifth Amendment rights.

Gouled v. United States
laws.findlaw.com/us/255/
298.html

Another limitation on the seizure of mere evidence of crime is that the evidence must aid in a particular apprehension or conviction. The Supreme Court stated the reason for this requirement:

> The requirements of the Fourth Amendment can secure the same protection of privacy whether the search is for "mere evidence" or for fruits, instrumentalities or contraband. There must, of course, be a nexus—automatically provided in the case of fruits, instrumentalities or contraband—between the item to be seized and criminal behavior. Thus, in the case of "mere evidence" probable cause must be examined in terms of cause to believe that the evidence sought will aid in a particular apprehension or conviction. In doing so, consideration of police purposes will be required. *Warden v. Hayden*, 387 U.S. 294, 306–07, 87 S.Ct. 1642, 1650, 18 L.Ed.2d 782, 792 (1967).

The U.S. Supreme Court held that law enforcement officers may seize "mere evidence" of a separate crime under a warrant authorizing "seizure of fruits, instrumentalities and evidence of crime at this (time) unknown" if the evidence of a separate crime can be used to show intent to commit the crime for which the warrant was issued. *Andresen v. Maryland*, 427 U.S. 463, 96 S.Ct. 2737, 49 L.Ed.2d 627 (1976).

An affidavit for a search warrant should indicate, for each item of property sought in the warrant, the type of seizable property under which the item is classified according to the law of the jurisdiction. This informs the magistrate that the items sought are connected with criminal activity. For the remainder of this chapter, items of property allowed to be seized under state or federal law are referred to as "items subject to seizure" or "seizable items."

Category 4 of Rule 41(b) deals with the search for and seizure of persons. This provision authorizing a search warrant to issue for a "person for whose arrest there is probable cause" covers the situation, discussed in Chapter 4, in which the person to be arrested is in the home of a third person. Officers must apply for a search warrant to satisfy the requirement of *Steagald v. United States*, 451 U.S. 204, 101 S.Ct. 1642, 68 L.Ed.2d 38 (1981), that a search warrant be obtained to justify entry into the home of any person other than the person to be arrested. Even when a search warrant would not be required to enter a place to search for a person, category 4 makes the warrant procedure available. Law enforcement officers are thus encouraged to resort to the pre-

Steagald v. United States
laws.findlaw.com/us/451/
204.html

ferred alternative of acquiring an objective judicial predetermination of probable cause that the person sought is at the place to be searched.

The provision making it possible for a search warrant to issue for a person "who is unlawfully restrained" is designed to provide the authorization of a warrant to search for victims of crimes such as kidnapping and criminal restraint. Although exigent circumstances, especially the need to act promptly to protect the life or well-being of the victim, will often justify an immediate warrantless search for the victim, this will not inevitably be the case.

PARTICULAR DESCRIPTION OF PLACE OR PERSON　　The affidavit supporting a request for a search warrant for a *place* must contain a description of the premises to be searched that points directly to a definitely ascertainable place to the exclusion of all others. The U.S. Supreme Court stated that "[i]t is enough if the description is such that the officer with a search warrant can with reasonable effort ascertain and identify the place intended." *Steele v. United States*, 267 U.S. 498, 503, 45 S.Ct. 414, 416, 69 L.Ed. 757, 760 (1925).

Steele v. United States
laws.findlaw.com/us/267/498.html

A correct street address is sufficient to identify the place to be searched. For example, in *United States v. Dancy*, 947 F.2d 1232 (5th Cir. 1991), officers executed a search warrant that described the place to be searched only as 5121 Rapido Drive, Houston, Texas. The court held:

> A correct street address in a search warrant, even if no other description is given, is particular enough to withstand constitutional scrutiny. The warrant must describe the place to be searched in enough detail for the executing officer (1) to locate the premises with reasonable effort, and (2) to be sure that the wrong premises are not mistakenly searched. . . . A correct street address meets both prongs of the test. 947 F.2d at 1234.

In *United States v. Turner*, 770 F.2d 1508, 1509–10 (9th Cir. 1985), the affidavit for search warrant and the search warrant itself described the house as follows:

> 2762 Mountain View, Escondido, California, and further described as a beige two-story stucco and adobe house with an attached two-car garage. The garage has entry doors on either side of a large garage door. The entry door located on the south side of the garage door has a brass-plated deadbolt lock installed. On the south side of this door are two windows covered by tinfoil. The doors and trim of the house are painted brown. The entry to the residence is located on the south side of the residence and the garage entry faces west. The driveway to the residence off of Mountain View Drive leads north from Mountain View Drive and is marked by three mailboxes numbered 2800, 2810 and 2756. This driveway leads past these three residences, the last identified by a residence marker of 2756, D.A. Mieir. The driveway then turns to concrete and dead ends at the 2762 Mountain View Drive residence. There is a farm road leading past 2762 Mountain View Drive and into an avocado grove. The driveway leads north from Mountain View Drive. Entry to the 2762 Mountain View Drive residence is located on the south side.

www.cybercrime.gov/searchmanual.htm#IIc
Federal guidelines for drafting a search warrant and affidavit to seize computer hardware and information

www.ndaa.org/apri/NCPCA/Update/apri_update_vol_12_no_9_1999.html
Article, "Search and Seizure in Cases of Computers and Child Pornography" by Susan Kreston

www.ndaa.org/apri/NCPCA/Update/apri_update_vol_13_no_4_2000.html
Article, "Exceptions to the Warrant Requirement in Computer Facilitated Child Sexual Exploitation Cases" by Susan Kreston

The description of the suspect house turned out to be correct except for the street number. The house that the agents had surveilled, intended to search, and actually did search was 2800 Mountain View Drive. Number 2762 Mountain View Drive was located approximately two-tenths of a mile away in a location that the agents did not know existed, and it did not resemble the description of the suspect house. The court held that the description in the search warrant was sufficiently particular despite the wrong street address. The court said:

> The verbal description contained in the warrant described the house to be searched with great particularity; no nearby house met the warrant's detailed description; the address in the warrant was reasonable for the location intended; the house had been under surveillance before the warrant was sought; the warrant was executed by an officer who had participated in applying for the warrant and who personally knew which premises were intended to be searched; and the premises that were intended to be searched were those actually searched. Under these circumstances, there was virtually no chance that the executing officer would have any trouble locating and identifying the premises to be searched, or that he would mistakenly search another house. 770 F.2d at 1511.

Officers should include detailed descriptions of the place to be searched (such as the one in the *Turner* case) in their affidavits to avoid errors and ensure that the particularity requirement is satisfied. In *United States v. Ellis*, 971 F.2d 701 (11th Cir. 1992), the warrant described the place to be searched as the "third mobile home on the north side" without any further description of its physical characteristics or mention of its occupant's name. The court found the description insufficiently particular.

The location of rural property is more difficult to describe, but there is also less chance that an error will be made in locating a specific piece of rural property. Therefore, a description of a farm or other rural property by the owner's name, the dwelling's color and style, and general directions will usually suffice. *Gatlin v. State*, 559 S.W.2d 12 (Ark. 1977).

When the place to be searched is a multiple-occupancy dwelling such as an apartment house, hotel, or rooming house, the affidavit must go beyond merely stating the location of the premises. In *Manley v. Commonwealth*, 176 S.E.2d 309 (Va. 1970), the affidavit on which the warrant was based read as follows:

> Place to be searched: 313 West 27th Street, a dwelling. The apartment of Melvin Lloyd Manley.

The defendant objected to the search on the ground that the apartment to be searched was not sufficiently described in the affidavit and warrant. The court held that the defendant's apartment was sufficiently described for the searching officers to locate it with very little effort:

> It has been generally held that a search warrant directed against a multiple-occupancy structure is invalid if it fails to describe the particular sub-unit to be searched with sufficient definiteness to preclude search of other units located in the larger structure and occupied by innocent persons. But there are exceptions to the general rule. Even though a search warrant against a multiple-occupancy structure fails to describe the particular sub-unit to be searched, it will ordinarily not be held invalid where it adequately specifies the name of the occupant of the sub-unit against which it is directed and provides the searching officers with sufficient information to identify, without confusion or excessive effort, such apartment unit. 176 S.E.2d at 314.

Whenever possible, however, information such as room number, apartment number, and floor should be included in the affidavit. If necessary, a diagram showing the location should be attached to the affidavit.

In another case involving a multiple-occupancy dwelling, the description in the warrant of the place to be searched (a four-building apartment complex) gave a wrong street address but correctly stated the apartment number. Since there was only one apartment with that number in the entire complex, the court held that the description was sufficient:

[T]he determining factor as to whether a search warrant describes the premises to be searched with sufficient particularity is not whether the description is technically accurate in every detail but rather whether the description is sufficient to enable the executing officer to locate and identify the premises with reasonable effort, and whether there is any reasonable probability that another premises might be mistakenly searched which is not the one intended to be searched under the search warrant. *United States v. Darensbourg*, 520 F.2d 985, 987 (5th Cir. 1975).

To obtain sufficiently descriptive information, an officer may need to view the premises, examine floor plans, or make inquiries of landlords, tenants, or others to determine the correct limits of the place to be searched. The U.S. Supreme Court said that "[t]he validity of the warrant must be assessed on the basis of the information that the officers disclosed, or had a duty to discover and to disclose, to the issuing magistrate." *Maryland v. Garrison*, 480 U.S. 79, 85, 107 S.Ct. 1013, 1018, 94 L.Ed.2d 72, 81 (1987). Nevertheless, the sufficiency of the description will be judged in light of the information available to the officer at the time he or she prepared the affidavit. The later discovery of facts demonstrating that a warrant was unnecessarily broad does not retroactively invalidate the warrant. In short, if an officer is diligent in gathering the information on which his or her description of the place to be searched is based, the warrant will be valid even though hindsight reveals that honest mistakes were made.

Maryland v. Garrison
laws.findlaw.com/us/480/
79.html

A warrant may be issued for the search of the premises of an innocent third party who is not suspected of any crime. In a case involving the search of newspaper offices, the U.S. Supreme Court said that search warrants are not directed at persons but at the seizure of things. "The critical element in a reasonable search is not that the owner of the property is suspected of crime but that there is reasonable cause to believe that the specific 'things' to be searched for and seized are located on the property to which entry is sought." *Zurcher v. The Stanford Daily*, 436 U.S. 547, 556, 98 S.Ct. 1970, 1977, 56 L.Ed.2d 525, 535 (1978). The *Zurcher* case involved a warrant to search a newsroom to obtain photographs of demonstrators who had injured several police officers. Note that Congress, in the Privacy Protection Act (1980), 42 U.S.C.A. § 2000aa, provided extensive protection against searches and seizures of not only the news media and newspeople but also others engaged in disseminating communications to the public, unless there is probable cause to believe the person possessing the materials has committed or is committing the criminal offense to which the materials relate.

Zurcher v. The Stanford Daily
laws.findlaw.com/us/436/
547.html

Complete text of 42 U.S.C. §
2000aa
caselaw.findlaw.com/scripts/
ts_search.pl?title=42&sec=
2000aa

A search warrant may also be issued to search a *person* for particular items of evidence, although the more common procedure is to arrest the person and conduct a search incident to arrest (see Chapter 8). Again, the standard for determining the validity of a warrant to search a person is whether the warrant describes the person to be searched with sufficient particularity to enable identification with reasonable certainty. Even though a person's name is unknown or incorrectly stated, a warrant may still be valid if a description of the person is included. *United States v. Ferrone*, 438 F.2d 381 (3d Cir. 1971). A law enforcement officer applying for a warrant for the search of a person should not only state the person's name, if known, but also give a complete description including weight, height, age, race, clothing, address, and any aliases. *State v. Tramantano*, 260 A.2d 128 (Conn. Super. 1969). If the name in the affidavit is incorrect, the supporting information will still enable the person to be identified.

Some courts hold that the Fourth Amendment prohibits any search of a person that requires surgery. *Adams v. State*, 299 N.E.2d 834 (Ind. 1973). Other courts require additional information in the affidavit to justify the issuance of a search warrant requiring surgery. The U.S. Supreme Court case of *Winston v. Lee*, 470 U.S. 753, 105 S.Ct. 1611,

Winston v. Lee
laws.findlaw.com/us/470/
753.html

84 L.Ed.2d 662 (1985), discussed the interests that must be balanced in determining whether a search requiring surgery is constitutional:

> The reasonableness of surgical intrusions beneath the skin depends on a case-by-case approach, in which the individual's interests in privacy and security are weighed against society's interests in conducting the procedure. In a given case, the question whether the community's need for evidence outweighs the substantial privacy interests at stake is a delicate one admitting of few categorical answers. 470 U.S. at 760, 105 S.Ct. at 1616, 84 L.Ed.2d at 669.

Among the factors to be weighed are the extent to which the procedure may threaten the safety or health of the individual and the extent of intrusion on the individual's dignitary interests in personal privacy and bodily integrity. Balanced against these individual interests is the community's interest in fairly and accurately determining guilt or innocence, the seriousness of the crime, the relevance and importance of the evidence sought, the likelihood of surgery's producing the evidence, and the available alternatives to surgery. In addition, a defendant may be entitled to an adversary hearing and an opportunity to appeal an order directing surgery. *United States v. Crowder*, 543 F.2d 312 (D.C.Cir. 1976).

The U.S. Supreme Court has established exceptions to the warrant requirement allowing certain carefully defined warrantless searches of motor vehicles (see Chapter 11). However, the basic rule remains that a warrant is required for the search of a motor vehicle. Since vehicles are considered *places* for search and seizure purposes, an affidavit is required to contain a description of the vehicle to be searched that is sufficiently particular that the vehicle can be located with reasonable certainty. Some courts have held that only the license plate number is necessary to sufficiently describe a motor vehicle for purposes of issuance of a warrant. "A vehicle search warrant ordinarily should include the license plate number on its face, but when this is not practicable a detailed description of the vehicle or a narrow geographical limit to the search may provide the requisite check on police discretion." *United States v. Vaughn*, 830 F.2d 1185 (D.C.Cir. 1987). A detailed description would include information such as the make, body style, color, year, location, and owner or operator of the vehicle.

Mail may also be considered a *place* for search and seizure purposes. Courts have ruled that first-class domestic mail may not be lawfully opened without a warrant. (Domestic mail is any letter or package traveling wholly within the United States.) Therefore, law enforcement officers must follow the same procedures to obtain a warrant to search first-class domestic mail as to search places, persons, and vehicles.

If a search warrant is sought to install a tracking device such as a beeper, a problem arises in describing the place to be searched, because the location of a place is usually what is sought to be discovered. The U.S. Supreme Court responded to this issue as follows:

> [I]t will still be possible to describe the object into which the beeper is to be placed, the circumstances that led agents to wish to install the beeper, and the length of time for which beeper surveillance is requested. In our view, this information will suffice to permit issuance of a warrant authorizing beeper installation and surveillance. *United States v. Karo*, 468 U.S. 705, 718, 104 S.Ct. 3296, 3305, 82 L.Ed.2d 530, 543 (1984).

United States v. Karo
laws.findlaw.com/us/468/
705.html

PARTICULAR DESCRIPTION OF THINGS   The affidavit supporting a request for a search warrant must contain a particular description of the items to be seized. The U.S. Supreme Court explained the reason for this requirement:

The requirement that warrants shall particularly describe the things to be seized makes general searches under them impossible and prevents the seizure of one thing under a warrant describing another. As to what is to be taken, nothing is left to the discretion of the officer executing the warrant. *Marron v. United States*, 275 U.S. 192, 196, 48 S.Ct. 74, 76, 72 L.Ed. 231, 237 (1927).

In general, the items to be seized must be described with sufficient particularity so that the officer executing the warrant (1) can identify the items with reasonable certainty and (2) is left with no discretion as to which property is to be taken. The primary concern of courts evaluating descriptions of things to be seized in affidavits for search warrants is to ensure that a person will not be deprived of lawfully possessed property by a seizure made under an imprecise warrant.

A description of items merely as "stolen goods," "obscene materials," or "other articles of merchandise too numerous to mention" is inadequate because it is imprecise. *Marcus v. Search Warrant*, 367 U.S. 717, 81 S.Ct. 1708, 6 L.Ed.2d 1127 (1961). When an item can be described in detail, all available information about it should be included in the affidavit. For example, number, size, color, weight, condition, brand name, and other distinguishing features of an item to be seized should be a part of the description where applicable. The affidavit should also indicate how the item is connected with criminal activity by stating the category of items subject to seizure within which the item falls.

A more general description may be allowed when specificity is impossible or difficult. For example, in a case involving the robbery of a post office, the court found sufficiently specific the description in a warrant directing the seizure of "a variety of items, including 'currency' and 'United States postage stock (stamps; envelopes; checks).'" The court said:

> At the time of the application and issuance of the warrant in the instant case, a more precise description of the stamps and currency taken during the robbery was unascertainable. Although the postal inspectors knew that stamps and currency had been stolen, no further information was available to more particularly describe the items in the warrant. We find that the description of the stamps and currency by generic classes was reasonably specific under the circumstances of this case. *United States v. Porter*, 831 F.2d 760, 764 (8th Cir. 1987).

A more general description may also be allowed when a large number of items to be seized are of a common nature and not readily distinguishable. In a case involving a stolen shipment of women's clothing, a search warrant authorized the seizure of "[c]artons of women's clothing, the contents of those cartons, lists identifying the contents of the cartons, and control slips identifying the stores intended to receive these cartons, such items being contraband and evidence of a violation of Title 18, United States Code, Section 659, Possession of Goods Stolen from Interstate Shipments." The court said:

> We recognize . . . that the overriding principle of the Fourth Amendment is one of reasonableness and on occasion have accepted general descriptions in warrants, holding that such descriptions are not always constitutionally infirm. . . . Such general descriptions are permissible only in "special contexts in which there [is] substantial evidence to support the belief that the class of contraband [is] on the premises and in practical terms the goods to be described [can] not be precisely described" [citation omitted]. In *United States v. Klein*, 565 F.2d 183 (1st Cir. 1977), we set forth two tests which in particular circumstances may help to illuminate whether this principle is satisfied: first,

Marron v. United States
laws.findlaw.com/us/275/
192.html

caselaw.findlaw.com/data/
constitution/amendment04/
02.html#4
Discussion (with annotations)
of the requirement of particular
description of things to be seized

Marcus v. Search Warrant
laws.findlaw.com/us/367/
717.html

www.cybercrime.gov/
searchmanual.htm
"Searching and Seizing Computers and Obtaining Electronic Evidence in Criminal
Investigations"; illustrates some
of the ways in which searching
a computer is different from
searching a desk, file cabinet, or
automobile
www.co.alameda.ca.us/da/pov/
web.htm
Article, "Computer Searches"
from the District Attorney's
Office in Alameda County,
California
www.usdoj.gov/criminal/
cybercrime/cryptfaq.htm
Frequently asked questions on
the United States Department
of Justice policy promoting the
development and use of strong
computer encryption that
enhances the privacy of communications and stored data while
preserving law enforcement's
ability to legally gain access to
evidence
washingtonpost.com/wp-srv/
local/feed/
a18401-1999dec5.htm
Article, "Computer Crime Cases
Test Limits of Legal Searches" by
Brooke A. Masters

the degree to which the evidence presented to the magistrate establishes reason to believe that a large collection of similar contraband is present on the premises to be searched, and, second, the extent to which, in view of the possibilities, the warrant distinguishes, or provides the executing agents with criteria for distinguishing, the contraband from the rest of an individual's possessions. *United States v. Fuccillo*, 808 F.2d 173, 176 (1st Cir. 1987).

The court found that government agents could have but did not obtain specific information, for presentment to the magistrate and inclusion in the warrant, that would have enabled the agents executing the search to differentiate contraband cartons of women's clothing from legitimate ones. The warrants were invalidated for failure to specify as nearly as possible the distinguishing characteristics of the goods to be seized.

Courts also allow a relaxation of the particularity requirement for search warrants seeking business records of businesses "permeated with fraud."

[W]here there is probable cause to believe that a business is "permeated with fraud," either explicitly stated in the supporting affidavit or implicit from the evidence therein set forth, a warrant may authorize the seizure of all documents relating to the suspected criminal area but may not authorize the seizure of any severable portion of such documents relating to legitimate activities. *United States v. Oloyede*, 982 F.2d 133, 141 (4th Cir. (1991).

The particular description of items to be seized was an issue in the case of *United States v. Upham*, 168 F.3d 532 (1st Cir. 1999) in which a search warrant was issued for "any and all computer software and hardware, computer disks, disk drives . . . [and] any and all visual depictions, in any format or media, of minors engaging in sexually explicit conduct." The Court held that the description of the items to be seized was not constitutionally overly broad. The Court said:

As a practical matter, the seizure and subsequent off-premises search of the computer and all available disks was about the narrowest definable search and seizure reasonably likely to obtain the images. A sufficient chance of finding some needles in the computer haystack was established by the probable-cause showing in the warrant application; and a search of a computer and co-located disks is not inherently more intrusive than the physical search of an entire house for a weapon or drugs. We conclude . . . that the first paragraph was not unconstitutionally overbroad.

Of course, if the images themselves could have been easily obtained through an on-site inspection, there might have been no justification for allowing the seizure of all computer equipment, a category potentially including equipment that contained no images and had no connection to the crime. But it is no easy task to search a well-laden hard drive by going through all of the information it contains, let alone to search through it and the disks for information that may have been "deleted." The record shows that the mechanics of the search for images later performed off site could not readily have been done on the spot. 168 F3d at 535.

A general description will usually not be allowed if a more specific description is possible. In *United States v. Townsend*, 394 F.Supp. 736 (E.D. Mich. 1975), a search warrant commanded the seizure of "Stolen firearms, app. ten (10), which are stored in the basement of the above location, and in bedrooms, and any and all other stolen items, contraband." The court held that the phrase "any and all other stolen items" was impermissibly vague. With respect to the description "10 firearms," the court said:

Firearms may be easily characterized by color, length, type and other defining attributes. Therefore, further description in the instant case is far from a "virtual impossibility," and the generic description in combination with the other defects in particularity, constitutes a violation of defendant's Fourth Amendment Guarantee. 394 F.Supp. at 747. . . .

Courts generally allow greater leeway in descriptions of contraband material.

If the purpose of the search is to find a specific item of property, it should be so particularly described in the warrant as to preclude the possibility of the officer seizing the wrong property; whereas, on the other hand, if the purpose is to seize not a specific property, but any property of a specified character, which by reason of its character is illicit or contraband, a specific particular description of the property is unnecessary and it may be described generally as to its nature or character. *People v. Schmidt,* 473 P.2d 698, 700 (Colo. 1970).

In *United States v. Spears,* 965 F.2d 262 (7th Cir. 1992), the warrant authorized a search for and seizure of "controlled substances and other drug related paraphernalia, and materials for packaging controlled substances." The court held:

The terms "controlled substances" and "materials for packaging controlled substances" are sufficiently specific on their face. The catch-all term "other drug related paraphernalia" also passes constitutional muster in that such items are easily identifiable and quickly found by drug law enforcement officers. A search warrant delineating those items generally, in combination with named contraband, sufficiently limits an officer's discretion to execute the warrant. 965 F.2d at 277.

In *United States v. Appoloney,* 761 F.2d 520, 524 (9th Cir. 1985), the court found the following description sufficient: "'wagering paraphernalia' such as betting slips, bottom sheets and owe sheets, and journals and schedules of sporting events."

General descriptions will not be allowed, however, if the items to be searched for or seized are books, films, recordings, or other materials that have not yet been adjudged obscene. Because these materials are presumed protected by the First Amendment, a very high degree of particularity is required in both the affidavit and the warrant. As the U.S. Supreme Court stated, "[T]he constitutional requirement that warrants must particularly describe the 'things to be seized' is to be accorded the most scrupulous exactitude when the 'things' are books, and the basis for their seizure is the ideas which they contain. . . . No less a standard could be faithful to First Amendment freedoms." *Stanford v. Texas,* 379 U.S. 476, 485–86, 85 S.Ct. 506, 511–12, 13 L.Ed.2d 431, 437 (1965). Therefore, in a case in which a magistrate viewed two films from the defendant's adult bookstore, concluded they were obscene, and issued a warrant authorizing the seizure of all other obscene materials, the U.S. Supreme Court held that the warrant was a prohibited general warrant:

Stanford v. Texas
laws.findlaw.com/us/379/
476.html

[T]he warrant left it entirely to the discretion of the officials conducting the search to decide what items were likely obscene and to accomplish their seizure. The Fourth Amendment does not permit such action. . . . Nor does the Fourth Amendment countenance open-ended warrants, to be completed while a seizure is being conducted and items seized or after the seizure has been carried out. *Lo-Ji Sales, Inc. v. New York,* 442 U.S. 319, 325, 99 S.Ct. 2319, 2324, 60 L.Ed.2d 920, 927–28 (1979).

On the other hand, a court found a warrant authorizing a search for child pornography materials sufficiently particular in a case in which

- the warrant quoted the statute that particularly described the sexually explicit conduct depicted in the materials that was prohibited, and
- there was only a small possibility that materials depicting child pornography could be protected by the First Amendment. *United States v. Koelling,* 992 F.2d 817 (8th Cir. 1993).

MULTIPLE AFFIDAVITS   A law enforcement officer applying for a search warrant may submit more than one affidavit to the magistrate. The officer or someone else may prepare the additional or supplemental affidavits.

> Since the object of the proceedings before the magistrate is to establish probable cause to justify issuance of a search warrant, law enforcement officers should not be hindered in their efforts to describe the basis for probable cause in supporting affidavits. So long as these affidavits are satisfactorily incorporated to all related documents necessary to the application for the warrant . . . the reviewing court will be assured of the simultaneous presence of these documents before the magistrate, and the search may be subjected to authoritative judicial review. *State v. Gamage,* 340 A.2d 1, 7 (Me. 1975).

The essential requirement is that all "affidavits are satisfactorily incorporated to all related documents necessary to the application for the warrant." The following procedure is suggested to ensure proper incorporation:

1. Entitle the first or primary affidavit "Affidavit and Request for Search Warrant."
2. Entitle all additional affidavits "Supplemental Affidavit 1," "Supplemental Affidavit 2," and so forth.
3. Include the following statement in the first or primary affidavit: "This request is also based on the information in the sworn statements in Supplemental Affidavit 1, Supplemental Affidavit 2, . . . which are attached." (The law requires that clear reference be made to all supplemental affidavits).
4. Securely attach all supplemental affidavits to the primary affidavit. Use a stapler or other semipermanent method of binding. A paper clip would be unsatisfactory because of its tendency to slip off.

By following these simple steps, the officer ensures that the magistrate will be simultaneously presented with all the information on which probable cause is to be based and that the appellate court will be able to effectively review the magistrate's decision.

Securing of Dwelling while Warrant Is Being Sought

When officers have probable cause to believe that evidence of criminal activity is in a dwelling, a temporary securing of the dwelling to prevent removal or destruction of evidence while a search warrant is being sought is not an unreasonable seizure of either the dwelling or its contents. The U.S. Supreme Court said:

> [T]he home is sacred in Fourth Amendment terms not primarily because of the occupants' *possessory* interests in the premises, but because of their *privacy* interests in the activities that take place within. . . . [A] seizure affects only possessory interests, not privacy interests. Therefore, the heightened protection we accord privacy interests is simply not implicated where a seizure of premises, not a search, is at issue. *Segura v. United States,* 468 U.S. 796, 810, 104 S.Ct. 3380, 3388, 82 L.Ed.2d 599, 612 (1984).

Segura v. United States
laws.findlaw.com/us/468/
796.html

Furthermore, the *Segura* case held that insofar as the *seizure* of the premises is concerned, it made no difference whether the premises were secured by stationing officers within the premises or by establishing a perimeter stakeout after a security check of the premises revealed that no one was inside. Under either method, officers control the premises pending arrival of the warrant. Both an internal securing and a perimeter stakeout interfere to the same extent with the possessory interests of the owners.

In *Illinois v. McArthur,* ___ U.S. ___, 121 S.Ct. 946, 148 L.Ed.2d 838 (2001), police officers, with probable cause to believe that the defendant had hidden marijuana in his home, prevented him from entering the home for about two hours while they obtained a warrant. Rather than employ a *per se* rule of unreasonableness, the U.S. Supreme Court balanced the privacy-related and law enforcement-related concerns and found the warrantless intrusion reasonable, and therefore lawful. First, the police had probable cause to believe that the defendant's home contained evidence of a crime and contraband, namely, unlawful drugs. Second, the police had good reason to fear that, unless restrained, the defendant would destroy the drugs before they could return with a warrant. Third, the police neither searched the home nor arrested the defendant, but imposed the significantly less restrictive restraint of preventing him from entering the home unaccompanied. Finally, the police imposed the restraint for a limited period of time, namely, two hours—the time reasonably necessary to obtain a warrant. "Given the nature of the intrusion and the law enforcement interest at stake, this brief seizure of the premises was permissible." ___ U.S. at ___, 121 S.Ct. at 953, 148 L.Ed.2d at 849.

Illinois v. McArthur
laws.findlaw.com/us/000/
99-1132.html

State courts have further refined the circumstances justifying the securing of a dwelling while a warrant is being sought. For example, the Virginia Court of Appeals held:

> To determine whether a warrantless entry for the limited purpose of securing the premises is reasonable, we must balance the law enforcement need to preserve evidence and protect its officers against the individual's privacy interest in maintaining the sanctity of the home. We find that the balance is weighted in favor of entry when, based on the totality of the circumstances, the following factors are present: (1) police officers have probable cause to believe evidence is on the premises; (2) delaying entry would create a substantial risk that evidence will be lost or destroyed or the critical nature of the circumstances prevents the use of any warrant procedure; and (3) the police must not be responsible for creating their own exigencies. . . .
>
> Once an entry has been justified under the three-pronged test enunciated above, in order to determine if anyone is present who might destroy evidence or pose a threat to police safety, police officers may conduct a limited security check in those areas where individuals could hide. If this security check reveals that no one is on the premises, the police have no legitimate reason to remain on the premises and should leave once they have secured the premises. If police suspect that others may soon arrive who would destroy evidence, they should then set up an external stakeout, which constitutes a lesser form of intrusion. *Crosby v. Commonwealth*, 367 S.E.2d 730, 735–36 (Va.App. 1988).

Anticipatory Search Warrants

An **anticipatory search warrant,** also called a prospective search warrant, is a warrant to search a particular place for a particular seizable item that has not yet arrived at the place where the search is to be executed. In recent years, law enforcement officers have applied for anticipatory search warrants in increasing numbers, especially in cases involving contraband in the mails and those involving informants or undercover officers. In general, courts have held that anticipatory warrants, if issued under proper circumstances, upon a proper showing, and with proper safeguards, do not violate the Fourth Amendment.

> [W]hen law enforcement personnel offer a magistrate reliable, independent evidence indicating that a delivery of contraband will very likely occur at a particular place, and when the magistrate conditions the warrant's execution for the search of that place on that delivery, the warrant, if not overbroad or otherwise defective, passes constitutional muster. That the contraband has not yet reached the premises to be searched at the time the warrant issues is not, in constitutional terms, an insuperable obstacle. *United States v. Ricciardelli,* 998 F.2d 8, 11 (1st Cir. 1993).

Although anticipatory search warrants are not constitutionally forbidden, a warrant conditioned on a future event presents a potential for abuse above and beyond that which exists in more traditional settings. Officers executing these warrants are inevitably called on to determine when and whether the triggering event specified in the warrant has actually occurred. Therefore, magistrates who are asked to issue anticipatory warrants must be particularly vigilant in ensuring that opportunities for exercising unfettered discretion are eliminated. To satisfy these concerns, the magistrate must set conditions governing the execution of an anticipatory warrant that are "explicit, clear, and narrowly drawn so as to avoid misunderstanding or manipulation by government agents." *United States v. Garcia,* 882 F.2d 699, 703–04 (2nd Cir. 1989).

> There are two particular dimensions in which anticipatory warrants must limit the discretion of government agents. First, the magistrate must ensure that the triggering event is both ascertainable and preordained. The warrant should restrict the officers' discretion in detecting the occurrence of the event to almost ministerial proportions, similar to a search party's discretion in locating the place to be searched. Only then, in the prototypical case, are the ends of explicitness and clarity served. Second, the contraband must be on a sure and irreversible course to its destination, and a future search of the destination must be made expressly contingent upon the contraband's arrival there. Under such circumstances, a number of courts have found anticipatory search warrants to be valid. *United States v. Ricciardelli,* 998 F.2d 8, 12 (1st Cir. 1993).

A search warrant was held invalid in *State v. Vitale,* 530 P.2d 394 (Ariz.App. 1975), because of failure to satisfy the "sure and irreversible course" requirement. In that case, a warrant to search the defendant's pawnshop was issued on the basis that a reliable informant had agreed to sell a stolen television set to the defendant at the pawnshop. The police had the television in their possession at the time they applied for the warrant. After the sale, the warrant was executed and the television was seized. The court held that there was no probable cause that a crime had been committed at the time the warrant was issued.

> The informant had not yet approached appellant regarding the television set at the time the . . . search warrant was issued; also there had not been any recent dealings between the informant and appellant. . . .
>
> In the instant case, no crime was in progress and it was a matter of speculation whether one would be committed in the future. The course of events strongly suggests that the duty to determine probable cause was improperly shifted from the magistrate to the police. 530 P.2d at 397–98.

If there had been some deal or arrangement between the informant and the defendant before the police applied for the warrant, the court might have found the warrant valid on the ground that a crime was in progress or at least was very likely to occur.

To ensure that a magistrate is provided with sufficient information to justify the issuance of an anticipatory search warrant, law enforcement officers should present strong evidence in an affidavit that the continuation of a process *already initiated* will result in seizable items arriving at a particular place at a particular time. To guard against premature execution of the warrant, the affidavit should carefully specify the time when the item to be seized will arrive at the place where the search is to occur and the time thereafter when the execution of the warrant is planned. This information will help satisfy the magistrate that the warrant will not be executed prematurely.

www.totse.com/en/law/
justice_for_all/anticser.html
Article, "Anticipatory Search
Warrants" by A. Louis Di Pietro

Redaction of Search Warrants

Search warrants may contain some clauses that are constitutionally sufficient and some that are not. Should courts suppress all evidence under these warrants, or only the evidence seized under the constitutionally insufficient clauses? To avoid the severe remedy of total suppression of all evidence under these warrants, many courts have adopted the theory of **redaction,** also called *partial suppression* and *severability*. Redaction involves invalidating clauses in a warrant that are constitutionally insufficient for lack of probable cause or particularity while preserving clauses that satisfy the Fourth Amendment.

Not all courts have adopted the concept of redaction, and the U.S. Supreme Court has not yet spoken on the issue. Those that have adopted redaction point out that it is not inconsistent with the deterrent effect of the exclusionary rule. Illegally seized evidence is still suppressed, thereby discouraging law enforcement officials from attempting to evade Fourth Amendment requirements and preventing the government from benefiting from its own wrongdoing. Yet redaction mitigates the heavy social costs of unnecessarily excluding legally seized evidence. As a further constitutional safeguard, courts have been careful not to use redaction when "the warrant, when read with the affidavit, is essentially general in character but as to some tangential items meets the requirement of particularity." *United States v. Cook,* 657 F.2d 730, 735 n.6 (5th Cir. 1981).

The Third Circuit Court of Appeals found that redaction is consistent with all five purposes of the warrant requirement:

> First, with respect to the search and seizure conducted pursuant to the valid portion of the redacted warrant, the intrusion into personal privacy has been justified by probable cause to believe that the search and seizure will serve society's need for law enforcement. Second, because it is a duly issued warrant that is being redacted, the objective of interposing a magistrate between law enforcement officials and the citizen has been attained. Third, even though it may not be coterminous with the underlying probable cause showing, the scope of a search pursuant to a particularized, overbroad warrant is nevertheless limited by the terms of its authorization. In the case of a warrant containing some invalid general clauses, redaction neither exacerbates nor ratifies the unwarranted intrusions conducted pursuant to the general clauses, but merely preserves the evidence seized pursuant to those clauses particularly describing items to be seized. Fourth, as to the valid portions of the warrant salvaged by redaction, the individual whose property is to be searched has received notification of the lawful authority of the executing officer, his need to search, and the limits of his power to search. Fifth, redaction does not affect the

Key Points

1. An issuing magistrate for a search warrant must be neutral, detached, and capable of determining whether probable cause exists for the requested search.

2. Before issuing a search warrant, the magistrate must have probable cause to believe that items subject to seizure are in a particular place or on a particular person at the time of the issuance of the warrant.

3. If a law enforcement officer knowingly and intentionally, or with reckless disregard for the truth, makes false statements in an affidavit supporting a request for a search warrant, the warrant may not issue or evidence seized under the warrant may be suppressed.

4. Probable cause to search for certain objects may become stale if there is too long a delay between the time when the information on which probable cause is based is gathered and the time when the search is executed. Depending on the nature of the object, the nature of the criminal activity, the criminal suspects, and other factors, there may no longer be good reason to believe that the property is still at the same location.

5. Generally, the types of property allowed to be seized under a search warrant are evidence of crime, contraband, fruits of crime, things otherwise criminally possessed, and instrumentalities of crime.

6. The affidavit supporting a request for a search warrant for a place must contain a description of the premises to be searched that points directly to a definitely ascertainable place to the exclusion of all others.

7. The affidavit supporting a request for a search warrant must contain a particular description of the items to be seized.

8. When law enforcement officers have probable cause to believe that evidence of criminal activity is in a dwelling, a temporary securing of the dwelling to prevent removal or destruction of evidence while a search warrant is being sought is not an unreasonable seizure of either the dwelling or its contents.

9. An *anticipatory* or *prospective* search warrant is a warrant to search a particular place for a particular seizable item that has not yet arrived at the place where the search is to be executed.

10. *Redaction* of search warrants, also called *partial suppression* and *severability,* involves invalidating clauses in a warrant that are constitutionally insufficient for lack of probable cause or particularity while preserving clauses that satisfy the Fourth Amendment.

generation of a record susceptible to subsequent judicial review. *United States v. Christine,* 687 F.2d 749, 758 (3d Cir. 1982).

Contents of the Warrant

Although search warrants vary among jurisdictions, most search warrants contain the following information:

- The caption of the court or division of the court from which the warrant issues
- A particular description of the place or person to be searched
- A particular description of the property to be seized
- The names of persons whose affidavits have been taken in support of the warrant
- A statement of grounds for issuance of the warrant
- The name of the officer or officers to whom the warrant is directed together with a command to search the person or place named for the property specified
- A specification of the time during the day when the search may be conducted

AO 93 (Rev. 6/92)   Search Warrant

United States District Court

DISTRICT OF

In the Matter of the Search of

(Name, address or brief description of person or property to be searched)

SEARCH WARRANT

CASE NUMBER:

TO: _____ and any Authorized Officer of the United States

Affidavit(s) having been made before me by _____ who has reason to

Affiant

believe that ☐ on the person of or ☐ on the premises known as (name, description and/or location)

in the _____ District of _____ there is now
concealed a certain person or property, namely (describe the person or property)

I am satisfied that the affidavit(s) and any recorded testimony establish probable cause to believe that the person
or property so described is now concealed on the person or premises above-described and establish grounds for
the issuance of this warrant.

YOU ARE HEREBY COMMANDED to search on or before _____

Date

(not to exceed 10 days) the person or place named above for the person or property specified, serving this warrant
and making the search (in the daytime — 6:00 A.M. to 10:00 P.M.) (at any time in the day or night as I find
reasonable cause has been established) and if the person or property be found there to seize same, leaving a copy
of this warrant and receipt for the person or property taken, and prepare a written inventory of the person or property seized and promptly return this warrant to _____
as required by law.   U.S. Judge or Magistrate Judge

_____ at _____
Date and Time Issued   City and State

_____   _____
Name and Title of Judicial Officer   Signature of Judicial Officer

A Typical Search Warrant Form, Page 1
■ EXHIBIT 5.2A

- ■ The name of the judicial officer to whom the warrant is to be returned
- ■ The date of issuance
- ■ The signature of the issuing magistrate together with a statement of the magistrate's official title

Exhibits 5.2 and 5.3 are typical search warrant forms.

AO 93A (Rev. 5/85) Search Warrant Upon Oral Testimony

RETURN

DATE WARRANT RECEIVED	DATE AND TIME WARRANT EXECUTED	COPY OF WARRANT AND RECEIPT FOR ITEMS LEFT WITH

INVENTORY MADE IN THE PRESENCE OF

INVENTORY OF PERSON OR PROPERTY TAKEN PURSUANT TO THE WARRANT

CERTIFICATION

I swear that this inventory is a true and detailed account of the person or property taken by me on the warrant.

_____

Subscribed, sworn to, and returned before me this date.

_____   _____

U.S. Judge or Magistrate Judge   Date

A Typical Search Warrant Form, Page 2
■ EXHIBIT 5.2B

Execution of the Warrant

The execution (also called service) of a search warrant is essentially the carrying out of the command or commands appearing on the face of the warrant itself. The U.S. Supreme Court stated that "the Fourth Amendment confines an officer executing a search warrant strictly within the bounds set by the warrant. . . ." *Bivens v. Six Unknown Named Agents,* 403 U.S. 388, 394 n.7, 91 S.Ct. 1999, 2004 n.7, 29 L.Ed.2d 619, 625

Bivens v. Six Unknown Named Agents
laws.findlaw.com/us/403/388.html

AO 93A (Rev. 5/85) Search Warrant Upon Oral Testimony

United States District Court

DISTRICT OF _____

In the Matter of the Search of

(Name, address or brief description of person or property to be searched)

SEARCH WARRANT UPON ORAL TESTIMONY

CASE NUMBER: _____

TO: _____ and any Authorized Officer of the United States

Sworn oral testimony has been communicated to me by _____

　　　　　　　　　　　　　　　　　　　　　　　　　　　　　Affiant

that ☐ on the person of or ☐ on the premises known as (name, description and/or location)

in the _____ District of _____ there is now concealed a certain person or property, namely (describe the person or property)

I am satisfied that the circumstances are such as to make it reasonable to dispense with a written affidavit and that there is probable cause to believe that the property or person so described is concealed on the person or premises above described and that grounds for application for issuance of the search warrant exist as communicated orally to me in a sworn statement which has been recorded electronically, stenographically, or in longhand and upon the return of the warrant, will be transcribed, certified as accurate and attached hereto.

YOU ARE HEREBY COMMANDED to search on or before _____

　　　　　　　　　　　　　　　　　　　　　　　　　　　　　Date

the person or place named above for the person or property specified, serving this warrant and making the search (in the daytime — 6:00 AM to 10:00 PM) (at anytime in the day or night as I find reasonable cause has been established) and if the person or property be found there to seize same, leaving a copy of this warrant and receipt for the person or property taken, and prepare a written inventory of the person or property seized and promptly return this warrant to _____

as required by law.　　　　　　　U.S. Judge or Magistrate Judge

_____ at _____
Date and Time Issued　　　　　　　　　　　City and State

_____　　　_____
Name and Title of Judicial Officer　　　　　Signature of Judicial Officer

I certify that on _____ at _____ ,
　　　　　　　　　　Date　　　　　　　　　　　　Time

_____ orally authorized the
U.S. Judge or Magistrate Judge

issuance and execution of a search warrant conforming to all the foregoing terms.

_____　　　_____　　　_____
Name of affiant　　　　　　　　　Signature of affiant　　　　　　　Exact time warrant executed

A Typical Form for a Search Warrant upon Oral Testimony, Page 1
■ EXHIBIT 5.3A

caselaw.findlaw.com/data/constitution/amendment04/02.html#7
Comprehensive discussion (with annotations) of execution of search warrants
www.ccdb.org/search.html
Article, "The Execution of Search Warrants" by H. Patrick Furman
www.bileta.ac.uk/99papers/maclean.html
Article, "Basic Considerations in Investigating Computer Crime, Executing Computer Search Warrants and Seizing High Technology Equipment" by John J. McLean

n.7 (1971). Furthermore, "a search which is reasonable at its inception may violate the Fourth Amendment by virtue of its intolerable intensity and scope. . . . The scope of the search must be 'strictly tied to and justified by' the circumstances which rendered its initiation permissible." *Terry v. Ohio*, 392 U.S. 1, 18, 88 S.Ct. 1868, 1878, 20 L.Ed.2d 889, 903–04 (1968). Although officers can determine many of their duties from simply reading the warrant, several aspects of the execution of search warrants need further explanation.

Terry v. Ohio
laws.findlaw.com/us/392/1.html

AO 93A (Rev. 5/85) Search Warrant Upon Oral Testimony

RETURN

DATE WARRANT RECEIVED	DATE AND TIME WARRANT EXECUTED	COPY OF WARRANT AND RECEIPT FOR ITEMS LEFT WITH

INVENTORY MADE IN THE PRESENCE OF

INVENTORY OF PERSON OR PROPERTY TAKEN PURSUANT TO THE WARRANT

CERTIFICATION

I swear that this inventory is a true and detailed account of the person or property taken by me on the warrant.

_____

Subscribed, sworn to, and returned before me this date.

_____   _____

U.S. Judge or Magistrate Judge   Date

A Typical Form for a Search Warrant upon Oral Testimony, Page 2
■ EXHIBIT 5.3B

Who May Execute

A search warrant is directed to a particular officer or class of officers. Only the named officer or a member of the named class of officers may execute or serve the warrant. If a warrant is directed to a particular officer such as a sheriff, a deputy may execute the warrant and the sheriff need not be present. Private persons may be enlisted to help in the execution of a warrant, but an officer to whom the warrant is directed must be personally present at the search scene. As with an arrest warrant, "it is a violation of the

Fourth Amendment for police to bring members of the media or other third parties into a home during the execution of a warrant when the presence of the third parties in the home was not in aid of the execution of the warrant." *Wilson v. Layne,* 526 U.S. 603, 614, 119 S.Ct. 1692, 1699, 143 L.Ed.2d 818, 830 (1999).

Wilson v. Layne
laws.findlaw.com/us/000/
98-83.html

Time Considerations

Three different aspects of time affect a law enforcement officer in the execution of a search warrant. First is the allowable delay between the warrant's issuance and its execution. In jurisdictions with no time limit fixed by statute, court rule, or judicial decision, a warrant must be executed within a reasonable time after issuance. Reasonableness depends on the facts and circumstances of each case.

The chief concern of the courts is that probable cause does not become stale before execution of the warrant. Some jurisdictions require that a search warrant be executed and returned within ten days after its date of issuance. Some of these jurisdictions also require that the warrant be executed "forthwith." To resolve this apparent ambiguity, courts require that the warrant be executed within a reasonable time after issuance, so long as it is executed within the statutory period. *United States v. Harper,* 450 F.2d 1032 (5th Cir. 1971). *Therefore, even though an officer executed the warrant within the statutory ten-day period, the search could still be held unlawful if there had been unnecessary delay resulting in legal prejudice to the defendant.*

Unnecessary delay is determined from the facts and circumstances of each case. In a case interpreting a statute with both a "ten-day" provision and a "forthwith" provision, a warrant for the seizure of equipment used to manufacture LSD was executed six days after its issuance. The court held that the execution was timely, as the premises were under daily surveillance, and no activity was noted until after the first five days. The court said:

> While it is desirable that police be given reasonable latitude to determine when a warrant should be executed, it is also necessary that search warrants be executed with some promptness in order to lessen the possibility that the facts upon which probable cause was initially based do not become dissipated.
>
> We adopt the reasoning of the Second Circuit in *Dunnings* to the effect that "forthwith" means any time within 10 days after the warrant is issued, provided that the probable cause recited in the affidavit continues until the time of execution, giving consideration to the intervening knowledge of the officers and the passage of time. *United States v. Nepstead,* 424 F.2d 269, 271 (9th Cir. 1970).

There are many justifications for delaying the execution of a search warrant. For example, weather conditions, long travel distances, traffic problems, and similar obstacles may prevent the prompt execution of the warrant. Delays may be necessary to gather sufficient human resources for the search, to protect the safety of the searching officers, to prevent the destruction of evidence, and to prevent the flight of a suspect. When the warrant is for the search of both a person and premises, the search may be delayed until the person is present on the premises. *People v. Stansberry,* 268 N.E.2d 431 (Ill. 1971).

Another aspect of time affecting the execution of a search warrant is the time of day during which the warrant may be executed. In general, search warrants should be executed in the daytime. Courts have always frowned on nighttime searches. The U.S. Supreme Court said that "it is difficult to imagine a more severe invasion of privacy than the nighttime intrusion into a private home. . . ." *Jones v. United States,* 357 U.S.

Jones v. United States
laws.findlaw.com/us/357/
493.html

493, 498, 78 S.Ct. 1253, 1257, 2 L.Ed.2d 1514, 1519 (1958). Furthermore, nighttime searches are more likely to be met with armed resistance. *State v. Brock,* 633 P.2d 805 (Or.App. 1981). As a result, to obtain a warrant authorizing a nighttime search, some jurisdictions require the affidavit to set forth specific facts showing a necessity for a nighttime search. Justification for a nighttime search has been found when a nighttime delivery of contraband was expected, when the property to be seized was likely to be removed promptly, and when part of a criminal transaction was to take place at night. *United States v. Curry,* 530 F.2d 636 (5th Cir. 1976).

Courts differ in their interpretations of when daytime and nighttime begin and end. A rule of thumb is that it is daytime when there is sufficient natural light to recognize a person's features. Otherwise, it is nighttime. Even if a nighttime search is not authorized, the execution of a search warrant that was begun in the daytime may be continued into the nighttime if it is a reasonable continuation of the daytime search. An officer is not required to cut short the reasonable execution of a daytime search warrant just because it becomes dark outside. *United States v. Joseph,* 278 F.2d 504 (3d Cir. 1960).

The third aspect of time, as it relates to the execution of a search warrant, is the amount of time allowed for the law enforcement officer to perform the search *once it is initiated.* The general rule was stated by the New Hampshire Supreme Court: "The police, in executing a search warrant for a dwelling, may remain on the premises only so long as it is reasonably necessary to conduct the search." *State v. Chaisson,* 486 A.2d 297, 303 (N.H. 1984). Furthermore, as stated by the Tenth Circuit Court of Appeals, "once a search warrant has been fully executed and the fruits of the search secured, the authority under the warrant expires and further governmental intrusion must cease." *United States v. Gagnon,* 635 F.2d 766, 769 (10th Cir. 1980). Therefore, after all the objects described in a warrant have been found, the warrant provides no authorization to search further. If, however, the executing officers have found some but not necessarily all of the described items, the search may lawfully continue.

Knock-and-Announce Requirement

Similar considerations apply to the entry of dwellings to search as apply to the entry of dwellings to arrest, as discussed in Chapter 4 under "Forced Entry." Law enforcement officers should knock and announce their authority and purpose before entering premises to execute a search warrant. Usually an announcement of identity as a law enforcement officer together with a statement that the officer has a search warrant is sufficient. A person may not refuse entry to an officer executing a warrant but must submit voluntarily. *State v. Valentine,* 504 P.2d 84 (Or. 1972). If entry is refused, the officer may enter using force, including breaking open doors and windows. The occupant must be given a brief opportunity to respond before entry is forced. Failure to respond or other behavior inconsistent with voluntary compliance is equivalent to refusal, however. Unoccupied premises may be entered, forcefully if reasonably necessary, as if officers had been refused entry. The sound of footsteps, whispers, or flushing toilets, indicating possible escape or destruction of evidence, may create exigent circumstances justifying an immediate forcible entry. *United States v. Mitchell,* 783 F.2d 971 (10th Cir. 1986).

The purposes of the so-called knock-and-announce requirements are as follows:

- To prevent violence to the police or other persons on the premises
- To protect the privacy of the occupants of the premises from unexpected intrusions
- To prevent property damage

■ To provide the occupant an opportunity to examine the warrant and point out a possible mistaken address or other errors

"Although a search or seizure of a dwelling might be constitutionally defective if police officers enter without prior announcement, law enforcement interests may also establish the reasonableness of an unannounced entry." *Wilson v. Arkansas,* 514 U.S. 927, 936, 115 S.Ct. 1914, 1919, 131 L.Ed.2d 976, 984 (1995). For example, the *Wilson* case recognized that the knock-and-announce requirement could give way under circumstances presenting a threat of physical violence or when law enforcement officers have reason to believe that evidence would likely be destroyed or concealed if advance notice were given. In *Richards v. Wisconsin,* 520 U.S. 385, 117 S.Ct. 1416, 137 L.Ed.2d 615 (1997), however, the Court refused to allow a blanket exception to the knock-and-announce requirement in felony drug cases. The Court said:

> [T]he fact that felony drug investigations may frequently present circumstances warranting a no-knock entry cannot remove from the neutral scrutiny of a reviewing court the reasonableness of the police decision not to knock and announce in a particular case. Instead, in each case, it is the duty of a court confronted with the question to determine whether the facts and circumstances of the particular entry justified dispensing with the knock-and-announce requirement. 520 U.S. at 394, 117 S.Ct. at 1421, 137 L.Ed.2d at 624.

The Court then established a "reasonable suspicion" standard for determining exceptions to the knock-and-announce requirement.

> In order to justify a "no-knock" entry, the police must have a reasonable suspicion that knocking and announcing their presence, under the particular circumstances, would be dangerous or futile, or that it would inhibit the effective investigation of the crime by, for example, allowing the destruction of evidence. This standard—as opposed to a probable cause requirement—strikes the appropriate balance between the legitimate law enforcement concerns at issue in the execution of search warrants and the individual privacy interests affected by no-knock entries. . . . This showing is not high, but the police should be required to make it whenever the reasonableness of a no-knock entry is challenged. 520 U.S. at 394–95, 117 S.Ct. at 1421–22, 137 L.Ed.2d at 624.

In *United States v. Fields,* 113 F.3d 313 (2d Cir. 1997), the court found that officers had reasonable suspicion to justify a forcible unannounced entry when police had been informed by a "known and reliable" informant that the defendant was engaged in a cocaine-bagging operation and would be leaving his premises soon, the defendant had a known potential for violence, the defendant had been alerted that police were in his rear yard, and the defendant could have easily disposed of the drug evidence.

In *United States v. Ramirez,* 523 U.S. 65, 71, 118 S.Ct. 992, 996, 140 L.Ed.2d 191, 198 (1998), the U.S. Supreme Court held that "whether . . . a 'reasonable suspicion' exists depends in no way on whether police must destroy property in order to enter." In that case, officers executing a no-knock search warrant broke a single pane of glass in the defendant's garage because they had been informed that a violent prison escapee was on the premises and might have access to a stash of weapons reported to be kept in the garage. The Court held that this police conduct was clearly reasonable and therefore did not violate the Fourth Amendment. Nevertheless, the Court cautioned that the reasonableness standard governs the method of execution of warrants. "Excessive or unnecessary destruction of property in the course of a search may violate the Fourth Amendment, even though the entry itself is lawful and the fruits of the search not subject to suppression." 523 U.S. at 71, 118 S.Ct. at 996, 140 L.Ed.2d at 198.

Wilson v. Arkansas
laws.findlaw.com/us/000/
u10280.html

Richards v. Wisconsin
laws.findlaw.com/us/000/
96-5955.html

United States v. Ramirez
laws.findlaw.com/us/000/
96-1469.html

Case in Point

Interpreting *Richards v. Wisconsin* and *United States v. Ramirez*

A court commissioner in Milwaukee County issued a search warrant for heroin and related drug paraphernalia for the lower unit of a two-story house in Milwaukee where Davis lived. The warrant authorized police officers to enter the unit without first announcing their presence. A police detective's affidavit in support of the warrant averred that an informant had recently purchased heroin from a young woman on the porch of the house.

In support of the no-knock aspect of the warrant, the detective's supporting affidavit averred, in its pre-printed portion, that "drug traffickers are frequently armed with weapons, [and] controlled substances are quickly and easily destroyed." Additionally, the detective hand-printed the following reasons specific to the residence for which the warrant was sought: "A large dog was observed on the porch with several lookouts. Affiant knows lookouts and dogs are used to warn the trafficker of the approach of police to provide time for the trafficker to destroy evidence, arm themselves, and/or escape." The detective's affidavit also averred that "an informant" had previously purchased heroin from a "male at the same residence." Davis concedes that the affidavit supported the warrant's authorization for a no-knock entry.

In the late afternoon of the day after the court commissioner issued the warrant, a police officer dressed in casual street clothes went to the house for which the warrant was issued to make an undercover drug buy and to get a lay of the land for the officers who were going to execute the warrant. Davis answered the door, and let him into a "little hallway section" in the front of the house. The undercover officer gave ten dollars to Davis, who, according to his testimony at the suppression hearing, then "proceeded to walk down the hallway and turned left into an unknown room area." The officer also testified that although he did not see any weapons and neither saw nor heard any dogs, he "could hear at least three or four other people inside the room that [Davis] went into." He later told this to the officers who were going to execute the search warrant. Davis returned to the hallway with the heroin after ten or fifteen seconds. The undercover officer then asked for more heroin. He explained to the trial court that he "was trying to gain a little more time to see if I could hear any more or see anything else that could be helpful for the entry team after I had made the buy."

Officers executed the warrant minutes after the undercover officer reported his observations to them. The lead detective on the warrant-execution team testified that he decided to have the officers execute the warrant without knocking and announcing themselves even though the undercover officer did not see any lookouts and did not see or hear a dog, because the undercover officer stayed in the front hall area, and thus was "unable to eliminate the risk factors" of lookouts or the dog.

The lead detective told the trial court that several days before the warrant was executed, he had seen a man come out of the house that was the subject of the search warrant with "a rather large dog," which he described as being "about a little over knee height" and weighing approximately 120 pounds with the musculature of "a pit bull or a terrier of some sort." The man walked the dog down the block and then returned to the house with the dog. He went back into the house, and the dog was tied up on the porch.

The lead detective noted that even though the undercover officer had not seen the dog, it "very well could have been on the other side of the doorway inside the living room from where [the undercover officer] was standing." He also explained that although the lookouts were not outside the house when the undercover officer made his controlled purchases of heroin shortly before the warrant was executed, they could have been observing the street from the inside of the house. The lead detective told the trial court that heroin was "easy to destroy" because it is "a very light, powdery substance" with "a consistency of even lighter than talcum powder. If you were to put it in your hand and blow hard, it would form a cloud that—that would dissipate." He also testified that if heroin were put into water, "unless we catch the water before it goes down the drain, it's—it's impossible to recover." In light of *Richards v. Wisconsin* and *United States v. Ramirez*, should the defendant's motion to suppress the evidence seized as a result of the search be granted? *State v. Davis*, 2000 WL 1665051, 2000 WI App 270 (Wis.App. 2000).

Read the court opinion at:
www.wisbar.org/WisCtApp2/4q00/99-2537.htm

Some courts allow an exception to the knock-and-announce requirement when entry is achieved by ruse or deception. In *United States v. Contreras-Ceballos*, 999 F.2d 432 (9th Cir. 1993), an officer executing a search warrant for drugs knocked on the defendant's door and replied "Federal Express" when asked who was there. When the door was opened, the officer pushed his way in and announced his authority and purpose. The court held that the use of force to keep the door open and to enter did not violate the knock-and-announce requirement because there was no "breaking." "To rule otherwise would dictate a nonsensical procedure in which the officers, after having employed a permissible ruse to cause the door to be opened, must permit it to be shut by the occupants so that the officers could then knock, reannounce, and open the door forcibly if refused admittance." 999 F.2d at 435.

Finally, knocking and announcing "is excused when the officers are justifiably and virtually certain that the occupants already know their purpose." *United States v. Eddy,* 660 F.2d 381, 385 (8th Cir. 1981). In *United States v. Tracy,* 835 F.2d 1267 (8th Cir. 1988), the court held that the officers' failure to announce their purpose after knocking did not invalidate the search. Surveillance of the premises to be searched for drugs revealed attempts to fortify the premises and indications that the occupants were monitoring the surrounding area. Under these circumstances, the officers could have justifiably believed that the defendants were anticipating their arrival and knew their purpose. Announcing their purpose would have been a useless gesture and, in addition, could have resulted in the destruction of evidence. Nevertheless, since compliance with the knock-and-announce requirement is simple and effortless, it is seldom wise for an officer to assume a defendant's knowledge and risk having evidence excluded because of noncompliance with the requirement. A defendant may know the officer's authority and purpose but may not know of the existence of a warrant.

Note that some states have enacted "no-knock" laws that permit magistrates to issue search warrants specifically authorizing officers to enter premises without knocking and announcing their authority and purpose. The officer applying for the warrant must convince the magistrate that unannounced entry is necessary to prevent destruction of evidence or to prevent harm to the executing officer or others. These no-knock warrants have been criticized on the ground that exigent circumstances can only be determined at the time of executing the warrant and cannot be prejudged at the time of applying for the warrant. *Parsley v. Superior Court,* 513 P.2d 611 (Cal. 1973).

A separate issue is whether law enforcement officers executing a search warrant may lawfully gain access to the area to be searched by entering areas not particularly described in the warrant. In general, courts have approved any means of gaining entry that was both reasonable and necessary. In *Dalia v. United States,* the U.S. Supreme Court approved a covert entry into a dwelling by officers attempting to install electronic surveillance equipment pursuant to a warrant. The Court said that it is generally left to the discretion of the executing officers to determine the details of conducting the search under the warrant. The Court added:

> Often in executing a warrant the police may find it necessary to interfere with privacy rights not explicitly considered by the judge who issued the warrant. For example, police executing an arrest warrant commonly find it necessary to enter the suspect's home in order to take him into custody, and they thereby impinge on both privacy and freedom of movement. . . . Similarly, officers executing search warrants on occasion must damage property in order to perform their duty. 441 U.S. 238, 257–58, 99 S.Ct. 1682, 1693–94, 60 L.Ed.2d 177, 193 (1979).

Therefore, officers executing a search warrant may use whatever method is reasonably necessary to gain access to premises to be searched, even to the extent of damaging property, if no reasonable alternative is available.

www.fbi.gov/publications/leb/
1997/may976.htm
Article, "Knock and Announce:
A Fourth Amendment Standard"
by Michael J. Bulzomi

www.findarticles.com/cf_0/
m1571/28_16/63940704/p1/
article.jhtml
Article, "Do Federal Police Need
Expanded Powers to Do No-
Knock Searches?" by Clifford S.
Fishman

www.pbx.org/9x/hp/FTPsites/
blackcrwl/survive/searches.txt
Article, "Emergency Searches of
Effects" by John Gales Sauls

www.cybercrime.gov/
searchmanual.htm#IIb5
Federal guidelines on no-knock
warrants in the search and
seizure of computers

Dalia v. United States
laws.findlaw.com/us/441/
238.html

Search and Seizure of Third Persons and Their Property

When a search warrant is issued for the search of a named person or a named person *and* premises, officers executing the warrant clearly can detain and search the person named. However, may a person on the premises but not named in the warrant be detained or searched? *The general rule is that the search warrant for premises gives a law enforcement officer no authority to search a person not named in the warrant who merely happens to be on the premises.* In *Ybarra v. Illinois*, 444 U.S. 85, 100 S.Ct. 338, 62 L.Ed.2d 238 (1979), the defendant was a mere patron in a bar and the police had a warrant to search the bar and the bartender. The U.S. Supreme Court held that the search of the defendant was illegal because the police did not have probable cause particularized with respect to the defendant.

Ybarra v. Illinois
laws.findlaw.com/us/444/85.html

> [A] person's mere propinquity to others independently suspected of criminal activity does not, without more, give rise to probable cause to search that person. . . . Where the standard is probable cause, a search or seizure of a person must be supported by probable cause particularized with respect to that person. This requirement cannot be undercut or avoided by simply pointing to the fact that coincidentally there exists probable cause to search or seize another or to search the premises where the person may happen to be. The Fourth and Fourteenth Amendments protect the "legitimate expectations of privacy" of persons, not places. 444 U.S. at 91, 100 S.Ct. at 342, 62 L.Ed.2d at 245.

The Court said that a warrant to search a place cannot normally be construed to authorize a search of each person in that place. Therefore, if an officer wishes to search a place and also specific persons expected to be at that place, the officer should obtain a search warrant to search the place and each specific person. To obtain such a warrant, the officer must establish in the affidavit probable cause to search the place and each specific individual.

Detention of persons present on premises to be searched under a warrant may be allowed in certain circumstances, however. In *Michigan v. Summers*, 452 U.S. 692, 101 S.Ct. 2587, 69 L.Ed.2d 340 (1981), the U.S. Supreme Court held that officers executing a valid search warrant for contraband may detain the occupants of the premises while the search is being conducted. The Court said that "[i]f the evidence that a citizen's residence is harboring contraband is sufficient to persuade a judicial officer that an invasion of the citizen's privacy is justified, it is constitutionally reasonable to require that citizen to remain while officers of the law execute a valid warrant to search his home." 452 U.S. at 704–05, 101 S.Ct. at 2595, 69 L.Ed.2d at 351. In explaining the justification for the detention, the Court emphasized the limited additional intrusion represented by the detention once a search of the home had been authorized by a warrant. The Court went on to say:

Michigan v. Summers
laws.findlaw.com/us/452/692.html

> In assessing the justification for the detention of an occupant of premises being searched for contraband pursuant to a valid warrant, both the law enforcement interest and the nature of the "articulable facts" supporting the detention are relevant. Most obvious is the legitimate law enforcement interest in preventing flight in the event that incriminating evidence is found. Less obvious, but sometimes of greater importance, is the interest in minimizing the risk of harm to the officers. Although no special danger to the police is suggested by the evidence in this record, the execution of a warrant to search for narcotics is the kind of transaction that may give rise to sudden violence or frantic efforts to conceal or destroy evidence. The risk of harm to both the police and the occu-

pants is minimized if the officers routinely exercise unquestioned command of the situation. . . . Finally, the orderly completion of the search may be facilitated if the occupants of the premises are present. Their self-interest may induce them to open locked doors or locked containers to avoid the use of force that is not only damaging to property but may also delay the completion of the task at hand. 452 U.S. at 702–03, 101 S.Ct. at 2594, 69 L.Ed.2d at 349–50.

An officer also has authority to conduct a limited patdown search or frisk for weapons of any person at the search scene who the officer reasonably believes is dangerous. The officer must be able to justify the frisk with specific facts and circumstances to support the belief that a particular person was dangerous. A mere suspicion or hunch that a person was dangerous will not justify a protective frisk. Nor will the unsupported premise of "officer safety" without individualized reasonable suspicion justify a protective frisk. (See Chapter 7 for details on conducting protective frisks.)

If an officer at a search scene obtains information constituting probable cause to make a felony arrest, or if a crime is being committed in the officer's presence, the officer may arrest the offender and search him or her incident to the arrest. (See Chapter 8 for details on search incident to arrest.)

Similar rules apply to the search and seizure of the *property* of third persons on the premises described in a warrant. For purposes of this discussion, a third person is a person who is not the target of the warrant and is not a resident of the target premises. In general, when a law enforcement officer executing a search warrant knows or reasonably should know that personal property located within the described premises belongs to a third person, the officer may not search or seize the property under authority of the warrant. In *State v. Lambert,* 710 P.2d 693 (Kan. 1985), a police officer executing a warrant for an apartment and its *male* occupant discovered three *women* in the kitchen of the apartment. The officers searched a purse lying on the kitchen table and found drugs. The court invalidated the search, finding that the officer had no reason to believe that the purse either belonged to the occupant of the premises or was part of the premises described in the search warrant. However, when officers neither know nor have reason to believe that property belongs to a third person, a search or seizure of the property will be upheld. In *Carman v. State,* 602 P.2d 1255 (Alaska 1979), the court upheld the search of a purse because the court found that the police did not know whether the purse belonged to a permanent resident of the apartment or a visitor.

Scope of the Search

A search warrant authorizing the search of particularly described premises justifies a search of the described land, all of the buildings on the land, and other things attached to or annexed to the land. *United States v. Meyer,* 417 F.2d 1020 (8th Cir. 1969). Courts have generally also allowed a search of any vehicles owned or controlled by the owner of the premises and found on the premises. *United States v. Percival,* 756 F.2d 600 (7th Cir. 1985). Searches of areas neighboring or adjacent to the particularly described premises are usually not allowed. However, if neighboring or adjacent areas are only nominally separate and actually used as a single living or commercial area, courts may allow the search of the entire area despite a limited warrant description. In *United States v. Elliott,* 893 F.2d 220 (9th Cir. 1990), the court held that the search of a storeroom behind an apartment did not exceed the scope of the warrant authorizing the search of the apartment. The storeroom was accessible through a hole cut in the wall of the suspect's bathroom and covered by a burlap bag. The court found that the unconventional means of access did not sever the room from the rest of the apartment. And in *United States v. Principe*, 499 F.2d 1135 (1st Cir. 1974), a search of a cabinet in a hallway several feet away from the apartment described in the search warrant was justified when the owner testified that the cabinet "went with the apartment."

Officers executing a search warrant may look only where the items described in the warrant might be concealed. The U.S. Supreme Court stated the general rule: "A lawful search of fixed premises generally extends to the entire area in which the object of the search may be found and is not limited by the possibility that separate acts of entry or opening may be required to complete the search." *United States v. Ross*, 456 U.S. 798, 820–21, 102 S.Ct. 2157, 2170–71, 72 L.Ed.2d 572, 591 (1982). The Court provided the following useful examples of the application of the rule:

United States v. Ross
laws.findlaw.com/us/456/
798.html

> [A] warrant that authorizes an officer to search a home for illegal weapons also provides authority to open closets, chests, drawers, and containers in which the weapon might be found. A warrant to open a footlocker to search for marijuana would also authorize the opening of packages found inside. A warrant to search a vehicle would support a search of every part of the vehicle that might contain the object of the search. When a legitimate search is under way, and when its purpose and its limits have been precisely defined, nice distinctions between closets, drawers, and containers, in the case of a home, or between glove compartments, upholstered seats, trunks and wrapped packages, in the case of a vehicle, must give way to the interest in the prompt and efficient completion of the task at hand. 456 U.S. at 821–22, 102 S.Ct. at 2171, 72 L.Ed.2d at 591.

Note that the U.S. Supreme Court extended the permissible scope of the search of an automobile in *Wyoming v. Houghton*, holding that "police officers with probable cause to search a car may inspect passengers' belongings found in the car that are capable of concealing the object of the search." 526 U.S. 295, 307 119 S.Ct. 1297, 1304, 143 L.Ed.2d 408, 419 (1999). The *Houghton* case is discussed in detail in Chapter 11.

Wyoming v. Houghton
laws.findlaw.com/us/000/
98-184.html

An inaccurate description of the premises to be searched may cause officers to exceed the scope of a warrant, especially with respect to multiple-occupancy dwellings. In *Maryland v. Garrison*, 480 U.S. 79, 107 S.Ct. 1013, 94 L.Ed.2d 72 (1987), officers obtained and executed a warrant to search the person of Lawrence McWebb and "the premises known as 2036 Park Avenue third floor apartment." The officers reasonably believed, on the basis of the information available, that only one apartment was located on the third floor. In fact, the third floor was divided into two apartments, one occupied by McWebb and one by the defendant. Before the officers discovered that they were in the wrong person's apartment, they had discovered contraband that led to the defendant's conviction.

Maryland v. Garrison
laws.findlaw.com/us/480/
79.html

The Court concluded that the officers had made a reasonable effort to ascertain and identify the place intended to be searched and that their failure to realize the overbreadth of the warrant was objectively understandable and reasonable. Nevertheless, the Court said:

> If the officers had known, or should have known, that the third floor contained two apartments before they entered the living quarters on the third floor, and thus had been aware of the error in the warrant, they would have been obligated to limit their search to McWebb's apartment. Moreover . . . they were required to discontinue the search of respondent's apartment as soon as they discovered that there were two separate units on the third floor and therefore were put on notice of the risk that they might be in a unit erroneously included within the terms of the warrant. 480 U.S. at 86–87, 107 S.Ct. at 1017–18, 94 L.Ed.2d at 82.

Therefore, although some latitude is allowed for honest mistakes in executing search warrants, officers may not rely blindly on the descriptions in a warrant but must make a reasonable effort to determine that the described place to be searched is the place *intended* to be searched.

Officers executing a search warrant must use only reasonable force in conducting the search. An otherwise reasonable search may be rendered unreasonable by the manner in which it is conducted. A search warrant gives officers authority to break into a house or other objects of search and to damage property if reasonably necessary to execute the warrant properly. In *United States v. Becker*, 929 F.2d 442 (9th Cir. 1991), the court found that the jackhammering of a concrete slab to execute a search warrant for drugs was reasonable, based on an examination of all the facts and circumstances: (1) officers had found evidence of the manufacture of methamphetamine in the shop next to the slab, (2) the concrete slab had been poured within the preceding forty-five days, and (3) the shop appeared to have been recently and hastily repainted and repaired. In a case involving a search of a vehicle for contraband, the U.S. Supreme Court said:

> An individual undoubtedly has a significant interest that the upholstery of his automobile will not be ripped or a hidden compartment within it opened. These interests must yield to the authority of a search, however. . . . *United States v. Ross*, 456 U.S. 798, 823, 102 S.Ct. 2157, 2172, 72 L.Ed.2d 572, 593 (1982).

Nevertheless, officers must exercise great care to avoid unnecessary damage to premises or objects. They must conduct a search in a manner designed to do the least damage possible, while still making a thorough examination of the premises. They should carefully replace objects that were necessarily moved or rearranged during the search. Generally, "[i]n executing a search warrant, to the extent possible, due respect should be given to the property of the occupants of the premises searched." *State v. Sierra*, 338 So.2d 609, 616 (La. 1976).

Finally, common decency and fair play mandate that officers executing a search warrant avoid any unnecessary injury to the feelings of persons present at the premises searched.

Seizure of Items Not Named in the Warrant

In *Coolidge v. New Hampshire,* the U.S. Supreme Court said that "[a]n example of the applicability of the 'plain view' doctrine is the situation in which the police have a warrant to search a given area for specific objects, and in the course of the search come across some other article of incriminating character." 403 U.S. 443, 465, 91 S.Ct. 2022, 2037, 29 L.Ed.2d 564, 582 (1971). This situation presented itself in *Cady v. Dombrowski,* 413 U.S. 433, 93 S.Ct. 2523, 37 L.Ed.2d 706 (1973), when police were investigating a possible homicide. The defendant informed the police that he believed there was a body lying near his brother's farm. The police found the body and the defendant's car at the farm. Looking in through the window of the car, the police observed a pillowcase, backseat, and briefcase covered with blood. Police then obtained a warrant to search the car for those items. While executing the warrant, police discovered, in "plain view" in the car, a blood-covered sock and floormat, which they seized. The defendant claimed that the sock and the floormat taken from his car were illegally seized since they were not specifically listed in the affidavit for the search warrant.

The Court held that the seizure of the items was constitutional. Since the warrant was validly issued and the car was the item designated to be searched, the police were authorized to search the car. Although the sock and floormat were not listed in the

Cady v. Dombrowski
laws.findlaw.com/us/413/
433.html

warrant, the officers discovered these items in plain view in the car while executing the warrant and therefore could constitutionally seize them without a warrant.

The U.S. Supreme Court did not elaborate on this decision. However, decisions of many courts since the *Dombrowski* decision have established the rule that *a law enforcement officer lawfully executing a valid search warrant may seize items not particularly described in the warrant that are found at the searched premises, if the seizure satisfies all the requirements of the plain view doctrine.* (See Chapter 10 for a complete discussion of the plain view doctrine.)

Duties after the Search Is Completed

Proper execution of a search warrant entails several duties after the actual search is completed. Most jurisdictions require that the officer conducting the search inventory all the property seized and leave a copy of the warrant and inventory with the occupants, or on the premises if no occupant is present. The warrant, together with a copy of the inventory, must be returned to the magistrate designated in the warrant. A typical form for the return and inventory (which is usually on the back of the search warrant) appears in Exhibits 5.2(b) and 5.3(b).

Courts unanimously hold that these postsearch duties are ministerial acts and that failure to perform them will not result in suppression unless the defendant demonstrates legal prejudice or shows that the failure was intentional or in bad faith. *United States v. Marx*, 635 F.2d 436 (5th Cir. 1981).

Key Points

11. In general, a search warrant should be executed in the daytime within a reasonable time after its issuance. Officers should remain on the searched premises only so long as is reasonably necessary to conduct the search.

12. Before law enforcement officers may lawfully force their way into a dwelling to execute a search warrant, they must first knock on the door, announce their authority and purpose, and then demand admittance. To justify an exception to this requirement, officers must have a reasonable suspicion that knocking and announcing their presence, under the particular circumstances, would be dangerous or futile or that it would inhibit the effective investigation of the crime by, for example, allowing the destruction of evidence.

13. A search warrant for premises gives a law enforcement officer no authority to *search* a person not named in the warrant who merely happens to be on the premises,

but an officer may *detain* such a person under certain circumstances.

14. A search warrant authorizing the search of particularly described premises justifies a search of the described land, all of the buildings on the land, and other things attached or annexed to the land.

15. A search authorized by a warrant for a particular object allows a search of the entire area in which the object may be found and allows the opening of closets, chests, drawers, and containers in which the object might be found.

16. A law enforcement officer lawfully executing a valid search warrant may seize items not particularly described in the warrant that are found at the searched premises, if the seizure satisfies all the requirements of the plain view doctrine.

Administrative Search Warrants

An **administrative search** is a routine inspection of a home or business by governmental authorities responsible for determining compliance with various statutes and regulations. An administrative search seeks to enforce fire, health, safety, and housing codes, licensing provisions, and the like. It differs from a criminal search in that a criminal search is directed toward gathering evidence to convict a person of a crime. An administrative search ordinarily does not result in a criminal prosecution.

Before 1967, courts consistently held that administrative searches were not subject to the restrictions of the Fourth Amendment and that a search warrant was not needed to inspect residential or commercial premises for violations of regulatory and licensing provisions. In 1967, in *Camara v. Municipal Court,* 387 U.S. 523, 87 S.Ct. 1727, 18 L.Ed.2d 930, involving the safety inspection of a dwelling, and *See v. City of Seattle,* 387 U.S. 541, 87 S.Ct. 1737, 18 L.Ed.2d 943, involving inspection of business premises for fire safety reasons, the U.S. Supreme Court reversed earlier decisions and held that administrative inspections were subject to the warrant requirement of the Fourth Amendment. The basis for both the *Camara* and *See* decisions was the Court's belief that a person's right of privacy should not be determined by the nature of the search. In *Camara,* the Court said, "It is surely anomalous to say that the individual and his private property are fully protected by the Fourth Amendment only when the individual is suspected of criminal behavior." 387 U.S. at 530, 87 S.Ct. at 1732, 18 L.Ed.2d at 936. In *See,* the Court said that a "businessman, like the occupant of a residence, has a constitutional right to go about his business free from unreasonable official entries upon his private commercial property. . . ." 387 U.S. at 543, 87 S.Ct. at 1739, 18 L.Ed.2d at 946. Nevertheless, the Court held that, because administrative searches differ in nature and purpose from criminal searches, the probable cause standard for administrative searches differs in nature and is less stringent than the standard for criminal searches.

> The warrant procedure is designed to guarantee that a decision to search private property is justified by a reasonable governmental interest. But reasonableness is still the ultimate standard. If a valid public interest justifies the intrusion contemplated, then there is probable cause to issue a suitably restricted search warrant. 387 U.S. at 539, 87 S.Ct. at 1736, 18 L.Ed.2d at 941.

The Court further explained the less stringent probable cause standard in *Marshall v. Barlow's, Inc.,* 436 U.S. 307, 320–21, 98 S.Ct. 1816, 1824–25, 56 L.Ed.2d 305, 316 (1978), a case involving a search of a business for occupational safety reasons.

> Probable cause in the criminal law sense is not required. For purposes of an administrative search such as this, probable cause justifying the issuance of a warrant may be based not only on specific evidence of an existing violation but also on a showing that "reasonable legislative or administrative standards for conducting an . . . inspection are satisfied with respect to a particular [establishment]" [citing *Camara*]. A warrant showing that a specific business has been chosen for an OSHA search on the basis of a general administrative plan for the enforcement of the Act derived from neutral sources such as, for example, dispersion of employees in various types of industries across a given area, and the desired frequency of searches in any of the lesser divisions of the area, would protect an employer's Fourth Amendment rights.

Exceptions to Warrant Requirement

Despite the less stringent probable cause standard, the U.S. Supreme Court and other courts have carved out various exceptions to the warrant requirement for administrative searches. Exceptions based on emergency, consent, plain view, and open fields are similar to exceptions to the warrant requirement for criminal searches discussed in

caselaw.findlaw.com/data/
constitution/amendment04/
01.html#7
Discussion (with annotations) of
searches and inspections in non-
criminal cases

Camara v. Municipal Court
laws.findlaw.com/us/387/
523.html

Marshall v. Barlow's, Inc.
laws.findlaw.com/us/436/
307.html

www.law.wfu.edu/faculty/wright/
Publications/YLJNote.htm
Article, "The Civil and Criminal
Methodologies of the Fourth
Amendment"

Part three of this book, but the standards are generally less stringent than those required for criminal searches. The Supreme Court has recognized another exception, allowing warrantless inspection of certain *licensed and closely regulated enterprises.* In *United States v. Biswell,* 406 U.S. 311, 92 S.Ct. 1593, 32 L.Ed.2d 87 (1972), the Court upheld a warrantless search of a gun dealer's storeroom licensed under the Gun Control Act of 1968. The Court said:

> [I]f inspection is to be effective and serve as a credible deterrent, unannounced, even frequent, inspections are essential. In this context, the prerequisite of a warrant could easily frustrate inspection; and if the necessary flexibility as to time, scope and frequency is to be preserved, the protections afforded by a warrant would be negligible.
>
> It is also plain that inspections for compliance with the Gun Control Act pose only limited threats to the dealer's justifiable expectations of privacy. When a dealer chooses to engage in this pervasively regulated business and to accept a federal license, he does so with the knowledge that his business records, firearms, and ammunition will be subject to effective inspection. 406 U.S. at 316, 92 S.Ct. at 1596, 32 L.Ed.2d at 92–93.

The Supreme Court held that inspections of licensed and closely regulated enterprises are reasonable only if they satisfy three criteria:

- a "substantial" government interest must support the regulatory scheme under which the inspection is made,
- the warrantless inspections must be necessary to further the regulatory scheme, and
- the regulatory statute must provide a constitutionally adequate substitute for a warrant by advising the owner of commercial premises that the search is being made pursuant to the law and has a properly defined scope and by limiting the discretion of the inspecting officers. *New York v. Burger,* 482 U.S. 691, 107 S.Ct. 2636, 96 L.Ed.2d 601 (1987).

In the *Burger* case, the Court found that a New York statute allowing warrantless inspection of automobile junkyards satisfied these criteria. The state had a substantial interest in regulating the automobile junkyard industry because motor vehicle theft had increased in the state and was associated with this industry. Warrantless inspections were necessary because frequent and unannounced inspections provide an element of surprise crucial to regulating the market in stolen cars and parts. Finally, the statute gave adequate notice to automobile junkyard operators and authorized inspections only during business hours and within a narrowly defined scope.

Distinction between Administrative and Criminal Search

Administrative search warrants and exceptions to the warrant requirement are not discussed in further detail because administrative searches are not conducted for purposes of the criminal law. However, the line between an administrative and a criminal search can sometimes become blurred. When an administrative search begins to take on the characteristics of a criminal search, the stricter standards applicable to criminal searches come into play. If these standards are not satisfied, any evidence obtained will be inadmissible in a criminal prosecution.

The line between administrative and criminal searches also may become obscured in fire investigation cases, because several different purposes may be served by a fire

United States v. Biswell
laws.findlaw.com/us/406/
311.html

New York v. Burger
laws.findlaw.com/us/482/
691.html

investigation and fire scenes present varying degrees of emergency. In addition, reasonable privacy expectations may remain in fire-damaged premises, thereby affecting the necessity to obtain a warrant.

> Privacy expectations will vary with the type of property, the amount of fire damage, the prior and continued use of the premises, and in some cases the owner's efforts to secure it against intruders. Some fires may be so devastating that no reasonable privacy interests remain in the ash and ruins, regardless of the owner's subjective expectations. The test essentially is an objective one: whether "the expectation [is] one that society is prepared to recognize as 'reasonable.'" . . . If reasonable privacy interests remain in the fire-damaged property, the warrant requirement applies, and any official entry must be made pursuant to a warrant in the absence of consent or exigent circumstances. *Michigan v. Clifford,* 464 U.S. 287, 292–93, 104 S.Ct. 641, 646, 78 L.Ed.2d 477, 483 (1984).

If a warrant is necessary, the purpose of the search determines the type of warrant required. If the primary purpose is to determine the cause and origin of a recent fire, only an administrative warrant is needed. To obtain an administrative warrant, "fire officials need show only that a fire of undetermined origin has occurred on the premises, that the scope of the proposed search is reasonable and will not intrude unnecessarily on the fire victim's privacy, and that the search will be executed at a reasonable and convenient time." *Michigan v. Clifford,* 464 U.S. 287, 294, 104 S.Ct. 641, 647, 78 L.Ed.2d 477, 484 (1984). If the primary purpose of the search is to gather evidence of criminal activity, a criminal search warrant may be obtained only on a showing of probable cause to believe that particularly described seizable property will be found in the place to be searched.

If evidence of criminal activity is discovered during the course of a valid administrative search, it may be seized under the plain view doctrine and used to establish probable cause to obtain a criminal search warrant. Fire officials may not, however, rely on this evidence to expand the scope of their administrative search without first satisfying an independent judicial officer that probable cause exists. The purpose of the search is important even if exigent circumstances exist.

> Circumstances that justify a warrantless search for the cause of a fire may not justify a search to gather evidence of criminal activity once that cause has been determined. If, for example, the administrative search is justified by the immediate need to ensure against rekindling, the scope of the search may be no broader than reasonably necessary to achieve its end. A search to gather evidence of criminal activity not in plain view must be made pursuant to a criminal warrant upon a traditional showing of probable cause. *Michigan v. Clifford,* 464 U.S. 287, 294–95, 104 S.Ct. 641, 647, 78 L.Ed.2d 477, 484–85 (1984).

An administrative search took on the characteristics of a criminal search in *Michigan v. Tyler,* 436 U.S. 499, 98 S.Ct. 1942, 56 L.Ed.2d 486 (1978), a case involving a late-night fire in a furniture store leased by the defendant. When the fire was reduced to smoldering embers, the fire chief, while investigating the cause of the fire, discovered two plastic containers of flammable liquid. The detective took several pictures, but because visibility was hindered by darkness, steam, and smoke, the investigators departed the scene at 4:00 A.M. and returned shortly after daybreak to continue the investigation. More evidence of arson was found and seized at that time. About a month later, a state police arson investigator made several visits to the fire scene and obtained evidence that was used at trial in convicting the defendant. At no time was any warrant or consent to search obtained.

www.interfire.com/res_file/
srchseiz.htm
Article, "Documentation of the Fire Scene: A Legal Perspective" by Guy E. Burnette

Michigan v. Clifford
laws.findlaw.com/us/464/
287.html

Michigan v. Tyler
laws.findlaw.com/us/436/
499.html

The Court held that the investigative activity on the date of the fire was legal but that the evidence-gathering activity a month after the fire was an illegal search and seizure.

> [W]e hold that an entry to fight a fire requires no warrant, and that once in the building, officials may remain there for a reasonable time to investigate the cause of the blaze. Thereafter, additional entries to investigate the cause of the fire must be made pursuant to the warrant procedures governing administrative searches. . . . Evidence of arson discovered in the course of such investigations is admissible at trial, but if the investigating officials find probable cause to believe that arson has occurred and require further access to gather evidence for a possible prosecution, they may obtain a warrant only upon a traditional showing of probable cause applicable to searches for evidence of crime. 436 U.S. at 511–12, 98 S.Ct. at 1951, 56 L.Ed.2d at 500.

Once a search is directed toward gathering evidence for a criminal prosecution, a criminal search warrant must be obtained. This requirement cannot be avoided by using other governmental officials to conduct searches under the guise of an administrative or regulatory inspection.

Key Points

17. An administrative search is a routine inspection of a home or business to determine compliance with various statutes and regulations, not to gather evidence for a criminal prosecution. Administrative searches are subject to the warrant requirement of the Fourth Amendment.

18. Because administrative searches differ in nature and purpose from criminal searches, the probable cause standard for administrative searches differs in nature and is less stringent than the standard for criminal searches.

19. Exceptions to the administrative warrant requirement based on emergency, consent, plain view, and open fields have less stringent standards than corresponding exceptions for criminal searches. Warrantless searches are also allowed for certain licensed and closely regulated enterprises.

20. If evidence of criminal activity is discovered during the course of a valid administrative search, it may be seized under the plain view doctrine and used to establish probable cause to obtain a criminal search warrant.

"Special Needs" Searches

The U.S. Supreme Court has also recognized an exception to warrant and probable cause requirements of the Fourth Amendment where "special needs" of the government, "beyond the normal need for law enforcement, make the warrant and probable-cause requirement impracticable." *Griffin v. Wisconsin*, 483 U.S. 868, 873, 107 S.Ct. 3164, 3168, 97 L.Ed.2d 709, 717 (1987). Under this exception, searches are evaluated under the "reasonableness" standard of the Fourth Amendment.

Griffin v. Wisconsin
laws.findlaw.com/us/483/
868.html

> To be reasonable under the Fourth Amendment, a search ordinarily must be based on individualized suspicion of wrongdoing. . . . But particularized exceptions to the main rule are sometimes warranted based on "special needs, beyond the normal need for law enforcement." . . . When such "special needs"—concerns other than crime detection—

are alleged in justification of a Fourth Amendment intrusion, courts must undertake a context-specific inquiry, examining closely the competing private and public interests advanced by the parties. *Chandler v. Miller,* 520 U.S. 305, 313–14, 117 S.Ct. 1295, 1301, 137 L.Ed.2d 513, 522–23 (1997).

Chandler v. Miller
laws.findlaw.com/us/000/
96-126.html

This requires balancing the nature and quality of the intrusion on the individual's Fourth Amendment interests against the importance of the governmental interests alleged to justify the intrusion.

Searches of Students

The U.S. Supreme Court created an exception to the warrant requirement, based on "special needs" for searches of students conducted by school officials. In *New Jersey v. T.L.O.,* 469 U.S. 325, 105 S.Ct. 733, 83 L.Ed.2d 720 (1985), the Court held that school officials carrying out searches and other functions pursuant to disciplinary policies act as representatives of the state and not merely as surrogates for parents and that they are therefore subject to the Fourth Amendment. However, in attempting to balance the students' legitimate privacy rights against the substantial interests of teachers and administrators in maintaining discipline in the classroom and on school grounds, the Court held that school officials need not obtain a warrant before searching students under their authority. The warrant requirement would unduly interfere with the maintenance of the swift and informal disciplinary procedures needed in the schools. Furthermore, rather than insist on strict adherence to the requirement that a search be based on probable cause to believe that the subject of the search has violated or is violating the law, "the legality of a search of a student should depend simply on the reasonableness, under all the circumstances, of the search." 469 U.S. at 341, 105 S.Ct. at 742, 83 L.Ed.2d at 734.

New Jersey v. T.L.O.
laws.findlaw.com/us/469/
325.html

www.keepschoolssafe.org/
leg.htm
Article, "Legal and Policy Issues
in Curbing Violence in Schools"
by Ann L. Majestic, Jonathan A.
Blumberg, Ruth T. Dowling, and
Tharrington Smith
www.keepschoolsafe.org/
check.htm
National Association of Attorneys General School Search
Checklists
attygen.state.ut.us/Utah%20
Search%20Manual%20for%20
Schools.htm
Utah School Search Manual
www.uncp.edu/home/
vanderhoof/sagan.html
List of several articles on school
searches
www.state.nj.us/lps/dcj/school/
New Jersey School Search
Policy Manual

Determining the reasonableness of any search involves an inquiry into (1) whether the action was justified at its inception and (2) whether the search as actually conducted was reasonably related in scope to the circumstances that justified the interference in the first place. The Court said:

> Under ordinary circumstances, a search of a student by a teacher or other school official will be "justified at its inception" when there are *reasonable grounds for suspecting* that the search will turn up evidence that the student has violated or is violating either the law or the rules of the school. Such a search will be permissible in its scope when the measures adopted are reasonably related to the objectives of the search and not excessively intrusive in light of the age and sex of the student and the nature of the infraction. 469 U.S. at 341–42, 105 S.Ct. at 744, 83 L.Ed.2d at 734–35. (Emphasis added.)

As indicated in the preceding quote, the school search approved in the *T.L.O.* case, while not based on probable cause, *was* based on individualized *suspicion* of wrongdoing. A similar standard was applied by the 7th Circuit Court of Appeals in *Willis v. Anderson Community School,* 158 F.3d 415 (7th Cir. 1998). That court held that to justify the search of a student, a student's conduct must "create a reasonable suspicion that a particular regulation or law has been violated, with the search serving to produce evidence of the violation." 158 F.3d at 418. The Fourth Amendment, however, imposes no irreducible requirement of individualized suspicion. In *Vernonia School District 47J v. Acton,* 515 U.S. 646, 115 S.Ct. 2386, 132 L.Ed.2d 564 (1995), the Court held that a public school's interest in deterring drug use by students constituted a "special need" justifying *suspicionless* random drug testing of students participating in

*Vernonia School District 47J
v. Acton*
laws.findlaw.com/us/000/
u10263.html

interscholastic athletics. The Court found that students in public schools have a decreased expectation of privacy because of the temporary custody, supervision, and control the school is required to exercise. Furthermore, student athletes have even less of a legitimate privacy expectation, because of the inherent elements of communal undress, physical examinations, and special rules regulating their conduct.

> Somewhat like adults who choose to participate in a "closely regulated industry," students who voluntarily participate in school athletics have reason to expect intrusions upon normal rights and privileges, including privacy. 515 U.S. at 657, 115 S.Ct. at 2393, 132 L.Ed.2d at 577.

Looking next to the character of the intrusion, the Court found that the search procedures were relatively unobtrusive, the conditions for the urine testing being nearly identical to those typically encountered in public rest rooms. Furthermore, the tests looked only for standard drugs, not medical conditions, and the test results were released to a limited group.

Finally, the Court found that deterring drug use by schoolchildren was clearly an important concern, noting that this program was directed more narrowly to drug use by school athletes, in which the risk of immediate physical harm to the drug user or other players is particularly high. As to the efficacy of the program for addressing the problem the Court found it "self-evident that a drug problem largely fueled by the 'role model' effect of athletes' drug use, and of particular danger to athletes, is effectively addressed by making sure that athletes do not use drugs." 515 U.S. at 663, 115 S.Ct. at 2395–96, 132 L.Ed.2d at 581.

The Court noted that the most significant element in approving this drug testing policy was that it was "undertaken in furtherance of the government's responsibilities, under a public school system, as guardian and tutor of children entrusted to its care." 515 U.S. at 665, 115 S.Ct. at 2396, 132 L.Ed.2d at 582. The Court cautioned against the assumption that suspicionless drug testing would readily pass constitutional muster in other contexts.

Searches of Government Employees

O'Connor v. Ortega
laws.findlaw.com/us/480/
709.html

In *O'Connor v. Ortega*, 480 U.S. 709, 107 S.Ct. 1492, 94 L.Ed.2d 714 (1987), the Supreme Court held that "special needs" may justify the search of a public employee's office by the employee's supervisor. The Court said that, in the case of searches conducted by a public employer, the invasion of the employee's legitimate expectations of privacy must be balanced against the government's need for supervision, control, and the efficient operation of the workplace. No search warrant is required for such searches.

> [R]equiring an employer to obtain a warrant whenever the employer wished to enter an employee's office, desk, or file cabinets for a work-related purpose would seriously disrupt the routine conduct of business and would be unduly burdensome. Imposing unwieldy warrant procedures in such cases upon supervisors, who would otherwise have no reason to be familiar with such procedures, is simply unreasonable. 480 U.S. at 722, 107 S.Ct. at 1500, 94 L.Ed.2d at 726.

www.co.alameda.ca.us/da/pov/
workplace.htm
Article, "Workplace Searches"
from the District Attorney's
Office in Alameda County,
California
www.fbi.gov/publications/leb/
1998/juneleb.pdf
Article, "The Workplace Privacy
of Law Enforcement and Public
Employees" by Michael J.
Bulzomi
(page 27 of the June 1998 *FBI
Law Enforcement Bulletin*)

The Court applied a reasonableness standard rather than a probable cause standard.

> [T]he "special needs, beyond the normal need for law enforcement make the . . . probable-cause requirement impracticable," . . . for legitimate work-related, noninvestigatory intrusions as well as investigations of work-related misconduct. A standard of rea-

sonableness will neither unduly burden the efforts of government employers to ensure the efficient and proper operation of the workplace, nor authorize arbitrary intrusions upon the privacy of public employees. We hold, therefore, that public employer intrusions on the constitutionally protected privacy interests of government employees for noninvestigatory, work-related purposes, as well as for investigations of work-related misconduct, should be judged by the standard of reasonableness under all the circumstances. Under this reasonableness standard, both the inception and the scope of the intrusion must be reasonable. . . . 480 U.S. at 725–26, 107 S.Ct. at 1502, 94 L.Ed.2d at 728.

The Court said that, given the great variety of work environments in the public sector, the question of whether an employee has a reasonable expectation of privacy must be determined on a case-by-case basis.

Governmental Drug Testing

The Court also used the "special needs" analysis to uphold warrantless governmental drug testing. *Skinner v. Railway Labor Executives' Ass'n.,* 489 U.S. 602, 109 S.Ct. 1402, 103 L.Ed.2d 639 (1989), upheld governmental regulations requiring railroad companies to test the blood and urine of employees involved in major train accidents and employees who violate particular safety rules. The Court found that the tests were not significant intrusions and that railroad workers have a diminished expectation of privacy because they work in a heavily regulated industry. The searches were held to be reasonable, despite the absence of individualized suspicion, because the government's significant special need to ensure public safety outweighed the employee's diminished privacy interest.

National Treasury Employees Union v. Von Raab, 489 U.S. 656, 109 S.Ct. 1384, 103 L.Ed.2d 685 (1989), upheld Customs Service regulations requiring employees seeking transfers or promotions to certain sensitive positions with the service to submit to urinalysis. The Court found that the government's special need to deter drug use outweighed the diminished privacy interests of the employees. Specifically, the Court emphasized the public interest in "ensuring that front-line interdiction personnel are physically fit, and have unimpeachable integrity and judgment" [and in] "prevent[ing] the promotion of drug users to positions that require the incumbent to carry a firearm, even if the incumbent is not engaged directly in the interdiction of drugs." 489 U.S. at 670, 109 S.Ct. at 1393, 103 L.Ed.2d at 705.

In *Chandler v. Miller,* 520 U.S. 305, 117 S.Ct. 1295, 137 L.Ed.2d 513 (1997), however, the U.S. Supreme Court struck down as unconstitutional a Georgia statute requiring candidates for designated state offices to certify that they have taken a drug test within thirty days prior to qualifying for nomination or election and that the test result was negative. The Court found that the alleged incompatibility of unlawful drug use with holding high state office was not sufficiently important to qualify as a special need for drug testing of candidates for state office.

> [T]he proffered special need for drug testing must be substantial—important enough to override the individual's acknowledged privacy interest, sufficiently vital to suppress the Fourth Amendment's normal requirement of individualized suspicion. 520 U.S. at 318, 117 S.Ct. at 1303, 137 L.Ed.2d at 526.

The need to deter unlawful drug users from attaining high state office was not considered a concrete danger demanding departure from the Fourth Amendment's main rule.

- There was no evidence of a drug problem among the state's elected officials.

caselaw.findlaw.com/data/
constitution/amendment04/
04.html#8
Discussion (with annotations) of
governmental drug testing

*Skinner v. Railway Labor
Executives' Ass'n*
laws.findlaw.com/us/489/
602.html

*National Treasury Employees
Union v. Von Raab*
laws.findlaw.com/us/489/
656.html

- Those officials did not perform high-risk, safety-sensitive tasks.
- The required certification of nondrug use did not immediately aid any drug interdiction effort.

The Court, therefore, concluded:

> [W]here the risk to public safety is substantial and real, blanket suspicionless searches calibrated to the risk may rank as "reasonable"—for example, searches now routine at airports and at entrances to courts and other official buildings. . . . But where . . . public safety is not genuinely in jeopardy, the Fourth Amendment precludes the suspicionless search, no matter how conveniently arranged. 520 U.S. at 323, 117 S.Ct. at 1305, 137 L.Ed.2d at 529.

Ferguson v. Charleston
laws.findlaw.com/us/000/
99-936.html

In *Ferguson v. Charleston*, ___ U.S. ___, 121 S.Ct. 1281, ___L.Ed.2d ___ (2001), the U.S. Supreme Court held unconstitutional a state hospital's policy involving warrantless, suspicionless, and nonconsensual testing of pregnant women for cocaine to obtain evidence for criminal prosecution. The policy, in which law enforcement authorities were extensively involved, used the threat of prosecution to coerce the patients into substance abuse treatment. The Court compared the case to the *Skinner, Von Raab, Acton,* and *Chandler* cases discussed earlier. The Court noted that the invasion of privacy in the *Ferguson* case was far more substantial than in the previous cases, in which there was no misunderstanding about the purpose of the test or the potential use of the test results, and there were protections against the dissemination of the results to third parties. Moreover, those cases involved disqualification from eligibility for particular benefits, a much less serious intrusion on privacy than the unauthorized dissemination of results to third parties. The critical difference, however, lies in the nature of the "special need" asserted as justification for the warrantless searches. In each of the previous cases, the special need was divorced from the State's general interest in law enforcement. "In this case, however, the central and indispensable feature of the policy from its inception was the use of law enforcement to coerce the patients into substance abuse treatment." ___ U.S. at ___, 121 S.Ct. at 1290, ___L.Ed.2d at ___ . The Court discussed the special needs doctrine further:

> While the ultimate goal of the program may well have been to get the women in question into substance abuse treatment and off of drugs, the immediate objective of the searches was to generate evidence for law enforcement purposes in order to reach that goal. The threat of law enforcement may ultimately have been intended as a means to an end, but the direct and primary purpose of MUSC's policy was to ensure the use of those means. In our opinion, this distinction is critical. Because law enforcement involvement always serves some broader social purpose or objective, under respondents' view, virtually any nonconsensual suspicionless search could be immunized under the special needs doctrine by defining the search solely in terms of its ultimate, rather than immediate, purpose. Such an approach is inconsistent with the Fourth Amendment. Given the primary purpose of the Charleston program, which was to use the threat of arrest and prosecution in order to force women into treatment, and given the extensive involvement of law enforcement officials at every stage of the policy, this case simply does not fit within the closely guarded category of "special needs."
>
> The fact that positive test results were turned over to the police does not merely provide a basis for distinguishing our prior cases applying the "special needs" balancing approach to the determination of drug use. It also provides an affirmative reason for enforcing the strictures of the Fourth Amendment. While state hospital employees, like other citizens, may have a duty to provide the police with evidence of criminal conduct

www.uakron.edu/lawrev/
ames.html
Article, "*Chandler v. Miller:*
Redefining 'Special Needs' for
Suspicionless Drug Testing under
the Fourth Amendment" by Joy
L. Ames
www.vaag.com/media%20
center/Opinions/
2000opns/an003.htm
Virginia Attorney General opinion regarding whether local
school boards may require drug
testing of students and employees

that they inadvertently acquire in the course of routine treatment, when they undertake to obtain such evidence from their patients for the specific purpose of incriminating those patients, they have a special obligation to make sure that the patients are fully informed about their constitutional rights, as standards of knowing waiver require. ___ U.S. at ___, 121 S.Ct. at 1291–92, ___L.Ed.2d at ___ .

Searches of Probationers

In *Griffin v. Wisconsin,* 483 U.S. 868, 107 S.Ct. 3164, 97 L.Ed.2d 709 (1987), the Supreme Court upheld a warrantless search of a probationer's home by probation officers under the authority of Wisconsin's probation regulation. The Court found that the probation system's necessity for nonadversarial supervision of probationers is a "special need" justifying lessened Fourth Amendment protection for the probationer. This special need makes the warrant requirement impracticable and justifies replacement of the probable cause standard by a "reasonable grounds" standard, as defined by the Wisconsin Supreme Court. The Court said:

> A warrant requirement would interfere to an appreciable degree with the probation system, setting up a magistrate rather than the probation officer as the judge of how close a supervision the probationer requires. Moreover, the delay inherent in obtaining a warrant would make it more difficult for probation officials to respond quickly to evidence of misconduct . . . and would reduce the deterrent effect that the possibility of expeditious searches would otherwise create. . . . 483 U.S. at 876, 107 S.Ct. at 3170, 97 L.Ed.2d at 719.

The probation search, however, should not serve as a subterfuge or ruse for a criminal investigation. "[A] parole search is unlawful when it is nothing more than a ruse for a police investigation. . . . Parole and police officers may work together, however, provided the parole officer is pursuing parole-related objectives and is not merely a stalking horse for the police." *United States v. McFarland,* 116 F.3d 316, 318 (8th Cir. 1997).

 **Key Points**

21. An exception to the warrant and probable cause requirements of the Fourth Amendment exists where "special needs" of the government, beyond the normal need for law enforcement, make the warrant and probable cause requirements impracticable.

22. "Special needs" exceptions are evaluated under the "reasonableness" standard of the Fourth Amendment requiring the balancing of the nature and quality of the intrusion on the individual's Fourth Amendment interests against the importance of the governmental interests alleged to justify the intrusion.

Warrants for Electronic Surveillance

Electronic surveillance through the use of wiretaps, bugs, or other devices to overhear conversations or obtain other kinds of information is a relatively recent concern of criminal and constitutional law. Certainly the Founding Fathers could not have even imagined the possibilities for gathering information on crime created by the marvels of

caselaw.findlaw.com/data/
constitution/amendment04/
05.html
Discussion (with annotations) of
electronic surveillance and the
Fourth Amendment
lawschool.lexis.com/emanuel/
web/crimpro/crimpro04.htm
General overview of the law
relating to electronic surveillance
www.uncp.edu/home/
vanderhoof/geolr.html#
Electronic
Summary of the law relating to
electronic surveillance

twentieth-century technology. Nor could they, when they drafted the Constitution, have contemplated the potential invasions of privacy brought about by the new technology. It is not surprising, then, that the Constitution gives little guidance for balancing privacy interests against the need for effective law enforcement in the area of electronic surveillance.

On the one hand, electronic listening, tracking, and recording devices provide a very powerful tool for law enforcement officials in investigating and prosecuting crime. On the other hand, the potential for the abuse of individual rights can be far greater with electronic surveillance than with any ordinary search or seizure. The task of resolving these competing interests has fallen on state legislatures, the United States Congress, and, ultimately, the courts. This section traces the early development of the law of electronic surveillance; examines legislative and judicial responses to the problem; and concludes with a discussion of Title III of the Omnibus Crime Control and Safe Streets Act of 1968, which provided authority for electronic surveillance pursuant to warrant.

History

Although electronic eavesdropping has been used as an information-gathering technique since the mid-1800s, the U.S. Supreme Court did not decide its first electronic eavesdropping case until 1928. In *Olmstead v. United States*, 277 U.S. 438, 48 S.Ct. 564, 72 L.Ed. 944 (1928), a case involving interception of telephone conversations by means of a wiretap, the Court held that wiretapping was not covered by the Fourth Amendment. One reason for this decision, as discussed in Chapter 3 under "Privacy," was that there was no search so long as there was no physical trespass into the defendant's premises. The other reason was that all the evidence had been obtained by hearing only, and since the Fourth Amendment referred only to the seizure of tangible items, the interception of a conversation could not qualify as a seizure. As shown in Chapter 3, *Katz v. United States* rendered invalid the first rationale of the *Olmstead* decision by changing the focus of Fourth Amendment analysis from a "property" approach to a "privacy" approach. The second rationale of the *Olmstead* decision was disposed of by *Berger v. New York*, 388 U.S. 41, 87 S.Ct. 1873, 18 L.Ed.2d 1040 (1967), which held that conversations were protected by the Fourth Amendment and that the use of electronic devices to capture conversations was a search within the meaning of the Fourth Amendment.

Once the premise was established that electronic surveillance is a search and seizure within the meaning of the Fourth Amendment, it became necessary for the U.S. Supreme Court to decide what kinds of electronic surveillance the Fourth Amendment allows. The Court also had to decide to what extent electronic surveillance is allowed and what kinds of electronic surveillance are prohibited, if any. The guidelines for these constitutional limits on electronic surveillance were worked out in a series of decisions in the mid-1960s.

This discussion begins with Justice William J. Brennan's dissent in *Lopez v. United States*, 373 U.S. 427, 83 S.Ct. 1381, 10 L.Ed.2d 462 (1963). In that dissent, Justice Brennan echoed the fears of law enforcement officials that if wiretaps were subjected to Fourth Amendment analysis, they would be completely prohibited, because they would be seen as inherently unreasonable searches. Brennan stated, "For one thing, electronic surveillance is almost inherently indiscriminate, so that compliance with the requirement of particularity in the Fourth Amendment would be difficult." 373 U.S. at 463, 83 S.Ct. at 1401, 10 L.Ed.2d at 485. He continued:

Olmstead v. United States
laws.findlaw.com/us/277/
438.html

Katz v. United States
laws.findlaw.com/us/389/
347.html

Berger v. New York
laws.findlaw.com/us/388/
41.html

Lopez v. United States
laws.findlaw.com/us/373/
427.html

If in fact no warrant could be devised for electronic searches, that would be a compelling reason for forbidding them altogether. The requirements of the Fourth Amendment . . . are the bedrock rules without which there would be no effective protection of the right to personal liberty. . . . Electronic searches cannot be tolerated in the name of law enforcement if they are inherently unconstitutional. 373 U.S. at 464, 83 S.Ct. at 1401, 10 L.Ed.2d at 485.

Despite his strong language, it is clear that Brennan left open the possibility that some forms of electronic surveillance might be constitutionally permissible.

The Supreme Court first explicitly considered the constitutionality of electronic surveillance conducted under authority of a warrant three years later in *Osborn v. United States*, 385 U.S. 323, 87 S.Ct. 429, 17 L.Ed.2d 394 (1966). In that case, federal law enforcement officials had information that labor leader Jimmy Hoffa's attorney was trying to bribe a prospective juror. The officials obtained a warrant authorizing an undercover agent with a concealed tape recorder to record a specific conversation with the attorney. The tape of the conversation was admitted at trial, and the attorney was convicted of attempting to bribe a juror. The Court upheld the conviction, emphasizing that "[t]he issue here is . . . the permissibility of using such a device under the most precise and discriminate circumstances. . . ." 385 U.S. at 329, 87 S.Ct. at 432–33, 17 L.Ed.2d at 399.

The Supreme Court's limited grant of constitutional permissibility for electronic surveillance was tested again the next year in *Berger v. New York*, 388 U.S. 41, 87 S.Ct. 1873, 18 L.Ed.2d 1040 (1967). In *Berger*, the issue was the constitutionality of a New York statute that authorized electronic surveillance pursuant to a judicial warrant. The New York law provided as follows:

An ex parte order for eavesdropping . . . may be issued by any justice . . . or judge . . . upon oath or affirmation of a district attorney, or of the attorney-general or of an officer above the rank of sergeant of any police department of the state . . . that there is reasonable ground to believe that evidence of crime may be thus obtained, and particularly describing the person or persons whose communications or discussions are to be overheard or recorded and the purpose thereof, and, in the case of a telegraphic or telephonic communication, identifying the particular telephone number or telegraph line involved. In connection with the issuance of such an order the justice or judge may examine on oath the applicant and any other witness he may produce and shall satisfy himself of the existence of reasonable grounds for the granting of such application. Any such order shall be effective for the time specified therein but not for a period of more than two months unless extended or renewed by the justice or judge who signed and issued the original order upon satisfying himself that such an extension or renewal is in the public interest. . . . N.Y.Code Crim.Proc. § 813–a.

The U.S. Supreme Court held the New York statute unconstitutional, primarily because it did not properly limit the nature, scope, or duration of the electronic surveillance. In so holding, the Court emphasized that the availability of an initial two-month surveillance period was "the equivalent of a series of intrusions, searches, and seizures pursuant to a single showing of probable cause." 388 U.S. at 59, 87 S.Ct. at 1883, 18 L.Ed.2d at 1052. The Court also stressed that the statute placed no termination requirement on the eavesdrop, even after the desired conversation had been obtained. Furthermore, the statute had two major deficiencies with respect to probable cause. First, an eavesdropping warrant could be issued without probable cause that a

mitpress.mit.edu/news/diffie/
wiretapping.html
Comprehensive history of
wiretapping

Osborn v. United States
laws.findlaw.com/us/385/
323.html

particular crime had been committed and without a particular description of "the property" (conversations in this context) to be seized. Second, an eavesdropping order could be extended or renewed without a showing of probable cause for continuation of the eavesdrop. Finally, in contrast to conventional search warrant procedures, the statute permitted electronic eavesdropping without prior notice or a showing of exigency excusing notice.

The Court's concern with the overbroad authorization of the New York statute is reflected in its comparison of the electronic search in the *Berger* case with the search in the *Osborn* case discussed earlier:

> The invasion [in Osborn] was lawful because there was sufficient proof to obtain a search warrant to make the search for the limited purpose outlined in the order of the judges. Through these "precise and discriminate" procedures the order authorizing the use of the electronic device afforded similar protections to those that are present in the use of conventional warrants authorizing the seizure of tangible evidence. Among other safeguards, the order described the type of conversation sought with particularity, thus indicating the specific objective of the Government in entering the constitutionally protected areas and the limitations placed upon the officer executing the warrant. Under it the officer could not search unauthorized areas; likewise, once the property sought, and for which the order was issued, was found the officer could not use the order as a passkey to further search. In addition, the order authorized one limited intrusion rather than a series or a continuous surveillance. And, we note that a new order was issued when the officer sought to resume the search and probable cause was shown for the succeeding one. Moreover, the order was executed by the officer with dispatch, not over a prolonged and extended period. In this manner no greater invasion of privacy was permitted than was necessary under the circumstances. Finally the officer was required to and did make a return on the order showing how it was executed and what was seized. Through these strict precautions the danger of an unlawful search and seizure was minimized. 388 U.S. at 57, 87 S.Ct. at 1882–83, 18 L.Ed.2d at 1051.

Despite the Supreme Court's disapproval of the New York statute in the *Berger* case, the possibility that a properly circumscribed warrant procedure for electronic surveillance could be created was left open. This possibility was given further credence by the landmark case of *Katz v. United States* (discussed in Chapter 3). In that case, FBI agents attached an electronic listening device to a public telephone booth and recorded the defendant's calls. The Court held that the interception was an unlawful search and seizure because there was no warrant. In discussing the warrant requirement, the Court said:

> [T]he surveillance was limited, both in scope and in duration, to the specific purpose of establishing the contents of the petitioner's unlawful telephonic communications. The agents confined their surveillance to the brief periods during which he [Katz] used the telephone booth, and they took great care to overhear only the conversation of the petitioner himself.
>
> Accepting this account of the Government's actions as accurate, it is clear that this surveillance was so narrowly circumscribed that a duly authorized magistrate, properly notified of the need for such investigation, specifically informed of the basis on which it was to proceed, and clearly apprised of the precise intrusion it would entail, could constitutionally have authorized, with appropriate safeguards, the very limited search and seizure that the Government asserts in fact took place. 389 U.S. 347, 354, 88 S.Ct. 507, 512–13, 19 L.Ed.2d 576, 583–84 (1967).

The possibility that a constitutionally permissible warrant procedure for electronic surveillance could be set up paved the way for congressional action in this area. In the year following the *Berger* and *Katz* opinions, Congress enacted the Omnibus Crime Control and Safe Streets Act of 1968. Title III of that act superseded earlier statutory prohibitions against intercepted communications and provided authorization for electronic surveillance pursuant to warrant.

Title III of the Omnibus Crime Control and Safe Streets Act of 1968

The passage of Title III of the Omnibus Crime Control and Safe Streets Act of 1968, following so closely on the heels of the *Berger* and *Katz* decisions, was not simply a result of Congress enacting legislation in response to the constitutional guidelines set out in those decisions. Concern had long been expressed about the inadequacy of existing electronic surveillance legislation. Besides the issues raised in various Supreme Court cases, defense lawyers and civil libertarians complained of governmental violations of the privacy rights of American citizens. On the other side, proponents of electronic surveillance argued that wiretapping and bugging were essential tools for law enforcement officials to combat the modern sophisticated criminal, especially in the area of organized crime.

In fact, the belief that electronic surveillance was the only way to deal with the unique problems of investigating and prosecuting organized crime prompted the President's Crime Commission to recommend legislation authorizing electronic surveillance. Political pressures were exerted in a national climate of fear brought about by intense social unrest and the assassinations of Martin Luther King Jr., and Robert F. Kennedy and crystallized in the "law and order" presidential campaign of Richard M. Nixon. The result was a bipartisan effort to balance modern society's conflicting demands for privacy and more effective law enforcement through the enactment of Title III in 1968.

The discussion now turns to an examination of Title III and cases interpreting it. Because of the length of the law, it is not possible to reproduce Title III's provisions verbatim. Therefore, this discussion is necessarily general in nature.

JUDICIAL SUPERVISION   One important characteristic of Title III, designed to protect against governmental abuses of citizens' privacy rights, is the law's provision for judicial supervision of all aspects of electronic surveillance. Federal law enforcement officials may not intercept wire, oral, or electronic communications without prior judicial approval. Before discussing the details of judicial supervision of electronic surveillance, definitions of important terms are necessary:

- *Intercept* is defined as "the aural or other acquisition of the contents of any wire, electronic, or oral communication through the use of any electronic, mechanical, or other device." 18 U.S.C.A. § 2510(4). (The 1986 amendments to Title III extended the law's coverage to include all forms of electronic communications and not just spoken conversations transmitted by telephone or overheard electronically.)
- *Wire communication* is defined as "any aural transfer made in whole or in part through the use of facilities for the transmission of communications by the aid of wire, cable, or other like connection between the point of origin and the point of reception (including the use of such connection in a switching station)

www.usdoj.gov/usao/eousa/foia_reading_room/usam/title9/7mcrm.htm
Department of Justice policy on the use of electronic surveillance
www4.law.cornell.edu/uscode/18/ch119.html
Title III in its entirety in a searchable format
www.rbs2.com/lt.htm
Article, "Response of Law to New Technology" by Ronald B. Standler; contains a section on wiretapping

Complete text of 18 U.S.C. § 2510
caselaw.findlaw.com/scripts/ts_search.pl?title=18&sec=2510

furnished or operated by any person engaged in providing or operating such facilities for the transmission of interstate or foreign communications or communications affecting interstate or foreign commerce and such term includes any electronic storage of such communication." 18 U.S.C.A. § 2510(1).

- An *aural transfer* is defined as "a transfer containing the human voice at any point between and including the point of origin and the point of reception." 18 U.S.C.A. § 2510(18).

- *Oral communication* is defined as "any oral communication uttered by a person exhibiting an expectation that such communication is not subject to interception under circumstances justifying such expectation, but such term does not include any electronic communication." 18 U.S.C.A. § 2510(2).

- *Electronic communication* is defined as "any transfer of signs, signals, writing, images, sounds, data, or intelligence of any nature transmitted in whole or in part by a wire, radio, electromagnetic, photoelectronic or photooptical system that affects interstate or foreign commerce but does not include (A) any wire or oral communication; (B) any communication made through a tone-only paging device; (C) any communication from a tracking device . . . ; or (D) electronic funds transfer information stored by a financial institution in a communications system used for the electronic storage and transfer of funds." 18 U.S.C.A. § 2510(12).

A court may issue an interception order only for specified crimes including espionage, treason, labor racketeering, murder, kidnapping, robbery, extortion, bribery of public officials, gambling, drug trafficking, escape, and counterfeiting. Note that the 5th Circuit has held that, for jurisdictional purposes, an interception of a wiretap takes place at both the location of the tapped telephone and the original listening post. Therefore, judges in either jurisdiction have authority under Title III to issue interception orders. *United States v. Denman*, 100 F.3d 399 (5th Cir. 1996). Before issuing an interception order, the court must find all of the following:

- Probable cause to believe that the person whose communication is to be intercepted has committed, is committing, or is about to commit one of the specified crimes. "The probable cause showing required . . . for electronic surveillance does not differ from that required by the fourth amendment for a search warrant." *United States v. Macklin*, 902 F.2d 1320, 1324 (8th Cir. 1990).

- Probable cause to believe that particular communications concerning that offense will be obtained through the interception.

- That normal investigative procedures have been tried and have failed, or reasonably appear to be unlikely to succeed if tried, or reasonably appear to be too dangerous. This condition is often referred to as the "necessity requirement" and is intended to ensure that electronic surveillance is not used unless normal investigative procedures are inadequate. For example, in *United States v. Wagner*, 989 F.2d 69 (1993), the necessity for a wiretap was established because (1) the rural location of the house and the presence of dogs made surveillance difficult, (2) the confidential informant was unable to determine the source of supply and method of delivery of marijuana, and (3) the government did not think it could infiltrate the marijuana distribution network with undercover agents.

- Probable cause to believe that the facilities from which, or the place where, the wire, oral, or electronic communications are to be intercepted are being used or are about to be used in connection with the commission of the specified offense, or are leased to, listed in the name of or commonly used by the suspect.

Other aspects of judicial supervision of electronic surveillance are the court's power to require, at any time, reports on the progress of the interception toward the achievement of authorized objectives, the requirement of court approval for any extension of the surveillance, and the requirement that the recordings of any communications be sealed under directions of the court immediately upon the order's expiration.

Judicial sanctions for violations of Title III include criminal penalties, penalties for contempt of court, and awards of civil damages. In addition, 18 U.S.C.A. § 2515 provides for the exclusion of evidence obtained in violation of Title III. In *United States v. Spadaccino*, 800 F.2d 292 (2d Cir. 1986), the court held that the good-faith exception to the exclusionary rule did not apply to violations of Title III. The court said that, when the legislature has spoken clearly on the issue, "it is appropriate to look to the terms of the statute and the intentions of the legislature, rather than to invoke judge-made exceptions to judge-made rules." 800 F.2d at 296.

> Complete text of 18 U.S.C. § 2515 caselaw.findlaw.com/scripts/ts_ search.pl?title=18&sec=2515

PROCEDURES FOR INTERCEPTION ORDERS   Title III establishes specific procedures for the application for, the issuance of, and the execution of court orders for the interception of wire, oral, or electronic communications.

Application   Application procedures for interception orders are governed by 18 U.S.C.A. § 2518(1), which is quoted here:

> Complete text of 18 U.S.C. § 2518 caselaw.findlaw.com/scripts/ts_ search.pl?title=18&sec=2518

§ 2518. Procedure for interception of wire, oral, or electronic communications
(1) Each application for an order authorizing or approving the interception of a wire, oral, or electronic communication under this chapter shall be made in writing upon oath or affirmation to a judge of competent jurisdiction and shall state the applicant's authority to make such application. Each application shall include the following information:
   (a) the identity of the investigative or law enforcement officer making the application, and the officer authorizing the application;
   (b) a full and complete statement of the facts and circumstances relied upon by the applicant, to justify his belief that an order should be issued, including (i) details as to the particular offense that has been, is being, or is about to be committed, (ii) except as provided in subsection (11) [roving taps], a particular description of the nature and location of the facilities from which or the place where the communication is to be intercepted, (iii) a particular description of the type of communications sought to be intercepted, (iv) the identity of the person, if known, committing the offense and whose communications are to be intercepted; (c) a full and complete statement as to whether or not other investigative procedures have been tried and failed or why they reasonably appear to be unlikely to succeed if tried or to be too dangerous;
   (d) a statement of the period of time for which the interception is required to be maintained. If the nature of the investigation is such that the authorization for interception should not automatically terminate when the described type of communication has been first obtained, a particular description of facts establishing probable cause to believe that additional communications of the same type will occur thereafter;

> www.usdoj.gov/usao/eousa/ foia_reading_room/usam/title9/ crm00029.htm "Electronic Surveillance—Title III Affidavits" *U.S. Attorneys Manual* instructions for preparing affidavits for electronic surveillance www.fbi.gov/publications/leb/ 2000/feb00leb.pdf Article, "Electronic Surveillance: A Matter of Necessity" by Thomas D. Colbridge (page 25 of the February 2000 *FBI Law Enforcement Bulletin*); focuses on the investigator's obligation to demonstrate the necessity for electronic surveillance before the court will authorize its use

(e) a full and complete statement of the facts concerning all previous applications known to the individual authorizing and making the application, made to any judge for authorization to intercept, or for approval of interceptions of, wire, oral, or electronic communications involving any of the same persons, facilities or places specified in the application, and the action taken by the judge on each such application; and

(f) where the application is for the extension of an order, a statement setting forth the results thus far obtained from the interception, or a reasonable explanation of the failure to obtain such results.

Only the U.S. attorney general or other federal attorneys specified by Title III may authorize an application for a federal interception order. Only a federal investigative or law enforcement officer, as defined by Title III, or an attorney authorized to prosecute Title III offenses, may make an application for a federal interception order. With respect to the requirement of identifying the person whose communications are to be intercepted, the U.S. Supreme Court held that the applicant must name all persons who the government has probable cause to believe are committing the offense for which the application is made. *United States v. Donovan*, 429 U.S. 413, 97 S.Ct. 658, 50 L.Ed.2d 652 (1977). The *Donovan* case also held, however, that failure to comply with this identification requirement did not require the exclusion of evidence obtained by the interception.

Section 2518(11) allows law enforcement officials to apply for authorization to conduct "roving taps." A roving tap targets a particular suspect's communications wherever they are made and dispenses with the normal requirement that interceptions be limited to a fixed location. *United States v. Petti*, 973 F.2d 1441 (9th Cir. 1991), held that roving taps do not violate the particularity requirement of the Fourth Amendment if the surveillance is limited to communications involving an identified speaker and relates to crimes in which the speaker is a suspected participant.

Issuance   If, on the basis of the application, the judge makes the required findings, the judge may issue an order authorizing or approving the interception of wire, oral, or electronic communications. Each order must specify all of the following:

- The identity, if known, of the person whose communications are to be intercepted
- The nature and location of the communications facilities as to which, or the place where, authority to intercept is granted
- A particular description of the type of communication sought to be intercepted, and a statement of the particular offense to which the communication relates
- The identity of the agency authorized to intercept the communications, and the identity of the person authorizing the application
- The period of time during which the interception is authorized, including a statement as to whether or not the interception shall automatically terminate when the described communication has been first obtained

Execution   Every order to intercept wire, oral, or electronic communications must be executed "as soon as practicable." In *United States v. Martino*, 664 F.2d 860 (2d Cir. 1981), however, the court held that delay in the execution of an interception order did not require the suppression of evidence obtained if the delay was not willful and if the information on which probable cause was based had not become stale. In *United States v. Gallo*, 863 F.2d 185 (2d Cir. 1988), the court held that suppression of the intercepted communications was not required because of a five-month delay in installing the interception devices, when the government adequately explained that the installation was extremely difficult and the crime was one of continuing conduct, in which probable cause was "freshened" by visual surveillance.

Title III requires that authorized interceptions be conducted in such a way as to minimize the interception of communications not otherwise subject to interception under Title III. This minimization effort must be objectively reasonable under the circumstances. In *Scott v. United States*, 436 U.S. 128, 98 S.Ct. 1717, 56 L.Ed.2d 168 (1978), the U.S. Supreme Court held an interception reasonable although only 40 percent of the intercepted conversations related to crimes specified in the order, because the remaining conversations were ambiguous and brief. *United States v. Smith*, 909 F.2d 1164 (8th Cir. 1990), held that minimization efforts were reasonable despite failure to minimize the defendant's sister's phone conversations with his ex-girlfriend, because the officers suspected the defendant's family of aiding in drug activities but did not know which family members were doing so.

Scott v. United States
laws.findlaw.com/us/436/
128.html

When a law enforcement officer intercepts communications relating to offenses other than those specified in the interception order, the officer must apply as soon as possible for judicial approval to disclose the evidence in court. Without judicial approval, the evidence may not be disclosed. In *United States v. Van Horn*, 789 F.2d 1492 (11th Cir. 1986), the court held that the judicial approval could take the form of the judge's granting an extension order after receiving progress reports and applications for extensions describing the nature of the conversations being intercepted.

Authorized interceptions must terminate upon attainment of the authorized objective, or in any event in thirty days. In *United States v. Carneiro*, 861 F.2d 1171 (9th Cir. 1988), the court held that suppression of communications intercepted after the discovery of a drug source was not required, because the objective of the wiretap was to investigate the entire drug operation, not merely to discover a drug source. Extensions of an interception order may be granted, but only upon reapplication in accordance with the same procedures as for an original application.

Immediately upon the expiration of an interception order, recordings are required to be delivered to the judge issuing the order and to be sealed under the judge's directions. The purposes of this requirement are to prevent tampering, aid in establishing the chain of custody, protect confidentiality, and establish judicial control over the surveillance. The statutory term *immediately* has been interpreted to mean without unnecessary or unreasonable delay. Failure to deliver the recordings or unjustifiable or unexplained late delivery may cause the recordings to be excluded from evidence. Before ordering suppression, however, courts will examine all the circumstances, including whether the defendant has been prejudiced by tampering or other governmental misconduct. *United States v. Rodriguez*, 786 F.2d 472 (2d Cir. 1986). If there is a delay in sealing, the "Government must explain not only why a delay occurred but also why it is excusable." *United States v. Ojeda Rios*, 495 U.S. 257, 265, 110 S.Ct. 1845, 1850, 109 L.Ed.2d 224, 236 (1990). Courts consider the following factors in determining whether the government has presented a satisfactory explanation for its failure to seal or delay in sealing:

United States v. Ojeda Rios
laws.findlaw.com/us/495/
257.html

> the length of any delay before sealing, the care taken in handling the recordings, prejudice to the defendants, any tactical advantage accruing to the government, and whether deliberate or gross dereliction of duty or honest mistake caused the failure to file. *United States v. Suarez*, 906 F.2d 977, 982 (4th Cir. 1990).

Finally, within a reasonable time, but not later than ninety days after the termination of the period of an order, an *inventory* must be served upon the persons named in

www.totse.com/en/law/
justice_for_all/judseal.htm/
Article, "The Judicial Sealing
Requirement in Electronic Surveillance: A Matter of Immediacy" by Robert A. Fiatal

the order and upon such other parties to intercepted communications as the judge may determine in the interest of justice. This inventory must also be served after emergency interceptions are carried out. It must include a notice of the fact of the order, the date of approval of the application, the period of the authorized interception, and a statement of whether or not wire, oral, or electronic communications were intercepted during the period. Failure to serve the inventory is not grounds for suppression unless the failure causes actual, incurable prejudice. *United States v. Harrigan,* 586 F.2d 860, 865 (1st Cir. 1978).

APPLICABILITY TO THE STATES   Title III specifically authorizes state law enforcement officials to apply for, obtain, and execute orders authorizing or approving the interception of wire, oral, or electronic communications. The procedures are similar to those governing federal interception orders. The primary difference is that the state procedure must be authorized by a separate state statute. If a state statute so authorizes, the principal prosecuting attorney of the state, or of a political subdivision of the state, may apply to a state court judge of competent jurisdiction for an interception order. In granting the order, the judge must comply with both the applicable state statute and Title III. The interception order may be granted only when the interception may provide

> evidence of the commission of the offense of murder, kidnapping, gambling, robbery, bribery, extortion, or dealing in narcotic drugs, marihuana or other dangerous drugs, or other crime dangerous to life, limb, or property, and punishable by imprisonment for more than one year, designated in any applicable State statute authorizing such interception, or any conspiracy to commit any of the foregoing offenses. 18 U.S.C.A. § 2516(2).

Complete text of 18 U.S.C. § 2516
caselaw.findlaw.com/scripts/ts_search.pl?title=18&sec=2516

"Generally speaking, insofar as wiretapping is concerned, states are free to superimpose more rigorous requirements upon those mandated by the Congress . . . but not to water down federally-devised safeguards." *United States v. Mora,* 821 F.2d 860, 863 n.3 (1st Cir. 1987). Federal courts are not obliged to adhere to more restrictive state laws, however, and will generally admit evidence that violates such a law, so long as the evidence was not obtained in violation of Title III. For example, in *United States v. Daniel,* 667 F.2d 783 (9th Cir. 1982), an interception of a conversation without a search warrant violated state law. Nevertheless, the evidence was held admissible in federal court because Title III does not require a warrant when one of the parties to the intercepted conversation consents to the interception.

SUPPRESSION   No contents of or evidence derived from electronic surveillance "may be received in evidence in any trial, hearing, or other proceeding in or before any court, grand jury, department, officer, agency, regulatory body, legislative committee, or other authority of the United States, a State, or a political subdivision thereof if the disclosure of that information would be in violation of this chapter." 18 U.S.C.A. § 2515. "Any aggrieved person in any trial, hearing, or proceeding in or before any court, department, officer, agency, regulatory body, or other authority of the United States, a State, or a political subdivision thereof, may move to suppress" the contents of or evidence derived from intercepts under Title III. 18 U.S.C.A. § 2518(10)(a). An *aggrieved person* is "a person who was a party to any intercepted wire, oral, or electronic communication or a person against whom the interception was directed." 18 U.S.C.A. § 2510(11).

The U.S. Supreme Court held that the term aggrieved person should be construed in accordance with existing standing rules. Therefore, "any petitioner would be entitled to the suppression of government evidence originating in electronic surveillance violative of his own Fourth Amendment right to be free of unreasonable searches and seizures. Such violation would occur if the United States unlawfully overheard conversations of a petitioner himself or conversations occurring on his premises, whether or not he was present or participated in those conversations." *Alderman v. United States,* 394 U.S. 165, 176, 89 S.Ct. 961, 968, 22 L.Ed.2d 176, 188 (1969). A violation of Title III does not require suppression of evidence, however, if the provision violated is not central to the statute's underlying purpose of guarding against unwarranted use of wiretapping or electronic surveillance. *United States v. Chavez,* 416 U.S. 562, 94 S.Ct. 1849, 40 L.Ed.2d 380 (1974). Therefore, suppression is seldom imposed for inadvertent, unavoidable, or unintentional violations.

EXCEPTIONS TO TITLE III   Many types of interceptions of wire, oral, or electronic communications are either not covered by provisions of Title III or specifically excepted from coverage. Some of the most important exceptions to Title III's requirement of an interception order are discussed here in general terms.

A party to an oral communication who has no reasonable expectation of privacy with respect to the communication is not protected by either Title III or the Fourth Amendment. In *State v. Salisbury,* 662 F.2d 738 (11th Cir. 1981), the court held that a party to a conversation has no legitimate expectation that another party to the conversation will not record the conversation or reveal its contents to authorities. In *United States v. Harrelson,* 754 F.2d 1153 (5th Cir. 1985), the court held that surreptitiously recorded conversations between a prison inmate and his wife did not qualify as oral conversations. The court found that the couple suspected eavesdropping and therefore could have had no reasonable expectation of privacy. "Mistaking the degree of intrusion of which probable eavesdroppers are capable is not at all the same thing as believing there are no eavesdroppers." 754 F.2d at 1170.

Sections 2511(2)(c) and 2511(2)(d) exclude consent surveillance from the regulatory scheme established by Title III for court-ordered surveillance. Therefore, when one party to a communication consents to the interception of the communication, neither Title III nor the Fourth Amendment prevents the use of the communication in court against another party to the communication. Thus, a law enforcement officer or a private citizen who is a party to a communication may intercept the communication or permit a law enforcement official to intercept the communication without violating Title III or the Fourth Amendment. This exception allows a law enforcement officer or agent to wear a body microphone, act as an undercover agent without being wired, or eavesdrop on a telephone conversation with the permission of the person receiving the call, without the knowledge of the person making the call. For example, in *United States v. Capo,* 693 F.2d 1330 (11th Cir. 1982), the government's interception of a conversation between a consenting informant and the defendant was held not to be a violation of the Fourth Amendment, since the defendant willingly projected his voice outside the privacy of his home and his voice was intercepted at the other end. A private citizen, however, may not intercept a communication "for the purpose of committing any criminal or tortious act in violation of the Constitution or laws of the United States or of any state." The absence of federal regulation or preemption regarding consent surveillance has left the states free to fashion their own approaches by statute or court decision.

Title III does not apply to the use of electronic devices emitting signals that enable law enforcement officials to track the location of objects and persons. Use of these devices, sometimes called transmitters or beepers, is governed solely by the Fourth Amendment. Since most of the legal issues involving these devices relate to the

Alderman v. United States
laws.findlaw.com/us/394/
165.html

United States v. Chavez
laws.findlaw.com/us/416/
562.htm

Complete text of 18 U.S.C.
§ 2511
caselaw.findlaw.com/scripts/ts_
search.pl?title=18&sec=2511

Smith v. Maryland
laws.findlaw.com/us/442/
735.html

Complete text of 18 U.S.C.
§ 3121
caselaw.findlaw.com/scripts/ts_
search.pl?title=18&sec=3121

www.hq.nasa.gov/office/oig/hq/
remote4.html
Article, "Remote Sensing and
the Fourth Amendment: A New
Law Enforcement Tool?"
www.sjsu.edu/faculty/kpnuger/
Privacyweb/HiTechSurv4th
%20am.htm
Article, "High-Tech Surveillance
Tools and the Fourth Amendment: Reasonable Expectations
of Privacy in the Technology
Age" by Richard S. Julie

Dalia v. United States
laws.findlaw.com/us/441/
238.html

www.loompanics.com/
Articles/Thermal.htm
Article, "Thermal Imaging:
Much Heat but Little Light"
by Thomas D. Colbridge
www.pegasus.rutgers.edu/
~record/drafts/flir.html
Article, "Reasonable Expectation
of Privacy" : Protecting Individual
Privacy in the Face of Intrusive
Surveillance Technology" by
James P. McGovern
www.mttlr.org/forum/
crisera_art.html
Article, "The Constitutionality of
FLIR-Device Searches Without a
Warrant" by Michael Crisera

attachment of the devices to vehicles and containers, these issues are discussed in Chapter 11, dealing with the warrantless search of vehicles and containers.

Similarly, Title III does not apply to trap-and-trace devices and pen registers. A trap-and-trace device traces the source of calls made to a particular telephone number. A pen register records all numbers dialed from a particular telephone number. In *Smith v. Maryland*, 442 U.S. 735, 99 S.Ct. 2577, 61 L.Ed.2d 220 (1979), the U.S. Supreme Court held that the installation and use of a pen register is not a search and is therefore not subject to the Fourth Amendment. The Court reasoned that the defendant had no reasonable expectation of privacy in the destination of his outgoing phone calls because the telephone company routinely monitors these calls to check billing, detect fraud, and prevent other violations of law. Federal courts have not yet addressed the Fourth Amendment implications of the use of trap-and-trace devices. Because telephone companies do not routinely monitor incoming calls, the rationale of the *Smith* case may not apply to the use of those devices. Since the *Smith* decision, Congress has enacted legislation (18 U.S.C.A. §§ 3121–3126) prohibiting the installation or use of a pen register or a trap-and-trace device except by court order.

Other electronic surveillance devices and techniques that do not invade a reasonable expectation of privacy are:

- Intercepted conversations on a cordless telephone. *United States v. Mathis*, 96 F.3d 1577 (11th Cir. 1996).
- Thermal infrared heat detectors. "In *United States v. Ford* we held that the ground surveillance of an unoccupied mobile home on leased land with a thermal infrared heat detector did not violate the Fourth Amendment. Three other circuits also have concluded that thermal infrared surveillance or FLIR is not an unconstitutional search." *United States v. Robinson*, 62 F.3d 1325, 1328 (11th Cir. 1995).
- Electronic pagers and the numbers in memory. *United States v. Ortiz*, 84 F.3d 977 (7th Cir. 1996).

Although law enforcement officials must obtain a judicial order to intercept wire, oral, or electronic communications, neither Title III nor the Fourth Amendment requires them to obtain judicial authorization to covertly enter premises to install a listening device. In *Dalia v. United States*, 441 U.S. 238, 99 S.Ct. 1682, 60 L.Ed.2d 177 (1979), a federal court authorized the interception of all oral communications concerning an interstate stolen-goods conspiracy at the defendant's office. Although the interception order did not explicitly authorize entry into the defendant's office, FBI agents secretly entered the office and installed a listening device in the ceiling. Six weeks later, after the surveillance had terminated, the agents reentered the office and removed the device. The defendant was convicted, partly on the basis of intercepted conversations. The Supreme Court considered the legislative history of Title III and concluded as follows:

[O]ne simply cannot assume that Congress, aware that most bugging requires covert entry, nonetheless wished to except surveillance requiring such entries from the broad authorization of Title III, and that it resolved to do so by remaining silent on the subject. On the contrary, the language and history of Title III convey quite a different explanation for Congress' failure to distinguish between surveillance that requires covert entry and that which does not. Those considering the surveillance legislation understood that, by authorizing electronic interception of oral communications in addition to wire communications, they were necessarily authorizing surreptitious entries. 441 U.S. at 252, 99 S.Ct. at 1691, 60 L.Ed.2d at 189.

With respect to the Fourth Amendment, the Court found that nothing in the language of the Fourth Amendment or the Court's decisions suggested that search warrants must include a specification of the precise manner in which those warrants must be executed. "On the contrary, it is generally left to the discretion of the executing officers to determine the details of how best to proceed with the performance of a search authorized by warrant—subject of course to the general Fourth Amendment protection 'against unreasonable searches and seizures.'" 441 U.S. at 257, 99 S.Ct. at 1693, 60 L.Ed.2d at 192.

Finally, Title III provides authority for designated federal or state officials to intercept wire, oral, or electronic communications without a prior interception order if (1) an emergency situation exists that involves immediate danger of death or serious physical injury to any person, conspiratorial activities threatening the national security interest, or conspiratorial activities characteristic of organized crime; and (2) an interception order cannot be obtained in sufficient time. The determination of emergency must be made by the U.S. attorney general or other governmental official specified in Title III. The law enforcement officer carrying out the emergency surveillance must apply for an interception order under Section 2518 within forty-eight hours after the interception has occurred or begins to occur. If an order is not obtained, the interception must immediately terminate when the sought-after communication is obtained or when the application is denied, whichever is earlier.

www.co.alameda.ca.us/da/pov/covert_entry.htm
Articled, "Covert Entry Warrants" from the District Attorney's Office in Alameda County, California

www.cdt.org/publications/lawreview/1997albany.shtml
Article, "Communications Privacy in the Digital Age: Revitalizing the Federal Wiretap Laws to Enhance Privacy" by James X. Dempsey

www.yale.edu/ynhti/curriculum/units/1983/4/83.04.07.x.html
Article, "Electronic Surveillance: Unlawful Invasion of Privacy or Justifiable Law Enforcement" by Willie J. Elder Jr.

www.aclu.org/congress/l040600a.html
ACLU statement before the House Judiciary Committee on the Fourth Amendment and the Internet

Key Points

23. Electronic surveillance by agents of the government is a search and seizure governed by the Fourth Amendment.

24. Electronic surveillance is permissible only if conducted pursuant to the authority of a warrant affording protections similar to those present in the use of conventional warrants authorizing the seizure of tangible evidence.

25. A warrant procedure authorizing electronic surveillance must carefully circumscribe the search in nature, scope, and duration and must not permit a trespassory invasion of the home or office by general warrant, contrary to the command of the Fourth Amendment.

26. Title III of the Omnibus Crime Control and Safe Streets Act balances the need to use electronic surveillance for effective law enforcement against the need to protect the privacy rights of individuals by providing for judicial supervision of all aspects of electronic surveillance and establishing warrant procedures similar to those required for the search and seizure of tangible objects.

27. Although a judicially issued interception order is required to intercept wire, oral, or electronic communications, judicial approval is not required to covertly enter premises to install a listening device.

Effect of Illegal Search and Seizure

www.aclu.org/issues/cyber/wiretap_brother.html
ACLU Special Report, "Big Brother in the Wires: Wiretapping in the Digital Age"

The most important effect of an illegal search or seizure is the exclusion of the evidence obtained from use in court against the person whose rights were violated. (The exclusionary rule is discussed in detail in Chapter 3.) When crucial evidence is suppressed, the prosecution's case may be lost, and the person charged with the crime may go free.

Another possible effect of an illegal search and seizure is the civil or criminal liability of the officer conducting the search and seizure. As with an illegal arrest, the consequences for the officer depend on the circumstances of each case, including the officer's good faith, the degree of care used, the seriousness of the violation, and the extent of injury or intrusion suffered by the defendant.

Summary

The general rule is that all searches and seizures conducted without a warrant are unreasonable and violate the Fourth Amendment to the U.S. Constitution. Although there are many well-defined exceptions to this rule, searches made under the authority of a warrant not only are greatly preferred by the courts but also give the law enforcement officer greater protection from liability.

A search warrant is a written order issued by a proper judicial authority (the magistrate) commanding a law enforcement officer to search for certain personal property and bring it before the judicial authority named in the warrant. An officer may obtain a search warrant by submitting to a magistrate a written application in the form of a sworn affidavit. The affidavit must state underlying facts and circumstances supporting probable cause to believe that particularly described items are located in a particularly described place or on a particularly described person. Only items connected with criminal activity, such as stolen property, contraband, and instrumentalities and evidence of crime, may be seized.

If a magistrate finds probable cause to search, he or she will issue a search warrant directing an officer or class of officers to execute the warrant. Officers must conduct the search within a reasonable time after the warrant's issuance and within any time period specified by law or court rule. Before entering premises by force to execute the warrant, officers must knock and announce their authority and purpose, unless this notice will result in the loss or destruction of evidence, the escape of a suspect, or danger to an officer or others. Persons on the premises may not be searched, unless the search warrant authorizes the search of a particular person. Property of persons who are not the target of the warrant and not residents of the target premises may not be seized. If officers are executing a warrant to search for contraband, persons on the premises may be detained during the course of the search. Any person on the premises whom officers reasonably believe to be dangerous may be frisked for weapons.

A search under authority of a search warrant may extend to the entire premises described in the warrant, but only to those parts of the premises where the items to be seized might be concealed. The search must be conducted in a manner to avoid unnecessary damage to the premises or objects. Items not named in the warrant may be seized if all elements of the plain view doctrine are satisfied. After the search is completed, the officer must leave at the searched premises a copy of the warrant and a receipt for property taken. The officer must return the warrant along with a written inventory of property seized to the judicial officer designated in the warrant.

An administrative search is a routine inspection of a home or business to determine compliance with codes and licensing provisions dealing with fire, health, safety, housing, and so on. Although administrative searches are not directed toward convicting a person of a crime, they are still subject to the warrant requirement of the Fourth Amendment. The probable cause standard for administrative searches is less stringent than the standard for criminal searches. If, however, an administrative search takes on the characteristics of a criminal search, the traditional probable cause standard applies. Exceptions to the administrative search warrant requirement are similar to the exceptions for a criminal search warrant with less stringent standards. Also, warrantless searches are allowed for certain licensed and closely regulated enterprises.

An exception to the warrant and probable cause requirements of the Fourth Amendment exists where "special needs" of the government, beyond the normal need for law enforcement, make the warrant and probable cause requirements impracticable. "Special needs" exceptions are evaluated under the "reasonableness" standard of the Fourth Amendment.

Electronic surveillance was originally considered beyond the coverage of the Fourth Amendment because it involved no trespass into the defendant's premises and no seizure of tangible items. In a series of U.S. Supreme Court decisions in the mid-1960s, the Court reversed this approach and held that electronic surveillance by agents of the government is a search and seizure governed by the Fourth Amendment. The leading case adopting this new approach was *Katz v. United States,* which held that the Fourth Amendment protects people, not places, thereby shifting the focus of the Fourth Amendment from property to privacy. In addition, the Court held that electronic surveillance is permissible only if conducted pursuant to a warrant that carefully limits the surveillance in nature, scope, and duration. In 1968, Congress enacted Title III of the Omnibus Crime Control and Safe Streets Act, which attempts to balance the need to use electronic surveillance for effective law enforcement against the need to protect individuals' privacy rights. Title III provides for judicial supervision of all aspects of electronic surveillance and establishes warrant procedures similar to those required for the search and seizure of tangible objects. These procedures are designed to limit who can authorize an application for an interception order, who can apply for an order, the duration of electronic surveillance allowed, and various aspects of the execution of an interception order.

The coverage of Title III has many exceptions. Title III does not protect a party to a conversation who has no reasonable expectation of privacy with respect to that conversation. Furthermore, if one party to a conversation consents to the interception of that conversation, the conversation may be used against the other party. Finally, Title III does not apply to the use of electronic devices such as beepers, trap-and-trace devices, and pen registers. Although an interception order is required to intercept wire, oral, or electronic communications, judicial approval is not required to covertly enter premises to install a listening device. Neither is an interception order

required to intercept wire, oral, or electronic communications in emergencies involving immediate danger of death or serious physical injury, or conspiracies threatening national security or involving organized crime, although an interception order must be applied for within forty-eight hours of the emergency interception.

An illegal search and seizure, whether caused by a failure to comply with warrant procedures or by a failure to satisfy one of the exceptions to the warrant requirement, will result in application of the exclusionary rule. The evidence seized during the search will be inadmissible in court, a situation often resulting in termination of the prosecution and release of the person charged. Furthermore, officers conducting an illegal search may be civilly or criminally liable for their actions.

Key Holdings from Major Cases

United States v. Jacobsen (1984). "A 'search' occurs when an expectation of privacy that society is prepared to consider reasonable is infringed. A 'seizure' of property occurs when there is some meaningful interference with an individual's possessory interests in that property." 466 U.S. 109, 113, 104 S.Ct. 1652, 1656, 80 L.Ed.2d 85, 94.

Johnson v. United States (1948). "The point of the Fourth Amendment, which often is not grasped by zealous officers, is not that it denies law enforcement the support of the usual inferences which reasonable men draw from evidence. Its protection consists in requiring that those inferences be drawn by a neutral and detached magistrate instead of being judged by the officer engaged in the often competitive enterprise of ferreting out crime." 333 U.S. 10, 13–14, 68 S.Ct. 367, 369, 92 L.Ed. 436, 440.

Shadwick v. City of Tampa (1972). "[A]n issuing magistrate must meet two tests. He must be neutral and detached, and he must be capable of determining whether probable cause exists for the requested arrest or search." 407 U.S. 345, 350, 92 S.Ct. 2119, 2123, 32 L.Ed.2d 783, 788.

Franks v. Delaware (1978). "[W]here the defendant makes a substantial preliminary showing that a false statement knowingly and intentionally, or with reckless disregard for the truth, was included by the affiant in the warrant affidavit, and if the allegedly false statement is necessary to the finding of probable cause, the Fourth Amendment requires that a hearing be held at the defendant's request. In the event that at the hearing the allegation of perjury or reckless disregard is established by the defendant by a preponderance of the evidence, and, with the affidavit's false material set to one side, the affidavit's remaining content is insufficient to establish probable cause, the search warrant must be voided and the fruits of the search excluded to the same extent as if probable cause was lacking on the face of

the affidavit." 438 U.S. 154, 155–56, 98 S.Ct. 2674, 2676–77, 57 L.Ed.2d 667, 672.

Andresen v. Maryland (1976). "[A]lthough the Fifth Amendment may protect an individual from complying with a subpoena for the production of his personal records in his possession because the very act of production may constitute a compulsory authentication of incriminating information, . . . a seizure of the same materials by law enforcement officers differs in a crucial respect—the individual against whom the search is directed is not required to aid in the discovery, production, or authentication of incriminating evidence." 427 U.S. 463, 473–74, 96 S.Ct. 2737, 2745, 49 L.Ed.2d 627, 638.

Gouled v. United States (1921). "There is no special sanctity in papers, as distinguished from other forms of property, to render them immune from search and seizure, if only they fall within the scope of the principles of the cases in which other property may be seized, and if they be adequately described in the affidavit and warrant." 255 U.S. 298, 309, 41 S.Ct. 261, 265, 65 L.Ed. 647, 652.

Warden v. Hayden (1967). "The requirements of the Fourth Amendment can secure the same protection of privacy whether the search is for 'mere evidence' or for fruits, instrumentalities or contraband. There must, of course, be a nexus—automatically provided in the case of fruits, instrumentalities or contraband—between the item to be seized and criminal behavior. Thus, in the case of 'mere evidence' probable cause must be examined in terms of cause to believe that the evidence sought will aid in a particular apprehension or conviction. In doing so, consideration of police purposes will be required." 387 U.S. 294, 306–07, 87 S.Ct. 1642, 1650, 18 L.Ed.2d 782, 792.

Steele v. United States (1925). "It is enough if the description [of the place to be searched] is such that the officer with a search warrant can with reasonable effort ascertain and identify the place intended." 267 U.S. 498, 503, 45 S.Ct. 414, 416, 69 L.Ed. 757, 760.

Zurcher v. The Stanford Daily (1978). "The critical element in a reasonable search is not that the owner of the property is suspected of crime but that there is reasonable cause to believe that the specific 'things' to be searched for and seized are located on the property to which entry is sought." 436 U.S. 547, 556, 98 S.Ct. 1970, 1977, 56 L.Ed.2d 525, 535.

Marron v. United States (1927). "The requirement that warrants shall particularly describe the things to be seized makes general searches under them impossible and prevents the seizure of one thing under a warrant describing another. As to what is to be taken, nothing is left to the discretion of the officer executing the warrant." 275 U.S. 192, 196, 48 S.Ct. 74, 76, 72 L.Ed. 231, 237.

Stanford v. Texas (1965). "[T]he constitutional requirement that warrants must particularly describe the 'things to be seized' is to be accorded the most scrupulous exactitude when the 'things' are books, and the basis for their seizure is the ideas which they contain." 379 U.S. 476, 485, 85 S.Ct. 506, 511–12, 13 L.Ed.2d 431, 437.

Segura v. United States (1984). "[W]here officers, having probable cause, enter premises, and with probable cause, arrest the occupants who have legitimate possessory interests in its contents and take them into custody and, for no more than the period here involved [nineteen hours], secure the premises from within to preserve the status quo while others, in good faith, are in the process of obtaining a warrant, they do not violate the Fourth Amendment's proscription against unreasonable seizures." 468 U.S. 796, 798, 104 S.Ct. 3380, 3382, 82 L.Ed.2d 599, 604.

"[S]ecuring a dwelling, on the basis of probable cause, to prevent the destruction or removal of evidence while a search warrant is being sought is not itself an unreasonable seizure of either the dwelling or its contents. . . . [A]bsent exigent circumstances, a warrantless search . . . is illegal." 486 U.S. at 810, 104 S.Ct. at 3388, 82 L.Ed.2d at 612.

Bivens v. Six Unknown Named Agents (1971). "[T]he Fourth Amendment confines an officer executing a search warrant strictly within the bounds set by the warrant. . . ." 403 U.S. 388, 394 n.7, 91 S.Ct. 1999, 2004 n.7, 29 L.Ed.2d 619, 625 n.7.

Wilson v. Layne (1999). "[I]t is a violation of the Fourth Amendment for police to bring members of the media or other third parties into a home during the execution of a warrant when the presence of the third parties in the home was not in aid of the execution of the warrant." 526 U.S. 603, 614, 119 S.Ct. 1692, 1699, 143 L.Ed.2d 818, 830.

Jones v. United States (1958). "[I]t is difficult to imagine a more severe invasion of privacy than the nighttime intrusion into a private home. . . ." 357 U.S. 493, 498, 78 S.Ct. 1253, 1257, 2 L.Ed.2d 1514, 1519.

Richards v. Wisconsin (1997). "In order to justify a 'no-knock' entry, the police must have a reasonable suspicion that knocking and announcing their presence, under the particular circumstances, would be dangerous or futile, or that it would inhibit the effective investigation of the crime by, for example, allowing the destruction of evidence." 520 U.S. 385, 394, 117 S.Ct. 1416, 1421, 137 L.Ed.2d 615, 624.

Dalia v. United States (1979). "Often in executing a warrant the police may find it necessary to interfere with privacy rights not explicitly considered by the judge who issued the warrant. For example, police executing an arrest warrant commonly find it necessary to enter the suspect's home in order to take him into custody, and they thereby impinge on both privacy and freedom of movement. . . . Similarly, officers executing search warrants on occasion must damage property in order to perform their duty." 441 U.S. 238, 257–58, 99 S.Ct. 1682, 1693–94, 60 L.Ed.2d 177, 193.

Ybarra v. Illinois (1979). "[A] person's mere propinquity to others independently suspected of criminal activity does not, without more, give rise to probable cause to search that person." 444 U.S. 85, 91, 100 S.Ct. 338, 342, 62 L.Ed.2d 238, 245.

Michigan v. Summers (1981). "If the evidence that a citizen's residence is harboring contraband is sufficient to persuade a judicial officer that an invasion of the citizen's privacy is justified, it is constitutionally reasonable to require that citizen to remain while officers of the law execute a valid warrant to search his home." 452 U.S. 692, 704–05, 101 S.Ct. 2587, 2595, 69 L.Ed.2d 340, 351.

United States v. Ross (1982). "A lawful search of fixed premises generally extends to the entire area in which the object of the search may be found and is not limited by the possibility that separate acts of entry or opening may be required to complete the search." 456 U.S. 798, 820–21, 102 S.Ct. 2157, 2170–71, 72 L.Ed.2d 572, 591.

Coolidge v. New Hampshire (1971). "An example of the applicability of the 'plain view' doctrine is the situation in which the police have a warrant to search a given area for specific objects, and in the course of the search come across some other article of incriminating character." 403 U.S. 443, 465, 91 S.Ct. 2022, 2037, 29 L.Ed.2d 564, 582.

Camara v. Municipal Court (1967). "The [administrative] warrant procedure is designed to guarantee that a decision to search private property is justified by a reasonable governmental interest. But reasonableness is still the ultimate standard. If a valid public interest justifies the intrusion contemplated, then there is probable cause to issue a suitably restricted search warrant." 387 U.S. 523, 539, 87 S.Ct. 1727, 1736, 18 L.Ed.2d 930, 941.

Michigan v. Clifford (1984). To obtain an administrative warrant to determine the cause and origin of a recent fire, fire officials need show only that "a fire of undetermined origin has occurred on the premises, that the scope of the proposed search is reasonable and will not intrude unnecessarily on the fire victim's privacy, and that the search will be executed at a reasonable and convenient time." 464 U.S. 287, 294, 104 S.Ct. 641, 647, 78 L.Ed.2d 477, 484.

"Circumstances that justify a warrantless search for the cause of a fire may not justify a search to gather evidence of criminal activity once that cause has been determined. . . . A search to gather evidence of criminal activity not in plain view must be made pursuant to a criminal warrant upon a traditional showing of probable cause." 464 U.S. at 294–95, 104 S.Ct. at 647, 78 L.Ed.2d at 484–85.

Chandler v. Miller (1997). "To be reasonable under the Fourth Amendment, a search ordinarily must be based on individualized suspicion of wrongdoing. . . . But particularized exceptions to the main rule are sometimes warranted based on 'special needs, beyond the normal need for law enforcement.' . . . When such 'special needs'—concerns other than crime detection—are alleged in justification of a Fourth Amendment intrusion, courts must undertake a context-specific inquiry, examining closely the competing private and public interests advanced by the parties." 520 U.S. 305, 313–14, 117 S.Ct. 1295, 1301, 137 L.Ed.2d 513, 522–23.

"[W]here the risk to public safety is substantial and real, blanket suspicionless searches calibrated to the risk may rank as 'reasonable'—for example, searches now routine at airports and at entrances to courts and other official buildings. . . . But where . . . public safety is not genuinely in jeopardy, the Fourth Amendment precludes the suspicionless search, no matter how conveniently arranged." 520 U.S. at 323, 117 S.Ct. at 1305, 137 L.Ed.2d at 529.

New Jersey v. T.L.O. (1985). "[T]he legality of a search of a student should depend simply on the reasonableness, under all the circumstances, of the search." 469 U.S. 325, 341, 105 S.Ct. 733, 742, 83 L.Ed.2d 720, 734.

"Under ordinary circumstances, a search of a student by a teacher or other school official will be 'justified at its inception' when there are reasonable grounds for suspecting that the search will turn up evidence that the student has violated or is violating either the law or the rules of the school. Such a search will be permissible in its scope when the measures adopted are reasonably related to the objectives of the search and not excessively intrusive in light of the age and sex of the student and the nature of the infraction." 469 U.S. at 341–42, 105 S.Ct. at 744, 83 L.Ed.2d at 734–35.

Vernonia School District 47J v. Acton (1995). "Somewhat like adults who choose to participate in a 'closely regulated industry,' students who voluntarily participate in school athletics have reason to expect intrusions upon normal rights and privileges, including privacy." 515 U.S. 646, 657, 115 S.Ct. 2386, 2393, 132 L.Ed.2d 564, 577.

Berger v. New York (1967). A warrant procedure authorizing electronic surveillance must carefully circumscribe the search in nature, scope, and duration and must not permit "a trespassory invasion of the home or office, by general warrant, contrary to the command of the Fourth Amendment." 388 U.S. 41, 64, 87 S.Ct. 1873, 1886, 18 L.Ed.2d 1040, 1055.

Alderman v. United States (1969). "[A]ny petitioner would be entitled to the suppression of government evidence originating in electronic surveillance violative of his own Fourth Amendment right to be free of unreasonable searches and seizures. Such violation would occur if the United States unlawfully overheard conversations of a petitioner himself or conversations occurring on his premises, whether or not he was present or participated in those conversations." 394 U.S. 165, 176, 89 S.Ct. 961, 968, 22 L.Ed.2d 176, 188.

Review and Discussion Questions

1. Why is time a more important factor in determining probable cause to search than it is in determining probable cause to arrest?

2. Formulate a set of circumstances in which there is probable cause to search but not probable cause to arrest; in which there is probable cause to arrest but not probable cause to search; in which there is probable cause both to arrest and to search.

3. Name three kinds of property that are unlikely to remain in a particular place for longer than a week. Name three kinds of property that are likely to remain in a particular place for longer than a week.

4. Why should law enforcement officers executing a search warrant refrain from asking the person against whom the search is directed to assist them in any way?

5. Assume that you are a law enforcement officer attempting to obtain a search warrant for urban premises, rural premises, a multiple-unit dwelling, and a motor vehicle. Describe, as you would in the affidavit, one of each of these places that is familiar to you. (For example, describe for purposes of a search warrant application a friend's farm in the country.)

6. Discuss three ways in which time affects a search warrant and an arrest warrant differently.

7. Law enforcement officers have a search warrant to search a house for heroin and to search the person of the house owners' eighteen-year-old daughter. When the officers arrive at the house to execute the warrant, the following persons are present:

   a. The owners

   b. The eighteen-year-old daughter

   c. The daughter's fifteen-year-old brother, who appears extremely nervous

   d. The daughter's boyfriend, whom the officers recognize as a local gang member who is known to carry a knife

   e. An unidentified elderly couple

   To what extent may the officers search or detain each person present?

8. A law enforcement officer has a search warrant to search the defendant's house for cameras stolen from a particular department store. May the officer

   a. look in desk drawers?

   b. search the defendant's body?

   c. seize a brown paper bag containing a white powder resembling heroin, found in a desk drawer?

   d. search the defendant's garage?

   e. look in the defendant's wife's jewelry box?

   f. break open a locked wall safe?

   g. seize a portable radio found on a table with a tag from the department store attached to it?

9. Is each of the following descriptions in a search warrant of items to be seized sufficiently particular?

   a. An unknown-make .38-caliber, blue steel, with wood grips, revolver. See *United States v. Wolfenbarger*, 696 F.2d 750 (10th Cir. 1982).

   b. Videotape and equipment used in a copyright infringement. See *United States v. Smith*, 686 F.2d 234 (5th Cir. 1982).

   c. All doctor's files concerning an accident patient. See *United States v. Hershenow*, 680 F.2d 847 (1st Cir. 1982).

   d. Plaques, mirrors, and other items. See *United States v. Apker*, 705 F.2d 293 (8th Cir. 1983).

   e. Items related to the smuggling, packing, distribution, and use of controlled substances. See *United States v. Ladd*, 704 F.2d 134 (4th Cir. 1983).

   f. Business papers that are evidence and instrumentalities of a violation of a general tax fraud statute. See *United States v. Cardwell*, 680 F.2d 75 (9th Cir. 1982).

10. Does a warrant to search a house authorize a search of a tent set up on the premises near the house? Does a warrant authorizing the seizure of stolen computers authorize the seizure of nonstolen computers commingled with them? Is the seizure of an entire book of accounts permissible when only two or three pages of the book are relevant to the specifications of the search warrant?

Real-Life Fact Situations

1 Before the police searched defendants' home, Lake County agent David Walsh filed a complaint for a search warrant pursuant to section 108-3(a) of the Code of Criminal Procedure of 1963 (725 ILCS 5/108-3(a) (West 1998)). In the complaint, Walsh named Bryan Burmeister and "2812 N. Elmwood, Waukegan" as the targets of the proposed search. Walsh did not allege that Bryan had any connection to the residence. Furthermore, Walsh mistakenly noted that the home is on the east side of the street when, in fact, it sits on the west side. A residence on the east side of the street, 2821 N. Elmwood, closely resembles the Burmeister residence.

Walsh stated that he had probable cause to believe that evidence of cocaine trafficking could be found in defendants' home. Walsh's suspicions were supported by tips from "anonymous sources" and an investigation by unnamed police officers. Garbage in defendants' neighborhood is collected weekly. On three consecutive trash days, the officers collected several black plastic garbage bags from the curb in front of the residence. The first search disclosed one 4½ -inch straw and "plastic baggies" containing a white powdery substance that field tested positive for cocaine. The second search disclosed "two clear plastic bags with the corners missing that had a white powdery residue which field tested for the presence of cocaine and indices." The third search disclosed one rolled-up tissue with residue that field tested positive for cocaine. Agent Walsh did not allege that he had any personal knowledge of the trash searches. Walsh applied for a warrant two days after the third search. After reviewing the complaint, Judge John Radosevich issued a search warrant for defendants' home. No evidence suggests that Walsh participated in the search of the residence.

The State offered no evidence at the hearing on defendants' motion to quash the arrests and suppress evidence. However, each defendant submitted an affidavit stating that he never used black trash bags to deposit garbage because the use of the bags was prohibited by the trash collection rules; defendants used only a large blue bin to deposit trash. Defendants introduced photographs of their home, adjacent homes, and the trash bin they used. The trial court granted defendants' motion, concluding that there was no probable cause to search defendants' home because the warrant application failed to establish a nexus between the curbside contraband and the residence. Should the defendant's motion to quash the arrests and suppress evidence be granted? *People v. Burmeister*, 728 N.E.2d 1260 (Ill.App. 2000).

Read the court opinion at:

www.state.il.us/court/Opinions/AppellateCourt/2000/
2ndDistrict/May/HTML/2990344.htm

2 Appellant was staying for an indefinite period of time at the home of James Meixner in rural Cass County. This particular house had been the object of a search pursuant to warrant in June 1997, three months previous to the October 1997 search at issue herein. In the June search numerous weapons and drugs were found on the premises.

A confidential reliable informant (CRI) visited Meixner on September 25, 1997. The CRI had previously purchased marijuana and methamphetamines from Meixner, and on this visit observed drug paraphernalia present. The informant told police that Meixner said someone named "Smiley" might have methamphetamines and possibly would stop by on September 27, 1997.

On September 26, 1997, a sheriff's deputy applied for a search warrant for Meixner's property, cars and Meixner himself. The application was based on the information from the CRI. The deputy also stated in the affidavit that he had personal knowledge that Meixner had two previous convictions for possession of controlled substances, including a conviction earlier that year. The deputy specifically requested a no-knock, nighttime entry. The affidavit stated that the nighttime search was sought because:

Your Affiant believes that entering onto the described property could be [sic] affected by law enforcement officers, if done under the cover of darkness, and therefore allowing for the security of property without endangering law enforcement officers or subjects who may be located within the residence or outbuildings. A [p]rior [s]earch [w]arrant was executed on the 27th of June 1997 and numerous weapons were removed [from] the residence.

The affidavit disclosed the unannounced entry was sought because:

Your Affiant knows that, through experience and training that often persons involved in narcotics trafficking and transactions carry firearms and/or other weapons to protect themselves and to protect their controlled substances.

Your Affiant further knows through experience that those involved with controlled substance[s] often attempt to destroy those substances if they should [fear] substances are in [jeopardy] of being confiscated by law enforcement officers.

The deputy testified at the omnibus hearing that most of this language was taken from other search warrant affidavits, and was commonly used in drug-related search warrant applications.

A district court judge signed the warrant application September 26 and it was executed at 9:30 P.M. on October 3, 1997. When executing the warrant the officers parked about a quarter of a mile from Meixner's house. Before entering, they observed Meixner and appellant, whom they did not recognize, sitting across from each other at a coffee table, playing what appeared to be a word game. One of the officers tried the front door, and found it unlocked. The officers, in camouflage, helmets and masks, entered with guns drawn, shouting, "police."

Meixner did not move other than raising his arms above his head. Appellant was startled by the entry, and tossed the dictionary he was holding into the air. He attempted to run out of the room, and did not obey officers' commands to keep his hands where they could be seen and to stand still. Appellant held his fist clenched, and then appeared to shove the contents of his fist down the front of his pants. Officers testified they thought appellant might be hiding a weapon. The officers eventually subdued him. Officers removed a buck knife from appellant's belt and two items containing methamphetamines—an inhaler and a plastic baggie.

Appellant was arrested and charged with fifth-degree controlled substance crime. See Minn.Stat. § 152.025, subd. 2(1) (1998). He moved to suppress all the evidence obtained during the execution of the warrant, claiming there was no basis for the unannounced search. Should the evidence be suppressed? *State v. Wasson*, 615 N.W.2d 316 (Minn. 2000).

Read the court opinion at:

www.finance-commerce.com/court/opinions/000807/
c799199.htm

3 Fish and Wildlife Trooper Danny Sides submitted the affidavit in support of the search warrant. The following facts are taken from the affidavit. Trooper Sides was investigating the illegal killing of a moose in the Point McKenzie area. On December 10, 1996, at 4:30 P.M., Trooper Sides interviewed Kenneth Webeck who told Trooper Sides that he saw a man illegally shoot and kill a bull moose in the Point McKenzie area. Webeck stated that the suspect had fired six to eight shots from an "assault" style rifle. The suspect was driving an older model Yamaha snow machine with a single headlight. He was accompanied by another rider who also had a snow machine with a single headlight. Neither man made any attempt to salvage the meat or antlers from the dead animal. Webeck stated he had picked up a spent cartridge from the scene which he gave Trooper Sides. Trooper Sides described the casing as a "point 30 cal. military, 7.62 NATO ([c]ivilian version is .308 cal.) round with 'CAVIM 92' stamped on the bottom of the brass."

Twenty minutes later, Trooper Sides contacted two suspects about one mile from the illegal moose kill. Trooper Sides examined the men's hunting licenses and tags. One of the men was Sherman R. Lewis Jr. and the other man was Robert L. Lemoine. Trooper Sides saw Lewis place an assault style rifle in a rifle case.

When he was talking with Lewis, Trooper Sides saw Lewis drop a cartridge on the ground. Trooper Sides picked up the cartridge and saw that it had "CAVIM 92" stamped on the bottom. Sides stated that Lewis was riding on an older model Yamaha snow machine with a single headlight and that Lemoine also had a snow machine with a single headlight. Sides also obtained the license number of the blue Ford Bronco which the men were driving and using to pull a trailer with the snow machines.

Trooper Sides then visited the site where the bull moose had been killed that morning. Sides described the moose as an illegal bull which had been killed by several rounds from a small caliber rifle.

The next day, Sides learned from computer records that Lewis had "a [f]elony conviction involving weapons." The records directed any law enforcement officer who had contact with Lewis to contact his probation officer. Trooper Sides contacted John Baiamonte, Lewis' probation officer. Baiamonte told Sides that Lewis was not allowed to be in possession of a firearm. He gave Sides Lewis' address. Fish and Wildlife Aide Larson went to the address and found the blue Ford Bronco and two snow machines.

Trooper Sides presented his affidavit to the magistrate to obtain a search warrant for evidence of the crimes of illegally taking a bull moose and wanton waste of the game. The magistrate issued a warrant authorizing the police to search Lewis' residence for evidence of these crimes. The warrant authorized the police to search for evidence of the game violations, including the assault style rifle and 7.62 caliber NATO military style ammunition with "CAVIM 92" stamped on the base of the bullet.

Based on comments made by Lewis' probation officer, Trooper Sides had reason to believe that Lewis was a heroin dealer. The warrants were executed on December 13, 1996 by Trooper Sides and six to eight other law enforcement officers. Probation Officer Baiamonte participated in the search. Trooper Sides knocked on Lewis' door and announced himself three times. He received no response, but heard scrambling noises inside. The officers then kicked the door in. The time between the first knock and the forced entry was about one minute. Upon entry, State Trooper Nashalook heard the toilet flush on the second level of the house. He ran upstairs and found Lewis sitting on the toilet with his shorts pulled up. Trooper Nashalook looked into the toilet bowl and saw a white substance dissolving rapidly. The trooper got a cup and scooped the white substance out of the toilet. He conducted a field test on the substance, which tested positive for cocaine. Troopers then obtained an additional warrant to search for evidence of a drug violation. Should the defendant's motion to suppress the evidence obtained as a result of the search be granted? *Lewis v. State,* 9 P.3d 1028 (Alaska App. 2000).

Read the court opinion at:
touchngo.com/ap/html/ap-1689.htm

4 On October 31, 1995, members of the Federal Bureau of Investigation's Caribbean Gang Task Force obtained a warrant to search 1437 East 116th Street, Cleveland, Ohio, for drug paraphernalia, and weapons. The warrant authorized a search of the "premises, curtilage, containers, and persons therein" at a location described as "1437 East 116th Street, Cleveland, Cuyahoga County, Ohio, and being more fully described as the downstairs unit in a two-family, two and one half story, white wood[-]sided dwelling with green trim."

Although the record is sparse, it appears that the "downstairs unit" is a five-room apartment consisting of a front room, two bedrooms, a kitchen, and a bathroom. One bedroom and the kitchen are located in the rear of the apartment. There is a door in the kitchen that leads to a common hallway. The hallway contains a door that leads into the building's basement. A person cannot directly access the basement from the downstairs unit. Defendants Kenneth and Kewin King lived in the downstairs unit.

On November 1, members of the Task Force executed the warrant. As the agents entered the downstairs unit, they observed defendants standing near the kitchen. Kenneth ran to the second floor but was apprehended by one of the agents. Both defendants were subsequently secured in the downstairs unit.

The officers searched the downstairs unit and found 60.6 grams of cocaine base in one bedroom and 16.65 grams in the other bedroom. One of the agents exited the downstairs unit and searched the building's basement where he discovered 443 grams of cocaine base. Should the defendants' motion to suppress the evidence seized from the basement be granted? *United States. v. King,* 227 F.3d 732 (6th Cir. 2000).

Read the court opinion at:
www.law.emory.edu/6circuit/sept97/97a0285p.06.html

5 Appellant was an eighth grade science teacher at Fork Union Military Academy (the Academy) in Fluvanna County. He resided in an apartment located in the middle school student barracks and served as a barracks supervisor. In 1997, Academy officials advised local and state police that appellant may have abused one or more of the Academy's students. One official told police that he had entered appellant's apartment to check a water leak. On two different occasions, he observed in appellant's apartment nude photographs depicting two named cadets, J.L. and H.L. Some of the photographs had been taken in appellant's apartment. He observed several journals containing "information about 'boys needing discipline and spanking.'" He also saw a "delinquency report completed on . . . 11th grader, [J.L.] with the consequences listed as '3 whacks on the bare behind'" and had information that J.L. had been seen leaving appellant's barracks at 10:00 P.M. in violation of school rules. The Academy had a written corporal punishment policy which provided that only the middle school commandant or headmaster could paddle middle school students. The policy also provided that such paddling could occur only while a student was fully clothed and required the parents' written permission. The Academy official opined that, because appellant taught middle school, appellant's relationship with 11th grader J.L. was "strange," and he opined that appellant's contact with an 8th grade student, which involved his constantly escorting the student to off-campus activities, exceeded the "normal student/teacher relationship" and was "unhealthy."

Using this information, police obtained a warrant to search appellant's barracks apartment. The warrant specifically listed as subject to seizure, *inter alia,* "photographs . . . depicting nudity and/or sexual activities involving children," "[w]ritten materials (letters, diaries) . . . related to sexual conduct between juveniles and adults," and "books . . . and photographs depicting nudity and/or sexual activities of juveniles." While executing the warrant, Deputy Hogsten scanned appellant's numerous handwritten journals looking for photographs and other materials specified in the warrant. If Hogsten observed an "explicit" photograph in a journal, he marked the journal and handed it to Trooper Watson, who assisted with the search. If no explicit photograph was immediately apparent in a journal, Hogsten scanned it "[to] see if [he] could find anything that was in the warrant [they] were looking for." After reviewing all appellant's journals in this fashion, Hogsten and Watson seized fourteen volumes and left behind two or three. Subsequently, Deputy Craig reviewed the seized journals in greater detail and decided which portions would be used as evidence.

A grand jury indicted appellant on sixteen counts of taking indecent liberties with two minors, J.L. and H.L. Appellant moved to suppress the excerpts taken from his diaries, arguing that the seizure of the diaries violated the Fourth Amendment's prohibition against general warrants. He also argued that admission of the excerpts into evidence would violate his Fourth and Fifth Amendment privilege against self-incrimination. Should the appellant's motion to suppress be granted? *Moyer v. Commonwealth,* 531 S.E.2d 580 (Va.App. 2000).

Read the court opinion at:
www.courts.state.va.us/txtops/2959972.txt

6 Simons was employed as an electronic engineer at the Foreign Bureau of Information Services (FBIS), a division of the Central Intelligence Agency (CIA). FBIS provided Simons with an office, which he did not share with anyone, and a computer with Internet access.

In June 1998, FBIS instituted a policy regarding Internet usage by employees. The policy stated that employees were to use the Internet for official government business only. Accessing unlawful material was specifically prohibited. The policy explained that FBIS would conduct electronic audits to ensure compliance:

Audits. Electronic auditing shall be implemented within all FBIS unclassified networks that connect to the Internet or other publicly accessible networks to support identification, termination, and prosecution of unauthorized activity. These electronic audit mechanisms shall . . . be capable of recording:

- Access to the system, including successful and failed login attempts, and logouts;
- Inbound and outbound file transfers;
- Terminal connections (telnet) to and from external systems;
- Sent and received e-mail messages;
- Web sites visited, including uniform resource locator (URL) of pages retrieved;
- Date, Time, and user associated with each event.

J.A. 125-26. The policy also stated that "[u]sers shall . . . [u]nderstand FBIS will periodically audit, inspect, and/or monitor the user's Internet access as deemed appropriate." J.A. 127.

FBIS contracted with Science Applications International Corporation (SAIC) for the management of FBIS' computer network, including monitoring for any inappropriate use of computer resources. On July 17, 1998, Clifford Mauck, a manager at SAIC, began exploring the capabilities of a firewall recently acquired by SAIC, because Mauck believed that SAIC needed to become more familiar with the firewall to service the FBIS contract properly. Mauck entered the keyword "sex" into the firewall database for July 14 and 17, 1998, and found a large number of Internet "hits" originating from Simons' computer. It was obvious to Mauck from the names of the sites that they were not visited for official FBIS purposes.

Mauck reported this discovery to his contact at FBIS, Katherine Camer. Camer then worked with another SAIC employee, Robert Harper, to further investigate the apparently unauthorized activity. Camer instructed Harper to view one of the websites that Simons had visited. Harper complied and found that the site contained pictures of nude women.

At Camer's direction and from his own workstation, Harper examined Simons' computer to determine whether Simons had downloaded any picture files from the Internet; Harper found over 1,000 such files. Again from his own workstation, Harper viewed several of the pictures and observed that they were pornographic in nature. Also at Camer's request and from his own workstation, Harper printed a list of the titles of the downloaded picture files. Harper was then asked to copy all of the files on the hard drive of Simons' computer; Harper accomplished this task, again, from his own workstation.

On or about July 31, 1998, two representatives from the CIA Office of the Inspector General (OIG), one of whom was a criminal investigator, viewed selected files from the copy of Simons' hard drive; the pictures were of minors. Later that day, Harper physically entered Simons' office, removed the original hard drive, replaced it with a copy, and gave the original to the FBIS Area Security Officer. The Security Officer turned it over to the OIG criminal investigator the same day. This last assignment was the only one that required Harper to physically enter Simons' office.

On August 5, 1998, FBI Special Agent John Mesisca viewed over 50 of the images on the hard drive that had been removed from Simons' office; many of the images contained child pornography. Mesisca, Harper, the two OIG representatives, and Assistant United States Attorney Tom Connolly worked together to prepare an application for a warrant to search Simons' office and computer. An affidavit from Mesisca supported the warrant application. The affidavit stated, *inter alia*, that Simons had connected a zip drive to his computer. The affidavit also expressed a "need" to conduct the search in secret. J.A. 140.

The warrant was issued on August 6, 1998. It stated that the executing officers were to leave at Simons' office a copy of the warrant and a receipt for any property taken. The warrant mentioned neither permission for, nor prohibition of, secret execution.

Mesisca and others executed the search during the evening of August 6, 1998, when Simons was not present. The search team copied the contents of Simons' computer; computer diskettes found in Simons' desk drawer; computer files stored on the zip drive or on zip drive diskettes; videotapes; and various documents, including personal correspondence. No original evidence was removed from the office. Neither a copy of the warrant nor a receipt for the property seized was left in the office or otherwise given to Simons at that time, and Simons did not learn of the search for approximately 45 days. When Mesisca reviewed the computer materials copied during the search, he found over 50 pornographic images of minors.

In September 1998, Mesisca applied for a second search warrant. The supporting affidavit, like the affidavit that supported the August application, stated that Simons had connected a zip drive to his computer. The September affidavit described the August application as an application for a surreptitious search warrant.

A second search warrant was obtained on September 17, 1998 and executed on September 23, 1998, with Simons present. Original evidence was seized and removed from the office. The executors left Simons with a copy of the warrant and an inventory of the items seized.

Simons subsequently was indicted on one count of knowingly receiving child pornography that had been transported in interstate commerce, *see* 18 U.S.C.A. § 2252A(a)(2)(A), and one count of knowingly possessing material containing images of child pornography that had been transported in interstate commerce, *see* 18 U.S.C.A. § 2252A(a)(5)(B). Simons moved to suppress the evidence, arguing that the searches of his office and computer violated his Fourth Amendment rights. Should the motion to suppress be granted? *United States v. Simons*, 206 F.3d 392 (4th Cir. 2000)

Read the court opinion at:
www.law.emory.edu/4circuit/feb2000/994238.p.html

Probable Cause

Outline

caselaw.findlaw.com/data/
constitution/amendment04/
02.html#3
Comprehensive discussion (with annotations) of probable cause
faculty.ncwc.edu/toconnor/
315/315lect06.htm
Article, "Probable Cause"; discusses all aspects of probable cause
majoritywhip.house.gov/
constitution/hints/
amendment4.asp
Excerpt, "Probable Cause" from "The Constitution of the United States of America: Analysis and Interpretation" by Johnny H. Killian and George A. Costello

For new and updated weblinks, go to www.wadsworth.com/
cj/ferdico0253

Carroll v. United States
laws.findlaw.com/us/267/
132.html
Brinegar v. United States
laws.findlaw.com/us/338/
160.html
Illinois v. Gates
laws.findlaw.com/us/462/
213.html

Probable cause is discussed to a limited extent in Chapter 3, as one of the basic underlying concepts of criminal procedure. It is also referred to in Chapters 4 and 5 as an essential element of the law dealing with arrests and search warrants. This chapter attempts to impart a practical working knowledge of all aspects of probable cause as it concerns both arrest and search and seizure. This chapter is therefore important for a complete understanding of Chapters 4 and 5 as well as of the later chapters in Part III on exceptions to the search warrant requirement.

Definition

Two different but similar definitions of probable cause are cited here, one for search and one for arrest, because different types of information are required to establish probable cause in each instance. An often-quoted definition of probable cause to search is that found in *Carroll v. United States,* 267 U.S. 132, 45 S.Ct. 280, 69 L.Ed. 543 (1925), in which the U.S. Supreme Court said that probable cause exists when "the facts and circumstances within their [the officers'] knowledge and of which they had reasonably trustworthy information [are] sufficient in themselves to warrant a man of reasonable caution in the belief that [seizable property would be found in a particular place or on a particular person]." 267 U.S. at 162, 45 S.Ct. at 288, 69 L.Ed. at 555. Paraphrasing the *Carroll* case, the Court defined probable cause to arrest in *Brinegar v. United States,* 338 U.S. 160, 175–76, 69 S.Ct. 1302, 1310–11, 93 L.Ed. 1879, 1890 (1949):

> Probable cause exists where the "facts and circumstances within their [the officers'] knowledge and of which they had reasonably trustworthy information [are] sufficient in themselves to warrant a man of reasonable caution in the belief that" an offense has been or is being committed [by the person to be arrested].

These definitions differ only in that the facts and circumstances that would justify an arrest may be different from those that would justify a search. This chapter is primarily concerned with the part of the definition of probable cause that is common to both arrests and searches—namely, the nature, quality, and amount of information necessary to establish probable cause. In this regard, another U.S. Supreme Court definition of probable cause may be helpful.

> "[T]he term 'probable cause,' according to its usual acceptation, means less than evidence which would justify condemnation. . . ." Finely tuned standards such as proof beyond a reasonable doubt or by a preponderance of the evidence, useful in formal trials, have no place in the magistrate's decision. While an effort to fix some general, numerically precise degree of certainty corresponding to "probable cause" may not be helpful, it is clear that "only the probability, and not a prima facie showing, of criminal activity is the standard of probable cause." *Illinois v. Gates,* 462 U.S. 213, 235, 103 S.Ct. 2317, 2330, 76 L.Ed.2d 527, 546 (1983).

This chapter is designed to clarify this definition by giving specific examples of information that law enforcement officers must have before they may arrest or search, with or without a warrant. *Effective criminal investigation and prosecution depend on the quality and quantity of the facts and circumstances gathered by law enforcement officers as well as their ability to communicate this information via reports, affidavits, and testimony.*

Information on which probable cause may be based can come to the attention of a law enforcement officer in two ways: (1) the officer may perceive the information, or

(2) someone else may perceive the information and relay it to the officer. These information sources are treated differently by the courts and are discussed separately here.

Key Points

1. Probable cause exists where the facts and circumstances within a law enforcement officer's knowledge and of which the officer has reasonably trustworthy information are sufficient in themselves to warrant a person of reasonable caution in the belief that a crime has been or is being committed by a particular person or that seizable property would be found in a particular place or on a particular person.

2. Only the fair probability, and not a *prima facie* showing, of criminal activity is the standard of probable cause.

Information Obtained through the Officer's Own Senses

Law enforcement officers applying for an arrest or search warrant must state *in writing* in the complaint or affidavit the underlying facts on which probable cause for the issuance of the warrant is based (see Chapters 4 and 5). All warrantless arrests and most warrantless searches must also be based on probable cause. Although no written document is required, officers must be prepared to justify a warrantless arrest or search with underlying facts if its validity is later challenged. Therefore, whether or not a warrant is sought, officers must have sufficient information supporting probable cause *before* conducting an arrest or search.

One type of information used to support probable cause is information from the officer's own senses. This includes what an officer perceives through the senses of sight, hearing, smell, touch, and taste. Furthermore, an officer's perceptions may be given additional credence because of personal experience or expertise in a particular area.

> [I]n some situations a police officer may have particular training or experience that would enable him to infer criminal activity in circumstances where an ordinary observer would not. . . . In such situations, when an officer's experience and expertise is relevant to the probable cause determination, the officer must be able to explain sufficiently the basis of that opinion so that it "can be understood by the average reasonably prudent person." *State v. Demeter*, 590 A.2d 1179, 1183–84 (N.J. 1991).

Indications of Criminal Activity Supporting Probable Cause

A law enforcement officer's perceptions of a crime being committed in his or her presence clearly provide probable cause to arrest the person committing the crime. Crimes are seldom committed in an officer's presence, however, and usually an officer must develop probable cause over time from perceptions of a variety of facts and circumstances. The following discussion focuses on specific facts and circumstances indicative of criminal activity, together with court cases explaining their relative importance in the probable cause equation.

www.law.wfu.edu/faculty/wright/Publications/YLJNote.htm
Article, "The Civil and Criminal Methodologies of the Fourth Amendment"; compares the "balancing" and "probable cause" approaches to deciding cases

lawschool.lexis.com/emanuel/web/crimpro/crimpro02.htm
Detailed outline explaining the basic principles of probable cause to arrest and to search

www.nedrud.com/rbA11.html
Article, "Arrest and Detention: Reasonable Grounds"; discusses probable cause to arrest, focusing on United States and Texas law

caselaw.findlaw.com/data/constitution/amendment04/01.html#2
Comprehensive discussion (with annotations) of the history and scope of the Fourth Amendment

www.tmcec.com/probcaus.htm
Article, "Probable Cause Affidavits for Search and Arrest Warrants" by Nigel Gusdorf

www.dep.state.pa.us/dep/deputate/polycomm/pressrel/97/afidavit.htm
Actual affidavit, "Affidavit of Probable Cause for Search Warrant" to find evidence of or instruments used for criminal violations of the Pennsylvania Solid Waste Management Act

FLIGHT   "[D]eliberately furtive actions and flight at the approach of strangers or law officers are strong indicia of mens rea [guilty mind], and when coupled with specific knowledge on the part of the officer relating the suspect to the evidence of crime, they are proper factors to be considered in the decision to make an arrest." *Sibron v. New York*, 392 U.S. 40, 66–67, 88 S.Ct. 1889, 1904–05, 20 L.Ed.2d 917, 937 (1968). In *United States v. Bell*, 892 F.2d 959 (10th Cir. 1989), the court found that the following facts gave a narcotics officer reasonable suspicion that the suspect was transporting illegal drugs, justifying his detention for investigation: The suspect disembarked from a flight originating in Hawaii and repeatedly went to a group of phones but did not appear to be talking; he had no luggage besides his shoulder bag and appeared visibly nervous; he met another person carrying a package and walked with him around the airport. The court held that, when the suspect dropped his bag and ran down the concourse in response to detention and questioning, the officer had probable cause to arrest him. Thus, flight *plus* other indications of criminal activity may provide probable cause to arrest.

Flight by itself, however, does not support a finding of probable cause. In *Wong Sun v. United States*, 371 U.S. 471, 83 S.Ct. 407, 9 L.Ed.2d 441 (1963), federal officers arrested a man named Hom Way at two o'clock in the morning and found narcotics in his possession. Hom Way told the officers that he had purchased an ounce of heroin from a person named Blackie Toy. At six o'clock that same morning, the officers went to a laundry operated by James Wah Toy. When Toy answered the door, one officer identified himself, whereupon Toy slammed the door and ran to his living quarters at the rear of the building. The officers broke in and followed Toy to his bedroom, where they arrested him.

The U.S. Supreme Court held that the arrest was made without probable cause. First, the officers had no basis in experience for confidence in the reliability of Hom Way's information. (The reliability of informants is discussed further later.) Second, the mere fact of Toy's flight did not provide a justification for a warrantless arrest without further information.

> Toy's refusal to admit the officers and his flight down the hallway thus signified a guilty knowledge no more clearly than it did a natural desire to repel an apparently unauthorized intrusion. . . .
>
> A contrary holding here would mean that a vague suspicion could be transformed into probable cause for arrest by reason of ambiguous conduct which the arresting officers themselves have provoked. 371 U.S. at 483–84, 83 S.Ct. at 415, 9 L.Ed.2d at 452–53.

FURTIVE CONDUCT   Law enforcement officers frequently observe persons engaged in secretive or furtive conduct, arousing suspicion of impending criminal activity or concealment of evidence of criminal activity. Usually, this conduct at least justifies an officer's further investigation to determine whether a crime is being or is about to be committed. (See Chapter 7 on stop and frisk.) Furtive conduct by itself, however, is usually insufficient to establish probable cause to arrest because the observed person may be making a totally innocent gesture, exhibiting a physical or mental problem, or reacting in fear to an officer's presence. A person's nervousness in the presence of a law enforcement officer does not alone amount to probable cause. The Supreme Court of Colorado stated that "[i]t is normal for law-abiding persons, as well as persons guilty of criminal activity, to be nervous when stopped by a policeman for a traffic offense." *People v. Goessl*, 526 P.2d 664, 665 (Colo. 1974). A person should not be subject to arrest or search on the basis of a mistaken interpretation of an innocent action.

Sibron v. New York
laws.findlaw.com/us/392/
40.html

Wong Sun v. United States
laws.findlaw.com/us/371/
471.html

In *United States v. Ingrao*, 897 F.2d 860 (7th Cir. 1990), the defendant was arrested because he carried a bag down a gangway previously used in a suspicious transaction and furtively looked around while crossing the street. The court held that, while furtive gestures are relevant to probable cause, more specific information connecting the defendant to criminal activity was needed to establish probable cause in that case.

When police have additional specific incriminating information, furtive conduct may be the deciding factor in determining probable cause to arrest. In *United States v. McCarty*, 862 F.2d 143 (7th Cir. 1988), officers had corroborated information from informants that the defendant was a convicted felon, that he was driving a tan compact car with Michigan license plates bearing the number 278, and that he was likely to be carrying a gun. While on routine patrol, officers saw the described car and followed it. The car attempted to evade the officers, and, when stopped, the driver was observed leaning to the right as if to hide something under the passenger seat. The officers arrested the defendant and seized a handgun found in his car. The court found probable cause to arrest the defendant for possession of a firearm by a convicted felon. "The fact that McCarty tried to evade [the officers] while they were following him, and his furtive gesture when he was stopped, reinforced the reasonableness of the officers' belief that McCarty had committed or was committing a crime." 862 F.2d at 147. Furtive conduct, therefore, is relevant to probable cause but must be evaluated in light of all the facts and circumstances, including time of day, setting, weather conditions, persons present, and nature of the crime.

REAL OR PHYSICAL EVIDENCE Officers may establish probable cause by the observation and evaluation of real or physical evidence. In *State v. Heald*, 314 A.2d 820 (Me. 1973), officers were summoned at 2:00 A.M. to a store that had recently been burglarized. The officers discovered two sets of footprints in fresh-fallen snow leading from the store to the tire tracks of an automobile. Since the tire tracks were identifiable by a distinctive tread, the officers followed them. After a short distance, the officers met another officer who had found a checkbook belonging to the store owner in the road. Farther down the road the officers found a bag containing electrical parts. Then the officers came upon a car parked in the middle of the road with its lights off—the only other vehicle the officers had seen since leaving the scene of the crime, except a vehicle driven by a person known to the officers. As the patrol car approached the parked car, the parked car's lights came on and the car was driven away. The officers stopped the car and arrested its two occupants for breaking and entering.

The court held that the items of real evidence found and the reasonable inferences drawn from the evidence, together with the highly suspicious circumstances, provided probable cause to arrest the defendants. The court added that "although the possibility of mistake existed, as it invariably does in a probable cause situation, they would have been remiss in their duty if they had not arrested the defendants promptly." 314 A.2d at 825.

ADMISSIONS A person's **admission** of criminal conduct to a law enforcement officer may provide probable cause to arrest. In *Rawlings v. Kentucky*, 448 U.S. 98, 100 S.Ct. 1556, 65 L.Ed.2d 633 (1980), a law enforcement officer, under authority of a search warrant, ordered the defendant's female companion (Cox) to empty the contents of her purse. Among those contents was a large quantity and variety of controlled substances. Upon pouring out these items, Cox told the defendant to take what was his. The defendant immediately claimed ownership of some of the controlled substances. The Court held that "[o]nce petitioner admitted ownership of the sizable quantity of

Rawlings v. Kentucky
laws.findlaw.com/us/448/
98.html

drugs found in Cox's purse, the police clearly had probable cause to place the petitioner under arrest." 448 U.S. at 111, 100 S.Ct. at 2564, 65 L.Ed.2d at 645.

FALSE OR IMPLAUSIBLE ANSWERS False or implausible answers to routine questions may be considered in determining probable cause, but usually they do not provide probable cause standing alone. In *United States v. Velasquez,* 885 F.2d 1076 (3d Cir. 1989), the court found that the following facts provided probable cause to arrest the defendant for interstate smuggling of contraband: (1) the defendant and her companion were on a long-distance trip from Miami, a major drug importation point, to the New York area; (2) the defendant and her companion had given the officer conflicting stories about the purpose of their trip and their relationship; (3) the defendant and her companion appeared nervous when answering the officer's questions; (4) the defendant had told the officer that the automobile she was driving belonged to her "cousin," but she could not give her cousin's name; and (5) the automobile she was driving had a false floor in its trunk and appeared specially modified to carry contraband in a secret compartment.

In *United States v. Anderson,* 676 F.Supp. 604 (E.D.Pa. 1987), the court held that police had probable cause to seize money found in a legally stopped car, based partially on the defendant's implausible statements.

> The officers knew that defendants were driving towards New York on a known drug route in a car owned by someone else, a procedure used by drug dealers to avoid forfeiture. The officers had found a large sum of money in small denominations, wrapped with rubber bands in small bundles. These bundles were in three bags. At the time of the stop, defendant Anderson stated that they won the money in Atlantic City and were on their way to Chester, however, the location where they were stopped and the way the money was packaged were not consistent with this story. Finally, a Chester police officer relayed that defendants were known drug pushers. Based on these facts, the police had probable cause to believe defendants were engaged in drug activity and that the money was drug-related. The money, therefore was properly confiscated. 676 F.Supp. at 608.

PRESENCE AT A CRIME SCENE OR IN A HIGH-CRIME AREA Mere presence at a crime scene or in a high-crime area does not alone constitute probable cause to arrest. In *Ker v. California,* 374 U.S. 23, 83 S.Ct. 1623, 10 L.Ed.2d 726 (1963), however, the Supreme Court found probable cause to arrest the wife of a drug suspect based on her presence at an apartment that she shared with her husband and that was being used as the base for his narcotics operation.

Ker v. California laws.findlaw.com/us/374/23.html

> Probable cause for the arrest of petitioner Diane Ker, while not present at the time the officers entered the apartment to arrest her husband, was nevertheless present at the time of her arrest. Upon their entry and announcement of their identity, the officers were met not only by George Ker but also by Diane Ker, who was emerging from the kitchen. Officer Berman immediately walked to the doorway from which she emerged and, without entering, observed the brick-shaped package of marijuana in plain view. Even assuming that her presence in a small room with the contraband in a prominent position on the kitchen sink would not alone establish a reasonable ground for the officers' belief that she was in joint possession with her husband, that fact was accompanied by the officers' information that Ker had been using his apartment as a base of operations for his narcotics activities. Therefore, we cannot say that at the time of her arrest there were not sufficient grounds for a reasonable belief that Diane Ker, as well as her husband, was committing the offense of possession of marijuana in the presence of the officers. 374 U.S. at 3637, 83 S.Ct. at 1631–32, 10 L.Ed.2d at 740.

Presence near the scene of a *recent* crime also provides a strong indication of probable cause. In *State v. Mimmovich*, 284 A.2d 282 (Me. 1971), an officer received a radio report that a break-in was in progress at a certain building. When the officer arrived at the building, he discovered that the rear window had been broken and metal bars over the window spread wide enough to permit the entrance of a person. He observed no suspects at the scene but heard voices coming from the second-floor porch of an adjoining building. The officer entered this building and went up to the roof, where he found the defendants, lightly clad on a cold night, attempting to conceal themselves. He arrested them, frisked them for weapons, and found coins that were later admitted into evidence. The court found that the radio warning that a break-in was in progress, the observations of the officer at the scene, the presence of the defendants near the scene of the crime, lightly clad on a cold winter night, and the defendants' attempt to conceal themselves were sufficient to give the officer probable cause to arrest the defendants.

Suspicious activity in a high-crime area may contribute to probable cause. For example, in *United States v. Green*, 670 F.2d 1148 (D.C.Cir. 1981), the court identified four factors that should be assayed in determining whether the "totality of the circumstances" provides probable cause in a drug case: (1) the presence of a suspect in a neighborhood notorious for drug trafficking or other crimes; (2) suspects engaging in a sequence of events typical of a drug transaction; (3) a suspect's flight after being confronted by police; and (4) a suspect's attempt to conceal the subject of his activities.

ASSOCIATION WITH OTHER KNOWN CRIMINALS   Association of a suspect with other known criminals may be considered in determining probable cause, but it is not alone sufficient to provide probable cause. In *United States v. Di Re*, 332 U.S. 581, 68 S.Ct. 222, 92 L.Ed. 210 (1948), the U.S. Supreme Court held that the defendant's presence in a car with others who illegally possessed counterfeit ration coupons did not provide probable cause to arrest the defendant, because no other information linked him to the crime.

United States v. Di Re
laws.findlaw.com/us/332/
581.html

> The argument that one who "accompanies a criminal to a crime rendezvous" cannot be assumed to be a bystander, forceful enough in some circumstances, is farfetched when the meeting is not secretive or in a suspicious hide-out but in broad daylight, in plain sight of passersby, in a public street of a large city, and where the alleged substantive crime is one which does not necessarily involve any act visibly criminal. If Di Re had witnessed the passing of papers from hand to hand, it would not follow that he knew they were ration coupons, and if he saw that they were ration coupons, it would not follow that he would know them to be counterfeit. . . . Presumptions of guilt are not lightly to be indulged from mere meetings. 332 U.S. at 593, 68 S.Ct. at 228, 92 L.Ed. at 219–20.

In *United States v. Lima*, 819 F.2d 687 (7th Cir. 1987), however, the court found probable cause to arrest a defendant who arrived on the scene of a drug transaction shortly after the other participants in the deal, parked directly behind the car of one of the known participants, and conversed with one of the participants who walked over to his car while the transaction was taking place. The court added that "any innocent interpretation is further undermined by the fact that neither [of the other principals] called off or postponed the delivery of the drugs despite [the defendant's] presence." 819 F.2d at 690.

An officer may use his or her experience, training, and knowledge in determining that probable cause connecting a defendant with criminal activity exists. *Texas v. Brown*, 460 U.S. 730, 103 S.Ct. 1535, 75 L.Ed.2d 502 (1983). For example, in *United States v. Munoz*, 738 F.Supp. 800 (S.D.N.Y. 1990), the court found that FBI agents'

Texas v. Brown
laws.findlaw.com/us/460/
730.html

observations, knowledge, and assumptions that a kidnapper would take several people along for security when he went to pick up ransom money were enough to establish probable cause to arrest an accomplice who was "observed doing nothing but sitting as a passenger in the Jeep." 738 F.Supp. at 802. But, in *Ybarra v. Illinois*, 444 U.S. 85, 100 S.Ct. 338, 62 L.Ed.2d 238 (1979), the U.S. Supreme Court held that the search of a patron in a bar that was the subject of a search warrant was in violation of the Fourth Amendment because the patron was not named in the warrant nor was there probable cause to tie the patron to the criminal activity at hand.

PAST CRIMINAL CONDUCT   The mere fact that a suspect has a known criminal record does not alone provide probable cause to arrest.

> We do not hold that the officer's knowledge of the petitioner's physical appearance and previous record was either inadmissible or entirely irrelevant upon the issue of probable cause. . . . But to hold that knowledge of either or both of these facts constituted probable cause would be to hold that anyone with a previous criminal record could be arrested at will. *Beck v. Ohio*, 379 U.S. 89, 97, 85 S.Ct. 223, 228, 13 L.Ed.2d 142, 148 (1964).

As the Court stated, however, prior criminal activity of a suspect is relevant to the determination of probable cause. In *United States v. McGlory*, 968 F.2d 309 (3d Cir. 1992), officers observed the defendant drive up to the residence of a known drug dealer. When the dealer entered the defendant's vehicle and handed the defendant money, the officers arrested the defendant. The court noted that the mere observation of the money exchange was not sufficient to support probable cause to arrest. However, the court still found probable cause to arrest because one of the arresting officers had personally observed the defendant's participation in a narcotics transaction nine months before.

FAILURE TO PROTEST   An arrested person's failure to protest an arrest cannot be used to infer probable cause to support that arrest.

> It is the right of one placed under arrest to submit to custody and to reserve his defenses for the neutral tribunals erected by the law for the purpose of judging his case. An inference of probable cause from a failure to engage in discussion of the merits of the charge with arresting officers is unwarranted. Probable cause cannot be found from submissiveness, and the presumption of innocence is not lost or impaired by neglect to argue with a policeman. It is the officer's responsibility to know what he is arresting for, and why, and one in the unhappy plight of being taken into custody is not required to test the legality of the arrest before the officer who is making it. *United States v. Di Re*, 332 U.S. 581, 594–95, 68 S.Ct. 222, 228, 92 L.Ed. 210, 220 (1948).

FACTS ARISING DURING INVESTIGATION OR TEMPORARY DETENTION   Probable cause to arrest or search may arise during routine investigation or questioning of a person. An officer may initially only be seeking information or investigating suspicious circumstances. Yet during the course of investigation, other facts may come to the officer's attention, either from the words or actions of a temporarily detained person or from other sources. For example, the detained person may give evasive answers, attempt to flee, or act in a furtive manner, or the officer may perceive any of the other indications of possible criminal activity discussed earlier. If the combination of facts and circumstances is sufficient to establish probable cause to arrest or search, the officer may act accordingly.

The most important precedent on this subject is the U.S. Supreme Court case of *Terry v. Ohio*, 392 U.S. 1, 88 S.Ct. 1868, 20 L.Ed.2d 889 (1968), the leading case on

Ybarra v. Illinois
laws.findlaw.com/us/444/
85.html

Beck v. Ohio
laws.findlaw.com/us/379/
89.html

Terry v. Ohio
laws.findlaw.com/us/392/1.html

stop and frisk. (In Chapter 7, the *Terry* case and other stop-and-frisk cases illustrate how probable cause to arrest or search may arise from routine investigation and questioning.)

Key Points

Information perceived by a law enforcement officer through any of the five senses may support probable cause.

An officer's perceptions may be given additional credence because of the officer's personal experience or expertise in a particular area.

The following facts and circumstances may be considered in determining probable cause: flight of a suspect; furtive conduct; physical evidence connecting a person with criminal activity; a suspect's admission of criminal conduct; false or implausible answers to routine questions; presence at a crime scene or in a high-crime area; association with other known criminals; past criminal conduct.

Information Obtained by the Officer through Informants

Most crimes are committed out of the presence of law enforcement officers. Therefore, officers must usually rely on information from sources other than their own perceptions to establish probable cause to arrest or search. This information must come from ordinary citizen informants or criminal informants who have themselves personally perceived indications of criminal activity. (The term **informant** is used in this chapter to refer to any person from whom a law enforcement officer obtains information on criminal activity.) The problem with using information from informants is ensuring that the information is trustworthy enough to be acted on. Over the years, courts have developed elaborate rules and procedures for establishing probable cause when the information comes from informants.

Illinois v. Gates

The method of establishing probable cause through the use of an informant's information is sometimes referred to as the *hearsay method,* as opposed to the direct observation method discussed previously. The hearsay method was the subject of a landmark decision by the U.S. Supreme Court in 1983. That decision, *Illinois v. Gates,* 462 U.S. 213, 103 S.Ct. 2317, 76 L.Ed.2d 527, abandoned an approach to determining probable cause through the use of informants that had been established by two previous Supreme Court decisions, *Aguilar v. Texas,* 378 U.S. 108, 84 S.Ct. 1509, 12 L.Ed.2d 723 (1964), and *Spinelli v. United States,* 393 U.S. 410, 89 S.Ct. 584, 21 L.Ed.2d 637 (1969). The *Aguilar* and *Spinelli* decisions had established specific requirements for law enforcement officers to follow in preparing complaints or affidavits when using information received from informants. The *Gates* decision abandoned rigid adherence to these specific requirements in favor of a "totality of the circumstances" approach to determining probable cause.

www.potbust.com/book.htm
Article, "Avoiding and Defending Potbusts in the 00's" by Jeffrey Steinborn; an extensive discussion of probable cause through use of informants written in layperson's language

www.fbi.gov/publications/leb/1998/nov98leb.pdf
Article, "Avoiding the Informant Trap: A Blueprint for Control: by James E. Hight

www.fbi.gov/publications/leb/2000/may00leb.pdf
Article, "Working with Informants: Operational Recommendations" by James E. Hight (page 6 of the May 2000 *FBI Law Enforcement Bulletin*)

washburnlaw.edu/wlj/39-1/articles/osth.pdf
Article, "Juvenile Informants— A Necessary Evil?" by Darci G. Osther

Aguilar v. Texas
laws.findlaw.com/us/378/108.html
Spinelli v. United States
laws.findlaw.com/us/393/410.html

Despite the changes brought about by the *Gates* decision, there are good reasons for discussing the *Aguilar* and *Spinelli* decisions in detail. First, the underlying rationales of these decisions and other cases interpreting them retain their vitality and help in analyzing the totality of the circumstances under *Gates*. Cases that affirm the vitality of the *Aguilar-Spinelli* two-pronged analysis include *Walden v. Carmack*, 156 F.3d 861 (8th Cir. 1998); *United States v. Allen*, 168 F.3d 293 (6th Cir. 1999); *United States v. McKinney*, 143 F.3d 325 (7th Cir. 1998); *United States v. Zayas-Diaz*, 95 F.3d 105 (1st Cir. 1996); and *United States v. Rucker*, 138 F.3d 697 (7th Cir. 1998).

Second, several states have rejected the *Gates* decision based on their state constitutions or statutes. These states still require complaints and affidavits to be prepared according to the *Aguilar* and *Spinelli* requirements. For example, in *People v. Griminger*, 529 N.Y.S.2d 55, 524 N.E.2d 409 (N.Y. 1988), the New York Court of Appeals held that, as a matter of state law, the *Aguilar-Spinelli* two-pronged test should be employed in determining the sufficiency of an affidavit submitted in support of a search warrant application. The court specifically found that the *Gates* test did not offer a suitable alternative to the *Aguilar-Spinelli* inquiry's satisfactory method of providing reasonable assurance that probable cause determinations are based on information derived from a credible source with firsthand information.

> Given the deference paid to the Magistrate's probable cause finding, and given the somewhat subjective nature of the probable cause inquiry, the aims of predictability and precision are again well served by providing the Magistrate with *Aguilar-Spinelli* concrete, structured guidelines. More importantly, this will also prevent the disturbance of the rights of privacy and liberty upon the word of an unreliable hearsay informant, a danger we perceive under the *Gates* totality-of-the-circumstances test. 529 N.Y.S.2d at 58, 524 N.E.2d at 412.

Therefore, this discussion of the hearsay method of determining probable cause begins with a detailed analysis of the *Aguilar-Spinelli* line of cases. It then evaluates the effect of the *Gates* totality-of-the-circumstances approach to the hearsay method of determining probable cause. The discussion concentrates on the situation in which a law enforcement officer is applying for a search warrant based on information from informants. This approach is used to help focus the discussion and to emphasize again that the officer should *write down* in the complaint or affidavit all the information on which probable cause is based. The same probable cause considerations are involved in arrest warrants and warrantless arrests and searches, except that the information will not be written down in an affidavit in the warrantless situation. It is important, however, that the officer reduce similar information in a warrantless situation to a written report.

Aguilar v. Texas

Before the *Gates* decision, the leading case on establishing probable cause under the hearsay method was the U.S. Supreme Court case of *Aguilar v. Texas*, 378 U.S. 108, 84 S.Ct. 1509, 12 L.Ed.2d 723 (1964). The *Aguilar* case set out a *two-pronged test* for determining probable cause when the information in an affidavit was either entirely or partially obtained from an informant:

1. The affidavit must describe underlying circumstances from which a neutral and detached magistrate may determine that the informant had a sufficient basis for his or her knowledge and that the information was not the result of mere rumor or suspicion.

Chapter 6: *Probable Cause*

2. The affidavit must describe underlying circumstances from which the magistrate may determine that the informant was credible or that the informant's information was reliable.

Both prongs of the *Aguilar* test had to be satisfied to establish probable cause. Each prong of the *Aguilar* test is discussed separately here, emphasizing the duties of the law enforcement officer in each case.

PRONG 1: INFORMANT'S BASIS OF KNOWLEDGE A law enforcement officer must demonstrate to the magistrate in the affidavit underlying circumstances enabling the magistrate to independently evaluate the accuracy of an informant's conclusion. This is usually done by showing how the informant knows the supplied information. To satisfy this requirement, the affidavit must show either that

- the informant personally perceived the information given to the officer or
- the informant's information came from another source, but there is good reason to believe it.

Informant's Information Is Firsthand If the informant came upon the information by personal perception, the law enforcement officer should have few problems in satisfying the first prong of the *Aguilar* test. The officer merely has to state, in the affidavit, *how, when,* and *where* the informant obtained the information furnished to the officer. In *State v. Daniels,* 200 N.W.2d 403 (Minn. 1972), the officer stated in the affidavit:

> For approximately the past two months I have received information from an informant whose information has recently resulted in narcotic arrests and convictions that a Gregory Daniels who resides at 929 Logan N, (down) has been selling marijuana, hashish and heroin. My informant further states that he has seen Daniels sell drugs, namely: heroin and further that he has seen Daniels with heroin on his person. The informant has seen heroin on the premises of 929 Logan N, (down) within the past 48 hours. 200 N.W.2d at 404.

The court said, "There seems to be no dispute that such personal observation satisfies that part of the *Aguilar* test which requires that the affidavit contain facts to enable the magistrate to judge whether the informant obtained his knowledge in a reliable manner." 200 N.W.2d at 406.

Stating in the affidavit the *time* when the informant obtained the information is very important, especially in applications for search warrants, because probable cause to search can become stale with time. In *United States v. Huggins,* 733 F.Supp. 445 (D.D.C. 1990), the court said, "[T]here is nothing in the affidavit from which the date of the controlled purchase can be determined and accordingly there was no way for the judicial officer to determine whether the information was stale. The controlled purchase could have occurred 'a day, a week, or months before the affidavit.'" 733 F.Supp. at 447.

Despite painstaking care by a law enforcement officer in establishing the basis of an informant's knowledge, courts will not find probable cause when errors in the informant's information result in serious injustice. In *United States v. Mackey,* 387 F.Supp. 1121 (D. Nev. 1975), officers detained the defendant for hitchhiking and sent his name through the computer at the National Crime Information Center (NCIC), a national clearinghouse for law enforcement agencies administered by the FBI. The computer reported that the defendant was wanted in another city for a parole violation. The officers arrested the defendant and subsequently found a gun in his possession. The NCIC report was later found to be false; the defendant had satisfied the parole violation five months earlier. The court ordered the suppression of all evidence resulting from the defendant's arrest.

> [A] computer inaccuracy of this nature and duration, even if unintended, amounted to a capricious disregard for the rights of the defendant as a citizen of the United States. The evidence compels a finding that the government's action was equivalent to an arbitrary arrest, and that an arrest on this basis deprived defendant of his liberty without due process of law. 387 F.Supp. at 1125.

Therefore, although the officers acted properly in all respects, the evidence was ruled inadmissible through no fault of their own. Note that "information received from the NCIC computer bank has been routinely accepted in establishing probable cause for a valid arrest." *United States v. Hines,* 564 F.2d 925 (10th Cir. 1977). Officers should ordinarily feel free to act on such information so long as they do so in good faith.

Informant's Information Is Hearsay   If the informant's information comes from a third person, that person and his or her information must satisfy both prongs of the *Aguilar* test. The officer preparing the affidavit must show how the third person knows the information furnished to the informant. For example, if the third person saw criminal activity taking place at a particular time, a statement in the affidavit to that effect would be sufficient to satisfy the first prong of the *Aguilar* test. The officer must, however, also satisfy prong 2 of the *Aguilar* test with respect to both the informant *and* the third person. (Prong 2 of *Aguilar* is discussed later in this chapter.)

Detailing Informant's Information   Courts recognize one other method of satisfying the first prong of the *Aguilar* test besides stating how, when, and where the informant came by the information provided. In the U.S. Supreme Court case of *Spinelli v. United States,* 393 U.S. 410, 89 S.Ct. 584, 21 L.Ed.2d 637 (1969), the Court said:

> In the absence of a statement detailing the manner in which the information was gathered, it is especially important that the tip describe the accused's criminal activity in sufficient detail that the magistrate may know that he is relying on something more substantial than a casual rumor circulating in the underworld or an accusation based merely on an individual's general reputation. 393 U.S. at 416, 89 S.Ct. at 589, 21 L.Ed.2d at 644.

Draper v. United States
laws.findlaw.com/us/358/
307.html

The *Spinelli* case cited another Supreme Court case, *Draper v. United States,* 358 U.S. 307, 79 S.Ct. 329, 3 L.Ed.2d 327 (1959), as an example of sufficient use of detail to satisfy the first prong of the *Aguilar* test. In the *Draper* case, the informant did not state the manner in which he had obtained his information. The informant did, however, report that the defendant had gone to Chicago the day before by train and that he would return to Denver by train with three ounces of heroin on one of two specified mornings. The informant went on to describe, with minute particularity, the clothes that the defendant would be wearing and the bag he would be carrying upon arrival at the Denver station. The Supreme Court said that "[a] magistrate, when confronted with such detail, could reasonably infer that the informant had gained his information in a reliable way." 393 U.S. at 417, 89 S.Ct. at 589, 21 L.Ed.2d at 644.

In *Soles v. State,* 299 A.2d 502 (Md.Spec.App. 1973), probable cause to conduct a warrantless search of an automobile was found even though the officer was unable to tell how, when, or where the informant obtained his information. The court held that the information given by the informant was sufficiently detailed to indicate that he had gained his information in a reliable way. Relevant parts of the officer's testimony at the motion to suppress hearing are quoted as follows, because the testimony indicates the type of detail that courts require to show that an informant spoke from personal knowledge.

The informant described the appellant in the following detail:

"A. The source described Mr. Soles. He gave—told me that the name of the subject was Soles. He didn't know any other name. Just Soles. He described Mr. Soles as being approximately five foot eight inches in height, approximately 160 pounds, as being a Negro male, approximately in his early 30s. I believe one age was 35 years of age. He said he had a receding hairline slightly, a small bush cut. He said his hair wasn't a big bush. He said it was short. He said he had a goatee and he was light skinned."

The informant described the appellant's automobile in the following detail:

"A. It was a late model blue convertible with a white top bearing New York tags, I believe WQ 9579, something like that; WX 9579. My recollection isn't real good on that."

The informant described the operation generally and the cocaine specifically in the following detail:

"THE WITNESS: The source called me at home and related to me that he had information about a male subject from New York who was a major distributor of cocaine to several known narcotics dealers in Washington. He related to me that this source was named Soles. He also indicated to me that he had given the tag number of Soles' car to my partner, Officer Robert Polzin, earlier that week, and in the conversation with this source he related to me that Soles had in excess of an eighth of a kilo of cocaine in his trunk of his car inside a briefcase. He said this cocaine would be inside a glass jar. He stated that Soles had several thousand dollars in cash on him, which were the assets from the sale of part of the cocaine he brought down from New York. He stated he was armed with a pistol, and stated that he would be leaving Washington for New York before three o'clock that evening."

The trial judge, "when confronted with such detail, could reasonably infer that the informant had gained his information in a reliable way," . . . that is, via first-hand observation. Upon our independent review, we draw such an inference. 299 A.2d at 507–08.

In summary, if a law enforcement officer does not know how, when, or where an informant obtained information, the officer can still satisfy the first prong of the *Aguilar* test by obtaining as much detail as possible from the informant and stating all of it in the affidavit.

PRONG 2: INFORMANT'S VERACITY   The second prong of *Aguilar* requires that the officer demonstrate to the magistrate in the affidavit underlying circumstances to convince the magistrate of the informant's veracity (that is, that the informant is credible or that the informant's information is reliable). In one of the few cases dealing with the reliability of an informant's information, the court found that information supplied by an unnamed street drug seller to one of his clients about a future drug "drop" was "reliable." The court said:

> Though from the criminal milieu, to be sure, he was not, wittingly at least, working with the police. He was not in the position of the "common informant . . . hidden behind a cloak of immunity from prosecution for his own misdeeds." . . . This street seller was, so far as he knew, engaged in a purely commercial venture for his own profit. He was

dealing with a regular and presumably valued customer. Being unable initially to satisfy his customer's demand, it was to his every advantage to assure the prompt return of that customer as soon as fresh merchandise was available for sale. He simply had no purpose in misleading his own clientele. The circumstances in which the seller passed on the information to a customer and confidant are replete, we think, with reasonable assurances of trustworthiness. Upon our constitutionally-mandated independent review, we believe the information furnished by this secondary informant to have been reliable, notwithstanding his utter lack of demonstrated credibility. *Thompson v. State,* 298 A.2d 458, 462 (Md. 1973).

Most cases have dealt with the "credibility" aspect of the informant's veracity rather than with the reliability of the informant's information. The amount and type of information required to establish credibility depends on whether the informant is an ordinary citizen informant or a criminal informant.

Ordinary Citizen Informant   An ordinary citizen informant is usually presumed credible and no further evidence of credibility need be stated in the affidavit beyond the informant's name and address and his or her status as a victim of, or witness to, a crime.

One cannot approach the problem of informants whose information may or may not be sufficient to create "probable cause" as if there was only two classes: reliable informants whose information has previously been tested by the police and "all others." A multitude of cases . . . attest to the fact that information from a citizen who purports to be the victim of or to have witnessed a crime may, under certain circumstances, provide a sufficient basis for an arrest. *People v. Griffin,* 58 Cal.Rptr. 707, 711 (Cal.App. 1967).

The reason behind this rule was stated by the Supreme Court of Wisconsin:

[A]n ordinary citizen who reports a crime which has been committed in his presence, or that a crime is being or will be committed, stands on much different ground than a police informer. He is a witness to criminal activity who acts with an intent to aid the police in law enforcement because of his concern for society or for his own safety. He does not expect any gain or concession for his information. An informer of this type usually would not have more than one opportunity to supply information to the police, thereby precluding proof of his reliability by pointing to previous accurate information which he has supplied. *State v. Paszek,* 184 N.W.2d 836, 843 (Wis. 1971).

Another reason for accepting the credibility of an ordinary citizen is the average person's fear of potential criminal or civil action for deliberately or negligently providing false information. *People v. Hicks,* 378 N.Y.S.2d 660, 341 N.E.2d 227 (N.Y. 1975).

Nevertheless, some courts have required additional information to establish the credibility of an ordinary citizen informant. For example, in *State v. White,* 396 S.E.2d 601, 603 (Ga.App. 1990), the court stated:

This court has always given the concerned citizen informer a preferred status insofar as testing the credibility of his information. . . . However, before an anonymous tipster can be elevated to the status of "concerned citizen," thereby gaining entitlement to the preferred status regarding credibility concomitant with that title, there must be placed before the magistrate facts from which it can be concluded that the anonymous tipster is, in fact, a "concerned citizen." . . . The affidavit in the case at bar contained no information from which it could be gleaned that the tipster was, in fact, a "concerned citizen." The magistrate was given nothing other than the affiant's conclusory statement that the tipster was a concerned citizen. That will not suffice.

In contrast, the Supreme Court of Virginia found an ordinary citizen informant credible when the affidavit stated that although the informant had not previously furnished information to the police concerning violations of the narcotics laws, he was steadily employed, was a registered voter, enjoyed a good reputation in his neighborhood, and had expressed concern for young people involved with narcotics. *Brown v. Commonwealth,* 187 S.E.2d 160 (Va. 1972). In another Virginia case, an officer's affidavit for a search warrant stated that the officer had known the ordinary citizen informant and his family for many years and that the informant was known to be credible. The court said:

> Although more extensive background information would be highly desirable, "a common sense and realistic" interpretation of the affidavit . . . leads us to the conclusion that it contains information reported by a first time citizen informer whose name was withheld by the affiant.
>
> Public-spirited citizens should be encouraged to furnish to the police information of crimes. Accordingly, we will not apply to citizen informers the same standard of reliability as is applicable when police act on tips from professional informers or those who seek immunity for themselves, whether such citizens are named . . . or, as here, unnamed. *Guzewicz v. Commonwealth,* 187 S.E.2d 144, 148 (Va. 1972).

These cases indicate that the more information provided in the affidavit about an ordinary citizen informant, the more likely the informant will be found to be credible. If, however, the informant appears in person before the magistrate and testifies under oath, subject to a charge of perjury if the information provided is false, no further evidence of credibility is needed. Personally testifying "provides powerful indicia of veracity and reliability." *United States v. Elliott,* 893 F.2d 220, 223 (9th Cir. 1990).

For certain crimes, the law enforcement officer must show not only that the informant is credible but also that the informant has some expertise in recognizing that a crime has been committed. In *United States v. Hernandez,* 825 F.2d 846 (5th Cir. 1987), the informant (Marone) told the police that the defendant (Hernandez) had attempted to pass a counterfeit twenty-dollar note. The court said:

> Generally, the reliability of an identified bystander or victim who witnesses crime need not be established. Hernandez challenges not Marone's motivation to tell the truth, but argues more narrowly that the Government has not shown that Marone possessed expertise in recognizing a bill as counterfeit. Nevertheless, it was known to the police that Marone was a carnival vendor who necessarily dealt with currency. Further, by immediately rejecting the bill once proffered and promptly notifying the police, Marone displayed confidence in his own ability to recognize the instant bill as counterfeit. Marone further conveyed this confidence by reporting to the police that the proffered paper was "an obviously counterfeit twenty dollar bill." We uphold the district court's determination that the circumstances would justify a reasonable law enforcement officer in believing there was a fair probability that a counterfeit note had been passed. 825 F.2d at 849–50.

Criminal Informant　Unlike the ordinary citizen's credibility, which may sometimes be presumed, the criminal informant's credibility must always be established by a statement of underlying facts and circumstances. Criminal informants may be professional police informants, persons with a criminal record, accomplices in a crime, or persons seeking immunity for themselves. Usually, criminal informants do not want their identities disclosed in an affidavit. The U.S. Supreme Court held that an informant's

McCray v. Illinois
laws.findlaw.com/us/386/
300.html

identity need not be disclosed if his or her credibility is otherwise satisfactorily established. In *McCray v. Illinois*, 386 U.S. 300, 306–07, 87 S.Ct. 1056, 1060, 18 L.Ed.2d 62, 68 (1967), the Court quoted the New Jersey Supreme Court with approval:

> If a defendant may insist upon disclosure of the informant in order to test the truth of the officer's statement that there is an informant or as to what the informant related or as to the informant's reliability, we can be sure that every defendant will demand disclosure. He has nothing to lose and the prize may be the suppression of damaging evidence if the State cannot afford to reveal its source, as is so often the case. And since there is no way to test the good faith of a defendant who presses the demand, we must assume the routine demand would have to be routinely granted. The result would be that the State could use the informant's information only as a lead and could search only if it could gather adequate evidence of probable cause apart from the informant's data. Perhaps that approach would sharpen investigatorial techniques, but we doubt that there would be enough talent and time to cope with crime upon that basis. Rather we accept the premise that the informer is a vital part of society's defensive arsenal. The basic rule protecting his identity rests upon that belief.

Whether or not the informant's identity is disclosed in the affidavit, a statement of underlying facts and circumstances supporting credibility must be included. The following facts and circumstances are relevant.

1. Informant has given accurate information in the past. The usual method of establishing the credibility of a criminal informant is by showing that the informant has in the past given accurate information that has led to arrests, convictions, recovery of stolen property, or some similar accomplishment. A law enforcement officer may not merely state in the affidavit the conclusion that the informant is credible because of proven credibility. The officer must state facts demonstrating that the informant has given accurate information in the past. This is sometimes referred to as establishing the informant's "track record."

United States v. Ventresca
laws.findlaw.com/us/380/
102.html

Magistrates are required to evaluate affidavits that attempt to establish the credibility of informants in a commonsense manner and not with undue technicality. *United States v. Ventresca*, 380 U.S. 102, 85 S.Ct. 741, 13 L.Ed.2d 684 (1965). The main concern of the magistrate is the *accuracy* of the information supplied by the informant in the past. In *People v. Lawrence*, 273 N.E.2d 637 (Ill.App. 1971), the court found the informant credible even though none of his prior tips had resulted in convictions.

> Convictions, while corroborative of an informer's reliability, are not essential in establishing his reliability. Arrests, standing alone, do not establish reliability, but information that has been proved accurate does. Arrestees may not be prosecuted; if prosecuted they may not be indicted; if indicted they may not be tried; if tried they may not be convicted. If a case is tried, the informer may never testify; his credibility may never be passed upon in court. The true test of his reliability is the accuracy of his information. 273 N.E.2d at 639.

In *United States v. Dunnings*, 425 F.2d 836, 839 (2d Cir. 1969), the court found sufficient a statement that the informant had "furnished reliable and accurate information on approximately 20 occasions over the past four years." In *State v. Daniels*, 200 N.W.2d 403, 406–07 (Minn. 1972), the court held that the credibility of the informant was sufficiently shown when the affidavit stated that the informant's information "has recently resulted in narcotic arrests and convictions." In *United States v. Smith*, 462 F.2d 456,

458 (8th Cir. 1972), the informant's credibility was established by an affidavit that specified:

> The informant has previously provided reliable information to agents of the Bureau of Narcotics and Dangerous Drugs. On one occassion [*sic*] within the last two weeks a search warrant was issued pursuant to the informants [*sic*] information and narcotics were seized. On another occassion [*sic*] within the last month the informant introduced me to an individual who he said was a dealer. I purchased heroin from the individual.

Generally, the more information provided about an informant's track record, the more likely the magistrate will find the informant credible. Types of information considered relevant are as follows:

- The time when previous information was furnished by the informant
- Specific examples of verification of the accuracy of the informant's information
- A description of how the informant's information helped in bringing about an arrest, conviction, or other result
- Documentation of the informant's consistency in providing accurate information
- Details of the informant's "general background, employment, personal attributes that enable him to observe and relate accurately, position in the community, reputation with others, personal connection with the suspect, any circumstances which suggest the probable absence of any motivation to falsify, the apparent motivation for supplying the information, the presence or absence of a criminal record or association with known criminals, and the like." *United States v. Harris*, 403 U.S. 573, 600, 91 S.Ct. 2075, 2090, 29 L.Ed.2d 723, 743 (1971) (dissenting opinion).

United States v. Harris
laws.findlaw.com/us/403/573.html

If an officer has no *personal* knowledge of circumstances demonstrating that an informant is credible, the officer may state in the affidavit information about the informant's credibility received from other law enforcement officers. *State v. Lambert,* 363 A.2d 707 (Me. 1976). The officer should state the names of other law enforcement officers and describe in detail how those officers acquired personal knowledge of the informant's credibility.

A dog trained to react to controlled substances may also be considered an informant. The dog's credibility can also be established by demonstrating the track record of the dog and its handler. In *United States v. Race,* 529 F.2d 12 (1st Cir. 1976), a dog reacted positively to two wooden crates in an airline warehouse containing some three hundred crates. The dog's reaction provided the basis for probable cause to arrest the defendant. The court said:

> We do not, of course, suggest that any dog's excited behavior could, by itself, be adequate proof that a controlled substance was present, but here the government laid a strong foundation of canine reliability and handler expertise. Murphy [the dog's handler] testified that the dog had undergone intensive training in detecting drugs in 1971, that he had at least four hours a week of follow-up training since then, as well as work experience, and that the strong reaction he had to the crates was one that in the past had invariably indicated the presence of marijuana, hashish, heroin or cocaine. 529 F.2d at 14.

2. Informant made admissions or turned over evidence against the informant's own penal interest. In *United States v. Harris,* 403 U.S. 573, 91 S.Ct. 2075, 29 L.Ed.2d 723 (1971), the U.S. Supreme Court held that an admission made by an informant against the informant's own penal interest is sufficient to establish the credibility of the informant.

www.uspcak9.com/caselaw/searchseizurelist.shtml
Article on the use of dogs to develop probable cause

People do not lightly admit a crime and place critical evidence in the hands of the police in the form of their own admissions. Admissions of crime, like admissions against proprietary interests, carry their own indicia of credibility—sufficient at least to support a finding of probable cause to search. That the informant may be paid or promised a "break" does not eliminate the residual risk and opprobrium of having admitted criminal conduct. 403 U.S. at 583–84, 91 S.Ct. at 2082, 29 L.Ed.2d at 734.

In *State v. Appleton*, 297 A.2d 363 (Me. 1972), the court held that an informant's turning over criminal evidence against the informant's penal interest was also strongly convincing evidence of credibility. The informant purchased certain drugs at the defendant's apartment and the same day brought those drugs to the police to be tested. A law enforcement officer applied for a warrant to search the defendant's apartment, stating both that the informant had purchased the drugs and that he had delivered them to the police. The court held that the informant's actions justified a belief in the credibility of his story. "An informant is not likely to turn over to the police such criminal evidence unless he is certain in his own mind that his story implicating the persons occupying the premises where the sale took place will withstand police scrutiny." 297 A.2d at 369.

Key Points

6. Probable cause may be based on information supplied to a law enforcement officer by ordinary citizen informants or criminal informants who have themselves personally perceived indications of criminal activity.

7. Under the *Aguilar* two-pronged test for determining probable cause when the information in an affidavit was either entirely or partially obtained from an informant, (1) the affidavit must describe underlying circumstances from which a neutral and detached magistrate may determine that the informant had a sufficient basis for his or her knowledge and that the information was not the result of mere rumor or suspicion, and (2) the affidavit must describe underlying circumstances from which the magistrate may determine that the informant was credible or that the informant's information was reliable.

8. An ordinary citizen informant is usually presumed credible, and no further evidence of credibility need be stated in the affidavit beyond the informant's name and address and his or her status as a victim or witness to crime.

9. A criminal informant's credibility is never presumed but must be established, usually by demonstrating the informant's "track record" of having given accurate information in the past.

10. A criminal informant's identity need not be disclosed if his or her credibility is otherwise satisfactorily established.

11. A dog trained to react to controlled substances may be considered an informant, and its credibility can be established by demonstrating the "track record" of the dog and its handler.

Corroboration

An officer may use **corroboration** to bolster information that is insufficient to satisfy either or both prongs of the *Aguilar* test. Corroboration means strengthening or confirming the information supplied by the informant with supporting information obtained by law enforcement officers. For example, an officer may receive a tip from an informant about criminal activity. Through surveillance or independent investigation, the officer or other officers may personally perceive further indications of criminal activity. By including this corroborating information in the affidavit with the informant's information directed toward satisfying the *Aguilar* test, the officer enables a magistrate to consider all facts that may bear upon probable cause, no matter what the source of the information.

The corroborative information provided by the law enforcement officer in the affidavit may work in three possible ways:

- The information obtained by the officer may *in itself* provide probable cause independent of the informant's information. (See "Indications of Criminal Activity Supporting Probable Cause" earlier in this chapter.) Corroborating information of this degree provides probable cause to search even if neither prong of the *Aguilar* test is met.
- The officer's information may confirm or verify the information provided by the informant. For example, if an officer cannot satisfy prong 2 of the *Aguilar* test, the corroborating information may provide the necessary verification of the informant's report. In other words, if some significant details of the informant's information are shown to be true by the independent observation of a law enforcement officer, the magistrate is more likely to be convinced of the informant's veracity.
- The officer's information may be added to an informant's information that meets *Aguilar* standards. Although neither standing alone is sufficient to establish probable cause, a combination of all the information may be sufficient.

Therefore, to ensure that a magistrate is presented with sufficient information on which to base a determination of probable cause, the affidavit should include the following:

- All information directed toward satisfying the *Aguilar* two-pronged test
- All information perceived by law enforcement officers that corroborates the informant's information
- All additional corroborating information perceived by law enforcement officers relating to the criminal activity for which the search warrant is being sought

To illustrate how courts deal with corroboration, two cases with similar fact situations but different results are discussed in detail below.

Spinelli v. United States

The U.S. Supreme Court case of *Spinelli v. United States,* 393 U.S. 410, 89 S.Ct. 584, 21 L.Ed.2d 637 (1969), is the leading case on corroboration. In that case, the defendant was convicted of traveling to St. Louis, Missouri, from a nearby Illinois suburb with the intention of conducting gambling activities prohibited by Missouri law. On appeal, the defendant challenged the validity of a search warrant that was used to obtain incriminating evidence against him. The affidavit in support of the search warrant contained the following allegations:

1. The FBI had kept track of the defendant's movements during five days in August 1965. On four of the five days, the defendant was seen crossing a bridge from Illinois to St. Louis between 11 A.M. and 12:15 P.M. and was seen parking his car in a lot used by residents of a certain apartment house between 3:30 P.M. and 4:45 P.M. On one day, the defendant was followed further and was seen to enter a particular apartment in the building.

2. An FBI check with the telephone company revealed that this apartment contained two telephones listed under the name of Grace Hagen and carried two different numbers.
3. The defendant was known to the officer preparing the affidavit (the affiant) and to federal law enforcement agents and local law enforcement agents as a "bookmaker, an associate of bookmakers, a gambler, and an associate of gamblers." 393 U.S. at 414, 89 S.Ct. at 588, 21 L.Ed.2d at 642.
4. The FBI had been informed by a confidential reliable informant that the defendant was operating a handbook and accepting wagers and disseminating wagering information by means of telephones assigned the same numbers as the phones in the previously mentioned apartment.

The Court first discussed in detail allegation 4, the information obtained from the informant. The Court said:

> The informer's report must first be measured against *Aguilar's* standards so that its probative value can be assessed. If the tip is found inadequate under *Aguilar,* the other allegations which corroborate the information contained in the hearsay report should then be considered. 393 U.S. at 415, 89 S.Ct. at 588, 21 L.Ed.2d at 643.

The Court found that prong 2 of *Aguilar* was not satisfied because the affiant merely stated that he had been informed by a "confidential reliable informant." This was a mere conclusion or opinion of the affiant, because no *underlying circumstances* were stated to show the magistrate that the informant was credible.

Nor was prong 1 satisfied. The affidavit failed to state sufficient *underlying circumstances* from which the informant concluded that the defendant was running a bookmaking operation. There was no statement as to how, when, or where the informant received his information—whether he personally observed the defendant at work or whether he ever placed a bet with him. If the informant obtained his information from third persons, there was no explanation as to why these sources were credible or how they obtained their information.

Finally, the affidavit did not describe the defendant's alleged criminal activity in sufficient detail to convince a magistrate that the information was more than mere rumor or suspicion. The only facts supplied were that the defendant was using two specified telephones to conduct gambling operations. As the Court said, this meager report could easily have been obtained from an offhand remark at a neighborhood bar.

The Supreme Court then considered allegations 1 and 2 of the affidavit to see whether they provided sufficient corroboration of the informant's information or probable cause in and of themselves. The Court found that these two items contained no suggestion of criminal conduct. The defendant's travels to and from the apartment building and his entry into a particular apartment could not be taken as indicative of gambling activity. And certainly nothing was unusual about an apartment containing two separate telephones. The Court, therefore, concluded:

> At most, these allegations indicated that Spinelli could have used the telephones specified by the informant for some purpose. This cannot by itself be said to support both the inference that the informer was generally trustworthy and that he had made his charge against Spinelli on the basis of information obtained in a reliable way. 393 U.S. at 417, 89 S.Ct. at 589, 21 L.Ed.2d at 644.

Finally, the Court considered allegation 3—that the defendant was "known" to the FBI and others as a gambler. The Court called this a bald and unilluminating assertion of police suspicion and said that it may not be used to give additional weight to allegations that would otherwise be insufficient.

Since the *Spinelli* decision, the Supreme Court has decided that the alleged criminal reputation of a suspect may be considered by a magistrate in evaluating an affidavit for a search warrant. *United States v. Harris,* 403 U.S. 573, 91 S.Ct. 2075, 29 L.Ed.2d 723 (1971). The Court said that criminal reputation could not be used in *Spinelli,* because *Spinelli* contained no factual indication of the defendant's past criminal activities that would support the assertion. The affiant in the *Harris* case stated in the affidavit that the defendant had a reputation for four years as a trafficker in illegal whiskey, that the officer had received information from all types of persons as to the defendant's activities, and that during this period a sizable stash of illegal whiskey had been found in an abandoned house under the defendant's control. The Court held that, when criminal reputation is supported by factual statements indicating prior criminal conduct, reputation can be considered along with other allegations.

The *Spinelli* case is instructive because it traces through all the *Aguilar* requirements for establishing probable cause using an informant's information and gives reasons why each test was not met by the affidavit. It then considers other information in the affidavit as corroboration of the informant's information and gives specific reasons why the corroborative information is inadequate.

Dawson v. State

Dawson v. State, 276 A.2d 680 (Md.Spec.App. 1971), is a case similar to the *Spinelli* case, except that the search warrant in *Dawson* was found to be valid. The discussion of the *Dawson* case centers on the differences between the two cases that caused the court in the *Dawson* case to reach a different conclusion.

In the *Dawson* case, the defendant was convicted of unlawfully maintaining premises for the purpose of selling lottery tickets and unlawfully betting, wagering, or gambling on the results of horse races. He appealed, claiming among other things that the search warrant of his home was illegal because probable cause was lacking. The affidavit for the warrant contained nine paragraphs. The first paragraph listed the investigative experience of the affiant and ended with his conclusion that gambling activities were at that time being conducted at the defendant's premises. The third through ninth paragraphs contained the direct observations of the affiant officer. (These paragraphs are considered later.) The second paragraph dealt with an informant's information and is quoted here:

> That on Thursday April 17, 1969 your affiant interviewed a confidential source of information who has given reliable information in the past relating to illegal gambling activities which has resulted in the arrest and conviction of persons arrested for illegal gambling activities and that the source is personally known to your affiant. That this source related that there was illegal gambling activities taking place at 8103 Legation Road, Hyattsville Prince George's County, Maryland by a one Donald Lee Dawson. That the source further related that the source would call telephone #577-5197 and place horse and number bets with Donald Lee Dawson. 276 A.2d at 685.

The court analyzed the second paragraph using the two-pronged *Aguilar* test. Considering the informant's basis of knowledge first, the court found that *Aguilar* was satisfied. The affidavit stated that the informant had personally called the phone number 577-5197 and had placed horse and number bets with the defendant. In contrast, in the *Spinelli* case, nothing was said about how the informant obtained his information.

The court found in *Dawson* that the information supplied about the credibility of the informant was barely sufficient. The affidavit stated that both arrests and convictions had resulted from the informant's information in the past, which was more than a mere conclusion or opinion of the affiant. The affidavit also went further to establish the informant's credibility than did the affidavit in *Spinelli*, where the informant was merely described as a "confidential reliable informant." The court implied that more specific information on the informant's credibility would have been desirable, but said:

> It may well be that the facts here recited are enough to establish the credibility of the informant. In view of the strong independent verification hereinafter to be discussed, however, it is unnecessary for the State to rely exclusively on such recitation. 276 A.2d at 686.

The court assumed for purposes of discussion that the credibility of the informant had *not* been adequately established and proceeded to discuss *corroboration,* making a concerted effort to compare the affidavit in this case with that in *Spinelli.*

Paragraphs 3 through 9 of the *Dawson* affidavit stated that a surveillance of the defendant's activities had been conducted during a six-day period in April 1969 and that the following information was obtained:

- The defendant was observed to be engaged in no apparent legitimate employment during the period.
- The defendant had two telephones in his residence with two separate lines, both of which had silent listings.
- One of the defendant's silent listings had been picked up in the course of a raid on a lottery operation three years earlier in another town.
- On each day of observation, the defendant was observed purchasing an *Armstrong Scratch Sheet,* which gives information about horses running at various tracks that day.
- On each morning of observation, the defendant was observed to leave his house between 9:02 and 10:20 A.M., to return to his house between 11:20 A.M. and 12:06 P.M., and to remain in his house until after 6:00 P.M. The affiant, who was experienced and expert in gambling investigations, stated that during the hours between noon and 6:00 P.M., horse and number bets can be placed and the results of betting become available.
- On each day of observation, the defendant was observed during his morning rounds stopping at a number of places, including liquor stores and restaurants, for very short periods. He never purchased anything from any of the stores, nor did he eat or drink at the restaurants. The affiant stated that such brief regular stops are classic characteristics of the pickup-man phase of a gambling operation: "He picks up the 'action' (money and/or list of bets) from the previous day or evening from prearranged locations—'drops.' At the same time, he delivers cash to the appropriate locations for the payoff of yesterday's successful players." 276 A.2d at 689.
- On one of the days, the defendant was observed in close association all day with another person who was known to have been arrested for alleged gambling violations three years before.
- Finally, the defendant had been arrested and convicted of gambling violations about three years before.

The court considered each allegation in detail. Although each allegation, taken separately, could admittedly have been consistent with innocent conduct on the defendant's part, the court refused to consider each allegation separately. Instead, the court said:

> [P]robable cause emerges not from any single constituent activity but, rather, from the overall pattern of activities. Each fragment of conduct may communicate nothing of significance, but the broad mosaic portrays a great deal. The whole may, indeed, be greater than the sum of its parts. 276 A.2d at 687.

Furthermore, the court relied heavily on the officer's experience in investigating gambling activities and the interpretations he was able to place on the defendant's conduct. The court, therefore, concluded:

> In reviewing the observations, the ultimate question for the magistrate must be[,] What is revealed by the whole pattern of activity? In the case at bar, the various strands of observation, insubstantial unto themselves, together weave a strong web of probable guilt. 276 A.2d at 689.

The court compared this case with the *Spinelli* case and explained why the affidavit here was sufficient to provide probable cause while the one in *Spinelli* was not.

- In *Spinelli*, there were no observations of the pickup-man type of activity.
- In *Spinelli*, there was no observed association with a previously arrested gambler.
- In *Spinelli*, there was no daily purchase of an *Armstrong Scratch Sheet* to evidence some daily interest in horse races.
- In *Spinelli*, neither Spinelli's nor Grace Hagen's phone number had been previously picked up in a raided gambling headquarters.
- In *Spinelli*, Spinelli was not a convicted gambler.
- Finally, and perhaps most important, the confidential informant's information in *Spinelli* was so inadequate under *Aguilar* as to lend no additional light or interpretation to the direct observations. In contrast, the confidential informant's information in the *Dawson* case was very substantial and significantly enhanced the direct observations.

  The hearsay information may, of course, reinforce the direct observation just as the direct observation may reinforce the hearsay information. There is no one-way street from direct observation to hearsay information. Rather, each may simultaneously cross-fertilize and enrich the other. 276 A.2d at 690.

The court's emphasis on analyzing the overall pattern of activities and the totality of facts and circumstances in the *Dawson* case was an early harbinger of the approach to probable cause taken in the landmark decision of the U.S. Supreme Court in *Illinois v. Gates*.

Key Points

12. *Corroboration* means strengthening the information supplied by the informant in the affidavit by stating supporting information obtained by the independent investigation of law enforcement officers.

13. Corroboration is a two-way street—direct observation of law enforcement officers may reinforce the hearsay information provided by the informant, and vice versa.

Totality-of-the-Circumstances Test

In the 1983 case of *Illinois v. Gates*, the U.S. Supreme Court abandoned the *Aguilar-Spinelli* two-pronged test for determining probable cause through the use of informants for a totality-of-the-circumstances test. More correctly, the Court abandoned a rigid adherence to the *Aguilar-Spinelli* test, since the elements of the *Aguilar-Spinelli* test remain important considerations under the new *Gates* test. This discussion of the *Gates* test begins with the facts of the case.

The *Gates* Decision

On May 3, 1978, the Bloomingdale, Illinois, Police Department received an anonymous letter that included statements that the defendants, a husband and wife, made their living selling drugs, that the wife would drive their car to Florida on May 3 and leave it to be loaded up with drugs, that the husband would fly down in a few days to drive the car back loaded with over $100,000 worth of drugs, and that the defendants had over $100,000 worth of drugs in the basement of their home. Acting on the tip, a police officer obtained the defendants' address and learned that the husband had made a reservation for a May 5 flight to Florida. The officer then made arrangements with a Drug Enforcement Administration (DEA) agent for surveillance of the May 5 flight. The surveillance revealed that the husband took the flight, stayed overnight in a motel room registered to his wife, and the next morning headed north with an unidentified woman toward Bloomingdale in a car bearing Illinois license plates issued to the husband. A search warrant for the defendants' residence and automobile was obtained, based on these facts and the anonymous letter. When the defendants arrived home, the police searched the car and the residence and found marijuana.

The Illinois Supreme Court found that the *Aguilar-Spinelli* two-pronged test had not been satisfied. First, the "veracity" prong was not satisfied because there was no basis for concluding that the anonymous person who wrote the letter to the police department was credible. Second, the "basis of knowledge" prong was not satisfied because the letter gave no information on how its writer knew of the defendants' activities. The court therefore concluded that no showing of probable cause had been made.

The U.S. Supreme Court said:

> We agree with the Illinois Supreme Court that an informant's "veracity," "reliability" and "basis of knowledge" are all highly relevant in determining the value of his report. We do not agree, however, that these elements should be understood as entirely separate and independent requirements to be rigidly exacted in every case, which the opinion of the Supreme Court of Illinois would imply. Rather . . . they should be understood simply as closely intertwined issues that may usefully illuminate the commonsense, practical question whether there is "probable cause" to believe that contraband or evidence is located in a particular place. *Illinois v. Gates*, 462 U.S. at 230, 103 S.Ct. at 2327–28, 76 L.Ed.2d at 543.

In effect, the Court said that the elements of the *Aguilar-Spinelli* two-pronged test are important considerations in determining the existence of probable cause, but they should be evaluated only as part of the ultimate commonsense determination and not as rigid rules to be applied mechanically. The Court believed that this totality-of-the-circumstances approach was more in keeping with the nature of probable cause as a fluid concept, which depends on probabilities arising from varying fact situations, and does not lend itself to a neat set of legal rules. The Court reiterated the following quotation from *Brinegar v. United States*, 338 U.S. 160, 175, 69 S.Ct. 1302, 1310, 93 L.Ed. 1879, 1890 (1949):

> In dealing with probable cause . . . as the very name implies, we deal with probabilities. These are not technical; they are the factual and practical considerations of everyday life on which reasonable and prudent men, not legal technicians, act.

The Supreme Court suggested that originally the two prongs of the *Aguilar-Spinelli* test were intended simply as guides to a magistrate's determination of probable cause, not as inflexible, independent requirements applicable in every case. The two prongs should be understood as

> relevant considerations in the totality of circumstances that traditionally has guided probable cause determinations: a deficiency in one may be compensated for, in determining the overall reliability of a tip by a strong showing as to the other, or by some other indicia of reliability. *Illinois v. Gates*, 462 U.S. at 233, 103 S.Ct. at 2329, 76 L.Ed.2d at 545.

The entire process of determining probable cause could, therefore, be simplified as follows:

> The task of the issuing magistrate is simply to make a practical, common-sense decision whether, given all the circumstances set forth in the affidavit before him, including the "veracity" and "basis of knowledge" of persons supplying hearsay information, there is a fair probability that contraband or evidence of a crime will be found in a particular place. And the duty of a reviewing court is simply to ensure that the magistrate had a "substantial basis for . . . conclud[ing]" that probable cause existed. 462 U.S. at 238–39, 103 S.Ct. at 2332, 76 L.Ed.2d at 548.

The *Gates* totality-of-the-circumstances test should cause little change in procedure for law enforcement officers applying for search warrants. If officers follow the advice in this chapter for preparing affidavits under the *Aguilar-Spinelli* test, the affidavits will have as good a chance or a better chance of satisfying the *Gates* test. The *Gates* emphasis on the value of corroborating information should, however, make it less difficult to obtain a search warrant based partially on information from an anonymous informant. As the *Gates* opinion indicated, overly rigid application of the two-pronged test tended to reject anonymous tips, because ordinary citizens generally do not provide extensive recitations of the basis of their everyday observations, and because the veracity of anonymous informants is largely unknown and unknowable. The Court said:

> [A]nonymous tips seldom could survive a rigorous application of either of the . . . prongs. Yet, such tips, particularly when supplemented by independent police investigation, frequently contribute to the solution of otherwise "perfect crimes." While a conscientious assessment of the basis for crediting such tips is required by the Fourth Amendment, a standard that leaves virtually no place for anonymous citizen informants is not. 462 U.S. at 237–38, 103 S.Ct. at 2332, 76 L.Ed.2d at 548.

With respect to the anonymous letter in the Gates case, the Supreme Court said that the corroboration of predictions that the defendants' car would be in Florida, that the husband would fly to Florida in a few days, and that the husband would drive the car back to Illinois indicated that the informant's other assertions were also true. The letter's accurate predictions of the defendants' future actions, especially, made it more likely that the informant also had access to reliable information of the defendants'

i2iorg/SuptDocs/Waco/
warrant3.htm
Article, "The Unwarranted Warrant: The Waco Search Warrant
and the Decline of the Fourth
Amendment" by David B. Kopel
and Paul H. Blackman (This reference is to Part III of the article
entitled "The Final Element of
Probable Cause." Links to the
other two parts appear at the
bottom of the file)

alleged illegal activities. Although the tip was corroborated only as to the defendants' seemingly innocent behavior, and although it by no means indicated with certainty that illegal drugs would be found, the Court believed that it sufficed:

> for the practical, common-sense judgment called for in making a probable cause deter-
> mination. It is enough, for purposes of assessing probable cause, that "corroboration
> through other sources of information reduced the chances of a reckless or prevaricating
> tale," thus providing "a substantial basis for crediting the hearsay." 462 U.S. at 244, 103
> S.Ct. at 2335, 76 L.Ed.2d at 552.

Application of the Test

In *United States v. Morales,* 171 F.3d 978, 98–1982 (5th Cir. 1999), the court held that "the totality of the circumstances test includes four factors: (1) the nature of the infor-
mation; (2) whether there has been an opportunity for the police to see or hear the matter reported; (3) the veracity and the basis of the knowledge of the informant; and (4) whether there has been any independent verification of the matters through police investigation." The following quotations from two drug cases illustrate the application of one or more of these factors in determining probable cause under the totality-of-
the-circumstances standard. The first case, *United States v. Cruz,* did not involve an informant.

> [W]e conclude that the law enforcement officers had probable cause to arrest Cruz at
> the time they stopped his truck on the New Jersey Turnpike. The determination of
> whether probable cause to arrest exists can be based on the collective knowledge of all
> of the officers involved in the surveillance efforts because the various law enforcement
> officers in this investigation were in communication with each other. . . . The information
> that the agents had available to them at the time of arrest included the results of the
> prior surveillance efforts of the DEA [Drug Enforcement Administration] agent which
> suggested that Cesar Cruz was involved with narcotics activity. In addition, the agents
> had observed the loading of the four heavy boxes into the trailer portion of the tractor
> trailer truck from Florida; the extensive construction activity performed on the trailer
> that led the agents to believe that a hiding place for the boxes was being prepared; the
> suspects' preoccupation with ensuring that the lights of the truck were functioning prop-
> erly, thus lessening the chances of being stopped by the police; Cruz's suspicious behav-
> ior in stopping his truck one mile after he had entered the New Jersey Turnpike, then
> turning off the truck's lights and standing by the cab of his truck for several minutes
> while he intently watched oncoming traffic; and Cruz's evasive driving when the police
> attempted to stop his truck. Although no single fact was sufficient by itself to establish
> probable cause, the totality of the circumstances as appraised by experienced drug
> enforcement agents was sufficient to support Cruz's arrest at the time the truck was
> stopped. 834 F.2d 47, 51 (2d Cir. 1987).

The second case, *United States v. De Los Santos,* did involve an informant.

> We believe that the officers had probable cause to believe that contraband would be
> found, and therefore they properly stopped and arrested De Los Santos. First, [DEA Spe-
> cial Agent] Castro knew that De Los Santos had dealt in heroin on previous occasions.
> He then received a tip from an informant who Castro knew and who had provided reli-
> able information in the past. The informant told Castro that De Los Santos would travel
> to a certain area to store drugs and would pick them up the next day at a certain time.

Cases in Point

Applying the "totality-of-the-circumstances test" of *Illinois v. Gates*

On May 1, 1997, United States Magistrate Judge Galvan issued a search warrant for Mr. Button's residence based on an affidavit DEA Special Agent James Baker submitted to him. The affidavit described an ongoing drug trafficking conspiracy dating from 1989, with three drug seizures linked to Stephen Michael Pollack and those working with Mr. Pollock. In a drug raid related to Mr. Pollock's alleged conspiracy, the police found Mr. Button's phone number next to Mr. Pollock's in a confiscated notebook. The affidavit also indicated that a cooperating source (CS2) had told agents Mr. Button was a courier of narcotics for Mr. Pollack. Among other details, the source stated that Mr. Pollack's conspiracy involved drug trafficking in Alamogordo, New Mexico, and Durango, Colorado. The affidavit showed police corroborated CS2's information by telephone records between Mr. Pollock and Mr. Button, agent surveillance of Mr. Button's car in Mr. Pollack's drive, information showing Mr. Button's residence in Alamogordo, New Mexico, and Mr. Pollack's residence in Durango, Colorado, and information provided by New Mexico state police that they had an informant who also said Mr. Button was a courier for Mr. Pollack.

Agents executed the warrant at Mr. Button's residence on May 2, 1997, and seized a semi-automatic pistol and a rifle. Mr. Button filed a motion to suppress evidence seized during the search, asserting the underlying affidavit to the warrant was defective. Applying the "totality-of-the-circumstances" test of *Illinois v. Gates*, should the motion to suppress be granted? *United States v. Button*, 166 F3d 1222 (10th Cir. 1999)

Read the court opinion at:
laws.findlaw.com/10th/972367.html

On March 7, 1999, Kentucky State Police detective Bill Riley inspected a rebuilt pickup truck that had been purchased from an auto sales store in London, Kentucky. Based on his long experience in investigating stolen cars and parts, his inspection revealed to him a truck made from stolen parts. Detective Riley then learned from the auto sales shop that the truck had been rebuilt for it by co-defendant Garnett Tuttle.

Detective Riley immediately conducted an independent investigation that included an interview of a London city police officer who had received information from an unidentified confidential informant indicating that the auto sales shop was currently selling cars and trucks assembled with stolen parts by Tuttle at a garage rented by Tuttle on property owned by co-defendant Larry Settle. The informant said that Tuttle's work was ongoing and that he was currently using the same place to rebuild other vehicles with stolen parts. The London city police officer specifically stated that

he had received information within the past week that the informant's information was still current.

Detective Riley memorialized the foregoing information in an affidavit submitted to a Kentucky state court judge, who issued a search warrant on March 8, 1996, authorizing the Kentucky State Police to search a white garage located on property owned by Settle and leased to Tuttle. The state court found that probable cause existed to believe that the garage was being used to house an illegal automobile "chop shop" operation. While executing the warrant on the white garage, the state police found and seized numerous items believed to be stolen property or evidence of crimes, including three autos, auto parts, VIN plates, boxes of records and receipts, and small amounts of marijuana and methamphetamine seized as contraband in plain view of the searching officers.

Based in part upon information obtained during the earlier search, the state court issued a second search warrant later that same day authorizing the search of a gray garage owned and controlled solely by Settle located on the same property near the white garage. Although nothing was seized from the gray garage, the state police observed a pickup truck with suspicious parts. Finally, several days later, a third and last search warrant was issued authorizing a search of both the white and gray garages. The state police found and seized additional auto parts, as well as other items believed to be stolen property and evidence of crimes.

The magistrate's report relied on by the district court to suppress the seized evidence characterized the affidavit in support of the first search warrant as lacking probable cause because there was nothing in the first paragraph of the affidavit that linked the white garage with any criminal activity or contraband. The paragraph only indicated that the seized truck was suspected of containing stolen parts and that it had been rebuilt by Tuttle. Furthermore, the magistrate found the second paragraph of the affidavit to be "fatally flawed" because it failed to establish the credibility of the confidential informant relied upon by the state police, as well as failed to provide any independent corroboration of the information relayed by the informant. The magistrate apparently believed that the affidavit for the warrant was insufficient under the rule of *Illinois v. Gates*, 462 U.S. 213 (1983), that an uncorroborated tip of an anonymous informant is insufficient to establish probable cause. Should the motion of the two defendants to suppress evidence seized under the three search warrants be granted? *United States v. Tuttle*, 200 F.3d 892 (10th Cir. 2000).

Read the court opinion at:
laws.findlaw.com/6th/00a0011p.html

As predicted by the informant, the next morning De Los Santos arrived in the neighborhood in the same vehicle he had been in before. The agents observed him go to a residence and stay there for only two to four minutes. This surveillance, therefore, corroborated information provided by the informant.

Moreover, Castro testified in camera as to other information that the informant supplied. This information also is supportive of probable cause. As in McCray:

> the officer[s] in this case described with specificity "what the informer actually said, and why the officer thought the information was credible." . . . The testimony of each of the officers informed the court of the "underlying circumstances from which the informant concluded that the narcotics were where he claimed they were, and some of the underlying circumstances from which the officer concluded that the informant . . . was 'credible' or his information 'reliable.'"

McCray, 386 U.S. at 304, 87 S.Ct. at 1059 (citations omitted). Thus, under the totality of the circumstances test, "[t]here can be no doubt upon the basis of the circumstances related by [Castro], that there was probable cause to sustain the arrest. . . ." 810 F.2d 1326, 1336 (5th Cir. 1987).

This case illustrates the continuing validity of the elements of the *Aguilar-Spinelli* two-pronged test in determining probable cause using information supplied by an informant.

In contrast, the *Gates* test was not satisfied in *United States v. Campbell*, 920 F.2d 793 (11th Cir. 1990):

> Here, we must first decide if there was probable cause to search Campbell's pickup truck when it was stopped at the Union 76 Truck Stop. Probable cause exists "when the facts and circumstances would lead a reasonably prudent [person] to believe that the vehicle contains contraband." . . . The Supreme Court echoed this analysis when it adopted the totality of the circumstances test for determining when information provided by an informant rises to the level of probable cause. *Illinois v. Gates*, 462 U.S. 213, 230, 103 S.Ct. 2317, 2328, 76 L.Ed.2d 527, 543 (1983). The totality of the circumstances do not suggest that the Montgomery police had probable cause to arrest the defendants, much less search the vehicle when they first encountered it at the truck stop. The district court found that the confidential informant was not reliable, but still found that the officers had probable cause to arrest the occupants of the pickup based on reliability of the information provided by the informant. The key to the district court's conclusion was that the informant provided the police with the approximate time of the vehicle's arrival and the location where it would stop. Campbell concedes that when the agents observed the pickup truck enter the Union 76 Truck Stop "they had reasonable suspicion to conduct a valid investigatory stop under *Terry v. Ohio*, 392 U.S. 1, 88 S.Ct. 1868, 20 L.Ed.2d 889 (1968) and its progeny." . . . Thus, under the holding of *Alabama v. White*, 496 U.S. 325, 110 S.Ct. 2412, 110 L.Ed.2d 301 (1990), the most that the Montgomery police had was a reasonable suspicion of illegal activity. In *White* the police kept the suspect under surveillance in order to corroborate the information. There was not the type of corroboration of criminal activity . . . to elevate it to the level of probable cause. 920 F.2d at 796–97.

See Chapter 7 for a discussion of *Terry v. Ohio* and *Alabama v. White*.

In *United States v. Brown*, 744 F.Supp. 558 (S.D.N.Y. 1990), the court held that, under the *Gates* standard, probable cause for the issuance of a search warrant could be based almost entirely on information received from a single confidential informant. In that case, the informant had provided highly reliable information in the past, had been providing information on the defendant for over a month, and had personal knowledge about the premises to be searched. The court said:

> The clear implication from the affidavit is that the informant had had a long relationship with law enforcement officials which had proved very reliable in the past. This information alone goes a long way to satisfying the totality of the circumstances test outlined in *Gates*. 744 F.Supp. at 567.

In another case involving a confidential informant, *United States v. Danhauer,* 229 F.3d 1002 (10th Cir. 2000), the court found insufficient facts to establish probable cause for the issuance of a warrant.

> The affidavit in this case failed to allege facts sufficient to establish probable cause. The affidavit contains repetitive statements regarding the physical description of the Danhauer residence and the identity of the occupants. Further, the affidavit contains statements about the criminal histories of both Dennis and Robbi Danhauer. The affidavit does not reveal, however, the informant's basis of knowledge or adequately verify the informant's most serious allegation, that the Danhauers were manufacturing methamphetamine. An affidavit replete with repetitive and tenuous facts does not provide a magistrate with a sufficient basis for drawing a reasonable inference that a search would uncover evidence of criminal activity.
>
> When there is sufficient independent corroboration of an informant's information, there is no need to establish the veracity of the informant. . . . In this case, however, the affiant neither established the veracity of the informant, nor obtained sufficient independent corroboration of the informant's information. The only police corroboration of the informant's information was the affiant's verification of the Danhauer residence's physical description, a records check to confirm that the Danhauers resided at the premises in question, an observation of Robbi Danhauer coming and going from the house to the garage, and a search of the Danhauers' criminal histories, which brought to light Robbi Danhauer's latest urinalysis revealing the presence of methamphetamine. The detective made little attempt to link methamphetamine to the Danhauer residence. *Cf. United States v. Le,* 173 F.3d 1258, 1266 (10th Cir. 1999) (concluding that affiant's search of suspect's trash and discovery of used bag with white powder residue confirmed to be methamphetamine helped corroborate information received from confidential sources). The only possible nexus between Danhauer's residence and the alleged criminal activity was his wife's urinalysis result. This is not the type of evidence that enables the state magistrate to draw a reasonable inference that the items subject to the search warrant would be located at Danhauer's residence. Such a nebulous connection does not give a magistrate a substantial basis for concluding that probable cause existed. 229 F.3d at 1006.

This case is notable, however, because the court found that the good-faith exception to the exclusionary rule applied because the officer's reliance on the search warrant was not "wholly unwarranted."

> Although the affidavit in support of the warrant did not establish probable cause, it was not so lacking in indicia of probable cause that the executing officer should have known the search was illegal despite the state magistrate's authorization. . . . Further, the absence of information establishing the informant's reliability or basis of knowledge does not necessarily preclude an officer from manifesting a reasonable belief that the warrant was properly issued, *see Bishop,* 890 F.2d at 217, particularly when the officer takes steps to investigate the informant's allegation. Detective McCarthy, who both obtained and

executed the search warrant, reasonably believed the fruits of his investigation into the informant's allegation sufficiently linked the manufacture of methamphetamine and Danhauer's residence. His affidavit contains more than conclusory statements based on the informant's allegation about the alleged criminal activity at Danhauer's residence.

This court concludes the search warrant failed to establish probable cause because the nexus between the alleged criminal activity and Danhauer's residence was insufficient. Nonetheless, the district court did not err in refusing to suppress the evidence seized because the officer acted in objectively reasonable, good-faith reliance on the warrant. 229 F.3d at 1007–08.

Key Points

14. Under the *Gates* totality-of-the-circumstances test, the task of the issuing magistrate is to make a practical, commonsense decision whether, given all the circumstances set forth in the affidavit, there is a fair probability that contraband or evidence of crime will be found in a particular place.

15. The elements of the *Aguilar-Spinelli* two-pronged test are important considerations in determining the existence of probable cause but should be evaluated only as part of the ultimate commonsense determination and not as rigid rules to be applied mechanically.

16. Corroboration of the details of an informant's tip by independent police investigation reduces the chances of a reckless or prevaricating tale and is a valuable means of satisfying the *Gates* totality-of-the-circumstances test for determining probable cause.

Summary

Probable cause exists when the facts and circumstances within a law enforcement officer's knowledge and of which the officer has reasonably trustworthy information are sufficient in themselves to warrant a person of reasonable caution in the belief either that

- a particular person has committed or is committing a crime or
- seizable items are located at a particular place or on a particular person.

Probable cause does not require certainty or proof beyond a reasonable doubt, but it does require something beyond mere suspicion. It is a practical, nontechnical, commonsense concept dealing with probabilities arising out of the varying facts and circumstances of everyday life. The U.S. Supreme Court has used the term "fair probability" to describe the probable cause standard.

Information on which probable cause is to be based may come to a law enforcement officer's attention in two possible ways:

- Through the officer's own perceptions
- Through the perceptions of an informant who relays the information to the officer

Some indications of criminal activity that may contribute to probable cause are as follows:

- Flight
- Furtive conduct
- Real or physical evidence such as fingerprints or weapons
- Incriminating admissions
- False or implausible answers
- Presence at a crime scene or in a high-crime area
- Association with other known criminals
- Past criminal conduct
- Facts arising during investigation or temporary detention

Standing alone, none of these indications of criminal activity may be sufficient to establish probable cause. However, when combined with other indications, each is a relevant factor in determining whether an arrest or a search is justified. Before law enforcement officers act, either to apply for a warrant or to conduct a warrantless arrest or search (in the proper circumstances), they should make sure that they have sufficient information on which to base their actions and that they can justify their actions before a magistrate or judge.

When information about criminal activity comes from an informant, an officer must satisfy the totality-of-the-circumstances test set out in the case of *Illinois v. Gates*. That test simply requires the officer to provide underlying facts and circumstances indicating a substantial basis for a magistrate to determine that probable cause to arrest or search exists. Highly relevant to this determination are the elements of the *Aguilar-Spinelli* two-pronged test. To satisfy this test, the officer must provide underlying circumstances indicating the basis of the informant's knowledge about the criminal activity and underlying circumstances from which the officer concluded that the informant was credible or that the information was reliable. These requirements need not be applied in a rigid, technical manner, but mere conclusions or opinions of the officer will not suffice to establish probable cause. The magistrate must be sat-isfied that the informant's information is not mere rumor, suspicion, or reckless or malicious fabrication. Corroboration of the details of an informant's tip by independent police work is a valuable means of satisfying the totality-of-the-circumstances test for determining probable cause.

Law enforcement officers applying for a warrant should include in the affidavit, in an orderly manner, the following:

- All information directed toward satisfying the *Aguilar-Spinelli* two-pronged test
- All information perceived by law enforcement officers to corroborate the informant's information
- All additional corroborating information perceived by law enforcement officers with respect to the criminal activity for which the search warrant is being sought

Key Holdings from Major Cases

Carroll v. United States (1925). Probable cause exists when "the facts and circumstances within their [the officers'] knowledge and of which they had reasonably trustworthy information [are] sufficient in themselves to warrant a man of reasonable caution in the belief that [seizable property would be found in a particular place or on a particular person]." 267 U.S. 132, 162, 45 S.Ct. 280, 288, 69 L.Ed. 543, 555.

Brinegar v. United States (1949). "In dealing with probable cause . . . as the very name implies, we deal with probabilities. These are not technical; they are the factual and practical considerations of everyday life on which reasonable and prudent men, not legal technicians, act." 338 U.S. 160, 175, 69 S.Ct. 1302, 1310, 93 L.Ed. 1879, 1890.

"Probable cause exists where the 'facts and circumstances within their [the officers'] knowledge and of which they had reasonably trustworthy information [are] sufficient in themselves to warrant a man of reasonable caution in the belief that' an offense has been or is being committed [by the person to be arrested]." 338 U.S. at 175–76, 69 S.Ct. at 1310–11, 93 L.Ed. at 1890.

United States v. Di Re (1948). "The argument that one who 'accompanies a criminal to a crime rendezvous' cannot be assumed to be a bystander, forceful enough in some circumstances, is farfetched when the meeting is not secretive or in a suspicious hide-out but in broad daylight, in plain sight of passersby, in a public street of a large city, and where the alleged substantive crime is one which does not necessarily involve any act visibly criminal. . . . Presumptions of guilt are not lightly to be indulged from mere meetings." 332 U.S. 581, 593, 68 S.Ct. 222, 228, 92 L.Ed. 210, 219–20.

"It is the right of one placed under arrest to submit to custody and to reserve his defenses for the neutral tribunals erected by the law for the purpose of judging his case. An inference of probable cause from a failure to engage in discussion of the merits of the charge with arresting officers is unwarranted. Probable cause cannot be found from submissiveness, and the presumption of innocence is not lost or impaired by neglect to argue with a policeman. It is the officer's responsibility to know what he is arresting for, and why, and one in the unhappy plight of being taken into custody is not required to test the legality of the arrest before the officer who is making it." 332 U.S. at 594–95, 68 S.Ct. at 228, 92 L.Ed. at 220.

Aguilar v. Texas (1964). "Although an affidavit may be based on hearsay information and need not reflect the direct personal observations of the affiant . . . the magistrate must be informed of some of the underlying circumstances from which the informant concluded that the narcotics were where he claimed they were, and some of the underlying circumstances from which the officer concluded that the informant, whose identity need not be disclosed . . . was 'credible' or his information 'reliable.' Otherwise, 'the inferences from the facts which lead to the complaint' will be drawn not 'by a neutral and detached magistrate,' as the Constitution requires, but instead, by a police officer 'engaged in the often competitive enterprise of ferreting out crime' . . . or, as in this case, by an unidentified informant." 378 U.S. 108, 114–15, 84 S.Ct. 1509, 1514, 12 L.Ed.2d 723, 729.

Note: This approach to determining probable cause when the information in an affidavit was either entirely or partially obtained from an informant is referred to as the *Aguilar* two-pronged test. Rigid adherence to this test was abandoned in favor of a totality-of-the-circumstances test in *Illinois v. Gates.*

Spinelli v. United States (1969). "The informer's report must first be measured against *Aguilar*'s standards so that its probative value can be assessed. If the tip is found inadequate under *Aguilar,* the other allegations which corroborate the information contained in the hearsay report should then be considered." 393 U.S. 410, 415, 89 S.Ct. 584, 588, 21 L.Ed.2d 637, 643.

Illinois v. Gates (1983). "We agree with the Illinois Supreme Court that an informant's 'veracity,' 'reliability' and 'basis of knowledge' are all highly relevant in determining the value of his report. We do not agree, however, that these elements should be understood as entirely separate and independent requirements to be rigidly exacted in every case. . . . Rather . . . they should be understood simply as closely intertwined issues that may usefully illuminate the common-sense, practical question whether there is 'probable cause' to believe that contraband or evidence is located in a particular place." 462 U.S. 213, 230, 103 S.Ct. 2317, 2327–28, 76 L.Ed.2d 527, 543.

The two prongs of *Aguilar* "are better understood as relevant considerations in the totality of circumstances that traditionally has guided probable cause determinations: a deficiency in one may be compensated for, in determining the overall reliability of a tip by a strong showing as to the other, or by some other indicia of reliability." 462 U.S. at 233, 103 S.Ct. at 2329, 76 L.Ed.2d at 545.

"'The term "probable cause," according to its usual acceptation, means less than evidence which would justify condemnation. . . .' Finely tuned standards such as proof beyond a reasonable doubt or by a preponderance of the evidence, useful in formal trials, have no place in the magistrate's decision. While an effort to fix some general, numerically precise degree of certainty corresponding to 'probable cause' may not be helpful, it is clear that 'only the probability, and not a prima facie showing, of criminal activity is the standard of probable cause.'" 462 U.S. at 235, 103 S.Ct. at 2330, 76 L.Ed.2d at 546.

"[I]t is wiser to abandon the 'two-pronged test' established by our decisions in *Aguilar* and *Spinelli.* In its place we reaffirm the totality of the circumstances analysis that traditionally has informed probable cause determinations. The task of the issuing magistrate is simply to make a practical, common-sense decision whether, given all the circumstances set forth in the affidavit before him, including the 'veracity' and 'basis of knowledge' of persons supplying hearsay information, there is a fair probability that contraband or evidence of a crime will be found in a particular place. And the duty of a reviewing court is simply to ensure that the magistrate had a 'substantial basis for . . . conclud[ing]' that probable cause existed." 462 U.S. at 238–39, 103 S.Ct. at 2332, 76 L.Ed.2d at 548.

Review and Discussion Questions

1. Why is it important for a law enforcement officer to write down in a complaint or affidavit the facts and circumstances on which probable cause is based?

2. Give an example of a strong indication of probable cause to arrest that is arrived at through each of the five senses: sight, hearing, smell, taste, and touch.

3. Give an example of a strong indication of probable cause to search that is arrived at through each of the five senses: sight, hearing, smell, taste, and touch.

4. List three possible strong indications of probable cause to arrest for each of the following crimes:
   a. Theft
   b. Assault
   c. Arson
   d. Breaking and entering
   e. Rape
   f. Driving to endanger

5. Discuss the significance in the probable cause context of the phrase "conduct innocent in the eyes of the untrained may carry entirely different 'messages' to the experienced or trained . . . observer." *Davis v. United States,* 409 F.2d 458, 460 (D.C.Cir. 1969). Discuss specifically in terms of drug offenses and gambling offenses.

6. Must law enforcement officers know exactly the elements and name of the specific crime for which they are arresting or searching to have probable cause? See *People v. Georgev,* 230 N.E.2d 851 (Ill. 1967).

7. What does corroboration mean, and why is it important to a law enforcement officer in establishing probable cause through the use of informants?

8. How did the U.S. Supreme Court case of *Illinois v. Gates* change the requirements for establishing probable cause through the use of informants? Does the *Gates* decision make the law enforcement officer's task easier or harder?

9. Mr. A walks into a police station, drops three wristwatches on a table, and tells an officer that Mr. B robbed a local jewelry store two weeks ago. Mr. A will not say anything else in response to police questioning. A quick investigation reveals that the three watches were among a number

of items stolen in the jewelry store robbery. Do the police have probable cause to do any or all of the following?

    a. Arrest Mr. A.

    b. Arrest Mr. B.

    c. Search Mr. A's home.

    d. Search Mr. B's home.

10. If you answered no to any of the items in question 9, explain why in detail. If you answered yes to any of them, draft the complaint or affidavit for a warrant, or explain why a warrant is not needed.

Real-Life Fact Situations

1 Leslie Boles was driving a truck eastbound when a Nebraska state trooper stopped him for bypassing a weighing station. After being pulled over, Mr. Boles informed the trooper that his driver's license had expired and that he was transporting his girl-friend's furniture from Texas to Chicago. He also claimed that his girlfriend had the truck's lease agreement, that her name was Sandra Caballero, and that she was driving ahead of him in a white Ford Bronco with New Mexico plates.

A consensual search of the truck uncovered over 1,000 pounds of marijuana. Mr. Boles was taken to the Nebraska State Patrol office where an investigator informed him of his *Miranda* rights before interviewing him. The investigator testified at the suppression hearing that Mr. Boles "decided that he would come clean and tell the truth." Mr. Boles admitted to knowing that his truck contained marijuana, told the investigator that Mr. Gonzales and Sandra Carrion were his accomplices, and provided a detailed description of the vehicle in which they were traveling.

Trooper William Leader testified at the suppression hearing that he and a colleague received information (ultimately derived from the investigator) that they were to look for a "red GM type pickup with New Mexico plates" headed eastbound on Interstate 80, that the vehicle had New Mexico license plate number 514 HMT, that there would be a male and a female in the vehicle, that the male was named Gonzales, and that there was a cell phone in the vehicle.

Trooper Leader also received information that the pickup was "escorting" another vehicle that had been stopped with a large quantity of marijuana. Trooper Leader thereafter identified and then stopped a vehicle headed eastbound on Interstate 80 that matched exactly the description that he had been given.

Sandra Carrion was driving, and Mr. Gonzales was the passenger. Trooper Leader asked for Ms. Carrion's driver's license and looked inside the vehicle, where he saw what he believed to be one marijuana cigarette on the passenger-side armrest. After asking Mr. Gonzales to exit the vehicle, Trooper Leader then saw what he believed to be two more marijuana cigarettes on the passenger-side armrest. Trooper Leader also saw a cell phone in the vehicle. Trooper Leader concluded that he had probable cause to arrest Mr. Gonzales and Ms. Carrion for their involvement in the distribution of controlled substances and therefore took them into custody.

Mr. Gonzales argues that Trooper Leader lacked reasonable suspicion for the initial stop, and that he had no probable cause justifying the arrest. Was there probable cause to arrest Gonzales? *United States v. Gonzales,* 220 F.3d 922 (8th Cir. 2000).

Read the court opinion at:
caselaw.findlaw.com/data2/circs/8th/001063P.pdf

2 On Saturday, April 10, 1999, Officer William Fuentes of the Union Township Police Department, was in uniform working off duty as a security guard at a local methadone clinic. He had performed this job on approximately fifty prior occasions and knew that the illegal sale of methadone was a constant problem, particularly on Saturdays when clinic patients received a bottle to take with them so that they would have a Sunday dosage. Fuentes had observed approximately thirty instances of illegal sales of methadone, although he did not specify over what period of time.

On the day in question, three of the clinic's patients told Fuentes there was a white male outside attempting to buy bottles of methadone. The officer knew each of these women from his work at the clinic, although he did not know their names. The third patient that approached him described the man attempting to purchase the drugs as a white male wearing a brown jacket, a plaid or "lumberjack" shirt and blue jeans. She further said he had a "scruffy" appearance. This woman "continued on line, got medicated" and then accompanied Fuentes outside where she pointed out defendant who was standing across the street. Defendant's appearance was consistent with the patient's description.

Fuentes approached defendant, who first tried to ignore the officer. As Fuentes got closer, defendant "was visibly nervous, shaking." In response to the officer's question, defendant denied attempting to purchase methadone. Fuentes informed defendant he was going to pat him down for his own safety. When he did so he felt the distinctive shape of two methadone bottles in defendant's pocket. Defendant then admitted possessing the drugs. Defendant was not a clinic patient. The woman who had pointed out defendant left the area without Fuentes ever asking her name.

On these facts the motion judge granted defendant's motion to suppress. The judge believed the officer was obligated to observe defendant in an effort to verify the information he received before approaching defendant, making inquiry of him and then patting him down. Was the motion judge correct? *State v. Sibilia*, 750 A.2d 149 (N.J. Super. A.D. 2000).

Read the court opinion at:
lawlibrary.rutgers.edu/courts/appellate/a2211-99.opn.html

3 During the execution of a state search warrant at 1007 North Fulbright in Springfield, Missouri, officers seized firearms that became the basis of a four-count federal indictment against Riccy Wells. The superseding indictment charges Wells with possession of stolen firearms, in violation of 18 U.S.C.§§ 922(j) and 924(a)(2); possession of a firearm with an obliterated serial number, in violation of 18 U.S.C. §§ 922(k) and 924(a)(1)(B); and possession of unlawful firearms while being an unlawful user of a controlled substance, in violation of 18 U.S.C. §§ 922(g)(3) and 924(a)(2). Wells filed a motion to suppress evidence on the ground that the search warrant was procured in violation of *Franks v. Delaware*, 438 U.S. 154, 98 S.Ct. 2674, 57 L.Ed.2d 667 (1978).

In relevant part, the affidavit in support of the search warrant states a belief that evidence relating to the crimes of first degree assault, unlawful use of a weapon, and armed criminal action would be found at 1007 North Fulbright in Springfield, Missouri. The affiant, Officer Darren Lane, stated that his division was assigned to investigate criminal street gangs, and in his experience, gang members often have access to firearms and ammunition that they use during the commission of crimes and trade among themselves.

The affidavit refers to three drive-by shootings. First, two vehicles had reportedly exchanged gunfire in the Big K superstore parking lot on February 26, 1999. A confidential informant reported that one of the vehicles (a white Oldsmobile convertible) had been driven by Zachary Wilson. Another informant reported that the other vehicle (a brown Chevrolet Suburban) was owned by Jerry and Mose Johnson.

The second drive-by shooting occurred on March 20, 1999, near the home of Jerry and Mose Johnson. A witness reported seeing "a dark-colored vehicle" leaving the area with its headlights off. (Appellant's Add. at 6.) One hour later, on March 21, 1999, a third drive-by shooting occurred at another location. The affidavit states that a witness reported shots had been fired from a " 'dark colored Lincoln' type vehicle." (Id.)

The affidavit asserted that two days later, the police department's crimestoppers hotline received two anonymous calls dealing with the shootings. The first, "a concerned citizen who wished to remain anonymous and confidential for his/her

safety," stated that he or she "had received information that" Riccy Wells, Zachary Wilson (known to the confidential informant as "Hennesse"), and "Joey" were responsible for the shootings. (Id.) The informant also stated that the vehicle and weapons used in the drive-by shootings were being kept hidden in the garage at 1007 North Fulbright, which was a duplex rented by Wells' girlfriend, "Misty." (Id.)

A second anonymous call came in "almost immediately" after the first call. (Id.) This anonymous caller stated that he or she had heard Zachary Wilson and Jose Rincon, known as "Joey," bragging about committing the recent shootings. Officer Lane also stated in the affidavit that an anonymous high school student had told him that he or she had heard that either Zachary Wilson or an associate of his had committed two of the drive-by shootings. (See id. at 7.)

Officer Lane stated that he corroborated through city utilities records that the account for 1007 North Fulbright was in the name of Misty Hardin. Springfield police department crimestoppers' records revealed that Misty and Wells were girlfriend and boyfriend. Police investigative files also note an association between Wells (an alleged member of the Gangster Disciples street gang), Zachary Wilson (allegedly involved in a narcotics distribution ring), and Jose Rincon (allegedly a member of the Mexican Mafia).

Finally, the affidavit states that when Officer Lane drove by the duplex at 1007 North Fulbright, he observed Wells washing a dark blue 1988 Buick Park Avenue automobile. In the affidavit, Officer Lane stated, "This vehicle matches the description given to us as the possible suspect vehicle in the above listed shootings." (Appellant's Add. at 8.) Lane also stated that in his experience, gang members often register their vehicles in the name of friends or family members. The 1988 Buick Park Avenue was registered to Dominic Stevens, who lived at an address that Zachary Wilson had once listed as his home address. Based on all of this information, Officer Lane applied for and received a state court-issued search warrant for 1007 North Fulbright, where the weapons were found that formed the basis for the federal indictment against Riccy Wells.

At the hearing on Wells' motion to suppress the evidence, Officer Lane testified, and the underlying police report demonstrates, that the witness to the March 21 shooting provided a detailed vehicle description of a new Lincoln, either dark green or black, with tint on all windows. (See Hearing Tr. at 29–30; Appellee's Add. at 2.) Officer Lane acknowledged that his description of the witness having reported seeing a " 'dark colored Lincoln' type vehicle" was a poor choice of words that greatly expanded what the witness really said as recited in the police report. The district court adopted the magistrate judge's report and recommendation, finding that the affidavit's description of the vehicle was central to the conclusion that the vehicle seen at 1007 North Fulbright matched that description, and that the misstatement or omission misled the judge who issued the warrant. The court further found that a properly reconstructed warrant lacked sufficient information to support a finding of probable cause that evidence of the shootings would be found at 1007 North Fulbright. The district court concluded Wells had established a *Franks* violation, and the district court granted Wells' motion to suppress the evidence found in the search of the duplex.

The government appeals, asserting that the search warrant affidavit supports a finding of probable cause, even absent the alleged misstatements and omissions. Should the motion to suppress be granted? *U.S. v. Wells*, 223 F.3d 835 (8th Cir. 2000).

Read the court opinion at:
caselaw.findlaw.com/data2/circs/8th/994213p.pdf

4 On October 22, 1998, Secord took his car to a Firestone garage for servicing. While the car was being inspected and repaired, a Firestone mechanic, Gary Voit, noticed that one of the taillights was not working. Voit called Secord for permission to fix the light, and Secord agreed. To fix the taillight, Voit opened the car's hatchback and saw what he thought was a box of child pornography videotapes, as well as some soft-cover child pornography books. Voit showed his manager, Randy Petersen, and another employee, Timothy Hanlin, what he had found. They did not remove any of the materials from the car. Secord picked up his car later that afternoon.

On October 28, 1998, Sergeant Bernie Martinson of the Sex Crimes Unit of the Minneapolis Police Department received a phone call from a Hennepin County probation officer. The probation officer told Martinson that a friend who worked at the Firestone garage had told him about suspected child pornography in Secord's car. That same day, Martinson called the garage and talked to Peterson, who told him that while servicing Secord's car, several employees saw what they thought was child pornography in the car. Martinson also spoke with Hanlin, who gave a description of Secord and his clothes.

Based on this information, Martinson applied for and received a search warrant to search Secord's car and residence. Martinson executed the search warrant on October 29, 1998. He seized the box of videotapes and the soft-cover books from Secord's car. Although some of the videotape titles suggested that they might be child pornography, none of them contained child pornography or photographic representations of sexual conduct involving minors within the meaning of the relevant statutes. The soft-cover books were not pornographic.

Martinson and another investigator also searched Secord's residence, where they seized pornographic tapes and magazines that did not contain child pornography or photographic representations of sexual conduct involving minors within the meaning of the relevant statutes. But Secord told the officers that he had used his computer to download "pictures of juveniles pos-

ing in sexual positions and having sex with adults." The officers seized the pictures.

Secord moved to suppress the materials seized from his residence on the grounds that the warrant was not supported by probable cause, did not establish a sufficient nexus to his residence to support a search of the residence, and contained misrepresentations. Should the motion to suppress be granted? *State v. Secord*, 614 N.W.2d 227 (Minn.App. 2000).

Read the court opinion at:
www.finance-commerce.com/court/opinions/000626/cx991721.htm

5 On October 11, 1995, Detective Gary Lomenick of the Chattanooga Police Department received a tip from a confidential informant ("CI") that a man called Red Dog, residing at 910 North Market Street, was in possession of cocaine. Red Dog was familiar to other officers, though not to Lomenick, as someone known to be involved with drugs, named Kenneth Allen. Based on the CI's information, Lomenick sought and obtained a search warrant that same day. The affidavit read in full as follows:

I, Gary Lomenick, a duly sworn Chattanooga Police Officer, hereby apply for a search warrant and make oath as follows:

1. I am a sworn Chattanooga Police Officer with the Narcotics Division, where I have been assigned for over 15 years, and a commissioned Special Deputy Sheriff for Hamilton County, Tennessee.

2. On the 11th day of October 1995 I, Gary Lomenick, received information from an informant, a responsible and credible citizen of the county and state, who I know to be a responsible and credible citizen because, I have known said informant for 5 years and said informant has given me information about individuals involved in criminal activity in the past that has proven to be reliable. Said informants's name whom I have this day disclosed to the Judge to whom this application is made, that [*sic*] John Doe (Alias) Red Dog who resides in or occupies and is in possession of the following described premises 910 North Market Street, apartment directly underneath carport located in Chattanooga, Hamilton County Tennessee, unlawfully has in his possession on said premises legend and/or narcotic drugs including Cocaine in violation of law made and provided in such cases.

3. On the 11th day of October 1995 said informant advised me that said informant was on the premises of the said John Doe (Alias) Red Dog located at 910 North Market Street, apartment directly underneath carport within seventy-two hours prior to our conversation on October 11th, 1995 and while there saw Cocaine in possession of the said John Doe (Alias) Red Dog[.]

WHEREFORE, as such officer acting in performance of my duty in the premises I pray that the Court issue a warrant authorizing the search of the said John Doe (Alias) Red Dog and the premises located at 910 North Market Street, apartment directly underneath the carport, for said legend and/or narcotic drugs including Cocaine and that such search be made either by day or by night.

Lomenick executed the warrant that day, with a team of other officers. When they approached the building, Allen, who was on a porch, saw them and fled inside. The officers gave chase. As Allen ran past a closet, the police heard a loud thump, and shortly thereafter found a 9-mm pistol on the floor of the closet. Allen left a trail of crack cocaine rocks behind him as he fled. When he was apprehended, more rocks of crack were found in his pockets, totaling 9.3 grams in all.

Allen was indicted on March 12, 1996. He was charged with (1) possession of cocaine base with intent to distribute, in violation of 21 U.S.C. § 841; (2) possession of a firearm in connection with a drug offense, in violation of 18 U.S.C. § 924(c); and (3) possession of a firearm by a convicted felon, in violation of 18 U.S.C. § 922(g). In a motion filed on April 18, 1996, he moved to suppress the evidence as illegally seized, alleging that the indictment was based on an insufficient affidavit, one that did not provide probable cause, since it did not claim or detail any expertise or previous reliability in narcotics contexts on the part of the CI. Should the motion to suppress be granted? *United States v. Allen*, 211 F.3d 970 (6th Cir. 2000).

Read the court opinion at:
laws.findlaw.com/6th/00a0157p.html

6 At the hearing on Cook's motion to suppress, Minneapolis Police Officer Michael Doran testified that on the morning of June 22, 1999, he received a telephone call from a CRI. Doran had worked with this particular CRI in the past and had met him in person. The CRI had previously provided Doran and other officers known to Doran with information that had led to at least 12 other convictions. The CRI was paid for his information. To Doran's knowledge, the CRI had never given any false information.

In the two weeks prior to June 22, the CRI told Doran that a man named Shilow Cook was dealing crack cocaine in the Minneapolis area. In the June 22 phone call, the CRI told Doran that Cook was selling crack cocaine at the YMCA located at 34th and Blaisdell in Minneapolis and that he had the crack cocaine in the waistband of his pants. The CRI further described Cook as a black male in his mid-40's, 5'6" tall, and weighing approximately 150 pounds. The CRI told Doran that Cook was wearing a red shirt, black pants, and a baseball cap. Finally, the CRI stated that Cook was driving a blue Lincoln with Minnesota license plate number 134PXH.

Within one hour, at approximately 11:30 A.M., Doran and other officers arrived at the YMCA. They saw a blue Lincoln with Minnesota license plate 134PXH parked in the lot. At approximately noon, the officers saw a man leave the YMCA. The man matched Cook's description as given by the CRI. The officers observed the man get into the driver's side of the blue Lincoln.

The officers approached the vehicle and placed the man under arrest. During a search, the officers found 7.2 grams of crack cocaine in the waistband of the man's pants and $1,186 in cash in his pockets. Cook was charged with a controlled substance crime in the second degree in violation of Minn.Stat. § 152.022, subd. 2(1) (1998) ("unlawfully possesses one or more mixtures of a total weight of six grams or more containing cocaine").

At the suppression hearing, Doran claimed that he did not obtain a search warrant prior to arresting Cook because there was insufficient time. Doran acknowledged that the CRI never indicated that he saw Cook selling drugs. Nor is there any evidence that the CRI ever claimed he had personally purchased drugs from Cook. Should the evidence be suppressed? *State v. Cook*, 610 N.W.2d 664 (Minn.App. 2000).

Read the court opinion at:
www.finance-commerce.com/court/opinions/000501/ c7991790.htm

Part III

Exceptions to Search Warrant Requirements

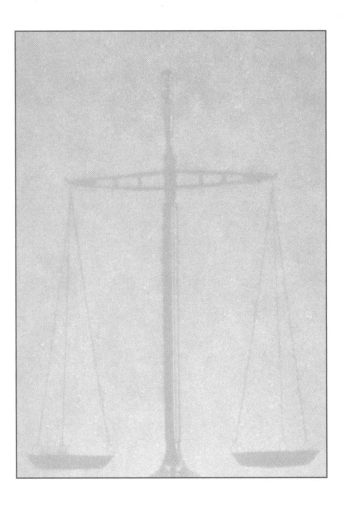

Chapter 7

Stop and Frisk

Outline

Objectives

■ **Understand the law's preference for search warrants and why exceptions to the warrant requirement are allowed.**

■ **Distinguish among a stop, a formal arrest, a seizure tantamount to an arrest, and minimal nonintrusive contact between a citizen and a law enforcement officer.**

■ **Understand the distinctions between a frisk and a full search.**

■ **Understand how to balance competing interests when determining the reasonableness of a stop and frisk.**

■ **Know what justifies a law enforcement officer in stopping a person and what interference with the person's freedom of action the law permits.**

■ **Know what justifies a law enforcement officer in frisking a person and the scope of the search the law permits.**

■ **Apply the legal principles governing stop and frisk to analogous situations such as detentions and examinations of luggage, mail, and other containers.**

Aguilar v. Texas
laws.findlaw.com/us/378/
108.html

The early chapters of this book emphasize the law's preference for warrants based on probable cause. Warrants are the chief means of balancing the need for efficient and effective law enforcement against the need to protect the rights of individual citizens to be secure against unreasonable searches and seizures. In *Aguilar v. Texas,* 378 U.S. 108, 84 S.Ct. 1509, 12 L.Ed.2d 723 (1964), the U.S. Supreme Court stated that the preference for warrants is so strong that less persuasive evidence will justify the issuance of a warrant than would justify a warrantless search or warrantless arrest.

> [W]hen a search is based upon a magistrate's, rather than a police officer's determination of probable cause, the reviewing courts will accept evidence of a less "judicially competent or persuasive character than would have justified an officer in acting on his own without a warrant," . . . and will sustain the judicial determination so long as "there was a substantial basis for [the magistrate] to conclude that [seizable evidence was] probably present. . . ." 378 U.S. at 111, 84 S.Ct. at 1512, 12 L.Ed.2d at 726.

The warrant procedure is preferred because it places responsibility for deciding the delicate question of probable cause with a neutral and detached judicial officer. Law enforcement is served, because law enforcement officers may search certain persons or places and seize certain persons or things when the officers can show reasonable grounds that a person, place, or thing is significantly connected with criminal activity. The Fourth Amendment rights of citizens are also served, because the decision to allow a search and seizure is removed from the hurried judgment of possibly overzealous law enforcement officers engaged in the competitive enterprise of investigating crime.

Situations often arise, however, in which the time and effort needed to obtain a warrant would unjustifiably frustrate enforcement of the laws. To ensure that the delicate balance between individual rights and law enforcement is maintained, courts have carved out various exceptions to the warrant requirement and have allowed warrantless searches and seizures in certain situations. One important exception is a stop and frisk.

In Chapter 4, a formal arrest was defined as "the taking of a person into custody for the commission of an offense as the prelude to prosecuting him for it." Also discussed were seizures tantamount to arrest, in which, although an officer has no intention of taking a person into custody and charging the person with a crime, the circumstances surrounding the detention are indistinguishable from an arrest in important respects. Stop and frisk involves an even less intrusive seizure of a person and a limited search of that person.

As a preliminary definition, stop and frisk is a police practice involving the temporary detention, questioning, and limited search of a person suspected of criminal activity. A stop may be initiated on a reasonable suspicion of crime amounting to less than probable cause for the purposes of crime prevention and investigation. A frisk is allowed for the protection of the law enforcement officer carrying out the investigation.

Stop and frisk should be distinguished from the common situation, also described in Chapter 4, in which the law enforcement officer approaches a person in a public place and asks whether the person is willing to answer questions. In this situation, the officer needs no justification or level of suspicion to approach the person, and the officer has no authority to detain the person, even momentarily, whether or not the person agrees to cooperate. However, if an initially friendly and neutral encounter somehow provides the officer with reason to suspect criminal activity or danger, the officer may be justified in making the more significant intrusion of a stop and frisk.

History

The law enforcement officer's power to detain and question suspicious persons dates back to the common law of England. Ancient statutes and court decisions gave constables the power to detain suspicious persons overnight to investigate their suspicious activities. In the United States, until the mid-1960s, police-initiated contacts with citizens not amounting to arrests were generally left to the discretion of individual officers and not subject to constitutional protections or judicial oversight. In the mid-1960s, a period of expanding constitutional rights for citizens, reformers called for the extension of constitutional protections to all police-citizen encounters and review of these encounters by the courts. This resulted in formalized procedures for many aspects of prearrest procedure and stirred up a controversy that continues to this day. Police and their supporters argued that, because of their experience and professionalism, street encounters should be subject to their discretion rather than formal rules. On the other hand, civil libertarians maintained that a free society requires that constitutional safeguards protect every citizen, especially minorities and dissidents, at all places and all times. In response, the U.S. Supreme Court adopted formal guidelines governing street encounters amounting to less than arrests or full searches in three cases decided in 1968. In those cases (*Terry v. Ohio, Sibron v. New York,* and *Peters v. New York*), the Court attempted to resolve the conflicting interests by applying a balancing test under the reasonableness clause of the Fourth Amendment.

Terry, Sibron, and *Peters*

The discussion of stop and frisk begins with summaries of *Terry v. Ohio,* 392 U.S. 1, 88 S.Ct. 1868, 20 L.Ed.2d 889 (1968), and *Terry*'s companion cases, *Sibron v. New York* and *Peters v. New York,* 392 U.S. 40, 88 S.Ct. 1889, 20 L.Ed.2d 917 (1968).

Terry v. Ohio

The facts of the case were stated by the U.S. Supreme Court.

> At the hearing on the motion to suppress this evidence, Officer McFadden testified that while he was patrolling in plain clothes in downtown Cleveland at approximately 2:30 in the afternoon of October 31, 1963, his attention was attracted by two men, Chilton and Terry, standing on the corner of Huron Road and Euclid Avenue. He had never seen the two men before, and he was unable to say precisely what first drew his eye to them. However, he testified that he had been a policeman for 39 years and a detective for 35 and that he had been assigned to patrol this vicinity of downtown Cleveland for shoplifters and pickpockets for 30 years. He explained that he had developed routine habits of observation over the years and that he would "stand and watch people or walk and watch people at many intervals of the day." He added: "Now, in this case when I looked over they didn't look right to me at the time."
>
> His interest aroused, Officer McFadden took up a post of observation in the entrance to a store 300 to 400 feet away from the two men. "I get more purpose to watch them when I seen their movements," he testified. He saw one of the men leave the other one and walk southwest on Huron Road, past some stores. The man paused for a moment and looked in a store window, then walked on a short distance, turned around and

faculty.ncsc.edu/toconnor/
serchrul.htm
Article, "Search and Seizure: A Guide to Rules, Requirements, Tests, Doctrines, and Exceptions"; overview of search and seizure law
lawschool.lexis.com/emanuel/
web/crimpro03.htm
General overview of law relating to warrantless searches

For new and updated weblinks, go to www.wadsworth.com/
cj/ferdico0253

Terry v. Ohio
laws.findlaw.com/us/392/1.html

walked back toward the corner, pausing once again to look in the same store window. He rejoined his companion at the corner, and the two conferred briefly. Then the second man went through the same series of motions, strolling down Huron Road, looking in the same window, walking on a short distance, turning back, peering in the store window again, and returning to confer with the first man at the corner. The two men repeated this ritual alternately between five and six times apiece—in all, roughly a dozen trips. At one point, while the two were standing together on the corner, a third man approached them and engaged them briefly in conversation. This man then left the two others and walked west on Euclid Avenue. Chilton and Terry resumed their measured pacing, peering and conferring. After this had gone on for 10 to 12 minutes, the two men walked off together, heading west on Euclid Avenue, following the path taken earlier by the third man.

By this time Officer McFadden had become thoroughly suspicious. He testified that after observing their elaborately casual and oft-repeated reconnaissance of the store window on Huron Road, he suspected the two men of "casing a job, a stick-up," and that he considered it his duty as a police officer to investigate further. He added that he feared "they may have a gun." Thus, Officer McFadden followed Chilton and Terry and saw them stop in front of Zucker's store to talk to the same man who had conferred with them earlier on the street corner. Deciding that the situation was ripe for direct action, Officer McFadden approached the three men, identified himself as a police officer and asked for their names. At this point his knowledge was confined to what he had observed. He was not acquainted with any of the three men by name or by sight, and he had received no information concerning them from any other source. When the men "mumbled something" in response to his inquiries, Officer McFadden grabbed petitioner Terry, spun him around so that they were facing the other two, with Terry between McFadden and the others, and patted down the outside of his clothing. In the left breast pocket of Terry's overcoat Officer McFadden felt a pistol. He reached inside the overcoat pocket, but was unable to remove the gun. At this point, keeping Terry between himself and the others, the officer ordered all three men to enter Zucker's store. As they went in, he removed Terry's overcoat completely, removed a .38-caliber revolver from the pocket and ordered all three men to face the wall with their hands raised. Officer McFadden proceeded to pat down the outer clothing of Chilton and the third man, Katz. He discovered another revolver in the outer pocket of Chilton's overcoat, but no weapons were found on Katz. The officer testified that he only patted the men down to see whether they had weapons, and that he did not put his hands beneath the outer garments of either Terry or Chilton until he felt their guns. So far as appears from the record, he never placed his hands beneath Katz' outer garments. Officer McFadden seized Chilton's gun, asked the proprietor of the store to call a police wagon, and took all three men to the station, where Chilton and Terry were formally charged with carrying concealed weapons. 392 U.S. at 5–7, 88 S.Ct. at 1871–72, 20 L.Ed.2d at 896–98.

Terry and Chilton were convicted of carrying concealed weapons. They appealed, claiming that the weapons were obtained by means of an unreasonable search and should not have been admitted into evidence at their trial. The U.S. Supreme Court affirmed the convictions. The Court said that, even though *stop and frisk* represented a lesser restraint than a traditional *arrest and search*, the procedure is still governed by the Fourth Amendment. However, stop and frisk is not subject to as stringent a limitation as is a traditional full arrest and search. Instead of applying the *probable cause* standard to stop and frisk, the Court applied the fundamental test of the Fourth

Amendment: the *reasonableness* in all the circumstances of the particular governmental invasion of a citizen's personal security.

In discussing the reasonableness of the officer's actions in this case, the Court first mentioned the long tradition of armed violence of American criminals and the number of law enforcement officers killed or wounded in action. In light of this, the Court recognized law enforcement officers' need to protect themselves when suspicious circumstances indicate possible criminal activity by potentially dangerous persons, even though probable cause for an arrest is lacking. In these situations, the Court felt it would be unreasonable to deny an officer the authority to take necessary steps to determine whether a suspected person is armed and to neutralize the threat of harm. The Court concluded that

> where a police officer observes unusual conduct which leads him reasonably to conclude in light of his experience that criminal activity may be afoot and that the persons with whom he is dealing may be armed and presently dangerous, where in the course of investigating this behavior he identifies himself as a policeman and makes reasonable inquiries, and where nothing in the initial stages of the encounter serves to dispel his reasonable fear for his own or other's safety, he is entitled for the protection of himself and others in the area to conduct a carefully limited search of the outer clothing of such persons in an attempt to discover weapons which might be used to assault him. 392 U.S. at 30, 88 S.Ct. at 1884–85, 20 L.Ed.2d at 911.

Sibron v. New York

The facts of the case were stated by the U.S. Supreme Court:

Sibron v. New York
laws.findlaw.com/us/392/
40.html

> At the hearing on the motion to suppress, Officer Martin testified that while he was patrolling his beat in uniform on March 9, 1965, he observed Sibron "continually from the hours of 4:00 P.M. to 12:00, midnight . . . in the vicinity of 742 Broadway." He stated that during this period of time he saw Sibron in conversation with six or eight persons whom he (Patrolman Martin) knew from past experience to be narcotics addicts. The officer testified that he did not overhear any of these conversations, and that he did not see anything pass between Sibron and any of the others. Late in the evening Sibron entered a restaurant. Patrolman Martin saw Sibron speak with three more known addicts inside the restaurant. Once again, nothing was overheard and nothing was seen to pass between Sibron and the addicts. Sibron sat down and ordered pie and coffee, and as he was eating, Patrolman Martin approached him and told him to come outside. Once outside, the officer said to Sibron, "You know what I am after." According to the officer, Sibron "mumbled something and reached into his pocket." Simultaneously, Patrolman Martin thrust his hand into the same pocket, discovering several glassine envelopes, which, it turned out, contained heroin. 392 U.S. at 45, 88 S.Ct. at 1893–94, 20 L.Ed.2d at 924–25.

Sibron was convicted of unauthorized possession of narcotics and appealed on the basis that the seizure was made in violation of his Fourth Amendment rights.

The Supreme Court found that the police officer in the *Sibron* case did not have probable cause to make an arrest and therefore could not justify the search as incident to arrest. The officer knew nothing of the conversations between Sibron and the others, and he saw nothing pass between them. All he had to go on was the fact that the others were addicts. This was not enough. "The inference that persons who talk to narcotics addicts are engaged in criminal traffic in narcotics is simply not the sort of reasonable inference required to support an intrusion by the police upon an individual's personal security." 392 U.S. at 62, 88 S.Ct. at 1902, 20 L.Ed.2d at 934. There was no basis to arrest until after the unlawful search.

Moreover, nothing in the record gave the slightest indication that the officer thought Sibron might be armed and dangerous. The officer, therefore, could not justify his actions on the grounds of self-protection. The *Terry* case did not authorize a routine frisk of everyone seen on the street or encountered by an officer. The officer in *Sibron* was apparently after narcotics and nothing else. His search was therefore unreasonable under the standards announced in the *Terry* case. Since there was neither probable cause to arrest nor sufficient justification to frisk, the heroin seized by the officer was not admissible in evidence, and Sibron's conviction was reversed.

Peters v. New York

Peters v. New York
laws.findlaw.com/us/392/40.html

The facts of the case were stated by the U.S. Supreme Court:

> Officer Samuel Lasky of the New York City Police Department testified . . . that he was at home in his apartment in Mount Vernon, New York, at about 1 P.M. on July 10, 1964. He had just finished taking a shower and was drying himself when he heard a noise at his door. His attempt to investigate was interrupted by a telephone call, but when he returned and looked through the peephole into the hall, Officer Lasky saw "two men tiptoeing out of the alcove toward the stairway." He immediately called the police, put on some civilian clothes and armed himself with his service revolver. Returning to the peephole, he saw "a tall man tiptoeing away from the alcove and followed by this shorter man, Mr. Peters, toward the stairway." Officer Lasky testified that he had lived in the 120-unit building for 12 years and that he did not recognize either of the men as tenants. Believing that he had happened upon the two men in the course of an attempted burglary, Officer Lasky opened his door, entered the hallway and slammed the door loudly behind him. This precipitated a flight down the stairs on the part of the two men, and Officer Lasky gave chase. His apartment was located on the sixth floor, and he apprehended Peters between the fourth and fifth floors. Grabbing Peters by the collar, he continued down another flight in unsuccessful pursuit of the other man. Peters explained his presence in the building to Officer Lasky by saying that he was visiting a girl friend. However, he declined to reveal the girl friend's name, on the ground that she was a married woman. Officer Lasky patted Peters down for weapons, and discovered a hard object in his pocket. He stated at the hearing that the object did not feel like a gun, but that it might have been a knife. He removed the object from Peters' pocket. It was an opaque plastic envelope, containing burglar's tools. 392 U.S. at 48–49, 88 S.Ct. at 1895, 20 L.Ed.2d at 926–27.

The Supreme Court affirmed Peters's conviction for possessing burglar's tools. The Court did not examine the officer's actions from a stop-and-frisk standpoint but, rather, found that the officer had probable cause to arrest and sufficient authority to search incident to the arrest. The Court's decision emphasized that the defendant's furtive action and his flight were significant considerations in establishing probable cause.

> It is difficult to conceive of stronger grounds for an arrest, short of actual eyewitness observation of criminal activity. . . . [D]eliberately furtive actions and flight at the approach of strangers or law officers are strong indicia of mens rea [criminal intent], and when coupled with specific knowledge on the part of the officer relating the suspect to

caselaw.findlaw.com/data/constitution/amendment04/03.html#2
Comprehensive discussion (with annotations) of detention short of arrest–stop and frisk

www.oag.state.ny.us/press/reports/stop_frisk/ch2_part1.html
Part 1 of the "Stop and Frisk" Report of the New York State Attorney General's Office; discusses Fourth Amendment standards

faculty.ncwc.edu/toconnor/frisk.htm
Article, "Stop and Frisk Law: A Guide to Doctrines, Tests, and Special Circumstances"

www.nolo.com/chapter/KYR/KYR_store_ch2_f.html
Discussion of the law relating to stop and frisk, with examples

the evidence of crime, they are proper factors to be considered in the decision to make an arrest. 392 U.S. at 66–67, 88 S.Ct. at 1904, 20 L.Ed.2d at 937.

Note that the Court in *Peters* found that the combination of the suspect's furtive actions, his flight at the approach of the officer, and the officer's knowledge relating the suspect to the evidence provided probable cause to arrest. Unprovoked flight, in and of itself, however, does not provide either probable cause to arrest or reasonable suspicion justifying a stop. See the discussion of *Illinois v. Wardlow*, 528 U.S. 119, 120 S. Ct. 673, 145 L. Ed. 2d 570 (2000), on pages 289–90 .

The remainder of this chapter discusses in detail the authority and scope of a law enforcement officer in conducting a stop and frisk.

Illinois v. Wardlow
laws.findlaw.com/us/000/
98-1036.html

The Reasonableness Standard

Stop-and-frisk procedures are serious intrusions on an individual's privacy. They are governed by the Fourth Amendment to the Constitution, which prohibits unreasonable searches and seizures.

> It is quite plain that the Fourth Amendment governs "seizures" of the person which do not eventuate in a trip to the station house and prosecution for crime—"arrests" in traditional terminology. It must be recognized that whenever a police officer accosts an individual and restrains his freedom to walk away, he has "seized" that person. And it is nothing less than sheer torture of the English language to suggest that a careful exploration of the outer surfaces of a person's clothing all over his or her body in an attempt to find weapons is not a "search." Moreover, it is simply fantastic to urge that such a procedure performed in public by a policeman while the citizen stands helpless, perhaps facing a wall with his hands raised, is a "petty indignity." It is a serious intrusion upon the sanctity of the person, which may inflict great indignity and arouse strong resentment, and it is not to be undertaken lightly. *Terry v. Ohio*, 392 U.S. at 16–17, 88 S.Ct. at 1877, 20 L.Ed.2d at 903.

Nevertheless, because a stop is more limited in scope than an arrest and because a frisk is more limited in scope than a full search, a stop and frisk may be judged by a less rigid standard than the probable cause standard applicable to an arrest and search. The *Terry* case made clear that stop and frisk is governed not by the warrant clause of the Fourth Amendment but by the reasonableness clause.

> [W]e deal here with an entire rubric of police conduct—necessarily swift action based upon the on-the-spot observations of the officer on the beat—which historically has not been, and as a practical matter could not be, subjected to the warrant procedure. Instead, the conduct involved in this case must be tested by the Fourth Amendment's general proscription against unreasonable searches and seizures. 392 U.S. 1, 20, 88 S.Ct. 1868, 1879, 20 L.Ed.2d 889, 905.

The question for the law enforcement officer then becomes whether it is reasonable, in a particular set of circumstances, for the officer to seize a person and subject the person to a limited search when there is no probable cause to arrest.

The determination of reasonableness involves a consideration of the competing interests involved in a stop-and-frisk situation. On one side are the individual's right to privacy and the individual's right to be free from unreasonable searches and seizures. As the Supreme Court said in *Terry*, "Even a limited search of the outer clothing for weapons constitutes a severe, though brief, intrusion upon cherished personal security, and it must surely be an annoying, frightening, and perhaps humiliating experience." 392 U.S. at 24–25, 88 S.Ct. at 1881–82, 20 L.Ed.2d at 908.

On the other side are the governmental interests involved. One of these is effective crime prevention and detection. The other governmental interest, with which the Court in *Terry* was most concerned, is the interest of police officers in taking steps to assure themselves that the person with whom they are dealing is not armed with a weapon that could unexpectedly be used against them:

> Certainly it would be unreasonable to require that police officers take unnecessary risks in the performance of their duties. American criminals have a long tradition of armed violence, and every year in this country many law enforcement officers are killed in the line of duty, and thousands more are wounded. 392 U.S. at 23, 88 S.Ct. at 1881, 20 L.Ed.2d at 907.

> Balancing these competing interests in a particular situation requires a consideration of

- whether *any* police interference at all is justified by the circumstances, and
- if so, *how extensive* an interference those circumstances justify.

In the following discussion, the stop aspect and the frisk aspect are considered separately because the stop and the frisk each have different purposes, different sets of circumstances that justify them, and different consequences for the person subjected to the procedure.

Key Points

1. The determination of the reasonableness of a stop and frisk involves balancing the individual's right to privacy and right to be free from unreasonable searches and seizures against the governmental interests of effective crime prevention and detection and the safety of law enforcement officers and others.

Determination of Whether to Stop

The U.S. Supreme Court recognized that stopping persons for the purpose of investigating possible criminal activity is necessary to the government's interest in effective crime prevention and detection:

> [I]t is this interest which underlies the recognition that a police officer may in appropriate circumstances and in an appropriate manner approach a person for purposes of investigating possibly criminal behavior even though there is no probable cause to make an arrest. *Terry v. Ohio*, 392 U.S. at 22, 88 S.Ct. at 1880, 20 L.Ed.2d. at 906–07.

What Is a Stop?

www.co.alameda.ca.us/da/pov/
Police.htm
Article, "Police Contacts" from
the District Attorney's Office in
Alameda County, California

Not every approach of a person by a law enforcement officer for purposes of investigating possible criminal activity will be considered a stop. In the *Terry* case, the Supreme Court noted:

Obviously not all personal intercourse between policemen and citizens involves "seizures" of persons. Only when the officer, by means of physical force or show of authority, has in some way restrained the liberty of a citizen may we conclude that a "seizure" has occurred. 392 U.S. at 19 n.16, 88 S.Ct. at 1879 n.16, 20 L.Ed.2d at 905 n.16.

A stop is the least intrusive type of seizure of the person governed by the Fourth Amendment. (More intrusive types of seizures—formal arrests and seizures tantamount to arrest—are discussed in Chapter 4.)

In *United States v. Mendenhall,* 446 U.S. 544, 100 S.Ct. 1870, 64 L.Ed.2d 497 (1980), the U.S. Supreme Court developed a test to be applied in determining whether a person has been seized within the meaning of the Fourth Amendment.

United States v. Mendenhall
laws.findlaw.com/us/446/544.html

> [A] person has been "seized" within the meaning of the Fourth Amendment only if, in view of all of the circumstances surrounding the incident, a reasonable person would have believed that he was not free to leave. Examples of circumstances that might indicate a seizure even where the person did not attempt to leave, would be the threatening presence of several officers, the display of a weapon by an officer, some physical touching of the person of the citizen, or the use of language or tone of voice indicating that compliance with the officer's request might be compelled. . . . In the absence of some such evidence, otherwise inoffensive contact between a member of the public and the police cannot, as a matter of law, amount to a seizure of that person. 446 U.S. at 554–55, 100 S.Ct. at 1877, 64 L.Ed.2d at 509.

In the *Mendenhall* case, the Court found no seizure (and therefore no stop) on the following facts:

> The events took place in the public concourse. The agents wore no uniforms and displayed no weapons. They did not summon the respondent to their presence, but instead approached her and identified themselves as federal agents. They requested, but did not demand to see the respondent's identification and ticket. Such conduct without more, did not amount to an intrusion upon any constitutionally protected interest. The respondent was not seized simply by reason of the fact that the agents approached her, asked her if she would show them her ticket and identification and posed to her a few questions. Nor was it enough to establish a seizure that the person asking the questions was a law enforcement official. In short, nothing in the record suggests that the respondent had any objective reason to believe that she was not free to end the conversation in the concourse and proceed on her own way, and for that reason we conclude that the agents' initial approach to her was not a seizure. 446 U.S. at 555, 100 S.Ct. at 1877–78, 64 L.Ed.2d at 510.

Cases since *Mendenhall* have established that, even when law enforcement officers have no basis for suspecting a particular person, they may ask questions of that person, including requests to examine identification or search luggage, and there is no seizure "as long as the police do not convey the message that compliance with their requests is required." *Florida v. Bostick,* 501 U.S. 429, 435, 111 S.Ct. 2382, 2386, 115 L.Ed.2d 389, 398–99 (1991).

Florida v. Bostick
laws.findlaw.com/us/501/429.html

"*Mendenhall* establishes that the test for existence of a 'show of authority' is an objective one: not whether the citizen perceived that he was being ordered to restrict his movement, but whether the officer's words and actions would have conveyed that to a reasonable person." *California v. Hodari D.,* 499 U.S. 621, 628, 111 S.Ct. 1547, 1551, 113 L.Ed.2d 690, 698 (1991). Application of this objective test was the basis for the

California v. Hodari D.
laws.findlaw.com/us/499/621.html

Michigan v. Chesternut
laws.findlaw.com/us/486/
567.html

Supreme Court's decision in *Michigan v. Chesternut*, 486 U.S. 567, 108 S.Ct. 1975, 100 L.Ed.2d 565 (1988). In that case, the Court said:

> The [*Mendenhall*] test is necessarily imprecise, because it is designed to assess the coercive effect of police conduct, taken as a whole, rather than to focus on particular details of that conduct in isolation. Moreover, what constitutes a restraint on liberty prompting a person to conclude that he is not free to "leave" will vary, not only with the particular police conduct at issue, but also with the setting in which the conduct occurs. 486 U.S. at 573, 108 S.Ct. at 1979, 100 L.Ed.2d at 572.

In the *Chesternut* case, officers in a patrol car chased the defendant after they observed the defendant run when he saw the patrol car. The chase consisted of a brief acceleration to catch up with the defendant followed by a short drive alongside the defendant. The Court held that no stop occurred, because the defendant could not have reasonably believed that he was not free to disregard the police presence and go about his business. The Court noted that the police did not activate a siren or flasher, did not command the defendant to halt, did not display any weapons, and did not operate the patrol car in an aggressive manner to block the defendant's course or otherwise control the direction or speed of the defendant's movement. The Court recognized that "[w]hile the very presence of a police car driving parallel to a running pedestrian could be somewhat intimidating, this kind of police presence does not, standing alone, constitute a seizure." 486 U.S. at 575, 108 S.Ct. at 1980, 100 L.Ed.2d at 573.

United States v. Dockter, 58 F.3d 1284 (8th Cir. 1995), held that defendants were not seized within the meaning of the Fourth Amendment when a deputy sheriff pulled his vehicle behind their automobile, which was parked off the traveled portion of the road and had its parking lights on, and activated his amber warning lights. The deputy sheriff did not block their vehicle in any manner to preclude them from leaving, did not draw his weapon, and spoke to them in a tone that was inquisitive rather than coercive. Nor was there a seizure when, in a different case, two law enforcement officers walked up to the defendant, who was seated on a bus, asked him a few questions, and asked whether they could search his bags. The U.S. Supreme Court said that, although the defendant may not have felt free to leave, his freedom of movement was restricted by a factor independent of police conduct.

> [T]he mere fact that Bostick did not feel free to leave the bus does not mean that the police seized him. Bostick was a passenger on a bus that was scheduled to depart. He would not have felt free to leave the bus even if the police had not been present. Bostick's movements were "confined" in a sense, but this was the natural result of his decision to take the bus; it says nothing about whether or not the police conduct at issue was coercive. *Florida v. Bostick,* 501 U.S. 429, 436, 111 S.Ct. 2382, 2387, 115 L.Ed.2d 389, 399 (1991).

Florida v. Bostick
laws.findlaw.com/us/501/
429.html

The Court stated:

> [I]n order to determine whether a particular encounter constitutes a seizure, a court must consider all the circumstances surrounding the encounter to determine whether the police conduct would have communicated to a reasonable person that the person was not free to decline the officers' requests or otherwise terminate the encounter. That rule applies to encounters that take place on a city street or in an airport lobby, and it applies equally to encounters on a bus. 501 U.S. at 439–40, 111 S.Ct. at 2389, 115 L.Ed.2d at 401–02.

Note that, for purposes of the Fourth Amendment, a seizure requires an *intentional* acquisition of physical control. For example, if a parked and unoccupied police car slips

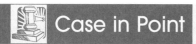

Case in Point

Interpreting *Sacramento v. Lewis*

Lucille Moreland, Demarrion Quintrell Jett, and Dominisha Lanae Jett appeal from the district court's grant of summary judgment in Appellees' favor on Appellants' 42 U.S.C. § 1983 and related state law claims arising from the shooting death of Damon Douglas. Appellants' central theory of this case is that Appellee Burns inadvertently shot the wrong man during a gunfight outside a Las Vegas bar and then he and his partner lied to cover up this mistake. . . .

This case stems from a gunfight that took place outside of a Las Vegas bar shortly after midnight on September 18, 1993. It is undisputed that when the smoke from this fight cleared, Damon Douglas ("Douglas") lay fatally wounded by a bullet fired by Appellee James Burns ("Burns"). Appellants are Douglas's mother and his two minor children. Appellees are the Las Vegas Metropolitan Police Department ("Metro") and two of its police officers, Burns and Jack Pope ("Pope").

Shortly after midnight on the night of September 17–18, 1993, Burns and Pope responded to a dispatch call indicating there was a fight in the parking lot of the Chances Arr bar in northwest Las Vegas. As Burns and Pope approached in their vehicle, they spotted a male standing beside a car in the parking lot, firing a semiautomatic handgun at individuals who were returning fire from the eastern side of the lot. Burns and Pope stopped their vehicle, illuminated the male with lights, and took cover behind a wall in a position approximately 45 feet behind and slightly to the right of the male. From this vantage point, Burns and Pope could see there were between 50 and 100 people trapped in the parking lot, many of whom were caught in the ongoing crossfire.

When the male failed to comply with the officers' orders to stop firing, Burns and Pope both fired at him. As each officer fired his final shot, the male fell to the ground and crawled away from the officers, toward the bar. After the shooting stopped, Burns and Pope looked for the male and found Douglas lying on the ground near the front of the bar. Douglas was taken to a local hospital and died shortly thereafter. An autopsy and forensics investigation determined that Douglas had been shot once by a bullet fired from Burns's gun that severed a major artery in Douglas's hip. No gun was found in Douglas's possession, but a semiautomatic pistol was found on the ground in front of the vehicle from which the male had been firing. Metro's fingerprint examiner excluded Douglas as the source of one of the two prints found on the gun, but could neither exclude nor identify Douglas as the source of the second print.

Burns and Pope gave statements to Metro investigators at the scene and later testified at the coroner's inquest that was held regarding the shooting of Douglas. In their inquest testimony and interviews at the scene, Burns and Pope identified Douglas as the man at whom they shot. Pope also testified that only the male's right side was exposed when he and Burns shot, while Burns stated that the male also exposed his left side to Burns as Burns fired his final shots. Additional inquest testimony and witness affidavits presented to the district court suggest Douglas may have been elsewhere in the parking lot for at least some part of the gunfight.

Appellants subsequently filed this lawsuit, asserting three causes of action against Appellees. The first cause of action was brought pursuant to 42 U.S.C. § 1983, based on four distinct theories of relief. The complaint also asserted state law wrongful death and intentional infliction of emotional distress causes of action. The district court ultimately granted Appellees' motions for summary judgment on all of Appellants' claims, and Appellants timely appealed. In light of *Sacramento v. Lewis*, should the appeal be granted? *Moreland v. Las Vegas Metropolitan Police Dept.*, 159 F.3d 365 (9th Cir. 1998).

Read the court opinion at:
laws.findlaw.com/9th/9717070v2.html

---

its brake and pins a passerby against a wall, it is likely that a tort has occurred but not a violation of the Fourth Amendment. And the situation would not change if the passerby happened, by lucky chance, to be a serial murderer for whom there was an outstanding arrest warrant—even if, at the time he was thus pinned, he was in the process of running away from two pursuing police officers. In *Brower v. County of Inyo*, 489 U.S. 593, 596–97, 109 S.Ct. 1378, 1381, 103 L.Ed.2d 628, 635 (1989), the Court said:

> [A] Fourth Amendment seizure does not occur whenever there is a governmentally caused termination of an individual's freedom of movement (the innocent passerby), nor even whenever there is a governmentally caused and governmentally *desired* termination

Brower v. County of Inyo
laws.findlaw.com/us/489/
593.html

www.fplc.edu/annsur97/
AS5.HTM
Article, "'What's In The Bag?'
Crack, Crooks, and Cops: *State v.
Quezada* and the Law of Seizure
in New Hampshire" by James S.
Cianci and Peter Cline

of an individual's freedom of movement (the fleeing felon), but only when there is a governmental termination of freedom of movement *through means intentionally applied.*

If the "show of authority" by a law enforcement officer does not result in a halting or submission by the person being confronted, there is no seizure. In *California v. Hodari D.*, 499 U.S. 621, 111 S.Ct. 1547, 113 L.Ed.2d 690 (1991), the defendant, who was fleeing the approach of an unmarked police car, was surprised when he confronted an officer on foot pursuing him from another direction. The defendant immediately tossed away a small rock and was soon thereafter tackled by the officer. The rock was recovered and proved to be crack cocaine. The Court held that, in the absence of any physical contact or submission to the officer's show of authority, the defendant was not seized until he was tackled. The cocaine abandoned while he was running was, therefore, not the fruit of a *seizure* and not subject to exclusion. Likewise, "no Fourth Amendment seizure would take place where a 'pursuing police car sought to stop the suspect only by the show of authority represented by flashing lights and continuing pursuit,' but accidentally stopped the suspect by crashing into him." *Sacramento v. Lewis*, 523 U.S. 833, 118 S.Ct. 1708, 140 L.Ed.2d 1043 (1998).

Sacramento v. Lewis
laws.findlaw.com/us/000/
96-1337.html

To summarize, three basic questions must be answered to determine if a seizure or stop has occurred for Fourth Amendment purposes. First, did the law enforcement officer's conduct constitute a "show of authority," as defined in *Mendenhall*? Second, under the totality of the circumstances, would a reasonable person believe that he was not free to leave? Finally, did the person submit to the police officers' "show of authority" as a result of means intentionally applied?

Authority to Stop

A law enforcement officer may stop and briefly detain a person for investigative purposes if the officer has a *reasonable suspicion* supported by articulable facts that criminal activity "may be afoot," even if the officer lacks probable cause. (Indications of criminal activity are discussed in Chapter 6.) Reasonable suspicion is "considerably less than proof of wrongdoing by a preponderance of the evidence" and "is obviously less demanding than that for probable cause." *United States v. Sokolow*, 490 U.S. 1, 7, 109 S.Ct. 1581, 1585, 104 L.Ed.2d 1, 10 (1989). The concept of reasonable suspicion, like probable cause, is not "readily, or even usefully, reduced to a neat set of legal rules." *Illinois v. Gates*, 462 U.S. 213, 232, 103 S.Ct. 2317, 2329, 76 L.Ed.2d 527, 544 (1983). In evaluating the validity of a stop, courts will consider the totality of the circumstances—the whole picture.

United States v. Sokolow
laws.findlaw.com/us/490/1.html

Illinois v. Gates
laws.findlaw.com/us/462/
213.html

[T]he totality of the circumstances—the whole picture—must be taken into account. Based upon that whole picture the detaining officers must have a particularized and objective basis for suspecting the particular person stopped of criminal activity. . . . The analysis proceeds with various objective observations, information from police reports, if such are available, and consideration of the modes or patterns of operation of certain kinds of lawbreakers. From these data, a trained officer draws inferences and makes deductions—inferences and deductions that might well elude an untrained person.

The process does not deal with hard certainties, but with probabilities. Long before the law of probabilities was articulated as such, practical people formulated certain common-sense conclusions about human behavior; jurors as fact-finders are permitted to do the same—and so are law enforcement officers. *United States v. Cortez*, 449 U.S. 411, 417–18, 101 S.Ct. 690, 695, 66 L.Ed.2d 621, 629 (1981).

United States v. Cortez
laws.findlaw.com/us/449/
411.html

The officer must be able to give reasons to justify any stop. As the Supreme Court said in *Terry*, "[I]n justifying the particular intrusion the police officer must be able to point to specific and articulable facts which, taken together with rational inferences from those facts, reasonably warrant that intrusion." 392 U.S. at 21, 88 S.Ct. at 1880, 20 L.Ed.2d at 906. A court will not accept an officer's mere statement or conclusion that criminal activity was suspected. The officer must be able to back up the conclusion by reciting the specific facts that led to that conclusion. For example, in *United States v. Pavelski*, 789 F.2d 485 (7th Cir. 1986), the court held that an officer who testified to a "gut feeling that things were really wrong" failed to articulate any objective facts indicative of criminal activity.

Furthermore, the officer's decision to initiate a stop will be judged against the following objective standard: "[W]ould the facts available to the officer at the moment of the seizure or the search 'warrant a man of reasonable caution in the belief' that the action taken was appropriate?" *Terry v. Ohio*, 392 U.S. at 21–22, 88 S.Ct. at 1880, 20 L.Ed.2d at 906. This objective standard is similar to the standard imposed on law enforcement officers in traditional search and seizure or arrest situations. For example, assume that an officer is attempting to obtain a warrant for a person's arrest. Since probable cause is required to obtain the warrant, the officer must produce specific facts sufficient to support a fair probability *that a specific crime has been or is being committed.* In the stop-and-frisk situation, no crime may have been committed—there is only a possibility that criminal activity is under way, perhaps only in the planning stage. However, the officer must still have specific facts indicating a *possibility of impending criminal activity* to justify the initial intrusion. The common element in the two situations is that officers must be able to justify their action with specific facts. The only difference is in the nature of the information to be given, and for an investigative stop, the officer need only show facts indicating the possibility that criminal behavior is afoot.

The officer's authority to stop is not limited to crimes about to be committed or crimes in the process of being committed. The U.S. Supreme Court has authorized the stop of a person whom officers suspected of being involved in a *completed* felony. The Court said:

> [W]here police have been unable to locate a person suspected of involvement in a past crime, the ability to briefly stop that person, ask questions, or check identification in the absence of probable cause promotes the strong government interest in solving crimes and bringing offenders to justice. Restraining police action until after probable cause is obtained would not only hinder the investigation, but might also enable the suspect to flee in the interim and to remain at large. Particularly in the context of felonies or crimes involving a threat to public safety, it is in the public interest that the crime be solved and the suspect detained as promptly as possible. The law enforcement interests at stake in these circumstances outweigh the individual's interest to be free of a stop and detention that is no more extensive than permissible in the investigation of imminent or ongoing crimes. *United States v. Hensley*, 469 U.S. 221, 229, 105 S.Ct. 675, 681, 83 L.Ed.2d 604, 612 (1985).

Note that an officer has the duty to discontinue the investigation and not make a *Terry*-type stop of a person when, by the time of the intended stop, justification for the initial suspicion has disappeared.

The scope of a policeman's inquiry and the permissibility of continuing to press the ongoing investigation necessarily depend upon the continuing flow of information coming

pegasus.rutgers.edu/~record/ columns/23rlr6/suspicion.html Article, "Reasonable and Articulable Suspicion in New Jersey" by James Graziano

United States v. Hensley laws.findlaw.com/us/469/ 221.html

to the officer's attention after the start of the originally undertaken investigation. If the officer discovers additional evidence of possible wrongdoing, he may expand his inquiry as suggested by this new information. . . . The converse proposition also holds true. An officer cannot continue to press his investigation when he discovers new evidence demonstrating that his original interpretation of his suspect's actions was mistaken. *State v. Garland*, 482 A.2d 139, 144 (Me. 1984).

Information from Informants

Adams v. Williams
laws.findlaw.com/us/407/
143.html

In *Adams v. Williams*, 407 U.S. 143, 92 S.Ct. 1921, 32 L.Ed.2d 612 (1972), a law enforcement officer on patrol in his cruiser was approached by a person known to him and was told that a man seated in a nearby vehicle had a gun at his waist and was carrying narcotics. The officer approached the vehicle, tapped on the window, and asked the occupant (the defendant) to open the door. When the defendant rolled down the window instead, the officer reached in, removed a pistol from the defendant's waistband, and then arrested the defendant. The U.S. Supreme Court held that the officer acted justifiably in responding to the informant's tip:

> The informant was known to him personally and had provided him with information in the past. This is a stronger case than obtains in the case of an anonymous telephone tip. The informant here came forward personally to give information that was immediately verifiable at the scene. Indeed, under Connecticut law, the informant herself might have been subject to immediate arrest for making a false complaint had Sgt. Connolly's investigation proven the tip incorrect. Thus, while the Court's decisions indicate that this informant's unverified tip may have been insufficient for a narcotics arrest or search warrant, the information carried enough indicia of reliability to justify the officer's forcible stop of Williams.
>
> In reaching this conclusion, we reject respondent's argument that reasonable cause for a stop and frisk can only be based on the officer's personal observation, rather than on information supplied by another person. Informants' tips, like all other clues and evidence coming to a policeman on the scene, may vary greatly in their value and reliability. One simple rule will not cover every situation. Some tips, completely lacking in indicia of reliability, would either warrant no police response or require further investigation before a forcible stop of a suspect would be authorized. But in some situations—for example, when the victim of a street crime seeks immediate police aid and gives a description of his assailant, or when a credible informant warns of a specific impending crime—the subtleties of the hearsay rule should not thwart an appropriate police response. 407 U.S. at 146–47, 92 S.Ct. at 1923–24, 32 L.Ed.2d at 617–18.

Under *Adams v. Williams*, an officer may stop a person based on an informant's tip if the tip carries "enough indicia of reliability" to provide reasonable suspicion of criminal activity. This standard is less than the probable cause standard discussed in Chapter 6. Nevertheless, the officer must be able to give specific reasons why the tip was believed to be reliable. As the quoted material indicates, an anonymous telephone tip might not be sufficiently reliable without corroboration.

Alabama v. White
laws.findlaw.com/us/496/
325.html

Alabama v. White, 496 U.S. 325, 110 S.Ct. 2412, 110 L.Ed.2d 301 (1990), illustrates the minimum level of corroboration needed to support an anonymous tip and provide reasonable suspicion to justify an investigatory stop. In that case, police received an anonymous telephone tip that the defendant would be leaving a particular apartment at a particular time in a particular vehicle, that she would be going to a particular motel, and that she would be in possession of cocaine. Police went immediately to the apartment building and saw a vehicle matching the caller's description. They observed the defendant leave the building and enter the vehicle, and they followed her along the most direct route to the motel, stopping her vehicle just short of the motel. A consensual search of the vehicle revealed marijuana, and after the defendant was arrested, cocaine was found in her purse.

The U.S. Supreme Court held that the anonymous tip, as corroborated by independent police work, exhibited sufficient indicia of reliability to provide reasonable suspicion to make the investigatory stop. The Court referred to the totality of the circumstances approach of *Illinois v. Gates* (see Chapter 6) in determining whether an informant's tip establishes probable cause.

> *Gates* made clear . . . that those factors that had been considered critical under *Aguilar* and *Spinelli*—an informant's "veracity," "reliability," and "basis of knowledge"—remain "highly relevant in determining the value of his report." . . . These factors are also relevant in the reasonable suspicion context, although allowance must be made in applying them for the lesser showing required to meet that standard. 496 U.S. at 328–29, 110 S.Ct. at 2415, 110 L.Ed.2d at 308.

The anonymous tip in this case, like the one in *Gates*, provided virtually nothing from which one might conclude that the caller is either honest or has reliable information, nor did the tip give any indication of the basis for the caller's predictions regarding the defendant's activities. As in *Gates*, however, in this case there was more than the tip itself. And although the tip was not as detailed and the corroboration not as complete, also as in *Gates*, the required degree of suspicion was not as high. The Court's rather lengthy discussion of reasonable suspicion is worthy of quotation:

> Reasonable suspicion is a less demanding standard than probable cause not only in the sense that reasonable suspicion can be established with information that is different in quantity or content than that required to establish probable cause, but also in the sense that reasonable suspicion can arise from information that is less reliable than that required to show probable cause. . . . Reasonable suspicion, like probable cause, is dependent upon both the content of information possessed by police and its degree of reliability. Both factors—quantity and quality are considered in the "totality of the circumstances—the whole picture," . . . that must be taken into account when evaluating whether there is reasonable suspicion. Thus, if a tip has a relatively low degree of reliability, more information will be required to establish the requisite quantum of suspicion than would be required if the tip were more reliable. The *Gates* Court applied its totality of the circumstances approach in this manner, taking into account the facts known to the officers from personal observation, and giving the anonymous tip the weight it deserved in light of its indicia of reliability as established through independent police work. The same approach applies in the reasonable suspicion context, the only difference being the level of suspicion that must be established. Contrary to the court below, we conclude that when the officers stopped the respondent, the anonymous tip had been sufficiently corroborated to furnish reasonable suspicion that respondent was engaged in criminal activity and that the investigative stop therefore did not violate the Fourth Amendment. 496 U.S. at 330–31, 110 S.Ct. at 2416, 110 L.Ed.2d at 309.

To better understand how corroboration works to supplement an anonymous tip in providing reasonable suspicion, it is worthwhile to discuss in detail the Court's analysis of corroboration. First, although not every detail mentioned by the tipster was verified—such as the name of the woman leaving the building or the precise apartment from which she left—the officers did corroborate that a woman left the building and got into the particularly described vehicle. Given that the officers proceeded to the building immediately after the call and that the defendant emerged not too long thereafter, it also appears that the defendant's departure was within the time frame predicted by the caller. Furthermore, since her four-mile route was the most direct way to the motel but nevertheless involved several turns, the caller's prediction of the defendant's destination was significantly corroborated even though she was stopped before she reached the motel. Moreover, the caller's ability to predict the defendant's future behavior demonstrated inside information—a special familiarity with her affairs. When significant aspects of the caller's predictions were verified, the officers had reason to believe not only that the caller was honest but also that he was well informed. Under the totality of the circumstances, the anonymous tip, as corroborated, exhibited sufficient indicia of reliability to justify the investigatory stop of the defendant's car.

Florida v. J.L.
laws.findlaw.com/us/000/
98-1993.html

In *Florida v. J.L.*, 529 U.S. 266, 120 S.Ct. 1375, 146 L.Ed.2d 254 (2000), the U.S. Supreme Court held that an anonymous tip that a person is carrying a gun is, without more, insufficient to justify a police officer's stop and frisk of that person. In the J.L. case, an anonymous caller reported to the police that a young black male standing at a particular bus stop and wearing a plaid shirt was carrying a gun. Soon thereafter, two officers arrived at the bus stop and saw three black males, one of whom was wearing a plaid shirt. Apart from the tip, the officers had no reason to suspect any of the three of illegal conduct. The officers did not see a firearm and J.L made no threatening or otherwise unusual movements. One of the officers approached J.L., told him to put his hands up, frisked him, and seized a gun from his pocket.

The U.S. Supreme Court found that contentions that the tip was reliable because its description of the suspect proved accurate misapprehended the reliability needed for a tip to justify a *Terry* stop.

> An accurate description of a subject's readily observable location and appearance is of course reliable in this limited sense: It will help the police correctly identify the person whom the tipster means to accuse. Such a tip, however, does not show that the tipster has knowledge of concealed criminal activity. The reasonable suspicion here at issue requires that a tip be reliable in its assertion of illegality, not just in its tendency to identify a determinate person. 529 U.S. at 272, 120 S.Ct. at 1379, 146 L.Ed.2d at 261.

The Court also rejected a so-called "firearm exception" under which a tip alleging an illegal gun would automatically justify a stop and frisk even if the tip failed standard reliability testing. Such an exception would enable any person seeking to harass another to set in motion an intrusive, embarrassing police search of the other person merely by placing an anonymous call falsely reporting that the person was carrying a gun. Also, the Court found that the *Terry* rule permitting protective police searches on the basis of reasonable suspicion adequately responded to the serious threat that armed criminals pose to public safety. The Court went on to say:

> The facts of this case do not require us to speculate about the circumstances under which the danger alleged in an anonymous tip might be so great as to justify a search even without a showing of reliability. We do not say, for example, that a report of a person carrying a bomb need bear the indicia of reliability we demand for a report of a person carrying a firearm before the police can constitutionally conduct a frisk. Nor do we hold that public safety officials in quarters where the reasonable expectation of Fourth

Case in Point

Interpreting *Florida v. J.L.*

On August 22, 1996, Metropolitan Police Sgt. Gregory Wilson received a call at his desk. Although Sgt. Wilson had been out of the particular police district since May 1994, he immediately recognized the caller as a tipster with whom he had personally spoken five or six times prior to May 1994, but whose name or other identifying characteristics he did not know. The caller told Sgt. Wilson that a tall, dark-complected black man, wearing dark shorts and a white tee-shirt, was "working" out of the trunk of a car parked at the intersection of Fourth and L Streets, S.E. Sgt. Wilson took this description to mean that the man was selling drugs. The informant described the car as a blue Datsun Z with damage to the left rear and District plates.

At Sgt. Wilson's direction, Officer Seth Weston and two other officers arrived at Fourth and L about fifteen minutes later and confirmed the innocent details of the tip, in particular the presence of a car matching the description and a man nearby matching the description. However, the man was not sitting in the car or involved in any suspicious activity when the officers arrived, and when he was unable to produce identification the officers decided not to detain him.

Soon thereafter, one of the officers asked loudly whether anyone owned the car and received no answer. The officers then searched the car. [The officers did not need to use force to access the car because it had an open top and the keys were lying inside on the floor.] Inside the trunk they found seventeen small bags of cocaine inside a larger bag. They immediately impounded the car.

Subsequently, during an inventory search, a Maryland learner's permit and District identification card belonging to appellant, the owner of the car, were recovered from the glove compartment. The officers recognized appellant's picture on the documents as portraying the man to whom they had spoken at the scene. The appellant moved to have the cocaine suppressed on the ground that the police lacked probable cause to search. In light of *Florida v. J.L.*, should the appellant's motion be granted? *Sanders v. United States*, 751 A.2d 952 (D.C.App. 2000).

Read the court opinion at:
www.dcbar.org/dcca/pdf/98cf1411.pdf

Amendment privacy is diminished, such as airports . . . and schools . . . cannot conduct protective searches on the basis of information insufficient to justify searches elsewhere. 529 U.S. at 273–74, 120 S.Ct. at 1380, 146 L.Ed.2d at 262.

Note that nothing in the *J.L.* decision limits the right of a law enforcement officer to observe, approach, or talk to a suspect, to observe a possible sign of a weapon such as a bulge in the clothing, or to ask for a suspect's consent to a search of his or her person or belongings.

In a case decided since *Florida v. J.L.*, the court held that police officers had reasonable suspicion to stop the defendant after an informant made a face-to-face report to police that he had seen a man fitting the description of the defendant moments before with a gun at 1:00 A.M. in a high-crime area known for shootings. *United States v. Valentine*, 232 F.3rd 350 (3rd Cir. 2000). Based on the report, two police officers stopped the defendant by force and found a gun. The Court found the informant's tip in this case to be distinguishable from the tip in *Florida v. J.L.* in several ways:

First, unlike *J.L.*, the officers in our case knew that the informant was reporting what he had observed moments ago, not what he learned from stale or second-hand sources. At the suppression hearing, Officer Woodard was asked, "Did [the informant] say how long ago that he saw the individual carrying a gun?" Woodard replied, "About—maybe a second ago, two seconds ago." . . . So the officers could expect that the informant had a

www.fbi.gov/publications/leb/2000/aug00leb.pdf
Article, "Anonymous Tips and Frisks: Determining Reasonable Suspicion" by Michael J. Bulzomi (page 28 of the August 2000 *FBI Law Enforcement Bulletin*)

www.cga.state.ct.us/2000/rpt/olr/htm/2000-R-0588.htm
Article, "Stop and Frisk Searches" by Gregory Joiner and Christopher Reinhart; discusses the case of *Florida v. J.L.* and other stop-and-frisk matters

www.jus.state.nc.us/NCJA/jl.htm
Discussion of *Florida v. J.L.* with advice to law enforcement officers from the North Carolina Justice Academy

reasonable basis for his beliefs. The Supreme Court has recognized the greater weight carried by a witness's recent report, such as when "the victim of a street crime seeks immediate police aid and gives a description of the assailant." *Adams v. Williams,* 407 U.S. at 147, 92 S.Ct. at 1924.

Second, the officers had more reason to believe that the informant was credible than the officers did in *J.L.,* for a tip given face to face is more reliable than an anonymous telephone call. As the Fourth Circuit recently explained, when an informant relates information to the police face to face, the officer has an opportunity to assess the informant's credibility and demeanor. *United States v. Christmas,* 222 F.3d 141, 144 (4th Cir. 2000). And when an informant gives the police information about a neighbor (as in *Christmas*) or someone nearby (as in our case), the informant is exposed to a risk of retaliation from the person named, making it less likely that the informant will lie. *Id.* Similarly, as the Fourth Circuit noted, "citizens who personally report crimes to the police thereby make themselves accountable for lodging false complaints." *Id.* (citing *Illinois v. Gates,* 462 U.S. at 233–34, 103 S.Ct. at 2329–30 (1983)). 232 F.3d at 354.

Officers may rely on a police radio dispatch to obtain facts to justify the stop of a person or vehicle. If, however, it is later determined that the person relaying the information over the radio had no factual foundation for the message, the stop will be ruled illegal. In *United States v. Robinson,* 536 F.2d 1298 (9th Cir. 1976), the court said:

> We recognize that effective law enforcement cannot be conducted unless police officers can act on directions and information transmitted by one officer to another and that officers, who must often act swiftly, cannot be expected to cross-examine their fellow officers about the foundation for the transmitted information. The fact that an officer does not have to have personal knowledge of the evidence supplying good cause for a stop before he can obey a direction to detain a person or a vehicle does not mean that the Government need not produce evidence at trial showing good cause to legitimate the detention when the legality of the stop is challenged. If the dispatcher himself had had founded suspicion, or if he had relied on information from a reliable informant who supplied him with adequate facts to establish founded suspicion, the dispatcher could properly have delegated the stopping function to Officer Holland. But if the dispatcher did not have such cause, he could not create justification simply by relaying a direction to a fellow officer to make the stop. 536 F.2d at 1299–1300.

Facts and Circumstances Determining Reasonableness

In *State v. King,* 499 N.W.2d 190 (Wis.App. 1993), the Wisconsin Supreme Court neatly summarized the types of facts and circumstances relevant in determining the reasonableness of a stop in its discussion of *State v. Guzy,* 407 N.W.2d 548 (Wis. 1987).

> The reasonableness of an investigatory stop . . . depends on all the facts and circumstances that are present at the time of the stop. . . . In *Guzy,* the police were alerted to a robbery committed by a suspect described as a white male, five feet five to five feet eight inches tall, with dark, shoulder-length hair and a beard, a slim build, wearing sunglasses and a blue vest with red stripes. Shortly thereafter, two officers followed a truck, which caught their attention because the passenger appeared to be a male with dark, shoulder-length hair, as described in the report. The only other specific and articulable

fact known to the officers was that the truck was spotted in the location at a time that would be consistent with a vehicle fleeing the crime scene.

In concluding that the officers acted reasonably by stopping the vehicle to further investigate, the *Guzy* court adopted Professor LaFave's six-factor analysis for use in making the determination of reasonableness:

(1) the particularity of the description of the offender or the vehicle in which he fled; (2) the size of the area in which the offender might be found, as indicated by such facts as the elapsed time since the crime occurred; (3) the number of persons about in that area; (4) the known or probable direction of the offender's flight; (5) observed activity by the particular person stopped; and (6) knowledge or suspicion that the person or vehicle stopped has been involved in other criminality of the type presently under investigation. . . .

The court also noted the following additional circumstances relevant in the determination of reasonableness: (1) alternative means available to the officer to investigate short of making the stop; (2) the opportunity for further investigation, if action was not taken immediately; and (3) whether the description of the individual known to the officer would allow him to quickly identify the individual so that there would be minimal intrusion. . . . Additionally, the severity or inherently dangerous nature of the criminal activity reported is a relevant consideration. 499 N.W.2d at 192–93.

Extent of Stop

Once an officer determines that the circumstances justify stopping an individual to investigate possible criminal activity, to what extent do those circumstances allow the officer to interfere? In other words, how long may the person be detained, how much force may be used, and to how much questioning may the person be subjected? In *Florida v. Royer*, 460 U.S. 491, 500, 103 S.Ct. 1319, 1325, 75 L.Ed.2d 229, 238 (1983), the U.S. Supreme Court said:

> The predicate permitting seizures on suspicion short of probable cause is that law enforcement interests warrant a limited intrusion on the personal security of the suspect. The scope of the intrusion permitted will vary to some extent with the particular facts and circumstances of each case. This much, however, is clear: an investigative detention must be temporary and last no longer than is necessary to effectuate the purpose of the stop. Similarly, the investigative methods employed should be the least intrusive means reasonably available to verify or dispel the officer's suspicion in a short period of time. . . . It is the State's burden to demonstrate that the seizure it seeks to justify on the basis of a reasonable suspicion was sufficiently limited in scope and duration to satisfy the conditions of an investigative seizure.

See page 109 for a detailed discussion of the *Royer* case.

An investigative stop can range from a friendly encounter with minimal intrusion to an angry confrontation accompanied by the use of force. Officers must be able to point to specific facts and circumstances to indicate that the extent of the interference with an individual was reasonable. This reasonableness determination involves a "weighing of the gravity of the public concerns served by the seizure, the degree to which the seizure advances the public interest, and the severity of the interference with individual liberty." *Brown v. Texas*, 443 U.S 47, 51, 99 S.Ct. 2637, 2640, 61 L.Ed.2d 357, 362 (1979).

Florida v. Royer
laws.findlaw.com/us/460/491.html

Brown v. Texas
laws.findlaw.com/us/443/47.html

www.fbi.gov/publications/leb/
1999/dec99leb.pdf
Article, "Vehicle Stops Involving
Extremist Group Members" by
James Kobolt (page 18 of the
December 1999 *FBI Law
Enforcement Bulletin*)

Pennsylvania v. Mimms
laws.findlaw.com/us/434/
106.html

Ohio v. Robinette
laws.findlaw.com/us/000/
u20042.html
Maryland v. Wilson
laws.findlaw.com/us/000/
95-1268.html

ORDERING DRIVER AND PASSENGERS OUT OF VEHICLE   An officer who has lawfully stopped a motor vehicle may, for personal safety reasons, order the driver out of the vehicle, even though he or she has no reason to suspect foul play from the particular driver at the time of the stop. The U.S. Supreme Court said:

> We think this additional intrusion can only be described as *de minimis*. The driver is being asked to expose to view very little more of his person than is already exposed. The police have already lawfully decided that the driver shall be briefly detained; the only question is whether he shall spend that period sitting in the driver's seat of his car or standing alongside it. Not only is the insistence of the police on the latter choice not a "serious intrusion upon the sanctity of the person," but it hardly rises to the level of a "'petty indignity.'" . . . What is at most a mere inconvenience cannot prevail when balanced against legitimate concerns for the officer's safety. *Pennsylvania v. Mimms*, 434 U.S. 106, 111, 98 S.Ct. 330, 333, 54 L.Ed.2d 331, 337 (1977).

Once the driver is out of the car, the officer may

- conduct a frisk, if the officer has reason to believe that the person is armed and dangerous, and
- request consent to search the car, whether or not the officer has a subjective intention to arrest or issue a traffic ticket. *Ohio v. Robinette*, 519 U.S. 33, 117 S.Ct. 417, 136 L.Ed.2d 347 (1996).

In *Maryland v. Wilson*, 519 U.S. 408, 415, 117 S.Ct. 882, 886, 137 L.Ed.2d 41, 48 (1997), the Court extended the rule of the *Mimms* case by holding that "an officer making a traffic stop may order *passengers* to get out of the car pending completion of the stop." (Emphasis added.) The Court found that the danger to an officer from a traffic stop is likely to be greater when there are passengers in addition to the driver in the stopped car. While there is not the same basis for ordering the passengers out of the car as there is for ordering the driver out, the additional intrusion on the passenger is minimal.

> [A]s a practical matter, the passengers are already stopped by virtue of the stop of the vehicle. The only change in their circumstances which will result from ordering them out of the car is that they will be outside of, rather than inside of, the stopped car. Outside the car, the passengers will be denied access to any possible weapon that might be concealed in the interior of the passenger compartment. It would seem that the possibility of a violent encounter stems not from the ordinary reaction of a motorist stopped for a speeding violation, but from the fact that evidence of a more serious crime might be uncovered during the stop. And the motivation of a passenger to employ violence to prevent apprehension of such a crime is every bit as great as that of the driver. 519 U.S. at 413–14, 117 S.Ct. at 886, 137 L.Ed.2d at 47–48.

Once the passenger is outside the car, if the officer has sufficient specific facts to support a belief that a dangerous situation exists, the officer may frisk the traffic offender's passengers for weapons. In *United States v. Tharpe*, 536 F.2d 1098 (5th Cir. 1976), the court found sufficient facts to justify such a frisk under the following circumstances: (1) the driver showed the officer a false license, (2) the driver admitted being the "bad check" suspect the officer had just been informed about by radio, (3) the officer recognized the two passengers as burglary suspects, (4) the officer was alone, and (5) the encounter occurred late at night.

By implication, an officer may also order a driver or passengers to remain in a vehicle or to get back into a vehicle. Oftentimes, an officer working alone will find it safer

www.fbi.gov/publications/leb/
1997/june976.htm
Article, "Extending the *Mimms*
Rule to Include Passengers" by
Lisa A Regini; discusses the case
of *Maryland v. Wilson*

for the driver and passengers to remain in a vehicle where the officer can perhaps more easily control the individuals for his or her own safety.

REASONABLE INVESTIGATIVE METHODS   An officer's initial questioning of a suspect may assure the officer that no further investigation is necessary. For example, a law enforcement officer in a patrol car observed a young man, carrying a flashlight and a small box, walking on the sidewalk of a residential street at 2:40 A.M. The officer drove past the young man and then stopped to ask him what he was doing. The young man replied that he was collecting nightcrawlers for fishing bait. The officer wished him luck and drove on.

On the other hand, the answers given by the stopped person may cause the officer to believe more strongly that something is amiss. In this situation, because the officer has developed new or additional reasonable suspicion based on evasive or implausible answers, the officer may investigate further or, if probable cause exists, arrest the person. For example, in *State v. Davis,* 517 A.2d 859 (N.J. 1986), an officer lawfully stopped the defendant and his companion on bicycles based on a reliable informant's tip that the men had been hanging around a closed gas station earlier at around midnight. The officer asked them whether they had been at the gas station and inquired as to their purpose. After receiving implausible answers, the officer asked for identification, and the companion produced a third person's automobile registration. After further implausible answers to the officer's questions, the officer got out of his police car and noticed a registration tag on one of the bicycles. When the officer radioed to determine whether the bicycles were stolen, both men admitted that they were stolen, and the officer arrested them. The court found that the officer's investigative techniques were reasonable under the circumstances.

> Once Officer D'Andrea stopped the individuals, he acted by using reasonably unintrusive techniques in a manner calculated to either verify or dispel his suspicions in a short period of time. He asked questions limited to the circumstances surrounding their presence at the gas station. Officer D'Andrea merely sought to ascertain if defendant and his companion had been "hanging around" the closed gas station at approximately midnight, as reported . . . and, if so, what they had been doing there. . . . As the questioning unfolded, Officer D'Andrea received answers that tended to strengthen his suspicions that the suspects were up to no good. For defendant and his compatriot not only failed miserably to dispel the officer's suspicions, they effectively talked themselves into the arrest at issue.
>
> Officer D'Andrea, as a reasonable police officer, could not have allowed defendant and his companion to pass, without, at the very least, asking them if they had been at the gas station, and, if so, why. He conducted the stop and the questioning in an efficient and unobtrusive manner. Hence, we conclude his conduct in stopping and questioning the defendant was reasonable and did not violate defendant's rights . . . to be free of unreasonable searches and seizures. 517 A.2d at 868–69.

During a traffic stop, "reasonable investigation includes asking for the driver's license and registration, requesting that the driver sit in the patrol car, and asking the driver about his destination and purpose." *United States v. Bloomfield,* 40 F.3d 910, 915 (8th Cir. 1994). Likewise, an officer may engage in similar routine questioning of the vehicle's passengers to verify information provided by the driver. Moreover, "if the responses of the detainee and the circumstances give rise to suspicions unrelated to the traffic offense, an officer may broaden his inquiry and satisfy those suspicions." *United States v. Barahona,* 990 F.2d 412, 416 (8th Cir. 1993). Once the purposes of an initial traffic stop are completed, however, the officer may not further detain the vehicle or its occupants unless something that occurs during the traffic stop generates necessary reasonable suspicion to justify further detention. *United States v. Mesa,* 62 F.3d 159 (6th Cir. 1995). The same rules apply at fixed vehicle checkpoints set up and conducted by the police. "When an officer seeks to expand the investigation of a motorist beyond the reasons stated for the checkpoint, he or she must have a particularized and objective basis for suspecting the particular person stopped of criminal activity." *United States v. Galindo-Gonzales,* 142 F.3d 1217, 1221 (10th Cir. 1998).

When a situation being investigated requires immediate action, the courts sometimes uphold extraordinary investigative methods. In *State v. Burgess,* 716 P.2d 948 (Wash.App. 1986), officers discovered an abandoned pickup truck about a block from an animal clinic that had sounded a silent alarm. By running a registration check, they discovered that the pickup belonged to the defendant and that he had burglarized the same animal clinic on a previous occasion. The officers flattened the vehicle's tires to secure it while they continued their investigation. The defendant argued that the officers had made an unreasonable "seizure" by deflating the tires of his truck. The court said:

> [T]he detention of the truck in this manner was valid as a reasonably limited intrusion into Burgess's right "to be secure" in his "effects" protected by the Fourth Amendment against "unreasonable searches and seizures." Warrantless seizures may be justified where police officers are faced with emergencies or exigencies which do not permit reasonable time and delay for a judicial officer to evaluate and act upon an application for a warrant. . . . Here, the officers deflated the truck tires during the time when several of them were in pursuit of a burglary suspect they believed was Burgess. The deflation of his truck tires, unaccompanied by any exploratory search at that time, was reasonably restricted in time and place and necessary to prevent the suspect from fleeing the scene of the burglary. If the officers had not deflated the tires, they would have been faced with the possibility that Burgess would remove the truck, taking its contents with him. 495 N.W.2d at 640.

TIME   "[T]he brevity of the invasion of the individual's Fourth Amendment interests is an important factor in determining whether the seizure is so minimally intrusive as to be justifiable on reasonable suspicion." *United States v. Place,* 462 U.S. 696, 709, 103 S.Ct. 2637, 2645, 77 L.Ed.2d 110 (1983). An investigative stop is not subject to any rigid time limitation, but at some point an extended stop that has not developed probable cause can no longer be justified as reasonable. In determining the reasonableness of the duration of a stop, courts consider the law enforcement purposes to be served by the stop as well as the time reasonably needed to effectuate those purposes. The U.S. Supreme Court said:

United States v. Place
laws.findlaw.com/us/462/
696.html

> In assessing whether a detention is too long in duration to be justified as an investigative stop, we consider it appropriate to examine whether the police diligently pursued a means of investigation that was likely to confirm or dispel their suspicions quickly, during which time it was necessary to detain the defendant. . . . A court making this assessment should take care to consider whether the police are acting in a swiftly developing situation and in such cases the court should not indulge in unrealistic second-guessing. . . . The question is not simply whether some other alternative was available, but whether the police acted unreasonably in failing to recognize or to pursue it. *United States v. Sharpe,* 470 U.S. 675, 686–87, 105 S.Ct. 1568, 1575–76, 84 L.Ed.2d 605, 615–16 (1985).

United States v. Sharpe
laws.findlaw.com/us/470/
675.html

In the *Sharpe* case, the Court approved a twenty-minute detention of a driver made necessary by the driver's own evasion of a drug agent and the decision of a state police officer, who had been called to assist in making the stop, to hold the driver until the agent could arrive on the scene. The Court found that it was reasonable for the state police officer to hold the driver for the brief period pending the drug agent's arrival because (1) the state police officer could not be certain that he was aware of all of the facts that had aroused the drug agent's suspicions, and, (2) as a highway patrolman, he lacked the agent's training and experience in dealing with narcotics investigations.

United States v. Hardy, 855 F.2d 753 (11th Cir. 1988), held that a canine sniff is the kind of brief, minimally intrusive investigation technique that may justify a *Terry* stop. The court noted that "a canine sniff does not require the opening of luggage and does not reveal intimate but noncontraband items to public view. . . . Nor does a canine sniff involve the time-consuming disassembly of luggage or an automobile frequently required in a thorough search for contraband." 855 F.2d at 759. Note, however, that stopping a vehicle and holding it for an extended period of time while awaiting the arrival of a canine could be deemed unreasonable under the Fourth Amendment.

Other reasons that might justify an officer's prolonging a suspect's detention are that the officer is attempting to obtain further information over the police radio or from other persons, summoning assistance, traveling to the scene of suspected criminal activity, caring for injured persons or responding to other emergency circumstances, and dealing with evasive tactics or other delays caused by the suspect. In *United States v. Quinn,* 815 F.2d 153 (1st Cir. 1987), the court held that the defendant's detention for investigation for twenty to twenty-five minutes did not transform the initial lawful *Terry* stop of the defendant into a seizure tantamount to arrest. Although several police officers were present, they made no threats, displayed no weapons, and exerted no physical restraint on the defendant. Moreover, the officers had a strong suspicion of criminal activity, and there was no way they could have greatly shortened the inquiry. Note that twenty to twenty-five minutes is probably the outside time limit beyond which a stop becomes a seizure tantamount to arrest, requiring a justification of probable cause.

Under ordinary circumstances, an officer who has a reasonable suspicion that a person may be engaged in criminal activity should initiate a stop of the person immediately. Nevertheless, a short delay in making the stop may be justified in certain situations. For example, in *State v. Cyr,* 501 A.2d 1303 (Me. 1985), an officer had grounds to stop a truck parked in an area of recent burglaries after observing the person in the driver's seat duck down to avoid detection. However, because the officer was transporting an arrested person, he continued driving slowly past the truck. In his rearview mirror, the officer observed the truck leave its parking place and follow his cruiser. After being informed that no other police unit was available to intercept the truck, the officer stopped the truck some two to three minutes after the first observation.

The court held that the suspicion had not evaporated because of the delay, since the truck remained within the officer's sight at all times and the delay resulted from the presence of an arrested person in the officer's vehicle. A longer delay, however, may cause a stop to be held illegal. For example, in *United States v. Posey,* 663 F.2d 37 (7th Cir. 1981), the court held that suspicion had evaporated when the defendant was stopped fifteen minutes after suspicion arose and fifteen miles away from the place where the defendant was originally seen.

FORCE When law enforcement officers make an investigative stop, they may take such steps as are "reasonably necessary to protect their personal safety and to maintain

www.fbi.gov/publications/leb/ 1999/aug99leb.pdf
Article, "Investigative Detentions: How Long Is Too Long?" by Jayme S. Walker (page 26 of the August 1999 *FBI Law Enforcement Bulletin*)

the status quo during the course of the stop." *United States v. Hensley,* 469 U.S. 221, 235, 105 S.Ct. 675, 684, 83 L.Ed.2d 604, 616 (1985). Use of force in making a stop is governed by the Fourth Amendment standard of reasonableness, judged from the perspective of a reasonable officer on the scene rather than from hindsight. The nature and quality of the intrusion on the suspect's Fourth Amendment interests must be balanced against the countervailing governmental interests at stake. The reasonableness inquiry is an objective one—whether the officers' actions are 'objectively reasonable' in light of the facts and circumstances confronting them, without regard to their underlying intent or motivation." *Graham v. Connor,* 490 U.S. 386, 397, 109 S.Ct. 1865, 1872, 104 L.Ed.2d 443, 456 (1989). Facts and circumstances that may be considered include the severity of the crime at issue, whether the suspect poses an immediate threat to the safety of the officers or others, and whether the suspect is actively resisting or attempting to evade the investigatory stop. Furthermore, "[t]he calculus of reasonableness must embody allowance for the fact that police officers are often forced to make split-second judgments—in circumstances that are tense, uncertain, and rapidly evolving—about the amount of force that is necessary in a particular situation." 490 U.S. at 396–97, 109 S.Ct. at 1872, 104 L.Ed.2d at 455–56.

The Eighth Circuit Court of Appeals listed factors to be considered in determining whether the amount and kind of force used was reasonable and consistent with an investigative stop. These include

> (1) the number of officers and police cars involved, (2) the nature of the crime and whether there is reason to believe the suspect is armed, (3) the strength of the officer's articulable, objective suspicions, (4) the need for immediate action by the officer, (5) the presence or lack of suspicious behavior or movement by the person under observation, and (6) whether there was an opportunity for the officer to have made the stop in less threatening circumstances. *United States v. Seelye,* 815 F.2d 48, 50 (8th Cir. 1987).

In *United States v. Bullock,* 71 F.3d 171 (5th Cir. 1995), the court held that law enforcement officers were justified in drawing their weapons on the defendant after stopping his vehicle for speeding. The officers had been informed over the radio that the defendant was a suspect in a bank robbery committed just hours before, and the officers were familiar with the defendant from previous encounters and knew him to be a dangerous man, one who had previously resisted arrest and threatened police. In *United States v. Melendez-Garcia,* 28 F.3d 1046, 1053 (10th Cir. 1994), however, the court held that it was unreasonable, after stopping drug suspects' vehicles, for officers to aim their guns at the suspects and handcuff them "when they outnumbered the defendants, executed the stop on an open highway during the day, had no tips or observations that the suspects were armed or violent, and the defendants had pulled their cars to a stop off the road and stepped out of their cars in full compliance with police orders."

See Exhibit 7.1 for a comparison of a stop and a formal arrest.

Graham v. Connor
laws.findlaw.com/us/490/
386.html

www.fbi.gov/publications/leb/
1998/mayleb.pdf
Article, "Investigative Detention:
Constitutional Constraints on
Police Use of Force" by John C.
Hall (page 26 of the May 1998
FBI Law Enforcement Bulletin)
www.icje.org/id72.htm
Article, "Does the use of handcuffs turn a temporary detention situation into an arrest?" by Robert T. Thetford

Key Points

2. A person has been "seized" within the meaning of the Fourth Amendment only if, in view of all of the circumstances surrounding the incident, a reasonable person would have believed that he or she was not free to leave. A "stop" is the least intrusive type of seizure of the person governed by the Fourth Amendment.

3. A Fourth Amendment seizure occurs only when there is a governmental termination of freedom of movement through means *intentionally* applied.

4. A law enforcement officer may stop and briefly detain a person for investigative purposes if the officer has a reasonable suspicion supported by articulable facts that criminal activity may be afoot.

5. A law enforcement officer's decision to initiate a stop will be judged against the objective standard: Would the facts available to the officer at the moment of the seizure or the search warrant a person of reasonable caution in the belief that the action taken was appropriate?

6. A law enforcement officer may stop a person based on an informant's tip if, under the totality of the circumstances, the tip, plus any corroboration of the tip by independent police investigation, carries enough indicia of reliability to provide reasonable suspicion of criminal activity.

7. Reasonable suspicion is a less demanding standard than probable cause, not only in the sense that reasonable suspicion can be established with information that is different in quantity or content than that required to establish probable cause, but also in the sense that reasonable suspicion can arise from information that is less reliable than that required to show probable cause.

8. An anonymous tip that a person is carrying a gun is not, without more information, sufficient to justify law enforcement officers in stopping and frisking that person.

9. An investigative stop must last no longer than reasonably necessary and must use the least intrusive methods reasonably available, to confirm or dispel the officer's suspicions of criminal activity.

10. An officer who has lawfully stopped a motor vehicle may order both the driver and passengers out of the vehicle pending completion of the stop.

11. An officer making an investigatory stop may use an objectively reasonable degree of force or threat of force to effect the stop.

Determination of Whether to Frisk

The law enforcement officer's determination of whether to frisk a suspect is a separate issue from the determination of whether to stop. It involves a different governmental interest to be served and a different set of factors to be considered by the officer. The governmental interest served by giving police the authority to frisk is that of protecting the officer and others from possible violence by persons being investigated for crime. "[W]e cannot blind ourselves to the need for law enforcement officers to protect themselves and other prospective victims of violence in situations where they may lack probable cause for an arrest." *Terry v. Ohio,* 392 U.S. at 24, 88 S.Ct. at 1881, 20 L.Ed.2d at 907–08.

Balanced against this interest is the citizen's right to privacy, which would necessarily be invaded by giving police the right to frisk suspects. The Supreme Court said, "We must still consider, however, the nature and quality of the intrusion on individual rights which must be accepted if police officers are to be conceded the right to search for weapons in situations where probable cause to arrest for crime is lacking." 392 U.S. at 24, 88 S.Ct. at 1881, 20 L.Ed.2d at 908. As noted earlier, the Court considers the stop-and-frisk procedure to be a serious intrusion on a person's rights, possibly inflicting great indignity and arousing strong resentment.

The Supreme Court considered these competing interests and set out a limited authority for a protective frisk by law enforcement officers in the following terms:

> Our evaluation of the proper balance that has to be struck in this type of case leads us to conclude that there must be a narrowly drawn authority to permit a reasonable search for weapons for the protection of the police officer, where he has reason to believe that

www.co.alameda.ca.us/da/pov/
car_searches.shtml
Article, "Pat Searches" from the
District Attorney's Office in
Alameda County, California

	STOP	**FORMAL ARREST**
Justification	Reasonable suspicion supported by articulable facts that criminal activity may be afoot.	Probable cause to believe that the person to be arrested has committed or is committing a crime.
Warrant	Not needed.	Preferred but not needed for arrests in public places. Arrest warrant is needed to enter suspect's home to arrest the suspect. Search warrant is needed to enter a third person's home to arrest the suspect.
Notice	None required.	Officer must give notice that the person is under arrest, notice of the officer's authority to arrest, and notice of the cause of arrest.
Force	Officer may use a reasonable degree of force judged from the perspective of a reasonable officer on the scene. Officer may never use deadly force. Officer must use the least intrusive methods reasonably available to confirm or dispel the officer's suspicions of criminal activity.	Officer may use any reasonably necessary nondeadly force to arrest for a felony or misdemeanor. Officer may use deadly force to arrest for a felony if the officer has probable cause to believe that the suspect poses a threat of serious physical harm either to the officer or others. Officer may never use deadly force to arrest for a misdemeanor.
Time limit	Must be temporary and last no longer than is necessary to effectuate the purpose of the stop.	Whatever time is reasonably needed to effectuate the arrest and bring the person into custody.
Search allowed	Protective patdown frisk of outer clothing for weapons, only if officer has reason to believe he or she is dealing with an armed and dangerous individual.	Full body search for weapons and evidence of arrestee and of the area into which the arrestee might reach in order to grab a weapon or evidentiary items.

Comparison of a Stop and a Formal Arrest
■ EXHIBIT 7.1

he is dealing with an armed and dangerous individual, regardless of whether he has probable cause to arrest the individual for a crime. 392 U.S. at 27, 88 S.Ct. at 1883, 20 L.Ed.2d at 909.

Limited Authority

The law enforcement officer's authority to frisk is a limited and narrowly drawn authority. An officer may not frisk everyone that the officer stops to investigate possible criminal activity. Before deciding to conduct any frisk, an officer must have "reason to believe that he is dealing with an armed and dangerous individual." The courts call this standard "reasonable suspicion." The officer need not be absolutely certain that the individual is armed. Rather, the issue, as stated in *Terry*, is "whether a reasonably prudent man in the circumstances would be warranted in the belief that his safety or that of others was in danger." 392 U.S. at 27, 88 S.Ct. at 1883, 20 L.Ed.2d at 909. Thus, frisks are governed by an objective standard similar to the standard governing stops. An officer must be able to justify a search or frisk of a person by pointing to specific facts and "specific reasonable inferences which he is entitled to draw from the facts in light of his experience." 392 U.S. at 27, 88 S.Ct. at 1883, 20 L.Ed.2d at 909.

Many factors may be considered in deciding whether it is appropriate to frisk a person. Some factors will carry more weight with one officer than with another because of differences in the officers' experience and knowledge. The following is a partial list of considerations in deciding to frisk a person:

- The suspected crime involves the use of weapons.
- The suspect is nervous or edgy about being stopped.
- There is a bulge in the suspect's clothing.
- The suspect's hand is concealed in his or her clothing.
- The suspect does not present satisfactory identification or an adequate explanation for suspicious behavior.
- The area in which the officer is operating is known to contain armed persons.
- The suspect exhibits belligerent behavior upon being stopped.
- The officer believes that the suspect may have been armed on a previous occasion.

Justification to frisk usually requires a combination of one or more of these factors or others, evaluated in the light of an officer's experience and knowledge.

Scope of Search

The U.S. Supreme Court requires a frisk to be "a *reasonable* search for weapons for the protection of the police officer." (Emphasis added.) *Terry v. Ohio*, 392 U.S. at 27, 88 S.Ct. at 1883, 20 L.Ed.2d at 909. Since the only justifiable purpose of a frisk is the protection of the officer and others, the search must be strictly "limited to that which is necessary for the discovery of weapons which might be used to harm the officer or others nearby." 392 U.S. at 26, 88 S.Ct. at 1882, 20 L.Ed.2d at 908. If the protective search goes beyond what is necessary to determine if the suspect is armed, it is no longer valid under *Terry*, and its fruits will be suppressed.

Therefore, the frisk must initially be limited to a patdown of the *outer* clothing. An officer has no authority to reach inside clothing or into pockets in the *initial* stages of a frisk. During the patdown, if the officer detects an object that feels like a weapon, the officer may then reach inside the clothing or pocket and seize it. If the object is not a weapon but is some other implement of crime (such as a burglar's tool), that implement is admissible in evidence for the crime to which it relates (for example, attempted burglary). The general principle under *Terry* is that, if the officer feels no weaponlike object during the course of the patdown, the officer can no longer have a reasonable fear that the person is armed. Any further search without probable cause would exceed the purpose of the frisk—namely, the protection of the officer and others—and would be unreasonable under the Fourth Amendment. Any evidence obtained from the search would be inadmissible.

The Supreme Court has approved an extension of the permissible scope of a protective search for weapons beyond the person of the suspect to include the passenger compartment of an automobile. In *Michigan v. Long,* 463 U.S. 1032, 103 S.Ct. 3469, 77 L.Ed.2d 1201 (1983), two police officers patrolling at night observed a car traveling erratically and at excessive speed. When the car swerved into a ditch, the officers stopped to investigate. The defendant, who was the only occupant of the car, met the officers at the rear of the car. He did not respond to initial requests to produce his license and registration, but after the request was repeated, he began walking toward the car to obtain the papers. Note that at this point, while the officers had sufficient grounds for a *Terry* stop, they did *not* have sufficient grounds to conduct a frisk for weapons. However, as the officers approached the car, they saw a hunting knife on the floorboard of the driver's side of the car. The Supreme Court held that the officers then had sufficient grounds to conduct a patdown search of the driver and a limited search of the passenger compartment of the car for weapons.

> [T]he search of the passenger compartment of an automobile, limited to those areas in which a weapon may be placed or hidden, is permissible if the police officer possesses a reasonable belief based on "specific and articulable facts which, taken together with the rational inferences from those facts, reasonably warrant" the officers in believing that the suspect is dangerous and the suspect may gain immediate control of weapons. 463 U.S. at 1049, 103 S.Ct. at 3480, 77 L.Ed.2d at 1220 (1983).

In reaching this decision, the Court recognized that roadside encounters between police and suspects are especially hazardous and that danger may arise from the possible presence of weapons in the area surrounding a suspect. The Court emphasized, however, that its decision does not mean that the police may conduct automobile searches whenever they conduct an investigative stop. Since the sole justification for a *Terry* search is the protection of police officers and others nearby, officers may conduct such a search only when they have a reasonable suspicion that the suspect is dangerous. Unlike a warrantless search incident to a lawful arrest (see Chapter 8), a *Terry* search is not justified by any need to prevent the disappearance or destruction of evidence of crime.

However, "[i]f, while conducting a legitimate *Terry* search of the interior of the automobile, the officer should . . . discover contraband other than weapons, he clearly cannot be required to ignore the contraband, and the Fourth Amendment does not require its suppression in such circumstances." *Michigan v. Long,* 463 U.S. 1032, 1050, 103 S.Ct. 3469, 3481, 77 L.Ed.2d 1201, 1220 (1983). In the *Long* case, one of the officers shined a flashlight into the car and saw a pouch protruding from under the armrest of the front seat. Since the pouch could have contained a weapon, the officer was justified in lifting the armrest, revealing an open pouch containing marijuana. Having discovered the marijuana pursuant to a legitimate *Terry* frisk, the officer was justified in seizing the marijuana under the **plain view doctrine.** Under that doctrine, "if police are lawfully in a position from which they view an object, if its incriminating charac-

Michigan v. Long
laws.findlaw.com/us/463/
1032.html

www.co.alameda.ca.us/da/pov/
car_searches.shtml
Article, "Protective Car
Searches" from the District
Attorney's Office in Alameda
County, California

ter is apparent, and if the officers have a lawful right of access to the object, they may seize it without a warrant." *Minnesota v. Dickerson,* 508 U.S. 366, 375, 113 S.Ct. 2130, 2136–37, 124 L.Ed.2d 334, 345 (1993). If, however, the police lack probable cause to believe that an object in plain view is contraband without conducting some further search of the object (such as manipulating the object to look for a serial number or some other identifying characteristic), the plain view doctrine cannot justify its seizure. The plain view doctrine is discussed in Chapter 10.

Minnesota v. Dickerson
laws.findlaw.com/us/508/
366.html

Relying on the plain view doctrine, the Supreme Court has also approved a so-called plain touch (or plain feel) exception to the rule allowing only the seizure of weapons or weaponlike objects in the course of a frisk. That exception allows the seizure of nonthreatening contraband if its identity as contraband is immediately apparent to the sense of touch as the result of the patdown search. *Minnesota v. Dickerson,* 508 U.S. 366, 113 S.Ct. 2130, 124 L.Ed.2d 334 (1993). This plain touch exception is discussed on pages 394 to 395 .

 Key Points

12. A law enforcement officer may conduct a reasonable limited protective search (frisk) for weapons when the officer has reasonable suspicion that he or she is dealing with an armed and dangerous person, regardless of whether the officer has probable cause to arrest.

13. A frisk must initially be limited to a patdown of the outer clothing. If a weaponlike object is detected or if a nonthreatening object's identity as contraband is immediately apparent to the officer's sense of touch,

the officer may reach inside the clothing or pocket and seize the object.

14. An officer may search the passenger compartment of a motor vehicle for weapons, if the officer has a reasonable, articulable suspicion that the vehicle's occupant is dangerous and that the occupant may gain immediate control of weapons. The officer may also seize contraband discovered in plain view during the course of such a search.

Specific Circumstances in Stop and Frisk

Stop and frisk encompasses an infinite variety of possible situations. A mere statement of general guidelines may not be sufficient to clearly indicate what behavior is or is not appropriate for a law enforcement officer in a given situation. Therefore, specific situations involving stop and frisk are presented here to show how courts throughout the United States deal with stop and frisk. Actual court decisions are discussed, and emphasis is placed on analyzing the courts' evaluations of the reasonableness of the actions of law enforcement officers. The cases are grouped under various headings indicating major factors influencing the courts' decisions.

Evasive Behavior

In *Illinois v. Wardlow,* 528 U.S. 119, 124, 120 S. Ct. 673, 676, 145 L. Ed. 2d 570, 576 (2000), the U.S. Supreme Court recognized that "nervous, evasive behavior is a pertinent factor in determining reasonable suspicion." The Court went on to say, "Headlong flight—wherever it occurs—is the consummate act of evasion: it is not necessarily indicative of wrongdoing, but it is certainly suggestive of such." In the *Wardlow* case, the defendant fled when he saw a caravan of police vehicles converge on his street in

Illinois v. Wardlow
laws.findlaw.com/us/000/
98-1036.html

Case in Point

Interpreting *Illinois v. Wardlow*

The only witness who testified at the suppression hearing was Officer Larry Gill, who conducted the investigatory stop and the patdown search of James. Officer Gill testified that, on February 17, 1995, about 6:00 P.M. or 6:30 P.M. he was patrolling Dauphin Island Parkway, a known high drug crime area, when he noticed a van pulled off on the shoulder of the road on Cedar Downs Drive located off Dauphin Island Parkway. Officer Gill observed "two or three subjects talking into the window of the van," but he could not see what the driver or the subjects were doing.

As Officer Gill approached the van, the "subjects" standing beside the van ran, and James, the driver of the van, drove away. Officer Gill followed the van and signaled his patrol lights for James to stop. After James pulled over at a Chevron gasoline station, he exited his van and met Officer Gill as he approached the van. Officer Gill told James he stopped him because Gill saw his van parked on the street "where those subjects ran from [his] van." Gill asked James whether he had any weapons in his possession, and James responded that he

did not. Nevertheless, Officer Gill informed James that he needed to conduct a patdown search of James for safety reasons. Officer Gill testified that, as he was conducting the patdown, James "went to put his hands in his left front pants pocket and I kind of tapped his hand and told him to pull his hand out and I put my hand in [James's] pocket after his hand coming out [and] I found the marijuana cigarettes in his pocket." Officer Gill testified that he did not patdown the outside of James's pants pocket before he reached into it and that he did not feel anything that appeared to be a weapon during his patdown of James. James moved to suppress the marijuana on the ground that the marijuana was seized during an illegal *Terry* stop and patdown search. In light of *Illinois v. Wardlow*, should his motion be granted? *Ex parte James*, 2000 WL 804442 (Ala. 2000).

Read the court opinion at:
www.birminghambar.org/SlipOpinions/SupCt/June/2000/1980820.htm

www.jus.state.nc.us/NCJA/
wardlow.htm
Article, "Reasonable Suspicion
to Stop" by Reece Trimmer and
Andrew Tallmer; discusses *Illinois v.
Wardlow* and provides advice for
law enforcement officers
www.forensic-evidence.com/
site/Police/Pol_Running.html
Article, "Running from the Police
. . . Is It Sufficient for a Stop?";
discusses *Illinois v. Wardlow*
www.fplc.edu/annsur97/
AS4.HTM
Article, "Two Perspectives on
Reasonable Suspicion after *Roach*
and *Vadnais*" by Jon Granoff and
Sue McGinnis; discusses federal
and New Hampshire law relating
to flight as reasonable suspicion

an area of Chicago known for heavy narcotics trafficking. Officers in one of the vehicles pursued the defendant and eventually cornered him on the street. One of the officers exited the vehicle, stopped the defendant, and immediately conducted a patdown search for weapons. The officer discovered a handgun and arrested the defendant.

The U.S. Supreme Court held that the stop of Wardlow by the officers was lawful because the suspect's presence in a high-crime area, coupled with his sudden flight, constituted reasonable suspicion to detain and investigate further.

Such a holding is entirely consistent with our decision in *Florida v. Royer,* 460 U.S. 491, 103 S.Ct. 1319, 75 L.Ed.2d 229 (1983), where we held that when an officer, without reasonable suspicion or probable cause, approaches an individual, the individual has a right to ignore the police and go about his business. . . . And any "refusal to cooperate, without more, does not furnish the minimal level of objective justification needed for a detention or seizure." *Florida v. Bostick,* 501 U.S. 429, 437, 111 S.Ct. 2382, 115 L.Ed.2d 389 (1991). But unprovoked flight is simply not a mere refusal to cooperate. Flight, by its very nature, is not "going about one's business"; in fact, it is just the opposite. Allowing officers confronted with such flight to stop the fugitive and investigate further is quite consistent with the individual's right to go about his business or to stay put and remain silent in the face of police questioning. 528 U.S. at 125, 120 S.Ct. at 676, 145 L.Ed.2d at 576.

Note that the Court made clear that neither presence in a high-crime area nor unprovoked flight, standing alone, would automatically provide reasonable suspicion to stop a suspect.

Relying on the *Wardlow* case, the court in *United States v. Jordan*, 232 F.3d 447 (5th Cir. 2000), held that the totality of the circumstances, including the defendant's "running at full sprint" from the direction of a nearby grocery store, his "looking back over his shoulder, left and right," the time (6:45 P.M. on a January evening), and place (a high-crime area), justified the officer's decision to stop the defendant. The court said:

> *Wardlow* did not establish a bright-line test in cases where a defendant is seen to be running. Instead, citing *Terry*, *Wardlow* examined the totality of circumstances to determine whether the officer had a "reasonable, articulable suspicion that criminal activity is afoot." . . . *Wardlow* noted that an individual's presence in a "high-crime area" is a relevant consideration, as is "nervous, evasive behavior." 232 F.3d at 449.

Observation of Bulge or Heavy Object

In *State v. Simmons*, 818 P.2d 787 (Idaho App. 1991), a sheriff's department notified local pawnshops to be alert for a described person suspected of burglary of a home and stealing silver dollars. When a pawnshop reported a person matching the description trying to sell silver dollars, detectives went to the pawnshop and saw the suspect apparently attempting to sell coins. He was wearing a long wool coat that seemed out of place for the day's weather, appeared nervous, and was sweating. One detective observed a bulge in an exterior pocket of the suspect's coat, and when the other detective frisked the suspect, he felt a hard object in the coat pocket that possibly felt like a small gun or knife. He reached his hand in and pulled out a pipe that appeared to be one used for smoking illegal drugs.

The court upheld both the stop and the frisk. The court found that the facts gave the detectives an articulable basis to believe that the person in the store was the burglar of the home. Consequently, they had sufficient grounds to make an investigative *Terry* stop of the suspect to inquire and confirm or dispel their suspicions. When they noticed the bulge in the suspect's overcoat pocket, they had reasonable grounds to be concerned for their safety and to conduct a frisk for weapons. The defendant claimed that wearing a long wool coat on a warm day and being nervous were not suspicious behaviors and that the officers had no reason to fear him. Nevertheless, the court said that "taken together . . . all of the information the police had about the case generated a reasonable, articulable suspicion, and a concern for their safety which warranted the intrusion." 818 P.2d at 792.

In *United States v. Barnes*, 909 F.2d 1059 (7th Cir. 1990), the court upheld the seizure of a pistol discovered as the result of a patdown search of a person lawfully stopped for having altered temporary license plates. The frisk was justified by the officer's observation of a "heavy object" protruding from the person's jacket and the person's attempt to reach for his pocket during the initial patdown.

Hand Concealed in Clothing; Force

In *United States v. Laing*, 889 F.2d 281 (D.C. Cir. 1989), a police emergency response team went to an apartment building shortly after midnight to execute a warrant to search apartment 202. From information supporting the warrant, the police believed the occupants were drug dealers armed with automatic weapons. Also, they recognized the apartment's neighborhood as a high-crime area. As police approached the building, they observed the defendant shove his hand into the front of his pants and run from the lobby to apartment 202. The officers reached him outside the apartment, and when he refused their order to lie down, they forced him to the floor and ordered him to remove his hand from his pants. When he refused that order, they forcibly removed his hand and ordered him to stretch out on the floor. When he complied, his pant legs rose up, revealing bags of cocaine in plain view.

The court found adequate justification for both the stop and the frisk of the defendant and found the use of force reasonable.

> The amount of force used to carry out the stop and search must be reasonable, but may include using handcuffs or forcing the detainee to lie down to prevent flight . . . or drawing guns where law officers reasonably believe they are necessary for their protection. . . . Factors that may justify an investigative stop, a search for weapons, or the escalated use of force include the time of day, the "high-crime" nature of the area, an informant's tips that persons might be armed, furtive hand movements, flight or attempted flight by the person sought to be detained, and a pressing need for immediate action. . . .
>
> The officers' treatment of Laing clearly falls within the *Terry* doctrine. Laing's hand movements and flight toward apartment 202, coupled with the time of day and the officers' knowledge of the area and their belief that those in the apartment were heavily armed, make it clear that the officers' actions were motivated by a genuine and well-founded fear that Laing was armed and were reasonable under the circumstances. 889 F.2d at 285.

Innocent Conduct

A series of individual lawful acts may provide reasonable suspicion of criminal activity sufficient to justify a stop, if the overall pattern of those acts is indicative of criminal activity. In *Reid v. Georgia,* the U.S. Supreme Court found no such overall pattern from the following facts: (1) the defendant had arrived from Fort Lauderdale, which a Drug Enforcement Administration (DEA) agent testified is a principal place of origin of cocaine sold elsewhere in the country; (2) the defendant arrived in the early morning, when law enforcement activity is diminished; (3) he and his companion appeared to the agent to be trying to conceal the fact that they were traveling together; and (4) they apparently had no luggage other than their shoulder bags.

> We conclude that the agent could not as a matter of law, have reasonably suspected the petitioner of criminal activity on the basis of these observed circumstances. Of the evidence relied on, only the fact that the petitioner preceded another person and occasionally looked backward at him as they proceeded through the concourse relates to their particular conduct. The other circumstances describe a very large category of presumably innocent travelers, who would be subject to virtually random seizures were the Court to conclude that as little foundation as there was in this case could justify a seizure. Nor can we agree, on this record, that the manner in which the petitioner and his companion walked through the airport reasonably could have led the agent to suspect them of wrongdoing. Although there could, of course, be circumstances in which wholly lawful conduct might justify the suspicion that criminal activity was afoot . . . this is not such a case. The agent's belief that the petitioner and his companion were attempting to conceal the fact that they were traveling together, a belief that was more an "inchoate and unparticularized suspicion or 'hunch,'" . . . than a fair inference in the light of his experience, is simply too slender a reed to support the seizure in this case. *Reid v. Georgia,* 448 U.S. 438, 441, 100 S.Ct. 2752, 2754, 65 L.Ed.2d 890, 894 (1980).

Reid v. Georgia
laws.findlaw.com/us/448/
438.html

In *United States v. Sokolow*, 490 U.S. 1, 109 S.Ct. 1581, 104 L.Ed.2d 1 (1989), however, the Court found an overall pattern indicating criminal activity from a similar but more specific and detailed set of facts. In that case, DEA agents stopped the defendant upon his arrival at Honolulu International Airport. The agents found 1,063 grams of cocaine in his carry-on luggage. When the defendant was stopped, the agents knew that (1) he paid $2,100 for two airplane tickets from a roll of $20 bills; (2) he traveled under a name that did not match the name under which his telephone number was listed; (3) his original destination was Miami, a source city for illicit drugs; (4) he stayed in Miami for only forty-eight hours, even though a round-trip flight from Honolulu to Miami takes twenty hours; (5) he appeared nervous during his trip; and (6) he checked none of his luggage. The Court found reasonable suspicion to justify the stop, even though there was no evidence of ongoing criminal activity. Applying a totality-of-the-circumstances test, the Court said that "[a]ny of these factors is not by itself proof of any illegal conduct and is quite consistent with innocent travel. But we think taken together they amount to reasonable suspicion." 490 U.S. at 9, 109 S.Ct. at 1586, 104 L.Ed.2d at 11.

In *United States v. Martinez*, 808 F.2d 1050 (5th Cir. 1987), the defendant purchased several chemicals, each with a legitimate use other than the manufacture of illegal drugs. A DEA officer stopped the defendant's car based on the officer's knowledge that there was no legitimate use for the particular *combination* of chemicals. The court held that the stop of the vehicle was justified and that, when the officer smelled an odor he recognized as characteristic of illegal drug manufacture, his temporary detention of the occupants of the car for further investigation was also justified. Therefore, the perception of totally innocent activity may provide to an officer with experience and knowledge about a particular type of crime a reasonable and articulable suspicion of criminal activity sufficient to justify a stop.

Admission by Defendant

The defendant's vehicle was stopped by a police officer for speeding. After stopping the vehicle, the officer walked up to it and the defendant got out, holding his right hand in the pocket of his knee-length coat. The pocket was baggy and sagging. The officer grabbed the defendant's arm and asked him whether he had a gun. The defendant answered yes. The officer then removed the gun and arrested the defendant.

The court assumed without discussion that the stop was reasonable because it was a routine traffic stop. In dealing with the frisk, the court cited *Terry v. Ohio*:

> *Terry v. Ohio* . . . tells us that when a police officer has reason to believe that he is dealing with an armed individual he has a right to search for weapons regardless of whether he has probable cause to arrest that individual for a crime. Here the officer did not merely think he was dealing with an armed person—he knew he was. *State v. Hall*, 476 P.2d 930, 931 (Or.App. 1970).

Traffic Stops and Roadblocks

An ordinary traffic stop is governed by the same standards as any other *Terry*-type investigative stop. "[A] traffic stop is valid under the Fourth Amendment if the stop is based on an observed traffic violation or if the police officer has reasonable articulable suspicion that a traffic or equipment violation has occurred or is occurring." *United States v. Botero-Ospina*, 71 F.3d 783, 787 (10th Cir. 1995). Since minor traffic or equipment violations are so common, law enforcement officers are often tempted to use such a violation to justify an investigation of a vague suspicion that the motorist may be engaging in more serious illegal activity. For example, an officer who observes a burned-out taillight, a cracked windshield, or failure to signal when changing lanes may stop the driver even if a hypothetical "reasonable officer" would not have been motivated to stop the car by a desire to enforce the traffic laws. A stop made under such pretenses is often called a "pretextual" stop.

In *Whren v. United States*, 517 U.S. 806, 116 S.Ct. 1769, 135 L.Ed.2d 89 (1996), plainclothes police officers patrolling a high-drug crime area in an unmarked vehicle observed a truck driven by the defendant waiting at a stop sign for an unusually long time. Suddenly, the truck turned without signaling and drove off at an unreasonable speed. One of the officers stopped the vehicle, supposedly to warn the driver about traffic violations, and upon approaching the truck, the officer observed plastic bags of crack cocaine in the defendant's hands. The defendant argued that the traffic stop was pretextual and that the evidence seized should be suppressed.

The U.S. Supreme Court held that police officers with *probable cause* to believe that a traffic violation has occurred may stop a vehicle even though the stop would seem to be a pretext to search for drugs. The Court emphasized that there is a significant difference between a pretextual stop based on probable cause that a traffic violation has occurred, and a stop that is not based on probable cause or even reasonable suspicion. The Court held that a motorist may be constitutionally stopped upon probable cause that the motorist has violated a traffic law regardless of the officer's subjective intent to stop the motorist upon suspicion of drug trafficking. The Court found that "[s]ubjective intentions play no role in ordinary, probable-cause Fourth Amendment analysis." 517 U.S. at 813, 116 S.Ct. at 1774, 135 L.Ed.2d at 98. The Court emphasized, however, the distinction between its holding in *Whren* and cases involving police intrusion without the probable cause that is the traditional justification for a seizure. The Court indicated its pretext analysis would not apply to such cases, which lack the "'quantum of individualized suspicion' necessary to ensure that police discretion is sufficiently contained." 517 U.S. at 817–18, 116 S.Ct. at 1776, 135 L.Ed.2d at 100. Therefore, pretext (the subjective motive for stopping a vehicle) is irrelevant when probable cause exists, but in regard to seizures made without probable cause, or even reasonable suspicion, there is no justification for a pretextual stop.

The *Whren* decision adopted the so-called *could* test and overrode previous law in some federal circuits that subscribed to the more narrow *would* test. In other words, the question for the officer is "*could* I stop the vehicle" (because there is probable cause to believe a traffic violation has occurred), not "*would* I stop the vehicle," (because, under normal circumstances, a stop would not be made for a minor violation). The *Whren* decision essentially legitimizes pretextual stops and disregards the subjective intent of the officer in favor of judging the constitutionality of a vehicle stop on the basis of objective data: was there probable cause to believe a violation of law occurred?

Random stops of vehicles, based on whim, hunch, or rumor, to check licenses, registrations, or equipment are not allowed, however. In *Delaware v. Prouse*, 440 U.S. 648, 663, 99 S.Ct. 1391, 1401, 59 L.Ed.2d 660, 673 (1979), the U.S. Supreme Court held

that except in those situations in which there is at least articulable and reasonable suspicion that a motorist is unlicensed or that an automobile is not registered, or that either the vehicle or an occupant is otherwise subject to seizure for violation of law, stopping an automobile and detaining the driver in order to check his driver's license and the registration of the automobile are unreasonable under the Fourth Amendment.

Whren v. United States
laws.findlaw.com/us/000/
u20005.html

www.fbi.gov/publications/leb/
1996/nov965.txt
Article, "Pretext Traffic Stops:
Whren v. United States" by John
C. Hall
www.w-dog.com/ltraf.htm
Article, "Traffic Stops: Police
Powers under the Fourth
Amendment; Application of the
Fourth Amendment"

Delaware v. Prouse
laws.findlaw.com/us/440/
648.html

The Court expressed its concern that random vehicle checks presented a potential danger of arbitrary or discriminatory enforcement of the law. Nevertheless, the Court's decision specifically held open the possibility for states to develop methods for spot checks that involve less intrusion or that do not involve the unconstrained exercise of discretion. The Court suggested as one possible alternative the questioning of all oncoming traffic at roadblock-type stops.

In *Michigan Department of State Police v. Sitz,* 496 U.S. 444, 110 S.Ct. 2481, 110 L.Ed.2d 412 (1990), the Supreme Court approved a highway sobriety checkpoint program with guidelines governing checkpoint operations, site selection, and publicity. During the only operation of the checkpoint at the time of the Court decision, 126 vehicles had passed through the checkpoint, the average delay per vehicle was twenty-five seconds, and two drivers were arrested for driving under the influence.

The Court found that a Fourth Amendment "seizure" occurs when a vehicle is stopped at a checkpoint. The Court used the balancing test of *United States v. Martinez-Fuerte,* 428 U.S. 543, 96 S.Ct. 3074, 49 L.Ed.2d 1116 (1976) (involving a fixed checkpoint designed to intercept illegal aliens) and *Brown v. Texas,* 443 U.S. 47, 99 S.Ct. 2637, 61 L.Ed.2d 357 (1979), to determine the reasonableness of such seizures under the Fourth Amendment. That test involves balancing "the gravity of the public concerns served by the seizure, the degree to which the seizure advances the public interest, and the severity of the interference with individual liberty." 443 U.S. at 51, 99 S.Ct. at 2640, 61 L.Ed.2d at 362. The Court found the magnitude of the drunken driving problem beyond dispute. In analyzing "the degree to which the seizure advances the public interest" the Court found in *Sitz* that this balancing factor was "not meant to transfer from politically accountable officials to the courts the decision as to which among reasonable alternative law enforcement techniques should be employed to deal with a serious public danger." 496 U.S. at 453, 110 S.Ct. at 2487, 110 L.Ed.2d at 422. That choice remains with the governmental officials who have a unique understanding of and a responsibility for limited public resources, including a finite number of police officers.

The Supreme Court found that the "objective" intrusion, measured by the duration of the seizure and the intensity of the investigation, was minimal. With respect to the "subjective" intrusion, the Court referred to the following language in *United States v. Ortiz,* 422 U.S. 891, 894–95, 95 S.Ct. 2585, 2587–88, 45 L.Ed.2d 623, 628 (1975).

> [T]he circumstances surrounding a checkpoint stop and search are far less intrusive than those attending a roving-patrol stop. Roving patrols often operate at night on seldom-traveled roads, and their approach may frighten motorists. At traffic checkpoints the motorist can see that other vehicles are being stopped, he can see visible signs of the officers' authority, and he is much less likely to be frightened or annoyed by the intrusion.

The Court noted that the "fear and surprise" to be considered are not the natural fear of one who has been drinking over the prospect of being stopped at a sobriety checkpoint but, rather, the fear and surprise engendered in law-abiding motorists by the nature of the stop. Other factors considered by the courts in determining whether a roadblock is reasonable are the following:

(1) The degree of discretion, if any, left to the officer in the field; (2) the location designated for the roadblock; (3) the time and duration of the roadblock; (4) standards set by superior officers; (5) advance notice to the public at large; (6) advance warning to the individual approaching motorist; (7) maintenance of safety conditions; (8) degree of fear or anxiety generated by the mode of operation; (9) average length of time each

Michigan v. Sitz
laws.findlaw.com/us/496/
444.html

United States v. Martinez-Fuerte
laws.findlaw.com/us/428/
543.html

www.fbi.gov/publications/leb/
1999/nov99leb.pdf
Article, "Drug Roadblocks" by
Kimberly A. Crawford (page 27
of the November 1999 *FBI Law
Enforcement Bulletin*)
www.pitt.edu/~lawrev/preprints/
english.htm
Article, "The Use of Sobriety
Checkpoints: What Has Happened to Sitz?" by James C.
English

United States v. Ortiz
laws.findlaw.com/us/422/
891.html

www.udayton.edu/~lawrev/
Book/Volume_24/24-1/
watson.html
Article, "When Individual Liberty and Police Procedure Collide: The Unconstitutionality of
High-Crime Area Checkpoints"
by Rachel R. Watson
www.fbi.gov/publications/leb/
1998/marleb.pdf
Article, "Checkpoints: Fourth
Amendment Implications of Limiting Access to High-Crime
Areas" by Kimberly A. Crawford
(page 27 of the March 1998 *FBI
Law Enforcement Bulletin*)

motorist is detained; (10) physical factors surrounding the location, type and method of operation; (11) the availability of less intrusive methods for combating the problem; (12) the degree of effectiveness of the procedure; and (13) any other relevant circumstances which might bear upon the test. *State v. Deskins*, 673 P.2d 1174, 1185 (Kan. 1983).

Indianapolis v. Edmond
laws.findlaw.com/us/000/
99-1030.html

In *Indianapolis v. Edmond*, 531 U.S. 32, 121 S.Ct. 447, 148 L.Ed.2d 333 (2000), the U.S. Supreme Court held that a highway checkpoint program the primary purpose of which was the discovery and interdiction of illegal narcotics violated the Fourth Amendment. What distinguished this checkpoint program from those previously approved by the Court is that its primary purpose was to detect evidence of criminal wrongdoing. The Court said:

> We have never approved a checkpoint program whose primary purpose was to detect evidence of ordinary criminal wrongdoing. Rather, our checkpoint cases have recognized only limited exceptions to the general rule that a seizure must be accompanied by some measure of individualized suspicion. We suggested in *Prouse* that we would not credit the "general interest in crime control" as justification for a regime of suspicionless stops. . . . Consistent with this suggestion, each of the checkpoint programs that we have approved was designed primarily to serve purposes closely related to the problems of policing the border or the necessity of ensuring roadway safety. Because the primary purpose of the Indianapolis narcotics checkpoint program is to uncover evidence of ordinary criminal wrongdoing, the program contravenes the Fourth Amendment. 531 U.S. at ___, 121 S.Ct. at 454, 148 L.Ed.2d at 343.

The Court said that without drawing the line at roadblocks designed to serve the general interest in crime control, law enforcement authorities could construct roadblocks for almost any conceivable law enforcement purpose and these intrusions could become a routine part of American life. Also, although the Court recognized the severe and intractable nature of the drug problem, "the gravity of the threat alone cannot be dispositive of questions concerning what means law enforcement officers may employ to pursue a given purpose. Rather, in determining whether individualized suspicion is required, we must consider the nature of the interests threatened and their connection to the particular law enforcement practices at issue. We are particularly reluctant to recognize exceptions to the general rule of individualized suspicion where governmental authorities primarily pursue their general crime control ends." 531 U.S. at ___, 121 S.Ct. at 455, 148 L.Ed.2d at 344. The Court was careful not to disturb its earlier decisions in the *Sitz*, *Martinez-Fuerte*, and *Prouse* cases.

> It goes without saying that our holding today does nothing to alter the constitutional status of the sobriety and border checkpoints that we approved in *Sitz* and *Martinez-Fuerte*, or of the type of traffic checkpoint that we suggested would be lawful in *Prouse*. The constitutionality of such checkpoint programs still depends on a balancing of the competing interests at stake and the effectiveness of the program. See *Sitz*, 496 U. S. at 450–455; *Martinez-Fuerte*, 428 U.S. at 556–564. When law enforcement authorities pursue primarily general crime control purposes at checkpoints such as here, however, stops can only be justified by some quantum of individualized suspicion.
>
> Our holding also does not affect the validity of border searches or searches at places like airports and government buildings, where the need for such measures to ensure public safety can be particularly acute. Nor does our opinion speak to other intrusions aimed primarily at purposes beyond the general interest in crime control. Our holding also does not impair the ability of police officers to act appropriately upon information that they

properly learn during a checkpoint stop justified by a lawful primary purpose, even where such action may result in the arrest of a motorist for an offense unrelated to that purpose. Finally, we caution that the purpose inquiry in this context is to be conducted only at the programmatic level and is not an invitation to probe the minds of individual officers acting at the scene. 531 U.S. at ___, 121 S.Ct. at 457, 148 L.Ed.2d at 347.

Racial Profiling

An issue causing great controversy and concern in recent years is the practice of racial profiling by law enforcement officers. Although definitions of racial profiling vary greatly, the following broad definition taken from a racial profiling study design guide produced for the U.S. Department of Justice is useful for a general discussion. Racial profiling is "any police-initiated action that relies upon: the race, ethnicity or national origin of an individual rather than [1] the behavior of that individual, or [2] information that leads the police to a particular individual who has been identified as being engaged in or having been engaged in criminal activity." One of the reasons racial profiling has become a volatile issue is the U.S. Supreme Court decision in *Whren v. United States* (discussed in the previous section) which gives police wide discretion in enforcing traffic laws so long as they have probable cause to believe that a traffic violation is occurring or has occurred. Under that decision, an officer who observes a minor traffic violation—a burned-out taillight, a cracked windshield, or failure to signal when changing lanes—may legally stop the driver even if the officer's actual subjective intent is to look for evidence of drug offenses or other more serious offenses. Because minor traffic violations are so common, some commentators have suggested that the *Whren* decision gives police virtually unlimited authority to stop any vehicle they wish to stop.

Many members of racial and ethnic groups and organizations that represent their interests claim that police are abusing their broad discretion by targeting members of these groups in the unequal enforcement of traffic laws. There has been a rash of articles, speeches, and other commentary condemning the practice of racial profiling and what have sarcastically been described as the "new" crimes of driving while black/brown (DWB) and, by extension, walking, idling, standing, shopping, and breathing while black/brown. The issue of racial profiling has engendered much anger, fear, resentment, and mistrust on the part of minorities and has contributed to disintegrating police-community relations in many areas of the country.

The extent of the racial profiling problem is in dispute. Recent studies and literature indicate that the majority of Americans, black and white, believe the problem is real and widespread. For example, an investigation of racial profiling by the Attorney General of New Jersey resulted in the conclusion that "minority motorists have been treated differently [by New Jersey State Troopers] than nonminority motorists during the course of traffic stops on the New Jersey Turnpike." Similar conclusions have resulted from surveys of police practices in Boston and Los Angeles. Some, however, continue to argue that racial profiling is more hype than substance.

To more accurately determine the extent of the problem, many state legislatures have enacted statutes providing for the collection of statistical data on racial profiling. These laws require law enforcement agencies to collect information on vehicle stops, including number of persons stopped, race and ethnicity of persons stopped, reasons for the stops, and actions taken by officers as a result of the stops. Also, a bill now before Congress, but not yet enacted, provides for the collection of similar data on racial profiling and reporting the results to Congress and the public. In 1999, President Clinton issued an executive order that declared that stopping or searching individuals on

www.aclu.org/profiling/report/
Article, "Driving While Black: Racial Profiling on Our Nation's Highways" by David A. Harris

www.fbi.gov/publications/leb/2000/nov00leb.pdf
Article, "Professional Police Traffic Stops: Strategies to Address Racial Profiling" by Grady Carrick (page 8 of the November 2000 *FBI Law Enforcement Bulletin*)

www.law.duke.edu/shell/cite.pl?50+Duke+L+J.+331
Article, "Why Modest Proposals Offer the Best Solution for Combating Racial Profiling" by Sean P. Trende

www.oag.state.ny.us/press/reports/stop_frisk/ch2_part2.html
Article, "The 14th Amendment Prohibition on Unequal or Discriminatory Stops"; part II of the "Stop and Frisk" Report of the New York State Attorney General's Office

www.aclu.org/issues/racial/bispeech99.html
Speech by ACLU's Ira Glasser, "American Drug Laws: The New Jim Crow"; focuses on how the drug wars fuel racial profiling

www.pegasus.rutgers.edu/~record/drafts/minorities.html
Article, "Why Minorities Run from the Police"

www1.umn.edu/irp/publications/racialprofiling.html
"Components of Racial Profiling Legislation" from the Institute on Race and Poverty

www.aele.org/losrace99.html
Article, "Race Relations in Police Operations: a Legal and Ethical Perspective" by Carl Milazzo

www.aele.org/losrace2000.html
Article, "Current Legal Issues in Racial Profiling: 2000 Update" by Aimee B. Anderson and Carl Milazzo

www.aele.org/zoufal.html
Article, "Developments in Racial Profiling Litigation: A Tale of Two Cities" by Donald R. Zoufal

www.totse.com/en/law/justice_for_all/ammerest.html
"Pagan's Guide to Dealing with Police Harassment"

the basis of race is not effective law enforcement policy, and is not consistent with this country's democratic ideals, especially the commitment to equal protection under the law for all persons. The president stated that such a practice "is neither legitimate nor defensible as a strategy for public protection. It is simply wrong." The executive order directs the Justice, Treasury, and Interior Departments to design and implement a system to collect and report statistics relating to race, ethnicity, and gender for law enforcement activities in the agencies. Throughout the country, local and state law enforcement agencies are establishing official policies against racial profiling and are integrating discussion about racial profiling into diversity and refresher training for their officers.

Stewart v. City and County of Denver, et al.
www.law.columbia.edu/
course_00F_L6419_001/
Racial%20Profiling.htm

Increasingly, citizens who claim to be the subjects of racial profiling are bringing lawsuits against the police in which they allege violations of their constitutional rights as guaranteed by the Fourth, Fifth, and Fourteenth Amendments. One example is *Stewart v. City and County of Denver, et al.*, an unpublished disposition of the Tenth Circuit Court of Appeals in January 2000. While the Court upheld the trial court's grant of summary judgment for the defendants—the police officers who made the stop and the municipality that employed them—the case indicates what is necessary to establish a claim of racial profiling. The plaintiff, an African American, argued that the police stopped him in Denver, Colorado, not because one of his vehicle's headlights was out as the police claimed, but because he was African American. The plaintiff raised claims of violations of his equal protection rights through racial discrimination, violation of his Fourth Amendment rights to be free from unlawful searches and seizures, and violation of his Fifth Amendment due process rights. The Circuit Court, though, upheld the finding of the trial court that the plaintiff was unable to make a specific showing of a police custom or practice to treat African Americans differently than others, beyond the vague testimony offered by the plaintiff and others that traffic stops in the particular neighborhood appeared to them to be racially motivated. In particular, the plaintiff failed to present sufficient evidence regarding the existence of a continuing, persistent, and widespread practice of unconstitutional conduct by the city's employees. In other words, the plaintiff's claims failed as a result of a lack of empirical evidence of racial profiling by the Denver police. The case is important, though, because it establishes a potential framework in which later successful suits may be brought by others aggrieved in a similar fashion.

In addition to individuals filing suits against the police for alleged racial profiling, there have also been a host of class-action suits filed by organizations (such as the ACLU and the NAACP) representing the constitutional rights of citizens; some of these suits seek significant monetary damages. Law enforcement officers must therefore be mindful that targeting an individual solely on the basis of that person's race or ethnicity may lead to civil liability or even, in certain circumstances, to the suppression of evidence. With that in mind, this discussion of racial profiling concludes with the entire concurring opinion of Judge Ireland of the Massachusetts Supreme Court in *Commonwealth v. Gonsalves*, 711 N.E.2d 108, 115–16 (Mass. 1999). That case held that the Massachusetts state constitution requires that a police officer, in a routine traffic stop, must have reasonable belief that the officer's safety, or the safety of others, is in danger before ordering the driver out of the motor vehicle.

I join in the opinion of the court and fully agree with its conclusion that, in the context of automobile exit orders, art. 14 of our State Constitution provides greater protection to Massachusetts citizens than the United States Constitution. As we were once reminded, "The right question . . . is not whether a state's guarantee is the same as or broader than its federal counterpart as interpreted by the Supreme Court. The right question is what the state's guarantee means and how it applies to the case at hand." . . . .

I write separately, however, to stress the dangers posed by unfettered police power to order individuals out of automobiles without any justification. The grant of such power is certainly, as the majority notes, "a clear invitation to discriminatory enforcement of the rule." This is precisely the type of power "that art. 14 was adopted to guard against," . . . because, in the words of James Otis, it " 'places the liberty of every man in the hands of every petty officer.' " . . .

The widespread public concerns about police profiling, commonly referred to as "DWB—driving while black," has been the subject of much discussion and debate both across the country and within the Commonwealth. See Black Drivers Describe Harassment by Police, *The Boston Globe*, Apr. 13, 1999, at A1. Statistics show that such racial profiling occurs throughout the nation. "In Florida, police documented 1,100 videotaped stops along Interstate 95 in the late 1980's. While blacks and Hispanics made up just 5 percent of the drivers, they made up eighty percent of those stopped and searched." Traffic Stops Discounted in Sentencing, *The Washington Post*, Dec. 17, 1998, at A8. One study found that seventy-three percent of cars stopped and searched on Interstate 95 in Maryland were driven by black people, while only fourteen percent of people who use the road are black. Seat Belt Push Raises Race Issue; Blacks Weigh Tolls of Safety vs. Bias, *The Washington Post*, Apr. 3, 1998, at A1. In addition, statistics presented to the United States House of Representatives indicate that "blacks, who make up about 14 percent of the population, account for 72 percent of drivers pulled over for routine traffic stops." House OKs Study of Car Searches, *The Boston Globe*, Mar. 25, 1998, at A12.

Indeed, the New Jersey Attorney General's Office has recently admitted that such racial profiling in traffic stops is "real, not imagined." Bradley Puts Race at Center of Campaign, *The Star-Ledger* (Newark, N.J.), Apr. 21, 1999, at 8. "Of the stops examined by the [New Jersey] Attorney General's Office, roughly 60 percent involved white drivers, 27 percent blacks, 7 percent Hispanics, and 4 percent Asians. Few of those stops[,] less than 1 percent [,] resulted in searches. But when they did, 77 percent of the searches involved blacks or Hispanics. Only 21 percent of the searches involved whites." Belated Acknowledgment an Essential First Step to Ending Racial Profiling, *The Record* (Northern N.J.), Apr. 22, 1999, at L8.

Other courts have also recognized racial profiling and "DWB" as a real cause for concern. See *United States v. Leviner*, 31 F.Supp.2d 23, 33 (D.Mass.1998); *State v. Valentine*, 132 Wash.2d 1, 28 n. 1, 935 P.2d 1294 (1997) (Sanders, J., dissenting).

As the court's opinion indicates, the rules in *Pennsylvania v. Mimms*, 434 U.S. 106, 98 S.Ct. 330, 54 L.Ed.2d 331 (1977), and *Maryland v. Wilson*, 519 U.S. 408, 117 S.Ct. 882, 137 L.Ed.2d 41 (1997), which permit automobile exit orders during any traffic stop "may also pose unique hardships on minorities" and could be a "clear invitation to discriminatory enforcement." Prohibiting the police from ordering people out of automobiles without any justification is a much-needed step in the right direction to cure such abuses.

Violent Crime

In *People v. Anthony*, 86 Cal.Rptr. 767 (Cal.App. 1970), police officers on patrol received a radio report of an armed robbery in their vicinity. The report came in at about 3:30 A.M., minutes after the robbery happened. The officers had seen only one moving car in the vicinity. They approached the car and noticed that one of the passengers fit the description of the robber given to them over the radio. The car was stopped and the two occupants were instructed to get out. No questions were asked, but one of the officers immediately began a patdown search of the defendant for weapons. Bullets were found, and the defendant was arrested.

The court held that both the stop and the frisk were justified.

> It is well established that circumstances short of probable cause to make an arrest may justify an officer's stopping motorists for questioning, and if the circumstances warrant it, the officer may in self-protection request a suspect to alight from an automobile and to submit to a superficial search for concealed weapons. . . . If the reason for the stop is an articulate suspicion of a crime of violence, and the officer has reason to fear for his personal safety, he may immediately proceed to make a patdown search for weapons without asking any prior questions. . . . "There is no reason why an officer, rightfully but forcibly confronting a person suspected of a serious crime, *should have to ask one question and take the risk that the answer might be a bullet.*" (Emphasis added.) 86 Cal.Rptr. at 773.

To summarize, an officer is not required to ask questions before frisking a suspect if the nature of the crime being investigated is violent and if the officer has a reasonable fear for his or her own safety.

Objects Felt in Frisk

In *People v. Navran,* 483 P.2d 228 (Colo. 1971), police had a certain residence under surveillance as a receiving point for marijuana shipments and had probable cause to arrest the occupant of the residence, although he was absent at the time. The defendants entered the driveway of the residence in a car, proceeded up the driveway, and were attempting to back out when the police stopped them. The officers knew that the defendants were not occupants of the residence, nor were they subjects of the investigation. Nevertheless, the officers caused the defendants to be spread-eagled against their car and searched. One of the officers patted down the defendants' outer and inner clothing. During the frisk of one defendant, the officer felt a lump in a shirt pocket. This lump was later disclosed to be a plastic bag containing marijuana seeds and a package of cigarette rolling papers. The court approved the stop:

> Admittedly the police officers would have been derelict in their duty had they not stopped the defendants' vehicle to determine whether the occupant of the residence, or any other known subject of the investigation, was in the car. Likewise, the officers could have detained the defendants long enough to ascertain why they were on the premises. 483 P.2d at 230.

However, the court found the *frisk* unreasonable:

> It is apparent that the search conducted herein was not the "reasonable search for weapons" contemplated by the *Terry* case. . . . The right to "stop and frisk" is not an open invitation to conduct an unlimited search incident to arrest or a means to effect a search to provide grounds for an arrest. Rather, it is a right to conduct a limited search for weapons. . . . The seeds and cigarette papers seized were not shown by any evidence produced at the hearing to have been taken from the defendants under circumstances which would permit a search for weapons. 483 P.2d at 232.

In another case involving objects felt in a frisk, an officer received a radio report that a murder had just been committed. The officer proceeded to the scene of the crime and observed the defendant, who fit the description that the officer had received on the radio. The officer stopped the defendant and conducted a frisk for weapons. Just after the officer started the search around the defendant's waistband, the defendant abruptly grabbed his outside upper jacket pocket. The officer moved the defendant's hand away from the pocket and from the outside felt a round cylindrical object that the officer surmised was a twelve-gauge shotgun shell. He reached into the pocket and removed the object, at the same time pulling out a marijuana cigarette. The cylindrical object was revealed to be a lipstick container. The defendant was convicted of unauthorized possession of marijuana.

The reasonableness of the stop was not in question. The officer clearly had a duty to investigate the defendant on the basis of the description given over the police radio. With respect to the reasonableness of the frisk, the court found that the officer could have reasonably believed that his safety was in danger and that the frisk was justified:

> Though there is some confusion in the record it is susceptible of the inference that at the moment the officer had not yet eliminated the possibility that defendant was hiding a relatively short shotgun under his jacket. In any event a shotgun was not necessarily the only object which, in combination with a shell, could be used as a weapon. The officer could reasonably believe that any sharp object could be used as a detonator. . . . Hindsight may suggest that, in order to combine maximum personal safety for the officer with a minimum invasion of defendant's privacy, the officer should first have ascertained what else defendant was carrying. We do not believe, however, that under the circumstances the officer was required to proceed in the coldly logical sequence which may suggest itself after the event. It appears from the record that his reaching into the pocket was almost a reflexive motion, provoked by defendant's sudden gesture toward the pocket and his own feeling of the contents. We cannot say that under all of the circumstances defendant's constitutional rights were violated. *People v. Atmore*, 91 Cal.Rptr. 311, 313–14 (Cal.App. 1970).

Collective Knowledge of Police

A law enforcement officer may stop a person on the basis of a wanted flyer indicating that another law enforcement agency has a reasonable suspicion that the person is or was involved in a crime. In *United States v. Hensley*, 469 U.S. 221, 232, 105 S.Ct. 675, 683–84, 83 L.Ed.2d 604, 614 (1985), the U.S. Supreme Court said: "[I]f a flyer or bulletin has been issued on the basis of articulable facts supporting a reasonable suspicion that the wanted person has committed an offense, then reliance on that flyer or bulletin justifies a stop to check identification . . . to pose questions to the person, or to detain the person briefly while attempting to obtain further information."

The *Hensley* case emphasized that, since criminal suspects are increasingly mobile and increasingly likely to flee across jurisdictional boundaries, police in one jurisdiction should be able to act promptly in reliance on information from another jurisdiction. If a flyer has been issued in the absence of a reasonable suspicion, however, a stop in objective reliance on it would violate the Fourth Amendment, although the officers making the stop would have a good-faith defense to any civil suit arising from the incident. Moreover, a stop made in reliance on a wanted flyer must not be significantly more intrusive than would have been permitted the agency that issued the flyer.

In *United States v. Rodriguez*, 831 F.2d 162 (7th Cir. 1987), the DEA was investigating a drug distribution network and had adequate suspicion to stop the defendant's car to check his identification. A DEA agent asked the state police to conduct the stop, and a state police officer did so. The defendant claimed that the state police officer who stopped his car had inadequate information to justify the stop. The court held as follows:

> [T]he officer making the investigatory stop might reasonably rely on the request of another investigator. The requesting DEA agent had good grounds for articulable suspicion and the detaining officer had a reasonable basis for believing the request to be well-founded—even though she did not personally know the facts giving rise to the suspicion. Unlike *Hensley*, here the automobile to be stopped with its occupant was pointed out specifically by the requesting officer, and the detaining officer knew the requesting officer was coordinating a large investigation with local agencies. The state trooper was therefore merely acting as an "extension" or agent of the DEA agent and she could act on the DEA agent's suspicions. 831 F.2d at 166.

High-Crime Area

In *Brown v. Texas*, 443 U.S. 47, 99 S.Ct. 2637, 61 L.Ed.2d 357 (1979), police on patrol in an area with a high incidence of drug traffic stopped the defendant in an alley while he was walking away from another person. The officer later testified that the situation "looked suspicious and we had never seen that subject in that area before." The U.S. Supreme Court held the stop illegal.

> The fact that appellant was in a neighborhood frequented by drug users, standing alone, is not a basis for concluding that appellant himself was engaged in criminal conduct. In short, the appellant's activity was no different from the activity of other pedestrians in that neighborhood. 443 U.S. at 52, 99 S.Ct. at 2641, 61 L.Ed.2d at 362–63.

In *Illinois v. Wardlow*, (discussed on page 289–90) the U.S. Supreme Court reiterated its holding in *Brown v. Texas*, but added that presence in a high-crime area combined with other specific suspicious information may provide a legally justifiable basis for a stop.

> An individual's presence in an area of expected criminal activity, standing alone, is not enough to support a reasonable, particularized suspicion that the person is committing a crime (citing *Brown v. Texas*). But officers are not required to ignore the relevant characteristics of a location in determining whether the circumstances are sufficiently suspicious to warrant further investigation. Accordingly, we have previously noted the fact that the stop occurred in a "high-crime area" among the relevant contextual considerations in a *Terry* analysis. 528 U.S. 119, 124, 120 S.Ct. 673, 676, 145 L.Ed.2d 570, 576.

In *United States v. Stanley*, 915 F.2d 54 (1st Cir. 1990), the court held that an officer was justified in making an investigatory stop of a suspect who was alone in his car, after midnight, in an area frequently used for illegal drug activities. The suspect was leaning over the car's center console, which was slightly illuminated, and appeared to be attempting to hide something when he saw the officer approaching. The court specifically stated that the reputation of the area was an appropriate factor in determining the reasonableness of an investigatory stop. The court also said that the circumstances of the case "are to be viewed through the eyes of a reasonable and cautious police officer on the scene, guided by his experience and training." 915 F.2d at 56.

Association with Known Criminals

In *United States v. Cruz,* 909 F.2d 422 (11th Cir. 1989), the court found adequate grounds, based partially on the suspect's association with known drug dealers, for both a stop and frisk of the suspect under the following circumstances:

> First, the appellant was seen walking together with a known drug dealer who had negotiated with one of the agents for the delivery of fifteen grams of cocaine. Second, the agents certainly understood that the crime of drug trafficking has a particularly violent nature. Finally, the appellant's male companion was seen speaking to one of the dealers whom the agents knew was present to exchange a kilogram of cocaine. While none of these factors, by themselves, necessarily justifies an investigative stop, they are each relevant in the determination of whether the agents had reasonable suspicion to stop the appellant. . . . Thus under all the circumstances known to the officers at the time of the stop, we hold that the officers had reasonable suspicion to stop the appellant who had walked away from the scene of the original arrests.
>
> Because the detective had reasonable suspicion to stop the appellant, she also had the right to make a limited protective search for concealed weapons in order to secure the safety of herself and the safety of those around her. The factors articulated above indicated that the appellant was likely involved in narcotics trafficking and, as is judicially recognized, such individuals are often armed. . . . In addition, in an area known for heavy drug trafficking, the appellant was walking down the street and stopping before a car of known dealers who were at the scene to exchange some cocaine. Under these circumstances, a limited protective search, including a search of the purse, was reasonable. 909 F.2d at 424.

Other Suspicious Circumstances

www.forensic-evidence.com/ site/Police/Pol_comm_care.html Article, "The Police Officer as a Community Caretaker"

In *Modesto v. State,* 258 A.2d 287 (Del.Super. 1969), after a high-speed chase, a law enforcement officer stopped the defendant's vehicle for speeding. The officer asked the defendant to get out of the vehicle. The defendant turned toward the officer and proceeded to take off his coat while he was still seated in the car. As he got out of the car, he dropped the coat on the passenger seat where he had been sitting. The officer thought it was peculiar for the defendant to remove his coat on a cold November night, so the officer grabbed the coat as the defendant was getting out. The officer noticed a pistol on the passenger seat, which had been covered by the coat, and the officer seized the pistol.

The court analyzed the reasonableness of both the stop and the frisk:

> The question then becomes whether or not the policeman acted legally when he reached into the car and picked up the defendant's coat. It should be noted that this case involves an incident where the police had a duty to act in stopping the vehicle. It is not a case of general exploratory investigation. Since the police had a duty to act, they also had a right to take reasonable measures to see that their safety was not endangered. . . . In view of the lateness of the hour, the high speed chase, the number of men in the car [3], the fact that the men had been drinking, the police acted reasonably in self protection in asking the gentlemen to get out of the car. Moreover, under these facts, it was reasonable for the police to conduct a limited patdown search for weapons. A person cannot avoid such a search of his clothing by removing his clothing when it necessarily remains in the general vicinity where he is to remain. The police do not have to risk watching three men to make sure that they did not at any time go back to

the clothing left in the car. And the mere fact that the coat was removed is another circumstance justifying a self protection frisk search. 258 A.2d at 288.

In another case, two police officers received information over the police radio that a shooting had occurred. The suspects were described as two black men in dark clothing and one Puerto Rican in light clothing. The officers proceeded to the scene of the shooting and observed a black man in dark clothing and a Puerto Rican in light clothing walking together near the scene, acting normally. The only reasons the police had to connect the two men with the reported shooting were that they were walking in the general area and they fit the limited description police had been given. The police had no information about the physical makeups or characteristics of the men they were seeking. The officers stopped the two men, frisked them on the spot, and found a gun in the defendant's belt.

The court discussed the stop and frisk aspects of the case together:

> A policeman may legally stop a person and question him. But he may not without a warrant restrain that person from walking away and "search" his clothing, unless he has "probable cause" to arrest that person or he observes such unusual and suspicious conduct on the part of the person who is stopped and searched that the policeman may reasonably conclude that criminal activity may be afoot, and that the person with whom he is dealing may be armed and dangerous. *Commonwealth v. Berrios*, 263 A.2d 342, 343 (Pa. 1970).

The court found that the circumstances of this case would *not* warrant a reasonably prudent person in the belief that his or her safety or the safety of others was in danger:

> If the policemen were constitutionally justified in searching Berrios under these circumstances, then every Puerto Rican wearing light clothing and walking with a negro in this area could likewise be validly searched. This, we cannot accept. 263 A.2d at 344.

In *United States v. $37,590.00*, 736 F.Supp. 1272 (S.D.N.Y. 1990), the court held that the mere facts that a person clutched his shoulder bags, refused to answer inquiries about them, and reached for them when asked what they contained, provided neither grounds for a stop nor an objective, reasonable, particularized suspicion that the person was armed and dangerous.

Key Points

15. A series of individual lawful acts may provide reasonable suspicion of criminal activity sufficient to justify a stop, if the overall pattern of those acts is indicative of criminal activity.

16. A law enforcement officer may not stop a motor vehicle and detain the driver to check license and registration unless the officer has reasonable, articulable suspicion of criminal activity or unless the stop is conducted in accordance with a properly conducted highway checkpoint program.

17. The test to determine the reasonableness of the stop of a vehicle at a highway checkpoint involves balancing the gravity of the public concerns served by the seizure, the degree to which the seizure advances the public interest, and the severity of the interference with individual liberty.

18. If a stop is made on a reasonable, articulable suspicion of a crime of violence, and the officer has reason to fear for his or her personal safety, the officer may immediately proceed to make a patdown search for weapons without asking any prior questions.

19. A law enforcement officer may stop a person on the basis of a wanted flyer indicating that another law enforcement agency has a reasonable suspicion that the person is or was involved in a crime.

Miscellaneous Issues in Stop and Frisk

This section discusses the following three issues related to stop and frisk: (1) whether *Miranda* warnings are required in the typical stop-and-frisk situation, (2) what considerations are raised by frisking persons of the opposite sex, and (3) how the principles already discussed apply to the investigative detention of containers and other property.

Stop and Frisk and *Miranda*

As discussed in Chapter 13, the *Miranda* warnings must be given before any interrogation of a person in custody or otherwise deprived of freedom of action in any significant way. Are the warnings required to be given before questioning in connection with a stop and frisk? The U.S. Supreme Court said no, holding that the ordinary *Terry*-type investigative stop and the ordinary traffic stop are noncustodial and do not require the administration of *Miranda* warnings. (See pages 476 to 477.)

If, however, circumstances develop out of an ordinary stop that create a coercive and compelling atmosphere resulting in a significant deprivation of a person's freedom of action, *Miranda* warnings would be required. For example, if the police outnumber the suspects, questioning is sustained and accusatory, force is used, or other coercive factors are present, alone or in combination, then it is very likely the warnings will be required. In other words, in determining custody for *Miranda* purposes, "the ultimate inquiry is simply whether there is a 'formal arrest or restraint on freedom of movement' of the degree associated with a formal arrest." *California v. Beheler,* 463 U.S. 1121, 1125, 103 S.Ct. 3517, 3520, 77 L.Ed.2d 1275, 1279 (1983). Since a stop is by definition a seizure of a lesser degree than a formal arrest, *Miranda* warnings are not required before questioning in connection with a stop.

California v. Beheler
laws.findlaw.com/us/463/
1121.html

Frisking Persons of the Opposite Sex

Frisking a person of the opposite sex presents a delicate situation for which few specific guidelines are available. On the one hand, in many situations a law enforcement officer could reasonably fear that a person of the opposite sex presented a danger to the officer or to other persons. On the other hand, if routine frisk procedures are used on a person of the opposite sex, an officer may be subjected to charges of assault or sexual misconduct. Therefore, an examination of the outer clothing of a person of the opposite sex should not be undertaken without some degree of certainty that the person is armed. The officer may ask a person to remove an overcoat or other covering, and the officer may squeeze handbags, shoulder bags, or other containers. Containers should not be opened unless a weaponlike object is felt. If the person is arrested, the search and seizure of clothing, pockets, bags, and bundles is governed by the law of search incident to arrest (see Chapter 8).

Containers and Other Property

The general rule regarding the investigatory detention of property was stated by the U.S. Supreme Court:

> Although the Fourth Amendment may permit the detention for a brief period of property on the basis of only "reasonable, articulable suspicion" that it contains contraband or evidence of criminal activity . . . it proscribes—except in certain well-defined

Smith v. Ohio
laws.findlaw.com/us/494/
541.html

circumstances—the search of that property unless accomplished pursuant to judicial warrant issued upon probable cause. *Smith v. Ohio,* 494 U.S. 541, 542, 110 S.Ct. 1288, 1289, 108 L.Ed.2d 464, 467 (1990).

In *United States v. Place,* 462 U.S. 696, 103 S.Ct. 2637, 77 L.Ed.2d 110 (1983), the Supreme Court held that the principles of the *Terry* case apply to the warrantless seizure and limited investigation of personal luggage. In that case, based on information from law enforcement officers in Miami, DEA agents at a New York airport believed that the defendant might be carrying narcotics. Upon the defendant's arrival at the airport, the agents approached him, informed him of their suspicion, and requested and received identification from him. When the defendant refused to consent to a search of his luggage, one of the agents told him that they were going to take the luggage to a federal judge to try to obtain a search warrant. The agents then took the luggage to another airport, where they subjected it to a "sniff test" by a trained narcotics detection dog, and the dog reacted positively to one of the bags. At this point, approximately ninety minutes had elapsed since the seizure of the luggage. The agents later obtained a search warrant for the luggage and, upon opening the luggage, discovered a large quantity of cocaine.

As in the *Terry* case, the Court balanced the nature and quality of the intrusion on the individual's Fourth Amendment interests against the importance of the governmental interests alleged to justify the intrusion. The court found a substantial governmental interest in detecting drug trafficking, a unique problem because it is highly organized and conducted by sophisticated criminal syndicates, the profits are enormous, and drugs are easily concealed. The Court said:

> The context of a particular law enforcement practice, of course, may affect the determination whether a brief intrusion on Fourth Amendment interests on less than probable cause is essential to effective criminal investigation. Because of the inherently transient nature of drug courier activity at airports, allowing police to make brief investigative stops of persons at airports on reasonable suspicion of drug-trafficking substantially enhances the likelihood that police will be able to prevent the flow of narcotics into distribution channels. 462 U.S. at 704, 103 S.Ct. at 2643, 77 L.Ed.2d at 119.

www.fbi.gov/publications/leb/
2000/jan00leb.pdf
Article, "Drug Detection Dogs:
Legal Considerations" by Michael
J. Bulzomi (page 27 of the January 2000 *FBI Law Enforcement
Bulletin*)
www.policek9.com/Case_Law/
Narcotics_Case_Law/
narcotics_case_law.html
Comprehensive index of cases
dealing with the Fourth Amendment implications of canine sniffs
for narcotics
www.uspcak9.com/training/
introsearchandseizure.shtml
Article, "The Dog Day Traffic
Stop: Basic Canine Search and
Seizure" by Ken Wallentine
uspcak9.com/caselaw/
searchseizurelist.shtml
"Search and Seizure Checklists"
for canine sniffs

With respect to the intrusion on Fourth Amendment rights, the Court found that seizures of property can vary in intrusiveness and that some brief detentions of personal effects may be so minimally intrusive that strong, countervailing governmental interests will justify a seizure based only on specific, articulable facts that the property contains contraband or evidence of a crime. The Court held that

> when an officer's observations lead him reasonably to believe that a traveler is carrying luggage that contains narcotics, the principles of *Terry* and its progeny would permit the officer to detain the luggage briefly to investigate the circumstances that aroused his suspicion, provided that the investigative detention is properly limited in scope. 462 U.S. at 706, 103 S.Ct. at 2644, 77 L.Ed.2d at 120.

In addition, the Court specifically found that the brief investigation of the luggage could include a "canine sniff" by a well-trained narcotics detection dog. This procedure was found to be uniquely limited in nature because it does not require opening the luggage, it does not expose noncontraband items to view, and it discloses only the presence or absence of narcotics, a contraband item.

Nevertheless, the Court found that the scope of the investigative detention of the luggage in the *Place* case exceeded the limits established in the *Terry* case, primarily because of the length of the detention. The Court said:

> Although the 90-minute detention of respondent's luggage is sufficient to render the seizure unreasonable, the violation was exacerbated by the failure of the agents to accurately inform respondent of the place to which they were transporting his luggage, of the length of time he might be dispossessed, and of what arrangements would be made for return of the luggage if the investigation dispelled the suspicion. In short, we hold that the detention of respondent's luggage in this case went beyond the narrow authority possessed by police to detain briefly luggage reasonably suspected to contain narcotics. 462 U.S. at 710, 103 S.Ct. at 2646, 77 L.Ed.2d at 122.

Although the Court did not establish any rigid time limitation on an investigative detention, it clearly indicated that efforts of officers to minimize the intrusion on Fourth Amendment rights would be considered in determining the reasonableness of the detention. (Time limitations on investigative detentions are discussed earlier under "Extent of Stop.")

Note that courts look differently upon detaining a person than detaining (or holding for further examination) an object. When, however, the object is something such as a person's passport, airline ticket, luggage, or driver's license, the person is not really free to leave, even though technically it is the object, not the person, being detained. Courts will more carefully scrutinize detentions of objects that actually detain persons.

In *United States v. Van Leeuwen*, 397 U.S. 249, 90 S.Ct. 1029, 25 L.Ed.2d 282 (1970), a case in which a person was not detained, a postal clerk advised a police officer that he was suspicious of two packages of coins that had just been mailed. The police officer immediately noted that the return address was fictitious and that the person who mailed the packages had Canadian license plates. Later investigation disclosed that the addresses on both packages (one in California, the other in Tennessee) were under investigation for trafficking in illegal coins. On this basis, a search warrant for both packages was obtained, but not until the packages had been detained for slightly more than a day. The defendants were convicted of trafficking in illegal coins.

United States v. Van Leeuwen laws.findlaw.com/us/397/249.html

The Court upheld the warrantless detention of the packages while the investigation was made, recognizing nevertheless that a detention of mail could at some point become an unreasonable seizure of "papers" or "effects" within the meaning of the Fourth Amendment. The Court emphasized, however, that the investigation was conducted promptly and that most of the delay was attributable to the fact that the Tennessee authorities could not be reached until the following day because of a time zone differential. As in the *Place* case, the length of time of the detention was an important determinant of the detention's reasonableness.

In *State v. Phaneuf,* 597 A.2d 55 (Me. 1991), the court held that a detention for several hours of a first-class package at the post office to allow a warrantless canine sniff to detect the presence of drugs was not so intrusive as to be unreasonable. In its decision, the court discussed *United States v. Thomas*, 757 F.2d 1359 (2d Cir. 1985), which excluded from evidence fruits of a search conducted under a warrant based on information obtained from a dog sniff of a door of a suspected drug dealer's apartment. In *Thomas*, the court found that a heightened expectation of privacy in residences prevented officers from bringing a trained dog to the door of the defendant's apartment to sniff for drugs. The Maine court, however, allowed the dog sniff of the package, rejecting the defendant's contention that the Fourth Amendment creates a *heightened* expectation of privacy in the mail akin to that in one's domicile.

Detention and search of carry-on luggage at airline security checkpoints are a special case because of the severe danger presented by allowing weapons or explosives on an airplane.

> Routine security searches at airport checkpoints pass constitutional muster because the compelling public interest in curbing air piracy generally outweighs their limited intrusiveness. . . . Consequently, all carry-on luggage can be subjected to initial x-ray screening for weapons and explosives without offending the Fourth Amendment. In the event the initial x-ray screening is inconclusive as to the presence of weapons or explosives, the luggage may be hand-searched as reasonably required to rule out their presence. . . . Other contraband inadvertently discovered during a routine checkpoint search for weapons and explosives may be seized and introduced in evidence at trial even though unrelated to airline security. *United States v. Doe,* 61 F.3d 107, 109–10 (1st Cir. 1995).

www.aclu.org/congress/
airtest.html
"Civil Liberties Implications of Airport Security Measures"; testimony of ACLU Legislative Counsel before the White House Commission on Aviation Safety and Security

On the other hand, lawful airline security searches of carry-on luggage may not be enlarged or tailored systemically to detect contraband (for instance, narcotics) unrelated to airline security. For example, in *United States v. $124,570 U.S. Currency,* 873 F.2d 1240, 1243–45 (9th Cir. 1989), the court upheld suppression of contraband unrelated to airline security where screeners were rewarded monetarily by law enforcement authorities for detecting such contraband in carry-on luggage.

In a case involving not a detention, but the equivalent of a "frisk" of luggage, the U.S. Supreme Court held that a law enforcement officer's physical manipulation of a bus passenger's carry-on luggage violated the Fourth Amendment's proscription against unreasonable searches. In *Bond v. United States,* 529 U.S. 334, 120 S.Ct. 1462, 146 L.Ed.2d 365 (2000), a border patrol agent boarded a bus in Texas to check the immigration status of its passengers. As the agent walked from the rear to the front of the bus, he squeezed the soft luggage that the passengers had placed in the overhead storage space above the seats. He squeezed a canvas bag above Bond's seat and noticed that it contained a "bricklike" substance. After Bond admitted ownership of the bag and consented to its search, the agent discovered a "brick" of methamphetamine.

Bond v. United States
laws.findlaw.com/us/000/
98-9349.html

The Court likened the level of intrusion of squeezing Bond's luggage to that of a frisk of his person. "Although Agent Cantu did not 'frisk' petitioner's person, he did conduct a probing tactile examination of petitioner's carry-on luggage. Obviously, petitioner's bag was not part of his person. But travelers are particularly concerned about their carry-on luggage; they generally use it to transport personal items that, for whatever reason, they prefer to keep close at hand." 529 U.S. at 337–38, 120 S.Ct. at 1464–65, 146 L.Ed.2d at 370.

The Court's reasoning in declaring the search unreasonable is worthy of quotation.

> Our Fourth Amendment analysis embraces two questions. First, we ask whether the individual, by his conduct, has exhibited an actual expectation of privacy; that is, whether he has shown that "he [sought] to preserve [something] as private." *Smith v. Maryland,* 442 U. S. 735, 740 (1979). . . . Here, petitioner sought to preserve privacy by using an opaque bag and placing that bag directly above his seat. Second, we inquire whether the individual's expectation of privacy is "one that society is prepared to recognize as reasonable." . . . When a bus passenger places a bag in an overhead bin, he expects that other passengers or bus employees may move it for one reason or another. Thus, a bus passenger clearly expects that his bag may be handled. He does not expect that other

Case in Point

Interpreting *Bond v. United States*

On May 16, 1996, between 10:00 and 11:15 A.M., Defendant-Appellant Michael Angelo Flowal was passing through the Greater Cincinnati-Northern Kentucky Airport on his way from Los Angeles, California, to Fort Wayne, Indiana. About this time, Lieutenant Gayle Blackburn, a drug task force officer, received word about a passenger who was on his way from Los Angeles to Fort Wayne and who matched a drug courier profile.

Lieutenant Blackburn, Officer Bauerle, also a drug task force officer, and Gary Curry, a Special Agent for the DEA, located two pieces of luggage matching the claim numbers 945197 and 198 at the airline baggage area. The luggage belonged to Flowal. Both pieces of luggage were locked. The officers shook the luggage to see if there was movement and pushed the sides of the luggage. They did not discover anything suspicious.

Lieutenant Blackburn stayed with the luggage in the baggage claim area while Officer Bauerle and Agent Curry returned to the airport terminal to locate Flowal. Officer Mike Evans, another drug task force officer, arrived in the luggage area with a drug-sniffing dog. The dog did not react or indicate that the luggage contained drugs. Officer Bauerle and Agent Curry knew this before talking to Flowal, but did not inform Flowal of the dog's reaction.

According to Officer Bauerle's testimony, Flowal started down the boarding ramp to board the airplane, and Officer Bauerle and Agent Curry followed and stopped him. Officer Bauerle identified himself to Flowal and told Flowal that he and Agent Curry had seen Flowal's luggage and that it looked suspicious. Officer Bauerle asked Flowal if he had packed the bags, to which Flowal responded he had. He then requested to search Flowal's luggage. Flowal consented. Officer Bauerle asked if Flowal had the key to the luggage. Flowal did not, but he again consented to the search of the luggage so long as the officers did not damage it.

Officer Evans searched Flowal's luggage and found five bundles of what appeared to be narcotics. Approximately a minute later, Lieutenant Blackburn returned to the terminal and arrested Flowal. Flowal was indicted on June 12, 1996, for possession with intent to distribute "approximately five point two (5.2) kilograms of cocaine." Flowal pled not guilty, but a jury found Flowal guilty of possession with intent to distribute cocaine. On appeal, Flowal argued that under the U.S. Supreme Court decision in *Bond v. United States*, the government's search of his luggage at an airport terminal violated his Fourth Amendment rights. Should his appeal be granted on this basis? *United States v. Flowal*, 234 F.3d 932 (6th Cir. 2000).

Read the court opinion at:

laws.findlaw.com/6th/00a0409p.html

---

passengers or bus employees will, as a matter of course, feel the bag in an exploratory manner. But this is exactly what the agent did here. We therefore hold that the agent's physical manipulation of petitioner's bag violated the Fourth Amendment. 529 U.S. at 338–39, 120 S.Ct. at 1465, 146 L.Ed.2d at 370.

Note that the *Bond* case does not prevent law enforcement officers from boarding buses or other means of public transportation and talking to passengers. Nor does it prevent officers from asking passengers for consent to search their belongings. The *Bond* case merely holds that it is illegal for a law enforcement officer to squeeze a passenger's belongings absent at least reasonable suspicion to believe a container has criminal evidence within it.

www.jus.state.nc.us/NCJA/jl.htm
Discussion of *Bond v. United States* with advice for law enforcement officers from the North Carolina Justice Academy

🔑 Key Points

20. *Miranda* warnings are not required before questioning in connection with an ordinary *Terry*-type investigative stop or an ordinary traffic stop.

21. A law enforcement officer may detain property for a brief time if the officer has a reasonable, articulable suspicion that the property contains contraband or evidence of criminal activity. The officer may not search

the property without a search warrant but may subject the property to a properly conducted "canine sniff."

22. A law enforcement officer's physical manipulation of a person's belongings absent at least reasonable suspicion that a container has criminal evidence within it is an unreasonable search under the Fourth Amendment.

Summary

A law enforcement officer may intrude on a person's freedom of action and stop the person for purposes of investigating possible criminal behavior even though the officer does not have probable cause to arrest the person. A stop is the least intrusive type of seizure of a person governed by the Fourth Amendment. Under that amendment, a person has been seized only if, in view of all the circumstances surrounding the incident, a reasonable person would have believed that he or she was not free to leave.

The officer making a stop must be able to justify the stop with specific facts and circumstances indicating possibly criminal behavior. This is sometimes called "reasonable, articulable suspicion of criminal activity." The investigative detention must last no longer than necessary to achieve its purpose, and the investigative methods used must be the least intrusive means reasonably available to verify or dispel the officer's suspicion. An officer who has lawfully stopped a motor vehicle may order both the driver and passengers out of the vehicle pending completion of the stop.

A law enforcement officer may, upon less than probable cause, intrude on a person's privacy for purposes of conducting a protective search for weapons, also called a frisk. A frisk is not automatically authorized whenever there is a stop. The officer

must be able to demonstrate, by specific facts and circumstances, reasonable suspicion that the person might be armed and dangerous. Furthermore, the frisk must be very strictly limited to a protective purpose and, therefore, will initially consist of a patdown search of outer clothing. If a weaponlike object is detected, or if a nonthreatening object's identity as contraband is immediately apparent to the officer's sense of touch, the officer may reach inside the clothing or pocket and seize the object. Evidence of crime seized as the result of a properly conducted frisk will be admissible in court.

The standard to be applied for both the stop and the frisk is whether the action taken by the officer was reasonable at its inception and limited in scope to what was minimally necessary for the accomplishment of the lawful purpose. This standard was developed by the U.S. Supreme Court as a result of a careful balancing of the needs of the police to prevent and investigate crime and to protect themselves and others from danger against the constitutional rights of individuals to their privacy, security, and freedom of action. Achieving an equitable balance in the infinite variety of encounters between police and citizens requires a careful consideration of the totality of the facts and circumstances.

Key Holdings from Major Cases

Terry v. Ohio (1968). "It is quite plain that the Fourth Amendment governs 'seizures' of the person which do not eventuate in a trip to the station house and prosecution for crime—'arrests' in traditional terminology. It must be recognized that whenever a police officer accosts an individual and restrains his freedom to walk away, he has 'seized' that person. And it is nothing less than sheer torture of the English language to suggest that a careful exploration of the outer surfaces of a person's clothing all

over his or her body in an attempt to find weapons is not a 'search.' Moreover, it is simply fantastic to urge that such a procedure performed in public by a policeman while the citizen stands helpless, perhaps facing a wall with his hands raised, is a 'petty indignity.' It is a serious intrusion upon the sanctity of the person, which may inflict great indignity and arouse strong resentment, and it is not to be undertaken lightly." 392 U.S. 1, 16–17, 88 S.Ct. 1868, 1877, 20 L.Ed.2d 889, 903.

"Obviously not all personal intercourse between policemen and citizens involves 'seizures' of persons. Only when the officer, by means of physical force or show of authority, has in some way restrained the liberty of a citizen may we conclude that a 'seizure' has occurred." 392 U.S. at 19 n.16, 88 S.Ct. at 1879 n.16, 20 L.Ed.2d at 905 n.16.

"[W]e deal here with an entire rubric of police conduct—necessarily swift action based upon the on-the-spot observations of the officer on the beat—which historically has not been, and as a practical matter could not be, subjected to the warrant procedure. Instead, the conduct involved in this case must be tested by the Fourth Amendment's general proscription against unreasonable searches and seizures." 392 U.S. at 20, 88 S.Ct. at 1879, 20 L.Ed.2d at 905.

"[I]n justifying the particular intrusion the police officer must be able to point to specific and articulable facts which, taken together with rational inferences from those facts, reasonably warrant that intrusion." 392 U.S. at 21, 88 S.Ct. at 1880, 20 L.Ed.2d at 906.

The police officer's decision to initiate a stop will be judged against the following objective standard: "[W]ould the facts available to the officer at the moment of the seizure or the search 'warrant a man of reasonable caution in the belief' that the action taken was appropriate?" 392 U.S. at 21–22, 88 S.Ct. at 1880, 20 L.Ed.2d at 906.

"[I]t is this interest [crime prevention and detection] which underlies the recognition that a police officer may in appropriate circumstances and in an appropriate manner approach a person for purposes of investigating possibly criminal behavior even though there is no probable cause to make an arrest." 392 U.S. at 22, 88 S.Ct. at 1880, 20 L.Ed.2d at 906–07.

"Certainly it would be unreasonable to require that police officers take unnecessary risks in the performance of their duties. American criminals have a long tradition of armed violence, and every year in this country many law enforcement officers are killed in the line of duty, and thousands more are wounded." 392 U.S. at 23, 88 S.Ct. at 1881, 20 L.Ed.2d at 907.

"[W]e cannot blind ourselves to the need for law enforcement officers to protect themselves and other prospective victims of violence in situations where they may lack probable cause for an arrest." 392 U.S. at 24, 88 S.Ct. at 1881, 20 L.Ed.2d at 907–08.

"Even a limited search of the outer clothing for weapons constitutes a severe, though brief, intrusion upon cherished personal security, and it must surely be an annoying, frightening, and perhaps humiliating experience." 392 U.S. at 24–25, 88 S.Ct. at 1881–82, 20 L.Ed.2d at 908.

"Our evaluation of the proper balance that has to be struck in this type of case leads us to conclude that there must be a narrowly drawn authority to permit a reasonable search for weapons for the protection of the police officer, where he has reason to believe that he is dealing with an armed and danger-

ous individual, regardless of whether he has probable cause to arrest the individual for a crime." 392 U.S. at 27, 88 S.Ct. at 1883, 20 L.Ed.2d at 909.

The issue in determining an officer's authority to frisk is "whether a reasonably prudent man in the circumstances would be warranted in the belief that his safety or that of others was in danger." 392 U.S. at 27, 88 S.Ct. at 1883, 20 L.Ed.2d at 909.

An officer must be able to justify a search or frisk of a person by pointing to specific facts and "specific reasonable inferences which he is entitled to draw from the facts in light of his experience." 392 U.S. at 27, 88 S.Ct. at 1883, 20 L.Ed.2d at 909.

"[W]here a police officer observes unusual conduct which leads him reasonably to conclude in light of his experience that criminal activity may be afoot and that the persons with whom he is dealing may be armed and presently dangerous, where in the course of investigating this behavior he identifies himself as a policeman and makes reasonable inquiries, and where nothing in the initial stages of the encounter serves to dispel his reasonable fear for his own or other's safety, he is entitled for the protection of himself and others in the area to conduct a carefully limited search of the outer clothing of such persons in an attempt to discover weapons which might be used to assault him." 392 U.S. at 30, 88 S.Ct. at 1884–85, 20 L.Ed.2d at 911.

Sibron v. New York (1968). "The inference that persons who talk to narcotics addicts are engaged in criminal traffic in narcotics is simply not the sort of reasonable inference required to support an intrusion by the police upon an individual's personal security." 392 U.S. 40, 62, 88 S.Ct. 1889, 1902, 20 L.Ed.2d 917, 934.

United States v. Mendenhall (1980). "[A] person has been 'seized' within the meaning of the Fourth Amendment only if, in view of all of the circumstances surrounding the incident, a reasonable person would have believed that he was not free to leave. Examples of circumstances that might indicate a seizure even where the person did not attempt to leave, would be the threatening presence of several officers, the display of a weapon by an officer, some physical touching of the person of the citizen, or the use of language or tone of voice indicating that compliance with the officer's request might be compelled. . . . In the absence of some such evidence, otherwise inoffensive contact between a member of the public and the police cannot, as a matter of law, amount to a seizure of that person." 446 U.S. 544, 554–55, 100 S.Ct. 1870, 1877, 64 L.Ed.2d 497, 509.

California v. Hodari D. (1991). "*Mendenhall* establishes that the test for existence of a 'show of authority' is an objective one: not whether the citizen perceived that he was being ordered to restrict his movement, but whether the officer's words and actions would have conveyed that to a reasonable person." 499 U.S. 621, 628, 111 S.Ct. 1547, 1551, 113 L.Ed.2d 690, 698.

Michigan v. Chesternut (1988). "The [*Mendenhall*] test is necessarily imprecise, because it is designed to assess the coercive effect of police conduct, taken as a whole, rather than to focus on particular details of that conduct in isolation. Moreover, what constitutes a restraint on liberty prompting a person to conclude that he is not free to 'leave' will vary, not only with the particular police conduct at issue, but also with the setting in which the conduct occurs." 486 U.S. 567, 573, 108 S.Ct. 1975, 1979, 100 L.Ed.2d 565, 572.

"While the very presence of a police car driving parallel to a running pedestrian could be somewhat intimidating, this kind of police presence does not, standing alone, constitute a seizure." 486 U.S. at 575, 108 S.Ct. at 1980, 100 L.Ed.2d at 573.

Florida v. Bostick (1991). "[N]o seizure occurs when police ask questions of an individual, ask to examine the individual's identification, and request consent to search his or her luggage—so long as the officers do not convey a message that compliance with their requests is required." 501 U.S. 429, 437, 111 S.Ct. 2382, 2388, 115 L.Ed.2d 389, 400.

"[I]n order to determine whether a particular encounter constitutes a seizure, a court must consider all the circumstances surrounding the encounter to determine whether the police conduct would have communicated to a reasonable person that the person was not free to decline the officers' requests or otherwise terminate the encounter. That rule applies to encounters that take place on a city street or in an airport lobby, and it applies equally to encounters on a bus." 501 U.S. at 439–40, 111 S.Ct. at 2389, 115 L.Ed.2d at 401–02.

Brower v. County of Inyo (1989). "[A] Fourth Amendment seizure does not occur whenever there is a governmentally caused termination of an individual's freedom of movement . . . nor even whenever there is a governmentally caused and governmentally desired termination of an individual's freedom of movement . . . but only when there is a governmental termination of freedom of movement through means intentionally applied." 489 U.S. 593, 596–97, 109 S.Ct. 1378, 1381, 103 L.Ed.2d 628, 635.

United States v. Sokolow (1989). Reasonable suspicion is "considerably less than proof of wrongdoing by a preponderance of the evidence" [and] "is obviously less demanding than that for probable cause." 490 U.S. 1, 7, 109 S.Ct. 1581, 1585, 104 L.Ed.2d 1, 10.

United States v. Hensley (1985). "[W]here police have been unable to locate a person suspected of involvement in a past crime, the ability to briefly stop that person, ask questions, or check identification in the absence of probable cause promotes the strong government interest in solving crimes and bringing offenders to justice. Restraining police action until after probable cause is obtained would not only hinder the investigation, but might also enable the suspect to flee in the interim and to remain at large. Particularly in the context of felonies or crimes involving a threat to public safety, it is in the public interest that the crime be solved and the suspect detained as promptly as possible. The law enforcement interests at stake in these circumstances outweigh the individual's interest to be free of a stop and detention that is no more extensive than permissible in the investigation of imminent or ongoing crimes." 469 U.S. 221, 229, 105 S.Ct. 675, 681, 83 L.Ed.2d 604, 612.

"[I]f a flyer or bulletin has been issued on the basis of articulable facts supporting a reasonable suspicion that the wanted person has committed an offense, then reliance on that flyer or bulletin justifies a stop to check identification . . . to pose questions to the person, or to detain the person briefly while attempting to obtain further information." 469 U.S. at 232, 105 S.Ct. at 683–84, 83 L.Ed.2d at 614.

Alabama v. White (1990). "*Gates* made clear . . . that those factors that had been considered critical under *Aguilar* and *Spinelli*—an informant's 'veracity,' 'reliability,' and 'basis of knowledge'—remain 'highly relevant in determining the value of his report.' . . . These factors are also relevant in the reasonable suspicion context, although allowance must be made in applying them for the lesser showing required to meet that standard." 496 U.S. 325, 328–29, 110 S.Ct. 2412, 2415, 110 L.Ed.2d 301, 308.

"Reasonable suspicion is a less demanding standard than probable cause not only in the sense that reasonable suspicion can be established with information that is different in quantity or content than that required to establish probable cause, but also in the sense that reasonable suspicion can arise from information that is less reliable than that required to show probable cause. . . . Reasonable suspicion, like probable cause, is dependent upon both the content of information possessed by police and its degree of reliability. Both factors—quantity and quality are considered in the 'totality of the circumstances—the whole picture,' . . . that must be taken into account when evaluating whether there is reasonable suspicion. Thus, if a tip has a relatively low degree of reliability, more information will be required to establish the requisite quantum of suspicion than would be required if the tip were more reliable. The *Gates* Court applied its totality of the circumstances approach in this manner, taking into account the facts known to the officers from personal observation, and giving the anonymous tip the weight it deserved in light of its indicia of reliability as established through independent police work. The same approach applies in the reasonable suspicion context, the only difference being the level of suspicion that must be established. Contrary to the court below, we conclude that when the officers stopped the respondent, the anonymous tip had been sufficiently corroborated to furnish reasonable suspicion that respondent was engaged in criminal activity and that the investigative stop therefore did not violate the Fourth Amendment." 496 U.S. at 330–31, 110 S.Ct. at 2416, 110 L.Ed.2d at 309.

Florida v. J.L. (2000). An anonymous tip that a person is carrying a gun is, without more, insufficient to justify a police officer's stop and frisk of that person. 529 U.S. 266, 120 S.Ct. 1375, 146 L.Ed.2d 254.

"An accurate description of a subject's readily observable location and appearance is of course reliable in this limited sense:

It will help the police correctly identify the person whom the tipster means to accuse. Such a tip, however, does not show that the tipster has knowledge of concealed criminal activity. The reasonable suspicion here at issue requires that a tip be reliable in its assertion of illegality, not just in its tendency to identify a determinate person." 529 U.S. at 272, 120 S.Ct. at 1379, 146 L.Ed.2d at 261.

Florida v. Royer (1983). "[A]n investigative detention must be temporary and last no longer than is necessary to effectuate the purpose of the stop. Similarly, the investigative methods employed should be the least intrusive means reasonably available to verify or dispel the officer's suspicion in a short period of time. . . . It is the State's burden to demonstrate that the seizure it seeks to justify on the basis of a reasonable suspicion was sufficiently limited in scope and duration to satisfy the conditions of an investigative seizure." 460 U.S. 491, 500, 103 S.Ct. 1319, 1325, 75 L.Ed.2d 229, 238.

Pennsylvania v. Mimms (1977). The additional intrusion of ordering the driver of a lawfully stopped vehicle out of the vehicle "can only be described as *de minimis*. The driver is being asked to expose to view very little more of his person than is already exposed. The police have already lawfully decided that the driver shall be briefly detained; the only question is whether he shall spend that period sitting in the driver's seat of his car or standing alongside it. Not only is the insistence of the police on the latter choice not a 'serious intrusion upon the sanctity of the person,' but it hardly rises to the level of a petty indignity. . . . What is at most a mere inconvenience cannot prevail when balanced against legitimate concerns for the officer's safety." 434 U.S. 106, 111, 98 S.Ct. 330, 333, 54 L.Ed.2d 331, 337.

Maryland v. Wilson (1997). "[A]n officer making a traffic stop may order passengers to get out of the car pending completion of the stop." 519 U.S. 408, 415, 117 S.Ct. 882, 886, 137 L.Ed.2d 41, 48.

United States v. Sharpe (1985). "In assessing whether a detention is too long in duration to be justified as an investigative stop, we consider it appropriate to examine whether the police diligently pursued a means of investigation that was likely to confirm or dispel their suspicions quickly, during which time it was necessary to detain the defendant. . . . A court making this assessment should take care to consider whether the police are acting in a swiftly developing situation and in such cases the court should not indulge in unrealistic second-guessing. . . . The question is not simply whether some other alternative was available, but whether the police acted unreasonably in failing to recognize or to pursue it." 470 U.S. 675, 686–87, 105 S.Ct. 1568, 1575–76, 84 L.Ed.2d 605, 615–16.

Graham v. Connor (1989). "The calculus of reasonableness must embody allowance for the fact that police officers are often forced to make split-second judgments—in circumstances that are tense, uncertain, and rapidly evolving—about the amount of force that is necessary in a particular situation." 490 U.S. 386, 396–97, 109 S.Ct. 1865, 1872, 104 L.Ed.2d 443, 455–56.

"[T]he 'reasonableness' inquiry in an excessive force case is an objective one: the question is whether the officers' actions are 'objectively reasonable' in light of the facts and circumstances confronting them, without regard to their underlying intent or motivation." 490 U.S. at 397, 109 S.Ct. at 1872, 104 L.Ed.2d at 456.

Michigan v. Long (1983). "[T]he search of the passenger compartment of an automobile, limited to those areas in which a weapon may be placed or hidden, is permissible if the police officer possesses a reasonable belief based on 'specific and articulable facts which, taken together with the rational inferences from those facts, reasonably warrant' the officers in believing that the suspect is dangerous and the suspect may gain immediate control of weapons." 463 U.S. 1032, 1049, 103 S.Ct. 3469, 3480, 77 L.Ed.2d 1201, 1220.

"If, while conducting a legitimate *Terry* search of the interior of the automobile, the officer should . . . discover contraband other than weapons, he clearly cannot be required to ignore the contraband, and the Fourth Amendment does not require its suppression in such circumstances." 463 U.S. at 1050, 103 S.Ct. at 3481, 77 L.Ed.2d at 1220.

Illinois v. Wardlow (2000). "[N]ervous, evasive behavior is a pertinent factor in determining reasonable suspicion. . . . Headlong flight—wherever it occurs—is the consummate act of evasion: it is not necessarily indicative of wrongdoing, but it is certainly suggestive of such." 528 U.S. 119, 124, 120 S. Ct. 673, 676, 145 L. Ed. 2d 570, 576.

"An individual's presence in an area of expected criminal activity, standing alone, is not enough to support a reasonable, particularized suspicion that the person is committing a crime. . . . But officers are not required to ignore the relevant characteristics of a location in determining whether the circumstances are sufficiently suspicious to warrant further investigation. Accordingly, we have previously noted the fact that the stop occurred in a 'high crime area' among the relevant contextual considerations in a *Terry* analysis." 528 U.S. 119, 124, 120 S.Ct. 673, 676, 145 L.Ed.2d 570, 576.

Whren v. United States (1996). A motorist may be constitutionally stopped upon probable cause that the motorist has violated a traffic law regardless of the officer's subjective intent to stop the motorist upon suspicion of a more serious offense. 517 U.S. 806, 116 S.Ct. 1769, 135 L.Ed.2d 89.

Delaware v. Prouse (1979). "[E]xcept in those situations in which there is at least articulable and reasonable suspicion that a motorist is unlicensed or that an automobile is not registered, or that either the vehicle or an occupant is otherwise subject to seizure for violation of law, stopping an automobile and detaining the driver in order to check his driver's license and the registration of the automobile are unreasonable under the Fourth

Amendment." 440 U.S. 648, 663, 99 S.Ct. 1391, 1401, 59 L.Ed.2d 660, 673.

California v. Beheler (1983). "Although the circumstances of each case must certainly influence a determination of whether a suspect is 'in custody' for purposes of receiving *Miranda* protection, the ultimate inquiry is simply whether there is a 'formal arrest or restraint on freedom of movement' of the degree associated with a formal arrest." 463 U.S. 1121, 1125, 103 S.Ct. 3517, 3520, 77 L.Ed.2d 1275, 1279.

Smith v. Ohio (1990). "Although the Fourth Amendment may permit the detention for a brief period of property on the basis of only 'reasonable, articulable suspicion' that it contains contraband or evidence of criminal activity . . . it proscribes—except in certain well-defined circumstances—the search of that property unless accomplished pursuant to judicial warrant issued upon probable cause." 494 U.S. 541, 542, 110 S.Ct. 1288, 1289, 108 L.Ed.2d 464, 467.

United States v. Place (1983). "The context of a particular law enforcement practice, of course, may affect the determination whether a brief intrusion on Fourth Amendment interests on less than probable cause is essential to effective criminal investigation. Because of the inherently transient nature of drug courier activity at airports, allowing police to make brief investigative stops of persons at airports on reasonable suspicion of drug-trafficking substantially enhances the likelihood that police will be able to prevent the flow of narcotics into distribution channels." 462 U.S. 696, 704, 103 S.Ct. 2637, 2643, 77 L.Ed.2d 110, 119.

"[W]hen an officer's observations lead him reasonably to believe that a traveler is carrying luggage that contains narcotics, the principles of *Terry* and its progeny would permit the officer to detain the luggage briefly to investigate the circumstances that aroused his suspicion, provided that the investigative detention is properly limited in scope." 462 U.S. at 706, 103 S.Ct. at 2644, 77 L.Ed.2d at 120.

"Although the 90-minute detention of respondent's luggage is sufficient to render the seizure unreasonable, the violation was exacerbated by the failure of the agents to accurately inform respondent of the place to which they were transporting his luggage, of the length of time he might be dispossessed, and of what arrangements would be made for return of the luggage if the investigation dispelled the suspicion. In short, we hold that the detention of respondent's luggage in this case went beyond the narrow authority possessed by police to detain briefly luggage reasonably suspected to contain narcotics." 462 U.S. at 710, 103 S.Ct. at 2646, 77 L.Ed.2d at 122.

United States v. Van Leeuwen (1970). "The rule of our decision certainly is not that first-class mail can be detained 29 hours after mailing in order to obtain the search warrant needed for its inspection. We only hold that on the facts of this case—the nature of the mailings, their suspicious character, the fact that there were two packages going to separate destinations, the unavoidable delay in contacting the more distant of the two destinations, the distance between Mt. Vernon and Seattle—a 29-hour delay between the mailings and the service of the warrant cannot be said to be 'unreasonable' within the meaning of the Fourth Amendment. Detention for this limited time was, indeed, the prudent act rather than letting the packages enter the mails and then, in case the initial suspicions were confirmed, trying to locate them en route and enlisting the help of distant federal officials in serving the warrant." 397 U.S. 249, 253, 90 S.Ct. 1029, 1032–33, 25 L.Ed.2d 282, 286.

Bond v. United States (2000). A law enforcement officer's physical manipulation of a person's belongings absent at least reasonable suspicion that a container has criminal evidence within it is an unreasonable search under the Fourth Amendment. 529 U.S. 334, 120 S.Ct. 1462, 146 L.Ed.2d 365.

Review and Discussion Questions

1. Name some of the factors that might distinguish a *Terry*-type investigative stop from a seizure tantamount to an arrest.

2. In determining whether he or she has a reasonable suspicion that criminal activity is afoot, must an officer have a particular crime in mind?

3. Is less evidence required to support an investigative stop for a suspected violent crime than for a minor misdemeanor?

4. Can a lawfully stopped suspect be transported by the police to a crime scene for identification by victims or witnesses?

Or would this action convert the stop into a seizure tantamount to arrest?

5. How does the indicia of reliability test for evaluating an informant's tip in the stop-and-frisk situation differ from the totality-of-the-circumstances test of the *Gates* case discussed in Chapter 6? Why should there be different tests?

6. Must there be an immediate possibility of criminal activity to justify a *Terry*-type investigative stop, or would a possibility of criminal activity at some time in the future suffice?

7. Assuming that a frisk of a person is warranted, how extensive a search is permitted? Can the officer look for razor blades, nails, vials of acid, or Mace containers? Can the officer look into briefcases, shopping bags, purses, hatbands, and other containers?

8. Should an officer conducting a roadblock-type stop to check licenses and registrations be allowed to order every driver stopped out of his or her vehicle? What factors might provide justification to frisk a driver or passengers in this situation?

9. Assuming that a law enforcement officer reasonably believes that a suspect is dangerous and may gain immediate control of weapons from an automobile, how extensive a protective search of the automobile may be made? May the officer look into suitcases and other containers?

10. If law enforcement officers have a reasonable suspicion that a package contains contraband, does the length of time that they may detain the package for investigation depend upon whether a person is carrying the package?

Real-Life Fact Situations

1 On June 29, 1999, at about 10:00 P.M., three Colorado Springs police officers responded to a disturbance at a mobile home park in the 3600 block of North Cascade. A neighbor had reported that men and women were yelling and screaming at that address. When they arrived at the scene, officers found a man heavily intoxicated, yelling and knocking on the door of the residence where the disturbance was reported. They placed the intoxicated man in one of the police cars. The officers then knocked on the residence door of the defendant, Kenneth Garcia (Garcia), to inquire about the reported disturbance. Garcia stepped approximately ten feet outside the residence to speak with the officers and left the door open behind him. The officers questioned Garcia. He denied there was any disturbance.

As the officers spoke with Garcia, they saw a small pipe on the ground next to him of a type used for smoking methamphetamine or crack cocaine. They also noticed a picture of a marijuana plant on the wall inside the residence.

The officers placed Garcia in the back seat of a different police car from where the intoxicated man was sitting. Officers testified at the suppression hearing that they had placed the intoxicated individual and Garcia in two separate police cars because they didn't know what was happening inside, if there are or were other individuals that were yelling—officer safety purposes. Officer testimony about Garcia's detention also included the following:

Q. And is there any reason that you could tell the Court why you decided to put him in the car versus having him stand outside?

A. Officer safety issues, that's the only reason he was in the patrol car.

The officers did not handcuff Garcia when they placed him in the police car, but he could not open the car doors from the inside. A cage separated Garcia from an officer who was sitting in the front seat of the police car. This officer told Garcia that he would be held in the police car during the investigation, and he asked Garcia whether there was anyone in the residence. Garcia replied that two women were inside.

While Garcia sat in the police car, the two women exited the residence. One of the women told the officers that Garcia offered her a blast from his crack pipe. Based on the pipe, the picture of the marijuana plant inside Garcia's residence, and the statement that Garcia had offered the woman crack to smoke, the officers decided to ask Garcia for consent to search his residence.

The officer who was sitting in the front of the police car with Garcia filled out the top portion of a search waiver form and handed it to him. Garcia read the search waiver aloud to the officer, then signed the bottom portion. The officers searched Garcia's residence and found several items of drug paraphernalia and crack cocaine. They then told Garcia that he was under arrest.

The prosecution charged Garcia with one count of possession of a schedule II controlled substance and one count of possession of drug paraphernalia. Garcia filed a motion to suppress evidence based on an illegal arrest. Should the motion to suppress be granted? *People v. Garcia,* 11 P.3d 449 (Colo. 2000).

Read the court opinion at:
www.cobar.org/coappcts/sc2000/sc1023c.htm

2 On September 22, 1995, a Greyhound bus on which Appellee was a passenger approached the tollbooth at the Delaware Water Gap interchange while traveling westbound on Interstate 80. Amid the traffic at the tollbooth, Agent Ronald Paret of the Pennsylvania Office of Attorney General and Officer Kirk Schwartz of the Delaware Water Gap Police Department approached the bus and requested that the driver pull to the side of the road after paying the toll. Both officers were wearing attire indicating that they were law enforcement officials. After paying the toll, the bus driver pulled over.

Agent Paret asked the driver if he could see the passengers' tickets. A review revealed one "quick turn" ticket from Cleveland to New York City and back, which indicated that the purchaser spent only about eight hours in New York. Agent Paret then boarded the bus, accompanied by Officer Schwartz. Officer Schwartz secured the bathroom on the bus, which revealed nothing, while Agent Paret approached Appellee, who had the other half of the quick turn ticket. Agent Paret asked Appellee for identification to which Appellee responded that he had none. Agent Paret then asked Appellee if he had any bags. Appellee stated that he did not.

The officers went on to match every bag on the bus with a passenger except for one, which Appellee then claimed as his. Agent Paret and Officer Schwartz then approached Appellee together and asked if they could search the bag. Appellee responded "okay," and Agent Paret located crack cocaine in the bag. Appellee was then arrested. Appellee filed a motion to suppress the evidence obtained by Officer Schwartz and Agent Paret. Should the motion to suppress be granted? *Commonwealth v. Polo,* 759 A.2d 372 (Pa. 2000).

Read the court opinion at:
caselaw.lp.findlaw.com/data2/pennsylvaniastatecases/supreme/j107-98mo.pdf

3 Officers Carlos Torres and Steven Stretmater of the United States Secret Service Uniform Division were stopped at the intersection of Columbia Road and Ontario Road, N.W., when they noticed appellant in the 1700 block of Columbia Road, a block Torres described as an "open air drug market," and where he had previously made drug-related arrests. They observed appellant and a homeless man engaged in what appeared to be a narcotics transaction. Torres witnessed appellant take two small plastic-wrapped objects from inside a larger piece of plastic in his cupped left hand and hand them to the homeless man, who inspected the objects. Torres testified that he had stopped this homeless person earlier that day after receiving a complaint that he was smoking narcotics in the 3100 block of 16th Street, N.W., and that the person had possessed a crack pipe at that time.

The officers proceeded through the light and made a U-turn when it was safe to do so. By the time they stopped, appellant had walked some distance along the street, and the homeless man had gone down an alley. The officers got out of their car and Officer Torres told appellant he wanted to talk to him. Appellant stopped. Officer Torres said: "Come over here." Appellant turned toward the officer and put his hands in his pants pockets, but did not come toward the officers. Officer Torres told appellant twice to take his hands out of his pockets, based on what Torres testified was a concern for his safety since appellant could have had a weapon in his pocket. Appellant eventually took his right hand out of his pocket. Torres then told appellant, in English and Spanish, to remove his other hand, and when appellant did not respond, the officers grabbed appellant and pulled him over to the police cruiser. After Torres again told appellant to take his left hand out of his pocket, appellant took his clenched left fist out of his pocket. The offi-

cers put appellant's hands on the car, and Torres told appellant to open his fist. At some point, a small bag of cocaine fell out of appellant's hand. Thereafter, appellant opened his left hand, revealing several small plastic wrappings containing a white-colored substance wrapped in a larger piece of clear plastic wrapping, and immediately stated that he had just purchased them and they were for his personal use. In total, appellant had in his possession thirty-three small packages of what tests later showed was crack cocaine. Should the appellant's motion to suppress the cocaine be granted? *Reyes v. United States,* 758 A.2d 35 (D.C. App. 2000).

Read the court opinion at:
www.dcbar.org/dcca/pdf/97cf1210.pdf

4 On the afternoon of March 4, 1998, in Laurens, South Carolina, Kenneth Burton was standing at a pay telephone outside the Green Street Mini-Mart when he was approached by four police officers who were in the area serving outstanding warrants. When one of the officers, Detective Tracy Burke, identified himself as a policeman and requested identification from Burton, Burton did not respond. The officers repeated their request several times, but Burton remained mute. The officers then asked Burton to remove his right hand from his coat pocket. When Burton failed to do so, the officers repeated their request. Burton still did not respond.

While the other officers remained facing Burton, Officer Burke moved behind Burton, reached around him, thrust his hand into Burton's coat, and grabbed his right hand. Burton resisted, and a struggle ensued, during which the officers wrestled Burton to the ground. While on the ground, Officer Burke claims that Burton "raised his left side of his body up" and pointed a handgun at Officer Burke, who was lying on top of him. Burton squeezed the trigger three or four times, but the gun was jammed and did not fire. The officers subdued Burton and removed the weapon.

Burton was indicted for unlawful possession of a firearm by a felon, in violation of 18 U.S.C. § 922(g). He moved to suppress the firearm as the fruit of an illegal search. At the evidentiary hearing before the district court, Officer Burke testified that at the time he approached Burton, he had no reason to suspect that Burton was engaged in criminal activity, but Burton's refusal to remove his hand from his coat made Officer Burke feel "uneasy about our safety being there with him with his hand and no response, you know, towards us." Officer Burke thought that Burton "possibly had a weapon in his pocket or in his hand or in his coat that he was holding on to. It could have been narcotics or maybe [an] alcoholic beverage or something." Should Burton's motion to suppress the firearm be granted? *United States v. Burton,* 228 F.3d 524 (4th Cir. 2000).

Read the court opinion at:
caselaw.lp.findlaw.com/scripts/getcase.pl?court=4th&navby=case&no=994465P

5 At 2:53 A.M., on August 17, 1998, Orono Police Officer William Sheehan watched a car drive into the Med Now parking lot and stop. Med Now is an emergency care medical facility that only operates during the day. Sheehan was concerned that the occupants of the car might be looking for emergency medical treatment. He followed the car into the lot, and parked about ten feet behind it. He did not activate his blue lights or his siren and did not block the vehicle's exit from the parking lot.

Upon approaching the car, Sheehan spoke briefly with the driver and asked if everything was okay. The driver, Tanner Gulick, responded that everything was fine and asked how far it was to Portland. Sheehan informed Gulick that the trip would take approximately two hours. He then asked to see Gulick's driver's license. Sheehan testified that, at the point that he requested Gulick's license, he was no longer concerned that Gulick or his passenger had a medical emergency.

Gulick did not have his license with him. Suspicious of Gulick's explanation for the missing license, Sheehan obtained Gulick's name and date of birth and checked on the status of Gulick's license to operate in Maine. Upon learning that Gulick's license was suspended, Sheehan issued him a summons for operating after suspension.

Gulick moved to suppress all evidence resulting from Sheehan's request for his license, pursuant to Rule 41A of the Maine Rules of Criminal Procedure, claiming that Sheehan lacked a reasonable articulable suspicion to justify detaining Gulick. Should the motion to suppress be granted? *State v. Gulick,* 759 A.2d 1085 (Me. 2000).

Read the court opinion at:
www.courts.state.me.us/00me170A.html

6 On February 12, 1997, at approximately noon, Sergeant Herman Badger of the New Haven police department received an anonymous telephone call from a citizen complaining about a drug transaction taking place on the steps of a church at 246 Dixwell Avenue. Badger was stationed at the police substation on Charles Street around the corner from the church when he received the call. The caller indicated that two black males, one taller than the other, were selling drugs. The caller also described the color of the jackets that the two individuals were wearing. The caller was excited and upset by the fact that drug dealing was occurring on the church steps. Badger was familiar with the area and testified that it was an area known for frequent drug transactions.

Badger contacted Officer Richard Zasciurinskas by radio and dispatched him in his patrol car to the area of the church to look for the suspects described in the anonymous tip. At the time that Zasciurinskas was dispatched, he was a very short distance from the area in a marked patrol car. Badger, accompanied by Officer Samuel Bagley, left the substation and walked approximately 100 to 200 feet to the intersection of Charles Street and Dixwell Avenue. All three officers were in full uniform. Just prior to reaching the intersection, Badger and Bagley observed two black males standing in front of the church. One male was taller than the other, and their jackets matched the description given by the caller. The officers did not observe any conduct indicating that a drug transaction was taking place. The two men, however, fled when they saw the officers approach.

The two men walked across Dixwell Avenue and proceeded north, away from the officers. Badger radioed Zasciurinskas and ordered him to stop the two individuals. Badger and Bagley then proceeded across Dixwell Avenue and followed the two men at a distance of approximately thirty to fifty feet. Zasciurinskas, who was traveling south on Dixwell Avenue, drove his car across the northbound lane of traffic in front of the suspects and partially blocked traffic. As Zasciurinskas exited his vehicle, the two suspects reacted by turning and proceeding south on Dixwell Avenue. Zasciurinskas yelled to them to stop. Zasciurinskas then observed one of them drop a bundle on the ground.

Zasciurinskas picked up the bundle, which consisted of nine glassine envelopes. On the basis of his almost twenty years of police experience, Zasciurinskas determined that the bags contained a possible narcotic substance. Badger and Bagley were about eight to ten feet from the two suspects, and Zasciurinskas was about ten to fifteen feet on the other side of them.

The two men were detained by Badger and Bagley, and transported to the police substation. There, the contents of one of the nine envelopes tested positive for the presence of heroin. The defendant was placed under arrest. A search of the defendant incident to the arrest revealed a single plastic bag containing a white powder also believed to be a narcotic substance. At the substation, the defendant indicated that the single bag of cocaine was for his personal use. Should the defendant's motion to suppress the evidence seized be granted? *State v. Hammond,* 759 A.2d 133 (Conn.App. 2000).

Read the court opinion at:
www.jud.state.ct.us/external/supapp/AROap/ap542.pdf

Chapter 8

Search Incident to Arrest

Outline

Chimel v. California

Another important exception to the Fourth Amendment warrant requirement is a **search incident to arrest.** Since 1969, the law of search incident to arrest has been controlled by the U.S. Supreme Court case of *Chimel v. California.* In that case, law enforcement officers arrived at the defendant's home with a warrant for his arrest for the burglary of a coin shop. The defendant was not at home, but his wife let the officers in to wait for him. When the defendant arrived, the officers handed him the warrant and asked whether they could look around. He objected, but the officers searched the entire house anyway on the basis of the lawful arrest. The officers found coins and other items that were later used in court to obtain a conviction against the defendant.

The U.S. Supreme Court found the search of the entire house unreasonable.

> When an arrest is made, it is reasonable for the arresting officer to search the person arrested in order to remove any weapons that the latter might seek to use in order to resist arrest or effect his escape. Otherwise, the officer's safety might well be endangered, and the arrest itself frustrated. In addition, it is entirely reasonable for the arresting officer to search for and seize any evidence on the arrestee's person in order to prevent its concealment or destruction. And the area into which an arrestee might reach in order to grab a weapon or evidentiary items must, of course, be governed by a like rule. A gun on a table or in a drawer in front of one who is arrested can be as dangerous to the arresting officer as one concealed in the clothing of the person arrested. There is ample justification, therefore, for a search of the arrestee's person and the area "within his immediate control"—construing that phrase to mean the area from within which he might gain possession of a weapon or destructible evidence.
>
> There is no comparable justification, however, for routinely searching any room other than that in which an arrest occurs—or, for that matter, for searching through all the desk drawers or other closed or concealed areas in that room itself. Such searches, in the absence of well-recognized exceptions, may be made only under the authority of a search warrant. 395 U.S. 752, 762–63, 89 S.Ct. 2034, 2040, 23 L.Ed.2d 685, 694.

The *Chimel* decision drastically changed the area allowed to be searched incident to arrest from that allowed under previous law. Under pre-*Chimel* law, an officer was allowed to search incident to arrest the area considered to be in the "possession" or under the "control" of the arrested person. These vague standards were interpreted by the courts to include areas that were not necessarily under the defendant's "physical control" but were within his or her "constructive possession." Under this interpretation, law enforcement officers could search an entire residence incident to an arrest made in the residence, and they had almost free reign in deciding what would be searched. Furthermore, because neither a written application for a warrant nor a demonstration of probable cause before a magistrate was required, the search incident to arrest was administratively more convenient and heavily used by law enforcement officers.

Although a warrant or probable cause is still not needed to conduct a search incident to arrest, the *Chimel* case has made it much more difficult for officers to obtain admissible evidence. This chapter discusses various ramifications of the limitations *Chimel* places on a law enforcement officer's power to search incident to arrest.

Objectives

■ **Understand the allowable purposes of a search incident to arrest as set forth in the holding of *Chimel v. California.***

■ **Know the limits on the allowable scope of a search incident to arrest with respect to the following: property that may be searched for and seized; search and seizure of the arrestee's body and items in or on the body or associated with or carried on the body; search of the area into which the arrestee might reach (1) motor vehicles; (2) other persons; search of other areas of the premises**

■ **Understand the other requirements of a valid search incident to arrest including: lawful custodial arrest; contemporaneous nature of arrest and search; who may conduct the search; limitations on use of force**

Chimel v. California
laws.findlaw.com/us/395/
752.html

Key Points

1. When an arrest is made, it is reasonable for the arresting officer to search the person arrested and the area within his or her immediate control—the area from within which the person might gain possession of a weapon or destructible evidence.

Scope

Generally, the allowable scope of a search incident to arrest depends on the allowable purposes of such a search. *Chimel* allows a law enforcement officer to search a person incident to arrest for only two purposes:

- To search for and remove weapons that the arrestee might use to resist arrest or effect an escape
- To search for and seize evidence to prevent its concealment or destruction. The following types of property may be seized:
  (1) property that constitutes evidence of the commission of a criminal offense; or (2) contraband, the fruits of crime, or things otherwise criminally possessed; or (3) property designed or intended for use or which is or has been used as the means of committing a criminal offense. F.R.Crim.P. 41(b).

In addition, an officer may seize evidence of crimes other than the crime for which the arrest was made. In *United States v. Simpson,* 453 F.2d 1028 (10th Cir. 1972), the defendant was arrested under a warrant for possessing and transporting explosives. During a search incident to the arrest, the arresting officer found a third person's Selective Service certificate and classification card, the possession of which was illegal. The court held that the certificate and card were admissible in court, even though they did not relate to the offense of possessing explosives.

> The general rule is that incident to a lawful arrest, a search without a warrant may be made of portable personal effects in the immediate possession of the person arrested. The discovery during a search of a totally unrelated object which provides grounds for prosecution of a crime different than that which the accused was arrested for does not render the search invalid. 453 F.2d at 1031.

Search of the Arrestee's Body

The *Chimel* case gives few guidelines as to the allowable extent of the search of an arrestee's body. However, the later cases of *United States v. Robinson,* 414 U.S. 218, 94 S.Ct. 467, 38 L.Ed.2d 427 (1973), and *Gustafson v. Florida,* 414 U.S. 260, 94 S.Ct. 488, 38 L.Ed.2d 456 (1973), held that a law enforcement officer may conduct a full search of a person's body incident to the **custodial arrest** of the person. In each case, the U.S. Supreme Court upheld an inspection of the contents of a cigarette package seized incident to the arrest of the defendant for a traffic violation. Illegal drugs were found in both cases. In the *Robinson* case, the Court said:

A police officer's determination as to how and where to search the person of a suspect whom he has arrested is necessarily a quick *ad hoc* judgment which the Fourth Amendment does not require to be broken down in each instance into an analysis of each step in the search. The authority to search the person incident to a lawful custodial arrest, while based upon the need to disarm and to discover evidence, does not depend on what a court may later decide was the probability in a particular arrest situation that weapons or evidence would in fact be found upon the person of the suspect. A custodial arrest of a suspect based on probable cause is a reasonable intrusion under the Fourth Amendment; that intrusion being lawful, a search incident to the arrest requires no additional justification. It is the fact of the lawful arrest which establishes the authority to search, and we hold that in the case of lawful custodial arrest a full search of the person is not only an exception to the warrant requirement of the Fourth Amendment, but is also a "reasonable" search under that Amendment. 414 U.S. at 235, 94 S.Ct. at 477, 38 L.Ed.2d at 441.

This language was quoted with approval in the *Gustafson decision,* 414 U.S. at 263–64, 94 S.Ct. at 491, 38 L.Ed.2d at 460. Therefore, under the *Robinson-Gustafson* rule, whenever an officer makes a lawful custodial arrest, the officer may make a full search of the arrestee's body incident to the arrest.

Full Search

What constitutes a full search of the arrestee's body? The following principles can be derived from court decisions dealing with this question.

- A full search of the arrestee's body allows the seizure of evidence on or in the body. Relatively nonintrusive seizures such as obtaining hair samples and fingernail clippings will usually be upheld if reasonable and painless procedures are employed. In *Commonwealth v. Tarver,* 345 N.E.2d 671 (Mass. 1975), the court upheld a seizure of hair samples from the head, chest, and pubic area of a person incident to arrest of that person for murder and sexual abuse of a child. More intrusive searches and seizures, such as obtaining blood samples or comparable intrusions into the body, require stricter limitations. *Schmerber v. California* (discussed in Chapter 4) teaches that a more intrusive search and seizure will be upheld only if (1) the process was a reasonable one performed in a reasonable manner (in *Schmerber,* blood was taken from a person arrested for drunk driving by a physician in a hospital environment according to accepted medical practices); (2) there was a clear indication in advance that the evidence sought would be found; and (3) there were exigent circumstances (in *Schmerber,* the blood test had to be taken before the percentage of alcohol in the blood diminished). If the purpose of obtaining blood had been to determine blood type, drawing the blood without a warrant would not have been permissible because there would be no exigent circumstances. *United States ex rel. Parson v. Anderson,* 354 F.Supp. 1060 (D.Del. 1972), order affirmed 481 F.2d 94 (3d Cir. 1973).
- A full search of the arrestee's body allows the *seizure* and *search* of items of evidence or weapons immediately associated with the arrestee's body, such as clothing, billfolds, jewelry, wristwatches, and weapons strapped or carried on the person. In this context, "immediately associated" means attached in a permanent or semipermanent way to the arrestee's body or clothing. In *State v. Smith,* 203 N.W.2d 348 (Minn. 1972), the court held that the seizure of the

defendant's boots at the time of booking was a valid seizure incident to arrest. A search of items seized might include going through the pockets of clothing; examining clothing for bloodstains, hair, or dirt; and examining weapons for bloodstains, fingerprints, or serial numbers. In *United States v. Molinaro,* 877 F.2d 1341 (7th Cir. 1989), the 7th Circuit Court of Appeals agreed with several other U.S. courts of appeals in holding that a person's wallet may be validly seized and its contents immediately searched incident to the arrest of the person, to prevent the destruction or concealment of evidence. In *United States v. Chan,* 830 F.Supp. 531 (N.D.Cal. 1993), Drug Enforcement Administration (DEA) agents arrested the defendant, seized an electronic pager in his possession, and, within minutes, searched the pager by activating its memory and retrieving certain telephone numbers stored in the pager. The court upheld the search as a valid search incident to arrest.

- A full search of the arrestee's body allows the seizure and search of other personal property and containers that are not immediately associated with the arrestee's body but that the arrestee is carrying or otherwise has under his or her immediate control. *United States v. Johnson,* 846 F.2d 279 (5th Cir. 1988). Property that might be seized and searched includes luggage, attaché cases, bundles, or packages.

Remoteness of Search

United States v. Chadwick
laws.findlaw.com/us/433/1.html

In *United States v. Chadwick,* 433 U.S. 1, 97 S.Ct. 2476, 53 L.Ed.2d 538 (1977), the U.S. Supreme Court held that the *search* of seized luggage or other personal property not immediately associated with the arrestee's body would not be allowed when the search is remote in time and place from the arrest, or when there is no exigency. In the *Chadwick* case, the defendants arrived in Boston from San Diego by train and loaded a large, double-locked footlocker, which they had transported with them, into the trunk of their waiting car. Federal narcotics agents, who had probable cause to arrest and to search the footlocker but no warrants, arrested the defendants. The agents took exclusive control over the footlocker and transported it and the defendants to the federal building in Boston. An hour and a half later, the agents, without the defendants' consent and without a search warrant, opened the footlocker and found large amounts of marijuana. The U.S. Supreme Court held that the search of the footlocker was illegal.

> The potential dangers lurking in all custodial arrests make warrantless searches of items within the "immediate control" area reasonable without requiring the arresting officer to calculate the probability that weapons or destructible evidence may be involved [citing *United States v. Robinson* and *Terry v. Ohio*]. However, warrantless searches of luggage or other property seized at the time of an arrest cannot be justified as incident to that arrest either if the "search is remote in time and place from the arrest," . . . or no exigency exists. Once law enforcement officers have reduced luggage or other personal property not immediately associated with the person of the arrestee to their exclusive control, and there is no longer any danger that the arrestee might gain access to the property to seize a weapon or destroy evidence, a search of that property is no longer an incident of the arrest.
>
> Here the search was conducted more than an hour after federal agents had gained exclusive control of the footlocker and long after respondents were securely in custody;

the search therefore cannot be viewed as incidental to the arrest or as justified by any other exigency. Even though on this record the issuance of a warrant by a judicial officer was reasonably predictable, a line must be drawn. In our view, when no exigency is shown to support the need for an immediate search, the Warrant Clause places the line at the point where the property to be searched comes under the exclusive dominion of police authority. Respondents were therefore entitled to the protection of the Warrant Clause with the evaluation of a neutral magistrate, before their privacy interests in the contents of the footlocker were invaded. 433 U.S. at 14–16, 97 S.Ct. at 2485–86, 53 L.Ed.2d at 550–51.

Footnotes to the *Chadwick* opinion indicate that the Court's decision was based in large part on its belief that the defendants' legitimate privacy interests were violated. In footnote 10 the Court said:

Unlike searches of the person, *United States v. Robinson,* 414 U.S. 218 (1973); *United States v. Edwards,* 415 U.S. 800 (1974), searches of possessions within an arrestee's immediate control cannot be justified by any reduced expectations of privacy caused by the arrest. Respondents' privacy interest in the contents of the footlocker was not eliminated simply because they were under arrest. 433 U.S. at 16 n.10, 97 S.Ct. at 2486 n.10, 53 L.Ed.2d at 551 n.10.

In footnote 8 the Court said:

Respondents' principal privacy interest in the footlocker was, of course, not in the container itself, which was exposed to public view, but in its contents. A search of the interior was therefore a far greater intrusion into Fourth Amendment values than the impoundment of the footlocker. Though surely a substantial infringement with respondents' use and possession, the seizure did not diminish respondents' legitimate expectation that the footlocker's contents would remain private. 433 U.S. at 13–14 n.8, 97 S.Ct. at 2485 n.8, 53 L.Ed.2d at 550 n.8.

To summarize, law enforcement officers may seize and search incident to arrest luggage and other personal property not immediately associated with the arrestee's body if that property is within the arrestee's immediate control and if the search is not remote in time and place from the arrest. Once officers have the property under their exclusive control, however, and there is no further danger that the arrestee might gain access to the property to seize a weapon or destroy evidence, officers may not search the property without a warrant or consent.

Emergencies

Of course, there may be other justifications for a warrantless search of luggage taken from a suspect at the time of his arrest; for example, if officers have reason to believe that luggage contains some immediately dangerous instrumentality, such as explosives, it would be foolhardy to transport it to the station house without opening the luggage and disarming the weapon. *United States v. Chadwick,* 433 U.S. 1, 15 n.9, 97 S.Ct. 2476, 2485 n.9, 53 L.Ed.2d 538, 551 n.9 (1977).

In *United States v. Johnson,* 467 F.2d 630 (2d Cir. 1972), police officers were notified by a reliable informant that a recent arrestee's suitcase containing a shotgun could be

www.fbi.gov/publications/leb/
1996/jan966.txt
Article, "Searching Locked Containers Incident to Arrest" by Edward M. Hendrie
www.fbi.gov/publications/leb/
1997/jan977.htm
Article, "Searching Pagers Incident to Arrest" by Lisa A. Regini
www.fletc.gov/legal/archive_dir.
htm
Article, "Electronic Pagers—May a Law Enforcement Officer Access the Memory During a Search Incident to Arrest?" by Bryan R. Lemons; third of three articles in the April 2, 2001 issue of *Quarterly Review: Legal Commentary for Federal Law Enforcement Officers*

found near the rear door of an apartment building. The officers knew that the building was located in a transient and high-crime area and that the suitcase was probably visible to passersby. The officers rushed to the apartment building, opened the suitcase, and found the shotgun. The court upheld both the seizure and search of the suitcase.

> [I]n opening the suitcases, the police were not acting in violation of the Fourth Amendment. The "exigencies of the situation made that course imperative." . . . The officers were holding a suitcase which they had probable cause to believe contained a contraband sawed-off shotgun. There was a substantial possibility the gun was loaded. As they stood in that transient and high crime area, their own safety and the safety of others required that they know whether they were holding a dangerous weapon over which they had no control. . . . Under these circumstances, we cannot hold that the police were required to carry the suitcase, unopened, to the police station to obtain a warrant or that an officer should have stood near or held the unopened suitcase as a warrant was obtained. The police were entitled to know what they were holding in their possession. 467 F.2d at 639.

State Departures from the *Robinson-Gustafson* Rule

The *Robinson* case has been criticized on the ground that it facilitates "pretext" or "subterfuge" arrests for minor offenses and searches incident to those arrests for evidence of more serious crimes for which probable cause to arrest is lacking. In *Whren v. United States,* 517 U.S. 806, 116 S.Ct. 1769, 135 L.Ed.2d 89 (1996), the U.S. Supreme Court clearly stated that an officer's ulterior motives do not invalidate the officer's conduct that is justifiable on the basis of probable cause to believe that a violation of law has occurred. Furthermore, such conduct is valid under the Fourth Amendment regardless of whether a "reasonable officer" would have been motivated to engage in such conduct. In short, if police conduct is justified by probable cause, subjective intent or pretext is irrelevant for Fourth Amendment purposes. The Court went on to say that

Whren v. United States
laws.findlaw.com/us/000/
u20005.html

> of course . . . the Constitution prohibits selective enforcement of the law based on considerations such as race. But the constitutional basis for objecting to intentionally discriminatory application of laws is the Equal Protection Clause, not the Fourth Amendment. Subjective intentions play no role in ordinary, probable-cause Fourth Amendment analysis. 517 U.S. at 813, 116 S.Ct. at 1774, 135 L.Ed.2d at 98.

Nevertheless, based on interpretations of their state constitutions, some state courts have refused to follow the *Robinson-Gustafson* rule allowing a full-body search incident to a lawful custodial arrest. Several states, including Alaska, Colorado, Hawaii, and Oregon, have placed various limitations on the *Robinson-Gustafson* rule. The Supreme Court of Hawaii limited the warrantless search of an arrestee's person incident to a lawful custodial arrest (1) to disarming the arrested person when there is reason to believe from the facts and circumstances that the person may be armed and (2) to discovering evidence related to the crime for which the person was arrested. *State v. Kaluna,* 520 P.2d 51, 60 (Hawaii 1974). Under this more restrictive rule, officers may not search for evidence incident to offenses that would not produce evidence (such as loitering and minor traffic offenses), and officers may not search for weapons unless they can point to specific facts and circumstances indicating the likelihood that the arrested person was armed and dangerous.

The California Supreme Court also refused to go along with the U.S. Supreme Court's decisions in the *Robinson* and *Gustafson* cases. In California, an officer may not conduct a full-body search of an arrested person when the arrest will be disposed of by a mere citation or the arrested person will be transported in a law enforcement vehicle to a police facility where the opportunity to post bond is available. Officers may, however, conduct a patdown frisk for weapons before placing an arrested person in a law enforcement vehicle for transportation to the station house. The court recognized the increased danger to law enforcement officers in this situation. *People v. Longwill,* 123 Cal.Rptr. 297, 538 P.2d 753 (Cal. 1975).

Key Points

2. The allowable purposes of a search incident to arrest are (1) to search for and remove weapons that the arrestee might use to resist arrest or effect an escape and (2) to search for and seize evidence to prevent its concealment or destruction.

3. A law enforcement officer may conduct a full search of a person's body incident to the arrest of the person.

4. A full search of the arrestee's body allows the seizure and search of weapons or evidence on, in, or immediately associated with the body.

5. A full search of the arrestee's body allows the *seizure* and *search* of other personal property *not* immediately associated with the arrestee's body but under the immediate control of the arrestee. This property may not be searched, however, if the search is remote in time and place from the arrest or no exigency exists.

6. If police conduct is justified by probable cause to believe that a violation of law has occurred, subjective intent or pretext is irrelevant for Fourth Amendment purposes.

Search of Area into Which the Arrestee Might Reach

And the area into which an arrestee might reach in order to grab a weapon or evidentiary items must, of course, be governed by a like rule. A gun on a table or in a drawer in front of one who is arrested can be as dangerous to the arresting officer as one concealed in the clothing of the person arrested. There is ample justification, therefore, for a search of the arrestee's person and the area "within his immediate control"—construing that phrase to mean the area from within which he might gain possession of a weapon or destructible evidence. 395 U.S. at 763, 89 S.Ct. at 2040, 23 L.Ed.2d at 694.

This passage from the *Chimel* case (also quoted at the start of this chapter) gives definite guidelines regarding the extent of the area around an arrestee that is "within his immediate control" and is therefore subject to search by an officer. This determination of the permissible area of search depends on several factors such as the size and shape of the room, the size and agility of the arrestee, whether the arrestee was handcuffed or otherwise subdued, the size and type of evidence being sought, the number of people arrested, and the number of officers present. This area is sometimes called the arrestee's "wingspan," "wingspread," or "grabbing distance."

The following cases illustrate the *Chimel* guidelines. In *James v. Louisiana,* 382 U.S. 36, 86 S.Ct. 151, 15 L.Ed.2d 30 (1965), the defendant, a suspected possessor of narcotics, was lawfully arrested on a downtown street corner. The officers then took him

James v. Louisiana
laws.findlaw.com/us/382/
36.html

to his home some distance away and conducted an intensive search that yielded narcotics. The Court held the search unreasonable:

> In the circumstances of this case . . . the subsequent search of the petitioner's home cannot be regarded as incident to his arrest on a street corner more than two blocks away. A search "can be incident to an arrest only if it is substantially contemporaneous with the arrest and is confined to the immediate vicinity of the arrest." 382 U.S. at 37, 86 S.Ct. at 151, 15 L.Ed.2d at 31 (1965).

For the same reason, the search of an arrestee's vehicle located a substantial distance from the doorstep of his home where he was arrested could not be justified as a search incident to arrest. *United States v. Lasanta*, 978 F.2d 1300 (2d Cir. 1992).

United States v. Tarazon, 989 F.2d 1045 (9th Cir. 1993), held that the drawers of the desk at which the defendant was sitting when he was arrested were clearly within the defendant's control and could be searched incident to the arrest moments after the arrest. In *People v. Spencer*, 99 Cal.Rptr. 681 (Cal.App. 1972), officers went to the defendant's trailer home to arrest him for participating in an armed robbery. They found him lying in bed. One officer immediately searched under the blankets for a gun as other officers attempted to subdue the defendant, who was resisting. Two revolvers were found in a box at the foot of the bed. The court held that this box was within the area of the defendant's reach and that the revolvers were admissible in evidence.

If it is necessary for an arrested person to go into a different area of the premises from that in which he or she was arrested, the officer may, for protective purposes, accompany the person and search if necessary. The following quotation from *Washington v. Chrisman* (discussed in Chapter 4) is worthy of repetition:

Washington v. Chrisman
laws.findlaw.com/us/455/1.html

> [I]t is not "unreasonable" under the Fourth Amendment for a police officer, as a matter of course, to monitor the movements of an arrested person, as his judgement dictates, following the arrest. The officer's need to ensure his own safety—as well as the integrity of the arrest—is compelling. Such surveillance is not an impermissible invasion of the privacy or personal liberty of an individual who has been arrested. 455 U.S. 1, 7, 102 S.Ct. 812, 817, 70 L.Ed.2d 778, 785 (1982).

In *Giacalone v. Lucas*, 445 F.2d 1238, 1247 (6th Cir. 1971), an arrest under authority of a warrant for conspiracy to commit extortion took place early in the morning when the arrested person was in his pajamas. An officer suggested that the defendant change into street clothes before leaving for the station. The defendant agreed and went to his bedroom, followed by the officers. As the defendant went to a chest of drawers to obtain clothing, one officer searched the drawer and found a blackjack and several other weapons. The defendant was convicted of illegal possession of a blackjack. The court held the search was lawful:

> Certainly, if immediately after a lawful arrest, the arrestee reads the arrest warrant and without coercion consents to go to his bedroom to change into more appropriate clothing, the arresting officers—incident to that arrest—may search the areas upon which the arrestee focuses his attention and are within his reach to gain access to a weapon or to destroy evidence. 445 F.2d at 1247.

Officers may not, however, deliberately move an arrested person near an object or place they want to search in order to activate the incident-to-arrest exception. *United States v. Perea*, 986 F.2d 633 (2d Cir. 1993).

Search of Motor Vehicles

In *New York v. Belton*, the leading U.S. Supreme Court case on search incident to arrest of motor vehicles, the facts were stated by the Court as follows:

New York v. Belton
laws.findlaw.com/us/453/
454.html

> On April 9, 1978, Trooper Douglas Nicot, a New York State policeman driving an unmarked car on the New York Thruway, was passed by another automobile traveling at an excessive rate of speed. Nicot gave chase, overtook the speeding vehicle, and ordered its driver to pull it over to the side of the road and stop. There were four men in the car, one of whom was Roger Belton, the respondent in this case. The policeman asked to see the driver's license and automobile registration, and discovered that none of the men owned the vehicle or was related to its owner. Meanwhile, the policeman had smelled burnt marihuana and had seen on the floor of the car an envelope marked "Supergold" that he associated with marihuana. He therefore directed the men to get out of the car, and placed them under arrest for the unlawful possession of marihuana. He patted down each of the men and "split them up into four separate areas of the Thruway at this time so they would not be in physical touching area of each other." He then picked up the envelope marked "Supergold" and found that it contained marihuana. After giving the arrestees the warnings required by *Miranda v. Arizona*, 384 U.S. 436, the state policeman searched each one of them. He then searched the passenger compartment of the car. On the back seat he found a black leather jacket belonging to Belton. He unzipped one of the pockets of the jacket and discovered cocaine. Placing the jacket in his automobile, he drove the four arrestees to a nearby police station. 453 U.S. 454, 455–56, 101 S.Ct. 2860, 2861–62, 69 L.Ed.2d 768, 772 (1981).

Belton was subsequently indicted for criminal possession of a controlled substance. In the trial court he moved that the cocaine the trooper had seized from the jacket pocket be suppressed. The Court held:

> [W]hen a policeman has made a lawful custodial arrest of the occupant of an automobile, he may, as a contemporaneous incident of that arrest, search the passenger compartment of that automobile.
>
> It follows from this conclusion that the police may also examine the contents of any containers found within the passenger compartment, for if the passenger compartment is within the reach of the arrestee, so also will containers in it be within his reach. . . . Such a container may, of course, be searched whether it is open or closed, since the justification for the search is not that the arrestee has no privacy interest in the container, but that the lawful custodial arrest justifies the infringement of any privacy interest the arrestee may have. 453 U.S. at 460–61, 101 S.Ct. at 2864, 69 L.Ed.2d at 75.

In a footnote, the Court defined a container as any object capable of holding another object. A container thus includes "closed or open glove compartments, consoles or other receptacles located anywhere within the passenger compartment, as well as luggage, boxes, bags, clothing, and the like." 453 U.S. at 460–61 n.4, 101 S.Ct. at 2684 n.4, 69 L.Ed.2d at 775 n.4. The Court also pointed out that only the interior of the passenger compartment of an automobile, and not the trunk, may be searched incident to arrest.

The 9th Circuit Court of Appeals described the practical effect of the *Belton* ruling:

www.nesl.edu/lawrev/vol30/
vol30-3/sheehan.htm
Article, "*State v. Pierce*: State
Constitutional Protection against
the *Belton* Search Incident to
Arrest Rule"

> [T]he underlying rationale of *Belton* was to provide a bright-line rule while balancing privacy and law enforcement interests. The protection of the Fourth . . . Amendment can only be realized if the police are acting under a set of rules which, in most instances, makes

it possible to reach a correct determination beforehand as to whether an invasion of privacy is justified in the interest of law enforcement . . . . Such rules are necessary because police officers engaged in an arrest on the highway have only limited time and expertise to reflect on and balance the social and individual interests involved in the specific circumstances they confront . . . . Because it is a bright-line rule that may be invoked regardless of whether the arresting officer has an actual concern for safety or evidence, we have held that the applicability of the *Belton* rule does not depend upon a defendant's ability to grab items in a car but rather upon whether the search is roughly contemporaneous with the arrest. *United States v. McLaughlin*, 170 F. 3d 889, 891–92 (9th Cir. 1999).

In *United States v. White*, 871 F.2d 41 (6th Cir. 1989), the court upheld a search of the defendant's automobile incident to his arrest in his vehicle, even though he was handcuffed and placed in the backseat of a police cruiser at the time of the search. The court said that

> even after the arrestee has been separated from his vehicle and is no longer within reach of the vehicle or its contents, the *Belton* rule allowing a police officer to search a vehicle incident to a lawful arrest applies, and such a search is valid. 871 F.2d at 44.

Likewise, in *United States v. Lacey*, 86 F.3d 956, 971 (10th Cir. 1996), the court held that "where an officer has made a lawful arrest of a suspect in an automobile, the officer may seize items of evidence found within the passenger compartment of the vehicle as part of a search incident to a lawful arrest, even when the suspect is outside of the vehicle and handcuffed." *United States v. Strahan*, 984 F.2d 159 (6th Cir. 1993), however, held that the *Belton* rule applies *only where the police initiate contact while the defendant is within his automobile.* In that case, the search of the vehicle incident to arrest was not allowed when the defendant was initially arrested not while within his vehicle but approximately thirty feet from his vehicle.

The *Belton* case deals only with the search-incident-to-arrest exception to the warrant requirement and has nothing to do with the so-called automobile exception under the *Carroll* doctrine (see Chapter 11). The U.S. Supreme Court in *Belton* specifically referred to the *Chimel* case, stating that articles inside the relatively narrow compass of the passenger compartment of an automobile are in fact generally, even if not inevitably, within "the area into which an arrestee might reach in order to grab a weapon or evidentiary item." 395 U.S. at 763, 89 S.Ct. at 2040, 23 L.Ed.2d at 694. Therefore, the holding in the *Belton* case does not apply unless there has been a custodial arrest of the occupant of an automobile. It is the custodial arrest that provides the justification for examining the contents of containers seized from the passenger compartment of the automobile. Moreover, as the previously quoted passage from the *Belton* case indicates, the searching of any containers found in the automobile must be substantially contemporaneous with the arrest of the automobile's occupant. If a container is seized and searched some time later, after it is in the exclusive control of the police, the *Chadwick* case requires that a warrant be obtained.

Search of Persons Other Than the Arrestee

When an arrest is made, other persons besides the arrested person are often in the vicinity. Courts generally allow a limited search or frisk of an arrestee's companion or companions in the immediate area of the arrest, when the arresting officer reasonably believes that these persons may present a danger or may destroy evidence. (See "Determination of Whether to Frisk" in Chapter 7.) The allowed search is limited to a patdown search of the companion's body and a search of the area within his or her immediate control for weapons or destructible evidence. "[A] search of items within the area of immediate control of a person who is present during a custodial arrest for a recent crime in which guns were used is reasonable when an objective probability of danger to law enforcement exists under the circumstances." *United States v. Simmons*, 567 F.2d 314, 320 (7th Cir. 1977).

Some courts apply a totality-of-the-circumstances test in determining whether a search of an arrestee's companions is justified. In *United States v. Flett*, 806 F.2d 823 (8th Cir. 1986), the court upheld a patdown search of an arrestee's companion, even though the companion made no threatening moves toward the officer and the officer noticed no bulge in the companion's clothing. The court said that the focus of the judicial inquiry was not whether the officer had an indication that the person was armed and dangerous but rather "whether the officer reasonably perceived the subject of the frisk as potentially dangerous." 806 F.2d at 828. The court found that the patdown search was justified by the following circumstances:

- The arrestee was the subject of an arrest warrant for narcotics violations.
- The arrestee was a known member of a national motorcycle gang with violent propensities.
- The arrestee was the "enforcer" of the local chapter of the motorcycle gang and had been previously charged with a firearms violation.
- The companion was in the arrestee's house, was dressed in attire similar to that of gang members, and physically resembled known gang members.
- The officer had fifteen years' experience in law enforcement.

The area within the reach of the defendant's companions is also subject to search. In *United States v. Lucas*, 898 F.2d 606 (8th Cir. 1990), the court held that a search of a cabinet in a small kitchen, immediately after officers had handcuffed the defendant and while they were removing him from the kitchen, was a valid search incident to arrest. The defendant had attempted to reach the cabinet door immediately before his struggle with the arresting officers. The court particularly noted that two of the defendant's friends, who had not been handcuffed, were still at the kitchen table when the search took place. A revolver found in the cabinet was held admissible in evidence against the defendant.

www.fletc.gov//legal/
review_archive.htm
Article, "Frisking the Companion of an Arrestee: The 'Automatic Companion' Rule" by Bryan R. Lemons; second of three articles in the October 2, 2000 issue of *Quarterly Review: Legal Commentary for Federal Law Enforcement Officers*

Key Points

7. When a law enforcement officer has made a lawful custodial arrest of an automobile's occupant, the officer may contemporaneously search the passenger compartment of that automobile and may also examine the contents of any containers found within the passenger compartment, whether the containers are open or closed.

8. A law enforcement officer may conduct a limited search or frisk of an arrestee's companion or companions in the immediate area of the arrest, when the arresting officer reasonably believes that these persons may present a danger or may destroy evidence.

Search of Other Areas of the Premises

Under the *Chimel* rule, officers may not conduct a full search of any areas of the premises other than the limited area within the arrestee's immediate control. Officers may, however, conduct a quick and limited search of a premises incident to an arrest to protect their own safety and the safety of others. This is sometimes referred to as a "protective sweep." Officers also may have to go through other rooms in entering or leaving the premises. These movements into other areas of the premises are not considered full-blown searches, because the officers are not looking for weapons or incriminating evidence. Nevertheless, an officer who observes a weapon or other seizable item lying open to view may seize it, and that item will be admissible in court if the requirements of the plain view doctrine are satisfied (see Chapter 10).

In *Maryland v. Buie*, 494 U.S. 325, 110 S.Ct. 1093, 108 L.Ed.2d 276 (1990), two men, one of whom was wearing a red running suit, committed an armed robbery. The same day, police obtained an arrest warrant for the defendant and his suspected accomplice and executed the warrant for the defendant at his house. The defendant was arrested as he emerged from the basement, after which one of the officers entered the basement "in case there was someone else" there and seized a red running suit lying in plain view.

In determining the reasonableness of the search of the basement leading to the plain view seizure, the U.S. Supreme Court balanced the officer's need to search against the invasion entailed by the search. Possessing an arrest warrant and probable cause to believe the defendant was in his home, the officers were entitled to enter and search anywhere in the house in which the defendant might be found. Once he was found, however, the search for him was over, and the officers no longer had that particular justification for entering any rooms that had not yet been searched. Those rooms, however, were not immune from entry simply because of the defendant's expectation of privacy with respect to them. That privacy interest must be balanced against the

> interest of the officers in taking steps to assure themselves that the house in which a suspect is being or has just been arrested is not harboring other persons who are dangerous and who could unexpectedly launch an attack. The risk of danger in the context of an arrest in the home is as great as, if not greater than, it is in an on-the-street or roadside investigatory encounter. 494 U.S. at 333, 110 S.Ct. at 1098, 108 L.Ed.2d at 285.

The Court held that the police officers had a limited right to conduct a protective sweep for their own protection.

> [A]s an incident to the arrest the officers could, as a precautionary matter and without probable cause or reasonable suspicion, look in closets and other spaces immediately adjoining the place of arrest from which an attack could be immediately launched. Beyond that, however, . . . there must be articulable facts which, taken together with the rational inferences from those facts, would warrant a reasonably prudent officer in believing that the area to be swept harbors an individual posing a danger to those on the arrest scene. 494 U.S. at 334, 110 S.Ct. at 1098, 108 L.Ed.2d at 286.

Thus, the standard to justify a protective sweep in conjunction with an in-home arrest is the same as the standard to justify an investigatory *Terry*-type stop: reasonable suspicion based on specific and articulable facts. The Supreme Court emphasized that a protective sweep of areas beyond the area immediately adjoining the place of arrest permits only a cursory inspection of those spaces where a person may be found; it does not permit a full search of the premises. The sweep may last no longer than is necessary to dispel the reasonable suspicion of danger and in any event no longer than it takes to complete the arrest and depart from the premises.

Maryland v. Buie
laws.findlaw.com/us/494/
325.html

www.textfiles.com/law/
search.txt
Article, "Searches of Premises
Incident to Arrest" by Louis
DiPietro
www.fbi.gov/publications/leb/
1998/julyleb.pdf
Article, "Protective Sweeps" by
Thomas D. Colbridge (page 25 of
the July 1998 *FBI Law Enforcement Bulletin*)

In *United States v. Soria,* 959 F.2d 855 (10th Cir. 1992), the court held a protective sweep of the defendant's auto shop proper when the defendant was arrested during a drug transaction close to the shop. The officers believed that drug dealing activities had taken place in the shop and that others may have been hiding inside. In *United States v. Hogan,* 38 F.3d 1148 (10th Cir. 1994), however, a protective sweep of the defendant's residence was held invalid in a case in which the defendant was arrested outside his residence. He was not home when the police first arrived, and the only possible danger to the police was the hypothetical possibility that the defendant's accomplice to the murder committed a month earlier might be in the residence.

Sometimes the events and circumstances surrounding an arrest will justify officers going into other parts of an arrestee's residence for reasons unrelated to their safety. In a bank robbery case, the defendant was arrested in his girlfriend's apartment. At the time of his arrest, the defendant was nude and the apartment was dark. An officer went to get clothing for the defendant and found two jackets of the type that had been described as having been worn by the bank robbers. On the way out of the apartment, an officer turned on the kitchen light so he could see his way. Money taken during the robbery was observed on the kitchen floor.

The court held that both the jackets and the money were admissible in evidence. Finding no violation of the *Chimel* rule, the court said:

> Since they were bound to find some clothing for Titus rather than take him nude to FBI headquarters on a December night, the fatigue jackets were properly seized under the "plain view" doctrine. Welch was entitled to turn on the kitchen lights, both to assist his own exit and to see whether the other robber might be about; when he saw the stolen money, he was permitted to seize it. Everything the agents took was in their "plain view" while they were where they had a right to be; there was no general rummaging of the apartment. *United States v. Titus,* 445 F.2d 577, 579 (2d Cir. 1971).

Key Points

9. Law enforcement officers may not conduct a full search of any areas of the premises other than the limited area within the arrestee's immediate control.

10. Incident to an arrest, the arresting officer may look in closets and other spaces immediately adjoining the place of arrest from which an attack could be immediately launched.

11. The Fourth Amendment permits a properly limited protective sweep in conjunction with an in-home arrest when the searching officer possesses a reasonable suspicion based on specific and articulable facts that the area to be swept harbors an individual posing a danger to those on the arrest scene.

Other Requirements for a Valid Search Incident to Arrest

Several other requirements for a valid search incident to arrest have been touched on in the previous discussion. This section treats each of these requirements in further detail.

www.fbi.gov/library/leb/1999/
may99leb.pdf
Article, "Search Incident to
Arrest: Another Look" by
Thomas D. Colbridge; focuses on
the case of *Knowles v. Iowa* (page
27 of the May 1999 *FBI Law
Enforcement Bulletin*)
www.jus.state.nc.us/NCJA/
knowles.htm
Discussion of *Knowles v. Iowa*
with advice for law enforcement
officers from the North Carolina
Justice Academy

Lawful Custodial Arrest

To justify a full search incident to arrest, an arrest must be a lawful *custodial arrest.* The word *custodial* is important here because in some states the term *arrest* is applied to situations in which an officer stops a person and issues a ticket, citation, or notice to appear in court, instead of taking the person into custody and transporting the person to a police station or other place to be dealt with according to the law. A full search would not be authorized in situations in which the officer merely issued a ticket, citation, or notice to appear. In other words, the officer must take the arrested person into custody to justify a full search. In *United States v. Parr,* 843 F.2d 1228 (9th Cir. 1988), the court found that when the defendant was stopped on suspicion of driving with a suspended driver's license and placed briefly in a patrol car, without any other restraint or questioning, there was no custodial arrest. Therefore, the search of the defendant's car could not be justified as a search incident to arrest. The court observed that "sitting in the patrol car for several minutes was merely a normal part of traffic police procedure for identifying delinquent drivers and did not constitute custodial arrest." 843 F.2d at 1230. The rule requiring a *custodial* arrest is based on the U.S. Supreme Court's observation

> that the danger to an officer is far greater in the case of the extended exposure which follows the taking of a suspect into custody and transporting him to the police station than in the case of the relatively fleeting contact resulting from the typical *Terry*-type stop. *United States v. Robinson,* 414 U.S. 218, 234–35, 94 S.Ct. 467, 476, 38 L.Ed.2d 427, 440.

Knowles v. Iowa
laws.findlaw.com/us/000/
97-7597.html

The U.S. Supreme Court reiterated its requirement of a lawful custodial arrest as a prerequisite to a search incident to arrest in *Knowles v. Iowa,* 525 U.S. 113, 119 S.Ct. 484, 142 L.Ed.2d 492 (1998). In that case a police officer with probable cause to believe the defendant was speeding stopped the defendant and issued a citation. The officer could have arrested the defendant because Iowa law permitted law enforcement officers to immediately arrest traffic violators and take them before a magistrate. Iowa law also permitted officers to issue a citation in lieu of arrest and provided that the issuance of such a citation "does not affect the officer's authority to conduct an otherwise lawful search." The officer searched the defendant's car, without probable cause or the defendant's consent, but based solely on Iowa's so-called search-incident-to-citation exception to the warrant requirement and found marijuana.

The Court held that Iowa's search-incident-to-citation exception to the Fourth Amendment was unconstitutional. The search-incident-to-arrest exception is a "bright-line rule," justified only by a lawful full custodial arrest. Mere probable cause to arrest, or the issuance of a citation alone, are not sufficient to justify the search. The Court noted the two historic rationales for a search incident to arrest. With respect to the first rationale, officer safety, the Court said:

> The threat to officer safety from issuing a traffic citation, however, is a good deal less than in the case of a custodial arrest. In *Robinson,* we stated that a custodial arrest involves "danger to an officer" because of "the extended exposure which follows the taking of a suspect into custody and transporting him to the police station." 414 U.S. at 234–235. We recognized that "[t]he danger to the police officer flows from the fact of the arrest, and its attendant proximity, stress, and uncertainty, and not from the grounds for arrest." *Id.,* at 234, n. 5. A routine traffic stop, on the other hand, is a relatively brief encounter and "is more analogous to a so-called '*Terry* stop' . . . than to a formal arrest." *Berkemer v. McCarty,* 468 U.S. 420, 437 (1984). . . . This is not to say that the concern

Case in Point

Interpreting *Knowles v. Iowa*

While on patrol in the early morning hours of December 30, 1997, Indiana State Police Trooper Rich Reynolds observed a car without a light illuminating its license plate. After deciding to investigate this infraction, Reynolds activated his lights and followed the car into the lot of a car wash establishment. The driver of the car drove into a bay and, although it was the middle of a winter night, he exited and picked up a spray nozzle as if he were going to wash the car. After Reynolds advised Leitch of the reason for the stop, he identified himself and told Reynolds that he "might be" a habitual traffic violator ("HTV"). Reynolds spoke with a State Police dispatcher, who confirmed that the Bureau of Motor Vehicles' computers indicated Leitch was indeed an HTV.

Based upon this information, Reynolds decided to arrest Leitch for operating a vehicle as an HTV. After a local marshal arrived to provide backup, Reynolds handcuffed Leitch, placed him in the police car, and advised him that he was under arrest for that offense. Because Leitch told Reynolds that his sister, the owner of the car, was in Florida, Reynolds then called for a wrecker to tow the car to an impoundment lot. While waiting for the wrecker to arrive, Reynolds and the marshal searched the car's passenger compartment. That search uncovered, among other things, 449 grams of marijuana in the glove compartment and 6.65 grams of amphetamine and methamphetamine in a tin on the front seat.

Leitch was charged with dealing in a schedule II controlled substance, possession of a schedule II controlled substance within 1,000 feet of school property, dealing in marijuana, possession of marijuana in excess of 30 grams, operating a vehicle as an HTV, and with being a habitual substance offender. Leitch filed two motions to suppress introduction of the marijuana and amphetamines into evidence. In light of *Knowles v. Iowa*, should his motions to suppress be granted? *Leitch v. State*, 736 N.E.2d 1284 (Ind.App. 2000).

Read the court opinion at:
www.ai.org/judiciary/opinions/archive/10300001.mpb.html

---

for officer safety is absent in the case of a routine traffic stop. It plainly is not. . . . But while the concern for officer safety in this context may justify the "minimal" additional intrusion of ordering a driver and passengers out of the car, it does not by itself justify the often considerably greater intrusion attending a full field-type search. 525 U.S. at 117, 119 S.Ct. at 487–88, 142 L.Ed.2d at __ .

With respect to the second rationale, the need to discover and preserve evidence, the Court said:

Once Knowles was stopped for speeding and issued a citation, all the evidence necessary to prosecute that offense had been obtained. No further evidence of excessive speed was going to be found either on the person of the offender or in the passenger compartment of the car. 525 U.S. at 118, 119 S.Ct. at 488, 142 L.Ed.2d at __ .

No further justification beyond that of a lawful custodial arrest is necessary to validate the seizure of an item in conjunction with a search incident to arrest. As stated by the 9th Circuit Court of Appeals, "For an item to be validly seized during a search incident to arrest, the police need not have probable cause to seize the item, nor do they need to recognize immediately the item's evidentiary nature." *United States v. Holzman*, 871 F.2d 1496, 1505 (9th Cir. 1989).

Contemporaneousness

A search "can be incident to an arrest only if it is substantially contemporaneous with the arrest and is confined to the immediate vicinity of the arrest." *James v. Louisiana*, 382 U.S. 36, 37, 86 S.Ct. 151, 151, 15 L.Ed.2d 30, 31 (1965). (The *James* case is

Note: After this book had gone to press, the U.S. Supreme Court held in *Atwater v. Lago Vista*, (decided April 24, 2001) that a law enforcement officer who perceives a person committing even a very minor criminal offense in the officer's presence may, without violating the Fourth Amendment, make a full custodial arrest of the person.
Read the court opinion at: laws.findlaw.com/us/000/99-1408.html

James v. Louisiana laws.findlaw.com/us/382/36.html

discussed on pages 325 to 326.) To be contemporaneous, a search must be conducted as close in time to the arrest as practically possible. The reason for this rule is that officers may search incident to arrest only (1) to protect themselves and (2) to prevent the destruction or concealment of evidence. A delayed search indicates that the officers were not concerned about either of these possibilities and that the search was conducted for another, impermissible, purpose. In *United States v. McLaughlin,* 170 F. 3d 889 (9th Cir. 1999), the court found that a search of the passenger compartment of a vehicle that occurred five minutes after the arrest of the driver was reasonable. The search was essentially contemporaneous with the arrest in that "the arrest, the filling out of the impound paperwork before searching the car, and the initial search were all one continuous series of events closely connected in time." 170 F.3d at 891.

Sometimes circumstances prevent an officer from conducting an immediate search incident to arrest. For example, body cavity searches and searches of persons of the opposite sex must usually be delayed. In these situations, the officer should remove the arrested person from the scene and conduct the search as soon as favorable circumstances prevail. In *United States v. Miles,* 413 F.2d 34 (3d Cir. 1969), an arrest for an armed bank robbery took place in a crowded hotel lobby, which was lit only by candles because of a power failure. The court held that under these circumstances it was proper for officers to make a cursory search for weapons at the hotel and to make a more thorough search later at the station.

Even though it is feasible to search an arrested person at the time of arrest, courts will allow a delay between the arrest and search under certain circumstances. The U.S. Supreme Court made such an exception to the general rule in the case of *United States v. Edwards,* 415 U.S. 800, 94 S.Ct. 1234, 39 L.Ed.2d 771 (1974). In that case, the defendant was arrested shortly after 11:00 P.M. for attempting to break into a building. The defendant was taken to jail. Law enforcement officials had probable cause to believe that the defendant's clothing contained paint chips from the crime scene. Since the police had no substitute clothing for the defendant, they waited until the next morning to seize his clothing without a warrant. Paint chips matching those at the break-in scene were found on the clothing.

The Court held that, despite the delay, the clothing was lawfully seized incident to the defendant's arrest. The administrative process and the mechanics of arrest had not yet come to a halt the next morning. The police had custody of the defendant and the clothing and could have seized the clothing at the time of arrest. It was reasonable to delay the seizure until substitute clothing was available.

> [O]nce the accused is lawfully arrested and is in custody, the effects in his possession at the place of detention that were subject to search at the time and place of his arrest may lawfully be searched and seized without a warrant even though a substantial period of time has elapsed between the arrest and subsequent administrative processing, on the one hand, and the taking of the property for use as evidence on the other. 415 U.S. at 807, 94 S.Ct. at 1239, 39 L.Ed.2d at 778.

The *Edwards* case does not allow law enforcement officers to delay a search incident to arrest for as long as they wish. Nor does the case sanction all delays in searching and seizing evidence incident to arrest. Officers must be able to provide good reasons for delaying a search incident to arrest, and the duration of a delay must be reasonable under the circumstances. Otherwise the search and seizure may be declared illegal.

The U.S. Supreme Court stated that "an incident search may not precede an arrest and serve as part of its justification." *Sibron v. New York,* 392 U.S. 40, 63, 88 S.Ct. 1889, 1902, 20 L.Ed.2d 917, 934–35 (1968). The Court reiterated this principle in

United States v. Edwards
laws.findlaw.com/us/415/
800.html

Sibron v. New York
laws.findlaw.com/us/392/
40.html

Smith v. Ohio, holding that the exception for searches incident to arrest "does not pe mit the police to search any citizen without a warrant or probable cause so long as arrest immediately follows." 494 U.S. 541, 543, 110 S.Ct. 1288, 1290, 108 L.Ed.2d 4(468 (1990). This does not necessarily mean that the arrest must always precede t search, although that is the usual sequence. The search may precede the arrest a still be a valid search incident to arrest, if

- probable cause to *arrest* existed at the time of the search and did not depend on the fruits of the search, and
- the "formal arrest followed quickly on the heels of the challenged search." *Rawlings v. Kentucky,* 448 U.S. 98, 111, 100 S.Ct. 2556, 2564, 65 L.Ed.2d 633, 645 (1980).

Rawlings v. Kentucky
laws.findlaw.com/us/448/
98.html

Who May Conduct the Search?

If possible, the law enforcement officer making the arrest should conduct the search incident to the arrest. If an officer makes an arrest and does not search the arrested person right away but later allows another officer to search the person, the later search may be held unlawful. It would not meet the requirement of contemporaneousness, nor would it indicate a concern for officer's protection or the prevention of the destruction or concealment of evidence.

Nevertheless, if the arresting officer transfers an arrested person to the custody of another officer, the second officer may again search the arrested person. This second search is allowed because the second officer is entitled to take personal safety measures and need not rely on the assumption that the arrestee has been thoroughly searched for weapons by the arresting officer. *United States v. Dyson,* 277 A.2d 658 (D.C.App. 1971).

Use of Force

Law enforcement officers searching a person incident to arrest may use the degree of force reasonably necessary to protect themselves, prevent escape, and prevent the destruction or concealment of evidence. Courts will review the use of force strictly, and officers should use as little force as is necessary to accomplish their legitimate purpose. In *Salas v. State,* 246 So.2d 621 (Fla.Dist.Ct.App. 1971), a seizure of drugs incident to arrest was upheld even though the arresting officer put a choke hold on the arrestee and forced him to spit out drugs he was attempting to swallow. However, before more intrusive measures are taken, such as pumping the stomach or probing body cavities, the following conditions must be satisfied:

- The officer must have good reason to believe that the person's body contains evidence that should be removed. For example, in *People v. Jones,* 97 Cal.Rptr. 492 (Cal.App. 1971), officers observed the defendant thrust drug capsules into his mouth and quickly swallow them.
- If possible, a doctor working under sanitary conditions and in a medically approved manner should perform the procedure.
- Only the amount of force reasonably necessary to make the person submit to the examination may be used. *Blackford v. United States,* 247 F.2d 745 (9th Cir. 1957).

Exhibit 8.1 shows a comparison of a frisk and a search incident to arrest.

Key Points

12. The lawful custodial arrest that justifies a search incident to arrest is an arrest that involves taking the person into custody and transporting him or her to a police station or other place to be dealt with according to the law. Mere probable cause to arrest, or the issuance of a citation alone, are not sufficient to justify a search incident to arrest.

13. In general, a search incident to arrest must be contemporaneous with the arrest and confined to the immediate vicinity of the arrest.

14. A search incident to arrest may not precede an arrest and serve as part of the arrest's justification.

15. Law enforcement officers searching a person incident to arrest may use the degree of force reasonably necessary to protect themselves, prevent escape, and prevent the destruction or concealment of evidence.

Search Incident to Detention

Cupp v. Murphy
laws.findlaw.com/us/412/291.html

In *Cupp v. Murphy*, 412 U.S. 291, 93 S.Ct. 2000, 36 L.Ed.2d 900 (1973), the U.S. Supreme Court decided that a law enforcement officer may conduct a limited warrantless search of a person merely detained for investigation. In that case, the defendant was notified of his wife's strangulation and then voluntarily came to the police headquarters and met his attorney there. Police noticed a dark spot on the defendant's finger and asked whether they could take a scraping from his fingernails. The defendant refused. Under protest and without a warrant, police proceeded to take the samples, which turned out to include particles of skin and blood of the defendant's wife and fabric from her clothing. The evidence was admitted at trial, and the defendant was convicted of second-degree murder.

The Court held that the momentary detention of the defendant to get the fingernail scrapings constituted a seizure governed by the Fourth Amendment. The Court, citing the *Chimel* case, also recognized that under prescribed conditions, warrantless searches incident to an arrest are constitutionally valid. In this case, however, without an arrest or search warrant, a full *Chimel* search of the defendant's body and the area within his immediate control would not have been permissible. Nevertheless, the Court validated the search under a limited application of the *Chimel* rule based on the unique facts of the case:

- The defendant was not arrested but was detained only long enough to take the fingernail scrapings.
- The search was very limited in extent, involving only the scraping of fingernails. (The Court was careful to point out that a full *Chimel* search would not have been justified without an arrest. The officers therefore could not have searched the defendant's body and the area within his immediate control.)
- The evidence—blood and skin on the fingernails—was readily destructible.
- The defendant made attempts to destroy the evidence, creating exigent circumstances.
- The officers had probable cause to arrest the defendant, even though he was not actually arrested.

All five of these conditions were essential to the Court's decision and must be satisfied to make a search incident to detention legal. Otherwise a warrant must be obtained before a search is conducted.

	FRISK	SEARCH INCIDENT TO ARREST
Justification	Officer must have reason to believe that the person to be searched is an armed and dangerous person.	Officer must make a lawful custodial arrest of the person to be searched.
Purpose	Protection of the officer and other prospective victims of violence.	1. To search for and remove weapons that the arrestee might use to resist arrest or effect an escape. 2. To search for and seize evidence in order to prevent its concealment or destruction.
Extent of search of person	Carefully limited search or patdown of the outer clothing in order to discover weapons that might be used to assault the officer.	Full body search and search of the area into which an arrestee might reach in order to grab a weapon or evidentiary item.
Extent of search of vehicle	Areas in the passenger compartment in which a weapon may be placed or hidden.	The entire passenger compartment and the contents of any containers found within the passenger compartment.
Items that may be seized	Weapons or weaponlike objects and nonthreatening contraband if its identity as contraband is immediately apparent to the touch.	Weapons and evidence.
Use of force	Only the force reasonably necessary to protect the officer and others.	Only the force reasonably necessary to protect the officer and others, to prevent the escape of the arrestee, and to prevent the destruction or concealment of evidence.

Comparison of a Frisk and a Seach Incident to Arrest

■ EXHIBIT 8.1

Summary

Search incident to arrest is a recognized exception to the warrant requirement of the Fourth Amendment. The U.S. Supreme Court case of *Chimel v. California* permits the search of a person who has been subjected to a lawful custodial arrest for the purposes of removing weapons and preventing the concealment or destruction of evidence. A full search for weapons and seizable evidence is permitted, whether or not there is any likelihood of danger or any reason to believe evidence will be found.

A search incident to arrest must be substantially contemporaneous with the arrest and may extend to the arrestee's body and to the area, and to all items and containers, within his or her immediate control—the area from which the arrestee might gain possession of a weapon or destructible evidence. Any weapon or seizable evidence found within this area may be seized. If, however, the item seized is luggage or other personal property not immediately associated with the person of the arrestee, a delayed search of the property, after it has come within the exclusive control of the police, may not be conducted without a warrant or exigent circumstances. A search incident to the arrest of an occupant of a motor vehicle may extend to the passenger area of the vehicle and may include a search of containers found in the vehicle, if the search is contemporaneous with the arrest.

Patdown searches of persons in the vicinity of the arrested person and searches of the areas within their immediate control may be conducted incident to the arrest, if reasonably necessary to remove weapons and prevent the concealment or destruction of evidence. Full searches of areas of the premises beyond the immediate control of the arrestee or companions may not be conducted. Nevertheless, an officer may look in closets and other spaces immediately adjoining the place of arrest from which an attack could be immediately launched. Also, an officer may conduct a properly limited protective sweep of the area beyond the spaces immediately adjoining the place of arrest when the officer reasonably suspects, based on specific and articulable facts, that the area to be swept harbors a person posing a danger to those on the arrest scene. Under the plain view doctrine, if police are lawfully in a position from which they view an object, if its incriminating character is apparent, and if the officers have a lawful right of access to the object, they may seize it without a warrant. Searches incident to arrest may be delayed in a variety of circumstances, but there must be good reason for a delay and the duration of the delay must be reasonable under the circumstances.

The U.S. Supreme Court has approved a limited warrantless search of a person merely detained for investigation. Law enforcement officers may conduct such a search, however, only if they have probable cause to arrest the suspect and if there is an imminent danger that crucial evidence will be destroyed if the search is not made immediately.

Key Holdings from Major Cases

Chimel v. California (1969). "When an arrest is made, it is reasonable for the arresting officer to search the person arrested in order to remove any weapons that the latter might seek to use in order to resist arrest or effect his escape. Otherwise, the officer's safety might well be endangered, and the arrest itself frustrated. In addition, it is entirely reasonable for the arresting officer to search for and seize any evidence on the arrestee's person in order to prevent its concealment or destruction. And the area into which an arrestee might reach in order to grab a weapon or evidentiary items must, of course, be governed by a like rule. A gun on a table or in a drawer in front of one who is arrested can be as dangerous to the arresting officer as one concealed in the clothing of the person arrested. There is ample justification, therefore, for a search of the arrestee's person and the area 'within his immediate control'—construing that phrase to mean the area from within which he might gain possession of a weapon or destructible evidence." 395 U.S. 752, 762–63, 89 S.Ct. 2034, 2040, 23 L.Ed.2d 685, 694.

United States v. Robinson (1973). "It is the fact of the lawful arrest which establishes the authority to search, and we hold that in the case of lawful custodial arrest a full search of the person is not only an exception to the warrant requirement of the Fourth Amendment, but is also a 'reasonable' search under that Amendment." 414 U.S. 218, 235, 94 S.Ct. 467, 477, 38 L.Ed.2d 427, 441.

United States v. Chadwick (1977). "Once law enforcement officers have reduced luggage or other personal property not immediately associated with the person of the arrestee to their exclusive control, and there is no longer any danger that the arrestee might gain access to the property to seize a weapon or destroy evidence, a search of that property is no longer an incident of the arrest." 433 U.S. 1, 15, 97 S.Ct. 2476, 2485, 53 L.Ed.2d 538, 551.

Whren v. United States (1996). An officer's ulterior motives do not invalidate the officer's conduct that is justifiable on the basis of probable cause to believe that a violation of law has occurred. 517 U.S. 806, 116 S.Ct. 1769, 135 L.Ed.2d 89.

New York v. Belton (1981). "[W]hen a policeman has made a lawful custodial arrest of the occupant of an automobile, he may, as a contemporaneous incident of that arrest, search the passenger compartment of that automobile.

"It follows from this conclusion that the police may also examine the contents of any containers found within the passenger compartment, for if the passenger compartment is within the reach of the arrestee, so also will containers in it be within his reach. . . . Such a container may, of course, be searched whether it is open or closed, since the justification for the search is not that the arrestee has no privacy interest in the container, but that the lawful custodial arrest justifies the infringement of any privacy interest the arrestee may have." 453 U.S. 454, 460–61, 101 S.Ct. 2860, 2864, 69 L.Ed.2d 768, 775.

Maryland v. Buie (1990). "[A]s an incident to the arrest the officers could, as a precautionary matter and without probable cause or reasonable suspicion, look in closets and other spaces immediately adjoining the place of arrest from which an attack could be immediately launched. Beyond that, however, . . . there must be articulable facts which, taken together with the rational inferences from those facts, would warrant a reasonably prudent officer in believing that the area to be swept harbors an individual posing a danger to those on the arrest scene." 494 U.S. 325, 334, 110 S.Ct. 1093, 1098, 108 L.Ed.2d 276, 286.

"The Fourth Amendment permits a properly limited protective sweep in conjunction with an in-home arrest when the searching officer possesses a reasonable belief based on specific and articulable facts that the area to be swept harbors an individual posing a danger to those on the arrest scene." 494 U.S. at 337, 110 S.Ct. at 1099–00, 108 L.Ed.2d at 288.

James v. Louisiana (1965). "A search 'can be incident to an arrest only if it is substantially contemporaneous with the arrest and is confined to the immediate vicinity of the arrest.'" 382 U.S. 36, 37, 86 S.Ct. 151, 151, 15 L.Ed.2d 30, 31.

United States v. Edwards (1974). "[O]nce the accused is lawfully arrested and is in custody, the effects in his possession at the place of detention that were subject to search at the time and place of his arrest may lawfully be searched and seized without a warrant even though a substantial period of time has elapsed between the arrest and subsequent administrative processing, on the one hand, and the taking of the property for use as evidence on the other." 415 U.S. 800, 807, 94 S.Ct. 1234, 1239, 39 L.Ed.2d 771, 778.

Cupp v. Murphy (1973). "Where there is no formal arrest, as in the case before us, a person might well be less hostile to the police and less likely to take conspicuous, immediate steps to destroy incriminating evidence on his person. Since he knows he is going to be released, he might be likely instead to be concerned with diverting attention away from himself. Accordingly, we do not hold that a full *Chimel* search would have been justified in this case without a formal arrest and without a warrant. But the respondent was not subjected to such a search.

"At the time Murphy was being detained at the station house, he was obviously aware of the detectives' suspicions. Though he did not have the full warning of official suspicion that a formal arrest provides, Murphy was sufficiently apprised of his suspected role in the crime to motivate him to attempt to destroy what evidence he could without attracting further attention. Testimony at trial indicated that after he refused to consent to the taking of fingernail samples, he put his hands behind his back and appeared to rub them together. He then put his hands in his pockets, and a 'metallic sound, such as keys or change rattling' was heard. The rationale of *Chimel*, in these circumstances, justified the police in subjecting him to the very limited search necessary to preserve the highly evanescent evidence they found under his fingernails. . . . On the facts of this case, considering the existence of probable cause, the very limited intrusion undertaken incident to the station house detention, and the ready destructibility of the evidence, we cannot say that this search violated the Fourth and Fourteenth Amendments." 412 U.S. 291, 296, 93 S.Ct. 2000, 2004, 36 L.Ed.2d 900, 906.

Review and Discussion Questions

1. Assume that while riding in the first-class section of an airplane, a person is legally arrested for transporting illegal drugs. Can the arresting officers immediately conduct searches of the following items and places incident to the arrest?

   a. The person's clothing

   b. The person's suitcase

   c. The entire first-class section of the airplane

   d. The person's body cavities

   If you approved any of the preceding searches, consider whether each search should be made. What are the possible alternatives?

2. If a defendant is arrested in an automobile for stealing the automobile, may the arresting officer search other passengers in the automobile incident to the defendant's arrest?

3. In a typical search-incident-to-arrest situation, the arrest is followed by a search and then by a seizure. Is a search followed by a seizure and then by an arrest valid? Is a seizure followed by an arrest and then by an additional search valid?

4. What problems relative to search incident to arrest arise when the individual arrested is a person of the opposite sex?

5. Does the nature of the offense arrested for have any effect on the scope of a search incident to arrest?

6. Assume that a defendant is arrested in his kitchen for the armed robbery of a bank earlier that day. The arresting officers have an arrest warrant but no search warrant. The defendant is one of three persons wanted in the robbery. The defendant's automobile, the suspected getaway car, is parked in his driveway. Indicate the full extent of the arresting officers' authority to search the defendant, his premises, and his automobile.

7. Assume the same facts as in question 6 except that the defendant is arrested while running from his house to his automobile. Indicate the full extent of the arresting officers' authority to search the defendant, his premises, and his automobile. What if the officers have only a search warrant for the defendant's house, and no arrest warrant? What if it is raining heavily?

8. Is the scope of a search incident to arrest affected by any of the following circumstances?

    a. The defendant is handcuffed and chained to a pole.
    b. The defendant is unconscious.
    c. The defendant is surrounded by a group of friends.
    d. The defendant is arrested on a dark street.

9. Since the search of containers in the passenger compartment of an automobile is now allowed incident to a custodial arrest under the ruling in *New York v. Belton*, should law enforcement officers wait until a defendant is in an automobile before making an arrest, when possible? Should officers make custodial arrests for offenses for which they would ordinarily not make custodial arrests?

10. Discuss the meaning of this statement: "It is not at all clear that the 'grabbing distance' authorized in the *Chimel* case is conditioned upon the arrested person's continued capacity 'to grab.'" *People v. Fitzpatrick*, 346 N.Y.S.2d 793, 797, 300 N.E.2d 139, 143 (N.Y. 1973).

Real-Life Fact Situations

1 West Virginia State Police in Rainelle, West Virginia, responded to a 911 dispatch during the early evening hours of May 10, 1998, which indicated that "a domestic altercation [was] in progress on Backus Mountain Road [in Meadow Bridge, West Virginia] with weapons involved." The 911 dispatcher had received a call from Anna Terry who stated: "[M]y daughter is living up there with a guy named Dennis Gwinn, and she just called me real fast and told me to call the police. . . . And she told me that he's got a gun in there by the door and he told her he was going to kill her." Terry also told the 911 dispatcher that her daughter had her baby with her.

State Trooper Ron Thomas was dispatched to respond to the call and was later joined by State Police Sergeant Scott Moore and another trooper. When Trooper Thomas arrived at 485 Backus Road, a remote location in Fayette County, he pulled his cruiser to within 25 yards of a small, "single-wide" trailer with a front porch. He drew his weapon from its holster and yelled for Dennis Gwinn to come out. Gwinn exited the trailer, wearing only a pair of blue jeans. Trooper Thomas conducted a pat-down search of Gwinn, handcuffed him, and placed him in the back seat of his cruiser. Trooper Thomas then asked Gwinn "where his wife was at so [Thomas] could speak to her." Gwinn responded that the woman was his girlfriend, not his wife, and that she was inside the trailer.

Trooper Thomas then entered the trailer—the door was open and the screen door shut—where he found Diane Harrah, crying and holding her baby. Sergeant Moore, who had just joined Trooper Thomas, conducted a protective sweep of the trailer while Thomas questioned Harrah. Harrah reported that Gwinn was drunk and had prevented her from leaving the trailer. She related that Gwinn had gone to the bedroom, obtained a pistol, and brandished it, telling her that "if you try to leave, I'll kill you." She described the handgun as a blue-colored pistol but did not know where Gwinn had put it. She had last seen him with it in the living room. Trooper Thomas and Sergeant Moore searched for the handgun, but discovered instead a loaded shotgun under the couch. They failed to find the handgun.

The officers left the trailer, placed the shotgun in the trunk of Trooper Thomas' cruiser, and prepared to transport Gwinn to the "regional jail." Because Gwinn was wearing no shirt or shoes, Trooper Thomas went back into the trailer and said to Harrah, "Where's his shoes? And we need to get a shirt for him." Harrah directed Thomas to Gwinn's boots in the living room, and she then went back to the bedroom to retrieve a shirt. While Harrah was getting the shirt, Trooper Thomas picked up Gwinn's mid-calf work boots, which "seemed awful[ly] heavy," and heard something "flop inside." When he opened the boot and looked inside, he discovered a pistol. He showed it to Harrah, and Harrah identified it as the weapon with which Gwinn had threatened her earlier that evening.

Gwinn was charged as a felon in possession of a Smith & Wesson .38 caliber revolver and a Winchester 12-gauge shotgun, in violation of 18 U.S.C. § 922. Gwinn moved to suppress the evidence of the two guns because they were obtained pursuant to a warrantless search. Should the guns be suppressed? *United States v. Gwinn*, 219 F.3d 326 (4th Cir. 2000).

Read the court opinion at:
law.findlaw.com/4th/994462p.html

2 Belfield police officer Michael Gant and Belfield police chief Eric Ahrens responded to a complaint from an employee of the Super Pumper Station Store in Belfield, North Dakota. The employee's complaint alleged a customer in the store's parking lot was making "fists gestures" at employees. When the officers arrived, they attempted to speak to Haverluk, who was seated in a car in the store's parking lot. Haverluk responded by cursing at the officers.

Officer Gant, who was stationed on the passenger side of Haverluk's vehicle, observed Haverluk place his right hand between the driver's seat and console. Gant informed Chief Ahrens of Haverluk's actions; the officers drew their weapons and ordered Haverluk to step out of the car.

The officers noticed several indications of intoxication and ultimately arrested Haverluk for being in actual physical control ("APC") of a motor vehicle while under the influence of intoxicating liquor, drugs, or other substances. Shortly after Haverluk was ordered out of the car, Gant entered the car and reached between the driver's seat and console, where he found a set of keys, one of which was the vehicle's ignition key. Ahrens advised Haverluk he was under arrest. Haverluk then struck Ahrens in the face.

After a preliminary hearing, Haverluk moved to suppress the keys, based on the testimony presented at the preliminary hearing. Should his motion to suppress be granted? *State v. Haverluk*, 617 N.W.2d 652 (N.D. 2000).

Read the court opinion at:
www.court.state.nd.us/court/opinions/20000077.htm

3 Canyon County Deputy Sheriff Donia Ballard received a call from dispatch shortly after 7 P.M. on a May evening. Dispatch relayed that a caller, who wished to remain anonymous, reported seeing a vehicle parked on a road in a field near the intersection of Farmway and Ustick Roads in early morning and late evenings several times in the preceding weeks. The caller reported that the vehicle was currently in the area and opined that its occupant might be "doing drugs," but did not articulate any reason for this suspicion.

Ballard responded to the dispatch and arrived in the area shortly before dusk. A vehicle was parked on a muddy dirt road surrounded by agricultural fields. The road paralleled a concrete irrigation ditch and came to a dead end in the fields of a farm belonging to Zelda Nickel. Three houses were in the general vicinity.

Ballard parked behind the vehicle. James Nickel was sitting in the driver's seat with the window rolled down. Ballard approached Nickel and explained that she had received a call about a suspicious vehicle and was checking out the report. Nickel told her his name and stated that he was "watching the corn grow." He told Ballard that he was on the property of his mother, Zelda Nickel, and pointed in the direction of his mother's house. Ballard later testified that she believed that

Nickel was under the influence of something because he was uncooperative, his eyes seemed wild, and he was shaky. Although Ballard knew that Zelda Nickel lived in the vicinity, she did not believe Nickel when he told her he was on his mother's property.

Ballard asked Nickel for identification, and he handed her a copy of an expired temporary permit, issued pursuant to Section 18-8002 of the Idaho Code. The record does not reveal how long Ballard kept the form or whether she returned it to Nickel. Nickel made no attempt to drive or walk away. Ballard returned to her patrol car and ran a check on Nickel's name. Her backup, Deputy William Adams, arrived about this time. The check with dispatch revealed an outstanding arrest warrant from the City of Caldwell. Ballard and Adams returned to the vehicle and Ballard asked Nickel to step out. He refused. After she asked several more times, Nickel eventually complied. Ballard then told him that he was under arrest. A brief scuffle ensued during which Adams used pepper spray to subdue Nickel.

After handcuffing Nickel, Ballard placed him in the back seat of her patrol car. As she was doing this, Adams searched the vehicle. On the passenger seat, Adams found a one-dollar bill wrapped around an off-white substance. The substance was removed from the vehicle. A field test indicated positive for methamphetamine; later tests at the Bureau of Forensic Services identified the substance as cocaine. Although Adams testified at the suppression hearing that his search of Nickel's vehicle was done as an inventory search, he did not fill out an inventory form. After the search, deciding that a tow truck would not be able to get the vehicle off the muddy road, Ballard and Adams decided to leave the vehicle where it was.

Ballard issued a misdemeanor citation to Nickel for resisting arrest. The Canyon County prosecutor filed a criminal information charging Nickel with possession of methamphetamine. Nickel pleaded not guilty to both charges. The district court later granted the State's motion to amend the information to charge Nickel with possession of cocaine. Nickel moved to suppress all evidence stemming from the search of the vehicle. Should his motion be granted? *State v. Nickel*, 7 P.3d 219 (Idaho 2000).

Read the court opinion at:
caselaw.findlaw.com/data2/idahostatecases/sc/1008/nickel5.pdf

4 The facts most favorable to the trial court's judgment reveal that on June 12, 1999, Sergeant John Cox brought his patrol car to a halt directly behind Gibson's van which was stopped at a red traffic light. Thereafter, Sergeant Cox conducted a random computer check of Gibson's license plate which indicated that Gibson had an outstanding warrant for his arrest from Brown County, Indiana. However, Sergeant Cox did not initiate a traffic stop of Gibson's van.

Instead, Sergeant Cox followed Gibson as he drove into the parking lot of a convenience store. As Gibson exited the van and walked toward the convenience store, Sergeant Cox got out of his patrol car, stopped Gibson, and requested his driver's license. After examining the driver's license, Sergeant Cox handcuffed Gibson. Thereafter, Officer Bradley Meyers, who had responded to Sergeant Cox's call for assistance, asked Gibson if he had any weapons or contraband in his van. Gibson informed Officer Meyers that marijuana was located in the center console of his van. Neither Sergeant Cox nor Officer Meyers informed Gibson of his *Miranda* rights prior to Officer Meyer questioning Gibson. A plastic bag containing a green leafy substance later determined to be marijuana was retrieved from Gibson's vehicle.

Consequently, the State charged Gibson with possession of marijuana, a Class A misdemeanor. Thereafter, Gibson filed with the trial court a motion to suppress the statements made by him after his arrest and the marijuana obtained from the warrantless search of his vehicle. Should his motion be granted? *Gibson v. State*, 733 N.E.2d 945 (Ind.App. 2000)

Read the court opinion at:
www.state.in.us/judiciary/opinions/archive/07310005.mgr.html

5 On the evening of September 26, 1995, three undercover Boston police officers were investigating drug activity in the Roxbury section of Boston. A woman attempted to flag down one of the officers, who was driving an unmarked vehicle. He did not stop, but reported by radio to nearby officers that he believed that the woman was interested in selling narcotics to him. He also communicated his location as well as the woman's description and requested backup.

When the other officers reported that they were in place, the officer returned to the street where he had seen the woman and stopped as she approached the vehicle. The woman asked him if he was "looking for something." The officer responded in the affirmative. She then asked him how many he wanted, and the officer said "a couple." The woman told him to wait, and she walked away from the rear of the officer's vehicle, which was parked on the side of the street. The woman crossed the street and met briefly with a black male, later identified as the defendant. The officer observed the woman and the defendant gesture to one another, then the woman put her hand to her mouth as she walked back toward him.

When the woman returned to the officer's vehicle, he indicated that he wanted two, at which point she opened her mouth and removed two small plastic bags. The officer told her that "they were too small" so he would purchase only one. He gave her two marked five dollar bills, and she handed to him a plastic bag that appeared to contain crack cocaine. The woman then walked away from the vehicle toward the defendant. As the officer drove off, he radioed to the other officers that the transaction was complete. He told them they should observe the defendant and the woman and retrieve the money.

One of the assisting officers saw the defendant and the woman standing on the steps of a building. He approached them to conduct a "field interrogation observation." The officer asked the defendant for his name and address. The officer then asked whether the defendant had any money on him. The defendant produced the two marked bills from his pocket. The officer placed the defendant under arrest.

The defendant was taken to a police station and booked. Immediately after booking, officers escorted the defendant to a corridor in the cellblock area to search him for weapons and contraband. As the defendant removed his pants and underpants, he reached behind his back and retrieved a plastic bag that appeared to contain crack cocaine. The officer then ordered the defendant to turn around and bend over. As the defendant did so, another plastic bag fell to the floor. The officer observed yet another plastic bag in the area between the defendant's buttocks and removed the bag.

In his motion to suppress, the defendant argued that the money was seized pursuant to an illegal stop. He further argued that the cocaine was seized as the fruit of his unlawful arrest and also as a result of an illegal strip search. Should the defendant's motion to suppress be granted? *Commonwealth v. Thomas*, 708 N.E.2d 669 (Mass. 1999).

Read the court opinion at:
www.socialaw.com/sjcslip/7839.html

6 On January 9, 1997, Tumwater Police Detective Anthony Gianesini observed Porter driving her van on Trosper Road in Tumwater. Porter's adult son, Charles, sat in the passenger seat next to her. Gianesini recognized both of them from prior incidents and he suspected that Charles had an outstanding warrant for his arrest. A computer warrants check confirmed Detective Gianesini's suspicion. Gianesini did not attempt to stop the van himself. At the time, he was dressed in civilian clothes and was driving an unmarked police car. Instead, he called for a uniformed Tumwater police officer to make the arrest.

Meanwhile, Porter drove to a gas station, legally parked the van next to a pay telephone, and got out to place a call. Gianesini then saw the two occupants go the rear of the van, do "something which [he] really couldn't see," and close the van doors. Report of Proceedings at 8. According to Gianesini, Porter and Charles looked directly at him. Charles then reentered the van, emerged with a leashed dog, and began walking along Trosper Road. Gianesini did not follow Charles. He chose to maintain his position, keeping both Charles and the van within sight.

A uniformed police officer arrived approximately 25–30 seconds later. The officer arrested Charles on the side of the road about 300 feet from the van. The officer searched Charles and discovered a small plastic bag containing methamphetamine. Charles was then handcuffed and placed in the back of the officer's patrol car. Porter observed the arrest and walked from the van to the arrest location. She retrieved the dog from Charles and continued to walk it along the road away from the van. She did not return to the van.

The uniformed officer then drove to Porter's van where Gianesini was waiting. Acting without a warrant, Gianesini opened the van and saw items consistent with the manufacture of methamphetamine. The van was impounded and later, based upon Gianesini's observations, a search warrant was obtained authorizing a full search. The subsequent search revealed glass vials and plastic bags, which were later found to contain amounts of pseudoephedrine, a precursor to methamphetamine.

The State charged Porter with possession of pseudoephedrine with the intent to manufacture methamphetamine. Porter moved to suppress the evidence seized from the van, arguing Gianesini's initial search could not be justified as a search incident to the arrest of her son. Should the motion to suppress be granted? *State v. Porter*, 6 P.3d 1245 (Wash. App. 2000).

Read the court opinion at:

www.cdlaw.com/cases/apps/09_00/24304-1.htm

Chapter 9

Consent Searches

Outline

Another well-established exception to the search warrant requirement is the **consent search.** A consent search occurs when a person voluntarily waives his or her Fourth Amendment rights and allows a law enforcement officer to search his or her body, premises, or belongings. The consenting person relinquishes any right to later protest the search on constitutional grounds, and any evidence seized as a result of the search is admissible in court, even though there was no warrant and no probable cause to search. A consent search can benefit a consenting party who is innocent of any wrongdoing.

> If the search is conducted and proves fruitless, that in itself may convince the police that an arrest with its possible stigma and embarrassment is unnecessary, or that a far more extensive search pursuant to a warrant is not justified. In short, a search pursuant to consent may result in considerably less inconvenience for the subject of the search, and, properly conducted, is a constitutionally permissible and wholly legitimate aspect of effective police activity. *Schneckloth v. Bustamonte,* 412 U.S. 218, 228, 93 S.Ct. 2041, 2048, 36 L.Ed.2d 854, 863 (1973).

Law enforcement officers use the consent search frequently because it is faster than warrant procedures and does not require the often difficult determination of whether there is probable cause, either to search or to arrest. Consent searches, however, present many opportunities for abuse of a person's Fourth Amendment rights by law enforcement officers. To protect those rights, courts closely examine the circumstances surrounding every consent search to determine whether the consent was truly voluntary. The U.S. Supreme Court said:

> [T]he Fourth and Fourteenth Amendments require that consent not be coerced, by explicit or implicit means, by implied threat or covert force. For, no matter how subtly the coercion were applied, the resulting "consent" would be no more than a pretext for the unjustified police intrusion against which the Fourth Amendment is directed. . . .
>
> The problem of reconciling the recognized legitimacy of consent searches with the requirement that they be free from any aspect of official coercion cannot be resolved by any infallible touchstone. To approve such searches without the most careful scrutiny would sanction the possibility of official coercion; to place artificial restrictions upon such searches would jeopardize their basic validity. Just as was true with confessions the requirement of "voluntary" consent reflects a fair accommodation of the constitutional requirements involved. In examining all the surrounding circumstances to determine if in fact the consent to search was coerced, account must be taken of subtly coercive police questions, as well as the possibly vulnerable subjective state of the person who consents. Those searches that are the product of police coercion can thus be filtered out without undermining the continuing validity of consent searches. In sum, there is no reason for us to depart in the area of consent searches, from the traditional definition of "voluntariness." *Schneckloth v. Bustamonte,* 412 U.S. 218, 228–29, 93 S.Ct. 2041, 2048–49, 36 L.Ed.2d 854, 864 (1973).

When the prosecuting attorney attempts to introduce into court evidence obtained as a result of a consent search, the court requires proof by "clear and convincing evidence" that the consent was voluntary and not the result of duress or coercion, express or implied. *United States v. Gonzales,* 842 F.2d 748, 754 (5th Cir. 1988). The prosecutor's proof will consist almost entirely of the law enforcement officer's testimony about the circumstances surrounding the obtaining of the consent and the conducting of the search. The remainder of this chapter is devoted to explaining in detail the meaning

Schneckloth v. Bustamonte
laws.findlaw.com/us/412/218.html

Objectives

- **Explain the benefits, to the law enforcement officer and to the person being searched, of a consent search.**
- **Understand the circumstances that are considered in determining whether a consent search is voluntary.**
- **Know the difference between a consent to enter premises and a consent to search the premises.**
- **Understand how the scope of a consent search is limited by: the person giving consent; the area to which consent to search is given; time, and; the expressed object of the search.**
- **Understand when a third person may be authorized to consent to a search of a person's property and how third-party consent is affected by the person's reasonable expectation of privacy.**

of the voluntariness requirement and providing guidelines for the law enforcement officer in conducting consent searches.

Key Points

1. Law enforcement officers may, without a warrant or probable cause, conduct a search based on a person's voluntary consent. Any evidence discovered during the search may be seized and admitted in court.

2. Before evidence seized as the result of a consent search may be admitted in court, the court must find from the totality of the circumstances that the consent was voluntary and not the result of duress or coercion, express or implied.

---

caselaw.findlaw.com/data/
constitution/amendment04/
04.html#1
Discussion (with annotations) of
consent searches
www.fbi.gov/publications/leb/
1996/aug967.txt
Article, "Consent Searches:
Guidelines for Officers" by Kimberly A. Crawford
lawschool.lexis.com/emanuel/
web/crimpro/crimpro03.htm
Chapter 3 contains an outline of
the law relating to consent
searches
www.mobar.net/journal/1999/
janfeb/swingle.htm
Article, "'Knock and Talk' Consent Searches: If Called by a Panther, Don't Anther" by H.
Morley Swingle and Kevin M.
Zoellner

*For new and updated weblinks,
go to* www.wadsworth.com/
cj/ferdico0253

Voluntariness Requirement

There are no set rules for determining whether a consent to search is voluntary. Courts will examine all the circumstances surrounding the giving of the consent in making this decision. The following examples illustrate the circumstances courts consider important in deciding the question of voluntariness of consent.

Force or Threat of Force

Courts usually find consent involuntary if law enforcement officers used force or threats of force in obtaining the consent. In *United States v. Al-Azzawy*, 784 F.2d 890 (9th Cir. 1985), the defendant gave permission to search his trailer as he was approached by numerous police officers with guns drawn while the defendant knelt outside his trailer with his hands on his head. The court found that, under these coercive conditions, the consent to search was not voluntary. And in *United States v. Hatley*, 999 F.2d 392 (9th Cir. 1993), the court found the defendant's consent to search involuntary because it was given after the officer threatened to take the defendant's child into custody. Lack of voluntary consent was also found when officers told the defendant that if he did not consent, the officers could and would get a search warrant that would allow them to tear the paneling off his walls and ransack his house. *United States v. Kampbell*, 574 F.2d 962 (8th Cir. 1978).

A mere statement by police that they will attempt to obtain a warrant if consent is withheld is usually not considered coercion. This is especially true if the officer indicates that he or she must apply for the warrant from a neutral and detached judicial authority and if the statement that a warrant can be obtained is well founded.

> One factor to be considered is whether a threat to obtain a search warrant will invalidate a subsequent consent. Courts have drawn distinctions where, on one hand, an officer merely says that he will attempt to obtain a search warrant or whether, on the other hand, he says he can obtain the search warrant, as if it were a foregone conclusion. However, consent is not likely to be held invalid where an officer tells a defendant that he could obtain a search warrant if the officer had probable cause upon which a warrant could issue. *United States v. Kaplan*, 895 F.2d 618, 622 (9th Cir. 1990).

Sometimes the initial encounter between a law enforcement officer and a suspect requires the officer to use force or threat of force for personal or public safety. Despite the coercive nature of the initial confrontation, an officer may still obtain a valid consent to search if the consent itself is obtained without coercion. In *United States v. Alfonso,* 759 F.2d 728 (9th Cir. 1985), police with guns drawn arrested the defendant in his motel room. After determining that no weapons or other persons were in the room, the officers holstered their guns. The officers informed the defendant of the purpose of their investigation, and the defendant, who was not handcuffed, responded that he had "nothing to hide." The court held that the defendant's consent to a search of his luggage was voluntary, despite the initial armed confrontation.

Submission to a Fraudulent or Mistaken Claim of Authority

A more subtle form of coercion is a law enforcement officer's assertion of a right to search when no such right exists. A person's submitting to a false assertion of authority and allowing a search does not constitute a voluntary consent. This is not an act of free will, but rather, a mistaken demonstration of respect for the law. This is true whether the officer's assertion of authority was mistaken or was deliberately designed to deceive the person. In *Bumper v. North Carolina,* 391 U.S. 543, 88 S.Ct. 1788, 20 L.Ed.2d 797 (1968), officers went to the home of a rape suspect to look for evidence. The home was owned and occupied by the defendant's grandmother. The officers told the grandmother that they had a search warrant, and she let them in. During the course of their search, a rifle was found. At the hearing on the motion to suppress the rifle as evidence, the prosecutor relied on the grandmother's consent rather than on the warrant to support the legality of the search. (In fact, no warrant was ever returned, nor was there any information about the conditions under which it was issued.)

Bumper v. North Carolina
laws.findlaw.com/us/391/543.html

The U.S. Supreme Court held that a search cannot be justified on the basis of consent when that consent has been given only after an announcement by the officers conducting the search that they have a search warrant:

> When a prosecutor seeks to rely upon consent to justify the lawfulness of a search, he has the burden of proving that the consent was, in fact, *freely and voluntarily given.* This burden cannot be discharged by showing no more than acquiescence to a claim of lawful authority. A search conducted in reliance upon a warrant cannot later be justified on the basis of consent if it turns out that the warrant was invalid. The results can be no different when it turns out that the State does not even attempt to rely upon the validity of the warrant, or fails to show that there was, in fact, any warrant at all.
>
> When a law enforcement officer claims authority to search a home under a warrant, he announces in effect that the occupant has no right to resist the search. The situation is instinct with coercion—albeit colorably lawful coercion. Where there is coercion there cannot be consent. (Emphasis added) 391 U.S. at 548–50, 88 S.Ct. at 1792, 20 L.Ed.2d at 802–03.

Misrepresentation or Deception

Coercion may also take the form of misrepresentation or deception on matters other than the officer's authority. A person's consent to search based on false impressions created by a law enforcement officer is not voluntary. In *Commonwealth v. Wright,* 190 A.2d 709 (Pa. 1963), officers arrested the defendant for robbery and murder and questioned him at police headquarters, but they obtained no incriminating statements. The next day officers, without a search warrant, went to the defendant's apartment to conduct a search. They falsely told the defendant's wife that the defendant had admitted the crime and had sent the police for the "stuff." The frightened and upset wife admitted the officers to the apartment and led them to money taken in the robbery. The court held that the consent given by the wife was not voluntary: "[I]t is well established that the consent may not be gained through stealth, deceit, or misrepresentation, and that if such exists this is tantamount to implied coercion." 190 A.2d at 709, 711.

If, however, the deceit is carried out by an undercover officer and concerns only the officer's identity as a governmental agent, a person's misplaced confidence in the agent will not make the person's consent involuntary.

> Entry of an undercover agent is not illegal if he enters a home for the "very purposes contemplated by the occupant." . . . If the occupant reveals private information to the visitor under such circumstances, he or she assumes the risk the visitor will reveal it. *United States v. Goldstein*, 611 F.Supp. 624, 626 (N.D. Ill. 1985).

In the *Goldstein* case, the undercover officer gained entrance to the defendant's home for the purpose understood by the defendant's wife: to discuss the possible purchase of a stolen emerald. The court held that the wife's voluntarily showing the officer the emerald was the result of her misplaced trust in the officer and did not implicate any Fourth Amendment privacy interest. "A government agent may obtain an invitation onto property by misrepresenting his identity, and if invited, does not need probable cause nor warrant to enter so long as he does not exceed the scope of his invitation." *United States v. Scherer*, 673 F.2d 176, 182 (7th Cir. 1982).

Arrest or Detention

United States v. Watson
laws.findlaw.com/us/423/
411.html

United States v. Mendenhall
laws.findlaw.com/us/446/
544.html

If the consenting party is in custody or detained, the voluntariness of the consent is still measured by the totality of the circumstances. In *United States v. Watson*, 423 U.S. 411, 96 S.Ct. 820, 46 L.Ed.2d 598 (1976), the U.S. Supreme Court held that a consent to search is not involuntary solely because the person giving the consent is under arrest or otherwise in custody. In *United States v. Mendenhall*, 446 U.S. 544, 100 S.Ct. 1870, 64 L.Ed.2d 497 (1980), the U.S. Supreme Court held that a person subjected to a legal *Terry*-type stop was capable of giving a valid consent to search. Nevertheless, courts tend to examine very carefully any consent given under circumstances of custody or detention. A person who has been taken into custody or arrested is believed to be "more susceptible to duress or coercion from the custodial officers." *United States v. Richardson*, 388 F.2d 842, 845 (6th Cir. 1968).

In general, it is more difficult to prove a consent was voluntary when the person giving the consent was in custody. However, if the person in custody is subjected to additional coercive action by a law enforcement officer, such as handcuffing, display of weapons, or incarceration, or if the officer interrogates the person without giving *Miranda* warnings, a subsequent consent to search is likely to be considered involuntary. In *United States v. Chan-Jimenez*, 125 F.3d 1324, 1327–28 (9th Cir. 1997), the court said:

> We agree with Chan-Jimenez that Officer Price's request for permission to search the truck with one hand resting on his gun was implicitly coercive. An officer's keeping his hand on his weapon throughout a colloquy with a suspect is clearly distinguishable from our decisions finding voluntary consent where an officer simply possessed a weapon. . . .

Combined with the fact that the incident took place on a desert highway, with nobody else in sight, Officer Price's actions would have been viewed by a reasonable person essentially as a command to allow a search of the truck. . . . Chan-Jimenez's failure to respond verbally to the officer's request further supports the conclusion that he did not voluntarily consent to a search of his vehicle. Instead, he silently and slowly unfastened the velcro that attached the tarp to the truck. A person's obedience to a show of authority is by itself insufficient to establish voluntary consent. . . . Although consent can be inferred from nonverbal actions, the government must show that consent was "unequivocal and specific" and "freely and intelligently given."

Evasive or uncooperative conduct on the part of the person in custody is also considered to indicate that the consent is not voluntary.

If the arrest or detention itself is *illegal,* courts will generally hold that any consent obtained by exploitation of the illegal conduct is "fruit of the poisonous tree" unless the causal chain between the illegal conduct and the obtaining of consent has been broken. In determining whether the causal chain has been broken, courts consider the time elapsed between the illegality and the giving of consent, the presence of intervening circumstances, and the purpose and flagrancy of the official conduct. *Brown v. Illinois,* 422 U.S. 590, 95 S.Ct. 2254, 45 L.Ed.2d 416 (1975). In *Florida v. Royer,* 460 U.S. 491, 103 S.Ct. 1319, 75 L.Ed.2d 229 (1983), the U.S. Supreme Court, after finding that the defendant was being illegally detained when he consented to the search of his luggage, held that the consent was tainted by the illegality and was ineffective to justify the search. In *United States v. Maez,* 872 F.2d 1444 (10th Cir. 1989), the consent to search was held invalid where the illegal arrest was such that it would cause surprise, fright, and confusion and where the defendant was in the custody of at least three officers for forty-five minutes between the arrest and the giving of consent. In *United States v. Wellins,* 654 F.2d 550 (9th Cir. 1981), however, despite an illegal arrest of the defendant, the court held that a consent to search obtained one and one-quarter hours after the illegal arrest was valid. Attenuating circumstances were found where the defendant was given *Miranda* warnings and allowed to consult with his attorney and codefendant before signing a consent form. Another court held that the passage of a significant amount of time and the lack of flagrant misconduct by police helped purge the taint of an illegal arrest. *United States v. Cherry,* 794 F.2d 201 (5th Cir. 1986).

Brown v. Illinois
laws.findlaw.com/us/422/590.html
Florida v. Royer
laws.findlaw.com/us/460/491.html

Knowledge of Right to Refuse Consent

Before the U.S. Supreme Court decision in *Schneckloth v. Bustamonte* (discussed earlier), some courts held that, to prove voluntary consent to search, the prosecution had to show that the person giving consent knew of the right to refuse consent. Other courts ruled that knowledge of the right to refuse consent was only one factor to be considered in determining voluntariness. In *Schneckloth v. Bustamonte,* the Supreme Court adopted the latter view:

[W]hen the subject of a search is not in custody and the State attempts to justify a search on the basis of his consent, the Fourth and Fourteenth Amendments require that it demonstrate that the consent was in fact voluntarily given, and not the result of duress or coercion, express or implied. Voluntariness is a question of fact to be determined from all the circumstances, and while the subject's knowledge of a right to refuse is a factor to be taken into consideration, the prosecution is not required to demonstrate such knowledge as a prerequisite to establishing a voluntary consent. 412 U.S. at 248–49, 93 S.Ct. at 2059, 36 L.Ed.2d at 875.

A law enforcement officer seeking to obtain a valid consent to search from a person not in custody need not give any warnings or otherwise ensure that the person is aware of the right to refuse consent.

Nevertheless, even though formal warnings are not required for noncustodial consent searches, the courts still consider a person's knowledge of the right to refuse consent as very persuasive evidence of voluntariness.

> [T]he . . . salutary practice of informing individuals that they are free to refuse consent to a search and to contact a lawyer . . . does not absolutely prove uncoerced consent, [but] it does in many instances assuage the fear of a court that an individual was intimidated into consent to a search. *United States v. Berry*, 670 F.2d 583, 597–98 (5th Cir. 1982).

For example, in *In re Joe R.*, 165 Cal.Rptr. 837, 612 P.2d 927 (Cal. 1980), the court found voluntary consent to search despite the presence of several officers with drawn guns, because officers had explained the right to refuse consent. But in *United States v. Jones*, 846 F.2d 358 (6th Cir. 1988), the court found the consent involuntary in similar circumstances, where the police failed to apprise the defendant of his *Miranda* rights or his right to refuse consent. In that case, the defendant, who had no formal education, had been stopped initially by three police cars and led by police to believe he was under arrest. Therefore, an officer may give a person formal warning of this right to increase the chances that the consent will be voluntary. Furthermore, since the courts have not yet decided whether knowledge of the right to refuse consent is necessary for a valid consent when the consenting person is in custody, officers should so inform persons under arrest or otherwise in custody. The following warning should adequately inform a person of the right to refuse consent:

> I am a law enforcement officer. I would like to request permission from you to search your premises (person, belongings).
>
> You have an absolute right to refuse to grant permission for me to search unless I have a search warrant.
>
> If you do grant permission to search, anything found can be used against you in a court of law. If you refuse, I will not make a search at this time.

A consent to search given by a person after receiving such a warning is likely to be considered voluntary by a court, assuming the officer did not use coercion.

If an officer has clear indications that the consenting person already knows of the right to insist on a search warrant, there is no need for the officer to give any warnings. In *United States v. Manuel*, 992 F.2d 272 (10th Cir. 1993), the court held that the defendant's steadfast, repeated refusals to consent to the search of a gift-wrapped package demonstrated his knowledge of the right to refuse consent. When he finally did consent under noncoercive circumstances, the court found the consent voluntary.

Some state courts have refused to follow the *Schneckloth v. Bustamonte* totality-of-the-circumstances test and have required that consenting persons be aware of their right to refuse consent in addition to requiring that the consent be voluntary. The New Jersey Supreme Court held that the state constitution demands that

> the validity of a consent to search, even in a noncustodial situation, must be measured in terms of waiver; i.e., where the state seeks to justify a search on the basis of consent it has the burden of showing that the consent was voluntary, an essential element of which is knowledge of the right to refuse consent. *State v. Johnson*, 346 A.2d 66, 68 (N.J. 1975).

Likewise, *Case v. State*, 519 P.2d 523 (Okla.Crim.App. 1974), held that officers must give *Miranda* warnings before obtaining consent.

Case in Point

Interpreting *Ohio v. Robinette*

On May 26, 1995, at approximately 12:40 A.M., a uniformed officer of the Upper Allen Township Police Department was on routine patrol in a marked vehicle, traveling on Fisher Road in a rural area, when he saw a car parked at the side of the road, alongside the lawn in front of a farmhouse and barn. Standing about fifteen feet from the parked car were two men who appeared to be urinating. The officer pulled in behind the parked car with the intent, as he explained at the suppression hearing, to ascertain what was happening and whether anything was wrong. He stepped out of his vehicle and approached the individuals, noticing, as he passed their car, that it contained a cooler containing unopened beer cans. When the officer asked the men what they were doing, they replied that they were coming from the races at the Williams Grove Speedway and had stopped to urinate. The officer asked to see their driver's licenses, which they produced, and returned to his vehicle to check on the validity of the licenses and to determine whether there were outstanding warrants for either of the men. As he was conducting the license check, a fellow officer arrived and parked his vehicle behind the patrol car. After verifying that the licenses were valid and that there were no warrants for either of the two men, the officer stepped back out of his cruiser; called defendant/appellant Brett Strickler (the owner and operator of the parked car) over to him; returned Strickler's driver's license to him; advised him that it was not appropriate to stop along the road and urinate on someone else's property; thanked him for his cooperation; and began walking toward his cruiser. At that point, he later testified, Strickler was free to go, although there is no evidence that he informed Strickler of that fact.

After taking a few steps toward his car, the officer turned around and asked Strickler if he had anything illegal in his car.

When Strickler answered that he did not, the officer then asked him "if he wouldn't mind if I took a look through his car." As the officer testified at the suppression hearing, he had no reason to suspect Strickler of having any form of contraband in the car.

Nevertheless, his reason for requesting Strickler's consent to search was "[t]o see if there was anything illegal in his car." In response to the request, [Strickler] hesitated. He stood there and looked at me and looked at [the officer] who assisted me at the scene, and I explained to him, you know, he didn't have to say yes, you know, and then I asked him again. After saying that, I said, Do you mind. Is it okay with you if we just take a quick search of your vehicle[?]

At that point, Strickler consented to a search. Upon searching the car, the officer found, between the console and the front passenger seat, an object that looked and smelled like a marijuana smoking pipe. Strickler was arrested and charged with possession of drug paraphernalia, 35 P.S. § 780–113(a)(32).

Strickler filed a pre-trial motion to suppress the marijuana pipe on the grounds that the arresting officer, having had no reasonable belief that a crime had occurred or was occurring, had impermissibly requested his consent to a search, and, in addition, that any search for drug paraphernalia was outside the scope of the consent that he gave. In light of *Ohio v. Robinette*, should Strickler's motion to suppress be granted? *Commonwealth v. Strickler*, 757 A.2d 884 (Pa. 2000).

Read the court opinion at:

www.courts.state.pa.us/opposting/supreme/out/j-256(b)-99mo.pdf

Informing Suspect That He or She Is Free to Go

In *Ohio v. Robinette*, 519 U.S. 33, 117 S.Ct. 417, 136 L.Ed.2d 347 (1996), the defendant was legally stopped for speeding and the officer asked for and was handed the defendant's license. The officer ran a computer check that indicated that the defendant had no previous violations. The officer then asked the defendant to step out of his car, turned on his mounted video camera, issued a verbal warning, and returned his license. After receiving a negative response to questions about the defendant's possession of drugs or weapons, the officer requested and received consent to search his car. In the car the officer found drugs. The defendant claimed that a lawfully seized defendant must be advised that he is "free to go" before his consent to search will be recognized as voluntary. The state supreme court agreed with the defendant, holding that both the state and federal constitutions required that citizens stopped for traffic

Ohio v. Robinette
laws.findlaw.com/us/000/
u20042.html

offenses be clearly informed by the detaining officer when they are free to go after a valid detention, before an officer attempts to engage in a consensual interrogation. The U.S. Supreme Court disagreed, holding that "just as it 'would be thoroughly impractical to impose on the normal consent search the detailed requirements of an effective warning,' . . . so too would it be unrealistic to require police officers to always inform detainees that they are free to go before a consent to search may be deemed voluntary." 519 U.S. at 39–40, 117 S.Ct. at 421, 136 L.Ed.2d at 355.

Suspect's Attitude about the Likelihood of Discovering Evidence

In *United States v. Crespo,* 834 F.2d 267 (2d Cir. 1987), the court found a voluntary consent to search based largely on the trial judge's finding that "having observed Jose Crespo, I believe he is arrogant and self-assured and that it is quite likely that he believed that the agents would not find the materials which were in a closet on a shelf hidden in a bag." 834 F.2d at 272. And in *United States v. Gonzalez-Basulto,* 898 F.2d 1011 (5th Cir. 1990), one of the considerations that led the court to find a voluntary consent was that the defendant "may well have believed that no drugs would be found because the cocaine was hidden in boxes toward the front of the trailer and there was little crawl space in the trailer." 898 F.2d at 1013.

Clearness and Explicitness of Consent

Another issue in determining the voluntariness of consent is whether the expression of consent is clear, explicit, and unequivocal. Hesitation or ambiguity in the giving of consent could indicate that the consent is not voluntary.

Both written and oral consent to search are equally effective in waiving a person's right to object later to the search on constitutional grounds. A signed and witnessed writing or a tape-recorded oral statement provides the best proof of a clear, voluntary waiver of a known right. A written or recorded consent is also the best way to refute any challenges later raised by the defendant. Exhibit 9.1 is a suggested form for obtaining a written consent to search.

Consent need not be expressed in words but may be implied from a person's gestures or conduct. For example, in *United States v. Benitez,* 899 F.2d 995 (10th Cir. 1990), the defendant never verbally consented to a search of his vehicle. Nevertheless, valid consent was found when the defendant exited his vehicle, opened the trunk, and opened a suitcase contained in the trunk. And in *United States v. Williams,* 754 F.2d 672 (1985), the court found indicative of voluntariness that the defendant assisted the officer in opening the suitcase by twice setting the tumbler on its combination lock.

Notification of Counsel

A defendant has no Sixth Amendment right to counsel until after the initiation of adversary judicial criminal proceedings. *Kirby v. Illinois,* 406 U.S. 682, 92 S.Ct. 1877, 32 L.Ed.2d 411 (1972). Thus, before the filing of formal charges, police are not required to notify retained counsel before soliciting a person's consent, even if the person is under arrest. However, the refusal by police to allow a person to consult with counsel upon request may be relevant to the determination of voluntariness of consent. By the same token, consent given after consultation with counsel will very likely be found to be voluntary. *Cody v. Solem,* 755 F.2d 1323, 1330 (8th Cir. 1985). Furthermore, it has

Kirby v. Illinois
laws.findlaw.com/us/406/
682.html

```
┌─────────────────────────────────────────────────────────────────┐
│                     CONSENT TO SEARCH                             │
│  I, _____, have been requested to        │
│  consent to a search of my _____, located at               │
│  _____. I have also been               │
│  advised of my constitutional rights to refuse consent and to     │
│  require that a search warrant be obtained prior to any search.   │
│  I have further been advised that if I do consent to a search,    │
│  any evidence found as a result of the search can be seized       │
│  and used against me in any court of law, and that I may          │
│  withdraw my consent to search at any time prior to the           │
│  conclusion of the search.                                        │
│                                                                   │
│         After having been advised of my constitutional rights     │
│  as stated above, I hereby waive those rights and consent to a    │
│  search and authorize _____ and _____ to      │
│  conduct a complete search of the above-described                 │
│  _____. This consent to search is being given by me    │
│  voluntarily and without threats or promises of any kind.         │
│                                                                   │
│                              _____        │
│                              Signature                            │
│                                                                   │
│                              _____        │
│                              Location and Date                    │
│                                                                   │
│  WITNESSES:                                                       │
│                                                                   │
│  _____                                    │
│  Signature, Title, and Date                                       │
│                                                                   │
│  _____                                    │
│  Signature, Title, and Date                                       │
└─────────────────────────────────────────────────────────────────┘
```

A Suggested Consent to Search Form
■ EXHIBIT 9.1

www.icje.org/id57.htm
Article, "Should Officers Use Written Consent to Search Forms?" by Robert T. Thetford

been suggested that when police have agreed with counsel (whenever retained) not to communicate with a suspect, a breach of that agreement may bar a valid consent. *Hall v. Iowa*, 705 F.2d 283, 289–90 (8th Cir. 1983).

Physical, Mental, Emotional, and Educational Factors

Voluntariness of consent may be affected by the physical, mental, or emotional condition of the person giving consent. These personal characteristics must be balanced against police pressures and tactics used to induce cooperation; the length of the police contact; the general conditions under which the contact occurs; excessive physical or psychological pressure; and inducements, threats, or other methods used to compel a response. If a person is sick, injured, mentally ill, under the influence of alcohol or drugs, or otherwise impaired, that person's vulnerability to subtle forms of coercion may affect the voluntariness of consent. Likewise, if a person is immature, inexperienced, mentally retarded, illiterate, or emotionally upset, the impairment of perception and understanding may render any consent to search a mere submission to authority. *United States v. Gallego-Zapata,* 630 F.Supp. 665 (D.Mass. 1986).

The existence of any one of these conditions or states of mind alone usually does not invalidate an otherwise uncoerced consent. "[T]he mere fact that one has taken drugs, or is intoxicated, or mentally agitated, does not render consent involuntary." *United States v. Rambo,* 789 F.2d 1289, 1297 (8th Cir. 1986). In *United States v. Gay,* 774 F.2d 368, 377 (10th Cir. 1985), the court said:

> The issue squarely put is whether Gay was so intoxicated that his consent to search was not the product of a rational intellect and a free will. . . . The question is one of mental awareness so that the act of consent was that of one who knew what he was doing. It is elementary that one must know he is giving consent for the consent to be efficacious.

In the *Gay case,* the court found voluntary consent to search the defendant's automobile glove compartment despite the defendant's intoxication, based on evidence that the defendant

- was able to answer questions addressed to him;
- produced his driver's license on request;
- responded when asked if he had been drinking;
- emptied his pockets upon request; and
- denied access to the automobile's trunk, which was found to contain cocaine in a later search.

Courts also consider a person's intelligence and educational level in determining the voluntariness of consent. In *United States v. Bates,* 840 F.2d 858 (11th Cir. 1988), the court found a valid consent when "[t]he defendant, an educated man, had 'been informed of [his] right to refuse to consent to such a search.'" 840 F.2d at 861. And in *United States v. Kaplan,* 895 F.2d 618 (9th Cir. 1990), one of the court's reasons for finding voluntary consent was that the defendant, a doctor, "was not a person lacking in education and understanding." 895 F.2d at 622.

Although a person's unfamiliarity with the English language is not an indication of intelligence or educational level, language barriers make determining voluntariness more difficult. In *State v. Xiong,* 504 N.W.2d 428, 432 (Wis.App. 1993), the court said:

> It is incumbent upon the police to effectively communicate their objectives when seeking consent to search. Merely providing an interpreter is not enough. The interpretation must convey what is intended to be communicated. Communication is effective only if it clearly and accurately relates all pertinent information to the listener. If effective communication is not provided, then that is a form of coercion.

Key Points

3. Consent to search given in submission to force, threats of force, or other show of authority is not voluntary.

4. Consent to search obtained by misrepresentation or deception is not voluntary, except that a person's misplaced trust in an undercover police agent will not alone invalidate an otherwise voluntary consent.

5. Knowledge of the right to refuse consent is only one factor among others to be considered in determining the voluntariness of a consent search.

6. The Fourth Amendment does not require that a lawfully seized person be advised that he or she is "free to go"

before the person's consent to search will be recognized as voluntary.

7. Voluntary consent to search may be given in writing, orally, or by a person's conduct so long as the expression of consent is clear and unequivocal.

8. Voluntariness of consent may be affected by the physical, mental, or emotional condition and the educational level of the person giving consent.

Scope

Determination of the allowable scope of a consent search involves issues of whether permission to actually search, rather than merely enter, has been given and what limits are placed on the search in terms of area, time, and expressed object of the search. Also included in this section is a discussion of revocation of consent.

Consent Merely to Enter

Although a person may give a valid consent to an officer's requests, it may not be a consent to *search*. The best example of this is a person's consent to allow an officer to *enter* his or her home in compliance with the officer's request for an interview. This does *not* automatically give the officer a right to search. There is a vital distinction between the granting of admission to one's home for the purposes of conversation and the granting of permission to thoroughly search the home.

In *Duncan v. State,* 176 So.2d 840 (Ala. 1965), officers investigating a murder knocked on the defendant's hotel room door and were invited in by the defendant. The defendant was not advised that they were police officers, nor did the officers make any request to search the defendant's room. Nevertheless, a search was conducted and incriminating evidence was found.

The court held that the invitation to enter his room, extended by the defendant to the person who knocked on the door, did not constitute a consent to search his room. Quoting from another case, the court said:

> To justify the introduction of evidence seized by a police officer within a private residence on the ground that the officer's entry was made by invitation, permission, or consent, there must be evidence of a statement or some overt act by the occupant of such residence sufficient to indicate his intent to waive his rights to the security and privacy of his home and freedom from unwarranted intrusions therein. An open door is not a waiver of such rights. 176 So.2d at 853.

Although an invitation to *enter* premises is not the equivalent of a consent to *search* the premises, an officer need not ignore contraband or other criminal evidence lying in plain view. Under the *plain view doctrine,* if police are lawfully in a position from which they view an object, if its incriminating character is apparent, and if the officers have a lawful right of access to the object, they may seize it without a warrant. In *Robbins v. Mackenzie,* 364 F.2d 45 (1st Cir. 1966), officers were investigating a robbery, and preliminary information led them to suspect a man named Albert. The officers went to Albert's apartment, knocked on the door, identified themselves, and were invited into the apartment by Albert, who opened the door and walked back into the room. The defendant was present in the apartment as Albert's guest. While talking to the two men, the officers noticed various objects fitting the description of items stolen in the robbery lying in plain view. They arrested the two men and seized the evidence observed.

The court held that the evidence seized was admissible against the defendant (Albert's guest). Because the officers were rightfully in the room by Albert's invitation, they were also rightfully there with respect to the defendant. Seeing what was patently and obviously open to view was therefore not a search, and seizing the evidence was not a violation of the defendant's rights. (The plain view doctrine is discussed in detail in Chapter 10.)

Area of Search

Florida v. Jimeno
laws.findlaw.com/us/500/
248.html

Assuming that an officer obtains a valid consent not only to *enter* premises but also to *search* the premises, "the standard for measuring the scope of a suspect's consent under the Fourth Amendment is that of 'objective reasonableness'—what would the typical reasonable person have understood by the exchange between the officer and the suspect?" *Florida v. Jimeno,* 500 U.S. 248, 251, 111 S.Ct. 1801, 1803–04, 114 L.Ed.2d 297, 302 (1991). In *People v. Cruz,* 40 Cal.Rptr. 841, 395 P.2d 889 (Cal. 1964), an officer obtained permission to "look around" an apartment. The court held that this did not authorize the officer to open and search boxes and suitcases that he had been informed were the property of persons other than the person giving consent. In other words, an officer can search only the parts of premises over which the person giving consent has some possessory right or control, and not personal property that the officer knows belongs to some other person. In *State v. Johnson,* 427 P.2d 705 (Wash. 1967), valid consent was given to officers to search the trunk of a car. The court held that this consent did not extend to search of the passenger area of the car and that evidence found in the passenger area was inadmissible in court. In another case, a consent to search form that authorized officers to search the defendant's car and remove "whatever documents or items of property whatsoever, which they deem pertinent to the investigation," was held to grant authority for a general and exploratory search. Therefore, officers did not exceed the scope of the consent by opening an unlocked suitcase found in the car's trunk. *United States v. Kapperman,* 764 F.2d 786 (11th Cir. 1985).

The limitation on the area of search allowed by consent applies equally to searches of the person as to searches of premises or vehicles. In a case involving both a nonverbal consent and a limitation on the area of the person allowed to be searched by consent, a police officer, while questioning the defendant with regard to narcotics, asked the defendant whether he was still using or carrying narcotics. When the defendant replied that he was not, the officer asked him whether he minded if he checked him for needle marks. The defendant said nothing but put his arms out sideways. The officer did not check the defendant's arms but instead patted down his coat and found marijuana cigarettes. The court held that the search went beyond the area to which the defendant had consented to allow a search:

> Bowens' putting out his arms sideways in response to a query whether he minded allowing the officer to check "if he had any marks on him" could hardly be said to be naturally indicative or persuasive of the giving of an intended consent to have the officer switch instead to a general search of his pockets—in which he had two marijuana cigarettes. *Oliver v. Bowens,* 386 F.2d 688, 691 (9th Cir. 1967).

As a general rule, if an officer asks for and obtains consent to search a specific area, whether in a place or on a person, the officer is limited to that specific area. If the search goes beyond that area, any evidence seized is likely to be held inadmissible in court.

Time

A consent to search may also be limited with respect to time. In *State v. Brochu*, 237 A.2d 418 (Me. 1967), officers investigating the death of the defendant's wife obtained a valid consent from the defendant to search his home. The officers conducted a search and found nothing. At that time, the defendant had not been accused of anything. However, later in the day, police received information giving them probable cause to arrest the defendant for his wife's murder and to obtain a search warrant for his premises. The defendant was arrested that evening, and the search warrant was executed the next day. The validity of the warrant was challenged, and the prosecution attempted to justify the second search on the basis that the defendant's earlier consent continued in effect after his arrest to the next day. The court rejected this contention.

> The officers entered the defendant's home on the 5th under the protection of his consent. By nightfall, however, the defendant had ceased to be the husband assisting in the solution of his wife's death and had become the man accused of his wife's murder by poison (and) held under arrest for hearing.
>
> When the defendant became the accused, the protective cloak of the Constitution became more closely wrapped around him. . . .
>
> The consent of December 5 in our view should be measured on the morning of the 6th by the status of the defendant as the accused. There is no evidence whatsoever that the consent of the 5th was ever discussed with the defendant at or after his arrest, or that he was informed of the State's intent to enter and search his home on the 6th on the strength of a continuing consent. We conclude, therefore, that consent of the defendant had ended by December 6, and accordingly the officers were not protected thereby on the successful search of the 6th. 237 A.2d 421.

If a significant period of time has passed since a consent to search was given, a new consent should be obtained before continuing to search, especially if intervening events suggest that a second consent might not be given so readily as the original consent. Otherwise, a search warrant should be obtained.

Object of Search

If the consenting person places no limit on the scope of a search, the scope is "generally defined by its expressed object." *Florida v. Jimeno*, 500 U.S. 248, 251, 111 S.Ct. 1801, 1804, 114 L.Ed.2d 297, 303 (1991). Therefore, a search may be as broad as the officer's previously acquired knowledge about the crimes likely to have been committed and the items of evidence likely to be discovered. *United States v. Sealey*, 630 F.Supp. 801 (E.D.Cal. 1986). In the *Jimeno* case, a police officer was following the defendant's car after overhearing the defendant arranging what appeared to be a drug transaction. The officer stopped the defendant's car for a traffic infraction and declared that he had reason to believe that the defendant was carrying narcotics in the car. The officer asked permission to search the car, the defendant consented, and the officer found cocaine inside a folded paper bag on the car's floorboard.

The Court held that a criminal suspect's Fourth Amendment right to be free from unreasonable searches is not violated when, after he gives a police officer permission to search his automobile, the officer opens a closed container found within the car that might reasonably hold the object. The Court said:

> We think that it was objectively reasonable for the police to conclude that the general consent to search respondent's car included consent to search containers within that car

www.fletc.gov/legal/
archive_dir.htm
Article, "Searching a Vehicle
without a Warrant: Consent
Searches" by Bryan R. Lemons;
first of three articles in the January 2, 2001 issue of *Quarterly
Review: Legal Commentary for
Federal Law Enforcement Officers*

which might bear drugs. A reasonable person may be expected to know that narcotics are generally carried in some form of a container. 500 U.S. at 251, 111 S.Ct. at 1804, 114 L.Ed.2d at 303.

United States v. Rodney, 956 F.2d 295 (D.C.Cir. 1992), held that a request to conduct a body search for drugs reasonably includes a request to conduct some search of the crotch area. The court noted that drug dealers frequently hide drugs near their genitals.

Note that the "objective reasonableness" standard depends on the facts of each case. A general consent to search a vehicle does not necessarily allow the search of all containers in a vehicle. For example, a consent to search the trunk of a car may not include authorization to pry open a locked briefcase found inside the trunk. As the U.S. Supreme Court noted in the *Jimeno* case, "[i]t is very likely unreasonable to think that a suspect, by consenting to the search of his trunk, has agreed to the breaking open of a *locked* briefcase within the trunk, but it is otherwise with respect to a closed paper bag." (Emphasis added.) 500 U.S. at 251–52, 111 S.Ct. at 1804, 114 L.Ed.2d at 303.

Of course, the consenting person may specifically limit the scope of a consent search to a search for a particular object. In *People v. Superior Court (Arketa),* 89 Cal.Rptr. 316 (Cal.App. 1970), a person gave officers consent to search his premises for a crime suspect. The officers conducted a thorough search of the house and its closets for a crowbar without advising the person that they wanted to look for a crowbar. The court invalidated the search because it went beyond the scope of the consent granted. In a case in which an individual consented to a search of his person for *weapons,* the court held that "the scope of the search consented to must be limited to the scope of the right of search asserted, unless it should clearly appear that free and voluntary consent was given to a general and exploratory search." *People v. Rice,* 66 Cal.Rptr. 246, 249 (Cal.App. 1968). In *Rice,* the seizure of marijuana in a plastic bottle in the defendant's pocket was held illegal as beyond the scope of the consent granted. Law enforcement officers should confine their search to only those areas where the object for which they have consent to search could possibly be located, taking into consideration the size, shape, and character of the object.

Revocation of Consent

Consent to search may be revoked or withdrawn at any time after the search has been partially completed. In *State v. Lewis,* 611 A.2d 69 (Me. 1992), after arresting the defendant for drunk driving and releasing him on personal recognizance, a state trooper offered to drive the defendant to a nearby motel. When the defendant retrieved a carry-on bag from his car, the trooper asked and received permission to check the bag for guns. The trooper immediately observed two large brown bags inside the carry-on bag, smelled marijuana, and asked permission to examine the bags. The defendant refused and attempted to return the carry-on bag to his car. The trooper intervened and searched the brown bags, finding marijuana. The court found that the defendant had revoked his consent to search the carry-on bag before the trooper opened the brown bags.

> Even though defendant consented to the trooper's looking inside his carry-on bag, he at no time consented to the trooper's looking into the brown bags contained therein. Rather, by expressly terminating his consent when the trooper requested to open the brown bags and by seeking to return them to his car, defendant most certainly manifested a subjective expectation of privacy with respect to those inside bags. Because those bags were always closed and their contents shielded from the trooper's view, society would regard defendant's expectation of privacy in them to be reasonable. 611 A.2d at 70.

In *United States v. Bily,* 406 F.Supp. 726 (E.D.Pa. 1975), the defendant consented to a search of his house for pornographic films. After an investigation of approximately two hours, during which certain films were discovered, the defendant stated, "That's enough, I want you to stop." The court held that this was a revocation of consent that took immediate effect. Only the seizures of films that took place before the revocation were held valid.

In *United States v. Ibarra,* 731 F.Supp. 1037 (D.Wyo. 1990), the court held that a motorist's closing and locking the trunk of his car after a police officer's consensual search of the trunk constituted a revocation of that consent and barred any further search.

Key Points

9. Although an invitation to *enter* premises is not the equivalent of a consent to *search* the premises, an officer invited onto premises need not ignore contraband or other criminal evidence lying in plain view.

10. The scope of a consent search depends on what the typical reasonable person would have understood by the exchange between the officer and the suspect.

11. A person giving consent to search may place a time limitation on the search.

12. If the consenting person places no limit on the scope of a consent search, the scope is generally defined by its expressed object.

13. Consent to search may be revoked or withdrawn at any time after the search has been partially completed.

Who May Give Consent

In general, the only person able to give a valid consent to a search is the person whose constitutional protection against unreasonable searches and seizures would be invaded by the search if it were conducted without consent. This means, for example, that when the search of a person's body or clothing is contemplated, only that person can consent to the search. The same rule applies to searches of property, except that when several people have varying degrees of interest in the same property, more than one person may be qualified to give consent to search.

In certain situations, the law recognizes authority in a third person to consent to a search of property even though he or she is not the person against whose interests the search is being conducted. In *United States v. Matlock,* 415 U.S. 164, 94 S.Ct. 988, 39 L.Ed.2d 242 (1974), the U.S. Supreme Court stated the test for determining whether a third person could consent to a search of premises or effects:

> [W]hen the prosecution seeks to justify a warrantless search by proof of voluntary consent, it is not limited to proof that consent was given by the defendant, but may show that permission to search was obtained from a third party who possessed *common authority over or other sufficient relationship to the premises or effects sought to be inspected.* (Emphasis added.) 415 U.S. 171, 94 S.Ct. 993, 39 L.Ed.2d 249–50.

The Court then defined "common authority":

> Common authority is, of course, not to be implied from the mere interest a third party has in the property. The authority which justifies the third-party consent does not rest

United States v. Matlock
laws.findlaw.com/us/415/
164.html

www.cybercrime.gov/
searchmanual.htm#Ic1
Excerpt from "Searching and Seizing Computers and Obtaining Electronic Evidence in Criminal Investigations," discusses consent searches

upon the law of property, with its attendant historical and legal refinements, . . . but rests rather on mutual use of the property by persons generally having joint access or control for most purposes, so that it is reasonable to recognize that any of the co-inhabitants has the right to permit the inspection in his own right and that the others have assumed the risk that one of their number might permit the common area to be searched. 415 U.S. at 171 n.7, 94 S.Ct. at 993 n.7, 39 L.Ed.2d at 250 n.7.

Furthermore, a warrantless entry and search is valid when based on the consent of a third party whom the police, at the time of the entry, *reasonably believe* to possess common authority over the premises but who *in fact* does not. This does not suggest that law enforcement officers may always accept a person's invitation to enter premises.

Even when the invitation is accompanied by an explicit assertion that the person lives there, the surrounding circumstances could conceivably be such that a reasonable person would doubt its truth and not act upon it without further inquiry. As with other factual determinations bearing upon search and seizure, determination of consent to enter must "be judged against an objective standard: would the facts available to the officer at the moment . . . 'warrant a man of reasonable caution in the belief'" that the consenting party had authority over the premises? . . . If not, then warrantless entry without further inquiry is unlawful unless authority actually exists. But if so, the search is valid. *Illinois v. Rodriguez,* 497 U.S. 177, 188–89, 110 S.Ct. 2793, 2801, 111 L.Ed.2d 148, 161 (1990).

Illinois v. Rodriguez
laws.findlaw.com/us/497/
177.html

The *Rodriguez* case has been construed as "appli[cable] to situations in which an officer would have had valid consent to search if the facts were as he reasonably believed them to be." *United States v. Whitfield,* 939 F.2d 1071, 1074 (D.C.Cir. 1991). *Rodriguez* would not validate, however, a search premised on an erroneous view of the law. For example, an investigator's erroneous belief that landladies are generally authorized to consent to a search of a tenant's premises could not provide the authorization necessary for a warrantless search.

The prosecution has the burden of showing that someone consented and that the person had the authority to do so. Therefore, law enforcement officers must provide sufficient evidence of both to the prosecuting attorney for presentation in court. Mutual authority generally comes from spouses and persons involved in similar partnerships, but also occurs in roommate, parent-child, employee-employer, and other relationships. The law enforcement officer should ask reasonable questions designed to show a relationship of such mutual authority that either party has the right to consent to the mutually shared real or personal property. And, of course, the answers received must reasonably show such a relationship. Reasonableness, not perfection, is the standard upon which the officer's behavior is measured. Officers are not required to be correct in their deductions, but they must act in good faith and reasonably, based on training and experience.

Note that a person with common authority may consent to a search only in the absence of other persons with equal or superior authority. In *State v. Leach,* 782 P.2d 1035 (Wash. 1989), a co-owner of a travel agency consented to a search of the agency office. The defendant, the other owner of the agency with a superior interest, was arrested at the office and was present during the search. His consent to search the office was not sought, however. The court invalidated the search.

Where the police have obtained consent to search from an individual possessing, at best, equal control over the premises, that consent remains valid against a cohabitant, who

www.jus.state.nc.us/NCJA/
legapr96.htm
Commentary on the case of
Illinois v. Rodriguez

also possesses equal control, only while the cohabitant is absent. However, should the cohabitant be present and able to object, the police must also obtain the cohabitant's consent. Any other rule exalts expediency over an individual's Fourth Amendment guarantees. Accordingly, we refuse to beat a path to the door of exceptions. 782 P.2d at 1040.

Questions of who may give valid consent are often confusing and complicated, and courts tend to carefully scrutinize any waiver of a person's constitutional rights. The remainder of this chapter examines examples of consent search situations in which the person giving the consent is not the person against whose interests the search is being conducted.

Persons Having Equal Rights or Interests in Property

It is well settled that, when two or more persons have substantially equal rights of ownership, occupancy, or other possessory interest in property to be searched or seized, any one of the persons may legally authorize a search, and any evidence found may be used against any of the other persons. In *United States v. Kelley,* 953 F.2d 562 (9th Cir. 1992), the court found authority to consent to a search of the defendant's bedroom and closet under the following circumstances: the person giving consent had rented the apartment together with the defendant and had signed the lease; she described herself as the defendant's roommate; and she had joint access not only to the common areas of the apartment but also to the defendant's separate bedroom, where the apartment telephone was located.

In determining whether a person is a joint occupant of premises, courts will consider whether the person paid rent, how long the person stayed, whether the person left belongings on the premises, whether the person possessed a key, and whether there was any written or oral agreement among other parties as to the person's right to use and occupy the premises. In *Illinois v. Rodriguez,* 497 U.S. 177, 110 S.Ct. 2793, 111 L.Ed.2d 148 (1990), the U.S. Supreme Court held that the defendant's former co-tenant did not have common authority to grant police consent to enter the defendant's premises without a warrant, even though she had some furniture and household effects in the premises and sometimes spent the night at the premises after moving out a month before the search at issue. Her name was not on the lease; she did not contribute to the rent; she was not allowed to invite others to the apartment on her own; she never went to the premises when the defendant was not at home; she had moved her clothing and that of her children from the premises; and she had taken a key to the premises without the defendant's knowledge.

Consent to search given by a person with common authority over the premises is not invalidated because that person gave consent with the expectation of receiving a reward. In *Bertolotti v. State,* 476 So.2d 130 (Fla. 1985), a woman who knew of the possibility of a reward through a crime watch program consented to a search of an apartment she shared with the defendant. The court said:

> A community-wide, regularly advertised program which rewards any citizen who provides information useful to the police in their criminal investigations is not tantamount to recruiting police agents; the state should not be penalized in the use of information so obtained. Mrs. Griest's consent to the search was not vitiated by the possibility of financial reward. 476 So.2d at 132.

In a case involving equal rights to *personal* property, the defendant, at his murder trial, objected to the introduction into evidence of clothing seized from his duffel bag. At the time of the seizure, the duffel bag was being used jointly by the defendant and his cousin and had been left in the cousin's home. When police arrested the cousin, they asked him whether they could have his clothing. The cousin directed them to the duffel bag, and both the cousin and his mother consented to its search. During the search, the officers came upon the defendant's clothing in the bag and seized it as well. The Court upheld the legality of the search over the defendant's objections.

> Since Rawls (the cousin) was a joint user of the bag, he clearly had authority to consent to its search. The officers therefore found evidence against petitioner while in the course of an otherwise lawful search [*plain view doctrine*]. . . . Petitioner argues that Rawls only had actual permission to use one compartment of the bag and that he had no authority to consent to a search of the other compartments. We will not, however, engage in such metaphysical subtleties in judging the efficacy of Rawls' consent. Petitioner, in allowing Rawls to use the bag and in leaving it in his house, must be taken to have assumed the risk that Rawls would allow someone else to look inside. We find no valid search and seizure claim in this case. *Frazier v. Cupp*, 394 U.S. 731, 740, 89 S.Ct. 1420, 1425, 22 L.Ed.2d 684, 693–94 (1969).

Frazier v. Cupp
laws.findlaw.com/us/394/
731.html

A third party who has common authority to use premises may give consent to a search of the premises even if not *actually* using the premises at the time of the search. In *United States v. Cook*, 530 F.2d 145 (7th Cir. 1976), the defendant's landlady consented to a search of a poultry house on her property. The poultry house consisted of a large room in which the landlady had segregated an area with wire fence for her exclusive use. She gave the defendant permission to use the remaining space, but she retained the right to use the space if necessary. The defendant claimed that since neither the landlady nor her family *actually* used the defendant's area, there was no common authority. The court upheld the search, however, ruling that the defendant had assumed the risk that the landlady would permit others to inspect the premises.

A third party cannot consent to a search of more than that over which he or she has common authority. In *United States v. Gilley*, 608 F.Supp. 1065 (S.D.Ga. 1985), the court held that a consent to search a home given by the home's occupant did not authorize a search of a guest's travel bag found in the living room. The guest had done nothing that diminished his natural expectation of privacy in the contents of the bag. The host lacked common authority over the bag, as she had not been authorized to open or use the bag, and she had not in fact opened the bag.

Landlord-Tenant

A landlord has *no* implied authority to consent to a search of a tenant's premises or a seizure of the tenant's property during the period of the tenancy, even though the landlord has the authority to enter the tenant's premises for the limited purposes of inspection, performance of repairs, or housekeeping services. *Chapman v. United States*, 365 U.S. 610, 81 S.Ct. 776, 5 L.Ed.2d 828 (1961). Once the tenant has abandoned the premises or the tenancy has otherwise terminated, however, and the landlord has the primary right to occupation and control of the premises, the landlord may consent to a search of the premises, even though the former tenant has left personal belongings on the premises. *United States v. Sledge*, 760 F.2d 854 (9th Cir. 1981). Furthermore, since a landlord clearly has joint authority over, and access to, common areas of an

Chapman v. United States
laws.findlaw.com/us/365/
610.html

apartment building, a landlord may give valid consent to search those areas. *United States v. Kelly,* 551 F.2d 760 (8th Cir. 1977).

Hotel Manager–Hotel Guest

The U.S. Supreme Court held that the principles governing a landlord's consent to a search of tenant's premises apply to consent searches of hotel rooms allowed by hotel managers. In *Stoner v. California,* 376 U.S. 483, 84 S.Ct. 889, 11 L.Ed.2d 856 (1964), police investigating a robbery went to the defendant's hotel. The defendant was not in his room, and police obtained permission from the hotel clerk to search the defendant's room. Items of evidence incriminating the defendant in the robbery were found in the room.

Stoner v. California
laws.findlaw.com/us/376/483.html

The Court held that the search was illegal and that the items seized could not be used against the defendant in court. The defendant's constitutional right was at stake here—not the clerk's or the hotel's. Therefore, only the defendant, either directly or through an agent, could waive that right. There was no evidence that the police had any basis whatsoever to believe that the night clerk had been authorized by the defendant to permit the police to search his room.

> It is true . . . that when a person engages a hotel room he undoubtedly gives "implied or express permission" to "such persons as maids, janitors or repairmen" to enter his room "in the performance of their duties." . . . But the conduct of the night clerk and the police in the present case was of an entirely different order. . . .
>
> No less than a tenant of a house, or the occupant of a room in a boarding house . . . a guest in a hotel room is entitled to constitutional protection against unreasonable searches and seizures. . . . That protection would disappear if it were left to depend upon the unfettered discretion of an employee of the hotel. 376 U.S. at 489–90, 84 S.Ct. at 893, 11 L.Ed.2d at 861.

When the term of a hotel guest's occupancy of a room expires, however, the guest loses his or her exclusive right to privacy in the room, whether or not the guest remains in the room. The hotel manager then has the right to enter the room and may consent to a search of the room and a seizure of items found in the room. *United States v. Larson,* 760 F.2d 852 (8th Cir. 1985).

Host–Guest

In general, the owner or primary occupant of the premises (the host) may validly consent to a search of the premises, and any evidence found would be admissible against a guest on the premises. In *United States v. Hall,* 979 F.2d 77 (6th Cir. 1992), the owner of a residence gave consent to search the room of the defendant, whom he had allowed to stay at his residence in exchange for farm work. The court held that the owner had authority to consent to the search when he owned all the furniture in the room, he had personal items stored in an adjacent room accessed through the defendant's room, the room was never locked, and there was no agreement between him and the defendant that he was not to go in the room.

If, however, the person against whom a search for evidence is directed is a long-term guest and has a section of the premises set aside for exclusive personal use, the host may not consent to a search of that area of the premises. *Reeves v. Warden,* 346 F.2d 915 (4th Cir. 1965). The host's authority to consent to a search of the guest's area of the premises depends on the length of time of the guest's stay, the exclusiveness of the guest's control of a particular area of the premises, and the guest's reasonable expectation of privacy in that area of the premises. Also, a host may not consent to a search of an item that is obviously the exclusive personal property of the guest. *State v. Edwards,* 570 A.2d 193 (Conn. 1990), held that although a lessee of an apartment could consent to a search of her apartment, she could not consent to a search of a guest's backpack:

> As "a common repository for one's personal effects, and therefore . . . inevitably associated with the expectation of privacy" . . . luggage may be lawfully searched, in general, only pursuant to a warrant. . . . We can discern no intrinsic constitutional distinction between a backpack and luggage. 570 A.2d at 202.

Employer–Employee

In general, an employer may consent to a search of any part of the employer's premises over which the employer has authority and control. In *State v. Robinson,* 206 A.2d 779 (N.J.Super. 1965), the court held that an employer could validly consent to the search of an employee's locker in the employer's plant. The employer not only owned the premises, but under the terms of a contract between the employer and the employee's union, the employer retained a master key to all employee's lockers. In *United States v. Carter,* 569 F.2d 801 (4th Cir. 1977), an employer's consent to search a company vehicle in an employee's custody was held valid. The employer not only owned the vehicle but could tell the employee what and what not to do with it and could designate any other use of it.

However, an employer may not effectively consent to a search of an area set aside for use by an employee and within the employee's exclusive control. In *United States v. Blok,* 188 F.2d 1019 (D.C.Cir. 1951), the court held that an employee's boss could not validly consent to a search of a desk assigned for the employee's exclusive use.

> In the absence of a valid regulation to the contrary, appellee was entitled to, and did keep private property of a personal sort in her desk. Her superiors could not reasonably search the desk for her purse, her personal letters, or anything else that did not belong to the government and had no connection with the work of the office. Their consent did not make such a search by the police reasonable. 188 F.2d at 1021.

An employee's ability to consent validly to a search of the employer's premises depends on the scope of the employee's authority. The average employee, such as a clerk, janitor, maintenance person, driver, or other person temporarily in charge, may not give such consent. *United States v. Block,* 202 F.Supp. 705 (S.D.N.Y. 1962). If, however, the employee is a manager or other person of considerable authority who is left in complete charge for a substantial period of time, the employee probably would be able effectively to consent to a search of the employer's premises. *United States v. Antonelli Fireworks Co.,* 155 F.2d 631 (2d Cir. 1946). In *People v. Litwin,* 355 N.Y.S.2d 646 (N.Y.App.Div. 1974), the court held that a baby-sitter has insufficient authority over the premises of his or her employer to give a valid consent to search the premises.

School Official–Student

The search by police of a high school student's locker, when consented to by a school official, is valid because of the relationship between the school authorities and the students. The school authorities have an obligation to maintain discipline over students, and usually they retain partial access to the students' lockers so that neither has an exclusive right to use and possession of the lockers. Thus, in a case in which the locker of a student suspected of burglary was opened by police with the consent of school authorities and incriminating evidence was found, the court said:

> Although a student may have control of his school locker as against fellow students, his possession is not exclusive against the school and its officials. A school does not supply its students with lockers for illicit use in harboring pilfered property or harmful substances. We deem it a proper function of school authorities to inspect the lockers under their control and to prevent their use in illicit ways or for illegal purposes. We believe this right of inspection is inherent in the authority vested in school administrators and that the same must be retained and exercised in the management of our schools if their educational functions are to be maintained and the welfare of the student bodies preserved. *State v. Stein,* 456 P.2d 1, 3 (Kan. 1969).

Consent searches of college dormitory rooms are treated similarly to searches of hotel rooms. In *Commonwealth v. McCloskey,* 272 A.2d 271 (Pa.Super. 1970), police, aided by the dean of men, searched the defendant's room at a university and found marijuana. The evidence was held to be inadmissible in court.

> A dormitory room is analogous to an apartment or a hotel room. It certainly offers its occupant a more reasonable expectation of freedom from governmental intrusion than does a public telephone booth. The defendant rented the dormitory room for a certain period of time, agreeing to abide by the rules established by his lessor, the University. As in most rental situations, the lessor, Bucknell University, reserved the right to check the room for damages, wear and unauthorized appliances. Such right of the lessor does not mean McCloskey was not entitled to have a "reasonable expectation of freedom from governmental intrusion," or that he gave consent to the police search, or gave the University authority to consent to such search. 272 A.2d at 273.

Principal–Agent

A person clearly may give someone else authority to consent to a search of the person's property. The person giving the authority is called the *principal;* the person acting for the principal is called his or her *agent.* For example, an attorney may consent to a search of a client's premises if the attorney has been specifically authorized to do so by the client. In *Brown v. State,* 404 P.2d 428 (Nev. 1965), a search of the defendant's premises and a seizure of his farm animals were upheld because consent to search had been given by the defendant's attorney after consultation with the defendant. Without a specific authorization to give consent to search, however, the mere existence of an attorney-client relationship gives an attorney no authority to waive a client's personal rights. In another example, *State v. Kellam,* 269 S.E.2d 197 (N.C.App. 1980), homeowners gave their next-door neighbor the key to their house with instructions to "look after their house" while the owners were away. The court held that the neighbor's consent to search the house was valid.

A principal has the power to limit the authority of his or her agent with respect to the principal's property. Therefore, for example, an employer could limit an employee's authority to show business records to certain persons and not to others. A principal may not, however, limit an agent's authority for the purpose of obstructing justice. Therefore, in a case in which a doctor told his employee to take business records and hide them from the authorities, the court said that "when an employer gives an

www.doj.state.wi.us/ss_manual/search.htm
Article, "Search and Seizure" discussing the Fourth Amendment as it applies to schools; focuses on Wisconsin law and includes extensive discussion of consent searches

employee access to documents intentionally and knowingly in order to obstruct justice, that employee is a custodian of those records for the purposes of a valid subpoena or seizure." *United States v. Miller,* 800 F.2d 129, 135 (7th Cir. 1986).

Husband-Wife

"Where two persons, such as a husband and wife, have equal rights to the use and occupation of certain premises, either may give consent to a search, and the evidence thus disclosed can be used against either." *United States v. Ocampo,* 492 F.Supp. 1211, 1236 (E.D.N.Y. 1980). In *Roberts v. United States,* 332 F.2d 892 (8th Cir. 1964), officers questioned the defendant's wife as part of a murder investigation. The wife volunteered information that the defendant had fired a pistol into the ceiling of their home some time ago. She later validly consented to a search for and seizure of the bullet in the ceiling.

The court sustained the search on the basis that the consent was voluntary, the place of the search was the home of the defendant's wife, and the premises were under the wife's immediate and complete control at the time of the search. Furthermore, the bullet could not be considered a personal effect of the husband, over which the wife would have no power to consent to search.

> It is not a question of agency, for a wife should not be held to have authority to waive her husband's constitutional rights. This is a question of the wife's own rights to authorize entry into premises where she lives and of which she had control. 332 F.2d at 896–97.

Some courts have even allowed estranged spouses to consent to the search of marital premises they have vacated. In *United States v. Long,* 524 F.2d 660 (9th Cir. 1975), the court held that an estranged wife, as a joint owner of a house she had vacated, could give consent to search the house even though her husband (the temporarily absent current occupant) had changed the locks on the doors.

Parent-Child

A parent's consent to search premises owned by the parent will usually be effective against a child who lives on those premises.

> Hardy's father gave his permission to the officers to enter and search the house and the premises which he owned and in which his son lived with him. Under the circumstances presented here the voluntary consent of Hardy's father to search his own premises is binding on Hardy and precludes his claim of violation of constitutional rights. *Commonwealth v. Hardy,* 223 A.2d 719, 723 (Pa. 1966).

A parent may not consent to a search of an area of the parent's home occupied by the child, however, if the child uses the room exclusively, has sectioned it off, has furnished it with his or her own furniture, pays rent, or otherwise establishes an expectation of privacy. *State v. Peterson,* 525 S.W.2d 599 (Mo.App. 1975). Furthermore, parents may not consent to a search of a child's room in their home if the child has already refused to grant such consent. "Constitutional rights may not be defeated by the expedient of soliciting several persons successively until the sought-after consent is obtained." *People v. Mortimer,* 46 A.D.2d 275, 277, 361 N.Y.S.2d 955, 958 (N.Y. 1974).

The Supreme Court of Georgia identified the following factors to be considered in determining whether a minor's consent to search family premises is valid:

> whether the minor lived on the premises; whether the minor had a right of access to the premises and the right to invite others thereto; whether the minor was of an age at which he or she could be expected to exercise at least minimal discretion; and whether officers acted reasonably in believing that the minor had sufficient control over the premises to give a valid consent to search. *Davis v. State,* 422 S.E.2d 546, 549 (Ga. 1992).

Bailor-Bailee

A bailee of personal property may consent to a search of the property if the bailee has full possession and control. (A bailee is a person in rightful possession of personal property by permission of the owner or bailor.) In *United States v. Eldridge,* 302 F.2d 463 (4th Cir. 1962), the defendant loaned his car to a friend for the friend's personal use. Police investigating a theft asked the friend for permission to search the trunk of the car. The friend opened the trunk, and the police found incriminating evidence against the defendant.

The court held that the search was legal and that the evidence found was admissible against the defendant. The friend had been given rightful possession and control over the automobile and could do with it whatever was reasonable under the circumstances. The defendant had reserved no exclusive right to the trunk when he gave his friend the key. The friend's opening of the trunk for the police was a reasonable exercise of his control over the car for the period during which he was permitted to use it.

If the bailee giving consent has only limited control over the property, such as for shipment, storage, or repair purposes, evidence found by law enforcement officers would not be admissible in court against the owner of the property. Thus, an airline could not consent to the search of a package that the defendant had wrapped, tied, and delivered to the airline solely for transportation purposes. *Corngold v. United States,* 367 F.2d 1 (9th Cir. 1966). Nor could the owner of a boat who had agreed to store certain of defendant's items on his boat give a valid consent to police to search and seize the items. *Commonwealth v. Storck,* 275 A.2d 362 (Pa. 1971). And *State v. Farrell,* 443 A.2d 438, 442 (R.I. 1982), held that "one who entrusts his automobile to another for the purposes of repair, or periodic inspection as required by law, does not confer the kind of mutual use or control which would empower that person to consent to a warrantless search and seizure."

In *United States v. Most,* 876 F.2d 191 (D.C.Cir. 1989), the court held that a store clerk who was asked by the defendant to watch a package could not give a legally valid consent to search the package. The court said, "We see no basis for holding that delivery people who *move* packages may not consent to a search, but that store clerks who *watch* packages may." 876 F.2d at 200 n.18.

Voluntary Production of Evidence

If a person voluntarily produces incriminating evidence, without any attempt by police to obtain consent and without coercion, deception, or other illegal police conduct, there is no search and seizure, and the evidence is admissible in court. In the U.S. Supreme Court case of *Coolidge v. New Hampshire,* 403 U.S. 443, 91 S.Ct. 2022, 29 L.Ed.2d 564 (1971), two officers went to the defendant's home, while the defendant

Coolidge v. New Hampshire
laws.findlaw.com/us/403/443.html

was at the police station under investigation for murder, to check out the defendant's story with his wife. The officers asked the wife whether the defendant owned any guns, and she replied, "Yes, I will get them in the bedroom." She then took four guns out of a closet and gave them to the officers. The officers then asked her what her husband had been wearing on the night in question, and she produced several pairs of trousers and a hunting jacket. The police seized all this evidence, and it was used against the defendant in court.

The Court found no objection to the introduction of the previously described evidence in court. In fact, the Court found that the actions of the police did not even amount to a search and seizure. Because the Court discussed in detail the significance of the actions of the police, and because of the importance of the issue, the Court's opinion is quoted here at length:

> [I]t cannot be said that the police should have obtained a warrant for the guns and clothing before they set out to visit Mrs. Coolidge, since they had no intention of rummaging around among Coolidge's effects or of dispossessing him of any of his property. Nor can it be said that they should have obtained Coolidge's permission for a seizure they did not intend to make. There was nothing to compel them to announce to the suspect that they intended to question his wife about his movements on the night of the disappearance or about the theft from his employer. Once Mrs. Coolidge had admitted them, the policemen were surely acting normally and properly when they asked her, as they asked those questioned earlier in the investigation, including Coolidge himself, about any guns there might be in the house. The question concerning the clothes Coolidge had been wearing on the night of the disappearance was logical and in no way coercive. Indeed, one might doubt the competence of the officers involved had they not asked exactly the questions they did ask. And surely when Mrs. Coolidge of her own accord produced the guns and clothes for inspection, rather than simply describing them, it was not incumbent on the police to stop her or avert their eyes. . . .
>
> In assessing the claim that this course of conduct amounted to a search and seizure, it is well to keep in mind that Mrs. Coolidge described her own motive as that of clearing her husband, and that she believed that she had nothing to hide. She had seen her husband himself produce his guns for two other policemen earlier in the week, and there is nothing to indicate that she realized that he had offered only three of them for inspection on that occasion. The two officers who questioned her behaved, as her own testimony shows, with perfect courtesy. There is not the slightest implication of an attempt to coerce or dominate her, or for that matter, to direct her actions by the more subtle techniques of suggestion that are available to officials in circumstances like these. To hold that the conduct of the police here was a search and seizure would be to hold, in effect, that a criminal suspect has constitutional protection against the adverse consequences of a spontaneous, good-faith effort by his wife to clear him of suspicion. 403 U.S. at 488–90, 91 S.Ct. at 2049–50, 29 L.Ed.2d at 596.

Reasonable Expectation of Privacy

Katz v. United States
laws.findlaw.com/us/389/347.html

Since the U.S. Supreme Court decision in *Katz v. United States*, 389 U.S. 347, 88 S.Ct. 507, 19 L.Ed.2d 576 (1967), courts have considered a person's reasonable expectation of privacy as a major factor in determining whether consent to search that person's property could be given by a third person. In *United States v. Novello*, 519 F.2d 1078 (5th Cir. 1975), the defendant rented an enclosed storage area that was accessible only to the rental agent and to those working with the agent. The defendant stored his truck containing marijuana in the area. Law enforcement officers, acting on an informant's tip, obtained consent to enter the enclosed area from one of the persons having access and discovered marijuana in the truck. The court held that the defendant had no reasonable expectation of privacy in the storage area and upheld the search. It said, "One who knows that others have of right general and untrammeled access to an area, a right as extensive as his own, can scarcely have much expectation of secrecy in it or confidence about whom they may let inspect it." 519 F.2d at 1080.

The Oregon Court of Appeals relied on a defendant's reasonable expectation of privacy to invalidate the search of a bedroom in a private residence that the defendant occupied under a rental agreement. A father and his two daughters leased and occupied the residence along with the defendant. The defendant was the only occupant of a private room under an agreement with the father. One of the daughters gave consent to search the defendant's room, where incriminating evidence was found. The court held that the daughter could not consent to a search of the defendant's room. The defendant had a reasonable expectation of privacy in the room because he rented it, was its sole occupant, and had never given anyone permission to enter it. *State v. Fitzgerald*, 530 P.2d 553 (Or.App. 1974).

Key Points

14. In general, the only person able to give a valid consent to a search is the person whose constitutional protection against unreasonable searches and seizures would be invaded by the search if it were conducted without consent.

15. A person may specifically authorize another to consent to a search of the person's property.

16. Consent to search may be obtained from a third party whom the police, at the time of entry, reasonably believe to possess common authority over or other sufficient relationship to the premises or effects sought to be inspected.

17. If a person voluntarily produces incriminating evidence, without any attempt by police to obtain consent and without coercion, deception, or other illegal police conduct, there is no search and seizure, and the evidence is admissible in court.

18. If a person establishes a reasonable expectation of privacy in property, another person may not consent to a search of the property.

Summary

A consent search occurs when a person allows a law enforcement officer to search his or her body, premises, or belongings. Consent searches are convenient for law enforcement officers, requiring no justification such as probable cause or a warrant, but consent searches present many opportunities for abuse. For this reason, courts exercise a strong presumption against consents to search and place a heavy burden on prosecutors to prove that a consent to search was voluntary. Voluntariness depends on the totality of circumstances surrounding the giving of consent. Among the circumstances considered are the following:

- Force or threat of force by police
- Fraudulent or mistaken claim of police authority
- Misrepresentation or deception by police

- Arrest or detention of consenting person
- Consenting person's awareness of the right to refuse consent to search
- Consenting person's attitude about the likelihood of discovery of evidence
- Clearness and explicitness of consent
- Physical, mental, emotional, and educational status of consenting person

The Fourth Amendment does not require that a lawfully seized person be advised that he or she is free to go before the person's consent to search will be recognized as voluntary.

A consent to *enter* premises is not the equivalent of a consent to *search* the premises. If, however, an officer who has been invited to enter premises observes criminal evidence lying open to view, the officer may seize the evidence if he or she complies with the requirements of the plain view doctrine.

The standard for measuring the scope of a suspect's consent is that of "objective reasonableness": what would the typical reasonable person have understood by the exchange between the officer and the suspect? The scope of a consent search may be limited in area, in time, and by the object for which the search is allowed. If the consenting person places no limit on the scope of a search, the scope is generally defined by its expressed object. Consent to search may be revoked by the person giving it at any time.

The constitutional right to refuse to consent to a search is a personal right of the individual against whom the search is directed. A person other than the person against whose interests the search is being conducted cannot effectively consent to a search of property unless (1) the person has been specifically authorized to do so, or (2) the person possesses common authority over, or has other sufficient relationship to, the premises or effects sought to be inspected. If a person establishes an exclusive reasonable expectation of privacy in property, another person may not consent to a search of the property.

Key Holdings from Major Cases

Schneckloth v. Bustamonte (1973). "In situations where the police have some evidence of illicit activity, but lack probable cause to arrest or search, a search authorized by a valid consent may be the only means of obtaining important and reliable evidence. . . . And in those cases where there is probable cause to arrest or search, but where the police lack a warrant, a consent search may still be valuable. If the search is conducted and proves fruitless, that in itself may convince the police that an arrest with its possible stigma and embarrassment is unnecessary, or that a far more extensive search pursuant to a warrant is not justified. In short, a search pursuant to consent may result in considerably less inconvenience for the subject of the search, and, properly conducted, is a constitutionally permissible and wholly legitimate aspect of effective police activity." 412 U.S. 218, 228, 93 S.Ct. 2041, 2048, 36 L.Ed.2d 854, 863.

"[T]he Fourth and Fourteenth Amendments require that consent not be coerced, by explicit or implicit means, by implied threat or covert force. For, no matter how subtly the coercion were applied, the resulting 'consent' would be no more than a pretext for the unjustified police intrusion against which the Fourth Amendment is directed. . . .

"The problem of reconciling the recognized legitimacy of consent searches with the requirement that they be free from any aspect of official coercion cannot be resolved by any infallible touchstone. To approve such searches without the most careful scrutiny would sanction the possibility of official coercion; to place artificial restrictions upon such searches would jeopardize their basic validity. Just as was true with confessions the requirement of 'voluntary' consent reflects a fair accommodation of the constitutional requirements involved. In examining all the surrounding circumstances to determine if in fact the consent to search was coerced, account must be taken of subtly coercive police questions, as well as the possibly vulnerable subjective state of the person who consents. Those searches that are the product of police coercion can thus be filtered out without undermining the continuing validity of consent searches. In sum, there is no reason for us to depart in the area of consent searches, from the traditional definition of 'voluntariness.'" 412 U.S. at 228–29, 93 S.Ct. at 2048–49, 36 L.Ed.2d at 864.

"[W]hen the subject of a search is not in custody and the State attempts to justify a search on the basis of his consent, the Fourth and Fourteenth Amendments require that it demonstrate that the consent was in fact voluntarily given, and not the result of duress or coercion, express or implied. Voluntariness is a question of fact to be determined from all the circumstances, and while the subject's knowledge of a right to refuse is a factor to be taken into consideration, the prosecution is not required to demonstrate such knowledge as a prerequisite to establishing a voluntary consent." 412 U.S. at 248–49, 93 S.Ct. at 2059, 36 L.Ed.2d at 875.

Bumper v. North Carolina (1968). "When a prosecutor seeks to rely upon consent to justify the lawfulness of a search, he has the burden of proving that the consent was, in fact, freely and voluntarily given. This burden cannot be discharged by showing no more than acquiescence to a claim of lawful authority. A search conducted in reliance upon a warrant cannot later be justified on the basis of consent if it turns out that the warrant was invalid. The results can be no different when it turns out that the State does not even attempt to rely upon the validity of the warrant, or fails to show that there was, in fact, any warrant at all.

"When a law enforcement officer claims authority to search a home under a warrant, he announces in effect that the occupant has no right to resist the search. The situation is instinct with coercion—albeit colorably lawful coercion. Where there is coercion there cannot be consent." 391 U.S. 543, 548–50, 88 S.Ct. 1788, 1792, 20 L.Ed.2d 797, 802–03.

Ohio v. Robinette (1996). "[I]t [would] be unrealistic to require police officers to always inform detainees that they are free to go before a consent to search may be deemed voluntary." 519 U.S. 33, 39–40, 117 S.Ct. 417, 421, 136 L.Ed.2d 347, 355.

Florida v. Jimeno (1991). "[T]he standard for measuring the scope of a suspect's consent under the Fourth Amendment is that of 'objective reasonableness'—what would the typical reasonable person have understood by the exchange between the officer and the suspect?" 500 U.S. 248, 251, 111 S.Ct. 1801, 1803–04, 114 L.Ed.2d 297, 302.

"If the consenting person places no limit on the scope of a search, the scope is 'generally defined by its expressed object.'" 500 U.S. at 251, 111 S.Ct. at 1804, 114 L.Ed.2d at 303.

"[I]t was objectively reasonable for the police to conclude that the general consent to search respondent's car included consent to search containers within that car which might bear drugs. A reasonable person may be expected to know that narcotics are generally carried in some form of a container." 500 U.S. at 251, 111 S.Ct. at 1804, 114 L.Ed.2d at 303.

United States v. Matlock (1974). "[W]hen the prosecution seeks to justify a warrantless search by proof of voluntary consent, it is not limited to proof that consent was given by the defendant, but may show that permission to search was obtained from a third party who possessed common authority over or other sufficient relationship to the premises or effects sought to be inspected." 415 U.S. 164, 171, 94 S.Ct. 988, 993, 39 L.Ed.2d 242, 249–50.

"Common authority is . . . not to be implied from the mere interest a third party has in the property. The authority which justifies the third-party consent does not rest upon the law of property, with its attendant historical and legal refinements, . . . but rests rather on mutual use of the property by persons generally having joint access or control for most purposes, so that it is reasonable to recognize that any of the co-inhabitants has

the right to permit the inspection in his own right and that the others have assumed the risk that one of their number might permit the common area to be searched." 415 U.S. at 171 n.7, 94 S.Ct. at 993 n.7, 39 L.Ed.2d at 250 n.7.

Illinois v. Rodriguez (1990). A warrantless entry and search is valid when based on the consent of a third party whom the police, at the time of the entry, reasonably believe to possess common authority over the premises, but who in fact does not. 497 U.S. 177, 110 S.Ct. 2793, 111 L.Ed.2d 148.

Chapman v. United States (1961). A landlord has no implied authority to consent to a search of a tenant's premises or a seizure of the tenant's property during the period of the tenancy, even though the landlord has the authority to enter the tenant's premises for the limited purposes of inspection, performance of repairs, or housekeeping services. 365 U.S. 610, 81 S.Ct. 776, 5 L.Ed.2d 828.

Stoner v. California (1964). "No less than a tenant of a house . . . a guest in a hotel room is entitled to constitutional protection against unreasonable searches and seizures. . . . That protection would disappear if it were left to depend upon the unfettered discretion of an employee of the hotel." 376 U.S. 483, 489–90, 84 S.Ct. 889, 893, 11 L.Ed.2d 856, 861.

Coolidge v. New Hampshire (1971). If a person voluntarily produces incriminating evidence, without any attempt by police to obtain consent and without coercion, deception, or other illegal police conduct, there is no search and seizure and the evidence is admissible in court. 403 U.S. 443, 91 S.Ct. 2022, 29 L.Ed.2d 564.

Review and Discussion Questions

1. If a person is deprived of freedom of action in a significant way by law enforcement officers, should the person be given warnings of the right to refuse consent before being asked for consent to search?

2. If a law enforcement officer asks a person for consent to search his or her home for stolen jewelry when the officer's real purpose is to look for marked money, is the consent voluntary?

3. Assume that law enforcement officers have obtained a valid consent to search an arrested defendant's automobile for drugs, and an initial search proves fruitless. Can the officers search the automobile again two hours later without obtaining a new consent to search? What about two days later? What about two weeks later? What changes in the defendant's status might render the initial consent no longer valid?

4. If, after giving consent to search, a person becomes nervous and revokes or limits the scope of the search, can this

reaction be used by the officers as an indication of probable cause to obtain a search warrant?

5. Are third-party consents to search the defendant's premises valid in the following circumstances?

   a. A husband, out of anger at his wife, the defendant, invites the police into the house and points out evidence incriminating the wife.

   b. The defendant's girlfriend, who lives with him part-time, consents to a search of the defendant's apartment.

   c. A wife disobeys the instructions of her husband, the defendant, not to allow a search of their home. Does it matter whether the police know of the instructions?

6. Is it proper for a law enforcement officer to deliberately avoid attempting to obtain consent to search from the defendant and instead attempt to obtain consent from someone with equal authority over the defendant's premises? Does it matter whether the law enforcement officer had an opportunity to attempt to obtain consent from the

defendant and deliberately failed to take it? What if the defendant was deliberately avoiding the police?

7. The dissenting opinion in *Florida v. Jimeno* stated, "Because an individual's expectation of privacy in a container is distinct from, and far greater than, his expectation of privacy in the interior of his car, it follows that an individual's consent to a search of the interior of his car cannot necessarily be understood as extending to containers in the car." 500 U.S. at 254, 111 S.Ct. at 1805, 114 L.Ed.2d at 305. Discuss.

8. Should a person be able to limit the number of officers conducting a consent search? Should a person be able to choose which officer or officers will conduct the consent search? Should a person be allowed to follow around the officer conducting the search?

9. Can the following persons give a valid consent to search?
   a. A highly intoxicated person
   b. A five-year-old, a seven-year-old, or a ten-year-old child
   c. A mentally retarded or senile person
   d. An emotionally upset person
   e. An uneducated person

10. Can the driver of a motor vehicle consent to a search of the vehicle even though a passenger objects? Can the owner of a store consent to a search of the store even though an employee objects? Can a parent consent to a search of his or her home even though a child objects?

Real-Life Fact Situations

1 On February 4, 1999, a bus containing about 25 to 30 passengers en route from Ft. Lauderdale to Detroit made a scheduled stop at a Greyhound bus station in downtown Tallahassee, Florida. During the stop, all of the passengers were required to exit the bus temporarily for reasons unrelated to law enforcement. As the passengers re-boarded, the driver checked their tickets before leaving to handle paperwork in the bus terminal office. Before the driver left for the terminal office, three members of the Tallahassee Police Department received permission from him for them to board the bus while the passengers were seated and waiting to depart. The officers were dressed casually and their badges were either hanging around their necks or held in their hands. They wore their guns in side-holsters, which were covered by either a shirt or jacket. There is no evidence to indicate that any passenger ever saw that the officers were armed.

Once on board the bus the officers did not make any general announcements to the passengers nor did they hold up their badges for all of the passengers to see. Officers Lang and Blackburn made their way to the back of the bus, while Officer Hoover knelt in the bus driver's seat, facing toward the rear of the bus in order to observe the passengers and ensure the safety of the other officers. In that position, Hoover could see the passengers and they could see him.

Officers Lang and Blackburn went to the back of the bus and started working their way forward, asking passengers where they were traveling from, and attempting to match passengers to the luggage in the overhead rack. The officers did not block the aisle, but instead stood next to or behind the passengers with whom they were talking. According to Lang's testimony, passengers who declined to have their luggage searched or who wished to exit the bus at any time would have been permitted to do so without argument. In similar bus searches conducted by Lang over the past year, five to seven passengers declined to have their luggage searched, and an unspecified number of other passengers exited the bus during the searches.

Defendants Drayton and Brown were seated next to each other a few rows from the rear of the bus on the driver's side, with Drayton in the aisle seat and Brown next to the window. After examining the rear of the bus, Lang approached the defendants from behind and leaned over Drayton's shoulder. He held up his badge long enough for the defendants to see that he was a police officer and, with his face 12–18 inches away from Drayton's face, Lang spoke in a voice just loud enough for the defendants to hear. He told them:

I'm Investigator Lang with the Tallahassee Police Department. We're conducting bus interdiction, attempting to deter drugs and illegal weapons being transported on the bus. Do you have any bags on the bus?

Both of the defendants responded by pointing to a green bag in the overhead luggage rack. Lang asked, "Do you mind if I check it?," to which Brown responded, "Go ahead." Lang handed the bag to Officer Blackburn to check. He did check it, and no contraband was found in the bag.

Officer Lang had noticed that both defendants were wearing heavy jackets and baggy pants despite the fact that it was a warm day, and he thought that they were overly cooperative during the search. So Lang requested and received permission from Brown to conduct a pat-down search of his person for weapons. Brown leaned up in his seat, pulled a cell phone out of his pocket, and opened up his jacket. Lang then reached across Drayton and patted down Brown's jacket and pockets, including his waist area, sides, and upper thighs. In both thigh areas, Lang detected hard objects which were inconsistent with human anatomy but similar to drug packages he had found on other occasions. Lang arrested and handcuffed Brown, and Officer Hoover escorted Brown off the bus.

Lang next turned to Drayton and asked, "Mind if I check you?" Drayton responded by lifting his hands approximately eight inches off of his legs. Lang conducted a similar patdown of Drayton's thighs. When Lang detected hard objects on Drayton's thighs similar to those he had felt on Brown, Drayton was arrested and escorted off the bus.

Once the defendants were off the bus, Lang unbuttoned their trousers and found plastic bundles of powder cocaine duct-taped between several pairs of boxer shorts. Drayton had two bundles containing 295 grams of cocaine, and Brown had three bundles containing 483 grams of cocaine. Should the defendants' motion to suppress the evidence be granted? *United States v. Drayton*, 231 F.3d 787 (11th Cir. 2000).

Read the court opinion at:
laws.findlaw.com/11th/9913814opn.html

2 On the evening of September 15, 1999, officers from the Muldrow, Oklahoma police department, accompanied by Damon Tucker, an Oklahoma Highway Patrol officer, established a checkpoint on Treat Road within the city limits of Muldrow. The impetus for establishing the checkpoint was the officers' suspicion that Holt, who lived in the area, was transporting illegal drugs along Treat Road.

At the checkpoint, the officers stopped all vehicles traveling along Treat Road and checked drivers' licenses. At approximately 10:30 P.M., Tucker observed a Ford Ranger truck approach the checkpoint. Tucker noted that the driver of the truck, defendant Holt, was not wearing a seatbelt. After asking to see Holt's driver's license, Tucker asked Holt why he was not wearing a seatbelt. Holt stated that he lived in the area and pointed toward his house. At some point thereafter, officers from the Muldrow police department informed Tucker that Holt was the person they were seeking. Tucker asked Holt to pull over to the side of the road and join Tucker in his patrol car.

After Holt got into the patrol car, Tucker asked for Holt's driver's license and proceeded to write a warning for the seatbelt violation. While doing so, Tucker asked Holt if "there was anything in [Holt's] vehicle [Tucker] should know about such as loaded weapons." App. at 40. According to Tucker, he asks that question "on a lot of [his] stops." Id. Holt stated there was a loaded pistol behind the passenger seat of his vehicle. Holt did not indicate whether he had a permit to carry a loaded gun (which was required under Oklahoma law), and Tucker did not ask whether Holt possessed such a permit. Tucker asked Holt if "there was anything else that [Tucker] should know about in the vehicle." Id. at 42. Holt stated, "I know what you are referring to" but "I don't use them anymore." Id. Upon further questioning by Tucker, Holt indicated that he had previously used drugs, but "hadn't been involved with them in about a year or

so." Id. at 43. Tucker then asked Holt for consent to search his vehicle. Holt agreed. It is unclear from the record whether Tucker issued the warning to Holt for the seatbelt violation at that point, or if Tucker ever returned Holt's driver's license to him. It is undisputed that Tucker had Holt's driver's license in his possession during the above-outlined questioning. According to Tucker, approximately three to four minutes elapsed between the time he and Holt got into the patrol car and the time that Holt consented to the search of his vehicle.

Tucker and Holt got out of the patrol car and Tucker again asked Holt if there was anything else in the vehicle. Holt responded that the gun was all that Tucker would find. Tucker proceeded to search the cab of the truck and, as described by Holt, found a loaded pistol behind the passenger seat. One of the Muldrow police officers, when informed by Tucker that Holt had given consent to have his vehicle searched, began looking through a camper shell on the back of the truck. During the course of his search, this officer found a small bag containing spoons, syringes, loose matches, and a white powdery substance in separate bags. Based upon the discovery of this evidence, Tucker arrested Holt and transported him to the Muldrow jail.

Shortly after Holt's arrest, Tucker contacted an assistant district attorney for Sequoyah County regarding the possibility of obtaining a search warrant for Holt's residence based upon the evidence recovered from Holt's vehicle. The assistant district attorney concluded the evidence was not sufficient to support a search warrant for Holt's residence. He did, however, advise Tucker to utilize "a knock and talk" technique. Id. at 48. In accordance with this advice, police officers went to Holt's residence and Holt's mother gave verbal consent to search the premises. During the search, officers found chemical glassware in a room where Holt stayed, as well as drugs and various drug-making equipment in an outbuilding. Should Holt's motions to suppress the evidence seized from his vehicle and from his residence be granted? *United States v. Holt*, 229 F.3d 931 (10th Cir. 2000).

Read the court opinion at:
www.kscourts.org/ca10/cases/2000/08/99-7150.htm

3 On June 29, 1999, at about 10:00 P.M., three Colorado Springs police officers responded to a disturbance at a mobile home park in the 3600 block of North Cascade. A neighbor had reported that men and women were yelling and screaming at that address. When they arrived at the scene, officers found a man heavily intoxicated, yelling and knocking on the door of the residence where the disturbance was reported. They placed the intoxicated man in one of the police cars. The officers then knocked on the residence door of the defendant, Kenneth Garcia (Garcia), to inquire about the reported disturbance. Garcia stepped approximately ten feet outside the residence to speak with the officers and left the door open behind him. The officers questioned Garcia. He denied there was any disturbance.

As the officers spoke with Garcia, they saw a small pipe on the ground next to him of a type used for smoking methamphetamine or crack cocaine. They also noticed a picture of a marijuana plant on the wall inside the residence.

The officers placed Garcia in the back seat of a different police car from where the intoxicated man was sitting. Officers testified at the suppression hearing that they had placed the intoxicated individual and Garcia in two separate police cars because they didn't know what was happening inside, if there are or were other individuals that were yelling—officer safety purposes. Officer testimony about Garcia's detention also included the following:

Q. And is there any reason that you could tell the Court why you decided to put him in the car versus having him stand outside?

A. Officer safety issues, that's the only reason he was in the patrol car.

The officers did not handcuff Garcia when they placed him in the police car, but he could not open the car doors from the inside. A cage separated Garcia from an officer who was sitting in the front seat of the police car. This officer told Garcia that he would be held in the police car during the investigation, and he asked Garcia whether there was anyone in the residence. Garcia replied that two women were inside.

While Garcia sat in the police car, the two women exited the residence. One of the women told the officers that Garcia offered her a blast from his crack pipe. Based on the pipe, the picture of the marijuana plant inside Garcia's residence, and the statement that Garcia had offered the woman crack to smoke, the officers decided to ask Garcia for consent to search his residence.

The officer who was sitting in the front of the police car with Garcia filled out the top portion of a search waiver form and handed it to him. Garcia read the search waiver aloud to the officer, then signed the bottom portion. The officers searched Garcia's residence and found several items of drug paraphernalia and crack cocaine. They then told Garcia that he was under arrest. Should Garcia's motion to suppress the evidence be granted? *People v. Garcia,* 11 P.3d 449 (Colo. 2000).

Read the court opinion at:
www.cobar.org/coappcts/sc2000/sc1023c.htm

4 On April 17, 1998, Jeff Thorp called the Lawrence Police Department and reported he was living at 1405 East 15th Street and that one of the other occupants of the residence was growing marijuana in the home. Thorp spoke with Dispatch Officer Tom Moore.

Officer Moore relayed the information to Officer David Axman who went to the residence to check out the tip. In his affidavit, Officer Axman related that Officer Moore told him that Thorp had said Lyzeme Savage was growing approximately 14 small marijuana plants on a window sill in the kitchen. Thorp also told Officer Moore that he had free access to the kitchen

area of the house and he would show a police officer the plants if they would come by.

When Officer Axman arrived at the residence, he knocked on the back door which led directly into the kitchen. Thorp answered the door. At the suppression hearing, evidence was presented that Thorp was 17 years old at the time of the search. Officer Axman asked the man his name, and he replied he was Jeff Thorp. Officer Axman asked Thorp if he lived at the residence and Thorp replied he did. Thorp stated he had lived there for approximately 2 months.

However, later in direct testimony, Officer Axman gave a slightly different sequence of the events. He testified that before he entered the residence, he identified himself as a Lawrence police officer, he asked Thorp his name, and then Thorp invited Officer Axman into the kitchen. It did not appear to Officer Axman that anyone else was present in the home. Officer Axman saw what appeared to be marijuana plants in the kitchen window sill. Officer Axman then asked Thorp if he lived at the residence and Thorp replied he did and had been there for approximately 2 months. Thorp told Officer Axman that he lived there with Savage, Savage's girlfriend Mary Thorp (Thorp's sister), and Mary Thorp's son. Thorp told Officer Axman that Mary and Savage slept in an upstairs bedroom and he slept on the couch in the living room.

Based on the information he gathered during his visit with Thorp, Officer Axman applied for a search warrant for 1405 East 15th Street. As additional information in his affidavit, Officer Axman stated that Thorp told him he had previously smoked marijuana at the residence, had seen Savage smoking marijuana at the residence, and that Savage had a small silver smoke pipe with a black-colored neck. The district judge granted a search warrant for the residence. As a result of the search, Savage was charged with cultivation of marijuana, individual counts of possession of marijuana, cocaine, methamphetamine, and two counts of possession of drug paraphernalia. Should Savage's motion to suppress the evidence obtained in the search be granted? *State v. Savage,* 10 P.3d 765 (Kan.App. 2000).

Read the court opinion at:
www.kscourts.org/kscases/ctapp/2000/20000901/83653.htm

5 On January 29, 1999, officers of the Madison, Wisconsin, police department arrested four men on charges of passing counterfeit dividend checks supposedly issued by the Johnson Controls Corporation. A search of their car turned up a receipt showing that a Rita Velasquez had rented Room 136 at a local Holiday Inn. Officers Louis Geblar and Bruce Frey, following up on that lead, drove to the hotel and went to the room in question. Joel Mejia responded to their knock on the door. He gave them permission to enter the room, where they found three other people: Celenia Mejia, Oscar Barrientos, and Jose Vasquez. Only Joel Mejia was fluent in English, and so the officers first asked him about the counterfeiting scheme, and then

had him serve as a translator for the others. Geblar asked everyone present for consent to search their wallets or purses, and everyone agreed.

After this exchange, three more women arrived at the room: Rita Velasquez herself, Marcella Hernandez, and the defendant Zoila Melgar. Geblar asked Velasquez to step into the hall, where he searched her purse and jacket, found a counterfeit check, and arrested her. (Velasquez told him that the check was a joke, but he obviously found that story implausible.) On a more serious note, Velasquez also told Geblar that she saw Melgar give Hernandez a large number of checks, and that Hernandez had placed these checks in her purse.

Geblar returned to the room and next summoned Hernandez into the hall with him. There he searched her purse, but he found nothing incriminating in it. When he asked Velasquez to offer an explanation, she indicated that the checks were in a second purse Hernandez owned (a black one), that was still in the room. Geblar held up that purse and asked everyone whose purse it was, but no one claimed ownership. He then opened it and found an envelope with Hernandez's name on it that contained fake Johnson Control checks. At that point, he arrested Hernandez.

Once again, Geblar then asked Velasquez to accompany him to the hall. This time he asked for her permission to search the room. His request was a general one; he did not specifically ask her if the police could search particular closed containers within the room, nor did he ask her which of the numerous people then in the room were actually staying there. Velasquez gave her permission, which she signified both orally and by signing a scrap of paper (since lost) on which Geblar had scribbled out a consent form. At that point, the officers arrested and handcuffed everyone who had not already been arrested (including Melgar) and sent them to the station house.

After they all departed, the officers began their search of the room. Between the mattress and box springs of one of the beds, Frey found a floral purse that had no personalized markings on the outside. He opened it, and found inside an identification form that bore Melgar's photograph and the name "Diana Lopez." He also found a counterfeit Johnson Controls check payable to Diana Lopez. It is this evidence that incriminated Melgar, and it is the district court's refusal to suppress this evidence on the ground that it was obtained in violation of the Fourth Amendment that Melgar challenges in this appeal. Was the district court correct in refusing to suppress the evidence? *United States v. Melgar,* 227 F.3d 1038 (7th Cir. 2000).

Read the court opinion at:
laws.findlaw.com/getclose/7th/case/993322&exact=1

6 On the evening of January 29, 1999, at about 11:30 P.M., the Jamestown Police Department responded to a call to investigate a loud party at an apartment in Jamestown. Officer Nagel was the first to arrive. He noticed an unusual number of cars parked nearby, as well as loud music and talking coming from the top floor apartment. Officer Nagel climbed the stairs to the upstairs apartment and knocked on the door. He heard people warning "It's the cops. The cops are here." By this time there were three officers around the apartment.

Officer Nagel continued to knock and could hear people scrambling around inside, he also heard people making comments, and what he believed to be a window breaking. He directed another officer to go and make sure no one was jumping out of the windows. By this time a fourth officer had arrived. Officer Nagel requested assistance from the county sheriff's department and continued to knock on the apartment door.

A young woman opened the door. Officer Nagel testified he could smell the odor of alcoholic beverage coming from inside the apartment and could see a number of young people inside. From the door, Officer Nagel could see a short hallway with three open doors to adjoining rooms. There is conflict in the testimony about whether or not Officer Nagel stepped into the apartment at this point. The trial court found the officer walked into the apartment once the door was opened. Officer Nagel asked the young woman who opened the door if she lived in the apartment, she said she did not. Officer Nagel asked if she knew who did live there and said he needed to talk to the person who lived in the apartment. The legal resident of the apartment, John Dardis, came out of the bedroom.

Officer Nagel told Dardis he could smell the odor of an alcoholic beverage and asked if anyone in the apartment was 21 years old or older, Dardis shook his head to indicate no. Dardis walked toward Officer Nagel and Officer Nagel established Dardis's breath smelled of alcohol. Officer Nagel asked for some identification from Dardis, who turned to go to another room and then turned back to answer loudly that he did not have any identification. Officer Nagel observed Dardis's eyes were heavily bloodshot.

At this point Officer Nagel testified Dardis became very obnoxious and disorderly. Dardis turned and walked away from Officer Nagel, who told Dardis to stop and come back. Officer Nagel repeated this twice and Dardis continued walking away. A young man grabbed hold of Dardis in an attempt to calm Dardis down, which Officer Nagel said resulted in a shoving match. Officer Nagel called for assistance. Dardis broke away from the young man and continued to walk away. At this point Officer Nagel stepped further into the apartment and grabbed hold of Dardis to stop him from walking away. Dardis grabbed hold of Officer Nagel's wrist. Officer Nagel told Dardis to let go of his hand, which he did. Officer Nagel then arrested Dardis for consumption of alcohol and disorderly conduct. Should Dardis's motion to suppress the evidence obtained from his apartment be granted? *City of Jamestown v. Dardis,* 618 N.W.2d 495 (N.D. 2000).

Read the court opinion at:
www.court.state.nd.us/court/opinions/20000109.htm

Chapter 10

The Plain View Doctrine

The **plain view doctrine** was simply stated by the U.S. Supreme Court in *Harris v. United States:* "It has been settled that objects falling in the plain view of an officer who has a right to be in a position to have that view may be introduced in evidence." 390 U.S. 234, 236, 88 S.Ct. 992, 993, 19 L.Ed.2d 1067, 1069 (1968). Under the doctrine, "if police are lawfully in a position from which they view an object, if its incriminating character is apparent, and if the officers have a lawful right of access to the object, they may seize it without a warrant." *Minnesota v. Dickerson,* 508 U.S. 366, 375, 113 S.Ct. 2130, 2136–37, 124 L.Ed.2d 334, 345 (1993).

The plain view doctrine permits law enforcement officers to observe and seize evidence without a warrant or other justification. It is a recognized exception to the warrant requirement of the Fourth Amendment, even though a plain view observation technically does not constitute a *search*. A search occurs only if there is an infringement of a person's reasonable expectation of privacy; a law enforcement officer's mere observation of an item of evidence from a position in which the officer has a right to be is ordinarily not an infringement of a person's privacy rights. But the Fourth Amendment prohibits unreasonable *seizures* as well as unreasonable searches.

> The right to security in person and property protected by the Fourth Amendment may be invaded in quite different ways by searches and seizures. A search compromises the individual interest in privacy; a seizure deprives the individual of dominion over his or her person or property. . . . The "plain view" doctrine is often considered an exception to the general rule that warrantless searches are presumptively unreasonable, but this characterization overlooks the important difference between searches and seizures. If an article is already in plain view, neither its observation nor its seizure would involve any invasion of privacy. . . . A seizure of the article, however, would obviously invade the owner's possessory interest. . . . If "plain view" justifies an exception from an otherwise applicable warrant requirement, therefore, it must be an exception that is addressed to the concerns that are implicated by seizures rather than by searches. *Horton v. California,* 496 U.S. 128, 133–34, 110 S.Ct. 2301, 2306, 110 L.Ed.2d 112, 120–21 (1990).

The theory of the plain view doctrine consists of extending to nonpublic places such as the home, where searches and seizures without a warrant are presumptively unreasonable, the long-standing authority of the police to make warrantless seizures in public places of incriminating objects such as weapons and contraband.

> [T]he practical justification for that extension is the desirability of sparing police, whose viewing of the object in the course of a lawful search is as legitimate as it would have been in a public place, the inconvenience and the risk—to themselves or to preservation of the evidence—of going to obtain a warrant. *Arizona v. Hicks,* 480 U.S. 321, 327, 107 S.Ct. 1149, 1153, 94 L.Ed.2d 347, 355 (1987).

Therefore, the plain view doctrine is not predicated on any sort of exigency, but is permitted in the interest of police convenience.

> The reason so light and transient a justification as police convenience is deemed reasonable is because of the absolutely minimal risk posed by the Plain View Doctrine to either of the two traditional Fourth Amendment values or concerns. . . . In terms of the initial intrusion or breach into the zone of privacy, the Plain View Doctrine, by definition, poses no threat whatsoever. It does not authorize the crossing of a threshold or other initiation of an intrusion. It does not even come into play until the intrusion is already a valid fait accompli. . . .
>
> In terms of the other traditional Fourth Amendment concern, preventing even a validly initiated search from degenerating into an exploratory fishing expedition or

Objectives

- **Understand** why the plain view doctrine is not a true exception to the search warrant requirement.

- **Distinguish** the plain view doctrine from the law of search incident to arrest.

- **Give** examples of prior valid intrusions into constitutionally protected areas.

- **Understand** how the plain view doctrine is affected by the reasonable expectation of privacy of the person against whom a search or observation is directed.

- **Know** the distinctions between: a plain view observation and probable cause to believe that an item of evidence is in a certain place and; a plain view observation and a search, especially with respect to closer examinations of items and examinations of containers.

- **Understand** the so-called "plain touch" or "plain feel" doctrine.

Harris v. United States
laws.findlaw.com/us/390/234.html
Minnesota v. Dickerson
laws.findlaw.com/us/508/366.html
Horton v. California
laws.findlaw.com/us/496/128.html
Arizona v. Hicks
laws.findlaw.com/us/480/321.html

general rummaging about, the Plain View Doctrine, again by definition, poses no threat whatsoever, for it authorizes not even the most minimal of further searching. It authorizes only the warrantless seizure by the police of probable evidence already revealed to them, with no further examination or searching being involved. *State v. Jones,* 653 A.2d 1040, 1045 (Md.Spec.App. 1995).

Requirements of the Plain View Doctrine

Despite the apparent simplicity and obviousness of its basic concept, the plain view doctrine does not give law enforcement officers a license to look around anywhere, any time, and under any circumstances and to seize anything they wish. The doctrine has carefully prescribed requirements developed through court decisions over the years. These requirements can be summarized as follows:

- The officer, as the result of a prior valid intrusion, must be in a position in which he or she has a legal right to be.
- The officer must not unreasonably intrude on any person's reasonable expectation of privacy.
- The incriminating character of the object to be seized must be immediately apparent to the officer.
- The discovery of the item of evidence by the officer need not be inadvertent.

Before the seizure of an item of evidence can be justified under the plain view doctrine, the law enforcement officer seizing the item must satisfy these requirements. The remainder of this chapter is devoted to a discussion of these requirements.

The Officer, as the Result of a Prior Valid Intrusion, Must Be in a Position in Which He or She Has a Legal Right to Be

The situations in which a law enforcement officer is in a position in which he or she has a legal right to be are too numerous to present an exhaustive listing. The U.S. Supreme Court gave several examples:

> What the "plain view" cases have in common is that the police officer in each of them had a prior justification for an intrusion in the course of which he came . . . across a piece of evidence incriminating the accused. The doctrine serves to supplement the prior justification—whether it be a warrant for another object, hot pursuit, search incident to lawful arrest, or some other legitimate reason for being present unconnected with a search directed against the accused—and permits the warrantless seizure. *Coolidge v. New Hampshire,* 403 U.S. 443, 466, 91 S.Ct. 2022, 2038, 29 L.Ed.2d 564, 583 (1971).

Coolidge v. New Hampshire
laws.findlaw.com/us/403/
443.html

For purposes of this chapter, a prior valid intrusion or a prior justification for an intrusion simply means that a law enforcement officer has made a legal encroachment into a constitutionally protected area or has otherwise legally invaded a person's reasonable expectation of privacy. Stated otherwise, "[i]t is . . . an essential predicate to any valid warrantless seizure of incriminating evidence that the officer did not violate the Fourth Amendment in arriving at the place from which the evidence could be plainly viewed." *Horton v. California,* 496 U.S. 128, 136, 110 S.Ct. 2301, 2308, 110 L.Ed.2d

112, 123 (1990). This section discusses several examples in which this requirement of the plain view doctrine has been applied.

EFFECTING AN ARREST OR SEARCH INCIDENT TO ARREST   A law enforcement officer may lawfully seize an object that comes into view during a lawfully executed *arrest* or a *search incident to arrest.* The law of search incident to arrest and the plain view doctrine must be clearly distinguished. Under the rule of *Chimel v. California* (see Chapter 8), a law enforcement officer may search a person incident to arrest only for weapons or to prevent the destruction or concealment of evidence. The extent of the search is limited to the arrestee's body and the area within the arrestee's immediate control, "construing that phrase to mean the area from within which he might gain possession of a weapon or destructible evidence." 395 U.S. at 763, 89 S.Ct. at 2040, 23 L.Ed.2d at 694.

Chimel v. California
laws.findlaw.com/us/395/752.html

The plain view doctrine does not extend the permissible area of search incident to arrest. In the *Chimel* case, the Court specifically said:

> There is no comparable justification, however, for routinely searching any room other than that in which an arrest occurs—or for that matter, for searching through all the desk drawers or other closed or concealed areas in that room itself. Such searches, in the absence of well-recognized exceptions, may be made only under the authority of a search warrant. 395 U.S. at 763, 89 S.Ct. at 2040, 23 L.Ed.2d at 694.

Nevertheless, the law of search incident to arrest does not require a law enforcement officer to ignore or avert his or her eyes from objects readily visible in the room where the arrest occurs. If the arresting officer observes an item of evidence open to view but outside the area under the immediate control of the arrestee, the officer may seize it, so long as the observation was made in the course of a lawful arrest or an appropriately limited search incident to arrest. The item of evidence is admissible in court if all requirements of the plain view doctrine are satisfied. The same rule applies to items of evidence observed during the course of a properly limited protective sweep (see Chapter 8).

CONDUCTING A STOP AND FRISK   A seizable item observed by an officer during the course of a lawful *stop and frisk* may also be seized without a warrant. (See Chapter 7 for a discussion of stop and frisk.) Again, the plain view doctrine does not extend the area of search permissible under stop-and-frisk law, but it does give the officer authority to seize readily visible objects. This authority extends to the passenger compartment of an automobile.

> If while conducting a legitimate *Terry* search of the interior of the automobile, the officer should . . . discover contraband other than weapons, he clearly cannot be required to ignore the contraband, and the Fourth Amendment does not require its suppression in such circumstances. *Michigan v. Long,* 463 U.S. 1032, 1050, 103 S.Ct. 3469, 3481, 77 L.Ed.2d 1201, 1220 (1983).

Michigan v. Long
laws.findlaw.com/us/463/1032.html

EXECUTING A SEARCH WARRANT   In the case of *Cady v. Dombrowski,* 413 U.S. 433, 93 S.Ct. 2523, 37 L.Ed.2d 706 (1973), the U.S. Supreme Court held that an officer executing a valid *search warrant* could legally seize items of evidence lying in plain view even though they were not particularly described in the warrant. For purposes of this discussion, law enforcement officers executing a valid search warrant are in a position in which they have a legal right to be. Once officers have discharged their duties under a search warrant, however, the warrant no longer provides a legitimate justification for

Cady v. Dombrowski
laws.findlaw.com/us/413/433.html

their presence on premises. Therefore, a seizure of items of evidence observed in plain view after a search warrant is fully executed is an illegal seizure. *United States v. Lima-toc,* 807 F.2d 792 (9th Cir. 1987).

MAKING CONTROLLED DELIVERIES   The U.S. government has the right to inspect all incoming goods from foreign countries at the port of entry. In addition, common carriers have a common-law right to inspect packages they accept for shipment, based on their duty to refrain from carrying **contraband.** Although the sheer volume of goods in transit prevents systematic inspection of all or even a large percentage of these goods, common carriers and customs officials inevitably discover contraband in transit in a variety of circumstances. When such a discovery is made, it is routine procedure to notify the appropriate authorities, so that the authorities may identify and prosecute the person or persons responsible for the contraband's movement. The arrival of law enforcement authorities on the scene to confirm the presence of contraband and to determine what to do with it does not convert the otherwise legal search by the common carrier or customs official into a government search subject to the Fourth Amendment. *United States v. Edwards,* 602 F.2d 458 (1st Cir. 1979). See also *United States v. Jacobsen,* 466 U.S. 109, 104 S.Ct. 1652, 80 L.Ed.2d 85 (1984).

United States v. Jacobsen
laws.findlaw.com/us/466/
109.html

Law enforcement authorities, rather than simply seizing the contraband and destroying it, will often make a so-called controlled delivery of the container, monitoring the container on its journey to the intended destination. The person dealing in the contraband can then be identified upon taking possession of and asserting control over the container. The typical pattern of a controlled delivery has been described as follows:

> They most ordinarily occur when a carrier, usually an airline, unexpectedly discovers what seems to be contraband while inspecting luggage to learn the identity of its owner, or when the contraband falls out of a broken or damaged piece of luggage, or when the carrier exercises its inspection privilege because some suspicious circumstance has caused it concern that it may unwittingly be transporting contraband. Frequently, after such a discovery, law enforcement agents restore the contraband to its container, then close or reseal the container, and authorize the carrier to deliver the container to its owner. When the owner appears to take delivery he is arrested and the container with the contraband is seized and then searched a second time for the contraband known to be there. *United States v. Bulgier,* 618 F.2d 472, 476 (7th Cir. 1980).

The U.S. Supreme Court, relying on the plain view doctrine, held that no protected privacy interest remains in contraband in a container once government officers have lawfully opened that container and identified its contents as illegal. Furthermore, the simple act of resealing the container to enable the police to make a controlled delivery does not operate to revive or restore the lawfully invaded privacy rights. The Court said:

> The plain view doctrine is grounded on the proposition that once police are lawfully in a position to observe an item first-hand, its owner's privacy interest in that item is lost; the owner may retain the incidents of title and possession but not privacy. . . . [O]nce a container has been found to a certainty to contain illicit drugs, the contraband becomes like objects physically within the plain view of the police, and the claim to privacy is lost. Consequently, the subsequent reopening of the container is not a "search" within the intendment of the Fourth Amendment. *Illinois v. Andreas,* 463 U.S. 765, 771–72, 103 S.Ct. 3319, 3324, 77 L.Ed.2d 1003, 1010 (1983).

Illinois v. Andreas
laws.findlaw.com/us/463/
765.html

In the *Andreas* case, the Court acknowledged that there are often unavoidable interruptions of control or surveillance of a container and that at some point after such an interruption, courts should recognize that the container may have been put to other uses, thereby reinstating the individual's legitimate expectation of privacy in the container. The Court decided that a workable, objective standard that limits the risk of intrusion on legitimate privacy interests when such an interruption occurs is whether there is a substantial likelihood that the contents of the container have been changed during the gap in surveillance. If there is no such likelihood, the officer may legally open the container without a warrant.

PURSUING A FLEEING SUSPECT   Law enforcement officers who are lawfully on premises in **hot pursuit** of a dangerous person may seize items of evidence observed open to their view. In *Warden v. Hayden*, 387 U.S. 294, 87 S.Ct. 1642, 18 L.Ed.2d 782 (1967), the police were informed that an armed robbery had taken place and that a suspect wearing a light cap and dark jacket had entered a certain house less than five minutes before the officers arrived. Several officers entered the house and began to search for the described suspect and weapons that he had used in the robbery and might use against them. One officer, while searching the cellar, found in a washing machine clothing of the type that the fleeing man was said to have worn. The Court held that the seizure of the clothing was lawful:

Warden v. Hayden
laws.findlaw.com/us/387/
294.html

> [T]he seizures occurred prior to or immediately contemporaneous with Hayden's arrest, as part of an effort to find a suspected felon, armed, within the house into which he had run only minutes before the police arrived. The permissible scope of search must, therefore, at the least, be as broad as may reasonably be necessary to prevent the dangers that the suspect at large in the house may resist or escape. 387 U.S. at 299, 87 S.Ct. at 1646, 18 L.Ed.2d at 787.

If, however, the suspect had already been taken into custody when the officer looked into the washing machine, the seizure of the clothing would have been unlawful. There no longer would have been any danger of the fleeing suspect's using a weapon against the officers and, therefore, no reason to look for weapons in the washing machine.

To summarize, officers who enter a constitutionally protected area in hot pursuit of a fleeing suspect are in a position in which they have a legal right to be and may seize items of evidence observed lying open to view during the hot pursuit and the protective search for weapons. Note that hot pursuit does not necessarily involve a violent crime or a dangerous person. The U.S. Supreme Court held that there was a hot pursuit when officers chased the defendant, who the officers had probable cause to believe had just purchased illegal drugs, from her doorway into her house. *United States v. Santana*, 427 U.S. 38, 96 S.Ct. 2406, 49 L.Ed.2d 300 (1976).

United States v. Santana
laws.findlaw.com/us/427/
38.html

RESPONDING TO AN EMERGENCY   Related to the hot pursuit situation is the situation in which an officer responds to an **emergency** and observes items of evidence open to view. In *United States v. Gillenwaters*, 890 F.2d 679 (4th Cir. 1989), a police officer responded to a report of a stabbing at the defendant's home. The victim was a visiting friend, and the officer arrived while paramedics were still tending the woman's wounds. The officer briefly questioned the woman and also observed several incriminating items open to view in the room where the victim lay. A search warrant was obtained partially on the basis of these observations. The court held that the observations were not an improper warrantless search.

> Hager [the officer] was responding to an emergency call; he arrived while the victim was still receiving emergency medical treatment on the scene; he attempted to obtain evidence from her concerning her assailant. His presence was unquestionably justified by

exigent circumstances, and his observations—made in the room where the victim lay bleeding—fall within the scope of the plain view doctrine. 890 F.2d at 682.

In *State v. Moulton*, 481 A.2d 155 (Me. 1984), police had probable cause to believe that a dangerous criminal suspect was on the premises of an auto repair complex. The officers believed that the suspect not only had stolen motor vehicles and parts but also had driven one vehicle into a lake and had set another on fire. The auto repair complex was large, with many exits, making it difficult to secure. The likely presence of tools, vehicles, and flammable liquids added to the danger, and the hour was late, adding to the difficulty of obtaining a warrant. Under these exigent circumstances, the court found that the officers were justified in entering the building without a search warrant for the suspect. Once inside the building, officers observed criminal evidence lying in plain view and seized it. These warrantless seizures were held reasonable under the Fourth Amendment, and a subsequent search warrant, obtained in part on the basis of the items found in plain view, was valid.

Police may thus enter premises and search without a warrant for a dangerous criminal suspect if

- the police have probable cause to believe that the dangerous criminal suspect is on the premises, and
- exigent circumstances preclude police from securing the premises long enough to obtain a search warrant.

Once police have made a valid intrusion into the premises, they may seize items of evidence lying in plain view.

Law enforcement officers may be tempted to justify otherwise illegal searches by resorting to this combination of the plain view doctrine and response to an emergency. Courts will carefully examine these situations and will invalidate a search if a genuine emergency does not exist, or if a search goes beyond what is necessary to respond to the emergency. In *Arizona v. Hicks,* summarized on pages 387–389, the search went beyond what was necessary to respond to the emergency. Therefore, in the absence of probable cause to justify the additional search and in the absence of probable cause to seize the object, the plain view doctrine did not apply. The U.S. Supreme Court stated that "a warrantless search must be 'strictly circumscribed by the exigencies which justify its initiation,' . . ." *Mincey v. Arizona,* 437 U.S. 385, 393, 98 S.Ct. 2408, 2414, 57 L.Ed.2d 290, 300 (1978). In the *Mincey* case, the prosecution attempted to justify an extensive four-day warrantless search of a murder victim's apartment on the basis of a "murder scene exception" to the warrant requirement. The search occurred when there was no emergency threatening life or limb and after all persons in the apartment had been located.

Mincey v. Arizona
laws.findlaw.com/us/437/
385.html

The Court said that police may make warrantless entries on premises where they reasonably believe that a person within needs immediate aid. Police may also make a prompt warrantless protective search of the area to see whether other potentially dangerous persons are still on the premises. Any evidence observed in plain view during the course of these legitimate emergency activities may be seized. However, the Court held that absent an emergency, "the 'murder scene exception' . . . is inconsistent with the Fourth and Fourteenth Amendments—that the warrantless search of Mincey's apartment was not constitutionally permissible simply because a homicide had recently occurred there." 437 U.S. at 395, 98 S.Ct. at 2414, 57 L.Ed.2d at 302. In *Thompson v. Louisiana,* 469 U.S. 17, 105 S.Ct. 409, 83 L.Ed.2d 246 (1984), the Court reiterated that even a limited two-hour, general, nonemergency search of a murder scene remains a significant intrusion on a person's privacy and may not be conducted without a war-

Thompson v. Louisiana
laws.findlaw.com/us/469/
17.html

Case in Point

Interpreting *Flippo v. West Virginia*

On March 22, 1997 at 1:00 A.M., while on patrol, Officer Edward Sousa of the Bloomfield Police Department was flagged down at the corner of Bloomfield and Belmont Avenues by an individual named Angelo DiGiacomo. Mr. DiGiacomo advised Officer Sousa that another party had broken into a garage located at 5 Columbus Street and left that location carrying a cardboard box. Mr. DiGiacomo then pointed down the street at the individual to which he was referring. Officer Sousa observed the individual to whom Mr. DiGiacomo was referring and stopped him at the corner of Bloomfield Avenue and North 10th Street. Upon walking up to the individual, later identified as Louis Gillick, Officer Sousa observed a cardboard box which Mr. Gillick was carrying. He noticed that the box was filled with car radios. Officer Sousa questioned Mr. Gillick about where he had found the radios. Mr. Gillick had responded that he found the box on the street corner, and then advised Officer Sousa that his brother worked in the garage. Since Officer Sousa had observed Mr. Gillick walking down the street with the box in hand, he determined that Mr. Gillick was a suspect in the burglary of the garage that Mr. DiGiacomo had previously discussed with Officer Sousa. At that time, Officer Sousa read Mr. Gillick his Miranda rights and Mr. DiGiacomo identified Mr. Gillick as the individual he saw leaving the garage. Officer Sousa then brought Mr. Gillick back to the exterior of the garage and Mr. Gillick was identified by a second witness, Mr. Edgar Villaneuva. Mr. Villaneuva had advised Officer Sousa that he had seen the light in the garage and had seen one person walking around inside. Both witnesses, Messrs. DiGiacomo and Villaneuva, lived at 7 Columbus, next door to the subject garage.

After Mr. Gillick was placed under arrest for burglary and theft, Officer Sousa went to the front of the garage. He observed that a door panel to the garage door had been pushed in, leading him to determine that there had been a forcible entry into the building. Officer Sousa, accompanied by Officers Dwyer and Motsch, who came to the scene pursuant to a burglary in progress call, entered the garage in search of additional suspects. Upon entering the garage, the officers observed a large number of car parts from what appeared to be newer model cars. The search did not produce any additional suspects and did not produce any cars being repaired. Based on Officer Sousa's six-month experience with the Auto

Theft Task Force and his fifteen (15) years with the Bloomfield Police Department, he believed that the parts were stolen and that the garage was being used as a "chop shop." Officer Sousa then wrote down the Vehicle Identification Numbers (VINs) for three (3) of the car doors which he observed in the garage and radioed those numbers to his dispatcher, who ran the numbers through the NCIC. As a result of the NCIC search, the dispatcher advised Officer Sousa that the car doors were from cars that had been reported stolen. Upon getting the results, Officer Sousa secured the garage as a crime scene and obtained a search warrant based on the information that he had gained from his entry into the building.

A few hours after the initial incident, at approximately 8:00 A.M. on March 22, 1997, a warrant to search the garage at 5 Columbus, Bloomfield, New Jersey, was obtained from Municipal Court Judge John Bukowsky. Officer Sousa participated in the search of the garage pursuant to the warrant and the auto parts that were housed at that location were seized. Additionally, during the search, a tool box which was believed to contain "other property connected with the crime of chop shop operation," as detailed in the warrant, was searched. The "other property" referenced in the warrant was interpreted by Officer Sousa to mean registrations, licenses, insurance policies and any other items that would show ownership of the cars to which the car parts went. In one of the drawers of the tool box, Officer Sousa found license plates which had been folded and placed in a small bag through which the contents could be seen. In continuing to search the tool box, Officer Sousa removed a black pouch from the tool box and, believing that other folded license plates and pieces of identification could be found inside the pouch, Officer Sousa opened the pouch and found a white powdery substance believed to be heroin along with green vegetation believed to be marijuana. These items were later tested and proved to be controlled dangerous substances. In light of *Flippo v. West Virginia*, should the motion of defendant Anthony Faretra for suppression of evidence seized by the police following the warrantless entry of a garage leased by him be granted? *State v. Faretra*, 750 A.2d 166 (N.J.Super. 2000).

Read the court opinion at:
lawlibrary.rutgers.edu/courts/appellate/a1990-99.opn.html

---

rant. In *Flippo v. West Virginia*, 528 U.S. 11, 120 S.Ct. 7, 145 L.Ed.2d 16 (1999), law enforcement officers remained for sixteen hours to conduct a warrantless search of a homicide scene. The Court, citing *Mincey*, rejected the trial court's finding that after

Flippo v. West Virginia
supreme.pub.findlaw.com/
supreme_court/decisions/
98-8770.2.html

the homicide crime scene was secured for investigation, a search of "anything and everything found within the crime scene area" was "within the law."

Key Points

1. The plain view doctrine allows the warrantless seizure of incriminating evidence observed after a prior justification for an intrusion, whether that justification be a warrant for another object, hot pursuit, search incident to arrest, an emergency, or some other legitimate reason.

2. Once police are lawfully in a position to observe an item firsthand, its owner's privacy interest in that item is lost,

   although the owner may retain the incidents of title and possession.

3. Absent a continuing emergency, a warrantless search of a murder scene is not constitutionally permissible simply because a homicide had recently occurred there.

www.fletc.gov/legal/
archive_dir.htm
Article, "A Murder Scene Exception to the Fourth Amendment Warrant Requirement" by Bryan R. Lemons; second of three articles in the July 6, 2000, issue of *Quarterly Review: Legal Commentary for Federal Law Enforcement Officers*
www.fbi.gov/publications/leb/
1999/jan99leb.pdf
Article, "Crime Scene Searches: The Need for Fourth Amendment Compliance" by Kimberley A. Crawford (page 26 of the January 1999 *FBI Law Enforcement Bulletin*)
www.jus.state.nc.us/NCJA/
flippo.htm
Article, "No Crime Scene Exception to the Fourth Amendment's Search Warrant Requirement"; discusses *Flippo v. West Virginia* and provides advice for law enforcement officers
www.co.alameda.ca.us/da/pov/
scene_searches.htm
Article, "Crime Scene Searches" from the Alameda County, California District Attorney's Office

The Officer Must Not Unreasonably Intrude on Any Person's Reasonable Expectation of Privacy

Not all observations made by law enforcement officers who are in a position in which they have a legal right to be will satisfy Fourth Amendment requirements. If an observation unreasonably intrudes on a person's reasonable expectation of privacy, it will be considered an illegal search unless it is supported by a warrant or falls within a recognized exception to the warrant requirement.

In a case illustrating this principle, a law enforcement officer observed the defendant and another man enter the men's room of a city park and remain there. After about five minutes, the officer entered the plumbing access area of the rest room and observed the men performing illegal sexual acts. The officer had observed no other suspicious acts by the defendant before the defendant entered the men's room. The court held that this was not a plain view observation by the officer but an illegal search.

> The People here urge us to hold that clandestine observation of doorless stalls in public rest rooms is not a "search" and hence is not subject to the Fourth Amendment's prohibition of unreasonable searches. This would permit the police to make it a routine practice to observe from hidden vantage points the rest room conduct of the public whenever such activities do not occur within fully enclosed toilet stalls and would permit spying on the "innocent and guilty alike." Most persons using public rest rooms have no reason to suspect that a hidden agent of the state will observe them. The expectation of privacy a person has when he enters a rest room is reasonable and is not diminished or destroyed because the toilet stall being used lacks a door.
>
> Reference to expectations of privacy as a Fourth Amendment touchstone received the endorsement of the United States Supreme Court in *Katz v. United States*, 389 U.S. 347, 88 S.Ct. 507, 19 L.Ed.2d 576 (1967). Viewed in the light of *Katz*, the standard for determining what is an illegal search is whether defendant's "reasonable expectation of privacy was violated by unreasonable governmental intrusion." *People v. Triggs*, 106 Cal.Rptr. 408, 412–13, 506 P.2d 232, 236–37 (Cal. 1973).

If, however, a person has no reasonable expectation of privacy in a place or an object, plain view observations of the place or object by law enforcement officers violate no

Fourth Amendment rights. In *New York v. Class*, 475 U.S. 106, 106 S.Ct. 960, 89 L.Ed.2d 81 (1986), a law enforcement officer stopped an automobile for a traffic infraction. After the driver voluntarily got out of the vehicle, the officer entered the vehicle and removed some papers from the dashboard in order to ascertain the vehicle identification number (VIN). (Federal law requires the VIN to be placed in the plain view of someone outside the automobile to facilitate the VIN's usefulness for various governmental purposes such as research, insurance, safety, theft prevention, and vehicle recall.)

The Court held that there was no reasonable expectation of privacy in the VIN because of the important role played by the VIN in the pervasive governmental regulation of the automobile and because of the efforts of the federal government to ensure that the VIN is placed in plain view. Furthermore, the placement of papers on top of the VIN was insufficient to create a privacy interest in the VIN, since efforts to restrict access to an area do not generate a reasonable expectation of privacy where none would otherwise exist. The mere viewing of the formerly obscured VIN was not, therefore, a violation of the Fourth Amendment. Moreover, since the officer's entry into the vehicle to uncover the VIN did not violate the Fourth Amendment, the officer had a legal right to be where he was when he saw a gun under the seat. The gun was thus in plain view, and, given the officer's probable cause that the gun was evidence of a crime, the officer could seize it under the plain view doctrine.

New York v. Class
laws.findlaw.com/us/475/
106.html

 **Key Points**

4. If a person has no reasonable expectation of privacy in a place or an object, plain view observations by law enforcement officers violate no Fourth Amendment rights.

The Incriminating Character of the Object to Be Seized Must Be Immediately Apparent to the Officer

This requirement of the plain view doctrine means that before an object may be seized, the police must have *probable cause* that the object is subject to seizure without conducting some further search of the object. *Arizona v. Hicks*, 480 U.S. 321, 107 S.Ct. 1149, 94 L.Ed.2d 347 (1987).

PROBABLE CAUSE   "If . . . the police lack probable cause to believe that an object in plain view is contraband without conducting some further search of the object—i.e., if 'its incriminating character [is not] "immediately apparent,"' . . . the plain-view doctrine cannot justify its seizure." *Minnesota v. Dickerson*, 508 U.S. 366, 375, 113 S.Ct. 2130, 2137, 124 L.Ed.2d 334, 345 (1993). The term *contraband*, as used in this quote, should be interpreted to include the categories of property subject to seizure as listed in Chapter 5:

1. Property that constitutes evidence of the commission of a criminal offense;
2. Contraband, the fruits of crime, or things otherwise criminally possessed; or
3. Property designed or intended for use or that is or has been used as the means of committing a criminal offense.

In *Coolidge v. New Hampshire,* 403 U.S. 443, 466, 91 S.Ct. 2022, 2038, 29 L.Ed.2d 564, 583 (1971), the U.S. Supreme Court said that a seizure of an item in plain view is justified "only where it is *immediately apparent* to the police that they have evidence before them." (Emphasis added.) The term *immediately apparent* has been broadly interpreted to give officers a reasonable time within which to make the probable cause determination. For example, in *United States v. Johnston,* 784 F.2d 416 (1st Cir. 1986), the court held that an item's incriminating nature need not be determined by the first officer who observes the item, but may be based on the collective knowledge of all officers lawfully on the premises after all have observed the item. In the *Johnston* case, an officer came across torn pages from a notebook while executing a search warrant for narcotics. Probable cause to seize the pages as incriminating evidence did not develop, however, until the team of searching officers completed a search of the rest of the premises and discovered related evidence of narcotics violations. So long as the officers had probable cause to believe the items were incriminating by the time of completion of the execution of the search warrant, the *immediately apparent* requirement was held to be satisfied.

> If the plain view doctrine's immediate apparency requirement were taken literally, it would mean that unless searching officers had probable cause to grasp the incriminating character of an item not specifically covered by a search warrant at the precise moment they first spotted it, its seizure would become unlawful for the duration of the search, regardless of information lawfully acquired later in the search. Such an approach would condition the lawfulness of a seizure on the fortuity of whether the item was discovered early or late in the search: if officers entered premises under a warrant, and first saw a kitchen knife and then a corpse with its throat slit, they could not take the knife; but they could if the sequence were reversed. Thus, although the phrase immediately apparent sounds temporal, its true meaning must be that the incriminating nature of the item must have become apparent, in the course of the search, without the benefit of information from any unlawful search or seizure. *United States v. Garces,* 133 F.3d 70, 75 (D.C. Cir. 1998).

In *State v. Mosher,* 270 A.2d 451 (Me. 1970), a Massachusetts police officer arrested the defendant and two companions for trespassing with their automobile on private property. While waiting for assistance, the officer observed articles of clothing wrapped in cellophane lying inside the car. Later, after the car had been removed to the police station, the officer learned through police channels that similar clothing had recently been stolen in Maine. He obtained a search warrant and seized the clothing.

The court found the search warrant defective but upheld the seizure because the items of clothing were in the officer's plain view. The court said:

> Even where . . . no search is necessary, the accompanying seizure must be accompanied by probable cause or reasonable grounds to believe that the property falls within a category which warrants the seizure. 270 A.2d at 453.

When the officer seized the items, he had probable cause to believe that the articles of clothing were *stolen* based on the report that similar articles had been stolen in Maine. If the officer had seized the articles of clothing when he first observed them, the seizure would have been illegal. At that time, he had no reason to believe that they were stolen or that they came under any other category of seizable property. It was only after he received the report that similar clothing had been stolen in Maine that he had probable cause to believe the property was seizable.

Officers may use their background and experience to evaluate the facts and circumstances in arriving at a probable cause determination. In *Texas v. Brown,* 460 U.S.

Texas v. Brown
laws.findlaw.com/us/460/
730.html

730, 103 S.Ct. 1535, 75 L.Ed.2d 502 (1983), an officer stopped the defendant's auto-mobile at night at a routine driver's license checkpoint, asked the defendant for his license, and shined a flashlight into the car. The officer observed an opaque green party balloon, knotted about one-half inch from the tip. After shifting his position, the offi-cer also observed several small vials, quantities of loose white powder, and an open bag of party balloons in the open glove compartment. The U.S. Supreme Court held that the officer had probable cause to believe that the balloon contained an illicit substance:

> [The officer] testified that he was aware, both from his participation in previous nar-cotics arrests and from discussions with other officers, that balloons tied in the manner of the one possessed by [the defendant] were frequently used to carry narcotics. This testimony was corroborated by that of a police department chemist who noted that it was "common" for balloons to be used in packaging narcotics. In addition, [the officer] was able to observe the contents of the glove compartment of [the defendant's] car, which revealed further suggestions that [the defendant] was engaged in activities that might involve possession of illicit substances. The fact that [the officer] could not see through the opaque fabric of the balloon is all but irrelevant: the distinctive character of the balloon itself spoke volumes as to its contents—particularly to the trained eye of the officer. 460 U.S. at 742–43, 103 S.Ct. at 1543, 75 L.Ed.2d at 514.

In *Shipman v. State*, 282 So.2d 700 (Ala. 1973), however, the object containing drugs was found to be insufficiently distinctive in character to justify its seizure. In that case, law enforcement officers detained several persons on a storeowner's complaint that they were acting in an unruly manner. An officer observed one of the persons move an object to the top of his boot. The object, though clearly not a weapon, was seized and was later determined to contain heroin. The court held that, even though the object was in plain view, its seizure was illegal because the officer did not have probable cause to believe it was contraband; in other words, its incriminating nature was not readily apparent.

> The reason for this rule is apparent. If the rule were otherwise, an officer acting on mere groundless suspicion, could seize anything and everything belonging to an individual which happened to be in plain view on the prospect that on further investigation some of it might prove to have been stolen or to be contraband. It would open the door to unreasonable confiscation of a person's property while a minute examination of it is made in an effort to find something criminal. Such practice would amount to the "general exploratory search from one object to another until something incriminating at last emerges" which was condemned in *Coolidge v. New Hampshire*. . . . Ex post facto justi-fication of a seizure made on mere groundless suspicion, is totally contrary to the basic tenets of the Fourth Amendment. . . .
>
> For an item in plain view to be validly seized, the officer must possess some judgment at the time that the object to be seized is contraband and that judgment must be grounded upon probable cause. 282 So.2d at 704.

In certain instances, an officer may have occasion to search rather than seize items found in plain view. In *Arizona v. Hicks,* 480 U.S. 321, 107 S.Ct. 1149, 94 L.Ed.2d 347 (1987) (discussed in further detail later), an officer conducting an emergency search of an apartment after a shooting incident observed stereo equipment that he suspected was stolen. He searched the equipment, moving it for closer examination, and obtained the serial numbers. He determined that the equipment was stolen and seized some immediately and some later under a warrant. The Court held that the same probable cause standard applies to plain view searches as applies to plain view seizures. Since the officer had only a suspicion that the stereo equipment was stolen, his search was not based on probable cause and was therefore unreasonable under the Fourth Amendment.

MECHANICAL OR ELECTRICAL AIDS   Although the plain view doctrine does not allow a law enforcement officer to conduct a further search of an object to determine its incriminating nature, it is well settled that an officer may use mechanical or electrical aids to assist in observing items of evidence. Of course, the officer must be in a position in which he or she has a legal right to be and must not intrude on someone's reasonable expectation of privacy. *Texas v. Brown*, 460 U.S. 730, 103 S.Ct. 1535, 75 L.Ed.2d 502 (1983). In *Marshall v. United States*, 422 F.2d 185 (5th Cir. 1970), when a law enforcement officer arrived at a drive-in restaurant, he was told that a car had been parked in the parking lot for an hour with its lights on and with a person lying in the back seat. The officer went over to the car to see whether anything was wrong. He shined a flashlight into the car and observed the defendant lying in the back with a sawed-off shotgun resting on the floorboard between his feet. He arrested the defendant and seized the shotgun.

The court held that the observation of the shotgun by the officer was not a search. The officer was in a position in which he had a legal right to be, and his use of the flashlight did not, in itself, make his observations unlawful:

> When the circumstances of a particular case are such that the police officer's observation would not have constituted a search had it occurred in daylight, then the fact that the officer used a flashlight to pierce the nighttime darkness does not transform his observation into a search. Regardless of the time of day or night, the plain view rule must be upheld where the viewer is rightfully positioned, seeing through eyes that are neither accusatory nor criminally investigatory. The plain view rule does not go into hibernation at sunset. 422 F.2d at 189.

Similarly, courts have generally approved of the use of binoculars to enhance natural observations so long as they are not used to see into an area that would otherwise be impossible to view with the naked eye. In *United States v. Grimes*, 426 F.2d 706 (5th Cir. 1970), an officer stationed himself in a field about fifty yards from the defendant's house and with the aid of binoculars watched the activities of the defendant, a known liquor violator. The officer observed the defendant place two large cardboard boxes (each of which contained six gallons of untaxed whiskey) into a 1961 Buick. The liquor was later found in the car while another person was driving the car on a public street. The court held that the officer's use of binoculars to observe the defendant's activities did not constitute an illegal search. A defendant's reasonable expectation of privacy was violated, however, in a case in which police looked into an eighth-floor window from a vantage point two to three hundred yards away using high-powered binoculars.

> We . . . view the test of validity of the surveillance as turning upon whether that which is perceived or heard is that which is conducted with a reasonable expectation of privacy and not upon the means used to view it or hear it. So long as that which is viewed or heard is perceptible to the naked eye or unaided ear, the person seen or heard has no reasonable expectation of privacy in what occurs. Because he has no reasonable expectation of privacy, governmental authority may use technological aids to visual or aural enhancement of whatever type available. However, the reasonable expectation of privacy extends to that which cannot be seen by the naked eye or heard by the unaided ear. While governmental authority may use a technological device to avoid detection of

its own law enforcement activity, it may not use the same device to invade the protected right. *People v. Arno*, 153 Cal.Rptr. 624, 627 (Cal.App. 1979).

(See the section, "Plain View, Open Fields, and Observations into Constitutionally Protected Areas" in Chapter 12.)

SHIFTING OF POSITION   In *Texas v. Brown*, 460 U.S. 730, 103 S.Ct. 1535, 75 L.Ed.2d 502 (1983), the U.S. Supreme Court held that a police officer's changing of position to get a better vantage point to look inside a vehicle did not invalidate an otherwise legal plain view observation.

> [T]he fact that [Officer] Maples "changed [his] position" and "bent down at an angle so [he] could see what was inside" Brown's car . . . is irrelevant to Fourth Amendment analysis. The general public could peer into the interior of Brown's automobile from any number of angles; there is no reason Maples should be precluded from observing as an officer what would be entirely visible to him as a private citizen. There is no legitimate expectation of privacy . . . shielding that portion of the interior of an automobile which may be viewed from outside the vehicle by either inquisitive passersby or diligent police officers. In short, the conduct that enabled Maples to observe the interior of Brown's car and of his open glove compartment was not a search within the meaning of the Fourth Amendment. 460 U.S. at 740, 103 S.Ct. at 1542, 75 L.Ed.2d at 512–13.

CLOSER EXAMINATION OF ITEMS   A difficult issue is how far an officer may go in examining an item more closely before the examination constitutes a search rather than a mere plain view observation. The U.S. Supreme Court gave some guidelines in a case in which police, investigating a shooting, entered the defendant's apartment to search for the shooter, other victims, and weapons. One officer noticed stereo components and, suspecting they were stolen, read and recorded their serial numbers, moving some of the equipment in the process. After checking with headquarters and learning that the components were stolen, the officer seized some of the components and obtained warrants for others. The Court analyzed the officer's actions in terms of search and seizure law.

> [T]he mere recording of the serial numbers did not constitute a seizure. . . . [I]t did not "meaningfully interfere" with respondent's possessory interest in either the serial numbers or the equipment, and therefore did not amount to a seizure. . . . Officer Nelson's moving of the equipment, however, did constitute a "search" separate and apart from the search for the shooter, victims, and weapons that was the lawful objective of his entry into the apartment. Merely inspecting those parts of the turntable that came into view during the latter search would not have constituted an independent search because it would have produced no additional invasion of respondent's privacy interest. . . . But taking action, unrelated to the objectives of the authorized intrusion, which exposed to view concealed portions of the apartment or its contents, did produce a new invasion of respondent's privacy unjustified by the exigent circumstance that validated the entry. *Arizona v. Hicks*, 480 U.S. 321, 324–25, 107 S.Ct. 1149, 1152, 94 L.Ed.2d 347, 353–54 (1987).

The lesson of the *Hicks* case is that an officer's examination of an item of property will be a *search* rather than a *plain view observation* if

- the officer produces a new invasion of the person's property by taking action that exposes to view concealed portions of the premises or its contents; and
- the officer's action is unrelated to, and unjustified by, the objectives of his or her authorized intrusion.

In *United States v. Silva*, 714 F.Supp. 693 (S.D.N.Y. 1989), an officer executing a search warrant for fruits and instrumentalities of the crime of bank robbery discovered a notebook in plain view. The government argued that once the notebook was in plain view, the officer was justified in opening and reading it to ascertain its value as evidence. The court rejected that contention, specifically referring to the *Hicks* case.

> This court can hardly imagine a less intrusive action than moving a stereo turntable to view its serial number. By comparison, the opening of a notebook or document is, if anything, a more significant intrusion since it is bound to reveal something of much greater personal value than the bottom of a turntable. Accordingly, the court is constrained to conclude that, after *Hicks*, even the minor investigation of a notebook beyond inspecting what is visible must constitute a search. 714 F.Supp. at 696.

The court further elaborated in a footnote:

> The court does not hold that an officer cannot read a document or book if it is plainly visible without opening or disturbing it in any way. The holding is limited to finding that if the incriminating nature of the document cannot be readily ascertained without moving or disturbing it, an officer may not, absent probable cause move or further search the book or document. 714 F.Supp. at 696 n.6.

Ordinarily, the opening and examination of a closed container by a government agent will be considered a search because of the serious invasion of privacy these actions usually entail. Nevertheless, courts have held these actions not to be searches when

- the contents of the container can be inferred from its outward appearance, distinctive configuration, transparency, or other characteristics (*United States v. Haley*, 669 F.2d 201 [4th Cir. 1982]); or
- the container has already been opened and its contents examined by a private party.

In *United States v. Eschweiler*, 745 F.2d 435 (7th Cir. 1984), the court held that the removal of a key from an envelope that said "safe-deposit box key" and had the name of the bank on it was not an additional search of the envelope, which was found in plain view.

> [A] container that proclaims its contents on the outside is not a private place. This point would be obvious if the envelope had been transparent; then its contents would have been literally in plain view. The inscription and other characteristics that unequivocally revealed its contents made it transparent in the contemplation of the law. 745 F.2d at 440.

In *United States v. Jacobsen*, 466 U.S. 109, 104 S.Ct. 1652, 80 L.Ed.2d 85 (1984), the U.S. Supreme Court allowed a warrantless examination of a partially closed container by government agents after the container had been opened and its contents examined by a private party. Employees of a freight carrier examined a damaged cardboard box wrapped in brown paper and found a white powdery substance in the innermost of four plastic bags that had been concealed in a tube inside the package. The employees notified the Drug Enforcement Administration (DEA), replaced the plastic bags in the tube, and placed the tube back in the box. A DEA agent arrived and removed the tube from the box and the plastic bags from the tube. When he saw the white powder, he opened the bags and removed a small amount of the white powder. He then subjected the powder to a field chemical test. The test indicated that the powder was cocaine.

The U.S. Supreme Court found that the initial invasion of the package by the freight carrier employees did not violate the Fourth Amendment, because it was a private rather than a governmental action. The Court then analyzed the additional invasions of privacy by the DEA agent in terms of the degree to which they exceeded the scope of the private search. The Court found that even if the white powder was not itself in plain view because it was enclosed in so many containers and covered with papers, the DEA agent could be virtually certain that nothing else of significance was in the package and that a manual inspection of the tube and its contents would not tell him anything more than the freight carrier employees had already told him. The agent's reexamination of the contents of the package merely avoided the risk of a flaw in the employees' recollection, rather than further infringing on someone's privacy. Had the DEA agent's conduct significantly exceeded that of the freight carrier's employees, then he would have conducted a new and different search that would have been subject to Fourth Amendment protections. The Court said:

> Respondents could have no privacy interest in the contents of the package, since it remained unsealed and since the Federal Express employees had just examined the package and had, of their own accord, invited the federal agent to their offices for the express purpose of viewing its contents. The agent's viewing of what a private party had freely made available for his inspection did not violate the Fourth Amendment. . . . Similarly, the removal of the plastic bags from the tube and the agent's visual inspection of their contents enabled the agent to learn nothing that had not previously been learned during the private search. It infringed no legitimate expectation of privacy and hence was not a "search" within the meaning of the Fourth Amendment. 466 U.S. at 119–20, 104 S.Ct. at 1659–60, 80 L.Ed.2d at 98.

The Court further held that the agent's assertion of dominion and control over the package and its contents was a seizure but that the seizure was reasonable, since it was apparent that the tube and plastic bags contained contraband and little else. The Court said that

> it is well-settled law that it is constitutionally reasonable for law enforcement officials to seize "effects" that cannot support a justifiable expectation of privacy without a warrant, based on probable cause to believe they contain contraband. 466 U.S. at 121–22, 104 S.Ct. at 1661, 80 L.Ed.2d at 99.

The Supreme Court then addressed the question of whether the additional intrusion occasioned by the field test, which had not been conducted by the freight carrier employees and therefore exceeded the scope of the private search, was an unlawful search or seizure within the meaning of the Fourth Amendment. The Court held that a chemical test that merely discloses whether or not a particular substance is cocaine, and no other arguably "private" fact, compromises no legitimate privacy interest. Furthermore, even though the test destroyed a quantity of the powder and thereby permanently deprived its owner of a protected possessory interest, the infringement was constitutionally reasonable. The Court reasoned that the law enforcement interests justifying the procedure were substantial and, because only a trace amount of material was involved, the seizure could have, at most, only a minimal effect on any protected property interest.

To summarize, a law enforcement officer may examine, without a warrant, a container the contents of which are not open to view, if any privacy interest in the contents of the container has already been compromised by a private party and information about the contents has been made available to the officer by the private party. In addition, it is constitutionally permissible for the officer to seize the contents of the container, if the officer has probable cause to believe the contents are contraband, and to conduct a chemical field test so long as only a trace amount of the substance is destroyed by the test.

Key Points

5. Before a law enforcement officer may seize an item of property that is observed open to view, the officer must have probable cause to believe that the property comes within one of the categories of property subject to seizure under state or federal law. An officer is allowed a reasonable time within which to make the probable cause determination, but the officer may not conduct a further search of the object to make the probable cause determination.

6. Law enforcement officers may use mechanical or electrical devices, such as binoculars and flashlights, to assist in observing items of evidence, so long as they do not intrude on someone's reasonable expectation of privacy.

7. An officer's examination of an item of property will be a search rather than a plain view observation if the officer produces a new invasion of the property by taking action that exposes to view concealed portions of the premises or its contents and the officer's action is unrelated to and unjustified by the objectives of his or her authorized intrusion.

8. A law enforcement officer may open and examine the contents of a closed container found in open view, if the contents of the container can be inferred from its outward appearance, distinctive configuration, transparency, or other characteristics.

9. A law enforcement officer may open and examine, without a warrant, a container the contents of which are not open to view, if any privacy interest in the contents of the container has already been compromised by a private party and information about the contents has been made available to the officer by the private party.

The Discovery of the Item of Evidence by the Officer Need Not be Inadvertent

In *Horton v. California*, 496 U.S. 128, 110 S.Ct. 2301, 110 L.Ed.2d 112 (1990), a police officer investigating an armed robbery determined that there was probable cause to search the defendant's home for the proceeds of, and weapons used in, the robbery. His affidavit for a search warrant referred to police reports that described both the weapons and the proceeds, but the warrant issued by the magistrate only authorized a search for the proceeds. In executing the warrant, the officer did not find the stolen property but did find the weapons in plain view and seized them. The officer testified that, while he was searching for the named stolen property, he was also interested in finding other evidence connecting the defendant to the robbery. Thus, the seized evidence was not discovered "inadvertently."

In holding that inadvertence was not a necessary condition of a legitimate plain view seizure, the Court discussed the 1971 case of *Coolidge v. New Hampshire*, 403 U.S. 443, 91 S.Ct. 2022, 29 L.Ed.2d 564. Justice Stewart's opinion in *Coolidge* stated that "the discovery of evidence in plain view must be inadvertent." 403 U.S. at 469, 91 S.Ct. at 2040, 29 L.Ed.2d at 585. Nevertheless, Justice Stewart's analysis of the plain view doctrine did not command a majority, and a plurality of the Court has since made clear that the discussion is not a binding precedent. Justice Stewart concluded that the inadvertence requirement was necessary to avoid a violation of the express constitutional requirement that a valid warrant must particularly describe the things to be seized. The Court in *Horton* found two flaws in this reasoning.

First, evenhanded law enforcement is best achieved by the application of objective standards of conduct, rather than standards that depend upon the subjective state of mind of the officer. The fact that an officer is interested in an item of evidence and fully expects to find it in the course of a search should not invalidate its seizure if the search is confined in area and duration by the terms of a warrant or a valid exception to the warrant requirement. If the officer has knowledge approaching certainty that the item will be found, we see no reason why he or she would deliberately omit a particular description of the item to be seized from the application for a search warrant. Specification of the additional item could only permit the officer to expand the scope of the search. On the other hand, if he or she has a valid warrant to search for one item and merely a suspicion concerning the second, whether or not it amounts to probable cause, we fail to see why that suspicion should immunize the second item from seizure if it is found during a lawful search for the first. . . .

Second, the suggestion that the inadvertence requirement is necessary to prevent the police from conducting general searches, or from converting specific warrants into general warrants, is not persuasive because that interest is already served by the requirements that no warrant issue unless it "particularly describ[es] the place to be searched and the persons or things to be seized," . . . and that a warrantless search be circumscribed by the exigencies which justify its initiation. . . . Scrupulous adherence to these requirements serves the interests in limiting the area and duration of the search that the inadvertence requirement inadequately protects. Once those commands have been satisfied and the officer has a lawful right of access, however, no additional Fourth Amendment interest is furthered by requiring that the discovery of evidence be inadvertent. If the scope of the search exceeds that permitted by the terms of a validly issued warrant or the character of the relevant exception from the warrant requirement, the subsequent seizure is unconstitutional without more. 496 U.S. at 138–40, 110 S.Ct. at 2308–09, 110 L.Ed.2d at 124–25.

In this case, the scope of the search was not enlarged in the slightest by the omission of any reference to the weapons in the warrant. In fact, if the items named in the warrant had been found or surrendered at the outset, no search for weapons could have taken place.

The prohibition against general searches and general warrants serves primarily as a protection against unjustified intrusions on privacy. But reliance on privacy concerns is misplaced when the inquiry concerns the scope of an exception that merely authorizes an officer with a lawful right of access to an item to seize it without a warrant.

Note that the great majority of state and federal courts adopted the inadvertence requirement in response to *Coolidge v. New Hampshire*. Although federal courts are bound by the *Horton* decision abandoning the inadvertence requirement, some state courts may retain the inadvertence requirement based on interpretations of their state constitutions. The reader must determine the state of the law in his or her state by consulting pertinent court decisions.

Key Points

10. Even though a law enforcement officer is interested in an item of evidence and fully expects to find it in the course of a search, a plain view seizure of the item is not invalidated if the search is confined in its scope by the terms of a warrant or a valid exception to the warrant requirement.

"Plain Touch" or "Plain Feel"

In *Minnesota v. Dickerson,* 508 U.S. 366, 113 S.Ct. 2130, 124 L.Ed.2d 334 (1993), the U.S. Supreme Court applied the principles of the plain view doctrine to a situation in which a law enforcement officer discovered contraband through the sense of touch during an otherwise lawful search. In the *Dickerson* case, officers on patrol observed the defendant leaving a building known for cocaine traffic. When the defendant attempted to evade the officers, they stopped him and ordered him to submit to a patdown search. The search revealed no weapons, but the officer conducting the search felt a small lump in the defendant's jacket. The officer examined the lump with his fingers, it slid, and the officer believed it to be a lump of crack cocaine in cellophane. The officer then reached into the pocket and retrieved a small plastic bag of crack cocaine.

The Court said:

> We think that this [plain view] doctrine has an obvious application by analogy to cases in which an officer discovers contraband through the sense of touch during an otherwise lawful search. The rationale of the plain view doctrine is that if contraband is left in open view and is observed by a police officer from a lawful vantage point, there has been no invasion of a legitimate expectation of privacy and thus no "search" within the meaning of the Fourth Amendment—or at least no search independent of the initial intrusion that gave the officers their vantage point. . . . The warrantless seizure of contraband that presents itself in this manner is deemed justified by the realization that resort to a neutral magistrate under such circumstances would often be impracticable and would do little to promote the objectives of the Fourth Amendment. . . . The same can be said of tactile discoveries of contraband. If a police officer lawfully pats down a suspect's outer clothing and feels an object whose contour or mass makes its identity immediately apparent, there has been no invasion of the suspect's privacy beyond that already authorized by the officer's search for weapons; if the object is contraband, its warrantless seizure would be justified by the same practical considerations that inhere in the plain view context. 508 U.S. at 375–76, 113 S.Ct. at 2137, 124 L.Ed.2d at 345–46.

In this case, however, the Court held the seizure of the package of cocaine illegal, because the contraband contents of the defendant's pocket were not immediately apparent to the officer. Only after the officer squeezed, slid, and otherwise manipulated the pocket's contents did he determine that it was cocaine. The Court found that the facts of this case were very similar to those of *Arizona v. Hicks* (discussed on pages 387–389, in which the Court invalidated the warrantless seizure of stolen stereo equipment found by police while executing a valid search warrant for other evidence.

> Although the officer was lawfully in a position to feel the lump in respondent's pocket, because *Terry* entitled him to place his hands upon respondent's jacket, the court below determined that the incriminating character of the object was not immediately apparent to him. Rather, the officer determined that the item was contraband only after conducting a further search, one not authorized by *Terry* or by any other exception to the warrant requirement. Because this further search of respondent's pocket was constitutionally invalid, the seizure of the cocaine that followed is likewise unconstitutional. 508 U.S. at 379, 113 S.Ct. at 2139, 124 L.Ed.2d at 348.

Therefore, to paraphrase the plain view doctrine, if police are lawfully in a position from which they feel an object, if its incriminating character is immediately apparent,

www.icje.org/id64.htm
Article, "Plain Feel, A Second Look: When Is It Used and What Should Officers Know before Using this Technique?"
www.juris.duq.edu/spring2000/plain.htm
Article, "Plain Feel, Probable Cause, and the Fourth Amendment" by Jarrod A. Caruso

and if the officers have a lawful right of access to the object, they may seize it without a warrant. If, however, the police lack probable cause to believe that the object felt is subject to seizure without conducting some further search of the object, its seizure is not justified.

Some courts have further expanded the analogy to the plain view doctrine to the other senses of smell, taste, and hearing. For example, *United States v. Haley*, 669 F.2d 201 (4th Cir. 1982), held that "[a]nother characteristic [of a container] which brings the contents into plain view is the odor given off by those contents." 669 F.2d at 203. The U.S. Supreme Court has not dealt with the senses of smell, taste, or hearing in the context of the plain view doctrine, and the question remains open whether these senses would be treated similarly to the sense of touch.

www.mobar.net/journal/1997/
julaug/plain.htm
Article, "The Plain Feel Doctrine
in Missouri: *State of Missouri v.
Shaun Rushing*" by Cynthia A.
Ruchefsky
www.icje.org/id78.htm
Article, "Plain Feel and Tic Tac
Boxes: Tic Tac or a Crook on
Crack" by Wynn Dee Allen

Key Points

11. If a law enforcement officer is lawfully in a position from which he or she feels an object, if the object's incriminating character is immediately apparent, and if the officer has a lawful right of access to the object, the officer may seize it without a warrant.

Summary

Under the plain view doctrine, an observation of items lying open to view by a law enforcement officer who has a right to be in a position to have that view is not a search, and the officer may seize the evidence without a warrant. The doctrine has four requirements, all of which must be satisfied before seizure of an item of evidence can be legally justified.

First, the officer, as a result of a prior valid intrusion, must be in a position in which he or she has a legal right to be. Some examples of situations in which an officer's intrusion is justified are effecting an arrest or search incident to an arrest, conducting a stop and frisk, executing a search warrant, making controlled deliveries, pursuing a fleeing suspect, and responding to an emergency.

Second, the officer must not unreasonably intrude on any person's reasonable expectation of privacy. To satisfy this requirement, the officer must use common sense to keep the investigation of crime within reasonable bounds.

Third, the incriminating character of the object to be seized must be immediately apparent to the officer. This simply means that before an object may be seized, the officer must have *probable cause* that the object is subject to seizure without conducting some further search of the object. An officer may use his or her experience and background to assist in determining whether a particular item is seizable. The officer may use mechanical or electrical aids, such as a flashlight or binoculars, to assist in observing an item, so long as this does not unrea-

sonably intrude on someone's reasonable expectation of privacy. The officer may also examine items more closely, unless

- the officer produces a new invasion of the person's property by taking action that exposes to view concealed portions of the premises or its contents; and
- the officer's action is unrelated to, and unjustified by, the objectives of his or her authorized intrusion.

Furthermore, the opening of a container to determine whether incriminating evidence is inside is prohibited unless

- the contents of the container can be inferred from its outward appearance, distinctive configuration, transparency, or other characteristics; or
- any privacy interest in the container's contents has already been compromised by a private party and information about the contents has been made available to the officer by the private party.

Fourth, the discovery of the item of evidence by the officer need not be inadvertent. Nevertheless, even though the officer is interested in finding a particular item of evidence, the officer may not expand the scope of the search beyond the original justification for the search, whether that justification is a search warrant for other items of evidence, an exception to the search warrant requirement, or some other justification.

Analogizing to the plain view doctrine, the U.S. Supreme Court has allowed the seizure of an object discovered through "plain touch" rather than "plain view." Therefore, if police are lawfully in a position from which they feel an object, if its incriminating character is *immediately apparent,* and if the officers have a lawful right of access to the object, they may seize it without a warrant. If, however, the police lack probable cause to believe that the object felt is subject to seizure without conducting some further search of the object, its seizure is not justified.

Key Holdings from Major Cases

Harris v. United States (1968). "It has been settled that objects falling in the plain view of an officer who has a right to be in a position to have that view may be introduced in evidence. . . ." 390 U.S. 234, 236, 88 S.Ct. 992, 993, 19 L.Ed.2d 1067, 1069.

Coolidge v. New Hampshire (1971). "What the 'plain view' cases have in common is that the police officer in each of them had a prior justification for an intrusion in the course of which he came . . . across a piece of evidence incriminating the accused. The doctrine serves to supplement the prior justification—whether it be a warrant for another object, hot pursuit, search incident to lawful arrest, or some other legitimate reason for being present unconnected with a search directed against the accused—and permits the warrantless seizure. Of course, the extension of the original justification is legitimate only where it is immediately apparent to the police that they have evidence before them." 403 U.S. 443, 466, 91 S.Ct. 2022, 2038, 29 L.Ed.2d 564, 583.

Michigan v. Long (1983). "If while conducting a legitimate *Terry* search of the interior of the automobile, the officer should . . . discover contraband other than weapons, he clearly cannot be required to ignore the contraband, and the Fourth Amendment does not require its suppression in such circumstances." 463 U.S. 1032, 1050, 103 S.Ct. 3469, 3481, 77 L.Ed.2d 1201, 1220.

Illinois v. Andreas (1983). "The plain view doctrine is grounded on the proposition that once police are lawfully in a position to observe an item firsthand, its owner's privacy interest in that item is lost; the owner may retain the incidents of title and possession but not privacy. . . . [O]nce a container has been found to a certainty to contain illicit drugs, the contraband becomes like objects physically within the plain view of the police, and the claim to privacy is lost. Consequently, the subsequent reopening of the container is not a 'search' within the intendment of the Fourth Amendment." 463 U.S. 765, 771–72, 103 S.Ct. 3319, 3324, 77 L.Ed.2d 1003, 1010.

New York v. Class (1986). "Because of the important role played by the VIN [vehicle identification number] in the pervasive governmental regulation of the automobile and the efforts by the Federal Government to ensure that the VIN is placed in plain view . . . there was no reasonable expectation of privacy in the VIN. . . . [W]here the object at issue is an identification number behind the transparent windshield of an automobile driven upon the public roads, we believe that the placement of the obscuring papers was insufficient to create a privacy interest in the VIN. The mere viewing of the formerly obscured VIN was not, therefore, a violation of the Fourth Amendment. 475 U.S. 106, 114, 106 S.Ct. 960, 966, 89 L.Ed.2d 81, 90–91.

"Police officers are not authorized 'to enter a vehicle to obtain a dashboard-mounted VIN when the VIN is visible from outside the automobile. If the VIN is in the plain view of someone outside the vehicle, there is no justification for governmental intrusion into the passenger compartment to see it.'" 475 U.S. at 119, 106 S.Ct. at 968–69, 89 L.Ed.2d at 94.

Texas v. Brown (1983). "[T]he use of artificial means to illuminate a darkened area simply does not constitute a search, and thus triggers no Fourth Amendment protection." 460 U.S. 730, 740, 103 S.Ct. 1535, 1542, 75 L.Ed.2d 502, 512.

United States v. Jacobsen (1984). "[I]t is well-settled law that it is constitutionally reasonable for law enforcement officials to seize 'effects' that cannot support a justifiable expectation of privacy without a warrant, based on probable cause to believe they contain contraband." 466 U.S. 109, 121–22, 104 S.Ct. 1652, 1661, 80 L.Ed.2d 85, 99.

Horton v. California (1990). "[E]ven though inadvertence is a characteristic of most legitimate 'plain view' searches, it is not a necessary condition." 496 U.S. 128, 130, 110 S.Ct. 2301, 2304, 110 L.Ed.2d 112, 118–19.

"The fact that an officer is interested in an item of evidence and fully expects to find it in the course of a search should not invalidate its seizure if the search is confined in area and duration by the terms of a warrant or a valid exception to the warrant requirement." 496 U.S. at 138, 110 S.Ct. at 2308, 110 L.Ed.2d at 124.

Minnesota v. Dickerson (1993). "If a police officer lawfully pats down a suspect's outer clothing and feels an object whose contour or mass makes its identity immediately apparent, there has been no invasion of the suspect's privacy beyond that already authorized by the officer's search for weapons; if the object is contraband, its warrantless seizure would be justified by the same practical considerations that inhere in the plain view context." 508 U.S. 366, 375–76, 113 S.Ct. 2130, 2137, 124 L.Ed.2d 334, 346.

Review and Discussion Questions

1. The dissent in the *Horton* case said that "there are a number of instances in which a law enforcement officer might deliberately choose to omit certain items from a warrant application even though he has probable cause to seize them, knows they are on the premises, and intends to seize them when they are discovered in plain view." 496 U.S. at 146, 110 S.Ct. at 2313, 110 L.Ed.2d at 129. Give examples with reasons.

2. If law enforcement officers are in a place in which they have a right to be and they observe bottles that appear to contain illegal drugs, may they open the bottles and examine the contents further? May law enforcement officers use their sense of smell, taste, or touch to determine whether items are subject to seizure when they are not sure?

3. Assume that law enforcement officers have a warrant to arrest the defendant for having stolen guns four months ago. The officers suspect that the guns are at the defendant's home, but that suspicion is based on stale information insufficient to obtain a search warrant. May the officers seize guns found in plain view when they arrest the defendant? Would it make any difference if the officers could have easily found out whether the guns were still at the defendant's home by contacting a reliable informant?

4. May law enforcement officers take an item off the shelf in an antique store and examine it to determine whether it is stolen? May officers do the same thing in a private home into which they have been invited by a person who does not know they are law enforcement officers?

5. Discuss the meaning of the following statement of the U.S. Supreme Court: "'Plain view' is perhaps better understood . . . not as an independent 'exception' to the warrant clause, but simply as an extension of whatever the prior justification for an officer's 'access to an object' may be." *Texas v. Brown*, 460 U.S. 730, 738–39, 103 S.Ct. 1535, 1540–41, 75 L.Ed.2d 502, 511 (1983).

6. What problems are presented by an officer executing a search warrant for specified obscene materials, who seizes some magazines that are in plain view and were not specified in the warrant?

7. What are the limits on protective searches? May officers routinely look throughout a house for other suspects whenever they make an arrest or search? May officers go into other buildings on the premises? May officers go into neighboring homes? If an arrest is made in the hallway of a motel, may officers conduct a protective search of all or any of the rooms of the motel?

8. Does the plain view doctrine authorize a warrantless entry into a dwelling to seize contraband visible from outside the dwelling? Why? What if an officer observes contraband from the hallway of a motel through the open door to one of the rooms? What if an officer observes contraband lying on the desk in someone's office?

9. Would it be proper for officers executing a search warrant for stolen property to bring along victims of the theft to aid the officers in seizing other stolen items not named in the warrant that might be in plain view? Why?

10. If law enforcement officers are legitimately on premises, may they record the serial numbers of any objects that they suspect are stolen property? May they take photographs of these objects?

Real-Life Fact Situations

1 Defendant lived in a house in north Portland. The front of the house faced North Michigan Avenue. Behind the house, and detached from it, was a garage that faced the opposite direction, fronting on a public alley that ran parallel to North Michigan Avenue. A chain-link fence, with a gate, separated the backyard from the alley. The configuration of defendant's property is generally illustrated by the following map:

The rear of defendant's property, including the alley-way, fence, gate, path, and garage, is shown in pictures, submitted as defense exhibits, which are reproduced in *Appendix* "A" to this opinion.

[NOTE: The map and pictures can be seen as part of the Internet reference below.]

In the late spring of 1997, an unknown informant told Portland Police Officer Peter McConnell that people were working on cars in defendant's garage "until all hours of the night" and that "they" were on methamphetamine. Several weeks later, at about 11:00 P.M. on the night of July 3, 1997, as McConnell and his partner drove down the alley behind defendant's house, they saw light coming out of the open side door of the garage. They stopped and got out of their car.

The officers walked through the gate in the chain-link fence and proceeded up the path adjacent to the side of the garage. As the officers passed the open side door of the garage, McConnell looked in and saw defendant in the corner of the garage "kneeling down and * * * lighting something beneath a glass flask that * * * had a piece of brown surgical tubing coming out of it." There was smoke or steam coming from around the glass. From what he saw, McConnell believed that defendant was operating a methamphetamine lab.

McConnell knocked on the open door and, when defendant turned around, defendant looked "worried." McConnell asked if he could come in, and defendant refused. Defendant then came outside to speak to McConnell, closing the door behind him. In response to McConnell's questions, defendant said that he had been heating up varnish for antlers. When McConnell suggested that defendant might be operating a methamphetamine lab and asked if he could confirm that the substance in the flask was varnish, defendant refused.

Defendant then said that he needed to use the bathroom, went into the house, and did not return. McConnell, concerned that the garage might explode, called in other officers. Five to 10 minutes after defendant entered the house, McConnell went to the back door of the house and knocked. Defendant's wife answered and told the officers that defendant was not at home. She agreed that the officers could search the house for defendant, but the ensuing search merely confirmed that defendant was gone.

Either during or after the search of the house, McConnell asked defendant's wife for consent to search the garage. She refused, saying that she did not have access to the garage and was afraid that defendant would learn that she had consented. McConnell then told defendant's wife that he believed that there was a methamphetamine laboratory in the garage; that such operations were highly dangerous; and that, if she did not consent, he could obtain a search warrant. Defendant's wife then consented to a search of the garage, which yielded evidence of methamphetamine production. Should the defendant's motion to suppress that evidence be granted? *State v. Somfleth*, 8 P.3d 221 (Or.App. 2000).

Read the court opinion at:
www.publications.ojd.state.or.us/A100841.htm

2 On February 12, 1999, Detective James Davis of the Emporia Police Department was advised that Dorothea Smith, a suspect in a forgery case he was investigating, was in a taxi en route to the bus station. Detective Davis arrived at the bus station and Officer Stormont also arrived at the same time in another vehicle. Upon arrival, the officers noticed a parked taxi occupied by two backseat passengers, Smith and the appellant.

Detective Davis approached the taxi, removed Smith, and arrested her. He then patted her down for weapons. He directed Officer Stormont to remove the appellant from the taxi and pat him down.

The officers testified that they had no reason to believe Smith was armed and dangerous or that any evidence of the forgery would be found in the taxi or on Smith's person. Further, the appellant was not a suspect in the forgery or any other investigation. The appellant complied peaceably and without resistance to Officer Stormont's direction that he get out of the taxi and submit to a pat-down search. Nothing was found on appellant's person as a result of the search. When the appellant was patted down, Smith was already under arrest and in handcuffs on the other side of the car.

After patting down the appellant, Officer Stormont reached into the taxi to retrieve the appellant's jacket. He intended to return the jacket to the appellant and allow him to go on his way. Before giving the jacket to the appellant, however, Officer Stormont felt it for weapons. In doing so, he felt something hard which was about the size of an ink pen. He testified at both the suppression hearing and at trial that he had no idea what the object was. He further testified that it was not immediately apparent to him that the object was either a weapon or contraband.

The object turned out to be three small metal pipes which later were determined to contain cocaine residue. The appellant was placed under arrest for possession of drug paraphernalia. He later admitted that the pipes belonged to him and that he had smoked them.

The appellant filed a motion to suppress, claiming the officer was not justified in searching him or his jacket. The trial court denied the motion to suppress. Was the trial court correct? *State v. Davis*, 11 P.3d 1177 (Kan.App. 2000).

Read the court opinion at:
www.kscourts.org/kscases/ctapp/2000/20001020/83403.htm

3 In mid-June 1995, Deputies Zwemke and Hartley learned that there was an outstanding arrest warrant for defendant for burglary. They received information from a confidential informant that defendant was staying in an apartment rented by Corinna Pasalles. On June 29, the deputies approached the apartment and noticed that a car known to be used by defendant was parked nearby. After calling for back up, the deputies entered the apartment and found a male and female on the couch in the front living room. The deputies then proceeded to a back bedroom where they found defendant hidden in a hole cut into the floor, covered by carpet. With guns drawn, they ordered defendant out of the hole and to put his hands in the air. As defendant crawled out of the hole, he reached his right hand between the mattress and box spring of a bed about two feet away. The deputies again told defendant to raise his hands. After a few moments, defendant complied. Deputy Zwemke then took defendant into custody and handcuffed him. In a search of defendant's person, Deputy Zwemke found a syringe in defendant's left front pocket. Deputy Zwemke then removed defendant to the apartment's living room. At about the same time, Deputy Hartley searched between the mattresses where defendant had put his hand and found a fully loaded .22 caliber pistol. After another officer arrived to watch defendant, Hartley and Zwemke went back into the bedroom and conducted a further search to ensure there were no additional unsecured weapons in that room. Ms. Pasalles was in the bedroom at the time. During this search, Deputy Zwemke noticed a purple tin on a shelf in the closet of the bedroom. Deputy Zwemke inspected the tin's contents and found five small plastic baggies, two containing cocaine residue and two containing methamphetamine residue. The tin also contained a scale-like object, two razor blades, and copies of defendant's birth certificate, social security card, and Utah identification card.

Defendant was charged with possession of a dangerous weapon by a convicted person, possession of methamphetamine, possession of cocaine, and possession of drug paraphernalia. At the preliminary hearing, Deputies Hartley and Zwemke explained the circumstances under which they had located defendant and found the gun between the mattresses. Deputy Zwemke explained that after the gun was found, he returned to the bedroom "to assist to locate any other weapons that might be concealed within the apartment in the bedroom area." While searching, he "found a small purple metal tin container in the closet which had assorted paraphernalia items and also five small plastic baggies with a white powdery salmon colored substance," and a copy of defendant's birth certificate. The tin was about three inches by four inches by two inches, and had no lid. "I was just making sure there wasn't any guns or anything." Defendant was handcuffed and in the front room at the time. Ms. Pasalles was standing behind Deputy Zwemke when he found the tin. Defendant filed a motion to suppress both the gun and the evidence found in the purple tin. Should the defendant's motion be granted? *State v. Gallegos*, 967 P.2d 973 (Utah App. 2000).

Read the court opinion at:
courtlink.utcourts.gov/opinions/appopin/gallegos1.htm

4 On August 15, 1998, Richmond police officers, Douglas P. Vilkowski and Jason A. Yarema, were on patrol and stopped a car with no front license plate. The car was driven by Jesse Hamlin, appellant's cousin. Calvin Hamlin, the appellant, occupied the front passenger seat, and Mathew Pitchford was a passenger in the rear seat.

Yarema saw appellant reaching down and forward in front of his seat, and believing that appellant might have a weapon, Yarema approached the passenger side of the vehicle to ask appellant to get out of the car. When appellant complied, Yarema briefly placed handcuffs on appellant and patted him down for weapons. He found none. Officer Yarema then looked into the vehicle and found a brown paper bag containing an open bottle of beer on the floorboard in front of the passenger seat. He then looked under the passenger seat for weapons and found none. Officer Yarema next asked appellant to get back

in the car, which appellant did. Yarema asked appellant and Pitchford for identification in order to investigate a possible open container violation, although he did not share his purpose with them. During this time, Vilkowski was charging Jesse Hamlin with driving on a suspended license.

After receiving identification from appellant and Pitchford, Officer Yarema walked to the rear of the stopped vehicle where he could keep the occupants in view while he communicated their identifying information to the dispatcher. Within fifteen to twenty seconds, Yarema noticed appellant again reaching down and forward in the vehicle. Yarema then walked back to the passenger side of the vehicle and shined his flashlight inside. He saw appellant holding a clear plastic bag with a white powder substance, in the process of placing it under the seat. Yarema told appellant to put his hands up and get out of the car. When appellant failed to comply, Yarema opened the door and physically removed appellant. After a brief struggle, Yarema and Officer Vilkowski placed him under arrest. Found in appellant's hand was a red pouch containing a digital scale, razor blades, tinfoil, cut squares of paper and mannitol (a cutting agent for narcotics). The white powder later tested positive for cocaine. Should the appellant's motion to suppress the evidence seized be granted? *Hamlin v. Commonwealth*, 534 S.E.2d 363 (Va.App. 2000).

Read the court opinion at:
www.lawyersweekly.com/vacoa/1412992.htm

5 Beginning in approximately 1992, George Blair and Connie Blair (aka Launa Miakowski) operated several prostitution houses in Detroit, Michigan. As a part of their operation, the Blairs sold drugs—typically crack cocaine or heroin—to the prostitutes who worked in the houses, most of whom had serious drug addictions. In addition to requiring the prostitutes to buy their drugs from them, the Blairs sold drugs to the prostitutes' clients. The Blairs also sold drug paraphernalia such as syringes and pipes at their houses. During a routine "shift" at a house, the Blairs sold approximately $1,000 worth of drugs.

In April 1997, IRS Special Agent Thomas Kraft, having information that the Blairs were engaged in narcotics trafficking, provided an affidavit in order to obtain a search warrant for the Blairs' residence and one of the prostitution houses. A federal magistrate judge issued the warrant, which authorized law enforcement agents to seize records "relating to the transportation, importation, ordering, sale, and distribution of controlled substances." Detroit police officers assisted in the execution of the warrant to search the Blairs' residence. In that capacity, a Detroit police officer who was also a DEA Task Force Agent, Sergeant James Raby, aided in the search. Raby observed on top of a dresser an open pill vial that contained a plastic bag in which there was "a white substance [that appeared] to be narcotics." Raby conducted a field test on the substance which revealed the presence of cocaine.

At this point, Raby left the Blairs' residence to obtain a state search warrant authorizing agents to seize "[a]ll suspected controlled substances, all items used in the [*sic*] connection with the sales, manufacture, use, storage, distribution, transportation, delivery or concealment of controlled substances." Raby then returned to the Blairs' residence with the state warrant. Law enforcement agents ultimately seized 350 grams of crack cocaine, 50 grams of heroin, drug paraphernalia, four loaded firearms and approximately $13,000 in cash. Should the defendant's motion to suppress the evidence seized during the search of their residence be granted? *United States v. Blair*, 214 F.3d 690 (6th Cir. 2000).

Read the court opinion at:
www.michbar.org/opinions/us_appeals/2000/052600/7191.html

6 Officer Robert Greenleaf and a fellow officer from the Bay City Police Department were dispatched to a residence in Bay City to investigate a possible trespass. When they arrived at the location, the officers observed a parked vehicle occupied by two individuals. Officer Greenleaf approached the vehicle in which Billy Holder and defendant were located and, suspecting that Holder, the driver of the vehicle, was intoxicated, asked him to turn off the ignition and step out of the vehicle. After determining that Holder was too intoxicated to drive, Officer Greenleaf advised Holder that he could either have his vehicle towed to an impound lot or back to his residence at his own expense. Holder elected to have the vehicle towed back to his residence in Mt. Pleasant. Officer Greenleaf asked Holder to demonstrate that he had sufficient funds to pay the cost of towing the vehicle. Holder retrieved a wad of money out of his pants pocket estimated at approximately $500 in mostly $10 and $20 bills, along with a small plastic bag that appeared to Officer Greenleaf to contain marijuana. Officer Greenleaf arrested Holder, searched him for weapons, and placed him in the patrol car. As he entered the patrol car, Holder yelled to defendant, "[d]on't tell them a f...... thing."

After Holder was secured in the police vehicle, Officer Greenleaf asked defendant to get out of the vehicle. Officer Greenleaf did not initially fear for his safety, but after discovering marijuana on Holder, he concluded, on the basis of his training and experience, that defendant could be armed and dangerous. Thus, in order to ensure his safety, and that of his partner, Officer Greenleaf conducted a patdown search of defendant for weapons and contraband. Officer Greenleaf also indicated that defendant was going to be transported to the police department for questioning and it was departmental policy that anyone being transported in a police vehicle was to be patted down for weapons or possible illegal substances.

During the patdown, Officer Greenleaf felt what he believed to be a two- by three-inch card of blotter acid in defendant's front pants pocket and he removed the item. Instead of a card of blotter acid, however, Officer Greenleaf found three Polaroid pictures and placed them facedown on top of the vehicle without inspecting them. No other items were found on defendant. After completing the patdown, Officer Greenleaf retrieved the pictures from the roof of the vehicle and examined them. The three photographs depicted (1) Holder carrying two one-pound bags of marijuana with additional one-pound bags of marijuana on a coffee table in front of him, (2) a number of one-pound bags of marijuana, and (3) Holder sitting in a chair next to a suitcase that contained numerous one-pound bags of marijuana. The photographs were seized and defendant was transported to the police station for questioning.

Detective Joseph Lanava, who arrived at the scene to assist in the investigation, contacted Detective Jesse Flores in Mt. Pleasant, where defendant resided, and provided him with three addresses in Mt. Pleasant to check in connection with a traffic stop where a controlled substance was discovered. Specifically, Detective Lanava asked Detective Flores to determine if any of the houses contained furnishings similar to those found in the photographs seized from defendant. When Detective Flores arrived at defendant's address, he peered into the house through the front window using a flashlight. He communicated a description of the room and the items he observed to the officers in Bay City. Detective Flores' observations were subsequently used to obtain a search warrant for defendant's house, from which approximately fifteen pounds of marijuana were seized. Should the defendant's motion to suppress the evidence seized from his house be granted? *People v. Custer*, 618 N.W.2d 75 (Mich.App. 2000).

Read the court opinion at:
www.lawyersweekly.com/micoa/218817.htm

Chapter 11

Search and Seizure of Vehicles and Containers

Outline

■ **Understand the rationale for and the scope of searches allowed under the *Carroll* doctrine (automobile exception to the search warrant requirement).**

■ **Understand what types of exigent circumstances will justify the search of a motor vehicle on the basis of probable cause.**

■ **Understand how the differences between a motor vehicle and a movable container with respect to expectation of privacy affect a law enforcement officer's warrantless search authority.**

■ **Understand the circumstances under which a motor vehicle may be impounded and the requirements that must be met before law enforcement officers may conduct an inventory of the vehicle's contents.**

■ **Be able to analyze any search and seizure situation involving a motor vehicle in terms of the reasonable expectation of privacy of the vehicle's owner and occupants.**

Carroll v. United States
laws.findlaw.com/us/267/
132.html

The same basic legal principles apply to the search of vehicles as apply to the search of fixed premises. For instance, it is well settled that an automobile is a personal effect, a place, or a thing within the meaning of the Fourth Amendment and is protected against unreasonable searches and seizures. Therefore, law enforcement officers should obtain a warrant whenever they want to search a motor vehicle unless the situation falls within one of the exceptions to the warrant requirement discussed in this chapter or in other chapters of this book. (Guidelines for obtaining a warrant can be found in Chapters 5 and 6.)

Courts have created exceptions to the warrant requirement for motor vehicles because of their unique nature. Among the unique characteristics of motor vehicles are their mobility, their use as transportation to and from crime scenes, and their employment in transporting dangerous weapons, stolen goods, contraband, and instrumentalities of crime. In addition, a person has a lesser expectation of privacy in a motor vehicle because (1) it travels public thoroughfares where its occupants and contents are open to view, (2) it seldom serves as a residence or permanent place for personal effects, (3) it is required to be registered and its occupant is required to be licensed, (4) it is extensively regulated with respect to the condition and manner in which it is operated on public streets and highways, (5) it periodically undergoes an official inspection, and (6) it is often taken into police custody in the interests of public safety. This chapter discusses the exceptions to the warrant requirement for searches and seizures of motor vehicles and also examines the search and seizure of movable containers, because similar considerations apply to both areas of the law.

The *Carroll* Doctrine

The **Carroll doctrine** holds that a warrantless search of a readily mobile motor vehicle by a law enforcement officer who has probable cause to believe that the vehicle contains items subject to seizure is not unreasonable under the Fourth Amendment. The *Carroll* doctrine originated in the case of *Carroll v. United States*, 267 U.S. 132, 45 S.Ct. 280, 69 L.Ed. 543 (1925), and is sometimes referred to as the *automobile exception* to the search warrant requirement. In the *Carroll* case, federal prohibition agents obtained information that the defendant and another person were bootleggers who frequently traveled a certain road in a certain automobile. The officers later unexpectedly encountered the two men driving on that road in that automobile. The officers pursued and stopped the automobile on the highway. They thoroughly searched the automobile, finding several bottles of illegal liquor concealed in its upholstery. No warrant had been obtained for the search.

The U.S. Supreme Court held:

> On reason and authority the true rule is that if the search and seizure without a warrant are made upon probable cause, that is upon a belief, reasonably arising out of circumstances known to the seizing officer, that an automobile or other vehicle contains that which by law is subject to seizure and destruction, the search and seizure are valid. The Fourth Amendment is to be construed in the light of what was deemed an unreasonable search and seizure when it was adopted, and in a manner which will conserve public interests as well as the interests and rights of individual citizens. 267 U.S. at 149, 45 S.Ct. at 283, 69 L.Ed. at 549.

Probable Cause

The controlling consideration in the warrantless search of a vehicle is probable cause to believe that the vehicle contains items that are connected with criminal activity and thus are subject to seizure. This was emphasized in the *Carroll* decision:

> Having thus established that contraband goods concealed and illegally transported in an automobile or other vehicle may be searched for without a warrant, we come now to consider under what circumstances such search may be made. It would be intolerable and unreasonable if a prohibition agent were authorized to stop every automobile on the chance of finding liquor, and thus subject all persons lawfully using the highways to the inconvenience and indignity of such a search. Travelers may be so stopped in crossing an international boundary because of national self-protection reasonably requiring one entering the country to identify himself as entitled to come in, and his belongings as effects which may be lawfully brought in. But those lawfully within the Country, entitled to use the public highways, have a right to free passage without interruption or search unless there is known to a competent official, authorized to search, probable cause for believing that their vehicles are carrying contraband or illegal merchandise. 267 U.S. at 153–54, 45 S.Ct. at 285, 69 L.Ed. at 551–52.

Probable cause is discussed in detail in Chapters 3 and 6. In vehicle search and seizure cases, probable cause depends on the particular circumstances of each situation. The law enforcement officer's determination of probable cause must be based on objective facts that could justify the issuance of a warrant by a magistrate and not merely on the subjective good faith of the officer. Evidence seized from a vehicle that is not seized on the basis of probable cause will be inadmissible in court.

Although the *Carroll* doctrine allows the warrantless *search* of a motor vehicle on the basis of probable cause to believe the vehicle contains items subject to seizure, the U.S. Supreme Court has allowed the warrantless *seizure* of the *vehicle itself* when police have probable cause to believe that the vehicle itself is contraband. In *Florida v. White,* 526 U.S. 559, 119 S.Ct. 1555, 143 L.Ed.2d 748 (1999), police officers on several occasions observed the defendant using his car to deliver cocaine. Therefore, they had probable cause to believe that his car was subject to forfeiture under the Florida Contraband Forfeiture Act. That act provided that any vehicle used in violation of the act "may be seized and shall be forfeited." The defendant was later arrested at his workplace on unrelated charges. At the same time the arresting officers seized his automobile in accordance with the provisions of the act. During a subsequent inventory search, the police found crack cocaine in the automobile. The Court held that the warrantless seizure of the automobile did not violate the Fourth Amendment.

> Although . . . the police lacked probable cause to believe that respondent's car contained contraband . . . they certainly had probable cause to believe that the vehicle *itself* was contraband under Florida law. Recognition of the need to seize readily movable contraband before it is spirited away undoubtedly underlies the early federal laws relied upon in *Carroll* . . . . This need is equally weighty when the *automobile,* as opposed to its contents, is the contraband that the police seek to secure. 526 U.S. 564–65, 119 S.Ct. 1559, 143 L.Ed.2d 754.

The Court also stated that because the police seized the vehicle from a public place— the defendant's employer's parking lot—the warrantless seizure did not invade the defendant's privacy. The Court noted that "our Fourth Amendment jurisprudence has

caselaw.findlaw.com/data/ constitution/amendment04/ 03html#4
Discussion (with annotations) of vehicular searches

www.loompanics.com/ Articles/motorveh.html
Article, "The Motor Vehicle Exception: When and Where to Search" by Lisa Regini

gladstone.uoregon.edu/~uofla/ Fall99/Katz.html
Article, "So What Ever Happened to the Fourth Amendment?: Incremental Evaporation of Motorist's Rights Under Automobile Exceptions" by Daniel Katz

lawschool.lexis.com/emanuel/ web/crimpro/crimpro03.htm
Outline of the law relating to automobile searches

For new and updated weblinks, go to www.wadsworth.com/ cj/ferdico0253

Florida v. White
laws.findlaw.com/us/000/ 98-223.html

www.techlawonline.com/
articles/scase_fn.htm
Article, "Searches and Seizures:
Expanding the Unchecked Discretion of the Police"; discusses
the case of *Florida v. White*
www.fear.org/weisholtz.html
Article, "The Forfeiture Exception: Warrantless Seizures
(and Searches) in the Wake
of *Florida v. White*" by Adam
Weisholtz

Chambers v. Maroney
laws.findlaw.com/us/399/
42.html

consistently accorded law enforcement officials greater latitude in exercising their duties in public places." 526 U.S. at 565, 119 S.Ct. at 1559, 143 L.Ed.2d at 754.

Delay in Search

If possible, warrantless searches under the *Carroll* doctrine should be conducted immediately at the scene where the vehicle is stopped. If, however, the surrounding circumstances make an immediate search on the highway unsafe or impractical, the vehicle may be removed to a more convenient location. If a search is conducted without unreasonable delay after the vehicle's arrival at the new location, the probable cause factor existing on the highway remains in force, and the warrantless search is constitutionally permissible.

In *Chambers v. Maroney*, 399 U.S. 42, 90 S.Ct. 1975, 26 L.Ed.2d 419 (1970), the police had information that armed robbers carrying the fruits of the crime had fled the robbery scene in a light blue compact station wagon. Four men were said to be in the vehicle, one wearing a green sweater and another wearing a trench coat. The police stopped a vehicle fitting the description, arrested the four occupants, and drove the vehicle to the police station. The vehicle was thoroughly searched at the station, and evidence was seized leading to the defendant's conviction.

The U.S. Supreme Court upheld the search:

> In enforcing the Fourth Amendment's prohibition against unreasonable searches and seizures, the Court has insisted upon probable cause as a minimum requirement for a reasonable search permitted by the Constitution. As a general rule, it has also required the judgment of a magistrate on the probable cause issue and the issuance of a warrant before a search is made. Only in exigent circumstances will the judgment of the police as to probable cause serve as a sufficient authorization for a search. *Carroll* . . . holds a search warrant unnecessary where there is probable cause to search an automobile stopped on the highway; the car is movable, the occupants are alerted, and the car's contents may never be found again if a warrant must be obtained. Hence an immediate search is constitutionally permissible.
>
> Arguably, because of the preference for a magistrate's judgment, only the immobilization of the car should be permitted until a search warrant is obtained; arguably, only the "lesser" intrusion is permissible until the magistrate authorizes the "greater." But which is the "greater" and which the "lesser" intrusion is itself a debatable question and the answer may depend on a variety of circumstances. For constitutional purposes, we see no difference between on the one hand seizing and holding a car before presenting the probable cause issue to a magistrate and on the other hand carrying out an immediate search without a warrant. Given probable cause to search either course is reasonable under the Fourth Amendment.
>
> On the facts before us, the blue station wagon could have been searched on the spot when it was stopped since there was probable cause to search and it was a fleeting target for a search. The probable cause factor still obtained at the station house and so did the mobility of the car unless the Fourth Amendment permits a warrantless seizure of the car and the denial of its use to anyone until a warrant is secured. In that event there is little to choose in terms of practical consequences between an immediate search without a warrant and the car's immobilization until a warrant is obtained. 399 U.S. at 51–52, 90 S.Ct. at 1981, 26 L.Ed.2d at 428–29.

Michigan v. Thomas, 458 U.S. 259, 102 S.Ct. 3079, 73 L.Ed.2d 750 (1982), upheld a warrantless search of an automobile stopped on the road and taken into police cus-

Michigan v. Thomas
laws.findlaw.com/us/458/
259.html

tody, even though a prior search had already been made. *Florida v. Meyers,* 466 U.S. 380, 104 S.Ct. 1852, 80 L.Ed.2d 381 (1984), upheld a warrantless search of an impounded automobile eight hours after it had been impounded. And *United States v. Johns,* 469 U.S. 478, 105 S.Ct. 881, 83 L.Ed.2d 890 (1985), upheld a warrantless search of an impounded vehicle three days after the vehicle had been impounded. Officers should obtain a warrant for searches to be made more than three days after impounding a vehicle. Note again that courts' preference for warrants is strong, and law enforcement officers should, when possible, consider applying for a warrant to search an automobile, especially when the facts and circumstances supporting probable cause may be weak or questionable.

Exigent Circumstances

In the passage just quoted, the Supreme Court said that "[o]nly in exigent circumstances will the judgment of the police as to probable cause serve as a sufficient authorization for a search." Some lower courts have taken this to mean that the police must be able to demonstrate specific facts establishing exigent circumstances, in addition to probable cause, before searching a vehicle stopped on the road. The U.S. Supreme Court, however, has made it clear that this is not necessary. In *United States v. Ross,* 456 U.S. 798, 809, 102 S.Ct. 2157, 2164–65, 72 L.Ed.2d 572, 584 (1982), the Court said that in cases in which there was probable cause to search a vehicle "a search is not unreasonable if based on facts that would justify the issuance of a warrant, even though a warrant has not been actually obtained." In *Michigan v. Thomas,* 458 U.S. 259, 261, 102 S.Ct. 3079, 3081, 73 L.Ed.2d 750, 753 (1982), the Court said:

> In *Chambers v. Maroney* . . . we held that when police officers have probable cause to believe there is contraband inside an automobile that has been stopped on the road, the officers may conduct a warrantless search of the vehicle, even after it has been impounded and is in police custody. We firmly reiterated this holding in *Texas v. White,* 423 U.S. 67, 96 S.Ct. 304, 46 L.Ed.2d 209 (1975). . . . It is thus clear that the justification to conduct such a warrantless search does not vanish once the car has been immobilized; nor does it depend upon a reviewing court's assessment of the likelihood in each particular case that the car would have been driven away, or that its contents would have been tampered with, during the period required for the police to obtain a warrant.

In short, the requirement that exigent circumstances must exist before the police's judgment as to probable cause will justify a warrantless search is automatically satisfied in the case of a motor vehicle that is "readily mobile." "If a car is readily mobile and probable cause exists to believe it contains contraband, the Fourth Amendment . . . permits police to search the vehicle without more." *Pennsylvania v. Labron,* 518 U.S. 938, 940, 116 S.Ct. 2485, 2487, 135 L.Ed.2d 1031, 1036 (1996). And most recently, in *Maryland v. Dyson,* 527 U.S. 465, 467, 119 S.Ct. 2013, 2014, 144 L.Ed.2d 442, 445 (1999), the Court held that the state appellate court's holding "that the 'automobile exception' requires a separate finding of exigency in addition to a finding of probable cause is squarely contrary to our holdings in *Ross* and *Labron.*" Some state courts, however, may interpret their own constitutions to require stricter standards than those of the U.S. Supreme Court.

When a motor vehicle is not readily mobile, the law enforcement officer must satisfy the exigent circumstances requirement in addition to the probable cause requirement before conducting a warrantless search or seizure. Usually, exigent circumstances are established by demonstrating specific facts showing either that the vehicle may be

Florida v. Meyers
laws.findlaw.com/us/466/
380.html
United States v. Johns
laws.findlaw.com/us/469/
478.html

civilliberty.about.com//library/
weekly/aa062899.htm
Article, "Cars and the Fourth
Amendment"; criticizes the U.S.
Supreme Court decision in
Maryland v. Dyson

Pennsylvania v. Labron
laws.findlaw.com/us/000/
u20034.html
Maryland v. Dyson
supct.law.cornell.edu/supct/
html/98-1062.ZPC.html

moved to an unknown location or out of the jurisdiction, making a search under authority of a warrant impossible, or that items subject to seizure may be removed from the vehicle and concealed or destroyed.

California v. Carney
laws.findlaw.com/us/471/
386.html

For example, in *California v. Carney*, 471 U.S. 386, 105 S.Ct. 2066, 85 L.Ed.2d 406 (1985), Drug Enforcement Agency (DEA) agents had probable cause to search a mobile motor home parked in a lot in a large city's downtown area. The Court applied the standard that a search of a vehicle is justified under the *Carroll* doctrine if the vehicle "is being used on the highways, or if it is readily capable of such use and is found stationary in a place not regularly used for residential purposes—temporary or otherwise." 471 U.S. at 392, 105 S.Ct. at 2070, 85 L.Ed.2d at 414. The warrantless search of this mobile home was upheld because the vehicle was readily mobile by the turn of the ignition key and was so situated that an objective observer would conclude that it was being used not as a residence but as a vehicle. In a footnote, the Court listed some factors that would indicate that a mobile home was being used as a residence. "Among the factors that might be relevant in determining whether a warrant would be required in such a circumstance is its location, whether the vehicle is readily mobile or instead, for instance, elevated on blocks, whether the vehicle is licensed, whether it is connected to utilities, and whether it has convenient access to a public road." 471 U.S. at 394 n.3, 105 S.Ct. at 2071 n.3, 85 L.Ed.2d at 415 n.3. In *United States v. Levesque*, 625 F.Supp. 428 (D.N.H. 1985), the court disallowed a warrantless search of a motor home that was not readily mobile:

> The trailer at issue . . . was situated in a trailer park and on a lot, objectively indicating that it was being used as a residence. Although the truck which tows the trailer was only a few feet from the trailer, the trailer was not readily mobile in light of the fact that one end of the trailer was elevated on blocks and that the trailer was connected to utilities at the campground, and also because of the three quarters of an hour lead time to connect the trailer and truck. The mobile home exception to the warrant requirement thus would appear to have no application herein. 625 F.Supp. at 450–51.

In *United States v. Tartaglia*, 864 F.2d 837 (D.C.Cir. 1989), police had probable cause to search a train roomette for drugs. Analogizing the train roomette to the readily mobile motor home in the *Carney* case, the court found exigent circumstances justifying a warrantless search of the roomette:

> Because the police did not have sufficient time to procure a warrant before train 98 left Union Station and because there was more than a reasonable likelihood that the train, and therefore the roomette and its contents, would be moved before a warrant could be obtained, the warrantless search of defendant's roomette was justified under the exigent circumstances exception to the warrant requirement of the Fourth Amendment. 864 F.2d at 843.

Cardwell v. Lewis
laws.findlaw.com/us/417/
583.html

In *Cardwell v. Lewis*, 417 U.S. 583, 94 S.Ct. 2464, 41 L.Ed.2d 325 (1974), the U.S. Supreme Court found exigent circumstances justifying the warrantless seizure of the defendant's automobile from a commercial parking lot in which the defendant had left it before his appearance at the police station, where he was arrested. The defendant had been fully aware that he was under investigation for several months, and he had told his attorney to see that his wife and family got the car. The Court based its finding of exigent circumstances on the possibility that the attorney or a family member might remove evidence from the car if the police delayed seizing it.

In *United States v. Forker*, 928 F.2d 365 (11th Cir. 1991), officers had probable cause to search a Cadillac for drugs and evidence of a drug distribution conspiracy. The Cadillac was parked in a motel parking lot, and police had recently arrested the defendant Forker, its driver. The court found that the following facts created exigent circumstances:

> The officers were not certain how many sets of keys to the Cadillac existed; they were not certain if the car would remain in the parking lot if they left to obtain a warrant. At the time Forker was stopped and arrested at the Holiday Inn parking lot, there were suspects in another hotel ten minutes away and Frawley, the suspected source of the cash as well as the known owner of the Cadillac driven by Forker, was inside the Holiday Inn. The agents had not apprehended all suspects and were not even aware of how many people were involved in the conspiracy. Further, the Cadillac was in the middle of a public parking lot, vulnerable to the efforts of cohorts of Forker's to seize the cash or destroy evidence. The agents were in the middle of a fast-moving series of events which prompted the search of the vehicle. The circumstances that prompted the search of the Cadillac were certainly exigent and as such, we find that the search of the vehicle was not violative of Forker and Frawley's fourth amendment rights. 928 F.2d at 369.

In a different case in which there were no indications of the potential mobility of an automobile, however, the court disallowed a warrantless search of a parked, unoccupied automobile:

> [A]ny search of an automobile that was parked, immobile and unoccupied at the time the police first encountered it in connection with the investigation of a crime must be authorized by a warrant issued by a magistrate or, alternatively, the prosecution must demonstrate that exigent circumstances other than the potential mobility of the automobile exist. Here, the prosecution failed to demonstrate any individualized exigent circumstances. *State v. Kock*, 725 P.2d 1285, 1287 (Or. 1986).

If a vehicle or its contents present a potential danger to public safety if not searched immediately, the *exigent circumstances* requirement of the *Carroll* doctrine may be satisfied, even though the car is immobile. In *United States v. Cepulonis*, 530 F.2d 238 (1st Cir. 1976), a law enforcement officer observed, through the window of an automobile, a sawed-off shotgun protruding from beneath the front seat. The court upheld the immediate warrantless seizure of the shotgun, finding probable cause and also finding that someone other than the car's owner (who was in custody) could have moved the car. The court went on to say:

> Moreover, a legitimate concern for public safety counselled against leaving the car, with a loaded shotgun visible through the window, unguarded in the Motel parking lot and "vulnerable to intrusion by vandals." . . . Under the circumstances the agents were faced with a choice whether to seize and hold the car while securing a warrant or to carry out an immediate warrantless search. 530 F.2d at 243.

In *Coolidge v. New Hampshire*, 403 U.S. 443, 91 S.Ct. 2022, 29 L.Ed.2d 564 (1971), the U.S. Supreme Court indicated that the exigent circumstances requirement would not be satisfied if there were no real possibility that someone would remove the car and conceal or destroy evidence within it. In the *Coolidge* case, the police had known for some time of the probable role of the defendant's automobile in a crime. The police went to the defendant's home, arrested him inside his house, and escorted his wife and

Coolidge v. New Hampshire
laws.findlaw.com/us/403/
443.html

Case in Point

Interpreting *Maryland v. Dyson*

On July 10, 1998, at approximately 8:00 P.M., a confidential informant met with Crookston Police Department Detective Gerardo Moreno, and other law enforcement officers. The informant stated that he or she had met with individuals the previous day at the Polk County Fair in Fertile, Minnesota, who stated they could supply the informant with controlled substances. The informant was supplied with $450 of "buy-money" and an electronic transmitter to record the purchase.

This informant met with Brian Christopher Johnson at the fair, and Johnson introduced the informant to Raymond Richard Krebs. Johnson and Krebs agreed to sell the informant two ounces of marijuana for $300 later in the evening.

The informant subsequently met with Krebs and Johnson. The three proceeded to a white four-door Dodge Spirit, which was registered to the appellant, Tamara Gay Pederson-Maxwell. Krebs entered the vehicle and told a female sleeping in the front seat (later identified as appellant) to open the trunk so he could get the "weed." Krebs instead grabbed a pair of boots from the back seat of the vehicle and took approximately two ounces of marijuana out of one of the boots.

The informant, Krebs, and Johnson then entered a different vehicle and drove around for a short time. The informant, after being dropped off, met with Deputy Helget. The informant told Deputy Helget that Krebs and Johnson smoked a marijuana joint while they were in the car, and that Krebs provided the informant with approximately two ounces of marijuana in exchange for $300.

A short time later, the informant identified Krebs to Detective Moreno as the man who sold him the marijuana. The informant also identified appellant as the woman who was sleeping in the Dodge Spirit when Krebs obtained the marijuana. Krebs and appellant were placed under arrest. Johnson was also subsequently arrested. The officers searched Krebs

and found $517 in cash, $290 of which was marked buy-money that the informant stated was paid in exchange for the marijuana. Appellant's purse was found to contain approximately two ounces of marijuana and $2,675 in cash. At trial, the evidence established that the actual amount of marijuana in appellant's purse totaled 39.9 grams.

Detective Moreno asked appellant for permission to search the Dodge Spirit, but she refused. Appellant agreed to allow Detective Moreno to drive the vehicle from the fairgrounds to the Fertile Police Department.

Once at the police department, a trained drug-detection dog reacted to the presence of controlled substances in the vehicle and in the trunk. The vehicle was impounded and transported to the Northwest Regional Corrections Center in Crookston.

On July 13, 1998, officers searched the Dodge Spirit without a warrant. Three Tupperware containers filled with marijuana, a weight scale, a cellular phone, a pager, a .380 caliber semi-automatic handgun and an ammunition clip, a .38 caliber semi-automatic handgun with one loaded and one unloaded ammunition clip, an interchangeable .45 caliber barrel, ammunition, and other items were found in the trunk of the vehicle.

Appellant was charged with, and convicted of, two counts of fifth-degree controlled substance crime and one count of failing to affix a controlled substance tax stamp. In light of *Maryland v. Dyson*, should the appellant's motion to suppress the evidence obtained in the search of her car be granted? *State v. Pederson-Maxwell*, 619 N.W.2d 777 (Minn.App. 2000).

Read the court opinion at:
www.state.mn.us/courts/library/archive/ctappub/0012/
c1992112.htm

children to another town to spend the night. No other adults resided in the house. The vehicle was unoccupied and in the defendant's driveway. Police towed the vehicle to the station house and searched it there without a warrant.

The Court held that the search of the automobile could not be justified under the *Carroll* doctrine because the car was not movable, nor were there any other exigent circumstances to justify the search.

> [S]urely there is nothing in this case to invoke the meaning and purpose of the rule of *Carroll v. U.S.*—no alerted criminal bent on flight, no fleeting opportunity on an open highway after a hazardous chase, no contraband or stolen goods or weapons, no confederates waiting to move the evidence, not even the inconvenience of a special police detail to guard the immobilized automobile. In short, by no possible stretch of the legal

imagination can this be made into a case where "it is not practicable to secure a warrant," . . . and the "automobile exception," despite its label, is simply irrelevant. 403 U.S. at 462, 91 S.Ct. at 2035–36, 29 L.Ed.2d at 580.

In *Lavicky v. Burnett,* 758 F.2d 468 (10th Cir. 1985), the automobile exception was held not to apply to the warrantless seizure and search of the defendant's truck, which was immobile because its engine was partially dismantled.

Entry onto Private Premises

When law enforcement officers, acting on probable cause and following closely behind a vehicle, would have been authorized to stop and search the vehicle while on a public way, they may properly follow the vehicle onto private property and conduct the search there. In *Scher v. United States,* 305 U.S. 251, 59 S.Ct. 174, 83 L.Ed. 151 (1938), an informant's tip and careful surveillance gave police officers probable cause to believe that a certain automobile contained contraband. The officers followed the auto until the defendant parked it in his garage. The Court held the subsequent warrantless search of the car in the garage valid.

Scher v. United States
laws.findlaw.com/us/305/251.html

> [I]t seems plain enough that just before he entered the garage, the following officers properly could have stopped petitioner's car and made search. . . .
>
> Passage of the car into the open garage closely followed by the observing officer did not destroy this right. 305 U.S. at 255, 59 S.Ct. at 176, 83 L.Ed. at 154.

Scope of Search

The scope of the search of a vehicle under the *Carroll* doctrine depends on whether the searching officer has probable cause to search the entire vehicle or whether the officer has probable cause only to search a particular container found in the vehicle.

SEARCH OF ENTIRE VEHICLE   The permissible scope of a warrantless search of a motor vehicle under the *Carroll* doctrine has been defined in the case of *United States v. Ross,* 456 U.S. 798, 102 S.Ct. 2157, 72 L.Ed.2d 572 (1982), a case involving the legitimate stopping of an automobile by police officers who had probable cause to believe that the automobile contained narcotics. During the search of the car, the searching officer found and opened a closed brown paper bag and a zippered leather pouch, discovering heroin in the bag and a large amount of money in the pouch. In holding the search legal, the U.S. Supreme Court said:

United States v. Ross
laws.findlaw.com/us/456/798.html

> [T]he scope of the warrantless search authorized by [the *Carroll*] exception is no broader and no narrower than a magistrate could legitimately authorize by warrant. If probable cause justifies the search of a lawfully stopped vehicle, it justifies the search of every part of the vehicle and its contents that may conceal the object of the search. 456 U.S. at 825, 102 S.Ct. at 2173, 72 L.Ed.2d at 594.

Emphasizing that the scope of a search under the *Carroll* doctrine depends entirely on the object of the search, the Supreme Court stated:

> The scope of a warrantless search of an automobile thus is not defined by the nature of the container in which the contraband is secreted. Rather, it is defined by the object of the search and the places in which there is probable cause to believe that it may be found. Just as probable cause to believe that a stolen lawnmower may be found in a

www.november.org/1226.html
Article, "Supreme Court Expands
Authority over Motorists and
Passengers"; discusses the case of
Wyoming v. Houghton
law.miningco.com/newsissues/
law/library/weekly/
aa040899.htm
Article, "Supreme Court Contin-
ues Its Activist Ways in Vehicle
Search Case"; discusses the case
of *Wyoming v. Houghton*
www.bc.edu/bc_org/avp/law/
lwsch/journals/bclawr/41_1/
02_TXT.htm
Article, "Privacy Takes a Back
Seat: Putting the Automobile
Exception Back on Track after
Several Wrong Turns" by Carol
A. Chase

United States v. Di Re
laws.findlaw.com/us/332/
581.html

Rakas v. Illinois
laws.findlaw.com/us/439/
128.html
Wyoming v. Houghton
laws.findlaw.com/us/000/
98-184.html

garage will not support a warrant to search an upstairs bedroom, probable cause to believe that undocumented aliens are being transported in a van will not justify a warrantless search of a suitcase. Probable cause to believe that a container placed in the trunk of a taxi contains contraband or evidence does not justify a search of the entire cab. 456 U.S. at 824, 102 S.Ct. at 2172, 72 L.Ed.2d at 593.

The scope of the warrantless search allowed under the *Carroll* doctrine may even extend to dismantling part of the vehicle. In *United States v. Zucco,* 71 F.3d 188 (5th Cir. 1995), police had probable cause to search an entire recreational vehicle because cocaine had been found in a cabinet in the vehicle as the result of a valid consent search. When a drug-sniffing dog alerted to another part of the vehicle, police were authorized to remove a wall panel, where they discovered a large cache of cocaine.

Furthermore, in *United States v. Johns,* 469 U.S. 478, 105 S.Ct. 881, 83 L.Ed.2d 890 (1985), the Court held that, when officers have probable cause to search a vehicle for a specific object, the search of a container in the vehicle that could contain that object need not be conducted at the same time as the seizure or search of the vehicle. Customs agents in the *Johns* case had seized and impounded a vehicle under the *Carroll* doctrine on the basis of probable cause to believe it contained marijuana. The Court approved a warrantless search, conducted three days later, of plastic bags found in the vehicle.

If an officer obtains probable cause to search a container after the container has been removed from a vehicle, the *Carroll* doctrine does not apply, even if the container is in the process of being returned to the vehicle. The officer must have probable cause to believe that items subject to seizure are contained *somewhere inside the vehicle.* As stated by the Maine Supreme Judicial Court in a case in which the defendant voluntarily retrieved from his car a carry-on bag containing two bags, and an officer searched the two bags after smelling the odor of marijuana, "the fact that the bags came from the car and were in the process of being returned to the car does not trigger the automobile exception." *State v. Lewis,* 611 A.2d 69, 71 (Me. 1992).

Officers may not conduct body searches of a vehicle's occupants under the *Carroll* doctrine. *United States v. Di Re,* 332 U.S. 581, 68 S.Ct. 222, 92 L.Ed. 210 (1948). However, passengers in a vehicle have no reasonable expectation of privacy in the vehicle's interior area. Therefore, a warrantless search based on probable cause of areas such as the glove compartment, the spaces under the seats, and the trunk is permissible. Such a search invades no Fourth Amendment interest of the passengers, even if it turns up evidence implicating the passengers. *Rakas v. Illinois,* 439 U.S. 128, 99 S.Ct. 421, 58 L.Ed.2d 387 (1978).

Furthermore, in *Wyoming v. Houghton,* 526 U.S. 295, 307 119 S.Ct. 1297, 1304, 143 L.Ed.2d 408, 419 (1999), the U.S. Supreme Court held that "police officers with probable cause to search a car may inspect passengers' belongings found in the car that are capable of concealing the object of the search." The Court found that passengers, like drivers, possess a reduced expectation of privacy with regard to property that they transport in motor vehicles. Police examination of an item of a passenger's personal property is unlikely to produce the annoyance, fear, and humiliation that a search of one's body is likely to produce. In contrast, the Court found the government's interests in inspecting passengers' belongings substantial.

Effective law enforcement would be appreciably impaired without the ability to search a passenger's personal belongings when there is reason to believe contraband or evidence of criminal wrongdoing is hidden in the car. As in all car-search cases, the "ready mobility" of an automobile creates a risk that the evidence or contraband will be permanently

Case in Point

Interpreting *Wyoming v. Houghton*

On May 8, 1997, the Sacramento Sheriff's Department received a report at about 1:30 A.M. that a Chevrolet van was parked in a residential area. The caller, a resident in the area, thought the van was suspicious and "believed that there was possible burglary activity about to take place." Deputy Donald Bricker and another deputy responded to a dispatch and went to investigate. Deputy Bricker observed the right front and rear tires of the van were on the sidewalk, in violation of Vehicle Code section 22500, subdivision (f). When he knocked on the side door of the van, the defendant opened the door. The deputy looked inside the van and saw the defendant (by the side door) and Scott LeBlanc (in the rear of the van). There was a bed in the rear of the van, and the deputy was concerned someone could have hidden under it.

Deputy Bricker asked the defendant and LeBlanc what they were doing in the neighborhood, but neither responded. He then asked for their identification to determine whether either was subject to an arrest warrant or had a valid license to drive the vehicle. The deputy was concerned about his safety because of the possibility of a concealed weapon. The defendant looked around on the floor of the van and stated she was searching for her identification. However, after she searched for several minutes without finding it, the deputy asked them to step out of the van. There was no indication the defendant was under the influence of alcohol or narcotics.

Deputy Bricker patted them down for weapons and placed them in the rear of the patrol car. The defendant gave the deputy her name and birth date and claimed ownership of the van. She told him her identification was in the van, either on the floorboard or in the visor, despite the fact that she had previously searched those areas. When Deputy Bricker told the defendant he was going to look in the van for her identification, she told him she did not want him to search the van. Choosing now to respond to Deputy Bricker's original inquiry as to her purpose in the neighborhood, she told Deputy Bricker that she and LeBlanc were "on a rendezvous because they didn't want to be seen together."

Deputy Bricker initially went into the van for just a moment, looking for weapons or other people, and saw a purse on the floor in the back of the van. After a discussion with the other deputy, he reentered the van and opened the purse. Inside, he found a glass pipe, marijuana, methamphetamine, and the defendant's California identification card. In light of *Wyoming v. Houghton*, should the defendant's motion to suppress the evidence seized from her van be granted? *People v. Hart*, 86 Cal.Rptr.2d 762 (Cal.App. 3d Dist. 1999).

Read the court opinion at:
freecaselaw.com/ca/C028605.htm

---

lost while a warrant is obtained. . . . In addition, a car passenger—unlike the unwitting tavern patron in *Ybarra*—will often be engaged in a common enterprise with the driver, and have the same interest in concealing the fruits or the evidence of their wrongdoing. Cf. *Maryland v. Wilson*, 519 U. S. 408, 413–414 (1997). A criminal might be able to hide contraband in a passenger's belongings as readily as in other containers in the car . . . perhaps even surreptitiously, without the passenger's knowledge or permission. 526 U.S. at 304–05, 119 S.Ct. at 1302–03, 143 L.Ed.2d at 417–18.

Of course, if an officer has probable cause to arrest one or more occupants of a motor vehicle, the officer may search all arrested occupants and the passenger compartment incident to the arrest. (See the discussion of *New York v. Belton* in Chapter 8.)

To summarize, under the *Carroll* doctrine, if officers have probable cause to search an entire vehicle for a specific seizable item, they may search to the same extent as if they had a warrant to search for that item, including the inspection of passengers' belongings found in the car that are capable of concealing the object of the search.

SEARCH OF CONTAINER FOUND IN VEHICLE   When officers have probable cause only to search a particular container placed in a vehicle, however, they may search that container without a warrant but not the entire vehicle. In *California v. Acevedo*, 500 U.S. 565, 111 S.Ct. 1982, 114 L.Ed.2d 619 (1991), police observed the defendant leave an

California v. Acevedo
laws.findlaw.com/us/500/
565.html

www.fletc.gov/legal/
archive_dir.htm
Article, "Locked Containers—
An Overview" by John Besselman; second of three articles in
the November 24, 1999 issue of
*Quarterly Review: Legal Commentary for Federal Law Enforcement
Officers*

apartment known to contain marijuana with a brown paper package the same size as marijuana packages they had seen earlier. He placed the bag in the trunk of his car and started to drive away. Fearing the loss of evidence, officers in an unmarked car stopped him. They opened the trunk and the bag and found marijuana.

The Court held that the Fourth Amendment does not compel separate treatment for an automobile search that extends only to a container within the vehicle. The Court said:

> The interpretation of the *Carroll* doctrine set forth in *Ross* now applies to all searches of containers found in an automobile. In other words, the police may search without a warrant if their search is supported by probable cause. The Court in *Ross* put it this way:
>
>> "The scope of a warrantless search of an automobile . . . is not defined by the nature of the container in which the contraband is secreted. Rather, it is defined by the object of the search and the places in which there is probable cause to believe that it may be found." 456 U.S. at 824, 102 S.Ct. at 2172.
>>
>> It went on to note: "Probable cause to believe that a container placed in the trunk of a taxi contains contraband or evidence does not justify a search of the entire cab." *Ibid.* We affirm that principle. In the case before us, the police had probable cause to believe that the paper bag in the automobile's trunk contained marijuana. That probable cause now allows a warrantless search of the paper bag. The facts in the record reveal that the police did not have probable cause to believe that contraband was hidden in any other part of the automobile and a search of the entire vehicle would have been without probable cause and unreasonable under the Fourth Amendment. 500 U.S. at 579–80, 111 S.Ct. at 1991, 114 L.Ed.2d at 634.

SEARCH OF CONTAINER NOT FOUND IN VEHICLE   The rationale justifying a warrantless search of an automobile believed to be transporting items subject to seizure arguably applies with equal force to any movable container believed to be carrying such an item. The U.S. Supreme Court, however, squarely rejected that argument. In *United States v. Chadwick*, 433 U.S. 1, 97 S.Ct. 2476, 53 L.Ed.2d 538 (1977), federal railroad officials became suspicious when they noticed that a large footlocker loaded onto a train was unusually heavy and leaking talcum powder, a substance often used to mask the odor of marijuana. Narcotics agents met the train at its destination, and a trained police dog signaled the presence of a controlled substance inside the footlocker. The agents did not seize the footlocker at that time. Instead, they waited until the defendant arrived and placed the footlocker in the trunk of his automobile. Before he started the engine, the officers arrested him and his two companions. The agents then removed the footlocker to a secure place, opened it without a warrant, and discovered a large quantity of marijuana.

The prosecution did not contend on appeal that the locker's brief contact with the automobile's trunk sufficed to make the *Carroll* doctrine applicable. Rather, the prosecution argued that the warrantless search was "reasonable" because a footlocker has some of the mobile characteristics that support warrantless searches of automobiles. The Supreme Court rejected the argument:

> The factors which diminish the privacy aspects of an automobile do not apply to respondents' footlocker. Luggage contents are not open to public view, except as a condition to a border entry or common carrier travel; nor is luggage subject to regular inspections and official scrutiny on a continuing basis. Unlike an automobile, whose primary function is transportation, luggage is intended as a repository of personal effects. In sum, a

United States v. Chadwick
laws.findlaw.com/us/433/1.html

person's expectations of privacy in personal luggage are substantially greater than in an automobile. 433 U.S. at 13, 97 S.Ct. at 2484, 53 L.Ed.2d at 549.

The Court noted that the practical problems associated with the temporary detention of a piece of luggage during the period of time necessary to obtain a warrant are significantly less than those associated with the detention of an automobile. In holding the warrantless search of the footlocker unjustified, the Court reaffirmed the general principle that closed packages and containers may not be searched without a warrant. Thus, the Court declined to extend the rationale of the automobile exception to permit a warrantless search of any movable container found in a public place. *California v. Acevedo*, 500 U.S. 565, 111 S.Ct. 1982, 114 L.Ed.2d 619 (1991). (See also the discussion of the *Chadwick* case in Chapter 8.)

OTHER CONTAINER SEARCHES   Inventory searches of containers are discussed in Chapter 4 and in this chapter pages 415–418. Investigatory detentions of containers are discussed in Chapter 7. Seizures and searches of containers incident to arrest are discussed in Chapter 8. Seizures and searches of containers under the plain view doctrine are discussed in Chapter 10. Seizures and searches of abandoned containers are discussed in Chapter 12.

Key Points

1. Under the *Carroll* doctrine, if a car is readily mobile and probable cause exists to believe it contains contraband, the Fourth Amendment permits police to search the vehicle without additional justification.

2. The justification to search a motor vehicle under the *Carroll* doctrine does not vanish once the vehicle has been immobilized, impounded, and taken into police custody; nor does it depend on the likelihood that the vehicle would have been driven away or that its contents would have been tampered with during the period required for the police to obtain a warrant.

3. To conduct a warrantless search of a vehicle that is not readily mobile, law enforcement officers must demonstrate exigent circumstances in addition to probable cause. Exigent circumstances are established by showing that the vehicle may be moved or that evidence in the vehicle may be concealed or destroyed, making a search under authority of a warrant impossible.

4. If an officer has probable cause to search an entire vehicle for a particular object under the *Carroll* doctrine, the officer may look anywhere in the vehicle in which there is probable cause to believe the object may be found, including containers that could hold the object.

5. Law enforcement officers with probable cause to search a motor vehicle may inspect passengers' belongings found in the vehicle that are capable of concealing the object of the search.

6. If an officer has probable cause to search only a particular container placed in a vehicle, the officer may search that container without a warrant but not the entire vehicle.

7. The *Carroll* doctrine does not permit the warrantless search of any movable container found in a public place, even if the searching officer has probable cause. Closed containers and packages may not be searched without a warrant or justification under some other exception to the warrant requirement.

Impoundment and Inventory of Vehicles

The police may **impound** motor vehicles for a variety of reasons. Accompanying a vehicle's impoundment, police routinely inventory the vehicle's contents for reasons of safety, liability, and convenience. This section explores the legal issues involved in impounding and inventorying motor vehicles.

Impoundment

In the interests of public safety and as part of what the Court has called "community caretaking functions," . . . automobiles are frequently taken into police custody. Vehicle accidents present one such occasion. To permit the uninterrupted flow of traffic and in some instances to preserve evidence, disabled or damaged vehicles will often be removed from the highways or streets in caretaking and traffic control activities. Police will also frequently remove and impound automobiles which violate parking ordinances and which thereby jeopardize both the public safety and the efficient movement of vehicular traffic. The authority of police to seize and remove from the streets vehicles impeding traffic or threatening public safety and convenience is beyond challenge. *South Dakota v. Opperman*, 428 U.S. 364, 368–69, 96 S.Ct. 3092, 3096, 49 L.Ed.2d 1000, 1005 (1976).

South Dakota v. Opperman
laws.findlaw.com/us/428/
364.html

Other reasons that may justify police **impoundment** of a vehicle are

- the driver has been arrested and taken into custody. *United States v. Lyles*, 946 F.2d 78 (8th Cir. 1991);
- the driver is incapacitated by intoxication, injury, illness, or some other condition. *United States v. Ford*, 872 F.2d 1231 (6th Cir. 1989);
- the vehicle is seized as evidence of or an instrument of a crime. *United States v. Cooper*, 949 F.2d 737 (5th Cir. 1991);
- the vehicle is forfeited pursuant to a state or federal forfeiture law. *United States v. Bizzell*, 19 F.3d 1524 (4th Cir. 1994);
- the vehicle has been reported stolen.

Note that in many jurisdictions, the right of police to impound vehicles is defined by statute or departmental policy or both. If an officer impounds a vehicle in violation of statute or policy, or for some other illegitimate reason such as harassment of the driver or conducting an investigatory search, the impoundment may be held illegal. *United States v. Ibarra*, 955 F.2d 1405 (10th Cir. 1992).

Impoundment procedure usually involves the police taking possession of the vehicle and moving it to a garage or police lot for safekeeping. The main justification for impoundment is that the vehicle would otherwise be left unattended on a public street or highway and would be an easy target for theft or vandalism, leaving the police open to potential liability.

Law enforcement officers are not constitutionally required to offer a defendant the opportunity to make other arrangements for the safekeeping of his or her vehicle, nor must they always choose methods of dealing with a defendant's vehicle that are less intrusive than impoundment. As stated by the U.S. Supreme Court, "[t]he reasonableness of any particular governmental activity does not necessarily or invariably turn on the existence of alternative 'less intrusive' means." *Illinois v. Lafayette*, 462 U.S. 640, 647, 103 S.Ct. 2605, 2610, 77 L.Ed.2d 65, 72 (1983). Therefore, nothing prohibits the exercise of police discretion to impound a vehicle rather than to lock and park it in a safe place, for instance, "so long as that discretion is exercised according to standard criteria and on the basis of something other than suspicion of evidence of criminal activity." *Colorado v. Bertine*, 479 U.S. 367, 375, 107 S.Ct. 738, 743, 93 L.Ed.2d 739, 748 (1987).

Illinois v. Lafayette
laws.findlaw.com/us/462/
640.html

Colorado v. Bertine
laws.findlaw.com/us/479/
367.html

Some states, however, require officers to consider reasonable alternatives to impoundment. "Although an officer is not required to exhaust all possibilities, the officer must at least consider alternatives; attempt, if feasible, to obtain a name from the driver of someone in the vicinity who could move the vehicle; and then reasonably conclude from this deliberation that impoundment is proper." *State v. Coss*, 943 P.2d

1126, 1130 (Wash.App. 1997). In the *Coss* case, impoundment of a stopped vehicle was found unreasonable and, therefore, unlawful when the driver had a suspended license but a properly licensed passenger could have driven the vehicle from the scene of the stop.

Inventory

Assuming that a vehicle has been lawfully impounded, may the vehicle then be searched for incriminating evidence without a warrant? Unless the situation satisfies the requirements of the *Carroll* doctrine, police have no authority to conduct a warrantless investigatory search of a lawfully impounded motor vehicle. In other words, police must obtain a search warrant to search an impounded vehicle unless they have probable cause to search the vehicle and

- the vehicle is readily mobile, or
- exigent circumstances make an immediate warrantless search necessary.

Nevertheless, in *South Dakota v. Opperman*, 428 U.S. 364, 96 S.Ct. 3092, 49 L.Ed.2d 1000 (1976), the U.S. Supreme Court approved a more limited search of a lawfully impounded motor vehicle: the routine practice of local police departments of securing and inventorying the vehicle's contents. This limited type of search is allowed to protect

- the owner's property while it remains in police custody;
- the police against claims or disputes over lost, stolen, or vandalized property; and
- the police from potential danger.

This **inventory** procedure is not considered to be a search for purposes of the Fourth Amendment because its object is not to find incriminating evidence as part of a criminal investigation. Rather, it is considered to be a routine administrative-custodial procedure and "must not be a ruse for a general rummaging in order to discover incriminating evidence." *Florida v. Wells*, 495 U.S. 1, 4, 110 S.Ct. 1632, 1635, 109 L.Ed.2d 1, 6 (1990). Nevertheless, an investigatory motive will not invalidate an inventory if there is also an administrative motive.

Florida v. Wells
laws.findlaw.com/us/495/1.html

> It would be disingenuous of us to pretend that when the agents opened Judge's bag, they weren't hoping to find some more evidence to use against him. But, they could have also reasonably had an administrative motive, which is all that is required under *Bertine*. While there are undoubtedly mixed motives in the vast majority of inventory searches, the constitution does not require and our human limitations do not allow us to peer into a police officer's "heart of hearts." *United States v. Judge,* 864 F.2d 1144, 1147 n.5 (5th Cir. 1989).

STANDARD PROCEDURES   Each law enforcement agency must have standard procedures for inventorying impounded vehicles, or the inventories will be declared an illegal search. In upholding the validity of an inventory of an impounded car in *South Dakota v. Opperman,* the U.S. Supreme Court emphasized that the police were using a standard inventory form pursuant to standard police procedures. The Court said, "The decisions of this Court point unmistakably to the conclusion reached by both federal and state courts that inventories pursuant to standard police procedures are reasonable." 428 U.S. at 372, 96 S.Ct. at 3092, 49 L.Ed.2d at 1007. The Ninth Circuit Court of Appeals invalidated an inventory of a legally impounded automobile because the local police department did not have a standard procedure regarding the inventorying of an impounded vehicle's contents.

www.fletc.gov/legal/archive_dir.htm
Article, "Searching a Vehicle Without a Warrant: Inventory Searches" by Bryan R. Lemons; second of three articles in the April 2, 2001 issue of *Quarterly Review: Legal Commentary for Federal Law Enforcement Officers*
www.totse.com/en/law/justice_for_all/search2.html
Article, "Inventory Searches: The Role of Discretion" by Austin A. Anderson

[E]ven if an investigatory motive was not shown, our decision would be the same because the inventorying of impounded cars was not shown to be a routine practice and policy of *this* police department, as was the case in *Opperman.* . . . It is the inventorying practice and not the impounding practice that, if routinely followed and supported by proper noninvestigatory purposes, could render the inventory a reasonable search under *Opperman.* The fact that other police departments routinely follow such a practice may give support to the proposition that such a practice, if locally followed, is reasonable. It does not, however, render reasonable a search where the inventorying practice is not locally followed and the search, thus, is a departure from local practice. *United States v. Hellman,* 556 F.2d 442, 444 (9th Cir. 1977).

Standard inventory procedures need not be written. In *United States v. Feldman,* 788 F.2d 544 (9th Cir. 1986), the court approved a procedure under which officers are instructed orally that stolen vehicles must be impounded and their contents inventoried on a standard printed form.

SCOPE   Officers should follow standard departmental procedures regarding the allowable scope of a vehicle inventory. The inventory should be restricted to accessible areas of the vehicle in which the owner's or occupant's personal belongings might be vulnerable to theft or damage. Areas covered by the inventory would usually include an unlocked glove compartment, an unlocked trunk, the sun visors, the front and rear seat areas, and other places where property is ordinarily kept. *People v. Andrews,* 85 Cal.Rptr. 908 (Cal.App. 1970). As a part of the inventory, a notation should be made of the vehicle identification number, the motor number, and the make, model, and license plate number of the car in order that the car may be easily identified later. *Cotton v. United States,* 371 F.2d 385 (9th Cir. 1967).

If officers dismantle the vehicle, look behind the upholstery, or in any other manner indicate that their purpose is other than to protect and secure the vehicle's contents, the courts will consider the inventory a pretext for a search designed to uncover evidentiary materials. The inventory will then be considered an illegal warrantless search, and the fruits of the search will be inadmissible in court. But when officers reasonably believe that the contents of an automobile or the contents of a locked compartment in an automobile present a danger to themselves or others, they may make as extensive a search as is necessary to end the danger.

The U.S. Supreme Court decision in *Colorado v. Bertine,* 479 U.S. 367, 107 S.Ct. 738, 93 L.Ed.2d 739 (1987), expanded the allowable scope of an inventory search to include the opening of closed containers found within the impounded vehicle and the examination of their contents. Standardized criteria must regulate the opening of containers found during inventory searches to narrow the latitude of individual police officers and prevent the inventory search from becoming a general rummaging to discover incriminating evidence.

> But in forbidding uncanalized discretion to police officers conducting inventory searches, there is no reason to insist that they be conducted in a totally mechanical "all or nothing" fashion. . . . A police officer may be allowed sufficient latitude to determine whether a particular container should or should not be opened in light of the nature of the search and characteristics of the container itself. Thus, while policies of opening all containers or of opening no containers are unquestionably permissible, it would be equally permissible, for example, to allow the opening of closed containers whose contents officers determine they are unable to ascertain from examining the containers' exteriors. The allowance of the exercise of judgment based on concerns related to the purposes of an

inventory search does not violate the Fourth Amendment. *Florida v. Wells*, 495 U.S. 1, 4, 110 S.Ct. 1632, 1635, 109 L.Ed.2d 1, 6–7 (1990).

The importance of following established department guidelines or procedures cannot be overstressed. For example, if department procedures prohibit searching inside of containers, any evidence obtained in that manner will be inadmissible in court. In *United States v. Ramos-Oseguera*, 120 F.3d 1028 (9th Cir. 1997), the court suppressed heroin found in the pockets of a pair of jeans discovered during an inventory search of an automobile. The court said:

> Inventory searches have been held constitutional if they are conducted in accordance with the standard procedures of the agency conducting the search or come under another exception to the Fourth Amendment warrant requirement. . . . These regulations specifically provide for cataloging and/or safekeeping visible property. They do not permit searching the inside of containers. The government argues that the jeans were visible and they might have contained something valuable. The regulations, however, do not provide authority to look inside of things to find valuable items. 120 F.3d at 1036.

In *United States v. Khoury*, 901 F.2d 948 (11th Cir. 1990), the court held that a second examination of a diary found in a briefcase during an inventory of the defendant's impounded car was an illegal search. The officer's initial examination consisted of flipping through a notebook to look for items of value. He determined that it was a diary but not that it had evidentiary value. Subsequently, he further examined the notebook and decided that it did have evidentiary value. The court said:

> [Agent] Simpkins' initial inspection of the notebook was necessary and proper to ensure that there was nothing of value hidden between the pages of the notebook. Having satisfied himself that the notebook contained no discrete items of value and having decided that the diary entries themselves would have intrinsic value to [the defendant], Simpkins had satisfied the requisites of the inventory search and had no purpose other than investigation in further inspecting the notebook. Such a warrantless investigatory search may not be conducted under the guise of an inventory. 901 F.2d at 959.

Note that, if the inventory of a vehicle is not completed, a court may consider it a mere subterfuge for an exploratory search and invalidate it. In *Bowen v. State*, 606 P.2d 589 (Okl.Cr. 1980), a so-called inventory of a vehicle by police was discontinued when a shotgun was found. The court said, "While the rationale for such procedures is to protect property from being stolen and to prevent false charges of theft against police officers, the search here was obviously not conducted for that purpose, since the spare tire, jack, battery, a blanket and other items in the trunk were not inventoried after the shotgun was removed." 606 P.2d at 592.

TIME   A vehicle inventory should be conducted as soon as possible after the impoundment, taking into consideration the police agency's personnel resources, facilities, workload, and other circumstances. An unreasonably delayed inventory indicates that police were not really concerned about safeguarding the owner's property or protecting themselves against claims or from danger but were primarily interested in looking for evidence.

> [T]he Fourth Amendment requires that, without a demonstrable justification based upon exigent circumstances other than the mere nature of automobiles, the inventory be conducted either contemporaneously with the impoundment or as soon thereafter as would be safe, practical, *and* satisfactory in light of the objectives for which this exception to the Fourth Amendment warrant requirement was created. In other words, to be

valid, there must be a sufficient temporal proximity between the impoundment and the inventory. When the inventory must be postponed, each passing moment detracts from the full effectuation of the objectives of the inventory, and indeed, disserves those objectives; at some point, the passage of time requires, to uphold the validity of the inventory, proof of some immediate and exigent circumstances (other than the mere nature of automobiles) the attention to which is more important than protecting the arrestee's property and protecting the police from false claims or danger associated with that property. *Ex parte Boyd*, 542 So.2d 1276, 1279 (Ala. 1989).

PLAIN VIEW DOCTRINE   Although an officer may not look for evidence of crime while conducting a bona fide inventory, if contraband or other items subject to seizure are observed open to view, those items may lawfully be seized and are admissible in evidence. Under the **plain view doctrine,** an officer lawfully conducting an inventory of a vehicle is in a position in which he or she has a legal right to be as the result of a prior valid intrusion. (See Chapter 10.) In both the *Opperman* and *Bertine* cases, officers discovered drugs in plain view while lawfully conducting inventories of impounded vehicles.

Exhibit 11.1 shows a comparison of a *Carroll* doctrine search and an inventory search.

Key Points

8. Police may impound motor vehicles when they impede traffic or threaten public safety and convenience, or when their drivers or owners are taken into custody or are incapacitated.

9. Police may inventory the contents of lawfully impounded vehicles according to standardized procedures to protect the owner's property; to protect the police against claims over lost, stolen, or vandalized property; and to protect the police from potential danger.

10. The allowable scope of an inventory search of an impounded vehicle extends to accessible areas of the vehicle in which the owner's or occupant's personal belongings might be vulnerable to theft or damage. It may include opening closed containers found within the vehicle and examining their contents.

11. Although an officer may not look for evidence of crime while conducting a bona fide inventory, if contraband or other items subject to seizure are observed open to view, those items may lawfully be seized under the plain view doctrine.

Expectation of Privacy

In recent years, courts have begun to analyze warrantless searches and seizures of vehicles to determine whether they intrude upon a person's reasonable expectation of privacy. In *Cardwell v. Lewis*, 417 U.S. 583, 94 S.Ct. 2464, 41 L.Ed.2d 325 (1974), the U.S. Supreme Court held that when probable cause exists, a warrantless examination of a car's exterior is not unreasonable under the Fourth and Fourteenth Amendments.

One has a lesser expectation of privacy in a motor vehicle because its function is transportation and it seldom serves as one's residence or as the repository of personal effects. A car has little capacity for escaping public scrutiny. It travels public thoroughfares where both its occupants and its contents are in plain view. . . . This is not to say that no part of the interior of an automobile has Fourth Amendment protection; the exercise of a desire to be mobile does not, of course, waive one's right to be free of unreasonable governmental intrusion. But insofar as Fourth Amendment protection extends to a motor

	SEARCH UNDER *CARROLL* DOCTRINE	INVENTORY SEARCH
Justification	Probable cause to search vehicle combined with exigent circumstances. (Exigent circumstances requirement is satisfied if vehicle is readily mobile.)	Impoundment of vehicle by police.
Purpose	To obtain evidence of crime	To protect the owner's property while it remains in police custody; to protect the police against claims or disputes over lost, stolen, or vandalized property; and to protect the police from potential danger.
Scope of search of entire vehicle	If there is probable cause to search the entire vehicle, the search may extend to every part of the vehicle and its contents that may conceal the object of the search, including the opening of containers. If there is probable cause to search only a container in the vehicle, then only the container and not the entire vehicle may be searched.	If standard departmental procedures are followed, inventory may extend to all areas of the vehicle in which the owner's or occupant's personal belongings might be vulnerable to theft or damage.
Scope of search of containers found in vehicle	If there is probable cause to search the entire vehicle, a container that may contain the object of the search may be searched. If there is probable cause to search only a container in a vehicle, then only the container may be searched.	If standard departmental procedures are followed, the inventory may include the opening of closed containers found within the vehicle and the examination of their contents.
Time	Search should be conducted without unreasonable delay, but vehicle may be removed to another location for the search, and searches up to three days later have been upheld.	Inventory should be conducted as soon as possible after the impoundment of the vehicle, taking into consideration the police agency's human resources, facilities, workload, and other circumstances, such as an emergency requiring the inventory to be delayed.
Plain view doctrine	If items subject to seizure other than the object of the search are observed open to view during a search under the *Carroll* doctrine, the items may be lawfully seized and are admissible in evidence. (The requirements of the plain view doctrine must be satisfied.)	If items subject to seizure are observed open to view during a bona fide inventory, the items may be lawfully seized and are admissible in evidence. (The requirements of the plain view doctrine must be satisfied.)

Comparison of a *Carroll* doctrine Search and an Inventory Search
■ EXHIBIT 11.1

vehicle, it is the right to privacy that is the touchstone of our inquiry. 417 U.S. at 590–91, 94 S.Ct. at 2469–70, 41 L.Ed.2d at 335.

In *South Dakota v. Opperman*, 428 U.S. 364, 96 S.Ct. 3092, 49 L.Ed.2d 1000 (1976), the Court approved the warrantless inventory of an automobile impounded for parking violations. The Court said:

> Besides the element of mobility, less rigorous warrant requirements govern because the expectation of privacy with respect to one's automobile is significantly less than that relating to one's home or office. In discharging their varied responsibilities for ensuring the public safety, law enforcement officials are necessarily brought into frequent contact with automobiles. Most of this contact is distinctly noncriminal in nature. . . . Automobiles, unlike homes, are subjected to pervasive and continuing governmental regulation and controls, including periodic inspection and licensing requirements. As an everyday occurrence, police stop and examine vehicles when license plates or inspection stickers have expired, or if other violations, such as exhaust fumes or excessive noise, are noted, or if headlights or other safety equipment are not in proper working order. 428 U.S. at 367–68, 96 S.Ct. at 3096, 49 L.Ed.2d at 1004.

Furthermore, a person does not have a greater expectation of privacy in a vehicle merely because the vehicle is capable of functioning as a home.

> In our increasingly mobile society, many vehicles used for transportation can be and are being used not only for transportation, but for shelter, i.e., as a "home" or "residence." To distinguish between respondent's motor home and an ordinary sedan for purposes of the vehicle exception would require that we apply the exception depending upon the size of the vehicle and the quality of its appointments. Moreover, to fail to apply the exception to vehicles such as a motor home ignores the fact that a motor home lends itself easily to use as an instrument of illicit drug traffic and other illegal activity. . . . We decline . . . to distinguish between "worthy" and "unworthy" vehicles which are either on the public roads and highways, or situated such that it is reasonable to conclude that the vehicle is not being used as a residence. *California v. Carney*, 471 U.S. 386, 393–94, 105 S.Ct. 2066, 2070, 85 L.Ed.2d 406, 414–15 (1985).

The quoted passages indicate that the courts are imposing fewer restrictions on law enforcement officers with regard to warrantless searches of vehicles. Nevertheless, even though the reasonable expectation of privacy in a vehicle is less than that in a home or office, law enforcement officers must not violate that expectation when conducting searches or inventories of vehicles. For example, the U.S. Supreme Court has stated that "a search, even of an automobile, is a substantial invasion of privacy. To protect that privacy from official arbitrariness, the Court always has regarded probable cause as the minimum requirement for a lawful search." *United States v. Ortiz*, 422 U.S. 891, 896, 95 S.Ct. 2585, 2588, 45 L.Ed.2d 623, 629 (1975).

United States v. Ortiz
laws.findlaw.com/us/422/891.html

Electronic Beepers

A **beeper** is a radio transmitter, usually battery operated, that emits periodic signals that can be picked up by a radio receiver. A beeper neither records nor transmits any sounds other than its signal, but the signal can be monitored by directional finders, enabling law enforcement officers to determine the beeper's location. The U.S. Supreme Court dealt with the Fourth Amendment implications of the use of beepers for the first time in *United States v. Knotts*, 460 U.S. 276, 103 S.Ct. 1081, 75 L.Ed.2d

United States v. Knotts
laws.findlaw.com/us/460/276.html

55 (1983). With the consent of a chemical company, officers installed a beeper in a five-gallon container of chloroform, a substance used to manufacture illicit drugs. One of the defendants purchased the container of chloroform and transported it by automobile to a codefendant's secluded cabin in another state. Law enforcement officers monitored the progress of the automobile carrying the chloroform all the way to its destination. After three days of visual surveillance of the cabin, officers obtained a search warrant, searched the cabin, and found evidence of the illegal manufacture of drugs.

The Court held that the warrantless monitoring of the beeper by law enforcement officers to trace the location of the chloroform container did not violate the defendant's legitimate expectation of privacy:

> The governmental surveillance conducted by means of the beeper in this case amounted principally to the following of an automobile on public streets and highways. . . . A person travelling in an automobile on public thoroughfares has no reasonable expectation of privacy in his movements from one place to another. When [the codefendant] travelled over the public streets he voluntarily conveyed to anyone who wanted to look the fact that he was travelling over particular roads in a particular direction, the fact of whatever stops he made, and the fact of his final destination when he exited from public roads onto private property. 460 U.S. at 281, 103 S.Ct. at 1085, 75 L.Ed.2d at 62.

Although the owner of the cabin and surrounding premises undoubtedly had a justifiable expectation of privacy within the cabin, the expectation did not extend to the visual observation of his codefendant's automobile arriving on his premises after leaving a public highway or to movements of objects such as the container of chloroform outside the cabin. That the officers relied not only on visual surveillance but also on the use of the beeper to locate the automobile did not alter the situation. "Nothing in the Fourth Amendment prohibited the police from augmenting the sensory faculties bestowed upon them at birth with such enhancement as science and technology afforded them in this case." 460 U.S. at 282, 103 S.Ct. at 1086, 75 L.Ed.2d at 63.

The Court emphasized the limited use the officers made of the signals from the beeper. There was no indication that the beeper signal was received or relied on after it had indicated that the chloroform container had ended its automotive journey at the defendant's camp. Moreover, there was no indication that the beeper was used in any way to reveal information as to the container's movement within the cabin or in any way that would not have been visible to the naked eye from outside the cabin.

The U.S. Supreme Court case of *United States v. Karo*, 468 U.S. 705, 104 S.Ct. 3296, 82 L.Ed.2d 530 (1984), addressed the question of whether the monitoring of a beeper in a private residence, a location not open to visual surveillance, violates the Fourth Amendment rights of those who have a justifiable interest in the privacy of the residence. In that case, government agents installed a beeper in a container of chemicals with the consent of the original owner, who sold the container to the defendant. The agents saw the defendant pick up the container from the owner, followed the defendant to his house, and determined that the container was inside the house where it was monitored. The Court found that the government's warrantless surreptitious use of an electronic device to obtain information it could not have obtained by observation from outside the curtilage of a house was the same, for purposes of the Fourth Amendment, as a law enforcement officer's warrantless surreptitious entry of the house to verify that the beeper was in the house. Even though the monitoring of a beeper inside a private residence is less intrusive than a full-scale search, it is illegal unless conducted under authority of a warrant. The Court said:

United States v. Karo
laws.findlaw.com/us/468/705.html

Requiring a warrant will have the salutary effect of ensuring that use of beepers is not abused, by imposing upon agents the requirement that they demonstrate in advance their justification for the desired search. This is not to say that there are no exceptions to the warrant rule, because if truly exigent circumstances exist no warrant is required under general Fourth Amendment principles. 468 U.S. at 717–18, 104 S.Ct. at 3305, 82 L.Ed.2d at 543.

Therefore, the warrantless monitoring of a beeper is permissible only if the beeper or its container could have been observed from outside the curtilage of a house, or if there is an emergency. Otherwise, the monitoring of a beeper located in a place not open to visual surveillance is illegal without a warrant.

Although the *monitoring* of the beeper was held illegal in the *Karo* case, the Court held that the warrantless *installation* of a beeper in a manner that does not violate reasonable expectations of privacy is generally permissible. "It is the exploitation of technological advances that implicates the Fourth Amendment, not their mere existence." 468 U.S. at 712, 104 S.Ct. at 3302, 82 L.Ed.2d at 539–40. Furthermore, in *United States v. Jones,* 31 F.3d 1304 (4th Cir. 1994), the court held that "the Fourth Amendment does not prohibit the placing of beepers in contraband and stolen goods because the possessors of such articles have no legitimate expectation of privacy in substances which they have no right to possess at all." 31 F.3d at 1311.

Searches by Dogs

In *United States v. Solis,* 536 F.2d 880 (9th Cir. 1976), the court held that the use of specially trained dogs to detect the smell of marijuana in a vehicle did not violate the reasonable expectation of privacy of the vehicle's owner. In that case, a drug agent suspected that marijuana was hidden in the floor of a certain semitrailer parked at the rear of a gas station. The agent went to the gas station and found the semitrailer with what appeared to be white talcum powder on its doors. The officer knew from his training and experience that marijuana was often smuggled in semitrailer floors and that talcum powder was often used to conceal marijuana's odor. The agent notified the customs office, which sent two customs officers with specially trained marijuana-sniffing dogs. The dogs, which were determined to be extremely reliable, reacted positively to marijuana in the semitrailer. A search warrant was obtained, and the marijuana was seized.

The court held that the use of the dogs to help the officers establish probable cause to search was reasonable and did not violate the defendant's reasonable expectation of privacy. The court said:

> The dogs' intrusion such as it was into the air space open to the public in the vicinity of the trailer appears to us reasonably tolerable in our society. There was no invasion of the "curtilage"—the trailer. No sophisticated mechanical or electronic devices were used. The investigation was not indiscriminate, but solely directed to the particular contraband. There was an expectation that the odor would emanate from the trailer. Efforts made to mask it were visible. The method used by the officers was inoffensive. There was no embarrassment to or search of the person. The target was a physical fact indicative of possible crime, not protected communications. We hold that the use of the dogs was not unreasonable under the circumstances and therefore was not a prohibited search under the fourth amendment. 536 F.2d at 882–83.

In *United States v. Stone,* 866 F.2d 359 (10th Cir. 1989), the court held that police use of a trained dog to sniff an automobile detained on reasonable suspicion that it

www.k9fleck.org/nlu06.htm
Outline and summary of vehicle
search cases involving dog sniffs

contained narcotics was not a search. The court analogized the situation to the detention of luggage at airports.

> Upon reasonable suspicion, police may temporarily detain luggage at an airport. Under such circumstances, police use of a narcotics dog to sniff the luggage is not a search. . . . Likewise, we think police may employ a narcotics dog to sniff an automobile which they have stopped upon reasonable suspicion to believe it contains narcotics. Under these circumstances, police use of a narcotics dog is not a search requiring a search warrant or probable cause. 866 F.2d 363.

However, the sniffing of *persons* by dogs may constitute a search protected by the Fourth Amendment.

> "[S]ociety recognizes the interest in the integrity of one's person, and the fourth amendment applies with its fullest vigor against any intrusion on the human body. . . . [W]e hold that sniffing by dogs on the students' persons . . . [i.e., sniffing around each child, putting his nose on the child and scratching and manifesting other signs of excitement in the case of an alert] . . . is a search within the purview of the fourth amendment." *Horton v. Goose Creek Indep. School Dist.*, 690 F.2d 470, 478–479 (5th Cir. 1982).

Note that the *Horton* case also held that dogs' sniffing of student lockers in public hallways and automobiles parked in public parking lots did *not* constitute a search.

Courts disagree over the search and seizure implications of the use of drug-detecting dogs. The safest procedure for law enforcement officers is to make sure drug-detecting dogs are reliable and to obtain a warrant before conducting a search based on a dog's reactions.

Key Points

12. The reasonable expectation of privacy in a motor vehicle is less than that in a home or office because it travels public thoroughfares where its occupants and contents are open to view, it seldom serves as a residence or permanent place for personal effects, and it is subject to pervasive and continuing governmental regulation and controls.

13. The warrantless monitoring of a beeper in a motor vehicle to trace the movement of the vehicle over public thoroughfares does not violate the reasonable expectation of privacy of the occupant of the vehicle.

14. The use of specially trained dogs to detect the smell of drugs in a vehicle does not violate the reasonable expectation of privacy of the vehicle's owner.

Summary

Although the search and seizure of motor vehicles are generally governed by the warrant requirement of the Fourth Amendment, courts have created certain exceptions to the warrant requirement for motor vehicles, based on the differences between a motor vehicle and fixed premises. A motor vehicle is mobile and is used to transport criminals, weapons, and fruits and instrumentalities of crime. It seldom serves as a residence or a permanent repository of personal effects. Furthermore, a person has a reduced expectation of privacy in a motor vehicle because the vehicle travels public thoroughfares where its occupants and contents are open to view, and because the vehicle is subject to extensive governmental regulation, including periodic inspection and licensing.

The most important exception to the warrant requirement is the so-called automobile exception as embodied in the *Carroll* doctrine. Under the *Carroll* doctrine, law enforcement officers may conduct a warrantless search of a motor vehicle if they have probable cause to believe that the vehicle contains items subject to seizure and if exigent circumstances make obtaining a warrant impracticable. If the vehicle is readily mobile, the exigent circumstances requirement is automatically satisfied and the police need not provide supporting facts and circumstances to establish the existence of exigent circumstances. A search under the *Carroll* doctrine need not be conducted immediately, but may be delayed for a reasonable time and may be performed even after the vehicle has been impounded and is in police custody. The scope of the search is defined by the object of the search and the places in which there is probable cause to believe the object may be found. If officers have probable cause to believe that a particular seizable item is located somewhere in a vehicle that is readily mobile, they may search the vehicle as if they had a search warrant for the item. This means they have the right to open and search closed, opaque containers, located inside the vehicle, in which the seizable item might be contained. Furthermore, officers with probable cause to search a vehicle may inspect passengers' belongings found in the vehicle that are capable of concealing the object of the search. If, however, police do not have probable cause to search the entire vehicle but only probable cause to search a particular container inside the vehicle, they may search only that container but not the entire vehicle.

Warrantless searches of movable, closed, opaque containers *unassociated with a vehicle* are not allowed under the rationale of the *Carroll* doctrine, even if there is probable cause to believe they contain items subject to seizure. Closed, opaque containers may only be searched under authority of a warrant or some other exception to the warrant requirement. For example, if a closed, opaque container is seized incident to the arrest of an occupant of a motor vehicle, the search and seizure of the contents of the container are governed by the case of *New York v. Belton* (discussed in Chapter 8).

Motor vehicles may be removed from the highways and streets and impounded in the interests of public safety and as part of a law enforcement agency's community caretaking function. An inventory search of an impounded vehicle may be conducted without a warrant. This procedure is not considered to be a search for Fourth Amendment purposes, but merely an administrative procedure. The officer making the inventory may not do so with the purpose of looking for incriminating evidence, but may be concerned only with protecting the owner's property, protecting the police against claims or disputes over lost or stolen property, and protecting the police from potential danger. The inventory of a vehicle must be limited in scope and intensity by the purposes for which it is allowed and must conform to standard police procedures. Nevertheless, evidence of crime found in plain view during the inventory may be seized and will be admissible in court.

Although courts are in disagreement, they generally approve the tracing of the location of a motor vehicle on public thoroughfares by means of an electronic beeper, and the detection of drugs in a motor vehicle by means of sniffing by specially trained dogs. Both these limited types of intrusion are allowed because of the reduced expectation of privacy in motor vehicles.

Key Holdings from Major Cases

Carroll v. United States (1925). "[I]f the search and seizure without a warrant are made upon probable cause, that is, upon a belief, reasonably arising out of circumstances known to the seizing officer, that an automobile or other vehicle contains that which by law is subject to seizure and destruction, the search and seizure are valid." 267 U.S. 132, 149, 45 S.Ct. 280, 283, 69 L.Ed.2d 543, 549.

Chambers v. Maroney (1970). "*Carroll* . . . holds a search warrant unnecessary where there is probable cause to search an automobile stopped on the highway; the car is movable, the occupants are alerted, and the car's contents may never be found again if a warrant must be obtained. Hence an immediate search is constitutionally permissible.

"Arguably, because of the preference for a magistrate's judgment, only the immobilization of the car should be permitted until a search warrant is obtained; arguably, only the 'lesser' intrusion is permissible until the magistrate authorizes the 'greater.' But which is the 'greater' and which the 'lesser' intru-sion is itself a debatable question and the answer may depend on a variety of circumstances. For constitutional purposes, we see no difference between on the one hand seizing and holding a car before presenting the probable cause issue to a magistrate and on the other hand carrying out an immediate search without a warrant. Given probable cause to search either course is reasonable under the Fourth Amendment." 399 U.S. 42, 51–52, 90 S.Ct. 1975, 1981, 26 L.Ed.2d 419, 428–29.

Michigan v. Thomas (1982). "In *Chambers v. Maroney* . . . we held that when police officers have probable cause to believe there is contraband inside an automobile that has been stopped on the road, the officers may conduct a warrantless search of the vehicle, even after it has been impounded and is in police custody. . . . It is thus clear that the justification to conduct such a warrantless search does not vanish once the car has been immobilized; nor does it depend upon a reviewing court's assessment of the likelihood in each particular case that the car would have been driven away, or that its contents would have been tampered with, during the period required for the police to obtain a warrant." 458 U.S. 259, 261, 102 S.Ct. 3079, 3081, 73 L.Ed.2d 750, 753.

Pennsylvania v. Labron (1996). "If a car is readily mobile and probable cause exists to believe it contains contraband, the Fourth Amendment . . . permits police to search the vehicle without more." 518 U.S. 938, 940, 116 S.Ct. 2485, 2487, 135 L.Ed.2d 1031, 1036.

California v. Carney (1985). A search of a vehicle (motor home) is justified under the *Carroll* doctrine if the vehicle "is being used on the highways, or if it is readily capable of such use and is found stationary in a place not regularly used for residential purposes—temporary or otherwise." 471 U.S. 386, 392, 105 S.Ct. 2066, 2070, 85 L.Ed.2d 406, 414.

Coolidge v. New Hampshire (1971). There were no exigent circumstances under the *Carroll* doctrine when there was "no alerted criminal bent on flight, no fleeting opportunity on an open highway after a hazardous chase, no contraband or stolen goods or weapons, no confederates waiting to move the evidence, not even the inconvenience of a special police detail to guard the immobilized automobile. In short, by no possible stretch of the legal imagination can this be made into a case where 'it is not practicable to secure a warrant,' . . . and the 'automobile exception,' despite its label, is simply irrelevant." 403 U.S. 443, 462, 91 S.Ct. 2022, 2035–36, 29 L.Ed.2d 564, 580.

United States v. Ross (1982). "[T]he scope of the warrantless search authorized by [the *Carroll*] exception is no broader and no narrower than a magistrate could legitimately authorize by warrant. If probable cause justifies the search of a lawfully stopped vehicle, it justifies the search of every part of the vehicle and its contents that may conceal the object of the search." 456 U.S. 798, 825, 102 S.Ct. 2157, 2172, 72 L.Ed.2d 572, 594.

United States v. Johns (1985). "*Ross* authorizes a warrantless search of packages several days after they were removed from vehicles that police officers had probable cause to believe contained contraband." 469 U.S. 478, 479, 105 S.Ct. 881, 883, 83 L.Ed.2d 890, 893–94.

United States v. Di Re (1948). Officers may not conduct body searches of the occupants of a vehicle under the *Carroll* doctrine. 332 U.S. 581, 68 S.Ct. 222, 92 L.Ed. 210.

Wyoming v. Houghton (1999). "[P]olice officers with probable cause to search a car may inspect passengers' belongings found in the car that are capable of concealing the object of the search." 526 U.S. 295, 307 119 S.Ct. 1297, 1304, 143 L.Ed.2d 408, 419.

California v. Acevedo (1991). "In the case before us, the police had probable cause to believe that the paper bag in the automobile's trunk contained marijuana. That probable cause now allows a warrantless search of the paper bag. The facts in the record reveal that the police did not have probable cause to believe that contraband was hidden in any other part of the

automobile and a search of the entire vehicle would have been without probable cause and unreasonable under the Fourth Amendment." 500 U.S. 565, 580, 111 S.Ct. 1982, 1991, 114 L.Ed.2d 619, 634.

United States v. Chadwick (1977). "The factors which diminish the privacy aspects of an automobile do not apply to respondents' footlocker. Luggage contents are not open to public view, except as a condition to a border entry or common carrier travel; nor is luggage subject to regular inspections and official scrutiny on a continuing basis. Unlike an automobile, whose primary function is transportation, luggage is intended as a repository of personal effects. In sum, a person's expectations of privacy in personal luggage are substantially greater than in an automobile." 433 U.S. 1, 13, 97 S.Ct. 2476, 2484, 53 L.Ed.2d 538, 549.

Illinois v. Lafayette (1983). "The reasonableness of any particular governmental activity does not necessarily or invariably turn on the existence of alternative 'less intrusive' means." 462 U.S. 640, 647, 103 S.Ct. 2605, 2610, 77 L.Ed.2d 65, 72.

South Dakota v. Opperman (1976). "The authority of police to seize and remove from the streets vehicles impeding traffic or threatening public safety and convenience is beyond challenge.

"When vehicles are impounded, local police departments generally follow a routine practice of securing and inventorying the automobiles' contents. These procedures developed in response to three distinct needs: the protection of the owner's property while it remains in police custody, . . . the protection of the police against claims or disputes over lost or stolen property, . . . and the protection of the police from potential danger, ... The practice has been viewed as essential to respond to incidents of theft or vandalism. . . . In addition, police frequently attempt to determine whether a vehicle has been stolen and thereafter abandoned." 428 U.S. 364, 369, 96 S.Ct. 3092, 3096, 49 L.Ed.2d 1000, 1005.

Colorado v. Bertine (1987). "Nothing prohibits the exercise of police discretion to impound a vehicle rather than to park and lock it in a safe place, for instance, so long as that discretion is exercised according to standard criteria and on the basis of something other than suspicion of evidence of criminal activity." 479 U.S. 367, 375, 107 S.Ct. 738, 743, 93 L.Ed.2d 739, 748.

The allowable scope of an inventory search of an impounded vehicle may include the opening of closed containers found within the vehicle and the examination of their contents. 479 U.S. 367, 107 S.Ct. 738, 93 L.Ed.2d 739.

Florida v. Wells (1990). "A police officer [conducting an inventory search] may be allowed sufficient latitude to determine whether a particular container should or should not be opened in light of the nature of the search and characteristics of the container itself. Thus, while policies of opening all containers or of opening no containers are unquestionably permissible, it would be equally permissible, for example, to allow the opening of closed containers whose contents officers determine they are unable to ascertain from examining the containers' exteriors.

The allowance of the exercise of judgment based on concerns related to the purposes of an inventory search does not violate the Fourth Amendment." 495 U.S. 1, 3, 110 S.Ct. 1632, 1635, 109 L.Ed.2d 1, 6–7.

Cardwell v. Lewis (1974). "One has a lesser expectation of privacy in a motor vehicle because its function is transportation and it seldom serves as one's residence or as the repository of personal effects. A car has little capacity for escaping public scrutiny. It travels public thoroughfares where both its occupants and its contents are in plain view. . . . This is not to say that no part of the interior of an automobile has Fourth Amendment protection; the exercise of a desire to be mobile does not, of course, waive one's right to be free of unreasonable governmental intrusion. But insofar as Fourth Amendment protection extends to a motor vehicle, it is the right to privacy that is the touchstone of our inquiry." 417 U.S. 583, 590–91, 94 S.Ct. 2464, 2469–70, 41 L.Ed.2d 325, 335.

United States v. Knotts (1983). "The governmental surveillance conducted by means of the beeper [located inside the vehicle] in this case amounted principally to the following of an automobile on public streets and highways. . . . A person travelling in an automobile on public thoroughfares has no reasonable expectation of privacy in his movements from one place to another. When [the codefendant] travelled over the public streets he voluntarily conveyed to anyone who wanted to look the fact that he was travelling over particular roads in a particular direction, the fact of whatever stops he made, and the fact of his final destination when he exited from public roads onto private property." 460 U.S. 276, 281, 103 S.Ct. 1081, 1085, 75 L.Ed.2d 55, 62.

United States v. Karo (1984). "Requiring a warrant will have the salutary effect of ensuring that use of beepers is not abused, by imposing upon agents the requirement that they demonstrate in advance their justification for the desired search. This is not to say that there are no exceptions to the warrant rule, because if truly exigent circumstances exist no warrant is required under general Fourth Amendment principles." 468 U.S. 705, 717–18, 104 S.Ct. 3296, 3305, 82 L.Ed.2d 530, 543.

Review and Discussion Questions

1. Are there any situations in which a warrant is required to search a motor vehicle? In reality, isn't the warrant requirement the exception rather than the rule in automobile cases?

2. Do the legal principles in this chapter apply to vehicles such as bicycles, rowboats, motor homes, trains, or airplanes?

3. If a law enforcement officer has probable cause to believe a vehicle contains small concealable items such as drugs, jewels, or rare coins, to what extent can he or she search the vehicle without a warrant under the *Carroll* doctrine? Can the upholstery be ripped open? Can the vehicle be dismantled? Can the tires be taken off to look inside them? Can pillows, radios, clothing, and other potential containers be dismantled or ripped apart?

4. Under the *Carroll* doctrine, an officer with probable cause to search a motor vehicle has the choice to either conduct the search immediately or impound the vehicle and search it later at the station house. What factors should be considered in making this choice?

5. Describe three situations in which there are exigent circumstances and probable cause to search a vehicle that is not readily mobile.

6. If the postal service turns over to the police plastic bags believed to contain illegal drugs, may the police conduct chemical tests on the contents of the bags without a warrant?

7. Assume that a person is arrested for drunken driving late at night while driving alone on a city street. He tells the police that he does not want his car impounded and that a friend will pick up the car some time the next day. He says he will sign a statement absolving the police from any liability for any loss of or damage to the car or its contents. Can the police still impound the car? Should they?

8. Under the *Carroll* doctrine, must the police have probable cause to search the vehicle at the time it is stopped on the highway in order to search it later at the station? Suppose a person is arrested on the highway for drunk driving and is told to accompany officers to the station to post bond. A routine check at the station reveals that the vehicle is stolen. May the officers search it without a warrant?

9. If officers have probable cause to search a vehicle stopped on the highway but no probable cause to arrest the passengers of the vehicle, can they search the passengers also? Are the passengers "containers" under the ruling of the *Ross* case? Does the answer depend on the nature of the evidence for which the officers are looking?

10. Is a warrantless installation of a beeper proper in any of the following circumstances?

    a. Attaching a beeper to the outside of an automobile

    b. Placing a beeper somewhere inside an automobile

    c. Opening a closed package or luggage to install a beeper

    d. Attaching a beeper to the outside of a package or luggage

    e. Placing a beeper with money taken in a bank robbery

Real-Life Fact Situations

1 Nebraska State Patrol Trooper Kyle Johansen was dispatched to the scene of a one-car accident, occurring earlier in the day near Byron, Nebraska, in rural Thayer County, after a passerby reported seeing a weapon in the car. Johansen had visited the accident scene earlier in the day and had a brief conversation with Thayer County Deputy Sheriff Gordon Downing about the accident. At that time, Johansen observed an individual in the back of Downing's car whom Downing identified as the driver of the car in the accident and whom Johansen later learned was Scovill. Johansen talked to Downing a second time about the accident while at the sheriff's station later that same day, but before Johansen was dispatched to the scene on the weapons call.

When Johansen responded to the dispatch, he looked inside and immediately observed a handgun on the front passenger seat. At the time he responded to the call, no one else was present at the accident scene. Johansen testified that he did not remember whether he reached through a broken window to pick up the gun but that he did eventually open the passenger door of the car. Upon closer examination of the gun, Johansen realized it was a BB gun. After making this determination, Johansen continued searching for other weapons and for the registration of the vehicle. He testified that while he had seen the person identified as the driver, he was curious as to who owned the car. Johansen opened the glove box and found the car's registration, which listed Scovill as the owner. He also found a piece of broken mirror and small medical forceps which were burnt on the ends, which Johansen believed were drug paraphernalia.

Johansen then searched the remainder of the car for contraband before turning the focus of his search to the items strewn about the accident scene. Johansen first found a Crown Royal whiskey bag about 30 feet in front of the vehicle, which he picked up and, upon feeling a small box inside, opened the bag and removed the box. He then opened the box and found a small grain scale. Johansen also found a closed six-pack cooler, which he opened. Inside the cooler was a cardboard tube, which Johansen also opened and found short plastic straws which he believed were used for inhaling illegal drugs. Finally, Johansen found a bong, a pipe used for smoking marijuana, in a corn row in the harvested corn field adjacent to the ditch which was "a considerable distance" from the other items that were strewn about.

Johansen collected the paraphernalia and other items strewn about the scene and placed the paraphernalia in his patrol car and the rest of the items in the trunk of Scovill's car. He then called Downing back to the scene to discuss what he had found. Downing informed Johansen that he could probably find Scovill at a truckstop in Hebron, Nebraska. While Downing remained at the scene, Johansen went to the truckstop and found Scovill leaning against an outside wall of the building.

Johansen testified that he, while in uniform, approached Scovill and asked if he was Scovill. After Scovill nodded that he was, he informed Johansen that he was the only occupant in the car at the time of the accident and that the items in the car belonged to him.

Johansen then explained to Scovill that he had found drug paraphernalia at the scene and then asked whether Scovill had any weapons or contraband on his person. Scovill stated that he did not have any weapons. Johansen patted Scovill down nonetheless. Specifically, Johansen testified that he conducted the pat-down search because, based on what Johansen had found at the scene, he believed Scovill "still could have had drugs on him or possibly a weapon." On cross-examination, Johansen admitted he conducted the pat down "basically to search him to see if [he] could find anything else." Johansen also testified that he did not have any reason to believe Scovill was armed and dangerous other than the fact that Johansen did not know him, a possibility that exists with virtually anyone. Johansen was also curious because Scovill only answered that he did not have any weapons and said nothing about whether he had any contraband. Johansen testified that he thought he could not have arrested Scovill at that point because he had only found drug paraphernalia which he knew to be an infraction which would justify only the delivery of a citation in lieu of arrest.

Johansen started with the right front pocket of Scovill's ski jacket and, without manipulation, felt what he believed to be a pipe used for smoking marijuana. He then asked Scovill to remove the item from his pocket, which he did, and Johansen found that it was a marijuana pipe which still had residue inside. Johansen next patted the right front change pocket of Scovill's jeans and felt a small bulge. Johansen manipulated the bulge a little to see if it was soft and then removed it from the pocket. Johansen discovered that the item was a wad of plastic wrap containing some marijuana. There was also a cellophane wrapper containing part of a pill later determined to be alprazolam.

As Johansen continued his pat-down search on the right side of Scovill's coat, he felt a pocket with a small rectangular box inside. Johansen asked Scovill what the box contained, to which Scovill replied, "[S]ome meth." Johansen then removed the box, opened it, and found a razor and a small baggie containing a yellowish white powder, which Johansen believed to be methamphetamine. Johansen testified that he did not arrest Scovill until he completed searching him and that then he placed Scovill under arrest for possession of methamphetamine, possession of marijuana, and possession of drug paraphernalia. Should Scovill's motion to suppress the drugs and paraphernalia be granted? *State v. Scovill*, 608 N.W.2d 623 (Neb.App 2000).

Read the court opinion at:
www.nol.org/home/ncpa/ctopinio/A99-154.htm

2 The facts most favorable to the trial court's judgment reveal that on June 12, 1999, Sergeant John Cox brought his patrol car to a halt directly behind Gibson's van which was stopped at a red traffic light. Thereafter, Sergeant Cox conducted a random computer check of Gibson's license plate which indicated that Gibson had an outstanding warrant for his arrest from Brown County, Indiana. However, Sergeant Cox did not initiate a traffic stop of Gibson's van.

Instead, Sergeant Cox followed Gibson as he drove into the parking lot of a convenience store. As Gibson exited the van and walked toward the convenience store, Sergeant Cox got out of his patrol car, stopped Gibson, and requested his driver's license. After examining the driver's license, Sergeant Cox handcuffed Gibson. Thereafter, Officer Bradley Meyers, who had responded to Sergeant Cox's call for assistance, asked Gibson if he had any weapons or contraband in his van. Gibson informed Officer Meyers that marijuana was located in the center console of his van. Neither Sergeant Cox nor Officer Meyers informed Gibson of his *Miranda* rights prior to Officer Meyer questioning Gibson. A plastic bag containing a green leafy substance later determined to be marijuana was retrieved from Gibson's vehicle.

Consequently, the State charged Gibson with possession of marijuana, a Class A misdemeanor. Thereafter, Gibson filed with the trial court a motion to suppress the statements made by him after his arrest and the marijuana obtained from the warrantless search of his vehicle. Should Gibson's motion to suppress be granted? *Gibson v. State*, 733 N.E.2d 945 (Ind.App. 2000).

Read the court opinion at:
www.ai.org/judiciary/opinions/archive/07310005.mgr.html

3 On August 21, 1997, Officer Alex Hodge pulled over a red Ford Taurus traveling at the rate of 75 mph in a 70 mph zone in Jones County. The driver of the vehicle was the appellant, James B. Millsap, and forty-six kilograms of marijuana were found in the trunk of his car. A trial was held on February 23, 1999, and Millsap was found guilty and sentenced to twenty years in the custody of the Mississippi Department of Corrections with eight years suspended and twelve years to serve.

The State's first witness was Officer Alex Hodge, a trooper for the Mississippi Highway Patrol. Lieutenant Tony Sarrow, a lieutenant with the Harrison County Sheriff's Department, was riding along with Officer Hodge on the day in question. Officer Hodge testified that he pulled Millsap over and asked him for his license and registration. Officer Hodge testified that he became suspicious when he noticed that the vehicle was a Hertz rental and Millsap's name did not appear on the rental contract. He asked Millsap if he had any handguns, contraband or dead bodies in the vehicle. Officer Hodge testified that Millsap's response was "Of course not. My father would kill me if I was involved in anything like that." Then Officer Hodge testified that he asked Millsap, "What are you talking about when you refer to that?" and stated that Millsap's response was "You

know, drugs and stuff." Then Officer Hodge asked if he could search the vehicle, and Millsap stated that he did not want the vehicle searched because the last time it was searched the police had damaged his vehicle. Officer Hodge testified that he took this statement as an indicator that Millsap did not want him searching his trunk. This caused him to get his patrol dog to do an exterior walk around the vehicle, which resulted in the dog making an aggressive alert to the back of the car by scratching on the trunk. The officer explained that at this point he asked Mr. Millsap if there would be any reason the dog would have indicated on the vehicle or if there were any illegal narcotics in the vehicle. He testified that Millsap's response was "Yes" and after asking how much Millsap responded with "A lot." Officer Hodge then asked what he meant by a lot, and Millsap responded with "Well, it should be between 104 and 106 pounds."

Officer Hodge stated that he handcuffed Millsap and the passenger in the car, Alicia Stone, in order to safely search the car. When he opened the trunk he found two duffel bags filled with a "green leafy substance, compressed and wrapped in clear plastic wrap," later determined to be marijuana with a weight of forty-six kilograms or approximately 101 pounds. Officer Hodge arrested Millsap and brought him to the Highway Patrol Office in Hattiesburg. At the station, Officer Don Sumrall advised Millsap of his *Miranda* rights and gave him his rights advisement form. Millsap signed the waiver and explained to the officers that he traveled from Savereville, Tennessee to Houston, Texas to pick up the marijuana.

Millsap testified that he was not speeding on the day in question and that he gave a phone number to the officer to verify that he was driving the rental car with his friend's permission. He stated that he did not want the officer to search the car because he had some personal items in the car and that he never stated anything about the trunk or any drugs. He further testified that he was not allowed to observe the dog sniff the vehicle. He also stated that Officer Hodge never asked him if he had any drugs, guns or weapons in the car. Millsap also testified that during the questioning he asked for a lawyer and the officer replied, "Everybody in jail has a lawyer," but did not provide him with one. Should Millsap's motion to suppress the evidence seized from his vehicle be granted? *Millsap v. State*, 767 So.2d 286 (Miss.App. 2000).

Read the court opinion at:
www.mslawyer.com/mssc/ctapp/20000912/9900540.html

4 Nevada State Trooper Scott Cobel heard a report over his police radio that shots had been fired at the Saddle West Hotel & Casino in Pahrump, Nevada. Trooper Cobel immediately responded to the casino where he was flagged down by a security guard, who gave a license plate number and description of the vehicle in which the shooting suspects had left.

Trooper Cobel proceeded southbound on State Route 160 until he caught up with the vehicle and pulled it over. Cobel drew his weapon and ordered the four occupants of the vehicle to raise their hands. At the time of the stop, appellant was sitting in the back seat of the vehicle, behind the driver. With the assistance of another Trooper, Cobel then conducted a felony traffic stop, wherein he ordered each of the vehicle's occupants at gunpoint to step out of the car, one at a time. As each occupant stepped out of the vehicle, Cobel performed a quick pat-down search, handcuffed the individual, and sat him or her down on the side of the road. Trooper Cobel then searched the vehicle for weapons. Cobel testified that when he searched the vehicle, officer safety was not an issue because the four suspects were temporarily restrained and had been patted down for weapons.

Beneath the driver's seat, Cobel found a Beretta semiautomatic handgun ("Beretta"). The Beretta was located behind a metal bar which adjusts the seat, with the barrel pointed towards the front of the car and the hammer pulled back. Cobel also found marijuana in a black duffel bag. A casino security guard reported seeing appellant outside the casino carrying a black duffel bag. Methamphetamine and a second handgun were also recovered by police, as well as a third handgun which was thrown from the vehicle prior to the stop, but appellant was only convicted on charges related to the Beretta and the marijuana.

Appellant and the other occupants of the vehicle were arrested. Sergeant Steve Huggins of the Nye County Sheriff's Office informed Trooper Cobel that the sheriff's office would be handling the case, including gathering the evidence, and asked Cobel to return the Beretta, marijuana, and other evidence to the vehicle. Cobel placed the evidence back inside the vehicle.

Appellant was charged and tried on three counts of being an ex-felon in possession of a firearm (one count for the Beretta and two counts for the other two handguns) and two counts of possession of a controlled substance (one count for the marijuana in the black duffel bag and one count for methamphetamine found in the car). Prior to trial, appellant filed a motion to suppress the evidence obtained in the warrantless search of the vehicle. Should the motion be granted? *Hughes v. State*, 12 P.3d 948 (Nev. 2000).

Read the court opinion at:
caselaw.findlaw.com/scripts/getcase.pl?court=nv&vol=116NvAdvOpNo105&invol=2

5 Early in the morning on July 19, 1998, two Philadelphia police officers noticed a car with its headlights on behind an abandoned building in Philadelphia. The officers investigated and found Prenice Bolden standing outside his car urinating. The officers asked Bolden for some identification. He reached into his car and removed a driver's license from above the driver's side sun visor.

While the officers checked the validity of Bolden's license they also determined that he was intoxicated. The officers conducted field sobriety tests, which Bolden failed. The officers noticed that Bolden had two containers of beer in the front seat of his car, one of which was open. The officers arrested Bolden for violation of Philadelphia's open container law. Bolden was not arrested for DUI because the officers had not seen him driving his car.

Bolden was arrested. One of the officers sought to secure any valuables that may have been in Bolden's car. The officers testified that this was standard policy for the police department in order to decrease liability for items that could be stolen from an unattended automobile. As the officer reached above the sun visor from which Bolden had removed his license, a clear bag containing what the officer thought was cocaine fell to the floorboard of the car.

After Bolden was taken to the police station, the officers informed him of his *Miranda* rights. He indicated that he understood them. Bolden was then asked where he had purchased the drugs. Bolden identified the street on which he bought the cocaine, as well as the make and color of the automobile of the person from whom he bought it and the amount he paid. Bolden was charged with possession of cocaine.

From his subsequent conviction for possession of the drugs, Bolden appeals asserting that the search of his car that revealed the cocaine was illegal and that he was unable to validly waive his *Miranda* rights because of his intoxicated state. Was the search legal? *Bolden v. State*, 767 So.2d 315 (Miss.App. 2000).

Read the court opinion at:
www.mslawyer.com/mssc/ctapp/20000912/9901297.html

6 Except as specifically noted, the following facts are uncontroverted. At about 11:00 on the morning of May 25, 1997, Stayton Police Officer Jim Krieger received a dispatch that an unidentified informant had called 911 to report that a car was driving erratically near Sublimity. The caller described the car and gave its license plate number, and a records check showed that the car was registered to defendant. Krieger waited for the car, saw it run a stop sign, and then made a traffic stop based on that infraction. Krieger asked defendant, who was driving, for his license, registration, and proof of insurance, and then ran another records check, which confirmed that the car was registered to defendant.

Krieger then returned defendant's documents, issued defendant a citation for failing to obey a traffic control device, ORS 811.265, and told defendant that he was free to leave. After serving the defendant with the citation, Krieger clearly informed him he did not have to remain at the scene of the stop. However, defendant agreed to remain there so officer Krieger could investigate further the citizen's report of the reckless and intoxicated operation of the vehicle. Before pursuing that investigation Krieger returned to his patrol car, turned off his overheads, confirmed with Stayton dispatch that a backup officer would be there in minutes and then recontacted the defendant and his passenger, both of whom had remained seated in the vehicle. In the ensuing discussion, the defendant acknowledged that he had been driving erratically due to mechanical problems. During that conversation, defendant and his passenger remained seated in the car.

As Krieger and defendant spoke, Sergeant Stai of the Marion County Sheriff's Office arrived to provide backup. After Stai arrived, Krieger asked defendant if he would consent to a search of his car, and, when defendant refused, Krieger walked away to confer with a third officer. Meanwhile, Stai, who had been standing on the passenger side of defendant's car, noted that the door lock on the passenger door was completely missing, as if it had been "punched out." Based on his experience investigating stolen vehicles, Stai became curious and suspicious that the car might be stolen: "[T]hat got my suspicions up and my curiosity and concern."

Stai, who was unaware that Krieger had already confirmed defendant's registration, asked defendant for his registration. After defendant complied, Stai then attempted to compare the Vehicle Identification Number (VIN) on the registration with the VIN on the car's dashboard by looking through the windshield, but was unable to see clearly. Stai then "advised the two occupants that I wanted them to step from the vehicle so that I could check the federal trade sticker on the driver's door post, which would be another location for a VIN."

After defendant and his passenger opened their doors and got out, Stai bent down to examine the now-visible VIN sticker on the driver's-side door post. From that vantage point through the open door, Stai saw a stack of credit cards on the center console. Stai's "suspicions were aroused because people don't normally carry credit cards unprotected, or unconcealed I should say." Stai asked defendant and his passenger whether the cards were theirs, and both denied any ownership of them. Stai then seized the cards, which proved to have been stolen during the theft and burglary with which defendant was subsequently charged. In the ensuing search of defendant's car, police found other items, including checks, a baseball autographed by Barry Bonds, and baseball caps, all of which had been stolen, like the credit cards, from the offices of the Salem-Keizer Volcanoes.

Before trial, defendant moved to suppress the items, including the credit cards, found in the car. Should the defendant's motion to suppress be granted? *State v. Finlay*, 12 P.3d 999 (Or.App. 2000).

Read the court opinion at:
www.publications.ojd.state.or.us/A102256.htm

Chapter 12

Open Fields and Abandoned Property

Objectives

■ **Understand how the concepts of "open fields," "curtilage," and "reasonable expectation of privacy" interrelate and their importance to the law of search and seizure.**

■ **Be able to analyze a fact situation involving a description of a place and determine whether the place is located in the open fields or is within the curtilage.**

■ **Know the differences among the open fields doctrine, the plain view doctrine, and observations into the curtilage from a vantage point in the open fields or a public place.**

■ **Know the factors considered by courts in determining whether premises, objects, or vehicles have been abandoned and the significance of abandonment in the law of search and seizure.**

The Fourth Amendment to the U.S. Constitution guarantees "the right of the people to be secure in their persons, *houses*, papers, and effects, against unreasonable *searches* and seizures . . ." (emphasis added). U.S. Const., Amend. 4. The words *houses* and *searches* are italicized because the meaning of open fields depends on court interpretation of the word *houses*, and the meaning of abandoned property depends on court interpretation of the word *searches*. The legal meanings of these terms and their interrelationships are introduced with a summary of *Hester v. United States*, 265 U.S. 57, 44 S.Ct. 445, 68 L.Ed. 898 (1924), which established the concepts of **open fields** and **abandoned property** in the law of search and seizure.

Hester v. United States

In *Hester v. United States,* revenue officers investigating suspected bootlegging went to the house of Hester's father. As they approached, they saw Henderson drive up to the house. The officers concealed themselves and observed Hester come out of the house and hand Henderson a quart bottle. An alarm was given. Hester went to a nearby car and removed a gallon jug, and he and Henderson fled across an open field. One of the officers pursued, firing his pistol. Henderson threw away his bottle, and Hester dropped his jug, which broke, retaining about one quart of its contents. A broken jar, still containing some of its contents, was found outside the house. The officers examined the jug, the jar, and the bottle and determined that they contained illicitly distilled whiskey. The officers had neither a search warrant nor an arrest warrant.

The defendant was convicted of concealing distilled spirits and contended on appeal that the testimony of the two officers was inadmissible because their actions constituted an illegal search and seizure. The U.S. Supreme Court said:

> It is obvious that even if there had been a trespass, the above testimony was not obtained by an illegal search or seizure. The defendant's own acts, and those of his associates, disclosed the jug, the jar and the bottle—and there was no seizure in the sense of the law when the officers examined the contents of each after it had been *abandoned*. . . . The only shadow of a ground for bringing up the case is drawn from the hypothesis that the examination of the vessels took place upon Hester's father's land. As to that, it is enough to say that, apart from the justification, the special protection accorded by the Fourth Amendment to the people in their "persons, houses, papers and effects," is not extended to the *open fields*. The distinction between the latter and the house is as old as the common law. (Emphasis added.) 265 U.S. at 58–59, 44 S.Ct. at 446, 68 L.Ed. at 900.

The remainder of this chapter is devoted to a discussion of the law of search and seizure applied to open fields and abandoned property, as this law has developed since the *Hester* case.

Open Fields

The basic open fields doctrine was stated by the U.S. Supreme Court in the *Hester* case: "[T]he special protection accorded by the Fourth Amendment to the people in their 'persons, houses, papers and effects' is not extended to the open fields." 265 U.S. at 59, 44 S.Ct. at 446, 68 L.Ed. at 900. The open fields doctrine allows law enforcement officers to search for and seize evidence in the open fields without a warrant, probable cause, or any other legal justification. Even if officers trespass on the land of another

Hester v. United States
laws.findlaw.com/us/265/
57.html

while searching the open fields, the evidence they seize will not be inadmissible by reason of trespass. *Oliver v. United States,* 466 U.S. 170, 104 S.Ct. 1735, 80 L.Ed.2d 214 (1984). Furthermore, the officers themselves will not be held liable for trespass in a civil suit if the trespass was required in the performance of their duties. *Giacona v. United States,* 257 F.2d 450 (5th Cir. 1958).

The key issue under the open fields doctrine is the determination of where the area protected by the Fourth Amendment ends and the open fields begin. The answer is found in court decisions interpreting the word *houses* in the Fourth Amendment. This term has been given a very broad meaning by the courts. The Fourth Amendment has been held to protect people in their homes, whether owned, rented, or leased. The term *houses* has also been held to include any quarters in which a person is staying or living, whether permanently or temporarily. Examples of protected living quarters are hotel and motel rooms, apartments, rooming and boarding house rooms, and even hospital rooms.

Furthermore, the protection of the Fourth Amendment extends to places of business. *See v. City of Seattle,* 387 U.S. 541, 87 S.Ct. 1737, 18 L.Ed.2d 943 (1967). The protection extended to places of business is limited, however, to areas or sections that are not open to the public:

> [A] private business whose doors are open to the general public is also to be considered open to entry by the police for any proper purpose not violative of the owner's constitutional rights—e.g., patronizing the place or surveying it to promote law and order or to suppress a breach of the peace. *State v. LaDuca,* 214 A.2d 423, 426 (N.J. Super. 1965).

For convenience, the word *house* is used in the remainder of this chapter to refer to either residential or commercial premises covered by the Fourth Amendment.

Courts have extended the meaning of *houses* under the Fourth Amendment to include the "ground and buildings immediately surrounding a dwelling house." *State v. Sindak,* 774 P.2d 895, 898 (Idaho 1989). This area is commonly known as the **curtilage.** The concept of curtilage is vital to the open fields doctrine because the open fields are considered to be all the space not contained within the curtilage. The following discussion focuses on the facts and circumstances that courts rely on in determining the extent of the curtilage.

Determination of Curtilage

To determine whether property to be searched falls within a house's curtilage, the law enforcement officer must consider "the factors that determine whether an individual reasonably may expect that an area immediately adjacent to the home will remain private." *Oliver v. United States,* 466 U.S. 170, 180, 104 S.Ct. 1735, 1742, 80 L.Ed.2d 214, 225 (1984). The Court described those factors in another case:

> [W]e believe that curtilage questions should be resolved with particular reference to four factors: *the proximity of the area claimed to be curtilage to the home, whether the area is included within an enclosure surrounding the home, the nature of the uses to which the area is put, and the steps taken by the resident to protect the area from observation by people passing by.* (Emphasis added.) *United States v. Dunn,* 480 U.S. 294, 301, 107 S.Ct. 1134, 1139, 94 L.Ed.2d 326, 334–35 (1987).

These factors are not intended to produce a finely tuned formula but rather are useful analytical tools to help determine whether the area in question should be placed under the same Fourth Amendment protection as the home. The Court emphasized that "the

Oliver v. United States
laws.findlaw.com/us/466/
170.html

caselaw.findlaw.com/data/
constitution/amendment04/
04.html#3
Discussion (with annotations) of
open fields.

***For new and updated weblinks,
go to*** www.wadsworth.com/
cj/ferdico0253

See v. City of Seattle
laws.findlaw.com/us/387/
541.html

United States v. Dunn
laws.findlaw.com/us/480/
294.html

primary focus is whether the area in question harbors those intimate activities associated with domestic life and the privacies of the home." 480 U.S. at 301 n.4, 107 S.Ct. at 1139 n.4, 94 L.Ed.2d at 335 n.4. The four factors are discussed here under several headings through an analysis of court decisions on the open fields doctrine.

RESIDENTIAL YARD   The backyard of a house has repeatedly been held to be within the curtilage of a house and thereby protected from a warrantless search under the Fourth Amendment. *United States v. Van Dyke*, 643 F.2d 992 (4th Cir. 1980). For example, in *United States v. Boger*, 755 F.Supp. 333, 338 (E.D.Wash. 1990), the court said:

> [I]t is clear that the area of Mr. Boger's backyard . . . is within the curtilage of the home. The area was enclosed with sight obscuring fences on the east and west, and by the house on the south. An unoccupied field was to the north. The area in question was obviously used by the resident as part of the home. An outside patio was located on the rear of the home and the backyard was in grass and landscaping. Clearly the resident had taken appropriate steps to protect the area from observation on three sides and an unoccupied open field was on the fourth side.

If, however, a residential yard is accessible to the public and the owner takes no steps to protect the area from observation, it may not qualify for Fourth Amendment protection. In *People v. Bradley*, 81 Cal.Rptr. 457, 460 P.2d 129 (Cal. 1969), an officer had received information that the defendant was growing marijuana under a fig tree outside his residence. The officer went to the defendant's residence to investigate. The premises were described by the court as a house that faced the street with a driveway that ran along the east of the house and terminated in a garage at the rear and east of the house. The defendant's residence was attached to the rear of the garage. The fig tree was about twenty feet from the defendant's door. The officer observed marijuana plants growing in a keg near the base of the tree, partially covered by the leaves and limbs of the tree. In finding the seizure of the plants legal, the court said:

> [T]hey were located a scant 20 feet from defendant's door to which presumably delivery men and others came, and the front house, as well as defendant's house, apparently had access to the yard. Under the circumstances it does not appear that defendant exhibited a subjective expectation of privacy as to the plants. Furthermore, any such expectation would have been unreasonable. 81 Cal.Rptr. at 459, 460 P.2d at 131.

Law enforcement officers should treat the residential yard of a house as part of the curtilage unless there are clear indications that the person residing in the house allowed members of the public access to the yard and had no reasonable expectation of privacy in the yard.

FENCES   If the area immediately surrounding a house is enclosed by a fence, the area within the fence is usually defined as the curtilage. In *United States v. Swepston*, 987 F.2d 1510 (10th Cir. 1993), the court found that a chicken shed located a hundred feet from the defendant's house was within the curtilage of the house. The shed and the house were enclosed by a barbed wire fence and *no fence separated the two structures.* In addition, the defendant maintained a path between the house and the shed and visited the shed regularly, neither the house nor the shed could be seen from a public road or adjoining property, and there was no evidence that the shed was not being used for intimate activities of the home. In contrast, in the same case, marijuana gardens located about three hundred feet from the codefendant's house were found to be outside the curtilage.

[A]lthough the gardens were encircled by a barbed wire fence, *they were outside the fence that encircled [the codefendant's] house, and they were separated from [his] house by the chain-link fence. . . .* [T]he area within the barbed wire fence contained numerous chickens and chicken huts and was used primarily for the raising of game chickens. These huts were visible to the . . . officers as they overflew the area, and indicated to them that the area was not being used for intimate activities of the home. Finally, [the codefendant] did little to protect the marijuana gardens from observation by those standing in the open fields surrounding [his] property. (Emphasis added.) 987 F.2d at 1515.

If a piece of land is already outside the curtilage, erecting fences around it or taking other steps to protect privacy in the land will not establish that the expectation of privacy in the land is legitimate and bring the land within the curtilage. In *Oliver v. United States,* to conceal their criminal activities, the defendants planted marijuana on secluded land and erected fences and "No Trespassing" signs around the property. The U.S. Supreme Court said:

[I]t may be that because of such precautions, few members of the public stumbled upon the marijuana crops seized by the police. Neither of these suppositions demonstrates, however, that the expectation of privacy was *legitimate* in the sense required by the Fourth Amendment. The test of legitimacy is not whether the individual chooses to conceal asserted "private" activity. Rather, the correct inquiry is whether the government's intrusion infringes upon the personal and societal values protected by the Fourth Amendment. . . . [W]e find no basis for concluding that a police inspection of open fields accomplishes such an infringement. 466 U.S. at 182–83, 104 S.Ct. at 1743, 80 L.Ed.2d at 227.

Also, whether a fence defines the curtilage may depend on the nature of the fence. In *United States v. Brady,* 734 F.Supp. 923 (E.D.Wash. 1990), the court found that the fence was not sufficient to define the curtilage.

There was no "no trespassing" sign posted on or near the gate. The fence was not a sight-obstructing fence. The fence did not completely enclose the property in that there was a wide gap on either side of the gate which could reasonably be construed to be a pedestrian path. The fence was not of a type which evidenced an intent to exclude strangers. 734 F.Supp. at 928.

DISTANCE FROM THE DWELLING   Some courts use a rule of thumb that the curtilage ends approximately seventy-five feet from the main dwelling. See *United States ex rel. Saiken v. Bensinger,* 546 F.2d 1292 (7th Cir. 1976). Other courts refuse to adopt a *per se* rule in determining the extent of the curtilage but use a totality-of-the-circumstances approach, with the distance from the dwelling as one of many factors to be weighed in making the determination. For example, in *State v. Silva,* 509 A.2d 659 (Me. 1986), the court held that a marijuana patch located roughly 250 feet behind the defendant's house was within the curtilage and was entitled to Fourth Amendment protection. The marijuana patch was within a cultivated lawn extending from the house to a tree-studded bog just beyond the patch; a swath of trees stood between the patch and the house but was not long enough to cut the back lawn completely in half; and the lawn was dotted with fruit trees, fruit bushes, two gardens, a shed, and flowers.

MULTIPLE-OCCUPANCY DWELLINGS   Multiple-occupancy dwellings are treated differently from single-occupancy dwellings for purposes of determining the extent of the curtilage. Most courts hold that the shared areas of multiple-occupancy buildings (such as common corridors, passageways, driveways, and yards) are not entitled to the protection of the Fourth Amendment because tenants do not have a reasonable expectation of privacy with respect to those areas. *United States v. Nohara*, 3 F.3d 1239 (9th Cir. 1993). Nevertheless, there are many different types of multiple-occupancy dwellings, and courts will examine all the facts and circumstances in determining the curtilage. In *Fixel v. Wainwright*, 492 F.2d 480 (5th Cir. 1974), two law enforcement officers who had been informed that narcotics were being sold on the defendant's premises observed the defendant's behavior at his residence in a four-unit apartment building. Over a forty-five-minute period, several people entered the defendant's apartment, and each time the defendant would go into his backyard and remove a shaving kit from beneath some rubbish under a tree. One officer then went into the backyard and seized the shaving kit while the other officer arrested the defendant. Chemical analysis revealed that the shaving kit contained heroin. The government argued that the defendant's backyard was an area common to, or shared with, other tenants and should not be entitled to the protection usually afforded the curtilage of a purely private residence. The court held, however, that the backyard was a protected area and that the seizure and search of the shaving kit were illegal:

> The backyard of Fixel's home was not a common passageway normally used by the building's tenants for gaining access to the apartments. . . . Nor is the backyard an area open as a corridor to salesmen or other businessmen who might approach the tenants in the course of their trade. . . . This apartment was Fixel's home, he lived there and the backyard of the building was completely removed from the street and surrounded by a chain link fence. . . . While the enjoyment of his backyard is not as exclusive as the backyard of a purely private residence, this area is not as public or shared as the corridors, yards or other common areas of a large apartment complex or motel. Contemporary concepts of living such as multi-unit dwellings must not dilute Fixel's right to privacy anymore than is absolutely required. We believe that the backyard area of Fixel's home is sufficiently removed and private in character that he could reasonably expect privacy. 492 F.2d at 484.

In contrast, a parking area adjacent to an apartment complex was held not to be within the curtilage in *United States v. Soliz*, 129 F.3d 499 (9th Cir. 1997).

First (proximity):

> The parking area was adjacent to the residence, although the record does not reveal the distance between the parked cars and the apartment units. . . . Proximity is not determinative as there is no fixed distance at which curtilage begins or ends. . . . Here, the proximity is certainly close enough to support a finding of curtilage, if other factors support such a finding. . . .

Second (enclosure):

> A fence surrounded the entire property. However, it was a chain link fence through which the public could easily see—it was not intended to shield the property from public view. The mere existence of such a fence does not necessarily demonstrate enclosure of curtilage. . . .

Third (use):

> The use factor is helpful in determining whether the parking lot was an area which contained activities associated with the "sanctity of a man's home and the privacies of life." . . . There is no evidence that the parking lot was used for private activities connected with the sanctity of the home. . . . Rather, it was a shared area used by the res-

idents and guests for the mundane, open and notorious activity of parking. This is not the type of area which we have determined in the past to have the requisite expectation of privacy required to bring it within the protections of the Fourth Amendment. . . . We doubt whether, in the absence of evidence of intimate activities, a shared common area in a multi-unit dwelling compound is sufficiently privacy oriented to constitute curtilage. . . .

Fourth (steps taken to prevent observation):

No steps were taken here to prevent outside observation of the parking area. The fence surrounding the property did not prevent people from peering in, the gate was strewn on the ground, and the property could be viewed from both the street and the alley. . . . Additionally, there were no "No Trespassing" signs posted. . . . Unlike the defendant in *Depew* who went to great lengths to ensure his privacy, Soliz took no such steps. See *Depew*, 8 F.3d at 1428 (defendant chose residence because it was in a remote, secluded area not visible from the highway; defendant maintained post office box in town and read his own meter so that no postal worker or meter reader came to his premises).

Analysis of the four factors supports the district court's finding that there was no violation of the curtilage in this case. 129 F.3d at 502–03.

Porches and fire escapes outside a person's apartment or unit in a multiple-occupancy dwelling fall within the curtilage of the apartment or unit.

Unlike public halls or stairs which are public areas used in common by tenants and their guests or others lawfully on the property, a fire escape in a non-fireproof building is required outside of each apartment as a secondary means of egress for the occupants of that apartment. While it is true that in the event of fire others might have occasion to lawfully pass over the fire escape of another, this would be the only time that one might be lawfully on the fire escape of another. *People v. Terrell*, 53 Misc.2d 32, 38–39, 277 N.Y.S.2d 926, 933 (N.Y. 1967).

GARAGES   Garages are usually held to be part of the curtilage, especially if they are near or attached to the dwelling house and used in connection with it. Therefore, in *Commonwealth v. Murphy*, 233 N.E.2d 5 (Mass. 1968), a case in which a garage and a house were surrounded on three sides by a fence and the garage was close to the house, fifty to seventy-five feet from the street, the garage was held to be within the curtilage. A garage not used by its owner in connection with the owner's residence, however, was held to be outside the curtilage. *People v. Swanberg*, 22 A.D.2d 902, 255 N.Y.S.2d 267 (N.Y. 1964). Furthermore, a garage used in connection with a multiunit dwelling was held to be outside the curtilage because it was used in common by many tenants of the dwelling. *People v. Terry*, 77 Cal.Rptr. 460, 454 P.2d 36 (Cal. 1969).

OTHER OUTBUILDINGS   In determining whether an outbuilding is part of the curtilage, courts consider factors such as distance from the dwelling house, presence and location of fences, family use of the building, and attempts to protect the area from observation. In *United States v. Dunn*, 480 U.S. 294, 107 S.Ct. 1134, 94 L.Ed.2d 326 (1987), a barn located fifty yards from a fence surrounding a house and sixty yards from the house itself was held to be outside the curtilage. The U.S. Supreme Court found that the owner had done little to protect the barn area from observation by those standing in the open fields. The Court also found it especially significant that law enforcement officials possessed objective data indicating that the barn was not being used for intimate activities of the home. Rather, they knew that a truck carrying a container of phenylacetic acid was backed up to the barn, a strong odor of the acid emanated from the barn, and the sound of a pumplike motor could be heard from within the barn.

In *United States v. Calabrese*, 825 F.2d 1342 (9th Cir. 1987), the court found that a structure located some fifty feet from a main residence and its two *attached* garages was not within the curtilage. Most significant in the court's determination was law enforcement officials' knowledge, obtained during a previous legal search, that the detached structure was being used to manufacture methamphetamine and not for domestic activities.

In *United States v. Van Damme*, 823 F.Supp. 1552 (D.Mont. 1993), the court held that a greenhouse compound located more than two hundred feet from the defendant's house and surrounded by a twelve-foot stockade fence was not part of the house's curtilage.

> [B]ecause of the isolation of the greenhouse compound from the rest of the property, the lack of nearby buildings or facilities, and the absence of any indicia of activities commonly associated with domestic life, the investigating officers had no reason to deem the greenhouse compound as part of the Defendant's home. Additionally, the citizen informant's report provided the officers with some "objective data indicating that the [compound] was not being used for intimate activities of the home." 823 F.Supp. at 1558.

In contrast, a barn was held to be within the curtilage in a case in which a driveway ran between the house and the barn, tracks of vehicles and footprints were visible in the snow leading to both the house and the barn, and no barriers separated the house and the barn. *Rosencranz v. United States*, 356 F.2d 310 (1st Cir. 1966).

UNOCCUPIED TRACTS   An unoccupied, uncultivated, remote tract of land is almost always held to be outside the curtilage and in the open fields. The U.S. Supreme Court stated that

> the term "open fields" may include any unoccupied or undeveloped area outside of the curtilage. An open field need be neither "open" nor a "field" as those terms are used in common speech. For example . . . a thickly wooded area nonetheless may be an open field as that term is used in construing the Fourth Amendment. *Oliver v. United States*, 466 U.S. 170, 180 n.11, 104 S.Ct. 1735, 1742 n.11, 80 L.Ed.2d 214, 225 n.11 (1984).

In *Maine v. Thornton*, the companion case to *Oliver v. United States*, police officers, after receiving a tip that marijuana was being grown in the woods behind the defendant's residence, entered the woods by a path between the residence and a neighboring house. They followed a path through the woods until they reached two marijuana patches fenced with chicken wire and displaying "No Trespassing" signs. Later, the officers, upon determining that the patches were on the defendant's property, obtained a search warrant and seized the marijuana. The U.S. Supreme Court held that the officers' actions were not an unreasonable search and seizure, because the area was an open field. In another case, the Wisconsin Supreme Court held that the Fourth Amendment did not apply to a local sheriff's warrantless digging in a field about 450 feet from the defendant's house to find the body of the defendant's wife, who had disappeared.

> Under the "open fields" doctrine, the fact that evidence is concealed or hidden is immaterial. The area [the open field] is simply not within the protection of the Fourth Amendment. If the field where the body was found does not have constitutional protection, the fact that the sheriff, rather than observing the evidence that might have been in plain view, dug into the earth to find the body and committed a trespass in so doing does not confer protection. *Conrad v. State*, 218 N.W.2d 252, 257 (Wis. 1974).

A difficult question is presented if the unoccupied area searched is not completely vacant but is being used as a building lot. In *People v. Grundeis,* 108 N.E.2d 483 (Ill. 1952), law enforcement officers received a complaint that lumber, sacks of cement, and a cart had been stolen. Investigation led the officers to suspect the defendant. They went to the defendant's property, where the defendant was laying the foundation for a house, searched the property without a warrant, and found some of the stolen items. The court held that the area searched came within the category of open fields, even though a house was in the process of construction on it:

> If the lot had been left completely untouched, there could be no doubt that it would fall within the ruling of the *Hester* case. That a large quantity of building material has been brought upon the lot and a foundation for a house dug out, or even completely laid, does not change the nature of the place. Not even the broad policy of protection against "invasion of 'the sanctity of a man's home and the privacies of life,'" . . . is infringed by what took place here. Defendant's constitutional rights were not violated. 108 N.E.2d at 487.

Reasonable Expectation of Privacy

In determining the legality of the search in many of the cases discussed previously, courts have considered whether the person owning or inhabiting the premises had a reasonable expectation of privacy in the area searched. In this sense, reasonable expectation of privacy could be considered just another one of the facts and circumstances used to determine the extent of the curtilage. Since the U.S. Supreme Court decision in *Katz v. United States,* 389 U.S. 347, 88 S.Ct. 507,19 L.Ed.2d 576 (1967), however, a person's reasonable expectation of privacy has taken on a whole new meaning and importance in the law of search and seizure.

In the *Katz* case, a landmark opinion involving electronic eavesdropping, the Supreme Court stated that "the Fourth Amendment protects people, not places." 389 U.S. at 351, 88 S.Ct. at 511, 19 L.Ed.2d at 582. A later court decision said that *Katz* "shifts the focus of the Fourth Amendment from 'protected areas' to the individual's expectations of privacy. Whether the government's activity is considered a 'search' depends upon whether the individual's reasonable expectations of privacy are disturbed." *Davis v. United States,* 413 F.2d 1226, 1232 (5th Cir. 1969).

In *Oliver v. United States,* a case involving a police seizure of marijuana from a secluded plot of land surrounded by fences and "No Trespassing" signs, the U.S. Supreme Court stated that "an individual may not legitimately demand privacy for activities conducted out of doors in fields, except in the area immediately surrounding the home." 466 U.S. 170, 178, 104 S.Ct. 1735, 1741, 80 L.Ed.2d 214, 224. The Court went on to say:

> [O]pen fields do not provide the setting for those intimate activities that the [Fourth] Amendment is intended to shelter from government interference or surveillance. There is no societal interest in protecting the privacy of those activities such as the cultivation of crops, that occur in open fields. Moreover, as a practical matter these lands usually are accessible to the public and the police in ways that a home, an office or commercial structure would not be. It is not generally true that fences or "No Trespassing" signs effectively bar the public from viewing open fields in rural areas. And . . . the public and police lawfully may survey lands from the air. For these reasons, the asserted expectation of privacy in open fields is not an expectation that "society recognizes as reasonable." 466 U.S. at 179, 104 S.Ct. at 1741, 80 L.Ed.2d at 224.

www.pegasus.rutgers.edu/ ~record/drafts/flir.html
Article, "Reasonable Expectation of Privacy: Protecting Individual Privacy in the Face of Intrusive Surveillance Technology" by James P. McGovern

www.sjsu.edu/faculty/kpnuger/ Privacyweb/ TechandPrivacy.htm
Article, "New Technology and the Right to Privacy: The Convergence of Surveillance and Information Privacy Concerns" by Thomas B. Kearns

www.sjsu.edu/faculty/kpnuger/ Privacyweb/VideoSurv.htm
Article, "Scowl Because You're on Candid Camera: Privacy and Video Surveillance" by Quentin Burrows

www.fumio.org/research/paper/ lj23/internet3_e.html
Article, "Cyberspace, General Searches, and Digital Contraband: The Fourth Amendment and the Net-Wide Search" by Michael Adler

Katz v. United States
laws.findlaw.com/us/389/ 347.html

www.spatial.maine.edu/tempe/
curry.html
Article, "In Plain and Open
View: Geographic Information
Systems and the Problem of Privacy" by Michael R. Curry

www.co.alameda.ca.us/da/pov/
police_surveillance.htm
Article, "Police Surveillance"
from the District Attorney's
Office in Alameda County,
California

www.co.alameda.ca.us/da/pov/
protect_surveillance.htm
Article, "Protecting Surveillance
Sites" from the District Attorney's Office in Alameda County,
California

Plain View, Open Fields, and Observations into Constitutionally Protected Areas

Law enforcement officers often confuse the open fields and plain view doctrines. The plain view doctrine states that if a law enforcement officer, as the result of a prior valid intrusion, is in a position in which he or she has a legal right to be, items of evidence lying open to view may be seized if their incriminating character is immediately apparent (see Chapter 10). Under the open fields doctrine, an officer need not be concerned with the validity of the prior intrusion into a constitutionally protected area or a person's reasonable expectation of privacy. Open fields are not a constitutionally protected area and do not support a reasonable expectation of privacy. Therefore the officer may not only seize items that are open to view but also may search for items hidden from view and seize them. Of course, all seizures must be based on probable cause that the items are property subject to seizure.

In addition, from a vantage point in the open fields or a public place, an officer may, without a warrant, make observations into constitutionally protected areas. "[A] law enforcement 'officer's observations from a public vantage point where he has a right to be' and from which the activities or objects he observes are 'clearly visible' do not constitute a search within the meaning of the Fourth Amendment." *United States v. Taylor,* 90 F.3d 903, 908 (4th Cir. 1996). These observations may be enhanced by electrical or mechanical means such as flashlights or binoculars. *United States v. Dunn,* 480 U.S. 294, 107 S.Ct. 1134, 94 L.Ed.2d 326 (1987). In *United States v. Taft,* 769 F.Supp. 1295 (D.Vt. 1991), the court found no constitutional violation when police, while standing in the open fields, observed the defendant's cabin from about fifty yards with the aid of binoculars. Information obtained from such observations may be used as a basis for probable cause to arrest or to obtain a search warrant.

Observations into constitutionally protected areas may not, however, violate the reasonable expectation of privacy of the person whose premises or activities are being observed. In *Raettig v. State,* 406 So.2d 1273 (Fla.App. 1981), a person in lawful possession of a camper truck was held to have established a reasonable expectation of privacy by painting over the windows, locking the doors, and refusing access to the police. That expectation was violated when an officer shined a flashlight through a minute crack to observe the contents of the truck. The defendant's failure to seal the crack "could hardly be regarded as an implied invitation to any curious passerby to take a look." 406 P.2d at 1278. Also in *State v. Ward,* 617 P.2d 568, 573 (Hawaii 1980), the court held that

> [t]he Constitution does not require that in all cases a person, in order to protect his privacy, must shut himself off from fresh air, sunlight and scenery. And as a corollary, neither does the Constitution hold that a person, by opening his curtains, thereby opens his person, house, papers and effects to telescopic scrutiny by the government.

Note: After this book had gone to press, the U.S. Supreme Court held in *Kyllo v. United States,* (decided June 11, 2001) that when the government uses a device that is not in general public use (a thermal imaging device), to explore details of a private home (relative amounts of heat) that would previously have been unknowable without physical intrusion, the surveillance is "search" under the Fourth Amendment and is presumptively unreasonable without a warrant.

Read the court opinion at:
laws.findlaw.com/us/000/
99-8508.html

California v. Ciraolo
laws.findlaw.com/us/476/
207.html

In the *Ward* case, the court found that the viewing with binoculars of a crap game in a seventh-story apartment from a vantage point an eighth of a mile away was an illegal search. "[If] the purpose of the telescopic aid is to view that which could not be seen without it, it is a constitutional invasion." 617 P.2d 573.

AERIAL OBSERVATIONS   In *California v. Ciraolo,* 476 U.S. 207, 106 S.Ct. 1809, 90 L.Ed.2d 210 (1986), the U.S. Supreme Court held that the Fourth Amendment was not violated by a warrantless aerial observation from an altitude of a thousand feet of a fenced-in backyard within the curtilage of a home. The Court, relying on *Katz v.*

United States, 389 U.S. 347, 88 S.Ct. 507, 19 L.Ed.2d 576 (1967), analyzed the case by means of a two-part inquiry: First, has the individual manifested a subjective expectation of privacy in the object of the challenged search? Second, is society willing to recognize that expectation as reasonable?

The Court found that the defendant clearly manifested his own subjective intent and desire to maintain privacy by placing a ten-foot fence around his backyard. His expectation of privacy from observation from the air was found not to be reasonable, however.

> That the area is within the curtilage does not itself bar all police observation. The Fourth Amendment protection of the home has never been extended to require law enforcement officers to shield their eyes when passing by a home on public thoroughfares. Nor does the mere fact that an individual has taken measures to restrict some views of his activities preclude an officer's observations from a public vantage point where he has a right to be and which renders the activities clearly visible. 476 U.S. at 213, 106 S.Ct. at 1812, 90 L.Ed.2d at 216.

Because the observations took place from public navigable airspace, from which any member of the public flying in that airspace could have observed everything the officers observed, the defendant's expectation that his backyard was protected from observation was not an expectation that society was prepared to honor.

> In an age where private and commercial flight in the public airways is routine, it is unreasonable for respondent to expect that his marijuana plants were constitutionally protected from being observed with the naked eye from an altitude of 1,000 feet. The Fourth Amendment simply does not require the police traveling in the public airways at this altitude to obtain a warrant in order to observe what is visible to the naked eye. 476 U.S. at 215, 106 S.Ct. at 1813, 90 L.Ed.2d at 218.

Applying the same reasoning, the Supreme Court held that police observation of the defendant's greenhouse from a helicopter flying at four hundred feet did not violate the defendant's reasonable expectation of privacy and was therefore not a search.

> [T]he helicopter in this case was *not* violating the law, and there is nothing in the record or before us to suggest that helicopters flying at 400 feet are sufficiently rare in this country to lend substance to respondent's claim that he reasonably anticipated that his greenhouse would not be subject to observation from that altitude. Neither is there any intimation here that the helicopter interfered with respondent's normal use of the greenhouse or of other parts of the curtilage. As far as this record reveals, no intimate details connected with the use of the home or curtilage were observed, and there was no undue noise, no wind, dust, or threat of injury. In these circumstances, there was no violation of the Fourth Amendment. *Florida v. Riley*, 488 U.S. 445, 451–52, 109 S.Ct. 693, 697, 102 L.Ed.2d 835, 843 (1989).

In *Dow Chemical Co. v. United States*, 476 U.S. 227, 106 S.Ct. 1819, 90 L.Ed.2d 226 (1986), the Court held that the Environmental Protection Agency's aerial photography of a chemical company's 2,000-acre outdoor industrial plant complex from navigable airspace was not a search prohibited by the Fourth Amendment.

> [T]he open areas of an industrial plant complex with numerous plant structures spread over an area of 2,000 acres are not analogous to the "curtilage" of a dwelling for purposes of aerial surveillance; such an industrial complex is more comparable to an open field and as such it is open to the view and observation of persons in aircraft lawfully

www.law.berkeley.edu/
journals/btlj/articles/06_2/
Steele/html/text.html
Article, "The View from on
High: Satellite Remote Sensing
Technology and the Fourth
Amendment" by Lisa J. Steele

www.sjsu.edu/faculty/kpnuger/
Privacyweb/
CrimeTechSympo.htm
Article, "Technologically
Assisted Physical Surveillance:
The American Bar Association's
Tentative Draft Standards" by
Christopher Slobogin

www.sjsu.edu/faculty/kpnuger/
Privacyweb/
HiTechSurv4th%20am.htm
Article, "High-Tech Surveillance
Tools and the Fourth Amendment: Reasonable Expectations
of Privacy in the Technological
Age" by Richard S. Julie

www.hq.nasa.gov/office/oig/hq/
remote4.html
Article, "Remote Sensing and
the Fourth Amendment: A New
Law Enforcement Tool?"

wings.buffalo.edu/law/
Complaw/CompLawPapers/
t.html
Article, "Thermal Surveillance:
Poised at the Intersection of
Technology and the Fourth
Amendment" by David Reed

www.loompanics.com/
Articles/Thermal.htm
Article, "Thermal Imaging:
Much Heat but Little Light" by
Thomas D. Colbridge

Florida v. Riley
laws.findlaw.com/us/488/
445.html

*Dow Chemical Co. v. United
States*
laws.findlaw.com/us/476/
227.html

in the public airspace immediately above or sufficiently near the area for the reach of cameras. 476 U.S. at 239, 106 S.Ct. at 1827, 90 L.Ed.2d at 238.

DRIVEWAYS AND OTHER MEANS OF ACCESS TO DWELLINGS   In *Lorenzana v. Superior Court of Los Angeles County,* 108 Cal.Rptr. 585, 511 P.2d 33 (Cal. 1973), a narcotics officer investigating a tip about heroin dealing went to the place where the dealing was said to be occurring. The place was a single-family dwelling, seventy feet from the sidewalk, with access from the west. There were no doorways or defined pathways on the east side of the house, and a strip of land covered with grass and dirt separated the east side of the house from the driveway of the apartment next door. The officer went to the east side of the house, peeked through a two-inch gap under the partially drawn shade of a closed window, and observed indications of criminal activity.

The court held that the officer's observations constituted an illegal search. The court initially analyzed the problem in terms of whether the officer was standing on a part of the property surrounding the house that had been opened, expressly or impliedly, to public use. Under the facts, the officer was found to have made his observations from a position in which he had no right to be. Because neither a warrant nor one of the established exceptions to the warrant requirement justified the intrusion, the intrusion was unlawful.

The court went on to discuss the officer's actions at length, in terms of the defendant's reasonable expectation of privacy:

> [T]he generic *Katz* rule permits the resident of a house to rely justifiably upon the privacy of the surrounding areas as a protection from the peering of the officer unless such residence is "exposed" to that intrusion by the existence of public pathways or other invitations to the public to enter upon the property. This justifiable reliance on the privacy of the property surrounding one's residence thus leads to the *particular* rule that searches conducted without a warrant from such parts of the property *always* are unconstitutional unless an exception to the warrant requirement applies. . . .
>
> Pursuant to the principles of *Katz,* therefore, we do not rest our analysis exclusively upon such abstractions as "trespass" or "constitutionally protected areas" or upon the physical differences between a telephone booth and the land surrounding a residence; we do, however, look to the conduct of people in regard to these elements. Taking into account the nature of the area surrounding a private residence, we ask whether that area has been opened to public use; if so, the occupant cannot claim he expected privacy from all observations of the officer who stands upon that ground; if not, the occupant does deserve that privacy. Since the eavesdropping officer in the case before us stood upon private property and since such property exhibited no invitation to public use, we find that the officer violated petitioner Lorenzana's expectations of privacy, and hence his constitutional rights. 108 Cal.Rptr. at 594, 511 P.2d at 42.

In general, if an officer gathers information while situated in a public place or in a place where an ordinary citizen with legitimate business might be expected to be, the officer will not be invading anyone's reasonable expectation of privacy. Therefore, an officer's observations from an ordinary means of access to a dwelling, such as a front porch or side door, will not ordinarily violate a person's reasonable expectation of privacy. *People v. Willard,* 47 Cal.Rptr. 734 (Cal.App. 1965). Once officers are in a place in which they have a legitimate right to be, they may look around and peer through windows or other openings.

Peering through a window or a crack in the door or a keyhole is not, in the abstract, genteel behavior, but the Fourth Amendment does not protect against all conduct unworthy of a good neighbor. . . . [I]t is the duty of a policeman to investigate, and *we cannot say that . . . the Fourth Amendment itself draws the blinds the occupant could have drawn and did not. People v. Berutko,* 77 Cal.Rptr. 217, 222, 453 P.2d 721, 726 (Cal. 1969).

Furthermore, so long as officers are where they have a right to be, they may listen at doors or gather evidence with their other senses. In *United States v. Perry,* 339 F.Supp. 209, 213 (S.D.Cal. 1972), the court said:

> The general rule is that information obtained by an officer using his natural senses, where the officer has a right to be where he is, is admissible evidence. The fact that the information is in the form of conversations emanating from a private space, such as a hotel room, is not a bar to its admissibility.

> Regardless of which sense an officer is using to detect criminal activity occurring in a constitutionally protected area, the officer does not have authority to enter into the area to make a search or seizure without a warrant. Only a search warrant gives this authority, unless there is an emergency or the situation falls within one of the other recognized exceptions to the search warrant requirement.

> An officer is not entitled to conduct a warrantless entry and seizure of incriminating evidence simply because he has seen the evidence from outside the premises. "Incontrovertible testimony of the senses that an incriminating object is on premises belonging to a criminal suspect may establish the fullest possible measure of probable cause. But even where the object is contraband, this Court has repeatedly stated and enforced the basic rule that the police may not enter and make a warrantless seizure," absent exigent circumstances. *United States v. Wilson,* 36 F.3d 205, 209 n.4 (1st Cir. 1994).

In a case in which both probable cause and exigent circumstances were found, an officer approached the defendant's front door, looked through his picture window adjacent to the door, and observed a large amount of money and what appeared to him to be illegal drugs on the defendant's dining room table. As the officer was looking through the window, someone inside the house quickly closed the blinds. Under these circumstances, the officer "had a reasonable basis for concluding that there was probable cause to believe that criminal activity was in progress in the house and that there was an imminent danger that evidence would be destroyed unless the officers immediately entered the house and took possession of it." *United States v. Taylor,* 90 F.3d 903, 909–10 (4th Cir. 1996).

Key Points

1. Law enforcement officers may search for items of evidence in the open fields without a warrant, probable cause, or any other legal justification and may seize items if they have probable cause to believe that the items are "property subject to seizure" under the law of the officers' jurisdiction.

2. Open fields is all the space that is not contained within the *curtilage* and need be neither "open" nor "fields." The curtilage is the area around the home that harbors those intimate activities associated with domestic life and the privacies of the home.

3. Whether an area falls within the curtilage is determined by considering four factors: the proximity of the area claimed to be curtilage to the home, whether the area is included within an enclosure surrounding the home, the nature of the uses to which the area is put, and the steps taken by the resident to protect the area from observation by people passing by.

4. Generally, if the area surrounding a house is enclosed by a fence, the area within the fence is defined as the curtilage.

5. Generally, the shared areas of multiple-occupancy buildings are not entitled to Fourth Amendment protection because the public has access to them.

6. Law enforcement officers may make warrantless observations into constitutionally protected areas from a vantage point in the open fields or the air, if the observations do not violate the reasonable expectation of privacy of the person whose premises or activities are being observed.

Abandoned Property

United States v. Jacobsen
laws.findlaw.com/us/466/109.html

The meaning of the term *abandoned property* depends on the interpretation given to the word *searches* in the Fourth Amendment. As defined earlier, a search occurs "when an expectation of privacy that society is prepared to consider reasonable is infringed." *United States v. Jacobsen,* 466 U.S. 109, 113, 104 S.Ct. 1652, 1656, 80 L.Ed.2d 85, 94 (1984). It follows that no search occurs when a law enforcement officer observes, examines, or inspects property whose owner has "voluntarily discarded, left behind, or otherwise relinquished his interest in the property in question so that he could no longer retain a reasonable expectation of privacy with regard to it. . . ." *United States v. Colbert,* 474 F.2d 174, 176 (5th Cir. 1973). Because there is no search under the Fourth Amendment, officers may lawfully seize abandoned property without a warrant or probable cause and may use it as evidence in court.

The main difference between the abandonment doctrine and the plain view doctrine turns on the nature of the place from which the officer seizes an object. Under the plain view doctrine, if a law enforcement officer, as the result of a prior valid intrusion into a constitutionally protected area or a prior valid invasion of a reasonable expectation of privacy, is in a position in which he or she has a legal right to be, items of evidence lying open to view may be seized. The plain view doctrine is applicable only after the law enforcement officer has made such a lawful intrusion. On the other hand, if a law enforcement officer, acting lawfully, seizes objects that have been discarded on the street, in a public park, or in some other *situation not protected by the Fourth Amendment to the Constitution,* the seizure is legal under the abandonment doctrine. Note that the abandonment doctrine, unlike the plain view doctrine, involves no prior intrusion into a constitutionally protected area or prior invasion of a reasonable expectation of privacy. Law enforcement officers must learn this distinction because, for officers to lawfully seize items that have been discarded within a constitutionally protected area, all elements of the plain view doctrine must be satisfied or any item of evidence seized will be inadmissible in court. When law enforcement officers attempt to justify a seizure of property on the ground that it was abandoned, they must be prepared to prove abandonment.

The remainder of this chapter is devoted to a discussion of specific facts and circumstances bearing on the issue of abandonment, as illustrated by decisions of courts throughout the United States. These facts and circumstances can be classified into three broad categories:

- Indications of intent to abandon property
- Lawfulness of police behavior
- Reasonable expectation of privacy in the property

These categories are not intended to be a rigid classification scheme, but are merely offered as a useful means for organizing the discussion of individual court decisions on abandonment. Abandonment is a subtle and flexible concept and is not susceptible to finely tuned formulas or bright-line rules. Courts, therefore, must consider all the relevant facts and circumstances in determining whether abandonment has occurred in a given case.

Indications of Intent to Abandon Property

An important consideration of courts in determining whether property has been abandoned is the intent of the person vacating or discarding the property to relinquish all title, possession, or claim to that property. "[I]ntent may be inferred from words spoken, acts done, and other objective facts." *United States v. Colbert*, 474 F.2d 174, 176 (5th Cir. 1973). Sometimes intent to abandon is easy to establish, such as when a person voluntarily throws an object away, without any inducement by the police. In many situations, however, a person's intent to abandon property is not so easily established. The following discussion highlights the various indications of intent relied on by the courts in determining abandonment. The discussion is divided into three parts—premises, objects, and motor vehicles—because intent to abandon is determined in different ways for each kind of property.

PREMISES   In *Abel v. United States*, 362 U.S. 217, 80 S.Ct. 683, 4 L.Ed.2d 668 (1960), officers of the Immigration and Naturalization Service arrested the defendant in his hotel room, under an administrative arrest warrant, and charged him with illegally being in the United States. Before he was escorted out of his room, the defendant was permitted to pack his personal belongings. He packed nearly everything in the room except for a few things that he left on a windowsill and that he put in a wastebasket. He then checked out of the hotel, turned in his keys, and paid his bill. Shortly thereafter, an FBI agent, with the permission of the hotel management, searched the defendant's room without a warrant. In the wastebasket, the FBI agent found a hollow pencil containing microfilm and a block of wood containing a "cipher pad." The Court held that the search for and seizure of the pencil and block of wood were legal:

Abel v. United States
laws.findlaw.com/us/362/
217.html

> These two items were found by an agent of the F.B.I. in the course of a search he undertook of petitioner's hotel room, immediately after petitioner had paid his bill and vacated the room. They were found in the room's wastepaper basket, where petitioner had put them while packing his belongings and preparing to leave. No pretense is made that this search by the F.B.I. was for any purpose other than to gather evidence of crime, that is, evidence of petitioner's espionage. As such, however, it was entirely lawful, although undertaken without a warrant. This is so for the reason that at the time of the search petitioner had vacated the room. The hotel then had the exclusive right to its possession, and the hotel management freely gave its consent that the search be made. Nor was it unlawful to seize the entire contents of the wastepaper basket, even though some of its contents had no connection with crime. So far as the record shows, petitioner had abandoned these articles. He had thrown them away. So far as he was concerned, they were bona vacantia. There can be nothing unlawful in the Government's appropriation of such abandoned property. . . . The two items which were eventually introduced in evidence were assertedly means for the commission of espionage, and were themselves seizable as such. These two items having been lawfully seized by the Government in connection with an investigation of crime, we encounter no basis for discussing further their admissibility as evidence. 362 U.S. at 241, 80 S.Ct. at 698, 4 L.Ed.2d at 687–88.

In another case involving a hotel room, a court found that the defendant had abandoned a room he had rented on March 23, when he failed to pay his bill on March 28 and did not return to or communicate with the hotel before his arrest on April 8. At the time he rented the room, the defendant said he intended to stay only one night. A search of the defendant's baggage left in the room was therefore held not to violate his property rights. *United States v. Cowan,* 396 F.2d 83 (2d Cir. 1968). In *State v. Oken,* 569 A.2d 1218 (Me. 1990), the Maine Supreme Judicial Court found that, at 8:30 A.M. on November 17, when the police searched room 48 of the Coachman Motor Inn, the defendant had abandoned the room. Even though the defendant still retained the room key and checkout time was not until 11:00 A.M. on the 17th, the court based its conclusion of abandonment on the following observations of the motion justice:

> [N]o later than five and one-half hours after he checked into the Coachman, he drove to Freeport and checked into the Freeport Inn. He left nothing in Room 48 except a bloody jersey, a half bottle of vodka and some orange juice. He left no luggage. According to the manager and according to common sense, this is consistent with a person who has left and does not intend to return. From the police logs at the scene of the crime, it is clear that defendant did not return to the Coachman prior to approximately 1:30 A.M. on the 17th. From the motel manager's observations, we know defendant was not at the Coachman at 4:45 A.M. There is no evidence that defendant returned to the Coachman between 1:30 A.M. and 4:45 A.M. The bed in Room 48 was not slept in. Defendant was still in Freeport at 10:00 A.M. on the 17th and was extending his stay. 569 A.2d at 1220–21.

In *United States v. Hoey,* 983 F.2d 890 (8th Cir. 1993), the court found that the following facts established abandonment of an apartment: the defendant personally told her landlord she was leaving, she was six weeks behind in her rent, she held a moving sale, and her neighbor saw her leave. Courts have found abandonment of an apartment even in cases in which the abandoning party had time left on the rental period:

> Baggett quit his job, received pay for one day's work, told several people that he was going to New Orleans to get a job, paid all bills that he owed except one, told his friends in Little Rock good-bye on the 11th, turned the apartment keys over to the owner, and took all personal belongings to New Orleans with him. Of course, had he returned within the two days before his rent came due, he could not have gone into his apartment for Ballard [the landlord] had the keys. The fact that the rent was paid up for three days after Baggett left does not mean that the apartment had not been abandoned. *Baggett v. State,* 494 S.W.2d 717, 719 (Ark. 1973).

The following quotation from a case involving a warrantless search of a house illustrates other indications of intent to abandon:

> [I]t was clearly established that even though the Mannings had rented the . . . house for thirty days, they departed after the first day leaving no personal belongings. The door was unlocked, food was on the table, and dishwater was in the sink. Thirty days later the same condition prevailed. Moreover, the decayed food created a stench, the grass was uncut, and the weeds had grown high.
>
> These circumstances strongly indicate that the Mannings had abandoned the house. . . . *United States v. Manning,* 440 F.2d 1105, 1111 (5th Cir. 1971).

The nonpublic areas of a business office come within the Fourth Amendment's protection against unreasonable searches and seizures. If the office is abandoned by its occupant, however, it no longer has this protection. The indications of intent to abandon for an office are similar to those for a room or house. In *Mullins v. United States*, 487 F.2d 581 (8th Cir. 1973), U.S. postal inspectors, without a warrant, searched for and seized business records from an office that had previously been rented by the defendant. The defendant claimed that the search and seizure were illegal because he did not intend to abandon the office and the records kept there. The court found that the facts indicated an intent to abandon. The search and seizure were made on June 12, 1972. The defendant had rented the office from May 1, 1971, through October 31, 1971, but had left the state in August 1971. No rent had been paid for the office beginning November 1, 1971, nor did the defendant, his wife, or any business associate or employee visit the office after November 1, 1971. Finally, the office had been padlocked by the U.S. District Attorney during February 1972.

The mere absence of a person from the premises does not make the premises abandoned, unless the person had an intent to abandon the premises. Therefore, in a case in which the defendant's absence from his apartment was involuntary because of his arrest and incarceration, the court held that the prosecution should bear an especially heavy burden of showing that he intended to abandon it. The prosecution did not satisfy this burden by merely showing the defendant's absence without showing any other indications of intent to abandon. *United States v. Robinson*, 430 F.2d 1141 (6th Cir. 1970).

OBJECTS   Intent to abandon objects involves many of the same considerations as intent to abandon premises. For example, a strong indication of a person's intent to abandon an object is leaving the object unattended and unclaimed for a long period of time. In *United States v. Gulledge*, 469 F.2d 713 (5th Cir. 1972), two men left a U-Haul trailer at a service station, asking permission to leave it there for two or three days. The men stated that "everything we own is in the trailer." Ten days later, the men not having returned, the service station attendant called law enforcement authorities. The trailer was searched without a warrant, and stolen whiskey was found. The court held that the search was legal because the property had been abandoned.

Another indication of intent to abandon an object is the defendant's own words of disclaimer of ownership or possession. "'Whether an abandonment has occurred is determined on the basis of objective facts available to the investigating officers, not on the basis of the owner's subjective intent.' . . . When considering whether the circumstances support a finding of abandonment, 'two important factors are denial of ownership and physical relinquishment of the property.'" *United States v. Landry*, 154 F.3d 897, 899 (8th Cir. 1998). In *United States v. Lee*, 916 F.2d 814 (2d Cir. 1990), the defendant on three separate occasions told officers he was traveling without luggage. When informed that a maroon suitcase was sitting unclaimed in the baggage area, he adamantly denied that it was his. The court held that the defendant intended to abandon his suitcase and thereby forfeited any legitimate expectation of privacy in it. Mere disclaimer of ownership *alone*, however, may not provide sufficient indication of intent to abandon.

> Perea's statement that the duffel bag did not belong to him was a truthful statement of fact that cannot alone provide a basis for inferring an intent on his part to abandon the bag. While he may have also intended to disassociate himself from the incriminating contents of the bag, Professor LaFave has cautioned that "a mere disclaimer of ownership in an effort to avoid making an incriminating statement in response to police questioning should not alone be deemed to constitute abandonment." . . . The question is whether the owner has "voluntarily discarded, left behind, or otherwise relinquished

his interest in the property in question so that he could no longer retain a reasonable expectation of privacy with regard to it at the time of the search." Thus, if a person lawfully arrested disclaims any interest in the container and declines to take it with him, his readiness to depart the scene and leave an object such as a suitcase or briefcase in the control of no one may fairly be characterized as abandonment. *United States v. Perea,* 848 F.Supp. 1101, 1103 (E.D.N.Y. 1994).

Smith v. Ohio
laws.findlaw.com/us/494/
541.html

In other cases involving warrantless searches and seizures of objects, the object is often picked up by a law enforcement officer immediately after it is dropped, thrown away, or otherwise discarded by a person. In these cases, courts cannot rely on the length of time the object has been left unattended to determine whether the object has been abandoned. Courts must look to other circumstances, such as the defendant's conduct and the manner of the object's disposal. In *Smith v. Ohio,* 494 U.S. 541, 110 S.Ct. 1288, 108 L.Ed.2d 464 (1990), officers in an unmarked police vehicle observed the defendant carrying a brown paper grocery bag. One of the officers asked the defendant to "come here a minute" and identified himself as a police officer. The defendant threw the bag he was carrying onto the hood of his car and turned to face the approaching officer. The officer rebuffed the defendant's attempt to protect the bag, opened it, and discovered drug paraphernalia. The U.S. Supreme Court said: "[A] citizen who attempts to protect his private property from inspection, after throwing it on a car to respond to a police officer's inquiry, clearly has not abandoned that property." 494 U.S. at 543–44, 110 S.Ct. at 1290, 108 L.Ed.2d at 468. In *People v. Anderson,* 298 N.Y.S.2d 698, 246 N.E.2d 508 (N.Y. 1969), a police officer approached the defendant without probable cause to make an arrest, and the defendant dropped a tin box to the ground. The officer immediately picked up the box, opened it, and found heroin. The court held that the evidence was insufficient to constitute an abandonment:

> There is no proof that the defendant threw it away or attempted to dispose of it in any manner which might have manifested the requisite intention to abandon. Moreover, the police officer's testimony reveals that he picked up the box so soon after it had been dropped that it is impossible to determine whether or not the defendant, if given the opportunity, would have picked up the box himself. Absent any such proof, the seizure of the tin box under the circumstances of this case cannot be sustained. *People v. Anderson,* 298 N.Y.S.2d 698, 699, 246 N.E.2d 508, 509 (N.Y. 1969).

When, however, the manner of disposal indicates that a defendant intended to relinquish possession or control of property because of consciousness of guilt or fear of potential apprehension, the courts usually find abandonment. In *United States v. Morgan,* 936 F.2d 1561 (10th Cir. 1991), the court found that the defendant voluntarily abandoned a gym bag based on the following facts and circumstances:

- When he saw police, the defendant threw the bag off a porch.
- He made no attempt to retrieve the bag or to request officers or anyone else to retrieve it for him.
- He made no attempt to protect the bag or its contents from inspection.
- He made no manifestations, verbal or otherwise, to indicate that he retained a reasonable privacy interest in the bag.

The court noted that "[w]hile an abandonment must be voluntary, '[t]he existence of police pursuit or investigation at the time of abandonment does not of itself render the abandonment involuntary.'" 936 F.2d at 1570.

In *United States v. Morris,* 738 F.Supp. 20 (D.D.C. 1990), the court held that, once the defendant stuffed a plastic bag containing vials into the crevice between bus seats, he surrendered any reasonable expectation of privacy he may have had in the contents of the bag prior to that time. The court pointed out that the defendant's intent to relinquish possession and control was most clearly evidenced by the defendant's decision not to return to the row of seats in which he had left his bag.

> The critical fact in this case is that the defendant made a decision to place his property in a location that was out of control and open to the public. At the time he placed the bag between the seats and then left the area, nothing precluded another passenger from occupying that seat or the one next to it. Indeed, nothing would have prevented such a passenger from placing his/her hand between the seats and discovering the bag. 738 F.Supp. at 23.

Some courts find an intent to abandon property when the defendant fails to object or take any other affirmative action but merely allows evidence to be seized in the ordinary course of events. In *United States v. Cox,* 428 F.2d 683 (7th Cir. 1970), the defendant was in jail after being arrested for bank robbery. He was given a haircut pursuant to routine jail procedures, and the hair clippings were turned over to the FBI, at their request, and used as evidence. In response to the defendant's claim of an illegal search and seizure, the court said:

> At no time has defendant objected to the legality of the prison procedures under which he received his haircut. He has never claimed that the haircut was illegally or improperly given. The thrust of his contention is rather that a warrant should have been obtained before the shorn locks were appropriated by the state officer for analysis. Cox, however, never indicated any desire or intention to retain possession of the hair after it had been scissored from his head. Clippings such as those preserved in the instant case are ordinarily abandoned after being cut. Cox in fact left his hair and has never claimed otherwise. The deputy sheriff was not obliged to inform him that, if abandoned, his hair would be taken and analyzed. Having voluntarily abandoned his property, in this case his hair, Cox may not object to its appropriation by the government. 428 F.2d at 687–88.

MOTOR VEHICLES   Motor vehicles are unique for purposes of the discussion of abandonment in that they are treated both as premises and as objects. In *United States v. Hastamorir,* 881 F.2d 1551 (11th Cir. 1989), the court held that the defendant's repeated disclaimers of knowledge of, or interest in, a vehicle or its contents ended any reasonable expectation of privacy in the vehicle and was an abandonment of the vehicle for Fourth Amendment purposes. In *Thom v. State,* 450 S.W.2d 550 (Ark. 1970), the defendant, who was tampering with a cigarette machine, left his car in the street and fled on foot to avoid apprehension by an officer. The court said:

> Sometimes an automobile takes on the characteristics of a man's castle. Other times an automobile takes on the characteristic of an overcoat—that is, it is movable and can be discarded by the possessor at will. If appellant in his endeavors to avoid the clutches of the law had discarded his overcoat to make his flight more speedy, no one would think that an officer was unreasonably invading his privacy or security in picking up the overcoat and searching it thoroughly. In that situation most people would agree that the fleeing suspect had abandoned his coat as a matter of expediency as well as any rights relative to its search and seizure. What difference can there be when a fleeing burglar abandons his automobile to escape the clutches of the law? We can see no distinction and consequently hold that when property is abandoned officers in making a search thereof do not violate any rights or security of a citizen guaranteed under the Fourth Amendment. 450 S.W.2d at 552.

In *United States v. Tate*, 821 F.2d 1328 (8th Cir. 1987), the court held that the defendant, who fled on foot from a stolen truck after shooting two troopers who had legally stopped the truck, abandoned the truck and its contents and any expectation of privacy he might have had in either.

Note that if an officer has probable cause to search a motor vehicle, he or she may also be able to justify a search of the vehicle under the *Carroll* doctrine (see Chapter 11).

Lawfulness of Police Behavior

"An abandonment that occurs in response to proper police activity has not been coerced in violation of the Fourth Amendment." *United States v. Miller*, 974 F.2d 953, 958 (8th Cir. 1992). The following are examples of cases in which a person discarded or disclaimed ownership of an object in response to the lawful activities of the police, and courts considered the object abandoned and therefore seizable without a warrant or other justification:

- An officer asked the defendant, a bus passenger, whether she owned a tote bag on a rack above her seat and she denied ownership. *United States v. Lewis*, 921 F.2d 1294 (D.C.Cir. 1990).
- As Drug Enforcement Administration (DEA) agents were approaching the defendant's car to lawfully arrest him, the defendant opened the passenger door and threw down a packet later determined to contain cocaine. *United States v. Koessel*, 706 F.2d 271 (8th Cir. 1983).
- Officers in a public place asked the defendant questions about suitcases in the trunk of a car, and the defendant abandoned them by denying ownership of them. *United States v. Karman*, 849 F.2d 928 (5th Cir. 1988).
- Officers, attempting to execute a valid search warrant, temporarily detained the defendant at the scene of the search, and the defendant discarded a package containing incriminating evidence. *State v. Romeo*, 203 A.2d 23 (N.J. 1964).

In a case involving only *attempted* unlawful police activity, a law enforcement officer, without probable cause or reasonable articulable suspicion, pursued the defendant on mere suspicion of involvement in a drug transaction. As the officer approached the defendant, the defendant tossed away a small rock. A moment later, the officer tackled the defendant. The rock he threw away was later determined to be crack cocaine. The court held that, although the seizure of the defendant was illegal, the defendant tossed away the crack cocaine *before* he was seized. Therefore, the abandonment of the cocaine did not occur as a result of *unlawful police activity,* and the cocaine was admissible in court.

> [A]ssuming that [Officer] Pertoso's pursuit in the present case constituted a "show of authority" enjoining Hodari to halt, since Hodari did not comply with that injunction he was not seized until he was tackled. The cocaine abandoned while he was running was in this case not the fruit of a seizure, and his motion to exclude evidence of it was properly denied. *California v. Hodari D.*, 499 U.S. 621, 629, 111 S.Ct. 1547, 1552, 113 L.Ed.2d 690, 699 (1991).

California v. Hodari D.
laws.findlaw.com/us/499/
621.html

"When an individual abandons an object in response to an officer's violation of his constitutional rights, the violation taints the abandonment making it involuntary." *United States v. Mendez*, 827 F.Supp. 1280, 1284 (S.D. Tex. 1993). A stop of two black occupants of a car parked with its engine running in a black neighborhood merely because the officer did not recognize the men was held illegal in *United States v. Beck*,

Case in Point

Interpreting *California v. Hodari D.*

On August 4, 1995, Officers Christopher Juba and Donald Heffner of the Harrisburg Police Bureau were patrolling the 1300 block of Market Street in the City of Harrisburg between 8 P.M. and 1 A.M. The officers testified that while travelling east on Market, in an unmarked car, they noticed three individuals on the corner. The individuals were engaged in conversation. The officers passed the group at a very slow rate, and they observed appellant take his left hand out of his front pocket in a fist position and reach toward one of the other individuals. The individual reached out toward appellant and attempted to receive the unidentified item from his hand. To further investigate this conduct, Officer Heffner made a U-turn and drove to the corner where the group was gathered. As soon as appellant spotted the officers and the car, he placed his hand back in his pocket and began backing away from the group. Officer Juba exited the car, identified himself as a Harrisburg police officer, and began walking toward the group. Appellant immediately began to run "in almost a dead sprint." Officer Juba chased the appellant, with Officer Heffner following in the vehicle.

During the course of the chase, Officer Juba witnessed appellant throw two pagers to the ground; Officer Heffner saw appellant pull a sandwich bag from his pocket and throw it into the yard of an abandoned house. Ultimately, Officer Heffner apprehended appellant and recovered the sandwich bag. The bag was discovered to contain eighteen large rocks of crack cocaine and $45 in cash. Appellant moved to suppress the evidence that was abandoned during the chase, by arguing that the evidence was obtained as a result of an illegal seizure. In light of *California v. Hodari D.*, should the motion to suppress be granted? *Commonwealth v.* Cook, 735 A.2d 673 (Pa. 1999).

Read the court opinion at:
dpg-law.com/opinions/pa-suprm/9907/1063-cook.html

602 F.2d 726 (5th Cir. 1979). The court found that the discarding of drugs and paraphernalia by the men in connection with the stop was not a voluntary abandonment:

> While it is true that a criminal defendant's voluntary abandonment of evidence can remove the taint of an illegal stop or arrest . . . it is equally true that for this to occur the abandonment must be truly voluntary and not merely the product of police misconduct. . . . In this case, it seems clear that the contraband was abandoned because of the illegal stop of the Chevrolet. After the stop was made, and while [Officer] Spears was pulling his patrol car in front of the Chevrolet, he observed the marijuana cigarette thrown out Beck's window. The bag containing marijuana and the syringe were presumably discarded at the same time. These acts of abandonment do not reflect the mere coincidental decision of Beck and his passenger to discard their narcotics; it would be sheer fiction to presume they were caused by anything other than the illegal stop. Had Spears observed these items inside the Chevrolet during an unlawful stop they would be suppressed . . . ; the fact that Beck and his passenger threw them out the window onto the ground after the commencement of an illegal stop and just prior to an unlawful arrest does not change this result. 602 F.2d at 729–30.

Reasonable Expectation of Privacy in the Property

As shown in the discussion of the open fields doctrine, since the U.S. Supreme Court decision in *Katz v. United States*, the courts increasingly have analyzed the legality of warrantless searches and seizures in terms of their intrusion upon the defendant's reasonable expectation of privacy. This trend has extended also to cases involving vacated or discarded property. The Minnesota Supreme Court explained:

> In the law of property, the question . . . is whether the owner has voluntarily, intentionally, and unconditionally relinquished his interest in the property so that another, having acquired possession, may successfully assert his superior interest. In the law of search and seizure, however, the question is whether the defendant has, in discarding the property, relinquished his reasonable expectation of privacy so that its seizure and search is reasonable within the limits of the Fourth Amendment. In essence, what is abandoned is not necessarily the defendant's property, but his reasonable expectation of privacy therein. *City of St. Paul v. Vaughn,* 237 N.W.2d 365, 370–71 (Minn. 1975).

In a case involving supposedly vacated premises, law enforcement officers were investigating a possible arson in a building gutted by fire. The fire occurred on April 14, 1968, and the officers entered the building, made observations, and took photographs on April 24, 1968. Evidence showed that the house had been boarded up on April 14. Thereafter the owner went to the house every day, and both she and the defendant kept some of their personal effects in the house. The defendant claimed that the observations and photographs of the officers were a product of an illegal search and seizure. The court said:

> The uncontradicted evidence before the court was that the building was not abandoned. On April 24, 1968, it still contained personal effects and had been boarded up to keep the public out.
>
> The test to be used in determining whether a place is a constitutionally protected area within the meaning of the Fourth Amendment is . . . "whether the person has exhibited a reasonable expectation of privacy, and, if so, whether that expectation has been violated by unreasonable governmental intrusion." In the instant matter the owner of the dwelling house clearly demonstrated her expectation of privacy as to the interior of the house and its contents by boarding up the doorways, which were damaged by fire. That expectation was violated by the intrusion of the police on April 24, 1968. *Swan v. Superior Court, County of Los Angeles,* 87 Cal.Rptr. 280, 282 (Cal. 1970).

Courts differ on the extent of a person's reasonable expectation of privacy in discarded objects. The controversy has centered around the search and seizure of trash or garbage by law enforcement officers. In a leading case in this area, law enforcement officers, acting without a warrant, found marijuana in a trash can in the open backyard area of the defendant's residence. The court held that the marijuana in the trash can was not abandoned for the following reasons:

> As we have seen, the trash can was within a few feet of the back door of defendants' home and required trespass for its inspection. It was an adjunct to the domestic economy. . . . Placing the marijuana in the trash can, so situated and used, was not an abandonment unless as to persons authorized to remove the receptacle's contents, such as trashmen. . . . The marijuana itself was not visible without "rummaging" in the receptacle. So far as appears defendants alone resided at the house. In the light of the combined facts and circumstances it appears that defendants exhibited an expectation of privacy, and we believe that expectation was reasonable under the circumstances of the case. We can readily ascribe many reasons why residents would not want their castaway clothing, letters, medicine bottles or other telltale refuse and trash to be examined by neighbors or others, at least not until the trash has lost its identity and meaning by becoming part of a large conglomeration of trash elsewhere. Half truths leading to rumor

www.rbs2.com/
privacy.htm#anchor666666
Article, "Privacy Law in the
USA" by Ronald B. Standler;
Section 6 extensively discusses
the privacy of garbage

and gossip may readily flow from an attempt to "read" the contents of another's trash. *People v. Edwards*, 80 Cal.Rptr. 633, 638, 458 P.2d 713, 718 (Cal. 1969).

Other courts have generally agreed with the holding in the *Edwards* case and have found a violation of a defendant's reasonable expectation of privacy when the trash searched or seized was located within the curtilage of the defendant's house. *Ball v. State*, 205 N.W.2d 353 (Wis. 1973). In *United States v. Certain Real Property*, 719 F.Supp. 1396 (E.D.Mich. 1989), a police officer, disguised as a trash collector, walked up the defendant's driveway and invaded the curtilage to retrieve trash bags placed by the doorway for collection. In holding the seizure illegal, the court said that "the government decided to do directly what it already could do indirectly, and that trip up the side driveway makes all the difference for fourth amendment purposes." 719 F.Supp. at 1407. In a footnote the court said that the police could have had the regular garbage collector deliver the garbage bags to them after they had been removed from the curtilage of the home.

Where garbage is left *outside* the curtilage of the home, however, the U.S. Supreme Court held that the Fourth Amendment does not prohibit the warrantless search and seizure of the garbage. In *California v. Greenwood*, 486 U.S. 35, 108 S.Ct. 1625, 100 L.Ed.2d 30 (1988), police suspected the defendant of narcotics trafficking, but did not have probable cause to search the defendant's house. Police obtained from the regular trash collector garbage bags left at the curb in front of the defendant's house. On the basis of items found in the bags, police obtained a search warrant for the home and discovered controlled substances.

California v. Greenwood
laws.findlaw.com/us/486/
35.html

The defendants claimed an expectation of privacy with respect to their trash, but the Court held that even if they had an expectation of privacy, it was not one that society was prepared to accept as reasonable.

> [R]espondents exposed their garbage to the public sufficiently to defeat their claim to Fourth Amendment protection. It is common knowledge that plastic garbage bags left on or at the side of a public street are readily accessible to animals, children, scavengers, snoops, and other members of the public. . . . Moreover, respondents placed their refuse at the curb for the express purpose of conveying it to a third party, the trash collector, who might himself have sorted through respondent's trash or permitted others, such as the police, to do so. Accordingly, having deposited their garbage "in an area particularly suited for public inspection and, in a manner of speaking, public consumption, for the express purpose of having strangers take it," . . . respondents could have had no reasonable expectation of privacy in the inculpatory items that they discarded. . . . [T]he police cannot reasonably be expected to avert their eyes from evidence of criminal activity that could have been observed by any member of the public. 486 U.S. at 40–41, 108 S.Ct. at 1628–29, 100 L.Ed.2d at 36–37.

In *United States v. Dunkel*, 900 F.2d 105 (7th Cir. 1990), the court found that the defendant, a dentist, had no reasonable expectation of privacy in a dumpster located off the parking lot of a building that he owned and that housed several other businesses. All used the same dumpster, and the parking lot and dumpster were accessible to patients, employees, and the general public. No warrant was needed to search for and seize financial records discarded in the dumpster. In *United States v. Walker*, 624 F.Supp. 99 (D.Md. 1985), law enforcement officers found a paper shopping bag out in the open alongside a road in a sparsely populated rural setting. No attempt had been made to protect the bag from damage from the elements, from removal by a passerby, or from disturbance by an animal. The court held that, despite the defendant's claim that he did not intend to abandon the bag, by leaving the bag in the manner he did, the defendant was no longer retaining a reasonable expectation of privacy.

Key Points

7. Property is abandoned, for purposes of the Fourth Amendment, if its owner has voluntarily discarded, left behind, or otherwise relinquished his or her interest in the property so as to no longer retain a reasonable expectation of privacy with regard to it. Such property may be searched and seized without a warrant or other justification and without violating the Fourth Amendment.

8. Leaving property unattended for a long period of time is a strong indication of intent to abandon property.

9. Disclaimer of interest in property accompanied by departing the scene, making no attempt to retrieve or protect the property, and leaving the property in the care of no one are strong indications of intent to abandon property.

10. Discarding property as a direct result of the unlawful activity of a law enforcement officer is not voluntary abandonment but a forced response to the unlawful police behavior.

11. A person who establishes a reasonable expectation of privacy in property has not abandoned that property, and the property may not be searched or seized without a warrant or other legal justification.

12. When a person leaves garbage outside the curtilage of a home, the person no longer has a reasonable expectation of privacy in the garbage and the Fourth Amendment does not prohibit the warrantless search and seizure of the garbage.

Summary

A law enforcement officer may search for items of evidence lying in the open fields without probable cause, a search warrant, or other legal justification without violating a person's Fourth Amendment rights and may seize items if he or she has probable cause to believe the items are "seizable" under the law of the officer's jurisdiction. An officer may also legally make observations from a vantage point in the open fields into constitutionally protected areas to detect criminal activity or evidence.

The open fields are the area lying outside the curtilage of a person's home or business. Whether a piece of land or building falls within the curtilage can be determined by consideration of the following factors: the proximity to the home of the area claimed to be curtilage, the inclusion of the area within an enclosure surrounding the home, the nature of the uses to which the area is put, and the steps taken by the resident to protect the area from observation by passersby.

Since the 1967 U.S. Supreme Court decision in *Katz v. United States,* which held that "the Fourth Amendment protects people, not places," courts have increasingly analyzed the legality of warrantless searches in terms of the defendants' reasonable expectation of privacy, in addition to the concepts of curtilage and open fields. Law enforcement officers, therefore, must be careful to avoid warrantless intrusions not only into

the curtilage of a person's house but also into any area that the person reasonably seeks to preserve as private.

A law enforcement officer, without probable cause, a warrant, or other legal justification, may retrieve items of evidence that have been abandoned by their owners without violating Fourth Amendment rights. Property has been abandoned when its owner has voluntarily discarded, left behind, or otherwise relinquished his or her interest in the property so as to no longer retain a reasonable expectation of privacy with regard to it. Among the factors that the courts rely on in determining whether a given object has been abandoned by its owner are the following:

■ *Indications of intent to abandon property.* Indications of intent to abandon *premises* can be divided into positive acts and omissions. Positive indications of intent to abandon include removing personal belongings, paying final rent and other bills, turning in keys, quitting local employment, and taking leave of friends. Omissions indicating intent to abandon include failing to pay rent for a long time, long absence from the premises, failure to communicate with anyone regarding the premises, and failure to attend to or care for the premises. Intent to abandon an *object* is indicated by leaving the object unattended for an unreasonable period of time, discarding the object out of consciousness of guilt or fear of apprehension, disclaiming interest in the object and leaving it unprotected in the care of no one, and allowing the object to be taken away in the ordinary course of events, without objection. Intent to abandon *vehicles* is determined by the same considerations as those for premises and objects.

■ *Lawfulness of police behavior.* Objects discarded as a direct result of the unlawful activity of a law enforcement officer will not be considered voluntarily abandoned.

■ *Reasonable expectation of privacy in the property.* Even though property has been vacated or thrown away,

under certain circumstances, a person may reasonably retain an expectation of privacy with respect to the property. Such property is not considered abandoned, and a search and seizure of it, without a warrant or probable cause, will be illegal.

Determining whether property is abandoned is similar to determining whether it is in the open fields, in that both require a consideration not only of a person's property rights but also of the person's rights of privacy. Such determinations will always be difficult for the courts as well as for law enforcement officers. In the absence of an emergency, officers should obtain a search warrant whenever possible.

Key Holdings from Major Cases

Hester v. United States (1924). "[T]he special protection accorded by the Fourth Amendment to the people in their 'persons, houses, papers and effects' is not extended to the open fields." 265 U.S. 57, 59, 44 S.Ct. 445, 446, 68 L.Ed. 898, 900.

Oliver v. United States (1984). "[A]n individual may not legitimately demand privacy for activities conducted out of doors in fields, except in the area immediately surrounding the home." 466 U.S. 170, 178, 104 S.Ct. 1735, 1741, 80 L.Ed.2d 214, 224.

"[O]pen fields do not provide the setting for those intimate activities that the [Fourth] Amendment is intended to shelter from government interference or surveillance. There is no societal interest in protecting the privacy of those activities such as the cultivation of crops, that occur in open fields. Moreover, as a practical matter these lands usually are accessible to the public and the police in ways that a home, an office or commercial structure would not be. It is not generally true that fences or 'No Trespassing' signs effectively bar the public from viewing open fields in rural areas. And . . . the public and police lawfully may survey lands from the air. For these reasons, the asserted expectation of privacy in open fields is not an expectation that 'society recognizes as reasonable.'" 466 U.S. at 179, 104 S.Ct. at 1741, 80 L.Ed.2d at 224.

To determine whether property to be searched falls within the curtilage of a house, the law enforcement officer must consider "the factors that determine whether an individual reasonably may expect that an area immediately adjacent to the home will remain private." 466 U.S. at 180, 104 S.Ct. at 1742, 80 L.Ed.2d at 225.

"[T]he term 'open fields' may include any unoccupied or undeveloped area outside of the curtilage. An open field need be neither 'open' nor a 'field' as those terms are used in common speech. For example . . . a thickly wooded area nonetheless may be an open field as that term is used in construing the Fourth

Amendment." 466 U.S. at 180 n.11, 104 S.Ct. at 1742 n.11, 80 L.Ed.2d at 225 n.11.

United States v. Dunn (1987). "[C]urtilage questions should be resolved with particular reference to four factors: the proximity of the area claimed to be curtilage to the home, whether the area is included within an enclosure surrounding the home, the nature of the uses to which the area is put, and the steps taken by the resident to protect the area from observation by people passing by." 480 U.S. 294, 301, 107 S.Ct. 1134, 1139, 94 L.Ed.2d 326, 334–35.

"[T]he primary focus [in determining curtilage] is whether the area in question harbors those intimate activities associated with domestic life and the privacies of the home." 480 U.S. at 301 n.4, 107 S.Ct. at 1139 n.4, 94 L.Ed.2d at 335 n.4 (1987).

California v. Ciraolo (1986). "That the area is within the curtilage does not itself bar all police observation. The Fourth Amendment protection of the home has never been extended to require law enforcement officers to shield their eyes when passing by a home on public thoroughfares. Nor does the mere fact that an individual has taken measures to restrict some views of his activities preclude an officer's observations from a public vantage point where he has a right to be and which renders the activities clearly visible." 476 U.S. 207, 213, 106 S.Ct. 1809, 1812, 90 L.Ed.2d 210, 216.

Dow Chemical Co. v. United States (1986). "[T]he open areas of an industrial plant complex with numerous plant structures spread over an area of 2,000 acres are not analogous to the 'curtilage' of a dwelling for purposes of aerial surveillance; such an industrial complex is more comparable to an open field and as such it is open to the view and observation of persons in aircraft lawfully in the public airspace immediately above or sufficiently near the area for the reach of cameras. . . . [T]he taking of aerial photographs of an industrial plant complex from navigable airspace is not a search prohibited by the Fourth Amendment." 476 U.S. 227, 239, 106 S.Ct. 1819, 1827, 90 L.Ed.2d 226, 238.

Florida v. Riley (1989). The defendant, who had left the sides and roof of his greenhouse partially open "could not reasonably have expected that his greenhouse was protected from public or official observation from a helicopter had it been flying within the navigable airspace for fixed-wing aircraft.

"Nor . . . does it make a difference for Fourth Amendment purposes that the helicopter was flying at 400 feet when the officer saw what was growing in the greenhouse through the partially open roof and sides of the structure. We would have a different case if flying at that altitude had been contrary to law or regulation. But helicopters are not bound by the lower limits of the navigable airspace allowed to other aircraft. Any member of the public could legally have been flying over Riley's property in a helicopter at the altitude of 400 feet and could have observed Riley's greenhouse." 488 U.S. 445, 449–53, 109 S.Ct. 693, 696–97, 102 L.Ed.2d 835, 842.

Abel v. United States (1960). "There can be nothing unlawful in the Government's appropriation of . . . abandoned property." 362 U.S. 217, 241, 80 S.Ct. 683, 698, 4 L.Ed.2d 668, 687.

Smith v. Ohio (1990). "[A] citizen who attempts to protect his private property from inspection, after throwing it on a car to respond to a police officer's inquiry, clearly has not abandoned that property." 494 U.S. 541, 543–44, 110 S.Ct. 1288, 1290, 108 L.Ed.2d 464, 468.

California v. Greenwood (1988). "[H]aving deposited their garbage 'in an area particularly suited for public inspection and, in a manner of speaking, public consumption, for the express purpose of having strangers take it,' . . . respondents could have had no reasonable expectation of privacy in the inculpatory items that they discarded. . . . [T]he police cannot reasonably be expected to avert their eyes from evidence of criminal activity that could have been observed by any member of the public." 486 U.S. 35, 40–41, 108 S.Ct. 1625, 1629, 100 L.Ed.2d 30, 36–37.

Review and Discussion Questions

1. Does the term *open fields* include any place that is public, including forests, lakes, city streets, and stadiums?

2. Which of the following, if any, would be considered a house for purposes of the Fourth Amendment?
   a. Tent
   b. Lean-to
   c. Motor home
   d. Sailboat
   e. Cave

3. The dissent in *California v. Hodari D.* said that "a police officer may now fire his weapon at an innocent citizen and not implicate the Fourth Amendment—as long as he misses his target." If a person throws away an item of criminal evidence after being illegally shot at by a police officer, is that item abandoned?

4. Would a person's Fourth Amendment rights be violated by law enforcement officers who, after illegally arresting the person, entered the person's fenced and posted rural property to observe a marijuana field surrounded by a forest?

5. Compare the plain view doctrine, the open fields doctrine, and the abandonment doctrine with respect to the reasonable expectation of privacy.

6. If a person abandons property inside the curtilage of someone else's property, may a law enforcement officer seize the abandoned property?

7. Is observing activities inside a house in the country by looking into a window with binoculars from a field or forest any different from observing activities in a tenth-story apartment from a window in an adjacent apartment building?

8. Does the value of an object have any bearing on the question of whether a person abandoned it? Can a person who runs away from his or her automobile to avoid apprehension by the police be said to give up all reasonable expectations of privacy in the vehicle? What if the person locks the vehicle before fleeing?

9. For each place listed in question 2, what indications of intent to abandon would give a law enforcement officer authority to search for and seize items left at that place?

10. If a person undergoes emergency surgery after being shot by police while driving a stolen automobile, which of the following, if any, has the person abandoned?
    a. Clothing worn at the time of the shooting
    b. Wallets and other items in the pockets of the clothing
    c. Bullets surgically removed
    d. The automobile

Real-Life Fact Situations

1 The evidence used to convict appellant was obtained during the execution of a search warrant that contained the following information. The Cambridge Police Department received information that appellant made a cash payment of $3,000 for repairs to her automobile. An officer went to the house that appellant was renting and, without a warrant, grabbed trash bags that appellant had placed out for collection. The bags were on appellant's front lawn, but close enough to the public street that the officer could reach them without walking onto appellant's property. When the bags were inspected, police found (1) several baggies with the bottom corners cut out and with cocaine residue on them, (2) letters addressed to appellant, and (3) a draft of her resume.

After conducting additional "trash runs" in a similar manner, the officers included the results of their investigation in an application for a warrant to search appellant's residence. The warrant was issued on November 12, 1997, and executed on November 22, 1997. Appellant and her boyfriend were in the master bedroom when the police entered. The search turned up (1) "a black film canister with crack cocaine and a baggie with seven packets of powdered cocaine" on top of a dresser in the master bedroom, and (2) $3,700 in cash, most of which was found in a man's boot underneath the bed.

Appellant contends that the "trash runs" conducted by the officers were unreasonable searches and seizures under the Fourth Amendment of the United States Constitution. Was the appellant correct? *Sampson v. State*, 744 A.2d 588 (Md.App. 2000).

Read the court opinion at:
www.courts.state.md.us/opinions/cosa/2000/1892s98.pdf

2 On December 22, 1996, DEA Agent Tim Trout reported to Agent Stanton C. Hayes of the Montana Narcotics Investigation Bureau that he had received an anonymous tip that Depew was growing marijuana in Montana, probably at a residence with one of two telephone numbers. Agent Trout also told Agent Hayes that Depew had previously been convicted of growing marijuana in Idaho, but that the conviction had been overturned on constitutional grounds. Further, Agent Trout informed Agent Hayes of the details surrounding Depew's Idaho grow operation, including that Depew had: (1) used a house similar to the one he rented in Montana, (2) placed plywood over the inside of the windows, making them look normal from the outside while preventing light from escaping, and (3) used an elaborate heat ventilating system.

Agent Hayes learned that one of the phone numbers that the informant provided was listed to a David Depre at a residence on East Lake Shore Drive ("East Lake Residence"), while the other phone number was listed to a Steve Scott at a residence on Tall Pine Court ("Tall Pine Residence"). Upon a pre-liminary view of the residences, Agent Hayes's investigation focused primarily on the East Lake Residence.

According to DEA Special Agent Richard S. Hicks's affidavit, the East Lake Residence, which was visible from the road, was located on the east side of the street. On the property, there was a single-story house, an unattached garage, and a cherry orchard in the backyard. Agent Hayes observed that the windows on the north side of the house had some kind of covering over them, and he never saw either the windows or blinds open. Further, Agent Hicks stated in his affidavit that Agent Hayes had repeatedly seen Depew at the residence but had not observed other activity indicating anyone actually lived there. In particular, he noted that agents had not observed any trash near the residence.

Agent Hayes showed Agent Trout pictures of the East Lake Residence. Agent Trout stated that the residence looked similar to the one Depew used in Idaho. He further told Agent Hayes that Depew had bypassed the electrical meter at the Idaho house.

On October 7, 1997, Agent Hicks provided Agent Hayes with an administrative subpoena to obtain power records for the East Lake Residence and to determine if the electrical meter had been bypassed. The power records indicated that the average monthly usage had increased from 689 KWH to 1824 KWH since 1994. To determine whether the electrical meter had been bypassed, a power employee had to enter onto the East Lake Residence property. For the employee's safety, Agent Hayes accompanied him. While on the property, the employee determined that the electrical meter had in fact been bypassed. To measure the actual amount of electricity used at the East Lake Residence, the employee attached a meter to a transformer located off the property. Agent Hicks stated in his affidavit that while on the East Lake Residence property, Agent Hayes observed duct piping lying on a table and a squirrel cage fan behind the garage, which Agent Hicks alleged are commonly used in grow operations.

On October 15, 1997, at 4:30 A.M., Agent Hayes used an Agema Therma Vision 210 ("Agema 210") thermal imager to observe the East Lake Residence. The thermal imager revealed that an unusual amount of heat was emanating from the house's chimney and the vents on the north side of the house. Agent Hicks stated in his affidavit that the heat patterns were consistent with growing marijuana under artificial light. In addition, the new meter placed on the transformer indicated that the East Lake Residence used 744 KWH of power in one week, or about 3,000 KWH per month, which is unusually high.

Based on the above information, the government obtained a search warrant for the East Lake Residence, where the agents discovered 126 mature marijuana plants. Depew was charged with one count of knowingly, willfully, and unlawfully manufacturing a controlled substance in violation of 21 U.S.C. § 841(a)(1).

Depew moved to suppress the marijuana plants. Should his motion be granted? *United States v. Depew,* 210 F.3d 1061 (9th Cir. 2000).

Read the court opinion at:
laws.findlaw.com/9th/9830196.html

3 Officer Richard Washburn saw Mr. Lemus make what the officer believed to be an improper lane change on a city street in Othello. Officer Washburn stopped Mr. Lemus's vehicle and asked for back-up, a standard procedure for nighttime traffic stops. Mr. Lemus told Officer Washburn he did not have insurance. Officer Washburn decided not to charge the improper lane change, but returned to his patrol car to prepare a Notice of Infraction (NOI) for no insurance.

Officer Troy Kelly arrived as back-up. Officer Washburn advised Officer Kelly that Mr. Lemus was a known drug trafficker based upon prior contacts with the Othello Police Department. Officer Washburn approached Mr. Lemus again from the driver's side of the car while Officer Kelly approached from the passenger side. To ensure officer safety, Officer Kelly illuminated the passenger compartment of the vehicle with his flashlight. Officer Kelly particularly focused his attention on Mr. Lemus's hands. Officer Washburn noticed Mr. Lemus appeared nervous, which the officer felt was inconsistent with his prior encounters with Mr. Lemus.

Officer Kelly observed that Mr. Lemus kept his right hand motionless on his pant leg. Officer Kelly noticed that when Mr. Lemus moved his right hand to accept a pen from Officer Washburn to sign the NOI, there was a white powdery substance on Mr. Lemus's pant leg that had been previously concealed from view by Mr. Lemus's right hand and arm. Officer Kelly immediately concluded the powder was "very possibly" cocaine. Officer Kelly told Officer Washburn about the powdery substance. Officer Washburn asked Mr. Lemus what the substance was and told him not to move his hands. Mr. Lemus responded by brushing the substance off his pant leg. Officer Washburn testified that based upon his training, the powder "resembled" cocaine.

When Officer Washburn returned to Mr. Lemus's car with the infraction notice he detected the odor of intoxicants on Mr. Lemus's breath that he had not initially noticed due to the smell of cigarette smoke. After learning of the powdery substance, Officer Washburn asked Mr. Lemus to exit the vehicle to perform field sobriety tests (FSTs).

During the FSTs, passed successfully by Mr. Lemus, Officer Voss arrived with the field testing kit and without a warrant removed a sample of the white powdery substance from Mr. Lemus's vehicle. It field-tested positive for cocaine. Officer Washburn then arrested Mr. Lemus. Also during the FSTs, Officer Washburn noticed a bulge in Mr. Lemus's left front pants pocket. Officer Washburn then conducted a pat-down search. During the search, Officer Washburn felt a pointed object, which he thought might be a weapon. The object turned out to

be a small scale of the type used by drug dealers, but there was no evidence the scale had been used. Later, at the station during a strip-search, approximately 13.7 grams of cocaine was discovered in Mr. Lemus's underwear. Should Mr. Lemus's motion to suppress the evidence seized from the car and from his person be granted? *State v. Lemus,* 11 P.3d 326 (Wash.App. 2000).

Read the court opinion at:
www.cdlaw.com/cases/apps/10_00/18861-2.htm

4 On January 24, 1996, Trooper Anthony Ravotti of the Pennsylvania State Police and Officer Gary Petruzzi of the Allegheny County Police Department were assigned to narcotics interdiction at the Pittsburgh International Airport. Their duties consisted, *inter alia,* of observing passengers on incoming flights from "source cities," such as Los Angeles and New York. While watching passengers disembark from a Los Angeles flight, Trooper Ravotti noticed Appellant, Paula Dowds ("Dowds"), a well-dressed African-American woman wearing a long black fur coat, who was the last person to leave the plane. This struck Trooper Ravotti as unusual, since the flight attendants generally exit after the passengers. Dowds was holding a large, powder blue carry-on bag that was stained with what appeared to be tar. Trooper Ravotti related his observations to Officer Petruzzi, and they began following Dowds as she slowly proceeded along the main concourse of the airport, scanning the area along the way, at one point dropping her bag and dragging it. The officers thought that this conduct was unusual considering Dowds' expensive attire. On several other occasions, Dowds stopped and appeared to perform a 360-degree scan of the area. When Dowds reached the connecting gate for New York's LaGuardia Airport, she used a payphone, making several calls of short duration, then stood at the payphone with her finger on the hang-up lever. Officer Petruzzi asked an airline attendant at the gate to check the passenger manifest for females with connecting flights from Los Angeles to New York, and was advised that only two individuals were listed, both males. Officer Petruzzi then went to the baggage matrix and discovered a suitcase for the New York flight with a computer-generated registration for "Paula Douds" and a handwritten tag for "Paula Dowds." Further, he asked an airline agent to re-check the New York flight's passenger list, and on this occasion was advised that a "Paula Douds" was listed and had registered a piece of luggage. An officer was stationed to watch Dowds' suitcase, and a canine officer was summoned.

At this point, Officer Petruzzi and Trooper Ravotti approached Dowds, identified themselves, explained that they worked in narcotics and contraband interdiction, and that they would like to talk to her, to which Dowds agreed, later testifying that Officer Petruzzi "was very kind." Officer Petruzzi and Trooper Ravotti were wearing plain clothes and carried no visible weapons. Dowds was asked to produce her airline ticket, which she did. The ticket indicated a last name of "Douds" and its folder evidenced a tear where a baggage claim tag is normally affixed. Dowds also produced a New York driver's license, showing her last name as "Dowds." When asked if she had checked a suitcase for her trip to New York, Dowds stated that she had not, and upon being told that there was a bag at the baggage claim area with tags indicating both spellings of her last name, Dowds denied ownership. Officer Petruzzi asked Dowds if they could look through the bag, to which she responded, "It's not my bag. You can look through it if you want." Trooper Ravotti remained with Dowds, while Officer Petruzzi returned to the baggage matrix to arrange a canine sniff of the suitcase. Thereafter, Dowds asked Trooper Ravotti if she could use the restroom, and he advised her, "Sure. You're not under arrest. We're not detaining you at this time. You can do what you want to do." Dowds used the ladies' room and returned to the gate. During the canine sniff, the dog alerted to Dowds' suitcase, indicating the presence of narcotics. Officer Petruzzi then brought the suitcase to the gate area where Dowds was sitting, at which point she again denied ownership and told the officers that they could look inside it. Dowds was advised that she would be detained until a search warrant could be secured. Upon receipt of the warrant, the police forcibly opened the suitcase, finding 32.76 pounds of marijuana, and Dowds was charged with possession with intent to deliver a controlled substance.

Prior to trial, Dowds moved to suppress, asserting that the police lacked either reasonable suspicion or probable cause when they initially approached her, and that she was stopped solely because of her race. Dowds thus argued that the subsequent search of the luggage was tainted by prior illegality. Should her motion be granted? *Commonwealth v. Dowds*, 761 A.2d 1125 (Pa. 2000).

Read the court opinion at:
caselaw.findlaw.com/data2/pennsylvaniastatecases/supreme/
j-49-2000mo.pdf

5 In August 1997, Joseph Basinski learned that the FBI was investigating him for jewel thefts and interstate transportation of stolen goods. Shortly thereafter, in an effort to keep incriminating documents from the government, Basinski entrusted a locked briefcase to William Friedman, who hid it in a barn at his summer home in Grand Marsh, Wisconsin. Basinski had every reason to trust Friedman, as they had grown up in the same Chicago neighborhood and had been friends for over thirty years. Their relationship may also have extended to criminal activity. From time to time Basinski reportedly gave Friedman diamonds and pieces of jewelry for Friedman to sell, and Basinski was always generous with cash when it came to Friedman. But Basinski's trust only went so far. He never told Friedman what was in the plastic briefcase, never gave him the combination to the lock, and never gave him permission to open it. Around March 1998, after Basinski learned that the FBI had tapped his telephone, he instructed Friedman to burn the

briefcase so that the FBI could never obtain its contents. When Friedman suggested that he could instead sink it in a lake, Basinski rejected that idea, stating that the FBI could still retrieve it. Friedman ultimately promised Basinski that he would burn the case.

As it turns out, Basinski's trust in Friedman was somewhat misplaced. Friedman decided not to burn the briefcase and instead left it hidden in the barn. When Basinski called him on several occasions to make certain that the case and its contents were destroyed, Friedman assured him that he had carried out Basinski's orders. To reassure himself that Friedman had carried out his commands, Basinski asked that Friedman tell him what was left of the briefcase and show him the remains. Friedman responded that only the handle and locking mechanism survived the fire, and that these were in a pile of burnt trash. When Friedman asked why he had to have the briefcase burned, Basinski told him he feared the FBI would otherwise obtain a passport and documents which contained Basinski's fingerprints. Basinski's fears were justified. After several interviews with the FBI and a grand jury subpoena, Friedman told the government about the briefcase and his belief that it contained evidence of Basinski's alleged crimes. On February 23, 1999, Friedman led FBI Agent Edward McNamara and Agent Craig Henderson to his locked barn where they retrieved the briefcase. Although the government almost certainly could have obtained a warrant to search the contents of the briefcase, it elected not to do so, and instead the agents pried open the briefcase with screwdrivers and a hammer. The briefcase contained names of wholesale jewelers and information that would be useful to a jewel thief, such as combinations for locks belonging to the jewelers.

A few days after the search, Friedman demonstrated his divided loyalties by having his daughter contact Basinski in Las Vegas to inform him that the FBI had the briefcase. Apparently concerned, Basinski then arranged to meet with Friedman in Chicago. During the meeting Friedman confirmed that the FBI had the briefcase, at which Basinski expressed his displeasure. Subsequently, on March 23, 1999, Basinski and his friend Leonard Turow allegedly paid a visit to Friedman's home in the middle of the night. After Friedman opened the door Basinski allegedly attacked him. Basinski fled only when Friedman's wife called the police. Based on the attack, a federal grand jury indicted Basinski for retaliating against a witness and obstruction of justice. 18 U.S.C. §§ 1513(b), 1503(a). Basinski moved to suppress any evidence concerning the contents of the briefcase based on his Fourth Amendment rights. The government argued that suppression would be improper because although it did not have a warrant for the search, it had Friedman's consent and, alternatively, Basinski had abandoned the briefcase. Should Basinski's motion to suppress be granted? *United States v. Basinski*, 226 F.3d 829 (7th Cir. 2000).

Read the court opinion at:
laws.lp.findlaw.com/7th/993933.html

6 The record before the circuit court reflects that on June 9, 1997, Brian Roush, a Price County Deputy Sheriff, learned of information conveyed by a confidential informant regarding drug activity occurring at the Martwick residence. On May 3, 1997, the informant apparently saw large amounts of processed and unprocessed marijuana, as well as live plants in Martwick's house. According to the informant, Martwick complained that he needed to keep his plants inside because the weather was too cold in May to transplant them outdoors.

After reviewing the written report with fellow Deputy Sheriff Chris Jarosinski, Deputy Roush inquired about the possibility of obtaining a search warrant of the residence with the assistance of the Price County District Attorney's office. District Attorney Patrick G. Schilling thought the confidential information was probably stale because the informant observed the marijuana at Martwick's residence in May. Because the district attorney was concerned about the information's potential staleness, Deputy Roush decided to investigate further by viewing Martwick's property himself.

Before even reading the confidential informant's report, Deputy Roush had suspected Martwick of growing marijuana. Two years before, a county drug officer told Deputy Roush that he had found remnants of old marijuana growth in the Town of Elk. Martwick's name appeared on the pails used to grow the marijuana. Then, during the summer of 1996 another small marijuana plant was found on property thought to belong to Martwick.

Deputy Roush and Deputy Jarosinski drove to Martwick's residence on June 9, and a neighbor gave them permission to park their squad car on the neighbor's property. The boundary lines of Martwick's property are unmarked. The property is one of a group of recreational and year-around homes located along the Wilson Flowage in Price County. Approximately 20 homes fall within a one-mile radius of Martwick's home, and Martwick's nearest neighbor lives directly across the road.

Martwick's 1.52-acre property is irregularly shaped. According to Martwick's hand-drawn diagram, his property is approximately 122 feet long on its eastern edge, 260 feet long on its western edge, 333 feet long on its northern edge, and 413 feet long on its southern edge. (Exhibit 26.) On this diagram, Martwick's house appears near the center of the property, approximately 100 feet from E. Wilson Flowage Road, the main road bounding his property. At the extreme edge of the property farthest from the road are two ginseng sheds. Martwick also raises worms near the ginseng sheds. A gravel driveway leads up to the house from the road.

Martwick does not cultivate a traditional mowed lawn. As defense counsel admitted to the circuit court, his "client's home would not win a Martha Stewart award." Instead, a twenty-foot clearing surrounds the house in which only low-lying weeds, brush, and wildflowers grow. Woods cover the remainder of the property past the clearing. A footpath begins within ten feet of the house and extends into the wooded section leading to the ginseng sheds. Martwick occasionally clears the path with a brush cutter.

After parking their squad car, the two deputies walked onto Martwick's property from the neighboring property. According to Martwick's hand-drawn diagram, the deputies entered his property from the southern edge at a point between the house and the ginseng sheds. (Exhibit 26.) In the woods, Deputy Roush tripped over what he thought was some sort of wire placed no more than one foot above the ground. Then, the deputies observed five marijuana plants in four five-gallon plastic pails. Deputy Roush estimated that the pails were located between 50 and 75 feet from the house along the path leading to the ginseng sheds. The plants were approximately two and one-half to three and one-half feet tall. Deputy Roush and Deputy Jarosinski cut a leaf slip off of one of the suspected marijuana plants and returned immediately to the district attorney's office to conduct a Duquenois-Levine test. The leaf slip produced a positive result indicating that it contained THC, the active ingredient in marijuana.

Based on their observations and the test results, that same day the deputies applied for and obtained a search warrant. Within approximately three hours the deputies executed the search warrant and seized the plastic pails with the five marijuana plants, 29 smaller marijuana plants, baggies with green plant material and marijuana seeds, and plant cultivation products, among other items. Deputy Roush also took photographs of Martwick's property. Deputy Roush testified that from the vantage point of the potted plants, he could see the top of Martwick's house in the distance. (Exhibit 27.) However, from the house, a person could not see the plants.

The state charged Martwick with manufacturing marijuana contrary to Wis. Stat. § 961.41(1)(h)2. On August 21, 1997, Martwick moved to suppress the evidence the deputy sheriffs obtained on the basis that the search warrant for his residence was not supported by probable cause, since the deputies improperly obtained evidence supporting probable cause to search the entire property by illegally entering the curtilage of his residence. Should the motion to suppress be granted? *State v. Martwick*, 604 N.W.2d 552 (Wis. 2000).

Read the court opinion at:
www.wisbar.org/Wis3/98-0101.htm

Part IV

Admissions and Confessions and Pretrial Identification

Admissions and Confessions

Outline

Miranda v. Arizona
laws.findlaw.com/us/384/
436.html

Since the U.S. Supreme Court decision in *Miranda v. Arizona,* 384 U.S. 436, 86 S.Ct. 1602, 16 L.Ed.2d 694 (1966), the name Miranda has become familiar to criminal justice personnel throughout the United States. The *Miranda* decision radically changed the course of law enforcement in the area of admissions, confessions, and interrogations. This chapter focuses on the *Miranda* decision and the multitude of other court decisions interpreting *Miranda.* Other aspects of the law governing admissions and confessions are also discussed.

Definitions of the terms *statement, admission,* and *confession,* as used in this chapter, will assist the reader in understanding the chapter. **Statement** is a broad term meaning simply any oral or written declaration or assertion. **Admission** means a statement or acknowledgment of facts by a person tending to incriminate that person, but not sufficient of itself to establish guilt of a crime. An admission, alone or in connection with other facts, tends to show the existence of one or more, but not all, elements of a crime. **Confession** means a statement or acknowledgment of facts by a person establishing that person's guilt of all elements of a crime.

Historical Background

To fully appreciate the effect and significance of the *Miranda* decision, one must understand the developments in the law leading up to that decision. This section discusses the important concept of voluntariness of admissions and confessions and the landmark case of *Escobedo v. Illinois.*

Voluntariness

Before 1964, the only test for the admissibility of a defendant's admission or confession was its "voluntariness." An involuntary statement was ruled inadmissible because it violated the due process clause of the Fifth and Fourteenth Amendments to the Constitution. Involuntary statements violate due process for the following reasons: First, an involuntary statement is considered to be inherently untrustworthy or unreliable, and convictions based on unreliable evidence violate due process. Second, coercive police practices are a violation of "fundamental fairness," an essential element of due process. Therefore, a confession coerced by the police violates due process, even if that confession is otherwise reliable. Third, free choice is an essential aspect of due process, and an involuntary confession cannot be the product of a person's free and rational choice. Finally, our system of justice is an accusatorial, not an inquisitorial, system. As stated by the U.S. Supreme Court:

> Our decisions under [the Fourteenth Amendment] have made clear that convictions following the admission into evidence of confessions which are involuntary, i.e., the product of coercion, either physical or psychological, cannot stand. This is so not because such confessions are unlikely to be true but because the methods used to extract them offend an underlying principle in the enforcement of our criminal law: that ours is an accusatorial and not an inquisitorial system—a system in which the State must establish guilt by evidence independently and freely secured and may not by coercion prove its charge against an accused out of his own mouth. . . . To be sure, confessions cruelly extorted may be and have been, to an unascertained extent, found to be untrustworthy. But the constitutional principle of excluding confessions that are involuntary does not rest on this consideration. Indeed, in many of the cases in which the command of the

Due Process Clause has compelled us to reverse state convictions involving the use of confessions obtained by impermissible methods, independent corroborating evidence left little doubt of the truth of what the defendant had confessed. *Rogers v. Richmond,* 365 U.S. 534, 540–41, 81 S.Ct. 735, 739–40, 5 L.Ed.2d 760, 766–67 (1961).

The voluntariness requirement was established in *Brown v. Mississippi,* 297 U.S. 278, 56 S.Ct. 461, 80 L.Ed. 682 (1936), in which the U.S. Supreme Court held that a confession coerced from a defendant by means of police brutality violated due process of law. Later cases established that various other forms of police coercive conduct, including the more subtle psychological pressures, might render a resulting confession involuntary and thus violative of due process. The test for voluntariness of a statement was stated in *Townsend v. Sain,* 372 U.S. 293, 307–08, 83 S.Ct. 745, 754, 9 L.Ed.2d 770, 782–83 (1963):

> If an individual's "will was overborne" or if his confession was not "the product of a rational intellect and a free will," his confession is inadmissible because coerced. These standards are applicable whether a confession is the product of physical intimidation or psychological pressure. . . . Any questioning by police officers which in fact produces a confession which is not the product of a free intellect renders that confession inadmissible.

The following kinds of police conduct have been found to violate due process:

- Threats of violence. *Beecher v. Alabama,* 389 U.S. 35, 88 S.Ct. 189, 19 L.Ed.2d 35 (1967).
- Confinement of the suspect in a small space until the suspect confessed. *United States v. Koch,* 552 F.2d 1216 (7th Cir. 1977).
- Continued interrogation of an injured and depressed suspect in a hospital intensive care unit. *Mincey v. Arizona,* 437 U.S. 385, 98 S.Ct. 2408, 57 L.Ed.2d 290 (1978).
- Deprivation of food or sleep. *Greenwald v. Wisconsin,* 390 U.S. 519, 88 S.Ct. 1152, 20 L.Ed.2d 77 (1968).
- Extended periods of incommunicado interrogation. *Ashcraft v. Tennessee,* 322 U.S. 143, 64 S.Ct. 921, 88 L.Ed. 1192 (1944); *Davis v. North Carolina,* 384 U.S. 737, 86 S.Ct. 1761, 16 L.Ed.2d 895 (1966).
- Trickery or deception. *Spano v. New York,* 360 U.S. 315, 79 S.Ct. 1202, 3 L.Ed.2d 1265 (1959). However, some courts have adopted the view that "[c]onfessions generally are not vitiated when they are obtained by deception or trickery, as long as the means employed are not calculated to produce an untrue statement." *Matter of D.A.S.,* 391 A.2d 255, 258 (D.C.App. 1978).
- Obtaining of a statement during a period of unnecessary delay between arrest and presentment. *McNabb v. United States,* 318 U.S. 332, 63 S.Ct. 608, 87 L.Ed. 819 (1943); *Mallory v. United States,* 354 U.S. 449, 77 S.Ct. 1356, 1 L.Ed.2d 1479 (1957). The *McNabb* and *Mallory* cases apply only to federal courts and hold that any admission or confession obtained during an unreasonable delay between arrest and first appearance before a magistrate will be inadmissible in court. This rule was developed pursuant to the Court's supervisory power over the lower federal courts and is not applicable to the states as a constitutional rule would have been. The Court, clearly concerned about incommunicado interrogation and coerced confessions, designed the rule to implement the guarantees of Rule 5 of the Federal Rules of Criminal Procedure. Rule 5, at the time of the *Mallory* decision, required prompt arraignment, notification of rights, and provision for terms of bail. The Court never

caselaw.findlaw.com/data/
constitution/amendment05/
09.html#1
Comprehensive discussion (with annotations) of confessions, including police interrogation, due process, and self-incrimination
lawschool.lexis.com/emanuel/
web/crimpro/crimpro05.htm
General overview of law relating to confessions and police interrogation
faculty.ncwc.edu/toconnor/
miranda.htm
Article, "*Miranda* Law: A Guide to the Privilege against Self-Incrimination"; brief discussion of *Miranda* requirements and exceptions
www.poco.org/rab/law/
summary/confessions.htm
Article dealing with constitutional considerations relating to confessions; focuses on Texas law

For new and updated weblinks, go to www.wadsworth.com/
cj/ferdico0253

Rogers v. Richmond
laws.findlaw.com/us/365/
534.html
Brown v. Mississippi
laws.findlaw.com/us/297/
278.html
Townsend v. Sain
laws.findlaw.com/us/372/
293.html
Beecher v. Alabama
laws.findlaw.com/us/389/
35.html
Mincey v. Arizona
laws.findlaw.com/us/437/
385.html
Greenwald v. Wisconsin
laws.findlaw.com/us/390/
519.html
Ashcraft v. Tennessee
laws.findlaw.com/us/322/
143.html
Davis v. North Carolina
laws.findlaw.com/us/384/
737.html
Spano v. New York
laws.findlaw.com/us/360/
315.html
McNabb v. United States
laws.findlaw.com/us/318/
332.html
Mallory v. United States
laws.findlaw.com/us/354/
449.html

Complete text of 18 U.S.C.
§ 3501
caselaw.findlaw.com/scripts/ts_
search.pl?title=18&sec=3501

www.lib.jjay.cuny.edu/cje/html/
sample1.html
Article, "Deception by Police" by
Jerome Skolnick; contains exten-
sive section, "Interrogatory
Deception"
www.law.ukans.edu/research/
frcriml.htm#II
Current version of Rule 5 of the
Federal Rules of Criminal
Procedure

attempted to specify a minimum time after which delay in presenting a suspect for arraignment would invalidate confessions. Congress, however, enacted 18 U.S.C. §3501(c), which "permits exclusion of a confession, regardless of vol-untariness, where the confession is made after six hours following arrest but prior to arraignment and where the delay between arrest and arraignment is unreasonable in light of the means of transportation and the distance traveled to the nearest available magistrate." *United States v. Wilbon,* 911 F.Supp. 1420, 1432 (D.N.M. 1995). Several states have adopted similar provisions.

In contrast, courts have found the following practices, standing alone and without additional evidence of a suspect's will being overborne, insufficiently coercive to con-stitute a violation of due process:

- Promises of leniency. "[A] confession is not involuntary merely because the suspect was promised leniency if he cooperated with law enforcement officials." *United States v. Guarno,* 819 F.2d 28, 31 (2d Cir. 1987).
- Encouragement to cooperate.

Encouraging a suspect to tell the truth and suggesting that his cohorts might leave him "holding the bag" does not, as a matter of law, overcome a confessor's will. . . . Neither is a statement that the accused's cooperation will be made known to the court a suffi-cient inducement so as to render a subsequent incriminating statement involuntary. . . . A truthful and noncoercive statement of the possible penalties which an accused faces may be given to the accused without overbearing one's free will. Such an account may increase the chance that one detained will make a statement. However, as long as the statement results from an informed and intelligent appraisal of the risks involved rather than a coercive atmosphere, the statement may be considered to have been voluntarily made. . . . [T]elling the appellant in a noncoercive manner of the realistically expected penalties and encouraging her to tell the truth is no more than affording her the chance to make an informed decision with respect to her cooperation with the government. *United States v. Ballard,* 586 F.2d 1060, 1063 (5th Cir. 1978).

- Misrepresentations. *Evans v. Dowd,* 932 F.2d 739 (8th Cir. 1991), found a confession voluntary even though the officer misstated the purpose of the investigation and falsely stated that he had eyewitnesses.
- Promises of psychological treatment. *United States v. McClinton,* 982 F.2d 278, 283 (8th Cir. 1992), found the defendant's confession voluntary even though police "told him that he was not a bad person and that he would receive help for his drug and alcohol problems if he talked to them."

Courts also examine the personal characteristics of defendants in determining the voluntariness of an admission or confession. Some of the characteristics considered important are age; mental capacity; education level; physical or mental impairment from illness, injury, or intoxication; and experience in dealing with the police. The U.S. Supreme Court said that these personal characteristics are "relevant only in establish-ing a setting in which actual coercion might have been exerted to overcome the will of the suspect." *Procunier v. Atchley,* 400 U.S. 446, 453–54, 91 S.Ct. 485, 489, 27 L.Ed.2d 524, 531 (1971). The Court elaborated in *Colorado v. Connelly,* stating that

Procunier v. Atchley
laws.findlaw.com/us/400/
446.html
Colorado v. Connelly
laws.findlaw.com/us/479/
157.html

while mental condition is surely relevant to an individual's susceptibility to police coer-cion, mere examination of the confessant's state of mind can never conclude the due process inquiry. . . . [C]oercive police activity is a necessary predicate to the finding that a confession is not "voluntary" within the meaning of the Due Process Clause of the

Fourteenth Amendment. 479 U.S. 157, 165–67, 107 S.Ct. 515, 521–22, 93 L.Ed.2d 473, 483–84 (1986).

Therefore, absent coercive conduct by the police, every confession is considered to be voluntary. "Absent police conduct causally related to the confession, there is simply no basis for concluding that any state actor has deprived a criminal defendant of due process of law." 479 U.S. at 164, 107 S.Ct. at 520, 93 L.Ed.2d at 482.

Of course, state courts may decide that their state constitutions provide greater protection than the U.S. Constitution with respect to determining the voluntariness of a confession. For example, in *State v. Rees,* 2000 ME 55, 748 A.2d 976, the Maine Supreme Judicial Court found that because the defendant suffered from dementia, his statements to police officers were not the product of the free exercise of his will and rational intellect. The court stressed that there was no finding of improper or incorrect conduct on the part of the police. The decision pointed out that the determination that the defendant's dementia rendered him incapable of making a voluntary statement under the circumstances, was based not on the Fifth or Fourteenth Amendment, but the Maine Constitution.

Determination of the voluntariness of an admission or confession under the Fifth and Fourteenth Amendments to the U.S. Constitution can be summarized as follows:

- If no police coercion occurred, any statement will be considered voluntary, regardless of the suspect's mental or physical condition.
- If police coercion occurred, the voluntariness of the statement will be evaluated on the basis of the totality of the circumstances surrounding the giving of the statement. Except for the use of physical violence by the police, no single fact or circumstance will be solely determinative.

Escobedo and *Miranda*

In 1964, a major change in the law took place. In the case of *Escobedo v. Illinois*, 378 U.S. 478, 84 S.Ct. 1758, 12 L.Ed.2d 977 (1964), the U.S. Supreme Court held that

> where . . . the investigation is no longer a general inquiry into an unsolved crime but has begun to focus on a particular suspect, the suspect has been taken into police custody, the police carry out a process of interrogations that lends itself to eliciting incriminating statements, the suspect has requested and been denied an opportunity to consult with his lawyer, and the police have not effectively warned him of his absolute constitutional right to remain silent, the accused has been denied "the Assistance of Counsel" in violation of the Sixth Amendment to the Constitution as "made obligatory upon the States by the Fourteenth Amendment," . . . and . . . no statement elicited by the police during the interrogation may be used against him at a criminal trial. 378 U.S. at 491, 84 S.Ct. at 1765, 12 L.Ed.2d at 986.

The *Escobedo* case was significant not only because it shifted the area of inquiry from due process to the Sixth Amendment but also because it did not follow a totality-of-the-circumstances approach. Instead, the Court took a single circumstance and made it the single determinative factor in all cases in which it occurred. The Court said that "when the process shifts from investigatory to accusatory—when its focus is on the accused and its purpose is to elicit a confession . . . the accused must be permitted to consult with his lawyer." 378 U.S. at 492, 84 S.Ct. at 1766, 12 L.Ed.2d at 987. This has come to be known as the *Escobedo focus of investigation test.*

www.forensic-evidence.com/
site/Police/Pol_voluntar.html
Article, "The Evolution of the 'Voluntariness' Standards" by Andre A. Moenssens

Escobedo v. Illinois
laws.findlaw.com/us/378/
478.html

Miranda v. Arizona, decided two years later in 1966, again rejected a totality-of-the-circumstances approach, extended the *Escobedo* decision, and shifted the area of inquiry to the Fifth Amendment. In short, the *Miranda* case held that "the prosecution may not use statements, whether exculpatory or inculpatory, stemming from custodial interrogation of the defendant unless it demonstrates the use of procedural safeguards effective to secure the privilege against self-incrimination." 384 U.S. at 444, 86 S.Ct. at 1612, 16 L.Ed.2d at 706. Such statements may not be used to prove the case against the defendant even if the statements were otherwise voluntary. If the statements were *not* voluntary, they will be inadmissible even though the *Miranda* requirements were satisfied. As the U.S. Supreme Court said in *Dickerson v. United States*, 530 U.S. 428, 444, 120 S.Ct. 2326, 2336, 147 L.Ed.2d 405, 420 (2000), "The requirement that *Miranda* warnings be given does not, of course, dispense with the voluntariness inquiry."

Dickerson v. United States
laws.findlaw.com/us/000/
99-5525.html

Satisfaction of *Miranda* requirements is a relevant consideration in the determination of the voluntariness of a confession, but, as the following quotations indicate, is not conclusive.

> We do not suggest that compliance with *Miranda* conclusively establishes the voluntariness of a subsequent confession. But cases in which a defendant can make a colorable argument that a self-incriminating statement was "compelled" despite the fact that the law enforcement authorities adhered to the dictates of *Miranda* are rare. *Berkemer v. McCarty*, 468 U.S. 420, 433 n.20, 104 S.Ct. 3138, 3147 n.20, 82 L.Ed.2d 317, 330 n.20 (1984).

Berkemer v. McCarty
laws.findlaw.com/us/468/
420.html

New York v. Quarles
laws.findlaw.com/us/467/
649.html

Furthermore, "[a]s the *Miranda Court* itself recognized, the failure to provide *Miranda* warnings in and of itself does not render a confession involuntary." . . . *New York v. Quarles*, 467 U.S. 649, 655 n.5, 104 S.Ct. 2626, 2631 n.5, 81 L.Ed.2d 550, 556 n.5 (1984).

Key Points

1. Coercive police activity is necessary for an admission or confession to be found involuntary. The totality of the circumstances surrounding the giving of the statement, including the defendant's mental or physical condition, must be evaluated to determine if the coercion overcame the defendant's will.

2. Satisfaction of *Miranda* requirements is a relevant consideration in determining the voluntariness of an admission or confession, but it is not conclusive.

3. Only voluntary admissions or confessions that are obtained in compliance with *Miranda* requirements will be admissible in court.

Facts and Holdings of *Miranda*

The U.S. Supreme Court's opinion in *Miranda v. Arizona* encompasses three other cases besides *Miranda*, all dealing with the admissibility of statements obtained from a person who is subjected to custodial police interrogation. A brief description of the facts of each case is presented to delineate the scope of the opinion.

In *Miranda v. Arizona* the defendant was arrested at his home for rape and taken to a police station, where the complaining witness identified him. The defendant was then interrogated and within two hours signed a written confession. At no time was the defendant informed of his right to consult with an attorney, his right to have an attorney present during the interrogation, or his right not to be compelled to incriminate himself.

In *Vignera v. New York* the defendant was apprehended in connection with a robbery and was taken to detective squad headquarters. The defendant was interrogated; he confessed and was then locked up. About eight hours later, the defendant was interrogated again and gave a written statement. At no time was the defendant informed of any of his rights.

In *Westover v. United States* the defendant was arrested by municipal police as a robbery suspect. The municipal police, and later the FBI, interrogated the defendant at the municipal police department. After two hours of questioning, the defendant signed two confessions. The Court noted that the FBI interrogation was conducted following the interrogation by municipal police in the same police station—in the same compelling surroundings.

In *California v. Stewart* the defendant was arrested at his home, where police found proceeds from a robbery. The defendant was then taken to a police station and placed in a cell where, over a period of five days, he was interrogated nine times. The Court noted that the defendant was isolated with his interrogators at all times except when he was being confronted by an accusing witness.

In each of these cases, the defendant was questioned by police officers, detectives, or a prosecuting attorney in unfamiliar surroundings, cut off from the outside world. In none of the cases was the defendant given a full and effective warning of his rights at the outset of the interrogation process. In all of the cases, the questioning elicited oral statements. In three of the cases, signed statements were also given, and those statements were admitted into evidence at trial. Thus, all the cases shared the features of incommunicado interrogation of a person in a police-dominated atmosphere, resulting in self-incriminating statements without full warnings of constitutional rights.

In the *Miranda* opinion, the Court reviewed the facts in each case and then discussed specific police interrogation techniques as prescribed in police manuals. In condemning those techniques, the Court said:

> It is obvious that such an interrogation environment is created for no purpose other than to subjugate the individual to the will of his examiner. This atmosphere carries its own badge of intimidation. To be sure, this is not physical intimidation, but it is equally destructive of human dignity. The current practice of incommunicado interrogation is at odds with one of our Nation's most cherished principles—that the individual may not be compelled to incriminate himself. Unless adequate protective devices are employed to dispel the compulsion inherent in custodial surroundings, no statement obtained from the defendant can truly be the product of his free choice. 384 U.S. at 457–58, 86 S.Ct. at 1619, 16 L.Ed.2d at 714.

The Court then established procedural safeguards to protect the privilege against self-incrimination. Those safeguards are the *Miranda* warnings so familiar to law enforcement personnel.

> [W]hen an individual is taken into custody or otherwise deprived of his freedom by the authorities in any significant way and is subjected to questioning, the privilege against self-incrimination is jeopardized. Procedural safeguards must be employed to protect the privilege and unless other fully effective means are adopted to notify the person of his right of silence and to assure that the exercise of the right will be scrupulously honored, the following measures are required. He must be warned prior to any question that he

Case in Point

Interpreting *Dickerson v. United States*

Richard Morris Stanga, Sr., and his wife, Judy, divorced in 1988 after thirty years of marriage. Stanga's long-standing alcoholism factored foremost in the breakdown of their relationship. Judy received the couple's home in the divorce. Nevertheless, hoping Stanga would eventually find sobriety and they would reconcile, she allowed him to stay at her home occasionally. But after years with no change, Judy "gave up on" reconciliation. She obtained a protection order forbidding Stanga from contacting her or coming to her home. He began living on the street, but stayed at a homeless shelter in Sioux Falls when sober.

In November 1998, Stanga spotted Judy with a male acquaintance at church. Upset, he telephoned her numerous times. Although the calls were a violation of the protection order, Judy did not report them to law enforcement. When she did not return his messages, he resorted to more direct contact. On the evening of November 16, Judy was home alone. She heard noises outside at 7:30 P.M. coming from the back porch. When she looked out the window, she saw Stanga with "something shiny in his hand that he took out of his pocket." She dialed 911 for emergency help.

While Judy was on the telephone, Stanga broke the front window with a rock and crawled through into the house. He grabbed the phone from her, threw it to the floor, and hit her repeatedly with his fists. He pulled off her glasses and flung them down. In the struggle, her necklace and earrings were broken off. Then he ordered her upstairs with the threat, "or I'll kill you right here." Grabbing the neck of her sweater and twisting it into a tight hold, he began dragging her up the stairs. All the while, the 911 operator remained on the line, recording the unfolding events.

In a few minutes the police arrived. They found five or six large landscaping rocks piled against the back door—an apparent attempt by Stanga to block Judy's escape. The officers entered the house through another door and came upon Stanga and Judy halfway up the stairwell. A belt was wrapped around his wrist. Concerned that he had a weapon, the officers did not attempt to seize him immediately but ordered him to show his hands and let Judy go. Still clutching Judy's sweater, Stanga would not relent. He kept putting his free hand inside his coat pocket. After a brief standoff, the officers grabbed his legs, dragged him down the stairs with Judy in tow, and pried him away from her. Officers later recovered various items Stanga had brought with him that night: a utility knife, razor blades, needle-nose pliers, a pair of blunt-nose scissors, and a roll of duct tape.

Stanga was taken to the Minnehaha County Jail. A blood sample was drawn for testing, which later showed that he had a blood alcohol content of 0.17. At 8:55 P.M. Detective Troy Lubbers began to interrogate him. The interview was recorded

has the right to remain silent, that anything he says can be used against him in a court of law, that he has the right to the presence of an attorney, and that if he cannot afford an attorney one will be appointed for him prior to any questioning if he so desires. Opportunity to exercise these rights must be afforded to him throughout the interrogation. After such warnings have been given, and such opportunity afforded him, the individual may knowingly and intelligently waive these rights and agree to answer questions or make a statement. But unless and until such warnings and waiver are demonstrated by the prosecution at trial no evidence obtained as a result of interrogation can be used against him. 384 U.S. at 478–79, 86 S.Ct. at 1630, 16 L.Ed.2d at 726.

Shortly after the *Miranda* decision, in 1968, Congress enacted 18 U.S.C. §3501, which in essence laid down a rule that the admissibility of a suspect's statement made during custodial interrogation should turn only on whether or not it was voluntarily made. In the intervening years, that provision of law had never been relied on to challenge the *Miranda* decision. In *Dickerson v. United States*, 166 F.3d 667 (4th Cir. 1999), however, the court found that although the defendant had not received *Miranda* warnings before custodial interrogation, his statement was admissible under Section 3501 because it was voluntarily made. The court concluded that the *Miranda* decision was

with a hidden video camera and microphone. Only Detective Lubbers and Stanga were in the room. At trial, the detective testified that he repeatedly lied to Stanga to induce him to confess. Stanga admitted during interrogation that he wanted to kill Judy, but also contradicted himself with remarks that he would "never hurt" her and that he only wanted to "talk" to her.

Before the interrogation began, Detective Lubbers identified himself as an officer and advised Stanga of his *Miranda* rights. After a little hesitancy, he agreed to give an interview, acknowledging that he knew he did not have to. Lubbers then began questioning in a conversational tone. Stanga admitted that he had been drinking and Lubbers concluded that Stanga was under the influence: his breath smelled of an alcoholic beverage, his intoxication was apparent by his behavior, and his slurred speech was difficult to understand at times. During the interview, Stanga did not ask for an attorney or for questioning to stop. He was responsive and displayed an awareness of details such as Judy's street address, the length of his marriage to her, and how long it had been since their divorce.

Lubbers said numerous times that he was there to listen, making comments such as "it's between you and me," "I'm here to listen to your side," and "you need to get this off your chest," all as part of his interrogation technique. Stanga said repeatedly that he went to the house to "talk" to Judy, but he also admitted hitting her, and then divulged having in mind a plan to kill her. Throughout the interview, he sought assurances on whether he could trust the detective—whether he could speak "straight up." When Stanga seemed to forget who he was talking to, Lubbers reminded him, "Well, I am the cop." At one point, Stanga told the detective, "I know you're here to get something against me." But Lubbers responded, "No, I'm here for you and I to talk." After hearing this, Stanga said, "Okay. I'm going to tell you straight up, and if it goes any further than me and you, then I won't tell. I don't know." Lubbers responded, "You can trust me straight up. Go ahead."

Still needing more assurance, Stanga asked, "What I say to you, suppose it goes to everybody?" As the videotape ran and as other officers watched unseen, Lubbers replied, "Between you and me. There's nobody else in the room here. It's between you and me." Stanga confided again that he was thinking about killing Judy when he broke into her home. Later, seeming to understand that his statement could be used against him, Stanga said, "I'll tell you the truth and you tell the judge." Yet at the end of the interview, Stanga repeated his earlier overture, "Don't tell anybody either." Lubbers responded, "No, I ain't telling anybody anything. . . ." In light of *Dickerson v. United States*, should Stanga's motion to suppress the statements obtained during the interview with Lubbers be granted? *State v. Stanga*, 617 N.W.2d 486 (S.D. 2000).

Read the court opinion at:
www.state.sd.us/state/judicial/opinions/Cases/2000/ 2000_129.htm

---

not a constitutional holding and that therefore Congress could by statute have the final say on the question of admissibility. The U.S. Supreme Court reversed:

> We hold that *Miranda*, being a constitutional decision of this Court, may not be in effect overruled by an Act of Congress, and we decline to overrule *Miranda* ourselves. We therefore hold that *Miranda* and its progeny in this Court govern the admissibility of statements made during custodial interrogation in both state and federal courts. *Dickerson v. United States*, 530 U.S. 428, 432, 120 S.Ct. 2326, 2329–30, 147 L.Ed.2d 405, 412 (2000).

Issues of *Miranda*

The *Miranda* decision has raised many questions, and the issues can generally be divided into two categories:

- The first category is whether *Miranda* requirements apply to the particular case. The issues here are whether the defendant was in custody, whether the defendant's statements were the result of interrogation, whether the

www.truthinjustice.org/ scmiranda.htm
Article, "'Dickerson' Leaves '*Miranda*' Stronger Than Ever" by Tony Mauro
www.fletc.gov/legal/ archive_dir.htm
Article, "The Newest Constitutional Right—The Right to *Miranda* Warnings" by Jacquelyn Kuhens; lead article in the July 6, 2000, issue of *Quarterly Review: Legal Commentary for Federal Law Enforcement Officers*
duke.tnstate.edu/cmcginnis/ twoviewsofMiranda.htm
"Two Views of Miranda"; two articles discussing *Dickerson v. United States*

- interrogator was a law enforcement officer or agent, and whether the seriousness of the offense has any bearing.
- The second category is whether *Miranda* requirements have been met in a case in which they apply. The issues here are whether the warnings were adequate, whether rights were clearly waived, whether the suspect was competent to waive the rights, and whether more than one interrogation is allowed under *Miranda*.

In short, the major issues of *Miranda* hinge on the meaning of four terms: *custody, interrogation, warning,* and *waiver.* The remainder of this chapter is devoted to a discussion of the meanings of these terms as well as a discussion of additional miscellaneous issues.

Custody

The warnings required by the *Miranda* case must be given before police question a person who is in **custody** or deprived of his or her freedom of action in any significant way.

> Although the circumstances of each case must certainly influence a determination of whether a suspect is "in custody" for purposes of receiving *Miranda* protection, the ultimate inquiry is simply whether there is a "formal arrest or restraint on freedom of movement" of the degree associated with a formal arrest. *California v. Beheler*, 463 U.S. 1121, 1125, 103 S.Ct. 3517, 3520, 77 L.Ed.2d 1275, 1279 (1983).

In other words, has there been a seizure tantamount to arrest? (See Chapter 4.) In answering this question, courts consider the totality of the circumstances under which the questioning occurred from the viewpoint of a reasonable person. The circumstances to be considered include:

> The time, the place and purpose of the encounter; the persons present during the interrogation; the words spoken by the officer to the defendant; the officer's tone of voice and general demeanor; the length and mood of the interrogation; whether any limitation of movement or other form of restraint was placed on the defendant during the interrogation; the officer's response to any questions asked by the defendant; whether directions were given to the defendant during the interrogation; and the defendant's verbal or nonverbal response to such directions. *People v. Horn*, 790 P.2d 816, 818 (Colo. 1990).

As stated by the U.S. Supreme Court, "the only relevant inquiry is how a reasonable man in the suspect's position would have understood his situation." *Berkemer v. McCarty*, 468 U.S. 420, 442, 104 S.Ct. 3138, 3151, 82 L.Ed.2d 317, 336 (1984). "The reasonable person through whom we view the situation must be neutral to the environment and to the purposes of the investigation—that is, neither guilty of criminal conduct and thus overly apprehensive nor insensitive to the seriousness of the circumstances." *United States v. Bengivenga*, 845 F.2d 593, 596 (5th Cir. 1988). The following discussion examines various factors considered by the courts in determining whether a person is in custody for *Miranda* purposes.

Focus of Investigation

The *Miranda* decision is generally understood to have abandoned the focus of investigation test of the *Escobedo* case to determine when an interrogated suspect is entitled to warnings. The U.S. Supreme Court specifically held that even though a suspect

California v. Beheler
laws.findlaw.com/us/463/
1121.html

www.co.alameda.ca.us/da/pov/
Miranda_Custody.htm
Article, "*Miranda* 'Custody'"
from the District Attorney's
Office in Alameda County,
California
www.uncp.edu/home/
vanderhoof/
geolr.html#Custodial
Short summary of the law relating to custodial interrogations

is clearly the focus of a criminal investigation, the suspect need not be given *Miranda* warnings if he or she is not otherwise in custody or deprived of freedom of action in any significant way. *Beckwith v. United States,* 425 U.S. 341, 96 S.Ct. 1612, 48 L.Ed.2d 1 (1976).

> Our cases make clear, in no uncertain terms, that any inquiry into whether the interrogating officers have focused their suspicions upon the individual being questioned (assuming those suspicions remain undisclosed) is not relevant for purposes of *Miranda.* *Stansbury v. California,* 511 U.S. 318, 326, 114 S.Ct. 1526, 1530, 128 L.Ed.2d 293, 301 (1994).

The focus concept may still have some vitality as one of the circumstances to be considered by a court in determining the custody issue, but only if an officer's views or beliefs were somehow manifested to the person under interrogation and would have affected how a reasonable person in that position would perceive his or her freedom to leave.

> An officer's knowledge or beliefs may bear upon the custody issue if they are conveyed, by word or deed, to the individual being questioned. . . . Those beliefs are relevant only to the extent they would affect how a reasonable person in the position of the individual being questioned would gauge the breadth of his or her "'freedom of action.'" . . . Even a clear statement from an officer that the person under interrogation is a prime suspect is not, in itself, dispositive of the custody issue, for some suspects are free to come and go until the police decide to make an arrest. The weight and pertinence of any communications regarding the officer's degree of suspicion will depend upon the facts and circumstances of the particular case. *Stansbury v. California,* 511 U.S. 318, 325, 114 S.Ct. 1526, 1530, 128 L.Ed.2d 293, 300 (1994).

Place of Interrogation

Court decisions interpreting *Miranda* hold that the place of interrogation is an important, but not conclusive, factor in determining custody. The following discussion analyzes cases that have relied heavily on the place of interrogation in determining the question of custody.

POLICE STATIONS   In all four of the cases decided by the *Miranda* opinion, the suspect was questioned in a police station after arrest. There is little question that custody exists in this type of situation. Other courts have held that even if a person is not under arrest but is present at a police station for questioning at the command of the police, the person is in custody for purposes of *Miranda. United States v. Pierce,* 397 F.2d 128 (4th Cir. 1968).

In *Oregon v. Mathiason,* 429 U.S. 492, 97 S.Ct. 711, 50 L.Ed.2d 714 (1977), however, the U.S. Supreme Court held that a suspect questioned in a police station is not necessarily in custody. In that case, the defendant, a parolee, was a suspect in a burglary. A state police officer asked him to come to the state police offices "to discuss something." When the defendant arrived, the officer took him into a closed office and told him that he was not under arrest. The officer then informed the defendant that he was a suspect in the burglary and falsely stated that the defendant's fingerprints had been found at the scene. Within five minutes, the defendant confessed to the burglary. He left the office one-half hour later.

The Court held that the *Miranda* warnings were not required because the defendant was not in custody.

Beckwith v. United States
laws.findlaw.com/us/000/
u10398.html

Stansbury v. California
laws.findlaw.com/us/000/
ul0398.html

Oregon v. Mathiason
laws.findlaw.com/us/429/
492.html

[T]here is no indication that the questioning took place in a context where respondent's freedom to depart was restricted in any way. He came voluntarily to the police station, where he was immediately informed that he was not under arrest. At the close of a ½-hour interview respondent did in fact leave the police station without hindrance. It is clear from these facts that Mathiason was not in custody "or otherwise deprived of his freedom of action in any significant way." . . . Any interview of one suspected of a crime by a police officer will have coercive aspects to it, simply by virtue of the fact that the police officer is part of a law enforcement system which may ultimately cause the suspect to be charged with a crime. But police officers are not required to administer *Miranda* warnings to everyone whom they question. Nor is the requirement of warnings imposed simply because the questioning takes place in the station house, or because the questioned person is one whom the police suspect. *Miranda* warnings are required only where there has been such a restriction on a person's freedom as to render him "in custody." It was that sort of coercive environment to which *Miranda* by its terms was made applicable, and to which it is limited. 429 U.S. at 495, 97 S.Ct. at 714, 50 L.Ed.2d at 719.

Mathis v. United States
laws.findlaw.com/us/391/1.html

PRISONS AND JAILS   In *Mathis v. United States*, 391 U.S. 1, 88 S.Ct. 1503, 20 L.Ed.2d 381 (1968), a person who was incarcerated in a penitentiary for one offense was held to be in custody for purposes of an interrogation conducted by IRS (Internal Revenue Service) agents with respect to another offense. However, in *United States v. Conley*, 779 F.2d 970, 972–73 (4th Cir. 1985), the court said:

We decline to read *Mathis* as compelling the use of *Miranda* warnings prior to all prisoner interrogations and hold that a prison inmate is not automatically always in "custody" within the meaning of *Miranda*. . . . A different approach to the custody determination is warranted in the paradigmatic custodial prison setting where, by definition, the entire population is under restraint of free movement. The Ninth Circuit has taken the position that "restriction" is a relative concept and that, in this context, it "necessarily implies a change in the surroundings of the prisoner which results in an added imposition on his freedom of movement." . . . We agree that this approach best reconciles *Mathis* and *Miranda* in the unique context of prisons and the problems peculiar to their administration.

Therefore, in *United States v. Cooper*, 800 F.2d 412 (4th Cir. 1986), the court found that questioning of a prisoner that took place in a disciplinary boardroom occurred in an inherently less restrictive area than the defendant's cell and that the questioning was therefore noncustodial.

HOMES   Ordinarily, interrogation of a person in that person's home is noncustodial because the person is in familiar surroundings and there is no "police-dominated atmosphere." For example, in *United States v. Gregory*, 891 F.2d 732 (9th Cir. 1989), the court concluded that the defendant was not in custody under the following circumstances:

[H]e consented to be interviewed in his house, he was interviewed in the presence of his wife, the interview lasted only a brief time, and no coercion or force was used. Although the agents initially drew their guns, they returned them to their holsters prior to the interview. They stated that they wanted to question Gregory about some robberies committed in Phoenix and they made no suggestion that Gregory would not be free to leave. The entire interview lasted only a few minutes. 891 F.2d at 735.

However, in *Orozco v. Texas*, 394 U.S. 324, 89 S.Ct. 1095, 22 L.Ed.2d 311 (1969), a suspect was questioned at 4:00 A.M. in his bedroom by four officers, one of whom later testified that the suspect was under arrest. The Court held that even though the questioning was brief and the suspect was in familiar surroundings, the interrogation was custodial. The key reasons for the decision were the time of the interrogation, the number of officers present, and the somewhat unclear evidence of formal arrest.

Orozco v. Texas
laws.findlaw.com/us/394/
324.html

In *Sprosty v. Buchler,* 79 F.3d 635 (7th Cir. 1996), the court held that the defendant was in custody even though he was in his home, in the presence of his mother and at least one family friend, and not handcuffed or otherwise physically restrained. The court found that the degree to which the police dominated the scene was more important than the familiarity of the surroundings:

- When the police arrived at the defendant's mobile home, they surrounded his car, blocked the driveway from his car to the street, and escorted him inside.
- Four officers searched for the incriminating photographs while another officer, who was armed and in uniform, remained with the defendant to guard him.
- During the nearly three-hour period that the officers searched the home, they repeatedly asked the defendant to tell them where the photographs were located.

PLACES OF BUSINESS   Interrogation of a person at his or her place of business is usually held to be noncustodial. Like the home, the place of business represents a familiar surrounding. *United States v. Venerable,* 807 F.2d 745 (8th Cir. 1986). However, in *United States v. Steele,* 648 F.Supp. 1375 (N.D.Ind. 1986), a postal employee who was approached at her work station, asked to accompany two postal inspectors to a small room in the post office, and questioned for an hour and forty-five minutes was found to be in custody. The court said:

> The defendant was not subjected to severe restraint on her physical freedom. She was not handcuffed nor locked in any type of detention facility. In addition, she was not faced with a large number of police officers. She was, however, placed in a closely confined area and confronted by two government agents. Because this was an environment in which the defendant had no control, the physical restraint used, and the show of authority made by the inspectors remain significant. 648 F.Supp. at 1379.

The court also noted that the postal inspectors represented not only law enforcement authority but the authority of the defendant's employer as well. The court found that "a reasonable person would not feel free to rebuff the inspectors out of fear of jeopardizing his or her job as well as encouraging criminal suspicion. Because the interrogators had the power to initiate criminal charges and to terminate the defendant's job, this situation involved coercion greater than the more common situation involving a suspect approached on the street by a police officer." 648 F.Supp. at 1378.

STORES, RESTAURANTS, AND OTHER PUBLIC PLACES   Public places such as stores, restaurants, bars, streets, and sidewalks are considered less familiar to a suspect than a home or office. Nevertheless, courts usually find that an interrogation conducted in these places is noncustodial, because the suspect is in a place of personal choice and is not isolated from the outside world. In addition, there is usually not a police-dominated atmosphere in a public place. In *United States v. Masse,* 816 F.2d 805 (1st Cir. 1987), brief, noncoercive questioning of the defendant on the public sidewalks by two nonuniformed Drug Enforcement Administration (DEA) agents was held to be noncustodial.

HOSPITALS   Questioning of a suspect who is confined in a hospital as a patient but not under arrest is usually held to be a noncustodial interrogation. *United States v. Martin,* 781 F.2d 671 (9th Cir. 1985). Factors supporting such a holding include a lack of a compelling atmosphere, the routine nature of the questioning, and a lack of any deprivation of the defendant's freedom by the police. In *State v. Lescard,* 517 A.2d 1158 (N.H. 1986), however, the court found that the defendant was clearly in custody, when he had been handcuffed at the scene of an accident and was attended by a police officer while at the hospital.

CRIME SCENES   In *Miranda,* the Court said that its decision was

> not intended to hamper the traditional function of police officers in investigating crime. . . . General on-the-scene questioning as to facts surrounding a crime or other general questioning of citizens in the fact-finding process is not affected by our holding. It is an act of responsible citizenship for individuals to give whatever information they may have to aid in law enforcement. In such situations the compelling atmosphere inherent in the process of in-custody interrogation is not necessarily present. 384 U.S. at 477–78, 86 S.Ct. at 1629–30, 16 L.Ed.2d at 725–26.

In *United States v. Wolak,* 923 F.2d 1193 (6th Cir. 1991), two police officers responded to a "disturbance" call at a store. They had no details on what was going on, if anything, before they arrived, and they did not know what to expect. One officer asked the defendant what happened, and the defendant replied that he had pulled a gun because he feared that another person was going to assault him. The court held that even though the officers were not letting anyone leave the store until they found out what was going on, this was not the type of "custody" envisioned by *Miranda.* The court said that, carried to its logical conclusion, applying *Miranda* in this type of situation "would require officers to announce *Miranda* warnings to everyone present immediately upon arriving at a possible crime scene before they knew what happened or before they could ask any questions." 923 F.2d at 1196.

Investigative and Traffic Stops

The ordinary *Terry*-type investigative stop and the ordinary traffic stop are noncustodial for purposes of *Miranda* and do not require the administration of *Miranda* warnings. The U.S. Supreme Court's discussion of the issue in *Berkemer v. McCarty* is illuminating:

> Two features of an ordinary traffic stop mitigate the danger that a person questioned will be induced "to speak where he would not otherwise do so freely" [citing *Miranda*]. First, detention of a motorist pursuant to a traffic stop is presumptively temporary and brief. The vast majority of roadside detentions last only a few minutes. A motorist's expectations, when he sees a policeman's light flashing behind him, are that he will be obliged to spend a short period of time answering questions and waiting while the officer checks his license and registration, that he may then be given a citation, but that in the end he most likely will be allowed to continue on his way. In this respect, questioning incident to an ordinary traffic stop is quite different from stationhouse interrogation, which frequently is prolonged, and in which the detainee often is aware that questioning will continue until he provides his interrogators the answers they seek. . . .
>
> Second, circumstances associated with the typical traffic stop are not such that the motorist feels completely at the mercy of the police. To be sure, the aura of authority surrounding an armed, uniformed officer and the knowledge that the officer has some

discretion in deciding whether to issue a citation, in combination, exert some pressure on the detainee to respond to questions. But other aspects of the situation substantially offset these forces. Perhaps most importantly, the typical traffic stop is public, at least to some degree. Passersby, on foot or in other cars, witness the interaction of officer and motorist. This exposure to public view both reduces the ability of an unscrupulous policeman to use illegitimate means to elicit self-incriminating statements and diminishes the motorist's fear that, if he does not cooperate, he will be subjected to abuse. The fact that the detained motorist typically is confronted by only one or at most two policemen further mutes his sense of vulnerability. In short, the atmosphere surrounding an ordinary traffic stop is substantially less "police dominated" than that surrounding the kinds of interrogation at issue in *Miranda* itself . . . and in the subsequent cases in which we have applied *Miranda*.

In both of these respects, the usual traffic stop is more analogous to a so-called "*Terry* stop," . . . than to a formal arrest. Under the Fourth Amendment . . . a policeman who lacks probable cause but whose "observations lead him reasonably to suspect" that a particular person has committed, is committing, or is about to commit a crime, may detain that person briefly in order to "investigate the circumstances that provoke suspicion." . . . "[T]he stop and inquiry must be 'reasonably related in scope to the justification for their initiation.'" . . . Typically, this means that the officer may ask the detainee a moderate number of questions to determine his identity and to try to obtain information confirming or dispelling the officer's suspicions. But the detainee is not obliged to respond. And, unless the detainee's answers provide the officer with probable cause to arrest him, he must then be released. The comparatively nonthreatening character of detentions of this sort explains the absence of any suggestion in our opinions that *Terry* stops are subject to the dictates of *Miranda*. The similarly noncoercive aspect of ordinary traffic stops prompts us to hold that persons temporarily detained pursuant to such stops are not "in custody" for the purposes of *Miranda*. Berkemer v. McCarty, 468 U.S. 420, 437–40, 104 S.Ct. 3138, 3149–50, 82 L.Ed.2d 317, 333–35 (1983).

In *United States v. Murray*, 89 F.3d 459, 462 (7th Cir. 1996), the court held that when other aspects of a traffic stop were noncustodial, "the fact that Murray was questioned while seated in the back of the squad car did not put him 'in custody' for purposes of Miranda warnings."

Time of Interrogation

An interrogation conducted during business hours is less likely to be considered custodial than is an interrogation conducted in the late evening or early morning. The time of the interrogation (4:00 A.M.) was a significant reason for holding the interrogation at the suspect's home to be custodial in the *Orozco* case (see earlier discussion under "Homes").

Presence of Other Persons

The *Miranda* decision expressly indicated a concern for the suspect who is "cut off from the outside world." 384 U.S. at 445, 86 S.Ct. at 1612, 16 L.Ed.2d at 707. Courts have interpreted this to mean that the presence of family, friends, or neutral persons during the interrogation of a suspect may render the interrogation noncustodial. *People v. Butterfield*, 65 Cal.Rptr. 765 (Cal.App. 1968). Correspondingly, deliberately removing a suspect from the presence of family and friends is indicative of custody.

A frequently recurring example of police domination concerns the removal of the suspect from the presence of family, friends, or colleagues who might lend moral support during the questioning and deter a suspect from making inculpatory statements, an established interrogation practice noted by the *Miranda* court. . . . Officers diminish the public character of, and assert their dominion over, an interrogation site by removing a suspect from the presence of third persons that could lend moral support. *United States v. Griffin*, 922 F.2d 1343, 1352 (8th Cir. 1990).

United States v. Carter, 884 F.2d 368 (8th Cir. 1989), found custody when the defendant was questioned at his place of employment but was removed from his work station, isolated from others that might have lent moral support, and not told that he was free to leave. Some courts speak of a "balance of power" and find custody to exist where the sheer number of police indicates a police-dominated atmosphere. *Orozco v. Texas*, 394 U.S. 324, 89 S.Ct. 1095, 22 L.Ed.2d 311 (1969).

Arrest or Restraint

A suspect who is told that he or she is under arrest is definitely in custody for *Miranda* purposes. *Duckett v. State*, 240 A.2d 332 (Md.Spec.App. 1968). Conversely, a suspect who is told that he or she is not under arrest and is free to leave at any time is usually not considered to be in custody for *Miranda* purposes. *United States v. Guarno*, 819 F.2d 28 (2d Cir. 1987). Nevertheless, a suspect who was questioned by an FBI agent while sitting handcuffed in the back of a police car was found to be in custody, even though he was told he was not under arrest. *United States v. Henley*, 984 F.2d 1040 (9th Cir. 1993).

"Physical restraint . . . is ordinarily associated with a custodial interrogation." *United States v. Levy*, 955 F.2d 1098, 1104 (7th Cir. 1992). By the same token, an absence of physical restraint has led courts to conclude that the defendant was not in custody. In *United States v. Hocking*, 860 F.2d 769 (7th Cir. 1988), questioning in the defendant's home was held to be noncustodial when no restraints were placed on the defendant's movements and he was free to leave the house or ask the officers to leave. "A person detained during the execution of a search warrant is normally not in custody for *Miranda* purposes." *United States v. Saadeh*, 61 F.3d 510, 520 (7th Cir. 1995). In the *Saadeh* case, the defendant was not handcuffed or physically restrained in any way and was not detained for an unreasonably long period of time.

If the physical restraint of a person is accomplished by someone other than a law enforcement officer, the restraint does not constitute custody for *Miranda* purposes. In *Wilson v. Coon*, 808 F.2d 688 (8th Cir. 1987), a brief restraint of the defendant by a medical technician for medical purposes was held not to constitute custody.

Police Coercion or Domination

Police use of force or other types or coercion and the creation of a police-dominated atmosphere are usually indicative of custody. If an officer holds a gun on a suspect, the officer clearly creates a custodial situation. "[A] 'reasonable person' in [the defendant's] position—crouched on the ground and held at gunpoint by a citizen and then by a police officer—would have understood the situation to constitute the requisite restraint on freedom of movement." *Fleming v. Collins*, 917 F.2d 850, 853 (5th Cir. 1990). However, if the suspect is also armed, a court is unlikely to find that the suspect was in custody. *Yates v. United States*, 384 F.2d 586 (5th Cir. 1967).

In *United States v. Longbehn,* 850 F.2d 450 (8th Cir. 1988), the court found custody requiring *Miranda* warnings when the defendant was detained at his place of employment beyond usual work hours; was compelled to accompany officers in a police vehicle to police headquarters and then to his residence; and was forced to open his home and submit to the execution of its search by five officers, during which he was continuously chaperoned and overtly interrogated by three separate officers. The entire process took between two and one-half and four hours.

In *People v. Horn,* 790 P.2d 816 (Colo. 1990), the court found questioning of the defendant custodial, even though the defendant came to the police station voluntarily. The interview was conducted in a small, windowless room in the basement of the police station with only one officer and the defendant present. More important, a transcript of the interview strongly revealed police coercion and domination:

> The transcript reveals that the defendant initially denied involvement in any sexual assaults. It further indicates that [officer] Galyardt accused the defendant of lying on at least five occasions and twice left the defendant alone in the interview room to "reconsider" his prior responses. During the course of the interview, the defendant was urged to take a polygraph exam and encouraged to confess for the "therapeutic" effect it would have on the victim, who was now in the juvenile justice system. Although the defendant was repeatedly told that he was free to leave and that he would not be arrested that day, he was also confronted with the evidence against him and informed that charges would be filed against him regardless of his interview responses. 790 P.2d at 818–19.

In *United States v. Jones,* 630 F.2d 613, 616 (8th Cir. 1980), the court found the lack of police coercion or domination indicative of the absence of custody.

> No strong arm tactics were used. The defendant had not previously been subjected to a police escort nor given commands by the interrogating agents intended to dictate the course of conduct followed by the defendant.

A probationer, although subject to a number of restrictive conditions governing various aspects of life, is not in custody for purposes of *Miranda* simply by reason of the probationer status. A probation interview, unlike a custodial arrest, is arranged by appointment at a mutually convenient time and is conducted in familiar, nonintimidating surroundings. It does not become custodial for *Miranda* purposes because the probation officer could compel attendance and truthful answers at the interview. *Minnesota v. Murphy,* 465 U.S. 420, 104 S.Ct. 1136, 79 L.Ed.2d 409 (1984).

Minnesota v. Murphy
laws.findlaw.com/us/465/420.html

Psychological Restraints

Even when a person is not physically restrained, psychological restraints may be so powerful as to create an atmosphere of coercion constituting custody for *Miranda* purposes. In *United States v. Beraun-Panez,* 812 F.2d 578 (9th Cir. 1987), the court said:

> Although not physically bound, Beraun-Panez was subjected to psychological restraints just as binding. Accusing Beraun-Panez repeatedly of lying, confronting him with false or misleading witness statements, employing good guy/bad guy tactics, taking advantage of Beraun-Panez's insecurities about his alien status, keeping him separated from his co-worker in a remote rural location, insisting on the "truth" until he told them what they sought, the officers established a setting from which a reasonable person would believe that he or she was not free to leave. 812 F.2d at 580.

Interview Initiated by Suspect

If a suspect summons the police or initiates the interview, or both, a court is likely to hold that subsequent police interrogation is noncustodial. In the *Miranda* case itself, the U.S. Supreme Court said, "By custodial interrogation, we mean questioning *initiated by law enforcement officers* after a person has been taken into custody or otherwise deprived of his freedom of action in any significant way." (Emphasis added.) *Miranda v. Arizona*, 384 U.S. 436, 444, 88 S.Ct. 1602, 1612, 16 L.Ed.2d 694, 706 (1966). In *United States v. Jonas*, 786 F.2d 1019 (11th Cir. 1986), the defendant learned indirectly that an FBI agent wanted to contact him. He called the agent, agreed to talk with the FBI, and appeared voluntarily at FBI offices. The interview was held to be noncustodial. And in *United States v. Dockery*, 736 F.2d 1232 (8th Cir. 1984), the court found no custody when the defendant initiated a second interview with officers and was advised that she did not have to answer any questions and was free to go.

Key Points

4. The determination of whether a suspect is in custody for purposes of receiving *Miranda* protection depends on whether there is a formal arrest or restraint on freedom of movement of the degree associated with a formal arrest.

5. A suspect questioned in a police station is not necessarily in custody if his or her freedom to depart is not restricted in any way.

6. Interrogation of a person at his or her home or place of business, or in a public place, is usually held to be noncustodial.

7. *Miranda* warnings are not required before general on-the-scene questioning as to facts surrounding a crime or other general questioning of citizens in the fact-finding process.

8. *Miranda* warnings are not required in connection with the ordinary *Terry*-type investigative stop and the ordinary traffic stop, because these stops are usually noncustodial for purposes of *Miranda*.

9. Police interrogation of a person after the person has summoned the police or otherwise initiated the conversation is usually found to be noncustodial.

Interrogation

Rhode Island v. Innis
laws.findlaw.com/us/446/
291.html

The *Miranda* requirements apply only if a person in custody is subjected to **interrogation.** In *Rhode Island v. Innis*, 446 U.S. 291, 100 S.Ct. 1682, 64 L.Ed.2d 297 (1980), the U.S. Supreme Court recognized that the term *interrogation* in the *Miranda* opinion involved something more than express questioning.

> The concern of the Court in *Miranda* was that the "interrogation environment" created by the interplay of interrogation and custody would "subjugate the individual to the will of his examiner" and thereby undermine the privilege against compulsory self-incrimination. . . . The police practices that evoked this concern included several that did not involve express questioning. For example, one of the practices discussed in *Miranda* was the use of line-ups in which a coached witness would pick the defendant as the perpetrator. This was designed to establish that the defendant was in fact guilty as a predicate for further interrogation. . . . A variation on this theme discussed in *Miranda* was the so-called "reverse line-up" in which a defendant would be identified by coached witnesses as the perpetrator of a fictitious crime, with the object of inducing

him to confess to the actual crime of which he was suspected in order to escape the false prosecution. . . . The Court in *Miranda* also included in its survey of interrogation practices the use of psychological ploys, such as to "posi[t]" "the guilt of the subject," to "minimize the moral seriousness of the offense," and "to cast blame on the victim or on society." . . . It is clear that these techniques of persuasion, no less than express questioning, were thought, in a custodial setting, to amount to interrogation. 446 U.S. at 299, 100 S.Ct. at 1688–89, 64 L.Ed.2d at 306–07.

The *Innis* Court went on to define interrogation for purposes of *Miranda*.

[T]he *Miranda* safeguards come into play whenever a person in custody is subjected to either express questioning or its functional equivalent. That is to say, the term "interrogation" under *Miranda* refers not only to express questioning, but also to any words or actions on the part of police (other than those normally attendant to arrest and custody) that the police should know are reasonably likely to elicit an incriminating response from the suspect. 446 U.S. at 300–01, 100 S.Ct. at 1689, 64 L.Ed.2d at 307–08.

The Supreme Court further refined the definition by stating that an incriminating response is any response—whether inculpatory or exculpatory—that the prosecution may seek to introduce at trial. As stated by the Ninth Circuit Court of Appeals, "It can be in the form of a denial, an admission, an alibi, or any other inculpatory or exculpatory conduct." *Shedelbower v. Estelle*, 885 F.2d 570, 573 (9th Cir. 1989). Although this definition of interrogation is broad, many situations in which a person converses with, or gives information to, a law enforcement officer are not considered to be interrogation for *Miranda* purposes and do not require *Miranda* warnings.

Volunteered Statements

The most obvious situation not constituting interrogation is a volunteered statement— a statement made of a person's own volition and not in response to questioning by a law enforcement officer. In the *Miranda* opinion, the Supreme Court stated that "[v]olunteered statements of any kind are not barred by the Fifth Amendment and their admissibility is not affected by our holding today." 384 U.S. at 478, 86 S.Ct. at 1630, 16 L.Ed.2d at 726.

Volunteered statements sometimes occur when a person, intentionally or unintentionally, makes an incriminating statement in the presence of a law enforcement officer. *United States v. Wright*, 991 F.2d 1180 (4th Cir. 1993), found no interrogation when the defendant, standing in the doorway to his bedroom while it was being legally searched and without any provocation by police, admitted that he had purchased a rifle. Volunteered statements occur more frequently, however, when a person is in custody, either before, during, or after interrogation. *Deck v. United States*, 395 F.2d 89 (9th Cir. 1968).

Volunteered statements may occur during interrogation when the suspect makes an incriminating statement that is not in response to an officer's question. For example, in *Parson v. United States*, 387 F.2d 944 (10th Cir. 1968), an officer asked the defendant where the key to his car was, so the car could be moved off the street and put in storage. The defendant replied that the car had been stolen. The court held that the statement that the car was stolen was not responsive to the inquiry about the key and was completely voluntary. In *United States v. Paskett*, 950 F.2d 705, 707 (11th Cir. 1992), the court held that the defendant's bribe, offered in response to questioning by a law enforcement officer, was a volunteered statement.

www.co.alameda.ca.us/da/pov/Miranda_interrogation.htm
Article, "*Miranda*: 'Interrogation'" from the District Attorney's Office in Alameda County, California

www.fbi.gov/publications/leb/1998/oct98leb.pdf
Article, "Conducting Successful Interrogations" by David Vessel (page 1 of the October 1998 *FBI Law Enforcement Bulletin*)
Article, "Magic Words to Obtain Confessions" by Michael R. Napier and Susan H. Adams (page 11 of the October 1998 *FBI Law Enforcement Bulletin*)

www.icje.org/id86.htm
Article, "What Officers Can Tell Custodial Subjects about Making Their Cooperation Known to Prosecutors" by Robert T. Thetford

www.commonwealthpolice.com/Free_Stuff/CrimminalProcedure312_388/1999_criminal_procedure_toc.htm
Massachusetts Criminal Procedure Textbook: Police Interrogations Section

This statement was totally unresponsive to [the officer's] question. It was not improperly compelled by the officer's question in a custodial setting but, on the contrary, was spontaneously volunteered by [the defendant] in a deliberate attempt to commit a totally separate crime—bribery of a law enforcement official. The safeguards of *Miranda* can not be extended that far. An attempt to commit another crime designed to interfere with a police officer's carrying out of his duties simply must be beyond the intent of *Miranda*. This spontaneously volunteered bribery attempt is admissible since it is exactly the type of statement which the Supreme Court excluded from the *Miranda* rule.

Law enforcement officers need not interrupt a volunteered statement to warn a suspect of *Miranda* rights. The *Miranda* decision specifically states that "[t]here is no requirement that police stop a person who enters a police station and states that he wishes to confess to a crime, or a person who calls the police to offer a confession or any other statement he desires to make." 384 U.S. at 478, 86 S.Ct. at 1630, 16 L.Ed.2d at 726.

Clarifying Questions

Because many volunteered statements are ambiguous, an officer hearing a statement may try to clarify what is being said. Courts have held that a statement is volunteered even if some questions are asked by police. The questions must not, however, be directed to expand on what the person originally intended to say but merely to clear up or explain the original statement. *People v. Sunday*, 79 Cal.Rptr. 752 (Cal.App. 1969).

In *People v. Savage*, 242 N.E.2d 446 (Ill.App. 1968), a man walked into a police station and said, "I done it; I done it; arrest me; arrest me." The officer asked him what he had done, and the man said he killed his wife. Then the officer asked him how, and the man replied, "With an axe, that's all I had." The court held that the officer's clarifying questions were not interrogation and that no *Miranda* warnings were required.

Routine Questions

In the determination of custody, routine questioning is usually indicative of a lack of custody. Courts have also held that routine questioning is not interrogation under *Miranda*, even if the suspect is in custody. Routine booking questions regarding a suspect's name, address, height, weight, eye color, date of birth, and current age to secure biographical data necessary to complete booking or pretrial services fall outside the protections of *Miranda*. *Pennsylvania v. Muniz*, 496 U.S. 582, 110 S.Ct. 2638, 110 L.Ed.2d 528 (1990). Likewise, in *United States v. Booth*, 669 F.2d 1231 (9th Cir. 1981), the court found no interrogation when a police officer investigating a robbery asked a person resembling the description of one of the perpetrators to state his name, age, and residence.

Routine questioning in connection with enforcement of implied consent laws is also not interrogation. For example, in *South Dakota v. Neville*, 459 U.S. 553, 565 n.15, 103 S.Ct. 916, 923 n.15, 74 L.Ed.2d 748, 759 n.15 (1983), the U.S. Supreme Court stated that "[i]n the context of an arrest for driving while intoxicated, a police inquiry of whether the suspect will take a blood-alcohol test is not an interrogation within the meaning of *Miranda*." Nor is police questioning of a suspect to determine whether a suspect understands instructions as to how physical sobriety tests or breathalyzer tests are to be performed. *Pennsylvania v. Muniz*, 496 U.S. 582, 110 S.Ct. 2638, 110 L.Ed.2d 528 (1990).

Pennsylvania v. Muniz
laws.findlaw.com/us/496/582.html

South Dakota v. Neville
laws.findlaw.com/us/459/553.html

When a police officer has reason to know that a suspect's answer may incriminate him or her, however, even routine questioning may amount to interrogation. Thus, although there is usually nothing objectionable about asking a detainee his place of birth, the same question assumes a completely different character when an Immigration and Naturalization Service (INS) agent asks it of a person he suspects is an illegal alien. *United States v. Gonzalez-Sandoval*, 894 F.2d 1043 (9th Cir. 1990), held that such a question was interrogation. Likewise, *United States v. Disla*, 805 F.2d 1340 (9th Cir. 1986), held that questioning a defendant as to his residence subjected him to interrogation, when the officer knew that a large quantity of cocaine and cash had been found at the defendant's apartment and that the residents of the apartment had not been identified. The officer suspected the defendant of cocaine possession and "should have known that the question regarding Disla's residence was reasonably likely to elicit an incriminating response." 805 F.2d at 1347.

Spontaneous Questions

When law enforcement officers ask questions spontaneously, impulsively, or in response to an emergency, the questions are usually held not to be interrogation. In *People v. Morse*, 76 Cal.Rptr. 391, 452 P.2d 607 (Cal. 1969), a jailer and a guard were called to a cell area where they found a prisoner near death from strangling. While tending to the injured prisoner, they asked the defendant, who was also a prisoner, about the incident and received incriminating replies. The court held that this questioning was couched in a context of "stupefied wonderment," not one of incisive inquiry, and that the questioning was not interrogation for purposes of *Miranda*.

In *Turner v. Sullivan*, 661 F.Supp. 535 (E.D.N.Y. 1987), a law enforcement officer asked, "What happened to you?" when the arrested defendant complained that his leg was hurting, and the defendant gave an incriminating response. The court held that there was no interrogation.

> [T]he officer's question was a natural response to petitioner's remark that his leg hurt. The statement at issue was part of a colloquy, initiated by petitioner, about his physical condition. The officer's inquiry was not an effort to elicit information, but rather evidenced the appropriate concern about petitioner's injuries. The officer could not have foreseen that the response might help the prosecution by placing defendant at the scene of the crime. Accordingly, because there was no interrogation and thus no *Miranda* violation, the statement was properly admitted. 661 F.Supp. at 538.

Questions Related to Public Safety

Closely related to spontaneous questions are questions asked by a law enforcement officer out of a concern for public safety. In *New York v. Quarles*, 467 U.S. 649, 104 S.Ct. 2626, 81 L.Ed.2d 550 (1984), two police officers were approached by a woman who told them that she had just been raped and that her assailant had entered a nearby supermarket and was carrying a gun. One of the officers entered the store and observed the defendant, who matched the description given by the woman. The officer pursued the defendant with a drawn gun and ordered him to stop and put his hands over his head. The officer frisked the defendant and discovered that he was wearing an empty shoulder holster. After handcuffing the defendant, the officer asked him where the gun was, and the defendant nodded toward some empty cartons and responded "the gun is over there."

Although the defendant was in police custody when he made his statements and the facts fell within the coverage of *Miranda*, the U.S. Supreme Court held that there was a "public safety" exception to the requirement that *Miranda* warnings be given before a suspect's answers may be admitted into evidence. The Court said:

> The police in this case, in the very act of apprehending a suspect, were confronted with the immediate necessity of ascertaining the whereabouts of a gun which they had every reason to believe the suspect had just removed from his empty holster and discarded in the supermarket. So long as the gun was concealed somewhere in the supermarket, with its actual whereabouts unknown, it obviously posed more than one danger to the public safety: an accomplice might make use of it, a customer or employee might later come upon it. 467 U.S. at 657, 104 S.Ct. at 2632, 81 L.Ed.2d at 557–58.

The Court concluded that the need for answers to questions in a situation posing a threat to the public safety outweighed the need to protect the Fifth Amendment's privilege against self-incrimination. Furthermore, the Court held that the availability of the public safety exception does not depend on the motivation of the individual officers involved. The Court recognized that in a spontaneous, emergency situation like the one in the *Quarles* case, most police officers act out of several different, instinctive motives: a concern for their own safety and that of others, and, perhaps, the desire to obtain incriminating evidence from the suspect. A rigid adherence to the *Miranda* rules is not required when police officers ask questions reasonably prompted by a concern for the public safety.

Finally, the Court acknowledged that the public safety exception lessens the clarity of the *Miranda* rule but expressed confidence that the police would instinctively respond appropriately in situations threatening the public safety.

> [W]e recognize here the importance of a workable rule "to guide police officers, who have only limited time and expertise to reflect on and balance the social and individual interests involved in the specific circumstances they confront." But we believe that the [public safety] exception lessens the necessity of that on-the-scene balancing process. The exception will not be difficult for police officers to apply because in each case it will be circumscribed by the exigency which justifies it. We think police officers can and will distinguish almost instinctively between questions necessary to secure their own safety or the safety of the public and questions designed solely to elicit testimonial evidence from a suspect. 467 U.S. at 658–59, 104 S.Ct. at 2633, 81 L.Ed.2d at 559.

Note that the ruling in the *Quarles* case is an exception to the *Miranda* rule, and as an exception, it must be construed narrowly.

As the *Quarles* Court indicated, the "public safety" exception applies only where there is "an objectively reasonable need to protect the police or the public from any immediate danger associated with [a] weapon." . . . Absent such circumstances posing an objective danger to the public or police, the need for the exception is not apparent, and the suspicion that the questioner is on a fishing expedition outweighs the belief that public safety motivated the questioning that all understand is otherwise improper. *United States v. Mobley*, 40 F.3d 688, 693 (4th Cir. 1994).

In the *Mobley* case, the court found no immediate danger requiring questioning regarding the presence of weapons when

■ the defendant answered the door to his apartment naked;

www.co.alameda.ca.us/da/pov/ Miranda_exceptions.htm Article, "*Miranda*: Exceptions" from the District Attorney's Office in Alameda County, California; one of the exceptions discussed is the "public safety" exception

- by the time he was arrested, the FBI had already made a protective sweep of the premises and found that he was the only one present; and
- the questioning took place as the defendant was being led away from his apartment.

In contrast, in *United States v. Shea*, 150 F.3d 44 (1st Cir. 1998), an officer's question whether the defendant had any weapons was held admissible under the public safety exception; the officer had just apprehended the defendant who was suspected of attempting to commit a violent crime, armed bank robbery.

Confrontation of Suspect with Evidence

In general, it is proper for a law enforcement officer to confront a suspect with evidence or other facts in a case being investigated. Often, after such a confrontation, a suspect may make incriminating statements. Are these incriminating statements voluntary, or are they the product of a form of "silent interrogation"?

Courts have decided the issue both ways depending on the circumstances of individual cases. When there is no verbal interrogation and the suspect is merely confronted with evidence, courts have held that incriminating statements made after the confrontation were not the product of interrogation. *People v. Doss*, 256 N.E.2d 753 (Ill. 1970). When, however, along with such a confrontation, an officer subtly attempts to get the suspect to talk, courts have found interrogation and have suppressed statements obtained without prior warnings. *State v. LaFernier*, 155 N.W.2d 93 (Wis. 1967). The crucial question under *Rhode Island v. Innis* (discussed earlier) is whether the officer's words or actions are reasonably likely to elicit an incriminating response. *Toliver v. Gathright*, 501 F.Supp. 148 (E.D.Va. 1980).

Confrontation of Suspect with Accomplice

In general, whether confronting a suspect with an accomplice to the crime is the functional equivalent of interrogation depends on what is done or said in connection with the confrontation. As the Third Circuit Court of Appeals stated:

> Confronting a suspect with his alleged partner and informing him that his alleged partner has confessed is very likely to spark an incriminating response from a suspect if that suspect is in fact guilty. Accordingly we conclude that if the police, or [the alleged partner] at the police's instruction, had already confronted Nelson [the defendant] with the confession, then this case falls squarely under *Innis's* prohibition of ploys reasonably likely to elicit an incriminating response. On the other hand, if Nelson had not been informed of the confession by the words or conduct of [the partner] or the police, then suppression of the remark was not required; we cannot say that merely placing a suspect in the same room with his partner in crime, without any additional stimulus, is reasonably likely to evoke an incriminating response. *Nelson v. Fulcomer*, 911 F.2d 928, 934 (3d Cir. 1990).

In *Shedelbower v. Estelle*, 885 F.2d 570 (9th Cir. 1989), however, the court found that it was not the functional equivalent of interrogation for an officer to correctly inform the defendant that a codefendant was in custody and to falsely add that the victim had identified his picture as one of the perpetrators. The court said that these were not the type of comments that would encourage the defendant to make some spontaneous incriminating remark.

Statements or Actions of Officers

A law enforcement officer may receive an incriminating response to his or her mere comment or statement or an action that is not a question. If the officer's words or actions were not such that "the police should know are reasonably likely to elicit an incriminating response from the suspect," they are not interrogation. In *Rhode Island v. Innis*, 446 U.S. 291, 100 S.Ct. 1682, 64 L.Ed.2d 297 (1980), a conversation between police officers in the presence of the defendant expressing concern that neighborhood children with disabilities might find a missing shotgun was held not to be interrogation.

> There is nothing in the record to suggest that the officers were aware that the respondent was peculiarly susceptible to an appeal to his conscience concerning the safety of handicapped children. Nor is there anything in the record to suggest that the police knew that the respondent was unusually disoriented or upset at the time of his arrest. . . .
>
> The case thus boils down to whether, in the context of a brief conversation, the officers should have known that the respondent would suddenly be moved to make a self-incriminating response. Given the fact that the entire conversation appears to have consisted of no more than a few off hand remarks, we cannot say that the officers should have known that it was reasonably likely that Innis would so respond. This is not a case where the police carried on a lengthy harangue in the presence of the suspect. Nor does the record support the respondent's contention that, under the circumstances, the officers' comments were particularly "evocative." It is our view, therefore, that the respondent was not subjected by the police to words or actions that the police should have known were reasonably likely to elicit an incriminating response from him. 446 U.S. 291, 302–03, 100 S.Ct. 1682, 1690–91, 64 L.Ed.2d 297, 309.

In general, a law enforcement officer's informational response to a suspect's inquiry about the reasons for an arrest or investigation does not constitute interrogation. For example, it was held not to be interrogation for an officer, in response to a suspect's question about the reason for her arrest, to reply, "You can't be growing dope on your property like that." *United States v. Taylor*, 985 F.2d 3 (1st Cir. 1993).

If, however, the officer's statement is deliberately directed toward eliciting incriminating information, courts will consider the statement as tantamount to interrogation. In *United States v. Montana*, 958 F.2d 516, 518 (2d Cir. 1992), the court held that the officer's "unsolicited statement informing the defendants that any cooperation would be brought to the attention of the Assistant United States Attorney constituted 'interrogation.'" (See also *Brewer v. Williams*, 430 U.S. 387, 97 S.Ct. 1232, 51 L.Ed.2d 424 [1977], discussed later in this chapter under the heading "Attempts after Defendant Is Formally Charged.")

Brewer v. Williams
laws.findlaw.com/us/430/387.html

In *United States v. Samuels*, 938 F.2d 210 (D.C.Cir. 1991), the removal by an officer of a photograph of the defendant's son from the defendant's bag was held not to be the functional equivalent of interrogation. The court found that the officer could not have known that his action was reasonably likely to elicit an incriminating response.

Interrogation by Private Citizens

The *Miranda* warning requirements apply only to custodial interrogations conducted by *law enforcement officers*. Therefore, incriminating statements made by a person in response to custodial interrogation by a private citizen will be admissible in court despite a lack of prior warnings. In *United States v. Pace*, 833 F.2d 1307 (9th Cir. 1987), the defendant's cellmate, acting on his own initiative and without prior arrangement with the government, elicited incriminating statements from the defendant. The court held that, since the cellmate was not the government's agent, the government did not participate in any custodial interrogation in obtaining the confession, and no *Miranda* warnings were required. Similarly, a statement made to a nurse during routine performance of medical duties in a hospital emergency room was held not to be the product of interrogation. *United States v. Romero,* 897 F.2d 47 (2d Cir. 1990).

Multiple Attempts at Interrogation

In the *Miranda* opinion, the Court said:

> Once warnings have been given, the subsequent procedure is clear. If the individual indicates in any manner, at any time prior to or during questioning, that he wishes to remain silent, the interrogation must cease. At this point he has shown that he intends to exercise his Fifth Amendment privilege; any statement taken after the person invokes his privilege cannot be other than the product of compulsion, subtle or otherwise. Without the right to cut off questioning, the setting of in-custody interrogation operates on the individual to overcome free choice in producing a statement after the privilege has been once invoked. If the individual states that he wants an attorney, the interrogation must cease until an attorney is present. At that time the individual must have an opportunity to confer with the attorney and to have him present during any subsequent questioning. If the individual cannot obtain an attorney and he indicates that he wants one before speaking to police, they must respect his decision to remain silent. 384 U.S. at 473–74, 86 S.Ct. at 1627–28, 16 L.Ed.2d at 723.

The quoted language commands that, once a suspect indicates either a desire to remain silent or a desire for an attorney, all questioning must stop, at least until the suspect confers with an attorney. Nevertheless, under certain circumstances, some courts have admitted statements obtained after multiple attempts to question suspects.

ATTEMPTS AFTER RIGHT TO SILENCE IS INVOKED　　The U.S. Supreme Court has, under limited conditions, allowed a second interrogation of a suspect who exercised the *Miranda* right of silence after being given warnings.

The *Mosley* Rule　　In *Michigan v. Mosley,* 423 U.S. 96, 96 S.Ct. 321, 46 L.Ed.2d 313 (1975), the defendant was arrested early in the afternoon in connection with certain robberies and was given the *Miranda* warnings by a police detective. After indicating that he understood the warnings, the defendant declined to discuss the robberies, and the detective ceased the interrogation. Shortly after 6:00 P.M. the same day, after giving another set of *Miranda* warnings, a different police detective questioned the defendant about a murder that was unrelated to the robberies. The defendant made an incriminating statement that was used against him at his trial. He was convicted of the murder.

The Court held that admitting the defendant's statement into evidence did not violate *Miranda* principles. Even though the *Miranda* opinion states that the interrogation must cease when the person in custody indicates a desire to remain silent, the Court in the *Mosley* case held that "neither this passage nor any other passage in the *Miranda* opinion can sensibly be read to create a per se proscription of indefinite duration upon any further questioning by any police officer on any subject, once the person in custody has indicated a desire to remain silent." 423 U.S. at 102–03, 96 S.Ct. at 326, 46 L.Ed.2d at 320–21. The Court then gave several reasons that it allowed the second interrogation in the *Mosley* case:

Michigan v. Mosley
laws.findlaw.com/us/423/
96.html

- The defendant's right to cut off questioning had been "scrupulously honored" by the first detective.
- The first detective ceased the interrogation when the defendant refused to answer and did not try to wear down his resistance by repeated efforts to make him change his mind.
- The second interrogation was directed toward a different crime with a different time and place of occurrence.
- And, the second interrogation began after a significant time lapse and after the defendant had been given a fresh set of warnings.

In *United States v. Olof,* 527 F.2d 752 (9th Cir. 1975), the court held that a second interrogation by federal agents, conducted three hours after the defendant had refused to make a statement after being given the *Miranda* warnings, violated the defendant's rights. Although the agents gave the defendant fresh warnings, they pressured him to cooperate and they questioned him about the same crime for which the first warnings were given. In *Jackson v. Dugger,* 837 F.2d 1469 (11th Cir. 1988), however, the court held that the defendant's invocation of the right to silence was scrupulously honored when the police discontinued questioning after each invocation of the right, more than six hours elapsed between the initial invocation of the right and the confession, fresh warnings were given before the confession, and there was no allegation of overbearing police conduct.

These cases suggest the following guidelines for conducting a second custodial interrogation of a person who has exercised the *Miranda* right to remain silent.

- Scrupulously honor the person's right to terminate questioning at the initial interrogation.
- Allow a significant amount of time to intervene between the first and second interrogation attempts.
- Give the person complete *Miranda* warnings again.
- Do not employ any pressure to cooperate or other illegal tactics.

Invocation of the Right to Silence   In *United States v. Mikell,* 102 F.3d 470 (11th Cir. 1996), the court ruled that a suspect must articulate his desire to end questioning with sufficient clarity so that a reasonable police officer would understand that statement to be an assertion of the right to remain silent. Relying on *Davis v. United States* (see pages 492–93), the court added that if the statement is ambiguous or equivocal, the police have no duty to clarify the suspect's intent, and they may proceed with the interrogation. No particular word or combination of words is required to invoke the Fifth Amendment right to remain silent. For example, a suspect who acknowledged that he understood his *Miranda* rights by nodding and then remained silent in response to all pedigree questions was held to have sufficiently asserted his right to remain silent. *United States v. Montana,* 958 F.2d 516 (2d Cir. 1992). However, the *Mikell* case held that a suspect's refusal to answer certain questions, but not others, is not tantamount to the invocation, either equivocal or unequivocal, of the constitutional right to remain silent and that questioning may continue until the suspect articulates in some manner that he wishes the questioning to cease.

ATTEMPTS AFTER RIGHT TO COUNSEL IS INVOKED   As the quotation at the beginning of this section indicates, *Miranda* created a rigid rule that an accused's request for an attorney is *per se* an invocation of Fifth Amendment rights, requiring that all interrogation cease. This rigid rule is based on an attorney's unique ability to protect the Fifth Amendment rights of a client undergoing custodial interrogation. Once an accused person indicates that he or she is not competent to deal with the authorities without legal advice, courts will closely examine any later choice to make a decision without counsel's presence. Therefore, although an accused may waive *Miranda* rights and submit to interrogation, the U.S. Supreme Court has recognized that additional safeguards are necessary after an accused has exercised the right to counsel.

The *Edwards* Rule   The Supreme Court established these safeguards in the case of *Edwards v. Arizona*, 451 U.S. 477, 101 S.Ct. 1880, 68 L.Ed.2d 378 (1981). In that case, the defendant voluntarily submitted to questioning but later stated that he wanted an attorney before the discussions continued. The following day, detectives accosted the defendant in the county jail, and when the defendant refused to speak with the detectives, he was told that he "had" to talk. The Court held that subsequent incriminating statements made without his attorney present violated the rights secured to the defendant by the Fifth and Fourteenth Amendments. The Court stated:

> [W]hen an accused has invoked his right to have counsel present during custodial interrogation, a valid waiver of that right cannot be established by showing only that he responded to further police-initiated custodial interrogation even if he has been advised of his rights. We further hold that an accused, such as [the defendant], having expressed his desire to deal with the police only through counsel, is not subject to further interrogation by the authorities until counsel has been made available to him, unless the accused himself initiates further communication, exchanges, or conversations with the police. 451 U.S. at 484–85, 101 S.Ct. at 1884–85, 68 L.Ed.2d at 386.

The requirement that counsel be "made available" refers to more than an opportunity to consult with an attorney outside the interrogation room. In *Minnick v. Mississippi*, 498 U.S. 146, 153, 111 S.Ct. 486, 491, 112 L.Ed.2d 489, 498 (1990), the U.S. Supreme Court held that

> a fair reading of *Edwards* and subsequent cases demonstrates that we have interpreted the rule to bar police-initiated interrogation unless the accused has counsel with him at the time of questioning. . . . [W]hen counsel is requested, interrogation must cease, and officials may not reinitiate interrogation without counsel *present*, whether or not the accused has consulted with his attorney. (Emphasis added.)

The *Minnick* rule has no time limitation and is effective as long as the suspect remains in custody. Therefore, once a defendant invokes the right to counsel, the police are forever barred from initiating further custodial interrogation of the defendant unless defense counsel is present at the interview. Moreover, the *Minnick* rule bars further police-initiated interrogation about unrelated charges unless counsel is present. *Arizona v. Roberson*, 486 U.S. 675, 108 S.Ct. 2093, 100 L.Ed.2d 704 (1988). In summary, unless counsel is present, or unless the accused initiates further conversations, a waiver of *Miranda* rights after invocation of the right to counsel is presumed involuntary. Incriminating statements obtained after such an involuntary waiver, regardless of their merit, will be suppressed.

Relying on the Sixth Amendment, the Supreme Court also prohibited further interrogation without counsel present after assertions of the right to counsel *made at or after the initiation of adversary judicial proceedings*. The Court held that "if police initiate interrogation after a defendant's assertion, at an arraignment or similar proceeding, of his right to counsel, any waiver of the defendant's right to counsel for that police-initiated interrogation is invalid." *Michigan v. Jackson*, 475 U.S. 625, 636, 106 S.Ct. 1404, 1411, 89 L.Ed.2d 631, 642 (1986). The Sixth Amendment right to counsel, however, unlike

Edwards v. Arizona
laws.findlaw.com/us/451/477.html

Minnick v. Mississippi
laws.findlaw.com/us/498/146.html

Arizona v. Roberson
laws.findlaw.com/us/486/675.html

www.totse.com/en/law/justice_for_all/8interro.html
Article, "Custodial Interrogation: Impact of *Minnick v. Mississippi*" by Kimberly A. Crawford

Michigan v. Jackson
laws.findlaw.com/us/475/625.html

www.co.alameda.ca.us/da/pov/
questions.htm
Article, "Questioning a Charged
Suspect" from the District Attor-
ney's Office in Alameda County,
California

McNeil v. Wisconsin
laws.findlaw.com/us/501/
171.html

Texas v. Cobb
laws.findlaw.com/us/000/
99-1702.html

the *Miranda* Fifth Amendment right to counsel, is *offense specific*. Invocation of the Sixth Amendment right bars police-initiated interrogation regarding only the offense at issue; it does not bar later police-initiated interrogation on an unrelated charge.

> The purpose of the Sixth Amendment counsel guarantee—and hence the purpose of invoking it—is to "protec[t] the unaided layman at critical confrontations" with his "expert adversary," the government, *after* "the adverse positions of government and defendant have solidified" with respect to a particular alleged crime. . . . The purpose of the *Miranda-Edwards* guarantee, on the other hand—and hence the purpose of invoking it—is to protect a quite different interest: the suspect's "desire to deal with the police only through counsel," . . . This is in one respect narrower than the interest protected by the Sixth Amendment guarantee (because it relates only to custodial interrogation) and in another respect broader (because it relates to interrogation regarding any suspected crime and attaches whether or not the "adversarial relationship" produced by a pending prosecution has yet arisen). To invoke the Sixth Amendment interest is, as a matter of *fact, not* to invoke the *Miranda-Edwards* interest. *McNeil v. Wisconsin,* 501 U.S. 171, 177–78, 111 S.Ct. 2204, 2208–09, 115 L.Ed.2d 158, 168 (1991).

In *Texas v. Cobb,* ___ U.S. ___, ___, 121 S.Ct. 1335, 1339, ___L.Ed.2d ___, ___ (2001), the U.S. Supreme Court held that "*McNeil v. Wisconsin* . . . meant what it said, and that the Sixth Amendment right is 'offense specific.' " In the *Cobb* case, the defendant confessed to a home burglary but denied knowledge of a woman and child's disappearance from the home. He was indicted for the burglary, and counsel was appointed to represent him on that charge. He later confessed to his father that he had killed the woman and child in the course of the burglary, and his father contacted the police. After police arrested him and administered *Miranda* warnings, he waived his *Miranda* rights and confessed to the murders. On appeal of his capital murder conviction, he argued that his confession should have been suppressed because it was obtained in violation of his Sixth Amendment right to counsel. He claimed that the right attached when counsel was appointed in the burglary case, which was "factually related" to the capital murder charge. The Court rejected this claim and held that, because burglary and capital murder are not the *same* offense under Texas law, and because the Sixth Amendment right to counsel is "offense specific," the failure to obtain the defendant's counsel's permission did not bar the police from interrogating him regarding the murders. His confession was therefore admissible.

The Court clarified the test for determining whether two offenses are the "same offense":

> Although it is clear that the Sixth Amendment right to counsel attaches only to charged offenses, we have recognized in other contexts that the definition of an "offense" is not necessarily limited to the four corners of a charging instrument. In *Blockburger v. United States,* 284 U. S. 299 (1932), we explained that "where the same act or transaction constitutes a violation of two distinct statutory provisions, the test to be applied to determine whether there are two offenses or only one, is whether each provision requires proof of a fact which the other does not." *Id.,* at 304. We have since applied the *Blockburger* test to delineate the scope of the Fifth Amendment's Double Jeopardy Clause, which prevents multiple or successive prosecutions for the "same offence." See, *e.g., Brown v. Ohio,* 432 U. S. 161, 164–166 (1977). We see no constitutional difference between the meaning of the term "offense" in the contexts of double jeopardy and of the right to counsel. Accordingly, we hold that when the Sixth Amendment right to counsel attaches, it does encompass offenses that, even if not formally charged, would be con-

sidered the same offense under the *Blockburger* test. ___ U.S. at ___, 121 S.Ct. at 1343, ___L.Ed.2d at ___

Interrogation or Its Functional Equivalent If police action after the suspect has invoked his or her right to counsel is not "interrogation" or the "functional equivalent" of interrogation, then neither the *Edwards* rule nor the *Jackson* rule apply, and the suspect's statements will be admissible. In *Arizona v. Mauro*, 481 U.S. 520, 107 S.Ct. 1931, 95 L.Ed.2d 458 (1987), the defendant, who was in custody on suspicion of murdering his son, indicated that he did not wish to be questioned further without a lawyer present, and the questioning then ceased. The defendant's wife, who was being questioned in another room, asked whether she could speak to her husband. They were allowed to speak, but an officer was present in the room, and the conversation was tape-recorded with the couple's knowledge. The recording was used against the defendant at his trial.

Arizona v. Mauro
laws.findlaw.com/us/481/
520.html

The U.S. Supreme Court held that the actions of the police were not the functional equivalent of police interrogation. No evidence indicated that the officers sent the wife in to see her husband for the purpose of eliciting incriminating statements. Nor was the officer's presence in the room improper, because there were legitimate reasons for his presence, including the wife's safety and various security considerations. Furthermore, it is improbable that the defendant would have felt he was being coerced to incriminate himself simply because he was told his wife would be allowed to speak to him. Even though the police knew there was a possibility that the defendant would incriminate himself, "[o]fficers do not interrogate a suspect simply by hoping that he will incriminate himself." 481 U.S. at 529, 107 S.Ct. at 1936, 95 L.Ed.2d at 468. The Court held that the officers acted reasonably and that the defendant's tape-recorded statements could be used against him at trial. "Police departments need not adopt inflexible rules barring suspects from speaking with their spouses, nor must they ignore legitimate security concerns by allowing spouses to meet in private." 481 U.S. at 530, 107 S.Ct. at 1937, 95 L.Ed.2d at 468.

The following actions by police have been held to be interrogation, or the functional equivalent of interrogation, in violation of the *Edwards* rule prohibiting further interrogation after the defendant's invocation of the right to counsel.

- Reinterrogation about a separate offense. "[T]he presumption raised by a suspect's request for counsel—that he considers himself unable to deal with the pressures of custodial interrogation without legal assistance—does not disappear simply because the police have approached the suspect, still in custody, still without counsel, about a separate investigation." *Arizona v. Roberson*, 486 U.S. 675, 683, 108 S.Ct. 2093, 2099, 100 L.Ed.2d 704, 715 (1988).
- Resubmitting a waiver of rights form (which the defendant previously refused to sign) accompanied by an announcement that a victim of a shooting had died and that the charge was now murder. (The waiver of rights form is discussed later in this chapter.) *State v. Iovino*, 524 A.2d 556 (R.I. 1987).
- Offering to explain the operation of the criminal justice system to the defendant. (The court noted that despite their seeming innocence, such explanations are often designed to inform a defendant that cooperation may be beneficial.) *United States v. Johnson*, 812 F.2d 1329 (11th Cir. 1986).
- Exhibiting an incriminating document to the defendant ten minutes after he had invoked his *Miranda* right to counsel. *United States v. Walker*, 624 F.Supp. 103 (D.Md. 1985).
- Calling the defendant by the nickname of the person believed to have committed the particular offense. *State v. Dellorfano*, 517 A.2d 1163 (N.H. 1986).

www.co.alameda.ca.us/da/pov/
invoc.htm
Article, "*Miranda* Invocations"
from the District Attorney's
Office in Alameda County,
California

Patterson v. Illinois
laws.findlaw.com/us/487/
285.html

Smith v. Illinois
laws.findlaw.com/us/469/
91.html

Davis v. United States
laws.findlaw.com/us/000/
u10366.html

- Confronting the defendant with an arrest warrant and photographs of his fingerprints taken at the crime scene. *Clark v. Marshall,* 600 F.Supp. 1520 (E.D.Ohio 1985).
- Questioning about the ownership of an automobile parked at the crime scene. *United States v. Monzon,* 869 F.2d 338 (7th Cir. 1989).

Other examples of what does and does not constitute interrogation appear on pages 480 through 487.

Invocation of the Right to Counsel   In *Patterson v. Illinois,* 487 U.S. 285, 108 S.Ct. 2389, 101 L.Ed.2d 261 (1988), the U.S. Supreme Court held that, under the *Edwards* rule, police-initiated interrogation will be barred only after the right to counsel is *invoked.* In that case, the defendant's Sixth Amendment right to counsel came into existence with his indictment, but, unlike the defendant in *Michigan v. Jackson,* he did not ask for counsel after receiving the *Miranda* warnings. The Court said that the interrogation of the defendant after indictment was indistinguishable from the interrogation of a person before indictment whose right to counsel is in existence and available to be exercised during questioning. The Court said:

> Preserving the integrity of an accused's choice to communicate with police only through counsel is the essence of *Edwards* and its progeny—not barring an accused from making an *initial* selection as to whether he will face the State's officers during questioning with the aid of counsel, or go it alone. If an accused "knowingly and intelligently" pursues the latter course, we see no reason why the uncounseled statements he then makes must be excluded at his trial. 487 U.S. at 291, 108 S.Ct. at 2394, 101 L.Ed.2d at 271–72.

In *Smith v. Illinois,* 469 U.S. 91, 105 S.Ct. 490, 83 L.Ed.2d 488 (1984), the Court held that, after an accused has invoked the right to counsel, courts will not allow an accused's responses to further interrogation to be used to cast retrospective doubt on the clarity of the initial request itself. The Court said, "No authority, and no logic, permits the interrogator to proceed . . . on his own terms and as if the defendant had requested nothing, in the hope that the defendant might be induced to say something casting retrospective doubt on his initial statement that he wished to speak through an attorney or not at all." 469 U.S. at 99, 105 S.Ct. at 494, 83 L.Ed.2d at 496.

Under *Edwards,* after a knowing and voluntary waiver of the *Miranda* rights, law enforcement officers may continue questioning until and unless the suspect clearly requests an attorney. Ambiguous or equivocal references to an attorney are insufficient to invoke a suspect's right to counsel.

> Although a suspect need not "speak with the discrimination of an Oxford don," . . . he must articulate his desire to have counsel present sufficiently clearly that a reasonable police officer in the circumstances would understand the statement to be a request for an attorney. If the statement fails to meet the requisite level of clarity, *Edwards* does not require that the officers stop questioning the suspect. *Davis v. United States,* 512 U.S. 452, 459, 114 S.Ct. 2350, 2355, 129 L.Ed.2d 362, 371 (1994).

Of course, when a suspect makes an ambiguous or equivocal statement, it will often be good police practice for the interviewing officers to clarify whether he or she actually wants an attorney.

> Clarifying questions help protect the rights of the suspect by ensuring that he gets an attorney if he wants one, and will minimize the chance of a confession being suppressed due to subsequent judicial second-guessing as to the meaning of the suspect's statement

regarding counsel. But we decline to adopt a rule requiring officers to ask clarifying questions. If the suspect's statement is not an unambiguous or unequivocal request for counsel, the officers have no obligation to stop questioning him. 512 U.S. at 461–62, 114 S.Ct. at 2356, 129 L.Ed.2d at 373.

In the *Davis* case, the court held that the suspect's remark, "Maybe I should talk to a lawyer" was not a clear request for a lawyer, and officers therefore were not required to stop questioning him.

Initiation of Further Communications   In *Oregon v. Bradshaw*, 462 U.S. 1039, 103 S.Ct. 2830, 77 L.Ed.2d 405 (1983), the U.S. Supreme Court attempted to explain what would constitute the initiation of further communication with the police:

> [T]here are undoubtedly situations where a bare inquiry by either a defendant or by a police officer should not be held to "initiate" any conversation or dialogue. There are some inquiries, such as a request for a drink of water or a request to use a telephone that are so routine that they cannot be fairly said to represent a desire on the part of an accused to open up a more generalized discussion relating directly or indirectly to the investigation. Such inquiries or statements, by either an accused or a police officer, relating to routine incidents of the custodial relationship, will not generally "initiate" a conversation in the sense in which that word was used in *Edwards*. 462 U.S. at 1045, 103 S.Ct. at 2835, 77 L.Ed.2d at 412.

In *Bradshaw*, the Court found that the defendant's question to a police officer, after the defendant had asked for an attorney, as to what was going to happen to him now "evinced a willingness and a desire for a generalized discussion about the investigation; it was not merely a necessary inquiry arising out of the incidents of the custodial relationship." 462 U.S. at 412, 103 S.Ct. at 2835, 77 L.Ed.2d at 412.

Waiver of Rights   The *Edwards* case also established a second prerequisite to police interrogation of an accused who has invoked the right to have counsel present during custodial interrogation. Once it is established that the accused "initiated" further conversation or dialogue with the police, the next inquiry is

> whether a valid waiver of the right to counsel and the right to silence had occurred, that is, whether the purported waiver was knowing and intelligent and found to be so under the totality of the circumstances, including the necessary fact that the accused, not the police, reopened the dialogue with the authorities. 451 U.S. at 486 n.9, 101 S.Ct. at 1885 n.9, 68 L.Ed.2d at 387 n.9.

In the *Bradshaw* case, the Court found a knowing waiver when the police made no threats, promises, or inducements to talk; the defendant was properly advised of his rights and understood them; and within a short time the defendant changed his mind and decided to talk without any impropriety on the part of the police. In *Wyrick v. Fields*, 459 U.S. 42, 44, 103 S.Ct. 394, 396, 74 L.Ed.2d 214, 218 (1982), the U.S. Supreme Court held that by waiving his right to counsel at a polygraph examination, the accused also validly waived his right to have counsel present at posttest questioning, "unless the circumstances changed so seriously that his answers no longer were voluntary, or unless he no longer was making a 'knowing and intelligent relinquishment or abandonment' of his rights." (See the discussion of waiver later in this chapter.)

To summarize, before a suspect in custody can be subjected to further uncounseled interrogation after requesting an attorney, there must first be a showing that the suspect initiated communication with the authorities. Once this is established, it is still

Oregon v. Bradshaw
laws.findlaw.com/us/462/
1039.html

www.lectlaw.com/files/
cri13.htm
Article, "Invoking the *Miranda* Right to Counsel: The Defendant's Burden" by Kimberly A. Crawford

www.law.fsu.edu/journals/
lawreview/frames/243/
mazztxt.html
Article, "Crucial Stages, Crucial Confrontations, and the Florida Criminal Defendant's Right to Counsel" by Anthony J. Mazzo

Wyrick v. Fields
laws.findlaw.com/us/459/
42.html

necessary to establish as a separate matter the existence of a knowing and intelligent waiver of the right to counsel and the right to silence. Once a valid waiver is made, interrogation may continue until the circumstances change so seriously that the answers are no longer voluntary or until the accused revokes the waiver.

ATTEMPTS AFTER RIGHTS ARE WAIVED   Often, a suspect may waive *Miranda* rights and submit to interrogation, and after an interval of time, police may wish to interrogate the suspect again. The general rule is that

> the *Miranda* rights "need not be repeated so long as the circumstances attending any interruption or adjournment of the process [are] such that the suspect has not been deprived of the opportunity to make an informed and intelligent assessment of his interest involved in the interrogation, including his right to cut off questioning." *Bivins v. State*, 642 N.E.2d 928, 939 (Ind. 1994).

The Supreme Court of Pennsylvania listed five significant factors in determining whether an accused must be reinformed of his or her *Miranda* rights:

> (1) the time lapse between the last *Miranda* warnings and the accused's statement; (2) interruptions in the continuity of the interrogation; (3) whether there was a change of location between the place where the last *Miranda* warnings were given and the place where the accused's statement was made; (4) whether the same officer who gave the warnings also conducted the interrogation resulting in the accused's statement; and (5) whether the statement elicited during the complained of interrogation differed significantly from other statements which had been preceded by *Miranda* warnings. *Commonwealth v. Wideman*, 334 A.2d 594, 598 (Pa. 1975).

When *Miranda* warnings are not repeated during an ongoing interrogation, the ultimate question is whether the defendant, with full knowledge of his or her legal rights, knowingly and intentionally relinquished those rights.

Oregon v. Elstad
laws.findlaw.com/us/470/298.html

ATTEMPTS AFTER AN UNWARNED ADMISSION   In *Oregon v. Elstad*, 470 U.S. 298, 105 S.Ct. 1285, 84 L.Ed.2d 222 (1985), a law enforcement officer investigating a burglary obtained an admission from the defendant in a custodial setting without first giving him the *Miranda* warnings. Shortly thereafter, at the station house, the defendant received complete *Miranda* warnings, waived his rights, and gave a written confession.

The U.S. Supreme Court held that, although the initial unwarned admission was inadmissible in court, the written confession was admissible. The Court reasoned that, despite the *Miranda* violation before the officer obtained the first admission, no coercion or other illegal means were used to break the defendant's will.

The Court then evaluated the written statement as follows:

> We must conclude that, absent deliberately coercive or improper tactics in obtaining the initial statement, the mere fact that a suspect has made an unwarned admission does not warrant a presumption of compulsion. A subsequent administration of *Miranda* warnings to a suspect who has given a voluntary but unwarned statement ordinarily should suffice to remove the conditions that precluded admission of the earlier statement. In such circumstances, the finder of fact may reasonably conclude that the suspect made a rational and intelligent choice whether to waive or invoke his rights. 470 U.S. at 314, 105 S.Ct. at 1296, 84 L.Ed.2d at 235.

For the law enforcement officer, the lesson from the *Elstad* case is that, after an admission is obtained as a result of interrogating a suspect, the officer should carefully comply with all *Miranda* procedures in all subsequent interrogations, before obtaining further statements, no matter how much time has elapsed between interrogations. This will ensure that, even if an earlier statement is ruled inadmissible because of a *Miranda* violation, later statements will have a better chance of being admitted. Furthermore, even if an officer believes that a statement has been obtained in violation of *Miranda,* the officer need not warn that the statement cannot be used against the suspect. "Police officers are ill equipped to pinch-hit for counsel, construing the murky and difficult questions of when 'custody' begins or whether a given unwarned statement will ultimately be held inadmissible." 470 U.S. at 316, 105 S.Ct. at 1297, 84 L.Ed.2d at 237.

In effect, the Court in the *Elstad* case refused to apply the traditional "fruit of the poisonous tree" doctrine developed in Fourth Amendment cases, even though a violation of *Miranda* is a violation of a constitutional rule, as the Court declared in *Dickerson v. United States,* 530 U.S. 428, 120 S.Ct. 2326, 147 L.Ed.2d 405 (2000). The "fruit of the poisonous tree" doctrine applies only if the previous *Miranda* violation is accompanied by deliberately coercive or improper tactics in obtaining the initial statement. The Court explained that the decision in the *Elstad* case "does not prove that *Miranda* is a nonconstitutional decision, but simply recognizes the fact that unreasonable searches under the Fourth Amendment are different from unwarned interrogation under the Fifth Amendment." 530 U.S. at 441, 120 S.Ct. at 2335, 147 L.Ed.2d at 418.

ATTEMPTS AFTER DEFENDANT IS FORMALLY CHARGED In *Massiah v. United States,* 377 U.S. 201, 84 S.Ct. 1199, 12 L.Ed.2d 246 (1964), after the defendant was indicted, federal agents obtained incriminating statements from the defendant in the absence of his counsel. While the defendant was free on bail, his codefendant, in cooperation with the federal agents, engaged the defendant in conversation in the presence of a hidden radio transmitter. The Court held that the statements were inadmissible because the defendant was denied the basic protection of his Sixth Amendment right to assistance of counsel.

The *Massiah* decision has become less significant in recent years because the *Miranda* decision has resulted in courts shifting their emphasis from the Sixth Amendment to the Fifth Amendment. Nevertheless, as stated by the Fifth Circuit Court of Appeals:

> [I]t [*Massiah*] retains its vitality and stands as a supplement to *Miranda: Massiah* teaches that although the government may properly continue to gather evidence against a defendant after he has been indicted, it may not nullify the protection *Miranda* affords a defendant by using trickery to extract incriminating statements from him that otherwise could not be obtained without first giving the required warnings. Today *Massiah* simply means that after indictment and counsel has been retained the Fifth Amendment prevents law enforcement authorities from deliberately eliciting incriminating statements from a defendant by the surreptitious methods used in that case. *United States v. Hayles,* 471 F.2d 788, 791 (5th Cir. 1973).

The U.S. Supreme Court affirmed the continuing validity of the *Massiah* case in *Brewer v. Williams,* 430 U.S. 387, 97 S.Ct. 1232, 51 L.Ed.2d 424 (1977). In that case, the defendant had been arrested, arraigned, and jailed in Davenport, Iowa, for abducting a ten-year-old girl in Des Moines, Iowa, and was being transported by police to Des Moines to talk to his lawyer there. Both the defendant's Des Moines lawyer and the lawyer at his Davenport arraignment advised the defendant not to make any statements until after he had consulted with his Des Moines lawyer. The police officers who were to accompany the defendant on the trip agreed not to question him during the trip. Nevertheless, one of the police officers, who knew that the defendant was a

Massiah v. United States
laws.findlaw.com/us/377/
201.html

www.fletc.gov/legal/
archive_dir.htm
Article, "The Sixth Amendment Right to Counsel and Its Instantaneous Attachment at the Moment of Indictment" by Jacquelyn J. Kuhens; lead article in the March 22, 2000, issue of *Quarterly Review: Legal Commentary for Federal Law Enforcement Officers*
caselaw.findlaw.com/data/
constitution/amendment06/
11.html#3
Discussion (with annotations) of the right to counsel at custodial interrogations

former mental patient and was deeply religious, suggested that the defendant reveal the location of the girl's body because her parents were entitled to a Christian burial for the girl, who was taken away from them on Christmas Eve. The defendant eventually made several incriminating statements during the trip and finally directed the police to the girl's body.

The Court, citing *Massiah,* held that a person against whom adversary proceedings have commenced has a right to legal representation when the government interrogates him or her. Because the officer's "Christian burial" speech was tantamount to interrogation and the defendant had been formally charged, the defendant was entitled to the assistance of counsel at the time he made the incriminating statements. The Court found that the defendant did not waive his right to counsel and therefore held any evidence relating to or resulting from his statements inadmissible.

United States v. Henry
laws.findlaw.com/us/447/
264.html

In *United States v. Henry,* 447 U.S. 264, 100 S.Ct. 2183, 65 L.Ed.2d 115 (1980), the Supreme Court held inadmissible statements made by an indicted and imprisoned defendant to a paid, undisclosed government informant who was in the same cell block. Although the informant did not question the defendant, the informant "stimulated" conversations with the defendant and developed a relationship of trust and confidence with the defendant. As a result, the defendant made incriminating statements without the assistance of counsel. This indirect and surreptitious type of interrogation was an impermissible interference with the defendant's right to the assistance of counsel in violation of *Massiah.* The Court emphasized the potential susceptibility of an incarcerated person to subtle influences of government undercover agents.

Maine v. Moulton
laws.findlaw.com/us/474/
159.html

Furthermore, even when a confrontation between an accused and a police agent is initiated by the accused, the government may not deliberately attempt to elicit information without counsel being present. In *Maine v. Moulton,* 474 U.S. 159, 106 S.Ct. 477, 88 L.Ed.2d 481 (1985), the Supreme Court said that the guarantee of the Sixth Amendment includes the government's affirmative obligation not to act in a manner that circumvents the protections accorded the accused who invokes his or her right to rely on counsel as a "medium" between the accused and the government. The Court continued:

> [T]he Sixth Amendment is not violated whenever—by luck or happenstance—the State obtains incriminating statements from the accused after the right to counsel has attached. . . . However, knowing exploitation by the State of an opportunity to confront the accused without counsel being present is as much a breach of the State's obligation not to circumvent the right to assistance of counsel as is the intentional creation of such an opportunity. Accordingly, the Sixth Amendment is violated when the State obtains incriminating statements by knowingly circumventing the accused's right to have counsel present in a confrontation between the accused and a state agent. 474 U.S. at 176, 106 S.Ct. at 487, 88 L.Ed.2d at 496.

The *Henry* and *Moulton* cases illustrate that courts will carefully examine any attempts to circumvent the right of any formally charged person to have counsel present at a confrontation between the person and police agents. But, as the first sentence of the preceding quotation indicates, the defendant's Sixth Amendment rights are not violated when an informant, either through prior arrangement or voluntarily, reports the defendant's incriminating statements to the police. "[T]he defendant must demonstrate that the police and their informant took some action, beyond merely listening, that was designed deliberately to elicit incriminating remarks." *Kuhlmann v. Wilson,* 477 U.S. 436, 459, 106 S.Ct. 2616, 2630, 91 L.Ed.2d 364, 384–85 (1986). In *United States v. Labare,*

Kuhlmann v. Wilson
laws.findlaw.com/us/477/
436.html

191 F.3d 60 (1st Cir. 1999), the court ruled that a defendant's incriminating statements to a cellmate were admissible when the cellmate simply reported the statements to federal authorities under a general agreement to report what he might hear from other prisoners about violations of law. "Where a jail mate simply agrees to report whatever he learns about crimes from other inmates in general, . . . there is not enough to trigger *Massiah*." 191 F.3d at 65–66.

This prohibition against attempts to elicit information in the absence of counsel is not intended to hamper police investigation of crimes other than the crime for which adversary proceedings have already commenced. The police need to investigate crimes for which formal charges have already been filed as well as new or additional crimes. Either type of investigation may require surveillance of persons already indicted. Moreover, police who are investigating a person suspected of committing one crime and formally charged with having committed another crime may seek to discover evidence useful at a trial of either crime. In seeking evidence relating to pending charges, however, police investigators are limited by the Sixth Amendment rights of the accused. Therefore, incriminating statements relating to pending charges will be inadmissible at the trial of those charges, even though police were also investigating other crimes if, in obtaining the evidence, the government violated the Sixth Amendment by knowingly circumventing the accused's right to the assistance of counsel. On the other hand, evidence relating to charges to which the Sixth Amendment right to counsel had not attached at the time the evidence was obtained will not be inadmissible merely because other charges were pending at the time. *Maine v. Moulton*, 474 U.S. 159, 106 S.Ct. 477, 88 L.Ed.2d 481 (1985).

Key Points

10. Interrogation, for purposes of *Miranda*, refers not only to express questioning but also to any words or actions on the part of police (other than those normally attendant to arrest and custody) that the police should know are reasonably likely to elicit an incriminating response from the suspect. An incriminating response is any response—whether inculpatory or exculpatory—that the prosecution may seek to introduce at trial.

11. Law enforcement officers need not interrupt a volunteered statement to warn a suspect of *Miranda* rights.

12. Routine booking questions regarding a suspect's name, address, height, weight, eye color, date of birth, and current age to secure biographical data necessary to complete booking or pretrial services are not considered interrogation for purposes of *Miranda*, and incriminating statements made in response to such questions are admissible.

13. Questions asked by law enforcement officers in situations posing a threat to public safety need not be preceded by *Miranda* warnings.

14. *Miranda* warning requirements apply only to custodial interrogations conducted by law enforcement officers and not to questioning by private citizens.

15. If, after receiving *Miranda* warnings, a person indicates a desire to remain silent, the interrogation must cease. If the person requests an attorney, the interrogation must cease until an attorney is present.

16. Generally, a second custodial interrogation of a person who has exercised the *Miranda* right of silence is permissible after a lapse of a significant time period, if the person's right to terminate questioning at the first interrogation was scrupulously honored, fresh *Miranda* warnings are given, and no pressure to cooperate or other illegal tactics are used.

17. Whether the right to counsel is invoked during custodial interrogation or at an arraignment or similar proceeding, at or after which the defendant's Sixth Amendment right to counsel has attached, police may not further interrogate the defendant without counsel present unless the defendant initiates further

communication with the police. If the defendant initiates further communication, interrogation may proceed if the defendant makes a voluntary, knowing, and intelligent waiver of the right to counsel and the right to silence.

18. If an initial statement was obtained in violation of *Miranda,* but without coercion or other illegal means to break the defendant's will, a subsequent statement obtained after warnings and a valid waiver of *Miranda* rights is admissible.

19. After a person has been indicted and has retained counsel, the Fifth Amendment prevents law enforcement authorities from deliberately eliciting incriminating statements from the person by surreptitious methods.

Warnings

The **warnings** that must be given to a suspect by a law enforcement officer before conducting a custodial interrogation are stated in the *Miranda* decision.

> He must be warned prior to any questioning that he has the right to remain silent, that anything he says can be used against him in a court of law, that he has the right to the presence of an attorney, and that if he cannot afford an attorney one will be appointed for him prior to any questioning if he so desires. 384 U.S. at 479, 86 S.Ct. at 1630, 16 L.Ed.2d at 726.

The *Miranda* warnings need not be given in the exact form described in the *Miranda* decision, so long as the warnings reasonably convey to a suspect his or her rights as required by *Miranda. California v. Prysock,* 453 U.S. 355, 101 S.Ct. 2806, 69 L.Ed.2d 696 (1981). For example, the standard *Miranda* warnings used by the Federal Bureau of Investigation provide as follows:

California v. Prysock
laws.findlaw.com/us/453/355.html

> Before we ask you any questions, you must understand your rights.
> You have the right to remain silent.
> Anything you say can be used against you in court.
> You have the right to talk to a lawyer for advice before we ask you any questions and to have a lawyer with you during questioning.
> If you cannot afford a lawyer, one will be appointed for you before any questioning if you wish.
> If you decide to answer questions now without a lawyer present, you will still have the right to stop answering at any time. You also have the right to stop answering at any time until you talk to a lawyer. *Duckworth v. Eagan,* 492 U.S. 195, 202 n.4, 109 S.Ct. 2875, 2879 n.4, 106 L.Ed.2d 166, 176 n.4 (1989).

Duckworth v. Eagan
laws.findlaw.com/us/492/195.html

Most law enforcement agencies distribute *Miranda* warning cards to their officers to be used when informing persons subjected to custodial interrogation of their rights.

Manner of Giving Warnings

Miranda warnings must be stated clearly and in an unhurried manner, so that the person warned understands his or her rights and feels free to claim them without fear. The warnings should not be given in a careless, indifferent, and superficial manner. When warnings are given to an immature, illiterate, or mentally impaired person, the warnings must be given in language that the person can comprehend and on which the person can knowingly act. If necessary, the officer should explain and interpret the warnings. The test is whether the words used by the officer, in view of the age, intelligence, and demeanor of the individual being interrogated, convey a clear understanding of all *Miranda* rights. *Anderson v. State,* 253 A.2d 387 (Md.Spec.App. 1969).

Does the Suspect Require Warnings?

Although some suspects arguably may not need to be informed of their *Miranda* rights, the safest procedure for police is to administer the warnings in situations in which they are required.

SUSPECT KNOWS HIS OR HER RIGHTS   The *Miranda* opinion made it clear that law enforcement officers are not to assume that any suspect knows his or her rights:

> The Fifth Amendment privilege is so fundamental to our system of constitutional rule and the expedient of giving an adequate warning as to the availability of the privilege so simple, we will not pause to inquire in individual cases whether the defendant was aware of his rights without a warning being given. Assessments of the knowledge the defendant possessed, based on information as to his age, education, intelligence, or prior contact with authorities, can never be more than speculation; a warning is a clearcut fact. More important, whatever the background of the person interrogated, a warning at the time of the interrogation is indispensable to overcome its pressures and to insure that the individual knows he is free to exercise the privilege at that point in time. 384 U.S. at 468–69, 86 S.Ct. at 1625, 16 L.Ed.2d at 720.

SUSPECT IS NOT INDIGENT   If a suspect is known to be financially able to afford a lawyer, officers need not give the warning that a lawyer will be appointed in case of indigency. However, a law enforcement officer may not always be able to determine a person's financial status correctly, and "the expedient of giving a warning is too simple and the rights involved too important to engage in ex post facto inquiries into financial ability when there is any doubt at all on that score." 384 U.S. at 473, n.43 86 S.Ct. at 1627, n.43 16 L.Ed.2d at 723 n.43. Therefore, officers should give the complete set of *Miranda* warnings before conducting any custodial interrogation.

SUSPECT HAS AN ATTORNEY PRESENT   The *Miranda* opinion implies that the warnings are not required to be given to persons who have an attorney present with them:

> The presence of counsel . . . would be the adequate protective device necessary to make the process of police interrogation conform to the dictates of the privilege. His presence would insure that statements made in the government-established atmosphere are not the product of compulsion. 384 U.S. at 466, 86 S.Ct. at 1623, 16 L.Ed.2d at 719.

Passage of Time

The mere passage of time does not compromise a *Miranda* warning. Courts have consistently upheld the integrity of *Miranda* warnings even in cases in which several hours have elapsed between the reading of the warning and the interrogation. In *United States v. Frankson,* 83 F.3d 79 (4th Cir. 1996), the defendant contended that *Miranda* requires the police to readvise suspects of their rights when the interrogation does not immediately follow the *Miranda* warning or when an interrogation in progress is delayed. The court held that the defendant's "initial *Miranda* warning was in no way compromised by the passage of two and one-half hours between the issuance of his warning and the point at which he began to confess his crimes and cooperate with the police." 83 F.3d at 83.

20. Before custodial interrogation of a person, he or she must be warned (1) of the right to remain silent; (2) that anything said can be used against the person in a court of law; (3) of the right to the presence of an attorney; and (4) that if he or she cannot afford an attorney, one will be appointed prior to any questioning.

21. *Miranda* warnings need not be given in the exact form described in the *Miranda* decision, so long as the warn-

ings reasonably convey to a suspect his or her rights as required by *Miranda*.

22. Law enforcement officers should give complete *Miranda* warnings before conducting custodial interrogations, even if they believe that the suspect knows his or her rights or that the suspect is not indigent.

www.co.alameda.ca.us/da/pov/
Miranda%20_waivers.htm
Article, "*Miranda* Waivers" from
the District Attorney's Office in
Alameda County, California

Waiver

The *Miranda* case stated that, after warnings of *Miranda* rights have been given to a person subjected to custodial interrogation and the opportunity to exercise the rights has been afforded the person, "the individual may knowingly and intelligently waive these rights and agree to answer questions or make a statement. But unless and until such warnings and waiver are demonstrated by the prosecution at trial no evidence obtained as a result of interrogation can be used against him." 384 U.S. at 478–79, 86 S.Ct. at 1630, 16 L.Ed.2d at 726. A **waiver** is a voluntary and intentional relinquishment of a known right. The *Miranda* decision held that the defendant may waive the rights conveyed in the *Miranda* warnings "provided the waiver is made voluntarily, knowingly and intelligently." 384 U.S. at 475, 86 S.Ct. at 1628, 16 L.Ed.2d at 724. The inquiry whether the defendant has made a full and effective waiver has two distinct dimensions. As stated by the U.S. Supreme Court:

> First the relinquishment of the right must have been voluntary in the sense that it was the product of a free and deliberate choice rather than intimidation, coercion or deception. Second, the waiver must have been made with a full awareness both of the nature of the right being abandoned and the consequences of the decision to abandon it. Only if "the totality of the circumstances surrounding the interrogation" reveal both an uncoerced choice and the requisite level of comprehension may a court properly conclude that the *Miranda* rights have been waived. *Moran v. Burbine*, 475 U.S. 412, 421, 106 S.Ct. 1135, 1141, 89 L.Ed.2d 410, 421 (1986).

Moran v. Burbine
laws.findlaw.com/us/475/
412.html

To satisfy this totality-of-the-circumstances test, law enforcement officers must know what constitutes a waiver and must follow recommended procedures in obtaining the waiver. They also must be aware of the legal concerns involved in the two-dimensional inquiry regarding the validity of a waiver: (1) voluntariness and (2) requisite level of comprehension.

Obtaining a Waiver

After the *Miranda* warnings have been administered, the law enforcement officer should first ask the suspect whether he or she understands the rights that have been explained. The officer should then ask the suspect whether he or she wishes to talk without first consulting a lawyer or having a lawyer present during questioning. If the officer receives an affirmative answer to both questions, the officer should carefully note the exact language in which the answer was given, preserving it for possible future use in court. The officer may then proceed with the interrogation.

If possible, the officer should always try to obtain a written waiver of rights from the suspect before questioning. A written waiver is almost always held to be sufficient if the suspect is literate and there is no evidence of police coercion. *Menendez v. United States*, 393 F.2d 312 (5th Cir. 1968). Exhibit 13.1 is a suggested form for obtaining a written waiver of *Miranda* rights.

Law enforcement officers may not always be able to obtain express written or oral waivers. The U.S. Supreme Court held that "an explicit statement of waiver is not invariably necessary to support a finding that the defendant waived the right to remain silent or the right to counsel guaranteed by the *Miranda* case." *North Carolina v. Butler*, 441 U.S. 369, 375–76, 99 S.Ct. 1755, 1759, 60 L.Ed.2d 286, 293–94 (1979).

North Carolina v. Butler
laws.findlaw.com/us/441/369.html

> An express written or oral statement of waiver of the right to remain silent or of the right to counsel is usually strong proof of the validity of that waiver, but is not inevitably either necessary or sufficient to establish waiver. The question is not one of form, but rather whether the defendant in fact knowingly and voluntarily waived the rights delineated in the *Miranda* case. As was unequivocally said in *Miranda*, mere silence is not enough. That does not mean that the defendant's silence, coupled with an understanding of his rights and a course of conduct indicating waiver, may never support a conclusion that a defendant has waived his rights. The courts must presume that a defendant did not waive his rights; the prosecution's burden is great; but in at least some cases waiver can be clearly inferred from the actions and words of the person interrogated. 441 U.S. at 373, 99 S.Ct. at 1757, 60 L.Ed.2d at 292.

The Court went on to say that the question of waiver must be determined "on the 'particular facts and circumstances surrounding that case, including the background, experience, and conduct of the accused.'" 441 U.S. at 374–75, 99 S.Ct. at 1758, 60 L.Ed.2d at 293. Suspects may express themselves through an infinite variety of words and actions, which courts may or may not determine to be valid waivers of *Miranda* rights. Some suspects may be indecisive and may never clearly claim or waive their rights. Nevertheless, the prosecution must prove waiver of *Miranda* rights by a preponderance of the evidence. *Colorado v. Connelly*, 479 U.S. 157, 107 S.Ct. 515, 93 L.Ed.2d 473 (1986). Moreover, the absence of any evidence of waiver will result in a finding of no waiver and the exclusion of any statement obtained. *Tague v. Louisiana*, 444 U.S. 469, 100 S.Ct. 652, 62 L.Ed.2d 622 (1980). Therefore, when no written waiver or unambiguous oral waiver can be obtained, law enforcement officers should write down all circumstances surrounding the attempt to obtain the waiver so that the prosecution will have evidence to prove that the waiver was voluntary, knowing, and intelligent.

Tague v. Louisiana
laws.findlaw.com/us/444/469.html

Some courts require officers to cease all questioning if a suspect's exercise of the right to counsel is ambiguous. These courts allow further questioning only after the suspect's intention is clarified and the right to counsel is unequivocally waived. *United States v. Nordling*, 804 F.2d 1466 (9th Cir. 1986). Questions may be asked only to clarify

Case File _____ Police Dept. _____

Date _____ Time _____ Place _____

STATEMENT OF RIGHTS

THE FOLLOWING SEVEN STATEMENTS MUST BE FULLY UNDER-STOOD BY YOU BEFORE WE CAN CONTINUE. IF YOU DO NOT UNDERSTAND A STATEMENT, ASK THAT IT BE EXPLAINED:

1. You have the right to remain silent.
2. Anything you say can and will be used against you in a court of law.
3. You have the right to talk to a lawyer and have the lawyer present with you while you are being questioned.
4. If you cannot afford to hire a lawyer, one will be appointed to represent you before any questioning, if you wish.
5. You can decide at any time to exercise these rights and not answer any questions or make any statements.
6. Do you understand each of these rights I have explained to you?
7. Having these rights in mind, do you wish to talk to us now without a lawyer present?

ACKNOWLEDGEMENT AND WAIVER OF RIGHTS

THE ABOVE STATEMENT OF MY RIGHTS HAS BEEN READ AND EX-PLAINED TO ME AND I FULLY UNDERSTAND WHAT MY RIGHTS ARE. KNOWING THIS I AM WILLING TO ANSWER QUESTIONS OR TO MAKE A STATEMENT WITHOUT A LAWYER PRESENT.

Witness _____ Signed _____
   (Advising Officer or Witness)   (Individual Advised of Rights)

Witness _____ Education _____
   (Officer or Witness)   (Name of school and last grade completed)

STATEMENT

Page No. _____ of _____ Page Statement

I have read the above statement, have signed each page of the statement, and acknowledge receipt of a true copy of the statement.

I give this statement without threat, coercion or promise of any kind.

Witness _____

Witness _____ Signed _____

Suggested Form for Waiver of *Miranda* Rights, Page 1
■ EXHIBIT 13.1A

Page No. _____ of _____ Page Statement   Date _____

Page No. _____ of _____ Page Statement

I have read the above statement, have signed each page of the statement, and acknowledge receipt of a true copy of the statement.

I give this statement without threat, coercion or promise of any kind.

Witness _____

Witness _____ Signed _____

Suggested Form for Waiver of *Miranda* Rights, Page 2

■ EXHIBIT 13.1B

www.prospect.org/archives/
V11-10/nguyen-a.html
Article, "The Assault on
Miranda" by Alexander Nguyen;
discusses police tactics to obtain
waivers of *Miranda* rights

the defendant's wishes with respect to the request for counsel. *United States v. Fouche*, 833 F.2d 1284 (9th Cir. 1987).

Words and Actions Indicating a Waiver

When a defendant has been fully informed of his or her *Miranda* rights, any comprehensible oral statement of understanding and willingness to speak is usually acceptable as a waiver of rights. Examples of valid waivers are cases in which a suspect said, "I might as well tell you about it," *United States v. Boykin*, 398 F.2d 483, 484 (3d Cir. 1968); "I'll tell you," *State v. Kremens*, 245 A.2d 313, 315 (N.J. 1968); and, "I know all that," *State v. Brown*, 202 So.2d 274, 279 (La. 1967). Courts have also approved nonverbal waivers such as nods, shrugs, or other body language. *United States v. Chapa-Garza*, 62 F.3d 118 (5th Cir. 1995). After receiving a waiver in any of these forms, the law enforcement officer may begin questioning.

Often a suspect will indicate an understanding of *Miranda* rights and then simply begin to make a statement without any other verbal or nonverbal indication of waiver. Most courts have held that, once the suspect has been informed of *Miranda* rights and indicates an understanding of those rights, choosing to speak without a lawyer present is sufficient evidence of a knowing and voluntary waiver of the rights. *United States v. Puig*, 810 F.2d 1085 (11th Cir. 1987). However, this rule is probably valid only if the statement of the suspect follows closely after the suspect indicates an understanding of the warnings. *Billings v. People*, 466 P.2d 474 (Colo. 1970). In *Watkins v. Callahan*, 724 F.2d 1038 (1st Cir. 1984), the court found a valid waiver when the defendant indicated he was ready to make a statement after calling his family instead of calling an attorney. A suspect who indicates a desire to talk to a lawyer at some time in the future but agrees to answer questions without a lawyer has waived the right to counsel. *Thompson v. State*, 235 So.2d 354 (Fla.App. 1970).

Fare v. Michael C.
laws.findlaw.com/us/442/
707.html

A request to see someone other than a lawyer is not considered to be an assertion of rights under *Miranda*, although a denial of such a request may have some bearing on the voluntariness of the statements. For example, in *Fare v. Michael C.*, 442 U.S. 707, 99 S.Ct. 2560, 61 L.Ed.2d 197 (1979), the U.S. Supreme Court held that a juvenile waived his *Miranda* rights even though he had been denied a request to speak to his probation officer. The Court found that the request, made by an experienced older juvenile with an extensive prior record, did not *per se* constitute a request to remain silent, nor was it tantamount to a request for an attorney. However, some states require a parent, guardian, or other interested adult to be notified before a juvenile may be found to have waived *Miranda* rights. A request for counsel made by a suspect to a friend or relative is not the same as a request to the police. Therefore, even if the police are aware of such a request, the request does not operate as an exercise of *Miranda* rights. *People v. Smith*, 246 N.E.2d 689 (Ill.App. 1969).

www.doj.state.wi.us/
ss_manual/question.htm
Article, "Questioning of Juveniles
by Law Enforcement Officers and
School Employees"

Connecticut v. Barrett
laws.findlaw.com/us/479/
523.html

Once a suspect has been given *Miranda* warnings, the suspect's refusal to give a written statement outside the presence of his or her attorney does not render ineffective the suspect's clear waiver of rights for the purpose of giving an oral statement. In *Connecticut v. Barrett*, 479 U.S. 523, 107 S.Ct. 828, 93 L.Ed.2d 920 (1987), the suspect, who was in custody on a sexual assault charge, was given the *Miranda* warnings and indicated to the police that he would not make a written statement outside the presence of his attorney. He then clearly expressed his willingness to speak with the police without an attorney and made an oral statement admitting his involvement in the sexual assault. The Court held that the defendant's exercise of his right to counsel was limited by its terms to the making of written statements and did not prohibit further police questioning leading to the oral confession. Although the settled approach to questions of waiver requires giving a broad rather than a narrow interpretation to a defendant's request for counsel, the Court said:

> Interpretation is only required where the defendant's words, understood as ordinary people would understand them, are ambiguous. Here, however, Barrett made clear his intentions, and they were honored by police. To conclude that respondent invoked his right to counsel for all purposes requires not a broad interpretation of an ambiguous statement, but a disregard of the ordinary meaning of respondent's statement. 479 U.S. at 529–30, 107 S.Ct. at 832, 93 L.Ed.2d at 928.

Other examples of valid selective waivers are a defendant's assertion that "it would depend on the questions and he would answer some questions if he thought it appropriate." . . . *United States v. Eaton,* 890 F.2d 511, 513 (1st Cir. 1989), and the defendant's statement, "Well, ask your questions and I will answer those I see fit." *Bruni v. Lewis,* 847 F.2d 561, 564 (9th Cir. 1988). When a suspect indicates, after giving a valid written or oral waiver, a desire not to have any notes taken, this may suggest that the suspect erroneously believes that oral statements cannot be used as evidence in court. The law enforcement officer should explain that oral statements could be used against the suspect in court. Otherwise, a court might invalidate the waiver. *Frazier v. United States,* 419 F.2d 1161 (D.C.Cir. 1969).

Voluntariness of the Waiver

In *Colorado v. Connelly,* 479 U.S. 157, 107 S.Ct. 515, 93 L.Ed.2d 473 (1986), the U.S. Supreme Court held that the voluntariness inquiry in the *Miranda* waiver context was the same as that in the Fifth Amendment confession context. The Court said:

> The sole concern of the Fifth Amendment, on which *Miranda* was based, is governmental coercion. . . . The voluntariness of a waiver of this privilege has always depended on the absence of police overreaching, not on "free choice" in any broader sense of the word. 479 U.S. at 170, 107 S.Ct. at 523, 93 L.Ed.2d at 486.

Therefore, absent evidence that a suspect's will was overborne and his or her capacity for self-determination critically impaired because of coercive police conduct, the suspect's waiver of *Miranda* rights will be considered voluntary. The *Connelly* case holds that, even if a suspect is compelled to waive *Miranda* rights for some psychological or other reason, if the compulsion did not flow from the police, the waiver will not be held involuntary.

Psychological tactics, such as playing on the defendant's sympathies or explaining that honesty is the best policy, have been variously interpreted by courts in determining the voluntariness of a defendant's waiver. Some courts apply a totality-of-the-circumstances test to determine whether the defendant's will was overborne or his or her capacity for self-determination was critically impaired. In *United States v. Pelton,* 835 F.2d 1067 (4th Cir. 1987), the court said:

> Agents may properly initiate discussions on cooperation, and may indicate that they will make this cooperation known. . . . General encouragement to cooperate is far different from specific promises of leniency. 835 F.2d at 1073.

With respect to the use of psychological tactics, the Third Circuit Court of Appeals said:

> These ploys may play a part in the suspect's decision to confess, but so long as that decision is a product of the suspect's own balancing of competing considerations the

confession is voluntary. The question . . . is whether . . . statements were so manipulative or coercive that they deprived [the defendant] of his ability to make an unconstrained, autonomous decision to confess. *Miller v. Fenton*, 796 F.2d 598, 605 (3d Cir. 1986).

Requisite Level of Comprehension

The requirement that a waiver must be made with full awareness of both the right being abandoned and the consequences of the decision to abandon that right is satisfied by careful administration of the *Miranda* warnings to a suspect. As stated by the U.S. Supreme Court:

> The Constitution does not require that a criminal suspect know and understand every possible consequence of a waiver of the Fifth Amendment privilege. . . . The Fifth Amendment's guarantee is both simpler and more fundamental: A defendant may not be compelled to be a witness against himself in any respect. The *Miranda* warnings protect this privilege by insuring that a suspect knows that he may choose not to talk to law enforcement officers, to talk only with counsel present, or to discontinue talking at any time. The *Miranda* warnings ensure that a waiver of these rights is knowing and intelligent by requiring that the suspect be fully advised of this constitutional privilege, including the critical advice that whatever he chooses to say may be used as evidence against him. *Colorado v. Spring*, 479 U.S. 564, 574, 107 S.Ct. 851, 857–58, 93 L.Ed.2d 954, 966 (1987).

Colorado v. Spring
laws.findlaw.com/us/479/
564.html

Patterson v. Illinois, 487 U.S. 285, 108 S.Ct. 2389, 101 L.Ed.2d 261 (1988), held that the *Miranda* warnings are also sufficient to inform a defendant of the right to have counsel present during *postindictment* questioning and the consequences of a decision to waive the Sixth Amendment right during such questioning.

> [W]hatever warnings suffice for *Miranda's* purposes will also be sufficient in the context of postindictment questioning. The State's decision to take an additional step and commence formal adversarial proceedings against the accused does not substantially increase the value of counsel to the accused at questioning, or expand the limited purpose that an attorney serves when the accused is questioned by authorities. With respect to this inquiry, we do not discern a substantial difference between the usefulness of a lawyer to a suspect during custodial interrogation, and his value to an accused at postindictment questioning. 487 U.S. at 298–99, 108 S.Ct. at 2398, 101 L.Ed.2d at 276.

SUSPECT'S NEED FOR ADDITIONAL USEFUL INFORMATION   Suspects often claim that their waivers of *Miranda* rights were involuntary because police or prosecutors failed to give them enough information on which to base the decision to waive or not waive the rights. In *Moran v. Burbine*, 475 U.S. 412, 106 S.Ct. 1135, 89 L.Ed.2d 410 (1986), the U.S. Supreme Court held that the police are not required to inform an uncharged suspect of an attorney's attempts to reach him or her, or to otherwise keep the suspect abreast of the status of his or her legal representation, before giving *Miranda* warnings and obtaining a waiver of *Miranda* rights. In the *Burbine* case, an attorney who was contacted by the suspect's sister (without the suspect's knowledge) attempted to telephone the suspect, who was in custody at the police station. The police assured the attorney that the suspect would not be questioned any further that day. Later that evening, however, police informed the suspect of his *Miranda* rights, the suspect executed a series of valid written waivers, and the suspect eventually confessed to a murder. At no point during the course of interrogation, which occurred before arraignment, did the suspect request an attorney.

The Court held that the police's failure to inform the suspect of the attorney's phone call did not deprive the suspect of information essential to his ability to knowingly waive his Fifth Amendment rights. The Court said:

> Events occurring outside the presence of the suspect and entirely unknown to him surely can have no bearing on the capacity to comprehend and knowingly relinquish a constitutional right. . . . Once it is determined that a suspect's decision not to rely on his rights was uncoerced, that he at all times knew he could stand mute and request a lawyer, and that he was aware of the state's intention to use his statements to secure a conviction, the analysis is complete and the waiver is valid as a matter of law. 475 U.S. at 422–23, 106 S.Ct. at 1141–42, 89 L.Ed.2d at 421–22.

Furthermore, whether the police conduct in the case was intentional or inadvertent, the Court held that the police's state of mind was irrelevant to the question of the intelligence and voluntariness of the suspect's election to abandon his rights. Finally, there was no violation of the suspect's Sixth Amendment right to counsel. The Court reasoned that if that right had attached, the police would have been prohibited from interfering with the attorney's efforts to assist the suspect. But because the interrogation took place *before* the initiation of adversary judicial proceedings, the right to counsel did not attach, and the suspect could not have his confession suppressed for a violation of a right he did not have.

The Court frowned upon the police's deception of the attorney, but it found that this conduct was not so offensive as to deprive the defendant of the fundamental fairness guaranteed by the due process clause of the Fourteenth Amendment. The Court specifically warned, however, that a more flagrant violation by the police might rise to the level of a due process violation. Therefore, the police should not interpret the *Burbine* case as generally approving dishonest or shady dealings with defense attorneys in interrogation situations occurring before the initiation of formal charges. In fact, some states have explicitly rejected the ruling in *Moran v. Burbine* based on state constitutional law. The California Supreme Court held as follows:

> [W]hether or not a suspect in custody has previously waived his rights to silence and counsel, the police may not deny him the opportunity, before questioning begins or resumes, to meet with his retained or appointed counsel who has taken diligent steps to come to his aid.
>
> If the lawyer comes to the station before interrogation begins or while it is still in progress, the suspect must promptly be told, and if he then wishes to see his counsel, he must be allowed to do so. Moreover, the police may not engage in conduct, intentional or grossly negligent, which is calculated to mislead, delay, or dissuade counsel in his efforts to reach his client. Such conduct constitutes a denial of a California suspect's *Miranda* rights to counsel, and it invalidates any subsequent statements. *People v. Houston*, 230 Cal.Rptr. 141, 149, 724 P.2d 1166, 1174–75 (Cal. 1986).

In *Colorado v. Spring*, 479 U.S. 564, 107 S.Ct. 851, 93 L.Ed.2d 954 (1987), the defendant contended that the failure of police to inform him of the potential subjects of interrogation constituted police trickery and deception as condemned in *Miranda*, and rendered his waiver of *Miranda* rights invalid. The U.S. Supreme Court declined to hold that "mere silence by law enforcement officials as to the subject matter of an interrogation is 'trickery' sufficient to invalidate a suspect's waiver of *Miranda* rights. . . ." 479 U.S. at 576, 107 S.Ct. at 858, 93 L.Ed.2d at 967. Citing *Moran v. Burbine*, the Court said that a valid waiver does not require that police supply a suspect with all useful information to help the suspect calibrate his or her self-interest in deciding whether to speak or to stand by his or her rights. The Court concluded as follows:

> This Court's holding in Miranda specifically required that the police inform a criminal suspect that he has the right to remain silent and that anything he says may be used against him. There is no qualification of this broad and explicit warning. The warning, as formulated in *Miranda,* conveys to a suspect the nature of his constitutional privilege and the consequences of abandoning it. Accordingly, we hold that a suspect's awareness of all the possible subjects of questioning in advance of interrogation is not relevant to determining whether the suspect voluntarily, knowingly, and intelligently waived his Fifth Amendment privilege. 479 U.S. at 577, 107 S.Ct. at 859, 93 L.Ed.2d at 968.

In *United States v. Tapp,* 812 F.2d 177 (5th Cir. 1987), the court held that the interrogating officer's failure to inform the defendant that he was the target of the investigation did not render the defendant's waiver of *Miranda* rights involuntary.

SUSPECT'S COMPETENCY   The inquiry as to whether the suspect has the requisite level of comprehension to validly waive *Miranda* rights is also directed at the competency of the suspect. In determining competency to waive *Miranda* rights, courts will examine the totality of the circumstances surrounding the waiver, with no single factor controlling. Among the factors to be considered are the defendant's

- education—*Stawicki v. Israel,* 778 F.2d 380 (7th Cir. 1985);
- intelligence—*Henry v. Dees,* 658 F.2d 406 (5th Cir. 1981);
- literacy—*United States v. Binder,* 769 F.2d 595 (9th Cir. 1985);
- familiarity with the criminal justice system—*United States v. Scarpa,* 897 F.2d 63 (2d Cir. 1990);
- physical and mental condition—*United States v. Lewis,* 833 F.2d 1380 (9th Cir. 1987);
- ingestion of drugs or alcohol—*United States v. D'Antoni,* 856 F.2d 975 (7th Cir. 1988);
- language barriers—*United States v. Boon San Chong,* 829 F.2d 1572 (11th Cir. 1987);
- age—*Woods v. Clusen,* 794 F.2d 293 (7th Cir. 1986).

In a case involving a juvenile, the U.S. Supreme Court stated:

> This totality of circumstances approach is adequate to determine whether there has been a waiver even where interrogation of juveniles is involved. . . . The totality approach permits—indeed, it mandates—inquiry into all the circumstances surrounding the interrogation. This includes evaluation of the juvenile's age, experience, education, background, and intelligence, and into whether he had the capacity to understand the warnings given him, the nature of his Fifth Amendment rights, and the consequences of waiving those rights. *Fare v. Michael C.,* 442 U.S. 707, 725, 99 S.Ct. 2560, 2572, 61 L.Ed.2d 197, 212 (1979).

Additional circumstances to be considered in determining a waiver of a juvenile's rights are as follows: (1) knowledge of the accused as to the substance of the charge, if any has been filed; (2) whether the accused is held incommunicado or allowed to consult with relatives, friends, or an attorney; (3) whether the accused was interrogated before or after formal charges had been filed; (4) method used in interrogation; (5) length of interrogations; and (6) whether the accused refused to voluntarily give statements on prior occasions. *West v. United States,* 399 F.2d 467 (5th Cir. 1968).

dpa.state.ky.us/library/
advocate/july00/Ill.htm
Article, "Breaking Through: Communicating And Collaborating with the Mentally Ill Defendant" by Eric Drogin

In general, the officer should carefully observe the suspect and take notes on all indications of the suspect's competence or incompetence to waive *Miranda* rights. In *State v. Addington*, 518 A.2d 449 (Me. 1986), the court found that the suspect's refusal to talk to officers and refusal to undergo certain tests supported the conclusion that his waiver of *Miranda* rights was voluntary, knowing, and intelligent. Unless an officer is positive that the suspect is incapable of understanding and waiving *Miranda* rights, the officer should not refrain from trying to obtain a lawful confession. It is the duty of the courts, not of the law enforcement officer, to determine finally whether there was a voluntary, knowing, and intelligent waiver and a voluntary and trustworthy confession.

🔑 Key Points

23. After warnings of *Miranda* rights have been given to a person subjected to custodial interrogation and the opportunity to exercise the rights has been afforded the person, the person may voluntarily, knowingly, and intelligently waive the rights and agree to answer questions or make a statement. But unless and until such warnings and waiver are demonstrated by the prosecution at trial, no evidence obtained as a result of interrogation can be used against the person.

24. To constitute a full and effective waiver of *Miranda* rights, (1) the relinquishment of the right must have been voluntary in the sense that it was the product of a free and deliberate choice rather than police intimidation, coercion, or deception; and (2) the waiver must have been made with a full awareness both of the nature of the right being abandoned and the consequences of the decision to abandon it. This second requirement is satisfied by careful administration of the *Miranda* warnings to a competent suspect.

25. A request to see someone other than a lawyer is not considered to be an assertion of rights under *Miranda*, although a denial of such a request may have some bearing on the voluntariness of the statements.

26. The police are not required to inform an uncharged suspect of an attorney's attempts to reach him or her, or to otherwise keep the suspect abreast of the status of his or her legal representation or of other information useful to the person's defense, before giving *Miranda* warnings and obtaining a waiver of *Miranda* rights.

Other *Miranda* Issues

This section discusses issues collateral to the four core issues of *Miranda*: custody, interrogation, warning, and waiver. Included here are the application of *Miranda* to nontestimonial evidence; Fourth Amendment considerations; application of *Miranda* to minor offenses and civil proceedings; and implications of the use of undercover agents.

Nontestimonial Evidence

The self-incrimination clause of the Fifth Amendment provides that no "person . . . shall be compelled in any criminal case to be a witness against himself." U.S. Const., Amend. 5. Although the text of the amendment does not set out the ways in which a person might be a "witness against himself," the U.S. Supreme Court has long held that the privilege does not protect a suspect from being compelled by the state to produce "real or physical evidence." Rather, the privilege "protects an accused only from being compelled to testify against himself, or otherwise provide the State with evidence of a testimonial or communicative nature. . . ." *Schmerber v. California*, 384 U.S. 757, 761, 86 S.Ct. 1826, 1830, 16 L.Ed.2d 908, 914 (1966). "[I]n order to be testimonial, an accused's communication must itself, explicitly or implicitly, relate a factual assertion

Schmerber v. California
laws.findlaw.com/us/384/757.html

Doe v. United States
laws.findlaw.com/us/487/
201.html

or disclose information. Only then is a person compelled to be a 'witness' against himself." *Doe v. United States,* 487 U.S. 201, 210, 108 S.Ct. 2341, 2347, 101 L.Ed.2d 184, 197 (1988). In *Pennsylvania v. Muniz,* 496 U.S. 582, 597, 110 S.Ct. 2638, 2648, 110 L.Ed.2d 528, 549 (1990), the Court elaborated further:

> Whenever a suspect is asked for a response requiring him to communicate an express or implied assertion of fact or belief, the suspect confronts the "trilemma" of truth, falsity, or silence and hence the response (whether based on truth or falsity) contains a testimonial component.

In the *Muniz* case, the defendant was arrested for driving under the influence and was asked a series of questions without being given the *Miranda* warnings. In responding, his confusion and failure to speak clearly indicated a state of drunkenness. The Court held that the defendant's responses were not rendered inadmissible by *Miranda* merely because the slurred nature of his speech was incriminating.

United States v. Dionisio
laws.findlaw.com/us/410/1.html

> Under *Schmerber* and its progeny . . . any slurring of speech and other evidence of lack of muscular coordination revealed by Muniz's responses to [the officer's] direct questions constitute nontestimonial components of those responses. Requiring a suspect to reveal the physical manner in which he articulates words, like requiring him to reveal the physical properties of the sound produced by his voice [see *United States v. Dionisio,* 410 U.S. 1, 93 S.Ct. 764, 35 L.Ed.2d 67 (1973)] does not, without more, compel him to provide a "testimonial" response for purposes of the privilege. 496 U.S. at 592, 110 S.Ct. at 2645, 110 L.Ed.2d at 546.

California v. Byers
laws.findlaw.com/us/402/
424.html

In *California v. Byers,* 402 U.S. 424, 431–32, 91 S.Ct. 1535, 1539–40, 29 L.Ed.2d 9, 19 (1971), the U.S. Supreme Court held that a state statutory requirement that a driver involved in an accident stop at the scene and give his or her name and address was not testimonial in the Fifth Amendment sense:

> The act of stopping is no more testimonial—indeed less so in some respects—than requiring a person in custody to stand or walk in a police lineup, to speak prescribed words, or to give samples of handwriting, fingerprints, or blood. *United States v. Wade,* 388 U.S. 218, 221–23, 87 S.Ct. 1926, 1929–30, 18 L.Ed.2d 1149 (1967); *Schmerber v. California,* 384 U.S. 757, 764 n.8, 86 S.Ct. 1826, 1832, 16 L.Ed.2d 908 (1966). . . . Disclosure of name and address is an essentially neutral act.

www.richmond.edu/~jolt/v2i1/
sergienko.html
Article, "Self-Incrimination and
Cryptographic Keys" by Gregory
Sergienko

Fourth Amendment Violations

For purposes of this chapter, when a law enforcement officer attempts to obtain a statement from a person, not only must the voluntariness and *Miranda* requirements be satisfied, but also the officer must not violate the person's reasonable expectation of privacy. Thus, even though a law enforcement officer has satisfied all the *Miranda* requirements in obtaining a statement from a person, the statement may still be inadmissible in court if it was obtained in violation of the person's Fourth Amendment rights.

Katz v. United States
laws.findlaw.com/us/389/
347.html

The leading case on this subject is *Katz v. United States,* 389 U.S. 347, 88 S.Ct. 507, 19 L.Ed.2d 576 (1967), in which the defendant, who was in a telephone booth, was eavesdropped on by federal agents, who had attached an electronic listening and recording device to the outside of the booth. The Court held that despite the lack of an intrusion into a constitutionally protected area, the defendant's statements were inadmissible in court because they were taken in violation of his reasonable expectation of privacy. The Court said that once it is recognized that the Fourth Amendment protects people—and not simply "areas"—against unreasonable searches and seizures, it becomes clear that the reach of that Amendment cannot turn upon the presence or absence of a physical intrusion into any given enclosure. 389 U.S. at 353, 88 S.Ct. at 512, 19 L.Ed.2d at 583.

In *Halpin v. Superior Court,* 101 Cal.Rptr. 375, 495 P.2d 1295 (Cal. 1972), the incarcerated defendant's wife visited him at the jail during regular visiting hours. A detective allowed the defendant and his wife to use his office to converse, and the detective left the office. The conversation was secretly taped and was used in court against the defendant. The court ruled the tapes inadmissible, stating that law enforcement officers may not deliberately create an expectation of privacy so that a prisoner and his or her visitor will be lulled into believing their conversations will be confidential.

In *United States v. Fisch,* 474 F.2d 1071 (9th Cir. 1973), law enforcement officers were investigating a narcotics smuggling operation. The officers obtained a motel room adjacent to that of the suspects, and, by listening at the door, the officers heard a discussion of criminal acts. The officers used no electronic devices and committed no trespass. The court ruled that the statements were admissible, holding that the defendants had no justifiable expectation of privacy in their conversations. The court emphasized that a person's interest in privacy must be balanced against the public's interest in the investigation and prosecution of crime:

> Upon balance, appraising the public and private interests here involved, we are satisfied that the expectations of the defendants as to their privacy, even were such expectations to be considered reasonable despite their audible disclosures, must be subordinated to the public interest in law enforcement. In sum, there has been no justifiable reliance, the expectation of privacy not being "one that society is prepared to recognize as 'reasonable.'" 474 F.2d at 1078–79.

Nature or Severity of Offense

The U.S. Supreme Court held that "a person subjected to custodial interrogation is entitled to the benefit of the procedural safeguards enunciated in *Miranda,* regardless of the nature or severity of the offense of which he is suspected or for which he was arrested." *Berkemer v. McCarty,* 468 U.S. 420, 434, 104 S.Ct. 3138, 3147, 82 L.Ed.2d 317, 331 (1984). The Court explained:

> The occasions on which the police arrest and then interrogate someone suspected only of a misdemeanor traffic offense are rare. The police are already well accustomed to giving *Miranda* warnings to persons taken into custody. Adherence to the principle that all suspects must be given such warnings will not significantly hamper the efforts of the police to investigate crimes. 468 U.S. at 434, 104 S.Ct. at 3147, 82 L.Ed.2d at 331.

Miranda has been held inapplicable to civil proceedings such as customs procedures, civil commitments, extradition proceedings, and license revocation proceedings.

Undercover Agents

Miranda was concerned with the inherently compelling pressures generated by a police-dominated atmosphere "which work to undermine the individual's will to resist and to compel him to speak where he would not otherwise do so freely." 384 U.S. at 467, 86 S.Ct. at 1624, 16 L.Ed.2d at 719. Coercion is determined from the perspective of the

www.co.alameda.ca.us/da/pov/Miranda_exceptions.htm
Article, "*Miranda*: Exceptions" from the District Attorney's Office in Alameda County, California; one of the exceptions discussed is the "undercover agent" exception

suspect. Conversations between suspects and undercover agents do not implicate the concerns underlying *Miranda,* because a suspect speaking to those whom he assumes are not officers would not feel compelled to speak by the fear of reprisal for remaining silent or in the hope of more lenient treatment should he or she confess.

Hoffa v. United States
laws.findlaw.com/us/385/
293.html

In *Hoffa v. United States,* 385 U.S. 293, 87 S.Ct. 408, 17 L.Ed.2d 374 (1966), the U.S. Supreme Court held that placing an undercover agent near a suspect to gather incriminating information was permissible under the Fifth Amendment. In *Hoffa,* while the defendant was on trial, he met often with a person named Partin, who, unbeknownst to Hoffa, was cooperating with law enforcement officials. Partin reported to officials that Hoffa had divulged his attempts to bribe jury members. The Court approved using Hoffa's statements at his subsequent trial for jury tampering, on the rationale that no claim had been or could have been made that his incriminating statements were the product of any sort of coercion, legal or factual. In addition, the Court found that the fact that Partin had fooled Hoffa into thinking that Partin was a sympathetic colleague did not affect the voluntariness of the statements.

Illinois v. Perkins
laws.findlaw.com/us/495/
292.html

In *Illinois v. Perkins,* 495 U.S. 292, 110 S.Ct. 2394, 110 L.Ed.2d 243 (1990), police placed undercover agent Parisi in a jail cell block with the defendant, who was incarcerated on charges unrelated to the murder that Parisi was investigating. When Parisi asked him whether he had ever killed anyone, the defendant made statements implicating himself in the murder. The Court said that

> [t]he only difference between this case and *Hoffa* is that the suspect here was incarcerated, but detention, whether or not for the crime in question, does not warrant a presumption that the use of an undercover agent to speak with an incarcerated suspect makes any confession thus obtained involuntary. 495 U.S. at 298, 110 S.Ct. at 2398, 110 L.Ed.2d at 252.

It is the premise of *Miranda* that the danger of coercion results from the interaction of custody and official interrogation. The Court rejected the argument that *Miranda* warnings are required whenever a suspect is in custody in a technical sense and converses with someone who happens to be a government agent. *Miranda* forbids coercion, not mere strategic deception by taking advantage of a suspect's misplaced trust in one he or she supposes to be a fellow prisoner.

> *Miranda* was not meant to protect suspects from boasting about their criminal activities in front of persons whom they believe to be their cellmates. . . . Respondent had no reason to feel that undercover agent Parisi had any legal authority to force him to answer questions or that Parisi could affect respondent's future treatment. Respondent viewed the cellmate-agent as an equal and showed no hint of being intimidated by the atmosphere of the jail. In recounting the details of the Stephenson murder, respondent was motivated solely by the desire to impress his fellow inmates. He spoke at his own peril. 495 U.S. at 298, 110 S.Ct. at 2398, 110 L.Ed.2d at 252.

www.lectlaw.com/files/
cri19.htm
Article, "A Constitutional Guide to the Use of Cellmate Informants" by Kimberly A. Crawford

 Key Points

27. The privilege against self-incrimination does not protect a suspect from being compelled by the state to produce real or physical evidence but only protects an accused from being compelled to testify against himself or herself, or otherwise provide the state with evidence of a testimonial or communicative nature. To be testimonial, an accused's communication must itself, explicitly or implicitly, relate a factual assertion or disclose information.

28. When a law enforcement officer attempts to obtain a statement from a person, not only must the voluntariness and *Miranda* requirements be satisfied, but also the officer must not violate the person's reasonable expectation of privacy.

29. *Miranda* requirements apply regardless of the nature or severity of the offense being investigated.

30. *Miranda* is inapplicable to civil proceedings such as customs procedures, civil commitments, extradition proceedings, and license revocation proceedings.

31. Undercover agents need not administer *Miranda* warnings to suspects before obtaining statements, unless the suspect is coerced in some way.

Effect of *Miranda* in Court

Statements taken in violation of *Miranda* requirements will be inadmissible in court as substantive evidence in the prosecution's case in chief to prove the defendant's guilt of crime. In recent years, however, courts have allowed the use of statements taken in violation of *Miranda* for purposes other than the proof of a defendant's guilt. In *Harris v. New York*, 401 U.S. 222, 91 S.Ct. 643, 28 L.Ed.2d 1 (1971), and *Oregon v. Hass*, 420 U.S. 714, 95 S.Ct. 1215, 43 L.Ed.2d 570 (1975), the Court admitted testimony of previous inconsistent statements taken from a defendant in violation of his *Miranda* rights solely for the purpose of impeaching the defendant's testimony at trial. Stressing that the trustworthiness of the defendant's earlier conflicting statements must satisfy legal standards, the Court in *Harris* said:

> The shield provided by *Miranda* cannot be perverted into a license to use perjury by way of a defense, free from the risk of confrontation with prior inconsistent utterances. We hold, therefore, that petitioner's credibility was appropriately impeached by use of his earlier conflicting statements. 401 U.S. at 226, 91 S.Ct. at 646, 28 L.Ed.2d at 5.

Similarly, a statement taken in violation of the rule of *Edwards v. Arizona* and *Michigan v. Jackson* (see pages 488 to 494)—that once a criminal defendant invokes the Fifth Amendment right to counsel at a custodial interrogation or the Sixth Amendment right to counsel at a postarraignment interrogation, a subsequent waiver of that right, even if voluntary, knowing, and intelligent under traditional standards, is presumed invalid if secured pursuant to police-initiated conversation—may be used to impeach a defendant's false or inconsistent testimony at trial, even though the same statement may not be used as substantive evidence. *Michigan v. Harvey*, 494 U.S. 344, 110 S.Ct. 1176, 108 L.Ed.2d 293 (1990). And in *Michigan v. Tucker*, 417 U.S. 433, 94 S.Ct. 2357, 41 L.Ed.2d 182 (1974), the U.S. Supreme Court held that a *Miranda* violation that resulted in the discovery of a witness did not preclude the government from later calling that witness to testify at trial. The witness was named in the defendant's alibi during an interrogation that followed incomplete *Miranda* warnings. The witness not only contradicted the defendant's alibi but also provided additional incriminating information. The Supreme Court denied the defendant's attempt to exclude the witness's testimony at trial, concluding that, although statements taken without benefit of full *Miranda* warnings generally could not be admitted at trial, identification of witnesses is an acceptable use of the statements.

Law enforcement officers should not interpret the *Harris*, *Hass*, *Harvey*, and *Tucker* cases as providing an opportunity to evade the requirements of the *Miranda*, *Edwards*, and *Jackson* cases. An admission or confession obtained in compliance with the latter

Harris v. New York
laws.findlaw.com/us/401/222.html
Oregon v. Hass
laws.findlaw.com/us/420/714.html

Michigan v. Harvey
laws.findlaw.com/us/494/344.html
Michigan v. Tucker
laws.findlaw.com/us/417/433.html

www.law.utah.edu/Cassell/uclamir.htm
Article, "Police Interrogation in the 1990's: An Empirical Study of the Effects of *Miranda*" by Paul G. Cassell and Bret S. Hayman

cases is much more valuable to the prosecution than is an illegally obtained voluntary statement to be used only for impeachment or discovery of witnesses. In addition, *involuntary* statements obtained from a defendant cannot be used for any purpose in a criminal trial. The U.S. Supreme Court stated that "*any* criminal trial use against a defendant of his *involuntary* statement is a denial of due process of law, 'even though there is ample evidence aside from the confession to support the conviction.'" *Mincey v. Arizona,* 437 U.S. 385, 398, 98 S.Ct. 2408, 2416, 57 L.Ed.2d 290, 303 (1978). The only exception to this rule allows admission of an involuntary statement if the admission is found to be harmless error. *Arizona v. Fulminante,* 499 U.S. 279, 111 S.Ct. 1246, 113 L.Ed.2d 302 (1991).

In *United States v. Hale,* 422 U.S. 171, 95 S.Ct. 2133, 45 L.Ed.2d 99 (1975), and *Doyle v. Ohio,* 426 U.S. 610, 96 S.Ct. 2240, 49 L.Ed.2d 91 (1976), the U.S. Supreme Court held that a defendant's silence after receiving the *Miranda* warnings could not be used against the defendant at trial for the purpose of impeaching his or her trial testimony. The Court quoted the *Hale* case in the *Doyle* case as follows:

> [W]hen a person under arrest is informed as *Miranda* requires, that he may remain silent, that anything he says may be used against him, and that he may have an attorney if he wishes, it seems to me that it does not comport with due process to permit the prosecution during the trial to call attention to his silence at the time of arrest and to insist that because he did not speak about the facts of the case at that time, as he was told he need not do, an unfavorable inference might be drawn as to the truth of his trial testimony. . . . 426 U.S. at 619, 96 S.Ct. at 2245, 49 L.Ed.2d at 98.

The *Doyle* rule does not apply, however, to a defendant's silence before *Miranda* warnings are given.

> [T]he Constitution does not prohibit the use for impeachment purposes of a defendant's silence prior to arrest . . . or after arrest if no *Miranda* warnings are given. . . . Such silence is probative and does not rest on any implied assurance by law enforcement authorities that it will carry no penalty. *Brecht v. Abrahamson,* 507 U.S. 619, 628, 113 S.Ct. 1710, 1716, 123 L.Ed.2d 353, 366 (1993).

Finally, since the U.S. Supreme Court's decision "that *Miranda* is a constitutional decision," (*Dickerson v. United States,* 530 U.S. 428, 438, 120 S.Ct. 2326, 2333, 147 L.Ed.2d 405, 416 [2000]), law enforcement officers are potentially liable in a civil action such as an action for deprivation of constitutional rights under 42 U.S.C. §1983 if they violate the *Miranda* requirements. To avoid such liability, whenever an encounter with a person constitutes a "custodial interrogation," as explained in this chapter, officers must be extra careful to fully and properly administer *Miranda* warnings.

Mincey v. Arizona
laws.findlaw.com/us/437/385.html

Arizona v. Fulminante
laws.findlaw.com/us/499/279.html

United States v. Hale
laws.findlaw.com/us/422/171.html

Doyle v. Ohio
laws.findlaw.com/us/426/610.html

www.fbi.gov/publications/leb/1997/aug976.htm
Article, "Intentional Violations of *Miranda*: A Strategy for Liability" by Kimberly A. Crawford
www.fbi.gov/publications/leb/1997/mar976.htm
Article, "Beyond *Miranda*" by Edward M. Hendrie

Brecht v. Abrahamson
laws.findlaw.com/us/507/619.html

Complete text of 42 U.S.C. § 1983
caselaw.findlaw.com/scripts/ts_search.pl?title=42&sec=1983

 **Key Points**

32. Statements taken in violation of *Miranda, Edwards,* and *Jackson* requirements are inadmissible in court as substantive evidence in the prosecution's case in chief to prove the defendant's guilt of crime, but they may be used for the purpose of impeaching the defendant's testimony at trial.

33. Involuntary statements obtained from a defendant cannot be used for any purpose in a criminal trial.

34. A defendant's silence after receiving the *Miranda* warnings may not be used against the defendant at trial for the purpose of impeaching his or her trial testimony.

Summary

An admission or confession obtained by a law enforcement officer is inadmissible in court unless (1) it is voluntary and (2) the requirements of the U.S. Supreme Court case of *Miranda v. Arizona* are satisfied. Courts find a statement involuntary if the statement is a product of police coercion, whether by force or by subtler forms of coercion, and if, in the totality of the circumstances, the statement is not the result of a person's free and rational choice. In making the determination of voluntariness, courts will consider the personal characteristics of the defendant, such as age, mental capacity, physical or mental impairment, and experience with the police, in establishing the setting in which coercion might operate to overcome the will of the defendant.

The *Miranda* case held that a statement obtained by police during a custodial interrogation of a defendant is inadmissible unless the police used certain procedural safeguards to secure the defendant's privilege against self-incrimination. Those procedural safeguards are the giving of warnings of rights and the obtaining of a valid waiver of those rights before an interrogation is begun. The major issues of *Miranda* can thus be broken down into four categories: custody, interrogation, warnings, and waiver.

A person is in custody if there is a formal arrest or restraint on freedom of movement of the degree associated with a formal arrest. Custody is determined by examining, from a reasonable person's point of view, the totality of facts and circumstances surrounding an encounter between a person and law enforcement authorities, including the place; the time; the presence of family, friends, or other persons; physical restraint; and coercion or domination by the police.

Interrogation refers not only to express questioning but also to any words or actions on the part of police that the police should know are reasonably likely to elicit an incriminating response. Nevertheless, clarifying questions, spontaneous questions, and routine questions are not considered to be interrogation for *Miranda* purposes. In addition, volunteered statements are not the product of interrogation and are not subject to the *Miranda* requirements. Multiple attempts at interrogation are permitted after a defendant's invocation of the right to silence, but the defendant's right to cut off questioning must be scrupulously honored, fresh warnings must be given, and no

coercion or other pressures may be employed. If the defendant has exercised the right to counsel, further interrogation without counsel may be conducted only upon the initiation of the defendant and the waiver of *Miranda* rights. After a defendant has been formally charged and has retained counsel, law enforcement authorities are prohibited from using any methods, however surreptitious or indirect, to elicit incriminating evidence from the defendant in the absence of counsel.

Before persons in custody may be subjected to interrogation, they must be given the familiar *Miranda* warnings:

- You have the right to remain silent.
- Anything you say can and will be used against you in a court of law.
- You have the right to consult with a lawyer and to have the lawyer present with you while you are being questioned.
- If you cannot afford to hire a lawyer, a lawyer will be appointed to represent you before any questioning, if you wish.

These warnings must be recited clearly and unhurriedly and must be carefully explained to immature, illiterate, or mentally impaired persons.

If a person waives the *Miranda* rights to remain silent and to have an attorney, that person may be questioned. To be effective, a waiver of *Miranda* rights must be voluntary and made with a full awareness of both the nature of the right being abandoned and the consequences of the decision to abandon that right. Waiver will not be inferred from mere silence but may be expressed by a great variety of words and gestures. If possible, an officer should obtain a written waiver of rights, because this provides the best evidence of a voluntary and intentional relinquishment of a known right.

Even though the voluntariness and *Miranda* requirements have been met, a statement may still be inadmissible if the officer violates a person's reasonable expectation of privacy in obtaining the statement. *Miranda* requirements apply regardless of the nature or severity of the offense being investigated. *Miranda* is inapplicable, however, to civil proceedings such as customs procedures, civil commitments, extradition proceedings, and license revocation proceedings.

Key Holdings from Major Cases

Brown v. Mississippi (1936). "[T]he trial . . . is a mere pretense where the state authorities have contrived a conviction resting solely upon confessions obtained by violence. The due process clause requires 'that state action, whether through one agency

or another, shall be consistent with the fundamental principles of liberty and justice which lie at the base of all our civil and political institutions.' . . . It would be difficult to conceive of methods more revolting to the sense of justice than those taken to procure the confessions of these petitioners [beatings and whippings], and the use of the confessions thus obtained as the basis for conviction and sentence was a clear denial of due process." 297 U.S. 278, 286, 56 S.Ct. 461, 465, 80 L.Ed. 682, 687.

Townsend v. Sain (1963). "If an individual's 'will was overborne' or if his confession was not 'the product of a rational intellect and a free will,' his confession is inadmissible because coerced. These standards are applicable whether a confession is the product of physical intimidation or psychological pressure. . . . Any questioning by police officers which in fact produces a confession which is not the product of a free intellect renders that confession inadmissible." 372 U.S. 293, 307–08, 83 S.Ct. 745, 754, 9 L.Ed.2d 770, 782–83.

Colorado v. Connelly (1986). "[W]hile mental condition is surely relevant to an individual's susceptibility to police coercion, mere examination of the confessant's state of mind can never conclude the due process inquiry. . . . [C]oercive police activity is a necessary predicate to the finding that a confession is not 'voluntary' within the meaning of the Due Process Clause of the Fourteenth Amendment." 479 U.S. 157, 165–67, 107 S.Ct. 515, 521–22, 93 L.Ed.2d 473, 483–84.

The prosecution must prove waiver of *Miranda* rights by a preponderance of the evidence. 479 U.S. 157, 107 S.Ct. 515, 93 L.Ed.2d 473.

"The sole concern of the Fifth Amendment, on which *Miranda* was based, is governmental coercion. . . . The voluntariness of a waiver of this privilege has always depended on the absence of police overreaching, not on 'free choice' in any broader sense of the word." 479 U.S. at 170, 107 S.Ct. at 523, 93 L.Ed.2d at 86.

Escobedo v. Illinois (1964). "[W]here . . . the investigation is no longer a general inquiry into an unsolved crime but has begun to focus on a particular suspect, the suspect has been taken into police custody, the police carry out a process of interrogations that lends itself to eliciting incriminating statements, the suspect has requested and been denied an opportunity to consult with his lawyer, and the police have not effectively warned him of his absolute constitutional right to remain silent, the accused has been denied 'the Assistance of Counsel' in violation of the Sixth Amendment to the Constitution as 'made obligatory upon the States by the Fourteenth Amendment,' . . . and . . . no statement elicited by the police during the interrogation may be used against him at a criminal trial." 378 U.S. 478, 491, 84 S.Ct. 1758, 1765, 12 L.Ed.2d 977, 986.

Miranda v. Arizona (1966) "[T]he prosecution may not use statements, whether exculpatory or inculpatory, stemming from custodial interrogation of the defendant unless it demonstrates the use of procedural safeguards effective to secure the privilege against self-incrimination. By custodial interrogation, we mean questioning initiated by law enforcement officers after a person has been taken into custody or otherwise deprived of his freedom of action in any significant way. As for the procedural safeguards to be employed, unless other fully effective means are

devised to inform accused persons of their right of silence and to assure a continuous opportunity to exercise it, the following measures are required. Prior to any questioning, the person must be warned that he has a right to remain silent, that any statement he does make may be used as evidence against him, and that he has a right to the presence of an attorney, either retained or appointed. The defendant may waive effectuation of these rights provided the waiver is made voluntarily, knowingly, and intelligently. If, however, he indicates in any manner and at any stage of the process that he wishes to consult with an attorney before speaking there can be no questioning. Likewise, if the individual is alone and indicates in any manner that he does not wish to be interrogated, the police may not question him. The mere fact that he may have answered some questions or volunteered some statements on his own does not deprive him of the right to refrain from answering any further inquiries until he has consulted with an attorney and thereafter consents to be questioned." 384 U.S. 436, 444–45, 86 S.Ct. 1602, 1612, 16 L.Ed.2d 694, 706–07.

"The presence of counsel . . . would be the adequate protective device necessary to make the process of police interrogation conform to the dictates of the privilege. His presence would insure that statements made in the government-established atmosphere are not the product of compulsion." 384 U.S. at 466, 86 S.Ct. at 1623, 16 L.Ed.2d at 719.

"The Fifth Amendment privilege is so fundamental to our system of constitutional rule and the expedient of giving an adequate warning as to the availability of the privilege so simple, we will not pause to inquire in individual cases whether the defendant was aware of his rights without a warning being given. Assessments of the knowledge the defendant possessed, based on information as to his age, education, intelligence, or prior contact with authorities, can never be more than speculation; a warning is a clearcut fact. More important, whatever the background of the person interrogated, a warning at the time of the interrogation is indispensable to overcome its pressures and to insure that the individual knows he is free to exercise the privilege at that point in time." 384 U.S. at 468–69, 86 S.Ct. at 1625, 16 L.Ed.2d at 720.

"[T]he expedient of giving a warning is too simple and the rights involved too important to engage in *ex post facto* inquiries into financial ability when there is any doubt at all on that score." 384 U.S. at 473 n.43, 86 S.Ct. at 1627 n.43, 16 L.Ed.2d at 723 n.43.

"Once warnings have been given, the subsequent procedure is clear. If the individual indicates in any manner, at any time prior to or during questioning, that he wishes to remain silent, the interrogation must cease. At this point he has shown that he intends to exercise his Fifth Amendment privilege; any statement taken after the person invokes his privilege cannot be other than the product of compulsion, subtle or otherwise. Without the right to cut off questioning, the setting of in-custody interrogation operates on the individual to overcome free choice in producing a statement after the privilege has been once invoked. If the individual states that he wants an attorney, the interrogation must cease until an attorney is present. At that time the individual must have an opportunity to confer with the attorney and to have him present during any subsequent questioning. If the individual cannot obtain an attorney and he indicates that he wants one before speaking to police, they must respect his decision to remain silent." 384 U.S. at 473–74, 86 S.Ct. at 1627–28, 16 L.Ed.2d at 723.

"There is no requirement that police stop a person who enters a police station and states that he wishes to confess to a crime, or a person who calls the police to offer a confession or any other statement he desires to make. Volunteered statements of any kind are not barred by the Fifth Amendment and their admissibility is not affected by our holding today." 384 U.S. at 478, 86 S.Ct. at 1630, 16 L.Ed.2d at 726.

"[W]hen an individual is taken into custody or otherwise deprived of his freedom by the authorities in any significant way and is subjected to questioning, the privilege against self-incrimination is jeopardized. Procedural safeguards must be employed to protect the privilege and unless other fully effective means are adopted to notify the person of his right of silence and to assure that the exercise of the right will be scrupulously honored, the following measures are required. He must be warned prior to any question that he has the right to remain silent, that anything he says can be used against him in a court of law, that he has the right to the presence of an attorney, and that if he cannot afford an attorney one will be appointed for him prior to any questioning if he so desires. Opportunity to exercise these rights must be afforded to him throughout the interrogation. After such warnings have been given, and such opportunity afforded him, the individual may knowingly and intelligently waive these rights and agree to answer questions or make a statement. But unless and until such warnings and waiver are demonstrated by the prosecution at trial no evidence obtained as a result of interrogation can be used against him." 384 U.S. at 478–79, 86 S.Ct. at 1630, 16 L.Ed.2d at 726.

Dickerson v. United States (2000). "[M]iranda, being a constitutional decision of this Court, may not be in effect overruled by an Act of Congress, and we decline to overrule *Miranda* ourselves. . . . *Miranda* and its progeny in this Court govern the admissibility of statements made during custodial interrogation in both state and federal courts." 530 U.S. 428, 432, 120 S.Ct. 2326, 2329–30, 147 L.Ed.2d 405, 412 (2000).

California v. Beheler (1983). "Although the circumstances of each case must certainly influence a determination of whether a suspect is 'in custody' for purposes of receiving *Miranda* protection, the ultimate inquiry is simply whether there is a 'formal arrest or restraint on freedom of movement' of the degree associated with a formal arrest." 463 U.S. 1121, 1125, 103 S.Ct. 3517, 3520, 77 L.Ed.2d 1275, 1279.

Stansbury v. California (1994). "[A]ny inquiry into whether the interrogating officers have focused their suspicions upon the individual being questioned (assuming those suspicions remain undisclosed) is not relevant for purposes of *Miranda*." 511 U.S. 318, 326, 114 S.Ct. 1526, 1530, 128 L.Ed.2d 293, 301.

Oregon v. Mathiason (1977). "Any interview of one suspected of a crime by a police officer will have coercive aspects to it, simply by virtue of the fact that the police officer is part of a law enforcement system which may ultimately cause the suspect to be charged with a crime. But police officers are not required to administer *Miranda* warnings to everyone whom they question. Nor is the requirement of warnings imposed simply because the questioning takes place in the station house, or because the questioned person is one whom the police suspect. *Miranda* warnings are required only where there has been such a restriction on a person's freedom as to render him 'in custody.' It was that sort of coercive environment to which *Miranda* by its terms was made applicable, and to which it is limited." 429 U.S. 492, 495, 97 S.Ct. 711, 714, 50 L.Ed.2d 714, 719.

Berkemer v. McCarty (1984). "Under the Fourth Amendment . . . a policeman who lacks probable cause but whose 'observations lead him reasonably to suspect' that a particular person has committed, is committing, or is about to commit a crime, may detain that person briefly in order to 'investigate the circumstances that provoke suspicion.' . . . '[T]he stop and inquiry must be "reasonably related in scope to the justification for their initiation."' . . . Typically, this means that the officer may ask the detainee a moderate number of questions to determine his identity and to try to obtain information confirming or dispelling the officer's suspicions. But the detainee is not obliged to respond. And, unless the detainee's answers provide the officer with probable cause to arrest him, he must then be released. The comparatively nonthreatening character of detentions of this sort explains the absence of any suggestion in our opinions that *Terry* stops are subject to the dictates of *Miranda*. The similarly noncoercive aspect of ordinary traffic stops prompts us to hold that persons temporarily detained pursuant to such stops are not 'in custody' for the purposes of *Miranda*." 468 U.S. 420, 439–40, 104 S.Ct. 3138, 3150, 82 L.Ed.2d 317, 334–35.

Rhode Island v. Innis (1980). "[T]he *Miranda* safeguards come into play whenever a person in custody is subjected to either express questioning or its functional equivalent. That is to say, the term 'interrogation' under *Miranda* refers not only to express questioning, but also to any words or actions on the part of police (other than those normally attendant to arrest and custody) that the police should know are reasonably likely to elicit an incriminating response from the suspect." 446 U.S. 291, 300–01, 100 S.Ct. 1682, 1689, 64 L.Ed.2d 297, 307–08.

South Dakota v. Neville (1983). "In the context of an arrest for driving while intoxicated, a police inquiry of whether the suspect will take a blood-alcohol test is not an interrogation within the meaning of *Miranda*." 459 U.S. 553, 565 n.15, 103 S.Ct. 916, 923 n.15, 74 L.Ed.2d 748, 759 n.15.

New York v. Quarles (1984). "[T]here is a 'public safety' exception to the requirement that *Miranda* warnings be given before a suspect's answers may be admitted into evidence, and . . . the availability of that exception does not depend upon the motivation of the individual officers involved." 467 U.S. 649, 655–56, 104 S.Ct. 2626, 2631, 81 L.Ed.2d 550, 557.

"[T]he need for answers to questions in a situation posing a threat to the public safety outweighs the need for the prophylactic rule protecting the Fifth Amendment's privilege against self-incrimination. We decline to place officers . . . in the untenable position of having to consider, often in a matter of seconds, whether it best serves society for them to ask the necessary questions without the *Miranda* warnings and render whatever probative evidence they uncover inadmissible, or for them to give the warnings in order to preserve the admissibility of evidence they might uncover but possibly damage or destroy their ability to obtain that evidence and neutralize the volatile situation confronting them." 467 U.S. at 657–58, 104 S.Ct. at 2632, 81 L.Ed.2d at 558.

Michigan v. Mosley (1975). Even though the *Miranda* opinion states that the interrogation must cease when the person in custody indicates a desire to remain silent, "neither this passage nor any other passage in the *Miranda* opinion can sensibly be read to create a per se proscription of indefinite duration upon any further questioning by any police officer on any subject, once the person in custody has indicated a desire to remain silent." 423 U.S. 96, 102–03, 96 S.Ct. 321, 326, 46 L.Ed.2d 313, 320–21.

Edwards v. Arizona (1981). "[W]hen an accused has invoked his right to have counsel present during custodial interrogation, a valid waiver of that right cannot be established by showing only that he responded to further police-initiated custodial interrogation even if he has been advised of his rights. We further hold that an accused . . . having expressed his desire to deal with the police only through counsel, is not subject to further interrogation by the authorities until counsel has been made available to him, unless the accused himself initiates further communication, exchanges, or conversations with the police." 451 U.S. 477, 484–85, 101 S.Ct. 1880, 1884–85, 68 L.Ed.2d 378, 386.

Minnick v. Mississippi (1990). "[W]hen counsel is requested, interrogation must cease, and officials may not reinitiate interrogation without counsel present, whether or not the accused has consulted with his attorney." 498 U.S. 146, 153, 111 S.Ct. 486, 491, 112 L.Ed.2d 489, 498.

Michigan v. Jackson (1986). "[I]f police initiate interrogation after a defendant's assertion, at an arraignment or similar proceeding, of his right to counsel, any waiver of the defendant's right to counsel for that police-initiated interrogation is invalid." 475 U.S. 625, 636, 106 S.Ct. 1404, 1411, 89 L.Ed.2d 631, 642.

McNeil v. Wisconsin (1991). "The purpose of the Sixth Amendment counsel guarantee—and hence the purpose of invoking it—is to 'protec[t] the unaided layman at critical confrontations' with his 'expert adversary,' the government, *after* 'the adverse positions of government and defendant have solidified' with respect to a particular alleged crime. . . . The purpose of the *Miranda-Edwards* guarantee, on the other hand—and hence the purpose of invoking it—is to protect a quite different interest: the suspect's 'desire to deal with the police only through counsel,' . . . This is in one respect narrower than the interest protected by the Sixth Amendment guarantee (because it relates only to custodial interrogation) and in another respect broader (because it relates to interrogation regarding any suspected crime and attaches whether or not the 'adversarial relationship' produced by a pending prosecution has yet arisen). To invoke the Sixth Amendment interest is, as a matter of *fact, not* to invoke the *Miranda-Edwards* interest." 501 U.S. 171, 177–78, 111 S.Ct. 2204, 2208–09, 115 L.Ed.2d 158, 168.

Arizona v. Mauro (1987). "Officers do not interrogate a suspect simply by hoping that he will incriminate himself." 481 U.S. 520, 529, 107 S.Ct. 1931, 1936, 95 L.Ed.2d 458, 468.

"Police departments need not adopt inflexible rules barring suspects from speaking with their spouses, nor must they ignore legitimate security concerns by allowing spouses to meet in private." 481 U.S. at 530, 107 S.Ct. at 1937, 95 L.Ed.2d at 468.

Arizona v. Roberson (1988). "[T]he presumption raised by a suspect's request for counsel—that he considers himself unable to deal with the pressures of custodial interrogation without legal assistance—does not disappear simply because the police have approached the suspect, still in custody, still without counsel, about a separate investigation." 486 U.S. 675, 683, 108 S.Ct. 2093, 2099, 100 L.Ed.2d 704, 715.

Patterson v. Illinois (1988). "Preserving the integrity of an accused's choice to communicate with police only through counsel is the essence of *Edwards* and its progeny—not barring an accused from making an *initial* selection as to whether he will face the State's officers during questioning with the aid of counsel, or go it alone. If an accused 'knowingly and intelligently' pursues the latter course, we see no reason why the uncounseled statements he then makes must be excluded at his trial." 487 U.S. 285, 291, 108 S.Ct. 2389, 2394, 101 L.Ed.2d 261, 271–72.

"[W]hatever warnings suffice for *Miranda's* purposes will also be sufficient in the context of postindictment questioning. The State's decision to take an additional step and commence formal adversarial proceedings against the accused does not substantially increase the value of counsel to the accused at questioning, or expand the limited purpose that an attorney serves when the accused is questioned by authorities. With respect to this inquiry, we do not discern a substantial difference between the usefulness of a lawyer to a suspect during custodial interrogation, and his value to an accused at postindictment questioning." 487 U.S. at 298–99, 108 S.Ct. at 2398, 101 L.Ed.2d at 276.

Smith v. Illinois (1984). "No authority, and no logic, permits the interrogator to proceed . . . on his own terms and as if the defendant had requested nothing, in the hope that the defendant might be induced to say something casting retrospective doubt on his initial statement that he wished to speak through an attorney or not at all." 469 U.S. 91, 99, 105 S.Ct. 490, 494, 83 L.Ed.2d 488, 496.

Davis v. United States (1994). "Although a suspect need not 'speak with the discrimination of an Oxford don,' . . . he must articulate his desire to have counsel present sufficiently clearly that a reasonable police officer in the circumstances would understand the statement to be a request for an attorney. If the statement fails to meet the requisite level of clarity, *Edwards* does not require that the officers stop questioning the suspect." 512 U.S. 452, 459, 114 S.Ct. 2350, 2355, 129 L.Ed.2d 362, 371.

Oregon v. Bradshaw (1983). "[T]here are undoubtedly situations where a bare inquiry by either a defendant or by a police officer should not be held to 'initiate' any conversation or dialogue. There are some inquiries, such as a request for a drink of water or a request to use a telephone that are so routine that they cannot be fairly said to represent a desire on the part of an accused to open up a more generalized discussion relating directly or indirectly to the investigation. Such inquiries or statements, by either an accused or a police officer, relating to routine incidents of the custodial relationship, will not generally 'initiate' a conversation in the sense in which that word was used in *Edwards*." 462 U.S. 1039, 1045, 103 S.Ct. 2830, 2835, 77 L.Ed.2d 405, 412.

Oregon v. Elstad (1985). "[A]bsent deliberately coercive or improper tactics in obtaining the initial statement, the mere fact that a suspect has made an unwarned admission does not warrant a presumption of compulsion. A subsequent administration of *Miranda* warnings to a suspect who has given a voluntary but unwarned statement ordinarily should suffice to remove the conditions that precluded admission of the earlier statement. In such circumstances, the finder of fact may reasonably conclude that the suspect made a rational and intelligent choice whether to waive or invoke his rights." 470 U.S. 298, 314, 105 S.Ct. 1285, 1296, 84 L.Ed.2d 222, 235.

Massiah v. United States (1964). "[T]he petitioner was denied the basic protections of [the Sixth Amendment guarantee to assistance of counsel] when there was used against him at his trial evidence of his own incriminating words, which federal agents had deliberately elicited from him after he had been indicted and in the absence of his counsel. . . . '[I]f such a rule is to have any efficacy it must apply to indirect and surreptitious interrogations as well as those conducted in the jailhouse. . . . Massiah was more seriously imposed upon . . . because he did not even know that he was under interrogation by a govern-ment agent.'" 377 U.S. 201, 206, 84 S.Ct. 1199, 1203, 12 L.Ed.2d 246, 250.

Brewer v. Williams (1977). "Whatever else it may mean, the right to counsel granted by the Sixth and Fourteenth Amendments means at least that a person is entitled to the help of a lawyer at or after the time that judicial proceedings have been initiated against him—'whether by way of formal charge, preliminary hearing, indictment, information, or arraignment.'" 430 U.S. 387, 398, 97 S.Ct. 1232, 1239, 51 L.Ed.2d 424, 436.

"[T]he clear rule of *Massiah* is that once adversary proceedings have commenced against an individual, he has a right to legal representation when the government interrogates him." 430 U.S. at 401, 97 S.Ct. at 1240, 51 L.Ed.2d at 438.

Maine v. Moulton (1985). "[T]he Sixth Amendment is not violated whenever—by luck or happenstance—the State obtains incriminating statements from the accused after the right to counsel has attached. . . . However, knowing exploitation by the State of an opportunity to confront the accused without counsel being present is as much a breach of the State's obligation not to circumvent the right to assistance of counsel as is the intentional creation of such an opportunity. Accordingly, the Sixth Amendment is violated when the State obtains incriminating statements by knowingly circumventing the accused's right to have counsel present in a confrontation between the accused and a state agent." 474 U.S. 159, 176, 106 S.Ct. 477, 487, 88 L.Ed.2d 481, 496.

Kuhlmann v. Wilson (1986). The defendant's Sixth Amendment rights are not violated when an informant, either through prior arrangement or voluntarily, reports the defendant's incriminating statements to the police. "[T]he defendant must demonstrate that the police and their informant took some action, beyond merely listening, that was designed deliberately to elicit incriminating remarks." 477 U.S. 436, 459, 106 S.Ct. 2616, 2630, 91 L.Ed.2d 364, 384–85.

Duckworth v. Eagan (1989). "Reviewing courts . . . need not examine *Miranda* warnings as if construing a will or defining the terms of an easement. The inquiry is simply whether the warnings reasonably 'conve[y] to [a suspect] his rights as required by *Miranda*.'" 492 U.S. 195, 203, 109 S.Ct. 2875, 2880, 106 L.Ed.2d 166, 177.

Moran v. Burbine (1986). The inquiry whether the defendant has made a full and effective waiver of *Miranda* rights has two distinct dimensions. "First, the relinquishment of the right must have been voluntary in the sense that it was the product of a free and deliberate choice rather than intimidation, coercion or deception. Second, the waiver must have been made with a full awareness both of the nature of the right being abandoned and the consequences of the decision to abandon it. Only if 'the totality of the circumstances surrounding the interrogation' reveal both an uncoerced choice and the requisite level of comprehension may a court properly conclude that the *Miranda* rights have been waived." 475 U.S. 412, 421, 106 S.Ct. 1135, 1141, 89 L.Ed.2d 410, 421.

"Events occurring outside the presence of the suspect and entirely unknown to him surely can have no bearing on the capacity to comprehend and knowingly relinquish a constitutional right. . . . Once it is determined that a suspect's decision not to rely on his rights was uncoerced, that he at all times knew he could stand mute and request a lawyer, and that he was aware of the State's intention to use his statements to secure a conviction, the analysis is complete and the waiver is valid as a matter of law." 475 U.S. at 422–23, 106 S.Ct. at 1141, 89 L.Ed.2d at 421–22.

Connecticut v. Barrett (1987). "It is undisputed that Barrett desired the presence of counsel before making a written statement. Had the police obtained such a statement without meeting the waiver standards of *Edwards,* it would clearly be inadmissible. Barrett's limited requests for counsel, however, were accompanied by affirmative announcements of his willingness to speak with the authorities. The fact that officials took the opportunity provided by Barrett to obtain an oral confession is quite consistent with the Fifth Amendment. *Miranda* gives the defendant a right to choose between speech and silence, and Barrett chose to speak." 479 U.S. 523, 529, 107 S.Ct. 828, 832, 93 L.Ed.2d 920, 928.

Colorado v. Spring (1987). "The Constitution does not require that a criminal suspect know and understand every possible consequence of a waiver of the Fifth Amendment privilege. . . . The Fifth Amendment's guarantee is both simpler and more fundamental: A defendant may not be compelled to be a witness against himself in any respect. The *Miranda* warnings protect this privilege by insuring that a suspect knows that he may choose not to talk to law enforcement officers, to talk only with counsel present, or to discontinue talking at any time. The *Miranda* warnings ensure that a waiver of these rights is knowing and intelligent by requiring that the suspect be fully advised of this constitutional privilege, including the critical advice that whatever he chooses to say may be used as evidence against him." 479 U.S. 564, 574, 107 S.Ct. 851, 857–58, 93 L.Ed.2d 954, 966.

"This Court's holding in *Miranda* specifically required that the police inform a criminal suspect that he has the right to remain silent and that anything he says may be used against him. There is no qualification of this broad and explicit warning. The warning, as formulated in *Miranda,* conveys to a suspect the nature of his constitutional privilege and the consequences of abandoning it. Accordingly, we hold that a suspect's awareness of all the possible subjects of questioning in advance of interrogation is not relevant to determining whether the suspect voluntarily, knowingly, and intelligently waived his Fifth Amendment privilege." 479 U.S. at 577, 107 S.Ct. at 859, 93 L.Ed.2d at 968.

Fare v. Michael C. (1979). "This totality of circumstances approach is adequate to determine whether there has been a waiver even where interrogation of juveniles is involved. . . . The totality approach permits—indeed, it mandates—inquiry

into all the circumstances surrounding the interrogation. This includes evaluation of the juvenile's age, experience, education, background, and intelligence, and into whether he had the capacity to understand the warnings given him, the nature of his Fifth Amendment rights, and the consequences of waiving those rights." 442 U.S. 707, 725, 99 S.Ct. 2560, 2572, 61 L.Ed.2d 197, 212.

Schmerber v. California (1966). The privilege against self-incrimination "protects an accused only from being compelled to testify against himself, or otherwise provide the State with evidence of a testimonial or communicative nature." . . . 384 U.S. 757, 761, 86 S.Ct. 1826, 1830, 16 L.Ed.2d 908, 914.

Doe v. United States (1988). "[I]n order to be testimonial, an accused's communication must itself, explicitly or implicitly, relate a factual assertion or disclose information. Only then is a person compelled to be a 'witness' against himself." 487 U.S. 201, 210, 108 S.Ct. 2341, 2347, 101 L.Ed.2d 184, 197.

Pennsylvania v. Muniz (1990). "Requiring a suspect to reveal the physical manner in which he articulates words, like requiring him to reveal the physical properties of the sound produced by his voice . . . does not, without more, compel him to provide a 'testimonial' response for purposes of the privilege." 496 U.S. 582, 592, 110 S.Ct. 2638, 2645, 110 L.Ed.2d 528, 546.

Illinois v. Perkins (1990). "[A]n undercover law enforcement officer posing as a fellow inmate need not give *Miranda* warnings to an incarcerated suspect before asking questions that may elicit an incriminating response." 496 U.S. 292, 300, 110 S.Ct. 2394, 2399, 110 L.Ed.2d 243, 253.

Harris v. New York (1971). "The shield provided by *Miranda* cannot be perverted into a license to use perjury by way of a defense, free from the risk of confrontation with prior inconsistent utterances. We hold, therefore, that petitioner's credibility was appropriately impeached by use of his earlier conflicting statements." 401 U.S. 222, 226, 91 S.Ct. 643, 646, 28 L.Ed.2d 1, 5.

Doyle v. Ohio (1976). "[W]hen a person under arrest is informed as *Miranda* requires, that he may remain silent, that anything he says may be used against him, and that he may have an attorney if he wishes, it seems to me that it does not comport with due process to permit the prosecution during the trial to call attention to his silence at the time of arrest and to insist that because he did not speak about the facts of the case at that time, as he was told he need not do, an unfavorable inference might be drawn as to the truth of his trial testimony. . . ." 426 U.S. 610, 619, 96 S.Ct. 2240, 2245, 49 L.Ed.2d 91, 98.

Brecht v. Abrahamson (1993). "[T]he Constitution does not prohibit the use for impeachment purposes of a defendant's silence prior to arrest . . . or after arrest if no *Miranda* warnings are given. . . . Such silence is probative and does not rest on any implied assurance by law enforcement authorities that it will carry no penalty." 507 U.S. 619, 628, 113 S.Ct. 1710, 1716, 123 L.Ed.2d 353, 366.

Review and Discussion Questions

1. Would any of the following actions cause a statement of a suspect to be involuntary?
   a. Making an appeal to the suspect's moral or religious beliefs
   b. Confronting the suspect with the deceased or seriously injured victim of the crime in question
   c. Starting an argument with, challenging, or baiting the suspect

2. Does a person need a lawyer to help decide whether to waive *Miranda* rights? Is the compelling atmosphere of a custodial setting just as likely to influence a person's decision to waive rights as it is to influence the decision to confess?

3. Is a person's giving of consent to search an inculpatory or exculpatory statement? Should a person in custody be given *Miranda* warnings before being asked for consent to search?

4. Assume that a person has been formally arrested for one crime, and police want to question that person about another, unrelated crime. Are *Miranda* warnings required to be given before the questioning? If the answer is no, what additional circumstances might cause *Miranda* warnings to be required?

5. It is reasonable to assume that a person under investigation for a crime might think that complete silence in the face of an accusation might not look good to a judge or a jury. Should the *Miranda* warnings include a statement that a person's silence may not be used against the person in any way?

6. Should suspects be told the nature and seriousness of the offense for which they are being interrogated? What if a person believes that he or she is being investigated for an accident caused by driving while intoxicated but does not know that a person in the other vehicle has died?

7. What would be the advantages and disadvantages of requiring law enforcement officers to tape-record the entire process of administration of *Miranda* warnings and the suspect's invocation or waiver of rights?

8. Is it proper for a law enforcement officer to inform a suspect who has just invoked the *Miranda* right to counsel that the case against the suspect is strong and that immediate cooperation with the authorities would be beneficial in the long run? If the suspect says, "What do you mean?" would this be considered an initiation of further communication by the suspect and a waiver of the right to counsel?

9. Considering the confusion and pressures associated with being arrested and transported to a police station, should arrested persons be advised, in addition to the *Miranda* warnings, of where they are being taken, what is going to happen to them, how long they will be held, and with whom they may communicate?

10. Would the *Massiah* rule be violated if conversations of an indicted and imprisoned person were obtained by means of a listening device installed in that person's cell?

Real-Life Fact Situations

1 Police officers in Phoenix, Arizona, stopped Defendant after receiving a complaint from a restaurant that he had paid for his food with a counterfeit $20 bill. Before questioning Defendant, Officer Kulesa read the *Miranda* rights to him in English. Defendant, speaking in English with a Japanese accent, said that he understood his rights. Then Kulesa questioned Defendant about his driver's license and the license plate on his car. During that conversation, Defendant told Kulesa that he is from Japan. The officers arrested Defendant when they learned that his driver's license was suspended and that the license plate on his car was stolen. During an inventory of Defendant's car, the lawfulness of which is not at issue here, the officers found $360 in counterfeit bills.

Officers took Defendant to a police precinct, where Special Agent Thurling of the Secret Service questioned him about the manufacture and use of counterfeit currency. Before that questioning began, Thurling advised Defendant again, in English, of the *Miranda* rights. Defendant then signed a standard-form waiver of *Miranda* rights. That form, which is printed in English, said that Defendant understood his rights and was willing to speak to the agent without having a lawyer present. Thereafter, Defendant made oral statements (in English) that he had made and used counterfeit currency and signed a written statement (also in English) to the same effect. Additionally, Defendant signed a form, which was printed in English, authorizing a search of his apartment.

Neither Kulesa nor Thurling informed Defendant of a right to contact the Japanese consulate. Neither of them asked Defendant whether he needed an interpreter. Both officers testified, however, that Defendant appeared to have no difficulty understanding and conversing in English. Moreover, Defendant did not request an interpreter at any time during Kulesa's or Thurling's questioning.

After obtaining written consent, the Secret Service searched Defendant's apartment. There they found computer equipment with which Defendant had made counterfeit bills, $13,000 in counterfeit bills, and schedules for making and passing counterfeit bills. Those schedules were written in English. The officers also discovered computer manuals and books written in English, as well as check registers in which notations had been made in English.

Defendant was indicted on two counts: manufacturing counterfeit obligations and uttering counterfeit obligations, in violation of 18 U.S.C. §§ 472 and 474. Defendant filed a motion to suppress his written statement and the evidence found during the search of his apartment. Should his motion be granted? *United States v. Amano*, 229 F.3d 801 (9th Cir. 2000).

Read the court opinion at:
laws.lp.findlaw.com/9th/9910607.html

2 On August 13, 1997, shortly after 5:00 A.M., an anonymous caller telephoned the Anchorage Police Department and reported that there was a dead body in Room 222 of the Mush Inn, an Anchorage motel. Anchorage Police Officers Kevin Iverson and Steven Hebbe responded to the call. When the officers arrived at the Mush Inn, the door to Room 222 was open. The officers told a security guard on the scene and Murray, the occupant of Room 222, that they were responding to the dead-body report. The officers asked to enter the room to look for the dead body. Murray consented. While the officers were checking the room, they told Murray to sit down on the bed with his hands in view. Someone at the Mush Inn front desk called the room to ask Murray about payment for the room charges. Murray asked to leave to take care of his bill, but the officers told Murray he had to wait until they were finished searching. The officers found no body.

The officers questioned Murray while they were in the room, but they did not advise him of the *Miranda* warnings or tell him he was free to leave. The officers questioned Murray for 20–30 minutes. Murray told the officers that: (1) he was on felony probation for a prior drug offense (Officer Iverson ran a check that confirmed this); (2) he had only recently returned to the room; (3) his housemate and girlfriend, Jeannie Joy, and two other people had been in the room earlier; (4) Joy was a drug user, but he did not know whether she had drugs; (5) he had given Joy money to buy cocaine; (6) he had consumed some cocaine, and a urinalysis for cocaine would probably be positive; and (7) Joy still had the cocaine and was driving his Chevy Blazer around town.

The officers asked to search the room for drugs and Murray agreed to a search of the room for that purpose. The officers

found a single-serving plastic alcohol bottle with a hole cut in it that could be used to smoke crack cocaine.

The officers departed to look for Joy. They left Murray behind. The officers hoped to recover the Blazer for Murray and to search it for drugs.

Officer Hebbe spotted Murray's Blazer and stopped it at Third Avenue and Ingra Street. Joy and another person were inside the Blazer. Officer Iverson returned to the Mush Inn and told Murray that the police found his Blazer and asked Murray for his consent to search the Blazer. Murray gave that consent. Officer Iverson relayed the consent to Officer Hebbe.

Meanwhile, Joy was talking with the police and reported (1) that there was marijuana in the Blazer; (2) that Murray had given her the marijuana to sell; (3) that Murray grew marijuana; and (4) that Murray owned a firearm and had a prior drug conviction. The officers searched the Blazer and found marijuana and a crack pipe. About this time, Murray drove to Third and Ingra in his truck and parked behind the line of vehicles.

The officers questioned Murray about Joy's claims. Murray admitted that he had given marijuana to Joy to sell and that he had about a quarter of a pound of marijuana and a handgun at his home.

Murray drove to his home and the officers followed. The officers asked Murray to consent to a search of his home. At first, Murray agreed, but when the officers presented him with a consent-to-search form he asked for an attorney.

Because Murray withdrew his consent, the officers obtained a search warrant for Murray's residence. During the execution of the warrant, the police found the following items: (1) a bag containing 170.9 grams (approximately 6 ounces) of "bud" marijuana in a living room closet; (2) a screening tin (used to separate "bud" from "shake") and a gram scale in the kitchen; (3) marijuana residue in a bedroom drawer and in the screening tin; (4) a loaded .44 magnum handgun inside a "fur-lined case" in the bedside table drawer; and (5) a gun cleaning kit and boxes of ammunition in a bucket in the bedroom. In the handgun case, the officers later found a marijuana "bud."

The grand jury indicted Murray for the following offenses: one count of fourth-degree misconduct involving a controlled substance for possession of one ounce of marijuana with intent to deliver; another count of fourth-degree misconduct involving a controlled substance for maintaining a dwelling for keeping or distributing controlled substances; one count of second-degree misconduct involving weapons for possession of the .44 magnum handgun during the commission of a felony drug offense; one count of third-degree misconduct involving weapons for being a felon in possession of a firearm capable of being concealed on one's person; and another count of third-degree misconduct involving weapons for being a convicted felon and living in a dwelling knowing that a firearm was present in the dwelling.

Murray moved to suppress the evidence acquired in Room 222, including his statements to the police, claiming that the police violated the Fourth Amendment and did not advise him of his *Miranda* rights. He also claimed that evidence obtained after the police left the room should be suppressed as the fruit of this police illegality. Should Murray's motion to suppress be granted? *Murray v. State*, 12 P.3d 784 (Alaska App. 2000).

Read the court opinion at:
touchngo.com/ap/html/ap-1698.htm

3 According to the uncontradicted testimony of the detectives, the defendant was arrested shortly after witnesses claimed that he assaulted a man with a bat, pointed a gun at the witnesses, and fired several rounds in their direction. He was taken into custody at the Greeley Police Department. Because he was a juvenile at the time, the defendant's father was contacted and asked to come to the police station. [By statute in Colorado, the Fifth Amendment privilege of juveniles is further protected by requiring the presence of a parent or guardian during custodial interrogation.] After arriving, the father was read a Spanish translation of the *Miranda* . . . rights, and the defendant was read his *Miranda* rights in English in his father's presence. Following a private consultation with his father, the defendant told Detective Connell that he wanted to speak with a lawyer because either way, . . . he was going to jail. Detective Connell then told the father that the defendant would in fact be going to jail and escorted the father out.

The defendant was rehandcuffed and left in the interviewing room while Detective Connell worked on the attendant bonding paperwork in his office. About ten minutes later, Connell gave the completed paperwork to Detective Schrimpf for the purpose of taking the defendant to jail. However, Schrimpf returned in a moment and notified Connell that the defendant wanted to tell his side of the story. Connell testified that he did not initially respond because the defendant's father had already left. However, after another five minutes and several more requests by the defendant, including shouting out to him by name, Connell went to the interview room. When Connell reached the doorway, the defendant asked him what charges were being filed.

The detective responded by reciting the charges, at which point the defendant began talking about the incident and continued for about thirty seconds. The defendant acknowledged that he was present at the confrontation and had a pellet gun, but he claimed that he wasn't shooting at anybody and was just trying to scare people. Detective Connell testified that he then tried to find the defendant's father because he wanted to pursue the defendant's statement with follow-up questions. When it was clear that the father was already gone, the defendant was taken to jail without being questioned. Should the

defendant's statements be suppressed? *People v. Rivas*, 13 P.3d 315 (Colo. 2000).

Read the court opinion at:
www.cobar.org/coappcts/sc2000/sc1023d.htm

4 At 4:00 A.M. on April 17, 1999, Officer Bradley Deaver of the Brookings Police Department was dispatched to the local emergency room. Taylor Roberts was being treated there for what appeared to be a severe beating. Roberts had cuts and abrasions on his face. His left eye was swollen shut. He had a deep wound on his forehead. According to the medical personnel, Roberts had a "blow out fracture of the left orbit with [a] buckle fracture of the left lateral sinus wall." Deaver thought Roberts' injuries had been caused by a blunt object.

Deaver attempted an interview, but Roberts could not remember much of what occurred. He told Deaver that he had been walking through Normandy Village, a Brookings trailer court, on his way to a friend's home when a white Chevy S-10 pickup pulled up alongside him. He recognized Keith Whitehead and recalled that Whitehead stepped from the vehicle and confronted him. After that, all he could remember was being on the ground, having been beaten.

Deaver returned to the police department and discussed the case with Officer Even. Even recalled that earlier he had seen Keith Whitehead speaking with an individual in a white "low-rider" pickup with Florida license plates. Another officer had run a license plate check on the white pickup. Deaver obtained the license plate number from the police dispatch log and ran another check on the vehicle: the white pickup truck was registered to Pedro Morato. Officer Even told Deaver that Keith Whitehead was living at 920 Southland Lane. Deaver had a patrol officer drive by the residence to see whether the white pickup with Florida license plates was parked there. It was.

Deaver and another officer drove to the apartment complex and looked through the truck window. They spotted a jack handle lying on the floor of the pickup. The two officers proceeded to Whitehead's apartment. A female answered the door. She told the officers that Keith was home and invited them in. As he walked into the apartment, Deaver saw a man sleeping in an easy chair. He asked the man who owned the pickup. The man, later identified as Morato, responded that it was his vehicle. Keith Whitehead came out of the bedroom, and the officers asked both men to accompany them outside. Morato was escorted to Deaver's patrol car while Whitehead was taken to another patrol car.

Once Deaver and Morato were seated in the car, Deaver started a tape recorder. In the initial moments of the recording the following exchange took place:

Deaver: Hey listen, man, I also want you to understand you don't have to talk to me if you don't want to, alright?

Morato: Yeah, I know, I know.

Deaver: You're free to leave, um you're not under arrest.

Morato: Well, I just can't even talk right now cause you know I'm probably still, you know, messed up and stuff and that's the way it is.

In addition to commenting on his intoxicated state, Morato said that he did not remember anything of an altercation the night before. Morato did not say that he wished to leave the car or that he refused to talk; instead, his comments indicated only an inability to talk at that time because he was "drunk or halfway drunk."

Deaver noticed an odor of alcoholic beverage on Morato and saw that his eyes were slightly bloodshot. Morato had no difficulty walking from the apartment to the car, however. Deaver later described Morato's speech as "slightly slurred," but explained that he did not know whether this was attributable to Morato's alcohol consumption or his unfamiliar accent. Deaver exited the vehicle for a few minutes leaving Morato alone in the car.

When Deaver returned, the following conversation took place:

Deaver: Pedro.

Morato: Yeah.

Deaver: Here's what's going to happen, Pedro. We're going to tow your truck. Okay? Cause we believe that you and Keith and John were involved in an assault last night, and we believe, uh, the weapon that was used to assault the subject is in that _____ vehicle right now. So, we're going to have to tow it, secure it, so we can obtain a search warrant and go through the vehicle. Okay? You understand?

Morato: Yeah.

Deaver: You know why we're doing this, right?

Morato: Yeah, I know.

Deaver: You know what happened last night?

Morato: Yeah, I know what happened.

Deaver: Okay. You wanna tell me about it?

At this point Morato explained that he used "the bar" to hit the victim because the victim took a swing at him: "I had to defend myself." After this admission Morato was told he was no longer free to leave. Deaver read Morato the *Miranda* warnings and Morato invoked his right to counsel. Deaver told Morato that he needed to remove the jack handle from the pickup and requested Morato's permission to obtain it. Morato responded that he had the keys in his pocket and indicated which key would unlock the vehicle. Should Morato's motion to suppress his statements and the jack handle be granted? *State v. Morato,* 619 N.W.2d 655 (S.D. 2000).

Read the court opinion at:
www.state.sd.us/state/judicial/opinions/Cases/2000/2000_149.htm

5 On March 12, 1999, law enforcement officers of the Tri-State Drug Task Force were conducting surveillance on a Louis

Chavez in the Walgreen Drug parking lot in downtown Sioux City, Iowa. Defendant Plummer was observed meeting with Chavez. However, when defendant Plummer recognized Tri-State Drug Task Force Officer Cheshier, with whom Plummer had previous run ins, he left the parking lot in his automobile at a high rate of speed. He was pursued by Officer Cheshier. Officer Cheshier observed defendant Plummer committing numerous traffic violations as he tried to elude the police. After abandoning his automobile at Marian Health Center parking lot, defendant Plummer was located at a relative's house on Seventh Street and arrested without incident. He was then transported to the Sioux City Police Station for questioning.

At the Sioux City Police Department, defendant Plummer was placed in an interview room. The interview room is approximately fifteen feet by ten feet with several chairs and a desk. The room has no two-way mirror but does have the capacity for audio and video monitoring. The room also has videotaping capabilities but no videotaping occurred here pursuant to the United States Drug Enforcement Agency's ("DEA") policy of not recording or videotaping interrogations. Defendant Plummer was advised of his constitutional rights, as required under *Miranda,* using a written rights advisory form. Officers Cheshier, Van Beest and Johnson were present in the interview room. Defendant Plummer was asked to sign a waiver of rights located on the bottom of the rights advisory form. Defendant Plummer refused to sign the waiver. He then told the officers that he did not wish to waive his rights.

The officers, nonplussed by defendant Plummer's declaration, left the interview room and Officer Van Beest telephoned Assistant United States Attorney Peter Deegan and requested instructions on whether they could proceed to interview defendant Plummer. Deegan said he would look into it and requested that Van Beest call him back shortly. When Van Beest called Deegan back he was instructed that the officers could proceed with the interview. The officers then returned to the interview room and began reviewing the events of the day with defendant Plummer. Defendant was told that his cooperation would be reported to the United States Attorney. The interview was conducted in normal conversational tones in a relaxed atmosphere. The officers made no threats or promises nor did they engage in any intimidation, shouting, or threatening gestures. Defendant Plummer subsequently made statements to the officers which implicated himself in drug trafficking. Should Plummer's motion to suppress the statements be granted? *United States v. Plummer,* 118 F.Supp.2d 945 (N.D. Iowa 2000).

Read the court opinion at:
www.iand.uscourts.gov/iand/decisions.nsf/0/512400CFC55CDAE3862569850068C06E/$File/Plummer.pdf

6 Portland Police Officer White, who was patrolling the area by bicycle, stopped defendant after watching him riding his skateboard in a dangerous manner on a crowded street. The officer determined from identifying information that defendant gave him that there was an outstanding warrant for defendant's arrest. As a crowd began to gather, Officer White handcuffed defendant and called for a back-up officer. The crowd included acquaintances of defendant.

After handcuffing defendant, White conducted a pat-down. He found a large pouch-like wallet on defendant's person. Defendant stated that it contained his rent money in the amount of $360 and asked White to give the wallet to a friend in the crowd, so that he wouldn't have to take it to jail with him. White briefly looked through the wallet, found that it did contain a large amount of money and gave it to the friend whom defendant designated. He did not count the money or otherwise disturb the contents. White also allowed the friend to take defendant's skateboard.

Officer Busse arrived as the wallet was being handed to the friend. As soon as he arrived, he took custody of defendant and moved him toward his patrol car. Defendant was wearing a shoulder bag. The bag was about 10 inches square in size and hung by a strap. The strap was attached to the bag on both ends,

and the bag could not be taken from defendant without either removing the handcuffs or destroying the strap. Defendant asked Busse to take off the handcuffs and to allow him to give the bag to a friend in the crowd. The officer decided not to remove the handcuffs, and instead, knowing that the bag would accompany defendant into the car, he opened it to inventory its contents. Inside, he found two knives and six small plastic baggies that contained 27.7 grams of marijuana. Defendant saw Busse remove the items from the shoulder bag and said spontaneously, "That's my medicine. I use it for healing purposes." Defendant was placed in the police car and while being transported, offered the statement that he was a "medicine man." His statement was not in response to any questioning.

Defendant moved to suppress the evidence of the contents of the wallet, the evidence seized from the shoulder bag and his statements made to White and Busse. Should his motion be granted? *State v. Komas*, 13 P.3d 157 (Or.App. 2000).

Read the court opinion at:
www.publications.ojd.state.or.us/A102759.htm

Chapter 14

Pretrial Identification Procedures

Outline

Pretrial confrontation of a suspected criminal with witnesses or victims has long been an accepted law enforcement technique to identify perpetrators of crime and also to clear from suspicion those who are innocent. In 1967, the U.S. Supreme Court decided three major cases governing this area of the law: *United States v. Wade*, 388 U.S. 218, 87 S.Ct. 1926, 18 L.Ed.2d 1149; *Gilbert v. California*, 388 U.S. 263, 87 S.Ct. 1951, 18 L.Ed.2d 1178; and *Stovall v. Denno*, 388 U.S. 293, 87 S.Ct. 1967, 18 L.Ed.2d 1199. These decisions provide the foundation for most of the law applicable to pretrial identification procedures today.

The discussion of the *Wade, Gilbert,* and *Stovall* cases uses the terms *showup, lineup,* and *confrontation* throughout. A **showup** is the presentation of a single suspect to a victim or witness of a crime for the purpose of identifying the perpetrator of the crime. A **lineup** is the presentation at one time of several persons, including a suspect, to a victim or witness of a crime for the purpose of identifying the perpetrator of the crime. A lineup gives the victim or witness several choices. A **confrontation** includes both showups and lineups and is *any* presentation of a suspect to a victim or witness of a crime for the purpose of identifying the perpetrator of the crime. These terms are also sometimes used in connection with photographic or voice identifications. Thus, for example, a photographic showup would be a presentation of a single photograph of a suspect to a victim or witness of a crime. And a photographic lineup (also called a photo array) is a presentation at one time of several photographs, including that of a suspect, to a victim or witness of a crime.

Requirement of Counsel— The *Wade-Gilbert* Rule

The *Wade-Gilbert* rule was succinctly stated by the U.S. Supreme Court in *Gilbert v. California*.

> We [in *United States v. Wade*] held that a post-indictment pretrial lineup at which the accused is exhibited to identifying witnesses is a critical stage of the criminal prosecution; that police conduct of such a lineup without notice to and in the absence of his counsel denies the accused his Sixth Amendment right to counsel and calls in question the admissibility at trial of the in-court identifications of the accused by witnesses who attended the lineup. *Gilbert v. California*, 388 U.S. 263, 272, 87 S.Ct. 1951, 1956, 18 L.Ed.2d 1178, 1186.

Furthermore, if the suspect is unable to afford a lawyer, he or she is entitled to have one appointed by the court. This ruling is an extension of the right of all accused persons to have the assistance of counsel for their defense at all critical stages of their criminal prosecution as guaranteed by the Sixth Amendment to the Constitution. (See pages 22 to 24.)

Basis of the Court's Decision

The Supreme Court's reasoning in the *Wade* and *Gilbert* cases was based on (1) the inherent unreliability of eyewitness identifications and (2) the possibility of improper suggestions being made to witnesses during the confrontation procedure. The Court said:

> [T]he confrontation compelled by the State between the accused and the victim or witnesses to a crime to elicit identification evidence is peculiarly riddled with innumerable

Objectives

- **Understand the terms** *showup, lineup,* **and** *confrontation.*

- **Understand why the presence of counsel is required at a pretrial confrontation with witnesses conducted after the initiation of adversary judicial proceedings.**

- **Know the proper procedures for conducting a lineup.**

- **Know when a law enforcement officer may use a one-person showup and the ways in which the inherent suggestiveness of the showup may be reduced.**

- **Know the factors that indicate accuracy or reliability of an identification even though the identification procedure was unnecessarily suggestive.**

- **Know the proper procedures for conducting a photographic identification procedure.**

United States v. Wade
laws.findlaw.com/us/388/218.html
Gilbert v. California
laws.findlaw.com/us/388/263.html
Stovall v. Denno
laws.findlaw.com/us/388/293.html

caselaw.findlaw.com/data/
constitution/amendment06/
11.html#4
Discussion (with annotations) of
the right to counsel at lineups
and in other identification
situations

lawschool.lexis.com/emanuel/
web/crimpro/crimpro06.htm
General overview of the law
relating to pretrial identifications

www.uncp.edu/home/
vanderhoof/geolr.html#ID
Short summary of the law
relating to identifications

faculty.ncwc.edu/toconnor/325/
325lect06.htm
Article, "Identification, Bail,
Asset Forfeiture, and Other Pretrial Procedures"

www.frontiernet.net/
~fpdnywro/news/1999-10.htm
Article, "Use of Expert Witnesses
to Discredit Eyewitness Identification Testimony" by Kimberly
Schechter

www.lawyers.com/lawyers-com/
executable/today/
lawstory.asp?10
Article, "Could This Happen to
Your Spouse or Child?—Wrongful Convictions and Eyewitness
Testimony" by Jeralyn Merritt

www.sado.org/
19cdn12.htm#19cdn12a
Article, "Expert Testimony on
Eyewitness Reliability" by Tobin
Miller and Fred Bell

www.abanet.org/journal/oct99/
10TRACE.HTML
Article, "Yes, I'm Sure That's
Him: Eyewitness Reliability
under Question by Experts,
Courts" by John Gibeaut

aux.lincoln.edu/departments/
sociology/criminaljustice/
cipsychology.htm
Article dealing with various
aspects of eyewitness
identification

abcnews.go.com/sections/us/
DailyNews/
eyewitness_testimony.html
Article, "It's Him—Or is It?:
Mistaken Identity Can Land
Innocent People in Jail" by Amy
Sinatra

*For new and updated weblinks,
go to* www.wadsworth.com/
cj/ferdico0253

dangers and variable factors which might seriously, even crucially, derogate from a fair trial. The vagaries of eyewitness identification are well-known; the annals of criminal law are rife with instances of mistaken identification. . . . The identification of strangers is proverbially untrustworthy. . . . A major factor contributing to the high incidence of miscarriage of justice from mistaken identification has been the degree of suggestion inherent in the manner in which the prosecution presents the suspect to witnesses for pretrial identification. A commentator has observed that "[t]he influence of improper suggestion upon identifying witnesses probably accounts for more miscarriages of justice than any other single factor—perhaps it is responsible for more such errors than all other factors combined." . . . Suggestion can be created intentionally or unintentionally in many subtle ways. And the dangers for the suspect are particularly grave when the witness's opportunity for observation was insubstantial, and thus his susceptibility to suggestion the greatest.

Moreover, "[i]t is a matter of common experience that, once a witness has picked out the accused at the line-up, he is not likely to go back on his word later on, so that in practice the issue of identity may (in the absence of other relevant evidence) for all practical purposes be determined there and then, before the trial." 388 U.S. at 228–29, 87 S.Ct. at 1933, 18 L.Ed.2d at 1158–59.

The Court was concerned that, as with secret interrogations, there would be serious difficulty determining what happened at a lineup or other identification confrontation conducted in secret.

[T]he defense can seldom reconstruct the manner and mode of lineup identification for judge or jury at trial. Those participating in a lineup with the accused may often be police officers; in any event, the participants' names are rarely recorded or divulged at trial. The impediments to an objective observation are increased when the victim is the witness. Lineups are prevalent in rape and robbery prosecutions and present a particular hazard that a victim's understandable outrage may excite vengeful or spiteful motives. In any event, neither witnesses nor lineup participants are apt to be alert for conditions prejudicial to the suspect. And if they were, it would likely be of scant benefit to the suspect since neither witnesses nor lineup participants are likely to be schooled in the detection of suggestive influences. Improper influences may go undetected by a suspect, guilty or not, who experiences the emotional tension which we might expect in one being confronted with potential accusers. Even when he does observe abuse, if he has a criminal record he may be reluctant to take the stand and open up the admission of prior convictions. Moreover any protestations by the suspect of the fairness of the lineup made at trial are likely to be in vain; the jury's choice is between the accused's unsupported version and that of the police officers present. In short, the accused's inability effectively to reconstruct at trial any unfairness that occurred at the lineup may deprive him of his only opportunity meaningfully to attack the credibility of the witness' courtroom identification. 388 U.S. at 230–32, 87 S.Ct. at 1934–35, 18 L.Ed.2d at 1159–60.

The Court believed that the presence of counsel at the pretrial confrontation with witnesses would prevent misconduct by those conducting the confrontation. In addition, counsel would have firsthand knowledge of events at the confrontation and could, therefore, conduct an intelligent cross-examination of witnesses at a later suppression hearing or trial and point out any improprieties that might have occurred. The Court said:

Since it appears that there is grave potential for prejudice, intentional or not, in the pretrial lineup, which may not be capable of reconstruction at trial, and since presence of counsel itself can often avert prejudice and assure a meaningful confrontation at trial, there can be little doubt that for Wade the post-indictment lineup was a critical stage of the prosecution at which he was "as much entitled to such aid [of counsel] . . . as at the trial itself." . . . Thus both Wade and his counsel should have been notified of the impending lineup, and counsel's presence should have been a requisite to conduct of the lineup, absent an "intelligent waiver." 388 U.S. at 236–37, 87 S.Ct. at 1937, 18 L.Ed.2d at 1162–63.

The Court's ruling recognized the realities of modern criminal prosecution and the defendant's need for assistance at critical stages of the prosecution, formal or informal, in court or out, when the absence of counsel might adversely affect the right to a fair trial.

When the Bill of Rights was adopted, there were no organized police forces as we know them today. The accused confronted the prosecutor and the witnesses against him, and the evidence was marshalled, largely at the trial itself. In contrast, today's law enforcement machinery involves critical confrontations of the accused by the prosecution at pretrial proceedings where the results might well settle the accused's fate and reduce the trial itself to a mere formality. In recognition of these realities of modern criminal prosecution, our cases have construed the Sixth Amendment guarantee to apply to "critical" stages of the proceedings. The guarantee reads: "In all criminal prosecutions, the accused shall enjoy the right * * * to have the Assistance of Counsel for his defence." The plain wording of this guarantee thus encompasses counsel's assistance whenever necessary to assure a meaningful "defence." 388 U.S. at 224–25, 87 S.Ct. at 1931, 18 L.Ed.2d at 1156.

Waiver of the Right to Counsel

Suspects may waive their right to the presence of counsel at a pretrial confrontation.

A waiver is ordinarily an intentional relinquishment or abandonment of a known right or privilege. The determination of whether there has been an intelligent waiver of right to counsel must depend, in each case, upon the particular facts and circumstances surrounding that case, including the background, experience, and conduct of the accused. *Johnson v. Zerbst,* 304 U.S. 458, 464, 58 S.Ct. 1019, 1023, 82 L.Ed. 1461, 1466 (1938).

Johnson v. Zerbst
laws.findlaw.com/us/304/458.html

Before suspects can intelligently and understandingly waive their right to presence of counsel, they should be clearly advised of their rights. The form appearing as Exhibit 14.1 is suggested for this purpose. In *United States v. Sublet,* 644 F.2d 737 (8th Cir. 1981), the court found an intelligent waiver of the right to counsel, even though the defendant refused to sign the waiver form. In that case, the defendant consented to being placed in the lineup after its purpose was explained. Furthermore, "[t]he fact that another suspect requested an attorney and the lineup was delayed until counsel arrived is strong evidence that Sublet was not denied his right to counsel." 644 F.2d at 741–42.

Substitute Counsel

If a suspect requests the advice and presence of his or her own lawyer and that lawyer is not immediately available, a substitute lawyer may sometimes be called for the purpose of the confrontation. *Zamora v. Guam,* 394 F.2d 815 (9th Cir. 1968). As stated in *United States v. Wade:*

Although the right to counsel usually means a right to the suspect's own counsel, provision for substitute counsel may be justified on the ground that the substitute counsel's presence may eliminate the hazards which render the lineup a critical stage for the presence of the suspect's own counsel. 388 U.S. at 237 n.9, 87 S.Ct. at 1938 n.9, 18 L.Ed.2d at 1163–64 n.9.

Key Points

1. A postindictment pretrial lineup at which the accused is exhibited to identifying witnesses is a critical stage of the criminal prosecution. Police conduct of such a lineup without notice to and in the absence of his counsel denies the accused his Sixth Amendment right to counsel and calls in question the admissibility at trial of the in-court identifications of the accused by witnesses who attended the lineup.

www.ncjrs.org/pdffiles1/nij/
178240.pdf
Article, "Eyewitness Evidence: A Guide for Law Enforcement" published by the National Institute of Justice

psych-server.iastate.edu/
faculty/gwells/
americanpsychologisthtml.htm
Article, "From the Lab to the Police Station: A Successful Application of Eyewitness Research"; discusses the "Guide" in the preceding Internet reference

www.ryerson.ca/psychweb/
guide.html
"A National Guide for Eyewitness Evidence in the U.S.: New Ideas for the Oldest Way to Solve a Case" by John Turtle and Gary Wells

psych-server.iastate.edu/faculty/
gwells/whitejune1998.html
Article, "Eyewitness Identification Procedures: Recommendations for Lineups and Photospreads"; an official scientific review paper of the American Psychology/Law Society

www.defgen.state.vt.us/
lawbook/ch04.htm
"Identification Procedures"; focuses on Vermont law

Guidelines for Lineup Identifications

In general, the decision to conduct a lineup is made at the discretion of the police or prosecution. Although the police, the prosecution, or the court may grant a suspect's request for a lineup, there is no requirement that such a request be granted. *United States v. Harvey,* 756 F.2d 636 (8th Cir. 1985). The following are guidelines for the law enforcement officer in conducting a lineup identification procedure.

Before the Lineup

- No lineup identification procedure should be conducted by a law enforcement officer without the officer discussing with the prosecuting attorney the legal advisability of the lineup.
- A lineup should be conducted as soon after the arrest of a suspect as is practicable. Promptly conducted lineups enable the release of innocent arrestees, guarantee the freshness of witnesses' memories, and ensure that crucial identification evidence is obtained before the suspect is released on bail or for other reasons. When possible, lineup arrangements (such as contacting witnesses and locating innocent participants) should be completed before the arrest of the suspect.
- A person in custody may be compelled to participate in a lineup without Fourth or Fifth Amendment rights being violated. Most courts hold that once a person is in custody, his or her liberty is not further infringed by that person's being presented in a lineup for witnesses to view. *People v. Hodge,* 526 P.2d 309 (Colo. 1974). Furthermore, "compelling the accused merely to exhibit his person for observation by a prosecution witness prior to trial involves no compulsion of the accused to give evidence having testimonial significance. It is compulsion of the accused to exhibit his physical characteristics, not compulsion to disclose any knowledge he might have." *United States v. Wade,* 388 U.S. 218, 222, 87 S.Ct. 1926, 1930, 18 L.Ed.2d 1149, 1154–55 (1967).

  Compelling persons who are not in custody to appear in a lineup involves a much greater intrusion on liberty and is usually done only by order of a court or grand jury, or by authority of statute in some states. Some courts have upheld the ordering of a person not in custody to appear in a lineup in serious cases in which the public interest in law enforcement outweighed the privacy interests of the person. *Wise v. Murphy,* 275 A.2d 205 (D.C.App. 1971). Other courts have held that a person not in custody cannot be ordered to participate in a lineup unless there is probable cause to arrest. *Alphonso C. v. Morgenthau,* 50 A.D.2d 97, 376 N.Y.S.2d 126 (N.Y. 1975).

- If the suspect has the right to counsel at the lineup, the suspect should be informed of that right. If the suspect chooses to waive the right to counsel, a careful record should be made of the suspect's waiver and agreement to voluntarily participate in the lineup. (See Exhibit 14.1.)

- If the suspect chooses to have an attorney present at the lineup proceedings, the lineup should be delayed a reasonable time to allow the attorney to appear. The attorney must be allowed to be present from the beginning of the lineup, or "the moment [the suspect] and the other lineup members were within the sight of witnesses." *United States v. LaPierre,* 998 F.2d 1460, 1464 (9th Cir. 1993). The attorney should be allowed to consult with the suspect before the lineup and be given every opportunity to observe all the proceedings, take notes, and tape-record the identification process in whole or in part. If the attorney has any suggestions that might improve the fairness of the proceedings, the officer in charge may follow them if they are reasonable and practicable. However, the attorney should not be allowed to control the proceedings in any way.

  Note that the suspect's attorney must be made aware that an identification is taking place. The attorney's mere presence will not satisfy the *Wade-Gilbert* rule. In a case in which the suspect and his attorney were unaware that witnesses had identified the suspect during his arraignment, the suspect's right to counsel was held to be violated. *Mason v. United States,* 414 F.2d 1176 (D.C.Cir. 1969). Counsel's purpose is to ensure that the identification is conducted fairly and to reconstruct the procedures at trial. Counsel can do neither if he or she is unaware that an identification is taking place.

- Even when the suspect's counsel is not required at a lineup (see the following section entitled "Exceptions to the *Wade-Gilbert* Rule"), the officer conducting the lineup should consider allowing counsel to be present to minimize subsequent challenges to the fairness of the lineup. *State v. Taylor,* 210 N.W.2d 873 (Wis. 1973).

- The names of all persons participating in the lineup, the names of the officers conducting the lineup, and the name of the suspect's attorney, if any, should be recorded and preserved.

- The witness or victim viewing the lineup should be advised of the purpose for which the lineup is being conducted, but the officer should not suggest that the suspect is one of those in the lineup or even that the suspect is in police custody. Moreover, all witnesses who are to view the lineup should be prevented from seeing the suspect in custody, particularly in handcuffs, or in any other circumstances that would indicate the identity of the suspect in question.

- If possible, witnesses should not be allowed to view photographs of the suspect before the lineup. If a witness has viewed photographs before the lineup, the officer conducting the lineup should inform the suspect's counsel and the court of any identification of the suspect's photograph, any failure to identify the suspect's photograph, and any identification of a photograph of someone other than the suspect.

Pretrial Identification Warning and Waiver

Name: _____   Address: _____

Age: _____   Place: _____

Date: _____   Time: _____

Warning

Before appearing at any confrontation with any witnesses being conducted by (Name of Police Department) in relation to (Description of Offense), you are entitled to be informed of your legal rights.

The results of the confrontation can and will be used against you in court.

You have the right to the presence and advice of an attorney of your choice at any such confrontation.

If you cannot afford an attorney and you want one, an attorney will be appointed for you at no expense, before any confrontation is held.

Waiver

I have been advised of my right to the advice of an attorney and to have an attorney present at any confrontation with witnesses, and that if I cannot afford an attorney, one will be appointed for me before any such confrontation occurs. I understand these rights.

I do not want an attorney and I understand and know what I am doing.

No promises have been made to me and no pressures of any kind have been used against me.

_____

Signature of Suspect

Certification

I, (Name of Officer), hereby certify that I read the above warning to (Name of Suspect) on (Date), that this person indicated an understanding of the rights, and that this person signed the WAIVER form in my presence.

_____

Signature of Officer

_____

Witness

Pretrial Identification Warning and Waiver
■ EXHIBIT 14.1

- Before viewing the lineup, each witness should be required to give to the officer in charge of the lineup a written description of the perpetrator of the crime. A copy should be made available to the suspect's counsel.

During the Lineup

- Insofar as possible, all persons in the lineup should be of the same general weight, height, age, and race; should have the same general physical characteristics; and should be dressed similarly. A suspect, and other participants in the lineup, may be required to wear particular kinds of clothing at the lineup. *United States v. King,* 433 F.2d 937 (9th Cir. 1970). In addition, a suspect may be required to shave, trim his or her hair, or even grow a beard before participating in a lineup. *United States v. O'Neal,* 349 F.Supp. 572 (N.D.Ohio 1972). If a suspect fails to cooperate with identification procedures or attempts to change his or her appearance, the officer conducting the lineup should keep a careful record of this behavior.
- The suspect should be allowed to choose his or her initial position in the lineup and to change that position after each viewing. This promotes fairness and eliminates any claim that the positioning of the suspect in the lineup was unduly suggestive.
- Nonsuspects participating in the lineup should be instructed not to act in any way that singles out the suspect.
- If any body movement or gesture is necessary, it should be made one time only by each person in the lineup and repeated only at the express request of the observing witness or victim. Again, the officer conducting the lineup should keep a careful record of any person's failure to cooperate.
- Lineup participants may be compelled to speak for purposes of voice identification. As stated by the U.S. Supreme Court in the *Wade* case, "[C]ompelling Wade to speak within hearing distance of the witnesses, even to utter words purportedly uttered by the robber, was not compulsion to utter statements of a 'testimonial' nature; he was required to use his voice as an identifying physical characteristic, not to speak his guilt." 388 U.S. at 222–23, 87 S.Ct. at 1930, 18 L.Ed.2d at 1155. Each person in the lineup should be asked to speak the same words.
- A color photograph or videotape (or both) of the lineup should be made, and copies should be provided to the suspect's counsel as soon as possible after the lineup.
- If more than one witness is called to view a lineup, the persons who have already viewed the lineup should not be allowed to converse with the persons who have not yet viewed the lineup. It is good practice to keep witnesses who have viewed the lineup in a room separate from witnesses who have not yet viewed the lineup. Furthermore, only one witness at a time should be present in the room where the lineup is being conducted.
- The officer conducting the lineup should not engage in unnecessary conversation with witnesses. Most important, the officer should not indicate by word, gesture, or otherwise his or her opinion as to the identity or guilt of the suspect. This means, especially, that the officer should not tell the witness that he or she has chosen the person suspected of the crime or has made the "correct" decision.

- The officer conducting the lineup should not allow unnecessary persons in the lineup room. A suggested group of people to include is the witness, the officer conducting the lineup, the prosecuting attorney, the suspect's attorney, and an investigator.

- Upon entering the room in which the lineup is being conducted, each witness should be handed a form for use in the identification. The form should be signed by the witness and the law enforcement officer conducting the lineup. A suggested form appears as Exhibit 14.2.

- A copy of the witness identification form should be given to the suspect's attorney at the time each witness completes his or her viewing of the lineup.

- Use of a one-way mirror in a lineup, so that the suspect is unable to know what occurs on the other side of the mirror, has been held to be a *prima facie* violation of constitutional due process. This means that a lineup identification in which a one-way mirror is so used will be illegal, unless the officer conducting the lineup can show that particularly compelling or exigent circumstances made the use of the mirror necessary. *State v. Northup*, 303 A.2d 1, 5 (Me. 1973). When the suspect's counsel is present, however, one-way mirrors may be permitted because counsel can observe the conduct of the lineup and preserve the suspect's rights. A one-way mirror may also be used to protect witnesses who fear retaliation. *Commonwealth v. Lopes*, 287 N.E.2d 118 (Mass. 1972).

After the Lineup

- The officer conducting the lineup should take complete notes of everything that takes place at the lineup and should prepare an official report of all the proceedings, to be filed in the law enforcement agency's permanent records. The report should include the time, location, identity of persons present, statements made, and photographs or videotapes of the lineup. A copy should be sent to the prosecuting attorney and made available to the suspect's attorney. The lineup identification form (see Exhibit 14.2) for each witness viewing the lineup should be included as part of the officer's report.

- A defendant has no right to have his or her counsel present at a postlineup police interview with an identifying witness. *Hallmark v. Cartwright*, 742 F.2d 584 (10th Cir. 1984).

- Any officer who observed a lineup must disclose to the court that reviews the lineup any evidence that might affect the accuracy of the identification, whether the evidence was observed before, during, or after the lineup. Failure to do so may be a violation of the suspect's due process rights.

- Multiple lineups involving the same suspect and witness are inherently suggestive and strongly discouraged. In *Foster v. California*, 394 U.S. 440, 89 S.Ct. 1127, 22 L.Ed.2d 402 (1969), the eyewitness was unable to make a positive identification at the first lineup in which Foster was placed with men considerably shorter than he. Even after the eyewitness met one-on-one with Foster, the identification was tentative with the eyewitness still indicating he was not sure Foster was the one. At a second lineup, the eyewitness was finally convinced Foster committed the crime and positively identified him. Foster was the only person who was used in both lineups. The U.S. Supreme Court reversed the conviction:

    The suggestive elements in this identification procedure made it all but inevitable that David would identify petitioner whether or not he was in fact

Foster v. California
laws.findlaw.com/us/394/
440.html

Lineup Identification Form for Witnesses

Your Name: _____   Date of Birth: _____

Address: _____

Telephone Number: _____   Case Number: _____

Place Viewed: _____   Officer: _____

Agency: _____

TO THE WITNESS: You have been asked to look at a lineup. This is either a presentation in person of several individuals or a presentation of several photographs. You may or may not be able to identify a person in the lineup. Please look at all the persons before making any choice. If you do not identify a person in the lineup, please indicate below. If you do identify a person, please indicate the number of the person on this form.

You must look at this display and make an independent identification *without assistance*. Do not ask any questions about the people being shown. You may, however, ask the officer to have persons in the lineup say certain words, do certain things, or wear certain clothing, if you think it will aid you. Do not ask anyone for help or discuss this with anyone except the officer. There is no "right" answer, so do not ask whether you have made the "right" choice.

Please mark your choice with an "X":

I do not identify anyone

I identify   1   2   3   4   5   6   7   8

COMMENTS: _____

_____

_____

_____

Thank you for your cooperation.

_____ Date and Time _____
Viewer's Signature

_____ Date and Time _____
Officer's Signature/Badge Number

Lineup Identification Form for Witnesses
■ EXHIBIT 14.2

"the man." In effect, the police repeatedly said to the witness, "This is the man." . . . This procedure so undermined the reliability of the eyewitness identification as to violate due process. 394 U.S. at 443, 89 S.Ct. at 1129, 22 L.Ed.2d at 407.

Exceptions to the *Wade-Gilbert* Rule

The *Wade* and *Gilbert* decisions have caused much controversy, generating many conflicting opinions in subsequent court decisions. Some lower courts have limited *Wade* and *Gilbert* to their particular facts. Others have created exceptions to the broad holdings implicit in the decisions. Several of those exceptions are discussed here.

Identifications Conducted before the Initiation of Adversary Judicial Proceedings

Most identification procedures take place before the defendant is indicted. The following discussion explains at what point in the judicial process the right to counsel attaches and what standards govern identification procedures conducted before the right to counsel attaches.

Kirby v. Illinois
laws.findlaw.com/us/406/
682.html

KIRBY V. ILLINOIS At what stage of a criminal proceeding does a suspect have a right to counsel at an identification procedure? The U.S. Supreme Court decided this issue in *Kirby v. Illinois*, 406 U.S. 682, 92 S.Ct. 1877, 32 L.Ed.2d 411 (1972). In the *Kirby* case, the Court held that the right to counsel attaches to lineups and showups conducted

> at or after the initiation of adversary judicial criminal proceedings—whether by way of formal charge, preliminary hearing, indictment, information or arraignment. . . .
>
> The initiation of judicial criminal proceedings is far from a mere formalism. It is the starting point of our whole system of adversary criminal justice. For it is only then that the government has committed itself to prosecute, and only then that the adverse positions of government and defendant have solidified. It is then that a defendant finds himself faced with the prosecutorial forces of organized society, and immersed in the intricacies of substantive and procedural criminal law. It is this point, therefore, that marks the commencement of the "criminal prosecutions" to which alone the explicit guarantees of the Sixth Amendment are applicable. 406 U.S. at 689–90, 92 S.Ct. at 1882, 32 L.Ed.2d at 417–18.

Therefore, a law enforcement officer need not warn a suspect of the right to counsel at a confrontation, if criminal proceedings have not been initiated.

Courts differ in their interpretations of when criminal proceedings are initiated. The Supreme Court of Pennsylvania, for example, affords an accused a right to counsel at all lineups held after arrest. *Commonwealth v. Richman*, 320 A.2d 351 (Pa. 1974). In *People v. Blake*, 361 N.Y.S.2d 881, 320 N.E.2d 625 (N.Y. 1974), the court concluded that a complaint for an arrest warrant triggers the right to counsel since it is an "accusatory instrument." Other courts have held that the filing of a complaint and issuance of an arrest warrant do not trigger the right to counsel. *United States v. Smith*, 778 F.2d 925 (2d Cir. 1985). And in *Ellis v. Grammer*, 664 F.Supp. 1292 (D.Neb. 1987), the court held that a defendant who has been formally charged for one offense does not have a right to counsel at a lineup conducted for a different offense of which the defendant is suspected. An officer conducting a confrontation with witnesses must determine at what point in the criminal justice process the right to counsel at pretrial identification procedures attaches under the law applicable to the officer's jurisdiction.

Even though a suspect has no right to counsel at a confrontation with witnesses held before the initiation of adversary judicial criminal proceedings, the suspect retains the right to have the identification procedure conducted in a fair and impartial manner. In the *Kirby* case, the Court said:

> What has been said is not to suggest that there may not be occasions during the course of a criminal investigation when the police do abuse identification procedures. Such abuses are not beyond the reach of the Constitution. As the Court pointed out in *Wade* itself, it is always necessary to "scrutinize *any* pretrial confrontation. . . ." 388 U.S. 227, 87 S.Ct. 1932. The Due Process Clause of the Fifth and Fourteenth Amendments forbids a lineup that is unnecessarily suggestive and conducive to irreparable mistaken identification. *Stovall v. Denno*, 388 U.S. 293, 87 S.Ct. 1967, 18 L.Ed.2d 1199; *Foster v. California*, 394 U.S. 440, 89 S.Ct. 1127, 22 L.Ed.2d 402. When a person has not been formally charged with a criminal offense, *Stovall* strikes the appropriate constitutional balance between the right of a suspect to be protected from prejudicial procedures and the interest of society in the prompt and purposeful investigation of an unsolved crime. 406 U.S. at 690–91, 92 S.Ct. at 1883, 32 L.Ed.2d at 418–19.

STOVALL V. DENNO   The case of *Stovall v. Denno*, 388 U.S. 293, 87 S.Ct. 1967, 18 L.Ed.2d 1199 (1967), mentioned in the previous quote from the *Kirby* case, held that the due process clause of the Fifth and Fourteenth Amendments to the Constitution forbids any pretrial identification procedure that is unnecessarily suggestive and conducive to irreparable mistaken identification. Furthermore, "a claimed violation of due process of law in the conduct of a confrontation depends on the totality of the circumstances surrounding it. . . ." 388 U.S. at 302, 87 S.Ct. at 1972, 18 L.Ed.2d at 1206. For the law enforcement officer, this simply means that *all* lineups and showups must be conducted in a fair and impartial manner. The word *all* is emphasized because the *Stovall* test applies whether or not a suspect is represented by an attorney at the identification procedure.

The *Stovall* case is particularly important with respect to confrontations occurring *before* the initiation of adversary judicial criminal proceedings against a suspect. Courts will carefully scrutinize identification procedures for fairness and impartiality in these instances, because suspects are without the benefit of an attorney to protect their rights. Therefore, when a law enforcement officer conducts a *lineup* to identify a suspect, before the suspect has been formally charged, the officer should carefully follow the recommended procedures in the section of this chapter entitled "Guidelines for Lineup Identifications."

When a *showup* rather than a lineup is used, the officer must exercise great care to ensure that identification procedures are not unnecessarily suggestive and conducive to irreparable mistaken identification. Unarranged spontaneous showups are not considered impermissibly suggestive. For example, in *United States v. Boykins*, 966 F.2d 1240 (8th Cir. 1992), an unaccompanied witness, while walking toward the courtroom on the day of trial, recognized the defendant as one of the armed intruders into her home. She told the prosecuting attorney, who accompanied her down the hall to confirm the identification. She later identified the defendant in court. The court allowed the in-court identification, finding that the witness recognized the defendant without any suggestion from the government. "While a lineup is certainly the preferred method of identification, a witness who spontaneously recognized a defendant should be allowed to testify to that fact." 966 F.2d at 1243.

Showups resulting from a crime victim or witness cruising the area of the crime in a police car also rarely present problems of suggestiveness. Cruising the area is an accepted investigative technique when police have no suspect of a crime that has just occurred. Witness memories are still fresh, and perpetrators are still likely to be in the area and not have had opportunity to change their clothes or appearance. Of course, police should not coach witnesses by suggesting that persons the witnesses observe look suspicious or have bad reputations.

A more common type of showup is the *on-the-scene showup,* in which a suspect is arrested or apprehended at or near the scene of a crime and is immediately brought before victims or witnesses by a law enforcement officer for identification purposes. Clearly, so long as adversary judicial criminal proceedings have not been initiated, the suspect has no right to counsel at this type of confrontation. But does an on-the-scene showup satisfy the *Stovall* requirements regarding suggestiveness?

Although courts differ on this question, the prevailing view is that practical considerations may justify a prompt on-the-scene showup under the *Stovall* test. In *Russell v. United States,* 408 F.2d 1280 (D.C. Cir. 1969), the court said that the delay required to assemble a lineup "may not only cause the detention of an innocent suspect; it may also diminish the reliability of any identification obtained." 480 F.2d at 1284. The court also suggested that only "fresh" on-the-scene identifications that occur within minutes of the witnessed crime would satisfy the *Stovall* standard. In *Johnson v. Dugger,* 817 F.2d 726 (11th Cir. 1987), the court said:

> Although show-ups are widely condemned . . . immediate confrontations allow identification before the suspect has altered his appearance and while the witness' memory is fresh, and permit the quick release of innocent persons. . . . Therefore, show-ups are not unnecessarily suggestive unless the police aggravate the suggestiveness of the confrontation. 817 F.2d at 729.

In *Bates v. United States,* 405 F.2d 1104 (D.C. Cir. 1968), the court said:

> There is no prohibition against a viewing of a suspect alone in what is called a "one-man showup" when this occurs near the time of the alleged criminal act; such a course does not tend to bring about misidentification but rather in some circumstances to insure accuracy. The rationale underlying this is in some respects not unlike that which the law relies on to make an exception to the hearsay rule, allowing spontaneous utterances a standing which they would not be given if uttered at a later point in time. An early identification is not error. Of course, proof of infirmities and subjective factors, such as hysteria of a witness, can be explored on cross-examination and in argument. Prudent police work would confine these on-the-spot identifications to situations in which possible doubts as to identification needed to be resolved promptly; absent such need the conventional lineup viewing is the appropriate procedure. 405 F.2d at 1106.

The following fact situation from *United States v. Watson,* 76 F.3d 4, 6 (1st Cir. 1996), illustrates the type of on-the-scene showup identification procedure that courts do not find unnecessarily suggestive.

> As Alexander Milette was bicycling home to the Cathedral Project, a Porsche drove past him and stopped in front of his house. Trevor Watson got out of the car, carrying a loaded pistol of the type favored by the Boston police, a Glock 9mm semi-automatic. After accusing Milette of liking "hitting on" women, Watson aimed the gun at Milette's stomach. Someone said "Don't shoot him."
>
> Instead, Watson pistol-whipped Milette's head, causing the gun to fire into a building and then to jam. Milette, bleeding, ran while Watson unjammed the gun and fired again, hitting the building Milette ran behind. Milette sought sanctuary at a friend's house and was helped with his bleeding head.

Watson had jumped back into the Porsche, only to have it stall out in a deep puddle. A nearby off-duty Boston Police officer, Officer Christopher Shoulla, heard the shots, drove to the project, and put out a call on his police radio. Officer Shoulla saw Watson and asked him to stop. Watson instead fled, clutching his right pocket, and, ironically, ran right past Milette and past another youth. Two other Boston officers arrived and gave chase. Watson threw the gun, as he ran, into a small garden. Officer Shoulla stopped Watson at gunpoint. When the officers patted down Watson and determined he had no gun, they retraced Watson's steps and found it within forty seconds.

One officer saw Milette, still holding a bloody towel to his head, and had the others bring Watson over. Watson was brought over by patrol car and Milette was asked by the police, "What's the story?" Milette looked, and identified Watson as his assailant. He later testified he was 100% sure of that identification. Watson was also identified by the other youth past whom he had run.

Law enforcement officers should use on-the-scene showups only when a suspect can be shown to a witness minutes after the crime has occurred. Furthermore, officers should not add in any way to the already inherent suggestiveness of the on-the-scene identification. For example, the officer should not say or do anything to lead the witness to believe that the suspect is believed to be the perpetrator or that the suspect has been formally arrested, has confessed, or has been found in possession of incriminating items. If there is a significant delay between the commission of the crime and the confrontation, officers should take the suspect to the station and conduct a lineup in accordance with suggested procedures in the section of this chapter entitled "Guidelines for Lineup Identifications."

NEIL V. BIGGERS Despite the advice in the preceding paragraph, law enforcement officers have often conducted showups several days, weeks, or even months after a crime has occurred. Before 1972, most courts, applying the standards of *Stovall v. Denno*, held that delayed one-on-one confrontations were impermissibly suggestive and violative of due process. Evidence obtained from identifications made under these circumstances was held inadmissible in court.

In 1972, however, the U.S. Supreme Court decided the case of *Neil v. Biggers*, 409 U.S. 188, 93 S.Ct. 375, 34 L.Ed.2d 401, in which the Court noted that "[i]t is the likelihood of misidentification that violates a defendant's right to due process. . . . Suggestive confrontations are disapproved because they increase the likelihood of misidentification, and unnecessarily suggestive ones are condemned for the further reason that the increased chance of misidentification is gratuitous." 409 U.S. at 198, 93 S.Ct. at 381–82, 34 L.Ed.2d at 410–11. Thus, the Court focused on whether the identification was accurate or reliable despite the suggestiveness of the identification procedure. *Neil v. Biggers* involved a defendant who had been convicted of rape on evidence consisting, in part, of the victim's visual and voice identification of the defendant at a station house showup seven months after the crime. At the time of the crime, the victim was in her assailant's presence for nearly a half hour, and the victim directly observed her assailant indoors and under a full moon outdoors. The victim testified at trial that she had no doubt that the defendant was her assailant. Immediately after the crime, she gave the police a thorough description of the assailant that matched the description of the defendant. The victim had also made no identification of others presented at previous showups or lineups or through photographs.

Despite its concern about the seven-month delay between the crime and the confrontation, the Court held that the central question was "whether under 'the totality

Neil v. Biggers
laws.findlaw.com/us/409/
188.html

of the circumstances' the identification was reliable even though the confrontation procedure was suggestive." 409 U.S. at 199, 93 S.Ct. at 382, 34 L.Ed.2d at 411. The Court listed the following five factors to be considered in evaluating the likelihood of misidentification:

1. Witness's opportunity to view the criminal at the time of the crime
2. Witness's degree of attention
3. Accuracy of the witness's prior description of the criminal
4. Level of certainty demonstrated by the witness at the confrontation
5. Length of time between the crime and the confrontation

Applying these considerations to the facts of the case, the Court found no substantial likelihood of misidentification and held the evidence of the identification to be admissible in court.

Manson v. Brathwaite
laws.findlaw.com/us/432/
98.html

MANSON V. BRATHWAITE   In *Manson v. Brathwaite*, 432 U.S. 98, 97 S.Ct. 2243, 53 L.Ed.2d 140 (1977), the U.S. Supreme Court reiterated the five reliability factors of *Biggers* and emphasized that they should be balanced against the corrupting effect of the suggestive identification itself. The *Brathwaite* case involved an undercover drug officer's viewing of a single photograph of a drug crime suspect that had been left in his office by a fellow officer. Two days had elapsed between the crime and the viewing of the photograph. After finding that the single photographic display was unnecessarily suggestive, the Court considered the five factors affecting the reliability of an identification set out in *Neil v. Biggers*. The Court found that the undercover officer was no casual observer but a trained police officer, that the officer had sufficient opportunity to view the suspect for two or three minutes in natural light, that the officer accurately described the suspect in detail within minutes of the crime, that the officer positively identified the photograph in court as that of the drug seller, and that the officer made the photographic identification only two days after the crime.

The Court's analysis of the five factors indicated that the undercover drug officer was able to make an accurate identification of the defendant. The Court did not end its discussion at this stage as it did in the *Biggers* case, however. Instead, it took the additional step of analyzing the corrupting effect of the suggestive identification and then weighing that against the factors indicating reliability. The Court said:

> Although identifications arising from single-photograph displays may be viewed in general with suspicion, . . . we find in the instant case little pressure on the witness to acquiesce in the suggestion that such a display entails. D'Onofrio had left the photograph at Glover's office and was not present when Glover first viewed it two days after the event. There thus was little urgency and Glover could view the photograph at his leisure. And since Glover examined the photograph alone, there was no coercive pressure to make an identification arising from the presence of another. The identification was made in circumstances allowing care and reflection. 432 U.S. at 116, 97 S.Ct. at 2254, 53 L.Ed.2d at 155.

Under the totality of the circumstances, the Court held that the identification was reliable and that evidence of the identification was admissible in court.

The following quotation from the *Brathwaite* case sets out the basic test for determining the admissibility of evidence of identifications that take place before the initiation of adversary judicial criminal proceedings:

> We therefore conclude that reliability is the linchpin in determining the admissibility of identification testimony for both pre- and post-*Stovall* confrontations. The factors to be

considered are set out in *Biggers*. 409 U.S. at 199–200, 93 S.Ct. at 382. These include the opportunity of the witness to view the criminal at the time of the crime, the witness' degree of attention, the accuracy of his prior description of the criminal, the level of certainty demonstrated at the confrontation, and the time between the crime and the confrontation. Against these factors is to be weighed the corrupting effect of the suggestive identification itself. 432 U.S. at 114, 97 S.Ct. at 2253, 53 L.Ed.2d at 154.

www.criminaljustice.org/
CHAMPION/ARTICLES/
98jan01.htm
Article, "No Confidence: A Step toward Accuracy in Eyewitness Trials" by James M. Doyle

The lesson of the *Biggers* and *Brathwaite* cases is that, even though an officer conducts an unnecessarily suggestive identification procedure, the evidence is not necessarily lost because it may still be admitted in court if the identification was otherwise reliable. However, these cases should not be interpreted as evidencing a lack of concern about conducting fair and impartial identification procedures. As the Court stated in the *Brathwaite* case:

> [I]t would have been better had D'Onofrio presented Glover with a photographic array including "so far as practicable . . . a reasonable number of persons similar to any person then suspected whose likeness is included in the array." . . . The use of that procedure would have enhanced the force of the identification at trial and would have avoided the risk that the evidence would be excluded as unreliable. 432 U.S. at 117, 97 S.Ct. at 2254, 53 L.Ed.2d at 155.

In *United States v. Thody*, 978 F.2d 625 (10th Cir. 1992), the court applied the *Biggers-Brathwaite* factors to find an identification of a bank robber reliable despite an impermissibly suggestive lineup.

> Each witness had an adequate opportunity to observe Thody closely during the two robberies. All three witnesses testified at the suppression hearing that at least once they were within a few feet of Thody, and that they were able to observe McIntosh and him for several minutes. Woods and Harshfield were within arm's reach of Thody while complying with his instructions. The light was good, and there is no question that the attention of these three employees was riveted on Thody and his companion. Dillard testified that she had been trained to remember the descriptions of robbers. When the second robbery took place Harshfield immediately recognized Thody from the July 12 robbery, exclaiming to Woods, "It's him!" The descriptions of the robbers given by Harshfield, Woods, and Dillard after the robberies also corroborated one another to the degree that descriptions of subtleties in nose size, presence or lack of facial hair, and hair color corresponded significantly.
>
> The witnesses were unequivocal in their testimony, both at trial and at the suppression hearing. Despite attempts by defense counsel to unearth inconsistencies, no significant inconsistencies materialized. Also, only one week separated the confrontation from the robbery. 978 F.2d at 629.

In contrast, *United States v. De Jesus-Rios*, 990 F.2d 672 (1st Cir. 1993), found that a boat captain's identification of a woman who had contracted for cargo transport was *not* otherwise reliable after an impermissibly suggestive one-person showup. The court had no problem with the first, second, and fifth *Biggers-Brathwaite* factors but was troubled by application of the third and fourth factors (the accuracy of the witness's prior description of the criminal, and the level of certainty the witness demonstrated at the confrontation):

> Agent Marti testified that, on the date the cocaine was discovered, February 8, 1991, Rivera [the boat captain] described the suspect as "white" and approximately five feet,

Case in Point

Interpreting *Manson v. Brathwaite*

Flores' arrest and conviction stem from his involvement in a methamphetamine distribution ring operating out of Colorado Springs, Colorado, from early 1994 through January 1995. Flores' involvement with the ring became known to the Government on December 5, 1994. On that date, an undercover federal agent, Scot Thomasson ("Agent Thomasson") arranged to meet with the alleged leader of the ring, James Maass ("Maass"), to purchase a large quantity of methamphetamine. They met that night in the lighted parking lot of the Penny Arcade in Manitou Springs. Although Agent Thomasson expected to meet only with Maass, two additional individuals, previously unknown to Agent Thomasson, were present and waiting. One of these individuals approached Agent Thomasson and Maass, and expressed concerns to Maass about the safety of dealing with Thomasson. After Maass showed the individual the money that Agent Thomasson had given him for the drugs and convinced him that Agent Thomasson was safe, the individual entered Maass' car, where he proceeded to conduct a methamphetamine transaction with Maass. Maass then sold the drugs to Agent Thomasson.

Agent Thomasson had been told by Maass that a local street gang known as "the Banditos" was a supplier of methamphetamine for Maass' distribution ring. Subsequent to the transaction at the Penny Arcade, Agent Thomasson learned that local police detectives had interviewed and photographed a number of the members of the Banditos during the course of an unrelated investigation. Agent Thomasson met with one of the detectives, who began laying out a stack of nine photos of Banditos members on a desk. Immediately upon viewing Flores' photo, Agent Thomasson identified him as the first unidentified individual he had encountered at the Penny Arcade transaction. Agent Thomasson apparently did not identify the second individual from the photos shown him.

[Flores] was convicted . . . of conspiracy to distribute, and possession with intent to distribute, methamphetamine. [On appeal Flores argued] that because Agent Thomasson initially identified him as the result of an unnecessarily suggestive photo line-up, his in-court identification of Flores should have been disallowed by the court. Flores argues that the photo line-up used to identify him was unnecessarily suggestive because (1) the photos were shown to Agent Thomasson one-by-one, not in a single layout display; (2) although all of the photos shown to the agent were of young Hispanic men, in his photograph the eyes are very distinctive from the other photographs; and (3) his is the only photo of a man with a goatee. In light of *Manson v. Brathwaite*, should the court have disallowed the in-court identification of Flores? *United States v. Flores*, 149 F.3d 1272 (10th Cir. 1998).

Read the court opinion at:
laws.findlaw.com/10th/961152.html

two inches tall. Rivera's testimony at the suppression hearing and Agent Dania's trial testimony revealed that during his February 11, 1991, interview with Agent Dania, Rivera again described her as "white." It was not until after the February 16, 1991, showup that Rivera described the suspect as having "light brown" skin. Moreover, Rivera also failed to provide an accurate description of her height (five feet, six inches) at either of his pre-showup descriptions.

The record also contains uncontroverted evidence that, despite having been asked at the February 16, 1991, showup to signal the agents when he positively identified Eva Rios, Rivera waited until after she approached the agents and began speaking with them (as scheduled) to signal. We hardly think that this constitutes a high degree of certainty on Rivera's part, particularly in light of the showup procedure at issue here. Prior to that showup, Rivera was informed that the agents were meeting the suspect in front of the customs building at a specific time. While a few other women also may have walked by the customs building that morning, only Eva Rios stopped to speak with the agents. 990 F.2d at 678.

Law enforcement officers have control over the conduct of the identification procedures, but they have little or no control over the five factors determining the reliability of the identification. Therefore, officers should conduct all identification procedures fairly and impartially. To avoid the risk that identification evidence will be excluded as unreliable, officers should follow the guidelines for lineup identifications set out earlier in this chapter. When photographs are used, officers should follow the guidelines for photographic identifications appearing later in this chapter.

Emergency Identifications

In an emergency, courts are more likely to condone one-person showups and violations of the *Wade* right-to-counsel rule, because an immediate identification by a witness may be the only identification possible. For identification purposes, an emergency can be defined as a witness in danger of death or blindness or a suspect in danger of death. The leading case on emergency identifications is *Stovall v. Denno*, 388 U.S. 293, 87 S.Ct. 1967, 18 L.Ed.2d 1199 (1967). In that case, the defendant was arrested for stabbing a doctor to death and seriously wounding his wife, who was hospitalized for major surgery. Without affording the defendant time to retain counsel, police arranged with the wife's surgeon to bring the defendant to her hospital room. The wife identified the defendant as her assailant. The court held that "a claimed violation of due process of law in the conduct of a confrontation depends on the totality of the circumstances surrounding it, and the record in the present case reveals that the showing of the defendant to the wife in an immediate hospital confrontation was imperative."

> Here was the only person in the world who could possibly exonerate Stovall. Her words, and only her words, "He is not the man" could have resulted in freedom for Stovall. The hospital was not far distant from the courthouse and jail. No one knew how long Mrs. Behrendt might live. Faced with the responsibility of identifying the attacker, with the need for immediate action and with the knowledge that Mrs. Behrendt could not visit the jail, the police followed the only feasible procedure and took Stovall to the hospital room. Under these circumstances, the usual police station line-up, which Stovall now argues he should have had, was out of the question. 388 U.S. at 302, 87 S.Ct. at 1972–73, 18 L.Ed.2d at 1206.

In *Trask v. Robbins*, 421 F.2d 773 (1st Cir. 1970), the defendant, who was being held in jail on a charge of robbing a store, was presented to a hospitalized victim of a separate assault and robbery offense that was under investigation. It was uncertain whether the defendant had retained a lawyer on the store robbery charge, and no lawyer was contacted for the identification proceeding in the separate assault and robbery crime. The defendant was transported to the hospital by a deputy sheriff. The victim spontaneously and positively identified the defendant as his assailant. The defendant claimed that he should have been represented by a lawyer at this pretrial confrontation with the victim.

Applying the *Stovall* totality-of-the-circumstances test, the court found that the circumstances surrounding the identification were not unnecessarily suggestive and conducive to irreparable mistaken identification: (1) no preliminary statements were made to the victim, (2) the victim's words of identification were spontaneous and positive, (3) the defendant said nothing in the presence of the victim, (4) the case was merely in the investigatory stage, and (5) the critically injured victim (thought to be dying) was about to be moved to a distant hospital. Under these emergency conditions, the fact that a lawyer was not present did not void the identification.

Note that identification procedures involving critically injured persons should only be conducted with the approval of medical authorities. The importance of obtaining an identification is secondary in importance to the treatment and care of an injured person.

Preparatory Steps

The *Wade* decision made clear that there is no right to counsel at preparatory steps in the gathering of the prosecution's evidence, such as "systematized or scientific analyzing of the accused's fingerprints, blood sample, clothing, hair, and the like."

> We think there are differences which preclude such stages being characterized as critical stages at which the accused has the right to the presence of his counsel. Knowledge of the techniques of science and technology is sufficiently available, and the variables in techniques few enough, that the accused has the opportunity for a meaningful confrontation of the Government's case at trial through the ordinary processes of cross-examination of the Government's expert witnesses and the presentation of the evidence of his own experts. The denial of a right to have his counsel present at such analyses does not therefore violate the Sixth Amendment; they are not critical stages since there is minimal risk that his counsel's absence at such stages might derogate from his right to a fair trial. 388 U.S. at 227–28, 87 S.Ct. at 1932–33, 18 L.Ed.2d at 1158.

Key Points

2. The suspect's right to counsel at a pretrial confrontation with witnesses attaches at or after the initiation of adversary judicial criminal proceedings—whether by way of formal charge, preliminary hearing, indictment, information, or arraignment.

3. Due process requires that the totality of the circumstances surrounding an identification must not be so overly suggestive as to cause a substantial likelihood of irreparable misidentification. All lineups and showups must be conducted in a fair and impartial manner.

4. The central question surrounding an identification is whether under the totality of the circumstances the identification was reliable even though the confrontation procedure was suggestive. Factors to be considered in evaluating the reliability of an identification are (1) the witness's opportunity to view the criminal at the time of the crime, (2) the witness's degree of attention, (3) the accuracy of the witness's prior description of the criminal, (4) the level of certainty demonstrated by the witness at the confrontation, (5) the length of time between the crime and the confrontation, and (6) the corrupting effect of the suggestive identification.

Photographic Identifications

Simmons v. United States
laws.findlaw.com/us/390/377.html

United States v. Ash
laws.findlaw.com/us/413/300.html

A common and accepted method of police investigation is the showing of mug shots or photographs to witnesses to aid in identifying or eliminating criminal suspects. In *Simmons v. United States*, 390 U.S. 377, 88 S.Ct. 967, 19 L.Ed.2d 1247 (1968), the U.S. Supreme Court approved this procedure, subject to the same standards of fairness set out in *Stovall v. Denno*. Furthermore, the Court held that there is no right to counsel at any photographic identification procedure, whether that procedure is held before or after the initiation of adversary judicial criminal proceedings. *United States v. Ash*, 413 U.S. 300, 93 S.Ct. 2568, 37 L.Ed.2d 619 (1973). The basic rationale of *Ash* is that "[s]ince the accused himself is not present at the time of the photographic display, . . . no possibility arises that the accused might be misled by his lack of familiarity with the law. . . ." 413 U.S. at 317, 93 S.Ct. at 2577, 37 L.Ed.2d at 631. In addition, the Court stated that the accused has sufficient opportunity at trial to contest the identification without being present at the time the photographs are shown. Therefore, unless at the pretrial stage there was involved the physical presence of the accused at a trial-like confrontation at which the accused requires the guiding hand of counsel, the Sixth Amendment does not guarantee the assistance of counsel.

Applying similar reasoning, the court in *United States v. Amrine*, 724 F.2d 84 (8th Cir. 1983), held that the defendant was not entitled to counsel at the showing of a videotaped lineup in which the defendant was one of the participants. The court said that the videotape was not to be considered an actual lineup but, rather, was more aptly categorized as a photographic display. And in *United States v. Dupree*, 553 F.2d 1189 (8th Cir. 1977), the court held that there was no right to counsel at the playing of a tape-recorded voice array.

Each case must be decided on the totality of the circumstances surrounding it, and the identification evidence will be excluded in court "only if the photographic identification procedure was so impermissibly suggestive as to give rise to a very substantial likelihood of irreparable misidentification" (390 U.S. at 384, 88 S.Ct. at 971, 19 L.Ed.2d at 1253), and if the identification fails to satisfy the basic reliability test set out in the previous discussion of *Manson v. Brathwaite*.

The following guidelines, based on the *Simmons* case, are suggested for photographic identifications:

- More than one photograph should be shown to a witness. In the *Simmons* case, six photographs were shown to several witnesses, and the Supreme Court suggested that even more than six would be preferable. "In the absence of exigent circumstances, presentation of a single photograph to the victim of a crime amounts to an unnecessarily suggestive photographic identification procedure." *United States v. Jones*, 652 F.Supp. 1561, 1570 (S.D.N.Y. 1986).

- The people appearing in the photographs should be of the same general age, height, weight, hair color, and skin color.

- No group of photographs should be arranged in such a way that the photograph of a single person recurs or is in any way emphasized. Furthermore, the officer conducting the photographic identification should do nothing to indicate which picture is that of the suspect. *Cikora v. Wainwright*, 661 F.Supp. 813 (S.D.Fla. 1987).

- If there are two or more suspects, no two should appear together in a group photo.

- Witnesses should be handled in a manner similar to that suggested in the guidelines for lineup identifications presented earlier in this chapter.

- If there are several witnesses, only some of them should be shown the photographs to obtain an initial identification. Then the suspect should be displayed to the remaining witnesses in a more reliable lineup. By following this procedure, the officer helps ensure that the perceptions of the witnesses at the lineup are not influenced by a viewing of the photographs.

- After the photographs have been shown to the witnesses, they should be numbered and preserved as evidence. The officer conducting the photographic identification should take careful notes of all remarks made by witnesses while viewing photos and of all positive identifications and all failures to identify the suspect. Proper record keeping is essential. The ability to exactly reconstruct a photographic identification procedure may help to counter defense claims of undue suggestiveness and to support the validity of a later in-court identification. Some courts hold that a photo array that is not preserved is presumed to be unduly suggestive.

By failing to show the defendant or the court the photos, the state virtually assures that the defendant will be unable to argue the suggestiveness of the photographs. Unless the witness or officer admits to the suggestiveness of the array, there will be no means available to contest the identification procedures. *Smith v. Campbell,* 781 F.Supp. 521, 527–28 (M.D.Tenn. 1991).

- It is good practice to have an identifying witness initial and date the back of the photograph selected. Care should be taken, however, to avoid allowing later witnesses to see an earlier witness's initials on the back of a photograph.
- After a witness selects a photograph from a photographic display, that witness should not be shown the same photograph in later displays. Such a procedure would tend to fix the image of the photograph in the witness's mind and blur the image actually perceived at the crime. *United States v. Eatherton,* 519 F.2d 603 (1st Cir. 1975).
- Photographs of suspects in the act of committing the crime (such as bank robbery surveillance photographs) do not present any problems of suggestiveness and mistaken identification. Courts have held that presenting such photographs to witnesses shows the actual perpetrator of the crime in the act rather than suggesting a number of possible perpetrators. The photographs refresh the witness's memory of the actual crime and thereby strengthen the reliability of the witness's in-court identification. *United States v. Browne,* 829 F.2d 760 (9th Cir. 1987).
- If possible, a mug shot of a suspect should not be displayed in a photographic array alongside ordinary photographs of other persons. Mug shots may prejudice the suspect by implying that he or she has a criminal record. Nevertheless, use of mug shots is often unavoidable. Therefore, it is suggested that only frontal views be used and that the photographs be presented in a manner that disguises their identity as mug shots. Of course, if police have no suspect, the display of a mug book to a witness or victim for identification purposes presents no problems of suggestivity. A reasonable number of photographs should be shown and careful records kept of all pictures shown and any pictures identified.
- A photograph in a photographic display may be altered (to show what the person would look like with a beard or a hat, for example) so long as all other photographs in the display are altered in the same way. *United States v. Dunbar,* 767 F.2d 72 (3d Cir. 1985).
- "Once law enforcement officers obtain from a witness a photographic identification of a suspect which is both untainted and positive, they may show other pictures of that properly and positively identified suspect to the witness without implicating the concerns of *Simmons* and its progeny." *United States v. Jones,* 652 F.Supp. 1561 (S.D.N.Y. 1986).
- Photographic identification should not be used once a suspect's identity is known and the suspect is in police custody. A lineup is preferable in these circumstances because lineups are normally more accurate than photographic identifications. *Simmons v. United States,* 390 U.S. at 386 n.6, 88 S.Ct. at 972 n.6, 19 L.Ed.2d at 1254 n.6 (1968).

These guidelines are only suggested; different circumstances may require different identification procedures. The law requires that the totality of the circumstances surrounding an identification must not be so overly suggestive as to cause a substantial likelihood of irreparable misidentification. As discussed earlier, courts will look beyond the mere fact of a suggestive photographic identification procedure in determining

www.icje.org/id77.htm
Article, "Question: Can a Department Legally Use Mug Shots or a 'Mug Book' for Identification Purposes?" by Robert T. Thetford

whether there was a substantial likelihood of irreparable misidentification. Courts will analyze each case with respect to the five factors determining the reliability of the identification as set out in *Neil v. Biggers*. Courts will then weigh those factors against the corrupting effect of the suggestive identification, as was done in *Manson v. Brathwaite*. Law enforcement officers should follow the guidelines for photographic identifications set out in this section to minimize the suggestiveness of identification procedures and to help ensure that identification evidence will not be excluded as unreliable.

www.mopca.com/members/
documents/vol2/modshowu.txt
"Showups, Photographic Identifications and Lineups: Model Policy"

Key Points

5. A suspect has no right to counsel at any photographic identification procedure, whether that procedure is held before or after the initiation of adversary judicial criminal proceedings.

Effect of an Improper Identification Procedure

To enforce the standards set out by the U.S. Supreme Court with respect to pretrial identifications, certain rules have been established for the admission of identification evidence in court. If a pretrial identification is made in violation of defendant's right to counsel, or if the identification is unreliable and thereby violates a defendant's right to due process of law, the court must exclude at trial

- any evidence of the pretrial identification presented as a part of the prosecutor's direct case and
- any identification of the perpetrator of the crime made by a witness in court.

If, however, the prosecution can establish by clear and convincing evidence that a witness has a source independent from the illegal confrontation for identifying the perpetrator of the crime, the court may allow in-court identification testimony. *Frisco v. Blackburn*, 782 F.2d 1353 (5th Cir. 1986). A court will find that an in-court identification has an *independent source* when the court is convinced that the identifying witness, by drawing on personal memory of the crime and observations of the defendant during the crime, has such a clear and definite image of the defendant that the witness can make an identification unaffected by the illegal confrontation. Some factors considered by judges in determining an independent source were set out in the *Wade* case.

> Application of [the independent source test] requires consideration of various factors; for example, the prior opportunity to observe the alleged criminal act, the existence of any discrepancy between any pre-lineup description and the defendant's actual description, any identification prior to the lineup of another person, the identification by picture of the defendant prior to lineup, failure to identify the defendant on a prior occasion, and the lapse of time between the alleged act and the lineup identification. It is also relevant to consider those facts which, despite the absence of counsel, are disclosed concerning the conduct of the lineup. 388 U.S. at 241, 87 S.Ct. at 1940, 18 L.Ed.2d at 1165.

In *McKinon v. Wainwright*, 705 F.2d 419 (11th Cir. 1983), the court found an independent source for the identification of the accused at trial when the witness had known the accused long before the crime was committed and had spent several hours with the accused on the day of the crime. Law enforcement officers should gather information on these factors from witnesses and record the information in their reports. Officers should obtain as much detail as possible because strong evidence of an independent source for identification of a criminal can salvage an improperly conducted identification procedure. Of course, if the defendant does not meet the threshold requirement of showing that the in-court identification was tainted by impermissible suggestiveness, then "independent reliability [of the in-court identification] is not a constitutionally required condition of admissibility . . . and the reliability of the identification is simply a question for the jury." *Jarrett v. Headley,* 802 F.2d 34, 42 (2d Cir. 1986).

The same independent-source factors are used by courts to determine the admissibility of in-court identifications that violate the defendant's Fourth Amendment rights. For example, in *United States v. Slater,* 692 F.2d 107 (10th Cir. 1982), the photograph used for an out-of-court identification had been obtained through an illegal arrest. The court held that the in-court identification of the defendant was admissible, however, because

> the witnesses . . . had each actually seen the crime committed at close hand, there was little discrepancy between the pretrial descriptions and the defendant's actual description, there was no identification of another person or failure to identify the defendant, and the person who committed the crime made no attempt to conceal his face. 692 F.2d at 108.

Summary

A criminal suspect has a right to counsel at all lineups and showups conducted *at* or *after* the initiation of adversary judicial criminal proceedings against the suspect. The emergency showup is the only possible exception to this rule. In every other case, the suspect should be warned of the right to counsel in accordance with the form appearing as Exhibit 14.1.

If a lineup or showup is conducted *before* adversary judicial criminal proceedings are initiated against a suspect, the suspect is *not* entitled to the presence or advice of counsel. Nevertheless, *all* pretrial identification procedures, whether lineups or showups, must be conducted in accordance with due process, which forbids any pretrial identification procedure that is unnecessarily suggestive and conducive to irreparable mistaken identification. As further interpreted by the U.S. Supreme Court, due process simply requires that all pretrial identifications be reliable in the totality of the circumstances, or evidence of the identification will be inadmissible in court. Factors to be considered in determining reliability are the witness's opportunity to view the criminal at the time of the crime, the witness's degree of attention, the accuracy of the witness's prior description of the criminal, the level of certainty demonstrated by the witness at the confrontation, and the length of time between the crime and the confrontation. These factors are to be weighed against the corrupting effect of any suggestive identification. Officers conducting lineups are advised to follow the guidelines for lineup identifications presented in this chapter.

A criminal suspect is not entitled to the presence or advice of counsel at *photographic* identification procedures no matter when those procedures are held. Nevertheless, such procedures must be conducted as fairly and impartially as possible, and identifications will be evaluated by the reliability test described in the preceding paragraph. Officers are advised to follow the guidelines for photographic identifications provided in this chapter.

Key Holdings from Major Cases

Gilbert v. California (1967). "[A] post-indictment pretrial lineup at which the accused is exhibited to identifying witnesses is a critical stage of the criminal prosecution; . . . police conduct of such a lineup without notice to and in the absence of his counsel denies the accused his Sixth Amendment right to counsel and calls in question the admissibility at trial of the in-court identifications of the accused by witnesses who attended the lineup." 388 U.S. 263, 272, 87 S.Ct. 1951, 1956, 18 L.Ed.2d 1178, 1186.

United States v. Wade (1967). "Since it appears that there is grave potential for prejudice, intentional or not, in the pretrial lineup, which may not be capable of reconstruction at trial, and since presence of counsel itself can often avert prejudice and assure a meaningful confrontation at trial, there can be little doubt that for Wade the post-indictment lineup was a critical stage of the prosecution at which he was 'as much entitled to such aid [of counsel] . . . as at the trial itself.' . . . Thus both Wade and his counsel should have been notified of the impending lineup, and counsel's presence should have been a requisite to conduct of the lineup, absent an 'intelligent waiver.'" 388 U.S. 218, 236–37, 87 S.Ct. 1926, 1937, 18 L.Ed.2d 1149, 1162–63.

Kirby v. Illinois (1972). "The initiation of judicial criminal proceedings is far from a mere formalism. It is the starting point of our whole system of adversary criminal justice. For it is only then that the Government has committed itself to prosecute, and only then that the adverse positions of Government and defendant have solidified. It is then that a defendant finds himself faced with the prosecutorial forces of organized society, and immersed in the intricacies of substantive and procedural criminal law. It is this point, therefore, that marks the commencement of the 'criminal prosecutions' to which alone the explicit guarantees of the Sixth Amendment are applicable.

"In this case we are asked to import into a routine police investigation an absolute constitutional guarantee historically and rationally applicable only after the onset of formal prosecutorial proceedings. We decline to do so. Less than a year after *Wade* and *Gilbert* were decided, the Court explained the rule of those decisions as follows: 'The rationale of those cases was that an accused is entitled to counsel at any "critical stage of the prosecution," and that a postindictment lineup is such a "critical stage."' We decline to depart from that rationale today by imposing a *per se* exclusionary rule upon testimony concerning an identification that took place long before the commencement of any prosecution whatever." 406 U.S. 682, 689–90, 92 S.Ct. 1877, 1882–83, 32 L.Ed.2d 411, 417–18.

Stovall v. Denno (1967). The Constitution forbids any identification procedure that is "so unnecessarily suggestive and conducive to irreparable mistaken identification that he was denied due process of law. This is a recognized ground of attack upon a conviction independent of any right to counsel claim. . . . The practice of showing suspects singly to persons for the purpose of identification, and not as part of a lineup, has been widely condemned. However, a claimed violation of due process of law in the conduct of a confrontation depends on the totality of the circumstances surrounding it. . . ." 388 U.S. 293, 302, 87 S.Ct. 1967, 1972, 18 L.Ed.2d 1199, 1206.

Manson v. Brathwaite (1977). "[R]eliability is the linchpin in determining the admissibility of identification testimony for both pre- and post-*Stovall* confrontations. The factors to be considered are set out in *Biggers*. 409 U.S. at 199–200, 93 S.Ct. at 382. These include the opportunity of the witness to view the criminal at the time of the crime, the witness' degree of attention, the accuracy of his prior description of the criminal, the level of certainty demonstrated at the confrontation, and the time between the crime and the confrontation. Against these factors is to be weighed the corrupting effect of the suggestive identification itself." 432 U.S. 98, 114, 97 S.Ct. 2243, 2253, 53 L.Ed.2d 140, 154.

Simmons v. United States (1968). Evidence obtained from a photographic identification procedure will be excluded "only if the photographic identification procedure was so impermissibly suggestive as to give rise to a very substantial likelihood of irreparable misidentification." 390 U.S. 377, 384, 88 S.Ct. 967, 971, 19 L.Ed.2d 1247, 1253.

Review and Discussion Questions

1. What circumstances might justify the use of a one-way mirror during a lineup procedure? What if a witness or victim refuses to view a lineup unless a one-way mirror is used?

2. Why should a person not have a right to demand an immediate lineup to clear himself or herself and avoid the many inconveniences associated with being arrested?

3. State three ways in which a law enforcement officer conducting a lineup can decrease the suggestibility of the lineup. State three ways in which a law enforcement officer can decrease the suggestibility of a one-person showup.

4. Assume that a suspect is about to be placed in a lineup and is told by a law enforcement officer that she has a right to counsel at the lineup. If the suspect asks, "Why do I need a lawyer?" what should the officer tell her?

5. Why should photographic identification procedures not be used when a physical lineup is contemplated? What arguments would a defense attorney make at a suppression hearing under each of the following circumstances?

    a. The witness identified the defendant's photograph at a pretrial photographic display but failed to identify the defendant at a later physical lineup.

    b. The witness failed to identify the defendant's photograph at a pretrial photographic display but identified the defendant at a later physical lineup.

c. The witness identified the defendant's photograph at a pretrial photographic display and also identified the defendant at a later physical lineup.

6. Is it possible to conduct a fair lineup when the suspect is unusually tall or short or has very distinctive features or deformities?

7. Would an emergency one-person showup be justified if the suspect and not the victim were seriously injured? In what ways could the suggestibility of the showup be decreased?

8. Would certain suggestive pretrial identification procedures be excusable in a small rural police department as opposed to a large urban police department? What procedures might be excusable, and why?

9. Discuss the following quotation from Justice William J. Brennan's dissenting opinion in *United States v. Ash*, 413 U.S. 300, 344, 93 S.Ct 2568, 2591, 37 L.Ed.2d 619, 646–47 (1973), in which the U.S. Supreme Court held that there is no right to counsel at any photographic identification procedure: "There is something ironic about the Court's conclusion today that a pretrial lineup identification is a 'critical stage' of the prosecution because counsel's presence can help to compensate for the accused's deficiencies as an observer, but that a pretrial photographic identification is not a 'critical stage' of the prosecution because the accused is not able to observe at all."

10. Would there be any need for counsel at a lineup if the entire lineup procedure were recorded on both audiotape and videotape?

Real-Life Fact Situations

1 On the night of March 18, 1997, Thomas Rund ("Rund"), a detective with the City of St. Louis Police Department, arrested Appellant for a misdemeanor capias warrant. At the time of his arrest, Rund verbally advised Appellant of his *Miranda* rights. Appellant indicated he understood those rights, and he did not ask for a lawyer.

After arriving at the police station, Rund informed Appellant about an investigation concerning five robberies occurring near the area in which Appellant was arrested. In particular, Rund questioned Appellant for about ten minutes regarding a robbery occurring the night before involving a victim named Bridgette Sinar ("Sinar"). Appellant stated that he did approach a woman at the robbery location and ask her for some money.

Subsequently, Rund contacted Sinar to request her presence at the police station to view a physical lineup. Rund selected four individuals with a similar description as Appellant who were already incarcerated in a holdover to participate in the lineup with Appellant. Rund informed Sinar that she would see five individuals in the lineup, and if she recognized one of the individuals as the person who approached her during the robbery in question, she should identify the individual by an assigned number.

Prior to the lineup, Rund advised Appellant that he was going to be placed in the lineup. At this time, approximately 1:30 A.M., Appellant provided Rund with the name of an attorney whom he requested Rund contact. Rund attempted to contact the attorney prior to the lineup, but he was unsuccessful. Later in the morning, after the lineup, Rund left a message with the attorney's secretary.

Initially, Appellant refused to stand up for the lineup, even after he was requested to do so. Thus, two officers brought Appellant to his feet, and during the lineup, they stood behind Appellant so that he could be viewed. Sinar identified Appellant as her assailant.

Following Sinar's identification of Appellant in the lineup, Rund again advised Appellant of his *Miranda* rights. Appellant completed a warning and waiver form, indicating that he understood and waived those rights. Appellant did not ask for a lawyer at this time. Part of the warning and waiver form included a written statement by Appellant confessing to the robberies. Appellant signed the form, which was dated March 19, 1997, at 2:30 A.M. No threats or promises were made to Appellant for completing this statement.

Subsequently, Rund conducted lineups for each of the other robbery victims, each of whom identified Appellant as their assailant. Should the Appellant's motion to suppress statements and motion to suppress identification be granted? *State v. Lanos*, 14 S.W.3d 90 (Mo.App. 2000).

Read the court opinion at:
www.lawyersweekly.com/mocoa/75693.htm

2 On March 31, 1999, a white male wearing sunglasses and a blue hat resembling those issued by the LaPrairie Mutual Insurance Company approached Denise Brown, the walk-up teller at Heritage Bank. He told Brown to remove all of the money from the drawer, but then, speaking in a low voice, he altered his instructions and indicated that he wanted only bundles and no

$1 bills. Brown later said that she paid close attention to his mouth and lower face, because she was concerned that the robber might become agitated if she had difficulty understanding him. In the 50-some seconds she had to observe him, she also formed the impression that he was lightly unshaven, between 5'6" and 5'8" tall, about 150 pounds, and between 35 and 45 years old. The other teller on duty, Karen Jones, was serving drive-up customers and thus caught only a glimpse of the robber; her description of him was similar to Brown's.

The next day, someone gave Peoria police officers and FBI agents a tip that a woman named Kim Salzman could help them. Salzman was cooperative. She told the officers that the person in the surveillance video from the bank strongly resembled her brother, Randy Downs. Her statement, along with her account that Downs's gambling problems had led him to break into her printing business and steal a compressor in order to pawn it, increased the suspicions of the investigators. They decided to assemble a photo array and show it to both Brown and Jones. They did so, but neither was able positively to identify Downs as the robber from the pictures. Brown suggested that it would be more helpful to see people wearing hats and sunglasses.

Later that day, the officers interviewed Downs himself, first on a gambling boat and then later in a security office. The next day, they talked to Richard Downs, his father. The elder Mr. Downs told the officers that he had given Randy a hat from LaPrairie Mutual Insurance very similar to the one that appeared on the video. He also volunteered that when he had refused to loan Randy $2,000, Randy had responded "you leave me little choice." After this, the officers searched Randy's apartment, with his consent; they found nothing there.

On April 5, the officers held the line-up that is the focus of this appeal. On that day, they had finally arrested Downs and brought him to the police station. One officer telephoned Jones and asked her to come to the station, and he informed Jones that they had arrested someone. Another officer called Brown and asked her to come, but it is unclear whether or not she was told there had been an arrest. For the line-up, each person was given a LaPrairie Mutual hat and a pair of sunglasses. They entered the room seriatim; each man stepped in, walked around, and said "No, put the money in the envelope, hurry." Downs was the second to walk in. As the exhibits Downs later introduced make crystal clear, the other four all sported heavy moustaches; only Downs had no facial hair at all. Otherwise (but it is a big "otherwise"), they were similar in body build.

At the line-up, both Brown and Jones identified Downs as the robber. Jones was not very confident in her choice, describing her certainty as a seven out of ten, if ten meant absolutely sure. Brown, in contrast, jumped behind one of the detectives the minute she saw Downs enter the room, and exclaimed "Oh my God, that's him." She was crying and trembling, according to the testimony of another officer. Brown then viewed the last three line-up participants, and at the end reiterated that she

was "positive" the robber was Downs, based on "the lower half of his face" and his "stocky upper body." Should Downs's motion to suppress both the line-up and any in-court identification by Brown or Jones be granted? *United States v. Downs,* 230 F.3d 272 (7th Cir. 2000).

Read the court opinion at:
laws.findlaw.com/7th/993760.html

3 On the morning of October 30, 1998, Tim Seese, a delivery man for Grady Sims d/b/a Sims Distributing Company, a distributor of Tom's snack foods, parked the company delivery van in front of Laird's Hospital in Union, Mississippi. Seese left the doors of the van open as he was inside of the hospital making an inventory of the snack machines and refilling them. Sherry Whinery and Faye Walker, two of the hospital's employees, approached Seese to inform him that they had witnessed two individuals take something from the delivery van driven by Seese. Upon returning to the van, Seese ascertained that between $500 to $600 in coins and one dollar bills was missing from the van.

Following a call to the police by the witnesses, an investigation of this incident took place. The investigation led to the questioning of Whinery and Walker. They provided a detailed description of the thieves to the police, including the fact that they were two black men. As well, Whinery and Walker gave a detailed description of the car in which the perpetrators drove away, including the make and color of the car, and the Alabama license plate number. A report was then radioed out to all nearby law enforcement agents. Soon after, the police pulled over a vehicle matching the description given by Whinery and Walker. The car was occupied by Stradford and Richards Burks. Burks and Stradford were immediately apprehended and a search of the vehicle ensued. No money was found in the car at the time of the search; however, it was later recovered by a highway maintenance worker along a roadside, apparently having been dumped there after the crime.

About two hours after Burks and Stradford were arrested, Whinery and Walker were shown photographs of six black men. At that time, they identified Burks and Stradford as the men they saw robbing the delivery van at the hospital. Before the trial began, Burks filed a motion to suppress the identification testimony of Whinery and Walker. [Stradford claims that the photographs of him and Burks were the only photographs where there was not present an identification tag worn by criminals who had been arrested.] At trial, both Burks and Stradford objected to this identification testimony. A hearing was conducted outside the presence of the jury regarding the motion and objections. The trial judge denied the motion and overruled the objections, allowing the testimony to be heard by the jury. Stradford cites error on the part of the trial court for failing to suppress such testimony. Should the court have suppressed the testimony? *Stradford v. State*, 771 So.2d 390 (Miss.App. 2000).

Read the court opinion at:
www.mslawyer.com/mssc/ctapp/20001107/9901755.html

4 As two female pedestrians were walking across the Duke Ellington Bridge from Adams Morgan to Connecticut Avenue shortly after midnight on August 23, 1996, a car approached. Men in the car made harassing comments to the women, which they ignored. As the women continued to walk away, the car cut in front of them. A man alighted from the vehicle, brandishing a weapon. One pedestrian, Ms. Moriconi, ran across the street to avoid the car, and hid behind a street light. But the other pedestrian, Ms. Dizon, remained and was faced by the assailant directly. The assailant pointed the gun at her and grabbed her clutch purse away from her. The man then hit her in the face with the gun, saying "I don't like your attitude, bitch," and got back into the car. The car drove away, passing within seven feet of Ms. Moriconi.

Police responded shortly thereafter and were given descriptions of the assailant and the driver, as well as the car they drove. The police broadcast a lookout for the car and for the two men, one of whom was said to be armed. In a matter of minutes, an officer spotted a car matching the description, heading the wrong way with its lights off on California Street, in the vicinity of the crime. The officer tried to pull the car over, but the car sped away. After a short chase, the car was eventually stopped by another police cruiser at Kalorama Circle. Several officers were on the scene as the car was stopped and the passenger, who was appellant Maddox, and the driver, who was appellant Davis, were removed from the vehicle.

While Maddox and Davis were secured, another officer, Officer Felicia Toronto, searched the car for weapons. The glove compartment was open, so the officer looked inside and removed a clutch purse that was obstructing her view of the compartment. The officer placed the purse on the passenger seat and continued to search, but did not find a weapon. She left the purse, apparently open, on the seat.

Detective Hugh Carew then came to the scene and observed, through the window of the car, the open purse and an exposed identification card of Debra Dizon. He called an officer at the scene of the crime to confirm whether one of the complainants' names matched that of the identification on the passenger seat. After finding that the identification did indeed match the name of the victim, he seized the purse.

While Ms. Dizon was taken to a local emergency room for treatment for a serious gash inflicted by the assailant's weapon which required at least 40 stitches, Ms. Moriconi was escorted from the crime scene to the spot where the car was stopped to determine whether the men stopped could be identified as the perpetrators. Prior to arriving, she was informed that two men

fitting her general description had been found. There, she identified appellant Maddox as the assailant and appellant Davis as the driver of the car involved in the incident. Approximately an hour later, the police brought Maddox to the hospital where Ms. Dizon was being treated. There, she identified Maddox as the assailant. Should appellants' motions to suppress evidence of these identifications by the two victims and to suppress the clutch purse and its identification card be granted? *Maddox v. United States*, 745 A.2d 284 (D.C.App. 2000).

Read the court opinion at:
www.dcbar.org/dcca/pdf/97cf1670.pdf

5 On April 6, 1993, at approximately 4:30 A.M., the victim drove to the Econo Foods supermarket in Iron Mountain, Michigan, in order to pick up doughnuts for the guests of the Super Eight Motel. After coming out of the supermarket, the victim was abducted by a man hiding in the back seat of her car. The man brandished a knife and instructed the victim to drive to a secluded spot along a dirt road, where he ordered her to climb into the back seat. The man then forced the victim to disrobe, to kiss him on the lips, and to perform oral sex. Shortly thereafter, the headlights of a police car appeared behind the victim's car. The man instructed the victim to put her shirt back on, climb back into the front seat, and drive away from the area.

After driving around for a while, the man instructed the victim to park along a residential street in Iron Mountain and once again had her climb into the back seat. This time he forced the victim to perform oral and vaginal intercourse. He then had her drive to a point near a gas station where he got out of the car. The victim returned to the Super Eight Motel and reported the incident to the police. She described her attacker as an unshaven, dark complexioned white man of medium build, about six feet tall, forty to fifty years old, with uncombed, dirty dishwater blond hair and odd looking lips. He had been drinking, smelled bad, and smoked a darker than normal cigarette.

The defendant ultimately became the prime suspect. The police took defendant into custody and arranged a corporal lineup. The victim tentatively identified the defendant as her assailant at the lineup. She made the following statement after the lineup:

I was called at 2:00 P.M. to come down to look at a line-up. I looked at eight people. Number six looked like him, but I can't be sure. His eyes and face fit, but his lips were what threw me off. His eyes really look like the eyes I remember. I can't be positive, but there is something about his eyes and face.

The police arrested and charged defendant with one count of kidnapping and two counts of third-degree CSC after the lineup. Later that evening, Officer Revord went to the victim's home to inform her that the police had arrested a suspect. During the visit, Officer Revord showed the victim a single photograph of the defendant. After seeing the photograph, she became sure that defendant was the one who attacked her. As she testified at the hearing on defendant's motion to suppress the identification:

When I was relaxed after the line-up and I was at home, Officer Revord came over and he showed me the picture and it was at that time that I had no doubts that it was him.

The trial court denied a motion by defendant to prohibit an in-court identification of defendant by the victim, holding that although the use of the photograph by Officer Revord was improper, there was a sufficiently independent basis for the victim to identify Mr. Gray at trial. Pursuant to his plea agreement, defendant appealed the denial of his motion. Should his appeal be granted? *People v. Gray*, 577 N.W.2d 92 (Mich. 2000).

Read the court opinion at:
www.lawyersweekly.com/misup/106442.htm

6 At approximately 10:00 P.M. on June 6, 1999, a man entered Eileen Olson's apartment through a patio door and robbed her. According to Olson, the man was in her apartment for about ten to fifteen minutes. The man hit Olson, cut her with a knife, and threatened to kill her. Olson described her assailant as a 45 year old white male wearing a baseball hat, a dark plaid shirt, and blue jeans. Olson was treated for her injuries at a Fargo hospital, where police officers showed her a picture of Norrid, a suspect they had detained and photographed near her apartment. Olson did not have her glasses at the hospital, and she was unable to positively identify Norrid as her assailant. After officers retrieved her glasses from her apartment, she was still unable to positively identify Norrid as her assailant, and she indicated "it was hard for me to look at those pictures cause my

glasses were so bent out of shape." At approximately 12:30 A.M., Olson was taken to a location near the scene of the crime to personally view Norrid. Olson indicated "[t]hey put a spot light on him and asked me if that was the man that had assaulted me. And I said I was 99 percent sure, I said I just—I just—I hated to think that I would get an innocent man or anything and I wanted to stay and make sure. So we sat for a long time until I was positive it was him."

Prior to Olson's identification of Norrid as her assailant, police officers detained him and gave him warnings required by *Miranda v. Arizona*, 384 U.S. 436, 86 S.Ct. 1602, 16 L.Ed.2d 694 (1966). After Olson identified Norrid, he was taken to the police station at approximately 3:00 A.M. and again given *Miranda* warnings. Detective Jim LeDoux interviewed Norrid at the police station. Norrid initially denied involvement in the incident, but at 6:15 A.M., he signed a written statement implicating himself in the incident.

The State charged Norrid with burglary, aggravated assault, and terrorizing. Norrid moved to suppress Olson's identification of him, arguing it was unduly suggestive and violated his due process rights under the Fourteenth Amendment of the United States Constitution. Norrid also moved to suppress statements he made to police officers, arguing the statements were extracted through deception and coercion and violated his privilege against self-incrimination under the Fifth and Fourteenth Amendments. Should Norrid's motions be granted? *State v. Norrid*, 611 N.W.2d 866 (N.D. 2000)

Read the court opinion at:
www.court.state.nd.us/court/opinions/990308.htm

GLOSSARY

dictionary.law.com
The Real Life Dictionary of the Law

www.lectlaw.com/def.htm
The 'Lectric Law Library's comprehensive legal dictionary

dictionary.findlaw.com
Findlaw Law Dictionary

www.nolo.com/dictionary/wordindex.cfm
Nolo's Legal Dictionary

www.wwlia.org/diction.htm
Duhaime's Law Dictionary

www.wld.com/conbus/orans/welcome.asp
Oran's Dictionary of the Law

fountcom.com/folio/glossary.html
CongressLink Glossary of Legal and Government Terms

www.uscourts.gov/understanding_courts/gloss.htm
Federal Judiciary Glossary of Terms

www.ncmd.uscourts.gov/glossary.htm
Glossary of Frequently-Used Terms in the Federal District Court System

dictionary.prisonwall.org
A Prisoner's Dictionary

www.numismaticrareuscoin.com/nbn/defs.html
Definitions of antiquated legal terms

www.1000dictionaries.com/legal_dictionaries_1.html
Links to free online dictionaries on all aspects of the law

Definitions for this glossary are taken from Ferdico's *Criminal Law and Justice Dictionary*, also published by Wadsworth Publishing Company.

Abandoned Property. Property whose owner has voluntarily discarded, left behind, or otherwise relinquished his or her interest in the property in question so that the owner could no longer retain a reasonable expectation of privacy with regard to it. Law enforcement officers may lawfully seize abandoned property without a warrant or probable cause because the Fourth Amendment is inapplicable.

Acquittal. A judgment of a court, based either on the verdict of a jury or of a judicial officer in a nonjury trial, that the defendant is not guilty of the offense for which he or she has been tried. An acquittal on all charges is a final court disposition terminating criminal jurisdiction over the defendant.

Administrative Search. A routine inspection of a home or business by governmental authorities responsible for determining compliance with various statutes and regulations. An administrative search seeks to enforce fire, health, safety, and housing codes, licensing provisions, and the like. It differs from a criminal search in that a criminal search is directed toward gathering evidence in order to convict a person of a crime. An administrative search ordinarily does not result in a criminal prosecution.

Admission. A statement or acknowledgment of a fact by a person tending to incriminate the person but not sufficient of itself to establish guilt of a crime. An admission, alone or in connection with other facts, tends to show the existence of one or more, but not all, of the elements of a crime. See **Confession.**

Affidavit. A written statement sworn to or affirmed before an officer authorized to administer an oath or affirmation. An affidavit may be distinguished from a deposition in some contexts in that an affidavit requires no notice to the adverse party or opportunity for cross-examination. In the criminal law, affidavits are used by law enforcement officers and others to provide information to a magistrate to establish probable cause for the issuance of an arrest warrant or a search warrant.

Anticipatory Search Warrant. A warrant to search a particular place for a particular seizable item that has not yet arrived at the place where the search is to be executed.

Appeal. An application to or proceeding in an appellate court for review or rehearing of a judgment, decision, or order of a lower court or other tribunal in order to correct alleged errors or injustices in the trial below. A successful appeal results in the reversal or modification of the lower court judgment, decision, or order. An appeal may be either on the record of the proceedings below or de novo. In an appeal on the record only, matters of law may be reviewed. In an appeal de novo, matters of fact as well as law may be reviewed.

Appellate Jurisdiction. Lawful authority or power of a court to review a decision made by a lower court or to hear an appeal from a judgment of a lower court.

Arraignment. The hearing before a court having jurisdiction in a criminal case, in which the identity of the defendant is established, the defendant is informed of the charge and of his or her rights, and the defendant is required to enter a plea. The defendant's entering of a plea is the crucial distinguishing element of the arraignment. Besides the pleas of guilty or not guilty, courts of many states and the federal courts permit pleas of nolo contendere and some accept pleas of not guilty by reason of insanity or former jeopardy.

Arrest. The taking of a person into the custody of the law for the purpose of charging the person with a criminal offense or a delinquent act or status offense. The basic elements necessary to constitute a formal arrest are:

1. a law enforcement officer's purpose or intention to effect an arrest;

2. a law enforcement officer acting under real or pretended authority;

3. an actual or constructive seizure or detention of the person to be arrested by an officer having the present power to control the person; and

4. understanding by the person to be arrested that it is the intention of the arresting officer then and there to arrest and detain him or her.

In order to make a lawful formal arrest without a warrant, a law enforcement officer must either have probable cause to believe that the person to be arrested is committing or has committed a felony or the person to be arrested must be committing a misdemeanor in the officer's presence.

Even though an officer does not intend to make a formal arrest, a court may find that the officer's actions are tantamount to an arrest if they are indistinguishable from an arrest in important respects. If an officer seizes (see **Seizure,** definition 1) or detains a person significantly, beyond a mere stop or other minor investigatory detention, the seizure or detention may nevertheless be considered an arrest for purposes of the Fourth Amendment, even if the officer does not comply with all the requirements of a formal arrest. As such, the seizure or detention will be ruled illegal unless it is supported by probable cause.

Arrest Warrant. A written order issued by a magistrate or other proper judicial officer, upon probable cause, directing a law enforcement officer to arrest a particular person. An arrest warrant is issued on the basis of a sworn complaint charging that the accused person has committed a crime. The arrest warrant must identify the person to be arrested by name and/or other unique characteristics and must describe the crime.

Attenuation of Taint. See **Fruit of the Poisonous Tree Doctrine.**

Automobile Exception. See *Carroll* **Doctrine.**

Bail. To obtain the release from custody of an arrested or imprisoned person by pledging money or other property as a guarantee of the person's appearance in court at a specified date and time. The purposes of bail are to prevent the imprisonment of an accused prior to trial and to ensure his or her appearance at trial. The court may or may not require that the pledge of money or property be secured. Pledges may be secured in several ways. The most common way is by employment of a bail bondsman, to whom a nonrefundable fee is paid. In other cases the court can require a deposit of money before the person is released. The requirement can be for the full amount pledged, or for a percentage of the amount pledged.

Beeper. A radio transmitter, usually battery operated, which emits periodic signals that can be picked up by a radio receiver.

Bench Trial. Same as **Nonjury Trial.**

Booking. A police administrative procedure officially recording an arrest in a police register. Booking involves, at the minimum, recording the name of the person arrested, the officer making the arrest, and the time of, place of, circumstances of, and reason for the arrest. The meaning of booking, however, is sometimes expanded to include other procedures that take place in the station house after an arrest. Booking may include a search of the arrested person, including in some cases a search of body cavities, fingerprinting, photographing, a lineup, or other identification procedures. Booking is usually completed before the arrested person is taken for his or her initial appearance before the magistrate.

Burden of Proof. The duty to establish a particular issue or proposition by the quantity of evidence required by law. The prosecution has the burden of proof to establish every element of the crime charged beyond a reasonable doubt.

***Carroll* Doctrine.** The search and seizure doctrine, originating in the case of *Carroll v. United States,* 267 U.S. 132, 45 S.Ct. 280, 69 L.Ed. 543 (1925), that a warrantless search of a motor vehicle under exigent circumstances by a law enforcement officer who has probable cause to believe that the vehicle contains items subject to seizure is not unreasonable under the Fourth Amendment. The doctrine is sometimes referred to as the automobile exception to the search warrant requirement. "As a general rule, [the

U.S. Supreme Court has] required the judgment of a magistrate on the probable cause issue and the issuance of a warrant before a search is made. Only in exigent circumstances will the judgment of the police as to probable cause serve as a sufficient authorization for a search." *Chambers v. Maroney,* 399 U.S. 42, 51, 90 S.Ct. 1975, 1981, 26 L.Ed.2d 419, 428 (1970). Usually, exigent circumstances are established by demonstrating specific facts showing either that the vehicle may be moved to an unknown location out of the jurisdiction, making a search under authority of a warrant impossible, or that items subject to seizure may be removed from the vehicle and concealed or destroyed. The U.S. Supreme Court has held, however, that this is not necessary and that the exigent circumstances requirement is automatically satisfied in the case of a readily mobile motor vehicle. "If a car is readily mobile and probable cause exists to believe it contains contraband, the Fourth Amendment . . . permits police to search the vehicle without more." *Pennsylvania v. Labron,* 518 U.S. 938, 940, 116 S.Ct. 2485, 2487, 135 L.Ed.2d 1031, 1036 (1996).

Challenge for Cause. A formal objection to a prospective juror directed toward the qualifications of that juror. The party exercising a challenge for cause has an unlimited number of such challenges. Each challenge for cause, however, must be supported by a satisfactory reason or the judge will not dismiss the challenged juror. A general challenge for cause is an objection that the prospective juror is unqualified to serve in any case because of conviction of crime, unsoundness of mind, etc. A special or particular challenge for cause is an objection that the juror is unqualified to serve in the case to be tried because the juror has formed an opinion in the case, has a bias toward one of the parties, etc.

Civil Rights. Generally, the constitutionally guaranteed rights of a person by virtue of the person's status as a member of civil society, except those rights involving participation in the establishment, support, or management of the government. Examples of civil rights are those rights to personal liberty established by the bill of rights and by the Thirteenth and Fourteenth Amendments to the Constitution and other congressional acts.

Closing Argument. The part of a trial after all the evidence has been presented and the jury has been instructed in which each party recapitulates the facts and evidence it has presented and attempts to convince the judge or jury of the correctness of its position.

Collateral Estoppel Doctrine. When an issue of ultimate fact has once been determined by a valid and final judgment, that issue cannot again be litigated between the same parties in any future lawsuit.

Common Law. The system of law, originated and developed in England, based on court decisions and on custom and usage, rather than on written laws created by legislative enactment. "The common law does not consist of absolute, fixed, and inflexible rules, but rather of broad and comprehensive principles based on justice, reason, and common sense. It is of judicial origin and promulgation. Its principles have been determined by the social needs of the community and have changed with changes in such needs. These principles are susceptible of adaptation to new conditions, interests, relations and usages as the progress of society may require." *Miller v. Monsen,* 37 N.W.2d 543, 547 (Minn. 1949).

Complaint. A sworn written statement presented to a magistrate or other proper judicial officer alleging that a specified person has committed a specified crime and requesting prosecution. The complaint must state the essential facts constituting the crime charged, including the time and place of its commission and the name or description of the defendant. If the defendant has been arrested without an arrest warrant, the complaint may serve as the charging document upon which the preliminary examination is held. If the defendant has not been arrested, the complaint serves as the basis for determining whether there is probable cause to justify the issuance of a warrant for the arrest. Most jurisdictions call the charging document filed in a misdemeanor case or at the first step of a felony case a complaint, and the document filed to initiate trial proceedings at the second step of a felony case an information. In some jurisdictions, the document filed to bind over a defendant until a grand jury decides whether or not to issue an indictment is also called a complaint.

Compulsory Process. Coercive means used by courts to procure the attendance in court of persons wanted as witnesses or otherwise. Examples of compulsory process are subpoenas and arrest warrants. The Sixth Amendment to the U.S. Constitution guarantees a defendant the right to have compulsory process to obtain witnesses in his or her favor. The right makes the subpoena power of the court available to a defendant only with respect to competent, material witnesses subject to the court's process, whose expected testimony will be admissible.

Confession. A statement whereby a person admits facts revealing his or her guilt as to all elements of a particular crime. See **Admission.**

Confrontation. 1. The right of confrontation is the right of an accused person to come face to face with an adverse witness in the court, so the accused person has the opportunity to object to the testimony of the witness and to cross-examine the witness. The Sixth Amendment to the U.S. Constitution guarantees the right of confrontation to defendants in federal criminal prosecutions. The due process clause of the Fourteenth Amendment makes this Sixth Amendment guarantee applicable to the states. 2. Any presentation of a suspect to a victim or witness of a crime for the purpose of identifying the perpetrator of the crime. The term confrontation includes both lineups and showups.

Consent Search. A search of a person's body, premises, or belongings conducted by a law enforcement officer with the person's permission. A consent search is lawful only if the totality of circumstances surrounding the search indicates that the consent was voluntary. A person may limit the scope of a consent search by words or actions and may revoke the consent to search at any time. A person may not consent to the search of a third person's premises or property unless the third person has specifically given the person authority to do so or the person possesses "common authority over or other sufficient relationship to the premises or effects sought to be inspected." Common authority rests "on mutual use of the property by persons generally having joint access or control for most purposes, so that it is reasonable to recognize that any of the coinhabitants has the right to permit the inspection in his own right and that the others have assumed the risk that one of their number might permit the common area to be searched." *United States v. Matlock*, 415 U.S. 164, 171 n.7, 94 S.Ct. 988, 993 n.7, 39 L.Ed.2d 242, 250 n.7 (1974).

Contraband. Goods the possession of which is prohibited.

Corroborate. To support or enhance the believability of a fact or assertion by presenting additional information that confirms or strengthens the truthfulness of the fact or assertion. A law enforcement officer applying for a search warrant or arrest warrant based on information from an informant may increase the likelihood of the warrant issuing by presenting in the affidavit information that corroborates the information provided by the informant.

Court of General Jurisdiction. Speaking only of criminal courts, a court that has trial jurisdiction over all criminal offenses, including all felonies, and that may or may not hear appeals. A court of general jurisdiction has original jurisdiction over all felonies and frequently has appellate jurisdiction over the decisions of a court of limited jurisdiction. The decisions of a court of general jurisdiction may be reviewed by an appellate court. Courts of general jurisdiction are commonly named superior court, district court, and circuit court. The factual determination of a court of general jurisdiction is final. Appeals are on the record and on matters of law rather than on matters of fact.

Court of Limited Jurisdiction. Speaking only of criminal courts, a court whose trial jurisdiction either includes no felonies or is limited to less than all felonies, and which may or may not hear appeals. A court of limited jurisdiction is limited to a particular class or classes of cases, and cannot try every felony. A court of limited jurisdiction often has jurisdiction over misdemeanor or traffic cases, over the initial setting of bail and preliminary examinations in felony cases, and occasionally over felony trials where the penalty prescribed for the offense is below a statutorily specified limit. In these cases, the courts of general jurisdiction maintain concurrent jurisdiction over those felonies that the courts of limited jurisdiction are also empowered to try. In some jurisdictions a court of general jurisdiction may hear appeals from a court of limited jurisdiction, and in some cases may review decisions of a court of limited jurisdiction de novo. In other jurisdictions, appeals from a court of limited jurisdiction are made directly to an appellate court, bypassing the court of general jurisdiction. With respect to civil actions, a court of limited jurisdiction may be limited to a certain type of case, or to cases where the amount in controversy is below a statutorily specified limit. Courts of limited jurisdiction are commonly named city court, county court, district court, domestic relations court, family court, justice court, magistrate court, municipal court, police court, probate court, small claims court, and traffic court.

Cross-Examination. The questioning of a witness by the party opposed to the party producing the witness. Cross-examination comes after direct examination of the witness by the party producing the witness. The purpose of cross-examination is to discredit the witness's information and impeach the witness's credibility as a means of testing the accuracy of his or her testimony. The scope of cross-examination is usually limited to matters covered during direct examination.

Curtilage. The ground and buildings immediately surrounding a dwelling and used for domestic purposes in connection with the dwelling. Under the Fourth Amendment to the U.S. Constitution, "[t]he right of the people to be secure in their persons, houses, papers, and effects, against unreasonable searches and seizures, shall not be violated. . . ." Courts have extended the meaning of houses under the Fourth Amendment to include the curtilage. To determine whether property falls within the curtilage of a house, one must consider "the factors that determine whether an individual reasonably may expect that an area immediately adjacent to the home will remain private." *Oliver v. United States*, 466 U.S. 170, 180, 104 S.Ct. 1735, 1742, 80 L.Ed.2d 214, 225 (1984). The U.S. Supreme Court described those factors in another case: "[W]e believe that curtilage questions should be resolved with particular reference to four factors: the proximity of the area claimed to be curtilage to the home, whether the area is included within an enclosure surrounding the home, the nature of the uses to which the area is put, and the steps taken by the resident to protect the area from observation by people passing by." *United States v. Dunn*, 480 U.S. 294, 301, 107 S.Ct. 1134, 1139, 94 L.Ed.2d 326, 334–35 (1987). The Court emphasized that "the primary focus is whether the area in question harbors those intimate activities associated with domestic life and the privacies of the home." 480 U.S. at 301 n.4, 107 S.Ct. at 1139 n.4, 94 L.Ed.2d at 335 n.4.

Custodial Arrest. An arrest in which the person arrested is taken into custody and not merely given a ticket, citation, or notice to appear. Whether or not an arrest is custodial is a determining factor in justifying a search incident to arrest. The U.S. Supreme Court held that "in the case of lawful custodial arrest, a full search of the person is not only an exception to the warrant requirement of the Fourth Amendment, but is also a 'reasonable' search under that Amendment." *United States v. Robinson*, 414 U.S. 218, 235, 94 S.Ct. 467, 477, 38 L.Ed.2d 427, 441 (1973).

Custody. 1. Legal or physical control of a person or thing; legal, supervisory or physical responsibility for a person or thing. The term custody has several degrees of meaning, depending on the context in which it is used, and may mean actual imprisonment or the mere power, legal or physical, to imprison or take into physical possession. It ranges from the clearest legal and physical control and responsibility, as when a legally arrested person is in the custody of a police officer, to physical control without legal justification, as when a jail holds prisoners in its custody who are legally under the jurisdiction of a state prison system. Custody also applies to physical objects, such as evidence taken into custody by law enforcement investigators. 2. A person is in custody for purposes of *Miranda v. Arizona* when the person is deprived of freedom of action in any significant way. The U.S. Supreme Court said: "Although the circumstances of each case must certainly influence a determination of whether a suspect is 'in custody' for purposes of receiving *Miranda* protection, the ultimate inquiry is simply whether there is a 'formal arrest or restraint on freedom of movement' of the degree associated with a formal arrest." *California v. Beheler*, 463 U.S. 1121, 1125, 103 S.Ct. 3517, 3520, 77 L.Ed.2d 1275, 1279 (1983).

Deposition. Out-of-court testimony of a witness, taken under oath prior to trial and reduced to writing. A deposition is taken either orally or upon written interrogatories with notice to the adverse party so that the adverse party may attend and cross-examine. If it appears that a prospective witness may be unable to attend or be prevented from attending a trial or hearing, that the witness's testimony is material, and that it is necessary to take the witness's deposition to prevent a failure of justice, the court may, upon motion and notice to the parties, order that the witness's testimony be taken by deposition. At the trial or hearing, the deposition, or any part of it, may be used if the court finds that:

- the witness is dead;
- the witness is out of the jurisdiction, unless the court finds that the absence of the witness was procured by the party offering the deposition;
- the witness is unable to attend or testify because of sickness or infirmity; or
- the party offering the deposition has been unable to procure the attendance of the witness by subpoena.

A deposition may also be used by any party for the purpose of contradicting or impeaching the testimony of the deponent as a witness.

Derivative Evidence. See **Fruit of the Poisonous Tree Doctrine.**

Direct Examination. The first interrogation or examination of a witness in a trial by the party on whose behalf the witness is called. The direct examination consists of specific questions asked by the attorney for the party calling the witness, and the witness is expected to give testimony favorable to the party calling the witness.

Discovery. A procedure by which a party obtains a legal right to compel the opposing party to allow him or her to obtain, inspect, copy, or photograph items within the possession or control of the opposing party. Among the items subject to discovery are tangible objects, tape recordings, books, and papers, including written or recorded statements made by the defendants or witnesses, and the results or reports of physical examinations and scientific tests, experiments, and comparisons. Information usually not subject to discovery includes investigators' notes, lawyers' work product, and anything that would violate the defendant's constitutional privilege against compelled self-incrimination.

The general purpose of discovery is "to promote the orderly ascertainment of the truth" during trial. Ordinarily, to obtain the right to discovery, a party must make a motion before the court and must show that the specific items sought may be material to the preparation of its case and that its request is reasonable. A recent development is automatic informal discovery for certain types of evidence, without the necessity for motions and court orders. The state of the law governing discovery is constantly changing, but the trend appears to be in favor of broadening the right of discovery for both the defense and the prosecution. The federal government and the states have varying statutes and rules relating to the nature and scope of the information required to be disclosed in the discovery process.

Double Jeopardy. A legal doctrine that "protects against a second prosecution for the same offense after acquittal, against a second prosecution for the same offense after conviction, and against multiple punishments for the same offense." *Justices of Boston Municipal Court v. Lydon*, 466 U.S. 294, 306–07, 104 S.Ct. 1805, 1812, 80 L.Ed.2d 311, 323 (1984). The Fifth Amendment to the U.S. Constitution prohibits placing a person in double jeopardy ("nor shall any person be subject for the same offense to be twice put in jeopardy of life or limb"). "Same offense," under two different tests, means either an offense requiring the same evidence to sustain a conviction or an offense arising from the same criminal act or transaction. The stage of the prosecution at which a person is considered to be in danger of conviction differs in different jurisdictions. Generally, however, an accused is in legal jeopardy in a trial at the moment the jury is sworn or, in nonjury trials, when the first witness is sworn. The constitutional protection against double jeopardy is extended to state prosecutions through the due process clause of the Fourteenth Amendment as a result of the U.S. Supreme Court decision in *Benton v. Maryland, 395 U.S. 784, 89 S.Ct. 2056, 23 L.Ed.2d 707 (1989).* Nevertheless, the double jeopardy clause does not bar a state prosecution of a defendant who was acquitted on a federal charge arising out of the same criminal act.

Dual Sovereignty Doctrine. The doctrine under which, "[w]hen a defendant in a single act violates the 'peace and dignity' of two sovereigns by breaking the laws of each, he has committed two distinct 'offences.' " *Heath v. Alabama, 474 U.S. 82, 88, 106 S.Ct. 433, 437, 88 L.Ed.2d 387 (1985).* The dual sovereignty doctrine is limited, by its own terms, to cases where the two entities that seek successively to prosecute a defendant for the same course of conduct can be termed separate sovereigns. This determination turns on whether the two entities draw their authority to punish the offender from distinct sources of power, not on whether they are pursuing separate interests. Double jeopardy does not arise when a single act exposes a defendant to prosecution by two separate sovereigns such as the federal government and a state government or the governments of two different states.

Due Process of Law. Another name for governmental fair play, i.e., laws and procedures that conform to the rules and principles established in our system of justice for the enforcement and protection of individual rights. Some of the essential elements of due process of law, with respect to criminal justice, are: a law creating and clearly defining the offense and punishment; an impartial tribunal having jurisdictional authority over the case; accusation in proper form; notice and opportunity to appear, to be heard, and to defend against charges; trial according to established procedure; and discharge from all restraints or obligations unless convicted. The Fifth Amendment to the U.S. Constitution provides that "nor [shall any person] be deprived of life, liberty, or property, without due process of law." This provision applies only to actions of the federal government. The due process requirement was made applicable to the states by the Fourteenth Amendment, Section 1, which states "nor shall any State deprive any person of life, liberty, or property, without due process of law." The meaning of due process of law is not fixed but changes with changing jurisprudential attitudes of fair play. In his concurring opinion in the 1951 case of *Joint Anti-Fascist Refugee Committee v. McGrath*, Justice Frankfurter said:

> The requirement of "due process" is not a fair weather or timid assurance. It must be respected in periods of calm and in times of trouble; it protects aliens as well as citizens. But "due process," unlike some legal rules, is not a technical conception with a fixed content unrelated to time, place and circumstances. Expressing as it does in its ultimate analysis respect enforced by law for that feeling of just treatment which has been evolved through centuries of Anglo-American constitutional history and civilization, "due process" cannot be imprisoned within the treacherous limits of any formula. Representing a profound attitude of fairness between man and man, and more particularly between the individual and government, "due process" is compounded of history, reason, the past course of decisions, and stout confidence in the strength of the democratic faith which we profess. Due process is not a mechanical instrument. It is not a yardstick. It is a process. It is a delicate process of adjustment inescapably involving the exercise of judgment by those whom the Constitution entrusted with the

unfolding of the process. 341 U.S. 123, 162–63, 71 S.Ct. 624, 643–44, 95 L.Ed. 817, 849.

In *Green v. State, 247 A.2d 117, 121 (Me. 1968),* the court said: Due process . . . does not restrict the State to any particular mode of procedure. It protects against the exercise of arbitrary governmental power and guarantees equal and impartial dispensation of law according to the settled course of judicial proceedings or in accordance with fundamental principles of distributive justice.

Duplicitous Indictment or Information. An indictment or information that unites two or more separate and distinct offenses in the same count. By obscuring the exact charge, duplicitous indictments or informations may violate the defendant's constitutional right to notice of charges and may impair the defendant's ability to plead double jeopardy in a subsequent prosecution.

Emergency. A serious situation developing suddenly and unexpectedly and demanding immediate action; a pressing necessity; an exigency; **exigent circumstances.**

Equal Protection of the Laws. The Fourteenth Amendment to the U.S. Constitution provides, in part, that no state shall "deny to any person within its jurisdiction the equal protection of the laws." This constitutional guarantee prohibits states from denying any person or class of persons the same protection of the law enjoyed by other persons or other classes of persons in similar circumstances. No state may adopt laws, regulations, or policies that establish categories of people receiving unequal treatment on the basis of race, religion, or national origin. Thus, racial segregation in public schools and other public places, laws that prohibit the sale or use of property to certain minority groups, and laws that prohibit interracial marriage have been struck down. Furthermore, the U.S. Supreme Court held that purely private acts of discrimination can be in violation of the equal protection clause if they are customarily enforced throughout the state, whether or not there is a specific law or other explicit manifestation of action by the state.

No specific equal protection clause applies to the federal government, but the federal government is prohibited from denying a person equal protection of federal laws by judicial interpretations of the due process clause of the Fifth Amendment.

Evidence. Anything offered to a court or jury through the medium of witnesses, documents, exhibits, or other objects, to demonstrate or ascertain the truth of facts in issue in a case; the means by which facts are proved or disproved in court.

Exclusionary Rule. A rule, developed by the U.S. Supreme Court, stating that evidence obtained in violation of a person's constitutional rights by law enforcement officers or agents will be inadmissible in a criminal prosecution against the person whose rights were violated. "The exclusionary rule prohibits introduction into evidence of tangible materials seized during an unlawful search, *Weeks v. United States, 232 U.S. 383, 34 S.Ct. 341, 58 L.Ed. 652 (1914),* and of testimony concerning knowledge acquired during an unlawful search, *Silverman v. United States, 365 U.S. 505, 81 S.Ct. 679, 5 L.Ed.2d 734 (1961).* Beyond that, the exclusionary rule also prohibits the introduction of derivative evidence, both tangible and testimonial, that is the product of the primary evidence, or that is otherwise acquired as an indirect result of the unlawful search, up to the point at which the connection with the unlawful search becomes 'so attenuated as to dissipate the taint,' *Nardone v. United States, 308 U.S. 338, 341, 60 S.Ct. 266, 268, 84*

L.Ed. 307 (1939)." *Murray v. United States,* 478 U.S. 533, 536–37, 108 S.Ct. 2529, 2532–33, 101 L.Ed.2d 472, 480 (1988). The purpose of the exclusionary rule is to deter law enforcement officers and other government officials from violating the constitutional rights of suspects by removing the incentive for obtaining illegally seized evidence. The rule does not apply to evidence obtained by persons other than government officials.

Exigent Circumstances. Generally, an emergency, a pressing necessity, or a set of circumstances requiring immediate attention or swift action. In the criminal procedure context, exigent circumstances means "an emergency situation requiring swift action to prevent imminent danger to life or serious damage to property, or to forestall the imminent escape of a suspect or destruction of evidence. There is no ready litmus test for determining whether such circumstances exist, and in each case the claim of an extraordinary situation must be measured by the facts known to the officers." *People v. Ramey,* 127 Cal.Rptr. 629, 637, 545 P.2d 1333, 1341 (Cal. 1976).

Ex Post Facto. Latin. "After the fact." An ex post facto law is "one which makes that criminal which was not so at the time the action was performed, or which increases the punishment, or, in short, in relation to the offense or its consequences, alters the situation of a party to his disadvantage." *Lindsey v. Washington,* 301 U.S. 397, 57 S.Ct. 797, 81 L.Ed. 1182 (1937). Ex post facto laws are prohibited by Article I, Sections 9 and 10, of the U.S. Constitution and similar provisions of state constitutions.

Extradition. The surrender of an accused or convicted person by one state (asylum state), to which the person has fled, to the state with jurisdiction to try or punish the person (demanding state), upon demand of the latter state, so that the person may be dealt with according to its laws. The demand occurs in the form of an extradition warrant issued by the governor of the demanding state. The delivery of the person to the demanding state will occur under the executive or judicial authorization of the asylum state. The U.S. Constitution, Article IV, Section 2, requires the officials of a state to arrest and return an accused fugitive to another state for trial upon demand of the governor of the latter state. Most states have adopted the Uniform Criminal Extradition Act, which provides uniform extradition procedures among the states.

Felony. In general, a crime of a more serious nature than those designated as misdemeanors. Felonies are distinguished from misdemeanors by place of punishment and possible duration of punishment as defined by statute. The statutory definition of felony may differ between states and between the federal government and various states. Typically a felony is a crime with a possible punishment of death or imprisonment in a state or federal prison facility for a period of one year or more.

Fresh Pursuit. Immediate pursuit of a fleeing criminal with intent to apprehend him or her. Fresh pursuit generally refers to the situation in which a law enforcement officer attempts to make a valid arrest of a criminal within the officer's jurisdiction, and the criminal flees outside the jurisdiction to avoid arrest, with the officer immediately pursuing. An arrest made in fresh pursuit will be legal if the pursuit was started promptly and maintained continuously. Many states have adopted the Uniform Act on Fresh Pursuit to govern fresh pursuits that take an arresting officer into a neighboring state.

Frisk. A modified search consisting of a careful exploration of the outer surfaces of a person's clothing all over his or her body in an attempt to find weapons. The 1968 U.S. Supreme Court case of *Terry v. Ohio* set out the limits on law enforcement officers' authority to frisk persons. "[T]here must be a narrowly drawn authority to permit a reasonable search for weapons for the protection of the police officer, where he has reason to believe that he is dealing with an armed and dangerous individual, regardless of whether he has probable cause to arrest the individual for a crime." 392 U.S. 1, 27, 88 S.Ct. 1868, 1883, 20 L.Ed.2d 889, 909. In a later case, the Court extended the permissible scope of a frisk to include the passenger compartment of an automobile. "[T]he search of the passenger compartment of an automobile, limited to those areas in which a weapon may be placed or hidden, is permissible if the police officer possesses a reasonable belief based on 'specific and articulable facts which, taken together with the rational inferences from those facts, reasonably warrant' the officers in believing that the suspect is dangerous and the suspect may gain immediate control of weapons." *Michigan v. Long,* 463 U.S. 1032, 1049, 103 S.Ct. 3469, 3480, 77 L.Ed.2d 1201, 1220 (1983).

Fruit of the Poisonous Tree Doctrine. The doctrine that evidence will be inadmissible in court if it was indirectly obtained by exploitation of some prior unconstitutional police activity (such as an illegal arrest or search or a coerced confession). The evidence indirectly obtained is sometimes called derivative evidence. The doctrine derives its name from the idea that once a tree is poisoned (illegal police activity), then the fruit of the tree (derivative evidence obtained by exploiting the illegal activity) is likewise poisoned or tainted and should not be used. If, however, evidence is obtained by means sufficiently distinguishable to be purged of the taint of the primary illegality, the primary illegality has not been exploited and the evidence will be admissible. Courts refer to this as attenuation or dissipation of the taint and require the prosecution to prove at least an intervening act by the defendant or a third party that breaks the causal chain linking the illegality and evidence in such a way that the evidence is not in fact obtained by exploitation of that illegality. *Example:* Assume that the police arrest a man illegally merely because he is walking in an area where a bank robbery has occurred. Then they take him to the bank and the teller identifies him as the robber. The derivative evidence of the teller's identification of the man at the bank would be "fruit of the poisonous tree" and would be inadmissible in court because the identification was obtained by exploitation of the prior illegal arrest. Assume further that the arrested person was arraigned and released on his own recognizance, but returned several days later to make a full confession of the robbery. The confession would be admissible because the connection between the arrest and the confession "had become so attenuated as to dissipate the taint." *Wong Sun v. United States,* 371 U.S. 471, 491, 83 S.Ct. 407, 419, 9 L.Ed.2d 441, 457 (1963).

Good-Faith Exception. An exception to the **exclusionary rule** for illegal searches conducted in good faith. Under this exception, whenever a law enforcement officer acting with objective good faith has obtained a search warrant from a detached and neutral judge or magistrate and acted within its scope, evidence seized pursuant to the warrant will not be excluded, even though the warrant is later determined to be invalid. In determining what is good faith on the part of an officer, the Court said that "our good-faith inquiry is confined to the objectively ascertainable question whether a reasonably well-trained officer would have known that the search was illegal despite the magistrate's authorization. In making this determination, all of the circumstances, including whether the warrant application has previously been rejected by a different magistrate, may be considered." *United States v. Leon,* 468 U.S. 897, 922–23 n.23, 104 S.Ct. 3405, 3421 n.23, 82 L.Ed.2d 677, 698 n.23 (1984). The good-faith exception has been extended to protect police who acted in good-faith reliance upon a statute (subsequently found invalid) that authorized warrantless administrative searches. *Illinois v. Krull,* 480 U.S. 340, 107 S.Ct. 1160, 94 L.Ed.2d 364 (1987).

Grand Jury. A jury, usually of 16 to 23 persons, selected according to law and sworn, whose duty is to receive criminal complaints, hear the evidence put forth by the prosecution, and find indictments when they are satisfied that there is probable cause that an accused person has committed a crime and should be brought to trial. Grand juries may also investigate criminal activity generally and investigate the conduct of public agencies and officials. In many states all felony charges must be considered by a grand jury before filing in the trial court. Ordinarily a prosecutor presents to the grand jury for its consideration a list of charges and evidence related to a specific criminal event. The grand jury may then, after deliberation, decide to indict or not to indict. The grand jury may call witnesses and may even compel witnesses to appear or produce documents by having them served with subpoenas. Grand jury proceedings are kept secret for the following reasons:

- to prevent an escape from the jurisdiction of someone who is not yet in custody but whose indictment may be contemplated;

- to provide the utmost freedom for the grand jury in its deliberations and to protect jury members from outside influences;

- to prevent tampering with witnesses who may testify before the grand jury and later appear at the trial of those indicted;

- to encourage the free and unrestrained disclosure of information by persons who have information on the commission of crimes; and

- to protect innocent persons who are exonerated of charges from disclosure of the fact that they were under grand jury investigation.

A trial jury is distinguished from a grand jury in that a trial jury hears a case in order to render a verdict of guilty or not guilty. A grand jury only decides whether there is sufficient evidence to cause a person to be brought to trial for a crime.

Habeas Corpus. The name of a writ issued by a court and directed to a person detaining or confining another (usually the superintendent of a confinement facility) commanding him or her to bring the body of the person detained before a judicial officer and to show cause whether the detention is legal. Article I, Section 9, Clause 2, of the U.S. Constitution provides that "[t]he privilege of the Writ of Habeas Corpus shall not be suspended, unless when in Cases of Rebellion or Invasion the public Safety may require it." The right of a person to the writ depends on the legality of the detention and not on the person's guilt or innocence. The major grounds for issuance of the writ are lack of jurisdiction of the court in which the prisoner was convicted and violation of the petitioner's constitutional rights. Habeas corpus is an extraordinary remedy to be used only in cases of special urgency and not when relief can be obtained by other adequate

remedies, such as a motion for a new trial or an appeal. The writ of habeas corpus is also called the great writ.

Hearsay Evidence. Evidence of a statement made other than by a witness testifying at a trial or hearing offered to prove the truth of the matter asserted. The statement may be oral or written or may be nonverbal conduct intended as a substitute for words.

Hearsay Rule. The hearsay rule, simply stated, is that **hearsay evidence** is inadmissible. The basis of the hearsay rule is that the credibility of the person making a statement is the most important factor in determining the truth of the statement. If a statement is made out of court, there is no opportunity to cross-examine the person making the statement or to observe the person's demeanor. Without these methods of determining the truth of the statement, the statement may not be admitted into evidence. Many exceptions to the hearsay rule allow the admission of hearsay evidence for various reasons of trustworthiness of the evidence and practical necessity.

Hot Pursuit. The immediate pursuit by a law enforcement officer of a person into a house or other constitutionally protected area in response to an emergency. Examples of emergencies that will justify a hot pursuit are escape of a fleeing felon or other dangerous person, avoidance of arrest by a person suspected of a crime, and prevention of the destruction or concealment of evidence. Once inside the house or other constitutionally protected area, officers may search the premises if necessary to alleviate the emergency and any items of evidence observed lying open to view may be legally seized under the plain view doctrine. *Warden v. Hayden,* 387 U.S. 294, 87 S.Ct. 1642, 18 L.Ed.2d 782 (1967).

Immunity. Freedom or exemption from prosecution granted to a witness to compel answers to questions or the production of evidence, which the witness might otherwise refuse to do on the grounds of the Fifth Amendment privilege against self-incrimination. Two types of immunity that may be granted are transactional immunity and use immunity. Under transactional immunity a witness may be compelled to testify despite the privilege against self-incrimination, but the witness is protected from any prosecution for crimes to which his or her compelled testimony relates. Under use immunity a witness may be compelled to testify despite the privilege against self-incrimination, but the witness is protected from the use of the compelled testimony and any evidence derived from it. Use immunity would still permit prosecution for related offenses based upon evidence derived from independent sources. A witness's failure to answer questions or produce evidence within the subject of the investigation as ordered by the court constitutes contempt of court.

Impound. To take a vehicle, document, or other object into the custody of the law or of a court or law enforcement agency for safekeeping or examination. The U.S. Supreme Court approved the impounding of motor vehicles under certain circumstances in *South Dakota v. Opperman.* "In the interests of public safety and as part of what the Court has called "community caretaking functions," automobiles are frequently taken into police custody. Vehicle accidents present one such occasion. To permit the uninterrupted flow of traffic and in some circumstances to preserve evidence, disabled or damaged vehicles will often be removed from the highways or streets at the behest of police engaged solely in care-taking and traffic-control activities. Police will also frequently remove and impound automobiles which violate parking ordinances and which thereby jeopardize both the public safety and the efficient movement of vehicular traffic. The authority of police to seize and remove from the streets vehicles impeding traffic or threatening public safety and convenience is beyond challenge." 428 U.S. 364, 368–69, 96 S.Ct. 3092, 3097, 49 L.Ed.2d 1000, 1005 (1976).

Independent Source. An exception to the **fruit of the poisonous tree doctrine** that allows the admission of tainted evidence if that evidence was also obtained through a source wholly independent of the primary constitutional violation. The independent source exception is compatible with the underlying rationale of the exclusionary rule: the deterrence of police misconduct. As stated by the U.S. Supreme Court, "The independent source doctrine teaches us that the interest of society in deterring unlawful police conduct and the public interest in having juries receive all probative evidence of a crime are properly balanced by putting the police in the same, not a worse, position than they would have been in if no police error or misconduct had occurred." *Nix v. Williams,* 467 U.S. 431, 443, 104 S.Ct. 2501, 2509, 81 L.Ed.2d 377, 387 (1984).

Indictment. A formal written accusation submitted by a grand jury to a court, alleging that a specified person has committed a specific offense. An indictment, like an **information,** is usually used to initiate a felony prosecution. In some jurisdictions, all felony accusations must be by indictment, but in others felony trials will ordinarily be initiated by the filing of an information by a prosecutor. Ordinarily, the prosecutor presents allegations and evidence (often called a bill of indictment) to the grand jury, which endorses on it "a true bill" if it decides that there is sufficient evidence to sustain the accusation and that a trial should be had. The indictment delivered to the court states the facts about the alleged crime as found by the grand jury and cites the penal code sections believed to have been violated. If the grand jury ignores the bill of indictment, it endorses "no true bill," "not a true bill," or "not found" on it. When a grand jury takes notice of an offense on its own initiative and delivers an indictment, it is sometimes called a grand jury original or a presentment.

Inevitable Discovery. A variation of the **independent source** doctrine allowing the admission of tainted evidence if it would inevitably have been discovered in the normal course of events. Under this exception, the prosecution must establish by a preponderance of the evidence that, even though the evidence was actually discovered as the result of a constitutional violation, the evidence would ultimately or inevitably have been discovered by lawful means, for example, as the result of the predictable and routine behavior of a law enforcement agency, some other agency, or a private person. "[I]f the government can prove that the evidence would have been obtained inevitably and, therefore, would have been admitted regardless of any overreaching by the police, there is no rational basis to keep that evidence from the jury in order to ensure the fairness of the trial proceedings. In that situation, the State has gained no advantage at trial and the defendant has suffered no prejudice. Indeed, suppression of the evidence would operate to undermine the adversary system by putting the State in a worse position than it would have occupied without any police misconduct." *Nix v. Williams,* 467 U.S. 431, 447, 104 S.Ct. 2501, 2511, 81 L.Ed.2d 377, 389–90 (1984).

Informant. A person who gives information to the police regarding criminal activity.

Information. A formal, written accusation submitted to a court by a prosecutor, without the approval or intervention of a grand jury, alleging that a specified person has committed a specific offense. An information is similar in nature and content to an **indictment** and serves as an alternative to the indictment in some jurisdictions to initiate usually felony prosecutions. Some jurisdictions initiate felony prosecutions only through indictment and others allow use of the information only after the defendant has waived an indictment.

Initial Appearance. The first appearance of an accused person in the first court having jurisdiction over his or her case. Various procedural steps may be taken during the initial appearance. In minor misdemeanor cases the initial appearance may be the only one, and judgment and penalty, if any, will be determined at that time. When the charge is more serious, the accused at initial appearance may be informed of the charges, a plea may be entered and bail set, or the accused may merely be informed of his or her rights and of the general nature of the proceedings and it may be determined whether he or she has counsel. In any given jurisdiction, the initial appearance may be characterized by the major step taken in that court at that point. Thus, it may be called a preliminary arraignment, preliminary examination, magistrate's preliminary hearing, or presentment. The timing of an initial appearance is largely determined by whether the defendant is in custody, and by the laws concerning the maximum period a person can be held in custody without court appearance. In most states an arrested person has a right to be brought forthwith before a court or magistrate for an initial appearance.

Instruction. A direction or explanation given by a trial judge to a jury informing them of the law applicable to the case before them. Attorneys for both sides normally furnish the judge with suggested instructions.

Interrogation. The questioning of a person suspected of a crime with the intent of eliciting incriminating admissions from the person. The U.S. Supreme Court explained the meaning of interrogation for purposes of the *Miranda v. Arizona* decision as follows: "[T]he *Miranda* safeguards come into play whenever a person in custody is subjected to either express questioning or its functional equivalent. That is to say, the term 'interrogation' under *Miranda* refers not only to express questioning, but also to any words or actions on the part of police (other than those normally attendant to arrest and custody) that the police should know are reasonably likely to elicit an incriminating response from the suspect." *Rhode Island v. Innis,* 446 U.S. 291, 300–01, 100 S.Ct. 1682, 1689, 64 L.Ed.2d 297, 307–08 (1980). The Court further refined the definition by stating that an incriminating response is any response, whether inculpatory or exculpatory, that the prosecution may seek to introduce at trial. Volunteered statements, questions directed at clarifying a suspect's statement, brief, routine questions, spontaneous questions, and questions necessary to protect the safety of the police and public are not considered interrogation for purposes of *Miranda.*

Inventory Search. The routine practice of police departments of securing and recording the contents of a lawfully impounded vehicle. In *South Dakota v. Opperman,* 428 U.S. 364, 96 S.Ct. 3092, 49 L.Ed.2d 1000 (1976), the U.S. Supreme Court approved this limited type of search for the purposes of protecting the vehicle owner's property while it remains in custody and protecting the police from potential danger and from claims or disputes over lost or stolen property. This inventory procedure is not considered to be a search for purposes of the Fourth Amendment because its object is not to find incriminating evidence as part of a criminal investigation. Rather, it is considered to be a routine administrative-custodial procedure, and it may not be used as a pretext to conduct an exploratory search for incriminating evidence in order to circumvent the warrant requirement. If, however, incriminating evidence is found under circumstances satisfying the plain view doctrine, that evidence may be seized and is admissible in court. The validity of an inventory search depends on whether the officers conducting the inventory followed standard inventory procedures of their law enforcement agency.

Items Subject to Seizure. Items for which a search warrant may be issued. Federal Rule of Criminal Procedure 41 (b) specifies that "[a] warrant may be issued under this rule to search for and seize any (1) property that constitutes evidence of the commission of a criminal offense; or (2) contraband, the fruits of crime, or things otherwise criminally possessed; or (3) property designed or intended for use or which is or has been used as the means of committing a criminal offense. . . ." Most states have similar rules.

Joinder. Generally, the uniting or combining of two or more persons, parties, charges, causes of action, etc. to be considered together. In criminal proceedings, joinder means the naming of two or more defendants and/or the listing of two or more charges in a single charging document.

Judgment. 1. The statement of a court's decision of conviction or acquittal of a person charged with a crime. The date of a judgment of conviction is an important item in calculations of elapsed time in those jurisdictions where a sentence must be pronounced within a time limit. The count begins the day the judgment is pronounced. Judgment is sometimes used to mean any court decision, such as a judgment of conviction, an acquittal, a court order, or a sentence. 2. Generally, the determination or decision of a court upon a matter within its jurisdiction; the final conclusion of a court as to matters of fact and law. Sometimes judgment is used only in the sense of a final or authoritative decision.

Judicial Review. "Judicial review is the exercise by courts of their responsibility to determine whether acts of the other two branches are illegal and void because those acts violate the constitution. The doctrine authorizes courts to determine whether a law is constitutional, not whether it is necessary or useful. In other words, judicial review is the power to say what the constitution means and not whether such a law reflects a wise policy. Adherence to the doctrine of judicial review is essential to achieving balance in our government. . . . Judicial review, coupled with the specified constitutional provisions which keep the judicial branch separate and independent of the other branches of government and with those articles of the constitution that protect the impartiality of the judiciary from public and political pressure, enables the courts to ensure that the constitutional rights of each citizen will not be encroached upon by either the legislative or the executive branch of the government." *State v. LaFrance*, 471 A.2d 340, 343–44 (N.H. 1983).

Jurisdiction. 1. The territory, subject matter, or person over which lawful authority may be exercised by a court or other justice agency, as determined by statute or constitution. *Example:* Criminal cases are not within the jurisdiction of the probate court. 2. The lawful authority or power of a court or an administrative agency to act upon or deal with a matter. *Example:* Police agencies do not have jurisdiction over most private disputes. 3. The jurisdiction of a court, more specifically, is the lawful authority or power to hear or act upon a case or question and to pass and enforce judgment on it. A particular court can have more than one kind of jurisdiction. *Example:* An appellate court has appellate jurisdiction over felony cases and original jurisdiction for the issuance of certain writs, but no jurisdiction to conduct trials.

Jury. A body of persons, selected and sworn according to law, to inquire into certain matters of fact and to render a verdict or true answer based on evidence presented before them.

Jury Nullification. The power of a jury to acquit regardless of the strength of the evidence against a defendant. Nullification usually occurs when the defendant is particularly sympathetic, or when the defendant is prosecuted for violating an unpopular law.

Jury Panel. The group of persons summoned to appear in court as potential jurors for a particular trial, or the persons selected from the group of potential jurors to sit in the jury box, from which second group those acceptable to the prosecution and the defense are finally chosen as the jury. The group of persons who are asked to sit in the jury box are usually selected by the court clerk by lot. As individuals are dismissed from the box for various reasons, replacements are chosen, also by lot.

Lineup. A **confrontation** (definition 2) involving the presentation at one time of several persons, including a person suspected of committing a crime, to a victim or witness of the crime for the purpose of identifying the perpetrator of the crime. The presentation is usually conducted by a law enforcement official or a prosecuting attorney. In *United States v. Wade*, 388 U.S. 218, 87 S.Ct. 1926, 18 L.Ed.2d 1149 (1967), the U.S. Supreme Court held that a pretrial confrontation is a critical stage in the legal proceedings against a suspect and that the suspect has a right to the presence of a lawyer at the lineup. Furthermore, if the suspect cannot afford a lawyer, he or she is entitled to have one appointed by the court. In *Kirby v. Illinois*, 406 U.S. 682, 689, 92 S.Ct. 1877, 1882, 32 L.Ed.2d 411, 417 (1972), the Court held that the right to counsel attaches only to lineups held "at or after the initiation of adversary judicial criminal proceedings, whether by way of formal charge, preliminary hearing, indictment, information or arraignment." Nevertheless, even though a suspect may not have a right to counsel at a confrontation, the due process clause of the Fifth and Fourteenth Amendments to the Constitution forbids any pretrial identification procedure that is unnecessarily suggestive and conducive to irreparable mistaken identification. *Stovall v. Denno*, 388 U.S. 293, 87 S.Ct. 1967, 18 L.Ed.2d 1199 (1967). If an officer conducts an unnecessarily suggestive identification procedure, the identification evidence will be inadmissible in court unless the identification is otherwise reliable under the totality of the circumstances. "[R]eliability is the linchpin in determining the admissibility of identification testimony for both pre- and post-*Stovall* confrontations. The factors to be considered are set out in *Biggers*. 409 U.S., at 199–200, 93 S.Ct., at 382. These include the opportunity of the witness to view the criminal at the time of the crime, the witness' degree of attention, the accuracy of his prior description of the criminal, the level of certainty demonstrated at the confrontation, and the time between the crime and the confrontation. Against these factors is to be weighed the corrupting effect of the suggestive identification itself." *Manson v. Brathwaite*, 432 U.S. 98, 114, 97 S.Ct. 2243, 2253, 53 L.Ed.2d 140, 154 (1977).

Magistrate. A judicial officer of a court of limited jurisdiction or with limited or delegated authority. Among the duties of a magistrate are the issuance of arrest warrants, search warrants, and summonses, the setting of bail, the ordering of release on bail, and the conduct of arraignments and preliminary examinations of persons charged with serious crimes. A magistrate may also have limited authority to try minor cases or to dispose of cases on a guilty plea. The authority of a magistrate in a particular jurisdiction depends on the statutes, rules, and customs of that jurisdiction.

Misdemeanor. In general, a crime of less serious nature than those designated as felonies. In jurisdictions that recognize the felony-misdemeanor distinction, a misdemeanor is any crime that is not a felony. Misdemeanors are usually punished by fine or by incarceration in a local confinement facility rather than a state prison or penitentiary. The maximum period of confinement that may be imposed for a misdemeanor is defined by statute and is usually less than one year. Court procedures for handling misdemeanors are usually different from those for felonies.

Motion. An oral or written request made to a court at any time before, during, or after court proceedings, asking the court to make a specified finding, decision, or order. In criminal proceedings the prosecution, the defense, or the court itself can make a motion.

Multiplicitous Indictment or Information. An indictment or information that charges the commission of a single offense in several counts. The evil of a multiplicitous indictment or information is that it may lead to multiple sentences for the same offense, or it may have some psychological effect upon a jury by suggesting that the defendant has committed more than one crime.

Nolo Contendere. Latin. "I do not wish to contest." A defendant's plea to a criminal charge in which the defendant states that he or she does not contest the charge, but neither admits guilt nor claims innocence. A plea of *nolo contendere* subjects the defendant to the same legal consequences as a guilty plea. Both pleas can be followed by a judgment of conviction without a trial or verdict, and by a sentencing disposition. The major difference between the two pleas is that a plea of nolo contendere cannot constitute evidence in a civil action that relevant facts have been admitted; a guilty plea can. A court may not accept a plea of *nolo contendere* unless the court is satisfied, after inquiry, that the defendant committed the crime charged and that the plea is made voluntarily with an understanding of the nature of the charge.

Nonjury Trial. A trial in which there is no jury and in which a judicial officer determines all issues of fact and law.

Open Fields. The portions of a person's premises lying outside the **curtilage** of his or her home or business. The open fields doctrine states that "the special protection accorded by the Fourth Amendment to the people in their 'persons houses, papers, and effects,' is not extended to the open fields. *Hester v. United States*, 265 U.S. 57, 59, 44 S.Ct. 445, 446, 68 L.Ed. 898, 900 (1924). This doctrine simply means that a law enforcement officer may search for and seize items of evidence lying in the open fields without probable cause or other legal justification without violating a person's Fourth Amendment rights.

Opening Statement. The part of a trial before the presentation of evidence in which the attorney for each party gives an outline of what that party intends to prove by the evidence it will present. The primary purpose of the opening statement is to acquaint the judge and jury in a general way with the nature of the case.

Original Jurisdiction. Jurisdiction of a court or administrative agency to hear or act upon a case from its beginning and to pass judgment on the law and the facts.

Peremptory Challenge. A formal objection to a prospective juror for which no reason need be given. The judge will automatically dismiss a juror to whom a peremptory challenge is made. The number of peremptory challenges available to each party is limited by statute or court rule.

Plain Feel Doctrine. Same as **Plain Touch Doctrine.**

Plain Touch Doctrine. The doctrine stating that if police are lawfully in a position from which they feel an object, if its incriminating character is immediately apparent, and if the officers have a lawful right of access to the object, they may seize it without a warrant. If, however, the police lack probable cause to believe that the object felt is subject to seizure without conducting some further search of the object, its seizure is not justified.

Plain View Doctrine. The doctrine stating that "if police are lawfully in a position from which they view an object, if its incriminating character is apparent, and if the officers have a lawful right of access to the object, they may seize it without a warrant." *Minnesota v. Dickerson*, 508 U.S. 366, 375, 113 S.Ct. 2130, 2136–37, 124 L.Ed.2d 334, 345 (1993). The plain view doctrine has four requirements, all of which must be satisfied before seizure of an item of evidence can be legally justified.

1. The officer, as the result of a prior valid intrusion, must be in a position in which he or she has legal right to be, such as effecting an arrest, executing a search warrant, or responding to an emergency.
2. The officer must not unreasonably intrude on any person's reasonable expectation of privacy.
3. The incriminating character of the object to be seized must be immediately apparent to the officer.
4. The discovery of the item of evidence by the officer need not be inadvertent.

Plea. A defendant's formal answer in court to the charge contained in a complaint, information, or indictment, that he or she is guilty or not guilty of the offense charged, or does not contest the charge. The pleas in a criminal case are guilty, nolo contendere, not guilty, and not guilty by reason of insanity.

Plea Bargaining. The exchange of prosecutorial or judicial concessions, or both, in return for a guilty plea. Common concessions include a lesser charge, the dismissal of other pending charges, a recommendation by the prosecutor for a reduced sentence, or a combination of these. The guilty plea arrived at through the process of plea bargaining is sometimes called a negotiated plea.

Plea bargaining has been approved by the U.S. Supreme Court and is governed by rules of court in federal and in many state courts. The U.S. Supreme Court stated: "The disposition of criminal charges by agreement between the prosecutor and the accused, sometimes loosely called "plea bargaining," is an essential component of the administration of justice. Properly administered, it is to be encouraged. If the criminal charge were subjected to a full-scale trial, the States and the Federal Government would need to multiply by many times the number of judges and court facilities.

Disposition of charges after plea discussions is not only an essential part of the process but a highly desirable part for many reasons. It leads to prompt and largely final disposition of most criminal cases; it avoids much of the corrosive impact of enforced idleness during pretrial confinement for those who are denied release pending trial; it protects the public from those accused persons who are prone to continue criminal conduct even while on pretrial release; and, by shortening the time between charge and disposition, it enhances whatever may be the rehabilitative prospects of the guilty when they are ultimately imprisoned. *Santobello v. New York*, 404 U.S. 257, 260–61, 92 S.Ct. 495, 498, 30 L.Ed.2d 427, 432 (1971).

Preliminary Examination. The proceeding before a judicial officer in which three matters must be decided: whether a crime was committed; whether the crime occurred within the territorial jurisdiction of the court; and whether there is probable cause to believe that the defendant committed the crime.

A chief purpose of the preliminary examination is to protect the accused from an inadequately based prosecution in felony cases by making a judicial test of the existence of probable cause early in the proceedings. In felony cases in states where a felony trial can be initiated by the filing of an information by the prosecutor, the preliminary examination (usually in a lower court) is a key step at which it is determined whether proceedings will continue. If the court does find probable cause, bail may be set or reset, and the defendant will be bound over or held to answer the charge in the trial court.

In felony cases in states where the grand jury indictment is used to initiate proceedings in the trial court, defendants often waive the preliminary examination, because the grand jury will make the probable cause determination. But some defendants request a preliminary examination because it affords opportunity to acquire information about the basis of the prosecution's case or to move for dismissal of the case.

Whether the defendant has the right to a preliminary examination in a misdemeanor case depends upon the jurisdiction.

Prima Facie Case. A case established by prima facie evidence, and which will prevail until contradicted and overcome by other sufficient evidence. Prima facie evidence is defined as "evidence sufficient to establish a given fact and which, if not rebutted or contradicted, will remain sufficient." *State v. Williams*, 400 So.2d 575, 579 (La. 1981).

Probable Cause. Probable cause exists when the facts and circumstances within a person's knowledge and of which he or she has reasonably trustworthy information are sufficient in themselves to justify a person of reasonable caution and prudence in believing that something is true. It means something less than certainty, but more than mere suspicion, speculation, or possibility. The U.S. Supreme Court defined probable cause to search as "a fair probability that contraband or evidence of a crime will be found in a particular place." *Illinois v. Gates*, 462 U.S. 213, 238, 103 S.Ct. 2317, 2332, 76 L.Ed.2d 527, 548 (1983).

Probable cause is required to justify the issuance of an arrest warrant or search warrant, all arrests made without a warrant, and most searches made without a warrant. The quality and amount of information needed to establish probable cause to arrest or search are the same in either case. The kind of information needed to justify an arrest, however, is different from that to justify a search. Probable cause to arrest arises from facts tending to show

that a specific crime has been or is being committed and that a particular person committed or is committing it. Probable cause to search arises from facts tending to show that the items searched for are items subject to seizure and that they will be located in a particular place at a particular time.

Information to establish probable cause may come to a person through any of his or her five senses or through a third person or informant. When the information comes through an informant, the information must satisfy the "totality of the circumstances" test set out in the U.S. Supreme Court case of *Illinois v. Gates*. Even though the *Gates* case dealt with a search warrant, the "totality of the circumstances" test must be satisfied to establish probable cause for a warrantless search and for arrests made both with and without a warrant.

Probable cause to believe that a particular person committed a particular crime is also required to initiate prosecution. In felony cases the existence of probable cause will be established in court in a hearing usually called a preliminary examination, or by a grand jury, before felony trial proceedings begin. Whether the defendant has the right to a preliminary examination in a misdemeanor case depends upon the jurisdiction.

Probation. The conditional freedom without imprisonment granted by a judicial officer to an alleged or adjudicated adult or juvenile offender, as long as the person meets certain conditions of behavior. Probation differs from parole, in that it is conditional freedom ordered by a court, whereas parole is conditional freedom granted by a paroling authority after commitment to a period of confinement. Probation is usually a continuation of freedom previously granted by the court during court proceedings. It may be granted after conviction, but also may be granted before adjudication, as when the defendant concedes guilt, prosecution is suspended, and the subject placed on probation.

Probation is usually granted to young offenders and first offenders who have committed minor crimes. Typical conditions of adult probation, as set forth by the court that granted the probation, frequently include maintaining regular employment, abstaining from drugs and alcohol, not associating with known offenders or other specified persons, regularly reporting to a probation officer or other designated person, and/or remaining within a designated geographic area. Not committing another offense is always a condition of probation. A grant of probation after conviction often includes another kind of sentencing disposition as a condition: confinement in jail, payment of restitution in the form of money or public service, a fine, etc. Conditions of probation unique to a person may also be imposed, such as payment of personal debts. Some courts commit offenders to prison with a period of probationary status, instead of parole, to follow. This is often called shock probation.

The limits of probationary periods are usually set by statute and can be longer than the maximum sentence of confinement, or series of sentences to confinement, provided by law for a given offense. Some jurisdictions limit probationary periods for felonies to the maximum possible period of imprisonment for the offense.

Violation of any of the conditions of probation may lead to probation revocation and the execution of a suspended sentence or the imposition and execution of a sentence if one has not already been imposed.

Juvenile probation is often designated as informal or formal, depending upon the authority granting it and the nature of the conditions. Juveniles may be placed on informal probation by a probation officer in lieu of the filing of a juvenile petition.

Reasonable Doubt. An accused person is presumed innocent until proven guilty beyond a reasonable doubt. Beyond a reasonable doubt requires little interpretation, although many courts have attempted to formulate somewhat involved definitions that add little to the plain meaning of the term. Some examples of these definitions are "fully satisfied," "entirely convinced," "reasonably certain," and "satisfied to a moral certainty." Suffice it to say that proof beyond a reasonable doubt requires that the fact be established to a reasonable, but not absolute or mathematical, certainty. A possibility or probability is not sufficient.

In the U.S. Supreme Court decision holding that due process required the use of the reasonable doubt standard in criminal prosecutions, Justice John M. Harlan concurred, writing: "I view the requirement of proof beyond a reasonable doubt in a criminal case as bottomed on a fundamental value determination of our society that it is far worse to convict an innocent man than to let a guilty man go free." *In re Winship,* 397 U.S. 358, 372, 90 S.Ct. 1068, 1077, 25 L.Ed.2d 368, 380 (1970). In the *Winship* decision, the Court also decided that the Fourteenth Amendment required proof beyond a reasonable doubt in state juvenile delinquency proceedings during the adjudicatory stage, when the juvenile was charged with an act that would constitute a crime if committed by an adult. Furthermore, the *Winship* decision held that due process requires "proof beyond a reasonable doubt of every fact necessary to constitute the crime with which [the defendant] is charged." 397 U.S. at 364, 90 S.Ct. at 1073, 25 L.Ed.2d at 375. This means that the prosecution must establish every element of the offense beyond a reasonable doubt.

Redaction. In evaluating the constitutional sufficiency of a search warrant, the practice of invalidating clauses in the warrant that are constitutionally insufficient for lack of probable cause or particularity while preserving clauses that satisfy the Fourth Amendment.

Redirect Examination. A reexamination of a witness by a prosecuting attorney in order to rehabilitate him or her after cross-examination.

Search. Under the Fourth Amendment prohibition against unreasonable searches and seizures, a search can be defined as an examination or inspection of a location, vehicle, or person by a law enforcement officer or other authorized person for the purpose of locating objects relating to or believed to relate to criminal activities or wanted persons. Mere observation of objects lying open to view by a law enforcement officer who is in a position in which he or she has a legal right to be does not constitute a search. In recent years courts have increasingly analyzed search and seizure issues in terms of violation of the right of privacy and have expanded the definition of search to include any official intrusion into matters and activities as to which a person has exhibited a reasonable expectation of privacy. "A 'search' occurs when an expectation of privacy that society is prepared to consider reasonable is infringed." *United States v. Jacobsen,* 466 U.S. 109, 113, 104 S.Ct. 1652, 1656, 80 L.Ed.2d 85, 94 (1984).

The general rule is that any search conducted without a search warrant is unreasonable. Courts have fashioned several well-defined exceptions to this rule, however. A warrant is not required, therefore, for a **search incident to arrest;** a **consent search;** an observation of evidence falling under the **plain view doctrine;**

an emergency search of a motor vehicle under the *Carroll* doctrine; searches conducted in the **open fields;** observations and seizures of **abandoned property;** and frisks conducted as a part of an investigative stop (see **Stop and Frisk**).

Search Incident to Arrest. A recognized exception to the search warrant requirement, allowing a law enforcement officer who legally arrests a person to conduct a warrantless search of that person contemporaneous with the arrest. The basic legal requirements of a search incident to arrest are stated in the 1969 U.S. Supreme Court case of *Chimel v. California:* "When an arrest is made, it is reasonable for the arresting officer to search the person arrested in order to remove any weapons that the latter might seek to use in order to resist arrest or effect his escape. Otherwise, the officer's safety might well be endangered, and the arrest itself frustrated. In addition, it is entirely reasonable for the arresting officer to search for and seize any evidence on the arrestee's person in order to prevent its concealment or destruction. And the area into which an arrestee might reach in order to grab a weapon or evidentiary items must, of course, be governed by a like rule. A gun on a table or in a drawer in front of one who is arrested can be as dangerous to the arresting officer as one concealed in the clothing of the person arrested. There is ample justification, therefore, for a search of the arrestee's person and the area "within his immediate control" construing that phrase to mean the area from within which he might gain possession of a weapon or destructible evidence." 395 U.S. 752, 762–63, 89 S.Ct. 2034, 2040, 23 L.Ed.2d 685, 694.

Search Warrant. An order in writing, issued by a magistrate or other proper judicial officer in the name of the people of a state or of the nation, directed to a law enforcement officer and commanding him or her to search a specified person or premises for specified property and to bring it before the judicial authority named in the warrant. Generally, the types of property for which a search warrant may be issued, as set out in statutes or rules of court, are weapons, contraband, fruits of crime, instrumentalities of crime, and other evidence of crime (see **Items Subject to Seizure**). The Fourth Amendment to the U.S. Constitution states that "no warrants shall issue, but upon probable cause, supported by Oath or affirmation, and particularly describing the place to be searched and the persons or things to be seized." The judicial officer, before issuing the warrant, must determine whether there is probable cause to search based on information supplied in an affidavit by a law enforcement officer or other person.

Seizable Items. Same as **Items Subject to Seizure.**

Seizure. 1. Under the Fourth Amendment prohibition against unreasonable searches and seizures, a seizure of the *person* can be defined as follows: "[A] person has been 'seized' within the meaning of the Fourth Amendment only if, in view of all of the circumstances surrounding the incident, a reasonable person would have believed that he was not free to leave. Examples of circumstances that might indicate a seizure even where the person did not attempt to leave, would be the threatening presence of several officers, the display of a weapon by an officer, some physical touching of the person of the citizen, or the use of language or tone of voice indicating that compliance with the officer's request might be compelled. . . . In the absence of some such evidence, otherwise inoffensive contact between a member of the public and the police cannot, as a matter of law, amount to a seizure of that person." *United States v. Mendenhall,* 446 U.S. 544, 554–55, 100 S.Ct. 1870, 1877, 64 L.Ed.2d 497, 509 (1980).

The least intrusive type of seizure of the person governed by the Fourth Amendment is the so-called *Terry*-type investigative stop (see **Stop and Frisk**). At a still higher level of intensity are police contacts with members of the public involving a detention or temporary seizure of a person that is more intrusive on a person's freedom of action than a brief investigatory stop, but that does not satisfy the four elements of a formal arrest. An example would be an officer's handcuffing a suspect and transporting him or her to the station for questioning without formally arresting the person. In this type of situation, a court may find that the officer's actions are tantamount to an arrest if they are indistinguishable from an arrest in important respects. The seizure or detention will be ruled illegal unless it is supported by probable cause. This type of seizure is sometimes referred to as a seizure tantamount to arrest or a *de facto* arrest.

The highest level of seizure of the person governed by the Fourth Amendment is the formal arrest.

2. Under the Fourth Amendment's prohibition against unreasonable searches and seizures, a seizure of *property* "occurs when there is some meaningful interference with an individual's possessory interests in that property." *United States v. Jacobsen,* 466 U.S. 109, 113, 104 S.Ct. 1652, 1656, 80 L.Ed.2d 85, 94 (1984). Usually a seizure involves the taking into custody by a law enforcement officer of an item of property relating to or believed to relate to criminal activity. Ordinarily property is seized after a search conducted pursuant to a search warrant or pursuant to one of the recognized exceptions to the warrant requirement. In certain situations, however, such as seizures of items under the plain view doctrine, seizures of items found in the open fields, and seizures of abandoned property, the seizure may be made without any preceding search. Because a search and seizure are often combined in one transaction, they are often referred to together by the term "search and seizure," and the legal principles applicable to searches and seizures are referred to as the law of search and seizure.

Sentence. The penalty imposed by a court upon a person convicted of a crime. The types of sentences are death, commitment to confinement, probation or a suspended sentence, and a fine. The determination of the sentence is perhaps the most sensitive and difficult decision the judge has to make because of the effect it will have on the defendant's life. For this reason, most states have laws directing and guiding the judge in this determination. A typical provision requires the judge to impose sentence without unreasonable delay. This protects the defendant from a prolonged period of uncertainty about the future. In addition, before imposing sentence, the judge is usually required to address the defendant personally and ask if the defendant desires to be heard before the imposition of sentence. The defendant may be heard personally or by counsel or both. The purpose of this provision is to enable the defendant to present any information that may be of assistance to the court in determining punishment.

Another typical statutory provision that is designed to assist the court in fixing sentence allows the court, in its discretion, to direct the state probation and parole board to make a presentence investigation and presentence report to the court before the imposition of sentence. This report will contain any prior criminal record of the defendant and such other information on personal characteristics, financial condition, and the circumstances affecting the defendant's behavior as may be helpful to the court in reaching its decision.

The court has a number of alternatives open to it with respect to sentencing, depending largely on individual state criminal statutes. Some criminal statutes have mandatory sentences, some have fixed maximum sentences, some have fixed minimum sentences, and others leave the matter of sentencing to the judge. Therefore, depending upon the offense for which the defendant has been convicted, the court may have a very broad discretion in fixing sentence, or no discretion whatsoever. In a few states, the jury has the power to fix the sentence as well as to determine guilt or innocence.

Showup. A **confrontation** (definition 2) involving the presentation of a single suspect to a victim or witness of a crime for the purpose of identifying the perpetrator of the crime.

Standing. The legal right of a person to judicially challenge the conduct of another person or the government. In general, standing depends on whether the person seeking relief has a legally sufficient personal interest at stake to obtain judicial resolution of merits of the dispute. The "gist of the question of standing" is whether the party seeking relief has "alleged such a personal stake in the outcome of the controversy as to assure that concrete adverseness which sharpens the presentation of issues upon which the court so largely depends for illumination of difficult constitutional questions." *Baker v. Carr,* 369 U.S. 186, 204, 82 S.Ct. 691, 703, 7 L.Ed.2d 663, 678 (1962).

To invoke the exclusionary rule to challenge the admissibility of evidence, a defendant must have standing. A defendant has standing when his or her own constitutional rights have been violated. "Fourth Amendment rights are personal rights which, like some other constitutional rights, may not be vicariously asserted." . . . A person who is aggrieved by an illegal search and seizure only through the introduction of damaging evidence secured by a search of a third person's premises or property has not had any of his Fourth Amendment rights infringed. . . . And since the exclusionary rule is an attempt to effectuate the guarantees of the Fourth Amendment, . . . it is proper to permit only defendants whose Fourth Amendment rights have been violated to benefit from the rule's protections." *Rakas v. Illinois,* 439 U.S. 128, 133–34, 99 S.Ct. 421, 425, 58 L.Ed.2d 387, 394–95 (1978). In determining whether a defendant's Fourth Amendment rights have been violated, courts will analyze whether the defendant had a reasonable expectation of privacy in the area searched or the item seized.

Stop and Frisk. A shorthand term for the law enforcement practice involving the temporary investigative seizure of a person and the patdown search of the person's outer clothing for weapons. A stop and frisk is a much less severe and less extensive restraint on a person than that of an arrest and search. A stop and frisk may be initiated on a lesser justification than probable cause for the purposes of crime prevention and investigation and for the protection of the law enforcement officer carrying out the investigation. In order to protect society's interest in effective crime prevention or detection, a law enforcement officer may stop or temporarily detain a person for the purpose of investigating possibly criminal behavior, even though there is no probable cause to make an arrest. The officer making the stop, however, must have an articulable suspicion—specific and articulable facts that, taken together with rational inferences from those facts, reasonably warrant that intrusion. Also, the extent of the officer's interference with the person must be reasonable under the circumstances.

In order to protect the officer and others from possible violence by persons being investigated for crime, a law enforcement officer may frisk or patdown the outer clothing of a person for weapons. The officer conducting the frisk must have reason to believe that he or she is dealing with an armed and dangerous person and must be able to justify the stop by pointing to specific facts and specific reasonable inferences that the officer is entitled to draw from the facts in light of his or her experience. Also, the frisk must be limited to what is minimally necessary for self-protection and the protection of others and therefore must be limited initially to a patdown of the outer clothing for weapons. If a weaponlike object is felt, the officer may seize it. If a weaponlike object is not felt, the officer must discontinue the search immediately.

The basic principles of the law of stop and frisk are discussed in the U.S. Supreme Court case of *Terry v. Ohio*, 392 U.S. 1, 88 S.Ct. 1868, 20 L.Ed.2d 889 (1968). Note that these basic principles have been applied to other limited detention and search situations involving objects such as motor vehicles and packages in the mail.

Subpoena. A written order issued by a judicial officer requiring a specified person to appear in a designated court at a specified time in order to testify in a case under the jurisdiction of that court, or to bring a document, piece of evidence or other thing for use or inspection by the court. A subpoena to serve as a witness is called a subpoena ad testificandum. A subpoena to bring a document, piece of evidence, or other thing into court is called a subpoena duces tecum. Subpoenas can be served in various ways. They may be served in person by a law enforcement officer, or by another person authorized to do so. In some jurisdictions some types of subpoenas may be served by mail or by telephone. Failure to obey a subpoena is contempt of court.

Summons. A written order issued by a judicial officer requiring a person accused of a criminal offense to appear in a designated court at a specified time to answer the charge or charges. Rules of court and statutes usually provide that if a defendant fails to appear in response to a summons, an arrest warrant will be issued for his or her arrest. The summons is usually used when the offense charged in a complaint is a violation of a municipal ordinance or some other misdemeanor or petty offense. If the offender is a citizen with "roots firmly established in the soil of the community," and thus can be easily found for service of a warrant if the summons is ignored, the summons procedure is a much easier and better way of inducing a defendant to appear in court than is arresting the defendant and taking him or her into custody.

Testimonial Communication. The Fifth Amendment protects a person against being incriminated by his or her own compelled testimonial communications. This protection is applicable to the states through the Fourteenth Amendment. *Malloy v. Hogan*, 378 U.S. 1, 84 S.Ct. 1489, 12 L.Ed.2d 653 (1964). To be testimonial, a "communication must itself, explicitly or implicitly, relate a factual assertion or disclose information" that is "the expression of the contents of an individual's mind." *Doe v. United States*, 487 U.S. 201, 210 n.9, 108 S.Ct. 2341, 2347 n.9, 101 L.Ed.2d 184, 197 n.9 (1988). Therefore, the privilege against self-incrimination is not violated by compelling a person to appear in a lineup, to produce voice exemplars, to furnish handwriting samples, to be fingerprinted, to shave a beard or mustache, or to take a blood-alcohol or breathalyzer test.

Trial *De Novo*. A new trial or retrial in which the whole case is gone into again as if no trial whatever had been held before. In a trial *de novo*, matters of fact as well as law may be considered, witnesses may be heard, and new evidence may be presented, regardless of what happened at the first trial.

Venue. The geographical area from which the jury is drawn and in which a court with jurisdiction may hear and determine a case. Venue is usually the county or district in which the crime is alleged to have been committed. The Sixth Amendment to the U.S. Constitution grants an accused "the right to a speedy and public trial, by an impartial jury of the State and district wherein the crime shall have been committed, which district shall have been previously ascertained by law. . . ."

Verdict. The decision made by a jury in a jury trial, or by a judicial officer in a nonjury trial, that a defendant is either guilty or not guilty of the offense for which he or she has been tried. In entering a judgment, a judicial officer has the power to reject a jury verdict of guilty, but must accept a jury verdict of not guilty. Thus a jury verdict of not guilty results in a judgment of acquittal, but a verdict of guilty does not necessarily result in a judgment of conviction.

***Voir Dire*.** French. "To speak the truth." 1. An examination conducted by the court or by the attorneys of a prospective juror or witness to determine if he or she is competent or qualified for service. 2. During a trial, a hearing conducted by the court out of the presence of the jury on some issue upon which the court must make an initial determination as a matter of law.

Waiver. "[T]he intentional relinquishment or abandonment of a known right or privilege." *Johnson v. Zerbst*, 304 U.S. 458, 464, 58 S.Ct. 1019, 1023, 82 L.Ed. 1461, 1466 (1938).

Warrant. A written order or writ issued by a judicial officer or other authorized person commanding a law enforcement officer to perform some act incident to the administration of justice.

Witness. 1. A person who directly sees or perceives an event or thing or who has expert knowledge relevant to a case. 2. A person who testifies to what he or she has seen or perceived or what he or she knows. 3. A person who signs his or her name to a document to attest to its authenticity. Such a person is sometimes called an attesting witness.

Writ of Assistance. A form of general warrant issued by the British Colonial courts against the American colonists in the mid-eighteenth century to enforce the Trade Acts. Writs of assistance authorized royal customs officers to search houses and ships at will in order to discover and seize smuggled goods or goods on which the required duties had not been paid. The reaction of the colonists against the writs of assistance was strong and was one of the major causes of the American Revolution.

Writ of *Certiorari*. A discretionary writ issued from an appellate court for the purpose of obtaining from a lower court the record of its proceedings in a particular case. In the U.S. Supreme Court, and in some states, this writ is the mechanism for discretionary review. A request for review is made by petitioning for a writ of certiorari, and granting of review is indicated by issuance of the writ.

TABLE OF CASES

SUBJECT INDEX